The Cambridge Handbook of Expertise and Expert Performance

This is the first handbook where the world's foremost "experts on expertise" review our scientific knowledge on expertise and expert performance and how experts may differ from non-experts in terms of their development, training, reasoning, knowledge, social support, and innate talent. Methods are described for the study of experts' knowledge and their performance of representative tasks from their domain of expertise. The development of expertise is also studied by retrospective interviews and the daily lives of experts are studied with diaries. In 15 major domains of expertise, the leading researchers summarize our knowledge of the structure and acquisition of expert skill and knowledge and discuss future prospects. General issues that cut across most domains are reviewed in chapters on various aspects of expertise, such as general and practical intelligence, differences in brain activity, self-regulated learning, deliberate practice, aging, knowledge management, and creativity.

K. Anders Ericsson is Conradi Eminent Scholar and Professor of Psychology at Florida State University. In 1976 he received his Ph.D. in Psychology from University of Stockholm, Sweden, followed by a postdoctoral fellowship at Carnegie-Mellon University. His current research concerns the structure and acquisition of expert performance and in particular how expert performers acquire and maintain their superior performance by extended deliberate practice. He has published many books, including *Toward a General Theory of Expertise: Prospects and Limits* and *The Road to Excellence: The Acquisition of Expert Performance in the Arts and Sciences, Sports, and Games.*

Neil Charness is Professor of Psychology at Florida State University and Research Associate at the Pepper Institute on Aging and Public Policy at Florida State University. He received his Ph.D.

(1974) in Psychology from Carnegie-Mellon University. His research on expertise focuses on how people develop and preserve high-level performance across the life span. He has published more than 100 articles and chapters on the topics of expert performance, age, and human factors. He is on the editorial boards of *Psychology and Aging*, the *Journal of Gerontology: Psychological Sciences*, and *Gerontechnology.*

Paul J. Feltovich is a Research Scientist at the Florida Institute for Human and Machine Cognition, Pensacola, Florida. He has conducted research and published on topics such as expert-novice differences in complex cognitive skills, conceptual understanding and misunderstanding for complex knowledge, and novel means of instruction in complex and ill-structured knowledge domains. Since joining FIHMC, he has been investigating coordination, regulation, and teamwork in mixed groups of humans and intelligent software agents. He has authored nearly 100 professional articles and two prior books.

Robert R. Hoffman, Ph.D., is a Research Scientist at the Florida Institute for Human and Machine Cognition, Pensacola, Florida. He is also an Adjunct Instructor at the Department of Psychology of the University of West Florida in Pensacola. His research has garnered him a designation as one of the pioneers of Expertise Studies. Hoffman has been recognized on an international level in at least five disciplines – remote sensing, meteorology, experimental psychology, human factors, and artificial intelligence. Within psycholinguistics, he has made pioneering contributions, having founded the journal *Metaphor & Symbol*, and having written extensively on the theory of analogy. He is coeditor of the regular department "Human Centered Computing" in the journal *IEEE: Intelligent Systems.*

The Cambridge Handbook
of Expertise and Expert Performance

Edited by

K. Anders Ericsson
Florida State University

Neil Charness
Florida State University

Paul J. Feltovich
Florida Institute for Human and Machine Cognition

Robert R. Hoffman
Florida Institute for Human and Machine Cognition

CAMBRIDGE UNIVERSITY PRESS
Cambridge, New York, Melbourne, Madrid, Cape Town, Singapore,
São Paulo, Delhi, Dubai, Tokyo

Cambridge University Press
32 Avenue of the Americas, New York, NY 10013-2473, USA

www.cambridge.org
Information on this title: www.cambridge.org/9780521600811

First published 2006
Reprinted 2007 (twice), 2009 (twice)

Printed in the United States of America

A catalog record for this publication is available from the British Library.

Library of Congress Cataloging in Publication Data

The Cambridge handbook of expertise and expert performance / edited by
K. Anders Ericsson... [et al.]...
  p. cm.
Includes bibliographical references and index.
ISBN-13: 978-0-521-84097-2 (hardcover)
ISBN-10: 0-521-84097-X (hardcover)
ISBN-13: 978-0-521-60081-1 (pbk.)
ISBN-10: 0-521-60081-2 (pbk.)
1. Expertise. 2. Ability. 3. Performance – Psychological aspects. I. Ericsson,
K. Anders (Karl Anders), 1947–
BF431.C26835 2006
153.9 – dc22   2006002825

ISBN 978-0-521-84097-2 Hardback
ISBN 978-0-521-60081-1 Paperback

Anders Ericsson would like to dedicate this Handbook to his wife, Natalie; to his two children Lina and Jens; and to his grandson, Jakob.

Neil Charness would like to dedicate this Handbook to his wife, Beth; to his two children, Michelle and Alan; and to his two grandchildren, Benjamin and Madeline.

Paul Feltovich would like to dedicate this Handbook to his wife, Joan, and to his three children, Ellen, Andrew, and Anne.

Robert Hoffman would like to dedicate this Handbook to his wife, Robin, and to his two children Rachel and Eric.

Contents

PART V.B

ARTS, SPORTS, & MOTOR SKILLS

PART V.C

GAMES AND OTHER TYPES OF EXPERTISE

PART VI

GENERALIZABLE MECHANISMS MEDIATING EXPERTISE AND GENERAL ISSUES

Acknowledgments

Anders Ericsson wants to gratefully acknowledge the financial support provided by the John D. and Catherine T. MacArthur Foundation, Grant #32005-0, which supported the planning and the invitation of handbook authors during his year as a Fellow at the Center for Advanced Study in the Behavioral Sciences. He also would like to credit the Conradi Eminent Scholar Endowment at the Florida State Foundation for its support during the editing phase of the work on the handbook.

Neil Charness gratefully acknowledges support from the National Institutes of Health / National Institute on Aging, Grants R01 AG13969 and 1P01 AG 17211, that permitted him both to edit and contribute to chapters in this handbook.

Paul Feltovich and Robert Hoffman would like to acknowledge the Florida Institute for Human and Machine Cognition for support during the preparation of the handbook.

We also want to thank M. Anne Britt (Northern Illinois University), Jamie I. D. Campbell (University of Saskatchewan, Canada), Randall Davis (MIT), Leo Gugerty (Clemson University), Alice F. Healy (University of Colorado), Anastasia Kitsantas, (George Mason University), Reinhold Kliegl (University of Potsdam, Germany), Ralf Th. Krampe (University of Leuven, Belgium), Richard E. Mayer (University of California, Santa Barbara), Daniel Morrow (University of Illinois at Urbana-Champaign), Kathleen Mosier (San Francisco State University), Gary D. Phye (Iowa State University), Mauro Pesenti (Universite Catholique de Louvain, Belgium), Pertti Saariluoma (University of Jyväskylä, Finland), Mike Saks (University of Lincoln, UK), John B. Shea (Indiana University), Dean Keith Simonton (University of California, Davis), J. Michael Spector (Florida State University), Janet L. Starkes (McMaster University, Canada), Gershon Tenenbaum (Florida State University), Oliver Vitouch (University of Klagenfurt, Austria), and Richard K. Wagner (Florida State University) for their full-length reviews of particular chapters, along with the numerous authors of chapters within the handbook itself, who provided insightful comments and suggestions for other chapters in this volume.

Contributors

PHILLIP L. ACKERMAN
School of Psychology
Georgia Institute of Technology

RAY J. AMIRAULT
Instructional Technology
Wayne State University

JASON S. AUGUSTYN
Department of Psychology
University of Virginia

MARGARET E. BEIER
Department of Psychology
Rice University

ROBERT K. BRANSON
Instructional Systems
College of Education
Florida State University

LEE R. BROOKS
Department of Psychology
McMaster University

BRUCE BUCHANAN
Computer Science Department
University of Pittsburgh

C. SHAWN BURKE
Department of Psychology
Institute for Simulation & Training
University of Central Florida

BRIAN BUTTERWORTH
Institute of Cognitive Neuroscience
University College London

NEIL CHARNESS
Psychology Department
Florida State University

MICHELENE T. H. CHI
Learning Research and Development Center
University of Pittsburgh

ANNA T. CIANCIOLO
Command Performance Research, Inc.

WILLIAM J. CLANCEY
NASA/Ames Research Center

RAJAL G. COHEN
Department of Psychology
Pennsylvania State University

JEAN CÔTÉ
School of Physical and Health Education,
Queen's University

ANDREW DATTEL
Department of Psychology
Texas Tech University

RANDALL DAVIS
Computer Science and Artificial Intelligence
    Laboratory
Massachusetts Institute of Technology

Janice Deakin
School of Physical and Health Education,
Queen's University

Frank T. Durso
Department of Psychology
Texas Tech University

Mica Endsley
SA Technologies

K. Anders Ericsson
Department of Psychology
Florida State University

Kevin Eva
Clinical Epidemiology and Biostatistics
Faculty of Health Sciences
McMaster University

Julia Events
School of Sociology & Social Policy
University of Nottingham

Edward A. Feigenbaum
Department of Computer Science
Stanford University

Ulrike Felt
Institut für Wissenschaftsforschung
Universität Wien

Paul J. Feltovich
Florida Institute for Human and Machine
Cognition (FIHMC)

Stephen M. Fiore
Institute for Simulation & Training
University of Central Florida

Fernand Gobet
Department of Human Sciences
Brunel University

Gerald F. Goodwin
U.S. Army Research Institute

Hans Gruber
Institute for Education
University of Regensburg

Stanley J. Hamstra
Department of Surgery
University of Toronto

Peter Hancock.
Department of Psychology and
Institute for Simulation and Training
University of Central Florida

Andrew Harvey
Department of Economics
St. Mary's University

Nicole Hill
Learning Research and Development
Center
University of Pittsburgh

Nicola J. Hodges
School of Human Kinetics
University of British Columbia

Robert R. Hoffman
Florida Institute for Human and Machine
Cognition (FIHMC)

John L. Horn
Department of Psychology
University of Southern California

Earl Hunt
Department of Psychology
University of Washington

Steven A. Jax
Moss Rehabilitation Research Institute

Ronald T. Kellogg
Department of Psychology
Saint Louis University

Gary Klein
Klein Associates Inc

Ralf Th. Krampe
Department of Psychology
University of Leuven

Andreas C. Lehmann
Hochschule fuer Musik Wuerzburg

Gavan Lintern
Advanced Information Engineering Services, Inc
A General Dynamics Company

Clare Macmahon
Department of Psychology
Florida State University

Hiromi Masunaga
Department of Educational Psychology,
Administration, and Counseling
California State University, Long Beach

Cynthia T. Matthew
PACE Center
Yale University

Harald A. Mieg
Geographisches Institut
Humboldt-Universität zu Berlin

Cornelia Niessen
Department of Psychology
University of Konstanz

Helga Noice
Department of Psychology
Elmhurst College

TONY NOICE
Department of Theatre
Elmhurst College

GEOFF NORMAN
Clinical Epidemiology and Biostatistics
Faculty of Health Sciences
McMaster University

MICHAEL J. PRIETULA
Goizueta Business School
Emory University

ROBERT W. PROCTOR
Department of Psychological Sciences
Purdue University

MICHAEL ROSEN
Department of Psychology and
Institute for Simulation and Training
University of Central Florida

DAVID A. ROSENBAUM
Department of Psychology
Pennsylvania State University

KAROL G. ROSS
Klein Associates Inc

EDUARDO SALAS
Department of Psychology and
Institute for Simulation and Training
University of Central Florida

WALTER SCHNEIDER
Learning Research and Development
Center
University of Pittsburgh

JAN MAARTEN SCHRAAGEN
TNO Defence, Security and Safety

JENNIFER L. SHAFER
Klein Associates Inc

DEAN KEITH SIMONTON
Department of Psychology
University of California, Davis

SABINE SONNENTAG
Department of Psychology
University of Konstanz

JANET L. STARKES
Department of Kinesiology
McMaster University

ROBERT J. STERNBERG
School of Arts and Sciences
Tufts University

MICHAEL TSCHIRHART
Department of Psychology
University of Michigan

ELIZABETH R. VALENTINE
Department of Psychology
Royal Holloway
University of London

JUDITH VOLMER
Department of Psychology
University of Konstanz

JAMES F. VOSS
Learning Research and Development
Center
University of Pittsburgh

KIM-PHUONG L. VU
Department of Psychology
California State University Long Beach

RICHARD K. WAGNER
Florida Center for Reading Research
Department of Psychology
Florida State University

PAUL WARD
Human Performance Laboratory
Learning Systems Institute
Florida State University

ROBERT W. WEISBERG
Department of Psychology
Temple University

JOHN. M. WILDING,
Department of Psychology
Royal Holloway
University of London

JENNIFER WILEY
Department of Psychology
University of Illinois

A. MARK WILLIAMS
Research Institute for Sport and Exercise
Sciences
Liverpool John Moores University

J. FRANK YATES
Department of Psychology & Ross School
of Business
University of Michigan

BARRY J. ZIMMERMAN
Doctoral Program in Educational
Psychology
City University of New York

Part I

INTRODUCTION AND PERSPECTIVE

CHAPTER 1

An Introduction to *Cambridge Handbook of Expertise and Expert Performance*: Its Development, Organization, and Content

K. Anders Ericsson

A significant milestone is reached when a field of scientific research matures to a point warranting publication of its first handbook. A substantial body of empirical findings, distinctive theoretical concepts and frameworks, and a set of new or adapted methods justify a unifying volume. The growth of this field is evident from the publication of a series of edited books on diverse sets of skills and expertise from many domains during the last several decades (Anderson, 1981; Bloom, 1985a; Chase, 1973; Chi, Glaser, & Farr, 1988; Ericsson, 1996a; Ericsson & Smith, 1991a; Feltovich, Ford, & Hoffman, 1997; Hoffman, 1992; Starkes & Allard, 1993; Starkes & Ericsson, 2003). And as in many other fields, the name of a branch of scientific study, in our case expertise and expert performance, often communicates the domain of studied phenomena.

Expert, Expertise, and Expert Performance: Dictionary Definitions

Encyclopedias describe an **Expert** as "one who is very skillful and well-informed in some special field" (*Webster's New World Dictionary*, 1968, p. 168), or "someone widely recognized as a reliable source of knowledge, technique, or skill whose judgment is accorded authority and status by the public or his or her peers. Experts have prolonged or intense experience through practice and education in a particular field" (Wikipedia, 2005). **Expertise** then refers to the characteristics, skills, and knowledge that distinguish experts from novices and less experienced people. In some domains there are objective criteria for finding experts, who are consistently able to exhibit superior performance for representative tasks in a domain. For example, chess masters will almost always win chess games against recreational chess players in chess tournaments, medical specialists are far more likely to diagnose a disease correctly than advanced medical students, and professional musicians can perform pieces of music in a manner that is unattainable for less skilled musicians. These types of superior reproducible performances of representative tasks capture the essence of the respective domains, and authors have been encouraged to refer to them as *Expert Performance* in this handbook.

In some domains it is difficult for non-experts to identify experts, and consequently researchers rely on peer-nominations by professionals in the same domain. However, people recognized by their peers as experts do not always display superior performance on domain-related tasks. Sometimes they are no better than novices even on tasks that are central to the expertise, such as selecting stocks with superior future value, treatment of psychotherapy patients, and forecasts (Ericsson & Lehmann, 1996). There are several domains where experts disagree and make inconsistent recommendations for action, such as recommending selling versus buying the same stock. For example, expert auditors' assessments have been found to differ more from each other than the assessments of less experienced auditors (Bédard, 1991). Furthermore, experts will sometimes acquire differences from novices and other people as a function of their repetitive routines, which is a consequence of their extended experience rather than a cause for their superior performance. For example, medical doctors' handwriting is less legible than that of other health professionals (Lyons, Payne, McCabe, & Fielder, 1998). Finally, Shanteau (1988) has suggested that "experts" may not need a proven record of performance and can adopt a particular image and project "outward signs of extreme self-confidence" (p. 211) to get clients to listen to them and continue to offer advice after negative outcomes. After all, the experts are nearly always the best qualified to evaluate their own performance and explain the reasons for any deviant outcomes.

When the proposal for this *Handbook* was originally prepared, the outline focused more narrowly on the structure and acquisition of highly superior (expert) performance in many different domains (Ericsson, 1996b, 2004). In response to the requests of the reviewers of that proposal, the final outline of the handbook covered a broader field that included research on the development of expertise and how highly expe-rienced individuals accumulate knowledge in their respective domains and eventually become socially recognized experts and masters. Consequently, to reflect the scope of the *Handbook* it was entitled the *Cambridge Handbook of Expertise and Expert Performance*. The current handbook thus includes a multitude of conceptions of expertise, including perspectives from education, sociology, and computer science, along with the more numerous perspectives from psychology emphasizing basic abilities, knowledge, and acquired skills. In this introductory chapter, I will briefly introduce some general issues and describe the structure and content of the *Handbook* as it was approved by Cambridge University Press.

Tracing the Development of Our Knowledge of Expertise and Expert Performance

Since the beginning of Western civilization there has been a particular interest in the superior knowledge that experts have in their domain of expertise. The body of knowledge associated with the domain of expertise in which a person is expert is a particularly important difference between experts and other individuals. Much of this knowledge can be verbally described and shared with others to benefit decision making in the domain and can help educate students and facilitate their progress toward expertise. The special status of the knowledge of experts in their domain of expertise is acknowledged even as far back as the Greek civilization. Socrates said that

> *I observe that when a decision has to be taken at the state assembly about some matter of building, they send for the builders to give their advice about the buildings, and when it concerns shipbuilding they send for the shipwrights, and similarly in every case where they are dealing with a subject which they think can be learned and taught. But if anyone else tries to give advice, whom they don't regard as an expert, no matter how handsome or*

wealthy or well-born he is, they still will have none of him, but jeer at him and create an uproar, until either the would-be speaker is shouted down and gives up of his own accord, or else the police drag him away or put him out on the order of the presidents. (Plato, 1991, pp. 11–12)

Aristotle relied on his own senses as the primary source of scientific knowledge and sought out beekeepers, fishermen, hunters, and herdsmen to get the best and most reliable information for his books on science (Barnes, 2000). He even tried to explain occasional incorrect reports from some of his informants about how offspring of animals were generated. For example, some of them suggested that "the ravens and the ibises unite at the mouth" (Aristotle, 2000, p. 315). But Aristotle notes: "It is odd, however, that our friends do not reason out how the semen manages to pass through the stomach and arrive in the uterus, in view of the fact that the stomach concocts everything that gets into it, as it does the nourishment" (pp. 315 & 317). Similarly, "those who assert that the female fishes conceive as a result of swallowing the male's semen have failed to notice certain points" (p. 311). Aristotle explains that "Another point which helps to deceive these people is this. Fish of this sort take only a very short time over their copulation, with the result that many fishermen even never see it happening, for of course no fishermen ever watches this sort of thing for the sake of pure knowledge" (p. 313). Much of Aristotle's knowledge comes, at least partly, from consensus reports of professionals.

Much later during the Middle Ages, craftsmen formed guilds to protect themselves from competition. Through arrangements with the mayor and/or monarch they obtained a monopoly on providing particular types of handcraft and services with set quality standards (Epstein, 1991). They passed on their special knowledge of how to produce products, such as lace, barrels, and shoes, to their students (apprentices). Apprentices would typically start at around age 14 and commit to serve and study with their master for around 7 years – the length of time varied depending on the complex-

ity of the craft and the age and prior experience of the apprentice (Epstein, 1991). Once an apprentice had served out their contract they were given a letter of recommendation and were free to work with other masters for pay, which often involved traveling to other cities and towns – they were therefore referred to as journeymen. When a journeyman had accumulated enough additional skill and saved enough money, he, or occasionally she, would often return to his home town to inherit or purchase a shop with tools and apply to become a master of the guild. In most guilds they required inspection of the journeyman's best work, that is, master pieces, and in some guilds they administered special tests to assess the level of performance (Epstein, 1991). When people were accepted as masters they were held responsible for the quality of the products from their shop and were thereby allowed to take on the training of apprentices (See Amirault & Branson, Chapter 5, and Chi, Chapter 2, on the progression toward expertise and mastery of a domain).

In a similar manner, the scholars' guild was established in the 12th and 13th century as "a *universitas magistribus et pupillorum,*" or "guild of masters and students" (Krause, 1996, p. 9). Influenced by the University of Paris, most universities conducted all instruction in Latin, where the students were initially apprenticed as arts students until they successfully completed the preparatory (undergraduate) program and were admitted to the more advanced programs in medicine, law, or theology. To become a master, the advanced students needed to satisfy "a committee of examiners, then publicly defending a thesis, often in the town square and with local grocers and shoemakers asking questions" (Krause, 1996, p. 10). The goal of the universities was to accumulate and explain knowledge, and in the process masters organized the existing knowledge (See Amirault & Branson, Chapter 5). With the new organization of the existing knowledge of a domain, it was no longer necessary for individuals to discover the relevant knowledge and methods by themselves.

Today's experts can rapidly acquire the knowledge originally discovered and accumulated by preceding expert practitioners by enrolling in courses taught by skilled and knowledgeable teachers using specially prepared textbooks. For example, in the 13th century Roger Bacon argued that it would be impossible to master mathematics by the then-known methods of learning (self-study) in less than 30 to 40 years (Singer, 1958). Today the roughly equivalent material (calculus) is taught in highly organized and accessible form in every high school.

Sir Francis Bacon is generally viewed as one of the architects of the Enlightenment period of Western Civilization and one of the main proponents of the benefits of generating new scientific knowledge. In 1620 he described in his book *Novum Organum* his proposal for collecting and organizing all existing knowledge to help our civilization engage in learning to develop a better world. In it, he appended a listing of all topics of knowledge to be included in *Catalogus Historiarum Particularium*. It included a long list of skilled crafts, such as "History of weaving, and of ancillary skills associated with it," "History of dyeing," "History of leather-working, tanning, and of associated ancillary skills" (Rees & Wakely, 2004, p. 483).

The guilds guarded their knowledge and their monopoly of production. It is therefore not surprising that the same forces that eventually resulted in the French revolution were directed not only at the oppression by the king and the nobility, but also against the monopoly of services provided by the members of the guilds. Influenced by Sir Francis Bacon's call for an encyclopedic compilation of human knowledge, Diderot and D'Alembert worked on assembling all available knowledge in the first *Encyclopedie* (Diderot & D'Alembert, 1966–67), which was originally published in 1751–80.

Diderot was committed to the creation of comprehensive descriptions of the mechanical arts to make their knowledge available to the public and to encourage research and development in all stages of production and all types of skills, such as tannery, carpentry, glassmaking, and ironworking (Pannabecker, 1994), along with descriptions of how to sharpen a feather for writing with ink, as shown in Figure 1.1. His goal was to describe all the raw materials and tools that were necessary along with the methods of production. Diderot and his associate contributors had considerable difficulties gaining access to all the information because of the unwillingness of the guild members to answer their questions. Diderot even considered sending some of his assistants to become apprentices in the respective skills to gain access to all the relevant information (Pannabecker, 1994). In spite of all the information and pictures (diagrams of tools, workspaces, procedures, etc., as is illustrated in Figure 1.2 showing one of several plates of the process of printing) provided in the *Encyclopedie*, Diderot was under no illusion that the provided information would by itself allow anyone to become a craftsman in any of the described arts and wrote: "It is handicraft that makes the artist, and it is not in Books that one can learn to manipulate" (Pannabecker, 1994, p. 52). In fact, Diderot did not even address the higher levels of cognitive activity, "such as intuitive knowledge, experimentation, perceptual skills, problem-solving, or the analysis of conflicting or alternative technical approaches" (Pannabecker, 1994, p. 52).

A couple of years after the French revolution the monopoly of the guilds as eliminated (Fitzsimmons, 2003), including the restrictions on the practice of medicine and law. After the American Revolution and the creation of the United States of America laws were initially created to require that doctors and lawyers be highly trained based on the apprenticeship model, but pressure to eliminate elitist tendencies led to the repeal of those laws. From 1840 to the end of the 19th century there was no requirement for certification to practice medicine and law in the United States (Krause, 1996). However, with time both France and America realized the need to restrict vital medical and legal services to qualified professionals and developed procedures for training and certification.

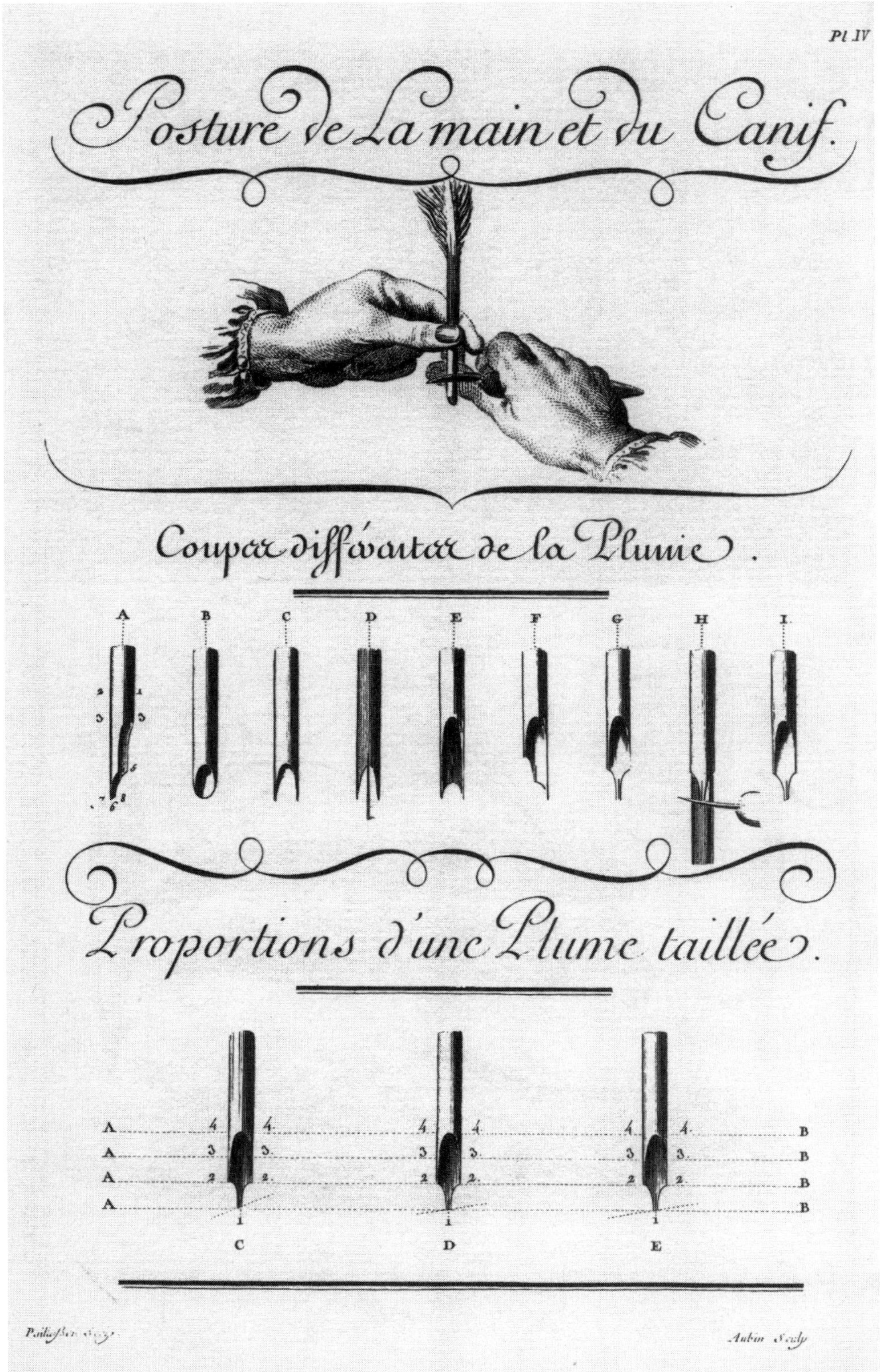

Figure 1.1. An illustration for how to sharpen a goose feather for writing with ink from Plate IV in the entry on "Ecriture" in the 23rd volume of *Encyclopedie ou dictionnare de raisonne des sciences, des artes et des métier* (Diderot & D'Alembert, 1966–67).

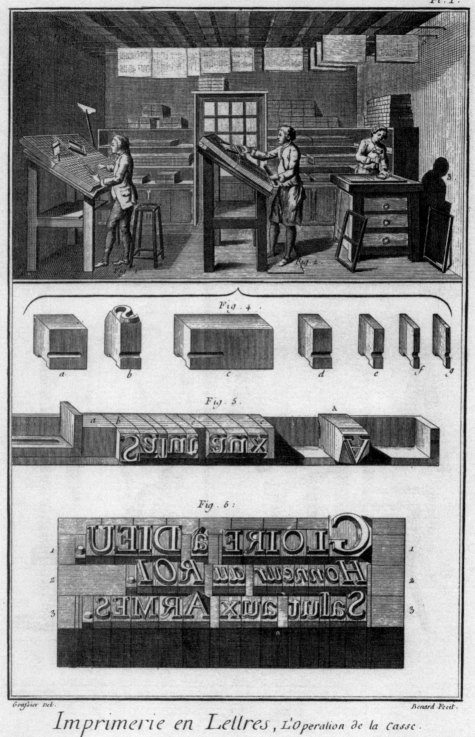

Figure 1.2. An illustration of the workspace of a printer with some of his type elements from Plate I in the entry on "Imprimerie" in the 28th volume of *Encyclopedie ou dictionnare de raisonne des sciences, des artes et des métier* (Diderot & D'Alembert, 1966–67).

Over the last couple of centuries there have been several major changes in the relation between master and apprentice. For example, before the middle of the 19th century children of poor families would often be taken on by teachers in exchange for a contractual claim for part of the future dancers', singers', or musicians' earnings as an adult (Rosselli, 1991). Since then the state has gotten more involved in the training of their expert performers, even outside the traditional areas of academia and professional training in medicine, law, business, and engineering. In the late 19th century, public institutions such as the Royal Academy of Music were established to promote the development of very high levels of skill in music to allow native students compete with better trained immigrants (Rohr, 2001). In a similar manner during the latter part of the 20th century, many countries invested in schools and academies for the development of highly skilled athletes for improved success in competitions during the Olympic Games and World Championships (Bloomfield, 2004).

More generally, over the last century there have been economic developments with public broadcasts of competitions and performances that generate sufficient revenue for a number of domains of expertise, such as sports and chess, to support professional full-time performers as well as coaches, trainers, and teachers. In these new domains, along with the traditional professions, current and past expert performers continue to be the primary teachers at the advanced level (masters), and their professional associations have the responsibility of certifying acceptable performance and the permission to practice. Accordingly, they hold the clout in thus influencing training in professional schools, such as law, medical, nursing, and business schools – "testing is the tail that wags the dog" (Feltovich, personal communication) – as well as continuing education training (see Evetts, Meig, & Felt, Chapter 7 on sociological perspectives on expertise). The accumulation of knowledge about the structure and acquisition of expertise in a given domain, as well as knowledge about the instruction and training of future professionals, has occurred, until quite recently, almost exclusively within each domain with little cross-fertilization of domains in terms of teaching, learning methods, and skill-training techniques.

It is not immediately apparent what is generalizable across such diverse domains of expertise, such as music, sport, medicine, and chess. What could possibly be shared by the skills of playing difficult pieces by Chopin, running a mile in less than four minutes, and playing chess at a high level? The premise for a field studying expertise and expert performance is that there are sufficient similarities in the theoretical principles mediating the phenomena and the methods for studying them in different domains that it would be possible to propose a general theory of expertise and expert performance. All of these domains of expertise have been created by humans. Thus the accumulated knowledge and skills are likely to reflect similarities in structure that reflect both human biological and psychological factors, as well as cultural factors. This raises many challenging problems for methodologies used to describe the organization of knowledge and mechanisms and reveals the mediating expert performance that generalizes across domains.

Once we know how experts organize their knowledge and their performance, is it possible to improve the efficiency of learning to reach higher levels of expert performance in these domains? It should also be possible to answer why different individuals improve their performance at different rates and why different people reach very different levels of final achievement. Would a deeper understanding of the development and its mediating mechanisms make it possible to select individuals with unusual potential and to design better developmental environments to increase the proportion of performers who reach the highest levels? Would it be possible even to facilitate the development of those rare individuals who make major creative contributions to their respective domains?

Conceptions of Generalizable Aspects of Expertise

Several different theoretical frameworks have focused on broad issues on attaining expert performance that generalize across different domains of expertise.

Individual Differences in Mental Capacities

A widely accepted theoretical concept argues that general innate mental capacities mediate the attainment of exceptional performance in most domains of expertise. In his famous book, "*Heriditary Genius,*" Galton (1869/1979) proposed that across a wide range of domains of intellectual activity the same innate factors were required to attain outstanding achievement and the designation of being a genius. He analyzed eminent individuals in many domains in Great Britain and found that these eminent individuals were very often the offspring of a small number of families – with much higher frequency than could be expected by chance. The descendents from these families were much more likely to make eminent contributions in very diverse domains of activity, such as becoming famous politicians, scientists, judges, musicians, painters, and authors. This observation led Galton to suggest that there must be a heritable potential that allows some people to reach an exceptional level in any one of many different domains. After reviewing the evidence that height and body size were heritable Galton (1869/1979) argued: "Now, if this be the case with stature, then it will be true as regards every other physical feature – as circumference of head, size of brain, weight of grey matter, number of brain fibres, &c.; and thence, a step on which no physiologist will hesitate, as regards mental capacity" (pp. 31–32, emphasis added).

Galton clearly acknowledged the need for training to reach high levels of performance in any domain. However, he argued that improvements are rapid only in the *beginning* of training and that subsequent increases become increasingly smaller, until "maximal performance becomes a rigidly determinate quantity" (p. 15). Galton developed a number of different mental tests of individual differences in mental capacity. Although he never related these measures to the objective performance of experts on particular real-world tasks, his views led to the common practice of using psychometric tests for admitting students into professional schools and academies for arts and sports with severely limited availability of slots. These tests of basic ability and talent were believed to identify the students with the capacity for reaching the highest levels.

In the 20th century scientists began the psychometric testing of large groups of experts to measure their powers of mental speed, memory, and intelligence. When the experts' performance was compared to control groups of comparable education, there was no evidence for Galton's hypothesis of a general superiority for experts because the demonstrated superiority of experts was found to be limited to specific aspects related to the particular domain of expertise. For example, the superiority of the chess experts' memory was constrained to regular chess positions and did not generalize to other types of materials (Djakow, Petrowski, & Rudik, 1927). Not even IQ could distinguish the best among chess players (Doll & Mayr, 1987) or the most successful and creative among artists and scientists (Taylor, 1975).

In a recent review, Ericsson and Lehmann (1996) found that (1) measures of basic mental capacities are not valid predictors of attainment of expert performance in a domain, (2) the superior performance of experts is often very domain specific, and transfer outside their narrow area of expertise is surprisingly limited, and (3) systematic differences between experts and less proficient individuals nearly always reflect attributes acquired by the experts during their lengthy training. The reader is directed to the chapter by Horn and Masunaga (chapter 34) and to comprehensive reviews in Sternberg and Grigorenko, 2003, and Howe, Davidson, and Sloboda. 1998.

Expertise as the Extrapolation of Everyday Skill to Extended Experience

A second general type of theoretical frameworks is based on the assumption that the same learning mechanisms that account for the acquisition of everyday skills can be extended to the acquisition of higher levels of skills and expertise. Studies in the 19th century proposed that the acquisition of high levels of skills was a natural consequence of extended experience in the domains of expertise. For example, Bryan and Harter (1899) argued that ten years of experience were required to become a professional telegrapher. The most influential and pioneering work on expertise was conducted in the 1940s by Adrian de Groot (1978), who invited international chess masters and skilled club players to "think aloud" while they selected the best move for chess positions. His analyses of the protocols showed that the elite players were able to recognize and generate chess moves that were superior to skilled club players by relying on acquired patterns and planning (see Gobet & Charness, chapter 30, and Ericsson, chapter 13, for a more detailed account). DeGroot's dissertation was later translated into English in the late 1960s and early 1970s (deGroot, 1978) and had substantial impact on the seminal theory of expertise proposed by Herb Simon and Bill Chase (Simon & Chase, 1973).

In the 1950s and 1960s Newell and Simon proposed how information-processing models of human problem solving could be implemented as computer programs, such as the General Problem Solver (Ernst & Newell, 1969). In their seminal book, *Human Problem Solving*, Newell and Simon (1972) argued that domain-general problem solving was limited and that the thinking involved in solving most tasks could be represented as the execution of a sequence of production rules – such as IF <pattern>, THEN <action> – that incorporated specific knowledge about the task environment. In their theory of expertise, Simon and Chase (1973) made the fundamental assumption that the same patterns (chunks) that allowed the experts to retrieve suitable actions from memory were the same patterns that mediated experts' superior memory for the current situation in a game. Instead of studying the representative task of playing chess, namely, selecting the best moves for chess positions (Ericsson & Smith, 1991b; Vicente & Wang, 1998), Chase and Simon (1973) redirected the focus of research toward studying performance of memory tasks as a more direct method of studying the characteristics of patterns that mediate improvement in skill. They found that there was a clear relation between the number of chess pieces recalled from briefly presented chess positions and the player's level of chess expertise. Grand masters were able to reproduce almost the entire chessboards (24 to 26 pieces) by recalling a small number of complex chunks, whereas novices could recall only around 4 pieces, where each piece was a chunk. The masters' superior memory was assumed to depend on an acquired body of many different patterns in memory because their memory for randomly rearranged chess configurations was markedly reduced. In fact in such configurations they could recall only around 5 to 7 pieces, which was only slightly better than the recall of novices.

Experts' superiority for representative but not randomly rearranged stimuli has since been demonstrated in a large number of domains. The relation between the mechanisms mediating memory performance and the mechanisms mediating representative performance in the same domains have been found to be much more complex than originally proposed by Simon and Chase (1973) (see Gobet & Charness, Chapter 30, and Wilding & Valentine, Chapter 31. See also Ericsson & Kintsch, 1995; Ericsson, Patel, & Kintsch, 2000; Gobet & Simon, 1996; Simon & Gobet, 2000; Vicente & Wang, 1998).

Expertise as Qualitatively Different Representation and Organization of Knowledge

A different family of approaches drawing on the Simon-Chase theory of expertise has focused on the content and organization of the experts' knowledge (Chi, Feltovich, & Glaser, 1981; Chi, Glaser, & Rees, 1982) and on methods to extract the experts knowledge to build computer-based models emulating the experts' performance (Hoffman, 1992). These approaches have studied experts, namely, individuals who are socially recognized as experts and/or distinguished by their extensive experience (typically over 10 years) and by knowledge of a particular subject attained through instruction, study, or practical experience. The work of Robert Glaser, Micheline Chi, and Paul Feltovich examined the representations of knowledge and problem solutions in academic domains, such as physics (See Chi, Chapters 3 and 10). Of particular importance, Chi studied children with extensive knowledge of chess and dinosaurs (See Chi, Chapter 10), and found these children displayed many of the same characteristics of the knowledge representation of adult experts. This work on expertise is summarized in Feltovich, Prietula, and Ericsson, Chapter 4, Chi, Chapter 10, and Hoffman and Lintern, Chapter 12, and in a couple of edited volumes (Chi, Glaser, & Farr, 1988; Starkes & Allard, 1993).

In a parallel development in the computer science of the late 1970s and early 1980s, Ed Feigenbaum and other researchers in the area of artificial intelligence and cognitive science have attempted to elicit the knowledge of experts (Hoffman, 1992) and to incorporate their knowledge in computer models (c.f. expert systems) that seek to replicate some of the decision making and behavior of experts (see Buchanan, Davis, & Feigenbaum, Chapter 6, and Hoffman & Lintern, Chapter 12). There has been a longstanding controversy over whether highly experienced experts are capable of articulating the knowledge and methods that control their generation of appropriate actions in complex situations.

The tradition of skill acquisition of Bryan and Harter (1899), Fitts and Posner (1967), and Simon and Chase (1973) assumed that expert performance was associated with automation and was virtually effortless performance based on pattern recognition and direct access of actions. However, Polanyi (1962, 1966) is generally recognized as the first critic who saw that nonconscious and intuitive mediation limits the possibility of eliciting and mapping the knowledge and rules that mediates experts' intuitive actions. Subsequent discussion of the development of expertise by Dreyfus and Dreyfus (1986) and Benner (1984) has argued that the highest levels of expertise are characterized by contextually based intuitive actions that are difficult or impossible to report verbally. Several chapters in this handbook propose methods for uncovering tacit knowledge about the successful development of expertise (Cianciolo, Matthew, Wagner, & Sternberg, Chapter 35), about methods of work through observation (Clancey, Chapter 8), Concept Mapping (Hoffman & Lintern, Chapter 12), similarity judgment (Chi, Chapter 10), and traditional psychometric analyses of individual differences in performance (Ackerman & Beier, Chapter 9) or simulated environments (Ward, Williams, & Hancock, Chapter 14). Other investigators argue that expert performers often continue to engage in deliberate practice in order to improve and that these performers have to actively retain and refine their mental representations for monitoring and controlling their performance. This retained ability to monitor performance allows them to give informative concurrent and retrospective reports about the mediating sequences of thoughts (see Ericsson, Chapter 13).

Expertise as Elite Achievement Resulting from Superior Learning Environments

There are other approaches to the study of expertise that have focused on objective achievement. There is a long tradition of influential studies with interviews of peer-nominated eminent scientists (Roe, 1952) and analyses of biographical data on Nobel Prize winners (Zuckerman, 1977) (see Simonton, Chapter 18, 1994, for a more extensive account). In a seminal study, Benjamin Bloom and his colleagues (Bloom, 1985a) interviewed international-level performers from six different domains of expertise ranging from swimming to molecular genetics. All of the 120 participants had won prizes at international competitions in their respective domains. They were all interviewed about their development, as were their parents, teachers, and coaches. For example, Bloom and his colleagues collected information on the development of athletes who had won international competitions in swimming and tennis. They also interviewed artists who have won international competitions in sculpting and piano playing and scientists who had won international awards in mathematics and molecular biology. In each of these six domains Bloom (1985b) found evidence for uniformly favorable learning environments for the participants. Bloom (1985b) concluded that the availability of early instruction and support by their family appeared to be necessary for attaining an international level of performance as an adult. He found that the elite performers typically started early to engage in relevant training activities in the domain and were supported both by exceptional teachers and committed parents. One of the contributors to the *Handbook*, Lauren Sosniak (1985a, 1985b, 1985c, 1985d), describes in Chapter 16 the main findings from the original study (Bloom, 1985a), along with more recent interview studies aimed to uncover the development of elite performers.

Expertise as Reliably Superior (Expert) Performance on Representative Tasks

It is difficult to identify the many mediating factors that might have been responsible for the elite performer to win an award and to write a groundbreaking book. When eminence and expertise is based on a singular or small number of unique creative products, such as books, paintings, or musical as compositions, it is rarely possible to identify and study scientifically the key factors that allowed these people to produce these achievements. Consequently, Ericsson and Smith (1991b) proposed that the study of expertise with laboratory rigor requires representative tasks that capture the essence of expert performance in a specific domain of expertise. For example, a world-class sprinter will be able to reproduce superior running performance on many tracks and even indoors in a large laboratory. Similarly, de Groot (1978) found that the ability to select the best move for presented chess positions is the best correlate of chess ratings and performance at chess tournaments – a finding that has been frequently replicated (Ericsson & Lehmann, 1996; van der Maas & Wagenmakers, 2005). Once it is possible to reproduce the reliably superior performance of experts in a controlled setting, such as a laboratory, it then becomes feasible to examine the specific mediating mechanisms with experiments and process-tracing techniques, such as think aloud verbal reports (see Ericsson, Chapter 13, and Ericsson & Smith, 1991b). The discovery of representative tasks that measure adult expert performance under standardized conditions in a controlled setting, such as a laboratory, makes it possible to measure and compare the performance of less-skilled individuals on the same tasks. Even more important, it allows scientists to test aspiring performers many times during their development of expertise, allowing the measurement of gradual increases in performance.

The new focus on the measurement of expert performance with standardized tasks revealed that "experts," that is, individuals identified by their reputation or their extensive experience, are not always able to exhibit reliably superior performance. There are at least some domains where "experts" perform no better than less-trained individuals and that sometimes experts' decisions are no more accurate than beginners' decisions and simple decision aids (Camerer & Johnson, 1991; Bolger & Wright, 1992). Most individuals who start as active professionals or as beginners in a domain change their behavior and increase their performance for a limited time until they reach an acceptable level. Beyond this point, however, further improvements appear to be unpredictable and the number of years of work and leisure experience in a domain is a poor predictor of attained performance (Ericsson & Lehmann, 1996). Hence, continued improvements (changes) in achievement are not automatic consequences of more experience, and in those domains where performance consistently increases, aspiring experts seek out particular kinds of experience, that is, deliberate practice (Ericsson, Krampe, & Tesch-Römer, 1993). Such activities are designed, typically by a teacher, for the sole purpose of effectively improving specific aspects of an individual's performance. A large body of research shows how deliberate practice can change mediating mechanisms and that the accumulated amounts of deliberate practice are related to the attained level of performance (see Ericsson, Chapter 38, and Deakin, Coté, & Harvey, Chapter 17, Zimmerman, Chapter 38, as well as the edited books by Ericsson [1996a] and Starkes & Ericsson [2003]).

General Comments

In summary, there are a broad range of approaches to the study of the structure and acquisition of expertise as well as expert performance. Although individual researchers and editors may be committed to one approach over the others, this *Handbook* has been designed to fairly cover a wide range of approaches and research topics in order to allow authors to express their different views. However, the authors have been encouraged to describe explicitly their empirical criteria for their key terms, such as "experts" and "expert performance." For example, the authors have been asked to report if the cited research findings involve experts identified by social criteria, criteria of lengthy domain-related experience, or criteria based on reproducibly superior performance on a particular set of tasks representative of the individuals' domain of expertise.

General Outline of the Handbook

The handbook is organized into six general sections. First, Section 1 introduces the *Handbook* with brief accounts of general perspectives on expertise. In addition to this introductory chapter that outlines the organization of the handbook, there are chapters by two of the pioneers of the study of cognitive skill and expertise. Michelene Chi (Chapter 2) describes two approaches to the study of expertise and Earl Hunt (Chapter 3) gives his general perspective on the principal factors related to expertise. In a recent book Hunt (1995) has made a convincing case for the increasing importance of high levels of skill in occupations of the future. He argues that with the development of technology to automate less complex jobs the most important occupations of the future will require creative design and planning that cannot be easily automated. He foresees a rapidly increasing need to train students to even higher levels of expertise to continue the development of our modern society. The key competitive differences between companies of the future may not have to do with raw materials and monetary resources but with human capital, namely, the abilities of the employees. The Nobel Prize winner Gary Becker has for a long time made the case for the critical role of education and human capital in our current industrialized world, and especially the crucial role of highly accomplished people. He (Becker, 2002) illustrated this claim by a quote from Microsoft founder Bill Gates: Take our 20 best people away and ... Microsoft would become an unimportant company" (Becker, 2002, p. 8).

The second section of the *Handbook* contains reviews of the historical development of the study of expertise in four major disciplines, namely, psychology, education, computer science, and sociology. Three pioneers in the psychological study of expertise, Paul Feltovich, Michael Prietula, and Anders Ericsson, describe the development of the study of expertise in psychology (Chapter 4). One of the pioneers in the development of instructional design, Robert Branson, has together with Ray Amirault (Chapter 5) described the role of expertise in the historical development of educational methods and theories. Three of the pioneers in the development of expert systems, Bruce Buchanan, Randall Davis, and Edward Feigenbaum (Chapter 6), describe the role of expertise in shaping contemporary approaches in computer science and artificial intelligence. Finally, Julia Evetts, Harald Mieg, and Ulrike Felt (Chapter 7) provide a description of the relevant approaches to the study of expertise from the point of view of sociology.

The next two sections of the *Handbook* review the core methods for studying the structure (Section 3) and acquisition (Section 4) of expertise and expert performance. Each of the chapters in Sections 3 and 4 has been written by one of the pioneering researchers who have developed these methods and approaches for use in research on expertise and expert performance. The chapters consist of a historical background, a detailed description of the recommended methodology with a couple of examples, and a general review of the type of empirical evidence that has been collected. In the first chapter of Section 3 William Clancey (Chapter 8) gives an overview of the ethnographic observational methods for studying the behavior of experts. Philip Ackerman and Margaret Beier (Chapter 9) review the use of psychometric methods for studying expertise. Michelene Chi (Chapter 10) describes how laboratory methods have been used to assess the structure of knowledge. Jan Maarten Schraagen (Chapter 11) describes how tasks presented to skilled and less-skilled individuals can be analyzed and how a task analysis can guide data analysis and theory construction. Robert Hoffman and Gavin Lintern (Chapter 12) review methods for how knowledge of experts can be elicited and represented by interviews, Concept Maps, and abstraction-decomposition diagrams. Anders Ericsson (Chapter 13) describes how the elicitation of "think-aloud" protocols can allow investigators to trace the thought processes of experts while they perform representative tasks from their domain. Finally, Paul Ward, Mark Williams, and Peter Hancock (Chapter 14) review how simulated environments can both be used to measure experts' representative performance as well as be used for training.

Section 4 contains chapters examining methods for studying how skill, expertise, and expert performance develop and are acquired through practice. In the first chapter, Robert Proctor and Kim-Phuon Vu (Chapter 15) describe how laboratory methods for the study of skilled performance can inform research on expertise and expert performance. Lauren Sosniak (Chapter 16) discusses how she and her colleagues used retrospective interviews to describe the development of expertise in the classic studies led by Benjamin Bloom (1985a), along with some recent extensions of that work. Janice Deakin, Jean Côté, and Andrew Harvey (Chapter 17) use diaries and describe different methods to study how expert performers spend their time and how experts allocate their practice time. In the final chapter of this section, Dean Simonton (Chapter 18) reviews the methods of historiometrics and how data about the development of eminent performers can be collected and analyzed.

Section 5 consists of fifteen chapters that review our current knowledge about expertise and expert performance in particular domains and represents the core of this *Handbook*. Each chapter has been written by internationally respected experts on the associated areas of expertise and contains a brief historic background followed by a review and future directions. The chapters in Section 5 have been broken down into three subsections. The first subsection is focused on different types of professional expertise, namely, medicine (Chapter 19 by Geoff Norman, Kevin Eva, Lee Brooks, and Stan Hamstra), transportation, such as driving, flying, and airplane control (Chapter 20 by Francis Durso and Andrew Dattel), software design (Chapter 21 by Sabine Sonnentag, Cornelia Niessen, and Judith Volmer), and writing (Chapter 22 by Ronald Kellogg). There are two chapters on various aspects of decision making, namely, judgments in dynamic situations (natural decision making, Chapter 23 by Karol Ross, Jennifer Shafer, and Gary Klein) and decision-making expertise (Chapter 24 by Frank Yates & Michael Tschirhart), followed by Chapter 25 by Eduardo Salas, Michael Rosen, Shawn Burke, Gerald Goodwin, and Stephen Fiore on research on expert teams. The second subsection contains chapters that review expert performance in music

(Chapter 26 by Andreas Lehmann and Hans Gruber) and in sports (Chapter 27 by Nicola Hodges, Janet Starkes, and Clare MacMahon), and expertise in other types of arts, such as acting, ballet, and dance (Chapter 28 by Helga Noice and Tony Noice). The final chapter in this subsection reviews research on perceptual-motor skills (Chapter 29 by David Rosenbaum, Jason Augustyn, Rajal Cohen, and Steven Jax). The third and final subsection covers the findings in a diverse set of domains of expertise, including games. The first chapter (Chapter 30 by Fernand Gobet and Neil Charness) describes the pioneering and influential work on expertise in the game of chess. The next chapter (Chapter 31 by John Wilding and Elizabeth Valentine) reviews research on exceptional memory, in particular for information that most people have difficulty remembering, such as numbers, names, and faces. The last two chapters review research on mathematical ability and expertise (Chapter 32 by Brian Butterworth) and expertise in history (Chapter 33 by Jim Voss and Jennifer Wiley) – an example of a knowledge-based domain.

In the last section of the *Handbook* we have invited some of the world's leading researchers on general theoretical issues that are cutting across different domains of expertise to review the current state of knowledge. In the first chapter John Horn and Hiromi Masunaga (Chapter 34) discuss the relation between general intelligence and expertise. In the following chapter Anna Cianciolo, Cynthia Mattew, Richard Wagner, and Robert Sternberg (Chapter 35) review the relation between expertise and central concepts, such as practical intelligence and tacit knowledge. Mica Endsley (Chapter 36) reviews evidence for situational awareness, namely, experts' superior ability to perceive and monitor critical aspects of situations during performance. The next three chapters focus on aspects of learning. Nicole Hill and Walter Schneider (Chapter 37) review the neurological evidence on physiological adaptations resulting from the acquisition of expertise. Anders Ericsson (Chapter 38) reviews the evidence

for the key role of deliberate practice in causing physiological adaptations and the acquisition of mechanisms that mediate expert performance. Finally, Barry Zimmerman (Chapter 39) describes the importance of self-regulated learning in the development of expertise. The last three chapters review general issues in expertise. Ralf Krampe and Neil Charness (Chapter 40) review the effects of aging on expert performance and how it might be counteracted. Harald Mieg (Chapter 41) reviews the importance of social factors in the development of expertise. Finally, Robert Weisberg (Chapter 42) discusses the relation between expertise and creativity.

Conclusion

This *Handbook* has been designed to provide researchers, students, teachers, coaches, and anyone interested in attaining expertise with a comprehensive reference to methods, findings, and theories related to expertise and expert performance. It can be an essential tool for researchers, professionals, and students involved in the study or the training of expert performance and a necessary source for college and university libraries, as well as public libraries. In addition, the *Handbook* is designed to provide a suitable text for graduate courses on expertise and expert performance. More generally, it is likely that professionals, graduate students, and even undergraduates who aspire to higher levels of performance in a given domain can learn from experts' pathways to superior performance in similar domains.

Many researchers studying expertise and expert performance are excited and personally curious about the established research findings that most types of expertise require at least a decade of extended efforts to attain the mechanisms mediating superior performance. There is considerable knowledge that is accumulating about generalizations across many domains about the acquisition and refinement of these mechanisms during an extended period of deliberate practice. The generalizable insights range from the characteristics of ideal training environments, to the methods for fostering motivation by providing both emotional support and attainable training tasks of a suitable difficulty level. This theoretical framework has several implications.

It implies that if someone is interested in the upper limits of human performance and the most effective training to achieve the highest attainable levels, they should study the training techniques and performance limits of experts who have spent their entire life maximizing their performance. This assumption also implies that the study of expert performance will provide us with the best current evidence on what is humanly possible to achieve with today's methods of training and how these elite performers are able to achieve their highest levels of performance. Given that performance levels are increasing every decade in most domains of expertise, scientists will need to work with elite performers and their coaches to discover jointly the ever-increasing levels of improved performance.

The framework has implications for education and professional training of performance for all the preliminary levels that lead up to the expert levels in professional domains of expertise. By examining how the prospective expert performers attained lower levels of achievement, we should be able to develop practice environments and foster learning methods that help people to attain the fundamental representations of the tasks and the self-regulatory skills that were necessary for the prospective experts to advance their learning to higher levels.

With the rapid changes in the relevant knowledge and techniques required for most jobs, nearly everyone will have to continue their learning and even intermittently relearn aspects of their professional skills. The life-long quest for improved adaptation to task demands will not be limited to experts anymore. We will all need to adopt the characteristics and the methods of the expert performers who continuously strive to attain and maintain their best level of achievement.

References

Anderson, J. R. (Ed.) (1981). *Cognitive skills and their acquisition*. Hillsdale, NJ: Erlbaum .

Aristotle (2000). *Generation of animals* (Translated by A. L. Pick and first published in 1942). Cambridge, MA: Harvard Univesity Press.

Barnes, J. (2000). *Aristotle: A very short introduction*. Oxford: Oxford University Press.

Becker, G. S. (2002). The age of human capital. In E. P. Lazear (Ed.), *Education in the twenty-first century* (pp. 3–8). Stanford,CA: Hoover Institution Press.

Bédard, J. (1991). Expertise and its relation to audit decision quality. *Contemporary Accounting Research*, 8, 198–222.

Benner, P. E. (1984). *From novice to expert – Excellence and power in clinical nursing practice*. Menlo Park, CA: Addison-Wesley.

Bloom, B. S. (Ed.) (1985a). *Developing talent in young people*. New York: Ballantine Books.

Bloom, B. S. (1985b). Generalizations about talent development. In B. S. Bloom (Ed.), *Developing talent in young people* (pp. 507–549). New York: Ballantine Books.

Bloomfield, J. (2004). *Australia's sporting success: The inside story*. Sydney, Australia: University of South Wales Press.

Bolger, F., & Wright, G. (1992). Reliability and validity in expert judgment. In G. Wright and F. Bolger (Eds.), *Expertise and decision support* (pp. 47–76). New York: Plenum.

Bryan, W. L., & Harter, N. (1899). Studies on the telegraphic language: The acquisition of a hierarchy of habits. *Psychological Review*, 6, 345–375.

Camerer, C. F., & Johnson, E. J. (1991). The process-performance paradox in expert judgment: How can the experts know so much and predict so badly? In K. A. Ericsson and J. Smith (Eds.), *Towards a general theory of expertise: Prospects and limits* (pp. 195–217). Cambridge: Cambridge University Press.

Chase, W. G. (Ed.) (1973). *Visual information processing*. New York: Academic Press.

Chase, W. G., & Simon, H. A. (1973). The mind's eye in chess. In W. G. Chase (Ed.), *Visual information processing* (pp. 215–281). New York: Academic Press.

Chi, M. T. H., Feltovich, P. J., & Glaser, R. (1981). Categorization and representation of physics problems by experts and novices. *Cognitive Science*, 5, 121–152.

Chi, M. T. H., Glaser, R., & Farr, M. J. (Eds.) (1988). *The nature of expertise*. Hillsdale, NJ: Erlbaum.

Chi, M. T. H., Glaser, R., & Rees, E. (1982). Expertise in problem solving. In R. S. Sternberg (Ed.). *Advances in the psychology of human intelligence* (Vol. 1, pp. 1–75). Hillsdale, NJ: Erlbaum.

De Groot, A. (1978). *Thought and choice in chess*. (Original by published in 1946). The Hague, the Netherlands: Mouton.

Diderot, D., & D'Alembert, J. L. R. (Eds.) (1966–67). *Encyclopedie ou dictionnaie de raisonne' des sciences, des artes et des métier [Encyclopedia or dictionary of the sciences, arts, and occupations]*. (Originally published 1751–80). Stuttgart-Bad Cannstatt, Gemany: Frommann.

Djakow, Petrowski, & Rudik (1927). *Psychologie des Schachspiels [Psychology of chess]*. Berlin: Walter de Gruyter.

Doll, J., & Mayr, U. (1987). Intelligenz und Schachleistung – eine Untersuchung an Schachexperten. [Intelligence and achievement in chess – a study of chess masters]. *Psychologische Beiträge, 29*, 270–289.

Dreyfus, H. L., & Dreyfus, S. E. (1986). *Mind over machine: The power of intuition and expertise in the era of the computer*. New York: The Free Press.

Epstein, S. A. (1991). *Wage, labor, & guilds in medieval Europe*. Chapel Hill, NC: North Carolina University Press.

Ericsson, K. A. (Ed.) (1996a). *The road to excellence: The acquisition of expert performance in the arts and sciences, sports, and games*. Mahwah, NJ: Erlbaum.

Ericsson, K. A. (1996b). The acquisition of expert performance: An introduction to some of the issues. In K. A. Ericsson (Ed.), *The road to excellence: The acquisition of expert performance in the arts and sciences, sports, and games* (pp. 1–50). Mahwah, NJ: Erlbaum.

Ericsson, K. A. (2004). Deliberate practice and the acquisition and maintenance of expert performance in medicine and related domains. *Academic Medicine, 10*, S70–S81.

Ericsson, K. A., & Kintsch, W. (1995). Long-term working memory. *Psychological Review, 102*, 211–245.

Ericsson, K. A., Krampe, R. T., & Tesch-Römer, C. (1993). The role of deliberate practice in the acquisition of expert performance. *Psychological Review, 100*, 363–406.

Ericsson, K. A., & Lehmann, A. C. (1996). Expert and exceptional performance: Evidence on maximal adaptations on task constraints. *Annual Review of Psychology, 47*, 273–305.

Ericsson, K. A., Patel, V. L., & Kintsch, W. (2000). How experts' adaptations to representative task demands account for the expertise effect in memory recall: Comment on Vicente and Wang (1998). *Psychological Review, 107*, 578–592.

Ericsson, K. A., & Smith, J. (Eds.) (1991a). *Toward a general theory of expertise: Prospects and limits*. Cambridge: Cambridge University Press.

Ericsson, K. A., & Smith, J. (1991b). Prospects and limits in the empirical study of expertise: An introduction. In K. A. Ericsson and J. Smith (Eds.), *Toward a general theory of expertise: Prospects and limits* (pp. 1–38). Cambridge: Cambridge University Press.

Ernst, G. W., & Newell, A. (1969). *GPS: A case study in generality and problem solving*. New York: Academic Press.

Feltovich, P. J., Ford, K. M., & Hoffman, R. R. (Eds.) (1997). *Expertise in context: Human and machine*. Cambridge, MA: AAAI/MIT Press.

Fitts, P., & Posner, M. I. (1967). *Human performance*. Belmont, CA: Brooks/Cole.

Fitzsimmons, M. P. (2003). *The night that the Old Regime ended*. University Park, PA: Pennsylvania State University Press.

Galton, F., Sir (1869/1979). *Hereditary genius: an inquiry into its laws and consequences*. (Originally published in 1869). London: Julian Friedman Publishers.

Gobet, F., & Simon, H. A. (1996). Templates in chess memory: A mechanism for recalling several boards. *Cognitive Psychology, 31*, 1–40.

Hoffman, R. R. (Ed.) (1992). *The psychology of expertise: Cognitive research and empirical AI*. New York: Springer-Verlag.

Howe, M. J. A., Davidson, J. W., & Sloboda, J. A. (1998). Innate talents: Reality or myth? *Behavioral and Brain Sciences, 21*, 399–442.

Hunt, E. B. (1995). *Will we be smart enough?* New York: Russell Sage Foundation.

Krause, E. A. (1996). *Death of guilds: Professions, states and the advance of capitalism, 1930 to the present*. New Haven, CT: Yale University Press.

Lyons, R., Payne, C., McCabe, M., & Fielder, C. (1998). Legibility of doctors' handwriting: Quantitative and comparative study. *British Medical Journal, 317*, 863–864.

Newell, A., & Simon, H. A. (1972). *Human problem solving*. Englewood Cliffs, NJ: Prentice-Hall.

Pannabecker, J. R. (1994). Diderot, the mechanical arts and the *encyclopedie*: In search of the heritage of technology education. *Journal of Technology Education*, 6, 45–57.

Plato (1991). *Protagoras* (Translated by C. C. W. Taylor). Oxford: Clarendon Press.

Polanyi, M. (1962). *Personal knowledge: Toward a post-critical philosophy* (Corrected edition). Chicago: The University of Chicago Press.

Polanyi, M. (1966). *The tacit dimension* (Reprinted in 1983). Gloucester, MA: Peter Smith.

Rees, G., & Wakely, M. (Eds.) (2004). *The instauratio magna, Part II: Novum organum and associated texts*. Oxford: Clarendon Press.

Roe, A. (1952). *The making of a scientist*. New York: Dodd, Mead & Company.

Rohr, D. (2001). *The careers and social status of British musicians, 1750–1850: A profession of artisans*. Cambridge: Cambridge University Press.

Rosselli, J. (1991). *Music & musicians in nineteenth-century Italy*. Portland, OR: Amadeus Press.

Shanteau, J. (1988). Psychological characteristics and strategies of expert decision makers. *Acta Psychologica*, 68, 203–215.

Simon, H. A., & Gobet, F. (2000). Expertise effects in memory recall: Comment on Vicente and Wang (1998). *Psychological Review*, 107, 593–600.

Simon, H. A, & Chase, W. G. (1973). Skill in chess. *American Scientist*, 61, 394–403.

Simonton, D. K. (1994). *Greatness: Who makes history and why*. New York: Guilford Press.

Singer, C. (1958). *From magic to science*. New York: Dover.

Sosniak, L. A. (1985a). Learning to be a concert pianist. In B. S. Bloom (Ed.), *Developing talent in young people* (pp. 19–67). New York: Ballantine Books.

Sosniak, L. A. (1985b). Becoming an outstanding research neurologist. In B. S. Bloom (Ed.), *Developing talent in young people* (pp. 348–408). New York: Ballantine Books.

Sosniak, L. A. (1985c). Phases of learning. In B. S. Bloom (Ed.), *Developing talent in young people* (pp. 409–438). New York: Ballantine Books.

Sosniak, L. A. (1985d). A long-term commitment to learning. In B. S. Bloom (Ed.), *Developing talent in young people* (pp. 477–506). New York: Ballantine Books.

Starkes, J. L., & Allard, F. (Eds.) (1993). *Cognitive issues in motor expertise*. Amsterdam: North Holland.

Starkes, J., & Ericsson, K. A. (Eds.) (2003). *Expert performance in sport: Recent advances in research on sport expertise*. Champaign, IL: Human Kinetics.

Sternberg, R. J., & Grigorenko, E. L. (Eds.) (2003). *Perspectives on the psychology of abilities, competencies, and expertise*. Cambridge: Cambridge University Press.

Taylor, I. A. (1975). A retrospective view of creativity investigation. In I. A. Taylor and J. W. Getzels (Eds.), *Perspectives in creativity* (pp. 1–36). Chicago, IL; Aldine Publishing Co.

Van der Maas, H. L. J., & Wagenmakers, E. J. (2005). A psychometric analysis of chess expertise. *American Journal of Psychology*, 118, 29–60.

Vicente, K. J., & Wang, J. H. (1998). An ecological theory of expertise effects in memory recall. *Psychological Review*, 105, 33–57.

Webster's New World Dictionary (1968). Cleveland, OH: The World Publishing Company.

Wikipedia. http://en.wikipedia.org/wiki/Expert

Zuckerman, H. (1977). *Scientific elite: Nobel laureates in the United States*. New York: Free Press.

Author Notes

This article was prepared in part with support from the FSCW/Conradi Endowment Fund of Florida State University Foundation. The author wants to thank Neil Charness, Paul Feltovich, Len Hill, Robert Hoffman, and Roy Roring for their valuable comments on earlier drafts of this chapter.

Two Approaches to the Study of Experts' Characteristics

Michelene T. H. Chi

This chapter differentiates two approaches to the study of expertise, which I call the "absolute approach" and the "relative approach," and what each approach implies for how expertise is assessed. It then summarizes the characteristic ways in which experts excel and the ways that they sometimes seem to fall short of common expectations.

Two Approaches to the Study of Expertise

The nature of expertise has been studied in two general ways. One way is to study truly exceptional people with the goal of understanding how they perform in their domain of expertise. I use the term *domain* loosely to refer to both informal domains, such as sewing and cooking, and formal domains, such as biology and chess. One could choose exceptional people on the basis of their well-established discoveries. For example, one could study how Maxwell constructed a quantitative field concept (Nersessian, 1992). Or one could choose contemporary scientists whose breakthroughs may still be debated, such as pathologist Warren and gastroenterologist Marshall's proposal that bacteria cause peptic ulcers (Chi & Hausmann, 2003; Thagard, 1998; also see the chapters by Wilding & Valentine, Chapter 31, Simonton, Chapter 18, and Weisberg, Chapter 42).

Several methods can be used to identify someone who is truly an exceptional expert. One method is retrospective. That is, by looking at how well an outcome or product is received, one can determine who is or is not an expert. For example, to identify a great composer, one can examine a quantitative index, such as how often his or her music was broadcast (Kozbelt, 2004). A second method may be some kind of concurrent measure, such as a rating system as a result of tournaments, as in chess (Elo, 1965), or as a result of examinations (Masunaga & Horn, 2000), or just measures of how well the exceptional expert performs his task. A third method might be the use of some independent index, if it is available. In chess, for example, there exists a task called the Knight's Tour that requires a player to move a Knight Piece across the rows of a chess board, using legal Knight Moves. The time it

Table 2.1. A proficiency scale (adapted from Hoffman, 1998).

Naive	One who is totally ignorant of a domain
Novice	Literally, someone who is new – a probationary member. There has been some minimal exposure to the domain.
Initiate	Literally, a novice who has been through an initiation ceremony and has begun introductory instruction.
Apprentice	Literally, one who is learning – a student undergoing a program of instruction beyond the introductory level. Traditionally, the apprentice is immersed in the domain by living with and assisting someone at a higher level. The length of an apprenticeship in the Craft Guilds depends on the domain, ranging from about one to 12 years in the Craft Guilds.
Journeyman	Literally, a person who can perform a day's labor unsupervised, although working under orders. An experienced and reliable worker, or one who has achieved a level of competence. Despite high levels of motivation, it is possible to remain at this proficiency level for life.
Expert	The distinguished or brilliant journeyman, highly regarded by peers, whose judgments are uncommonly accurate and reliable, whose performance shows consummate skill and economy of effort, and who can deal effectively with certain types of rare or "tough" cases. Also, an expert is one who has special skills or knowledge derived from extensive experience with subdomains.
Master	Traditionally, a master is any journeyman or expert who is also qualified to teach those at a lower level. Traditionally, a master is one of an elite group of experts whose judgments set the regulations, standards, or ideals. Also, a master can be that expert who is regarded by the other experts as being "the" expert, or the "real" expert, especially with regard to sub-domain knowledge.

takes to complete the moves is an indication of one's chess skill (Chi, 1978). Although this task is probably not sensitive enough to discriminate among the exceptional experts, a task such as this can be adapted as an index of expertise. In short, to identify a truly exceptional expert, one often resorts to some kind of measure of performance. The assessment of exceptional experts needs to be accurate since the goal is to understand their superior performance. Thus, this approach studies the remarkable few to understand how they are distinguished from the masses.

Though expertise can be studied in the context of "exceptional" individuals, there is a tacit assumption in the literature that perhaps these individuals somehow have greater minds in the sense that the "global qualities of their thinking" might be different (Minsky & Papert, 1974, p. 59). For example, they might utilize more powerful domain-general heuristics that novices are not aware of, or they may be naturally endowed with greater memory capacity (Pascual-Leone, 1970; Simonton, 1977). This line of reasoning is extended to cognitive

functioning probably because genetic inheritance does seem to be a relevant component for expertise in music and sports. In short, the tacit assumption is that greatness or creativity arises from chance and unique innate talent (Simonton, 1977). Let's call this type of work in psychology the study of exceptional or *absolute* expertise.

A second research approach to expertise is to study experts in comparison to novices. This *relative* approach assumes that expertise is a level of proficiency that novices can achieve. Because of this assumption, the definition of expertise for this contrastive approach can be more relative, in the sense that the more knowledgeable group can be considered the "experts" and the less knowledgeable group the "novices." Thus the term "novices" is used here in a generic sense, in that it can refer to a range of non-experts, from the naives to the journeymen (see Table 2.1 for definitions).

Proficiency level can be grossly assessed by measures such as academic qualifications (such as graduate students vs. undergraduates), seniority or years performing the task, or consensus among peers. It can also be assessed at a more fine-grained level, in terms of domain-specific knowledge or performance tests.

One advantage of this second approach, the study of "relative expertise," is that we can be a little less precise about how to define expertise since experts are defined as relative to novices on a continuum. In this relative approach, a goal is to understand how we can enable a less skilled or experienced persons to become more skilled since the assumption is that expertise can be attained by a majority of students. This goal has the advantage of illuminating our understanding of learning since presumably the more skilled person became expert-like from having acquired knowledge about a domain, that is, from learning and studying (Chi & Bassok, 1989) and from deliberate practice (Ericsson, Chapter 38; Ericsson, Krampe, & Tesch-Römer, 1993; Weisberg, 1999). Thus, the goal of studying relative expertise is not merely to describe and identify the ways in which experts excel. Rather, the goal is to understand how experts became that way so that others can learn to become more skilled and knowledgeable.

Because our definition characterizes experts as being more knowledgeable than non-experts, such a definition entails several fundamental theoretical assumptions. First, it assumes that experts are people who have acquired more knowledge in a domain (Ericsson & Smith, 1991, Table 2.1) and that this knowledge is organized or structured (Bedard & Chi, 1992). Second, it assumes that the fundamental capacities and domain-general reasoning abilities of experts and non-experts are more or less identical. Third, this framework assumes that differences in the performance of experts and non-experts are determined by the differences in the way their knowledge is represented.

Manifestations of Experts' Skills and Shortcomings

Numerous behavioral manifestations of expertise have been identified in the research literature and discussed at some length (see edited volumes by Chi, Glaser, & Farr, 1988; Ericsson & Smith, 1991; Ericsson, 1996; Feltovich, Ford, & Hoffman, 1997; Hoffman, 1992). Most of the research has focused on how experts excel, either in an absolute context or in comparison to novices. However, it is equally important to understand how experts fail. Knowing both how they excel and how they fail will provide a more complete characterization of expertise. This section addresses both sets of characteristics.

Ways in which Experts Excel

I begin by very briefly highlighting seven major ways in which experts excel because this set of findings have been reviewed extensively in the literature, followed by a slightly more elaborate discussion of seven ways in which they fall short.

GENERATING THE BEST

Experts excel in generating the best solution, such as the best move in chess, even under time constraints (de Groot, 1965), or the best solution in solving problems, or the best design in a designing task. Moreover, they can do this faster and more accurately than non-experts (Klein, 1993).

DETECTION AND RECOGNITION

Experts can detect and see features that novices cannot. For example, they can see patterns and cue configurations in X-ray films that novices cannot (Lesgold et al., 1988). They can also perceive the "deep structure" of a problem or situation (Chi, Feltovich, & Glaser, 1981).

QUALITATIVE ANALYSES

Experts spend a relatively great deal of time analyzing a problem qualitatively, developing a problem representation by adding many domain-specific and general constraints to the problems in their domains of expertise (Simon & Simon, 1978; Voss, Greene, Post, & Penner, 1983).

MONITORING

Experts have more accurate self-monitoring skills in terms of their ability to detect errors and the status of their own comprehension. In the domain of physics, experts were more accurate than novices in judging the difficulty of a problem (Chi, Glaser, & Rees, 1982). In the domain of chess, expert (Class B) chess players were more accurate than novices in predicting the number of pieces they thought they could recall immediately or the number of times they thought they needed to view a chess position in order to recall the entire position correctly. Moreover, the experts were significantly more accurate in discriminating their ability to recall the randomized (positions with the pieces scrambled) from the meaningful chess positions, whereas novices thought they could recall equal number of pieces from the randomized as well as the meaningful positions (Chi, 1978).

STRATEGIES

Experts are more successful at choosing the appropriate strategies to use than novices. For example, in solving physics problems, the instructors tend to work forward, starting from the given state to the goal state, whereas students of physics tend to work backwards, from the unknown to the givens (Larkin, McDermott, Simon, & Simon, 1980). Similarly, when confronted with routine cases, expert clinicians diagnose with a data-driven (forward-working) approach by applying a small set of rules to the data; whereas less expert clinicians tend to use a hypothesis-driven (backward chaining) approach (Patel & Kaufman, 1995). Even though both more-expert and the less-expert groups can use both kinds of strategies, one group may use one kind more successfully than the other kind. Experts not only will know which strategy or procedure is better for a situation, but they also are more likely than novices to use strategies that have more frequently proved to be effective (Lemaire & Siegler, 1995).

OPPORTUNISTIC

Experts are more opportunistic than novices; they make use of whatever sources of information are available while solving problems (Gilhooly et al., 1997) and also exhibit more opportunism in using resources.

COGNITIVE EFFORT

Experts can retrieve relevant domain knowledge and strategies with minimal cognitive effort (Alexander, 2003, p. 3). They can also execute their skills with greater automaticity (Schneider, 1985) and are able to exert greater cognitive control over those aspects of performance where control is desirable (Ericsson, Chapter 13).

Ways in which Experts Fall Short

An equally important list might be ways in which experts do not excel (Sternberg, 1996; Sternberg & Frensch, 1992). Because much less has been written about experts' handicaps, I present a slightly more extensive discussion of seven ways in which experts do not surpass novices. This list also excludes limitations that are apparent in experts, but in fact novices would be subjected to the same limitations if they have the knowledge. For example, experts often cannot articulate their knowledge because much of their knowledge is tacit and their overt intuitions can be flawed. This creates a science of knowledge elicitation to collaboratively create a model of an expert's knowledge (Ford & Adams-Webber, 1992). However, this shortcoming is not listed below since novices would most likely have the same problem except that their limitation is less apparent since they have less knowledge to explicate.

DOMAIN-LIMITED

Expertise is domain-limited. Experts do not excel in recall for domains in which they have no expertise. For example, the chess master's recall of randomized chess board positions is much less accurate than the recall for actual positions from chess games (Gobet & Simon, 1996), and the engineer's attempt to recall the state of affairs of thermal-hydraulic processes that are not physically meaningful is much less successful than attempts to recall such states that are meaningfull (Vicente, 1992). There are a number of demonstrations from various other domains that show experts' superior recall compared to novices for representative situations but not for randomly rearranged versions of the same stimuli (Ericsson & Lehmann, 1996; Vicente & Wang, 1998). Thus, the superiority associated with their expertise is very much limited to a specific domain.

Of course there are exceptions. For example, expert chess players can display a reliable, but comparatively small, superiority of memory performance for randomized chess positions when they are briefly presented (see Gobet & Charness, Chapter 30), or when the random positions are presented at slower rates (Ericsson, Patel, & Kinstch, 2000). Nevertheless, in general, their expertise is domain-limited.

OVERLY CONFIDENT

Experts can also miscalibrate their capabilities by being overly confident. Chi (1978) found that the experts (as compared to both the novices and the intermediates) overestimated the number of chess pieces they could recall from coherent chess positions (see Figure 9, left panel, Chi, 1978). Similarly, physics and music experts overestimated their comprehension of a physics or music text, respectively, whereas novices were far more accurate (Glenberg & Epstein, 1987). It seems that experts can be overly confident in judgments related to their field of expertise (Oskamp, 1965). Of course, there are also domains, such as weather forecasting, for which experts can be cautious and conservative (Hoffman, Trafron, & Roebber 2005).

GLOSSING OVER

Although experts surpass novices in understanding and remembering the deep structure of a problem, a situation, or a computer program, sometimes experts fail to recall the surface features and overlook details. For example, in recalling a text passage describing a baseball game, individuals with high baseball knowledge actually recalled fewer baseball-irrelevant sentences than individuals with low baseball knowledge (Voss, Vesonder, & Spilich, 1980), such as sentences containing information about the weather and the team. But high-knowledge individuals do recall information that is relevant to the goal structure of the game, as well as changes in the game states. Similarly, in answering questions about computer programs, novices are better than experts for concrete questions, whereas experts are better than novices for abstract questions (Adelson, 1984).

In medical domains, after the presentation of an endocarditic case, 4th and 6th year medical students recalled more propositions about the case than the internists (Schmidt & Boshuizen, 1993). Moreover, because the internists' biomedical knowledge was better consolidated with their clinical knowledge, resulting in "short cuts," their explanations thus made few references to basic pathophysiological processes such as inflammation. In short, it is as if experts gloss over details that are the less relevant features of a problem.

CONTEXT-DEPENDENCE WITHIN A DOMAIN

The first limitation of expertise stated above is that it is restricted to a specific domain. Moreover, within their domain of expertise, experts rely on contextual cues. For example, in a medical domain, experts seem to rely on the tacit enabling conditions of a situation for diagnosis (Feltovich & Barrows, 1984). The enabling conditions are background information such as age, sex, previous diseases, occupation, drug use, and so forth. These circumstances are not necessarily causally related to diseases, but physicians pick up and use such correlational knowledge from clinical practice. When expert physicians were presented the complaints associated with a case along with patient charts and pictures of the patients, they were 50% more accurate than the novices in their diagnoses, and they were able to reproduce a large amount of context information that was directly relevant to the patient's problem (Hobus, Schmidt, Boshuizen, & Patel, 1987). The implication is that without the contextual enabling information, expert physicians might be more limited in their ability to make an accurate diagnosis.

Experts' skills have been shown to be context-dependent in many other studies, such as the failure of experienced waiters to indicate the correct surface orientation of liquid in a tilted container, despite their experience in the context of wine glasses (Hecht & Proffitt, 1995), and the inaccuracies of wildland fire fighters in predicting the spread of bush fire when the wind and slope are opposing rather than congruent, which is an unusual situation (Lewandowsky, Dunn, Kirsner, & Randell, 1997).

INFLEXIBLE

Although Hatano and Inagaki (1986) have claimed that exceptional (versus routine) experts are adaptive, sometimes experts do have trouble adapting to changes in problems that have a deep structure that deviates from those that are "acceptable" in the domain. For example, Sternberg and Frensch (1992) found that expert bridge players suffered more than novice players when the game's bidding procedure was changed. Similarly, expert tax accountants had more difficulty than novice tax students in transferring knowledge from a tax case that disqualified a general tax principle (Marchant, Robinson, Anderson, & Schadewald, 1991). Perhaps the experts in these studies are routine experts; but they nevertheless showed less flexibility than the novices.

Inflexibility can be seen also in the use of strategies by Brazilian street vendors who can be considered "experts" in "street mathematics" (Schliemann & Carraher, 1993). When presented with a problem in a pricing context, such as "If 2 kg of rice cost 5 cruzeiros, how much do you have to pay for 3 kg?," they used mathematical strategies with 90% accuracies. However, when presented with a problem in a recipe context ("To make a cake with 2 cups of flour you need 5 spoonfuls of water; how many spoonfuls do you need for 3 cups of flour?"), they did not adapt their mathematical strategies. Instead, they used estimation strategies, resulting in only 20% accuracies.

INACCURATE PREDICTION, JUDGMENT, AND ADVICE

Another weakness of experts is that sometimes they are inaccurate in their prediction of novice performance. For example, one would expect experts to be able to extrapolate from their own task-specific knowledge how quickly or easily novices can accomplish a task. In general, the greater the expertise the worse off they were at predicting how quickly novices can perform a task, such as using a cell phone (Hinds, 1999). In tasks requiring decision under uncertainty, such as evaluating applicants for medical internships (Johnson, 1988) or predicting successes in graduate school (Dawes, 1971), it has been shown consistently that experts fail to make better judgments than novices. Such lack of superior decision making may be limited to domains that involve predicting human behavior, such as parole decisions, psychiatric judgment, and graduate school successes (Shanteau, 1984).

An alternative interpretation of experts' inaccuracies in making predictions is to postulate that they cannot take the perspectives of the novices accurately. Compatible with this interpretation is the finding that students are far more able to incorporate feedback from their peers than from their expert instructor in a writing task (Cho, 2004).

BIAS AND FUNCTIONAL FIXEDNESS

Bias is probably one of the most serious handicaps of experts, especially in the medical profession. Sometimes physicians are biased by the probable survival or mortality rates of a treatment. Christensen, Heckerling, Mackesy, Berstein, and Elstein (1991) found that residents were more susceptible to let the probable survival outcome determine options for treatment, whereas novice students were not. Fortunately, experienced physicians were not affected by the mortality rates either. In another study, however, my colleagues and I found the experienced physicians to manifest serious biases. We presented several types of cases to specialists, such as hematologists, cardiologists, and infectious disease specialists. Some were hematology cases and others were cardiology cases. We found that regardless of the type of specialized case, specialists tended to generate hypotheses that corresponded to their field of expertise: Cardiologists tended to generate more cardiology-type hypotheses, whether the case was one of a blood disease or an infectious disease (Hashem, Chi, & Friedman, 2003). This tendency to generate diagnoses about which they have more knowledge clearly can cause greater errors. Moreover, experts seem to be more susceptible to suggestions that can bias their choices than novices (Walther, Fiedler, & Nickel, 2003).

Greater domain knowledge can also be deleterious by creating mental set or functional fixedness. In a problem-solving context, there is some suggestion that the more knowledgeable participants exhibit more functional fixedness in that they have more difficulty coming up with creative solutions. For example, in a remote association task, three words are presented, such as *plate*, *broken*, and *rest*, and the subject's task is to come up with a fourth word that can form a familiar phrase with each of the three words, such as the word *home* for *home plate* (a baseball term), *broken home*, and *rest home*. A "misleading" set of three words can be *plate*, *broken*, and *shot*, in which the correct solution is *glass*. High baseball knowledge subjects were less able than low baseball knowledge subjects to generate correct solutions to the misleading type of problems because the first word *plate* primed their baseball knowledge so that it caused functional fixedness (Wiley, 1998).

In conclusion, the two sections above each summarized seven ways in which experts excel and seven ways in which they fall short. Although much more research has been carried out focusing on ways in which experts' greater knowledge allows them to excel, it is equally important to know ways in which their knowledge is limiting. The facilitations and limitations of knowledge can provide boundary conditions for shaping a theory of expertise.

References

Adelson, B. (1984). When novices surpass experts: The difficulty of a task may increase with expertise. *Journal of Experimental Psychology: Learning, Memory, and Cognition*, 10, 483–495.

Alexander, P. A. (2003). Can we get there from here? *Educational Researcher*, 32, 3–4.

Bedard, J., & Chi, M. T. H. (1992). Expertise. *Current Directions in Psychological Science*, 1, 135–139.

Chi, M. T. H. (1978). Knowledge structure and memory development. In R. Siegler (Ed.), *Children's thinking: What develops?* (pp. 73–96). Hillsdale, NJ: Erlbaum.

Chi, M. T. H., & Bassok, M. (1989). Learning from examples via self-explanations. In L. B. Resnick (Ed.), *Knowing, learning, and instruction: Essays in honor of Robert Glaser* (pp. 251–282). Hillsdale, NJ: Erlbaum.

Chi, M. T. H., Feltovich, P., & Glaser, R. (1981). Categorization and representation of physics problems by experts and novices. *Cognitive Science*, 5, 121–152.

Chi, M. T. H., Glaser, R., & Farr, M. J. (Eds.) (1988). *The nature of expertise*. Hillsdale, NJ: Erlbaum.

Chi, M. T. H., Glaser, R., & Rees, E. (1982). Expertise in problem solving. In R. Sternberg (Ed.), *Advances in the Psychology of Human Intelligence* (Vol. 1, pp. 7–76). Hillsdale, NJ: Erlbaum.

Chi, M. T. H., & Hausmann, R. G. M. (2003). Do radical discoveries require ontological shifts? In L. V. Shavinina (Ed.), *International handbook on innovation* (pp. 430–444). New York: Elsevier Science Ltd.

Cho, K. (2004). When experts give worse advice than novices: The type and impact of feedback given by students and an instructor on student writing. Unpublished dissertation, University of Pittsburgh.

Christensen, C., Heckerling, P. S., Mackesy, M. E., Berstein, L. M., & Elstein, A. S. (1991). Framing bias among expert and novice physicians. *Academic Medicine*, 66 (suppl): S76–S78.

Dawes, R. M. (1971). A case study of graduate admissions: Application of three principles of human decision making. *American Psychologist*, 26, 180–188.

De Groot, A. (1965). *Thought and choice in chess.* The Hague: Mouton.

Elo, A. E. (1965). Age changes in master chess performance. *Journal of Gerontology*, 20, 289–299.

Ericsson, K. A. (1996). The acquisition of expert performance: An introduction to some of the issues. In K. A. Ericsson (Ed.)*The road to excellence: The acquisition of expert performance in the arts and sciences, sports, and games* (pp. 1–50). Mahwah, NJ: Erlbaum.

Ericsson, K. A., Krampe, R. T., & Tesch-Römer, C. (1993). The role of deliberate practice in acquisition of expert performance. *Psychological Review*, 100, 363–406.

Ericsson, K. A., & Lehmann, A. C. (1996). Expert and exceptional performance: evidence on maximal adaptations on task constraints. *Annual Review of Psychology*, 47, 273–305.

Ericsson, K. A., Patel, V. L., & Kinstch, W. (2000). How experts' adaptations to representative task demands account for the expertise effect in memory recall: Comment on Vincente and Wang (1998). *Psychological Review*, 107, 578–592.

Ericsson, K. A., & Smith, J. (1991). Prospects and limits of empirical study of expertise: An introduction. In K. A. Ericsson & J. Smith (Eds.). *Toward a general theory of expertise: Prospects and limits* (pp. 1–38).Cambridge: Cambridge University Press.

Feltovich, P. J., & Barrows, H. S. (1984). Issues of generality in medical problem solving. In H. G.Schmidt & M. L.de Volder (Eds.), *Tutorials in problem-based learning* (pp. 128–142). Maaastricht, Netherlands: Van Gorcum.

Feltovich, P. J., Ford, K. M., & Hoffman, R. R. (Eds.) (1997). *Expertise in context.* Cambridge, MA: The MIT Press.

Ford, K. M., & Adams-Webber, J. R. (1992). Knowledge acquisition and constuctivist epistemology. In R. R. Hoffman (Ed.), *The psychology of expertise: Cognitive research and empirical AI* (pp. 121–136). New York: Springer-Verlag.

Gilhooly, K. J., McGeorge, P., Hunter, J., Rawles, J. M., Kirby, I. K., Green, C., & Wynn, V. (1997). Biomedical knowledge in diagnostic thinking: the case of electrocardiogram (ECG) interpretation. *European Journal of Cognitive Psychology*, 9, 199–223.

Glenberg, A. M., & Epstein, W. (1987). Inexpert calibration of comprehension. *Memory and Cognition*, 15, 84–93.

Gobet, F., & Simon, H. A. (1996). Recall of rapidly presented random chess positions is a function of skill. *Psychonomic Bulletin and Reviews*, 3, 159–163.

Hashem, A., Chi, M. T. H., & Friedman, C. P. (2003). Medical errors as a result of specialization. *Journal of Biomedical Informatics*, 36, 61–69.

Hatano, G., & Inagaki, K. (1986). Two courses of expertise. In H. Stevenson, H. Azmuma, & K. Hakuta (Eds.), *Child development and education in Japan* (pp. 262–272). New York, NY: W. Y. Freeman and Company .

Hecht, H., & Proffitt, D. R. (1995). The price of expertise: Effects of experience on the water-level task. *Psychological Science*, 6, 90–95.

Hinds, P. J. (1999). The curse of expertise: The effects of expertise and debiasing methods on prediction of novice performance. *Journal of Experimental Psychology: Applied*, 5, 205–221.

Hobus, P. P. M., Schmidt, H. G., Boshuizen, H. P. A., & Patel, V. L. (1987). Context factors in the activation of first diagnostic hypotheses: Expert-novice differences. *Medical Education*, 21, 471–476.

Hoffman, R. R. (Ed.) (1992). *The psychology of expertise: Cognitive research and empirical AI.* Mahwah, NJ: Erlbaum.

Hoffman, R. R. (1998). How can expertise be defined?: Implications of research from cognitive psychology. In R. Williams, W. Faulkner, & J. Fleck (Eds.), *Exploring expertise* (pp. 81–100). New York: Macmillan.

Hoffman, R. R., Trafton, G., & Roebber, P. (2005). *Minding the weather: How expert forecasters think.* Cambridge, MA: MIT Press.

Johnson, E. J. (1988). Expertise and decision under uncertainty: Performance and process. In M. T. H. Chi, R. Glaser, & M. J. Farr (Eds.), *The nature of expertise* (pp. 209–228). Hillsdale, NJ: Erlbaum.

Klein, G. A. (1993). A recognition primed decision (RPD) model of rapid decision making. In G. A. Klein, J. Orasanu, R. Calderwood, & C. E. Zsambok (Eds.), *Decision-making in action: Models and methods* (pp. 138–147). Norwood, NJ: Ablex.

Kozbelt, A. (2004). Creativity over the lifespan in classical composers: Reexamining the equal-odds rule. Paper presented at the 26th Annual Meeting of the Cognitive Science Society.

Larkin, J. H., McDermott, J., Simon, D. P., & Simon, H. A. (1980). Models of competence in solving physics problems. *Cognitive Science*, 4, 317–345.

Lemaire, P., & Siegler, R. S. (1995). Four aspects of strategic change: Contributions to children's learning of multiplication. *Journal of Experimental Psychology: General*, 124, 83–97.

Lesgold, A., Rubinson, H., Feltovich, P., Glaser, R., Klopfer, D., & Wang, Y. (1988). Expertise in a complex skill: Diagnosing X-ray pictures. In M. T. H. Chi, R. Glaser, M. J. Farr (Eds.), *The nature of expertise* (pp. 311–342). Hillsdale, NJ: Erlbaum.

Lewandowsky, S., Dunn, J. C., Kirsner, K., & Randell, M. (1997). Expertise in the management of bushfires: Training and decision support. *Australian Psychologist*, 32(3), 171–177.

Marchant, G., Robinson, J., Anderson, U., & Schadewald, M. (1991). Analogical transfer and expertise in legal reasoning. *Organizational Behavior and Human Decision Making*, 48, 272–290.

Masunaga, H., & Horn, J. (2000), Expertise and age-related changes in components of intelligence. *Psychology & Aging*, Special Issue: Vol. 16(2), 293–311.

Minsky, M., & Papert, S. (1974). *Artificial intelligence*. Condon Lectures, Oregon /State System of Higher Education, Eugene, Oregon.

Nersessian, N. J. (1992). How do scientists think? Capturing the dynamics of conceptual change in science. In R. N. Giere (Ed.), *Cognitive models of science: Minnesota studies in the philosophy of science*, Vol. XV (pp. 3–44). Minneapolis, MN: University of Minnesota Press.

Oskamp, S. (1965). Overconfidence in case-study judgments. *Journal of Consulting Psychology*, 29, 261–265.

Pascual-Leone, J. (1970). A mathematical model for the decision rule in Piaget's developmental stages. *Acta Psychologica*, 32, 301–345.

Patel, V. L., & Kaufman, D. R. (1995). Clinical reasoning and biomedical knowledge: implications for teaching. In J. Higgs & M. Jones (Eds.), *Clinical reasoning in the health professions* (pp. 117–128). Oxford, UK: Butterworth-Heinemann Ltd.

Schliemann, A. D., & Carraher, D. W. (1993). Proportional reasoning in and out of school. In P. Light & G. Butterworth (Eds.), *Context and cognition: Ways of learning and knowing* (pp. 47–73). Hillsdale, NJ: Erlbaum.

Schmidt, H. G., & Boshuizen, P. A. (1993). On acquiring expertise in medicine. *Educational Psychology Review*, 5, 205–220.

Schneider, W. (1985). Training high performance skills: Fallacies and guidelines. *Human Factors*, 27(3), 285–300.

Shanteau, J. (1984). Some unasked questions about the psychology of expert decision makers. In M. El Hawaray (Ed.), *Proceedings of the 1984 IEEE conference on systems, man, and cybernetics*. New York: Institute of Electrical and Electronics Engineers, Inc.

Simon, D. P., & Simon, H. A. (1978). Individual differences in solving physics problems. In R. Siegler (Ed.), *Children's thinking: What develops?* (pp. 325–348). Hillsdale, NJ: Erlbaum.

Simonton, D. K. (1977). Creative productivity, age, and stress: A biographical time-series analysis of 10 classical composers. *Journal of Personality and Social Psychology*, 35, 791–804.

Sternberg, R. J. (1996). Costs of expertise. In K. A. Ericsson (Ed.), *The road to excellence: The acquisition of expert performance in the arts and sciences, sports, and games* (pp. 347–354). Hillsdale, NJ: Erlbaum.

Sternberg, R. J., & Frensch, P. A. (1992). On being an expert; A cost-benefit analysis. In R. R. Hoffman (Ed.), *The psychology of expertise: Cognitive research and empirical AI* (pp. 191–203). New York: Springer Verlag.

Thagard, P. (1998). Ulcers and bacteria I: Discovery and acceptance. *Studies in History and Philosophy of Science*, 29, 107–136.

Vicente, K. J. (1992). Memory recall in a process control system: A measure of expertise and display effectiveness. *Memory and Cognition*, 20, 356–373.

Vicente, K. J., & Wang, J. H. (1998). An ecological theory of expertise effects in memory recall. *Psychological Review*, 105, 33–57.

Voss, J. F., Greene, T. R., Post, T., & Penner, B. C. (1983). Problem solving skill in the social sciences. In G. Bower (Ed.), *The psychology of learning and motivation*. (pp. 165–213). New York: Academic Press.

Voss, J. F., Vesonder, G., & Spilich, H. (1980). Text generation and recall by high-knowledge and low-knowledge individuals. *Journal of Verbal Learning and Verbal Behavior*, 19, 651–667.

Walther, E., Fiedler, K., & Nickel, S. (2003). The influence of prior knowledge on constructive biases. *Swiss Journal of Psychology*, 62(4), 219–231.

Weisberg, R. W. (1999). Creativity and knowledge: A challenge to theories. In R. J. Sternberg (Ed.), *Handbook of Creativity* (pp. 226–250). Cambridge, UK: Cambridge University Press.

Wiley, J. (1998). Expertise as mental set: The effects of domain knowledge in creative problem solving. *Memory and Cognition*, 26, 716–730.

Author Notes

The author is grateful for support provided by the Pittsburgh Science of Learning Center. Reprints may be requested from the author or downloaded from the WEB, at www.pitt.edu/~chi

CHAPTER 3

Expertise, Talent, and Social Encouragement

Earl Hunt

Introduction

There have literally been volumes of studies of expertise (Chi, Glaser, & Farr, 1988; Ericsson, 1996; Ericsson & Smith, 1991; Sternberg & Grigorenko, 2001). The fields covered range from medicine to amateur wrestling. In spite of this diversity, regular themes emerge.

Experts know a lot about their field of expertise. This is hardly surprising; an ignorant expert would be an oxymoron. Experts work at becoming experts. The revealed wisdom is that this takes at least ten years (Richman et al., 1996). In some fields the time is spent perfecting the minutiae rather than in the fun of solving problems or winning games. Amateur musicians spend a great deal of time playing pieces, whereas professional musicians spend a great deal of time practicing sequences of movements (Ericsson, Krampe, & Tesch-Römer, 1993). Chess masters do not just play a lot of chess, they read a lot of the chess literature.

Because practice is so important, some psychologists have minimized the contribution of talents developed before starting on the path to expertise (Ericsson et al., 1993; Sloboda, 1996). This position is consistent with well-established laboratory findings showing that under certain circumstances extended practice can lead to improvements in performance by an order of magnitude, along with a huge reduction in the range of interindividual differences (Schneider & Shiffrin, 1977).

In this chapter I explore the relation between studies of expertise and a few selected results from different areas of psychology and economics. I shall argue that different types of expertise make different types of cognitive demands. Accordingly the balance between talent and practice may vary with the field, but it will vary in a predictable way. In addition, acquiring expertise is not solely a cognitive matter. Personal interests and social support are also very important.

Intelligence, Cognition, and Experience

Any discussion of the role of talent versus experience has to begin with an analysis of the role of intelligence. Operationally, intelligence is usually defined by scores on tests of cognitive abilities. Based on the distributions of test scores, modern psychometricians have largely agreed on a hierarchical model of intelligence, originally due to Cattell (1971), in which general intelligence "*g*" is inferred from positive correlations between sets of broadly applicable but distinct cognitive abilities. These include a generalized reasoning ability ("fluid intelligence-Gf"), the possession and use of knowledge to solve problems ("crystallized intelligence-Gc"), spatial-visual reasoning, a general ability to think quickly, and several other broad factors (Carroll, 1993).

The distinction between *g*, Gf, and Gc often drops out in discussions of the relation between intelligence and social outcomes. This is unfortunate, for Gf and Gc are measured by different instruments. The Wechsler Adult Intelligence Scale (WAIS) confounds Gf and Gc (Horn, 1985). Two group tests that are widely used in industrial and academic settings, the Armed Services Vocational Aptitude Battery (ASVAB) and the Scholastic Assessment Test (SAT) are essentially tests of Gc, based on the general knowledge and problem-solving skills that one expects an American high school graduate to have (Roberts et al., 2000). The best tests of Gf, by contrast, are tests in which an examinee must detect patterns in abstract and unusual material (Jensen, 1998).

The definition of Gc ensures that any Gc test is culture specific. Cattell (1971) anticipated this when he noted that within a person Gc consists of two components, a general ability to use knowledge and the possession of specific knowledge. He even suggested that the proper evaluation of Gc would require separate tests for every profession. The same spirit can be found in the research of Sternberg et al. (2000) on "practical intelligence," which is evaluated by tests of culture- or subgroup-specific knowledge.

Gf and Gc are correlated, which makes it possible to speak reasonably about *g*. However, the correlations between measures of different types of cognitive abilities are highest toward the low end of the general intelligence scale, and markedly lower at the high end (Detterman & Daniel, 1989; Deary et al., 1996). This is important, as expertise is generally associated with high levels of performance.

Measures of Gf have substantial correlations with measures of the performance of working memory. A high-Gf person is probably good at keeping track of several things at once and of concentrating his or her attention in the face of distractions (Engle, Kane & Tulhoski, 1999; Kyllonen & Christal, 1990). These talents are good to have during the learning phase of most psychomotor activities (e.g., skiing, riding a bicycle, playing tennis). However, they are much less needed once an activity has been learned. Laboratory studies of how people learn to do psychomotor tasks have shown that intelligence is a reasonably good predictor of performance early in learning but does not predict asymptotic levels of learning very well (Ackerman 1996; Fleishman, 1972).

An important study by Ackerman and Cianciolo (2000) modifies this conclusion. Ackerman and Cianciolo reasoned that if a task taxes working memory after it has been learned, the correlation with tests of reasoning should remain. They then trained people on two different, greatly reduced versions of an air traffic controller's task. One could be solved by memorizing a not-too-complicated set of rules. To solve the more complicated task the participant had to develop orderly patterns of traffic in the area near a terminal. Participants practiced the tasks for several days. The correlation between the first task and a measure of fluid intelligence decreased over practice from .45 to .30. The correlations between the intelligence measure and performance increased from .40 to .55 over the training period.

There are obvious parallels between this study and the general study of expertise. Some aspects of expertise, such as swinging a golf club, require learning a constant relationship between stimulus and response. Others aspects, such as the analogical reasoning typical of the law, involve varied mappings, the development of mental models of a situation, and extensive knowledge. Demands on both Gf and Gc never cease.

A second important observation is based on studies of natural decision making. By definition, experts make better decisions than novices. However, this does not mean that experts become better decision makers in the sense that they learn to avoid the mistakes that have been documented in laboratory studies of decision making (Kahneman, 2003). Instead, experienced real-life decision makers rely on analogical reasoning and schematic techniques for selecting and monitoring a plan of action (Klein, 1998). This kind of decision making depends on two things: having the experiences on which the analogies can be based and encoding those experiences in a way that makes information accessible when needed. Gc again!

Findings from Industrial-Organizational Psychology

Although laboratory studies offer the advantage of control, they cannot replicate the very long periods of time over which expertise is acquired in the workplace. The appropriate studies are the domain of industrial-organizational, rather than cognitive, psychology.

In the late 1980s the US military evaluated various predictors of the performance of enlisted men and women (Wigdor & Green, 1991) in military occupations ranging from artillerymen to cooks. Performance increased with experience, but appeared to asymptote after about three years. Asymptotic level of performance was related to scores on a test of mental skills, the Armed Forces Qualifying Test (AFQT), taken at time of enlistment, but there was an interaction.[1] Enlisted personnel with high scores reached asymptotic performance in a year, personnel with lower test scores took longer. Differences in performance could be related to the AFQT after more than three years of service, but the differences were less than half those for personnel with only a year's service. (See Hunt [1995] for a further

discussion of the general issue of intelligence and workplace performance.)

Similar observations have been made in the civilian sector. Scores on tests of cognitive competence are related to workplace performance, and the correlations are somewhat higher during training than during performance after training (Schmidt & Hunter, 1998).[2]

The conclusions just offered were drawn from analyses of jobs that might be characterized as "blue collar" or "lower level white collar." Although the data base is more limited, the same thing seems to be true of upper-level professional jobs. One large, particularly well-designed study of managers found a correlation of .38 between cognitive scores obtained at the outset of employment and level of management reached after more than fifteen years on the job (Howard & Bray, 1988).

Evidently intelligence-as-reasoning and working memory are always important during the early stages of learning, well before the expert level is reached. A task analysis is necessary to determine the extent to which performance depends on reasoning and working memory after the expert level has been reached.

Specialized knowledge will always be important if expertise depends largely on the execution of psychomotor sequences, as in ball-striking in golf. The sports example is obvious. Psychomotor sequences are important in other areas, including medicine and piloting high-performance aircraft. In other cases (e.g., the law, physics), expertise requires the development of schema that can guide problem solving. To some extent the use of such schema can reduce the burden on working memory, thus shifting the balance between the Gf-and Gc-aspects of intelligence.

Different types of expertise can be characterized by their location on the psychomotor/mental-modeling-and problem-solving/use-of-experience dimensions. Almost every task in which expertise can be illustrated contains some elements of each dimension.

Will we ever be able to test people at the outset of their experience, say early in high school, and predict who would become experts solely on the basis of their talents? Probably not, for we have not yet considered the social-personality aspect of expert development.

Why Become an Expert?

Sternberg (1996) has observed that intelligence is successful to the extent that it has been used to meet one's goals. It does not make sense to do the work that it takes to be an expert unless you want to be one. In order to understand expertise we have to understand interests.

Ackerman and his colleagues (Ackerman & Beier, 2001; Ackerman & Rolfhus, 1999; Rolfhus & Ackerman, 1999) have shown that within American society interests fall into three definable clusters:science and mathematics, intellectual and cultural activity, and social activities. People have knowledge bases that correspond to their interests. They also show markedly different personality profiles. Most important for our concerns here, the amount of knowledge a person has within his or her own interest area is best predicted by measures of Gc, or the extent to which a person has picked up knowledge of the society in general.

Because intelligence is differentiated at the upper end, one would expect differential patterns of ability to be particularly predictive of career choices of the gifted. They are. Lubinski, Benbow, and their colleagues have conducted longitudinal studies of gifted students who, at age 13, were in the top ten-thousandth of examinees on tests of verbal and mathematical skill (Lubinski, Webb, Morelock, & Benbow, 2001). They differentiated between students who had significantly higher verbal scores than mathematics scores, or the reverse, and students who were "high flat," that is, verbal and mathematical scores were essentially the same. It is important to remember that in this group a "low" score corresponds to above average performance in the general population.

Overall the gifted students did very well. Several had doctorates at age 23 or less;

many others were attending some of the most prestigious graduate schools in the country. Some had made substantial contributions outside of academia. The type of achievement differed by group. Students whose mathematics scores were higher than their verbal scores at age 13 gravitated to mathematics and science courses in college, students whose verbal scores were highest gravitated toward the humanities and social sciences, and students with a flat profile (very high scores everywhere) showed a more even distribution of interests. Preferences appeared relatively early. Reports of favorite class in high school mirrored later professional specialization.

Talents are channeled by interests. In general, people are more interested in things they are good at than things they find difficult. The combination of talent and interest leads to specialized knowledge, and knowledge produces expertise. Society reacts to the combination of talent and interest by offering support, which leads to further specialization.

Social Encouragement and Expertise

Because the acquisition of expertise requires substantial effort, the social support provided during the learning phase is extremely important. Chess experts begin early, often by participation in chess clubs (Charness, Krampe, & Mayr, 1996). Lubinski et al.'s gifted students made substantial use of advanced placement courses in high school and other educational acceleration programs. If we look at individual cases, the amount of social support can be dramatic. Gardner's (1993) biographic study of exceptional contributors to society, such as Einstein and Picasso, stresses how these great contributors were able to be single-minded because they were supported by family, friends, and colleagues, often at considerable expense. At a less earthshaking level of expertise, the 2004 winner of the Wimbledon woman's tennis tournament, Maria Sharapova, received a scholarship to a tennis academy at age eight!

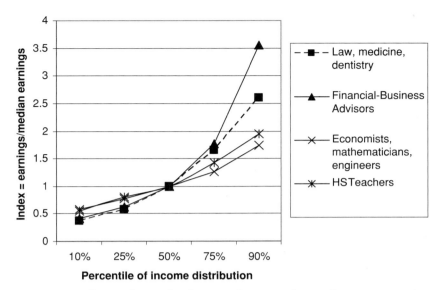

Figure 3.1. Differential reward indices as a function of type of occupation and the percentile of the income distribution. Data derived from US Census 2000 income reports.

Because expertise requires motivation and support, society has considerable leverage in deciding what types of expertise will be developed, by varying the extent to which rewards and support are offered for expert compared to journeyman performance.[3] Where does our own society reward expertise?

Rewarding expertise has to be distinguished from rewarding an entire occupation. This can be done by defining the *differential reward index,* $D_{occ}(x)$ for the xth percentile of an occupation, as

$$D_{occ}(x) = \frac{Income_{occ}(x)}{MedianIncome} \qquad (3.1)$$

Where $D_{occ}(x)$ is the value of the reward index at the xth percentile of the income distribution in occupation "occ," $Income_{occ}(x)$ is the income at the xth percentile, and *MedianIncome* is the median income for the occupation. To illustrate, in 1999 the median income for a physician or surgeon $(Income_{physician}(50))$ was $120,000, while $Income_{physician}(75)$ was $200,000. Therefore, for physicians and surgeons $D_{phsyician}(75)$ was 1.67. For people who made their living fishing, $Income_{fisher}(50)$ was $25,000, far less than the median income of physicians.

However, $Income_{fisher}(75)$ was $40,000, so $D_{fisher}(75) = 1.6$. Society rewarded physicians, as a group, far more than society rewarded fishers, but within each group the relative rewards for expert compared to journeyman performance were about the same.

Figure 3.1 shows the differential reward indices for four groups of occupations within our society. Financial business advisors (including stock brokers) represent a group whose compensation is closely tied to their success. Three professions (physician-surgeons, lawyers [excluding judicial officers], and dentists) generally derive income on a fee-for-service basis, including participation in joint practices. Subgroups of professionals who develop specialized expertise (e.g., neurosurgeons, orthodontists, trial lawyers) usually receive larger incomes than general practitioners. Mathematicians (outside of academia) and aerospace engineers also have high degrees of specialization, and could, in principle, be rewarded for expertise. Finally, high school teachers receive income from salaries that are almost entirely determined by their location of work and years of seniority. Therefore they serve as a control group.

The differential reward index varied markedly across occupations. Financial and business advisors in the 90th percentile of their profession earned 3.5 times the median income for their profession, whereas those at the 10th percentile earned half the median income. A similar but not-so-drastic acceleration was shown for the physician-dentist-lawyer group. The differential reward function for mathematicians and engineers was almost identical to that for high school teachers. In all groups acceleration occurred at the top. The differential reward functions were virtually linear from the 10th to the 50th percentile.

These data suggest, but certainly do not prove, that our society encourages the development of expertise in business, law, and the biomedical professions. The figures do not suggest very much encouragement for the development of expertise in mathematics and engineering. It is of interest to note that as of 2004 educators and policy makers were deploring the dearth of American students in engineering and mathematics, the biomedical fields were prosperous, and business schools were booming.

Bleske-Recheck, Lubinski, and Benbow (2004) make a related point. They observed that extremely gifted mathematics students reported liking Advanced Placement classes because it gave them an opportunity to study with, and proceed at the pace of, their academic peers. Bleske-Recheck et al. then asked whether a well-documented trend toward opening up Advanced Placement classes to a greater range of students, in order to encourage participation by students from a wider spectrum of society, might actually make these classes less attractive to the very gifted, and therefore channel talented individuals away from the areas where they might maximize their contributions. This is not the place to debate the overall social merits of opening up opportunities to non-traditional students versus offering special nurturance to the gifted. (Bleske-Recheck et al. acknowledge that such benefits exist.) What is relevant here is that experiences relatively early in adolescence do motivate students to make particular career choices.

If we need experts in some field we must encourage people to acquire appropriate expertise and reward them when they have done so.

Closing Remarks

In order to understand the development of expertise we have to distinguish between expertise in perceptual-motor tasks and expertise in cognitive activities. Perceptual-motor expertise requires automation in the literal sense. Cognitive expertise requires experience, and probably depends to some extent on automated "nonconscious" thought. It also depends very much on the acquisition of knowledge.

Working memory and attention are generally considered to be the intellectual bottlenecks on human thought. These are the processes most taxed in the early stages of either perceptual-motor learning or knowledge acquisition. Therefore it is harder to become an expert than to be one! Nevertheless, in some areas of expert performance working memory demands, and hence demands for high fluid intelligence, appear to extend beyond the learning period.

This conclusion does not deny the importance of practice. Becoming an expert in almost anything requires literally years of work. People will do this only if they have some initial success, enjoy the work, and are supported by the social climate. Expertise is not solely a cognitive affair.

Footnotes

1. The AFQT is a subset of the ASVAB, and therefore a test of Gc.
2. Schmidt and Hunter refer to tests of general cognitive competence. However, the tests that they list appear to be tests mainly of Gc.
3. My claim is not that expertise is the sole determiner of income. That would be silly. I do claim, however, that expertise is one of the determinants of income. Therefore the differential distribution of income within an occupation partly reflects payment for expertise and partly reflects other features, such as seniority.

References

Ackerman, P. L. (1996). A theory of adult intellectual development: Personality, interests, and knowledge. *Intelligence*, 22, 227–257.

Ackerman, P. L., & Beier, M. E. (2001). Trait complexes, cognitive investment, and domain knowledge. In R. J. Sternberg & E. L. Grigorenko (Eds.), *The Psychology of abilities, competences, and expertise* (pp. 1–30). Cambridge: Cambridge University Press.

Ackerman, P. L., & Cianciolo, A. T. (2000). Cognitive, perceptual-speed, and psychomotor determinants of individual differences during skill acquisition. *Journal of Experimental Psychology: Applied*, 6, 33–60.

Ackerman, P. L., & Rolfhus, E. L. (1999). The locus of adult intelligence: Knowledge, abilities, and non-ability traits. *Journal of Educational Psychology*, 91, 511–526.

Bleske-Rechek, A., Lubinski, D., & Benbow, C. P. (2004). Meeting the educational needs of special populations: Advanced placement's role in developing exceptional human capital. *Psychological Science*, 15, 217–224.

Carroll, J. B. (1993). *Human cognitive abilities*. Cambridge: Cambridge University Press.

Cattell, R. B. (1971). *Abilities: Their structure, growth, and action*. Boston, MA: Houghton Mifflin.

Charness, N., Krampe, R. Th., & Mayr, U. (1996). The role of practice and coaching in entreprenurial skill domains: An international comparison of life-span chess skill acquisition. In K. A. Ericsson (Ed.), *The road to excellence: The acquisition of expert performance in the arts and sciences, sports, and games* (pp. 51–80). Mahwah, NJ: Erlbaum.

Chi, M. T. H., Glaser, R., & Farr, M. J. (Eds.) (1988). *The nature of expertise*. Hillsdale, NJ: Erlbaum.

Deary, I. J., Egan, V., Gibson, G. J., Austin, E. J., Brand, C. R., & Kellaghan, T. (1996). Intelligence and the differentiation hypothesis. *Intelligence*, 23, 105–132.

Detterman, D. K., & Daniel, M. H. (1989). Correlations of mental tests with each other and with cognitive variables are highest in low IQ groups. *Intelligence*, 13, 349–360.

Engle, R. W., Kane, M. J., & Tulhoski, S. W. (1999). Individual differences in working memory and what they tell us about controlled attention, general fluid intelligence, and functions of the prefrontal cortex. In A. Miyake & P. Shah (Eds.), *Models of working memory: Mechanisms of active maintenance and executive control* (pp. 102–154). New York: Cambridge University Press.

Ericsson, K. A. (Ed.) (1996). *The road to excellence: The acquisition of expert performance in the arts and sciences, sports, and games*. Mahwah, NJ: Erlbaum.

Ericsson, K. A., Krampe, R. Th., & Tesch-Römer, C. (1993). The role of deliberate practice in the acquisition of expert performance. *Psychological Review*, 100, 363–406.

Ericsson, K. A., & Smith, J. (Eds.) (1991). *Towards a general theory of expertise*. Cambridge: Cambridge University Press.

Fleischman, E. A. (1972). On the relation between abilities, learning, and human performance. *American Psychologist*, 27, 1017–1032.

Gardner, H. (1993). *Creating minds: An anatomy of creativity seen through the lives of Freud, Einstein, Picasso, Stravinsky, Eliot, Graham, and Gandhi*. New York: Basic Books.

Horn, J. L. (1985). Remodeling old models of intelligence. In B. B. Wolman (Ed.), *Handbook of intelligence: Theories, measurements, and applications* (pp. 267–300). New York: Wiley.

Howard, A., & Bray, D. W. (1988) *Managerial lives in transition: Advancing age and changing times*. New York: Guilford Press.

Hunt, E. (1995). *Will we be smart enough? A cognitive analysis of the coming workforce*. New York: Russell Sage.

Jensen, A. R. (1998) *The g factor: The science of mental ability*. Westport, CT: Praeger Publishers/Greenwood Publishing Group.

Kahneman, D. (2003). A perspective on judgment and choice: Mapping bounded rationality. *American Psychologist*, 58, 697–720.

Klein, G. (1998). *Sources of power: How people make decisions*. Cambridge, MA: MIT Press.

Kyllonen, P. C., & Christal, R. E. (1990). Reasoning ability is (little more than) working memory capacity? *Intelligence*, 14, 389–433.

Lubinski, D., Webb, R. M., Morelock, M. J, & Benbow, C. P. (2001). Top 1 in 10,000: A 10-year follow-up of the profoundly gifted. *Journal of Applied Psychology*. 861, 718–729.

Richman, H. B., Gobet, F., Staszewski, J. J., & Simon, H. A. (1996). Perceptual and memory processes in the acquisition of expert performance: The EPAM model. In K. A. Ericsson (Ed.), *The road to excellence: The acquisition of expert performance in the arts and sciences, sports, and games* (pp 167–188). Mahwah, NJ: Erlbaum.

Roberts, R. D., Goff, G. N., Anjoul, F., Kyllonen, P. C., Pallier, G., & Stankov, L. (2000). The Armed Services Vocational Aptitude Battery (ASVAB): Little more than acculturated learning (Gc)!? *Learning and Individual Differences*, 12, 81–103.

Rolfhus, E. L., & Ackerman, P. L. (1999). Assessing individual differences in knowledge: Knowledge, intelligence, and related traits. *Journal of Educational Psychology*, 91, 511–526.

Schmidt, F. L., & Hunter, J. E. (1998). The validity and utility of selection methods in personnel psychology: Practical and theoretical implications of 85 years of research findings. *Psychological Bulletin*, 124, 262–274.

Schneider, W., & Shiffrin, R. M. (1977). Controlled and automatic processing: I. Detection, search, and attention. *Psychological Review*, 84, 1–66.

Sloboda, J. A. (1996). The acquisition of musical performance expertise: Deconstructing the "Talent" account of individual differences in musical expressivity. In K. A. Ericsson (Ed.), *The road to excellence: The acquisition of expert performance in the arts and sciences, sports, and games* (pp 107–126). Mahwah, NJ: Erlbaum.

Sternberg, R. J. (1996). *Successful intelligence: How practical and creative intelligence determine success in life*. New York: Simon & Schuster.

Sternberg, R. J., Forsythe, G. B., Hedlund, J., Horvath, J. A., Wagner, R. K., Williams, W. M., Snook, S. A., & Grigorenko, E. L. (2000). *Practical intelligence in everyday life*. New York: Cambridge University Press.

Sternberg, R. J., & Grigorenko, E. L. (Eds.) (2001). *The psychology of abilities, competencies, and expertise*. Cambridge: Cambridge University Press.

Wigdor, A. K., & Green, B. F., Jr. (1991). *Performance assessment in the workplace*. Washington, DC: National Academy Press.

Part II

OVERVIEW OF APPROACHES TO THE STUDY OF EXPERTISE – BRIEF HISTORICAL ACCOUNTS OF THEORIES AND METHODS

CHAPTER 4

Studies of Expertise from Psychological Perspectives

*Paul J. Feltovich, Michael J. Prietula,
& K. Anders Ericsson*

Introduction

The study of expertise has a very long history that has been discussed in several other chapters in this handbook (Ericsson, Chapter 1; Amirault & Branson, Chapter 5). This chapter focuses on the influential developments within cognitive science and cognitive psychology that have occurred over the last three decades. Our chapter consists of two parts. In the first part we briefly review what we consider the major developments in cognitive science and cognitive psychology that led to the new field of expertise studies. In the second part we attempt to characterize some of the emerging insights about mechanisms and aspects of expertise that generalize across domains, and we explore the original theoretical accounts, along with more recent ones.

The Development of Expertise Studies

In this handbook there are several pioneering research traditions represented that were brought together to allow laboratory studies of expertise, along with the development of formal models that can reproduce the performance of the experts. One early stream was the study of thinking using protocol analysis, where participants were instructed to "think aloud" while solving everyday life problems (Duncker, 1945), and experts were asked to think aloud while selecting moves for chess positions (de Groot, 1946/1965; Ericsson, Chapter 13). Another stream developed out of the research on judgment and decision making, where researchers compared the judgments of experts to those of statistical models (Meehl, 1954; Yates & Tschirhart, Chapter 24). The most important stream was one inspired by describing human performance with computational methods, in particular, methods implemented as programs on the computer, such as Miller, Galanter, and Pribram (1960), Reitman (1965), and Newell and Simon, (1972).

In this chapter we emphasize a period of research roughly from the mid 1950s into the 1970s, when empirical experimental studies of thinking in the laboratory were combined with theoretical models of human thought processes that could reproduce the observable performance. Even though there was important earlier work on expertise, this was the period when a number of forces came together to provide enough traction for the field to "take off." There were three main sources to this impetus: artificial intelligence, psychology, and education. We will survey these briefly.

Early computer models developed by Herbert Simon and Allen Newell demonstrated that it is relatively easy for computational devices to do some things worthy of being considered "intelligent." This breakthrough at Carnegie-Mellon was based on the confluence of two key realizations that emerged from the intellectual milieu that was developing between Carnegie and Rand at the time (Prietula & Augier, 2005). First, they (Al Newell, Cliff Shaw, and Herb Simon) envisioned that computers could be used to process "symbols and symbol structures." To explore this, they necessarily developed what was to become the first list-processing computer language, IPL, which afforded them the ability to create arbitrarily complex list structures and manipulate them recursively. Second, they incorporated the concept of "levels of abstraction" in articulating their theories and, consequently, their programs. These allowed them to address two critical technical problems: the "specification problem," in which the components and processes of the target system are sufficiently specified to capture the characteristics of interest, and the "realization problem," in which the specification can be implemented in an actual physical system to enable synthesis (Newell & Simon, 1956). The seeds of viewing humans and machines as complex information-processing systems had been sown.

During these early years, the first artificial intelligence program, called the Logic Theorist (Newell & Simon, 1956), was written. The Logic Theorist (LT) was coded in IPL. Significantly, it was able to prove theorems in the predicate calculus in a manner that mimics human adults (Newell & Simon, 1972). Of particular relevance to expertise,

LT was able to create some novel proofs. The heuristics from LT were later generalized into a model that could solve problems in many different domains, the General Problem Solver (Ernst & Newell, 1969). There were also other computer models that were built, not as simulations of human problem solving, but based on effective computation designed to represent artificial methods for producing intelligent action. For example, Samuel's (1959) checker-playing program was able to challenge and beat excellent human checker players. These early, along with subsequent, successes spawned some themes regarding expertise pertinent to the present chapter.

First, the idea that computation could support intelligent behavior reinforced the growing idea that computers and their programs could stand as formal models of human cognition. This grew into a pervasive stance toward human and machine cognition, the "information processing" model that is still widely held. Cognitive psychology and computer science merged into a very close collaboration (along with linguistics and a few other fields) that was later named Cognitive Science. These computational models and theories provided at least alternatives to the "behaviorist" (stimulus-response, no internal mental mechanisms) approaches that had dominated psychology for the prior half a century (more on this in our treatment of psychology and expertise below). Newell and Simon, two pioneers of the information-processing viewpoint, asserted this forcefully:

> *As far as the great debates about the empty organism, behaviorism, intervening variables, and hypothetical constructs are concerned, we take these simply as a phase in the development of psychology. Our theory posits internal mechanisms of great extent and complexity, and endeavors to make contact between them and the visible evidences of problem solving. That is all there is to it. (Newell & Simon, 1972, pp. 9–10)*

As we will address in our treatment of psychological influences, it is quite difficult to imagine what a field of studying expertise could have looked like if behaviorism had continued to hold sway.

The second theme has to do with alternative basic approaches to achieving intelligence in a computational device, what have been termed "weak and strong methods" (Newell, 1973). The earliest successful AI programs utilized weak reasoning and problem-solving methods that were drawing on descriptions of human thought processes. Indeed, at one point Newell termed artificial intelligence the "science of weak methods," at least as one characterization of AI (Newell, 1973, page 9). *Weak* methods are highly portable, generalizable methods that do not depend on the particular content of the domain of problem solving but, in being so, are less capable of finding solutions. Examples are "generate and test" (produce and apply all possible known next steps, and see if any of them yields success) and "means-ends analysis" (represent the goal state, what you are trying to achieve; represent where your progress has brought you right now; and try to find some currently available computational operator that can decrease some aspect of the distance between these. Repeat until done. *Strong* methods are more heavily dependent on rich knowledge of the problem-solving area and an understanding of what kinds of operations are likely to be successful in encountered situations. They are domain specialists, not generalists.

When early AI was being applied in relatively simple and well-structured areas, such as elementary games like checkers, weak methods fared fairly well. As the field developed and researchers started to address richer, complex, and knowledge-laden task environments, such as medicine (Pauker, Gorry, Kassirer, & Schwartz, 1976; Shortliffe, 1976) and chemical spectral analysis (Buchanan & Feigenbaum, 1978), the need for ever-stronger methods became clear. Portability across task domains had to be sacrificed in favor of capability, but narrowly restricted capability. The highly successful "expert systems" industry that eventually developed (Buchanan, Davis, & Feigenbaum, Chapter 6) is in large part testimony to the efficacy of strong methods. As related to this chapter, this is important because a similar progression unfolded in other kinds of investigations of expertise, including those in psychology (see later sections in this chapter on *"Expertise Is Limited in Its Scope and Elite Performance Does Not Transfer"; and "Knowledge and Content Matter Are Important to Expertise"*).

Behaviorism was the school of psychology that eschewed resorting to unobservable mental constructs, structural or process, of any kind. Only the observable environment (the stimulus) and an organism's overt reaction (the response) were considered the legitimate purview of a psychological science. Behaviorism had dominated psychology for much of the first half of the twentieth century. During the reign of behaviorism, considerable success was obtained in analyzing complex skills in terms of acquired habits, that is, as a large collection of stimulus-response pairs in the form of learned reactions associated to specific situations. The principle difficulties of this approach were associated with explaining the acquisition of abstract rules, creative use of language, general mental capacities, and logical reasoning in unfamiliar domains. It was around the middle of the century that this hold on the field began to loosen. There was both a push side and a pull side to this development.

On the push side, as we have noted, stimulus-response models were facing great difficulty in trying to account for complex human processes such as language, reasoning, and abstractions that were independently coming under increasing investigation. In this respect, the work of the linguist Chomsky (1957) was critical. The findings and theorizing out of linguistics were affecting psychology, in exposing what seemed to be significant inadequacies in accounting for complex psychological processes. A notable volume (Jakobovits & Miron, 1967), not surprisingly focusing on language, brought the camps head to head in their explanatory systems for complex human activity. The Herculean effort by Osgood (1963), reprinted in that volume, to save S-R theory in the face of discoveries about language, just served in its cumbersomeness to prove the inadequacies of S-R theories to account for language.

On the pull side, theories, mechanisms, and constructs were arising that showed promise for providing an infrastructure to support a new kind of psychology. These included the development of the information-processing viewpoint in psychology, along with the platform to support it, the computer. Electrical engineer Newell and economist/philosopher Simon believed that what they were doing was psychology (see earlier quote)! In fact, they predicted in 1958 that "within ten years most theories in psychology will take the form of computer programs, or of qualitative statements about the characteristics of computer programs" and discussed the nature of heuristic search and ill-structured problems (Simon & Newell, 1958, p. 7). In his landmark volume titled "Cognitive Psychology," Ulric Neisser (1967) engaged information-processing language and the computer metaphor as advances that helped enable the creation of a cognitive psychology, and he acknowledged the contributions of Newell, Shaw, and Simon in this regard (Neisser, 1967, pp. 8–9).

Additionally, and often not independently, researchers were progressively encroaching the realm of the mental, studying such things as planning (Miller, Galanter, & Pribram, 1960), thinking (Bartlett, 1958; Bruner, Goodnow, & Austin, 1956), and mental structures and their functioning (Bartlett, 1932; Miller, 1956). Not surprisingly, groundbreaking progress in this regard came from the information-processing camp in their studies of problem solving (Newell & Simon, 1972), especially in their studies (following de Groot, 1946, 1965) of expertise in chess (Chase & Simon, 1973a, 1973b; See also Gobet & Charness, Chapter 30). The clear, surprising, and even enchanting findings (two people looking at the very same "stimulus" can see totally different things, even things that are not actually there!) arising from this research about the cognitive differences between experts and novices stimulated others to

conduct such studies (Charness, 1976, 1979, 1981; Chi, 1978; Chi, Feltovich, & Glaser, 1981; Elstein, Shulman, & Sprafka, 1978; Larkin, McDermott, Simon, & Simon, 1980), and the rest, as they say, is history. The existence of this Cambridge *Handbook* is its own best evidence for the subsequent development and tremendous expansion of the field of "Expertise Studies" into its current myriad forms.

It is interesting to think about whether a field of expertise studies could have emerged at all – and if so, what it could possibly have looked like – if alternatives to behaviorism had not emerged. For instance, would we have discovered that experts do not just complete tasks and solve problems faster and better than novices, but often attain their solutions in qualitatively different ways? Would we have discovered that experts frequently spend a greater proportion of their time in initial problem evaluation compared to novices (e.g., Glaser & Chi, 1988, regarding "Experts spend a great deal of time analyzing a problem qualitatively"; Lesgold et al., 1988; see also Kellogg's Chapter 22 on planning by professional writers and Noice & Noice's Chapter 28 on the deep encoding by professional actors as they study their lines)?

We will, of course, never know, but there was considerable interest in complex thought processes among some of the behaviorists. For example, John B. Watson (1920) was the first investigator to study problem solving by instructing a participant to think aloud while the participant figured out the function of an object (Ericsson, Chapter 13). Neo-behaviorists, such as Berlyne (1965), proposed stimulus-response accounts for complex goal-directed thought and cognitive development. Today, behavior analysts recommend the collection of think-aloud protocols to better understand complex performance (Austin, 2000). Given the broad divide in the theoretical mechanisms used by cognitive and behavioral researchers, it is interesting that researchers are converging on methods of collecting observable process indicators and have mutual interest in large, reproducible differences in performance.

The last peg in the story of expertise studies that we consider is education and educational psychology. There are at least two dimensions in the evolution of education that are related to expertise studies, and that we have also seen in the other influences we have considered. First, like psychology, educational theory and practice was under the influence of behaviorism in and around the mid century (Skinner, 1960; Watson, 1913). Both learning and teaching centered around establishing appropriate stimulus-response connections. "Programmed learning" and "teaching machines" were in vogue. A representative example is the landmark volume co-edited by Robert Glaser (Lumsdaine & Glaser, 1960), who would go on to play a central role in newer incarnations of educational and psychological theory and practice. Essentially, a teaching machine, in doing programmed learning, would present questions or problems to learners, one by one, and depending on the student's response either reinforce a correct response or note an incorrect one (and perhaps also provide some remedial guidance). This process was believed to establish stable connections between problematic situations and appropriate situational responses. What would expertise look like under such a worldview? It is interesting in this regard to examine a statement about this made by one of Behaviorism's founders:

> Mathematical behavior is usually regarded not as a repertoire of responses involving numbers and numerical operations, but as evidence of mathematical ability or the exercise of the power of reason. It is true that the techniques which are emerging from the experimental study of learning are not designed to "develop the mind" or to further some vague "understanding" of mathematical relationships. They are designed, on the contrary, to establish the very behaviors which are taken to be evidences of such mental states or processes. (Skinner, 1960, pp. 111)

In this view, it seems expertise would be a matter of responding well in challenging situations. Although modern views of expertise retain this criterion of superior performance, there is also considerable interest

and theorizing about mediating processes and structures that support, and can be developed to produce, these superior performances (see later sections in this chapter on "Expertise Involves Larger and More Integrated Cognitive Units"; and "Expertise Involves Functional, Abstracted Representations of Presented Information"). Interestingly, however, current theorizing about the critical role of deliberate practice in the development of expertise emphasizes mechanisms not incompatible with these earlier theories, in particular the need for clear goals, repeated practice experiences, and the vital role of feedback about the quality of attempts (Ericsson, Krampe, & Tesch-Römer, 1993). In addition, it is possible that discoveries from behaviorist research about different "schedules of reinforcement" (e.g., Ferster & Skinner, 1957), and their relation to sustaining motivation and effort over long periods of time, might contribute to our understanding of how some people manage to persevere through the very long periods of practice and experience, involving both successes and inevitably many failures, that we now know are so essential to the development of expert levels of skill. How to scaffold sustained, consistent, purposeful effort, over very long periods of time and despite inevitable setbacks, appears at this time to be one of the great puzzles to be solved in developing a science of human excellence (see Hunt, Chapter 3, for a discussion).

With the emergence of the cognitive turn in psychology and educational psychology, a new role for expertise studies also emerged. Expert cognition was conceived as the "goal state" for education, the criterion for what the successful educational process should produce, as well as a measure by which to assess its progress. In this regard, advanced methods have now been developed for eliciting and representing the knowledge of experts (see Hoffman & Lintern, Chapter 12) and for observing and describing experts' work practices in natural settings (see Clancey, Chapter 8). Novice cognition (as well as that of various levels of intermediates) could serve as "initial states," as models of the starting place for the educational process. In a sort of means-ends analysis, the job of education was to determine the kinds of operations that could transform the initial conditions into the desired more expertlike ones (Glaser, 1976). Although it is tempting to believe that upon knowing how the expert does something, one might be able to "teach" this to novices directly, this has not been the case (e.g., Klein & Hoffman, 1993). Expertise is a long-term developmental process, resulting from rich instrumental experiences in the world and extensive practice. These cannot simply be handed to someone (see the later section in this chapter on "*Simple Experience Is Not Sufficient for the Development of Expertise*").

One venue in which expertise as "goal state" has gained considerable use is in intelligent computer-based education, for example, "intelligent tutoring systems." (e.g., Clancey & Letsinger, 1984; Forbus & Feltovich, 2001; Sleeman & Brown, 1982). Such systems often utilize an "expert model," a representation of expert competence in a task, and a "student model," a representation of the learner's pertinent current understanding. Discrepancy between the two often drives what instructional intervention is engaged next. Another educational approach is to build tools for enhancing and accelerating experience (e.g., Klein & Hoffman, 1993; Spiro, Collins, Thota, & Feltovich, 2003), and this is closely related to methods for analyzing the representative tasks to be mastered (see Schraagen, Chapter 11).

Some early research on the difference between experts and novices led directly to the creation of new methods of instruction. This is particularly true in medical education, where early expert-novice studies (Barrows, Feightner, Neufeld, & Norman, 1978; Elstein, Shulman, & Sprafka, 1978) led to the creation of "problem-based learning" (Barrows & Tamblyn, 1980). Over a long period of time, PBL (and variants) has come to pervade medical education, as well as making significant inroads into all types of education, including K-12, university, and every sort of professional education (see Ward, Williams, & Hancock, Chapter 14, for a review of the use of simulation in training).

A second theme related to expertise studies that also appears in education, as well as in the other contributors we have discussed, is related to weak and strong methods (Amirault & Branson, Chapter 5). As long as there has been education, there has been controversy about what constitutes an educated person, what such a person should know and be able to do, and how to bring such a person about. Examination of the history of education as it relates to expertise (Amirault & Branson, Chapter 5) reveals the ebb and flow between understanding the object of education (expertise) to be the generalist (sound reasoning, broad knowledge, critical thinking) or the specialist (one who has undergone a great amount of training and experience in a limited domain of activity and has acquired a vast knowledge base specifically tailored for that activity). As with the development of artificial intelligence, our modern educational and psychological conception of expertise seems to favor the specialist and specialized skills, honed over many years of extensive training and deliberate practice (Ericsson, Chapter, 38). The notion of an "expert generalist" is difficult to capture within the current explanatory systems in expertise studies (e.g., Feltovich, Spiro, & Coulson, 1997; see also the discussion of the preparation for creative contributions by Weisberg, Chapter 42).

Toward Generalizable Charactistics of Expertise and Their Theoretical Mechanisms

From the kinds of beginnings just discussed, expertise studies have become a large and active field. Fortunately, periodic volumes have served to capture its state of development over time (Anderson, 1981; Bloom, 1985; Chase, 1973; Chi, Glaser, & Farr, 1988; Clancey & Shortliffe, 1984; Ericsson, 1996a; Ericsson & Smith, 1991a; Feltovich, Ford, & Hoffman, 1997; Hoffman, 1992; Starkes & Allard, 1993; Starkes & Ericsson, 2003).

The remainder of the current chapter attempts to crystallize the classic and enduring findings from the study of expertise. It will draw on generalizable characteristics of expertise identified in earlier reviews (Glaser & Chi, 1988; Chi, Chapter 2) and discuss them and other aspects in the light of the pioneering research that uncovered them. We will also discuss the original theoretical accounts for these findings. However, where pertinent, we will also present more recent challenges and extensions to these classic accounts, including pertinent findings and theoretical treatments reviewed in the chapters of this handbook.

Expertise Is Limited in Its Scope and Elite Performance Does Not Transfer

There is a general belief that talented people display superior performance in a wide range of activities, such as having superior athletic ability and superior mental abilities. However, if we restrict the claims to individuals who can perform at very high levels in a domain, then it is clear that people hardly ever reach an elite level in more than a single domain of activity (Ericsson & Lehmann, 1996). This has proven to be one of the most enduring findings in the study of expertise (see Glaser & Chi, 1988, Characteristic 1). There is little transfer from high-level proficiency in one domain to proficiency in other domains – even when the domains seem, intuitively, very similar.

For example, in tasks similar to those used in the Simon and Chase chessboard studies, Eisenstadt and Kareev (1979) studied the memory for brief displays for expert GO and Gomoko players. Even though these two games are played on the same board and use the same pieces, GO players showed quite poor performance on Gomoko displays, and vice versa. In tasks involving political science, for example, devising plans for increasing crop production in the Soviet Union, Voss and colleagues (Voss, Greene, Post, & Penner, 1983; Voss, Tyler, & Yengo, 1983) found that experts in chemistry (chemistry professors) performed very much like novices in political science, in comparison to political science experts (see Voss & Wiley, Chapter 33, and Endsley, Chapter 36, for more recent examples). Task specificity

is also characteristic of expertise involving perceptual-motor skills (e.g., Fitts & Posner, 1967; Rosenbaum, Augustyn, Cohen, & Jax, Chapter 29), as exemplified in many chapters in this handbook, but in particular in perceptual diagnosis and surgery (Norman, Eva, Brooks, & Hamstra, Chapter 19), sports (Hodges, Starkes, & MacMahon, Chapter 27), and music (Lehmann & Gruber, Chapter 26).

Some of the most solid early evidence for specificity in expertise came from expert-novice difference studies in medicine, investigating the clinical reasoning of practitioners (Barrows et al., 1978; Elstein et al., 1978). These studies showed that the same physician can demonstrate widely different profiles of competence, depending on his or her particular experiential history with different types of cases. Indeed, in modern medical education, where assessment of clinical skill is often evaluated by performance on real or simulated cases, it has been found that because of the case-specificity of clinical skill, a large number of cases (on the order of fourteen to eighteen) are needed to achieve an acceptably reliable assessment of skill (Petrusa, 2002; Norman et al., Chapter 19).

Knowledge and Content Matter Are Important to Expertise

In and around the late 1960s and the 1970s, maintaining a traditional distinction between domain-specific skills and general cognitive abilities was becoming less tenable. In research studies, knowledge was no longer seen as a "nuisance variable" but as a dominant source of variance in many human tasks. In particular, Newell and Simon (1972) found that problem solving and skilled performance in a given domain were primarily influenced by domain-specific acquired patterns and associated actions. Domain-specific skills and knowledge were also found to influence even basic cognitive abilities. For example, Glaser and others (Pellegrino & Glaser, 1982a, 1982b) investigated basic foundations of intelligence, including induction, and found evidence that even these were strongly influenced by a person's knowledge in the operative domain (for example, a person's conceptual knowledge about numbers in number analogy and number series tasks).

Acquired knowledge in a domain was found to be associated with changes in fundamental types of cognitive processing. For example, drawing on the expert-novice paradigm, Chi (1978) compared experienced chess-playing children with other children in their performance on memory and learning tasks related to chess. The differences in experience, knowledge, and skill in chess produced differences, in favor of the chess players, in such basic learning processes as the spontaneous use of memory strategies (like grouping and rehearsal), the ability to use such strategies even under experimental prompting, and the amount of information that could be held in short-term memory (Chi, 1978).

Voss and colleagues (Chiesi, Spilich, & Voss, 1979; Spilich, Vesonder, Chiesi, & Voss, 1979) extended this kind of research into other forms of learning. Studying high- and low-knowledge individuals with regard to the game of baseball, they found that, compared to the low-knowledge individuals, high-knowledge ones exhibited superior learning for materials from that and only that particular domain. In particular, high-knowledge individuals had greater recognition and recall memory for new material, could make useful inferences from smaller amounts of partial information, and were better able to integrate new material within a coherent and interconnected framework (organized, for instance, under a common goal structure).

Some studies showed reasoning itself to be dependent on knowledge. Wason and Johnson-Laird (1972) presented evidence that individuals perform poorly in testing the implications of logical inference rules (e.g., if p then q) when the rules are stated abstractly. Performance greatly improves for concrete instances of the same rules (e.g., "every time I go to Manchester, I go by train"). Rumelhart (1979), in an extension of this work, found that nearly five times as many participants were able to test cor-

rectly the implications of a simple, single-conditional logical expression when it was stated in terms of a realistic setting (e.g., a work setting: "every purchase over thirty dollars must be approved by the regional manager") versus when the expression was stated in an understandable but less meaningful form (e.g., "every card with a vowel on the front must have an integer on the back").

These kinds of studies in the psychology of learning and reasoning were mirrored by developments within artificial intelligence. There was an evolution from systems in which knowledge (declarative) and reasoning (procedural) were clearly separated, to systems in which these components were indistinct or at least strongly interacted. For example, early computer systems, such as Green's QA3 (Green, 1969) and Quillian's TLC (Quillian, 1969), utilized databases of declarative knowledge and a few general-purpose reasoning algorithms for operating on those knowledge bases. Such systems were progressively supplanted by ones in which the separation between knowledge and reasoning was not nearly as distinct, and in which general reasoning algorithms gave way to more narrowly applicable reasoning strategies, embedded in procedures for operating within specific domains of knowledge (e.g., Norman, Rumelhart, & LNR, 1979; Sacerdoti, 1977; VanLehn & Seely-Brown, 1979; Winograd, 1975).

It was within this kind of context that studies of expertise and expert-novice differences, along with the growth of knowledge-intense "expert systems" in artificial intelligence (e.g., Shortliffe, 1976; Buchanan, Davis, & Feigenbaum, Chapter 6), began also to emphasize the criticality of knowledge. This was evident in the progression in AI from weak to strong methods, and within psychology in the growing recognition of the role in expertise of such knowledge-based features as perceptual chunking, knowledge organization, knowledge differentiation, and effective perceptual-knowledge coupling.

This research clearly rejects the classical views on human cognition, in which general abilities such as learning, reasoning, problem solving, and concept formation correspond to capacities and abilities that can be studied independently of the content domains. In fact, inspired by the pioneering work by Ebbinghaus (1885/1964) on memory for nonsense syllables, most laboratory research utilized stimulus materials for which the prior experience of participants was minimized, in order to allow investigators to study the cognitive processes of learning, reasoning, and problem solving in their "purest" forms. This kind of research, some examples of which were discussed earlier in this section, showed that participants, when confronted with unfamiliar materials in laboratory tasks, demonstrated surprisingly poor performance. In contrast, when tested with materials and tasks from familiar domains of everyday activity, people exhibited effective reasoning, learning, and problem solving. Similarly, the performance of experts is superior to novices and less-skilled individuals primarily for tasks that are representative of their typical activities in their domain of expertise – the domain specificity of expertise (see the earlier section "Expertise Is Limited").

In the expert-performance approach to expertise, researchers attempt to identify those tasks that best capture the essence of expert performance in the corresponding domain, and then standardize representative tasks that can be presented to experts and novices. By having experts repeatedly perform these types of tasks, experimenters can identify, with experimental and process-tracing techniques, those complex mechanisms that mediate their superior performance (Ericsson, Chapter 13 and Chapter 38). The experts' superior performance on tasks related to their domain of expertise can be described by psychometric factors (expert reasoning and expert working memory) that differ from those general ability factors used to describe the performance of novices (Horn & Masunaga, Chapter 34, and see Ackerman & Beier, Chapter 9, for a review of individual differences as a function of level of expertise). In short, knowledge matters (Steier & Mitchell, 1996).

Expertise Involves Larger and More Integrated Cognitive Units

With increased experience and practice, most people cognitively organize the perceptually available information in their working environment into larger units. This is a classic and one of the best-established phenomenon in expertise (Glaser & Chi, 1988, Characteristic 2). It is supported by a long line of research, but was first discovered in the game of chess (see also Gobet & Charness, Chapter 30).

In the 1960s and early 1970s, de Groot (1965) and Chase and Simon (1973a, 1973b) studied master-level and less-accomplished chess players. In the basic experimental task, participants were shown a chess board with pieces representing game positions from real games. Participants were shown the positions for only five seconds, and they were then asked to reproduce the positions they had seen.

After this brief glance, an expert was able to reproduce much more of the configuration than a novice. In the studies by Chase and Simon (1973a, 1973b) noted earlier, the expert recalled four to five times the number of pieces recalled by the novice. In the similar studies by de Groot, the recall performance by world-class players was nearly perfect (for 25-piece boards). In contrast, novices were able to reproduce about five pieces, or about the number of items that can be maintained in short-term memory exclusively by rehearsal.

The original, classical explanation by Chase and Simon (Simon & Chase, 1973; Chase & Simon, 1973a, 1973b) for expert superiority involved "chunking" in perception and memory. With experience, experts acquire a large "vocabulary," or memory store, of *board patterns involving groups of pieces*, or what were called chunks. A chunk is a perceptual or memory structure that bonds a number of more elementary units into a larger organization (e.g., the individual letters "c", "a," and "r" into the word "car"). When experts see a chess position from a real game, they are able to rapidly recognize such familiar patterns. They can then associate these patterns with moves stored in memory that have proven to be good moves in the past. Novices do not have enough exposure to game configurations to have developed many of these kinds of patterns. Hence they deal with the board in a piece-by-piece manner. Similarly, when experts are presented with chess boards composed of randomly placed pieces that do not enable the experts to take advantage of established patterns, their advantage over novices for random configurations amounts to only a few additional pieces.

These basic phenomena attributed to chunking were replicated many times, in chess but also in other fields (e.g., the games of bridge, Engle & Bukstel, 1978; GO, Reitman, 1976; and electronics, Egan & Schwartz, 1979). In many such studies, it is the chunk *size* that is larger for experts. Both the novice and the expert are constrained by the same limitations of short-term (or working) memory (Cowan, Chen, & Rouder, 2004; Miller 1956). However, expert chunks are larger. A chess novice sees a number of independent chess pieces; the expert recognizes about the *same number* of *larger* units. For example, one chunk of chess pieces for an expert might be a "king defense configuration," composed of a number of individual chess pieces.

As we have just discussed, it was originally believed that experts develop larger chunks and that these enable the expert to functionally expand the size of short-term or working memory. However, in the mid-1970s, Charness (1976) showed that expert chess players do not rely on a transient short-term memory for storage of briefly presented chess positions. In fact, they are able to recall positions, even after the contents of their short-term memory have been completely disrupted by an interfering activity. Subsequent research has shown that chess experts have acquired memory skills that enable them to encode chess positions in long-term working memory (LTWM, Ericsson & Kintsch, 1995). The encoding and storage of the chess positions in LTWM allow experts to recall presented chess positions after disruptions of short-term memory, as well as

being able to recall multiple chess boards presented in rapid succession (see Ericsson, Chapter 13, and Gobet & Charness, Chapter 30, for an extended discussion of new theoretical mechanisms accounting for the experts' expanded working memory). The experts' superior ability to encode representative information from their domain of expertise and store it in long-term memory, such that they can efficiently retrieve meaningful relations, provides an alternative to the original account of superior memory in terms of larger chunks stored in STM. There is another, similar characteristic of expertise. It has to do with the *nature* and *organization* of the perceptual encoding and memory structures experts develop and use. This is discussed next.

Expertise Involves Functional, Abstracted Representations of Presented Information

Some studies, utilizing methods similar to the Simon and Chase chessboard paradigm, examined the *nature* of expert and novice cognitive units, such as chunks or other knowledge structures. Chase and Simon (1973a, 1973b) themselves analyzed the characteristics of the chess pieces their experts grouped together as they reproduced a chess position after a brief presentation. Expert configurations of chess pieces were based largely on strategic aspects of the game, for example, configurations representing elements of threat or opportunity. It was not clear how novice units were organized. Glaser and Chi (1988) identified a related general characteristic, namely, that "Experts see and represent a problem in their domain at a deeper (more principled) level than novices; novices tend to represent a problem at a superficial level" (p. xviii). Our characterization for expert representations, "functional and abstracted" as elaborated next, simply seeks to provide a bit more insight into the nature of "deep" (see Chi, Chapter 10, for a review of research on assessments of experts' cognitive representations).

Early studies involving bridge (Charness, 1979, Engle & Bukstel, 1978) and electronics

(Egan & Schwartz, 1979), patterned after the Chase and Simon procedure, showed similar results. In the bridge studies, experts and novices were briefly presented depictions of four-handed bridge deals, and they were required to reproduce these deals. Experts reproduced the cards by suit, across hands. They remembered cards of the same suit from three hands and inferred the fourth; this is an organization useful in playing the game of bridge. Novices recalled the cards by order of card rank within hands, an organization *not* useful to supporting strategic aspects of the game. In electronics, subjects were shown an electronic circuit diagram, which they were then to reproduce. Experts grouped individual diagram components into major electronic components (e.g., amplifiers, filters, rectifiers). Novice organization was based largely on the spatial proximity of symbols appearing in the diagram.

Similar results have been shown from yet other fields, using somewhat different methodologies that compared the performance of groups of adults who differ in their knowledge about a given domain. For example, Voss and colleagues (Spilich et al., 1979) studied ardent baseball fans and more casual baseball observers. Participants were presented a colorful description of a half-inning of baseball and were then asked to recall the half-inning. Expert recall was structured by major goal-related sequences of the game, such as advancing runners, scoring runs, and preventing scoring. Novices' recall contained less integral components, for example, observations about the weather and the crowd mood. Novice recall did not capture basic game-advancing, sequential activity nearly as well. More recent research on fans that differ in their knowledge about soccer and baseball has found that comprehension and memory for texts describing games from these sports is more influenced by relevant knowledge than by verbal IQ scores (see Hambrick & Engle, 2002, for a recent study and a review of earlier work).

Two early studies of computer programming produced similar results. McKeithen,

Reitman, Reuter, and Hirtle (1981) presented a list of 21 commands in the ALGOL language to ALGOL experts, students after one ALGOL course, and students at the beginning of an ALGOL course. Participants were given 25 recall trials after they initially learned the list. The organization of the recalled items by pre-ALGOL students was by surface features of commands (e.g., commands with the same beginning letter or same length of command name) and groups of commands forming natural language segments (e.g., "STRING IS NULL BITS") that have no conceptual meaning within the language. Experts, in contrast, grouped commands that formed mini ALGOL algorithms (e.g., formation of loops) or constituted types of ALGOL data structures. Students, after an ALGOL course, produced groupings that were a mixture of surface-related and meaningful ALGOL organizations.

In a similar study, Adelson (1981) presented a list of programming commands, constituting three intact computer programs, scrambled together and out of order, to expert and novice programmers. Participants were required to recall the list. Over recall trials, experts reconstructed the original three algorithms. The organization of novice recall was by syntactic similarities in individual command statements, regardless of the embedded source algorithms. Sonnentag, Niessen, and Volmer (Chapter 21) provide a review of the more recent research on knowledge representations and superior performance of software experts.

Other pertinent findings came from early work in physics (Chi et al., 1981) and medicine (Feltovich, Johnson, Moller, & Swanson, 1984; Johnson et al., 1981). In the basic task from the physics study, problems from chapters in an introductory physics text were placed on individual cards. Expert (professors and advanced graduate students) and novice (college students after their first mechanics course) physics problem solvers sorted the cards into groups of problems they would "solve in a similar manner." The finding was that experts created groups based on the major physics principles (e.g., conservation and force laws) applicable in the problems' solutions. Novice groupings were organized by salient objects (e.g., springs, inclined planes) and features contained in the problem statement itself. Similarly, in studies of expert and novice diagnoses within a subspecialty of medicine, expert diagnosticians organized diagnostic hypotheses according to the major pathophysiological issue relevant in a case (i.e., constituting the "Logical Competitor Set" of reasonable alternatives for the case, e.g., lesions involving right-sided heart volume overload), whereas novice hypotheses were more isolated and more dependent on particular patient cues.

Zeitz (1997) has reviewed these and more recent studies of this type, investigating what she calls experts' use of "Moderately Abstracted Conceptual Representations"(MACRs), which are representational abstractions of the type just discussed. She proposes numerous ways in which such abstraction aids the efficient utilization of knowledge and reasoning by experts. These include: (a) the role of abstracted representations in retrieving appropriate material from memory (e.g., Chi et al., 1981); (b) the schematic nature of MACRs in integrating information and revealing what information is important, (c) providing guidance for a line of action and supporting justification for such a line of approach (e.g., Phelps & Shanteau, 1978; Schmidt et al., 1989; Voss et al., 1983); (d) aiding productive analogical reasoning (e.g., Gentner, 1988); and (e) providing abstract representations that support experts' reasoning and evaluation of diagnostic alternatives (e.g., Patel, Arocha, & Kaufman, 1994).

The functional nature of experts' representations extends to entire activities or events. Ericsson and Kintsch (1995) proposed that experts acquire skills for encoding new relevant information in LTWM to allow direct access when it is relevant and to support the continual updating of a mental model of the current situation – akin to the situational models created by readers when they read books (see Endsley, Chapter 36, on the expert's superior ability to monitor the current situation – "situational

awareness"). This general theoretical framework can account for the slow acquisition of abstract representations that support planning, reasoning, monitoring, and evaluation (Ericsson, Patel, & Kintsch, 2000). For example, studies of expert fire fighters have shown that experts interpret any scene of a fire dynamically, in terms of what likely preceded it and how it will likely evolve. This kind of understanding supports efforts to intervene in the fire. Novices interpret these scenes in terms of perceptually salient characteristics, for example, color and intensity (Klein, 1998, and see Ross, Shafer, & Klein, Chapter 23). Studies of expert surgeons have shown that some actions within a surgery have no real value for immediate purposes, but are made in order to make some later move more efficient or effective (Koschmann, LeBaron, Goodwin, & Feltovich, 2001). The research on expert chess players shows consistent evidence for extensive planning and evaluation of consequences of alternative move sequences (See Ericsson, Chapter 13, and Gobet & Charness, Chapter 30). Furthermore, there is considerable evidence pertaining to experts' elaborated encoding of the current situation, such as in situational awareness (Endsely, Chapter 36), mental models (Durso & Dattel, Chapter 20), and LTWM (Noice & Noice, Chapter, 28).

In summary, research conducted in the last thirty or so years indicates that expert performers acquire skills to develop complex representations that allow them immediate and integrated access to information and knowledge relevant to the demands of action in current situations and tasks. These acquired skills can account also for the their superior memory performance when they are given a task, such as recalling a briefly presented chess position, as in the studies by Chase and Simon (1973a, 1973b). Novices, on the other hand, lack such knowledge and associated representations and skills, and thus perform these tasks with the only knowledge and skills they have available. They try to impose organization and meaningful relations, but their attempts are piecemeal and less relevant to effectively functioning in the task domain, organized, for example, by items named in a situation, current salient features, proximity of entities to others, or superficial analogies.

Expertise Involves Automated Basic Strokes

Most people considered to be experts are individuals with extreme amounts of practice on a circumscribed set of tasks in their work environment. For example, some expert radiologists estimated they had analyzed more than half a million radiographs (X-rays) in their careers (Lesgold et al., 1988). Such experience, appropriately conducted, can yield effective, major behavioral and brain changes (Hill & Schneider, Chapter 37).

Research on the effects of practice has found that the character of cognitive operations changes after even a couple of hours of practice on a typical laboratory task. Operations that are initially slow, serial, and demand conscious attention become fast, less deliberate, and can run in parallel with other processes (Schneider & Shiffrin, 1977). With enough practice, one can learn how do several tasks at the same time. Behavioral studies of skill acquisition have demonstrated that automaticity is central to the development of expertise, and practice is the means to automaticity (Posner & Snyder, 1975, see also Proctor & Vu, Chapter 15). Through the act of practice (with appropriate feedback, monitoring, etc.), the character of cognitive operations changes in a manner that (a) improves the speed of the operations, (b) improves the smoothness of the operations, and (c) reduces the cognitive demands of the operations, thus releasing cognitive (e.g., attentional) resources for other (often higher) functions (e.g., planning, self-monitoring; see also Endsley Chapter 36). Automatic processes seem resistant to disruption by reduced cognitive capacity and, to a limited degree, are largely resource insensitive (Schneider & Fisk, 1982). Interestingly, fMRI studies have demonstrated that shifts to automaticity reveal a shift (decrease) in activity in a certain part of the brain, but not a shift in anatomical loci (Jansma, Ramsey, Slagter, & Kahn, 2001; Hill & Schneider, Chapter 37).

There are many examples in the early expertise-related literature of the effects of practice on dual-task performance of experts. For example, expert typists can type and recite nursery rhymes at the same time (Shaffer, 1975). Skilled abacus operators can answer routine questions ("What is your favorite food?") without loss of accuracy or speed in working with the abacus (Hatano, Miyake, & Binks, 1977). After six weeks of practice (one hour per day), college students could read unfamiliar text while simultaneously copying words read by an experimenter, without decrement in reading speed or comprehension (Spelke, Hirst, & Neisser, 1976).

Automaticity is important to expertise. It appears it has at least two main functions. The first has to do with the relationship between fundamental and higher-order cognitive skills, and the second has to do with the interaction between automaticity of processes and usability of available knowledge.

With regard to the first, in complex skills with many different cognitive components, it appears that some of the more basic ones (e.g., fundamental decoding, encoding of input) must be automated if higher-level skills such as reasoning, comprehension, inference, monitoring, and integration are ever to be proficient (e.g., Logan, 1985; Endsley, Chapter 36). For example, in a longitudinal study, Lesgold and Resnick (1982) followed the same group of children from their initial exposure to reading in kindergarten through third and fourth grade. They found, for example, that if basic reading skills do not become automated, such as the decoding and encoding of letters and words, comprehension skills will not substantially develop. Furthermore, the relationship seems to be causal; that is, speed increases in word skills predict comprehension increases later on, whereas increases in comprehension do not predict increases in word facility. However, subsequent pertinent research has accentuated the complex-nature of the relationship between automated basic processes and higher-order deliberate ones and point to the need for continued research (Hill & Schneider, Chapter 37).

There is also a possible interaction between automaticity of processes and the usability of available knowledge. Investigators (e.g., Feltovich et al., 1984; Jeffries et al., 1981) have suggested that a major limitation of novices is their inability to access knowledge in relevant situations, even when they can retrieve the same knowledge when explicitly cued by the experimenter. Problems in knowledge usability may be associated with overload or inefficiency in using working (or short-term) memory. The usable knowledge of experts may, in turn, result from the subordination of many task components to automatic processing, which increases capability for controlled management of memory and knowledge application (cf. Perfetti & Lesgold, 1979).

An alternative proposal about usability of knowledge has subsequently been made by Ericsson and Kintsch (1995), in which experts acquire skills that are designed to encode relevant information in long-term memory (LTM) in a manner that allows automatic retrieval from LTM when later needed, as indicated by subsequent activation of certain combinations of cues in attention. They argued that experts acquire LTWM skills that enable them, when they encounter new information (such as a new symptom during an interview with a patient), to encode the relevant associations such that when yet other related information is encountered (such as subsequent information reported by the patient), the expert will automatically access relevant aspects of the earlier information to guide encoding and reasoning. The key constraint for skilled encoding in LTM is that the expert be able to anticipate potential future contexts where the encountered information might become relevant. Only then will the expert be able to encode encountered information in LTWM in such a way that its future relevance is anticipated and the relevant pieces of information can be automatically activated when the subsequent rele-

vant contexts are encountered. In this model of the experts' working memory storage in LTM, the large capacity of LTM allows the expert to preserve access to a large body of relevant information without any need to actively maintain the information in a limited general capacity STM (Ericsson, Chapter 13; Gobet & Charness, Chapter 30; Noice & Noice, Chapter 28; Wilding & Valentine, Chapter 31).

Expertise Involves Selective Access of Relevant Information

Within the classical expertise framework based on chunking, questions about access to task-relevant information are important issues, and a critical aspect of intelligence (Sternberg, 1984). Given the functional nature of expert representations, how are they properly engaged in the context of solving a problem? To what kind of problem features do experts attend? How are these features "linked up" to the significant concepts in memory? In a sense, having a trace laid down in memory is not a sufficient condition for use. Extant traces must be accessed and important non-extant traces must be inferred or otherwise computed.

This characteristic of expertise addresses the critical problem of accessing knowledge structures. This development overcomes (at least) two difficulties for expertise as a "big switch" (Newell, 1973) between the recognition of familiar events and application of experience associated with those events (see also Ross, Shafer, & Klein, Chapter 23, "recognition-primed decision making). The first of these is related to the variability in events; one cannot "step into the same river twice." The useful utilization of events as familiar requires a degree of appropriate abstraction, both in the event features utilized and in the memory organization imposed on the memory models themselves. The former adaptation is reflected in expert utilization of abstracted features for problem classification, features whose loci in a problem statement are not apparent (Chi et al., 1981). The latter adaptation is reflected in the development of hierarchical organizations, which characterize expert or experienced memory (e.g., Feltovich et al., 1984; Patil, Szolovits, & Schwartz, 1981).

Critical to this characteristic is selectivity. Selectivity is based on the attribution of differential importance or, broadly conceived, a separation of signal from noise either in the features extracted from events or on internal cognitive processes themselves (see also Hill & Schneider, Chapter 37). Selectivity, as a means of task adaptation, is assumed to be forced on the human based on their limited cognitive capacity. With regard to events, selectivity involves the abstraction of invariances of the discriminating cues that define types of situations or are otherwise integral to a task. Expertise, then, involves learning which information is most useful and which is tangential or superfluous (e.g., Chi et al., 1981; Hinsley et al., 1978; Patel & Groen, 1991; Spilich et al., 1979). In certain types of "stable" environments, the important invariance is well defined and the task is sufficiently constrained so that the mechanisms linking selectivity and performance can be explicated. For example, as consistent with the LTWM hypothesis, skilled typists appear to achieve subordination, usability, and access by developing integrated representations of letters and key presses that facilitate translation between perception and response (Rieger, 2004).

This theme of expertise also reflects the general problem of knowledge inversion; that is, the notion of moving from a concept-centered mode of reasoning to a mode that must somehow scan the problem features for regularities, incorporate abstraction, integrate multiple cues, and accept natural variation in patterns to invoke aspects of the relevant concept. We find this in many fields. For example, medical students acquire much specific "disease-centered" knowledge – given disease X, this is the underlying pathophysiology, these are the variations, and these are the classic manifestations. When faced with a patient, however, they are presented with just the opposite situation: Given a patient, what is the disease? Recent developments in medical education focus on case-oriented learning in which medical students are given early exposure to representative clinical situations. This type of training forces learners to develop mental representations and an LTWM that support medical reasoning under real-time, representative constraints (Norman, Eva, Brooks, & Hamstra, Chapter 19; Ericsson, Chapter 13; Endsley, Chapter 36).

Expertise Involves Reflection

Another challenge to the traditional information processing view, with its severe constraints on cognitive capacity, concerns the experts' ability not just to perform effectively but also to be able to reflect on their thought processes and methods (Glaser & Chi, 1988, Characteristic 7 (see also Zimmerman, Chapter 39). Metacognition is knowledge about one's own knowledge and knowledge about one's own performance (Flavell, 1979). It is what an individual knows about his or her own cognitive processes. Its relevance to expertise is derived, in part, from the observation that experts are graceful in their reasoning process. As Bartlett (1958) notes, "Experts have all the time in the world." There is an element of unencumbered elegance in expert performance, the underpinnings of which are based on the efficient management and control of the adaptive processes. A source for this might be in abstracted layers of control and planning.

The traditional (classical) account of metacognition within the information-processing model is that abstract descriptions of plans and procedures enable an individual to operate on or manipulate problem-solving operations, for example, to modify and adjust them to context. They also provide a general organizational structure that guides and organizes the details of application, so that a general line of reasoning can be maintained despite low-level (detailed) fluctuations and variations. Novice physics problem solvers, in contrast to experts, have no abstract or meta-level descriptions for their basic problem-solving operators, which for them are physics equations (Chi et al., 1981). Rather, operators are tied directly to problem details, show little modifiability, and can only organize problem-solving activity locally (i.e., at the level of isolated problem components present).

In addition to abstraction in control and planning, there must also be mechanisms for maintaining information to allow efficient back-tracking or starting over when lines of reasoning need to be modified or abandoned. Largely, the traditional view proposes that experts deal with the severe working-memory demands required by backtracking by minimizing the need for it. For example, experts can attempt to withhold decisions until they are sufficiently constrained to restrict the options. In other cases when decisions are under-constrained, experts can rely on abstract solution descriptions and conditions for solution (constraints) that both guide the search for solutions and help eliminate alternatives.

The traditional information procesing view has difficulties in accounting for the possibility that experts might be disrupted or otherwise forced to restart their planning. More recent research has shown that experts are far more able to maintain large amounts of information in working memory. For example, chess masters are able to play chess games with a quality that approaches that of normal chess-playing under blindfolded conditions in which perceptual access to chess positions is withheld (for a review see Ericsson et al., 2000; Ericsson & Kintsch, 2000). Chess masters are able to follow multiple games when they are presented move by move and can recall the locations of all pieces with high levels of accuracy. Chess masters are also able to recall a series of different chess positions when they are briefly presented (5 seconds per position). In studies of expert physicians (e.g., Feltovich, Spiro, & Coulson, 1997), it was found that when experts do not know the correct diagnosis for a patient, they often can give a plausible description of the underlying pathophysiology of a disease; that is, they are able to reason at levels that are more fundamental and defensible in terms of the symptoms presented. When novices fail to reach a diagnosis for a patient, their rationale for possible alternatives is generally incompatible with the symptoms presented. Experts fail gracefully; novices crash. Vimla Patel and her colleagues (Groen & Patel, 1988; Patel & Groen, 1991) have found that medical experts are able to explain their diagnoses by showing how the presented symptoms are all explained by the proposed integrated disease state, whereas less advanced medical students have a more piece-meal representation that is less well integrated.

Metacognition, then, is important for people to test their own understanding and partial solutions to a problem. This kind of monitoring prevents blind alleys, errors, and the need for extensive back-up and retraction, thus ensuring overall progress to a goal. In addition, these same kinds of monitoring behaviors are critical throughout the process of acquiring knowledge and skills on which expertise depends. The mental representations developed by aspiring experts have multiple functions. They need to allow efficient and rapid reactions to critical situations, and they need to allow modifiability, mechanisms by which a skilled performer, for instance, adjusts his performance to changed weather conditions, such as a tennis player dealing with rain or wind, or adjusts to unique characteristics of the place of performance, such as musicians adjusting their performance to the acoustics of the music hall. Furthermore, these representations need to be amenable to change so aspiring expert performers can improve aspects and gradually refine their skills and their monitoring representations.

Experts, for the most part, work in the realm of the familiar (familiar *for them*, not for people in general) and may often be able to generate adequate actions by rapid recognition-based problem solving (Klein, 1998). The same experts are also the individuals called on to address the subtle, complicated, and novel problems of their field. They need to recognize when the task they are facing is not within their normal, routine domain of experience and adjust accordingly (Feltovich et al., 1997); this is just one of many pertinent aspects of metacognitive activity in the function of expertise.

If the view is maintained that metacognition (in the broadest sense) is enabled by metacognitive knowledge, and metacognitive knowledge is, in fact, "knowledge," should we not expect it to be subject to the same demands and possess the same properties as "regular" knowledge, albeit in a slightly different context? Evidence exists, for example, that metacognition can be automatic (Reder & Shunn, 1996), thus avoiding Tulving's (1994) consciousness requirement for metacognitive judgement. There is also indication that metacognitive strategies are explicitly learnable in rather general contexts (Kruger & Dunning, 1999), as well as in special contexts such as reading (Paris & Winograd, 1990) and nursing (Kuiper & Pesut, 2004). Accordingly, metacognitive activities, perhaps in a variety of ways and forms, both explicit and implicit, afford and support the developmental and performance dynamics of expertise.

Expertise Is an Adaptation

In this section, we advance an argument that the development of expertise is largely a matter of amassing considerable skills, knowledge, and mechanisms that monitor and control cognitive processes to perform a delimited set of tasks efficiently and effectively. Experts restructure, reorganize, and refine their representation of knowledge and procedures for efficient application to their work-a-day environments (See also Ericsson & Lehmann, 1996). Experts certainly know more, but they also know differently. Expertise is appropriately viewed not as simple (and often short-term) matter of fact or skill acquisition, but rather as a complex *construct* of adaptations of mind and body, which include substantial self-monitoring and control mechanisms, to task environments in service of representative task goals and activities. As we shall argue, the nature of the adaptations reflects differential demands of the task environment and mediates the performance evidenced by

highly skilled individuals. Adaptation matters (Hill and Schneider, Chapter 37).

The classical theory of expertise (Simon & Chase, 1973) focused on the fundamental architectural limits imposed on human information-processing capacities. Early investigators assumed that complex cognition must occur within surprisingly rigidly constrained parameters. Many of these limits are not singular, but are considered collectively as a statement of associated (related) constraints. Furthermore, the architecture underlying these constraints is not specified, other than the fact that it is physical. Thus, the constraints of the architecture could be realized as a symbol system (e.g., Newell & Simon, 1976), perhaps grounded in modalities (Barsalou, 1999; Barsalou et al., 2003), or as a dynamic phase space (e.g., van Gelder & Port, 1995).

In particular, under the traditional theme, three specific reasoning limits are important to explaining performance of typical novices on traditional laboratory tasks (e.g., Prietula & Simon, 1989). First, there is a *limit of attention* (Shipp, 2004). We can focus on solving only one problem (or making only one decision) at a time when performing an unfamiliar task. However, we sometimes share our attentional resources by shifting rapidly from thinking about a given task to another different task. In addition, perceptual limits on what can be detected with the eye (and the eye-brain) exist, situating the perception in scale bands of size (of objects), time (speed of movement), distance, and spectra. Our perceptual and attention resources have evolved to handle a region of time, a region of space, a region of distance, and a region of spectra. We act in, and react with, a highly constrained perceptual environment, balancing attention and awareness (Lamme, 2003).

Related to this single-mindedness is a *limit of working memory*. There is a difference between long-term memory, our large, permanent repository for knowledge and working memory, which is much smaller in capacity and restricted to holding information about the particular task at hand, involving multiple components that mediate between long-term memory and the environment (Baddeley, 2000, 2002). When focusing attention on making a particular decision or solving a particular problem, three types of events occur that are critical for effective reasoning: (1) we seek (and perceive) data from the environment, (2) we bring relevant knowledge to bear from our long-term memory to working memory and, by reviewing the data in the presence of relevant knowledge retrieved from long-term memory, (3) we draw inferences about what is going on – which may lead to seeking more data and activating more knowledge.

Finally, there is a *limit of long-term memory access.* To what extent we truly forget things is uncertain, so there may not actually be an arbitrary size constraint on this aspect of our long-term memory. That, however, is not the issue. What is certain is that we lose access to (or the power to evoke) the knowledge stored. A typical demonstration of this is the "tip of the tongue" phenomenon – in which you know that you know something, but cannot retrieve it (Brown 1991; Brown & McNeill 1966). Therefore, even though we may scan the right data in an analysis, there is no guarantee that we will be able to trigger the appropriate knowledge in long-term memory to allow us to make correct inferences from those data. In practice, a large part of expert problem solving is being able to access relevant knowledge, at the right time, for use in working memory.

This traditional approach to expertise was founded on the powerful theoretic assumption that experts' cognitive processes, such as generating, representing, and using knowledge, had to conform to these severe limits. This theory proposed many mechanisms by which experts would be able to functionally adapt to these constraints to produce superior performance. The expert chunking mechanism, for example, permits a vocabulary that is much more robust and complex than the novice can invoke. Although both the expert and the novice have the same working-memory constraints, the expert sees the world in larger and more diverse units. In effect, chunking, permits expanding the functional size of working memory and increasing the efficiency of search. This phenomenon has been experimentally demonstrated across a remarkably wide variety of domains.

The role and function of automaticity within expertise is important in this regard also. Automaticity seems to be entwined with functional organization, chunking, and conditions of application. They work in concert to adapt to the demands of the task, under the constraints of both the task and their own capabilities to make appropriate use of our memory. Automaticity, then, is intricately bound with the overall adaptation of the system through knowledge reorganization and refinement.

The general argument is that expert knowledge structures and procedures are reorganized in directions that enable effective application to task demands of a working environment. As we have discussed, most of these changes are adaptations that enable utilization of large amounts of information in the context of limited internal-processing resources (in particular those imposed by the small capacity of short-term or working memory). Grouping or chunking on information structures and procedure components functionally increases the size of working memory and its efficiency. More information can be considered for each "unit" in working memory. Expert selectivity, discrimination, and abstraction (discussed earlier) insure that only the most useful information is thrown into competition for resources. Automaticity is a means of restructuring some procedures so that working memory is largely circumvented, freeing resources for other cognitive chores. It is a tension between high information load and limited internal resources that encourages the development of strategies for the efficient use of knowledge and processing.

This pioneering theory of expertise (Simon & Chase, 1973) has been and remains very influential and has been extended with additional mechanisms to explain experts' greatly expanded working memory (Gobet & Simon, 1996; Richman, Gobet, Staszewski, & Simon, 1996). At the same time there have been many arguments raised against the claims that the computational architecture remains fixed and thus presents an invariant constraint on skilled and expert processing.

One of the most general criticisms is that the laboratory – produced empirical evidence for capacity constraints of attention and STM are based on an operational definition of chunks in terms of independent pieces of information, no matter how small or large the individual chunks (see Cowan, 2001, and Ericsson & Kirk, 2001). It is relatively easy to design experimental materials for memory experiments that are made of independent pieces and measure experts' and novices' memory in terms of chunks. However, when one analyzes the information processed by experts when they perform representative tasks in their domain of expertise, then all the heeded and relevant information has relations to the task and other pieces of information. If the encountered information can be encoded and integrated within a model of the current context, then how many independent chunks are stored or maintained in attention and working memory? Similarly, when experts encounter representative tasks situations where beginners perceive several independent tasks, the aspiring experts are able to develop skills and encodings that allow them to integrate the different tasks into a *more general task* with more diversified demands. More recent research has shown how in laboratory studies, participants performing dual tasks that are believed to contain immutable bottlenecks of processing can, after training, perform them without any observable costs of the dual task (Meyer & Kieras, 1997; Schumacher et al., 2001, but see Proctor & Vu, Chapter 15, for an alternative account). If the definition of chunks and tasks requires independence for imposing limits on information processing, then it seems that the acquisition of expertise entails developing integrated representations of knowledge and coordination of initially separate tasks that make the fundamental information-processing limits inapplicable or substantially attenuated.

The second general criticism of the traditional theory of expertise comes from a rejection of the premise that expertise is an extension of the processes observed in everyday skill acquisition (Fitts & Posner, 1967). According to this model, the acquisition of skill proceeds in stages, and during the first stage people acquire a cognitive representation of the task and how to react in typical situations so they can avoid gross errors. During the subsequent stages, the performance of sequences of actions becomes smoother and more efficient. In the final stage, people are able to perform with a minimal amount of effort, and performance runs essentially automatically without active cognitive control. In an edited book on general theories of expertise (Ericsson & Smith, 1991a), several researchers raised concerns about explaining expertise as an extension of this general model (Ericsson & Smith, 1991b; Holyoak, 1991; and Salthouse, 1991). Ericsson and Smith (1991b) found evidence that experts maintain their ability to control their performance and are able to give detailed accounts of their thought processes that can be validated against other observable performance and process data. Ericsson and Smith reviewed evidence that complex cognitive representations mediate the performance and continued learning by experts, which has been confirmed by subsequent reviews (Ericsson, 1996b, 2003, Chapter 13).

The third and final type of criticism comes from the emerging evidence that extended focused practice has profound effects on, and can influence virtually every aspect of, the human body, such as muscles, nerve systems, heart and circulatory system, and the brain. Several chapters in this handbook review the structural changes resulting from practice, such as Butterworth, Chapter 32, on mathematical calculation; Ericsson, Chapter 38; Lehmann and Gruber, Chapter 26, on music performance; Proctor and Vu, Chapter 15, on adaptations in skill acquisition; and Hill and Schneider, Chapter 37, with an overview of changes in the structure and function of the brain with extended practice and the development of expertise.

Simple Experience Is Not Sufficient for the Development of Expertise

Most everyday skills are relatively easy to acquire, at least to an acceptable level. Adults often learn to drive a car, type, play chess, ski, and play (bad) golf within weeks or months. It is usually possible to explain what an individual needs to know about a given skill, such as rules and procedures, within a few hours (see also Hoffman & Lintern, Chapter 12). Once individuals have learned the underlying structure of the activity and what aspects they must attend to, they often focus on attaining a functional level of performance. This is often attained in less than 50 hours of practice. At this point, an acceptable standard of performance can be generated without much need for more effortful attention and execution of the everyday activity has attained many characteristics of automated performance (Anderson, 1982, 1987; Fitts & Posner, 1967; Shiffrin & Schneider, 1977) and requires only minimal effort.

In their seminal paper, Simon and Chase (1973) pointed to similarities between the decade-long mastery of one's first language and the need for extended experience to master complex domains of expertise, such as chess and sports. They made a strong argument for a long period of immersion in active participation in activities in the domain, making the claim that even the best chess players needed to spend over ten years studying chess before winning at the international level. The necessity for even the most talented performers to spend ten years working and practicing was later converted into an equivalence, namely, that ten years of experience in a domain made somebody an expert. However, for chess, tennis, and golf, everyone knows examples of excited recreational players who regularly engage in play for years and decades, but who never reach a very skilled level.

Reviews of the relation between the amount of experience and the attained level of performance show consistently that once an acceptable level is attained, there are hardly any benefits from the common kind of additional experience. In fact, there are many domains where performance decreases as a function of the number of years since graduation from the training institution (Ericsson, Chapter 38).

Several research methods have been developed to describe the development paths of expert performers, such as analysis of the historical record of eminent performers (Simonton, Chapter 18), retrospective interviews (see Sosniak, Chapter 16), and diary studies of practice (See Deakin, Côté, & Harvey, Chapter 17). Research with these methods has shown that additional experience appears to make performance less effortful and less demanding, but to improve performance it is necessary to seek out practice activities that allow individuals to work on improving specific aspects, with the help of a teacher and in a protected environment, with opportunities for reflection, exploration of alternatives, and problem solving, as well as repetition with informative feedback.

In this handbook several chapters discuss the effectiveness of this type of deliberate practice in attaining elite and expert levels of performance (Ericsson, Chapter 38; Zimmerman, Chapter 39), in software design (Sonnentag, Niessen, & Volmer, Chapter 21), in training with simulators (Ward, Williams, & Hancock, Chapter 14), in maintaining performance in older experts (Krampe & Charness, Chapter 40), and in creative activities (Weisberg, Chapter 42). Other chapters review evidence on the relationship between deliberate practice and the development of expertise in particular domains, such as professional writing (Kellogg, Chapter 22), music performance (Lehmann & Gruber, Chapter 26), sports (Hodges, Starkesi & MacMohan, Chapter 27), chess (Gobet & Charness, Chapter 30), exceptional memory (Wilding & Valentine, Chapter 31), and mathematical calculation (Butterworth, Chapter 32).

Concluding Remarks

The theoretical interest in expertise and expert performance is based on the assumption that there are shared psychological constraints on the structure and acquisition of expert performance across different domains. The theory of Simon and Chase (1973) proposed that the invariant limits on information processing and STM severely constrained how expert skill is acquired and proposed a theory based on the accumulation through experience of increasingly complex chunks and pattern-action associations. This theory emphasized the acquired nature of expertise and focused on the long time required to reach elite levels and the learning processes sufficient to gradually accumulate the large body of requisite patterns and knowledge. This view of expertise offered the hope that it would be possible to extract the accumulated knowledge and rules of experts and then use this knowledge to more efficiently train future experts and, thus, reduce the decade or more of experience and training required for elite performance. Efforts were made even to encode the extracted knowledge in computer models and to build expert systems that could duplicate the performance of the experts (Bachanan et al., Chapter 6).

Subsequent research on extended training revealed that it is possible to acquire skills that effectively alter or, at least, circumvent the processing limits of attention and working memory. Studies of expertise focused initially on the expert's representation and memory for knowledge. As research started to examine and model experts' superior performance on representative tasks, it became clear that their complex representations and mechanisms that mediate performance could not be acquired by mere experience (Ericsson, Chapter 38). Research on what enabled some individuals to reach expert performance, rather than mediocre achievement, revealed that expert and elite performers seek out teachers and engage in specially designed training activities (deliberate practice). The future expert performers need to acquire representations and mechanisms that allow them to monitor, control, and evaluate their own performance, so they can gradually modify their own mechanisms while engaging in training tasks that provide feedback on performance, as well as opportunities for repetition and gradual refinement.

The discovery of the complex structure of the mechanisms that execute expert performance and mediate its continued improvement has had positive and negative implications. On the negative side, it has pretty much dispelled the hope that expert performance can easily be captured and that the decade-long training to become an expert can be dramatically reduced. All the paths to expert performance appear to require substantial extended effortful practice. Effortless mastery of expertise, magical bullets involving training machines, and dramatic shortcuts, are just myths. They cannot explain the acquisition of the mechanisms and adaptations that mediate skilled and expert performance. Even more important, the insufficiency of the traditional school system is becoming apparent. It is not reasonable to teach students knowledge and rules about a domain, such as programming, medicine, and economics, and then expect them to be able to convert this material into effective professional skills by additional experience in the pertinent domain. Schools need to help students acquire the skills and mechanisms for basic mastery in the domain, and then allow them gradually to take over control of the learning of their professional skills by designing deliberate practice activities that produce continued improvement.

On the positive side, the discovery of effective training methods for acquiring complex cognitive mechanisms has allowed investigators to propose types of training that appear to allow individuals to acquire levels of performance that were previously thought to be unobtainable, except for the elite group of innately talented. The study of the development of expert performers provides observable paths for how they modified or circumvented different types of psychological and physiological constraints. It should be possible for one type of expert in one domain, such as surgery, to learn from how other experts in music or sports, for instance, have designed successful training procedures for mastering various aspects of perceptual-motor procedures, and to learn the amount of practice needed to reach specified levels of mastery. If someone is interested, for instance, in whether a certain type of perceptual discrimination can ever be made reliably, and how much and what type of training would be required to achieve this, then one should in the future be able to turn to a body of knowledge of documented expert performance. Our vision is that the study of expert performance will become a science of learning and of the human adaptations that are possible in response to specialized extended training. At the same time that our understanding of the real constraints on acquiring high levels of performance in any domain becomes clearer, and the similarities of those constraints across many different domains are identified, the study of the acquisition of expert performance will offer a microcosm for how various types of training can improve human performance and provide insights into the potential for human achievement.

The study of expert performance is not concerned only with the ultimate limits of performance, but also with earlier stages of development through which every future performer needs to pass. There is now research emerging on how future expert performers will acquire initial and intermediate levels of performance. Attaining these intermediate levels may be an appropriate goal for people in general and for systems of general education (e.g., recreational athletes, patrons of the arts). However, knowing how to achieve certain goals is no guarantee that people will be successful, as we know from studies of dieting and exercise. On the other hand, when the goal is truly elite achievement, the study of expert performance offers a unique source of data that is likely to help us understand the necessary factors for success, including the social and motivational factors that push and pull people to persevere in the requisite daunting regimes of training.

References

Adelson, B. (1981). Problem solving and the development of abstract categories in programming languages. *Memory and Cognition, 9*, 422–433.

Anderson, J. R. (Ed.) (1981). *Cognitive skills and their acquisition*. Hillsdale, NJ: Erlbaum.

Anderson, J. R. (1982). Acquisition of cognitive skill. *Psychological Review, 89*, 369–406.

Anderson, J. R. (1987). Skill acquisition: Compilation of weak-method problem situations. *Psychological Review, 94*, 192–210.

Austin, J. (2000). Performance analysis and performance diagnostics. In J. Austin & J. E. Carr (Eds.), *Handbook of applied behavior analysis* (pp. 321–349). Reno, NV: Context Press.

Baddeley, A. (2000). Short-term and working memory. In E. Tulving & F. Craik (Eds.), *The Oxford handbook of memory* (pp. 77–92). Oxford, UK: Oxford University Press.

Baddeley, A. (2002). Is working memory still working? *European Psychologist, 7*(2), 85–97.

Barrows, H. S., Feightner, J. W., Neufeld, V. R., & Norman, G. R. (1978). *Analysis of the clinical methods of medical students and physicians*. Final Report, Ontario Department of Health Grants ODH-PR-273 & ODH-DM-226. Hamilton, Ontario: McMaster University.

Barrows, H. S., & Tamblyn, R. M. (1980). *Problem-based learning: An approach to medical education*. New York: Springer.

Barsalou, L. W. (1999). Perceptual symbol systems. *Behavioral and Brain Sciences, 22*, 577–660.

Barsalou, L. W., Simmons, W. K., Barbey, A. K., & Wilson, C. D. (2003). Grounding conceptual knowledge in modality-specific systems. *TRENDS in Cognitive Sciences, 7*(2), 84–91.

Bartlett, F. (1932). *Remembering*. Cambridge, UK: Cambridge University Press.

Bartlett, F. (1958). *Thinking*. New York: Basic Books.

Berlyne, D. E. (1965). *Structure and direction in thinking*. Oxford, UK: Wiley.

Bloom, B. (Ed.) (1985). *Developing talent in young people*. New York: Ballentine.

Brown, A. (1991). A review of the tip-of-the-tongue experience. *Psychological Bulletin, 109*, 204–223.

Brown, R. W., & MacNeill, D. (1966). The "tip of the tongue" phenomenon. *Journal of Verbal Learning and Verbal Behavior, 5*, 325–337.

Bruner, J. S., Goodnow, J. J., & Austin, G. A. (1956). *A study of thinking*. New York: John Wiley and Sons.

Buchanan, B. G., & Feigenbaum, E. A. (1978). DENDRAL and MetaDENDRAL: Their applications dimension. *Artificial Intelligence*, *11(1)*, 5–24.

Charness, N. (1976). Memory for chess positions: Resistance to interference. *Journal of Experimental Psychology: Human Learning and Memory*, *2*, 641–653.

Charness, N. (1979). Components of skill in bridge. *Canadian Journal of Psychology*, *33*, 1–50.

Charness, N. (1981). Search in chess: Age and skill differences. *Journal of Experimental Psychology: Human Perception and Performance*, *7*, 467–476.

Chase, W. G. (Ed.) (1973). *Visual information processing*. New York: Academic Press.

Chase, W. G., & Simon, H. A. (1973a). The mind's eye in chess. In W. G. Chase (Ed.), *Visual information processing*. New York: Academic Press.

Chase, W. G., & Simon, H. A. (1973b). Perception in chess. *Cognitive Psychology*, *1*, 33–81.

Chi, M. T. H. (1978). Knowledge structures and memory development. In R. S. Siegler (Ed), *Children's thinking: What develops?* (pp. 73–96). Hillsdale, NJ: Erlbaum.

Chi, M. T. H., Feltovich, P., & Glaser, R. (1981). Categorization and representation of physics problems by experts and novices. *Cognitive Science*, *5*, 121–152.

Chi, M. T. H., Glaser, R., & Farr, M. J. (Eds.) (1988). *The nature of expertise*. Hillsdale, NJ: Erlbaum.

Chiesi, H. L., Spilich, G. J., & Voss. J. F. (1979). Acquisition of domain-related information in relation to high and low domain knowledge. *Journal of Verbal Learning and Verbal Behavior*, *18*, 257–274.

Chomsky, N. (1957). *Syntactic structures*. The Hague: Mouton.

Clancey, W. J. & Letsinger, R. (1984). NEOMYCIN: Reconfigure a rule-based expert system for application to teaching. In W. J. Clancey & E. H. Shortliffe, (eds.), *Readings in medical artificial intelligence* (pp. 361–381). Readings Addision.

Clancey, W. J., & Shortliffe, E. H. (1984). *Readings in medical artificial intelligence: The first decade*. Reading, MA: Addison-Wesley.

Cowan, N. (2001). The magical number 4 in short-term memory: A reconsideration of mental storage capacity. *Behavioral and Brain Sciences*, *24*, 87–185.

Cowan, N., Chen, Z., & Rouder, J. (2004). Constant capacity in an immediate serial-recall task: A logical sequel to Miller (1956). *Psychological Science*, *15 (9)*, 634–640.

de Groot, A. (1946). *Het denken van den schaker.* Amsterdam: Noord-Hllandsche Uit. Mij.

de Groot, A. (1965). *Thought and choice in chess, 1st Edition*. The Hague: Mouton.

Duncker, K. (1945). On problem solving. *Psychological Monographs*, *58* (Whole No. 270), 1–113.

Ebbinghaus, H. (1885/1964). *Memory: A contribution to experimental cognitive psychology* (Henry A. Ruger & Clara E. Bussenius, Trans.). New York: Dover.

Egan, D. E., & Schwartz, B. J. (1979). Chunking in recall of symbolic drawings. *Memory and Cognition*, *7*, 149–158.

Eisenstadt, M., & Kareev, Y. (1979). Aspects of human problem solving: The use of internal representations. In D. A. Norman & D. E. Rumelhart (Eds.), *Exploration in cognition*. San Francisco: W. H. Freeman.

Elstein, A. S., Shulman, L. S., & Sprafka, S. A. (1978). *Medical problem solving*. Cambridge, MA: Harvard University Press.

Engle R. W., & Bukstel, L. (1978). Memory processes among bridge players of differing expertise. *American Journal of Psychology*, *91*, 673–89.

Ericsson, K. A. (Ed.) (1996a). *The road to excellence: The acquisition of expert performance in the arts and sciences, sports, and games.* Mahwah, NJ: Erlbaum.

Ericsson, K. A. (1996b). The acquisition of expert performance: An introduction to some of the issues. In K. A. Ericsson (Ed.), *The road to excellence: The acquisition of expert performance in the arts and sciences, sports, and games* (pp. 1–50). Mahwah, NJ: Erlbaum.

Ericsson, K. A. (2003). The acquisition of expert performance as problem solving: Construction and modification of mediating mechanisms through deliberate practice. In J. E. Davidson & R. J. Sternberg (Eds.), *Problem solving* (pp. 31–83). New York: Cambridge University Press.

Ericsson, K. A., & Kintsch, W. (1995). Long-term working memory. *Psychological Review*, *102*, 211–245.

Ericsson, K. A., & Kintsch, W. (2000). Shortcomings of generic retrieval structures with slots of the type that Gobet (1993) proposed and modeled. *British Journal of Psychology*, *91*, 571–588.

Ericsson, K. A., & Kirk, E. P. (2001). The search for fixed generalizable limits of "pure STM" capacity: Problems with theoretical proposals based on independent chunks. *Behavioral and Brain Sciences*, *24*, 120–121.

Ericsson, K. A., Krampe, R. T., & Tesch-Römer, C. (1993). The role of deliberate practice in the acquisition of expert performance. *Psychological Review, 100,* 363–406.

Ericsson, K. A., & Lehmann, A. C. (1996). Expert and exceptional performance: Evidence on maximal adaptations on task constraints. *Annual Review of Psychology, 47,* 273–305.

Ericsson, K. A., Patel, V. L., & Kintsch, W. (2000). How experts' adaptations to representative task demands account for the expertise effect in memory recall: Comment on Vicente and Wang (1998). *Psychological Review, 107,* 578–592.

Ericsson, K. A., & Smith, J. (Eds.) (1991a). *Toward a general theory of expertise: Prospects and limits.* Cambridge, MA: Cambridge University Press.

Ericsson, K. A., & Smith, J. (1991b). Prospects and limits in the empirical study of expertise: An introduction. In K. A. Ericsson and J. Smith (Eds.), *Toward a general theory of expertise: Prospects and limits* (pp. 1–38). Cambridge, MA: Cambridge University Press.

Ernst, G., & Newell, A. (1969). *GPS: A case-study in generality and problem solving.* New York: Academic Press.

Feltovich, P., Ford, K. M., & Hoffman, R. R. (Eds.) (1997). *Expertise in context: Human and Machine.* Menlo Park, CA: AAAI Press.

Feltovich, P. J., Johnson, P. E, Moller, J., & Swanson, D. (1984). The role and development of medical knowledge in diagnostic reasoning. In. W. Clancey & E. Shortliffe (Eds.), *Readings in medical artificial intelligence: The first decade* (pp. 275–319). Reading, MA: Addison Wesley.

Feltovich, P., Spiro, R., & Coulson, R. (1997). Issues of expert flexibility in contexts characterized by complexity and change. In P. Feltovich, K. Ford, & R. Hoffman (Eds.), *Expertise in context: Human and machine.* Menlo Park, CA: AAAI Press.

Ferster, C. B., & Skinner, B. F. (1957). *Schedules of reinforcement.* New York: Appleton-Century-Crofts.

Fitts, P. M., & Posner, M. I. (1967). *Human performance.* Belmont, CA: Brookes Cole.

Flavell, J. (1979). Metacognition and cognition monitoring: A new area of cognitive-developmental inquiry. *American Psychologist, 34,* 906–911.

Forbus, K. D. & Feltovich, P. J. (2001), *Smart machines in education.* Menlo PK, CA: AAAI/ MIT Press.

Gentner, D. (1988). Metaphor as structure-mapping: The relational shift. *Child Development, 59,* 47–59.

Glaser, R. (1976). Cognition and instructional design. In D. Klahr (Ed.), *Cognition and instruction* (pp. 303–315). Hillsdale, NJ: Erlbaum.

Glaser, R., & Chi, M. T. H. (1988). Overview. In M. T. H., Chi, R., Glaser, & M. J., Farr (Eds.), *The nature of expertise* (pp. xv-xxviii). Hillsdale, NJ: Erlbaum.

Gobet, F., & Simon, H. A. (1996). Templates in chess memory: A mechanism for recalling several boards. *Cognitive Psychology, 31,* 1–40.

Green, C. (1969). *The application of theorem proving to question-answering systems.* Doctoral dissertation Dept. of Electrical Engineering, Stanford University. Also Standford Artificial Intelligence Project Memo AI-96, June 1969.

Groen, G. J., & Patel, V. L. (1988). The relationship between comprehension and reasoning in medical expertise. In M. T. H. Chi, R. Glaser, & M. J. Farr (Eds.), *The nature of expertise* (pp. 287–310). Hillsdale, NJ: Erlbaum.

Hambrick, D., & Engle, R. (2002). Effects of domain knowledge, working memory capacity, and age on cognitive performance: An investigation of the knowledge-is-power hypothesis. *Cognitive Psychology, 44,* 339–387.

Hatano, G., Miyake, Y., & Binks, M. B. (1977). Performance of expert abacus operators. *Cognition, 5,* 57–71.

Hinsley, D., Hayes, J., & Simon, H. A.(1978). From words to equations: Meaning and representation in algebra word problems. In M. Just & P. Carpenter (Eds.), *Cognitive processes in comprehension.* Hillsdale, NJ: Erlbaum.

Hoffman, R. R. (Ed.) (1992). *The psychology of expertise.* New York: Springer-Verlag.

Holyoak, K. J. (1991). Symbolic connectionism: toward third generation theories of expertise. In K. A. Ericsson & J. Smith (Eds.), *Toward a general theory of expertise: Prospects and limits* (pp. 301–335). Cambridge, MA: Cambridge University Press.

Jakobovits, L. A. & Miron, M. S. (1967). *Readings in the Psychology of language.* Englewood, cliffs, NJ: Prentice-Hall.

Jansma, J., Ramsey, N., Slagter, H., & Kahn, R. (2001). Functional anatomical correlates of controlled and automatic processing. *Journal of Cognitive Neuroscience, 13* (6), 730–743.

Jeffries, R., Turner, A. A., Polson, P. G, & Atwood, M. E. (1981). The processes involved in software design. In J. R. Anderson (Ed.), *Cognitive skills and their acquisition*. Hillsdale, NJ: Erlbaum.

Johnson, P. E., Duran, A. S., Hassebrock, F., Moller, J., Prietula, M. J., Feltovich, P. J., & Swanson, D. B. (1981). Expertise and error in diagnostic reasoning. *Cognitive Science*, 5, 235–283.

Klein, G. A. (1998). *Sources of power: How people make decisions*. Cambridge, MA: MIT Press.

Klein, G. A., & Hoffman, R. R. (1993). Seeing the invisible: Perceptual-cognitive aspects of expertise. In M. Rabinowitz (Ed.), *Cognitive science foundations of instruction*. Hillsdale, NJ: Erlbaum.

Koschmann, T. D., LeBaron, C., Goodwin, C., & Feltovich, P. J. (2001). Dissecting common ground: Examining an instance of reference repair. In *Proceedings of the 23rd Conference of the Cognitive Science Society*. Mahwah, NJ: Erlbaum.

Kruger, J., & Dunning, D. (1999). Unskilled and unaware of it: How difficulties in recognizing one's own incompetence lead to inflated self-assessments. *Journal of Personality and Social Psychology*, 77, 1121–1134.

Kuiper, R., & Pesut, D. (2004). Promoting cognitive and metacognitive reflective reasoning skills in nursing practice: Self-regularities learning theory. *Journal of Advanced Nursing*, 45, 381–391.

Larkin, J., McDermott, J., Simon, D. & Simon, H. A. (1980). Expert and novice performance in solving physics problems. *Science*, 208, 1335–1342.

Lamme, V. (2003). Why visual attention and awareness are different. *Trends in Cognitive Sciences*, 7(1), 12–18.

Lesgold, A. M., & Resnick, L. (1982). How reading difficulties devlop: Perspectives from a longitudinal study. In J. Das, R. Mulcahey, & A. wall (Eds.), *Theory and research in learning disabilities* (pp. 155–187). New York: Plenum Press.

Lesgold, A. M., Rubinson, H., Feltovich, P. J., Glaser, R., Klopfer, D., & Wang, Y. (1988). Expertise in a complex skill: Diagnosing x-ray pictures. In M. T. H. Chi, R. Glaser, & M. J. Farr (Eds.), *The nature of expertise* (pp. 311–342). Hillsdale, NJ: Erlbaum.

Logan, G. (1985). Skill and automaticity: Relations, implications and future directions. *Psychological Review*, 95, 492–527.

Lumsdaine, A. A., & Glaser, R. (1960). *Teaching machines and programmed learning: A source book*. Washington, DC: National Education Assoc.

McKeithen, K. B., Reitman, J. S., Reuter, H. H., & Hirtle, S. C., (1981). Knowledge organization and skill differences in computer programmers. *Cognitive Psychology*, 13, 307–325.

Meehl, P. E. (1954). *Clinical versus statistical prediction: A theoretical analysis and a review of the evidence*. Minneapolis: University of Minnesota Press.

Meyer, D. E., & Kieras, D. E. (1997). A computational theory of executive cognitive processes and multiple-task performance: Part 2. Accounts of psychological refractory-period phenomena. *Psychological Review*, 104, 749–791.

Miller, G. A. (1956). The magical number seven plus or minus two: Some limits on our capacity for processing information. *Psychological Review*, 63, 81–97.

Miller, G. A., Galanter, E., & Pribram, K. H. (1960). *Plans and the structure of behavior*. New York: Holt, Rinehart & Winston.

Neisser, U. (1967). *Cognitive psychology*. New York: Appleton-Century-Crofts.

Newell, A. (1973). Artificial intelligence and the concept of mind. In R. C. Schank & K. M. Colby (Eds.), *Computer models of language and thought* (pp. 1–60). San Franciso: W. H. Freeman.

Newell, A., & Simon, H. A. (1956). The logic theory machine: A complex information processing system. *IRE Transactions on Information Theory*, Vol IT-2, No. 3, 61–79.

Newell, A., & Simon, H. A. (1972). *Human problem solving*. Englewood Cliffs, NJ: Prentice Hall.

Newell, A., & Simon, H. A. (1976). Computer science as empirical inquiry: Symbols and search. *Communications of the ACM*, 19(3), 113–126.

Norman, D. A., Rumelhart, D. E., & the LNR group (1979). *Explorations in cognition*. San Francisco: W. H. Freeman.

Osgood, C. E. (1963). On understanding and creating sentences. *American Psychologist*, 18, 735–751.

Paris, S., & Winograd, P. (1990). How metacognition can promote academic learning and instruction. In B. Jones & L. Idol (Eds.), *Dimensions of thinking and cognitive instruction* (pp. 15–51). Hillsdale, NJ: Erlbaum.

Patel, V. L., Arocha, J. F., & Kaufman, D. R. (1994). Diagnostic reasoning and medical expertise. In D. Medin (Ed.), *The psychology of learning and motivation.* Vol. 30 (pp. 187–251). New York: Academic Press.

Patel, V. L., & Groen, G. J. (1991). The general and specific nature of medical expertise: A critical look. In K. A. Ericsson & J. Smith (Eds.), *Toward a general theory of expertise* (pp. 93–125). Cambridge, MA: Cambridge University Press.

Patil, R. S., Szolovitz, P., & Schwartz, W. B. (1981). Causal understanding of patient illness in medical diagnosis. In *Proceedings of the seventh international conference on artificial intelligence.* Vol. 2 (pp. 893–899). Los Altos, CA: William Kaufman.

Pauker, S. G., Gorry, G. A., Kassirer, J. P., & Schwartz, W. B. (1976). Towards simulation of clinical cognition: Taking a present illness by computer. *American Journal of Medicine, 60,* 981–996.

Pellegrino, J. W., & Glaser, R. (1982a). Improving the skills of learning. In D. K. Detterman & R. J. Sternberg (Eds.), *How much and how can intelligence be increased.* Norwood, NJ: Ablex.

Pellegrino, J. W., & Glaser, R. (1982b). Analyzing aptitudes for learning: Inductive reasoning. In R. Glaser (Ed.), *Advances in instructional psychology.* Vol. 2 (pp. 269–345). Hillsdale, NJ: Erlbaum.

Perfetti, C. A., & Lesgold, A. M. (1979). Coding and comprehension in skilled reading. In L. B. Resnick & P. Weaver (Eds.), *Theory and practice of early reading.* Hillsdale, NJ: Erlbaum.

Phelps, R. H., & Shanteau J. (1978). Livestock judges: How much information can an expert use? *Organizational Behavior and Human Performance, 21,* 209–219.

Petrusa, E. R. (2002). Clinical performance assessments. In G. R. Norman, C. P. M. van der Vleuten, & D. I. Neuble (Eds.), *International handbook of research in medical education.* Dordrecht: Kluwer Academic Publishers.

Posner, M., & Snyder, C. (1975). Attention and cognitive control. In R. L. Solso (Ed.), *Information processing and cognition: The Loyola symposium.* Hillsdale, NJ: Erlbaum.

Prietula, M., & Augier, M. (2005). Adventures in software archeology: Seeking (ABTOF) theory in the code. *Proceedings of the 2005 Annual Academy of Management Meeting,* August 5–10, Honolulu HI.

Prietula, M., & Simon, H. (1989). The experts in your midst. *Harvard Business Review,* Jan–Feb, 120–124.

Quillian, R. (1969). The teachable language comprehender: A Simulation program and theory of language. *Communications of the ACM, 12* 459–476.

Reder, L., & Shunn, C. (1996). Metacognition does not imply awareness: Strategy choice is governed by implicit learning and memory. In L. Reder (Ed.), *Implicit memory and metacognition.* Mahwah, NJ: Erlbaum.

Reitman, J. (1976). Skilled perception in GO: Deducing memory structure from interresponse times. *Cognitive Psychology, 8,* 336–356.

Reitman, W. R. (1965). *Cognition and thought.* New York: Wiley.

Richman, H. B., Gobet, F., Staszewski, J. J., & Simon, H. A. (1996). Perceptual and memory processes in the acquisition of expert performance: The EPAM model. In K. A. Ericsson (Ed.), *The road to excellence: The acquisition of expert performance in the arts and sciences, sports, and games* (pp. 167–187). Mahwah, NJ: Erlbaum.

Rieger, M. (2004). Automatic keypress activation in skilled typists. *Journal of Experimental Psychology: Human Perception and Performance, 3,* 555–565.

Rumelhart, D. E. (1979). *Analogical processes and procedunal representations.* CHIP Report # 81. Center for Human Information Processing, Univ. California, San Diego: February, 1979.

Sacerdoti, E. D. (1977). *A structure for plans and behavior.* New York: Elsevier-North Holland Publishing.

Salthouse, T. A. (1991). Expertise as the circumvention of human processing limitations. In K. A. Ericsson and J. Smith (Eds.), *Toward a general theory of expertise: Prospects and limits* (pp. 286–300). Cambridge, MA: Cambridge University Press.

Samuel, A. L. (1959). Some studies in machine learning using the game of checkers. *IBM Journal of Research and Development, 3,* 210–229.

Schneider, W., & Fisk, A. (1982). Concurrent automatic and controlled visual search: Can processing occur without resource cost? *Journal of Experimental Psychology, 8,* 261–278.

Schneider, W., & Shiffrin, R. M. (1977). Controlled and automatic human information processing: 1. Detection, search and attention. *Psychological Review, 84*, 1–66.

Schmidt, J. A., McLaughlin, J. P., & Leighton, P. (1989). Novice strategies for understanding paintings. *Applied Cognitive Psychology, 3*, 65–72.

Schumacher, E. H., Seymour, T. L., Glass, J. M., Fencsik, D. E., Lauber, E. J., Kieras, D. E., & Meyer, D. E. (2001). Virtually perfect time sharing in dual-task performance: Uncorking the central cognitive bottleneck. *Psychological Science, 12*, 101–108.

Shaffer, L. H. (1975). Multiple attention in continuous verbal tasks. In P. M. A. Rabbitt & S. Dornic (Eds.) *Attention and performance V.* New York: Academic Press.

Shiffrin, R. M., & Schneider, W. (1977). Controlled and automatic human information processing: II. Perceptual learning, automatic attending and a general theory. *Psychological Review, 84*, 127–189.

Shipp, S. (2004). The brain circuitry of attention. *Trends in Cognitive Sciences. 8*, 223–230.

Shortliffe, E. H. (1976). *Computer-based medical consultations: MYCIN.* New York: American Elsevier.

Simon, H. A., & Chase, W. G. (1973). Skill in chess. *American Scientist, 61*, 394–403.

Simon, H. A., & Newell, A. (1958). Heuristic problem solving: The next advance in operations research. *Operations Research, 6*, 1–10.

Skinner, B. F. (1960). The science of learning and the art of teaching. In A. A. Lumsdaine & R. Glaser (Eds.), *Teaching machines and programmed learning: A source book* (pp. 99–113). Washington, DC: National Education Assoc.

Sleeman, D., & Brown, J. S. (1982). *Intelligent tutoring systems.* New York: Academic Press.

Spelke, E., Hirst, W., & Neisser, U. (1976). Skills of divided attention. *Cognition, 4*, 215–30.

Spilich, G. J., Vesonder, G. T., Chiesi, H. L., & Voss, J. F. (1979). Text processing of domain-related information for individuals with high and low domain knowledge. *Journal of Verbal Learning and Verbal Behavior, 14*, 506–522.

Spiro, R. J., Collins, B. P. Thota, J. J., & Feltovich, P. J. (2003). Cognitive flexibility theory: Hypermedia for complex learning, adaptive knowledge application, and experience acceleration. *Educational technology, 44*, 5–10.

Starkes, J. L., & Allard, F. (Eds.) (1993). *Cognitive issues in motor expertise.* Amsterdam: North Holland.

Starkes, J., & Ericsson, K. A. (Eds.) (2003). *Expert performance in sport: Recent advances in research on sport expertise.* Champaign, IL: Human Kinetics.

Steier, D., & Mitchell, T. (Eds) (1996). *Knowledge matters: A tribute to Allen Newell.* Mahwah, NJ: Erlbaum.

Sternberg, R. (1984). Toward a triarchic theory of human intelligence. *Behavioral and Brain Sciences, 7*, 269–287.

Tulving, E. (1994). Forward. In J. Metcalfe & A. Shimamura (Eds.), *Metacognition: Knowing about knowing.* Cambridge, MA: MIT Press.

Van Gelder, T., & Port, R. (1995). It's about time: An overview of the dynamical approach to cognition. In T. van Gelder & R. Port (Eds.), *Mind as motion* (pp 1–43). Cambridge, MA: MIT Press.

VanLehn, K., & Brown, J. S. (1979). Planning nets: A representation for formalizing analogies and semantic models of procedural skills. In R. E. Snow & W. E. Montague (Eds.), *Aptitude, learning and instruction: Cognitive process analyses.* Hillsdale, NJ: Erlbaum.

Voss, J. F., Greene, T. R., Post, T. A., & Penner, B. C. (1983). Problem solving skill in the social sciences. In G. H. Bower (Ed.), *The psychology of learning and motivation: Advances in research theory.* Vol. 17 (pp. 165–213). New York: Academic Press.

Voss, J. F., Tyler, S., & Yengo, L. (1983). Individual differences in the solving of social science problems. In R. Dillon & R. Schmeck (Eds.), *Individual differences in cognition* (pp. 205–232). New York: Academic Press.

Wason, P. M., & Johnson-Laird, P. N. (1972). *Psychology of reasoning: Structure and content.* Cambridge, MA: Harvard University Press.

Watson, J. B. (1913). Psychology as the behaviorist views it. *Psychological Review, 20*, 158–77.

Watson, J. B. (1920). Is thinking merely the action of language mechanisms? *British Journal of Psychology, 11*, 87–104.

Winograd, T. (1975). Frame representations and the declarative procedural controversy. In D. G. Bobrow & A. M. Collins (Eds.), *Representation and understanding.* New York: Academic Press.

Zeitz, C. M. (1997). Some concrete advantages of abstraction: How experts' representations facilitate reasoning. In P. J. Feltovich, K. M. Ford, & R. R. Hoffman (Eds.), *Expertise in context: Human and machine* (pp. 43–65). Menlo PK, CA: AAAI/MIT Press.

CHAPTER 5

Educators and Expertise: A Brief History of Theories and Models

Ray J. Amirault & Robert K. Branson

Introduction

This chapter presents a brief historical account of educators' views about the nature of expertise and the roles experts have played in educational models to improve human performance. We provide a listing of historically relevant educators and a descriptive summary of the various learning theories and mechanisms advocated as fundamental components of high skill development. We also describe some of the methods used through history by which expertise and expert performance have been assessed from an educational standpoint.

In categorizing the historical record to undertake this task, it is apparent that the absence of definitions of, and the lack of differentiation between, terms such as *experts*, *expertise*, and *expert performers*, particularly in early and medieval contexts, presents a challenge to historical synthesis. In many historical writings, for example, terms such as "masters," "teachers," and "professors" are commonly used to denote highly skilled individuals, and any referent to "expertise" is often general in nature. The empirical

descriptions provided by systematic investigation into the mechanisms underlying expertise and expert performance did not begin to appear in the historical account until the late nineteenth century, when operationalized definitions for performance phenomena were first developed and tested by the pioneering psychologists of that era.

The lack of empirical specificity in the earlier record does not preclude, however, the review and synthesis of either the role experts have played in past educational efforts or the historically prescribed techniques for the development of highly skilled performance. Rather, it requires that the historical investigator become attuned to terms, phrases, and descriptions that align with what today's theorists and practitioners might more precisely refer to as either "expertise" or "expert performance." It requires that the reader, too, be able to consider descriptions of past situations and individuals and recognize common threads in the historical record as it relates to all types and views of skills development.

As we shall see, the salient characteristic of the historical record over some two and a half millennia from Socrates (ca. 400 BC) to Gagné (ca. 1970 AD) is an *increasingly constrained view toward the study and development of expertise*. The earliest recorded educators, including Plato and Socrates, often viewed expertise in what can be described as a "whole man" approach, a holistic view that included aspects of knowledge, skills, and morality to achieve "virtue" in the learner. Medieval European educators, describing new educational programs such as the *trivium* and the *quadrivium*, and implementing those paradigms within novel institutions such as the *cathedral schools* and the *university*, constrained the focus of skills development to more specialized areas, including geometry and the Latin language, resulting in greater codification of educational systems and their attendant instructional techniques. In the most recent period, twentieth-century educational psychologists, working in scientifically based learning paradigms, further constrained the focus of skills development and expertise, specifying detailed and empirically based models for the acquisition of the highest levels of skill within highly specific domain areas (e.g., concert violin performance, professional golfing, and tournament-level chess competition). This trend, broad and imperfect as it may be, will nevertheless serve nicely to trace the general outlines of our history.

It is beneficial at the outset of our review to make note of some key historical trends that will be presented in this chapter and that have impacted educators' views of expertise throughout the centuries. Among these, we will see

1. The progression from largely *individualized instruction* in the ancient context to *mass education* in later periods (finding culmination in the mass production educational techniques of the nineteenth and twentieth centuries),
2. The progression of a model of *education for the few* in ancient times to *education for the many* after the Industrial Revolution (a function of the decreasing cost of educating a learner via mass production techniques),

3. The changing role of the instructor, juxtaposing at various points in history between *subject matter expert* and *expert in educational techniques* (reflecting current views on how to best achieve learning in students), and
4. A shift in skills assessment from *informal and oral assessment* in the ancient context to *formal, objective, and measurable assessment* in the Twentieth century (reflecting the increasing desire to objectively measure expertise).

These trends, all of which can be seen in "seed" form in the ancient context, laid the foundation for, and sometimes the boundaries circumscribing, later attempts to study the nature and development of highly skilled individuals.

We commence our review by looking first at the ancient views of skill building and expertise. We then move on to examine the evolution of these views through the Early and High Middle Ages. We then examine some of the modern salient influential theories of learning and skills building that affect theories of expertise, culminating with the most recent attempt to quantify and objectively measure skills in specific domain areas, Ericsson's *expert performance* model (Ericsson, 1996; Chapter 38).

The Ancient Context

Education as a discipline has never suffered a shortage of divergent views, and it comes as little surprise that we immediately witness in the ancient period an early demarcation between two positions on its purpose: one that focused on the holistic development of the individual, and one that focused on applied skills building. These two early philosophies of education played a direct role in the manner in which expertise was defined and measured. Regardless of the position, however, the assumption was that the instructor should be an expert in the area in which he taught. This placed the teacher at the focal point of all education, with students building expertise via transmission from the expert, the instructor himself.

Socrates, Plato, and the Sophists

Socrates (469–399 BC), one of history's earliest educators, was born in Athens of a stonemason, but grew to become one of the most influential educators of his time. His student, Plato (428–347 BC), was the recorder of Socrates' words and shared many of Socrates' philosophical positions. Much of what we know about Socrates' spoken words comes from the Platonic writings. Plato has been often cited as producing the most long-lived and influential views impacting western education, and his beliefs are still referenced and debated today.

Socrates did not promote a formalized educational system consisting of schools that delivered and assessed learning outcomes; rather, he viewed education as a process of developing the inner state of individuals through dialogue and conversation (Jeffs, 2003). Now referred to as the *Socratic method*, the teacher employing this method would not transmit knowledge or practical skills (*techne*), but would engage the student in a dialogical process that brought out knowledge believed to be innate within the student (Gardner, 1987). Instruction in the Socratic context, therefore, was conducted by means of interactive questioning and dialog, without concern for fixed learning objectives, and with the goal of developing "virtue" and achieving truth (Rowe, 2001). Socrates similarly assessed his students via informal, dialectic questioning, his quest always to find some person who knew more than he (Rowe, 2001).

Plato, generally sharing Socratic views, had some specific recommendations concerning the education of younger learners, which can be found in his classic work, *The Republic*. For example, Plato states that future Guardians of the State should pursue math-related studies for a period of ten years before advancement to subjects such as rhetoric or philosophy (Cooper, 2001). Plato also emphasized the importance of abstract disciplines, such as philosophy and mathematics, but also believed that only a very few individuals possessed the "natural abilities" required for pursuit of such subjects (Cooper, 2001). Thus, we witness in Plato an early belief in the presence of *natural ability* based on some form of genetic endowment, a prototypical concept foreshadowing all the way to Sir Francis Galton's nineteenth-century attempts to measure a generalized, inheritable intelligent quotient, *g* (Galton, in Ericsson, 2004; Horn & Masunaga, Chapter 34).

Socrates and Plato did not seem strongly concerned with the development of applied skills and actually seemed to demonstrate an aversion to practical skills training when devoid of what they viewed as the deeper meanings of education (Johnson, 1998). Further, neither viewed education's primary role as the transmission of information to students: education was viewed as *inherently* valuable as an intellectual exploration of the soul. This position therefore provided a definition of expertise as a *general set of inner ethical and knowledge-based traits that was informally and orally assessed by the instructor.*

In notable opposition to the "whole man" educational approach advocated by Plato and Socrates were the *Sophists*. The name "Sophist" itself implies the orientation: the Greek word *sophia* denotes skill at an applied craft (Johnson, 1998), and Sophist educators focused on the development of specific applied skills for individuals studying to become lawyers or orators (Elias, 1995).

Much of what we know about the Sophists anticipates today's professional or vocational training movement. Sophists were freelance teachers who charged a fee for their services and were generally in competition with one another for teaching positions (Saettler, 1968). Sophists taught *arete*, a skill at a particular job, using a carefully prepared lecture/tutorial approach in what could be conceived as an early attempt at mass instruction (Johnson, 1998). Sophist instructional methodologies were systematic, objective in nature, and made use of student feedback (Saettler, 1968). It was the applied skills-building aspect of Sophism that Plato rejected, accusing the Sophists of turning education into "a marketable bag of tricks" (Johnson, 1998).

Sophists would likely have defined expertise as *the presence of highly developed and comprehensive rhetorical and applied skills* that spanned the knowledge base of the era, a definition quite distinct from the notions of Socrates or Plato. Central to Sophism was the belief that there was a single base skill – rhetoric – that once learned could be transferred to any subject (Johnson, 1998). Rhetoric therefore proved to be the chief subject of Sophist instruction, the educational goal being the development of what today we might call a *polymath*, an individual who had mastered many subjects and whose knowledge was "complete" (Saettler, 1968). Sophist methods attempted to transfer rhetorical skill into all types of subject domains, including geography, logic, history, and music, through the acquisition of cognitive rules for each domain (Saettler, 1968). The systematic nature of sophist instructional techniques ensured that students clearly understood learning objectives and assisted learners in gauging their own progress in achieving those objectives (Saettler, 1968). This approach, then, moved educational assessment slightly more towards an objective standard than the informal, oral techniques of Socrates and Plato.

Summary: Expertise in the Ancient Period

We witness in the ancient context two unfolding views toward expertise, each vested in a philosophical view of the nature and purpose of education. If one subscribed to the notion that education held innate worth and that its goal was the development of the "inner man" (as did Plato and Socrates), then "expertise" could be seen as *the attainment of a general set of inner traits that made one wise, virtuous, and in harmony with truth*. If one subscribed to the value of applied skills development (as did the Sophists), then "expertise" could be viewed as the *attainment of a set of comprehensive practical abilities*. Regardless of the position, the emphasis on rhetorical skills and the individualized nature of instruction in this period proscribed a generally informal assessment of expertise based on the judgment of the teacher, not strictly on objectively defined performance measures.

The Medieval Context

Medieval Educational Structures

Much of the knowledge from the ancient school was carried through to the medieval context, but medieval institutions increasingly codified and delineated that knowledge. Subject matter was also acquiring an increasingly practical application that would serve the medieval church: *geometry* was required to design new church buildings, *astronomy* was required for calculating the dates for special observances, and *Latin* was required for conducting religious services and interpreting ancient texts (Contreni, 1989). Latin was the central focus of nearly all education, and mastery of the language was required in order for one to be deemed "educated."

A key event in the development of educational practice in medieval Europe occurred with the ascent of the Frank leader Charlemagne (742–814 AD), who established the Frankish Empire, later to evolve into the *Holy Roman Empire*, across a large portion of Europe. Charlemagne had a deep and abiding interest in education, implementing educational reform in law through a device called the *capitularies*, a collection of civil statues (Cross & Livingstone, 1997). Charlemagne's motivation for education centered around two concerns: he felt an educated populace was necessary for the long-term well-being of the empire, but also understood that the medieval church required highly trained individuals to conduct all facets of the institution's business, both secular and religious (LeGoff, 2000). Charlemagne set in motion a movement toward formalized education that was to shape education in western Europe for centuries (Rowland-Entwistle & Cooke, 1995).

The University

The emphasis Charlemagne placed on formalized education in continental Europe was both long-lived and influential. By the thirteenth century, the *university* had become a focal point for intellectual development, and with it came a systematized curriculum called the *seven liberal arts* (Cross & Livingstone, 1997). The curriculum was divided into an initial four-to-seven year period of study in Latin, rhetoric, and logic called the *trivium* (leading to the baccalaureate), followed by a second period of advanced studies in arithmetic, astronomy, geometry, and music called the *quadrivium* (leading to the masters or doctorate). It was by progression through these curricula that students acquired expertise and status as a master. University courses were delivered in traditional didactic manner, with the instructor presenting material that the students would assimilate, grammatically analyze, and restate to the instructor via written and oral dialogue (Contreni, 1989).

The increased formalization and structure of the medieval university amplified the performance demands placed on students. Students – who sat on the floor while taking notes from the master's lectures – were forced to develop a battery of mnemonic devices to remember lecture material, much of which was extemporaneously delivered because of prohibitions against a master reading from notes (Durant, 1950). Further adding to the demand placed on students was the fact that many students could not afford textbooks. Still handmade at this point, books were rare and costly artifacts, making oral lectures the primary source of information (Durant, 1950).

Formalization of medieval educational structures also affected the amount of time required to achieve a degree. It could, for example, take up to 16 years to achieve the doctorate in theology or philosophy at the University of Paris, and as little as five percent of students ever reached this level (Cantor, 2004). Most students left the system in far shorter time (usually five to ten years), taking lesser degrees that allowed them to function successfully as cathedral canons (Cantor, 2004).

The assessment techniques applied to medieval university students is described in detail in volume five of Durant's classic 11-volume text, *The Story of Civilization* (1950). Durant's history reveals that no formalized examinations took place during a medieval student's initial course of study. Instead, students engaged in oral discussion and debate with and between themselves and the master for purposes of improving intellectual and rhetorical skills, as well as weeding out students. After a period of some five years, a committee formed by the university presented the student with a preliminary examination consisting of two parts: a series of private questions (*responsio*) followed by a public dispute (*determinatio*). If the student successfully defended both parts of the exam, he was awarded *baccalarii* status and was able to function with a master as an assistant teacher. Should a *baccalarii* decide to continue studies under the guidance of a master, the would-be doctoral candidate would, after many years of additional study, be presented an examination by the chancellor of the university. Completion of this examination, which included reports on the "moral character" of the student, led to the awarding of the doctoral degree. A newly awarded master would then give his inaugural lecture (*inceptio*), which was also called "commencement" at Cambridge University (Durant, 1950).

Expertise and specialization among teaching faulty was also a salient element of the university system. The abbey of St-Victor of Paris, for example, was well known for a series of highly acclaimed teaching faculty, and John of Salisbury, teaching at the cathedral school of Chartres, was held in esteem for his knowledge of political theory (Jordan, 2003). This trend evolved to a point where institutions themselves developed reputations for excellence in specific areas based on the faculty: among many others, Bologna for law, Paris for theology, and Cambridge for natural philosophy and theology (Jordan, 2003). The expertise represented by such institutions drew a steadily increasing number of students, many having costs defrayed by scholarships (Durant, 1950). This trend reflected both the extent to which expertise was valued within the education community, as well as the increasing domain specialization of instructors, whose domain knowledge was regarded as a critical component for mastering any topic.

Medieval Instructional Techniques

The medieval period saw the birth of a number of teaching techniques that were applied at the various universities, cathedral schools, and monasteries throughout Europe. It was through these techniques that learners were expected to master grammar, rhetoric, and language, all of which were the bedrock requirement for mastery of higher education, and reflected the continuing importance of communication skills carried over from the ancient context.

Typical of such techniques was *Scholasticism*, an eleventh-century innovation greatly influenced by the questioning techniques of Abelard (1079–1142 AD) and later fully described by Aquinas (1225–1274 AD). Scholasticism was a syllogistic learning and teaching technique that investigated apparent contradictions in ancient texts (Cross & Livingstone, 1997). Assessment under the Scholastic method was conducted by the master's review of student responses to such apparently contradictory source material: the student was required to apply the rules of logic in an exacting technique, with the goal of being able either to defend the "contradictory" statements as not actually containing contradiction, or to otherwise craft a convincing statement positing the human inability to resolve the contradiction (i.e., the "contradiction" was a divine truth). These interactions followed a set ritual (*scholastica disputatio*), whereby a master's question required from the student first a *negative* answer and defense, followed by a *positive* answer and defense, and finally a reasoned set of responses to any objections[1] (Durant, 1950). Thus, it can be seen that the ancient topics of rhetoric and oratory still held powerful sway in the medieval curriculum.

There were also other instructional approaches employed in the medieval university: Comenius (1592–1670 AD), for example, taught by using visuals embedded within instructional texts, such as his *Orbus Pictus* (Saettler, 1968), and Isidore of Seville (560–636 AD) applied grammatical rules to a wide variety of fields of study in an attempt to view all knowledge through the lens of language and its structure (Contreni, 1989). But the techniques demonstrate how an expert teacher, with highly-developed domain knowledge, sought to inculcate that knowledge in students and, over time, develop highly proficient individuals who would someday take over the teaching task.

The Craft Guilds

A fascinating parallel to the formalized academic systems found in medieval schools and universities were the craft guilds (Icher, 1998) that targeted development of the highest levels of expertise in their members. Begun around the tenth century, the craft guilds represented an applied-skills movement that eventually covered a wide range of building and manufacturing trades. The example of the European cathedral builders reveals such trades as *masons, stone cutters, carpenters, plasterers,* and *roofers* (Icher, 1998). By the thirteenth century, a total of 120 craft corporations were catalogued with over 5,000 members. This number swelled to 70,000 members in 1650, consisting of 20,000 masters and the rest apprentices and journeyman (Cole, 1999).

In contrast to the general intellectually oriented emphasis of the medieval university, craftsmen progressed through a hands-on apprenticeship of some seven-to-ten years within a specialized area. Craftsmen were defined, even within groups, as "superior" and "less important" based on abilities (Icher, 1998). The craft guilds movement emphasized exacting performance within each discipline, all under the watchful eyes of a hierarchy of fellow artisans who both formally and informally critiqued ongoing work. The rule for being a master craftsman was "*Whosoever wishes to practice the craft as master, must know how to do it in all points, by himself, without advice or aid from another, and he must therefore be examined by the wards of the craft*" (Cole, p. 50). In many respects, because of the emphasis placed on the development of specific skills, the extended period of training, and the reproducibility of performance, an argument can be made that these medieval craftsmen conformed loosely to our modern understanding of *expert performance* (cf. Ericsson & Smith, 1991; Ericsson, Chapter 38).

Summary: Expertise in the Middle Ages

Three primary factors characterized the development of expertise in the medieval period, all continuing to proffer the notion of *teacher as expert*. First, the formalization and systemization of educational structures such as the *university* and *cathedral schools* helped to strengthen and codify knowledge that could then be studied and mastered by topic. Second, the implementation of new instructional techniques, typified by the *Scholastic method*, moved educators away from *ad hoc* instruction into analyzing learning processes in a more systematic manner and establishing sequences of instruction to improve learning outcomes. Finally, the appearance of the *craft guilds* established a skills-based, performance-assessed, and domain-specific learning community that mastered the artisan trades under the direct guidance and supervision of experts.

Medieval assessment continued to make use of informal, rhetorically based techniques. Although medieval educational structures increasingly moved assessment toward formalization, informal assessment nevertheless continued to prevail. The craft guilds were the exception, where skills were developed and assessed to a high level of specificity and were routinely measured and formally assessed by the guild masters.

The Modern Context

Impact of Modernization on Education

One of the most significant historical events to impact education was the Industrial Revolution, a period commencing in Britain in the eighteenth century as a result of a variety of economic and technological developments (Roberts, 1997). European transformation from an agrarian society into towns with seemingly innumerable factories and mills placed new demands on existing educational systems. Prior to this, education was restricted to privileged groups, including males, religious clerics, nobility, and those with the means to afford it. Even the craft guilds often charged large sums of money for admittance, restricting membership to a select pool of potential apprentices. This left education at a fundamental disconnect with the common classes, leaving them to learn what they could outside formal systems (Contreni, 1989).

The role of privilege and gender as it pertained to education greatly diminished with the Industrial Revolution. As a country's economic situation improved because of the new industries, the demand for supplying a continual stream of skilled industry workers forced educational structures to evolve in order to keep pace with that demand. This contributed in part to the ever-increasing enrollment rates that were seen in many European schools, eventually resulting in essentially universal enrollment in portions of Europe (Craig, 1981). In some countries, free, state-based education became compulsory (Roberts, 1997), and basic primary education became available to both girls and boys (Davies, 1996).

The postindustrial educational model therefore represents a significant shift in the development of human skill. In ancient times, learners spent time with the instructor on an individual basis, engaging in interactive dialogue and questioning. Later, in medieval times, although educational formalization was increasingly present, students still moved to the location of their master of choice, working with the master to achieve educational goals.

After the industrial revolution, however, mass-production techniques from industry were applied to the educational world, employing *large instructional classes and many teachers*. In such an environment, the *upper limit construct*, the upper performance bounding of such a massed, classroom-based learning environment, began to come into play (cf. Branson, 1987). Learners were now taught basic skills such as reading, writing, and basic math, and the goal was the development of competent industry workers (Madsen, 1969). Removing learners even further from the one-on-one and personalized instruction of the ancient context, and no longer focused on the development of expertise in any one particular area, this "industrial" education model can be seen in many settings until the current day (e.g., in liberal arts vs. engineering education).

Further, the notion of the development of a true polymath, an educational goal tracing its roots all the way back to the ancient context (and later revived in the Renaissance in the concept of a "Renaissance man"), became increasingly disregarded in the Industrial context. Indeed, the move toward industrialization was not the only factor at play: as the amount of available knowledge exploded with the Renaissance, it became increasingly apparent that no one person would ever master *in toto* such a collection of knowledge. *Specialization by field* was now becoming the dominant paradigm when moving beyond the basic skills demanded by industry. Van Doren (1991) notes that

> The failure of the Renaissance to produce successful "Renaissance men" did not go unnoticed. If such men as Leonardo, Pico, Bacon, and many others almost as famous could not succeed in their presumed dream of knowing all there was to know about everything, then lesser men should not presume to try. The alternative became self-evident: achieve expertise in one field while others attained expertise in theirs. *(Van Doren, 1991) (emphasis added)*

Thus, the goal of developing expertise in all fields had been fully abandoned by the time of the Industrial Revolution. If any person was to become an expert, that recognition was likely to be gained in a single field or domain of study.[2] (See Feltovich et al., Chapter 4, for a comparision of this trend from generality to specificity in the concept of expertise.)

Education Becomes a "Science"

By the late nineteenth century, the subject of "Education" became institutionalized in the universities as a distinct field, no longer the forte of the various specialized disciplines. Universities at this point were transitioning into research institutions, and calls for the application of a science-based approach to education were becoming increasingly common (Lagemann, 2000). Harvard professor Josiah Royce wrote his influential piece, *Is There a Science of Education?*, in which he said there was "no universally valid science of pedagogy" (Royce, in Lagemann, p. ix). John Dewey (1859–1952) was another of the early players in the attempt to apply science to education, writing a 1929 work, *The Sources of a Science of Education* (Lagemann, 2000). Much of the subsequent work in education was spearheaded by psychologists who had recently undergone the division of their field from philosophy, and the discipline of *educational psychology* soon came into existence. Carrying on from the pioneering work of the Wundt laboratory at Leipzig in 1879 and subsequent work by Ebbinghaus and others, *learning was to be scientifically and empirically investigated as a distinct psychological process* (Boring, 1950).

The impact of this extraordinary shift in approach can hardly be overstated: every aspect of the learning process, including learner characteristics, instructional methodologies, psychological processes, and even physiological factors were now to be scrutinized, quantified, and aggregated into what would eventually become *learning theories*. This approach was also highly significant in that it threatened to remove teaching from the exclusive control of domain experts: the field of education would now seek to develop generalized scientific approaches for teaching and learning any subject, and the joint efforts of educators and psychologists would develop these approaches (Lagemann, 2000).

These investigations would play a dominant role in the manner in which researchers viewed expertise. If a science-based and empirically validated theory of learning could describe the psychological process of learning, then the development of expertise, that is, learning taken to its ultimate realization, would similarly be described. It was often assumed that expertise was developed by successive application of the prescriptive methods built from each theory until the specified performance level was achieved. Some of the more prominent of these theories and models are now briefly presented.

Programmed Instruction and Teaching Machines

Programmed instruction was one of the first technologies of instruction that used a psychological theory (i.e., behaviorism) as a rationale for its technique (Saettler, 1968; Feltovich et al., Chapter 4). Sidney L. Pressey, a psychologist at Ohio State University, developed the technique in the 1920s, though presaged much earlier by Comenius, Montessori, and others. Skinner, seeing the educational potential of the approach, popularized the technique a few decades later, even using the method to teach his own classes at Harvard University in the 1950s (Saettler, 1968).

The technique used a mechanical or paper-based device, called a *teaching machine*, to control the presentation of a programmed sequence of highly structured questions to the learner. The learner's understanding was shaped by providing immediate feedback as the learner answered questions embedded in the material, branching to appropriate places based on learner response (Garner, 1966). This allowed students to perform self-assessment through the instructional sequence, branching either forward or backward in the sequence depending on the correctness of particular responses. The methodology was found to be highly effective in a number of cases, prompting a large programmed instruction movement in the United States

during the 1960s, including use in the U.S. military (Gardner, 1987).

World War II, the Military, and Performance

World War II, much like the Industrial Revolution, brought new performance demands to the educational establishment. The requirements for consistent and competent performance under battle conditions required that new theories and techniques be applied within military educational structures. In reaction to these demands, *general systems theory* was applied to a variety of practical military problems. Because many psychologists were involved in military training and selection programs, these individuals began to adopt systems thinking in approaching military-related human resources issues.

Robert B. Miller (1962) first formalized the relationships among various psychological approaches to create expertise in military jobs. Both the Army's Human Resources Research Organization (HumRRO) and the Air Force Human Resources Laboratory were major contributors to this effort (Ramsberger, 2001). Much of the theory surrounding this history is captured in Gagné's (1966) *Psychological Principles in System Development*, which contains material by the leading advocates of performance development through application of systems thinking.

In the late 1960s, the Army's Continental Army Command (now TRADOC) issued a regulation that set forth the major functions of training design, development, and implementation (*The Systems Engineering of Training*, 1968). Beginning in the early 1970s, the term "systems engineering" was gradually replaced by *instructional systems development* in the training community, and all branches of the military service formally adopted that term with the publication of the *Interservice Procedures for Instructional Systems Development* (Branson, 1978). Because a substantial number of military tasks were highly consequential, a demand for expertise in a wide variety of jobs was both desirous and necessary.

Such military-related jobs had historically been trained through standard "schoolhouse platform" instruction. The introduction of increasingly effective simulators and part-task trainers, coupled with a complete instructional design process based on systems theory, made training more efficient and effective across all jobs.

Fundamental, too, for success in military training was the research effort that supported the development of new practices and the continuing commitment to use systems- and evidence-based approaches to training. Increasingly complex jobs and missions required increasingly sophisticated training approaches, and the implementation of highly capable simulators made possible the practice necessary for success. Through the process of distributed interactive simulation, full missions could now be rehearsed in advance until a criterion performance level was met. The capabilities contained in such simulated systems included a full range of "what-if" scenarios and set the early stage for the introduction of computerized simulators with real-time, software-based programming in the later part of the twentieth century (Ward, Williams, & Hancock, Chapter 14).

The Rise of Cognitivism

Behaviorism had posited that learners were essentially blank slates, changed by their environment and learning through the mechanisms of stimulus and response. In this view the learner was a *passive* recipient of knowledge, waiting for imprinting of new learning. Over time, the new stimulus-response patterns would be strengthened and become automatic: learning was then said to have occurred. Expertise could be viewed as *the development of many automatized stimulus-response patterns fully imprinted within the learner.*

By the mid-twentieth century, however, a number of theorists were raising questions about the ability of behaviorism to explain all learning and psychological processes.

Questions surrounding the ability of learners to organize information and solve problems, for example, seemed to be left unaddressed by raw behavioral theory (Tuckman, 1996). This led to the development of a number of new learning theories that pointedly included mental operations as part of the description of learning. Among these were the information processing theory of Atkinson and Shiffrin (Matlin, 2002) and the cognitive approach of Robert M. Gagné (1989).

Learning Hierarchies

Robert M. Gagné (1916–2002), a leading educational psychologist at the University of California at Berkeley and subsequently at Florida State University, conducted extensive investigations into the nature of learning as a psychological process, leading him to the development of a concept he termed *learning hierarchies.* As implied by the name, a learning hierarchy is a set of specified abilities having an ordered relationship to one another, generally depicted in graphical format (Gagné, 1989). The learning hierarchy, then, depicts a skill and its component subskills requisite for performing the skill. Gagné simultaneously categorized skills with regard to their placement within a learning outcome taxonomy consisting of *psychomotor skills, verbal information, intellectual skills, cognitive strategies,* and *attitudes* (Gagné, Briggs, & Wager, 1992). The hierarchy is often constructed in conjunction with a *task analysis,* a detailed specification of the mental and physical processes involved in task performance (Smith & Ragan, 1999; Schraagen, Chapter 11).

Carroll's Model of School Learning

Harvard University professor John B. Carroll (1916–2003) in 1963 proposed his *model of school learning* (Carroll, 1963). Carroll's model, although not a learning theory *per se*, nevertheless demonstrated a practical equation for how individual task mastery is attained and also challenged traditional notions of *student aptitude* (Guskey, 2001). Carroll's system used five variables, three internal to the learner (amount of time required for learning the task, ability to understand instruction, and time willing to be spent on learning) and two external (time allowed for learning and quality of instruction). Carroll combined these five elements into a ratio that results in the degree of learning: degree of learning = (time actually spent on learning) / (time needed for learning) (Carroll, 1963). Challenging the traditional notion of student aptitude as *ability* (see also Horn & Masunaga, Chapter 34), Carroll said that aptitude was more accurately a measure of *learning rate,* or the time an individual student requires to master a new learning task. Carroll's model depicted acquisition of expertise, therefore, as primarily a function of *time*: time required for learning (called *aptitude*), time willing to be spent on learning (called *perseverance*), and time allowed for learning (called *opportunity*). Carroll's work influenced a number of "individualized" instruction methodologies, including *Individually Prescribed Instruction* (Glaser, 1966), *Individually Guided Education* (Klausmeier, 1971), and others (Guskey, 2001).

Mastery Learning

One of the key results of Carroll's model was the interest it stirred for Benjamin Bloom (1921–1999) in suggesting methods to improve school outcomes. Bloom was an educational research and policy analyst from the University of Chicago interested in improving the effectiveness and quality of educational methods. Bloom believed that virtually all students could excel and master most any subject, given the proper learning conditions (Bloom, 1968). Bloom had predicted that, given such conditions, 90% of students could perform to levels previously only reached by the top 10% (Kulik, Kulik, & Bangert-Drowns, 1990).

Carroll's work stimulated Bloom to extend the work to encompass a new model of teaching and learning called *mastery learning.* Bloom laid out the theory in his 1976 work, *Human Characteristics and School Learning*, in which he theorized that the combination of cognitive entry behaviors,

affective entry characteristics, and quality of instruction could account for up to 90% of achievement variation in students (Guskey, 2001). Noting the inadequacies of traditional instructional methods, Bloom investigated two types of processes: the processes involved in pairing students with excellent tutors, and the practices and strategies of academically successful students. Bloom's resultant instructional methodology included two principal components: first, feedback, corrective, and enrichment processes; and second, instructional alignment (Guskey, 2001). These were combined into a self-paced, individualized learning system to give each student the specific instruction and adequate time needed for mastery of the instructional task (Kulik et al., 1990). Numerous studies have confirmed the efficacy of the mastery learning model (see Kulik et al., 1990, for a meta-analysis), and the technique remains in use today.

The relationship of Bloom's model to the development of expertise lies within the theorized percentage of students mastering a topic when using the method: Bloom claimed that the outcome of such a mastery approach could alter the "normal" performance curve frequently witnessed in educational settings. Such normal performance curves, Bloom posited, were actually what might be witnessed with *no instructional intervention present*, and with student aptitude alone determining learning outcomes (Smith & Ragan, 1999). The implication was that *expertise in this model lay well within the grasp of a majority of students, not simply a small percentage of those with "natural" aptitude.*

Objectives

In the early 1960s, Mager sought a method that would enable teachers and trainers to operationalize their instructional intentions. Mager's widely read book, *Preparing Objectives for Programmed Instruction* (1962), influenced the systematic design of instruction probably more than any other text. Mager intended that all instructors should state in advance the precise behaviors that they intended to cause and then measure the accomplishment of those behaviors with criterion-referenced procedures. Instructional outcome specifications and measurement to absolute standards gradually became the norm for training critical tasks in a variety of domains.

Learning Outcomes

In the mid-1960s, Gagné published his monumental work, *The Conditions of Learning* (1965), in which he integrated research and theory to provide a comprehensive approach to instruction. Although Gagné was principally focused on the learning of school subjects, his work was widely used in other arenas. It was Gagné's interest in school subjects that led him to conceptualize the construct of the *learning hierarchy*. He recognized three major relationships between initial and subsequent learning:

- The learning of A was independent of the learning of B, and no sequence was implied,
- The learning of A facilitated the learning of B, thus suggesting a favored sequence, and
- The learning of B could not occur unless A had first been learned, thus requiring a correct sequence.

These relationships are substantially incorporated into Gagné's *Nine Events of Instruction* (1965). From the research literature, Gagné defined five possible learning outcomes:

- *Motor skills* encompass the totality of the perceptual-motor domain.
- *Verbal information* is declarative knowledge about a domain.
- *Intellectual skills* are required to apply principles and rules to a domain.
- *Cognitive strategies* are higher-order processes for learning and problem solving.
- *Attitudes* are choices that a learner makes about future behavior.

Designing instruction appropriate for the domain could facilitate each learning outcome. Most domains contain multiple outcomes.

Considering expertise from another perspective, one can think of a student being an expert third-grader. For hierarchically ordered intellectual skills such as mathematics, learners must achieve behavioral fluency at one level before they can successfully progress to the next level (Binder & Watkins, 1990). Binder and Watkins argue that behavioral fluency is similar to automaticity and that the best dependent variables for assessing learning are the response time required to recall and use any fact or relationship (e.g., solving equations) and the accuracy of the response. Thus, those students with the shortest times and highest accuracy scores are the experts. Binder and Watkins have made a strong case that instruction should be designed to cause behavioral fluency in all students (Binder & Watkins, 1990).

Constant Time of Exposure Model vs. Criterion Referenced Instruction

As in the ancient context, the twentieth century witnessed the development of two distinct educational philosophies and their related instructional practices that were in tension with one another. The vast majority of public schools, universities, and many military schools applied the traditional *constant time of exposure model*. The constant-time model produces learner results that vary much as the normal curve, establishing the basis for grading students and causing winners and losers. Because many situations and occupations require constant, competent performance, the constant time model does not meet the requirements for many learners.

Consistent with the work of Carroll and Bloom, who demonstrated that providing different amounts of time to learn produced a much larger proportion of students that reached criterion, Glaser and Klaus (1962) elaborated the practice of *criterion referenced testing*. For any level of expertise, *subject matter experts developed criterion performances that could be reliably judged by those proficient in the domain*. Instruction was designed to accommodate a distribution of time-to-completion measures that resembled the normal curve of performance scores found in traditional settings. The intention was to identify the level of performance that was required by the authentic situation and measure the performance of individuals compared to the standard or criterion. It was deemed particularly important to use criterion performances to judge competence in highly consequential tasks.

In the majority of education and training environments, the goal is usually to develop competence in large numbers of people. The overlap between "competence" and "expertise" might be illustrated by comparing naval aviators and concert violinists. The Naval Aviation flight training community strives to have every cadet become competent at carrier landings. Thus, each landing must be made according to defined standards for approach and touchdown. Each landing is highly consequential and when done incorrectly, the result is immediately and publicly known. For the world-class concert violinist, only a small portion of the audience would ever know that the performance given was not up to the violinist's high expectations. Rarely would an average performance be consequential to an expert violinist.

Instructional Systems

A number of the aforementioned theory and research efforts coalesced with the Instructional Systems Development (ISD) movement in the late twentieth century. Making simultaneous use of *performance objectives* (Mager), *the events of instruction* (Gagné), *instruction with feedback* (Skinner), *criterion-referenced instruction* (Mager), and *learning hierarchies* (Bloom, Gagné), the systems approach to instructional design is a methodology rooted in both educational research and applied experience, whose goal is the development of effective, quality instructional materials. The ISD methodology is differentiated from others in that it applies basic concepts from *systems theory* (Katz & Kahn, 1978) to the design of instruction. Each stage of the ISD process is viewed as input to another stage as well as output from a previous stage, with feedback loops

to allow the process to adjust and improve (Rothwell & Kazanas, 1992). The result is an objective, tightly controlled, and research-grounded process that is easily applied to a wide variety of learning situations.

Instructional Systems and Experts

A significant characteristic of the ISD approach relating to expertise is the manner in which it makes use of domain experts. Because the use of learning hierarchies predicates an understanding of the skills and sub-skills required for task performance, ISD employs domain experts *as a source of accurate information on how specific tasks should be conducted*. In addition, the use of domain experts to inform instructional decisions in the ISD approach means that the desired outcome for instruction is aligned with how *experts*, not novices, perform a task (Feltovich et al., Chapter 4, "expertise as goal state for learning"). Although ISD is frequently used to train novices in a subject area and the stated goal is often described as "competency," ISD's use of criterion-aligned performance against an expert standard implies that the goal is to develop learners who do not stop at competence, but continue on the path to expertise. The ISD educational approach is therefore unique in its view of experts: *domain experts are now seen as a source of information for informing the learning process, but not necessarily as designers of instruction*.

Curriculum Reform: Using Domain Experts to Design Instruction

Interestingly, there was a concurrent series of curriculum reform efforts in the United States alongside the Instructional Systems movement that applied an *opposite* approach toward the use of experts in education. The movement included such now-famous efforts as the "new math," and encompassed a wide variety of disciplines including physics, history, and mathematics. This movement is documented in Lagemann's *An Illusive Science: The Troubling History of Educational Research* (2000). These curricular reforms were aimed at reinfusing "discipline-based scholarship" into the design of educational materials in reaction to what was considered the poor results of "educators," who had assumed responsibility for teaching such subjects with the rise of "education" as a discipline. The claim was that domain experts, including physicists, mathematicians, and historians, would be able to bring academic "rigor" to their subjects, and improve classroom materials. This heavily funded movement lasted more than a decade, and with the results of the approach contested from all sides, produced no clear consensus of its impact (Lagemann, 2000).

Constructivism

As implied by our history, each generation has found ways to reject prior wisdom and strike out on a new direction. Psychology has seen many such excursions in which the current fad or fashion is considered to be the truth. There were the *structuralists*, the *behaviorists*, and then the *radical behaviorists*, each group vociferously marking out intellectual territory. Parallel to these positions was a generic empirical psychology that sought to find answers to basic questions from a theory and research base. This group included those who sought empirical methods to improve military training and ways of increasing performance. In that group can be found Gagné (1989) and Glaser (1966), among others.

Many of these viewpoints had their own research agenda and methods of collecting data. Few would challenge the empirical findings of Skinner and his colleagues who detailed the results of schedules of reinforcement, that were primarily described from animal research and were demonstrated to apply in the same manner to rats, pigeons, and humans. For decades, psychologists have known that a stimulus event, followed by a behavior, followed by a consequence would lead to a change in the probability of that behavior occurring at the next presentation of the cue stimulus. Skinner and his students and colleagues refined this generalization over the years. This school of thought is

now represented by the *Society for the Analysis of Behavior*.

Around 1970, cognitive psychologists began to provide data and theory suggesting that humans were subject to acquiring behavior that was best explained from an Information processing perspective. Cognition was again considered a legitimate source of data, depending on the experimental methodology that established it. Sensation and perception, as well as other functions of the nervous system, were important areas of study.

Another approach appeared on the scene with the advent of *constructivism*. Beginning around 1985 – although some would argue that the date was much earlier – a number of educational researchers began to elaborate the tenets of constructivism. Based primarily on the study of school subjects, as constructivist literature is almost exclusively tied to the development of learning environments within school settings (Tobin, 1993), constructivists posited that students could learn only if they effectively mapped new information onto prior knowledge and experience. Stated another way, learners were said to construct their *own* knowledge, which may or may not map to what *others* consider objective reality.

Limiting the bounds of constructivism to the study of school subjects is a productive effort. As previously mentioned, systems psychologists recognize that the traditional model of schooling long ago reached the upper limit of its capability. Therefore, the design of constructivist learning environments in schools can be a significant step forward. Early research (Scardamalia & Bereiter, 1994) indicates that students can greatly improve their knowledge acquisition skills using technologies and constructs based on information processing.

Students advancing their learning in constructivist learning environments represent one level of achievement. However, they do not represent promising options for developing the two kinds of expertise mentioned earlier. Earlier in this chapter, we attempted to classify development that leads to expertise into two major categories: instruction that enables a large number of trainees to reach an acceptable performance criterion and perhaps be "certified" (i.e., pilots, surgeons, ship captains); and instruction that enables a select few individuals to achieve high levels of independent learning via the mechanism of peer-critique. Given these conditions, there are three areas that have differing learning requirements: *school subjects*, *criterion performance*, and *outstanding expertise*.

Sometimes the difference in learning requirements is presented as a conflict between "instructivist" perspectives and "constructivist" perspectives. Our view is that both conceptualizations are useful, depending on the kinds and stages of learning that must be accomplished. It is hard to imagine a constructivist environment that would reliably prepare one for adequate entry level into the Army *Rangers* or Navy *SEALS*. Conversely, if an objective of education is to prepare students for future lifelong self-directed learning, then constructivist learning environments appear to be far more promising than the standard classroom instruction (Hannafin & Hill, 2002). Stated another way, one instructional approach does not fit every learning situation.

One example where traditional instructional design techniques have been challenged by recent researchers includes the work of Spiro, Feltovich, Jacobson, and Coulson (1991), who have focused research on the deficiencies of past educational techniques and made recommendations for adjustments in instructional design to improve educational outcomes and preparation for continued learning. These researchers have made a case that real-world situations are much more complex and ill-structured than most instructional systems reflect, and that these underlying biases and assumptions in the design of instruction lead to poor learning. Spiro and colleagues recommend a constructivist learning environment that emphasizes the real world complexity and ill-structured nature of many areas of learning (Spiro et al., 1991) and capitalizes on the modern computer as a flexible device for meeting such demands. The result

is an instructional system that emphasizes cognitive flexibility and nonlinear instruction, and is suited for progressively advanced knowledge acquisition as well as transfer of learning (Spiro et al., 1991).

In summary on this modern issue, the history of psychology suggests that there is no one "truth" about how to accomplish learning and instruction. An examination of the conflict between the traditionalists and the constructivists clearly fits the historic perspective described in this chapter.

Educational Exploration of Expertise as a Phenomenon

As the twentieth century unfolded, the acquisition of expertise became an increasingly targeted subject of scientific inquiry, particularly among cognitive psychologists who were attempting to describe the internal mechanisms responsible for mediating superior human performance. Among these, K. Anders Ericsson authored a salient line of empirical research investigating *expert performance*, a term he used to describe consistent, measurable, and reproducible performance of the world's premier performers in a wide variety of domains (Ericsson, 1996; Ericsson, chapter 38). Ericsson's model of expert performance differentiated from earlier expertise models such as Fitts and Posner (1967) and Chi and Glaser (1982) in its proposition that time and/or practice alone could not produce the highest levels of human performance. Ericsson proposed that a particular type of exercise that he termed *deliberate practice*, a technique involving a learner's full mental engagement and oriented on the goal of overcoming current performance boundaries, is required for such achievement (Ericsson, 1996). Further developing the model, Ericsson and Delaney (1998) provided an expanded description on the specialized techniques expert performers employ for both circumventing the limitations of short-term memory and rapidly accessing long-term memory. This line of research has investigated viability of the expert performance model across a wide variety of performance domains, including memory, sports, chess, and music. Ericsson's model, with its emphasis on objective and verifiable assessment of skill levels, remains a leading empirical explanation of the acquisition of expert performance in a wide variety of performance domains.

Conclusion

The historic evolution of views concerning skills development, commencing with the informal and individualized instruction of Socrates and Plato and continuing to the empirically measured and formally assessed instruction of today, has resulted in the modern attempt at building a common, empirically based understanding of the attainment of expertise and expert performance. To achieve this goal, a transdisciplinary group of scholars, including educational researchers, cognitive psychologists, domain experts, and many others, work together to build a shared understanding of high-performance phenomena. The standard, too, is now higher: empirical performance measures, reproducibility of results within and between learners, and theoretical models that withstand the rigors of experimental validation are all a part of this quest. Advances in these fields provide evidence that empirically verifiable models, encompassing all of the variables surrounding the phenomenon of learning, are still a worthy goal for educators.

Footnotes

1. This instructional technique bore loose resemblance to an older teaching methodology traced as far back as the ninth century called the *Quaestio method*, in which the master embedded questions to be answered by the scholar at selected points within the instructional material (Contreni, 1989).
2. Van Doren posits that the segmentation of the university into "departments" helped facilitate the shift towards specialization, the "uni" in the term "university" having been abandoned (p. 141). Van Doren points to World War II as the point at which undergraduate university programs totally abandoned the idea of a liberal education, at which point "...the liberal curriculum was abandoned almost everywhere, and the departmental organization of the educational establishment was installed at all levels below the university, even in many elementary schools" (p. 142).

References

Binder, C., & Watkins, C. L. (1990). Precision teaching and direct instruction: Measurably superior instructional technology in schools. *Performance Improvement Quarterly*, 3(4), 74–96.

Bloom, B. S. (1968). Learning for mastery. *Evaluation Comment*, 1(2), 1–5.

Boring, E. G. (1950). *A history of experimental psychology*. New York: Appleton-Century-Crofts, Inc.

Branson, R. K. (1978). The interservice procedures for instructional systems development. *Educational Technology*, 26(3), 11–14.

Branson, R. K. (1987). Why the schools can't improve: The upper limit hypothesis. *Journal of Instructional Development*, 10(4), 15–26.

Cantor, N. F. (2004). *The last knight: The twilight of the middle ages and the birth of the modern era*. New York: Free Press.

Carroll, J. B. (1963). A model of school learning. *Teachers College Record*, 64, 723–733.

Chi, M. T. H., & Glaser, R. (1982). Expertise in problem solving. In R. S. Sternberg (Ed.), *Advances in the psychology of human intelligence* (Vol. 1, pp. 1–75). Hillsdale, NJ: Erlbaum.

Cole, R. (1999). *A traveller's history of Paris* (3rd ed.). Gloucestershire: The Windrush Press.

Contreni, J. J. (1989). Learning in the early middle ages: New perspectives and old problems. *The International Journal of Social Education (official journal of the Indiana Council for the Social Studies)*, 4(1), 9–25.

Cooper, D. E. (2001). Plato. In J. A. Palmer (Ed.), *Fifty major thinkers on education from Confucius to Dewey* (pp. 10–14). London: Routledge.

Craig, J. E. (1981). The expansion of education. *Review of Research in Education*, 9, 151–213.

Cross, F. L., & Livingstone, E. A. (Eds.). (1997). *The Oxford dictionary of the Christian church*. New York: Oxford University Press.

Davies, N. (1996). *Europe: A history*. New York: Oxford University Press.

Durant, W. (1950). *The age of faith*. New York: MJF Books.

Elias, J. L. (1995). *Philosophy of education: Classical and contemporary*. Malabar, FL: Krieger Publishing Company.

Ericsson, K. A. (1996). The acquisition of expert performance: An introduction to some of the issues. In K. A. Ericsson (Ed.), *The road to excellence: The acquisition of expert performance in the arts and sciences, sports, and games*. Mahwah, NJ: Erlbaum.

Ericsson, K. A. (2004). Deliberate practice and the acquisition and maintenance of expert performance in medicine and related domains. *Academic Medicine, 79*(10), S70–S81.

Ericsson, K. A., & Delaney, P. F. (1998). Long-term working memory as an alternative to capacity models of working memory in everyday skilled performance. In A. Miyake & P. Shah (Eds.), *Models of working memory: Mechanisms of active maintenance and executive control* (pp. 257–297). Cambridge, England: Cambridge University Press.

Ericsson, K. A., & Smith, J. (1991). Prospects and limits of the empirical study of expertise: An introduction. In K. A. Ericsson & J. Smith (Eds.), *Toward a general theory of expertise: Prospects and Limits* (pp. 1–38). New York: Cambridge.

Fitts, P., & Posner, M. I. (1967). *Human performance*. Belmont, CA: Brooks/Cole.

Gagné, R. M. (1965). *The conditions of learning*. New York: Holt, Rinehart & Winston.

Gagné, R. M. (1966). *Psychological principles in system development*. New York: Holt, Rinehart & Winston.

Gagné, R. M. (1989). *Studies of learning: 50 years of research*. Tallahassee, FL: Learning Systems Institute.

Gagné, R. M., Briggs, L. J., & Wager, W. W. (1992). *Principles of instructional design* (4th ed.). Fort Worth: Harcourt Brace Jovanovich.

Gardner, H. (1987). *The mind's new science*. New York: Basic Books.

Garner, W. L. (1966). *Programmed instruction*. New York: Center for Applied Research in Education.

Glaser, R. (1966). *The program for individually prescribed instruction*. Pittsburgh, PA: University of Pittsburgh.

Glaser, R. & Klaus, D. J. (1962). *Proficiency measurement*: Assessing human performance. In R. M. Gagné (Ed.), *Psychological principles in systems development*. New York: Holt, Rinehort & Winston.

Guskey, T. R. (2001). *Benjamin S. Bloom's contributions to curriculum, instruction, and school learning*. Paper presented at the Annual Meeting of the American Educational Research Association, Seattle, WA.

Hannafin, M. J., & Hill, J. R. (2002). Epistemology and the design of learning environments. In R. A. Reiser (Ed.), *Trends and issues in instructional design and technology*. Upper Saddle River, NJ: Merrill/Prentice-Hall.

Icher, F. (1998). *Building the great cathedrals* (A. Zielonka, Trans.). New York: Harry N. Abrams, Inc.

Jeffs, T. (2003). Quest for knowledge begins with a recognition of shared ignorance. *Adults Learning, 14*, 28.

Johnson, S. (1998). Skills, Socrates and the Sophists: Learning from history. *British Journal of Educational Studies, 46*(2), 201–213.

Jordan, W. C. (2003). *Europe in the high middle ages* (Vol. 3). New York: Penguin Putnam Inc.

Katz, D., & Kahn, R. (1978). *The social psychology of organizations* (2nd ed.). New York: Wiley.

Klausmeier, H. J. (1971). Individually guided education in the multi-unit school: Guidelines for implementation. *Phi Delta Kappan, 53*(3), 181–184.

Kulik, C.-L. C., Kulik, J. A., & Bangert-Drowns, R. L. (1990). Effectiveness of mastery learning programs: A meta-analysis. *Review of Educational Research, 60*(2), 265–299.

Lagemann, E. C. (2000). *An elusive science: The troubling history of education research*. Chicago: The University of Chicago Press.

LeGoff, J. (2000). *Medieval civilization: 400–1500*: Barnes & Noble Books.

Madsen, D. (1969). History and philosophy of higher education. In H. E. Mitzel (Ed.), *Encyclopedia of educational research* (5th ed., Vol. 2, pp. 795–803). New York: Macmillan Publishing Co, Inc.

Mager, R. F. (1962). *Preparing objectives for programmed instruction*. Belmont, CA: Fearon.

Matlin, M. W. (2002). *Cognition*: Harcourt College Publishers.

Miller, R. B. (1962). Task description and analysis. In R. M. Gagne (Ed.), *Psychological principles in system development* (pp. 353–380). New York: Holt, Rinehart & Winston.

Ramsberger, P. F. (2001). *HumRRO: The first 50 years*. Alexandria, VA: Human Resources Research Organization.

Roberts, J. M. (1997). *A history of Europe*. New York: Allen Lane/The Penguin Press.

Rothwell, W. J., & Kazanas, H. C. (1992). *Mastering the instructional design process: A systematic approach*. San Francisco: Jossey-Bass, Inc.

Rowe, C. J. (2001). Socrates. In J. A. Palmer (Ed.), *Fifty major thinkers on education from Confucius to Dewey* (pp. 5–10). London: Routledge.

Rowland-Entwistle, T., & Cooke, J. (1995). *Great rulers of history: A biographical history*. Barnes & Noble Books.

Saettler, P. (1968). *A history of instructional technology*. New York: McGraw-Hill.

Scardamalia, M., & Bereiter, C. (1994). Computer support for knowledge-building communities. *Journal of the Learning Sciences*, 3(3) 265–283.

Smith, P. L., & Ragan, T. J. (1999). *Instructional design* (2nd ed.). Upper Saddle River, NJ: Merrill/Prentice Hall.

Spiro, R. J., Feltovich, P. J., Jacobson, M. J., & Coulson, R. L. (1991). Cognitive flexibility, constructivism, and hypertext: Random access instruction for advanced knowledge acquisition in ill-structured domains. *Educational Technology*, 11(5), 24–33.

The Systems Engineering of Training. (1968). Army Continental Army Command, U.S. Army.

Tobin, K. (1993). *The practice of constructivism in science education*. American Association for Advancement of Science.

Tuckman, B. W. (1996). *Theories and applications of educational psychology*. New York: McGraw-Hill, Inc.

Van Doren, C. (1991). *A history of knowledge: Past, present, and future*. New York: Ballantine Books.

CHAPTER 6

Expert Systems: A Perspective from Computer Science

Bruce G. Buchanan, Randall Davis,
& Edward A. Feigenbaum

Expert systems are computer programs that exhibit some of the characteristics of expertise in human problem solving, most notably high levels of performance. Several issues are described that are relevant for the study of expertise and that have arisen in the development of the technology. Moreover, because expert systems represent testable models that can be manipulated in laboratory situations, they become a new methodology for experimental research on expertise. The main result from work on expert systems has been demonstrating the power of specialized knowledge for achieving high performance, in contrast with the relatively weak contribution of general problem solving methods.

AI and Expert Systems: Foundational Ideas

A science evolves through language and tools that express its concepts, mechanisms, and issues. The science of studying expertise evolved largely in the second half of the 20th century. It is not accidental that

this coincides with the development of the digital stored-program computer, computer programming, artificial intelligence (AI) research, and information-processing models of human cognition (Feltovich, Prietula, & Ericsson, Chapter 4). The language of cognitive information processing was developed by the same AI researchers and cognitive psychologists that had adopted computation as the basis for models of thought (Anderson, 1982; Feigenbaum & Feldman, 1963; Newell & Simon, 1972; VanLehn, 1996).

AI's scientific goal is to understand intelligence by building computer programs that exhibit intelligent behavior and can be viewed as models of thought. One core of the AI science is concerned with the concepts and methods of symbolic inference, or reasoning, by a computer, and how the knowledge used to make inferences will be represented inside the computer. The term *intelligence* covers many cognitive skills, including the ability to solve problems, perceive, learn, and understand language. AI scientists study and model all of those.

Some AI research came to focus on the modeling of world-class human problem solving behavior (i.e., the behavior of experts). This research, and its subsequent applications, became known as "expert systems." One of the most important contributions of expert systems to the study of expertise has been to provide tools for building testable models and thus determining characteristics of expert problem solvers (Elstein et al., 1978; Larkin et al., 1980; Pauker & Szolovits, 1977).

Expert systems were developed in the mid-1960s as a type of computer/AI program that uses codified (hence, more or less formalized) human expertise in order to solve complex problems. As with human experts whose expertise is in cognitive skills, as opposed to motor skills, an expert system is expected to exhibit the following four abilities:

1. Problem solving at high levels of ability, well above the performance levels of competent practitioners and novices, even in the face of incomplete or incorrect descriptions of problems.
2. A capacity to explain the relevant factors in solving a problem and to explain items in its knowledge base.
3. The ability to separate facts about the subject matter domain from procedures and strategies that use those facts (declarative vs. procedural knowledge).
4. A capacity to modify its knowledge base (KB) and to integrate new knowledge into the KB.

Expert systems have brought new methods and new questions into the study of expertise and into the science and engineering of artificial intelligence. Some of the questions addressed by this work are:

1. Can expert-level performance be achieved by a computer program without intentionally simulating experts' knowledge structures and reasoning methods?
2. If some of what an expert knows is tacit knowledge, how can it be made explicit?

3. How does someone without specialized knowledge elicit an expert's knowledge of a problem area?
4. What general representation of knowledge is simple enough to be manageable and complex enough to express the relevant expertise of a specialist?
5. Are some types of knowledge more critical to high performance than other?
6. What experiments can measure accurately a computer's, or person's, level of expertise?

Some interesting questions arise in the course of defining an expert system in the first place. For instance, is performance alone sufficient to call a system (or a person) an expert?[1] How much does the speed of performance matter in the definition of expertise, even though it has been noted that experts do in fact solve problems faster than novices (Anderson, 1982; Arocha & Patel, 1995)? Again, though it has been noted that experts use different problem solving strategies than novices and select relevant information better (Shanteau, 1988), how much do these characteristics define expertise? Asking lay persons to characterize intelligent behavior (Berg & Sternberg, 1992) resulted in characteristics that also suggest questions about the nature of expertise, which we have used to help define intelligent systems (Buchanan, 1994). Because expert systems rely essentially on explicitly articulated knowledge, the terms "expert system" and "knowledge-based system" are often used synonymously, suggesting still further questions about the role of knowledge in human expertise.

The area of human intellectual endeavor to be captured in an expert system is called the *task domain*. *Task* refers to some goal-oriented, problem solving activity. *Domain* refers to the subject area within which the task is being performed. Typical tasks are diagnosis, planning, scheduling, configuration, and design. Examples of task domains (just a few of thousands) are troubleshooting an automobile engine, scheduling aircraft crews, and determining chemical structure from physical data.

Example: The PUFF Expert System for Diagnosing Lung Disease

PUFF is an early expert system that provides a useful concrete example of the concept (Rutledge et al., 1993). In the domain of pulmonary medicine one important task is the diagnosis of specific lung disorder(s). A patient is asked to breathe through a mask connected to an airflow meter. Data on expiration and inhalation flows versus time are captured by a device called a spirometer. The data, combined with other information from the patient's history and examination, are interpreted by a relatively simple inference process that uses a knowledge base (KB) of about 400 IF-THEN rules. The rules relate patient data and information to intermediate or final disease diagnoses. PUFF outputs a paragraph of diagnostic statements in a stylized English that uses the common terminology of pulmonary physiologists doing diagnoses in this domain. Note the key role of specialization: the knowledge is domain-specific (see also, Feltovich et al., Chapter 4). It is just that domain-specific knowledge that provides the power, in much the same way that the specialized training of human medical specialists allows them to provide expertise not often present in general practitioners.

The 400 rules of domain-specific knowledge were elicited by a computer scientist who worked closely with an expert physician over a period of several weeks.[2] Together they carefully examined hundreds of actual cases from the physician's files, codifying expertise into rules expressed in the domain's vocabulary, and therefore understandable to the physician and his peers.

This encoding of knowledge in the domain vocabulary and its consequent comprehensibility is another key attribute of expert systems. Because they reason using a vocabulary familiar to people, expert systems can explain their reasoning simply by playing back the sequence of rules applied to specific cases. This notion of *transparency* is another characteristic that distinguishes expert systems from other computational approaches to problem solving. (Consider by contrast having a dynamic programming algorithm play back its sequence of operations. Would that provide a comprehensible account of why its answer was correct?)

Because the program's rationale for each diagnosis can be explained by the program in the expert's own vocabulary, the expert can find the causes of errors quite readily. The process of eliciting knowledge, testing cases, and refining the knowledge base is called knowledge engineering. The process stops when, in the judgment of the expert (physician in the case of PUFF), the performance of the system (PUFF) is at expert level (or better). With PUFF, the medical research institute at which the work was done later licensed the knowledge base to a commercial firm that makes and sells spirometers. The firm rewrote PUFF in an industrial strength version that it sells with its instruments.

A Brief History of AI and Expert Systems

Expert systems are based on the computational techniques of artificial intelligence (AI). From its beginnings as a working science in 1956, AI has been a growing collection of ideas about how to build computers that exhibit human-level intelligence. One important branch of AI sought to understand and faithfully simulate the problem solving methods of humans (the psychology branch of AI). A second major branch sought to invent methods that computers could use for intelligent problem solving, whether or not humans used them (the engineering branch of AI). In both branches of the science, the primary source of data and inspiration was the human problem solver, and both have contributed to the study of expert systems.

In the earliest phase of AI, roughly 1950–1965, there was much emphasis on defining efficient symbol manipulation techniques, finding efficient means to search a problem space, and defining general-purpose heuristics for pruning and evaluating branches of a search tree. The early programs were demonstrations of these core ideas in problem areas that were acknowledged to require intelligence and skill. For example, in 1956–57, Newell, Shaw, and Simon's (1957) Logic Theory Program found two novel and interesting proofs to theorems in Whitehead and Russell's *Principia Mathematica*; in 1957–58, Gelernter's Geometry Theorem Proving Program showed superb performance in the New York State Regents Examination in Plane Geometry; and by 1963 Samuel's Checker Playing program had beaten one of the best checker players in the United States (Samuel, 1959). Samuel's work is especially interesting, given the expert-systems work that was to come, because he chose the components of the feature vector used to evaluate the goodness of a board position by extensively interviewing master checker players.

Some researchers have pursued general methods of cognition that were relatively knowledge-free (e.g., Newell and Simon's General Problem Solver, McCarthy's advocacy of methods from mathematical logic, and Robinson's Resolution Theorem Proving Method that advanced that part of the science). In this line of research (weak methods), expertise is seen to reside in the power of *reasoning methods* such as search, means-end analysis, backtracking, and analogical reasoning. Others experimented with *knowledge-rich* programs (strong methods) in a quest for powerful behavior. With knowledge-rich programs, expertise is seen to lie in the domain-specific and common-sense facts, assumptions, and heuristics in a program's knowledge base: in the knowledge lies the power. The reasoning methods in these programs are quite simple, often little more than modus ponens (If A, and A implies B, then B).

Theorem proving was a major focus in AI in the 1960s. It appeared to be a universal method for solving problems in any task domain. To some, it seemed that the main problem of creating intelligent computers had been solved (Nilsson, 1995) because in all of this early work, expert-level performance was considered to be due more to the *methods* than to the *knowledge*.

However, the research focused on knowledge-based methods continued, in the quest to make programs into smart and useful aids to humans. For example, this was done in the domains of symbolic algebra and calculus (e.g., the work of Hearn [Hearn, 1966]; and of Moses and an MIT team [Moses, 1971]). Knowledge of mathematical specialists was sought and used, though no attempt was made to separate the mathematical knowledge base from the inference methods.

The Emergence of the Expert Systems Focus in AI Research in the Period 1965–75

Beginning in 1965, the DENDRAL research project (Lindsay et. al., 1980) at Stanford University was exploring several big questions in AI using the experimental method of modeling-by-programming. The aim of the project was to emulate the analytic expertise of world-class chemists who could hypothesize organic chemical structures from spectral data. The AI questions were similar to those mentioned earlier:

1. Could the methods-based approach of earlier AI work be augmented by domain-specific knowledge to model human expertise in difficult tasks of hypothesis induction?

2. For programs that achieved expert levels of performance, what was the source of their power? Relatively speaking, was the power in the knowledge used, or in the reasoning method used?

3. How could the domain-specific knowledge be represented in a way that was modular, easily understandable to both system-builders and end-users, efficient at the engineering stage of knowledge acquisition, and efficient at run time when reasoning programs were using the knowledge?

4. Were there any new AI methods, or combinations of old methods, to discover in relation to the induction task?

The task of analyzing data from a mass spectrometer on an unknown chemical sample was unusual in AI at the time because it was recognized to require expertise not held by the programmer: it was performed by chemists with doctoral degrees; it was taught in graduate courses; and postdoctoral trainees sought out a handful of chemists with experience who were acknowledged experts. In addition it was a task from empirical science where some hypotheses are better than others but none has a proof of correctness. Most researchers at the time were choosing to study problem solving in the context of games, puzzles, and mathematics where a suggested solution was either correct or not and little knowledge of a specific subject area was required.

By 1977, the DENDRAL project and its siblings in chemistry, medicine, and other areas of expertise (e.g., see Buchanan & Shortliffe, 1984; Michie, 1979) resulted in what was called by two MIT researchers (Goldstein & Papert, 1977) a shift to the knowledge-based paradigm in AI because its results indicated that the wellspring of high levels of performance is specialized knowledge, not general inference methods.

It is important to note that the domains chosen for AI research were small and bounded in comparison with everything an expert knows. This no doubt was a contributing factor to making it possible to encode enough of the relevant expertise to achieve expert-level performance.

Production systems – collections of conditional sentences with an interpreter no more complex than modus ponens – were in use to build psychological simulations of people solving problems of various types (Davis & King, 1984). These were suitable for encoding DENDRAL's specialized chemistry knowledge (of mass spectrometry) because they were highly modular and allowed use of the experts' vocabulary. Each rule, then, could be understood singly and within groups of similar rules both as declarative statements and as steps within the interpretive process.

The DENDRAL project continued for an extraordinary 18 years, becoming integrated with the chemistry research of Professor Carl Djerassi at Stanford. Over the years, its knowledge model became quite broad within its domain. The modularity and effectiveness of its rule-based representation of knowledge enabled a learning program, Meta-DENDRAL, to discover new rules of mass spectrometry that were subsequently published in the refereed literature of chemistry (Buchanan et al., 1976).

The Methodology of Expert Systems and Knowledge Engineering

Building an expert system is as much an epistemological enterprise as it is a computer science task. The specialists who do this work (sometimes computer scientists, sometimes domain experts) are called knowledge engineers. For each expert system, the knowledge engineer must choose and use a *knowledge representation* (the symbolic form of the knowledge, e.g., conditional rules, or expressions in mathematical logic). The knowledge engineer also chooses and uses a compatible *reasoning method* (e.g., modus ponens, as in rule-based systems, or reductio ad absurdum, as in resolution theorem proving). There are many software development tools to assist with these jobs. Above all, the knowledge engineer is a patient and careful epistemologist.

The Building Blocks of Expert Systems

Every expert system consists of two principal parts: the knowledge base and the reasoning, or inference, engine. Both are implemented within a conceptual framework, or model, that defines the overall problem solving strategy.

The *knowledge base* of expert systems contains both factual and heuristic knowledge.

Factual knowledge is that knowledge of the task domain that is widely shared, typically found in textbooks or journals, and commonly agreed upon by those knowledgeable in the particular field.

Heuristic knowledge is the less rigorous, more experiential, more judgmental knowledge of performance (see also Cianciolo et al., Chapter 35). In contrast to factual knowledge, heuristic knowledge is rarely discussed and is largely individualistic. It is the knowledge of good practice, good judgment, and plausible reasoning in the domain. It is the knowledge that underlies the art of good guessing (Polya, 1954). Although Polanyi (1962) and others have asserted that much expertise relies on tacit knowledge that cannot be articulated, the working view of knowledge engineering is that tacit knowledge is explicable.

The *knowledge representation* formalizes and organizes the knowledge. One widely used representation is the *production rule*, or simply *rule*. A rule consists of an antecedent (IF part) and a consequent (THEN part), also called a *condition* and an *action*. The IF part lists a set of conditions in some logical combination. When the IF part of the rule is satisfied, the THEN part can be concluded, or its problem solving action taken.

A production rule is a somewhat broader concept than a conditional sentence in logic. First, it may carry a degree of certainty that allows the program to draw a plausible conclusion that is less than certain from premises that are themselves uncertain. Second, both the condition and action parts may name functions – which may be primitive concepts in the task domain but complex functions from an information-processing point of view. These allow the program to check whether the result of the condition function is true (or "true enough") and, if it is, to execute the function in the action rather than merely assert the truth of a statement in logic. Expert systems whose knowledge is represented in rule form are called *rule-based systems* (Buchanan & Shortliffe, 1984).

Another widely used representation, called the *structured object* (also known as *frame, unit, schema,* or *list structure)* is based on a more passive view of knowledge. Such a unit is an assemblage of associated symbolic knowledge about an entity to be represented (Minsky, 1981) including its place in a taxonomic hierarchy, its most common properties, and its defining criteria. Typically, a unit consists of a list of properties of the entity and associated values for those properties.

Since every task domain consists of many entities that stand in various relations, the properties can also be used to specify relations, and the values of these properties are the names of other units that are linked according to the relations. One unit can also represent knowledge that is a special case of another unit, or some units can be parts of another unit. Structured objects are especially convenient for representing taxonomic knowledge and knowledge of prototypical cases.

The *problem solving model* (or framework, problem solving architecture, or paradigm) organizes and controls the steps taken to solve the problem. These problem solving methods are built into program modules we earlier referred to as *inference engines* (or *inference procedures*) that use knowledge in the knowledge base to form a line of reasoning. Whereas human experts probably use combinations of these, and more, expert systems have been successful following each of these strategies singly.

One common but powerful paradigm involves the chaining of IF-THEN rules to form a line of reasoning. If the chaining starts from a set of conditions and moves toward some conclusion, the method is called *forward chaining*. If the conclusion is known (for example, a goal to be achieved) but the path to that conclusion is not known, then reasoning backwards is called for, and the method is *backward chaining*. Data interpretation problems tend to call for forward chaining. Diagnostic problems, however, often call for backward chaining because goals (and subgoals) direct the collection of relevant data.

The *blackboard model* of reasoning (Engelmore & Morgan, 1988; Erman et al., 1980) is opportunistic in that the order of inferences in problem solving is dictated by the items that seem most relevant in the problem description, in the partial solution, or in the knowledge base. This model can be used effectively to combine the judgments of multiple expert systems with specialized knowledge in different parts of the problem.

Still another paradigm, which emphasizes the power of experiential knowledge, is *case-based* or *analogical reasoning* (Kolodner, 1993; Leake, 1996). In a case-based reasoning system, previously solved problems (cases) are stored in memory. A new problem is matched against those and the closest matches are retrieved to suggest solutions for the new problem.

The Tools Used

Today there are presently two ways to build expert systems. They can be built from scratch, or built using a piece of development software known as a tool or a shell.

PROGRAMMING LANGUAGES

The fundamental working hypothesis of AI is that intelligent behavior can be precisely described as symbol manipulation and can be modeled with the symbol-processing capabilities of the computer. In the late 1950s, special programming languages were invented that facilitate this kind of modeling. The most prominent is called LISP (LISt Processing) and has been extensively used in expert-systems development. In the early 1970s another AI programming language, called PROLOG (PROgramming in LOGic), was invented in France. LISP has its roots in one area of mathematics (lambda calculus), PROLOG in another (first-order predicate calculus).

SHELLS, TOOLS

Only a small number of AI methods have been developed in enough detail to be useful in building expert systems. Currently, there are only a handful of ways in which to represent knowledge, to make inferences, or to generate explanations. As a consequence, software infrastructure can be built that contains these useful methods and formalisms; then the domain-specific knowledge model can be added. Such software tools are known as shells, or simply AI tools (e.g., CLIPS, 2004).

Building expert systems by using shells offers significant advantages. A system can be built to perform a unique task by entering into a shell all the necessary knowledge about a task domain. The inference engine is itself part of the shell. If the program is not very complicated and if experts have had some training in the use of a shell, the experts can enter the knowledge

themselves, without the assistance of knowledge engineers.

Two other properties of expert systems are important and are commonly built into the shell system: reasoning with *uncertainty*, and *explanation* of the line of reasoning.

Facts about people and things in the world are almost always incomplete and uncertain. Expertise must include knowledge and methods for dealing with facts that are uncertain or missing altogether. An expert, or expert system, may fill in reasonable defaults by looking at prototypes or by inferring plausible features from others that are known. Or it may be possible to ignore the missing information and deal just with available data. Knowing how to treat incomplete descriptions is a small, but important, part of high performance and expertise.

Inference is also typically uncertain – few inferences outside of mathematics are absolutely true. To deal with uncertain inference, a rule may have associated with it a *confidence factor* or a weight. The set of methods for using uncertain knowledge in combination with uncertain data in the reasoning process is called *reasoning with uncertainty*. One important method for reasoning with uncertainty combines probability statements using Bayes' Theorem to infer the probabilities associated with events or outcomes of interest. Whereas Tversky and Kahneman (1974) have shown that even expert decision makers fail to combine probability statements rationally (i.e., according to Bayes' Theorem and other laws of probability), a program makes no such errors. This helps emphasize the point that expert systems are normative models of human expertise as it ought to be applied, not descriptive computational models of observed human performance (with all of its foibles).

The Applications of Expert Systems

Expert systems are widely used today as surrogate experts and decision-making assistants – in business, manufacturing, and service industries, in health care, education, finance, science, space exploration, and defense (see also, Chapters 19–33). The benefits of expert systems derive from a few basic facts:

1. Computers process information faster and more reliably than people.
2. Computer software can be replicated cheaply and easily.
3. Expertise is scarce.

Because of these facts, the major benefits become:

1. A speed-up of human professional or semi-professional work – typically by a factor of ten and sometimes by a factor of a hundred or more.
2. Improved quality of decision making. In some cases, the quality or correctness of decisions evaluated after the fact show a ten-fold improvement.
3. Major internal cost savings. Savings within companies can result from quality improvement or more efficient production of goods and information, and provide a major motivation for using expert systems.
4. Preservation of expertise. Expert systems are used to preserve scarce know-how in organizations, to capture the expertise of individuals who are retiring, and to preserve corporate know-how so that it can be widely distributed to other factories, offices, or service centers of the company (Hoffman & Lintern, Chapter 12).
5. Wide spectrum of applications. Applications of expert systems find their way into most areas of knowledge work and are as varied as helping salespersons sell modular factory-built homes to helping NASA plan the maintenance of a space shuttle in preparation for its next flight. In general terms, the applications tend to cluster into the following six major classes.

Diagnosis and Troubleshooting of Devices and Systems

This class comprises systems that diagnose faults and suggest corrective actions for a malfunctioning device or process. Medical diagnosis was one of the first knowledge areas to which expert-systems technology was applied (see e.g., Shortliffe 1976, Norman et al., Chapter 19), but diagnosis of engineered systems quickly became important commercialy. There are probably more diagnostic applications of expert systems (including telephone help desks and equipment troubleshooting) than any other type. The diagnostic problem can be stated in the abstract as: given the evidence presenting itself, what is the underlying problem/reason/cause?

Planning and Scheduling

Systems that fall into this class analyze a set of one or more potentially complex and interacting goals in order to determine a set of actions to achieve those goals, and/or provide a detailed temporal ordering of those actions, taking into account personnel, materiel, and other constraints (see also Durso & Dattel, Chapter 20). This class has great commercial impact. Examples involve airline scheduling of flights, personnel, and gates; cargo loading and unloading for multiple ships in a port; manufacturing job-shop scheduling; and manufacturing process planning.

Configuration of Manufactured Objects from Subassemblies

Configuration is historically one of the most important of expert system applications and involves synthesizing a solution to a problem from a set of elements related by a set of constraints. Configuration applications were pioneered by computer companies as a means of facilitating the manufacture of semi-custom minicomputers (McDermott, 1982). The technique has found its way into use in many different industries, for example, modular home building, telecommunications, manufacturing, and other areas involving complex engineering design and manufacturing.

Financial Decision Making

The financial services industry has been a vigorous user of expert-system techniques. Early applications were in credit card fraud detection software. Advisory programs have been created to assist bankers in determining whether to make loans to businesses and individuals. Insurance companies have used expert systems to assess the risk presented by a customer and to determine a price for the insurance. In the financial markets, foreign-exchange trading is an important expert-system application.

Knowledge Publishing

The primary function of the expert system is to deliver knowledge that is relevant to the user's problem, in the context of that problem. Two widely distributed expert systems are in this category: an advisor that counsels a user on appropriate grammatical usage in a text, and a tax advisor that accompanies a tax preparation program and advises the user on tax strategy, tactics, and individual tax policy. Note that in both cases the role of the system is to find and then present the user with knowledge relevant to a decision the user has to make.

Process Monitoring and Control

Systems in this class analyze real-time data from physical devices with the goal of noticing anomalies, predicting trends, and controlling for both optimality and failure correction. Examples of real-time systems that actively monitor processes can be found in steel making, oil refining, and even the control of space probes for space exploration (Nayak & Williams, 1998).

Issues about Expertise Arising from Work on Expert Systems

As one would expect, the two main areas for research on expert systems are also central issues in AI: knowledge representation and reasoning. In addition, three other major lines of work take on extra importance in dealing with expert systems: knowledge acquisition, explanation, and validation. Within each of these areas many issues have been explored in both psychology and AI; for some of them there have been

substantial results (e.g., Chi et al., 1988; Feltovich et al., 1997), whereas for others these issues are driving new research.

Knowledge Representation

In knowledge representation, the key topics are concepts, languages, and standards for knowledge representation (see also Chi, Chapter 10; Hoffman & Lintern, Chapter 12). There are many issues involved in scaling up expert systems: defining the problems encountered in the pursuit of large knowledge bases; developing the infrastructure for building and sharing large knowledge bases; and actually accumulating a large body of knowledge, for example, commonsense knowledge or engineering and technical knowledge. Moreover, expertise involves an efficient organization of knowledge: a disparate collection of unrelated facts does not constitute expertise.

As with human experts, problem solving by computer requires an efficacious representation of a problem and of the knowledge needed to solve it (Davis et al., 1993). IF-THEN rules, for example, seem "natural" for stating the inferential knowledge needed to diagnose the causes of many medical problems or for classifying loan applicants into levels of credit risk. However, work on expert systems has shown that a single representation can be insufficient for different tasks in the same domain (Clancey, 1985). For example, teaching about a subject domain requires different knowledge and skills from solving problems in the domain. Moreover, work has shown that different representations may be used equally well for the same task in a domain (Aikins, 1983). Diagrams are known to be useful for human problem solving (Polya, 1954) but their use by computer is still only partially understood.

Experts' knowledge is not homogeneous and can be categorized along at least two dimensions: formal versus informal knowledge, and public versus private (Forsythe, Osheroff, Buchanan, & Miller, 1991). Knowledge encoded in textbooks and journals is formal and public, heuristics shared among members of a lab tend to be informal and private. Paradoxically, when some private knowledge (e.g., of how to get around an institution's rules) is made public, it loses its value (because administrators change the rules).

Strategic knowledge is important because of its power: experts use more efficient problem solving strategies than novices. This capability is replicated to some extent in an expert system through meta-level knowledge (Hayes-Roth et al., 1983). For example, MYCIN's diagnostic strategy was predominantly backward chaining: starting with the goal of recommending therapy for a patient with an infection, MYCIN works backward to what it needs to know to do that – recursively until the answers to what it needs to know can be found by asking a doctor or nurse. This conveys a sense of purpose to the doctor or nurse using the program. However, MYCIN was also given meta-knowledge to direct the lines of reasoning even further, For example, to indicate the order in which to pursue different goals. Meta-knowledge in the program, as with experts, also told MYCIN whether enough information was available on a case to warrant a conclusion or whether it had enough knowledge relevant to a case to attempt solving it at all (Davis, 1980).

Knowledge Use

Knowledge, once codified, should be useful for solving different kinds of problems within different reasoning paradigms. Research on knowledge use, or problem solving, involves the development of new methods for different kinds of reasoning, such as causal models, analogical reasoning, reasoning based on probability theory and decision theory, and reasoning from case examples. At present, each of these reasoning paradigms uses a specialized representation of knowledge even for the same problem domain. As with human problem solvers, communication is difficult when programs are working in different conceptual frameworks.

The first generation of expert systems was characterized by knowledge bases that were narrow. Hence, their performance was brittle: when the boundary of a system's knowledge was traversed, the system's behavior went from extremely competent to incompetent very quickly (Davis, 1989a, 1989b). To overcome such brittleness, researchers are now focusing on reasoning from models, principles, and causal mechanisms. Thus, a knowledge-based system will not have to know everything about an area, as it were, but can reason with a broader base of knowledge by using the models, the principles, and the causal mechanisms.

As mentioned above, experts and expert systems must be able to reason under uncertainty (Tversky & Kahneman, 1974). Several methods have been introduced for assessing the strength of evidence and of the conclusions it supports within expert systems (e.g., Zadeh, 1965; Pearl, 2002; Buchanan & Shortliffe, 1984; Weiss et al., 1978; and Gordon & Shortliffe, 1985). One of the lessons learned from these investigations is that rough estimates of uncertainty often support expert-level performance. Moreover, rough estimates do not create the illusion of knowing facts with more precision than they are actually known.

As a result of the line of research starting with the classic study by Simon and Chase (1973), it is now recognized that expertise is truly task specific and does not transfer from one domain to another (see also Feltovich et al., Chapter 4). Expertise depends on well-organized, specialized knowledge much more than on either superior memory skills (which would transfer) or general problem solving ability (which also would transfer).

Knowledge Acquisition (KA)

Experience is a prerequisite to human expertise (Ericsson, Chapter 38). In expert systems, expertise gained through experience can be codified in the knowledge base (as rules and heuristics, definitions, taxonomies, prototypes, etc.), in the statistics of prior associations, in a library of previously solved cases, and in a library of prototypical cases.

Knowledge acquisition refers to the task of giving an expert system its knowledge (i.e., eliciting and codifying it), a task usually performed by knowledge engineers (Hoffman & Lintern, Chapter 12). Unfortunately, most KA is still done manually (and slowly), although the process is now better understood than before (Scott et al., 1991; Hoffman et al., 1995). In addition, interactive tools have been developed to assist in conceptualizing and encoding expertise (Boose, 1989) and to assist in the process of knowledge base refinement (Davis, 1979; Pazzani & Brunk, 1991).

With some expert systems, previously solved cases are stored in a library and used to check new additions to the KB for consistency. If an addition causes inappropriate or inaccurate behavior when applied to previous cases, then either the addition needs to be modified (the simplest explanation) or modifications need to be made in the knowledge or in the cases previously considered to be correct. Some of the strategies for acquiring and modifying expertise are explored in (Davis, 1979).

Iterative refinement of a knowledge base using case presentations has been found to be a successful method for eliciting knowledge from an expert that might otherwise appear to be inexplicable. Interviewing alone is not as successful as interactive discussions of specific problems. However, the entire elicitation process is a social process (Forsythe & Buchanan, 1992) and can fail when the knowledge engineer fails to deal with this fact.

Knowledge engineers find that some types of knowledge are easier to elicit and encode than others (Hoffman & Lintern, Chapter 12). Troubleshooting procedures that are given to untrained persons at central help desks, for example, are natural starting places for discussions with an expert. On the other hand, in general, knowledge required for perceptual tasks is harder to make precise. For example, it is more difficult to elucidate heuristics that refer to what something "looks like," as in whether (or how much) a patient "looks sick" or the slurry from an oil well "looks too thick."

Continued maintenance of a knowledge base is a key to continuing success. Since most interesting tasks requiring expertise are not static, the knowledge base requires frequent updating. Organizing a body of knowledge within a conceptual framework that is familiar to an expert makes it easier to manage and easier to maintain (Bennett, 1985). Machine learning has matured to the point that knowledge bases for expert systems can sometimes be learned from stored descriptions of prior cases (Rulequest, 2005; Buchanan, 1989; Buchanan & Wilkins, 1993). However, both a system's performance and the understandability of its knowledge are improved after an expert reviews and modifies the learned information (Davis, 1979; Richards & Compton, 1998; Ambrosino & Buchanan, 1999). In any case, the vocabulary and conceptual framework in which the experiential data are described are critical to the success of automated systems that search for associations in the data, just as they are when experts are looking for patterns in data.

Explanation

Experts can explain and justify their reasoning. Although they may leap to a conclusion without consciously stepping through a chain of inferences, they can, after the fact, explain where their conclusions come from. We expect them to be able to teach apprentices how to reason about hard cases and critique their own and others' use of knowledge. We would expect an expert system to have some of the same capabilities. After all, in order to commit resources to a recommended action, we want to know the justification for it.

Expert systems have demonstrated the ability to show how they reach a conclusion by showing the rules that connect inferential steps linking primary facts about a case with the program's conclusions, for example, its recommendations for how to fix a problem (e.g., in the MYCIN program [Buchanan & Shortliffe, 1984]). They can also explain why some pieces of knowledge (facts and inferential rules) were used and others not used.

And they allow users to query and browse the knowledge base in order to see the scope and limits of what the system knows.

However, expertise in a program rests on implicit assumptions (Clancey, 1985). In some contexts, for example, training, it is important to be able to convey the assumptions and strategies, and even describe the mechanisms on which they rest. Each task and problem solving context dictates the amount of detail that has to be made explicit. But there will always be unstated assumptions.

Evaluation

It became obvious that measuring a system's level of expertise by the size of its knowledge base was misleading because the grain size of the primitive concepts used can vary widely. For example, in MYCIN the concept of degree of sickness could either be a primitive, whose value would be filled in by a physician or nurse, or it could be inferred from rules using the values of several other primitives such as temperature and heart rate.

Rather than measuring the size of the knowledge base, MYCIN's level of expertise was measured through a series of evaluations that compared its performance to that of humans (Buchanan & Shortliffe, 1984). Because expertise in medical diagnosis, as in all other areas, is not precisely defined, MYCIN's performance was ranked by a panel of acknowledged outside experts against the performance of several persons, called the practitioners, whose presumed expertise ranged from novice (a medical student) to competent practitioner (physicians without subspecialty training) to local expert (faculty providing the subspecialty training). The practitioners were asked to look at descriptions of randomly selected cases of infections and provide therapy recommendations. MYCIN was given information from the same descriptions. Then the panel of the outside experts was asked whether each of the recommendations – from the practitioners and (anonymously)

from MYCIN – agreed or disagreed with their own recommendation for these cases. Based on the number of times the outside experts said that MYCIN's recommendation was acceptable, compared with numbers of acceptable recommendations among the practitioners, MYCIN's performance was found to be indistinguishable from that of the local experts, and better than the performance of the competent practitioners and novice.

In this and other task domains for which there is no gold standard of correctness, using acknowledged experts to judge the relative expertise of an expert system has become a widely used method of evaluation. Numerous other methods for judging the appropriateness and correctness of knowledge bases have also been proposed (see the bibliography in Buchanan, 1995).

Future Directions and Main Result Regarding Expertise

Although work on expert systems has elucidated many issues regarding expertise and, perhaps most important, has provided tools for building testable models, can we say what some important future directions are, and what the most important thing we have learned is, from all of these experiments?

Future Directions

Except for Internist (Pople et al., 1975) and a few other programs, most expert systems have been narrow in the scope of their domain because knowledge acquisition has been difficult and costly. A consequence is that continuing knowledge maintenance of an expert system is also difficult and costly. Research directions in expert systems and, more generally, in AI are seeking to widen the scope and size of KBs and facilitate knowledge acquisition.

VERY LARGE KNOWLEDGE BASES

If knowledge is the source of power for intelligent systems (as we have argued), then it is a reasonable bet that more knowledge will enable greater intellectual power. In particular, in the mid-1980s Lenat envisioned that a very large KB, encoding and representing millions of items about the ordinary world in which ordinary people live and act, would enable commonsense behavior in AI programs (Lenat & Guha, 1990). Although common sense is not sufficient for expert behavior in specialized areas, it is unquestionably necessary.

Lenat's research team, CYC, now a company (CYC Corp.), has built such a large knowledge base. (They have also made an important subset of the CYC KB, called OpenCYC, available to the research community.) The CYC KB is a tour de force of knowledge representation and knowledge elicitation at both the heuristic and the logical levels. It has been, and continues to be, manually constructed by a trained cadre of researchers who are, essentially, applied epistemologists. One hypothesis is that the manually encoded core of the CYC KB will eventually enable powerful machine-learning processes (Lenat & Feigenbaum, 1987). Testing that hypothesis experimentally is one of the most important of current issues.

Another effort to encode a large body of commonly held knowledge is being undertaken by the Openmind project (www.openmind.org). It solicits participation of any willing user of the World Wide Web in the task of accumulating knowledge about all the things an average person knows but takes for granted, because they are so obvious. In contrast with the extremely careful knowledge engineering of CYC, this effort works on the premise that a sufficiently large body of "good enough" common sense will still be powerful. By enlisting users all over the world to help build it they hope to accumulate a very large knowledge base in a relatively short time.

EXTRACTING KNOWLEDGE FROM THE WEB
AND FROM OTHER LARGE DATABASES

Much of the world's knowledge, especially that being newly generated, already has a computer-based form, as textual or graphical entries in the World Wide Web. A substantial international effort is under way to define, and later distribute, semantic markup languages that would empower those who create Web or database entries to give some meaning to their text or graphics. The flow of research communications about the so-called semantic web (Berners-Lee et al. 2001) are on the web site www.semanticweb.org. The technology for traversing the Web to infer knowledge from the semantic markups is complex, in part because it involves semantic structures called ontologies, and needs some human assistance (at least for the foreseeable future).

When prior observations and experience are codified in structured database, induction methods can extract useful patterns. These methods range from statistical regression to knowledge-based rule learning (Mitchell, 1997). Additional research on extracting knowledge from existing sources will address the issues of reading and understanding textbooks, diagrams (Hammond & Davis, 2004), learning from large databases, learning by watching (Wilkins, Clancey, & Buchanan, 1987), learning by doing, and learning from unrestricted dialogues.

KNOWLEDGE SHARING

Considerable effort could be saved if expert systems working in related domains were able to share their knowledge (Borron et al., 1996). For example, partial knowledge of insects is common to many expert systems dealing with agricultural pests, yet each specific expert system currently requires representing that overlapping knowledge in its own framework. The goal of knowledge-sharing research is to overcome the isolation of first-generation expert systems, which rarely interchanged any knowledge. Hence, the knowledge bases that were built for expert systems in the 1980s were not cumulative. In addition to sharing among expert systems, large organizations must share knowledge among people within their organisations and their customers. Knowledge management systems (Smith & Farquhar, 2000) enable the distribution of corporate-wide information and knowledge efficiently and effectively.

Main Result: The Knowledge-Is-Power Theme

The most important ingredient in any expert system is knowledge. The power of expert systems resides in the specific, high-quality knowledge they contain about task domains. AI researchers will continue to explore and add to the current repertoire of general knowledge representation and reasoning methods. In the knowledge resides the power.

For an AI program (including an expert system) to be capable of behavior at high levels of performance on a complex intellectual task, perhaps surpassing the highest human level, the program must have extensive knowledge of the domain. Knowledge means things like terms for entities, descriptions of those entities and procedures for identifying them, relationships that organize the terms, and entities for reasoning, symbolic concepts, abstractions, symbolic models of basic processes, fundamental data, a large body of remembered instances, analogies, and heuristics for good guessing, among many other things. These, we believe, are the essential inqredients of expertise.

In contrast, programs that are rich in general inference methods – some of which may even have some of the power of mathematical logic – but poor in domain-specific knowledge can behave expertly on almost no tasks. The experimental literature on the study of human expertise (Feltovich et al., Chapter 4) is understood in the same way; for example, the classic study showing chess masters (vs. novices) bring to bear about fifty thousand things in their recognition of chess situations (Simon & Chase, 1973).

Because of the importance of knowledge in expert systems and because current knowledge-acquisition methods are slow and tedious, much of the future of expert systems depends on breaking the knowledge-acquisition bottleneck and on codifying and representing a large knowledge infrastructure (Chi, Chapter 10; Hoffman & Lintern, Chapter 12).

Footnotes

1. The Deep Blue chess program (Deep Blue, 2005) is a case in point. Although it won a celebrated match against the reigning world champion, its success was probably due more to the number of possibilities it could consider at each move than to its knowledge of chess.

2. This development time was atypically short in our experience. Some of the fast development may be due to a good fit between the expert's reasoning processes and the conceptual framework of the program, the well-defined nature of the pulmonary diagnosis task from the start, and the skill and motivation of the development team.

3. The literature on expert systems is vast. Several good starting places are listed among the specific references, but we also suggest perusing conference proceedings, journals, and web sites found by searching the web for "expert systems." One current source in particular bears mentioning: http://www. aaai. org/aitopics/ html/expert.html.

References[3]

Aikins, J. S. (1983). Prototypical knowledge for expert systems. *Artificial Intelligence, 20,* 163–210.

Ambrosino, R. & Buchanan, B. G. (1999). The use of physician domain knowledge to improve the learning of rule-based models for decision-support. *Proceedings of the 1999 American Medical Informatics Association (AMIA).*

Anderson, J. R. (1982). Acquisition of cognitive skill. *Psychological Review, 89,* 369–406.

Arocha, J. F. & Patel, V. L. (1995). Novice diagnostic reasoning in medicine: Accounting for evidence. *The Journal of the Learning Sciences, 4,* 355–384.

Bennett, J. S. (1985). ROGET: A knowledge-based system for acquiring the conceptual structure of a diagnostic expert system. *Journal of Automated Reasoning, 1,* 49–74.

Berg, C. A. & Sternberg, R. J. (1992). Adults' conception of intelligence across the adult life span. *Psychology and Aging*, 7, 221–231.

Berners-Lee, Hendler, T., J., & Lassila, O. (2001). The semantic web. *Scientific American*, 284, 34–43.

Borron, J., Morales, D., & Klahr, P. (1996). Developing and deploying knowledge on a global scale. *AI Magazine*, 17, 65–76.

Boose, J. H. (1989). A survey of knowledge acquisition techniques and tools. *Knowledge Acquisition*, 1, 39–58.

Buchanan, B. G. (1989). Can machine learning offer anything to expert systems? *Machine Learning*, 4, 251–254.

Buchanan, B. G. (1994). The role of experimentation in artificial intelligence. *Philosophical Transactions of the Royal Society*, 349, 153–166.

Buchanan, B. G. (1995). Verification and validation of knowledge-based systems: A representative bibliography. http://www.quasar.org/21698/tmtek/biblio.html.

Buchanan, B. G. & Shortliffe, E. H. (Eds.) (1984). *Rule-based expert systems: The MYCIN experiments of the Stanford heuristic programming project*. Reading, MA: Addison-Wesley.

Buchanan, B. G., Smith, D. H., White, W. C., Gritter, R. J., Feigenbaum, E. A., Lederberg, J., & Djerassii, C. (1976). Application of artificial intelligence for chemical inference XXII: Automatic rule formation in Mass Spectrometry by means of the Meta-DENDRAL program. *Journal of the American Chemical Society*, 98, 61–68.

Buchanan, B. G. & Wilkins, D. C. (1993). *Readings in knowledge acquisition and learning*. San Mateo, CA: Morgan Kaufmann.

Chi, M., Glaser, R., & Farr, M. J. (Eds) (1988). *The nature of expertise*. Hillsdale, NJ: Erlbaum.

Clancey, W. J. (1985). Heuristic classification. *Artificial Intelligence*, 27, 289–350.

CLIPS web site. (2004). http://www.ghg.net/clips/CLIPS.html.

Davis, R. (1979). Interactive transfer of expertise: Acquisition of new inference rules. *Artificial Intelligence*, 12, 121–157.

Davis, R. (1980). Meta-rules: Reasoning about control. *Artificial Intelligence*, 15, 179–222.

Davis, R. (1989a). Expert systems: How far can they go? Part I. *AI Magazine*, 10, 61–67.

Davis, R. (1989b). Expert systems: How far can they go? Part II. *AI Magazine*, 10, 65–67.

Davis, R. & King, J. (1984). The origin of rule-based systems in AI. In B. G. Buchana & E. H. Shortliffe (Eds.), Rule-based expert systems: The MYCIN experiments of the stanford heuristic programming project reading. MA: Addison-Wesley.

Davis, R., Shrobe, H. E., & Szolovits, P. (1993). What is a knowledge representation? *AI Magazine*, 14, 17–33.

Deep Blue (2005). Web site http://www.research.ibm.com/deepblue/.

Elstein, A. S., Shulman, L. S., & Sprafka, S. A. (1978). *Medial problem solving: An analysis of clinical reasoning*. Cambridge, MA: Harvard University Press.

Engelmore, R. & Morgan, T. (1988). *Blackboard systems*. Reading, MA: Addison-Wesley.

Erman, L., Hayes-Roth, F., Lesser, V., & Reddy, D. R. (1980). The Hearsay-II speech-understanding system: Integrating knowledge to resolve uncertainty, *ACM Computing Surveys*, 12, 213–253.

Feigenbaum, E. A. & Feldman, J. (1963). *Computers and thought*. New York: McGraw-Hill.

Feltovich, P. J., Ford, K. M., & Hoffman, R. R. (Eds.) (1997). *Expertise in context: Human and machine*. Menlo Park, CA and Cambridge, MA: AAAI Press/MIT Press.

Forsythe, D. E., Osheroff, J. A., Buchanan, B. G., & Miller, R. A. (1991). Expanding the concept of medical information: An observational study of physicians' needs. *Computers & Biomedical Research*, 25, 181–200.

Forsythe, D. E. & Buchanan, B. G. (1992) Non-technical problems in knowledge engineering: Implications for project management. *Expert Systems with Applications*, 5, 203–212.

Goldstein, I. & Papert, S. (1977). Artificial intelligence, language and the study of knowledge. *Cognitive Science*, 1, 84–123.

Gordon, J. & Shortliffe, E. H. (1985). A method for managing evidential reasoning in a hierarchical hypothesis space. *Artificial Intelligence*, 26, 323–357.

Hammond, T. & Davis, R. (2004). Automatically transforming symbolic shape descriptions for use in sketch recognition. *Proceedings of the Nineteenth National Conference on Artificial Intelligence, USA*, 450–456.

Hearn, A. C. (1966). Computation of algebraic properties of elementary particle reactions using a digital computer. *Communications of the ACM*, 9, 573–577.

Hoffman, R. R., Shadbolt, N. R., Burton, A. M., & Klein, G. (1995). Eliciting knowledge from experts: A methodological analysis. *Organizational Behavior and Human Decision Processes*, 62, 129–158.

Kolodner, J. (1993). *Case-based reasoning.* San Mateo, CA: Morgan Kaufmann.

Larkin, J., McDermott, J., Simon, D. P., & Simon, H. A. (1980). Expert and novice performance in solving physics problems. *Science*, 208, 1335–1342.

Leake, D. B. (Ed.) (1996). *Case-based reasoning: Experiences, lessons, and future directions.* Menlo Park, CA: AAAI Press /MIT Press.

Lenat, D. & Feigenbaum E. A. (1987). On the thresholds of knowledge. *Proceedings of the Tenth International Joint Conference on Artificial Intellingence, Italy*, 1173–1182.

Lenat, D. B. & Guha, R. V. (1990). *Building large knowledge-based systems: Representation and inference in the Cyc project.* Reading, MA: Addison-Wesley.

Lindsay, R. K., Buchanan, B. G., Feigenbaum, E. A., & Lederberg, J. (1980). *Applications of artificial intelligence for chemical inference: The DENDRAL project.* New York: McGraw-Hill.

McDermott, J. (1982). A rule-based configurer of computer systems. *Artificial Intelligence*, 19, 39–88.

Michie, D. (Ed.) (1979). *Expert systems in the micro-electronic age.* Edinburgh: Edinburgh University Press.

Minsky, M. (1981). A framework for representing knowledge. In J. Haugland (Ed.), *Mind design: Philosophy, psychology, artificial intelligence* (pp. 95–128). Montgomery, VT: Bradford Books.

Mitchell, T. *Machine learning.* New York: McGraw Hill, 1997.

Moses, J. (1971). Symbolic integration: The stormy decade. *Communications of the ACM*, 14, 548–560.

Nayak, P. & Williams, B. C. (1998). Model-directed autonomous systems. *AI Magazine*, 19, 126.

Newell, A., Shaw, J. C., & Simon, H. A. (1957). Empirical explorations with the logic theory machine. Reprinted in Feigenbaum & Feldman (1963).

Newell, A. & Simon, H. (1972). *Human problem solving.* Englewood Cliffs, NJ: Prentice-Hall.

Nilsson, N. J. (1995). Eye on the prize. *AI Magazine*, 16, 9–17.

Pauker, S. P. & Szolovits, P. (1977). Analyzing and simulating taking the history of the present illness: Context formation. In W. Schneider and A. L. Sagvall-Hein (Eds.), *IFIP working congress on computational linguistics in medicine* (pp. 109–118). Amsterdam: North-Holland.

Pazzani, M. J., & Brunk, C. A. (1991). Detecting and correcting errors in rule-based expert systems: An integration of empirical and explanation-based learning. *Knowledge Acquisition*, 3, 157–173.

Pearl, J. (2002). Reasoning with cause, effect. *AI Magazine*, 23, 95–112.

Polanyi, M. (1962). *Personal knowledge.* Chicago: University of Chicago Press.

Polya, G. (1954). *Mathematics and plausible reasoning* (Vols. I & II). Princeton: Princeton University Press.

Pople, H. E., Myers, J., & Miller, R. (1975). DIALOG: A model of diagnostic logic for internal medicine. *Proceedings of the Fourth International Joint Conference on Artificial Intelligence, USSR*, 848–855.

Richards, D. & Compton, P. (1998). Taking up the situated cognition challenge with ripple down rules. *International Journal of Human Computer Studies*, 49, 895–926.

Rutledge, G., Thomsen, G. E., Farr, B. R., Tovar, M. A., Polaschek, J. X., Beinlich, I. A. Sheiner, L. B., & Fagan, L. M. (1993). The design and implementation of a ventilator-management advisor. *Artificial Intelligence in Medicine*, 5, 67–82.

Samuel, A. (1959). Some studies in machine learning using the game of checkers. *IBM Journal of Research and Development*, 3(3) 211–229. Reprinted in (Feigenbaum & Feldman, 1963).

Scott, A. C., Clayton, J. E., & Gibson, E. L. (1991). *A practical guide to knowledge acquisition.* Boston: Addison-Wesley Longman.

Shanteau, J. (1988). Psychological characteristics and strategies of expert decision makers. *Acta Psychologica*, 68, 203–215.

Shortliffe, E. H. (1976). *Computer-based medical consultation.* MYCIN. New York: American Elsevier.

Simon, H. A. & Chase, W. G. (1973). Skill in chess. *American Scientist*, *62*, 394–403.

Smith, R. & Farquhar, A. (2000). The road ahead for knowledge management: An AI perspective. *AI Magazine*, *21*, 17–40.

Tversky, A. & Kahneman, D. (1974). Judgment under uncertainty: Heuristics and biases. *Science*, *185*, 1124–1131.

VanLehn, K. (1996). Cognitive skill acquisition. *Annual Review of Psychology*, *47*, 513–539.

Weiss, S. M., Kulikowski, C. A., Amarel, S., & Safir, A. (1978). A model-based method for computer-aided medical decision making. *Artificial Intelligence*, *11*, 145–172.

Wilkins, D. C., Clancey, W. J., & Buchanan, B. G. (1988). Knowledge base refinement by monitoring abstract control knowledge. *International Journal of Man-Machine Studies*, *27*, 281–293.

Zadeh, L. (1965). Fuzzy sets. *Information and Control*, *8*, 338–353.

CHAPTER 7

Professionalization, Scientific Expertise, and Elitism: A Sociological Perspective

Julia Evetts, Harald A. Mieg, & Ulrike Felt

Introduction

A key principle of sociology is that the lives of individuals cannot be understood without considering the social contexts in which the individuals live. Sociology is both a science and humanistic discipline that examines explanations based on structure, culture, discourse, and action dimensions in order to understand and interpret human behavior, beliefs, and expectations. This chapter will therefore examine the social contexts for, and different interpretations of, expertise, particularly within the context of professional work, science, and politics.

From a psychological point of view, expertise may be studied without respect to social contexts (Feltovich, Prietula, & Ericsson, Chapter 4). In contrast to this, sociology concerns itself with contextual conditions of the development of expertise and its functions in modern societies. From a sociological point of view, expertise and experts are relational notions: to be an expert always means to be an expert in contrast to non-experts, that is, to laypersons (see also Mieg, Chapter 41). The dichotomy between

experts and laypersons often implies not only a gradient of expertise, but also gradients in other social dimensions, such as prestige, privileges, and power. *Sociological* propositions about experts and expertise generally refer to this dichotomy.

Section One of this chapter deals with professions as the main form of an institutionalization of expertise in industrialized countries, the most prominent being lawyers and the medical profession. As we will see, professions can be analyzed as a generic group of occupations based on knowledge and expertise, both technical and tacit. Professions are essentially the *knowledge-based* category of occupations that usually follow a period of tertiary education and vocational training and experience. As Abbott puts it, professionalism has the "quality of institutionalizing expertise in people" (Abbott, 1988, p. 323). There exists a long line of theorizing on professions that also includes Marxist and Weberian interpretations. Today, professionalism is being used as a *discourse* to promote and facilitate particular occupational changes in service work organizations. Therefore, the study of professions includes the analysis of how the discourse on professionalism operates at occupational/organizational (macro) and individual/employee (micro) levels.

Section Two of this chapter is concerned with the sociology of science. Scientists are regarded as experts par excellence, and science is the expert system par excellence. From a sociological perspective, science as an expert system is based on specific *practices of knowledge production* that have gained social and cultural authority.

Section Three deals with the relationship between experts and *elites*. Notions of "elite" imply not only power, prestige, and privileges as key components, but also the idea of excellence in a field of activity that may be seen as an intersection with notions of "expert." From a political point of view, "expert power" (Turner, 2001) is a problem because it violates the equality conditions presupposed by democratic accountability. We will have to ask: What role do experts play in the formation and functioning of elites, and what role does expertise play in the acquisition of legitimacy and the establishment of elite positions?

As we will see, the golden thread running through the sociological discussion on experts is *social closure* (Murphy, 1988): professions, sciences, and expert elites are forms of exclusion, separating experts from nonexperts. Sociology studies the structure, culture, discourse, and action dimensions underlying this process of social closure.

Professional Expertise: The Sociology of Professional Groups

One way of operationalizing and analyzing the concept of expertise in sociology is by means of its formation and utilization in different professional occupational groups. This will be addressed in this section where the focus is the history, concepts, and theories of the sociology of professional groups. This intellectual field has a long and complex history. It is clearly linked and closely

associated with the sociologies of work and occupation, where Anglo-American sociologists began to differentiate particular occupations (such as law and medicine) in terms of their aspects of service orientation and "moral community," and hence their contribution to the stability and civility of social systems. In Europe generally, the influence of the study of work and occupations on the analysis of professions has been strong. The focus has been wide, including occupational identity and socialization (Dubar, 2000), but also the analysis of professional elites or "cadres" (Gadea, 2003) and the consideration of the professions as employment in public sector organizations (Svensson, 2003).

The study of the sociology of organizations is also strongly influencing analysis of professions because even the traditional professions of law, and particularly medicine, increasingly involve employment in work organizations; hence, the differences in the professional practitioners' employment relations (compared with other employees) are reducing or disappearing. Indeed it is sometimes claimed that professions, as a special (privileged) category of service-sector occupations, are in decline. Professions, as a category, have been criticized as not being a generic occupational type (Crompton, 1990) and have been perceived as under threat from organizational, economic, and political changes (e.g., Greenwood & Lachman, 1996; Reed, 1996). Professions are portrayed as experiencing a reduction in autonomy and dominance (Freidson, 1988; Mechanic, 1991; Allsop & Mulcahy, 1996; Harrison, 1999; Harrison & Ahmad, 2000); a decline in their abilities to exercise the occupational control of work (Freidson, 1994); and a weakening of their abilities to act as self-regulating occupational groups (MacDonald, 1995), able to enter into "regulative bargains" (Cooper, Lowe, Puxty, Robson, & Willmott, 1988) with states.

Many other researchers, often from non-Anglo-American societies, have argued that knowledge-based occupations are the expanding employment categories and the growth sectors of labor markets in developed (Lyotard, 1984; Perkin, 1988; Reed, 1996; Frenkel, Korczynski, Donoghue, & Shire, 1995), transitional (Buchner-Jeziorska, 2001; Buchner-Jeziorska & Evetts, 1997) and developing societies (Hiremath & Gudagunti, 1998; Sautu, 1998). This interpretation has focused on the expansion of occupations based on knowledge (Murphy, 1988), whether or not the concept of profession is used, and the growing capacity of higher education systems in most societies to produce workers who are educated and trained. It is also the case in Europe that in the common market of the European Union (EU) there are changes in the political and economic environment for professions. There are attempts both to harmonize professional service provision, on the one hand, and to deregulate, on the other. In 2003, the EU Commission invited the European professional federations to take part in the process of defining vocational qualifications for their members on a European level (Evetts, 2001; Evetts & Dingwall, 2002), which could refocus the emphasis on knowledge work as the new wealth of nations. The sociology of professional groups, however, has its own intellectual history.

The Early Years: Professionalism as a Normative and Functional Value

The earliest analyses and interpretations of professional groups tended to focus on and to utilize the concept of professionalism, and for the most part these analyses referred to professionalism as providing a normative value and emphasized its meanings and functions for the stability and civility of social systems.

Durkheim (1992) assessed professionalism as a form of moral community based on occupational membership. Tawney (1921) perceived professionalism as a force capable of subjecting rampant individualism to the needs of the community. Carr-Saunders and Wilson (1933) saw professionalism as a force for stability and freedom against the threat of encroaching industrial and governmental bureaucracies. Marshall (1950) emphasized altruism or the "service" orientation of professionalism and how professionalism might form a bulwark against threats to stable democratic processes.

The best-known, though perhaps the most frequently misquoted, attempt to clarify the special characteristics of professionalism and its central normative and functional values was that of Parsons (1951). Indeed, Dingwall has claimed (Dingwall & Lewis, 1983) that research in the sociology of the professions is largely founded on the contributions of Parsons, as well as the work of Hughes. Parsons tried to clarify the importance of professionalism through "a theoretical base in the sociology of knowledge, in terms of a socially-grounded normative order" (Dingwall & Lewis, 1983, p. 2). Parsons recognized, and was one of the first theorists to show, how the capitalist economy, the rational-legal social order (of Weber), and the modern professions were all interrelated and mutually balancing in the maintenance and stability of a fragile normative social order. He demonstrated how the authority both of the professions and of bureaucratic organizations rested on the same principles (for example, of functional specificity, restriction of the power domain, application of universalistic, impersonal standards). The professions, however, by means of their collegial organization and shared identity, demonstrated an alternative approach to the hierarchy of bureaucratic organizations, towards the shared normative end.

Whereas Parsons distinguished between professions and occupations, Hughes regarded the differences between professions and occupations as differences of degree, rather than kind, in that all occupational workers have expertise (Mieg, Chapter 41 – "relative experts"). For Hughes (1958), professions and occupations not only presume to tell the rest of their society what is good and right for it, they also determine the ways of thinking about problems that fall in their domain (Dingwall & Lewis, 1983, p. 5). Professionalism in occupations and professions implies the importance of expertise but also trust in economic relations in modern societies with an advanced division of labor. In other words, lay people *must* place their trust in professional workers (electricians and plumbers as well as lawyers and doctors) and, as a result, some professionals acquire confidential knowledge. Professionalism requires professionals to be worthy of that trust, that is, to maintain confidentiality and to protect private knowledge and not exploit it for self-serving purposes. In return for this professionalism in relations with clients, professionals are granted authority, rewards, and high status.

Professions as Institutions: Defining the Field

For a period in the 1950s and 1960s, researchers shifted focus to the concept of profession as a particular kind of occupation, or as an institution with special characteristics. The difficulties of defining these special characteristics and clarifying the differences between professions and occupations have long troubled analysts and researchers. For a period the "trait" approach occupied sociologists who struggled to define the special characteristics of professional (compared with other occupational) work. For example, Greenwood (1957) and Wilensky (1964) argued that professional work had a number of characteristics: it required a long and expensive education and training in order to acquire the necessary knowledge and skill; professionals were autonomous and performed a public service; they were guided in their decision making by a professional ethic or code of conduct; they were in special relations of trust with clients; and they were altruistic and motivated by universalistic values. In the absence of such characteristics, the label "occupation" was deemed to be more appropriate, and for occupations having some but not all of the characteristics, the term "semi-profession" was suggested (Etzioni, 1969).

The "trait" approach is now seen largely as inadequate in that it did nothing to assist our understanding of the power of particular occupations (such as law and medicine, historically) or of the appeal of "being a professional" in all occupational groups. It no longer seems important to draw a hard line between professions and occupations. Instead, sociologists regard both as similar social forms that share many common characteristics.

Researchers now handle the definitional problem in different ways. Some avoid giving a definition of profession and instead offer a list of relevant occupational groups (e.g., Hanlon, 1998, claimed to be following Abbott, 1988). Others have used the disagreements and continuing uncertainties about precisely what a profession *is* to dismiss the separateness of professions as a field, although not necessarily to dispute the relevance of current analytical debates. Crompton (1990), for example, considered how paradoxes and contradictions within the sociological debates about professions actually reflected wider and more general tensions in the sociologies of work, occupations, and employment.

Hence, professions can be analyzed as a generic group of occupations based on knowledge and expertise, both technical and tacit. Professions are essentially the knowledge-based category of occupations that usually follow a period of tertiary education and vocational training and experience. Another way of differentiating these occupations is to see professions as the structural, occupational, and institutional arrangements for dealing with work associated with the uncertainties of modern lives in risk societies. Professionals are extensively engaged in dealing with risk, and with risk assessment, and, through the use of expert knowledge, in enabling customers and clients to deal with uncertainty (also Mieg, Chapter 41). To paraphrase and adapt a list in Olgiati, Orzack, and Saks (1998), professions are involved in birth, survival, physical and emotional health, dispute resolution and law-based social order, finance and credit information, educational attainment and socialization, physical constructs and the built environment, military engagement, peacekeeping and security, entertainment and leisure, and religion and our negotiations with the next world.

Professionalization: The Professional Project

During the 1970s and 1980s, when sociological analysis of professions was dominated by various forms of professionalism as ideological theorizing and by the influence of Marxist interpretations, one concept that became prominent was the "professional project." The concept was developed by Larson (1977) and included a detailed and scholarly historical account of the processes and developments whereby a distinct occupational group both sought a monopoly in the market for its service as well as status and upward mobility (collective as well as individual) in the social order. The idea of a professional project was developed in a different way by Abbott (1988), who examined the carving out and maintenance of a jurisdiction through competition, as well as the requisite cultural and other work that was necessary to establish the legitimacy of a monopoly practice.

Larson's work is still frequently cited, and MacDonald's textbook on professions (1995) continues to use and to support Larson's analysis in the examination of the professional field of accountancy. The outcome of the successful professional project was a "monopoly of competence legitimized by officially sanctioned 'expertise,' and a monopoly of credibility with the public" (Larson, 1977, p. 38). Larson's interpretation has not gone unchallenged. Freidson (1982) preferred market "shelters" to complete monopolies in characterizing the provision of professional service, which indicated the incomplete nature of most market-closure projects. It is also the case that Larson's careful analysis has been oversimplified by enthusiastic supporters, such that some researchers talk about *the* professional project, as if professions and professional associations do nothing else apart from protecting the market monopoly. One aspect of Larson's work is of particular interest in this

section, however. Larson asked why and how a set of work practices and relations that characterized medicine and law become a rallying call for a whole set of knowledge-based occupations in very different employment conditions. This question points to the importance of the appeal and attraction of the concept of professionalism to skilled workers in all types of modern society.

Another version of the "professionalization as market closure" has been the notion of professions as *powerful* occupational groups who not only close markets and dominate and control other related occupations, but also "capture" states and negotiate "regulative bargains" (Cooper et al., 1988) with states in the interests of their own practitioners. Again, this was an aspect of theorizing about professions in Anglo-American societies that began in the 1970s (e.g., Johnson, 1972), was influenced by Marxist interpretations, and focused on medicine and law. It has been a particular feature of analyses of the medical profession (e.g., Larkin, 1983), where researchers have interpreted relations among health professionals as an aspect of medical dominance as well as gender relations (e.g., Davies, 1995).

Since the mid-1980s, the flaws in the more extreme versions of the "professional project" have become apparent. Annandale (1998) has investigated aspects of medical dominance and has linked this with diversity, restratification, and growing hierarchy within the medical profession itself – namely, only *some* doctors can become dominant, along with *some* nurses and *some* midwives. More generally, it has turned out that governments could successfully challenge the professions. Professions do sometimes initiate projects and influence governments, but as often professions are *responding* to external demands for change, which can be political, economic, cultural, and social. This has resulted in a reappraisal of the historical evidence, which is still incomplete. One line of development has been the view that the demand-led theory of professionalization needs to be complemented by an understanding of the supply side (Dingwall, 1996). Instead of the question "How do professions capture states?" it is suggested that the central question should be "Why do states create professions, or at least permit professions to flourish?" This has resulted in a renewed interest in the interpretation of professionalism as providing normative and functional values. It has also spawned new interest in the historical evidence about the parallel processes of the creation of modern nation-states in the second half of the 19th century and the development of modern professions in the same period. It is suggested, for example, that professions might be one aspect of a state founded on liberal principles, one way of regulating certain spheres of risky life without developing an oppressive central bureaucracy.

Professionalism: As Discourse of Occupational Control

In the 1990s researchers began to reassess the significance of professionalism and its positive (as well as negative) contributions for customers and clients, as well as for social systems. To an extent this indicates the same return to professionalism as normative and functional value, but in addition there are new directions in the analysis.

REAPPRAISAL

One result of this return and reappraisal is a more balanced assessment of professionalism as providing normative value. In addition to protecting their own members' market position through controlling the license to practice and protecting their elite positions, professionalism might also represent a distinctive form of decentralized occupational control that is important in civil society (see Durkheim, 1992). It has been argued also that the public interest and professional self-interest are not totally at odds and that the pursuit of self-interest may be compatible with advancing the public interest (Saks, 1995). Professionalism might work also to confer distinct professional values or moral obligations that restrain excessive competition and encourage cooperation (Dingwall, 1996).

The claim is now being made (e.g., Freidson, 1994, 2001) that professionalism is a unique form of occupational control of work that has distinct advantages over market, organizational, and bureaucratic forms of control. In assessing the political, economic, and ideological forces that are exerting enormous pressure on the professions today, Freidson (1994) has defended professionalism as a desirable way of providing complex, discretionary services to the public. He argues that market-based or organizational and bureaucratic methods impoverish and standardize the quality of service to consumers and provide disincentives to practitioners. Thus, professions might need to close markets in order to be able to endorse and guarantee the education, training, expertise, and tacit knowledge of licensed practitioners, but once achieved, the profession might then concentrate more fully on developing service-oriented and performance-related aspects (Halliday, 1987; Evetts, 1998). The process of occupational closure will also result in monopoly in the supply of the expertise and the service, and probably also to privileged access to salary and status. However, as has been noted, the pursuit of private interests is not always in opposition to the pursuit of the public interest, and indeed both can be developed simultaneously (Saks, 1995).

In general, then, some recent Anglo-American analyses of professions have involved the reinterpretation of the concept of professionalism as a normative and functional value in the socialization of new workers, in the preservation and predictability of normative social order in work and occupations, and in the maintenance and stability of a fragile normative order in state and increasingly international markets. The result is now a more balanced and cautious appraisal in which, for example, a possible benefit is recognized in some professional groups wanting to promote professionalism as normative value. This latest interpretation involves a reevaluation of the importance of trust in client/practitioner relations (Karpik, 1989), of discretion (Hawkins, 1992), of the importance of risk management (Grelon,

1996), and of the value of expert judgment (Milburn, 1996; Trépos, 1996). It also includes a greater valuing of *quality* of service and of professional *performance* in the best interests of both customers (in order to avoid further standardization of service provision) and practitioners (in order to protect discretion in service work decision making) (Freidson, 1994).

NEW DIRECTIONS

A different interpretation of the concept of professionalism is also developing, and this involves examination of professionalism as a discourse of occupational change and control. This interpretation would seem to have greatest relevance in the analysis of occupational groups in organizations where the discourse is increasingly applied and utilized.

There is now extensive use of the concept of professionalism in an increasingly wide range of work, occupational, organizational, and institutional contexts. It is used as a marketing slogan in advertising to appeal to customers (Fournier, 1999) and in campaigns to attract prospective recruits. It is used in company mission statements and organizational aims and objectives to motivate employees, and also in policy procedures and manuals. It is an appealing prospect for an occupation to be identified as a profession and for occupational workers and employees to be labeled as professionals. The concept of professionalism has entered the managerial literature and CPD (Continuing Professional Development) procedures. The discourse of professionalism is also claimed by both sides in disputes and political and policy arguments, and in disagreements between practitioners and governments – particularly with respect to proposed changes in funding and organizational and administrative arrangements within health and education (Crompton, 1990).

In trying to account for such wide-ranging appeal and attraction of the discourse of professionalism, a different interpretation is required. It is suggested that professionalism is being used as a discourse to promote and facilitate particular occupational changes in service work organizations. This includes the analysis of how the discourse operates at both occupational/organizational (macro) and individual worker (micro) levels.

The occupational, organizational, and worker changes entailed by this new conception have been summarized by Hanlon (1999, p. 121), who stated that "in short the state is engaged in trying to redefine professionalism so that it becomes more commercially aware, budget-focused, managerial, entrepreneurial and so forth." Hanlon emphasized the state because he was discussing the legal profession. When this analysis is applied to the use of the discourse of professionalism in other occupational groups, the state might be less directly involved, and the service company, firm, organization, and perhaps pertinent regulatory bodies would probably be the constructors, promoters, and users of the professional discourse.

It is necessary to clarify and operationalize the concept of discourse. Here discourse refers to the ways in which workers themselves are accepting, incorporating, and accommodating the concepts of "profession," and particularly "professionalism," in their work. It will also become apparent that in the case of many, if not most, occupational groups the discourse of professionalism is in fact being constructed and used by the managers, supervisors, and employers of workers, and it is being utilized in order to bring about occupational change and rationalization, as well as to (self-) discipline workers in the conduct of their work. It is argued that this use of the discourse is very different from the earlier (historical) constructions and uses of "professionalism" within medicine and law – from where the discourse originated.

At the level of individual actors, the appeal to professionalism can be seen as a powerful motivating force of control "at a distance" (Miller & Rose, 1990; Burchell, Gordon, & Miller, 1991). At the level of systems, such as occupations, the appeal to professionalism can be seen also as a mechanism for promoting social change. In these cases, however, the appeal is to a myth or an ideology of professionalism that includes aspects such as exclusive ownership of an area of expertise, autonomy and discretion in work practices, and occupational control of work. However, the reality of the new professionalism is very different. The appeal to professionalism most often includes the substitution of organizational for professional values; bureaucratic, hierarchical, and managerial controls rather than collegial relations; budgetary restrictions and rationalizations; and performance targets, accountability, and increased political control. In this sense, then, it can be argued that the appeal to professionalism is in effect a mechanism of social control at micro, meso, and macro levels.

The Sociology of Professional Groups: Theories and Results

When returning to the question of the appeal of professionalism, it is necessary to understand how professionalism as a discourse is now being increasingly used in modern organizations, institutions, and places of work as a mechanism to facilitate and promote occupational change. Why, and in what ways, have a set of work practices and relations that historically characterized medicine and law in Anglo-American societies resonated first with engineers, accountants, and teachers, and now with pharmacists, social workers, care assistants, computer experts, and law enforcement agencies in different social systems around the world?

The discourse of professionalism that is so appealing to occupational groups and their practitioners includes aspects such as exclusive ownership of an area of expertise and knowledge, and the power to define the nature of problems in that area, as well as the control of access to potential solutions. It also includes an image of collegial work relations, of mutual assistance and support rather than hierarchical, competitive, or managerialist control. Additional aspects of the discourse and its appeal are autonomy in decision making and discretion in work practices, decision making in the public interest fettered only marginally by financial constraints, and in some cases (for example the medical profession historically) even self-regulation or the occupational control of work (Freidson, 1994).

The reality of professionalism in most service and knowledge-based occupational contexts is very different, however, and even medicine and law in Anglo-American social systems are no longer exempt. Fiscal crises have been features of most states, and such crises have been explained by governments as resulting from the rising costs of welfare states and particularly social service professionalism. Remedial measures to contain the fiscal crises have been taken (sometimes motivated, as in the UK, by a New Right ideology), and these have included cut backs in funding and increases in institutional efficiency measures, as well as the promotion of managerialist/organizational cultures in the professional public service sector (including medicine).

Accountability and audit, targets, and performance indicators have now become fundamental parts of the new professionalism (Evetts, 2003). Professionals of all kinds and the institutions in which they work are subject to achievement targets to justify their receipt of public expenditure. These, in turn, enable the performance of particular organizations (such as schools, universities, and hospitals), and the professionals who work in them, to be measured, assessed, and compared. Accountability has been operationalized as audit. Work organizations specify such targets and sometimes, by means of devolved budgets, are requiring all budgetary units to clarify and maximize income streams while controlling expenditures.

It is also important to consider the appeal of professionalism as a discourse of disciplinary control at the micro level. Fournier (1999, p. 290) has demonstrated how the reconstitution of employees as professionals involves more than just a process of relabeling, "it also involves the delineation of 'appropriate work identities' and potentially allows for control at a distance by inscribing the disciplinary logic of professionalism within the person of the employee so labelled." In new and existing occupational and organizational contexts, service and knowledge workers and other employees are having to, and indeed choosing to, reconstitute themselves in organizational and occupational forms that incorporate career development for the self-managing and self-motivated employee (Grey, 1994; Fournier, 1998). In other words, those who as workers act like "professionals" are self-controlled and self-motivated to perform in ways the organization defines as appropriate. In return, those who achieve the targets will be rewarded with career promotion and progress.

In trying to understand how the discourse is used differently between occupational groups, it might be useful to turn to McClelland's categorization (1990, p. 170) of "professionalization 'from within' (successful manipulation of the market by the group) and 'from above' (domination of forces external to the group)." This categorization was intended to differentiate Anglo-American and German forms of professionalization, but instead it might be used to indicate and explain the various usages of, and indeed the appeal of, professionalism in different occupational groups. Where the appeal to professionalism is made and used by the occupational group itself, "from within," then the returns to the group can be substantial. In these cases, historically, the group has been able to use the discourse in constructing its occupational identity, promoting its image with clients and customers, and in bargaining with states to secure and maintain its (sometimes self-) regulatory responsibilities. In these instances the occupation is using the discourse partly in its own occupational and practitioner interests, but sometimes also as a way of promoting and protecting what it would claim to be the public interest.

In the case of most contemporary service occupations, however, professionalism is being imposed "from above," and for the most part this means from the employers and managers of the service organizations in which these "professionals" work. Here the discourse of dedicated service and autonomous decision making are part of the appeal of professionalism. In these cases,

however, the discourse is being used to promote and facilitate occupational change and as a disciplinary mechanism used by autonomous subjects to ensure appropriate conduct. The discourse is grasped by the occupational group since it is perceived to be a way of improving the occupation's status and rewards collectively and individually. However, the realities of professionalism "from above" are very different.

When professionalism is constructed and demanded "from within," *and* it corresponds with a (supply-side) state's willingness and perception that the delegation of professional powers is in the state's best interest, then the aspects of normative and functional values of professionalism can be paramount in the discourse. The professional group constructs and controls the discourse that it continues to use in its own as well as in the public's interest. The historically powerful professions of medicine and law have sometimes demonstrated opposition to "moral conduct" and "appropriate behavior" mechanisms, however, particularly in their development of alternative interpretations of the public interest.

The willingness by states to concede professional powers and regulatory responsibilities (and for occupational groups to construct and demand professionalism "from within") is now universally in decline. The consequence of this is still diversity in the use and construction of the discourse between different occupational groups – although this diversity might be in decline. The legal profession now (in contrast to medicine) is perhaps the best example of an occupational group in a relatively privileged position and still able to construct professionalism "from within." There are, however, numerous occupational groups within the profession of law, and in general it is those occupations categorized as social service law, rather than entrepreneurial law professions (Hanlon, 1999), who are publicly funded. Hence, the discourse is constructed and controlled by others. The medical professions are similarly highly stratified and differentially powerful in the sense of being able to construct and demand professionalism "from within." It is also interesting to observe that the professional groups who are becoming powerful in international markets (for example some accountancy and legal professions) might be in a better position to construct and demand professionalism "from within."

In summary, the sociological analysis of expertise has always been closely linked with the analysis of professions and professionalism. However, unlike in the past, it seems that increasingly the discourse of professionalism is being used to convince, cajole, and persuade employees, practitioners, and other workers to perform and behave in ways that the organization or the institution deem to be appropriate, effective, and efficient. And "professional" workers are very keen to grasp and lay claim to the normative values of professionalism. But professional expertise now needs to be measured, assessed, regulated, and audited. From a discourse controlled and constructed by practitioners, professionalism is now increasingly used in work organizations and occupations as an instrument of managerial control and occupational change. The discourse includes normative elements, but not in the sense of increasing occupational powers. Organizational professionalism is very different in control and relationship terms from the historical and idealized image of the independent, semi-autonomous practitioner of the liberal professions – very different from the "third logic" analyzed by Freidson (2001). It becomes even more important, therefore, for sociologists to understand the appeal of professionalism in new and old occupations, and how the discourse is being used to promote and facilitate occupational change and social control.

Professional groups have been one main form of the institutionalization of expertise in industrialized countries, and the sociological analysis of professions has provided different, and sometimes contrasting, interpretations of professionalism and expertise over time. We now turn to the sociology of science and consider the processes and procedures in science as an alternative form (to professions) of the institutionalization of expertise. Scientists are regarded as experts, and science is the prime example of an expert system with its own checks, validation procedures, recognition and authority processes, and hence claims to legitimacy. From a sociological perspective, science as an expert system is based on specific practices of knowledge production that have gained social and cultural authority. The sociological analysis of science as an institutionalized form and social practice has varied over time and offers different (sometimes contrasting) interpretations of expertise.

Scientific Experts: The Social Study of Science

When trying to trace and understand the creation and performance of scientific expertise and the role of scientific experts from the perspective of social studies of science, a look from at least three different complementary angles seems necessary. First, the question of the construction and protection of the boundaries between the science system – both as a knowledge system and as a social territory – and other forms of expertise present in society need to be addressed. In a second step the social conditions and practices of knowledge production on a more micro-sociological level have to be considered as being an important manifestation of what gets defined as, or is (to be) understood as, scientific expertise. Finally, the picture will be completed by taking a gender-sensitive approach to the question of the construction of expertise and experts.

The Shaping of Scientific Expertise: A Historical Perspective

In trying to understand the place of modern science in contemporary societies, a closer look has to be taken at the processes and procedures that play a part in constructing the boundary around the territory labeled "science" (Gieryn, 1995). This demarcation is meant not only to delimit science from other forms of cultural knowledge-producing activities, but also to secure the authority of scientific expertise in the larger societal setting and to be able to legitimately claim autonomy over the definition of the science system's internal structures, rules, and practices. The very construction of this knowledge system as an expert system, how it continually performs deliberations about which claims or practices are to be regarded as scientific and which not, but also the ways in which this expertise manages to become accepted and gains a certain esteem, both within the system but also in society at large, has to be considered. In that sense, we have to see what repertoire of activities has been established in order to be able to meet challenges to scientific authority, and thus to threats to credibility, power, and prestige.

It seems crucial to take different aspects into account. The first is linked to the development of institutional structures in which scientific knowledge was first demonstrated and negotiated (as in the framework of the Royal Society), and in later phases also to how it was produced. From a historical perspective one realizes that the production of scientific knowledge gradually moved out of the private context into specific settings where the procedures, practices, and internal rules of this production were increasingly standardized. Institutionalization, however, served also to define who had access to these places where scientific expertise was developed and negotiated (Shapin & Schaffer, 1985).

Along with the creation of scientific institutions and the growth of a community of those involved in activities that we would today label "science and technology" went the development of a formalized communication system. This became the second major factor in building the demarcation line around science and in shaping what is understood as scientific expertise. From a collection of narrative, nonstandardized accounts of diverse scientific observations written by the editor of the first scientific journal, the system gradually evolved into one where scientists wrote the accounts of the empirical and theoretical considerations themselves and where colleagues working in similar domains were involved in deciding about whether or not certain scientific

papers would be published (Bazerman, 1989). In that sense being part of this expert community and publishing one's findings in the specialized journals were closely intertwined. Besides this phenomenon, one also has to realize that scientific knowledge was no longer transmitted by publicly showing an experiment, but increasingly by reading about the empirical observations of other researchers. Thus, the empiricist processes of knowledge production and the spatial separateness of the members of this nascent community led to the problem of trust that necessarily arises when some people have direct access and others – the large majority – only in a mediated way. Institutionalization and the formation of a scientific community gradually led to a professionalization process: the notion "scientist" was coined and career paths began to structure the field.

But changes did not take place only on the institutional and social levels, but also on the epistemic level. Implementing the notion of objectivity, and claiming the universal validity of epistemic claims made by scientists (once validated by the science system), did also stress the fundamental difference and superior quality of scientific knowledge as compared to other forms of cultural knowledge (Daston, 1992).

Along with these developments, scientific expertise, the procedures through which knowledge was produced as well as those who were the producers of this knowledge, gained social and cultural authority. This meant that particular explanations and definitions of reality increasingly managed to be established as more valid than others. Although this role of the science system as an expert system was exerted within society only in rather informal ways in earlier periods, the 20th century witnessed a growing intertwinedness among the scientific, economic, and political systems.

This development explains partly why science as a professional occupation moved into the focus of sociologists' interest. In a first step the sociologist of sciences Robert K. Merton developed in the 1940s his normative framework for the conduct of science based on universalism, communalism, disinterestedness, and organized skepticism. These norms were supposed to form a strong basis for the construction of mutual trust and professional identity (Merton, 1942/1973). With these norms it seemed possible to draw a clear line between what should be regarded as professional, ethical practice and what not. Though this approach became rather influential, it simultaneously triggered rather strong critique from the side of those sociologists who turned away from an idealised picture of consensus among scientists and instead became preoccupied with studying scientific debate and disagreement (Mulkay, 1976). They conceptualised science much more as a practice and culture and showed the ambiguities and the continuous shifts in what is regarded as widely acceptable in professional terms. However, in spite of the theoretical and empirical weakness of describing science in terms of norms, the norms themselves retain rhetorical support among many scientists.

Scientific expertise in many ways became an important resource in rethinking and developing contemporary societies. However, at the same time a growing ambivalence toward this exclusive and exclusionary role played by scientific expertise and by scientific experts can also be witnessed. Today the question is posed increasingly about whether or not the demarcation of science from other forms of knowledge is sufficient for justifying the hierarchy that was automatically assumed between these forms of knowledge. Claims for more public participation and arguments that other forms of expertise should gain more weight, once societal decisions have to be taken, are but one rather visible consequence of this growing ambivalence towards the exclusive role of scientific expertise (Wynne, 1995).

An Ethnographical Approach to Expertise: Science as Practice

Complementing the processes of boundary drawing and differentiation, which we have just described, it is also necessary to see how this newly created space for science was allowed to develop and refine procedures through which knowledge, on the basis of which expertise can be claimed, is produced. Through taking an ethnographic look at the way life in laboratories is organized, we have come to understand the scientists' repertoire of possible actions within the laboratory, and how they build their arguments and impose certain views of the physical world (Knorr-Cetina, 1981; Latour & Woolgar, 1979/1986 (see also Clancey, Chapter 8)). We have learned that the laboratory is more than the place where empirical work is conducted and where organizational as well as social structures become visible, but that it is precisely a hybrid manifestation of all of them. Laboratories are places where both the objects of science, those entities that are to be investigated, as well as the subjects (the scientists, lab-assistants, etc.) are being reconfigured, where both do not exist in any "pure" form, but are defined by each other and by the spatial and temporal setting in which they are bound. These studies have tried to break with the asymmetry of the social and the natural, implicitly assumed in traditional descriptions of science, and rather convincingly show the inextricable linkage between the epistemic production of science and the social world. These investigations hinted at the idea that there was no fundamental epistemic difference between the pursuit of knowledge and that of power, and that much of what happened epistemologically in a lab was due to complicated negotiation procedures that also involve technical, social, economic, and political aspects. Furthermore, the use of particular techniques of representation had an important impact on the way expertise was shaped; that is, although science would claim universal validity, local laboratory cultures would play an important role, and "facts" needed long construction and acceptance procedures and were not simply unveiled.

Scientific expertise is thus not something easy to delimit or to clearly define, but it is always a temporarily confined outcome of certain constellations. In that sense the tensions between the role of individual competences and the image of science as a collective endeavor become visible in the laboratory. It is the individual that contributes its creativity and intellectual capacities, while at the same time the collective is the setting in which research has to be realized, procedures and outcomes have to be negotiated, and results validated.

Scientific Expertise From a Gender Perspective

The third perspective from which the creation and performance of scientific expertise/experts has to be considered is that of gender relations. Two aspects appear to be of particular relevance. The first concerns the question of scientific careers (Zuckerman, Cole, & Bruer, 1991) and the fact that women – even though they now have had access to academic institutions for more than 100 years – are still largely underrepresented in the group of scientific experts, at higher levels in particular. This fact holds even though numerous actions have been taken on the policy level, both nationally and internationally, over recent years in order to improve the situation. Without wanting to claim that women can be regarded as a homogeneous group, one that would necessarily act and need to be considered in standardized ways, it has so far remained unclear in what institutional environment – working conditions, daily practices, and policies – women could attain significant opportunities to perform in scientific careers. Drawing on studies of the historical dimension of this exclusion process (Schiebinger, 1989), it becomes obvious how strongly scientific expertise and the expert role was and is intertwined with power relationships within society (Rose, 1994; Haraway, 1989). In that sense "keeping women (or any other group) out of science" would also mean keeping the power over those societal domains where scientific expertise plays an important and shaping role.

Second, gender has an impact also on the epistemic level and thus on what counts as expertise and how it takes shape. The very way in which the universality and objectivity of scientific knowledge was, and

partly still is, claimed has been put in question by feminists from the 1980s onwards. In their view, behind the very concept of objectivity lies the idea of the "sacrifice of the self for the collective," thereby, delivering knowledge that would go far beyond the individual standpoint and could make more powerful and far-reaching claims for validity. However, the fact was "overlooked" that these "collectives" represented possible standpoints only in a rather selective way, namely, by excluding female actors to a large degree (Keller, 1985). Recent examples, such as the case study on the way grants were attributed by a medical research council in Sweden, as well as the MIT report on the difficult position of women scientists in this elite institution, clearly suggest the multiple and subtle mechanisms and values that implicitly define not only who is to be regarded as a scientific expert, but also what kind of scientific expertise is worthy of support (Wenneras & Wold, 1997; Members of the first and second Committees on Women Faculty in the School of Science, 1999).

Experts, Elites, and Political Power

The existence of experts and expertise plays an important role in the constitution and functioning of elites. There is no standard definition of "elite" in social science. But current definitions generally have some core features in common:

- Elites are small groupings of persons who are endowed with a high degree of potential power.
- This power may be due to the tenure of a formal position within an organization, or it may be due to the "charisma" of a person.
- Being a member of an elite entails successfully passing through a process of selection (Carlton, 1996; Dogan, 1989).

The notion of "elite" has been introduced by the three Italian classics of sociology, Pareto (1935), Mosca (1939), and Michels (1915), as an alternative concept to Marxist egalitarian concepts. With reference to the ancient idea of aristocracy ($\alpha\rho\iota\sigma\tau o\varsigma$ = the best), Pareto defined elites as those who are most capable in any area of activity (1935, § 2026 et seqq.). This ideal type definition of elite has a direct link to the notion of expertise and experts. But in present-day definitions of "elite," the emphasis is placed on power, not on excellence (Etzioni-Halevy, 2001). The power of elites is based on the possession and/or control of various resources or "capitals." As Bourdieu (1984) puts it,

> economic capital: money; any tradable property; means of production.
> social capital: tenure of leading positions in organizations; being interlocked in social networks supplying informal support (Granovetter, 1973); (privileged) access to institutions of training, sources of information, etc.; reputation.
> human capital: any esteemed knowledge and ability; charisma, ambition, stamina, etc.

We know three main historic mechanisms of transferring elite positions from one generation to the next: heredity, charisma, and merit (Weber, 1979). Charisma ($\chi\alpha\rho\iota\sigma\mu\alpha$) means "gift out of (divine) favor" and thus a qualification that cannot be generated systematically by training. Mainly in the sphere of politics, it remains a source of legitimization alternative to expertise, but in modern democracies its function is restricted to being a (populist) ferment in the process of political decision making. In the course of history the complexity of societies increased, and the skills needed for adequate governance and economic success grew more and more demanding and specialized. Hence, for lack of selectivity towards skills, the principle of heredity in elites became increasingly inappropriate and has largely been replaced by a principle of merit, mainly based on expertise (Elias, 1982).

In the course of rationalization of governmental and economic functions, experts try to monopolize the access to their respective field of activity by founding new professions. Professionalization in this strong sense means that a group of experts claims jurisdiction over the skills needed to be duly qualified to practice in the respective field. In cooperation with state authorities, they aim to transform their claims into a legal restriction of access to the respective field of activity for people who have undergone a certain vocational training, accounted for by formal credentials. In short, groups of experts strive to install mechanisms of social inclusion and exclusion to protect certain privileges against potential competitors.

Rationalization thus brings about a shift from collective mechanisms of social closure – that is, social exclusion on the basis of race, gender, religion, ethnicity, or language – to individual mechanisms of social inclusion and exclusion as a result of individual performance in standardized competitions on the basis of formal equality of opportunities (Murphy, 1988). This shift towards a principle of merit changes the rules of reproduction of social standing within families: Parents who hold an elite position due to professional expertise cannot bequeath this status directly to their children. They can only provide cultural capital that matches the requirements of the educational system and also mobilize financial and social capital to improve the starting conditions of their offspring. Statistically, these mechanisms of reproduction of elite positions due to expertise are still quite successful (Bourdieu, 1984, and plenty of subsequent studies based on this classic), but in many cases they fail – the link between the social standing of parents and that of their children is no longer deterministic as it was to a large extent in premodern societies, but it has grown stochastic with culturally specific biases. Thus, the safeguarding of privileges usually associated with elite positions based on expertise has become two-stage: families try to reproduce *access* to *any* field of distinguished expertise in their children, and groups of experts try to establish and have legally protected privileges by placing emphasis on the functional importance of their services for clients and society as a whole. It is characteristic for modern societies that these two contexts of reproduction are completely independent of each other. This disentanglement brings about an increase in societal rationality. It makes it possible for children of experts, who want to reproduce the parental expert status, not to be forced to choose the same field of expertise as their parents, but the field they are most talented for. This, on the other hand, allows for higher selectivity in the staffing of elite positions. It fuels competition among aspirants and thus aggravates the problem of reproduction of high social status in families.

In order to get a deeper insight into these structures, it is adequate to go back to some postulates of the Enlightenment and the French Revolution that amplified the functional importance of expertise, namely,

- Perfectability of societies: social structures are not an inalterable fate, but may be the subject of well-directed moulding through progress in each field of human activity.
- Democracy: as a precondition of democratic control, governments and bureaucracies are accountable to the public for their settlement of public affairs.
- Merit principle: privileges need legitimization through outstanding achievements in a field of activity.
- Equal opportunities: children should have equal access to all educational institutions regardless of their social background, and their advancement within these institutions should depend exclusively on their achievements.

As social developments since the 18th century show, there is a conflict between the first two postulates: The idea of perfectability of human affairs was a stimulus – inter alia – for exceeding expansion and differentiation of expertise and its application. But as expertise is not easily comprehensible for lay citizens, democratic control of the expanding activities of experts in contemporary societies is more questionable than ever (Feyerabend, 1978; Etzioni-Halevy, 1993). On the other hand, as long as elites as a

whole respond more or less to the demands of the public, discontent with the state of society remains a phenomenon of individuals and marginalized anomic groups and does not give rise to upheavals apt to overthrow the social order (Etzioni-Halevy, 1999). In order to maintain the capability to meet public demands and an equilibrium between public and particular interests, elites have to admit talented members of the nonelite and to dispose of those doing damage to their reputation by incapability, violation of public morality, and excessive parasitism on public goods. This process of self-purification is called "circulation of elites" (Kolabinska, 1912), and it is particularly characteristic for American elites (Lerner, Nagai, & Rothman, 1996).

The emergence of *counter-elites*: Societies have to cope with unintended undesirable side effects of human activities and with newly emerged natural dangers. In many cases single experts or small groups of experts first anticipate or perceive such a problem, make research on it, and try to initiate public discussions. But as it is hard to call public attention to displeasing things, such problem awareness normally remains confined for a long time to small circles of specifically interested or heavily affected people. The issue will grow into a matter of public concern and an item of the political agenda only if it is picked up by the mass media – most frequently on the occasion of an event apt to be scandalized. Seeking means for dissemination of their premonitions, experts may try – and indeed have often tried – to incite and lead a social movement or to support an already existing social movement by supplying expertise and expert respectability. In the case in which an issue passes successfully through such a process, marginalized views become common sense, and formerly nameless or even ill-reputed experts may grow respectable and gain fame. During periods of controversy the apologist experts constitute a counter-elite to established elites that are still reluctant to recognize the issue as a problem or the solutions recommended. Counter-elites play a decisive role in the generation of cultural change in modern societies and as an element of their checks and balances. If the issue as a matter of public concern gets undisputable and its solutions standardized, the counter-elite becomes a new established elite, and parts of old elites may be forced to resign (Imhof & Romano, 1994). A prominent example of the long latency of a matter in circles of experts is ecology and the "green issue." The environmental movement and subsequent social change created the demand for environmental expertise to grow rapidly and provided a basis for a new elite of risk professionals (Dietz & Rycroft, 1987).

On a *global* level the interplay between political, bureaucratic, and military elites of different states and the economic elites of transnational corporations promotes processes of globalization and the increase of societal complexity (Bornschier, 1989, 1996). The prosperity of the members of political, bureaucratic, and military elites depends on the success of the economies in their countries, and this success in turn depends on the degree of legitimacy of the social order, that is, on the extent to which the social order meets the needs of the citizens and fosters or hampers their vocational capabilities and achievement motivation. A prominent example of a pact of bureaucratic and economic elites is the constitution of the unified market in Europe (Nollert, 2000): The plans for this giant project were generated chiefly by expert bureaucrats of Brussels, that is, by an expert elite whose members have no or only very indirect democratic legitimization, whereas the role of the democratically legitimized European Council remained more or less confined to formal approval of already elaborated plans.

The coherence of plans and public projects may increase if they are worked out by experts without the fear of being voted out of their position. A disadvantage of purely expert-driven projects is their tendency to evolve too far from common sense and to jeopardize themselves through insufficient responsiveness to public concerns and objections. This example may be taken as illustration for a general problem in the evolution of modern state societies: The institutional frame of modern societies has grown so widely ramified and differentiated that only experts can overview its parts in full complexity – each expert able to focus on only one small section – and propose advancements. Therefore, contemporary states are forced to cede a great portion of institutional change to experts. This makes democratic engagement and control difficult (Turner, 2001), and in parts of the society it entails alienation and disorientation that may result in social unrest. It is impossible to foretell what this kind of social evolution will bring about in the long run, in particular with respect to the stability of societies, an area where the notion of expertise has its roots. But there is little doubt that experts and expertise will be highly in demand as long as modern societies keep evolving towards higher complexity, as they have done in recent centuries – despite the fact that there have always been antimodernist movements that challenge the role of expertise and experts in society by trying to revert to simpler structures of understanding and control, such as faith-based ones.

References

Abbott, A. (1988). *The system of professions: An essay on the division of expert labor.* Chicago: University of Chicago Press.

Allsop, J., & Mulcahy, L. (1996). *Regulating medical work: Formal and informal controls.* Buckingham: Open University Press.

Annandale, E. (1998). *The sociology of health and medicine.* Cambridge: Polity Press.

Bazerman, C. (1989). *Shaping written knowledge.* Madison: University of Wisconsin Press.

Bornschier, V. (1989). Legitimacy and comparative success at the core of the world system. *European Sociological Review,* 5(3), 215–230.

Bornschier, V. (1996). *Western society in transition.* New Brunswick, NJ: Transaction.

Bourdieu, P. (1984). *Distinction.* Cambridge, MA: Harvard University Press.

Buchner-Jeziorska, A. (2001). *Price of knowledge: the market of intellectual work in Poland in the 90s.* Paper presented in Professions Network of SASE Conference, Amsterdam, June 28–July 1.

Buchner-Jeziorska, A., & Evetts, J. (1997). Regulating professionals: The Polish example. *International Sociology, 12* (1), 61–72.

Burchell, G., Gordon, C., & Miller. P. (Eds.). (1991). *The Foucault effect: Studies in governmentality.* Hemel Hempstead: Harvester Wheatsheaf.

Carlton, E. (1996). *The few and the many: A typology of elites.* Brookfield, VT: Scolar Press.

Carr-Saunders, A. M., & Wilson, P. A. (1933). *The professions.* Oxford: The Clarendon Press.

Cooper, D., Lowe, A., Puxty, A., Robson, K., & Willmott, H. (1988). Regulating the U.K. accountancy profession: Episodes in the relation between the profession and the state. Paper presented at ESRC Conference on Corporatism at the Policy Studies Institute, London, January 1988.

Crompton, R. (1990). Professions in the current context. *Work, Employment and Society, Special Issue,* 147–66.

Daston, L. J. (1992). Objectivity and the escape from perspective. *Social Studies of Science, 22,* 597–618.

Davies, C. (1995). *Gender and the professional predicament in Nursing.* Buckingham: Open University Press.

Dietz, T. M., & Rycroft, R. W. (1987). *The risk professionals.* New York: Russell Sage Foundation.

Dingwall, R., (1996). Professions and social order in a global society. Plenary presentation at ISA Working Group 02 Conference, Nottingham, 11–13 September.

Dingwall, R., & Lewis, P. (Eds.). (1983). *The sociology of the professions: Doctors, lawyers and others.* London: Macmillan.

Dogan, M. (1989). *Pathways to power: Selecting rulers in pluralist democracies.* Boulder, CO: Westview Press.

Dubar, C. (2000). *La crise des identités: L'interprétation d'une mutation.* Paris: Presses Universitaires de France.

Durkheim, E. (1992). *Professional ethics and civic morals.* London: Routledge.

Elias, N. (1982). *The civilizing process, Vol. II: Power and civility.* New York: Pantheon Books.

Etzioni, A. (1969). *The semi-professionals and their organization: Teachers, nurses and social workers.* New York: Free Press.

Etzioni-Halevy, E. (1993). *The elite connection: Problems and potential of western democracy.* Cambridge, MA: Polity Press.

Etzioni-Halevy, E. (1999). Inequality and the quality of democracy in ultramodern society. *International Review of Sociology, 9* (2), 239–250.

Etzioni-Halevy, E. (2001). Elites: Sociological aspects. In N. Smelser (Ed.), *International encyclopedia of the social & behavioral sciences* (pp. 4420–4424). Amsterdam: Elsevier.

Evetts, J., & Dingwall, R. (2002). Professional occupations in the UK and Europe: Legitimation and governmentality. *International Review of Sociology, 12* (2), 159–171.

Evetts, J. (1998). Analysing the projects of professional associations: National and international dimensions. Unpublished paper presented at ISA Congress, Montreal, 26 July – 1 August.

Evetts, J. (2001). Professions in European and UK markets: The European professional federations. *International Journal of Sociology and Social Policy, 20* (11/12), 1–30.

Evetts, J. (2003). Professionalization and professionalism: Explaining professional performance initiatives. In H. A. Mieg & M. Pfadenhauer (Eds.), *Professionelle Leistung – Professional Performance: Positionen der Professionssoziologie* (pp. 49–69). Konstanz: UVK.

Feyerabend, P. (1978). *Science in a free society.* London: NLB.

Fournier, V. (1998). Stories of development and exploitation: Militant voices in an enterprise culture. *Organization, 5* (1), 55–80.

Fournier, V. (1999). The appeal to professionalism as a disciplinary mechanism. *Social Review, 47* (2), 280–307.

Freidson, E. (1982). Occupational autonomy and labor market shelters. In P. L. Steward & M. G. Cantor (Eds.), *Varieties of work* (pp. 39–54). Beverley Hills: Sage.

Freidson, E. (1988 [1970]). *Profession of medicine: A study in the sociology of applied knowledge.* Chicago: University of Chicago Press.

Freidson, E. (1994). *Professionalism reborn: Theory, prophecy and policy.* Cambridge: Polity Press.

Freidson, E. (2001). *Professionalism: The third logic.* London: Polity.

Frenkel, S., Korczynski, M., Donoghue, L., & Shire, K. (1995). Re-constituting work: Trends towards knowledge work and info-normative control. *Work, Employment and Society, 9* (4), 773–796.

Gadea, C. (Ed.). (2003). Sociologie des cadres et sociologie des professions: Proximités et paradoxes. *Knowledge, Work & Society, 1,* 1.

Gieryn T. (1995). Boundaries of science. In S. Jasanoff, G. E. Markle, J. C. Petersen, & T. Pinch (Eds.), *Handbook of science and technology studies* (pp. 393–443). Thousand Oaks: Sage.

Granovetter, M. S. (1973). The strength of weak ties. *American Journal of Sociology, 78*(6), 1360–1380.

Greenwood E. (1957). Attributions of a profession. *Social Work, 2,* 44–55.

Greenwood, R., & Lachman, R. (1996). Change as an underlying theme in professional service organizations: An introduction. *Organization Studies, 17*(4), 563–572.

Grelon, A. (1996). Ingenieurs et risques technologiques dans la chimie industrielle en France. Paper presented at ISA Working Group 02 Conference, Nottingham, 11–13 September.

Grey, C. (1994). Career as a project of the self and labour process discipline. *Sociology, 28,* 479–497.

Halliday, T. C. (1987). *Beyond monopoly: Lawyers, state crises and professional empowerment.* Chicago: University of Chicago Press.

Hanlon, G. (1998). Professionalism as enterprise: Service class politics and the redefinition of professionalism. *Sociology, 32*(1), 43–63.

Hanlon, G. (1999). *Lawyers, the state and the market: Professionalism revisited.* Basingstoke: Macmillan.

Haraway, D. (1989). *Primate visions: Gender, race and nature in the world of modern science.* London: Routledge.

Harrison, S. (1999). Clinical autonomy and health policy: Past and futures. In M. Exworthy & S. Halford (Eds.), *Professionals and the new managerialism in the public sector.* Buckingham: Open University Press.

Harrison, S., & Ahmad, W. (2000). Medical autonomy and the UK state 1975 to 2005. *Sociology, 34*(1), 129–146.

Hawkins, K. (Ed.). (1992). *The uses of discretion.* Oxford: Clarendon Press.

Hiremath, S. L., & Gudagunti, R. (1998). Professional commitment among Indian executives. Paper presented at ISA Congress Montreal, July 26–Aug 1.

Hughes, E. C. (1958). *Men and their work.* New York: Free Press.

Imhof, K., & Romano, G. (1994). *Die Diskontinuität der Moderne. Zur Theorie des sozialen Wandels* [The discontinuity of modernity: On the theory of social change]. Frankfurt a. M.: Campus.

Johnson, T. (1972). *Professions and power.* London: Macmillan.

Karpik, L. (1989). Le désintéressement. *Annales, Economies Sociétés Civilisations, 3* (May–June), 733–751.

Keller, E. F. (1985). *Reflections on gender and science.* New Haven: Yale University Press.

Knorr-Cetina, K. (1981). *The manufacture of knowledge: An essay on the constructivist and contextual nature of science.* Oxford: Pergamon.

Kolabinska, M. (1912). *La circulation des élites en France.* Lausanne: Imp. réunies.

Larkin, G. (1983). *Occupational monopoly and modern medicine.* London: Tavistock.

Larson, M. S. (1977). *The rise of professionalism.* Barkeley: University of California Press.

Latour, B., & Woolgar, S. (1986 [1979]). *Laboratory life. The (social) construction of scientific facts.* Beverly Hills, CA: Sage.

Lerner, R., Nagai, A. K., & Rothman, S. (1996). *American elites.* New Haven: Yale University Press.

Lyotard, J. F. (1984). *The post-modern condition: A report on knowledge.* Manchester: Manchester University Press.

MacDonald, K. M. (1995). *The sociology of the professions.* London: Sage.

Marshall, T. H. (1950). *Citizenship and social class and other essays.* Cambridge: Cambridge University Press.

McClellend, C. E. (1990). Escape from freedom? Reflections on German professionalization 1870–1933. In R. Torstendahl & M. Burrage (Eds.), *The formation of professions: Knowledge, state and strategy* (pp. 97–113). London: Sage.

Mechanic, D. (1991). Sources of countervailing power in medicine. *Journal of Health Politics, Policy and Law, 16,* 485–498.

Members of the first and second Committees on Women Faculty in the School of Science (1999). A study of the status of women faculty in science at MIT, to be found at http://web.mit.edu/fnl/women/women.html.

Merton, R. K. (1973 [1942]). The normative structure of science. In N. W. Storer (Ed.), *The sociology of science* (pp. 267–278). Chicago: University of Chicago Press.

Michels, R. (1915). *Political parties*. New York: Hearst's International Library.

Milburn, P. (1996). Les territoires professionnels et la négociation experte du réel: Compatibilité des modèles théoriques. Paper presented at ISA Working Group 02 Conference, Nottingham, 11–13 September.

Miller, P., & Rose, N. (1990). Governing economic life. *Economy and Society*, 19(1), 1–31.

Mosca, G. (1939). *The ruling class*. New York: McGraw-Hill.

Mulkay, M. (1976). Norms and ideology in science. *Social Science Information*, 15, 637–656.

Murphy, R. (1988). *Social closure: The theory of monopolization and exclusion*. Oxford: Clarendon Press.

Nollert, M. (2000). Lobbying for a Europe of big business: The European roundtable of industrialists. In V. Bornschier (Ed.), *State-building in Europe: The revitalization of Western European integration* (pp. 187–209). Cambridge: Cambridge University Press.

Olgiati, V., Orzack, L. H., & Saks, M. (Eds.). (1998). *Professions, identity and order in comparative perspective*. Onati: The International Institute for the Sociology of Law.

Pareto, V. (1935). *The mind and society: A treatise on general sociology* (ed. by A. Livingstone). New York: Harcourt, Brace & Co.

Parsons, T. (1951). *The social system*. New York: Free Press.

Perkin, H. (1988). *The rise of professional society*. London: Routledge.

Reed, M. (1996). Expert power and control in late modernity: An empirical review and theoretical synthesis. *Organization Studies*, 17(4), 573–597.

Rose, H. (1994). *Love, power and knowledge: Towards a feminist transformation of the sciences*. Cambridge: Polity Press.

Saks, M. (1995). *Professions and the public interest*. London: Routledge.

Sautu, R. (1998). The effect of the marketization of the Argentine economy on the labor market: Shifts in the demand for university trained professionals. Paper presented at ISA Congress, Montreal, July 26–Aug 1.

Schiebinger, L. (1989). *The mind has no sex?: Women in the origins of modern science*. Boston: Harvard University Press.

Shapin, S., & Schaffer, S. (1985). *Leviathan and the air-pump*. Princeton, NJ: Princeton University Press.

Svensson, L. (2003). Market, management and Professionalism: Professional work and changing organisational contexts. In H. A. Mieg & M. Pfadenhauer (Eds.), *Professionelle Leistung – Professional Performance: Positionen der Professionssoziologie* (pp. 313–355). Konstanz: UVK.

Tawney, R. H. (1921). *The acquisitive society*. New York: Harcourt Bruce.

Trépos, J. (1996). Une modelisation des jugements d'experts: Catégories et instruments de mesure. Paper presented at ISA Working Group 02 Conference, Nottingham, 11–13 September.

Turner, S. (2001). What is the problem with experts? *Social Studies of Science*, 31(1), 123–149.

Weber, M. (1979). *Economy and society* (trans. by G. Roth & C. Wittich). Berkeley, CA: University of California Press.

Wilensky, H. L. (1964). The professionalization of everyone? *The American Journal of Sociology*, 70(2), 137–158.

Wenneras C., & Wold, A. (1997). Nepotism and sexism in peer review. *Nature*, 387, 341–343.

Wynne, B. (1995). Public understanding of science. In S. Jasanoff, G. E. Markle, J. C. Petersen, & T. Pinch (Eds.), *Handbook of science and technology studies* (pp. 361–388). Thousand Oaks: Sage.

Zuckerman, H., Cole, J., & Bruer, J. (Eds.). (1991). *The outer circle: Women in the scientific community*. New York: Norton.

Part III

METHODS FOR STUDYING THE STRUCTURE OF EXPERTISE

CHAPTER 8

Observation of Work Practices in Natural Settings

William J. Clancey

Keywords: Ethnography, Workplace Study, Practice, Participant Observation, Ethnomethodology, Lived Work

Introduction

Expertise is not just about inference applied to facts and heuristics, but about being a social actor. Observation of natural settings begins not with laboratory behavioral tasks – problems fed to a "subject" – but with how work methods are adapted and evaluated by experts themselves, as situations are experienced as problematic and formulated as defined tasks and plans. My focus in this chapter is on socially and physically located behaviors, especially those involving conversations, tools, and informal (ad hoc) interactions. How an observer engages with practitioners in a work setting itself requires expertise, including concepts, tools, and methods for understanding other people's motives and problems, often coupled with methods for work systems design.

By watching people at work in everyday settings (Rogoff & Lave 1984) and observing activities over time in different circumstances, we can study and document *work practices*, including those of proficient domain practitioners. This chapter introduces and illustrates a theoretical framework as well as methods for observing work practices in everyday (or natural) settings in a manner that enables understanding and possibly improving how the work is done.

In the first part of this chapter, I explain the notion of work practices and the historical development of observation in natural settings. In the middle part, I elaborate the perspective of ethnomethodology, including contrasting ways of viewing people and workplaces, and different units of analysis for representing work observations. In the final part, I present methods for observation in some detail and conclude with trends and open issues.

What are Work Practices in a Natural Setting?

Every setting is "natural" for the people who frequent it. A laboratory is a natural work setting for some scientists, whereas expedition base camps are natural for others. The framework provided here is intended to be applicable to any setting, including school playgrounds, churches, interstate highways, and so on. But we focus on workplaces, where people are attempting to get some work done, for which they have been prepared, and have sufficient experience to be acknowledged as experts by other people with whom they interact. This can be contrasted with studies of everyday people being expert at everyday things (e.g., jumping rope, car driving) or events purposely arranged by a researcher in a laboratory.

In studying natural settings, one views them broadly: Consider a teacher in a school within a community, not just a classroom. Seek to grasp an entire place, with its nested contexts: Rather than focusing on a physician in a patient exam room, study the clinic, including the waiting room.

Heuristically, one can view an expert's performance as a play, identifying the stage, the "acts," roles, and the audience. But also view the play as having a history, whose nature is changing in today's performance: What are the actors' long-term motives? How is this performance challenging or influenced by the broader *community of practice* (Wenger 1998) (e.g., other clinics and nurses)?

Also inquire more locally about the chronology and flow of a performance: How do people prepare, who assists them (think of actors), how do they get information about today's work, when and where do they review and plan their work, how are events scheduled? Look for informal places and off-stage roles – backrooms and preparation areas, dispatchers, janitors, and support personnel. All of this is part of the expertise of getting a job done, and multiple parts and contributions need to be identified if the fundamental question about work is to be answered: What affects the quality of this performance? What accounts for its success? As a heuristic, to capture these contextual effects, one might frame a study as being

"a day in the life" of the people – and that means 24 hours, not the nominal work day.

Thus, a study of work practices is actually a study of a setting; this context makes the observed behavior understandable. For example, consider understanding clowns:

> If we had a film of a clown doing somersaults, and nothing else (i.e., we knew nothing about circuses, about the history of clowns and so on), then the film would not tell us what we need to know to make sense of what the clown was doing. . . . One would need to know something about how they are part and parcel of circuses, and how their somersaulting is viewed [by many observers] as a kind of sentimental self-mockery. (Harper 2000, pp. 244–245; attributed to Gilbert Ryle)

To understand a setting, it is useful to view all workers (not just performers on stage) as social actors. When we say that work is *socially recognized* as "requiring special skills or knowledge derived from extensive experience" (Hoffman, 1998, p. 86), we mean that people are visibly demonstrating competency, in how they make interpretations, conduct business, and produce results that are "recognizably accountable" (of agreeable quality) to institutional and public audiences (Heritage 1984; Dourish & Button 1998). This perspective has the dual effect for expertise studies of considering the worker as an agent who, with other agents, coconstructs what constitutes a problem to be solved and how the product will be evaluated. Methods for applying this theoretical perspective, called *ethnomethodology*, are presented in this chapter.

Observing people in a natural setting is commonly called *fieldwork*. Besides watching and recording and asking questions, fieldwork may include interviewing, studying documents, and meeting with the people being studied to analyze data together and present findings (Forsythe 1999, p. 128). Fieldwork is most often associated with the broader method of study called *ethnography* (Spradley 1979; Fetterman 1998 Harper 2000, p. 239), literally, the written study of a people or culture. Neither fieldwork nor ethnography are specific to any discipline. Originally associated most strongly with anthropology, the methods today are commonly used by linguists, sociologists, computer scientists, and educational psychologists.

The actual methods of observation – spending time in a natural setting and recording what occurs – may at first appear as the defining characteristic of an ethnographic study, but the difficult and less obvious part is being able to understand work practice. For example, outsiders are often unaware of the inherent conflicts of a work setting (e.g., to physicians, dying people are a source of money; to police, crime statistics a source of political trouble), which limit what can be done, making it necessary to creatively interpret procedures and regulations.

This chapter focuses on how to see what is happening, how to apply ethnomethodology concepts to analyzing everyday actions. Starting the other way around – with camera at hand and a poor theoretical background – could be like bringing an aquarium fish net to the deep sea, collecting a hodgepodge of anecdotes, narratives, and interesting photographs, with little understanding of people's practices (Button & Harper 1996, p. 267). Furthermore, a planned *analytic program* is important when studying work practice for design, "otherwise observations can be merely invoked at will for particular purposes such as, for example, to legitimize design decisions already made" (p. 267).

An observational study is itself modulated by the observer's purpose and relation to the organizational setting. Intending to transform the setting (e.g., as a consultant) requires engaging as an observer in a particular way, not merely recording and note taking. A helpful, reflective activity called *participatory design* (Greenbaum & Kyng 1991, p. 7; Beyer & Holtzblatt 1998) involves negotiating and codiscovering with the workers what is to be investigated (e.g., setting up a "task force group"; Engeström 1999, pp. 71–73). In settings such as hospitals and business offices, this developmental perspective commonly focuses on software engineering and organizational change.

Historical and Contemporary Perspectives

This section reviews how observation in natural settings developed and was shaped, especially by photographic tools, and how it relates to the psychological study of expertise.

Scientific Observation in Natural Settings

In studies of culture, surveying "informants" on site goes back to the earliest days of 19th-century anthropology (Bernard 1998, p. 12). Several articles and books provide excellent summaries of the theoretical background and methods for observation in natural settings, including especially *Direct Systematic Observation of Behavior* (Johnson & Sackett 1998) and *Participant Observation* (Spradley 1980; Dewalt & Dewalt 2002).

As the ethnomethodologist stresses, observation in natural settings is inherent in social life, for it is what people themselves are doing to organize and advance their own concerns. But perhaps the tacit, uncontrollable, and mundane aspect of everyday life led psychologists to set up experiments in laboratories and anthropologists to set up camp in exotic third-world villages. Moving studies of knowledge and expertise to modern work settings developed over a long period of time, starting with cognitive anthropologists and socio-technical analysts (Emery 1959), and progressing to the "Scandinavian approach" to information system design (Ehn 1988; Greenbaum & Kyng 1991). But today's methods of observation began with the invention of – and motivations for – photography.

Visual Anthropology

Photographs and video are indispensable for recording behavior for later study. The visual record allows studying how people structure their environment, providing clues about how they are relating to each other and structuring their work life. Using photography for close observation dates to the late 19th century. Eadweard Muybridge's famous early motion pictures (*Galloping Horse* [1878], *Ascending Stairs* [1884]) demonstrate the early motivation of using film to study animal and human movements whose speed or structure elude direct observation.

Margaret Mead and Gregory Bateson pioneered the use of film for capturing nonverbal behavior. Their work was influential in treating photography as primary data, rather than as only illustrations (El Guindi 1998, p. 472). Today the use of photographic methods is fundamental in observation of natural settings, and is termed video ethnography or *interaction analysis* (Jordan & Henderson 1995).

An integral part of any observational study in a natural setting considers how physical space, including furniture and designed facilities, is used "as a specialized elaboration of culture" (Hall 1966), called *proxemics*. This study broadly relates ethology (Lorenz 1952) to analyses of physical-perceptual experience (e.g., *kinesics*, Birdwhistell 1952), including "body language" (Scheflen 1972), personal and public kinds of space, nonverbal communication (Hall 1959), and culture differences. Using time-lapse video, Whyte (1980; PPS 2004) studied how people used public plazas at lunchtime, a striking everyday application of proxemics for architectural design.

Visual analysis considers posture, gestures, distance and orientation of bodies, territoriality, habitual use of space (e.g., movement during the day), relation of recreational and work areas, preferences for privacy or indirect involvement (open doors), and so on. For example, referring to Figure 8.1, how would you group the people, given their posture and behavior? What activities occur in this space? What do body positions reveal about people's sense of timing or urgency? Even a single image can reveal a great deal, and will provide evidence for broader hypotheses about relationships, complemented by living with these people for several weeks.

Figure 8.1. "The area between the tents" at the Haughton-Mars Base Camp 1999.

The Development of Natural Observation in Expertise Studies

Analysts seeking improved efficiency in procedures and designing automation studied workplaces throughout the 20th century. Developmental psychology primarily focused on schools, whereas organizational learning (Senge 1990) chose business settings. Computer scientists brought domain specialists into their labs to develop expert systems in the model-building process called *knowledge acquisition* (Buchanan & Shortliffe 1984). Human-factors psychologists took up the same analytic concepts for decomposing work into formal diagrams of goals and methods, called *cognitive task analysis* (Vicente 1999), and characterized decision making as probabilistic analyses of situations and judgmental rules (Chi et al. 1988). At the same time, social scientists were being drawn by colleagues designing computer systems, motivated largely by labor forces in Europe (Ehn 1988), forming subfields such as business anthropology and workplace studies (Luff et al. 2000).

By the 1990s, industrial engineers and social scientists already in the workplace were joined by computer scientists and psychologists, who had transitioned from laboratory interviews and experiments to "design in the context of use" (Greenbaum & Kyng

1991). The work of studying knowledge and learning moved to everyday settings such as supermarkets (Lave 1988), insurance offices, and weather bureaus (Hoffman et al. 2000). The discipline of human-computer interaction (HCI) became a large, specialized subfield, a consortium of graphics artists, social theorists, psychology modelers, and software engineers (Nardi 1996; Blum 1996; Kling & Star 1998).

Broadly speaking, HCI research has progressed from viewing people as computer *users* – that is, asking questions such as "What happens if people are in the loop?" – to viewing people, computers, documents, facilities, and so on as a *total system*, and understanding the processes holistically. In some respects, this approach began with socio-technical systems analysis in the 1950s–1970s (Corbet et al. 1991, p. 9ff). Hutchins (1995) provides especially well-developed examples of how tools, interfaces, and distributed group interactions constitute a work system.

Expertise in Context: Learning to See

Observing and systematically studying a work place is sometimes treated as easy by non-social-scientists, who might perform the work sketchily or not actually analyze practices (Forsythe 1999). The spread of the anthropological and social perspectives to cognitive science was at first limited, at best shifting the analysis to include the social context. For example, only one chapter in *Expertise in Context* (Feltovich et al. 1997) explicitly involved an observational study of a natural setting (Shalin's video analysis in a hospital). Ericsson and Charness used diaries for studying violinists, without investigating their home setting. Other researchers considered experts as socially selected (Agnew et al. 1997) and more broadly serving and part of market, organization, or community networks (Stern 1997); or viewed expertise as part of cultural construction (Collins 1997, Clancey 1997).

An edited volume from a decade earlier, *The Nature of Expertise* by Chi et al. (1988), focused even more narrowly on mental processing of text: Documents were provided to subjects to read, to judge, to type, or learn from. Expertise was viewed not about competence in settings (i.e., situated action), but decision making, reasoning, memory retrieval, pattern matching – predominantly aspects of the assumed internal, mental activity occurring in the brain. For example, a study of restaurant waiters (p. 27) was reduced to a study of memory, not the "lived work" of being a waiter. A study of typing concerned timing of finger movements, nothing about office work. Of the twelve studies of experts, only one included "naturalistic observation" to "fashion a relatively naturalistic task" (Lesgold et al. 1988; p. 313), namely, dictating X-ray interpretations.

This said, one of the most influential analyses of the contextual aspects of behavior, Suchman's (1987) *Plans and Situated Actions*, also did not involve the study of practice. Suchman studied two people working together who had never used a photocopier before (p. 115) – a form of puzzle solving in which a predefined task is presented in "the real world" (p. 114). Suchman's study is an example of *ethnomethodological analysis* because it focuses on mutual, visible construction of understanding and methods, but it is not carried out using the *ethnographic method* (Dourish and Button 1998, p. 406) because this was not a study of established practices in a familiar setting.

In summary, a participatory design project uses ethnography to study work practice, which may be analyzed from an ethnomethodological perspective (Heritage 1984). More generally, ethnography may involve many other analytic orientations, emphasizing different phenomena, topics, and issues (Dourish & Button 1998, p. 404). Ethnographic observation involves a rigorous commitment to confronting the worlds of people as they experience everyday life, to understand how problematic situations actually arise and are managed. Workplace studies, contrasted with the study of knowledge and experts in the 1970s and 1980s (Chi et al. 1988), signify a dramatic change in how expertise is viewed and studied, often with entirely different motivations, methods, and partnerships, and having a significant affect on the design of new technologies.

Work Systems Design Project Examples

Here I present two representative examples of work systems design projects to illustrate the relation of methods and the results achieved.

A three-year ethnographic study of a reprographics store was conducted to improve customer service (Whalen et al. 2004).[1] The data were collected in three phases. First, the researchers made ethnographic observations, shadowing and interviewing employees as they worked. Second, the team collected over 400 hours of video recordings in the store from multiple simultaneously recording cameras. The videotapes were digitized and divided into distinct episodes, consisting of more than 500 customer-employee interactions, some of which were transcribed and analyzed. Finally, three research team members became participant observers in the stores, working as employees, serving customers, and operating the printing and copying equipment.

The study resulted in the development of a "customer service skill set," a set of web-based instructional modules designed to raise employees' awareness of the organization of customer-employee interactions. Topics include how to listen to what the customer wants during initial order taking, how to talk about price, and the importance of taking the time to review the completed job with the customer. The modules were co-developed by the research team and six store employees who met once a week for two months. For example, the common question "When do you need it?" is practically unanswerable by the customer because they don't know the work load and scheduling constraints of the store, so they reply, "When can you have it?" The employees were asked to experiment with ways of opening up the discussion about due time (e.g., "Is this an urgent job?" or "Would you like to pick this up tomorrow afternoon?"), and they noticed a useful change in customer responses. These

analyses inform further reconsideration of the burden placed on customers in justifying the need for "full service" and the delicate balance of providing assistance to "self-service" customers.

The second example illustrates systematic design and adaptation to most aspects of a work system – organization, facilities, processes, schedules, documents, and computer tools. For three-and-a-half years, NASA Ames' researchers worked closely with the Mars Exploration Rover (MER) science and operations support teams at the Jet Propulsion Laboratory, in Pasadena, California. The project included the design and training phase of the mission (starting January 2001), as well as the surface operations phase that began after the successful landing of two rovers on the Martian surface (January 2004). Observation focused on the interactions between the scientists, computer systems, communication network (e.g., relay via Mars satellites), and the rovers, using ethnography to understand the successes, gaps, and problem areas in work flows, information flows, and tool design in operations systems.

Research data included field notes, mission documents and reports, photographs, video, and audiotape of the work of mission participants. Two to four researchers were present during all of the premission tests (2001–2003), all but one of the science team's twice-yearly meetings (2001–2003), and the majority of the science team's weekly conference calls. Learning the intricacies of the rover instruments and their operation was necessary to understand the telerobotic work. Ongoing findings in the form of "lessons learned" with recommendations for improving mission work processes were presented to operations teams several times each year. Data analysis focused on the learning of the science team as a work practice developed that moved the daily rover-operations plan from team to team across the three-shift mission timeline. The researchers identified and categorized types of information and working groups, and defined work flows, communication exchanges, scientists' work practice and scientific reasoning process, and the interactions of work practice between scientists and rover engineers. Over time many scientists and managers became informally involved in assisting the observation and documentation process and refining design recommendations.

The researchers developed a naming convention and ontology for objects on Mars, a prioritization scheme for planning rover activities, and a method of documenting the scientific intent of telerobotic operations to facilitate communication between operations shifts and mission disciplines. They trained MER scientists in these procedures and associated tools during simulated missions. During the mission in 2004, two researchers moved to Pasadena; six researchers rotated to cover the shifts that moved forty minutes later each day in synchrony with local Mars time. The team then developed operations concepts for an "extended mission phase," during which scientists worked from their home cities, and rover planning was compressed and simplified to reduce work on nights and weekends.

Overall, this work systems design project helped define and enhance the telerobotic scientific process and related mission surface operations, including design of facilities for science meetings. Researchers contributed to the design of four computer systems used for rover planning and scientific collaboration that were being developed simultaneously by NASA Ames colleagues and JPL. The MER work systems design and the methods employed are influencing operations concepts and system architectures for subsequent missions.

Ethnomethodology's Analytic Perspective

In this section, I explain how the "methodology" being studied in a workplace is not just a technical process for accomplishing a task, but incorporates social values and criteria for judging the quality of the work. This idea originated in Garfinkel's discovery

in the mid-1950s of jurors' "methodological" issues:

> ... such as the distinction between "fact" and "opinion," between "what we're entitled to say," "what the evidence shows," and "what can be demonstrated" ... These distinctions were handled in coherently organized and "agree-able" ways and the jurors assumed and counted on one another's abilities to use them, draw appropriate inferences from them and see the sense of them ... common-sense considerations that "anyone could see." (Heritage 1984, p. 4)

Ethnomethodology thus emphasizes the commonsense knowledge and practices of ordinary members of society, as they "make sense of, find their way about in, and act on the circumstances in which they find themselves" (p. 4). However, formalizing these assumptions, values, and resulting procedures is not necessarily easy for people without training (Forsythe 1999).

Ethnomethodology has led researchers to reconceive how knowledge and action are framed, "wresting ... preoccupation with the phenomenon of error" prevalent in human factors research (Heritage 1984). The focus shifts to how people succeed, how they construct the "inherent intelligibility and accountability" of social activity, placing new emphasis on the knowledge people use "in devising or recognizing conduct" (p. 5). Button and Harper (1996) provide a cogent example about how "Decisions about what crimes are reported by police are intimately tied up with questions of what is *practical* for the reporting officer and what is in the *interests* of the police organization as a whole" (p. 275).

Contrasted with technical knowledge (Schön 1987), this aspect of work methods is reflective and social, concerning how one's behavior will be viewed, through understood norms and social consequences. Ethnomethodology thus provides a kind of logical, systemic underpinning to how activity becomes coordinated – "how the actors come to share a common appraisal of their empirical circumstances" (Heritage 1984, p. 305) – that is, the process by which they come to cooperate and their methods for resolving conflicts.

The idea of "intelligibility and accountability" means that the work activity is "organized so that it can be rationalized" (Dourish & Button 1998, p. 415), that is, so that it appears rational. For example, the Mars Exploration Rover's (MER) operations (Squyres et al. 2004) were planned and orchestrated by the science team so the exploration could be recognizable to others in perpetuity as being science, especially through the method of justifying instrument applications in terms of hypothesis testing. In practice, geologists will often just strike a rock to see what is inside. In MER, the application of the rock abrasion tool was often explained within the group and to the public as looking for something specific. As the mission continued on for many months, the need for such rationalization diminished, but as the scientists were bound at the hip, with one rover to command (at each site), they continued to justify to each other why they would hit a particular rock and not another – something that would be inconceivable in their activity of physically walking through such a site with a hammer and hand lens. Thus, the practice of geology changed during the MER mission to adapt to the circumstances of a collective, historical, public, time-pressured activity; and production of accounts of what should be demonstrably scientific action were adapted to fit this situation (cf. Dourish & Button 1998, p. 416).

One must avoid a misconception that technical knowledge is just being selectively applied in social ways. Rather, what counts as expertise – the knowledge required to identify and solve problems – reflectively develops *within the setting*, which Collins calls "the mutual constitution of the social and conceptual" (Collins 1997, p. 296). During the MER mission, a cadre of scientists and engineers capable of doing science with rovers has developed new expertise and methods of working across disciplines in a time-pressured way.

In summary, expertise is more than facts, theories, and procedures (e.g., how to be a geologist or policeman); it includes practical, setting-determined know-how in being a recognizably competent social actor. Ethnomethodology reveals the reflective work of constructing *observable* (nonprivate) categorizations (e.g., deciding which Mars rocks to investigate). Thus, an essential task for the outside observer is to learn to see the ordered world of the community of practice: "Human activity exhibits a methodical orderliness . . . that the co-participants can and do realize, procedurally, at each and every moment. . . . The task for the analyst is to demonstrate just how they do this" (Whalen et al. 2004, p. 6). The following section provides some useful frameworks.

What People Do: Contrasting Frameworks

Social-analytic concepts for understanding human behavior in natural settings are contrasted here with information processing concepts that heretofore framed the study of knowledge and expertise (Newell & Simon 1972).

Practice vs. Process

Practice concerns "work as experienced by those who engage in it" (Button & Harper 1996, p. 264), especially, how "recognizable categories of work are assembled in the real-time actions and interactions of workers" (p. 264), memorably described by Wynn (1991):

> The person who works with information deals with an "object" that is more difficult to define and capture than information flow charts would have us imagine. These show "information" in little blocks or triangles moving along arrows to encounter specific transformations and directions along the diagram. In reality, it seems, all along the arrows, as well as at the nodes, that there are people helping this block to be what it needs to be – to name it, put it under the heading where it will be seen as a recognizable variant, deciding whether to leave it in or take it out, whom to convey it to. (pp. 56–57).

Button and Harper (1996, p. 265) give the example of people analyzing interviews: "The coders would resort to a variety of *practices* to decide what the coding rules actually required of them and whether what they were doing was actually (or virtually) in correspondence with those rules."

Practice is also called "lived work" – "what work consists of as it is lived as part of organizational life by those who do it" (Button & Harper 1996, p. 272). Practice is to be contrasted with formal *process specification* of what work is to be done. In the workplace itself, processes are often idealized and constitute shared values – "crimes should be reported to the bureau as soon as possible" (p. 277). Narratives that people record or present to authorities cater to these avowed policies or preferences, creating an *inherent conflict* in the work system between what people do and what they say they do. The point is not just that the documents and behavior may disagree, but rather, for example, the records may reveal workers' understanding of how their practices must be represented to appear rational.

Two fundamental concepts related to the practice–process distinction are behavior–function and activity–task. Process models (e.g., information processing diagrams) are idealized functional representations of the tasks that people in certain roles are expected to do. Practice concerns chronological, located behaviors, in terms of everyday activities, for example, "reading email," "meeting with a client," and "sorting through papers." Activities are how people "chunk" their day, how they would naturally describe "what I am doing now." Tasks are discovered, formulated, and carried out within activities, which occur on multiple levels in parallel (Clancey 2002).

Putting these ideas together, one must beware of identifying a formalized *scenario* (cf. Feltovich et al. 1997, p. 117) with the physical, interactive, social context in which work occurs. The work context is fundamentally conceptual (i.e., it cannot be exhaustively inventoried in descriptions or diagrams) and dynamically interpreted, in which the actor relates constraints of location, timing, responsibility, role, changing

organization, and so on. Scenarios used for studying expertise often represent an experimenter's idealized notion of the "inputs," and thus working a scenario may be more like solving a contrived puzzle than interacting with the flow of events that an actor naturally experiences.

Invisible vs. Overt Work

Observing work is not necessarily as easy as watching an assembly line. Work may be invisible (Nardi & Engeström 1999, p. 2) to an observer because of biases, because it occurs "back stage," or because it is tacit, even to the practitioners. These three aspects are discussed here.

First, preconceptions and biased methods may prevent the ethnographer from seeing what workers accomplish. For example, in a study of telephone directory operators, the researchers' a priori "notion of the 'canonical call' rendered the variability of actual calls invisible and led to a poor design for a partially automated directory assistance system" (p. 3). A related presumption is that people with authority are the experts (Jordan 1992). For example, the Mycin program (Buchanan & Shortliffe 1984) was designed in the 1970s to capture the expertise of physicians, but no effort was made to understand the role of nurses and their needs; in the study of medical expertise, nurses were "non-persons" (Goffman 1969; Star & Strauss 1999, p. 15).

The second aspect of invisibility arises because "many performers – athletes, musicians, actors, and arguably, scientists – keep the arduous process of preparation for public display well behind the scenes" (Star & Strauss 1999, p. 21), which Goffman called "back stage." One must beware of violating autonomy or not getting useful information because of members' strategic filtering or hiding of behavior (Star & Strauss 1999, p. 22).

The third form of invisible work is tacit "articulation work" – "work that gets things back 'on track' in the face of the unexpected, and modifies action to accommodate unanticipated contingencies." (Star & Strauss 1999, p. 10). These may be steps that people take for granted, such as a phone call to a colleague, which they wouldn't necessarily elevate to being a "method."

Participatory design handles the various forms of invisible work by using ethnography to identify stakeholders and then involving them in the work systems design project (e.g., see the examples in Greenbaum & Kyng 1991).

Members' Documentation vs. Literal Accounts

The production of documentation is part of the lived work of most business, government, and scientific professions. To deal with the nonliteral nature of documentation mentioned previously, one should study the activity of reporting "involved in sustaining an account of the work as a formal sequential operation" (Button & Harper 1996, p. 272) as a situated action with social functions. For example, in Mars habitat simulations (Clancey 2002, in press), one can learn from daily reports what the crew did. But one must also inquire how the reporting was accomplished (e.g., contingencies such as chores, fatigue, power failure, etc. that made reporting problematic), what accountability concerned the crew (e.g., the public image of the Mars Society; hence what was emphasized or omitted), and why reporting was given such priority (e.g., to adhere to scientific norms). What people write may not be what they actually did, and interviews may present yet another perspective on why the reports even exist.

Managing Inherent Conflicts vs. Applying Knowledge

One view of expertise is that people apply knowledge to accomplish goals (Newell & Simon 1972). Yet, goals are not simply the local statement of a task, but relate to long-term social-organizational objectives, such as later "work load and responsibilities" (Button & Harper 1996, p. 277). For example, the chair of NASA's Mission Management Team during the Columbia mission (which was destroyed on re-entry by wing tiles damaged by broken tank insulation foam during launch) didn't classify foam damage on the prior mission, STS-112 in December 2002, as an "in-flight anomaly" – the established practice. Doing so could have delayed a subsequent mission in February that she would manage (CAIB 2003, p. 138–139). Thus, a recurrent consideration in how work is managed is "what-this-will-mean-for-me-later-on" besides "what-can-I-do-about-it-now." The organizational context of work, not just the facts of the case, affects reporting a mishap event (Button & Harper 1996, p. 277).

In summary, the view of rationality as "applying knowledge" can be adapted to fit natural settings, but the goal of analysis must include broad organizational factors that include role, identity, values, and long-term implications. The expert as agent (actor, someone in a social setting) is more than a problem solver, but also an expert problem finder, avoider, delegator, prioritizer, reformulater, communicator, and so on.

We have now considered several contrasts between information processing and social-analytic concepts for understanding human behavior in natural settings. But how does one apply an analytic perspective systematically?

Unit of Analysis: The Principle of Multiple Perspectives

A fundamental aspect of ethnography is to triangulate information received from different sources at different times, including reinterpreting one's own notes in light of later events, explicitly related to previous studies and analytic frameworks (Forsythe 1999, pp. 127–128). In conventional terms, to make a study systematic, one gathers data to model the work from several related different perspectives:

- Flows: Information, communication, product
- Independent variables: Time, place, person, document
- Process influences: Tool, organization/ role, facility, procedure

To provide a suitable social framing and organization of these data categories, this section suggests the following units of analysis: activity system, temporality, and collectives.

Activity System

Activity theory (Leont'ev 1979) provides essential analytic concepts for understanding what is happening in a natural setting (Lave 1988; Nardi 1996; Engeström 2000). Psychologically, activity theory suggests how motives affect how people conceptually frame situations and choose problem-solving methods (Schön 1979). People broadly understand what they are doing as identity-related activities (e.g., "exploring an Arctic crater as if we were on Mars"). Career, social, or political motives and identities may influence how procedures are interpreted and tasks enacted. Engeström (1999) provides an exemplary activity theory analysis of a hospital setting.

Temporality: Phases, Cycles, Rhythm

A second unit of analysis is temporality: How does the work unfold during the course of a day or a week? Does it vary seasonally? Is a given day typical? One might observe an individual at different times and settings, and look for disparities between interviews and what people say about each other (Forsythe 1999, p. 138). An essential, recurrent organizing conception is the separating of work into categories such as "'someone-now,' 'me-when-I-can,' 'what-is-mine,' and 'everyone's-concern' to prioritise...work" (Button & Harper 1996, p. 276). Thus, expertise transcends how individual tasks are accomplished, to involve how time is made accountably productive.

Collectives

The third unit of analysis is the *collective*, the people who are interacting in a setting, as well as the conceptualized audience of clients, managers, and the community of practice. The collective might consist of people who don't directly know each other: "The occupational community [of photo-copy machine technicians] shares few cultural values with the corporation; technicians from all over the country are much more alike than a technician and a salesperson from the same district" (Orr 1996, p. 76).

How is the study of a collective related to individual expertise? Lave (1988) contrasts the view that culture is a collection of value-free factual knowledge with the view that society and culture "shape the particularities of cognition and give it content" (p. 87). Thus, the study of culture is inseparable from a study of how expertise is identified, developed, exploited, organized, and so on. Orr's study reveals that "The technicians are both a community and a collection of individuals, and their stories celebrate their individual acts, their work, and their individual and collective identities" (p. 143), such that storytelling has a social-psychological function with many practical and institutional effects.

Methods for Observation in Natural Settings

In considering methods of observation, one should not rush to the recording paraphernalia, but first focus on how the study is framed, the nature of engagement of the observer in the setting, and the work plan. This section of this chapter surveys useful handbooks, then summarizes key considerations and methods.

Handbooks for Observing Natural Settings

The following handbook-style guides are suggested for learning more about how to observe natural settings. These fall on a spectrum from observational science to rigorous engineering design.

Handbook of Methods in Cultural Anthropology (Bernard 1998) provides a balanced treatment of the history and methods of anthropology, with tutorial-style chapters on epistemological grounding, participant observation, systematic observation, structured interviewing, discourse and text analysis, and visual analysis.

Design at Work: Cooperative Design of Computer Systems (Greenbaum & Kyng 1991) is a primer of examples, theory, and methods for participatory design. It represents especially well the Scandinavian perspectives that have defined change-oriented observational studies of workplaces as a morally driven, industrially funded, and theoretically grounded activity.

Contextual Design (Beyer & Holtzblatt 1998) may be used as a beginner's guidebook for conducting a "contextual inquiry," including how to observe and work with customers (with unusually detailed advice about how to conduct interviews); how to model work (organizational flow, task sequences, artifacts such as documents, culture/stakeholders, and physical environment); and how to redesign work (including storyboards, paper prototypes).

Cognitive Work Analysis (Vicente 1999) provides another program for designing computer-based information systems, based on detailed mapping of information flows, task constraints, and control processes. This book presents the methodology and perspective of Jens Rasmussen and his colleagues (Rasmussen, Pejtersen, & Goodstein 1994): Work models must be detailed for tool design, and hence observation must be systematically organized to understand the *domain* (see also Jordan 1996). In particular, analysis of fields – the physical-conceptual spaces for possible action – is generalized from observations of particular trajectories or behaviors in this space (Vicente 1999, p. 179).

Framing the Study: Purpose, Genre, Timing, and Biases

Every study of expertise occurs in its own context, which shapes the observer's interests, targeted product (a publication? a design document?), and the pace of work. Researchers therefore find it useful to have a variety of different approaches that can be adapted, rather than imposing one rigorous method on every setting.

Observation of expertise in natural settings has been undertaken as a scientific endeavor (studying decision making, creativity, etc.); to develop training strategies; or, typically, to redesign the workplace by automating or facilitating the work processes (Blomberg et al. 1993; Nardi & Engeström 1999; Jordan 1993, 1997; Ross et al. Chapter 23).

Dourish & Button (1998) summarize the relation of ethnography and ethnomethodology to technological design, emphasizing human-computer interaction. Luff, Hindmarsh, and Heath (2000) provide an updated collection of detailed workplace studies related to system design. More generally, workplace studies may be part of a broader interest in organizational development (Engeström 1999; Nardi & Engeström 1999, p. 4).

Before a study begins, one should make explicit one's interests, partly to approach the work systematically, and partly to expose biases so others may better evaluate and use the results (e.g., provide a comparative survey of related studies, Clancey in press). Throughout a study, one should also question conventional metaphors that predefine what is problematic. For example, the term "homelessness" could lead to focusing on housing, rather than studying how such people view and organize their lives (Schön 1979). The underlying nature of a setting may clarify as change is attempted (Engeström 1999, p. 78).

Observer Involvement

For many researchers, participant observation is the ideal way to study people, informally learning by becoming part of the group and learning by watching and asking questions. But participant observation is not necessary and may not be possible, for instance, in highly technical or risky work such as air traffic control (Harper 2000, p. 258).

Observation should be a *programmatic study* (p. 240–241), with demonstrated sincerity and probity (p. 251). Ethnography is not a haphazard hanging around or shadowing, as if anything is of interest (p. 254).

Rather, the observational work must be a systematic investigation, with some sequential order (though often dynamically replanned) that covers a related set of roles, places, situations, and timelines. For example, in studying MER rover operations mentioned previously, the researchers were confronted with a 24-hour operation in three floors of a building, involving three shifts of distinct engineering and scientist teams. Given access constraints, the group focused on one room at first, where the scientists met three times during the day and worked out from that group and place to understand how instructions were prepared for the rover's next-day operations and then how Mars data was received and stored for the scientists to access.

To stimulate inquiry and make learning progressive, the observer should keep a journal and review it periodically for issues to revisit. Another method is to review photographs and ask about every object, "What is that? What is it for? Who owns it? Where is it used and stored?" This can be done effectively via email with colleagues who are not at the study site, encouraging them to ask questions about what they see in the photos.

The ideal in participatory design is to find at least one person in the setting who can be a champion for the inquiry, explaining the study to others, getting access, and making the observational activity legitimate. By this conception, people in the workplace are partners in a cooperative activity, and not referred to as "subjects," "users," or "operators" (Wynn 1991, p. 54). Probably no other philosophical stance is more fundamental to the observer's success. Data are discussed with the workers (in appropriate forums); report outlines are circulated for comment; related local expertise responsible for modeling the workplace is solicited for advice; documents about the work may even be coauthored with organizational champions.

Program of Work

For an observational study to be systematic, there must be an explicit program or plan for what, where, and how to study the setting (Harper 2000, p. 248). For example:

- Map out the key processes of the organization.
- Understand the diversities of work.
- Understand how different sets of persons depend on one another.
- Determine salient junctures in the information life cycle.

A plan will specify particular kinds of records kept over a certain period, and how they will be created, as described in subsequent sections.

Person, Object, Setting, Activity, Time-oriented Records

To be systematic, the observer must deliberately adopt a perspective and keep records organized accordingly. Jordan (1996) suggests the perspectives person, object (e.g., documents), setting, and task or process. More generally, an activity-oriented record includes any recurrent behavior, including both predefined work tasks (e.g., processing an order) and behaviors that may not be part of a job description (e.g., answering a phone call). Time is an orthogonal dimension. For example, one could check to see what people in a work area are doing every 15 minutes or observe a given setting at the same time every day. Time-lapse video can be used to record when people enter and leave a particular place (Clancey 2001).

Anthropologists make a distinction between two kinds of data: Emic categories (after phon*emic*) are used by participants; etic categories (after phon*etic*) are formal distinctions from an analyst's perspective (Jordan 1996). The basic systematic units mentioned in this section are etic: activities, roles, objects, persons, places, durations, etc.; in Western European and North American business settings these often fit emic distinctions.

Study Duration

Observational studies may last from weeks to years. The duration depends on the logistics and natural rhythm of the setting, technical complexity, and the study's purpose. Generally speaking, long-term involvement is preferable to follow the development of work practice. However, a few months of regular observation can be sufficient; a few weeks of daily participation usually enables a proficient analyst to form an understanding that can be a launching point for more focused interviews and design sessions. Indeed, one aspect of a study is to identify periodicities and historical developments, that is, to locate observations within overarching cycles and trends.

Recording Methods and Logistics

Data from natural settings is recorded using tools varying from paper and pen to electronic tracking devices. The standard media are texts (e.g., field notes, documents found in the setting), video and audio recordings, photographs, and computer models (e.g., the Brahms work practice simulation system, Clancey et al. 1998; Sierhuis 2001). Recording has enabled "repeated and detailed examination of the events of an interaction ... permits other research to have direct access to the data about which claims are being made ... can be reused in a variety of investigations and can be re-examined in the context of new findings" (Heritage 1984, p. 238). Having a body of such data is the sine qua non for being a researcher who studies natural settings.

Recordings must be labeled, indicating at least the setting, date, and time. Experienced ethnographers suggest the following procedures: Collect photographs in a computer catalog, where they can be sorted by categories into folders. Transcribe field notes (not necessarily journals) in an electronic form so that they can be shared and searched. Organize computer files in folders, separating preparatory/logistic information, miscellaneous graphics, documents acquired, photographs, field notes, presentations and reports, press stories, email, and so on.

When recording outdoors, wireless microphones can be used to avoid wind interference. An audio mixer with several microphones enables combining different sources (e.g., computer speech output, "ambient" remarks, radio or telephone conversations). Typically, observation reveals settings where interpersonal interaction occurs, from which one chooses "hot spots" (Jordan 1996) for systematic video recording. The following methods are suggested: Use a tripod and wide angle lens, and multiple cameras for different view points if possible. Take systematic photographic records (e.g., the same place each day, such as a whiteboard) or take a rapid sequence to create a "film strip" that captures changing postures and positions as people interact with materials and each other. Interviews can be audio recorded, but video (on a tripod off to the side) provides more information.

Written records can include a pocket notebook (for jotting down phrases or noting things to do), a daily journal (often handwritten) that describes one's personal experience, and field notes (perhaps using an outline-based note-taker), with different sections to elaborate on observations, raise questions, and interpret what is happening. Surveys given before, during, and after observation are recommended. View a survey as a way to prompt conversations and to encourage people to reflect with you on what is important, including their sense of accountability and how they evaluate their own performance (see Clancey, in press). Finally, if the circumstances of privacy and intellectual property allow, one may learn a great deal from documents found in garbage cans.

Data Analysis

Experienced researchers suggest flexible use of computer tools for representing work (Engeström 1999, pp. 85–90). Analysis methods are detailed in the handbooks cited above. Key pointers are provided here.

First, video data must be inventoried or will probably never be analyzed. Use a spreadsheet or outline to list the general content for each recording, and as you watch loosely transcribe material of special interest. For an extensive video collection of very different settings, create a catalog of illustrative frames. Video to be analyzed should be reformatted if necessary with the time and date displayed.

Social scientists often use some form of *conversational analysis* (CA), including gaze and gestures (Heritage 1984, p. 233). This method has revealed that behavior in "naturally occurring interactions" is strongly organized to great levels of detail. In pure form, CA eschews uses of interviews, field notes, and set-up situations in real world environments (p. 236). CA emphasizes "conversation as social action, rather than as the articulation of internal mental states" (Dourish & Button 1998, p. 402; Whalen et al. 2004).

Video-based *interaction analysis* (Greenbaum & Kyng 1991; Jordan 1996; Jordan & Henderson 1995) is a method for examining data in which scientists from different disciplines may spend hours discussing a carefully chosen, transcribed five to ten minute segment.

Besides narratives and verbal analyses, data may be collected in spreadsheets (e.g., time vs. person/place/activity), flowcharts, concept networks, timelines, and graphs (generated from the spreadsheets) (Clancey 2001, in press). If the data have been gathered systematically, it will be possible to calculate summary statistics (e.g., how long people did various activities in different places). Such information may prompt further questioning and reveal patterns that were not noticed by the ethnographer on site.

Social scientists use a wide variety of metrics. However, some studies never measure or count anything, as statistics are viewed merely as an attempt to quantify everything (Forsythe 1999, p. 139) or as being misleading (Nardi & Engeström 1999, p. 1). Researchers engaged in design projects are more likely to seek a balance. The real issue is whether the measurements are meaningful (Bernard 1998, p. 17). As a stimulus for further inquiry, it may be useful to quantify members' concerns (e.g., "I'm interrupted too much").

Perspective: Improving Ethnographic Practice

Observation in natural settings is a valuable, and some say necessary, way to systematically learn about practical knowledge, that is, to understand how people, places, activities, tools, facilities, procedures, and so on relate. One can learn about technical knowledge from textbooks or lectures, or even get important insights from surveys or by designing experiments in a laboratory. But expertise has a subjective, improvisatory aspect whose form changes with the context, which is always changing. This context includes the workers' conception of personal and organizational identity (including motives and avowed goals), economic trends, physical environment, and so on.

Observation in natural settings may be arduous because of the time required, equipment maintenance, the amount of data that is often generated, personal involvement with the people being studied, and political and power concerns of the organizational setting. Some conflicts are inherent, with no easy solution:

- Ethics, privacy, and confidentiality
- Distribution and simultaneity of collective work
- Long-cycle phases and off-hours commitments
- Representativeness and systematicity of the data (vs. details of specific situations)
- Exposing invisible work (e.g., practices deviate from legally proscribed routines)
- Point-of-view and authoritative biases

Using ethnography for design of work systems is problematic: One often seeks a large-scale system design, but the study focuses on the "small-scale detail of action" (Dourish & Button 1998, p. 411). Observation naturally focuses on what is; how does one move to what might be? (see Greenbaum & Kyng 1991; Dekker, Nyce, & Hoffman 2003.)

Just like other work, ethnographies in practice do not always measure up to the espoused ideal: "Social scientists have for one reason or another failed to depict the core practices of the occupational worlds which they have studied" (Heritage 1984, p. 300). For example, the MER mission study was limited in practice by the number of observers and their stamina. Outside the defined workflow of mission operations, the scientists were also participating in parallel activities of grant writing, public affairs, paper preparation, and so forth. Some of these unobserved activities directly affected science operations (e.g., preparing a comparative graph for a conference presentation might require additional data from Mars).

The role of simulation for driving observation and formalizing data is unclear (Sierhuis 2001; Seah et al. 2005). As one delves into individual behaviors of specialists, are approaches recurrent or just idiosyncratic? To what extent does a collective have uniform methods? Should a simulation be broad (e.g., several weeks) or deep (e.g., modeling computer system interfaces)?

Finally, social scientists, like other workers, may find it difficult to articulate their own methods: There is "no stable lore of tried and trusted procedures through which, for example, taped records . . . can be brought to routine social scientific description" (Heritage 1984, p. 301). Researchers often have different disciplinary interests, so a group of ethnographers at one site might not collaborate until they write a report for the host organization. At this point, the problem of indexing and sharing data becomes visible, both within the group and to others seeking to better understand a study. Effectively, in documenting observational studies, the work practice researcher is caught up in all the familiar issues of lived work, accountability, and contingent methods.

Acknowledgments

I am especially indebted to my colleagues at the Institute for Research on Learning (1987–1997) for demonstrating through their work the ideas presented here. The MER Human-Centered Computing ethnography team from NASA/Ames included Roxana Wales, Charlotte Linde, Zara Mirmalek (University of California, San Diego), Chin Seah, and Valerie Shalin (Wright State University). Topic suggestions and editorial advice for this chapter were also provided by Robert Hoffman, Patty Jones, Brigitte Jordan, Mike Shafto, Maarten Sierhuis, Marilyn Whalen, and Judith Orasanu. This work has been supported in part by NASA's Computing, Communications, and Information Technology Program.

Footnote

1. The description of this project has been provided by Peggy Szymanski at PARC.

References

Bernard, H. R. (Ed.). (1998). *Handbook of methods in cultural anthropology*. Walnut Creek, CA: AltaMira Press.

Beyer, H. & Holtzblatt, K. (1998). *Contextual design: Defining customer-centered systems*. San Francisco: Morgan-Kaufmann.

Birdwhistell, R. (1952). *Introduction to kinesics*. Louisville: University of Louisville Press.

Blomberg, J., Giacomi, J., Mosher, A. & Swenton-Wall, P. (1993). Ethnographic field methods and their relation to design. In D. Schuler & A. Namioka (Eds.), *Participatory design: Principles and practices*, (pp. 123–155). Hillsdale, NJ: Erlbaum.

Blum, B. I. (1996). *Beyond programming: To a new era of design*. New York: Oxford University Press.

Buchanan, B. G., & Shortliffe, E. H. (Eds.). (1984). *Rule-based expert systems: The MYCIN experiments of the Heuristic Programming Project*. Reading, MA: Addison Wesley.

Button, G., & Harper, R. (1996). The relevance of "work-practice" for design. *Computer Supported Cooperative Work*, 4, 263–280.

Chi, M. T. H., Glaser, R., & Farr, M. J. (1988). *The nature of expertise*. Hillsdale, NJ: Erlbaum.

Clancey, W. J. (2001). Field science ethnography: Methods for systematic observation on an arctic expedition. *Field Methods*, 13, 223–243. August.

Clancey, W. J. (2002). Simulating activities: Relating motives, deliberation, and attentive coordination. *Cognitive Systems Research*, 3, 471–499.

Clancey, W. J. (in press). Participant observation of a Mars surface habitat mission simulation. To appear in *Habitation*.

Clancey, W. J., Sachs, P., Sierhuis, M., & van Hoof, R. (1998). Brahms: Simulating practice for work systems design. *Int. J. Human-Computer Studies*, 49, 831–865.

Collins, H. M. (1997). Rat-Tale: Sociology's contribution to understanding human and machine cognition. In P. J. Feltovich, K. M. Ford, & R. R. Hoffman (Eds.), *Expertise in context* (pp. 293–311). Cambridge, MA: MIT Press.

Columbia Accident Investigation Board (CAIB). (2003). *CAIB Report, Volume 1.* NASA. [August 2005] http://CAIB.NASA. GOV/news/report/volume1/default.html.

Corbet, J. M., Rasmussen, B., & Rauner, F. (1991). *Crossing the border: The social and engineering design of computer integrated manufacturing systems.* London: Springer-Verlag.

Dekker, S. W. A., Nyce, J. M., & Hoffman, R. R. (2003). From contextual inquiry to designable futures: What do we need to get there? *IEEE Intelligent Systems*, March–April, 74–77.

Dewalt, K. M., & Dewalt, B. R. (2002). *Participant observation.* Lanham, MD: Rowman & Littlefield.

Dourish, P., & Button, G. (1998). On "technomethodology": Foundational relationships between ethnomethodology and system design. *Human-computer interaction*, 13, 395–432.

Ehn, P. (1988). *Work oriented design of computer artifacts.* Stockholm: Arbetslivscentrum.

Emery, F. E. (1959). *The emergence of a new paradigm of work.* Canberra, Australia: Australian National University, Centre for Continuing Education.

El Guindi, F. (1998). From pictorializing to visual ethnography. In H. R. Bernard (Ed.), *Handbook of methods in cultural anthropology* (pp. 459–511). Walnut Creek, CA: AltaMira Press,

Engeström, Y. (1999). Expansive visibilization of work: An activity-theoretical perspective. *Computer Supported Cooperative Work*, 8, 63–93.

Engeström, Y. (2000). Activity theory as a framework for analyzing and redesigning work. *Ergonomics*, 43, 960–974.

Feltovich, P., Ford, K., & Hoffman, R. (Eds.). (1997). *Human and machine expertise in context.* Menlo Park, CA: The AAAI Press.

Fetterman, D. M. (1998). *Ethnography* (2nd Ed.). Thousand Oaks: Sage Publications.

Forsythe, D. E. (1999). "It's just a matter of common sense": Ethnography as invisible work. *Computer Supported Cooperative Work*, 8, 127–145.

Goffman, E. (1969). *The presentation of self in everyday life.* London: Allen Lane.

Greenbaum, J., & Kyng, M. (Eds.). (1991). *Design at work: Cooperative design of computer systems.* Hillsdale, NJ: Erlbaum.

Hall, Edward, T. (1966). *The hidden dimension.* New York: Doubleday.

Hall, Edward, T. (1959). *The silent language.* New York: Doubleday.

Harper, R. H. R. (2000). The organisation of ethnography: A discussion of ethnographic fieldwork programs in CSCW. *Computer Supported Cooperative Work*, 9, 239–264.

Heritage, J. (1984). *Garfinkel and ethnomethodology.* Cambridge, UK: Polity Press.

Hoffman, R. R. (1998). How can expertise be defined? Implications of research from cognitive psychology. In R. Williams, W. Faulkner, & J. Fleck (Eds.), *Exploring expertise* (pp. 81–100). New York: Macmillan.

Hoffman, R. R., Coffey, J. W., & Ford, K. M. (2000). *STORM-LK: System to organize representations in meteorology.* Deliverable on the contract, "Human-centered system prototype," National Technology Alliance.

Hutchins, E. (1995). *Cognition in the wild.* Cambridge: MIT Press.

Johnson, A., & Sackett, R. (1998). Direct systematic observation of behavior. In H. R. Bernard (Ed.), *Handbook of methods in cultural anthropology.* Walnut Creek: AltaMira Press, pp. 301–331.

Jordan, B. (1992). Technology and social interaction: Notes on the achievement of authoritative knowledge in complex settings. IRL Technical Report No. 92-0027. [December 2004] http:// www. lifescapes. org/ Writeups. htm.

Jordan, B. (1993). Ethnographic workplace studies and computer supported cooperative work. *Proceedings of the interdisciplinary workshop on informatics and psychology.* Schärding, Austria, June. Amsterdam: North Holland.

Jordan, B. (1996). Ethnographic workplace studies and computer supported cooperative work. In D. Shapiro, M. Tauber, & R.Traunmüller (Eds.), *The design of computer-supported cooperative work and groupware systems* (pp. 17–42). Amsterdam: North Holland/Elsevier Science.

Jordan, B. (1997). Transforming ethnography – reinventing research. *Cultural Anthropology Methods,* 9, 12–17, October.

Jordan, B., & Henderson, A. (1995). Interaction analysis: Foundations and practice. *The Journal of the Learning Sciences,* 4, 39–103.

Kling, R., & Star, S. L. (1998). Human centered systems in the perspective of organizational and social informatics. *Computers and Society,* 28, 22–29, March.

Lave, J. (1988). *Cognition in practice.* Cambridge: Cambridge University Press.

Leont'ev A. N. (1979). The problem of activity in psychology. In Wertsch, J. V. (Ed.), *The concept of activity in soviet psychology,* Armonk, NY: M. E. Sharpe, (pp. 37–71).

Lesgold, A., Rubinson, H., Feltovich, P., Glaser, R., Klopfer, D., & Wang, Y. (1988). Expertise in a complex skill: Diagnosing x-ray pictures. In M. T. H. Chi, R. Glaser, and M. J. Farr, (Eds.), *The nature of expertise.* (pp. 311–342) Hillsdale, NJ: Erlbaum,

Lorenz, K. (1952). *King Solomon's ring.* New York: Crowell.

Luff, P., Hindmarsh, J., & Heath, C. (Eds.). (2000). *Workplace studies: Recovering work practice and informing system design.* Cambridge: Cambridge University Press.

Nardi, B. (1995). *Context and consciousness: Activity theory and human-computer interaction.* Cambridge, MA: MIT Press.

Nardi, B., & Engeström, Y. (Eds.) (1999). A web on the wind: The structure of invisible work. *Computer Supported Cooperative Work,* 8(1–2), 1–8.

Newell, A., & Simon, H. A. (1972). *Human problem solving.* Englewood Cliffs, NJ: Prentice-Hall, Inc.

Orr, J. E. (1996). *Talking about machines. An ethnography of a modern job.* Cornell University Press.

PPS ("Project for Public Spaces"). [December 2004] http://www.pps.org/info/placemaking tools/placemakers/wwhyte.

Rogoff, B., & Lave, J. (1984). *Everyday cognition.* Cambridge: Harvard University Press.

Rasmussen, J., Pejtersen, A. M., & Goodstein, L. P. (1994). *Cognitive systems engineering.* New York: Wiley.

Scheflen, A. E. (1972). *Body language and the social order.* Englewood Cliffs: Prentice-Hall.

Schön, D. A. (1979). Generative metaphor: A perspective on problem-setting in social polity. In A. Ortony (Ed.), *Metaphor and thought* (pp. 254–283). Cambridge: Cambridge University Press,

Schön, D. A. (1987). *Educating the reflective practitioner: Toward a new design for teaching and learning in professions.* San Francisco: Jossey-Bass.

Seah, C., Sierhuis, M., & Clancey, W. J. (2005). Multi-agent modeling and simulation approach for design and analysis of MER mission operations. *Proceedings of 2005 international conference on human-computer interface advances for modeling and simulation (SIMCHI'05),* ISBN 1-56555-288-1.

Senge, P. M. (1990). *The fifth discipline: The art and practice of the learning organization.* New York: Doubleday.

Sierhuis, M. (2001). Modeling and simulating work practice. Ph.D. thesis, Social Science and Informatics (SWI), University of Amsterdam, The Netherlands, ISBN 90-6464-849-2.

Spradley, J. P. (1979). *The ethnographic interview.* New York: Holt, Rinehart and Winston.

Spradley, J. P. (1980). *Participant observation.* Fort Worth: Harcourt Brace College Publishers.

Squyres, S. W., Arvidson, R. E., Bell III, J. F., et al. (2004). The Spirit Rover's Athena science investigation at Gusev Crater, Mars, *Science,* 305, 794–800.

Star, S. L., & Strauss, A. (1999). Layers of silence, arenas of voice: The ecology of visible and invisible work. *Computer Supported Cooperative Work,* 8, 9–30.

Suchman, L. A. (1987). *Plans and situated actions: The problem of human-machine communication.* Cambridge: Cambridge University Press.

Vicente, K. J. (1999). *Cognitive work analysis: Toward safe, productive, and healthy computer-based work.* Mahwah, NJ: Erlbaum.

Webster's Third New International Dictionary, Unabridged. Merriam-Webster, 2002. http://unabridged. merriam-webster. com (13 Dec. 2004).

Wenger, E. (1998). *Communities of practice: Learning, meaning, and identity.* New York: Cambridge University Press.

Whalen, M., Whalen, J., Moore, R., Raymond, G., Szymanski, M., & Vinkhuyzen, E. (2004). Studying workscapes as a natural observational discipline. In P. LeVine & R. Scollon (Eds.), *Discourse and technology: Multimodal discourse analysis.* Washington, DC: Georgetown University Press (pp. 208–229).

Whyte, W. H. (1980). *The social life of small urban spaces.* Washington, DC: The Conservation Foundation.

Wynn, E. (1991). Taking practice seriously. In J. Greenbaum & M. Kyng (Eds.), *Design at work: Cooperative design of computer systems.* Hillsdale, NJ: Erlbaum, pp. 45–64.

CHAPTER 9

Methods for Studying the Structure of Expertise: Psychometric Approaches

Phillip L. Ackerman & Margaret E. Beier

"Psychometrics" refers to the scientific discipline that combines psychological inquiry with quantitative measurement. Though psychometric theory and practice pertain to all aspects of measurement, in the current context, psychometric approaches to expertise pertain to the measurement and prediction of individual differences and group differences (e.g., by gender, age) and, in particular, high levels of proficiency including expertise and expert performance. The scientific study of expertise involves several important psychometric considerations, such as reliability and validity of measurements, both at the level of predictors (e.g., in terms of developing aptitude measures that can predict which individuals will develop expert levels of performance), and at the level of criteria (the performance measures themselves). We will discuss these basic aspects of psychometric theory first, and then we will provide an illustration of psychometric studies that focus on the prediction of expert performance in the context of tasks that involve the development and expression of perceptual-motor skills, and tasks that involve predominantly cognitive/

intellectual expertise. Finally, we will discuss challenges for future investigations.

Before we start, some psychological terms need to be defined. The first terms are "traits" and "states." Traits refer to relatively broad and stable dispositions. Traits can be physical (e.g., visual acuity, strength) or psychological (e.g., personality, interests, intelligence). In contrast to traits, states represent temporary characteristics (e.g., sleepy, alert, angry). The second set of terms to be defined are "interindividual differences" and "intraindividual differences." Interindividual differences refer to differences between individuals, such as the difference between the heights of students in a classroom or the speed of different runners in a race. Intraindividual differences refer to differences within individuals, such as the difference between the typing speed of an individual measured at the beginning of typing class and that same individual's typing speed at the end of a year of practice in typing. Studies of the development of expertise during skill training can focus on interindividual differences (e.g., the rank ordering of a group of trainees), intraindividual differences (e.g., measuring the transition of performance for given individuals from novice to expert levels of performance), or a combination of the two (e.g., interindividual differences in intraindividual change – or more colloquially, which of the trainees learned the most or the least during the course of training).

General Aspects of Psychometric Approach: Predictors

There are two fundamental aspects of measurement that transcend psychology and other scientific inquiries, namely, reliability and validity. The first consideration of any measurement is reliability, because without reliable measurements, there would be no basis for establishing validity of the measures. However, even with reliable measurements, one may or may not have a valid measure for a particular application or theory. Thus, we will follow up our discussion of reliability with a review of the critical considerations of validity. The final part of this section will consider issues of reliability and validity in terms of predicting individual differences in expert-level performance, especially in the context of base-rate concerns.

Reliability

At a general level, the definition of psychometric reliability is not very different from a commonsense meaning of the term. If your coworker shows up for work at nearly the same time every day, you might say that her attendance is reliable. If another coworker is often late or even sometimes early, but you can rarely predict when she will actually walk through the door of the office, you might consider her to be unreliable in attendance. The psychometric concept of reliability concerns a similar accounting of consistency and precision, except in this case we ordinarily refer to the reliability of measures or tests, rather than individuals. A test or other form of assessment is considered to yield reliable results when a group of individ-

uals can be consistently rank-ordered over multiple measuring occasions.

There are many different ways to measure reliability; some approaches are more or less suitable to particular occasions than others. For example, a test of running speed might involve measuring how fast a group of runners can complete a 10-km race. One way to estimate the reliability of such a test is called the test-retest method, and it involves administering the same test again immediately after the first test. In the case of a running speed test given immediately at the conclusion of a race, performance might be very different across the two tests, because of differential fatigue. Such results might erroneously suggest that the test is not very reliable. Rather, a more suitable method for assessing the reliability of the running-speed test would be to administer the same test, but delayed in time a week after the first test. An index of reliability computed from these two scores would be more appropriate (because fatigue would be less likely to figure into any performance differences between the two occasions). Also, the state of the individual (e.g., mood, amount of sleep the previous night, etc.) is less likely to be the same on measurement occasions that are separated by a week or longer, and so the reliability of the test would be less influenced by state effects on performance, and more likely to be a function of the underlying trait of running speed.

In the example above, the same test is administered to the participants on more than one occasion (test-retest reliability). Although this strategy is both practical and reasonable for some physical performance measures, problems sometimes occur when considering the reliability of more cognitive or affective (i.e., personality) traits. There are two main problems for using test-retest procedures for estimating reliability of psychological traits. The first problem is memory – humans may remember how they responded to a survey or test across occasions, unless the tests are separated by a very long time (and sometimes, even this is insufficient). The second problem pertains mostly to performance measures, such as aptitude, ability, and skill assessments. This problem is learning – that is, examinees often learn either explicitly or implicitly during the test. Tests ranging in difficulty from simple arithmetic problems to complex simulations typically show significant and sometimes substantial improvements in performance from one occasion to the next, either because examinees have learned the correct responses, or they have become more skilled at performing the basic operations required by the test. Under these conditions, a more appropriate method of assessing the reliability of the test is to use what is known as an "alternate form." An alternate form is typically a test that is designed in a very similar fashion to the first test, but one that differs in terms of the actual items presented to the examinee. When fatigue is not an important consideration, alternate forms of a test can be administered one right after the other. Otherwise, alternate forms can be administered after a delay, just like in the test-retest procedure described above.

A final type of reliability that is relevant to the study of expertise is inter-observer reliability. This is an index of agreement between different judges, when performance cannot be objectively evaluated (e.g., gymnastics, diving, art, music). When judges have high agreement in rank-ordering individuals, there is high inter-observer reliability; but when there is little agreement, reliability of the judgements is low.

Reliability of a measure is the first hurdle that must be passed for it to be scientifically or practically useful. Without reliability, a test has little or no utility. But, just having a consistent rank-ordering of individuals on a test says nothing about whether or not the test actually measures what it sets out to measure. For that assessment, we have the concept of validity.

Validity

Validity is a property of an instrument that refers to whether it measures what it sets out to measure. Thus, a test of baseball skill is valid to the degree it actually provides a measurement of the trait defined as "baseball skill." There are three different aspects of a test that need to be considered in evaluating validity: content validity, construct validity, and criterion-related validity. Content validity refers to the underlying content of the trait under consideration. For baseball, the content of the skill would include batting, running, fielding, and other aspects. A test of baseball skill that focused on all relevant components of these tasks to the same degree that they are important would have high content validity. Generally, content validity is established through judgments of subject-matter experts and is not directly assessed in a quantitative fashion.

Construct validity refers to the relationship between a measure of a particular trait or state and the underlying theoretical concept or construct. Establishing the construct validity of a measure usually involves evaluating the correlation between the measure and other assessments of the same or similar constructs. Generally, in order for a measure to have high construct validity, it must correlate substantially with other measures of the same or similar constructs (this is called "convergent validity"), and the measure should not correlate substantially with measures of different constructs (this is called "discriminant validity"). For example, a measure of general baseball skill might be expected to have high correlations with a measure of baseball strategy knowledge (convergent validity), but low correlations with a measure of football strategy knowledge (discriminant validity).

Especially important in terms of the application of psychometric measures is criterion-related validity. The key to criterion-related validity is prediction; it refers to the degree to which the measure can predict individual differences in some criterion measure. For an intelligence test, criterion validity is frequently demonstrated by the degree to which scores on the intelligence test correlate with a criterion of academic performance, such as grade point average or academic promotion from one grade to the next. The typical application-oriented goal is to use a test or other assessment measure as an aid in selection, such as for educational or training opportunities or for a job or to be a team member. Ideally, criterion-related validity is assessed by administering the test to a group of individuals who are *all* selected for the educational or occupational opportunity. Criterion performance is then measured at a later time, such as after training, or after a period of job performance. This kind of assessment is called "predictive validity" and it provides the most precise estimate of the relationship between the measure and the criterion, unless there are individuals who leave the program prior to the time that criterion measurement is obtained.

When it is not possible to use such a procedure (such as when there is some selection procedure already in place, or when the cost of training is high), an investigator can perform a concurrent-validation assessment. In this procedure, the measure is administered to incumbents (e.g., current employees, current students, current team members), and their criterion performance is also assessed. Given that one can usually assume that incumbents are more restricted in range on the key traits for performance than are applicants (through either existing selection procedures, through self-selection, or through attrition associated with training or performance failures), establishing the validity of a new measure is more difficult using concurrent-validity procedures than it is for predictive-validity procedures. Procedures exist for estimating the predictive validity of a test when assessed in a concurrent-validity study, especially when there are data concerning the differences between incumbents and applicants (e.g., see Thorndike, 1949). For example, aptitude tests such as the SAT show only relatively modest concurrent validity correlations with college grade point average at selective colleges and universities. However, an institution can estimate the predictive validity of the SAT, given knowledge of the test score distributions of both applicants and incumbents.

Special Considerations of Measurement in the Prediction of Expert Performance

By its very nature, the study of expertise is associated with several specific measurement problems. We consider four of the most important problems: measurement of change, restriction of range, base rates, and interdependence issues.

Measurement of Change

From early in the 1900s, psychologists interested in individual differences in learning and skill acquisition (e.g., Thorndike, 1908; see Ackerman, 1987; Adams, 1987 for reviews) have attempted to evaluate which individuals learn the most during task practice or from training interventions. There are two fundamental issues that arise in assessing the amount of change during learning: measurement artifacts related to regression-to-the-mean effects, and the underlying nature of individual differences in learning. Regression-to-the-mean is a statistical phenomenon, not a set of causal effects. When measurements (in this case, initial performance on a task) are not perfectly reliable, those individuals with extreme scores on the first occasion are likely to obtain scores closer to the respective mean for the second occasion (after task practice). This means that, *ceteris paribus* (i.e., if everything else is equal), individuals with below average scores at initial performance measurement will have relatively higher scores at the second occasion, and individuals with above average scores on the first occasion will have relatively lower scores on the second occasion. Again, this is a statistical phenomenon, but it results in a potentially critical artifact that can be misinterpreted.

The deeper problem occurs when a researcher attempts to evaluate the relationship between initial task performance and the amount of learning (or gain in performance) after practice or training. Given the nature of the regression-to-the-mean phenomenon, the expected correlation between initial performance and later performance will be negative (simply as a function of the regression to the mean). An unsuspecting researcher might be tempted to conclude that a training program has the effect of "leveling" individual differences in performance, in that the poor performers get relatively better and the good performers get relatively worse (McNemar, 1940). Ultimately, it is a bad idea to attempt to measure individual differences in learning by correlating initial performance with performance after practice or training (e.g., see Cronbach & Furby, 1970).

A second issue related to measuring individual differences in learning is the nature of interindividual variability during learning or skill acquisition. Because the magnitude of interindividual variability is associated with changes in the reliability and validity of predictor measures, it is important to take account of factors that might lead to changes in interindividual variability. For skills that can be acquired by all or nearly all learners, interindividual variability tends to decline with task practice or training (e.g., see Ackerman, 1987). Frequently, the changes in variability can be substantial. For tasks with substantial motor or perceptual-motor components, such as typing or golf, there are extremely large interindividual differences in initial performance, but after extensive training, performance variability is much smaller. One reason for this is that there are physical limitations on performance at high levels of expertise. The most expert typist can type only as rapidly as one keystroke every 100 ms, and the most expert golfer is likely to perform a handful of strokes under par. In contrast, there are few limits at the other end of the performance continuum – there are many more ways that an individual can perform a task poorly than there are ways that a task can be performed at an expert level. Thus, when it comes to comparing the learning rates of a group of individuals, it is the poorest performing learners that have the most to gain, and the highest initial performers who have the least to gain from task practice or training.

It is important to emphasize that these substantial changes in interindividual variability are typically found only for tasks that are within the capabilities of nearly all learners. When tasks are complex or inconsistent in information-processing demands, interindividual variability may not change over task practice (Ackerman, 1987, 1992; Ackerman & Woltz, 1994), or there may be a Matthew effect (e.g., see Stanovich, 1986). A Matthew effect refers to the phenomenon of the "rich getting richer," essentially a positive association between initial standing and the amount of learning. (The term derives from Jesus' "Parable of the Talents," *Matthew*, XXV:29, "For unto every one that hath shall be given, and he shall have abundance: but from him that hath not shall be taken away even that which he hath.") Such effects have been found in reading skills and in other cognitive or intellectual tasks (Lohman, 1999). For example, expertise in mathematics is likely to show a Matthew effect, as many learners effectively drop out of the learning process at different stages along the way to developing expertise (e.g., at the level of acquiring skill at algebra, at calculus, or beyond). Across normal development, the differences between experts and non-experts in mathematics will become more pronounced, which will be manifest as larger interindividual variability in performance after practice or education.

A few laboratory-based examples may help illustrate the nature of the development of expert performance with the context of changing mean performance and changes in interindividual variability (as expressed in the between-individual standard deviation of performance). Figure 9.1a–c shows three different tasks, which are reasonably well defined, but differ in the nature of the task demands and the effects of practice on task performance. The first graph is from a skill-acquisition experiment with a simplified air traffic controller (ATC) task (the Kanfer-Ackerman Air Traffic Controller task; Ackerman & Cianciolo, 2000; for a

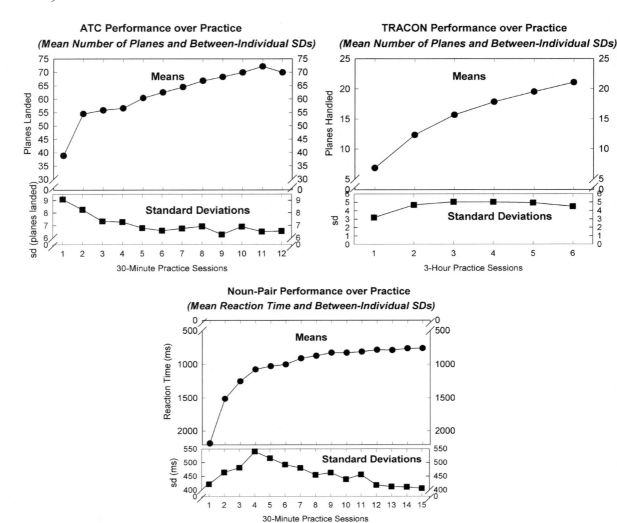

Figure 9.1a–c. Performance means and between-individual standard deviations over task practice. Panel a. Kanfer-Ackerman Air Traffic Controller task (data from Ackerman & Cianciolo, 2000); Panel b. Noun-Pair Lookup task (data from Ackerman & Woltz, 1994); Panel c. Terminal Radar Approach Control task (data from Ackerman & Kanfer, 1993).

more extensive description of the task, see Kanfer & Ackerman, 1989). The task is difficult for participants when they first perform it. Cognitive/intellectual abilities (discussed below) are substantially related to individual differences in initial task performance. However, the task has only seven rules, and all task operations can be accomplished with just four different keys on the computer keyboard. As a result, within five or six hours of practice, nearly all of the learners become expert performers. Figure 9.1 Panel a shows

how mean performance increases quickly in the early sessions of practice, but becomes asymptotic as most learners develop high levels of skills. Between-individual standard deviations start off high (when there are large differences between those learners who easily grasp the task demands early in practice, and those learners who must struggle to keep up), then decline as the slower learners ultimately acquire the skills necessary to perform the task at an expert level. At the end of six hours of practice, the magnitude of between-individual standard deviations has changed from 9.08 to 6.55, a reduction of about 28%.

In the second example, a more high-fidelity air traffic control task was used. In contrast to the previous task, this one (called TRACON, for Terminal Radar Approach Control; see Ackerman & Kanfer, 1993) involves sustained and focused attention, continuous sampling of the visual radar screen, short-term memory, problem-solving abilities, and spatial visualization. There are many more commands to learn, and each 30-minute task trial involves novel configurations of airplanes that the learner must handle in real-time. Few participants perform very well on the first few trials, and in general, it takes much longer to acquire skills on TRACON than it does for the simpler Kanfer-Ackerman ATC task. For TRACON, many learners do not reach expert levels of performance, even after extensive task practice. Figure 9.1b shows that while mean performance markedly increases over 18 hours of task practice, there is a slow rise in between-individual standard deviations in performance. From the initial to final practice sessions, standard deviations have changed from 3.19 to 4.49, an increase of 41%.

The third example illustrates what happens when learners adopt different learning or performance strategies. The task for this example is a simple lookup task, where the learner is presented with nine pairs of nouns on the upper part of a the computer display, and a test probe (which either has one of the matching pairs of words, or has two words that do not match) on the lower part of the computer display (Ackerman & Woltz, 1994). What happens in this task is that some individuals simply look up the words on each task trial, which is a strategy that minimizes effort on the individual trial level. We called these individuals "scanners." Performing with this strategy rarely can be accomplished in less than about 1 sec/trial (1000 msec). Other individuals, however, work to memorize the word pairs while they are also looking up the words for each trial. Their efforts are greater at the individual

trial level, but very quickly these individuals get quite a bit faster than their scanner counterparts because they can retrieve the word pairs from memory much faster than it takes to scan the display. Thus, we called these individuals "retrievers." Retrieving the items from memory can be very fast, and expert retrievers performed about twice as fast as the best scanners (e.g., about 500 msec/trial). Eventually (i.e., after several hundred task trials), the scanners learn at least some of the word pairs, almost incidentally, and get faster at the task.

When one looks at the overall performance and interindividual variability (Figure 9.1c), there is a general mean improvement in the speed of responding, as would be expected. However, there is an initial increase in between-individual variability as practice proceeds, since the retrievers are getting much better at task performance, and the scanners are profiting much less from each practice trial. Eventually, between-individual variability decreases, as even the scanners begin to memorize the word pairs. That is, an initial SD level of 421 msec increases to 521 msec (an increase of 24%) before declining to 406 ms. At the end of 1,350 task trials, there has been an overall decline in between-individual SD of only 4%.

Restriction of Range

When interindividual variability declines with the development of expertise, a group of expert performers can be expected to show much smaller differences between them than do novices. The psychometric problem associated with such a restriction in range of performance is that correlations with measures of limited variability attenuate (i.e., they get closer to zero). This can make it very difficult to find tests that can predict individual differences in performance, simply because there is relatively little variance to account for by the predictor measures. Of course, this makes betting on the winner of competitive sports competitions a highly speculative activity, whether one is wagering money on the outcome of the competition or predicting the rank order of individuals when validating an ability or personality test. In the final analysis, it is much easier to predict which individuals will develop expertise in a task that shows a Matthew effect with practice than it is to predict which individuals will develop expertise in a task that evidences a decline in interindividual variability.

Base Rate Issues

In addition to restriction of range in performance, there is a more fundamental problem for developing valid predictors of performance, namely, the problem of extreme base rates (i.e., the rate at which a behavior is exhibited in the population). It has been shown (e.g., Meehl & Rosen, 1955) that as a behavior becomes less likely to occur (such as when only 1 in 100 college athletes ultimately end up playing professional sports), a test to predict the likelihood of reaching the professional teams must have extremely high validity to be practically useful. Thus, when expert performance on a task is a rare phenomenon, it may not be practically feasible to develop a selection measure that provides valid inferences for which individual is going to succeed.

Interdependence of Performance

Another difficulty that arises in the study of expert performance in some tasks is that performance is not solely dependent on the efforts of the individual performer. In many occupations, ranging from sports (such as team efforts, or when there are other individual competitors, as in tennis or auto racing) to scientific discovery or technological research and development, performance success depends to a nontrivial degree on the actions or behaviors of others, or depends on environmental influences outside of the control of the performer (Ed: see Salas, et al., Chapter 25, this volume). Thus, a baseball player's batting performance is dependent on the skill level of the pitcher, perhaps nearly as much as it does on the skill of the batter. Or, the scientific contribution of a

scientist may depend on how many other researchers are working toward the same goal – getting to the goal a few days or months ahead of the competition may signal the difference between fame and fortune on the one hand, and relative obscurity on the other hand (e.g., see the discussion by Watson, 2001, on the race to discover the structure of DNA).

When expert performance is interdependent with the performance of others, the ideal measurement of an individual's performance would be an average of multiple measures taken with as divergent a set of other performers as possible. For some types of expert performance, a round-robin type tournament would be one means toward accomplishing this goal; however, this kind of procedure is not practical in many different domains. Race car drivers do not compete in cars from all competitor manufacturers, football players cannot be assigned willy-nilly to different teams every week, and research professors cannot be easily moved around from one institution to another. When random assignment is not possible, more complicated statistical designs are needed to attempt to disentangle the effects of the team or other performers on the performance of the individual. Sometimes, however, this is simply impossible to accomplish. Under these circumstances, the only acceptable solution is to create an artificial environment (such as a laboratory experiment with simulations) in which the individual's performance can be evaluated in the absence of other performers (Ed: see Ward, et al. Chapter 14, this volume). Although these procedures can provide the needed experimental control, the risk is that the performance measurements taken under artificial laboratory conditions may not be valid representations of the actual real-world task (e.g., see Hoffman, 1987).

Trait Predictors of Expertise

One of the most universal findings regarding individual differences in task performance over practice or education is that as the time between measurements increases, the correlations between measurements attenuate, though the correlations rarely drop all the way to zero. Sometimes, when the task is simple and skills are rapidly acquired, the decline in correlations between initial task performance and performance on later task trials is extremely rapid (e.g., see Ackerman, 1987; Fleishman & Hempel, 1955; Jones, 1962). When tasks are more complex, there is still a pattern of declining correlations, but it is much less steep. Intelligence test performance for children older than about age 5, for example, is very stable from one occasion to the next. Test-retest correlations with a lag of less than a year for an omnibus IQ test are in the neighborhood of .90. Correlations with a lag of a long time, such as age 6 to age 18, are indeed lower ($r = .80$ or so, see Honzik, MacFarlane, & Allen, 1948), but are still substantial.

The important aspect of this general phenomenon (which is called a simplex-like effect, after Guttman, 1954; see Humphreys, 1960) is that when the correlations are low between initial task performance and performance after extensive practice, *the determinants of initial task performance cannot be the same as the determinants of final task performance*. The critical questions, from a psychometric perspective, are what are the trait predictors of initial task performance, what are the trait determinants of expert level performance, and what is the difference between the two?

From the time of Immanuel Kant (e.g., 1790/1987), philosophers and psychologists have referred to three major families of traits: cognitive, affective, and conative. Cognitive traits refer to abilities, such as intelligence, or domain-specific knowledge and skills. Affective traits refer to personality characteristics (such as impulsivity, conscientiousness, extroversion). Conative traits refer to motivation, interests, or more generally "will." In addition, there are other traits that do not fit neatly into the tripartite breakdown, such as self-concept or self-efficacy. We briefly discuss these families of traits and

their validity for predicting individual differences in expert performance, or in the development of expertise.

Cognitive Traits

Perhaps the most pervasive evidence for the validity of psychological measurements in predicting individual differences in the development of expertise is found for measures of cognitive or intellectual ability (e.g., see Jensen, 1998; Terman, 1926). Cognitive ability measures can be very general (such as IQ, or general intelligence); they can be broad (such as verbal, numerical, and spatial ability); or they can be quite specific (such as verbal fluency, computational math, or spatial visualization). From the first introduction of the modern test of intelligence (Binet & Simon, 1973), it has been clearly demonstrated that IQ measures can provide a highly reliable and highly valid indicator of academic success or failure. In fact, over the past 100 years, IQ testing is probably the single most important application of psychological research in the western world. IQ tests have the highest validity for the purpose for which they were developed – namely, prediction of academic performance of children and adolescents. They provide significant and substantial predictive validity here, but somewhat less so for predictions of adult academic and occupational performance. Narrower tests, such as verbal, numerical, and spatial-content abilities, when properly matched with the task to be predicted, can have somewhat higher validities for adults than general intelligence.

However, the general pattern found across many different investigations is that general and broad measures of cognitive/intellectual abilities are the most important predictors of performance early in training or learning. When tasks are within the capabilities of most performers, and declining interindividual variability is observed, broad ability measures tend to show lower validity for predicting performance over task practice and instruction (e.g., see Ackerman, 1988; Barrett, Alexander, & Doverspike,

1992). That is, what appears to limit performance early in task practice (i.e., for novices) are the same abilities that are tapped by broad measures of intelligence, such as memory and reasoning. Individual differences in these abilities can determine how well a learner understands what is required in the task situation, and how effective the learner is in forming strategies and plans for task accomplishment. But, as we mentioned earlier in connection with interindividual variability, a learner who quickly grasps the essence of the task has an advantage early in practice that diminishes as slower learners eventually begin to catch up over time. Skills such as driving a car provide a good example of this kind of learning situation. Some learners grasp the procedures of scanning the various instruments and operating the controls quickly, and others more slowly, but after a few months of training and practice, the role of reasoning and memory in determining individual differences in performance is substantially diminished.

There has been some evidence to suggest that when tasks are relatively simple and highly dependent on speed of perception and response coordination, there is an increase in the predictive validity of perceptual speed and psychomotor abilities for task performance as expertise is developed (e.g., see Ackerman, 1988, 1990; Ackerman & Cianciolo, 2000). That is, after extensive practice where most individuals become reasonably skilled at the task (such as driving a car or typing), performance is limited by more basic and narrow abilities (such as visual acuity and manual dexterity). Under these circumstances, the best ability predictors for individual differences in expert performance may be those measures that are associated with the limiting determinants of performance, rather than those abilities that are associated with reasoning and problem solving.

When attempting to select applicants for training or for job performance, one needs to take account of both the cognitive/intellectual ability correlations with initial task performance and the narrow ability correlations with performance after extensive practice. If training is a long, expensive process (such as training individuals to fly airplanes), it may make more sense to focus on using broad measures of cognitive/intellectual abilities for selection purposes, so as to minimize the number of trainees that wash out of a training program. If training is less involved (such as in the selection of fast-food service workers or grocery-store checkout clerks), it may be more effective for the organization to base selection on perceptual speed and psychomotor measures to maximize the number of expert performers in the long run. More elaborate selection procedures can be used, such as a "multiple-hurdle" approach. This procedure would provide tests of both cognitive and psychomotor measures, and applicants would be selected only if they pass a threshold score on both measures. Such a procedure maximizes both the likelihood of training success and the likelihood of high levels of expert job performance.

When the tasks are not within the capabilities of many performers, or the task is highly cognitively demanding even after extensive task practice, general and broad content ability measures may maintain high levels of validity for predicting individual differences in performance long after training (e.g., for a discussion and examples, see Ackerman, 1992; Ackerman, Kanfer, & Goff, 1995). Most real-world jobs that are highly cognitively demanding have substantial domain knowledge prerequisites (e.g., the jobs of air traffic controller, neurosurgeon, software developer). One aspect that differentiates these tasks from other kinds of knowledge work are the strong demands of the tasks in handling novel information. Expert performance on these tasks is thus jointly influenced by individual differences in domain knowledge and by broad intellectual abilities (both general and content abilities, such as spatial abilities for air traffic controllers).

Although domain knowledge can partly compensate for ability shortcomings when memory and reasoning abilities decline with age, world-class performance for such tasks generally remains the province of relatively younger adults (e.g., see Simonton, 1994). In contrast, for jobs that are predominantly associated with domain knowledge rather than the ability to deal with novelty, domain knowledge and skills appear to be relatively more influential than current levels of general and broad content abilities (e.g., see Chi, Glaser, & Rees, 1982). Such jobs include author, lawyer, radiologist, and so on. In such cases, the additional domain knowledge obtained through experience more than compensates for declines in general abilities with age, at least into middle age, and sometimes into early old age. Predictors of expert performance in these jobs appear to be those measures that tap the breadth and depth of relevant domain knowledge and skills (e.g., see Willingham, 1974). For a classification of job types along these lines, see Warr (1994).

In general, across both motor-dependent tasks and knowledge or cognitive tasks, the key ingredient in maximizing the correlations between predictors and criteria is the concept of Brunswik Symmetry (Wittmann & Süß, 1999) – named after Egon Brunswik's Lens Model (Brunswik, 1952). That is, the content and especially the breadth of both predictor and criterion need to match. When a criterion is relatively narrow (e.g., specific task performance or a component of task performance), the best ability predictors will be those that are matched in both content (e.g., spatial, verbal, numerical, perceptual-motor) and breadth (in this example, a relatively narrow criterion would merit development of a relatively narrow ability battery for prediction purposes). Thus, predicting the typing speed of a typist is much more likely to be better predicted from a dexterity test (narrow) than an IQ test (broad).

Affective Traits

Affective, or personality, traits represent an area of great promise for prediction of the development and expression of expertise, but this area has little substantive evidence to date. Generally speaking, one can readily predict that serious affective psychopathol-ogy (e.g., schizophrenia, endogenous depression) is negatively correlated with development of expertise (all other things being equal), *ceteris paribus*, simply because these patterns of personality are associated with the ability to manage oneself in society. It is noteworthy, though, that there are many counterexamples of experts who have had serious psychopathology (such as the Nobel Laureate mathematician, John Forbes Nash Jr., the Russian dancer Vaslav Nijinsky, Sir Isaac Newton, Robert Schumann, and many others). The unanswered, and perhaps unanswerable question, is whether these and other such individuals would have developed their respective levels of world-class expertise if they had not suffered from these affective disorders.

In the realm of normal personality traits, one of the most promising constructs for predicting expertise has been need for Achievement (nAch), proposed by Murray et al. (1938). McClelland and his colleagues (McClelland & Boyatzis, 1982; see Spangler, 1992 for a review), performed several studies that provided various degrees of validation for nAch in predicting successful performance in a variety of different occupations, but especially in the domain of managerial success. Other personality traits (e.g., openness to experience, conscientiousness, extroversion) have been moderately linked to success in several different occupations (e.g., see meta-analyses by Barrick & Mount, 1991). However, in contrast to cognitive-ability predictors of expertise, the direction and magnitude of personality trait measure correlations with success appear to be more highly dependent on the occupational context. That is, even when some ability traits are not directly relevant to a particular job or task, correlations between ability predictors and criterion performance measures are almost always positive, even if not particularly substantial. In contrast, for example, extroversion may be reliably higher among experts in jobs that require interpersonal skills and leadership (e.g., politics, senior management), but the same trait may be relatively lower for experts in domains that require intensive individual efforts (e.g., mathematician, chess player). As a result, one perhaps might not expect that there will be particular personality traits that are associated with expertise across divergent domains.

Conative Traits

Some researchers have argued that the need for achievement (nAch) falls more in the domain of conation or will instead of personality, but this issue illustrates one of the more enduring issues in the field of personality research and theory – the problem of parsing the sphere of individual traits, when they do not really exist in isolation. nAch and many other conative traits, such as vocational interests, have clear and sometimes substantial overlap with personality traits (e.g., see Ackerman & Heggestad, 1997 for a review).

In the 1950s, vocational-psychology researchers converged on a set of core interest themes on which individuals reliability differ (e.g., see Guilford et al., 1954; Holland, 1959; Roe, 1956). Perhaps the most widely adopted framework from this research has been Holland's "RIASEC" model – which is an acronym for six major vocational interest themes, namely: Realistic, Investigative, Artistic, Social, Enterprising, and Conventional (e.g., see Holland, 1997). It is possible to match these vocational interest themes with characteristics of jobs, so that individuals can be guided by vocational counselors to occupations that best match their underlying interests. It is possible that one could identify areas of expert performance within each of these different interest themes. There is a body of research that would support the notion that if individuals and jobs are matched on these themes, individuals are more likely to develop expertise (along with job satisfaction) than if there is a mismatch between the individual's interests and the job characteristics (e.g., see Dawis & Lofquist, 1984; Super, 1940). However, a match between the direction of interests and job characteristics is not in itself suffi-

cient for predicting which individuals will develop expertise.

The concept of "occupational level" (Holland, 1997), which represents how much challenge an individual desires in the task, is probably at least as important as the direction of interests is to the prediction of expertise. Occupational level is considered to represent a complex function of both an individual's abilities and his/her self-concept, which is the individual's estimation of his/her own abilities. There is probably more to this construct than self-concept and objective ability, in the sense that some individuals have both high aptitude for attaining expertise, and have high estimation of their own aptitude, but lack the motivational drive to develop expertise. Kanfer (1987) has referred to this last component as the "utility of effort," that is, the individual's desired level of effort expenditures in a work context.

SELF-CONCEPT AND SELF-EFFICACY

Self-concept is a relatively broad set of constructs that parallel abilities (e.g., general intelligence, verbal, spatial, numerical abilities, etc.). Self-efficacy refers to task-specific confidence in one's abilities to accomplish particular levels of performance (Bandura, 1977). From a Brunswik Symmetry perspective (Wittmann & Süß, 1999), predictions of expert performance from self-efficacy measures are likely to show higher criterion-related validity for performing specific tasks, mainly because of a closer match of breadth of predictor to breadth of criterion. For example, a self-efficacy measure might ask a golfer to provide a confidence estimate for making a specific putt, whereas a self-concept measure might ask the golfer to provide an estimate of his/her competence in putting, overall. There is also a motivational component to self-efficacy that entails what an individual "will do" in a task, in addition to what the individual "can do." Existing data suggest that when the task is well defined, and when individuals have some experience with a task, self-efficacy measures can provide significant predictions of expert performance (e.g., Feltz, 1982).

Communality among Predictors and Trait Complexes

In terms of assessing and predicting individual differences in expertise, we have discussed how cognitive, affective, and conative traits all appear to play a role, at least to a greater or lesser extent. We would be remiss if we did not also note that whereas many researchers have only considered one or another of these trait families in predicting expertise, there is important shared variance among these traits. In terms of predictive validity, common variance between predictors means that their effects in a regression equation are not independent, and thus the total amount of variance accounted for in the criterion measure will ordinarily be less than would be obtained by adding the contributions of each trait family. Such common variance among trait families has even more important implications for theoretical considerations of the determinants of individual differences in expertise, in the sense that synergies across trait families may help us understand why individuals are oriented more toward some domains than others, or why some individuals succeed in developing expertise, whereas others develop only moderate or poor levels of task performance.

Trait Complexes

Ackerman and Heggestad (1997) reviewed the literature on the commonalities among abilities, personality, and interests. In the context of a meta-analysis, they found that there appeared to be at least four broad constellations of traits that appeared to hang together, which they called "trait complexes" (after Snow's concept of aptitude complexes; Snow, 1989). The underlying theoretical premise regarding these trait complexes is that they may represent configurations of traits that operate synergistically, in being either facilitative or impeding of the development of domain-specific knowledge,

skills, and ultimately expert performance. The four trait complexes derived by Ackerman and Heggestad are shown in Figure 9.2, in a spatial representation that overlays ability and personality traits with Holland's hexagonal model of interests. The four trait complexes were described as follows:

> The first trait complex shows no positive communality with ability measures, and is made up of a broad "Social" trait complex. It includes Social and Enterprising interests, along with Extroversion, Social Potency, and Well-Being personality traits. The remaining trait complexes do include ability traits. A "Clerical/Conventional" trait complex includes Perceptual Speed abilities, Conventional interests, and Control, Conscientiousness, and Traditionalism personality traits. The remaining trait complexes overlap to a degree, the third trait complex "Science/Math" is not positively associated substantially with any personality traits, but includes Visual Perception and Math Reasoning Abilities, and Realistic and Investigative interests. The last trait complex, "Intellectual/Cultural" includes abilities of Gc and Ideational Fluency, personality traits of Absorption, TIE [Typical Intellectual Engagement], and Openness, as well as Artistic and Investigative interests." (Ackerman & Heggestad, 1997, p. 238)

These trait complexes lie at the heart of Ackerman's (1996) investment theory of adult intellectual development. The theory, called PPIK, for intelligence-as-Process, Personality, Interests, and intelligence-as-Knowledge, along with a set of different outcome knowledge domains is illustrated in Figure 9.3. Briefly, the theory describes how individual investments of fluid intellectual abilities (processes like memory and reasoning) are guided by trait complexes that are facilitative (e.g., science/math and intellectual/cultural) and impeding (e.g., social) constellations of personality, self-concept, and interest traits. These investments, in turn, affect both the development of domain-specific knowledge (such as science or humanities knowledge), and general crystallized abilities. In this framework,

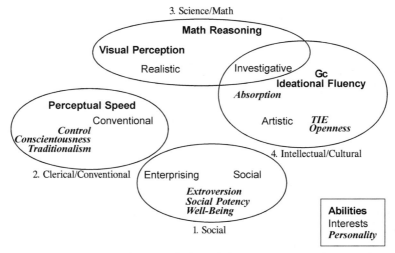

Figure 9.2. Trait complexes, including abilities, interests, and personality traits showing positive commonalities. Shown are: (1) Social, (2) Clerical/Conventional, (3) Science/Math, and (4) Intellectual/Cultural trait complexes. From Ackerman & Heggestad (1997). Copyright American Psychological Association. Reprinted by permission.

expert knowledge is obtained when there is a confluence of high intellectual abilities and high levels of affective and conative traits that are aligned with the particular knowledge domain. When abilities are moderate or low, but personality and interests are well aligned with the knowledge domain, some compensation is possible through investments of greater time and effort. However, even when suitable abilities are high for a particular domain, lower levels of matching personality and interests will likely tend to preclude development of expert levels of performance.

In several studies (e.g., Ackerman, 2000; Ackerman, Bowen, Beier, & Kanfer, 2001; Ackerman & Rolfhus, 1999) these trait complexes (and a few others) have been shown to be useful predictors of individual differences in domain knowledge among college students and middle-aged adults. Such results support the broader tenets of the PPIK investment approach, but they also show that the panoply of possible trait predictors across cognitive, affective, and conative variables could very well be reduced to a manageable set of complexes

for practical predictive purposes. Although the trait complex approach has yet to be explored in terms of predicting individual differences in expertise within a single job classification or task performance, this approach appears to have promise both for improving understanding of what factors determine ultimate expert performance achievement and for providing a small number of predictors that could be used diagnostically in expertise development contexts.

Classification Issues

One of the fields of psychometric applications that has been less explored outside of vocational counseling and large-scale selection (e.g., military placement) is the concept of "classification." Whereas occupational/educational selection starts with a larger number of applicants than positions to fill, and focuses on which candidates will be the most likely to succeed, classification starts with the assumption that most, if not all, of the applicants will be selected, and the goal is to match the applicant with the

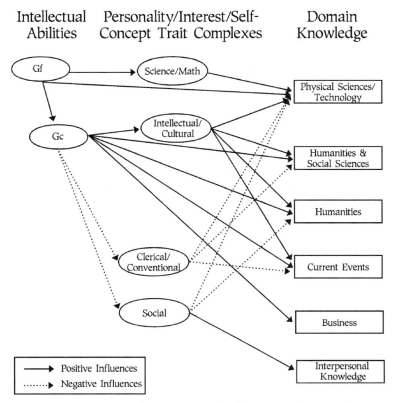

Figure 9.3. Illustration of constructs and influences in the PPIK theory (Ackerman, 1996). Gf (fluid intelligence) represents "intelligence-as-process;" Gc = crystallized intelligence. From Ackerman, Bowen, Beier, & Kanfer (2001). Copyright American Psychological Association. Reprinted by permission.

most suitable vocational/educational opportunities. Guidance counselors often try to operate in the classification context in that a major goal is to find the most suitable vocational path for each individual. From a psychometric perspective, attention is focused not specifically to *level* of ability, but rather to the pattern of strengths and weaknesses, so that the individual can effectively optimize the congruence of his/her characteristics and the *relative* demands of the occupation or educational opportunity. In this context, profiles of trait complexes have potential for predicting which educational and occupational opportunities will best match the individual's relative strengths and weaknesses.

Also, information about the individual's knowledge structures (i.e., the patterns of domain-specific knowledge and skills that the individual has) can also be used in the classification context, mainly because of the extensive body of research that has demonstrated that transfer-of-training from existing knowledge to new knowledge is more effective than novel learning. Thus, a psychometric approach to assessing the existing knowledge and skills of individuals might provide for more effective educational and vocational guidance, especially when this information is integrated with measurement of the cognitive/affective/conative trait complexes that indicate the individual's dispositions toward or away from particular domains. Ultimately, the classification goal is to maximize the *congruence* between the individual's characteristics and the characteristics of the job or educational program.

Discussion and Challenges for Future Research

In this chapter we have reviewed how psychometrics plays an important role in measuring the development of expertise and the prediction of individual differences in expert performance. Concepts of reliability and validity are central to all aspects of quantitative psychological research, but these concepts are too often implicit in experimental research, often to the detriment of the usefulness of the research. In the study of individual differences, reliability and validity are explicitly considered as integral to both theory and application. Special issues of measuring change and the problems associated with restriction of range in performance were reviewed, as these present challenges to many studies of expert performance.

Over the past century, there have been hundreds of studies that have focused on predicting individual differences in the performance of laboratory tasks, achievement in educational settings, and occupational performance. We have described only a few illustrative examples of theory and empirical results from these investigations, as they relate to cognitive, affective, and conative traits. Two general sets of findings are noted below, along with a third domain of expertise that presents both opportunities and further challenges to theory and application, as follows:

1. For tasks that require significant perceptual and motor components, most of the existing literature focuses on the effectiveness of ability predictors of individual differences in the development and expression of expert performance. General and broad cognitive abilities are most effective in predicting success with novel tasks, but perceptual and psychomotor abilities are often just as effective, if not more so, in predicting expert performance after extensive task practice. When the tasks are straightforward and accessible to most learners, cognitive abilities generally show lower predictive validity as expertise develops.

2. For tasks that are predominantly based on domain knowledge and skills, we reviewed some of the findings for various trait predictors of expertise. It appears that a heuristically useful approach to understanding and predicting individual differences in the development and expression of expertise in domain-knowledge tasks is one that focuses on the long-term investment of cognitive (intellectual) resources, through a small number of trait complexes (made up of cognitive, affective, and conative traits), leading to differences in the breadth and depth of domain knowledge and skills. Two trait complexes (science/math and intellectual/cultural) appear to be facilitative in the development of knowledge about different domains, whereas other trait complexes (e.g., Social) may impede the development of traditional domains of expert knowledge (e.g., academic and occupational knowledge).

3. In addition to these two types of expert performance, there is another one that has not received anywhere near the same level of attention – namely, expertise in interpersonal tasks. As noted by Hunt (1995), in the United States, there has been an increase in the number of jobs that are highly dependent on interpersonal skills – mostly in the service industries (e.g., child care worker, customer service representative) – an increase that has been concomitant with declines in the manufacturing and traditionally blue-collar jobs. To date, there is too little available information on even how to identify and describe expert performance in this domain. We can speculate that there are affective and conative traits that may be effective predictors of expertise in this domain. There is both historical (e.g.,

Ferguson, 1952) and current research (e.g. Barrick & Mount, 1991) that is consistent with this speculation. There is much more theory and research needed on the criterion side of the equation, along with a need for additional predictors on the cognitive/predictor side of the equation, before it will be possible to evaluate how well we can predict expertise in the interpersonal domain.

References

Ackerman, P. L. (1987). Individual differences in skill learning: An integration of psychometric and information processing perspectives. *Psychological Bulletin, 102*, 3–27.

Ackerman, P. L. (1988). Determinants of individual differences during skill acquisition: Cognitive abilities and information processing. *Journal of Experimental Psychology: General, 117*, 288–318.

Ackerman, P. L. (1990). A correlational analysis of skill specificity: Learning, abilities, and individual differences. *Journal of Experimental Psychology: Learning, Memory, and Cognition, 16*, 883–901.

Ackerman, P. L. (1992). Predicting individual differences in complex skill acquisition: Dynamics of ability determinants. *Journal of Applied Psychology, 77*, 598–614.

Ackerman, P. L. (1996). A theory of adult intellectual development: Process, personality, interests, and knowledge. *Intelligence, 22*, 229–259.

Ackerman, P. L. (2000). Domain-specific knowledge as the "dark matter" of adult intelligence: gf/gc, personality and interest correlates. *Journal of Gerontology: Psychological Sciences, 55B*, P69–P84.

Ackerman, P. L., Bowen, K. R., Beier, M. B., & Kanfer, R. (2001). Determinants of individual differences and gender differences in knowledge. *Journal of Educational Psychology, 93*, 797–825.

Ackerman, P. L., & Cianciolo, A. T. (2000). Cognitive, perceptual speed, and psychomotor determinants of individual differences during skill acquisition. *Journal of Experimental Psychology: Applied, 6*, 259–290.

Ackerman, P. L., & Heggestad, E. D. (1997). Intelligence, personality, and interests: Evidence for overlapping traits. *Psychological Bulletin, 121*, 219–245.

Ackerman, P. L., & Rolfhus, E. L. (1999). The locus of adult intelligence: Knowledge, abilities, and non-ability traits. *Psychology and Aging, 14*, 314–330.

Ackerman, P. L., & Kanfer, R. (1993). Integrating laboratory and field study for improving selection: Development of a battery for predicting air traffic controller success. *Journal of Applied Psychology, 78*, 413–432.

Ackerman, P. L., Kanfer, R., & Goff, M. (1995). Cognitive and noncognitive determinants and consequences of complex skill acquisition. *Journal of Experimental Psychology: Applied, 1*, 270–304.

Ackerman, P. L., & Woltz, D. J. (1994). Determinants of learning and performance in an associative memory/substitution task: Task constraints, individual differences, and volition. *Journal of Educational Psychology, 86*, 487–515.

Adams, J. A. (1987). Historical review and appraisal of research on the learning, retention, and transfer of human motor skills. *Psychological Bulletin, 101*, 41–74.

Bandura, A. (1977). Self-efficacy: Toward a unifying theory of behavioral change. *Psychological Review, 84*, 191–215.

Barrett, G. V., Alexander, R. A., & Doverspike, D. (1992). The implications for personnel selection of apparent declines in predictive validities over time: A critique of Hulin, Henry, and Noon. *Personnel Psychology, 45*, 601–617.

Barrick, M. R., & Mount, M. K. (1991). The Big Five personality dimensions and job performance: A meta-analysis. *Personnel Psychology, 1991, 44*, 1–26.

Binet, A., & Simon, Th. (1973). *The development of intelligence in children.* Trans. by Elizabeth Kite. New York: Arno Press.

Brunswik, E. (1952). *The conceptual framework of psychology.* Chicago: University of Chicago Press.

Chi, M. T. H., Glaser, R., & Rees, E. (1982). Expertise in problem solving. In R. J. Sternberg (Ed.), *Advances in the psychology of human intelligence* (Vol. 1, pp. 7–76). Hillsdale, NJ: Erlbaum.

Cronbach, L. J., & Furby, L. (1970). How we should measure "change" – or should we? *Psychological Bulletin, 74*, 68–80.

Dawis, R. V., & Lofquist, L. H. (1984). *A psychological theory of work adjustment: An individual differences model and its applications.* Minneapolis, MN: University of Minnesota Press.

Feltz, D. L. (1982). Path analysis of the causal elements in Bandura's theory of self-efficacy and anxiety-based model of avoidance behavior. *Journal of Personality and Social Psychology, 42(4),* 764–781.

Ferguson, L. W. (1952). A look across the years 1920 to 1950. In L. L. Thurstone (Ed.), *Applications of psychology* (pp. 1–17). New York: Harper & Brothers.

Fleishman, E. A., & Hempel, W. E., Jr. (1955). The relation between abilities and improvement with practice in a visual discrimination reaction task. *Journal of Experimental Psychology, 49,* 301–312.

Guilford, J. P., Christensen, P. R., Bond, N. A., Jr., & Sutton, M. A. (1954). A factor analysis study of human interests. *Psychological Monographs, 68,* (4, Whole No. 375).

Guttman, L. (1954). A new approach to factor analysis: The radex. In P. F. Lazarsfeld (Ed.), *Mathematical thinking in the social sciences* (pp. 258–348). Glencoe, Illinois, The Free Press.

Hoffman, R. R. (1987, Summer). The problem of extracting the knowledge of experts from the perspective of experimental psychology. *The AI Magazine, 8,* 53–67.

Holland, J. L. (1959). A theory of vocational choice. *Journal of Counseling Psychology, 6,* 35–45.

Holland, J. L. (1997). *Making vocational choices: A theory of vocational personalities and work environments (3rd Edition).* Odessa, FL: Psychological Assessment Resources.

Honzik, M. P., MacFarlane, J. W., & Allen, L. (1948). The stability of mental test performance between two and eighteen years. *Journal of Experimental Education, 17,* 309–324.

Humphreys, L. G. (1960). Investigations of the simplex. *Psychometrika, 25,* 313–323.

Hunt, E. (1995). *Will we be smart enough?: A cognitive analysis of the coming workforce.* New York: Russell Sage Foundation.

Jensen, A. R. (1998). *The g factor: The science of mental ability.* Westport, CT: Praeger.

Jones, M. B. (1962). Practice as a process of simplification. *Psychological Review, 69,* 274–294.

Kanfer, R. (1987). Task-specific motivation: An integrative approach to issues of measurement, mechanisms, processes, and determinants. *Journal of Social and Clinical Psychology, 5,* 251–278.

Kanfer, R., & Ackerman, P. L. (1989). Motivation and cognitive abilities: An integrative/aptitude-treatment interaction approach to skill acquisition. *Journal of Applied Psychology – Monograph, 74,* 657–690.

Kant, I. (1790/1987). *Critique of judgment.* Trans. by Werner S. Pluhar. Indianapolis, IN: Hackett Publishing Co.

Lohman, D. F. (1999). Minding our p's and q's: On finding relationships between learning and intelligence. In P. L. Ackerman, P. C. Kyllonen, & R. D. Roberts (Eds.), *Learning and individual differences: Process, trait, and content determinants* (pp. 55–76). Washington, DC: American Psychological Association.

McClelland, D. C., & Boyatzis, R. E. (1982). Leadership motive pattern and long-term success in management. *Journal of Applied Psychology, 67,* 737–743.

McNemar, Q. (1940). A critical examination of the University of Iowa studies of environmental influences upon the IQ. *Psychological Bulletin, 37,* 63–92.

Meehl, P. E., & Rosen, A. (1955). Antecedent probability and the efficiency of psychometric signs, patterns, or cutting scores. *Psychological Bulletin, 52,* 194–216.

Murray, H. A. et al. (1938). *Explorations in personality: A clinical and experimental study of fifty men of college age.* New York: Oxford University Press.

Roe, A. (1956). *The psychology of occupations.* New York: Wiley & Sons.

Simonton, D. K. (1994). *Greatness: Who makes history and why.* New York: Guilford Press.

Snow, R. E. (1989). Aptitude-treatment interaction as a framework for research on individual differences in learning. In P. L. Ackerman, R. J. Sternberg, & R. Glaser (Eds.), *Learning and individual differences: Advances in theory and research* (pp. 13–59). New York: W. H. Freeman.

Spangler, W. D. (1992). Validity of questionnaire and TAT measures of need of achievement: Two meta-analyses. *Psychological Bulletin, 112(1),* 140–154.

Stanovich, K. E. (1986). Matthew effects in reading. Some consequences of individual differences in the acquisition of literacy. *Reading Research Quarterly, 21,* 360–406.

Super, D. E. (1940). *Avocational interest patterns: A study in the psychology of avocations*. Stanford, CA: Stanford University Press.

Terman, L. M. (1926). *Genetic studies of genius: Mental and physical traits of a thousand gifted children*. Stanford, CA: Stanford University Press.

Thorndike, E. L. (1908). The effect of practice in the case of a purely intellectual function. *American Journal of Psychology, 19*, 374–384.

Thorndike, R. L. (1949). *Personnel selection*. New York: John Wiley & Sons.

Warr, P. (1994). Age and employment. In H. C. Triandis, M. D. Dunnette, et al. (Eds), *Handbook of industrial and organizational psychology*, Vol. 4 (pp. 485–550). Palo Alto, CA: Consulting Psychologists Press.

Watson, J. D. (2001). *The double helix: A personal account of the discovery of the structure of DNA*. New York: Simon & Schuster.

Willingham, W. W. (1974). Predicting success in graduate education. *Science, 183*, 273–278.

Wittmann, W. W., & Süß, H.-M. (1999). Investigating the paths between working memory, intelligence, knowledge, and complex problem-solving performances via Brunswik symmetry. In P. L. Ackerman, P. C. Kyllonen, & R. D. Roberts (Eds.), *Learning and individual differences: Process, trait, and content determinants* (pp. 77–108). Washington, DC: American Psychological Association.

CHAPTER 10

Laboratory Methods for Assessing Experts' and Novices' Knowledge

Michelene T. H. Chi

Introduction

Expertise, by definition, refers to the manifestation of skills and understanding resulting from the accumulation of a large body of knowledge. This implies that in order to understand how experts perform and why they are more capable than non-experts, we must understand the representation of their knowledge, that is, how their knowledge is organized or structured, and how their representations might differ from those of novices. For example, if a child who is fascinated with dinosaurs and has learned a lot about them correctly infers attributes about some dinosaurs that was new to them by reasoning analogically to some known dinosaurs (e.g., the shape of teeth for carnivores versus vegetarians), we would not conclude that the "expert" child has a more powerful analogical reasoning strategy is available to all children, but that novice children might reason analogically to some other familiar domain, such as animals

(rather than dinosaurs), as our data have shown (Chi, Hutchinson, & Robin, 1989). Thus, the analogies of domain-novice are less powerful not necessarily because they lack adequate analogical reasoning strategies, although they may, but because they lack the appropriate domain knowledge from which analogies can be drawn. Thus, in this framework, a critical locus of proficiency lies in the representation of their domain knowledge.

This chapter reviews several methods that have been used to study experts in the laboratory, with the goal of understanding how each method reveals the structure of experts' knowledge, in contrast to that of novices. The theoretical assumption is that the structure or representation of experts' knowledge is a primary determiner of how experts learn, reason, remember, and solve problems.

This chapter has three sections. It starts by briefly reviewing the historical background to studies of the experts' representations. The second section describes four general types of methods that have been commonly used to study expert knowledge. Finally, I briefly summarize what these methods can uncover about differences in the knowledge representations of experts and novices.

A Brief History on Representation in the Study of Expertise

The studies of representation in expertise have historically been intimately related to the type of problems being used. In early research on problem solving, the study of representation was carried out in the context of insight-type problems, such as Duncker's (1945) candle problem. The goal of this problem is to mount three candles at eye level on a door. Available to use for this problem are some tacks and three boxes. Participants were presented with the tacks either contained in the three boxes or outside of the boxes so that the boxes were empty. The solution requires that one re-represents the function of the boxes not as a container but as a platform that can be mounted on a wall to hold a candle. All the participants presented with the empty boxes could solve the problem, whereas less than half of the participants given the full boxes could solve it.

The key to all of these kinds of insight problems is to re-represent the problem in a way to either release a constraint that is commonly assumed, or to think of some new operator, that is again not the conventional one. So in the case of the candle problem, one could say that the conventional functional attribution that one applies to boxes is use as a container. Solving the problem requires thinking of a new function or affordance for boxes, in this case, as objects that can hold things up rather than hold certain kinds of things inside.

Although insight problems investigated the role of representation in the understanding phase of problem solving (i.e., how the elements, constraints, and operators of a problem are encoded and interpreted), insight problems did not lend themselves well to the study of expertise. That is, since expertise is defined as the accumulation of a large storehouse of domain knowledge, it is

not clear how and/or what domain knowledge influences the solution of insight problems.

A next generation of problem-solving research explored both knowledge-lean (puzzle-like) problems (such as the Tower of Hanoi) as well as knowledge-rich problems (such as in chess). Even though chess is arguably more knowledge-rich than the Tower of Hanoi problem, it shares similarities with puzzles and other "toy" domains in that the understanding phase of the representation had been assumed to be straightforward (But see Ericsson, Chapter 13, and Gobet and Charness, Chapter 30). That is, for a domain such as chess, the understanding phase of the representation needs to include the chess pieces, the permissible operators (or moves) for each kind of chess piece, and the goal state of checking and winning. In short, the understanding phase of the representation had been assumed to not clearly discriminate experts from novices.

If understanding is not the phase that affects the choice of efficient moves, then what is? One obvious answer is how effectively a solver can search for a solution. The classical contribution by Newell and Simon (1972) put forth the idea that what differentiates experts from novices is the way they search through "problem spaces." A problem space includes not only the elements, the operators, but also all the possible or permissible "states" created by the application of operators to the elements, which are entailed by the permissible strategies for guiding the search through this problem space. In this perspective, a representation is a model of the search performance of a solver on a specific problem (Newell & Simon, 1972). Thus, a "problem representation" consists of:

1. An understanding phase – the phase in which information about the initial state, the goal state, the permissible operators, and the constraints is represented (so for chess, that would be the pieces and their positions on the chess board, the moves allowed and disallowed for each kind of chess piece, etc.), and

2. A search phase – the phase in which a step-by-step search path through the problem space is represented.

Because the understanding phase had been assumed to be straightforward, differences between experts and novices are assessed via comparing differences in the search phase. A variety of different search heuristics have been identified, such as depth-first versus breadth-first searches, backward versus forward searches, exhaustive versus reduced problem-space searches, and so forth.

This view – that differences in search strategies or heuristics accounted for differences in expertise – was also applied to knowledge-rich domains for which the understanding phase may not be so straightforward. A perfect example is the work of Simon and Simon in the domain of physical mechanics. In this research, Simon and Simon (1978) compared the problem-solving skills of an expert and a novice by representing their solution paths in terms of a sequence of equations (a set of productions or condition-action rules) that they used to solve a physics problem. Based on this sequencing, the expert's representation was characterized as a forward-working search (working from initial state toward the desired end state in a series of steps), whereas the novice's representation was characterized as a backward-working search (working from the desired end state back to the initial state). Thus, the postulated representational difference between the expert and the novice was restricted to the search phase, even though the understanding phase may be a more crucial component for this knowledge-rich domain.

The revelation that search may not be the entire story came from the work of de Groot (1966). He found that world-class chess players did not access the best chess moves from an extensive search; rather, they often latched onto the best moves immediately after the initial perception of the chess positions. For example, de Groot could not find any differences in the number of moves considered, the search heuristics, or the

depth of search between masters and less-experienced (but proficient) players. What he did find was that the masters were able to reconstruct a chess position almost perfectly after viewing it for only 5 seconds. This ability could not be attributed to any superior general memory ability, for when the chess positions were "randomized," the masters performed just about as poorly as the less-experienced players. This finding suggests that the masters' superior performance with meaningful positions must have arisen from their ability to perceive structure in such positions and encode them in chunks.

The findings that chess experts can perceive coherent structures in chess positions and rapidlly come up with an excellent choice of moves suggest that the understanding phase must be more than merely the straightforward encoding of the elements and permissible operators to apply to the elements. Moreover, the application of different search heuristics cannot be the characterization that differentiates the experts from the novices in the search phase. Thus, what differentiated the experts and the novices' problem representation is determined by the representation of their domain knowledge, of chess in this case. This recognition led Chase and Simon (1973a, b) to the identification and characterization of the structures or chunks of meaningful chess patterns in memory. Thus, the work of de Groot (1966) and Chase and Simon (1973a, b) represented a first attempt at representing not just a *problem* solution, but knowledge of the *domain*. Subsequent work on expertise attempted to focus on how domain knowledge is represented in a way that leads to better solutions.

For example, we have shown that expert physicists' representation of their domain is more principle based, whereas novices' representations are more situation or formula based (Chi, Feltovich, & Glaser, 1981). Thus, the expertise work in the '80s reemphasized the understanding phase of representation, but it differed from the earlier work on insight and other knowledge-lean problems in that the focus was on the structure and organization of domain knowledge, and not merely the structure of the problem.

The next challenge for researchers is to combine the understanding phase and the search phase of a representation in order to understand how it differentiates experts from novices. In addition, new challenges are also presented when expertise is being investigated in real-world domains. Many complexities are involved when one studies expertise in real-world domains, where problems are complex and dynamic, so that the "space" is constantly changing with contextual dependencies and contingencies. In this kind of real-world scenarios, the space-search model of problem solving does not always apply as an explanatory mechanism. It is also essentially mute about problem finding, which is a main phenomenon in real-world problem-solving (see Klein, Pliske, Crandall, & Woods, 2005).

Empirical Methods to Uncover Representational Differences

The nature of expertise can be ascertained in two general ways. One way is to see how they perform in tasks that are familiar or *intrinsic* to their domain of expertise. For example, selecting the best chess move, generating the optimal blueprint, or detecting a cancerous mass on X-rays are tasks that are intrinsic to the domains of chess playing, on being an expert architect, and on being an experienced radiologist. This has been referred to as the study of performance at "familiar tasks" (Hoffman, 1987; Hoffman, Shadbolt, Burton, & Klein, 1995). Although these tasks might be abridged or in many ways adapted for empirical investigation under conditions of experimental control and the manipulation of variables, they are nevertheless more-or-less representative of what the domain experts do when they are doing their jobs.

Alternatively, one can use *contrived* tasks (Hoffman, 1987; Vicente & Wang, 1998) that are likely to be either unfamiliar to the practitioner, or that depart more radically from their familiar intrinsic tasks. Contrived tasks serve different purposes so that there is a continuum of contrived tasks, based on the degree of modifications to the familiar task in order to "bring the world into the laboratory," as it were (Hoffman et al., 1995). However, there is a set of standard tasks that are commonly undertaken in psychological laboratories, such as recall. Recall of chess positions, for example, can be considered a contrived task since chess experts' primary skill is in the selection of the best moves, not in recalling chess patterns. Although experts do recall games for a number of reasons (e.g., knowledge sharing), asking them to recall chess patterns can be thought of as a contrived task.

It is often the case that asking experts to perform in their familiar intrinsic tasks will show only that they are faster, more error free, and in general better in all ways than the novices. Their efficiency and speed can often mask how their skills are performed. Asking experts to perform contrived tasks, on the other hand, can have several advantages. First, a contrived task is often one that can be undertaken just as competently by a novice as an expert. Thus, it is not merely the completion, efficiency, or correctness of performance at a contrived task that is being evaluated, but rather, what the performance reveals about the knowledge structure of the individual, whether an expert or a novice. More importantly, a contrived task can shed light on experts' shortcomings (see Chi, Chapter 2), whereas an intrinsic task will not, by definition of expertise. A key limitation of contrived tasks, however, is that if the contrived task departs too much from the familiar task (e.g., lacks ecological validity and/or representativeness), then the model of performance that comes out may be a model of how the person adapts to the task, not a model of their expertise.

In this section, I describe four contrived tasks that have been used most extensively in laboratory studies of expertise with the goal of uncovering representational differences. The four methods are: recalling, perceiving, categorizing, and verbal reporting. Studies using these four methods are grouped on the basis of the tasks that were presented to the participants, and not the responses that they gave. For example, one could present a perceptual task and ask for verbal reports as responses. However, such a task would be classified here as a perceptual task and not a verbal reporting task. Clearly there are many combinations of methods and many optional ways to classify a task used in a specific study. The choice here reflects only the organization of the presentation in this chapter. Moreover, many studies use a combination of several methods.

RECALL

One of the most robust findings in expertise studies comes from using the method of free recall. Experts excel in recalling materials from their domain of expertise, such as better, faster, and more accurate recall, in domains ranging from static chess positions (Chase & Simon, 1973a) to dynamic computer-simulated thermal-hydraulic process plant (Vicente, 1992). The classic study by de Groot (1966) in the domain of chess involved presenting chess players with meaningful chess boards for a brief interval, such as 5 seconds, to see how many pieces they could recall by reproducing the arrangements of the pieces on a blank board. Chess masters were able to recall the positions almost perfectly (consisting of around 25 pieces). Less experienced players, on the other hand, typically recall only about 5 to 7 pieces (Chase & Simon, 1973a). However, when de Groot (1966) asked the players to find the best move, the masters and the less experienced players did not differ significantly in the number of moves they searched nor the depth of their search, even though the masters were always able to find and select the best move. Likewise, Klein, Wolf, Militello, and Zsambok (1995) found that the first move that expert chess players consider is significantly better than chance. Furthermore, chess experts do not differ from class-C players in the percentage of blunders and poor moves during regulation games, but do differ during blitz games. In fact, the experts showed very little increase in rate of blunders/poor moves from regulation to blitz, but the class-C players showed a big difference (Calderwood, Klein, & Crandall, 1988).

These findings suggest that it is not the experts' superior search strategies that helped them find the best move. Neither can the master players' superior recall be attributed to any differences in the memory capacities of the master and less experienced players, since masters can only recall a couple more pieces when the pieces are randomly placed on the chess board (Chase & Simon, 1973a).

This same pattern of results was also obtained when Go (or Gomoku) players were asked to recall briefly presented Gomoku (or Go) board patterns. Both Go and Gomoku utilize the same lattice-like board with two different colored stones, but the object of the two games is very different: In Go the goal is to surround the opponent's stone and in Gomoku it is to place five stones in a row (Eisenstadt & Kareev, 1975). The success of players in recalling board configurations suggests that it is the meaningfulness of the configurations that enables the strong players' better recall.

In order to understand how experts and novices might organize their knowledge to result in differential recall, Chase and Simon (1973a,b) incorporated two additional procedures in conjunction with their recall procedure, both aimed at segmenting the sequence in which players place the chess pieces during recall. The first procedure tape-recorded players as they reproduced chess pieces from memory and used the pauses in their placement of pieces to segment the sequence of placements. The second procedure was to modify the task from a recall to a visual memory task. In this modified visual task, players were simply asked to copy chess positions. The head turns they made to view the positions in order to reproduce the chess positions were used to segment the sequence of placements, that is, to reveal how the game arrays were "chunked." The results showed that players recalled positions in rapid bursts followed by relatively longer pauses (i.e., > 2 seconds), and they reproduced a meaningful cluster of pieces after a head turn. Because the master players recalled and reproduced a greater number of pieces before a long pause and a head turn, respectively, these two results, together, suggest that chess experts had many more recognizable configurations of chess patterns in their knowledge base, and these configurations (based on power in controlling regions of the board) were comprised of a greater number of pieces. The representational differences between the masters and less proficient players were that the masters had a greater number of recognizable patterns (or chunks) in memory, and each pattern on average contained a greater number of pieces.

More important, when memory performance was reanalyzed in terms of experts and non-expert chunks, the number of chunks recalled by experts and non-experts were now about the same, implying that their basic memory capacity is not that different after all, validating the finding of the depressed expert-recall performance for randomized board arrangements. The findings of equivalent recall for randomized positions and equivalent recall in terms of number of patterns, together, confirm that both expert and non-expert players are subject to the same short-term memory capacity limitations, but the limitation is not the point. The point is how people come to create meaningful chunks.

The recalled chess patterns (as determined by segregated pauses and head turns), when analyzed in detail, showed that they tended to consist of commonly occurring patterns that are seen in regular routine playing of chess, such as clusters in attack and defense positions. It seems obvious that such "local" patterns may be used to form representations at a higher level of familiar "global" patterns. Direct evidence of such a hierarchical representation can be seen also in the domain of architecture. Using the same recall procedure, looking at pauses, Akin (1980) uncovered a hierarchical representation of blueprints, with such things as doors and walls at the lowest level and rooms at a higher level, and clusters of room at the highest level.

The chunking of patterns into a hierarchical representation applies not only to games and architecture, but to other domains, such as circuit fault diagnosis. Egan and Schwartz (1979) found that expert circuit technicians chunk circuit elements together according to the function, such as chunking resistors and capacitors because together they perform the function of an amplifier. Here too, chunking leads to superior recall for experts as compared to non-experts. Moreover, the skilled electronic technicians' pattern recall was faster and more accurate, again suggesting that the local patterns formed higher-order patterns.

The recall superiority of experts can be captured not only in visual tasks, but also in verbal tasks. Looking at a practical domain, Morrow, Mernard, Stine-Morrow, Teller, and Bryant (2001) asked expert pilots and some non-pilots to listen to Air Traffic Control messages that described a route through an air space. Participants were then asked to read back each message and answer a probe question about the route. Expert pilots were more accurate in recalling messages and in answering the question than non-experts.

In sum, several different types of recall-related contrived tasks provide some insight into the experts' and non-experts' representation of their domain, such as patterns of familiar chunks, clusters of circuit elements with related function, and hierarchical organization of chunks.

PERCEIVING

Perception tasks address the issue of what experts versus non-experts perceive in a given amount of time (Chase & Chi, 1981). A good example of a perceptual task is examining X-ray films. Although the goal of examining X-ray films is usually to diagnose disease, one can also determine what experts and novices see (literal stimulus features) and perceive (meanings of the features or patterns of features). Lesgold et al. (1988) asked four expert radiologists with 10 or more years of experience after residency, and eight first-to-fourth year residents to examine X-ray films for as long as they wished, commenting on what they saw as well as verbally expressing their diagnoses. Although diagnosis is the familiar intrinsic task, the participants were also asked to undertake a more contrived task, which was to draw contours on the films showing what they believed to be the problematic areas, as a way of identifying the relevant features they saw. (The films showed diseases such as multiple tumors or collapsed lung.) Two of the four experts, but only one of the eight residents, diagnosed the collapsed lung film accurately. Did they see the features in the films differently? Both experts and residents saw the main feature, which was the collapse of the middle lobe, producing a dense shadow. However, this feature can lead only to a tumor diagnosis; the correct diagnosis of collapsed lung must require seeing the displaced lobe boundaries or hyperinflation of the adjacent lobes. Residents did not see the more subtle cues and the relations among the cues.

In addition to the accuracy of the diagnoses, the researchers looked at two kinds of coding of the protocols. The first coding was the diagnostic findings, which referred to the attribution of specific diagnostic properties in the film. For example, one finding might be "spots in the lungs." The second coding was the meaningful clusters. A cluster is a set of findings that had a meaningful path or reasoning chain from each finding to every other finding within the set. That is, the participants would relate the features logically to entail a diagnostic explanation. For example, if the participants commented that such spots might be produced by blood pooling, which in turn could have been produced by heart failure, then such a reasoning chain would relate the findings into a cluster. The results showed that the experts identified around three more findings per film, and had about one more cluster than the residents. This suggests that the experts not only saw more critical features on a film than the residents, but perceived more interrelations among the features.

Moreover, experts had finer discriminations. For example, the tumor film showed a patient with multiple tumors. For this tumor film, residents tended to merge local features (the tumors) as "general lung haziness." That is, they interpreted the hazy spots in the lungs as indicating fluid in the lungs, suggesting congestive heart failure, whereas experts saw multiple tumors. Residents also saw the heart as enlarged, while the experts did not. Residents also interpreted the cues or features they saw rather literally. For example, a large size heart shadow implied an enlarged heart, whereas experts might adjust their evaluation of the heart to other possibilities, such as a curvature in the spine.

The results of this study show basically that experts perceive things differently from non-experts. There are many other studies that show the same kind of results (see Klein & Hoffman, 1992). This includes the perception tasks of reproducing chess board patterns as discussed earlier. Reitman (1976) also replicated the Chase and Simon (1973a) study for the game of Go. In addition to asking participants to reproduce patterns of Go stones as quickly and accurately as possible while the stimulus board pattern remained exposed throughout the trial, she also asked the Go experts to draw circles (on paper transcriptions of the real game positions) showing stones that were related, and if appropriate, to indicate which groups of stones were related on yet a higher strategic level. The results showed that the experts partitioned the patterns not into a strictly nested hierarchy, but rather into overlapping subpatterns, as one might expect given the nature of Go – a given stone can participate in, or play a strategic role in, more than one cluster of stones. Although there were no novice data on penciled partitioning, the expert's partitioning into overlapping structures suggests this more interrelated lattice-like (versus strictly hierarchical) representation.

The perceptual superiority of experts applies to dynamic situations as well, such as perception of satellite infrared image loops in weather forecasting (Hoffman, Trafton, & Roebber, 2005), or watching a videotape of classroom lesson (Sabers, Cushing, & Berliner, 1991). For example, when expert and novice teachers were asked to talk out loud while watching a videotaped classroom lesson that showed simultaneous events occurring throughout the classroom, the experts saw more patterns by inferring what must be going on (such as "the students' note taking indicates that they have seen sheets like this . . . "), whereas the non-expert teachers saw less, saying that "I can't tell what they are doing. They are getting ready for class." In short, the explanations experts and non-experts can give reveal the features and meaningful patterns they saw and perceived.

A related task is detection of the presence of features or events accompanied by measurement of reaction times. For example, Alberdi et al. (2001) asked some more- and some less-experienced physicians to view traces on a computer screen showing five physiological measurements, such as heart rate, transcutaneous oxygen, etc. The traces represented both key events, such as developing pneumothorax, as well as more secondary but still clinically noteworthy events. Although the less-experienced physicians were almost as good in detecting and identifying the key events, they were significantly worse than the more-experienced physicians in detecting the secondary events. The more-experienced physicians were also significantly better at detecting artifacts. This suggests that they were not only better at detecting secondary events, but that they also made finer discriminations between meaningful events versus literal stimulus features.

It should perhaps be pointed out that such results do not arise from experts having better visual acuity. Nor do the results mean that the experts' perceptual superiority is necessarily visual (vs. analytical). That is, expertise involves perceiving more, not just seeing more. To deny the first interpretation, one can show that novices' visual acuity is just as good as experts in some other domain for which they have no expertise. However, expertise can enhance sensitivity to critical cues, features, and dimensions. Snowden, Davies, and Roling (2000) found expert radiologists to be more sensitive to low contrast dots and other features in X-rays. This increased sensitivity

can be driven "top down" by more developed schemas (rather than a better developed acuity) since greater experience with films means they have more familiarity with both under- and overexposed films. To disprove the second interpretation – that perceptual superiority is necessarily visual – one can show that experts can excel in perception even if the materials are not presented visually, as in the case of chess masters playing blindfolded chess (Campitelli & Gobet, 2005) and expert counselors forming an accurate model of a client from listening to a transcript of a counseling session (Mayfield, Kardash, & Kivlighan, 1999).

In sum, this section summarized perception tasks and related contrived tasks such as asking experts and novices to circle Go patterns or draw contours of X-ray films. The point of these studies is not merely to show *whether* experts are superior in performing these kinds of tasks, but to uncover their underlying representations and skills that derive from practice and perceptual learning, such as more interrelated clustering of findings on X-ray films and their representation of secondary events.

CATEGORIZING

Sorting instances according to categories is a simple and straightforward task that can be readily undertaken by experts and non-experts. One procedure is to ask participants to sort problem statements (each problem typed on a 3 × 5 card) into categories on the basis of similarities in the solution or some other functional categories. Chi et al. (1981) solicited the participation of physics graduate students (who technically would be apprentices or perhaps journeymen on the proficiency scale, but probably not fully expert) and undergraduate students (who had completed a semester of mechanics with an A grade, making them "initiates" and not really novices). They were asked to sort 24 physics problems twice (for consistency), and also to explain the reasons for their sorting. One would not necessarily expect quantitative differences in the sortings produced by the two skill groups, such as the number of groups, or the number of problems in the groups – since anyone could sort problems on any of a nearly boundless number of dimensions or criteria. The real interest lies in the nature of the sortings. Based on analyses of both the problems that the participants categorized into the same groups as well as their explanations for the sortings, it became apparent that the undergraduates grouped problems very differently from the graduate students. The undergraduates were more likely to base their sorting on literal surface features, such as the presence of inclined planes or concepts such as friction, whereas the graduate students were much more likely to base their sorting on domain principles that would be critical to the solutions (e.g., such as problems that involve Newton's Second Law or the laws of thermodynamics such as conservation of energy). This finding was further replicated by a specially designed set of problems that had either the same surface features but different deep principles, or different surface features but the same deep principles. The same results emerged, namely, that undergraduates sorted according to the surface features and graduates tended to sort according to the deep principles.

One interpretation of such results is that the undergraduates' schemas of problems are based on physical entities and literal formulas, whereas experts' schemas are more developed and organized around the principles of mechanics. This means that the explicit words or terminologies and diagrams used in the problem statements are connected (in experts' reasoning) to the basic principles. However, that connection is not necessarily direct. For instance, an inclined plane per se does not by itself indicate a Newton's-Second-Law problem for an expert physicist. An additional study asking participants to cite the most important features in a problem statement showed that the words in the problem statements are mediated by some intermediate concepts, such as a "before and after situation." Thus, the words in a problem interact to entail concepts, and experts' solutions may be based on these higher-level concepts (Chi et al, 1981; Chi & Ohlsson, 2005).

Much research followed that replicated the basic finding of shallow versus deep representations for novices versus experts. For example, when expert and novice programmers were asked to sort programming problems, the experts sorted them according to the solution algorithms, whereas the novices sorted them according to the areas of applications, such as creating a list of certain data types (Weiser & Shertz, 1983). Similarly, when expert and novice counselors were asked to categorize client statements from a counseling script as well as to map the relationships among the categories, novices tended to categorize and map on the basis of superficial details, such as the temporal order of the client statements (Mayfield et al., 1999), whereas the expert counselors tended to categorize and map on the basis of more abstract, therapeutically relevant information. Similarly, Shafto and Coley (2003) found that commercial fishermen sorted marine creatures according to commercial, ecological, or behavioral factors, whereas undergraduates sorted them according to the creatures' appearance.

Many variations of the sorting task have also been used. One variation is to ask participants to subdivide their groups further, to collapse groups, or to form multiple and differing sortings in order to shed light on the hierarchical structure of their knowledge representations (Chi, Glaser, & Rees, 1982). For example, by asking a young dinosaur "expert" to collapse his initial categories formed about different types of dinosaurs, the child would collapse them into two major superordinate categories– meat-eaters and plant-eaters (Chi & Koeske, 1983)– suggesting that the superordinate categories are somewhat well defined.

Another variation is a speeded category-verification task. In such a task, a category name appears first, followed by a picture. Participants press "true" if the picture matched the word, such as a picture of a dog with the term "animal," and "false" if it does not match, and reaction latencies can be measured. Moreover, the words can refer to a superordinate category such as "animals," a basic-object-level category such as "dog," or a subordinate category such as "dachshund." The basic-object level is normally the most accessible level for categorizing objects, naming objects, and so forth (Rosch, Mervis, Gray, Johnson, & Boyes-Braem, 1976). It has a privileged status in that it reflects the general characteristics of the human perceiver and the inherent structure of objects in the world (i.e., frequency of experience and word use). The basic-object level is also the first level of categorization for object recognition and name retrieval.

Dog experts showed the typical pattern of responses for their non-expert domain, such as birds, in that their reaction times were faster at the basic level than at the superordinate or the subordinate levels (Tanaka & Taylor, 1991; Tanaka, 2001). However, in their domain of expertise, the experts were just as fast at categorizing at the subordinate level as they are at categorizing at the basic-object level. For example, dog experts can categorize a specific dog as a dachshund as fast as they can categorize a dachshund as a dog. This downward shift in the creation of a second, more specific basic level in a hierarchy means that the experts' hierarchies are more differentiated even at the subordinate level (see also Hoffman, 1987). Moreover, this finer subordinate-level discrimination is evident even in child "experts" (Johnson & Eilers, 1998).

In sum, the categorization tasks described here, consisting of sorting and category verification, can reveal the structure of experts' knowledge, showing how it is more fully developed and differentiated at both the subordinate levels and the superordinate levels.

VERBAL REPORTING

One of the most common methods in the study of expertise is to elicit verbal reports. (It should be kept in mind that verbal reporting and introspection are different in important ways. Verbal reporting is task reflection as participants attend to problems. It is problem centered and outward looking. Introspection is to give judgments concerning one's own thoughts and perceptions.) Verbal reporting, as a category of task, can

be done either as an ongoing think-aloud protocol (Ericsson & Simon, 1984; see Ericsson, Chapter 13), as answers to interview questions (Cooke, 1994), or as explanations (Chi, 1997).

These three techniques are quite different. For concurrent think-aloud protocols, the participants are restricted to verbalize the problem information to which they are attending. In interviews, especially structured interviews, the questions are usually carefully crafted (i.e., to focus on a specific topic or scenario) and are often sequenced in a meaningful order (see Hoffman & Lintern, Chapter 12). Explanations, on the other hand, are given sometimes to questions generated by a peer, by oneself, or by an experimenter. Explanations can be retrospective and reflective. (Differences between think-aloud protocols and explanations are elaborated in Chi, 1997.) Not only are there different ways to collect verbal reports, but there are other important issues that are often debated. One issue, for example, concerns whether giving verbal reports actually changes one's processing of the task (Nisbett & Wilson, 1977), and another issue is whether different knowledge elicitation methods elicit different "kinds" of knowledge from the participants – the "differential access hypothesis" (Hoffman et al., 1995).

Not only can verbal reports be collected in several different ways, but they can be collected within the context of any number of other tasks, such as a perception task, a memory task, or a sorting task, as some of our earlier examples have shown. Thus, providing verbal reports can be a task in its own right – as in the case of a free-flowing, unstructured interview (Cullen & Bryman, 1988), or simply asking the participant to say what he or she knows about a concept (Chi & Koeske, 1983). But a verbal protocol can also be solicited in the context of some other task (such as solving problems or analyzing documents). However, to be consistent with the heuristic of this chapter, the studies below are grouped in this section according to the main task presented to the participants. In this regard it is worth noting that in some domains, giving a concurrent or retrospective verbal report is part of the familiar intrinsic task (e.g., coroner's audio record during autopsies; and during weather forecasting briefings, forecasters think aloud as they examine weather data).

The most difficult aspect of verbal report methods is data analysis. That is, how does one code and analyze verbal outputs? Again there are many methods; they can only be alluded to here (see Chi, 1997; Ericsson & Simon, 1984, for explicit techniques, and Ericsson, Chapter 13). Typically, think-aloud protocols are analyzed in the context of the cognitive task, which requires a cognitive task analysis in order to know the functional problem states that are to be used to categorize individual statements. The goal of protocol analysis then is to identify which sequence of states a particular participant progresses through, and perhaps a computational model is built to simulate those steps and the solution procedures. For explanations, coding methods involve segmenting and judging the content of the segments in terms of issues such as whether it is substantive or non-substantive (Chi, Siler, Jeong, Yamauchi, & Hausmann, 2001), principle oriented (deep) or entity oriented (shallow) (Chi et al., 1981). Note that an analysis of verbal data means that the content of the data is not always taken literally or word-for-word. That is, we are not asking experts and novices their subjective assessment of how they performed, or how they have performed. This is because much of expert knowledge is not explicit nor subject to introspection.

How people perform can be captured by the coding scheme. A study by Simon and Simon (1978) provides a good example. They collected concurrent protocols from an expert and a novice as they were solving physics problems. The researchers coded only the equation-related parts of the protocols. By examining what equations were articulated, and when, the researchers were able to model (using a production-system framework) each participant's problem-solving procedure and strategy. The researchers showed that the expert solved the problems in a forward-working strategy, whereas the novice worked back-

ward from the goal (as one would predict on the basis of studies described earlier in this chapter). The same forward-backward search patterns were obtained also in the domain of genetics with experts and novices (Smith & Good, 1984).

In a different kind of domain and task, Wineburg (1991) asked historians and history students to give think-aloud protocols while they constructed understanding of historical events from eight written and three pictorial documents. The participants' task was to decide which of the three pictures best depicted what happened during the Battle of Lexington at the start of the Revolutionary War, the event presented in the documents. Statements in the participants' picture-evaluation protocols were coded into four categories: description, reference, analysis, and qualification. Both experts and students provided descriptive statements, but the experts made more statements that fell into the other three categories. This is not surprising since the experts obviously had more to say, being more knowledgeable. What is more interesting is to identify the first category for which both the experts and novices described the picture using the same number of statements. The quality of those descriptions was different. Historians noted 25 of the 56 possible key features in the paintings that had a bearing on the historical accuracy of the paintings, whereas the students noted only four features on average. Moreover, in selecting the most accurate painting, historians did so on the basis of the correspondence between the visual representations and the written documents, whereas the students often chose on the basis of the quality of the artwork, such as its realism and detail. This suggests that the experts' representations were much more meaningfully integrated.

Interviewing techniques can include both open-ended questions and more direct questions. For example, Hmelo-Silver and Pfeffer (2004) asked experts and students both direct questions about aquaria, such as *"What do fish do in an aquarium?"* and open-ended questions, such as thinking out loud while attempting to *"Draw a picture of anything you can think is in an aquarium.*" Since biological systems and devices often can be characterized by their structure, behavior, or function (Gellert, 1962; Chi, 2000, p. 183; Goel et al., 1996), the protocols were coded according to statements relating to those three categories. There were no differences between the experts and the novices in the number of statements referring to the structures, but there were predictable and significant differences in the number of statements referring to behaviors and functions. The novices often did not offer additional behavioral or functional information even when probed. This suggests that the experts represent the deeper features (i.e., behavior and function), whereas novices think in terms of literal features (i.e., the structure).

In sum, the goal of these verbal reporting methods is to capture the underlying representations of the experts and novices, such as whether their searches are forward versus backward, whether their understanding of pictures and text are integrated versus literal, or whether their understanding manifest deep (behavioral and functional) versus shallow (structural) features.

Representational Differences

If the difference in representation (reflecting the organization of knowledge and not just the extent of knowledge) is one key to understanding the nature of expertise, then in what ways do the representations of experts and novices differ? In this section, I briefly address dimensions of representational differences, as captured by the empirical tasks of recalling, perceiving, categorizing, and verbal reporting described above. Each of these tasks has revealed ways in which representations of experts and novices differ.

KNOWLEDGE EXTENT

An obvious dimension of difference is that experts have more knowledge of their domain of expertise. More knowledge must be measured in terms of some units. Without being precise, a "bit" of knowledge can be a factual statement, a chunk/familiar pattern, a strategy, a procedure, or a schema. Chase and Simon (1973a, b) estimated an expert chess (master-level) player to know between 10,000 and 100,000 chunks or patterns, whereas a good (Class-A) player has around 1000 chunks; and Miller (1996, pp. 136–138) estimated college-educated adults to know between 40,000 to 60,000 words. Hoffman et al., (in press; Hoffman, Trafton, & Roebber, 2006) estimate that it would take thousands of propositions to capture the expert weather forecaster's knowledge just about severe weather in one particular climate. Regardless of how one wishes to quantify it, clearly, one can expect experts to know more than non-experts (including journeymen and especially compared to apprentices, initiates, and novices). Indeed, this is one definition of expertise. The recall task summarized earlier also revealed how the number of chunks and the chunk sizes differ for experts versus non-experts.

Aside from the sheer number of "bits" (however these are defined) in their knowledge base, a related concept to the dimension of size is *completeness*. Completeness has a different connotation than the idea of merely greater amount or extent of knowledge. In real-world domains knowledge is always expanding. Any notion of "completeness" becomes very slippery.

In terms of frame theory, one can conceive of completeness in terms of the availability or number of slots, or necessary slots. For example, a tree expert might have slots for "susceptibility to different diseases" with knowledge about potential diseases (values) for each kind of trees, whereas a novice might not have such slots at all. The earlier-described finding from a perception task showed that the more- (but not the less-) experienced physicians were able to recognize secondary events on traces of physiological measurements (Alberdi et al., 2001), can be interpreted to indicate that the more-experienced physicians had more complete frames or schemas. Greater amount of knowledge might also refer to more details in the experts' representation than in novices', for a particular domain.

Another way to discuss knowledge extent is in terms of the *content*. Experts might not have just more production systems than non-experts for solving problems, but they might have different production systems, as shown by Simon and Simon's (1978) study of physicists using a verbal-reporting task. For example, experts might have rules relevant to the principles, whereas novices might have rules relevant to the concrete entities in the problem statement (Chi et al., 1981). This can mean that the experts' production systems are deeper and more generalizable.

In sum, differences in the size or extent of the knowledge as a function of proficiency level can be uncovered in a number of contrived tasks that have been discussed in this chapter.

THE ORGANIZATION OF KNOWLEDGE

The hierarchical representation of knowledge can be inferred from the way experts cluster in their recall, as in the case of recalling architectural plans (Akin, 1980) and circuit diagrams (Egan & Schwartz, 1979). If we therefore assume that representations are sometimes hierarchical (depending on the domain), then in what further ways are the experts' representations different from novices?

One view is that non-experts might have missing intermediate levels. For example, using a recall task, Chiesi, Spilich, and Voss (1979) found that individuals with high or low prior knowledge of baseball were equally capable at recalling individual sentences that they had read in a baseball passage. However, the experts were better at recalling sequences of baseball events because they were able to relate each sequence to the high-level goals such as winning and scoring runs. This suggests that the basic actions described in the individual sentences were not connected to the high-level goals in the novices' understanding. Perhaps such connections have to be mediated by intermediate goals, which may be missing in novices' hierarchical structure. The same pattern of results was found in chil-

dren's representation of knowledge about "Star Wars." The "Star Wars" game can be represented in a hierarchical structure, containing high-level goals such as military dominance, subgoals such as attack/destroy key leaders, and basic actions, such as going to Yoda (Means & Voss, 1985).

Similar findings have been obtained also in studies of medical domains, in which physician's diagnostic knowledge has been represented in terms of hierarchical levels (Patel & Arocha, 2001). In such a representation, studies using a perception task show that physical observations are interpreted in terms of *findings*, which are observations that have medical significance and must be clinically accounted for. At the next level are *facts*, which are clusters of findings that suggest prediagnostic interpretation. At the highest level are *diagnoses*. Novices' and experts' representation can differ in that novices can be missing some intermediate-level knowledge, so that decisions are then made on the basis of the *findings* level, rather than the *facts* level.

A third way to conceive of differences in hierarchical representations of experts and novices is a in the level of the hierarchy that is most familiar or preferred for domains in which the hierarchical relationships is one of class-inclusion. Expert versus non-expert differences arise from the preferred level within the hierarchy at which experts and novices operate or act on. According to Rosch et al. (1976), to identify objects, people in general prefer to use basic-object-level names (bird, table) to superordinate-level names (e.g., animals, furniture). People are also generally faster at categorizing objects at the basic-object level than at the superordinate or subordinate levels (e.g., robin, office chair). Experts, however, are just as facile at naming and verifying the subordinate-level objects as the basic-level, suggesting that the overall preferential treatment of the basic level reflects how knowledge about the levels are structured, and not that the basic level imposes a certain structure that is more naturally perceived. Using a sorting task, this differentiated preference for experts and novices has been replicated in several domains, such as birds (Tanaka & Taylor, 1991), faces (Tanaka, 2001), dinosaurs (Chi et al., 1989), and geological and archaeological classification (Burton et al., 1987, 1988, 1990).

Just as the notion of knowledge extent can be slippery (because knowledge is never static), so too the notion of hierarchical memory organization can be slippery. For example, instead of conceiving of non-experts' memory representation as missing the intermediate levels, another view is that their representations are more like lattices than hierarchies (Chi & Ohlsson, 2005). (Technically, a lattice would involve cross connections that would be "category violations" in a strict hierarchy or "is-a" tree.) It is valuable to look at an extreme, that is, domains where everything can be causally related to everything else, and neither hierarchies, lattices, nor chains suffice to represent either the world or knowledge of the world, such as the weather forecaster's understanding of atmospheric dynamics (e.g., thunderstorms cause outflow, which in turn can trigger more thunderstorms). We do not yet have a clear understanding of how dynamic systems are represented (Chi, 2005). On the other hand, for a domain such as terrain analysis in civil engineering, much of the expert's knowledge is very much like a hierarchy, highly differentiated by rock types, subtypes, combinations of layers of subtypes, types of soils, soil-climate interactions, etc. (Hoffman, 1987).

In sum, although any inferences about knowledge representation need to be anchored in the context of a specific domain, contrived tasks such as recalling, perceiving, and categorizing can allow us to differentiate the ways experts' and novices' knowledge is organized.

"DEPTH" OF KNOWLEDGE

Representational differences can be characterized not only by extent and organization, but also by dimensions such as deep versus shallow, abstract versus concrete, function versus structure, or goal-directed versus taxonomic. Such differences have been revealed using a sorting task, to show, for example, that physicists represent

problems at the level of principles, whereas novices represent them at the concrete level of entities or superficial features (Chi et al., 1981), or that landscaping experts sort trees into goal-derived categories (e.g., shade trees, fast-growing trees, etc.), whereas taxonomists sort trees according to biological taxa (Medin, Lynch, Coley, & Atran, 1997).

Such differences can be revealed also in perception tasks. For example, a patient putting his hands on his chest and leaning forward as he walks slowly is interpreted by novices merely as someone having back pain (a literal interpretation), whereas a more expert physician might interpret the same observation as perhaps suggesting that the patient has some unspecified heart problem (Patel & Arocha, 2001). Differences can also be revealed in a verbal reporting task, such as explaining the behavior/function of fish in an aquarium versus explaining the structure of fish (Hmelo-Silver & Pfeffer, 2004). Differences can be revealed in a task that involves explaining causal relationships – a novice's explanations might focus on the time and place of an historical event, whereas an expert's explanations might focus on using the time to reconstruct other events (Wineburg, 1991).

In short, all four of the task types reviewed here can reveal differences between experts' and novices' representations in terms of depth.

CONSOLIDATION AND INTEGRATION

A fourth dimension of representational differences between experts and non-experts is that the experts' representation may be more *consolidated*, involving more efficient and faster retrieval and processing. A related way to characterize it might be the integratedness or coherence of a representation, that is, the degree to which concepts and principles are related to one another in many meaningful ways (e.g., Falkenhainer, Forbus, & Gentner, 1990; Schvaneveldt et al., 1985). One interpretation of integratedness is the interaction of features. Evidence for this interpretation can be seen in physics experts' and non-experts' representations (Chi et al., 1981), in which they identify features that are combined or integrated to form higher-level concepts in a sorting task, as well as in physicians' ability to form clusters of observations for their prediagnostic interpretation in a perception task (Patel & Arocha, 2001).

For example, given a physics problem statement and asked to identify the features that determine their basic approach to the solution, novices will solve a problem on the basis of the explicit concrete entities mentioned in the statement, whereas experts will solve a problem on the basis of derivative features (such as a "before and after" situation), in which the interactions of the concrete entities in the problem statement are integrated to describe the problem situation as "before and after" (see Chi et al., 1981, Table 11). Tabulating the frequencies with which the two experts and novices cited concrete entities (such as spring, friction) versus higher-level dynamic features (such as a "before and after" situation, or a physical state change), there were 74 instances in which the experts cited dynamic features versus 21 references to concrete entities, whereas the reverse was true for novices, who cited 39 instances of concrete entities versus only two instances of dynamic features. The more integrated nature of the experts' knowledge base was also reflected in the reasoning chains that expert radiologists manifested in their diagnoses, cited earlier (Lesgold et al., 1988).

In short, recall, perception, and categorization tasks can all reveal differences in the consolidation and integration of representations.

Conclusion

The goal of this chapter was to describe and illustrate the kind of laboratory methods that can be used to study the nature of expertise. The four general types reviewed – recall, perception, categorization, and verbal reports – are domain independent, or contrived tasks. These are tasks that are not necessarily expressive of the skills of the experts because they do not precisely mimic the tasks the experts usually perform. But these tasks, used often in the laboratories or

under controlled conditions (although they can be used also in cognitive field research), are suggestive of the ways that the mental representations of experts and novices can differ. The recall paradigm has revealed the differences in experts' and novices' representations in terms of chunks (coherent patterns) and organized structure; perception tasks have revealed phenomena of perceptual learning and differences in the salience of relevant features and the interrelatedness or integration of cues into meaningful patterns; and both the sorting and verbal reporting tasks have revealed differences in the depth and structure of knowledge representations.

There are of course important deeper and lingering issues that this chapter has not covered. A key issue is how exactly do the experts' knowledge representations facilitate or inhibit their performance for a specific skill. Some treatment of this issue just for the task of memory recall can be gleaned from papers by Ericsson, Delaney, Weaver, and Mahadevan (2004) and Vicente and Wang (1998). Moreover, although our interest focuses on understanding "relative expertise" (see Chi, Chapter 2), with the assumption that novices can become experts through learning and practice, in this chapter I have said little about another important issue of *how* one can translate differences in the representations of novices and experts into instruction and training (i.e., how we can train novices to become experts).

Acknowledgement

The author is grateful for the support provided by the Pittsburgh Science of Learning Center.

References

Akin, O. (1980). *Models of architectural knowledge.* London: Pion.

Alberdi, E., Becher, J. C., Gilhooly, K., Hunter, J., Logie, R., Lyon, A., McIntosh, N., & Reiss, J. (2001). Expertise and the interpretation of computerized physiological data: Implications for the design of computerized monitoring in neonatal intensive care. *International Journal of Human-Computer Studies, 55*, 191–216.

Burton, A. M., Shadbolt, N. R., Hedgecock, A. P., & Rugg, G. (1987). A formal evaluation of knowledge elicitation techniques for expert systems: Domain 1. In D. S. Moralee (Ed.), *Research and development in expert systems, Vol. 4.* (pp. 35–46). Cambridge: Cambridge University Press.

Burton, A. M., Shadbolt, N. R., Rugg, G., & Hedgecock, A. P. (1988). Knowledge elicitation techniques in classification domains. In Y. Kodratoff (Ed.), *ECAI-88: Proceedings of the 8th European Conference on Artificial Intelligence* (pp. 85–93). London: Pittman.

Burton, A. M., Shadbolt, N. R., Rugg, G., & Hedgecock, A. P. (1990). The efficacy of knowledge elicitation techniques: A comparison across domains and levels of expertise. *Journal of Knowledge Acquisition, 2*, 167–178.

Calderwood, R., Klein, G. A., & Crandall, B. W. (1988). Time pressure, skill, and move quality in chess. *American Journal of Psychology, 101*, 481–493.

Campitelli, G., & Gobet, F. (2005). The mind's eye in blindfold chess. *European Journal of Cognitive Psychology, 17*, 23–45.

Chase, W. G., & Chi, M. T. H. (1981). Cognitive skill: Implications for spatial skill in large-scale environments. In J. Harvey (Ed.), *Cognition, social behaviors, and the environment* (pp. 111–136). Hillsdale, NJ: Erlbaum.

Chase, W. G., & Simon, H. A. (1973a). Perception in chess. *Cognitive Psychology, 4*, 55–81.

Chase, W. G., & Simon, H. A. (1973b). The mind's eye in chess. In W. G. Chase (Ed.), *Visual information processing* (pp. 215–281). New York: Academic Press.

Chi, M. T. H. (1997). Quantifying qualitative analyses of verbal data: A practical guide. *Journal of the Learning Sciences, 6*, 271–315.

Chi, M. T. H. (2000). Self-explaining expository texts: The dual processes of generating inferences and repairing mental models. In R. Glaser (Ed.), *Advances in instructional psychology* (pp. 161–238). Hillsdale, NJ: Erlbaum.

Chi, M. T. H. (2005). Common sense conceptions of emergent processes: Why some misconceptions are robust. *Journal of the Learning Sciences, 14*, 161–199.

Chi, M. T. H., Feltovich, P., & Glaser, R. (1981). Categorization and representation of physics problems by experts and novices. *Cognitive Science, 5*, 121–152.

Chi, M. T. H., Glaser, R., & Rees, E. (1982). Expertise in problem solving. In R. J. Sternberg (Ed.), *Advances in the psychology of human intelligence, Vol. 1* (pp. 7–75). Hillsdale, NJ: Erlbaum.

Chi, M. T. H., Hutchinson, J., & Robin, A. F. (1989). How inferences about novel domain-related concepts can be constrained by structured knowledge. *Merrill-Palmer Quarterly, 35*, 27–62.

Chi, M. T. H., & Koeske, R. (1983). Network representation of a child's dinosaur knowledge. *Developmental Psychology, 19*, 29–39.

Chi, M. T. H., & Ohlsson, S. (2005). Complex declarative learning. In K. J. Holyoak, & R. G. Morrison, (Eds.), *The Cambridge handbook of thinking and reasoning* (pp. 371–399). Cambridge: Cambridge University Press.

Chi, M. T. H., Siler, S. A., Jeong, H., Yamauchi, T., & Hausmann, R. G. (2001). Learning from human tutoring. *Cognitive Science, 25*, 471–533.

Chiesi, H. L, Spilich, G. J., & Voss, J. F. (1979). Acquisition of domain-related information in relation to high and low domain knowledge. *Journal of Verbal Learning and Verbal Behavior, 18*, 257–273.

Cooke, N. J. (1994). Varieties of knowledge elicitation techniques. *International Journal of Human-Computer Studies, 41*, 801–849.

Cullen, J., & Bryman, A. (1988). The knowledge acquisition bottleneck: A time for reassessment? *Expert Systems, 5*, 216–225.

De Groot, A. (1966). Perception and memory versus thought: Some old ideas and recent findings. In B. Kleinmuntz (Ed.), *Problem solving: Research, method, and theory* (pp. 19–50). New York: Wiley.

Duncker, K. (1945). On problem-solving. (L. S. Lees, Trans.). *Psychological monographs, 58* (Whole No. 270). (Original work published, 1935.)

Egan, D. E., & Schwartz, B. J. (1979). Chunking in recall of symbolic drawings. *Memory & Cognition, 7*, 149–158.

Eisenstadt, M., & Kareev, Y. (1975). Aspects of human problem solving: The use of internal representations. In D. A. Norman & D. E. Rumelhart (Eds.), *Exploration in cognition* (pp. 308–346). San Francisco: Freeman.

Ericsson, K. A., Delaney, P. F., Weaver, G., & Mahadevan, R. (2004). Uncovering the structure of a memorist's superior "basic" memory capacity. *Cognitive Psychology, 49*, 191–237.

Ericsson, K. A., & Simon, H. A. (1984). *Protocol analysis*. Cambridge, MA: MIT Press.

Falkenhainer, B., Forbus, K. D., & Gentner, D. (1990). The structure-mapping engine: Algorithm and examples. *Artificial Intelligence, 41*, 1–63.

Gellert, E. (1962). Children's conception of the structure and function of the human body. *Genetic Psychology Monographs, 65*, 193–405.

Goel, A. K., Gomez de Silva Garza, A., Grue, N., Murdock, J. W., Recker, M. M., & Govinderaj, T. (1996). Towards designing learning environments. In C. Frasson, G. Gauthier, & A. Lesgold (Ed.), *Intelligent tutoring systems: Lecture notes in computer science* (pp. 493–501). Berlin: Springer-Verlag.

Hmelo-Silver, C. E., & Pfeffer, M. G. (2004). Comparing expert and novice understanding of a complex system from the perspective of structures, behaviors, and function. *Cognitive Science, 28*, 127–138.

Hoffman, R. R. (1987, Summer). The problem of extracting the knowledge of experts from the perspective of experimental psychology. *The AI Magazine, 8*, 53–67.

Hoffman, R. R., Coffey, J. W., Ford, K. M., & Novak, J. D. (in press). A method for eliciting, preserving, and sharing the knowledge of expert forecasters. *Weather & Forecasting*.

Hoffman, R. R., Shadbolt, N. R., Burton, A. M., & Klein, G. (1995). Eliciting knowledge from experts: A methodological analysis. *Organizational Behavior and Human Decision Processes, 62*, 129–158.

Hoffman, R. R., Trafton, G., & Roebber, P. (2006). *Minding the weather: How expert forecasters think*. Cambridge, MA: MIT Press.

Johnson, K., & Eilers, A. T. (1998). Effects of knowledge and development on subordinate level categorization. *Cognitive Development, 13*, 515–545.

Klein, G., Pliske, R. M., Crandall, B., & Woods, D. (2005). Problem detection. *Cognition, Technology, and Work, 7*, 14–28.

Klein, G. A., & Hoffman, R. R. (1992). Seeing the invisible: Perceptual-cognitive aspects of expertise. In M. Rabinowitz (Ed.), *Cognitive science foundations of instruction* (pp. 203–226). Mahwah, NJ: Erlbaum.

Klein, G., Wolf, S., Militello, L., & Zsambok, C. (1995). Characteristics of skilled option generation in chess. *Organizational Behavior and Human Decision Processes, 62*, 63–69.

Lesgold, A., Rubinson, H., Feltovich, P., Glaser, R., Klopfer, D., & Wang, Y. (1988). Expertise in a complex skill: Diagnosing X-ray pictures. In M. Chi, R. Glaser, & M. Farr (Eds.), *The nature of expertise* (pp. 311–342). Hillsdale, NJ: Erlbaum.

Mayfield, W. A., Kardash, C. M., & Kivlighan, D. M. (1999). Differences in experienced and novice counselors' knowledge structures about clients: Implications for case conceptualization. *Journal of Counseling Psychology, 46*, 504–514.

Means, M. L., & Voss, J. F. (1985). Star Wars: A developmental study of expert and novice knowledge structures. *Journal of Memory and Language, 24*, 746–757.

Medin, D. L., Lynch, E. B., Coley, J. D., & Atran, S. (1997). Categorization and reasoning among tree experts: Do all roads lead to Rome? *Cognitive Psychology, 32*, 49–96.

Miller, G. A. (1996). *The science of words*. New York: McGraw-Hill.

Morrow, D. G., Menard, W. E., Stine-Morrow, E. A. L., Teller, T., & Bryant, D. (2001). The influence of expertise and task factors on age differences in pilot communication. *Psychology & Aging, 16*, 31–46.

Newell, A., & Simon, H. A. (1972). *Human problem solving*. Englewood Cliffs, NJ: Prentice-Hall.

Nisbett, R. E., & Wilson, T. D. (1977). Telling more than we can know: Verbal reports on mental processes. *Psychological Review, 84*, 231–259.

Patel, V. L., & Arocha, J. F. (2001). The nature of constraints on collaborative decision-making in health care settings. In E. Salas, & G. A. Klein (Eds.), *Linking expertise and naturalistic decision making* (pp. 383–405). Mahwah, NJ: Erlbaum.

Reitman, J. S. (1976). Skilled perception in Go: Deducing memory structures from interresponse times. *Cognitive Psychology, 8*, 336–356.

Rosch, E., Mervis, C. B., Gray, W. D., Johnson, D. M., & Boyes-Braem, P. (1976). Basic objects in natural categories. *Cognitive Psychology, 8*, 382–439.

Sabers, D. S., Cushing, K. S., & Berliner, D. C. (1991). Differences among teachers in a task characterized by simultaneity, multidimensionality, and immediacy. *American Educational Research Journal*, 28, 63–88.

Schvaneveldt, R. W., Durso, F. T., Goldsmith, T. E., Breen, T. J., Cooke, N. M., Tucker, R. G., & DeMaio, J. C. (1985). Measuring the structure of expertise. *International Journal of Man-Machine Studies*, 23, 699–728.

Shafto, P., & Coley, J. D. (2003). Development of categorization and reasoning in natural world: Novices to experts, naïve similarity to ecological knowledge. *Journal of Experimental Psychology: Learning, Memory, and Cognition*, 29, 641–649.

Simon, D. P., & Simon, H. A. (1978). Individual differences in solving physics problems. In R. Siegler (Ed.), *Children's thinking: What develops?* (pp. 325–348). Hillsdale, NJ: Erlbaum.

Smith, M. U., & Good, R. (1984). Problem solving and classical genetics: Successful versus unsuccessful performance. *Journal of Research in Science Teaching*, 21, 895–912.

Snowden, P. T., Davies, I. R. L., & Roling, P. (2000). Perceptual learning of the detection of features in X-ray images: A functional role for improvements in adults' visual sensitivity? *Journal of Experimental Psychology: Human Perception and Performance*, 26, 379–390.

Tanaka, J. W. (2001). The entry point of face recognition: Evidence for face expertise. *Journal of Experimental Psychology: General*, 130, 534–543.

Tanaka, J. W., & Taylor, M. (1991). Object categories and expertise: Is the basic level in the eye of the beholder? *Cognitive Psychology*, 23, 457–482.

Vicente, K. J. (1992). Memory recall in a process control system: A measure of expertise and display effectiveness. *Memory and Cognition*, 20, 356–373.

Vicente, K. J., & Wang, J. H. (1998). An ecological theory of expertise effects in memory recall. *Psychological Review*, 105, 33–57.

Weiser, M., & Shertz, J. (1983). Programming problem representation in novice and expert programmers. *International Journal of Man-Machine Studies*, 14, 391–396.

Wineburg, S. S. (1991). Historical problem solving: A study of the cognitive processes used in the evaluation of documentary and pictorial evidence. *Journal of Educational Psychology*, 83, 73–87.

CHAPTER 11

Task Analysis

Jan Maarten Schraagen

Introduction

Analyses of tasks may be undertaken for a wide variety of purposes, including the design of computer systems to support human work, the development of training, the allocation of tasks to humans or machines, or the development of tests to certify job competence. Task analysis is, therefore, primarily an applied activity within such diverse fields as human factors, human–computer interaction, instructional design, team design, and cognitive systems engineering. Among its many applications is the study of the work of expert domain practitioners.

"Task analysis" may be defined as what a person is required to do, in terms of actions and/or cognitive processes, to achieve a system goal (cf. Kirwan & Ainsworth, 1992, p. 1). A more recent definition, which at first sight has the merit of being short and crisp, is offered by Diaper (2004, p. 15): "Task analysis is the study of how work is achieved by tasks." Both definitions are deceptively simple. They do, however, raise further issues, such as what a "system" is, or a "goal," or

"work," or "task." Complicating matters further, notions and assumptions have changed over time and have varied across nations. It is not my intention in this chapter to provide a complete historical overview of the various definitions that have been given for task analysis. The reader is referred to Diaper and Stanton (2004), Hollnagel (2003), Kirwan and Ainsworth (1992), Militello and Hoffman (2006), Nemeth (2004), Schraagen, Chipman, and Shalin (2000), and Shepherd (2001).

It is important, however, in order to grasp the subtle differences in task-analytic approaches that exist, to have some historical background, at least in terms of the broad intellectual streams of thought. Given the focus of this handbook, this historical overview will be slightly biased toward task analysis focused on professional practitioners, or experts. After the historical overview, the reader should be in a better position to grasp the complexities of the seemingly simple definitions provided above. Next, I will focus on some case studies of task analysis with experts. This should give the reader an understanding of how particular methods were applied, why they were applied, and what their strengths and weaknesses were. As the field is evolving constantly, I will end with a discussion of some open avenues for further work.

Historical Overview

Task analysis is an activity that has always been carried out more by applied researchers than by academic researchers. Academic psychology often involves research in which the experimenters create the tasks. Conversely, applied researchers look into their world to investigate the tasks that people perform in their jobs. Indeed, task analysis originated in the work of the very first industrial psychologists, including Wundt's student Hugo Münsterberg (see Hoffman & Deffenbacher, 1992). For instance, early research conducted by the so-called "psychotechnicians" (Münsterberg, 1914) involved studies of the tasks of railway motormen, and for that research, one of the very first simulators was created.

The applied focus and origins may be because the ultimate goal of task analysis is to improve something – be it selection, training, or organizational design. Given the applied nature of task analysis, one may hypothesize that there is a close connection between the focus of task analysis and current technological, economical, political, and cultural developments. One fairly common characterization of the past 100 years is the following breakdown in three periods (Freeman & Louçã, 2001; Perez, 2002):

1. The age of steel, electricity, and heavy engineering. Leading branches of the economy are electrical equipment, heavy engineering, heavy chemicals, and steel products. Railways, ships, and the telephone constitute the transport and communication infrastructure. Machines are manually controlled. This period, during which industrial psychology emerged (e.g., Viteles, 1932), lasted from approximately 1895–1940.

2. The age of oil, automobiles, and mass production. Oil and gas allow massive motorization of transport, civil economy, and war. Leading branches of the economy are automobiles, aircraft, refineries, trucks, and tanks. Radio, motorways, airports, and airlines constitute the transport and communication infrastructure. A new mode of control emerged: supervisory control, characterized by monitoring displays that show the status of the machine being controlled. The "upswing" in this period lasted from 1941 until 1973 (Oil Crisis). The "downswing" of this era is still continuing.

3. The age of information and telecommunications. Computers, software, telecommunication equipment, and biotechnology are the leading branches of the economy. The internet has become the major communication infrastructure. Equipment is "cognitively" controlled, in the sense that users need to draw on extensive knowledge of the environment and the equipment. Automation gradually takes on the form of intelligent cooperation. This period started around 1970 with the emergence of "cognitive engineering," and still continues.

Each of these periods has witnessed its typical task-analysis methods, geared toward the technology that was dominant during that period. In the historical overview that follows, I will use the breakdown into three periods discussed above.

The Age of Steel

Around 1900, Frederick Winslow Taylor observed that many industrial organizations were less profitable than they could be because of a persistent phenomenon that he termed "soldiering," that is, deliberately working slowly (Taylor, 1911/1998). Workers in those days were not rewarded for working faster. Therefore, there was no reason to do one's best, as Taylor noted. Workers also developed their own ways of working, largely by observing their fellow workers.

This resulted in a large variety of informal, rule-of-thumb-like methods for carrying out their work. Taylor argued that it was the managers' task to codify this informal knowledge, select the most efficient method from among the many held by the workers, and train workers in this method. Managers should specify in detail not only what workers should be doing but how their work should be done and the exact time allowed for doing their work. This is why Taylor called his analysis "time study." Workers following these instructions in detail should be rewarded with 30 to 100 percent wage increases, according to Taylor (1911/1998, p. 17). In this way, Taylor was certain he would eliminate the phenomenon of working slowly. Another approach, pioneered by Frank Gilbreth, was called "motion study" and consisted of studying every movement involved in a task in detail. Gilbreth proposed to eliminate all unnecessary movements and to substitute fast for slow motions.

Taylor's approach has the modern ring to it of what we now call "knowledge management." One should recognize, however, that the tasks he and others such as Gilbreth considered consisted primarily of repetitive manual operations, such as shoveling, pig iron loading, bricklaying, and manufacturing/assembly tasks. "Cognitive tasks" involving planning, maintaining situation awareness, and decision making were not directly addressed by this approach. Taylor was, sometimes unjustly, criticized because of his deterministic account of work, his view of humans as machines, his notion that humans are motivated only by monetary rewards, and the utter lack of discretion granted to workers.

Taylor's lasting influence on task analysis has been his analytical approach to decomposing complex tasks into subtasks, and the use of quantitative methods in optimizing task performance. By asserting that management should develop an ideal method of working, independent of workers' intuitions (or their "rule-of-thumb" method, as Taylor called them), he foreshadowed contemporary discussions on the value of using experts as sources of information. Indeed, to understand various manufacturing jobs, Taylor would first find people who were very good ("experts") and then bring them into a laboratory that simulated their workplace so that their activity might be studied. Taylor's time study continued to exert an influence on determining optimal work layout for at least half a century (Annett, 2000), and it still is a major approach to job design (Medsker & Campion, 1997).

Although World War I stimulated the development of more sophisticated equipment, particularly in the area of avionics, there was little attention to controls and displays. Rather, the main focus was on pilot selection and training (Meister, 1999). This line of research resulted in the development of the method of job analysis in the 1930s by the U.S. Department of Labor (Drury et al., 1987). Job analysis was devised to establish a factual and consistent basis for identifying personnel qualification requirements. A *job* consists of a *position* or a group of similar positions, and each position consists of one or more *tasks* (Luczak, 1997). Therefore, there is a logical distinction between *job analysis* and *task analysis*: the techniques employed in job analysis address a higher level of aggregation than the techniques employed in task analysis.

For instance, in a typical job analysis an analyst would rate, on a scale, whether a particular job element, such as "decision making and reasoning," would be used very often or very infrequent, and whether its importance is very minor or extreme. In a typical task analysis, on the other hand, an analyst would decompose decision making into its constituent elements, for instance, "plausible goals," "relevant cues," "expectancies," and "actions" (Klein, 1993). Furthermore, the goals and cues would be spelled out in detail, as would be the typical difficulties associated with particular cues (e.g., Militello & Hutton, 1998). Similarly, when analyzing the interaction between a human and a machine, job analysis would rate the extent and importance of this interaction, whereas task analysis would specify in detail how the human interacts with the machine, perhaps even down to the level of individual keystrokes (e.g., Card, Moran, & Newell, 1983). Job analysis and task analysis may use the same methods, for instance, interviews, work observation, and critical incidents. However, as mentioned above, these methods address different levels of aggregation.

The Age of Oil

It was not until after World War II that task analysis and human factors (the preferred term in North America) or ergonomics (the preferred term in Europe) began to take on a decidedly more "cognitive" form. This was initiated by the development of information-processing systems and computing devices, from the stage of *manual control* to the stage of *supervisory control* (Hollnagel & Cacciabue, 1999). Although Tayloristic approaches to task analysis were still sufficient in most of the work conducted in the first half of the twentieth century (when machines were manually controlled), the development of instrumented cockpits, radar displays, and remote process control forced the human into a supervisory role in which knowledge and cognition were more important than manual labor, and conditional branchings of action sequences were more important than strictly linear sequences of actions. Experience in World War II had shown that systems with well-trained operators were not always working. Airplanes with no apparent mechanical failures flew into the ground, and highly motivated radar operators missed enemy contacts. Apparently, the emphasis on testing and training had reached its limits, as had Taylor's implicit philosophy of designing the human to fit the machine. Now, experimental psychologists were asked to design the machine to fit the human.

MILLER: TASK DESCRIPTION AND TASK ANALYSIS

In 1953, Robert B. Miller had developed a method for task analysis that went beyond merely observable behavior (Miller, 1953; 1962). Miller proposed that each task be decomposed into the follow-

ing categories: cues initiating action, controls used, response, feedback, criterion of acceptable performance, typical errors. The method was of general applicability, but was specifically designed for use in planning for training and training equipment. Miller adopted a systems approach to task analysis, viewing the human as part of the system's linkages from input to output functions.

In his task-analysis phase, Miller included cognitive concepts such as "goal orientation and set," "decisions," "memory storage," "coordinations," and "anticipations." These "factors in task structure," as he called the concepts, are, to different degrees, inevitable parts of every task. The task analyst needs to translate the set of task requirements listed in the task description into task-structure terms. The next step would be to translate the task-structure terms into selection procedures, training procedures, and human engineering. Take, for instance, the task of troubleshooting. Miller provided some "classical suggestions" on how to train the problem-solving part of troubleshooting. One suggestion was to "indoctrinate by concept and practice to differentiate the function from the mechanism that performs the function" (Miller, 1962, p. 224). Although too general to be useful as a concrete training suggestion, this example predates later concepts such as the "abstraction hierarchy" introduced by Jens Rasmussen in 1979 (see Vicente, 2001).

FLANAGAN: CRITICAL INCIDENT TECHNIQUE

The applied area of human-factors engineering was less reluctant to adopt cognitive terminology than mainstream North American academic psychology, which at that time was still impacted by behaviorism. We have already seen how Miller's (1953) approach to task analysis included cognitive concepts. In 1954, Flanagan published his "critical incident technique" (Flanagan, 1954). This is a method for collecting and analyzing observed incidents having special significance. Although the modern-day reader may associate incidents with severe disasters, this was not Flanagan's primary definition.

During World War II, he and his coworkers studied reasons for failure in learning to fly, disorientation while flying, failures of bombing missions, and incidents of effective or ineffective combat leadership. After the war, the method was also applied to nonmilitary jobs, such as dentistry, bookkeeping, life insurance, and industry. These incidents were collected by interviewing hundreds of participants, resulting in thousands of incident records. Alternative methods of data collection were group interviews, questionnaires, and written records of incidents as they happened. These incidents were then used to generate critical job requirements, which in turn were used for training purposes, job design, equipment design, measures of proficiency, and to develop selection tests. Flanagan (1954) did not provide much detail on the reliability and validity of his technique, although he emphasized the importance of the reporting of facts regarding behavior rather than resting solely on subjective impressions. His technique demonstrates the importance of using domain experts as informants about any behavior that makes a significant contribution to the work that is carried out.

HIERARCHICAL TASK ANALYSIS

Although R. B. Miller had used cognitive concepts in his method for task analysis, his task descriptions were still tied very much to actual human–machine interaction. His task descriptions would therefore basically be lists of physical activities. His concept of user goals had more to do with the criteria of system performance that the user had to meet, than with a nested set of internal goals that drives user performance. A method for task analysis that began by identifying the goals of the task was developed in the 1960s by Annett and Duncan under the name of Hierarchical Task Analysis (HTA) (Annett & Duncan, 1967). In accordance with the dominant industries during this period (the Age of Oil), HTA was originally developed for training process-control tasks in the steel and petrochemical industries. These process-control tasks involved

significant cognitive activity such as planning, diagnosis, and decision making.

In the 1950s and 1960s, manual-control tasks had been taken over by automation. Operators became supervisors who were supposed to step in when things went wrong. The interesting and crucial parts of supervisory-control tasks do not lie with the observable behavior, but rather with unobservable cognitive activities such as state recognition, fault finding and scheduling of tasks during start-up and shutdown sequences. Training for these tasks therefore needed to be based on a thorough examination of this cognitive activity. Annett and Duncan felt the existing methods for task analysis (such as time and motion study and Miller's method) were inadequate to address these issues. Also, they were more clear about the need for task descriptions to involve hierarchies (i.e., conditional branchings versus linear sequences.) Hence *hierarchical* task analysis. Complex systems are designed with goals in mind, and the same goals may be pursued by different routes. Hence, a direct listing of activities may be misleading (they may be sufficient for routine repetitive tasks, though). The analyst therefore needs to focus on the goals.

Goals may be successively unpacked to reveal a nested hierarchy of goals and subgoals. For example, thirst may be the condition that activates the goal of having a cup of tea, and subgoals are likely to include obtaining boiling water, a teapot with tea, and so on. We may answer the question *why* we need boiling water by referring to the top-level goal of having a cup of tea. The analyst needs to ask next *how* to obtain boiling water. Whether the analyst needs to answer this question is dependent on the purpose of the analysis. If the purpose is to train someone who has never before made a cup of tea, then the subgoal of obtaining boiling water itself needs to be unpacked further, for instance: pour water in container, heat water, look for bubbles.

Since a general purpose of HTA is to identify sources of actual or potential performance failure, Annett and Duncan (1967) formulated the following *stop rule*: stop with

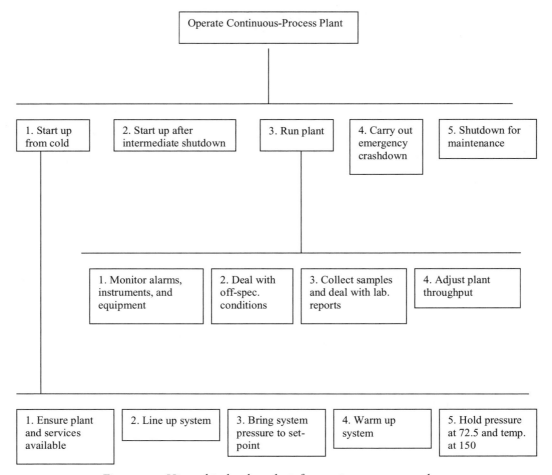

Figure 11.1. Hierarchical task analysis for continuous-process plant.

the analysis when the product of the probability of failure (p) and the cost of failure (c) is judged acceptable. In the example above, if we needed to train a child in making a cup of tea, we might judge the product of p and c to be acceptable for the subgoals of pouring water in the container and looking for bubbles. However, we may have some doubts about the subgoal of heating the water: a child may not know how to operate the various devices used for boiling water (probability of failure is high); moreover, the cost of failure may be high as well (burning fingers and worse). The analyst will therefore decide to further decompose this subgoal, but not the other subgoals. By successively decomposing goals and applying the $p \cdot c$ criterion at each step, the analyst can dis-

cover possible sources of performance failure and solutions can be hypothesized. For instance, one may discover that heating water with an electrical boiler in fact requires fairly extensive knowledge about electricity and the hazards associated with the combination of water and electricity. Based on current literature on training, and in particular training children, the analyst may finally suggest some ways of educating children in the dangers of using electrical boilers when making a cup of tea.

To take a more complex example than that of making a cup of tea, and illustrating the output of HTA in a graphical format, consider part of the HTA in Figure 11.1 for operating a continuous-process chemical plant (after Shepherd, 2001).

This example is deliberately simplified in that it does not show the order in which subgoals are pursued. A typical HTA would include a *plan* that does specify that order.

HTA may best be described as a generic problem-solving process. It is now one of the most familiar methods employed by ergonomics specialists in the United Kingdom (Annett, 2004). However, evaluation studies have shown that HTA can be very time intensive compared to other methods such as observation and interview. HTA is certainly far from simple and takes both expertise and practice to administer effectively (Annett, 2003). There is also a good deal of variability in the application of HTA. The reader may have had different thoughts than the writer of this chapter when reading about the particular decomposition of the subgoal of obtaining boiling water: why not describe a particular procedure for a particular way of boiling (e.g., pour water in pan, put pan on stove, turn on stove, wait until water boils)? One obvious reply would be that this description is less general than the one offered above because that description talks about "containers" in general. Furthermore, the actions are less precise (does one need to set the stove to a particular setpoint?), and the conditions indicating goal attainment are vague (how does one see that the water boils?). If there can be disagreement with such a simple example, imagine what problems an analyst can run into when dealing with a complex process-control task, such as the example above of the chemical plant.

One of the pitfalls in applying HTA is the fact that one may lose sight of the problem-solving nature of the task analysis itself. This is not a critique of HTA as such, but rather a cautionary note that analysts need to keep the purpose of the study in sight throughout the analysis.

The Age of Information Processing

In the early 1970s, the word "cognitive" became more acceptable in American academic psychology, though the basic idea had been established at least a decade earlier by George Miller and Jerome Bruner (see Gardner, 1985; Hoffman & Deffenbacher, 1992; Newell & Simon, 1972 for historical overviews). Neisser's *Cognitive psychology* had appeared in 1967, and the scientific journal by the same name first appeared in 1970. It took one more decade for this approach to receive broader methodological justification and its practical application. In 1984, Ericsson and Simon (1984) published *Protocol analysis: Verbal reports as data*. This book reintroduced the use of think-aloud problem-solving tasks, which had been relegated to the historical dustbin by behaviorism even though it had some decades of successful use in psychology laboratories in Germany and elsewhere in Europe up through about 1925. In 1983, Card, Moran, and Newell published *The psychology of human–computer interaction*. This book helped lay the foundation for the field of cognitive science and presented the GOMS model (Goals, Operators, Methods, and Selection rules), which was a family of analysis techniques, and a form of task analysis that describes the procedural, how-to-do-it knowledge involved in a task (see later section and Kieras, 2004, for a recent overview).

Task analysis profited a lot from the developments in artificial intelligence, particularly in the early 1980s when expert systems became commercially interesting (Hayes-Roth, Waterman, & Lenat, 1983). Since these systems required a great deal of expert knowledge, acquiring or "eliciting" this knowledge became an important topic (see Hoffman & Lintern, Chapter 12). Because of their reliance on unstructured interviews, system developers soon viewed "knowledge elicitation" as the bottleneck in expert-system development, and they turned to psychology for techniques that helped elicit that knowledge (Hoffman, 1987). As a result, a host of individual techniques was identified (see Cooke, 1994, for a review of 70 techniques), but no single overall method for task analysis that would guide the practitioner in selecting the right technique for a given problem resulted from this effort. However, the interest in the knowledge structures underlying expertise proved to be one of the approaches to what is now known as *cognitive task analysis* (Hoffman & Woods, 2000; see Hoffman & Lintern, Chapter 12; Schraagen, Chipman, & Shalin, 2000).

With artificial intelligence coming to be a widely used term in the 1970s, the first ideas arose about applying artificial intelligence to cockpit automation. As early as 1974, the concepts of adaptive aiding and dynamic function allocation emerged (Rouse, 1988). Researchers realized that as machines became more intelligent, they should be viewed as "equals" to humans. Instead of Taylor's "designing the human to fit the machine," or the human factors engineering's "designing the machine to fit the human," the maxim now became to design the joint human–machine system, or, more aptly phrased, the joint cognitive system (Hollnagel, 2003). Not only are cognitive tasks everywhere, but humans have lost their monopoly on conducting cognitive tasks, as noted by Hollnagel (2003, p. 6).

Again, as in the past, changes in technological developments were followed by changes in task-analysis methods. In order to address the large role of cognition in modern work, new tools and techniques were required "to yield information about the knowledge, thought processes, and goal structures that underlie observable task performance" (Chipman, Schraagen, & Shalin, 2000, p. 3).

Cognitive task analysis is not a single method or even a family of methods, as are Hierarchical Task Analysis or the Critical Incident Technique. Rather, the term denotes a large number of different techniques that may be grouped by, for instance, the type of knowledge they elicit (Seamster, Redding, & Kaempf, 1997) or the process of elicitation (Cooke, 1994; Hoffman, 1987). Typical techniques are observations, interviews, verbal reports, and conceptual techniques that focus on concepts and their relations. Apart from the expert-systems thread, with its emphasis on knowledge elicitation, cognitive task analysis has also been influenced by the need to understand expert decision making in naturalistic, or field, settings.

A widely cited technique is the Critical Decision Method developed by Klein and colleagues (Klein, Calderwood, & Macgregor, 1989; see Hoffman, Crandall, & Shadbolt, 1998, for a review, and see Hoffman & Lintern, Chapter 12, Ross, et al, Chapter 23). The Critical Decision Method is a descendent of the Critical Incident Technique developed by Flanagan (1954). In the CDM procedure, domain experts are asked to recall an incident in detail by constructing a time line, assisted by the analyst. Next, the analyst asks a set of specific questions (so-called *cognitive probes*) about goals, cues, expectancies, and so forth. The resulting information may be used for training or system design, for instance, by training novices in recognizing critical perceptual cues.

Despite, and perhaps because of, its rich and complex history, cognitive task analysis is still a relatively novel enterprise, and a number of major issues remain to be resolved. One is the usability of the products of cognitive task analysis, an issue that applies not only to cognitive task analysis, but to task analysis in general. Diaper, for instance, has argued since the beginning of the 1990s that a gulf exists between task analysis and traditional software-engineering approaches (Diaper, 2001). When designing systems, software engineers rarely use the task-analysis techniques advocated by psychologists. Conversely, as Lesgold (2000, p. 456) rightfully noted, "psychologists may have ignored the merits of object-based formalisms at least as often as analysts on the software engineering side have ignored human learning and performance constraints." Both groups can learn a lot from each other. Several attempts have been made to bridge the gulf (Diaper and Stanton's 2004 handbook lists a number of these), but none has been widely applied yet, possibly because of differences in background and training between software engineers and cognitive psychologists.

Another major challenge for cognitive task analysis is to deal with novel systems. For the most part, the existing practice of cognitive task analysis is based on the premise that one has existing jobs with experts and existing systems with experienced users to be analyzed. However, new systems for which there are no experts are being developed with greater frequency, and urgency.

These issues have been taken up by the *cognitive systems engineering* approach. At its core, cognitive systems engineering "seeks to understand how to model work in ways *directly useful for design* of interactive systems" (Eggleston, 2002, p. 15). Eggleston's useful overview of the field distinguishes three phases in the development of cognitive systems engineering: (1) a conceptual foundations period that occurred largely in the 1980s, (2) an engineering practice period that dominated the 1990s, and (3) an active deployment period that started around 2000. Cognitive task analysis figures prominently in the engineering practice period of cognitive systems engineering. However, whereas "traditional" cognitive task analysis focuses primarily on understanding the way people operate in their current world, cognitive systems engineering focuses also on understanding the way the world works and the way in which new "envisioned worlds" might work (Potter, Roth, Woods, & Elm, 2000).

With the discussion of cognitive task analysis and cognitive systems engineering, we have reached the present-day status of task analysis. The next section will describe a number of case studies that exemplify the use of task analysis methods.

Case Studies

In this section, I will describe various case studies on task analysis, with the aim, first, to provide the reader with some ideas on how to carry out a task analysis, and second, to note some of the difficulties one encounters when carrying out a task analysis in complex domains.

Improving the Training of Troubleshooting

The first case study is in the domain of troubleshooting. Schaafstal (1993), in her studies of expert and novice operators in a paper mill, found evidence for a structured approach to troubleshooting by experts. She presented experts and novices with realistic alarms on paper and asked them to think aloud. Consider the following protocol by a novice when confronted with the alarm: "conveyor belt of pulper 1 broke down":

> I would ... I would stop the pulper to start with and then I would halt the whole cycle afterwards and then try to repair the conveyor belt ... but you have to halt the whole installation, because otherwise they don't have any stock anymore.

An expert confronted with the same problem reacted as follows:

> OK. Conveyor belt of pulper 1 broke down ... conveyor belt of pulper 1 ... if that one breaks down ... yeah ... see how long that takes to repair ... not postponing the decision for very long, to ensure we don't have to halt the installation.

The novice starts repairs that are not necessary at all given the situation, whereas the expert first judges the seriousness of the problem. These and similar statements led to the inclusion of the category "judging the seriousness of the problem" in the expert's task structure of the diagnostic task. As novices rarely showed this deliberation, this category did not appear in their task structure.

The complete task structure is as follows (see Figure 11.2).

Experts in a paper mill first start by making a judgment about the seriousness of the problem. If the problem is judged to be serious, the operator will immediately continue with the application of a global repair, followed by an evaluation whether the problem has been solved. This process may be followed by a more thorough diagnosis in order to determine the correct local repair, ensuring a solution "once and for all." If the problem is not a very serious one, the expert will consider possible faults one by one and test them, until a likely one is found. This is then followed by a determination of repairs, their consequences, an ordering of repairs

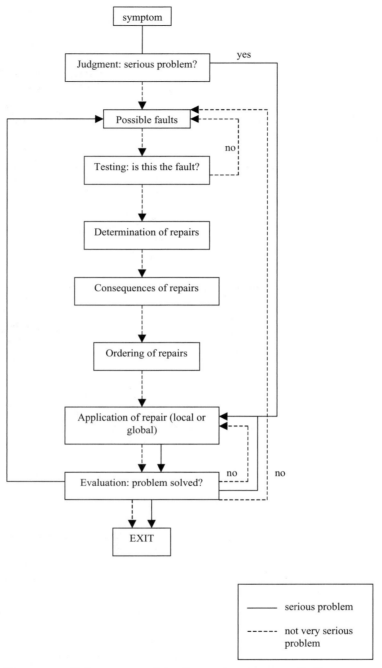

Figure 11.2. Task structure of the diagnostic strategy applied by expert operators (Schaafstal, 1991)

(if necessary), application of repairs, and an evaluation whether the problem has been solved. If the problem has not been solved, the expert might do two things: either try another repair, or back up higher in the tree –

he may realize that he has not yet spotted the actual fault, and therefore the problem has not been solved. In case no possible faults are left, or the operator cannot think of any other faults than the ones he already tested, he will be inclined to use a global repair to alleviate the problem.

Inexperienced operators show a far more simple diagnostic strategy. They don't judge the seriousness of the problem, they don't consider the consequences of repairs, and they don't evaluate whether the problem has been solved. Also, novices jump much more quickly to repairs without realizing whether a certain repair actually is right for a certain situation.

We applied this expert task structure to another area of troubleshooting (Schaafstal, Schraagen, & Van Berlo, 2000). Around 1990, complaints started to emerge from the Dutch fleet concerning the speed and accuracy of weapon engineers, who carry out both preventive and corrective maintenance onboard naval vessels. There were a number of reasons for the suboptimal performance of the troubleshooters. First, expertise was not maintained very well. Engineers shifted positions frequently, left military service for more lucrative jobs in the civilian world, or were less interested in a technical career in the first place. Second, a new generation of highly integrated systems was introduced, and this level of integration made troubleshooting more demanding. Third, the training the troubleshooters received seemed inadequate for the demands they encountered onboard ships.

We conducted a field study with real faults in real systems that showed that military technical personnel who had just completed a course and passed their exam diagnosed only 40% of the malfunctions correctly. We also obtained scores on a knowledge test, and found that the junior technicians scored only 55% correct on this test. Of even more importance was the low correlation (0.27) between the scores on the knowledge test and the actual troubleshooting performance. This cast doubt on the heavy emphasis placed on theory in the training courses.

Our suspicions about the value of theory in the training courses were further raised after having conducted a number of observational studies (see Schraagen & Schaafstal, 1996: Experiment 1). In these studies, we used both experts and novices (trainees who had just finished a course) in order to uncover differences in the knowledge and strategies employed. Our task-analysis method was to have technicians think aloud while troubleshooting two malfunctions in a radar system. The resulting verbal data were analyzed by protocol analysis, that is, by isolating and categorizing individual propositions in the verbal protocol.

The categories we used for classifying the propositions were derived from the expert task structure as shown in Figure 11.2. The radar study showed that a theory instructor who was one of our participants had difficulties troubleshooting this radar system. This turned our attention to a gap between theoretical instruction and practice. We also observed virtually no transfer of knowledge from one radar system to the other, as witnessed by the unsuccessful troubleshooting attempts of two participants who were experienced in one radar system but not in the radar system we studied. This turned our attention to the content of the training courses, which were component oriented instead of functionally oriented. Finally, the verbal protocols showed the typical unsystematic approach to troubleshooting by the novice participant in our study.

These studies provided a glimpse of what was wrong with the courses in troubleshooting. They were highly theoretical, component oriented, with little practice in actual troubleshooting. On the basis of our observations and experiments, we decided to change the courses. Basically, we wanted to teach the students two things: (1) a systematic approach to troubleshooting, (2) a functional understanding of the equipment they have to maintain. In our previous study (Schraagen & Schaafstal, 1996), we had found that the systematic approach to troubleshooting could not be taught independently of a particular context. In order to be able to search selectively in the enormous problem space of possible causes, it is essential that the representation of the system be highly structured.

One candidate for such a structuring is a functional hierarchical representation, much like Rasmussen's (1986) *abstraction hierarchy* (see Hoffman & Lintern, Chapter 12). For a course on a computer system, we decomposed the system into four levels, from the top-level decomposition of a computer system into power supply, central processor, memory, and peripheral equipment, down to the level of electrical schemata. We stopped at the level of individual replaceable units (e.g., a printed circuit board). In this way, substantial theoretical background that was previously taught could be eliminated. We replaced this theory with more practice in troubleshooting itself. Students were instructed to use a troubleshooting form as a job aid. This form consisted simply of a sheet of paper with four different steps to be taken in troubleshooting (problem description, generate causes, test causes, repair and evaluate). These four steps were a high-level abstraction of the diagnostic task structure previously identified in the papermill study by Schaafstal (1993). In this way, the systematic approach to troubleshooting was instilled in the practice lessons, while at the same time a functional understanding of the system was instilled in the theory sessions. Theory and practice sessions were interspersed such that the new theoretical concepts, once mastered, could then be readily applied to troubleshooting the real system.

We demonstrated to the Navy the success of this approach in a one-week add-on course: the percentage of problems solved went up from 40% to 86%. Subsequently, we were asked to completely modify the computer course according to our philosophy. Again, we evaluated this new course empirically by having students think aloud while solving four problems, and rating their systematicity of reasoning and level of functional understanding. Results were highly favorable for our modified course: 95% of malfunctions were correctly solved (previously 40%), and experts rated the students' systematicity and level of functional understanding each at 4.8 on a 1–5 scale (whereas these numbers were 2.6 and 2.9, respectively, for the old course). These results were most satisfying, especially considering the fact that the new course lasted four weeks instead of six weeks.

The Naval Weapon Engineering School, convinced by the empirical results, subsequently decided to use this method as the basis for the design of all its function courses. We have helped them with the first few courses, and subsequently wrote a manual specifying how to develop new courses based on our philosophy, but gradually the naval instructors have been able to modify courses on their own. Course length for more than 50 courses has on average been reduced by about 30%.

As far as task analysis is concerned, the reader may have noted that little mention has been made of any extensive task decomposition. Yet, this project could not have been as successful as it was without a cognitive task analysis of troubleshooting on the part of highly proficient domain practitioners. Troubleshooting is first and foremost a cognitive task. Little can be observed from the outside, just by looking at behavior. Observations and inferences are all knowledge based. We therefore almost always used think-aloud problem solving followed by protocol analysis as the data analysis method.

Shore-based Pilotage

In 1992, Rotterdam Municipal Port Management, with cooperation by the Rotterdam Pilots Corporation, ordered an investigation into the possibilities of extending shore-based pilotage (Schraagen, 1993). Normally, a pilot enters a ship and "conns" the ship from the sea to the harbor entrance. The expertise of a pilot lies in his or her extensive knowledge of the particular conditions of a specific harbor or port. The expertise of the ship's captain lies primarily in his or her extensive knowledge of a specific ship. Because of rough seas, situations sometimes arise where it is too dangerous for the pilot to board the ship himself. In those situations, either the pilot is brought on board by a helicopter, or the ship is piloted by a pilot ashore. The latter is called "shore-based pilotage." Extending shore-based pilotage would reduce costs for shipping companies since shore-based pilotage, at least at the time of the study, was cheaper than being served by a helicopter or waiting in a harbor for better weather. However, cost reduction should be weighed against decreased levels of safety as a result of the pilot not being on the bridge himself. In particular, in bad weather conditions, the captain has no overview of the traffic image in relation to the environment. Sometimes, large drift angles are seen by the captain. These angles are sometimes not accepted by the captain and advice given by the pilot is not followed up. The problem is that the captain may not be familiar with the local situation.

One important element in the study was to specify the extra information required by pilots if shore-based pilotage would be extended to ships exceeding 170 m in length. Ideally, a simulator study would be required in which one could systematically vary the information available to the pilot, variables such as ship length and height, traffic density, wind, current, and visibility conditions, and the quality of interaction between pilot and captain. However, this kind of study exceeded the project's budget, so we actually undertook a literature study, a comparison with air traffic control, a study of vessel-based systems, and a task analysis. The purpose of the task analysis was to find out what information pilots used onboard the ships.

The selection of expert pilots that participated in the task analysis was largely determined by the Pilots Corporation, based on a few constraints that we put forward. First, we needed pilots with at least ten years of practical experience. Second, we needed pilots who were proficient communicators, so they could explain what they were doing.

The task analysis consisted of two parts (see Schraagen, 1994, for more details): (1) observation and recording of pilot activities on eleven trips on ships, (2) paper and pencil tasks given to seven pilots who had also

cooperated during the trips. During the trips onboard ships, an extensive array of measurements was taken:

(a) Pilots were instructed to talk aloud; their verbalizations were tape-recorded.

(b) Pilot decisions and communication were timed with a stopwatch.

(c) Pilots were asked about their plans before entering the ship and were interviewed afterwards about the trip made.

(d) The ships' movements and positions were recorded.

(e) Recordings were made of the movements of ship traffic (via radar).

(f) Photographs of the view ahead were taken from the vantage point of the helm: photographs were taken every five minutes in order to obtain a running record of the pilot's perceptual input.

After the trips had been made, seven pilots participated in follow-up sessions. The primary aim was to obtain more detailed information on pilot information usage than had been possible during the trips (detailed interviews were impossible, of course, since pilots were doing their jobs). A secondary benefit was that data could be compared, in contrast to the trip data that differed in terms of ship, weather, and traffic conditions. In the follow-up session, pilots were asked to carry out the following tasks:

(a) Reconstruct the exact rudder advice given during a trip using fragments of video recordings as input (fragments of curved situations lasting four to ten minutes were presented on a TV monitor).

(b) Indicate on a map of the trajectory they were familiar with at what points course and speed changes were made.

(c) Draw on a map the course over ground together with acceptable margins under various wind and current conditions for the entrance into Hook of Holland.

These tasks represent what Hoffman (1987) has called "limited-information tasks." Limited-information tasks are similar to the task the expert is familiar with, but the amount or kind of information that is available to the expert is somehow restricted. For example, the video recordings were taken from a fixed point in the middle of the bridge, whereas pilots would normally stand at the righthand side of the bridge looking at the starboard side of the river. Although experts may initially feel uncomfortable with limited-information tasks, the tasks can be informative in revealing practitioner reasoning (Hoffman, Shadbolt, Burton, & Klein, 1995).

The task analysis yielded a wealth of information on the kinds of information pilots actually use when navigating. The most important references used were pile moorings, buoys, and leading lines. Several unexpected results emerged. First, pilots develop highly individualized references both to initiate course and speed changes and to check against the ship's movements. Although all pilots rely on pile moorings, buoys, and leading lines, which of these they use differs greatly among them. This is perhaps due to their individualized way of training. Second, one might hypothesize that the decision points mentioned by pilots on paper constitute only a fraction of, or are different in nature from, the decision points used during actual pilotage onboard a ship. This latter possibility turned out not to be the case. Decision points used in actual practice were all covered by the decision points mentioned on paper. This implies that this kind of knowledge is not "tacit" or difficult to verbalize.

More interesting than the precise results of the task analysis, at least for this chapter's purposes, are the lessons learned. First, this was a politically very sensitive project. It turned out that the sponsor, Rotterdam Port Authorities, had a different political agenda than the Rotterdam pilots. The Port Authorities wanted to reduce shipping costs in order to increase total amount of cargo handling. The pilots, on the other hand, publicly said they were afraid of jeopardizing safety in case shore-based pilotage was extended. They therefore offered their full assistance by allowing us to follow them on

their trips, so that they could convince us of the added value of having experts on board.

In another project that was to have started a year later, their knowledge of how to conn a ship into the harbor was required for "proficiency testing," that is, training captains of ships to conn their own ships into the harbor without the assistance of a pilot. Pilot participation in this project was withdrawn after a few months and the entire project was cancelled. In the end, this project may have been used by the Port Authorities to pose a threat to the pilots: if you don't lower your rates for helicopter assistance (the helicopter was leased by the pilots), we will extend shore-based pilotage. It seems that this threat worked. Shore-based pilotage was not extended, hence the results of this study were not implemented.

By spending time with the pilots, it would be easy for the researchers to develop loyalties with them and their organization, rather than with the Port Authorities who remained at a distance. In general, the task analyst who is studying expertise in context needs to be aware of these agenda issues.

A second lesson learned is that obtaining too many data can be counterproductive. In this project, for instance, the video recordings that were made of the synthetic radar image in the Harbor Coordination Center were never analyzed afterwards, although it seemed potentially valuable at the time we started. Second, the timing of the pilot decisions with a stopwatch, although laudable from a quantitative point of view, was really unnecessary given the focus of the project on the qualitative use of categories of information. Hindsight is always 20/20, but the general lesson for task analysts is to think twice before recording massive amounts of information just because the gathering of certain data types might be possible. Information gathering should be driven by the goals of the research.

Finally, the paper and pencil tasks were received with downright hostility by the pilots. They had been forced to spend their spare time on this exercise, and when they noted certain inadequacies in the information provided to them on paper, they became uncooperative and very critical. This required some subtle people-handling skills on the part of the task analyst. In retrospect, it would have been better to first talk through the materials with an independent pilot in order to remove the inadequacies. This confirms a conclusion already drawn in 1987 by Hoffman that "experts do not like it when you limit the information that is available to them (...). It is important when instructing the expert to drive home the point that the limited-information task is not a challenge of their ego or of their expertise" (Hoffman, 1987, p. 56).

In another cognitive task analysis, geared toward discovering the search strategies employed by forensic analysts, we also used limited-information tasks, this time without encountering resistance (Schraagen & Leijenhorst, 2001). This may have been due to the fact that the cases that were presented to the experts were developed in close cooperation with a forensic analyst who was not part of the study participants. Also, their familiar task, by definition, involves working with limited information.

Conclusions and Future Work

Where do we stand? Although it may be too early to tell, we may have shifted from the age of information to the age of knowledge sharing or innovation. Task analysis now has a focus of understanding expert knowledge, reasoning, and performance, and leveraging that understanding into methods for training and decision support, to amplify and extend human abilities to know, perceive, and collaborate. To do this, we have an overarching theory – macrocognition – (Klein, et al., 2003), and a rich palette of methods, with ideas about methods' strengths and limitations, and methods combinatorics. Task analysis, and cognitive task analysis in particular, are both useful and necessary in any investigation of expertise "in the wild."

Despite this generally positive outlook, there are several lingering issues that deserve future work. First, the issue of bridging the gulf between task analysis and systems design is still a critical one. Recently, interesting work has been carried out on integrating task analysis with standard software-engineering methods such as Unified Modeling Language (UML) (see Diaper & Stanton, 2004, Part IV).

A second issue regarding the gulf between task analysis and design concerns the development of systems that do not yet exist. Task analyses generally work well when experts can be interviewed who are experienced with current systems. However, with novel systems, there are no experts. If introducing new technology changes tasks, the analysis of a *current* task may be of limited use in the design of new sociotechnical systems (Woods & Dekker, 2000). Therefore, a somewhat different set of techniques is required for exploring the envisioned world, including storyboard walkthroughs, participatory design, and high-fidelity simulations using future scenarios.

References

Annett, J. (2000). Theoretical and pragmatic influences on task analysis methods. In J. M. Schraagen, S. F. Chipman, & V. L. Shalin (Eds.), *Cognitive task analysis* (pp. 25–37). Mahwah, NJ: Lawrence Erlbaum Associates.

Annett, J. (2003). Hierarchical task analysis. In E. Hollnagel (Ed.), *Handbook of cognitive task design* (pp. 17–35). Mahwah, NJ: Lawrence Erlbaum Associates.

Annett, J. (2004). Hierarchical task analysis. In D. Diaper & N. Stanton (Eds.), *The handbook of task analysis for human–computer interaction* (pp. 67–82). Mahwah, NJ: Lawrence Erlbaum Associates.

Annett, J., & Duncan, K. D. (1967). Task analysis and training design. *Occupational Psychology, 41,* 211–221.

Card, S. K., Moran, T. P., & Newell, A. (1983). *The psychology of human–computer interaction.* Hillsdale, NJ: Lawrence Erlbaum Associates.

Chipman, S. F., Schraagen, J. M., & Shalin, V. L. (2000). Introduction to cognitive task analysis. In J. M. Schraagen, S. F. Chipman, & V. L. Shalin (Eds.), *Cognitive task analysis* (pp. 3–23). Mahwah, NJ: Lawrence Erlbaum Associates.

Cooke, N. J. (1994). Varieties of knowledge elicitation techniques. *International Journal of Human–Computer Studies, 41*, 801–849.

Diaper, D. (2001). Task Analysis for Knowledge Descriptions (TAKD): A requiem for a method. *Behavior and Information Technology, 20*, 199–212.

Diaper, D. (2004). Understanding task analysis for human–computer interaction. In D. Diaper & N. Stanton (Eds.), *The handbook of task analysis for human–computer interaction* (pp. 5–47). Mahwah, NJ: Lawrence Erlbaum Associates.

Diaper, D., & Stanton, N. (2004). Wishing on a sTAr: The future of task analysis. In D. Diaper & N. Stanton (Eds.), *The handbook of task analysis for human–computer interaction* (pp. 603–619). Mahwah, NJ: Lawrence Erlbaum Associates.

Drury, C. G., Paramore, B., Van Cott, H. P., Grey, S. M., & Corlett, E. N. (1987). Task analysis. In G. Salvendy (Ed.), *Handbook of human factors* (pp. 371–401). New York: John Wiley & Sons.

Eggleston, R. G. (2002). Cognitive systems engineering at 20-something: Where do we stand? In M. D. McNeese & M. A. Vidulich (Eds.), *Cognitive systems engineering in military aviation environments: Avoiding cogminutia fragmentosa!* (pp. 15–78). Wright-Patterson Air Force Base, OH: Human Systems Information Analysis Center.

Ericsson, K. A., & Simon, H. A. (1984). *Protocol analysis: Verbal reports as data.* Cambridge, MA: MIT Press.

Flanagan, J. C. (1954). The critical incident technique. *Psychological Bulletin, 51*, 327–358.

Freeman, C., & Louçã, F. (2001). *As time goes by: From industrial revolutions to the information revolution.* Oxford: Oxford University Press.

Gardner, H. (1985). *The mind's new science: A history of the cognitive revolution.* New York: Basic Books.

Hayes-Roth, F., Waterman, D. A., & Lenat, D. B. (Eds.). (1983). *Building expert systems.* Reading, MA: Addison-Wesley Publishing Company.

Hoffman, R. R. (1987, Summer). The problem of extracting the knowledge of experts from the perspective of experimental psychology. *AI Magazine, 8*, 53–67.

Hoffman, R. R., & Deffenbacher, K. (1992). A brief history of applied cognitive psychology. *Applied Cognitive Psychology, 6*, 1–48.

Hoffman, R. R., Shadbolt, N. R., Burton, A. M., & Klein, G. (1995). Eliciting knowledge from experts: A methodological analysis. *Organizational Behavior and Human Decision Processes, 62*, 129–158.

Hoffman, R. R., Crandall, B. W., & Shadbolt, N. R. (1998). A case study in cognitive task analysis methodology: The critical decision method for elicitation of expert knowledge. *Human Factors, 40*, 254–276.

Hoffman, R. R., & Woods, D. D. (2000). Studying cognitive systems in context: Preface to the special section. *Human Factors, 42*, 1–7 (Special section on cognitive task analysis).

Hollnagel, E. & Cacciabue, P. C. (1999). Cognition, technology & wrok: An introduction. *Cognition, Technology & Work, 1(1)*, 1–6.

Hollnagel, E. (2003). Prolegomenon to cognitive task design. In E. Hollnagel (Ed.), *Handbook of cognitive task design* (pp. 3–15). Mahwah, NJ: Lawrence Erlbaum Associates.

Kieras, D. (2004). GOMS models for task analysis. In D. Diaper & N. A. Stanton (Eds.), *The handbook of task analysis for human–computer interaction* (pp. 83–116). Mahwah, NJ: Lawrence Erlbaum Associates.

Kirwan, B., & Ainsworth, L. K. (Eds.). (1992). *A guide to task analysis.* London: Taylor & Francis.

Klein, G. (1993). A recognition-primed decision (RPD) model of rapid decision making. In G. Klein, J. Orasanu, R. Calderwood, & C. E. Zsambok (Eds.), *Decision making in action: Models and methods* (pp. 138–147). Norwood, NJ: Ablex.

Klein, G. A., Calderwood, R., & Macgregor, D. (1989). Critical decision method for eliciting knowledge. *IEEE Transactions on Systems, Man, and Cybernetics, 19*, 462–472.

Klein, G., Ross, K. G., Moon, B. M., Klein, D. E., Hoffman, R. R., & Hollanagel, E. (May/June 2003). Macrocognition. *IEEE Intelligent Systems*, pp. 81–85.

Lesgold, A. (2000). On the future of congnitive task analysis. In J. M. Schraagen, S. F. Chipman, & V. L. Shalin (Eds.), *Cognitive task analysis* (pp. 451–465). Mahwah, NJ: Lawrence Erlbaum Associates.

Luczak, H. (1997). Task analysis. In G. Salvendy (Ed.), *Handbook of human factors and ergonomics* (2nd ed.) (pp. 340–416). New York: John Wiley & Sons.

Medsker, G. J., & Campion, M. A. (1997). Job and team design. In G. Salvendy (Ed.), *Handbook of human factors and ergonomics* (2nd ed.) (pp. 450–489). New York: John Wiley & Sons.

Meister, D. (1999). *The history of human factors and ergonomics*. Mahwah, NJ: Lawrence Erlbaum Associates.

Militello, L. G., & Hoffman, R. R. (2006). Perspectives on cognitive task analysis. Cambridge: MIT Press.

Militello, L. G., & Hutton, R. J. B. (1998). Applied cognitive task analysis (ACTA): A practitioner's toolkit for understanding cognitive task demands. *Ergonomics, 41*, 1618–1641.

Miller, R. B. (1953). *A method for man–machine task analysis*. Dayton, OH: Wright Air Development Center (Technical Report 53–137).

Miller, R. B. (1962). Task description and analysis. In R. M. Gagné (Ed.), *Psychological principles in system development* (pp. 187–228). New York: Holt, Rinehart and Winston.

Münsterberg, H. (1914). *Psychotechnik*. Leipzig: J. A. Barth.

Nemeth, C. P. (2004). *Human factors methods for design: Making systems human-centered*. Boca Raton: CRC Press.

Newell, A., & Simon, H. A. (1972). *Human problem solving*. Englewood Cliffs, NJ: Prentice-Hall.

Perez, C. (2002). *Technological revolutions and financial capital: The dynamics of bubbles and golden ages*. Cheltenham: Edward Elgar.

Potter, S. S., Roth, E. M., Woods, D. D., & Elm, W. C. (2000). Bootstrapping multiple converging cognitive task analysis techniques for system design. In J. M. Schraagen, S. F. Chipman, & V. L. Shalin (Eds.), *Cognitive task analysis* (pp. 317–340). Mahwah, NJ: Lawrence Erlbaum Associates.

Rasmussen, J. (1986). *Information processing and human–machine interaction: An approach to cognitive engineering*. Amsterdam: Elsevier.

Rouse, W. B. (1988). Adaptive aiding for human/computer control. *Human Factors, 30*, 431–443.

Schaafstal, A. M. (1991). Diagnostic skill in process operation: A comparison between experts and novices. Unpublished dissertation. University of Groningen, The Netherlands.

Schaafstal, A. M. (1993). Knowledge and strategies in diagnostic skill. *Ergonomics, 36*, 1305–1316.

Schaafstal, A. M., Schraagen, J. M., & van Berlo, M. (2000). Cognitive task analysis and innovation of training: The case of structured troubleshooting. *Human Factors, 42*, 75–86.

Schraagen, J. M. C. (1993). What information do river pilots use? In *Proceedings of the International Conference on Marine Simulation and Ship Manoeuvrability MARSIM '93* (Vol. II, pp. 509–517). St. John's, Newfoundland: Fisheries and Marine Institute of Memorial University.

Schraagen, J. M. C. (1994). What information do river pilots use? (Report TM 1994 C-10). Soesterberg: TNO Institute for Human Factors.

Schraagen, J. M. C., & Leijenhorst, H. (2001). Searching for evidence: Knowledge and search strategies used by forensic scientists. In E. Salas & G. Klein (Eds.), *Linking expertise and naturalistic decision making* (pp. 263–274). Mahwah, NJ: Lawrence Erlbaum Associates.

Schraagen, J. M. C., & Schaafstal, A. M. (1996). Training of systematic diagnosis: A case study in electronics troubleshooting. *Le Travail Humain, 59*, 5–21.

Schraagen, J. M., Chipman, S. F., & Shalin, V. L. (2000). *Cognitive task analysis*. Mahwah, NJ: Lawrence Erlbaum Associates.

Seamster, T. L., Redding, R. E., & Kaempf, G. L. (1997). *Applied cognitive task analysis in aviation*. London: Ashgate.

Shepherd, A. (2001). *Hierarchical task analysis*. London: Taylor & Francis.

Taylor, F. W. (1998). *The principles of scientific management* (unabridged republication of the volume published by Harper & Brothers, New York and London, in 1911). Mineola, NY: Dover Publications.

Vicente, K. J. (2001). Cognitive engineering research at Risø from 1962–1979. In E. Salas (Ed.), *Advances in human performance and cognitive engineering research* (Vol. 1, pp. 1–57). New York: Elsevier.

Viteles, M. S. (1932). *Industrial psychology*. New York: W. W. Norton.

Woods, D. D., & Dekker, S. (2000). Anticipating the effects of technological change: A new era of dynamics for human factors. *Theoretical Issues in Ergonomics Science, 1*, 272–282.

CHAPTER 12

Eliciting and Representing the Knowledge of Experts

Robert R. Hoffman & Gavan Lintern

Keywords: knowledge elicitation, expert systems, intelligent systems, methodology, Concept Maps, Abstraction-Decomposition, critical decision method

Introduction

The transgenerational transmission of the wisdom of elders via storytelling is as old as humanity itself. During the Middle Ages and Renaissance, the Craft Guilds had well-specified procedures for the transmission of knowledge, and indeed gave us the developmental scale that is still widely used: initiate, novice, apprentice, journeyman, expert, and master (Hoffman, 1998). Based on interviews and observations of the workplace, Denis Diderot (along with 140 others, including Emile Voltaire) created one of the great works of the Enlightenment, the 17 volume *Encyclopedie* (Diderot, 1751–1772), which explained many "secrets" – the knowledge and procedures in a number of tradecrafts. The emergent science of psychology of the 1700s and 1800s also involved research that, in hindsight, might legitimately be regarded as knowledge elicitation (KE). For instance, a number of studies of reasoning were conducted in the laboratory of Wilhelm Wundt, and some of these involved university professors as the research participants (Militello & Hoffman, forthcoming). In the decade prior to World War I, the stage was set in Europe for applied and industrial psychology; much of that work involved the systematic study of proficient domain practitioners (see Hoffman & Deffenbacher, 1992).

The focus of this chapter is on a more recent acceleration of research that involves the elicitation and representation of expert knowledge (and the subsequent use of the representations, in design). We lay out recent historical origins and rationale for the work, we chart the developments during the era of first-generation expert systems, and then we proceed to encapsulate our modern understanding of and approaches to the elicitation, representation, and sharing of expert knowledge. Our emphasis in this chapter is on methods and methodological issues.

Where This Topic Came From

The Era of Expert Systems

The era of expert systems can be dated from about 1971, when Edward Feigenbaum and his colleagues (Feigenbaum, Buchanan, & Lederberg, 1971) created a system in which a computable knowledge base of domain concepts was integrated with an inference engine of procedural (if-then) rules. This "expert system" was intended to capture the skill of expert chemists regarding the interpretation of mass spectrograms. Other seminal systems were MYCIN (Shortliffe, 1976), for diagnosing bacterial infections and PROSPECTOR (Duda, Gaschnig, & Hart, 1979), for determining site potential for geological exploration.

It seemed to take longer for computer scientists to elicit knowledge from experts than to write the expert system software. This "knowledge acquisition bottleneck" became a salient problem (see Hayes-Roth, Waterman, & Lenat, 1983). It was widely discussed in the computer science community (e.g., McGraw & Harbison-Briggs, 1989; Rook & Croghan, 1989). An obvious suggestion was that computer systems engineers might be trained in interview techniques (Forsyth & Buchanan, 1989), but the bottleneck also spawned the development of automated knowledge acquisition "shells." These were toolkits for helping domain experts build their own prototype expert systems (for a bibliography, see Hoffman, 1992).

By use of a shell, experts entered their expert knowledge about domain concepts and reasoning rules directly into the computer as responses to questions (Gaines & Boose, 1988). Neale (1988) advocated "eliminating the knowledge engineer and getting the expert to work directly with the computer" (p. 136) because human-on-human KE methods (interviews, protocol analysis) were believed to place an "unjustified faith in textbook knowledge and what experts say they do" (p. 135).

The field of expert systems involved literally thousands of projects in which expert knowledge was elicited (or acquired)

(Hoffman, 1992), but serious problems soon arose. For example, software brittleness (breakdowns in handling atypical cases) and explanatory insufficiency (a printout of cryptic procedural rules fails to clearly express to non-programmers the reasoning path that was followed by the software) were quickly recognized as troublesome (for reviews that convey aspects of the history of this field, see David, Krivine, & Simmons, 1993; Raeth, 1990). At the same time, there was a burgeoning of interest in expertise on the part of cognitive psychologists.

Expertise Studies in Psychology

The application of cognitive science and the psychology of learning to topics in instructional design led to studies of the basis for expertise and knowledge organization at different stages during acquisition of expertise (Lesgold, 1994; Means & Gott, 1988). In the early 1970s, a group of researchers affiliated with the Learning Research and Development Center at the University of Pittsburgh and the Psychology Department at Carnegie-Mellon University launched a number of research projects on issues of instructional design in both educational contexts (e.g., elementary-school-level mathematics word problems; college-level physics problems) and technical contexts of military applications (e.g., problem solving by electronics technicians) (e.g., Chi, Feltovich, & Glaser, 1981) Lesgold et al., 1981. The research emphasized problem-solving behaviors decomposed as "learning hierarchies" (Gagné & Smith, 1962), that is, sequences of learning tasks arranged according to difficulty and direction of transfer.

Interest in instructional design quickly became part of a larger program of investigation that generated several foundational notions about the psychology of expertise (see Glaser, 1987). A number of researchers, apparently independently of one another, began to use the term "cognitive task analysis" both to refer to the process of identifying the knowledge and strategies that make up expertise for a particular domain and task as well as to distinguish the process from so-called behavioral task analysis (e.g., Glaser et al., 1985; see Schraagen, this volume). A stream of psychological research evolved that shifted emphasis from studies with naive, college-aged "subjects" who participated in artificial tasks using artificial materials (in service of control and manipulation of variables) to studies in which highly skilled, domain-smart participants engaged in tasks that were more representative of the complexity of the "real world" in which they practiced their craft (Chi, Glaser, & Farr, 1988; Hoffman, 1992; Knorr-Cetina & Mulkay, 1983; Shanteau, 1992).

Investigators began to shift their attention from cataloging biases and limitations of human reasoning in artificial and simple problems (e.g., statistical reasoning puzzles, syllogistic reasoning puzzles) to the exploration of human capabilities for making decisions, solving complex problems, and forming mental models (Gentner & Stevens, 1983; Klahr & Kotovsky, 1989; Klein & Weitzenfeld, 1982; Scribner, 1984; Sternberg & Frensch, 1991). The ethnographic research of Lave (1988) and Hutchins (1995) revealed that experts do not slavishly conduct "tasks" or adhere to work rules or work procedures but instead develop informal heuristic strategies that, though possibly inefficient and even counterintuitive, are often remarkably robust, effective, and cognitively economical. One provocative implication of this work is that expertise results in part from a natural convergence on such strategies during engagement with the challenges posed by work.

Studies spanned a wide gamut of topics, some of which seem more traditional to academia (e.g., physics problem solving), but many that would traditionally not be fair game for the academic experimental psychologist (e.g., expertise in manufacturing engineering, medical diagnosis, taxicab driving, bird watching, grocery shopping, natural navigation). Mainstream cognitive psychology took something of a turn toward applications (see Barber, 1988), and today the phrase "real world" seems to no longer require scare quotes (see Hollnagel, Hoc, &

Cacciabue, 1996), although there are remnants of debate about the utility and scientific foundations of research that is conducted in uncontrolled or non-laboratory contexts (e.g., Banaji & Crowder, 1989; Hoffman & Deffenbacher, 1993; Hoffman & Woods, 2000).

The Early Methods Palette

Another avenue of study involved attempts to address the knowledge-acquisition bottleneck, the root cause of which lay in the reliance on unstructured interviews by the computer scientists who were building expert systems (see Cullen & Bryman, 1988). Unstructured interviews gained early acceptance as a means of simultaneously "bootstrapping" the researcher's knowledge of the domain, and establishing rapport between the researcher and the expert. Nevertheless, the bottleneck issue encouraged a consideration of methods from psychology that might be brought to bear to widen the bottleneck, including methods of structured interviewing (Gordon & Gill, 1997). Interviews could get their structure from preplanned probe questions, from archived test cases, and so forth.

In addition to interviewing, the researcher might look at expert performance while the expert is conducting their usual or "familiar" task and thinking aloud, with their knowledge and reasoning revealed subsequently via a protocol analysis (see Chi et al., 1981; Ericsson & Simon, 1993, Chapter 38, this volume). In addition, one could study expert performance at "contrived tasks," for example, by withholding certain information about the case at hand (limited-information tasks), or by manipulating the way the information is processed (constrained-processing tasks). In the "method of tough cases" the expert is asked to work on a difficult test case (perhaps gleaned from archives) with the idea that tough cases might reveal subtle aspects of expert reasoning, or particular subdomain or highly specialized knowledge, or aspects of experts' metacognitive skills, for example, the ability to reason about their own reasoning or create new procedures or conceptual categories "on the fly."

Empirical comparisons of KE methods, conducted in the late 1980s, were premised on the speculation that different methods might yield different "kinds" of knowledge – the "differential access hypothesis." (These studies are reviewed at greater length in Hoffman et al., 1995, and Shadbolt & Burton, 1990.) Hoffman worked with experts at aerial photo interpretation for terrain analysis, and Shadbolt and Burton worked with experts at geological and archaeological classification. Both research programs employed a number of knowledge-elicitation methods, and both evaluated the methods in terms of their yield (i.e., the number of informative propositions or decision/classification rules elicited as a function of the task time).

The results were in general agreement. Think-aloud problem solving, combined with protocol analysis, proved to be relatively time-consuming, having a yield of less than one informative proposition per total task minute. Likewise, an unstructured interview yielded less than one informative proposition per total task minute. A structured interview, a constrained processing task, and an analysis of tough cases were the most efficient, yielding between one and two informative propositions per total task minute.

The results from the studies by and Shadbolt and Burton and also showed that there was considerable overlap of knowledge elicited by two of the main techniques they used – a task in which domain concepts were sorted into categories and a task in which domain concepts were rated on a number of dimensions. Both of the techniques elicited information about domain concepts and domain procedures. Hoffman as well as Shadbolt and Burton concluded that interviews need to be used in conjunction with ratings and sorting tasks because contrived techniques elicit specific knowledge and may not yield an overview of the domain knowledge.

An idea that was put aside is that the goal of KE should be to "extract" expert knowledge. It is far more appropriate to refer to knowledge elicitation as a collaborative process, sometimes involving "discovery" of knowledge (Clancey, 1993; Ford & Adams-Webber, 1992; Knorr-Cetina, 1981; LaFrance, 1992). According to a transactional view, expert knowledge is created and maintained through collaborative and social processes, as well as through the perceptual and cognitive processes of the individual. By this view, a goal for cognitive analysis and design is to promote development of a workplace in which knowledge is created, shared, and maintained via natural processes of communication, negotiation, and collaboration (Lintern, Diedrich, & Serfaty, 2002).

The foundation for this newer perspective and set of research goals had been laid by the work of Gary Klein and his associates on the decision making of proficient practitioners in domains such as clinical nursing and firefighting (See Ross, Shafer, & Klein, Chapter 23; Klein et al., 1993). They had laid out some new goals for KE, including the generation of cognitive specifications for jobs, the investigation of decision making in domains involving time pressure and high risk, and the enhancement of proficiency through training and technological innovation. It became clear that the methodology of KE could be folded into the broader methodology of "cognitive task analysis" (CTA) (Militello & Hoffman, forthcoming; Schraagen, Chapter 11), which is now a focal point for human-factors and cognitive-systems engineering.

The Era of Cognitive Task Analysis

Knowledge engineering (or cognitive engineering) typically starts with a problem or challenge to be resolved or a requirement to be satisfied with some form of information processing technology. The design goal influences the methods to be used, including the methods of knowledge elicitation, and the manner in which they will be adapted. One thing that all projects must do is identify who is, and who is not, an expert.

Psychological research during the era of expert systems tended to define expertise somewhat loosely, for instance, "advanced

Table 12.1. Some Alternative Methods of Proficiency Scaling

Method	Yield	Example
In-depth career interviews about education, training, etc.	Ideas about breadth and depth of experience; Estimate of hours of experience	Weather forecasting in the armed services, for instance, involves duty assignments having regular hours and regular job or task assignments that can be tracked across entire careers. Amount of time spent at actual forecasting or forecasting-related tasks can be estimated with some confidence (Hoffman, 1991).
Professional standards or licensing	Ideas about what it takes for individuals to reach the top of their field.	The study of weather forecasters involved senior meteorologists of the US National Atmospheric and Oceanographic Administration and the National Weather Service (Hoffman, 1991). One participant was one of the forecasters for Space Shuttle launches; another was one of the designers of the first meteorological satellites.
Measures of performance at the familiar tasks	Can be used for convergence on scales determined by other methods.	Weather forecasting is again a case in point since records can show for each forecaster the relation between their forecasts and the actual weather. In fact, this is routinely tracked in forecasting offices by the measurement of "forecast skill scores" (see Hoffman & Trafton, 2006).
Social Interaction Analysis	Proficiency levels in some group of practitioners or within some community of practice (Mieg, 2000; Stein, 1997)	In a project on knowledge preservation for the electric power utilities (Hoffman & Hanes, 2003), experts at particular jobs (e.g., maintenance and repair of large turbines, monitoring and control of nuclear chemical reactions, etc.) were readily identified by plant managers, trainers, and engineers. The individuals identified as experts had been performing their jobs for years and were known among company personnel as "the" person in their specialization: *If there was that kind of problem I'd go to Ted. He's the turbine guy.*"

graduate students" in a particular domain. In general, identification of experts was not regarded as either a problem or an issue in expert-system development. (For detailed discussions, see Hart, 1986; Prerau, 1989.) The rule of thumb based on studies of chess (Chase & Simon, 1973) is that expertise is achieved after about 10,000 hours of practice. Recent research has suggested a qualification on this rule of thumb. For instance, Hoffman, Coffey, and Ford (2000) found that even junior journeymen weather forecasters (individuals in their early 30s) can have had as much as 25,000 hours of experience. A similar figure seems appropriate for the domain of intelligence analysis (Hoffman, 2003a).

Concern with the question of how to define expertise (Hoffman, 1998) led to an awareness that determination of who an expert is in a given domain can require effort. In a type of *proficiency-scaling* procedure, the researcher determines a domain and organizationally appropriate scale of proficiency levels. Some alternative methods are described in Table 12.1.

Social Interaction Analysis, the result of which is a sociogram, is perhaps the lesser known of the methods. A sociogram, which represents interaction patterns between people (e.g., frequent interactions), is used to study group clustering, communication patterns, and workflows and processes. For Social Interaction Analysis, multiple individuals within an organization are interviewed. Practitioners might be asked, for example, "If you have a problem of type x, who would you go to for advice?" Or they might be asked to sort cards bearing the names of other domain practitioners into piles according to one or another skill dimension or knowledge category.

Hoffman, Ford, and Coffey (2000) suggested that proficiency scaling for a given project should be based on at least two of the methods listed in Table 12.1. It is important to employ a scale that is both domain and organizationally appropriate, and that considers the full range of proficiency. For instance, in the project on weather forecasting (Hoffman, Coffey, & Ford, 2000), the proficiency scale distinguished three levels: experts, journeymen, and apprentices, each of which was further distinguished by three levels of seniority.

The expanded KE methods palette and the adoption of proficiency scaling represented the broadening of focus beyond expert systems to support for the creation of intelligent or knowledge-based systems of a variety of forms.

Foundational Methods of Cognitive Engineering

In North America, methods for CTA were developed in reaction to limitations of traditional "behavioral task analysis," as well as to limitations of the early AI knowledge acquisition techniques (Hollnagel & Woods, 1983; Rasmussen, 1986). CTA also emerged from the work of researchers who were studying diverse domains of expertise for the purpose of developing better methods for instructional design and enhancing human learning (see the chapters by Greeno, Gregg, Resnick, and Simon & Hayes in Klahr, 1976). Ethnographers, sociologists of science, and cognitive anthropologists, working in parallel, began to look at how new technology influences work cultures and how technology mediates cooperative activity (e.g., Clancey, Chapter 8; Hutchins, 1995,

Knorr-Cetina & Mulkay, 1983; Suchman, 1987).

The field of "Work Analysis," which has existed in Europe since the 1960s, is regarded as a branch of ergonomics, although it has involved the study of cognitive activities in the workplace. (For reviews of the history of the research in this tradition see De Keyser, Decortis, & Van Daele, 1998 Militello & Hoffman, forthcoming; Vicente, 1999.) Work Analysis is concerned with performance at all levels of proficiency, but that of course entails the study of experts and the elicitation of their knowledge. Seminal research in Work Analysis was conducted by Jens Rasmussen and his colleagues at the Risø National Laboratory in Denmark (Rasmussen, Petjersen, & Goodstein, 1994; Rasmussen, 1985). They began with the goal of making technical inroads in the safety-engineering aspects of nuclear power and aviation but concluded that safety could not be assured solely through technical engineering (see Rasmussen & Rouse, 1981). Hence, they began to conduct observations in the workplace (e.g., analyses of prototypical problem scenarios) and conduct interviews with experts.

The theme to these parallel North American and European efforts has been the attempt to understand the interaction of cognition, collaboration, and complex artifacts (Potter, Roth, Woods, & Elm, 2000). The reference point is the field setting, wherein teams of expert practitioners confront significant problems aided by technological and other types of artifacts (Rasmussen, 1992; Vicente, 1999).

The broadening of KE, folding it into CTA, has resulted in an expanded palette of methods, including, for example, ethnographic methods (Clancey, 1993, Hutchins, 1995; Orr, 1996; Spradley, 1979). An example of the application of ethnography to expertise studies appears in Dekker, Nyce, and Hoffman (2003). In this chapter we cannot discuss all of the methods in detail. Instead, we highlight three that have been widely used, with success, in this new era of CTA: the Critical Decision Method, Work Domain Analysis, and Concept Mapping.

Table 12.2. A Sample of a Coded CDM Protocol (Adapted from Klein et al., 1989)

Appraisal	This is going to be a tough fire,
Cue	and we may start running into heat exhaustion problems.
Cue	It is 70 degrees now and it is going to get hotter.
Action	The first truck, I would go ahead and have them open the roof up,
Action	and the second truck I would go ahead and send them inside and
Action	have them start ventilating, start knocking the windows out and working
Elaboration	with the initial engine crew, false ceilings, and get the walls opened up.
Action	As soon as I can, order the second engine to hook up to supply and pump to engine 1.
Anticipation	I am assuming engine 2 will probably be there in a second.
Cue-deliberation	I don't know how long the supply lay line is,
Anticipation	but it appears we are probably going to need more water than one supply line is going to give us.
Metacognition	So I would keep in mind,
Contingency	unless we can check the fire fairly rapidly.
Contingency	So start thinking of other water sources.
Action-Deliberation	Consider laying another supply line to engine 1.

The Critical Decision Method

The Critical Decision Method (CDM) involves multi-pass retrospection in which the expert is guided in the recall and elaboration of a previously experienced case. The CDM leverages the fact that domain experts often retain detailed memories of previously encountered cases, especially ones that were unusual, challenging, or in one way or another involved "critical decisions." The CDM does not use generic questions of the kind "Tell me everything you know about x," or "Can you describe your typical procedure?" Instead, it guides the expert through multiple waves of re-telling and prompts through the use of specific probe questions (e.g., "What were you seeing?") and "what-if" queries (e.g., "What might someone else have done in this circumstance?"). The CDM generates rich case studies that are often useful as training materials. It yields time-lined scenarios, which describe decisions (decision types, observations, actions, options, etc.) and aspects of decisions that can be easy or difficult. It can also yield a list of decision requirements and perceptual cues – the information the expert needs in order to make decisions.

An example of a coded CDM transcript appears in Table 12.2. In this example, events

in the case have been placed into a timeline and coded into the categories indicated in the leftmost column. As in all methods for coding protocols, multiple coders are used and there is a reliability check.

Given its focus on decision making, the strength of the CDM is its use in the creation of models of reasoning (e.g., decisions, strategies). Detailed presentations of the method along with summaries of studies illustrating its successful use can be found in Crandall, Klein, and Hoffman (2006) and Hoffman, Crandall, and Shadbolt (1998).

Work Domain Analysis

Unlike the CDM, which focuses on the reasoning and strategies of the individual practitioner, Work Domain Analysis (WDA) builds a representation of an entire work domain. WDA has most frequently been used to describe the structure of human-machine systems for process control, but it is now finding increasing use in the analysis and design of complex, systems (Burns & Hajdukiewicz, 2004; Chow & Vicente, 2002; Lintern, Miller, & Baker, 2002; Naikar & Sanderson, 2001).

An Abstraction-Decomposition matrix represents a work domain in terms of

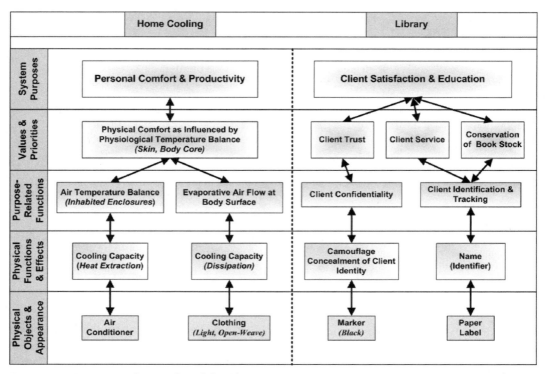

Figure 12.1. Two tutorial examples of the Abstraction-Decomposition representation, a primarily technical system (Home Cooling, left panel) and a sociotechnical system (Library Client Tracking, right panel).

"levels of abstraction," where each level is a distinctive type of constraint. Figure 12.1 presents matrices for two systems, one designed predominantly around physical laws and the other designed predominantly around social values. The library example grapples with a pervasive social issue, the need for individual identification balanced against the desire for personal confidentiality. These tutorial examples demonstrate that the Abstraction-Decomposition format can be used with markedly different work domains. In both of these matrices, entries at each level constitute the means to achieve ends at the level above. The intent is to express means-ends relations between the entries of adjacent levels, with lower levels showing how higher-level functions are met, and higher levels showing why lower-level forms and functions are necessary.

Work domains are also represented in terms of a second dimension: "levels of decomposition," from organizational con-

text, down to social collectives (teams), down to individual worker or individual component (e.g., software package residing on a particular workstation).

Typically, a work-domain analysis is initiated from a study of documents, although once an Abstraction-Decomposition matrix is reasonably well developed, interviews with domain experts will help the analyst extend and refine it. Vicente (1999) argues that the Abstraction-Decomposition matrix is an activity-independent representation and should contain only descriptions of the work domain (the tutorial examples of Figure 12.1 were developed with that stricture in mind). However, Vicente's advice is not followed universally within the community that practices WDA; some analysts include processes in their Abstraction-Decomposition matrices (e.g., Burns & Hajdukiewicz, 2004).

It is possible to add activity to the representation yet remain consistent with Vicente (1999) by overlaying a trajectory derived from a description of strategic reasoning undertaken by experts. Figure 12.2 presents a fragment of a structural description of a weather-forecasting work domain, and Figure 12.3 presents the same structural description with an activity overlay developed from a transcript of an expert forecaster's description of jobs, roles, and tools involved in forecasting (Hoffman, Coffey, & Ford, 2000). Activity statements (shown as callouts in Figure 12.3) were coded as falling into one or another of the cells, and the temporal sequence of the activity was represented by the flow of arrows as connectors to show how forecasters navigate opportunistically through an abstraction-decomposition space as they seek the information to diagnose and solve the problems.

When used in this manner, the matrix captures important propositions as elicited from domain experts concerning their goals and reasoning (see, e.g., Burns, Bryant, & Chalmers, 2001; Rasmussen, 1986; Schmidt & Luczak, 2000; Vicente, Christoffersen, & Pereklita, 1995) within the context of collaboration with larger collectives and organizational goals.

Concept Mapping

The third CTA method we will discuss is also one that has been widely used and has met with considerable success. Unlike Abstraction-Decomposition and its functional analysis of work domains, and unlike the CDM and its focus on reasoning and strategies, Concept Mapping has as its great strength the generation of models of knowledge.

Concept Maps are meaningful diagrams that include concepts (enclosed in boxes) and relationships among concepts or propositions (indicated by labeled connections between related concepts). Concept Mapping has foundations in the theory of Meaningful Learning (Ausubel, Novak, & Hanesian, 1978) and decades of research and application, primarily in education (Novak, 1998). Concept Maps can be used to show gaps in student knowledge. At the other end of the proficiency scale, Concept Maps made by domain experts tend to show high levels of agreement (see Gordon, 1992; Hoffman, Coffey, & Ford, 2000). (Reviews of the literature and discussion of methods

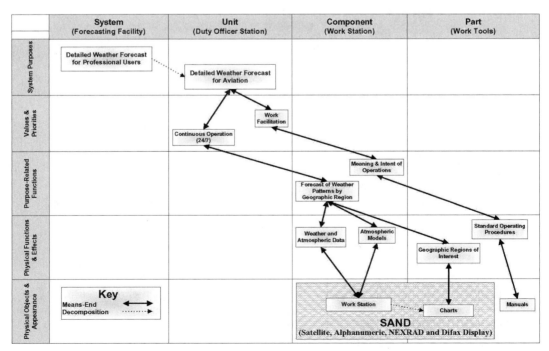

Figure 12.2. An Abstraction-Decomposition matrix of a fragment of a weather-forecasting work domain.

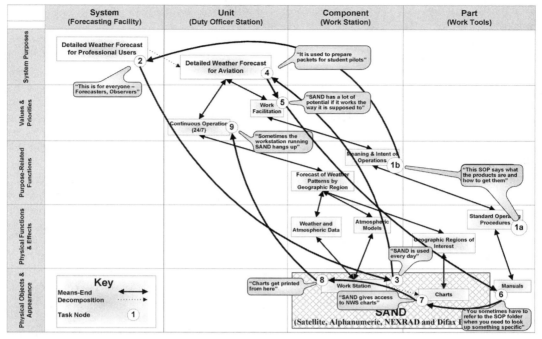

Figure 12.3. An Abstraction-Decomposition matrix of a fragment of a weather-forecasting work domain with an activity overlay (statements in callouts are quotes from a forecaster).

for making Concept Maps can be found in Cañas et al., 2004; and Crandall, Klein, & Hoffman, 2006.) Figure 12.4 is a Concept Map that lays out expert knowledge about the role of cold fronts in the Gulf Coast (Hoffman, Coffey, & Ford, 2000).

Although Concept Maps can be made by use of paper and pencil, a white board, or Post-Its, the Concept Maps presented here were created by use of CmapTools, a software suite created at the Institute for Human and Machine Cognition (free download at http://ihmc.us). In the KE procedure involving an individual expert, one researcher stands at a screen and serves as the facilitator while another researcher drives the laptop and creates the Concept Map that is projected on the screen. The facilitator helps the domain expert build up a representation of their domain knowledge, in effect combining KE with knowledge representation. (This is one reason the method is relatively efficient.) Concept Mapping can also be used by teams or groups, for purposes other than KE (e.g., brainstorming, consen-

sus formation). Teams can be structured in a variety of ways and can make and share Concept Maps over the world-wide web (see Cañas et al., 2004).

The ability to hyperlink digital "resources" such as text documents, images, video clips, and URLs is another significant advantage provided by computerized means of developing Concept Maps (Cmap-Tools indicate hyperlinks by the small icons underneath concept nodes). Hyperlinks can connect to other Concept Maps; a set of Concept Maps hyperlinked together is regarded as a "knowledge model." Figure 12.5 shows a screen shot from the top-level Concept Map in the System To Organize Representations in Meteorology (STORM), in which a large number of Concept Maps are linked together. In Figure 12.5, some of the resources have been opened for illustrative purposes (real-time satellite imagery, computer weather forecasts, and digital video in which the domain expert provides brief explanatory statements for some of the concepts throughout the model).

All of the STORM Concept Maps and resources can be viewed at http://www.ihmc.us/research/projects/STORMLK/

Knowledge models structured as Concept Maps can serve as living repositories of expert knowledge to support knowledge sharing as well as knowledge preservation. They can serve also as interfaces for intelligent systems where the model of the expert's knowledge becomes the interface for a performance support tool or training aid. (Ford et al., 1996).

Methodological Concepts and Issues

Research and various applied projects conducted since the seminal works on KE methodology have left some ideas standing and have led to some new and potentially valuable ideas. One recent review of CTA methods (Bonacteo & Burns, forthcoming)

lists dozens of methods. Although not all of them are methods that would be useful as knowledge-elicitation or knowledge-representation procedures, it is clear that the roster of tools and methods available to cognitive engineers has expanded considerably over the past two decades. We look now to core ideas and tidbits of guidance that have stood the test of time.

Where the Rubber Meets the Road

(1). In eliciting expert knowledge one can: (a) Ask people questions, and (b) Observe performance. Questions can be asked in the great many forms and formats for interviewing, including unstructured interviews, the CDM procedure, and Concept Mapping, as well as many other techniques (e.g., Endsley & Garland, 2000). Performance can be observed via ethnographic studies of patterns of communication in the workplace,

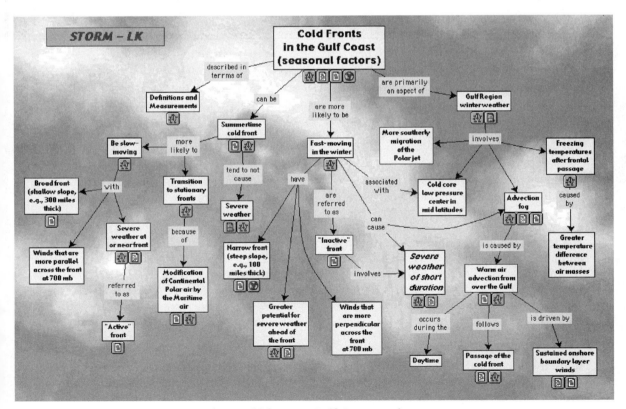

Figure 12.4. A Concept Map about cold fronts in Gulf Coast weather.

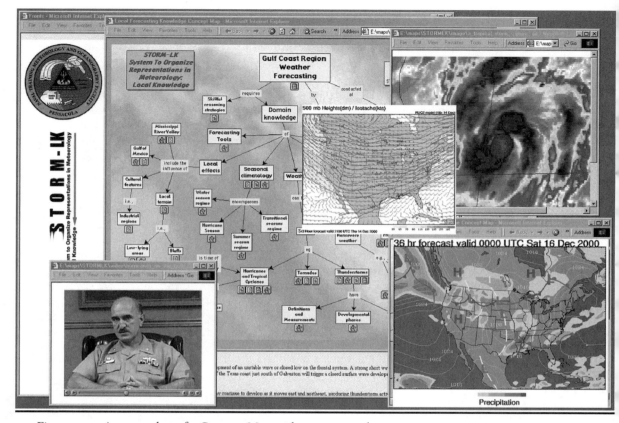

Figure 12.5. A screen shot of a Concept Map with some opened resources.

evaluations in terms of performance measures (e.g., the accuracy of weather forecasts), or evaluations of recall, recognition, or reaction-time performance in contrived tasks or think-aloud problem solving tasks.

(2). In eliciting expert knowledge one can attempt to create models of the work domain, models of practitioner knowledge of the domain, or models of practitioner reasoning. Models of these three kinds take different forms and have different sorts of uses and applications. This is illustrated roughly by the three methods we have described here. The CDM can be used to create products that describe practitioner reasoning (e.g., decision types, strategies, decision requirements, informational cues). The Abstraction-Decomposition matrix represents the functional structure of the work domain, which can provide context for an overlay of activity developed from interview protocols or expert narratives. Concept

Mapping represents practitioner knowledge of domain concepts such as relations, laws, and case types.

(3). Knowledge elicitation methods differ in their relative efficiency. For instance, the think-aloud problem solving task combined with protocol analysis has uses in the psychology laboratory but is relatively inefficient in the context of knowledge elicitation. Concept Mapping is arguably the most efficient method for the elicitation of domain knowledge (Hoffman, 2002). We see a need for more studies on this topic.

(4). Knowledge-elicitation methods can be combined in various ways. Indeed, a recommendation from the 1980s still stands – that any project involving expert knowledge elicitation should use more than one knowledge-elicitation method. One combination that has recently become salient is the combination of the CDM with the two other procedures we have discussed.

Concept-Mapping interviews almost always trigger in the experts the recall of previously encountered tough cases. This can be used to substitute for the "Incident Selection" step in the CDM. Furthermore, case studies generated by the CDM can be used as resources to populate the Concept-Map knowledge models (see Hoffman, Coffey, & Ford, 2000). As another example, Naikar and Saunders (2003) conducted a Work Domain Analysis to isolate safety-significant events from aviation incident reports and then employed the CDM in interviews with authors of those reports to identify critical cognitive issues that precipitated or exacerbated the event.

(5). The gold is not in the documents. Document analysis is useful in bootstrapping researchers into the domain of study and is a recommended method for initiating Work Domain Analysis (e.g., Lintern et al., 2002), but experts possess knowledge and strategies that do not appear in documents and task descriptions. Cognitive engineers invariably rely on interactions with experts to garner implicit, obscure, and otherwise undocumented expert knowledge. Even in Work Domain Analysis, which is heavily oriented towards Document Analysis, interactions with experts are used to confirm and refine the Abstraction-Decomposition matrices.

In the weather-forecasting project (Hoffman, Coffey, & Ford, 2000), an expert told how she predicted the lifting of fog. She would look out toward the downtown and see how many floors above ground level she could count before the floors got lost in the fog deck. Her reasoning relied on a heuristic of the form, "If I cannot see the 10th floor by 10 AM, pilots will not be able to take off until after lunchtime." Such a heuristic has great value but is hardly the sort of thing that could be put into a formal standard operating procedure. Many observations have been made of how engineers in process control bend rules and deviate from mandated procedures so that they can do their jobs more effectively (see Koopman & Hoffman, 2003). We would hasten to generalize by saying that all experts who work in complex sociotechnical contexts possess knowledge and reasoning strategies that are not captured in existing procedures or documents, many of which represent (naughty) departures from what those experts are supposed to do or to believe (Johnston, 2003; McDonald, Corrigan, & Ward, 2002).

Discovery of these undocumented departures from authorized procedures represents a window on the "true work" (Vicente, 1999), which is cognitive work independent of particular technologies, that is, it is governed only by domain constraints and by human cognitive constraints. Especially after an accident, it is commonly argued that experts who depart from authorized procedures are, in some way, negligent. Nevertheless, the adaptive process that generates the departures is not only inevitable but is also a primary source of efficient and robust work procedures (Lintern, 2003). In that these windows are suggestive of leverage points and ideas for new aiding technologies, cognitive engineers need to pay them serious attention.

(6). Differential access is not a salient problem. The first wave of comparative KE methodology research generated the hypothesis that different "kinds" of knowledge might be more amenable to elicitation by particular methods (Hoffman, 1987), and some studies suggested the possibility of differential access (Cooke & MacDonald, 1986, 1987; Evans, Jentsch, Hitt, Bowers, & Salas, 2001). Tasks involving the generation of lists of domain concepts can in fact result in lists of domain concepts, and tasks involving the specification of procedures can in fact result in statements about rules or procedures. However, some studies have found little or no evidence for differential access (e.g., Adelman, 1989; Shadbolt & Burton, 1990), and we conclude that a strong version of the differential-access hypothesis has not held up well under scrutiny. All of the available methods *can* say things about so-called declarative knowledge, so-called procedural knowledge, and so forth.

All KE methods can be used to identify leverage points – aspects of the organization or work domain where even a modest infusion of supporting technologies might have positive results (e.g., redesign of interfaces, redesign of the workspace layout, creation of new functionalities for existing software, and ideas about entirely new software systems.) Again we can use the project on expert weather forecasting as an example (Hoffman, Coffey, & Ford, 2000). That project compared a number of alternative knowledge-elicitation methods including protocol analysis, the CDM, the Knowledge Audit (Militello & Hutton, 1998; see Ross, Shafer and Klein, this volume), an analysis of "Standard Operating Procedures" documents, the Recent Case Walkthrough method (Militello & Hutton, 1998), a Workspace and Workpatterns analysis (Vicente, 1999), and Concept Mapping. All methods yielded data that spoke to practitioner knowledge and reasoning and all also identified leverage points.

(7). "Tacit" knowledge is not a salient problem. Without getting into the philosophical weeds of what one means by "kinds" of knowledge, another concern has to do with the possibility that routine knowledge about procedures or task activities might become "tacit," that is, so automatic as to be inexpressible via introspection or verbal report. This hangover issue from the heyday of Behaviorism remains to this day a non-problem in the practical context of eliciting knowledge from experts. For one thing, it has never been demonstrated that there exists such a thing as "knowledge that cannot be verbalized in principle," and the burden of proof falls on the shoulders of those who make the existence claim. Again sidestepping the philosophical issues (i.e., if it cannot be articulated verbally, is it really knowledge?), we maintain that the empirical facts mitigate the issue. For instance, in Concept-Mapping interviews with domain experts, experience shows that almost every time the expert will reach a point in making a Concept Map where s/he will say something like, *"Well, I've never really thought about that, or thought about it in this way, but now that you mention it ...,"* and what follows will be a clear specification on some procedure, strategy, or aspect of subdomain knowl-

edge that had not been articulated up to that point.

(8). Good knowledge elicitation procedures are "effective scaffolds." Although there may be phenomena to which one could legitimately, or at least arguably, append the designation "tacit knowledge," there is no indication that such knowledge lies beyond the reach of science in some unscientific netherworld of intuitions or unobservables. Over and over again, the lesson is not that there is knowledge that experts literally cannot articulate, nor is it the hangover issue of whether verbalization "interferes" with reasoning. Rather, the issue is whether the KE procedure provides sufficient scaffolding to support the expert in articulating what they know. Support involves the specifics of the procedure (e.g., probe questions), but it also involves the fact that knowledge elicitation is a collaborative process. There is no substitute for the skill of the elicitor (e.g., in framing alternative suggestions and wordings). Likewise, there is no substitute for the skill of the participating practitioner. Some experts will have good insight, but others will not. Though it might be possible for someone to prove the existence of "knowledge" that cannot be uncovered, knowledge engineers face the immediate, practical challenges of designing new and better sociotechnical systems. They accomplish something when they uncover useful knowledge that might have otherwise been missed.

New Ideas

Recent research and application efforts have also yielded some new ideas about the knowledge elicitation methods palette.

(1). The (hypothetical) problem of differential access has given way to a practical consideration of "differential utility." Any given method might be more useful for certain purposes, might be more applicable to certain domains, or might be more useful with experts having certain cognitive styles. In other words, each knowledge-elicitation method has its strengths and weaknesses. Some of these are more purely

methodological or procedural (e.g., transcription and protocol analysis takes a long time), but some relate to the content of what is elicited. The CDM has as its strength the elicitation of knowledge about perceptual cues and patterns, decision types, and reasoning strategies. The strength of Concept Mapping lies in the creation of knowledge models that can be used in the creation of knowledge bases or interfaces. Work Domain Analysis, which maps the functional structure of the work domain, can provide a backdrop against which the knowledge and skills of the individual expert can be fitted into the larger functional context of the organization and its purposes. Products from any of these procedures can support the design of new interfaces or even the redesign of workplaces and methods of collaboration.

(2). *Methodology benefits from opportunism.* It can be valuable during a knowledge-elicitation project to be open to emerging possibilities and new opportunities, even opportunities to create new methods or try out and evaluate new combinations of methods. In the weather-forecasting project (Hoffman, Coffey, & Ford, 2000), Concept-Mapping interviews demonstrated that practitioners were quite comfortable with psychologists' notion of a "mental model" because the field has for years distinguished forecaster reasoning ("conceptual models") from the outputs of the mathematical computer models of weather. Indeed, the notion of a mental model has been invoked as an explanatory concept in weather forecasting for decades (see Hoffman, Trafton, & Roebber, forthcoming). Practitioners were quite open to discussing their reasoning, and so a special interview was crafted to explore this topic in detail (Hoffman, Coffey, & Carnot, 2000).

(3). *Knowledge elicitation is not a one-off procedure.* Historically, KE was considered in the context of creating intelligent systems for particular applications. The horizons were expanded by such applications as the preservation of organizational or team knowledge (Klein, 1992). This notion was recently expanded even further to

the idea of "corporate knowledge management," which includes capture, archiving, application to training, proprietary analysis, and other activities (e.g., Becerra-Fernandez, Gonzalez, & Sabherwal, 2004; Davenport & Prusak, 1998). A number of government and private sector organizations have found a need to capture expert knowledge prior to the retirement of the experts and also the need, sometimes urgent, to reclaim expertise from individuals who have recently retired (Hoffman & Hanes, 2003). Instantiation of knowledge capture as part of an organizational culture entails many potential obstacles, such as management and personnel buy-in. It also raises many practical problems, not the least of which is how to incorporate a process of ongoing knowledge capture into the ordinary activities of the experts without burdening them with an additional task.

Recognition of the value of the analysis of tough cases led to a recommendation that experts routinely make notes about important aspects of tough cases that they encounter (Hoffman, 1987). This idea has been taken to new levels in recent years. For instance, because of downsizing in the 1980s, the electric power utilities face a situation in which senior experts are retiring and there is not yet a cohort of junior experts who are primed to take up the mantle (Hoffman & Hanes, 2003). At one utility, a turbine had been taken off line for total refitting, an event that was seen as an opportunity to videotape certain repair jobs that require expertise but are generally only required occasionally (on the order of once every 10 or more years).

Significant expertise involves considerable domain and procedural knowledge and an extensive repertoire of skills and heuristics. Elicitation is rarely something that can be done easily or quickly. In eliciting weather-forecasting knowledge for just the Florida Gulf Coast region of the United Sates, about 150 Concept Maps were made about local phenomena involving fog, thunderstorms, and hurricanes. And yet, dozens more Concept Maps could have been made on additional topics, including the use of the new weather radar systems and the use of the many computer models for weather forecasting (Hoffman, Coffey, & Ford, 2000). A current project on "knowledge recovery" that involves reclamation of expert knowledge about terrain analysis from existing documents such as the Terrain Analysis Database (Hoffman, 2003b) has generated over 150 Concept Maps containing more than 3,000 propositions.

Although knowledge elicitation on such a scale is daunting, we now have the technologies and methodologies to facilitate the elicitation, preservation, and sharing of expert knowledge on a scale never before possible. This is a profound application of cognitive science and is one that is of immense value to society.

Practice, Practice, Practice

No matter how much detail is provided about the conduct of a knowledge-elicitation procedure, there is no substitute for practice. The elicitor needs to adapt on the fly to individual differences in style, personality, agenda, and goals. In "breaking the ice" and establishing rapport, the elicitor needs to show good intentions and needs to be sensitive to possible concerns on the part of the expert that the capture of his/her knowledge might mean the loss of their job (perhaps to a machine). To be good and effective at knowledge-elicitation, one must attempt to become an "expert apprentice" – experienced at, skilled at, and comfortable with going into new domains, boostrapping efficiently and then designing and conducting a series of knowledge-elicitation procedures appropriate to project goals. The topic of how to train people to be expert apprentices is one that we hope will receive attention from researchers in the coming years (see Militello & Quill, forthcoming).

Acknowledgments

The senior Author's contribution to this chapter was supported through his participation in the National Alliance for Expertise Studies, which is supported by the "Sciences of Learning" Program of the National Science Foundation, and his participation in The Advanced Decision Architectures Collaborative Technology Alliance, which is sponsored by the US Army Research Laboratory under cooperative agreement DAAD19-01-2-0009.

References

Adelman, L. (1989). Management issues in knowledge elicitation. *IEEE Transactions on Systems, Man, and Cybernetics, 19*, 483–488.

Ausubel, D. P., Novak, J. D., & Hanesian, H. (1978). *Educational psychology: A cognitive view*, 2nd ed. New York: Holt, Rinehart and Winston.

Banaji, M. R., & Crowder, R. G. (1989). The bankruptcy of everyday memory. *American Psychologist, 44*, 1185–1193.

Barber, P. (1988). *Applied cognitive psychology*. London: Methuen.

Becerra-Fernandez, I., Gonzalez, A., & Sabherwal, R. (2004). *Knowledge management: challenges, solutions, and technologies*. Upper Saddle River, NJ: Prentice-Hall.

Bonaceto, C., & Burns, K. (forthcoming). Mapping the mountains: A survey of cognitive engineering methods and uses. In R. R. Hoffman (Ed.), *Expertise out of context: Proceedings of the Sixth International Conference on Naturalistic Decision Making*. Mahwah, NJ: Erlbaum.

Burns, C., & Hajdukiewicz, J. R. (2004). *Ecological interface design*. Boca Raton, FL: CRC Press.

Burns, C. M., Bryant, D., & Chalmers, B. (2001). Scenario mapping with work domain analysis. In *Proceedings of the Human Factors and Ergonomics Society 45th Annual Meeting* (pp. 424–428). Santa Monica, CA: Human Factors and Ergonomics Society.

Cañas, A. J., Hill, G., Carff, R., Suri, N., Lott, J., Eskridge, T., Gómez, G., Arroyo, M., & Carvajal, R. (2004). CmapTools: A Knowledge Modeling and Sharing Environment. In A. J. Cañas, J. D. Novak, & F. M. González (Eds.), *Concept Maps: Theory, Methodology, Technology, Proceedings of the 1st International Conference on Concept Mapping* (pp. 125–133). Pamplona, Spain: Universidad Pública de Navarra.

Chase, W. G., & Simon, H. A. (1973). Perception in chess. *Cognitive Psychology, 4*, 55–81.

Chi, M. T. H., Feltovich, P. J., & Glaser, R. (1981). Categorization and representations of physics problems by experts and novices. *Cognitive Science*, 5, 121–152.

Chi, M. T. H., Glaser, R., & Farr, M. L. (Eds.) (1988). *The nature of expertise*. Hillsdale, NJ: Erlbaum.

Chow, R., & Vicente, K. J. (2002). A field study of emergency ambulance dispatching: Implications for decision support. In *Proceedings of the Human Factors and Ergonomics Society 46th Annual Meeting* (pp. 313–317). Santa Monica, CA: Human Factors and Ergonomics Society.

Clancey, W. J. (1993). The knowledge level reinterpreted: Modeling socio-technical systems. In K. M. Ford & J. M. Bradshaw (Eds.), *Knowledge acquisition as modeling* (pp. 33–49, Pt. 1). New York: Wiley.

Cooke, N. M., & McDonald, J. E. (1986). A formal methodology for acquiring and representing expert knowledge. *Proceedings of the IEEE* 74, 1422–1430.

Cooke, N. M., & McDonald, J. E. (1987). The application of psychological scaling techniques to knowledge elicitation for knowledge-based systems. *International Journal of Man-Machine Studies*, 26, 533–550.

Crandall, B., Klein, G., & Hoffman, R. R. (2006). *Working Minds: A practitioner's guide to cognitive task analysis*. Cambridge, MA: MIT Press.

Cullen, J., & Bryman, A. (1988). The knowledge acquisition bottleneck: Time for reassessment? *Expert Systems*, 5, 216–225.

David, J.-M., Krivine, J.-P., & Simmons, R. (Eds.) (1993). *Second-generation expert systems*. Berlin: Springer Verlag.

Davenport, T. H., & Prusak, L. (1998). *Working knowledge: How organizations manage what they know*. Cambridge, MA: Harvard Business School Press.

De Keyser, V., Decortis, F., & Van Daele, A. (1998). The approach of Francophone ergonomy: Studying new technologies. In V. De Keyser, T. Qvale, & B. Wilpert (Eds.), *The meaning of work and technological options* (pp. 147–163). Chichester, England: Wiley.

Dekker, S. W. A., Nyce, J. M., & Hoffman, R. R. (March–April 2003). From contextual inquiry to designable futures: What do we need to get there? *IEEE Intelligent Systems*, pp. 74–77.

Diderot, D. (with d'Alembert, J.) (Eds.) (1751–1772). *Encyclopédie ou Dictionnaire raisonné des sciences, des arts et des métiers, par une Société de Gens de lettere*. Paris: Le Breton. *Compact Edition* published in 1969 by The Readex Microprint Corporation, New York. Translations of selected articles can be found at http://www.hti.umich.edu/d/did/.

Duda, J., Gaschnig, J., & Hart, P. (1979). Model design in the PROSPECTOR consultant system for mineral exploration. In D. Michie (Ed.), *Expert systems in the micro-electronic age* (pp. 153–167). Edinburgh: Edinburgh University Press.

Endsdley, M. R., & Garland, D. L. (2000). *Situation awareness analysis and measurement*. Hillsdale, NJ: Erlbaum.

Ericsson, K. A., & Simon, H. A. (1993). *Protocol analysis: Verbal reports as data, 2nd ed*. Cambridge, MA: MIT Press.

Evans, A. W., Jentsch, F., Hitt, J. M., Bowers, C., & Salas, E. (2001). Mental model assessments: Is there a convergence among different methods? In *Proceedings of the Human Factors and Ergonomics Society 45th Annual Meeting* (pp. 293–296). Santa Monica, CA: Human Factors and Ergonomics Society.

Feigenbaum, E. A., Buchanan, B. G., & Lederberg, J. (1971). On generality and problem solving: A case study using the DENDRAL program. In B. Meltzer & D. Michie (Eds.), *Machine intelligence 6* (pp. 165–190). Edinburgh: Edinburgh University Press.

Ford, K. M., & Adams-Webber, J. R. (1992). Knowledge acquisition and constructive epistemology. In R. Hoffman (Ed.), *The cognition of experts: Psychological research and empirical AI* (pp. 121–136). New York: Springer-Verlag.

Ford, K. M., Coffey, J. W., Cañas, A., Andrews, E. J., & Turne, C. W. (1996). Diagnosis and explanation by a nuclear cardiology expert system. *International Journal of Expert Systems*, 9, 499–506.

Forsyth, D. E., & Buchanan, B. G. (1989). Knowledge acquisition for expert systems: Some pitfalls and suggestions. *IEEE Transactions on Systems, Man, and Cybernetics*, 19, 345–442.

Gaines, B. R., & Boose, J. H. (Eds.) (1988). *Knowledge acquisition tools for expert systems*. London: Academic Press.

Gagné, R. M., & Smith, E. C. (1962). A study of the effects of verbalization on problem solving. *Journal of Experimental Psychology*, 63, 12–18.

Gentner, D., & Stevens, A. L. (Eds.) (1983). *Mental models*. Mahwah, NJ: Erlbaum.

Glaser, R. (1987). Thoughts on expertise. In C. Schooler & W. Schaie (Eds.), *Cognitive functioning and social structure over the life course* (pp. 81–94). Norwood, NJ: Ablex.

Glaser, R., Lesgold, A., Lajoie, S., Eastman, R., Greenberg, L., Logan, D., Magone, M., Weiner, A., Wolf, R., & Yengo, L. (1985). "Cognitive task analysis to enhance technical skills training and assessment." Report, Learning Research and Development Center, University of Pittsburgh, Pittsburgh, PA.

Gordon, S. E. (1992). Implications of cognitive theory for knowledge acquisition. In R. R. Hoffman (Ed.), *The psychology of expertise: Cognitive research and empirical AI* (pp. 99–120). Mahwah, NJ: Erlbaum.

Gordon, S. E., & Gill, R. T. (1997). Cognitive task analysis. In C. Zsambok and G. Klein (Eds.), *Naturalistic decision making* (pp. 131–140). Mahwah, NJ: Erlbaum.

Hart, A. (1986). *Knowledge acquisition for expert systems*. London: Kogan Page.

Hayes-Roth, F., Waterman, D. A., & Lenat, D. B. (1983). *Building expert systems*. Reading, MA: Addison-Wesley.

Hoffman, R. R. (1987, Summer). The problem of extracting the knowledge of experts from the perspective of experimental psychology. *AI Magazine*, 8, 53–67.

Hoffman, R. R. (1991). Human factors psychology in the support of forecasting: The design of advanced meteorological workstations. *Weather and Forecasting*, 6, 98–110.

Hoffman, R. R. (Ed.) (1992). *The psychology of expertise: Cognitive research and empirical AI.* Mahwah, NJ: Erlbaum.

Hoffman, R. R. (1998). How can expertise be defined?: Implications of research from cognitive psychology. In R. Williams, W. Faulkner, & J. Fleck (Eds.), *Exploring expertise* (pp. 81–100). New York: Macmillan.

Hoffman, R. R. (2002, September). An empirical comparison of methods for eliciting and modeling expert knowledge. In *Proceedings of the 46th Meeting of the Human Factors and Ergonomics Society* (pp. 482–486). Santa Monica, CA: Human Factors and Ergonomics Society.

Hoffman, R. R. (2003a). "Use of Concept Mapping and the Critical Decision Method to support Human-Centered Computing for the intelligence community." Report, Institute for Human and Machine Cognition, Pensacola, FL.

Hoffman, R. R. (2003b). "Knowledge recovery." Report, Institute for Human and Machine Cognition, Pensacola, FL.

Hoffman, R. R., Coffey, J. W., & Carnot, M. J. (2000, November). Is there a "fast track" into the black box?: The Cognitive Modeling Procedure. Poster presented at the 41st Annual Meeting of the Psychonomics Society, New Orleans, LA.

Hoffman, R. R., Crandall, B., & Shadbolt, N. (1998). A case study in cognitive task analysis methodology: The Critical Decision Method for the elicitation of expert knowledge. *Human Factors*, 40, 254–276.

Hoffman, R. R., & Deffenbacher, K. (1992). A brief history of applied cognitive psychology. *Applied Cognitive Psychology*, 6, 1–48.

Hoffman, R. R., & Deffenbacher, K. A. (1993). An analysis of the relations of basic and applied science. *Ecological Psychology*, 5, 315–352.

Hoffman, R. R., Coffey, J. W., & Ford, K. M. (2000). "A case study in the research paradigm of Human-Centered Computing: Local expertise in weather forecasting." Report to the National Technology Alliance on the Contract, "Human-Centered System Prototype." Institute for Human and Machine Cognition, Pensacola, FL.

Hoffman, R. R., Ford, K. M., & Coffey, J. W. (2000). "The handbook of human-centered computing." Report, Institute for Human and Machine Cognition, Pensacola, FL.

Hoffman, R. R., & Hanes, L. F. (2003/July–August). The boiled frog problem. *IEEE: Intelligent Systems*, pp. 68–71.

Hoffman, R. R., Shadbolt, N. R., Burton, A. M., & Klein, G. (1995). Eliciting knowledge from experts: A methodological analysis. *Organizational Behavior and Human Decision Processes*, 62, 129–158.

Hoffman, R. R., Trafton, G., & Roebber, P. (2006). *Minding the weather: How expert forecasters think*. Cambridge, MA: MIT Press.

Hoffman, R. R., & Woods, D. D. (2000). Studying cognitive systems in context. *Human Factors*, 42, 1–7.

Hoc, J.-M., Cacciabue, P. C., & Hollnagel, E. (1996). Expertise and technology: "I have a feeling we're not in Kansas anymore." In J.-M. Hoc, P. C. Cacciabue, & E. Hollnagel (Eds.), *Expertise and technology: Cognition and human-computer cooperation* (pp. 279–286). Mahwah, NJ: Erlbaum.

Hollnagel, E., & Woods, D. D. (1983). Cognitive systems engineering: New wine in new bottles. *International Journal of Man-Machine Studies, 18*, 583–600.

Johnston, N. (2003). The paradox of rules: Procedural drift in commercial aviation. In R. Jensen (Ed.), *Proceedings of the Twelfth International Symposium on Aviation Psychology* (pp. 630–635). Dayton, OH: Wright State University.

Hutchins, E. (1995). *Cognition in the wild.* Cambridge, MA: MIT Press.

Klahr, D. (Ed.) (1976). *Cognition and instruction.* Hillsdale, NJ: Erlbaum.

Klahr, D., & Kotovsky, K. (Eds.) (1989). *Complex information processing: The impact of Herbert A. Simon.* Mahwah, NJ: Erlbaum.

Klein, G. (1992). Using knowledge elicitation to preserve corporate memory. In R. R. Hoffman (Ed.), *The psychology of expertise: Cognitive research and empirical AI* (pp. 170–190). Mahwah, NJ: Erlbaum.

Klein, G. A., Calderwood, R., & MacGregor, D. (1989). Critical decision method for eliciting knowledge. *IEEE Transactions on Systems, Man, and Cybernetics, 19*, 462–472.

Klein, G., Orasanu, J., Calderwood, R., & Zsambok, C. E. (Eds.) (1993). *Decision making in action: Models and methods.* Norwood, NJ: Ablex Publishing Corporation.

Klein, G., & Weitzenfeld, J. (1982). The use of analogues in comparability analysis. *Applied Ergonomics, 13*, 99–104.

Knorr-Cetina, K. D. (1981). *The manufacture of knowledge.* Oxford: Pergamon.

Knorr-Cetina, K. D., & Mulkay, M. (1983). *Science observed.* Berkeley Hills, CA: Sage.

Koopman, P., & Hoffman, R. R. (2003/November–December). Work-arounds, makework, and kludges. *IEEE: Intelligent Systems,* pp. 70–75.

LaFrance, M. (1992). Excavation, capture, collection, and creation: Computer scientists' metaphors for eliciting human expertise. *Metaphor and Symbolic Activity, 7*, 135–156.

Lave, J. (1988). *Cognition in practice: Mind, mathematics, and culture in everyday life.* Cambridge: Cambridge University Press.

Lesgold, A. M. (1984). Acquiring expertise. In J. R. Anderson & S. M. Kosslyn (Eds.), *Tutorials in learning and memory: Essays in honor of Gordon Bower* (pp. 31–60). San Francisco, CA: W. H. Freeman.

Lesgold, A., Feltovich, P. J., Glaser, R., & Wang, M. (1981). "The acquisition of perceptual diagnostic skill in radiology." Technical Report No. PDS-1, Learing Research and Development Center, University of Pittsburgh, Pittsburgh, PA.

Lintern, G. (2003). Tyranny in rules, autonomy in maps: Closing the safety management loop. In R. Jensen (Ed.), *Proceedings of the Twelfth International Symposium on Aviation Psychology* (pp. 719–724). Dayton, OH: Wright State University.

Lintern, G., Diedrich, F. J. & Serfaty, D. (2002). Engineering the community of practice for maintenance of organizational knowledge. *Proceedings of the IEEE 7th Conference on Human Factors and Power Plants* (pp. 6.7–6.13). New York: IEEE.

Lintern, G., Miller, D., & Baker, K. (2002). Work centered design of a USAF mission planning system. In *Proceedings of the 46th Human Factors and Ergonomics Society Annual Meeting* (pp. 531–535). Santa Monica, CA: Human Factors and Ergonomics Society.

McDonald, N., Corrigan, S., & Ward, M. (2002). Cultural and organizational factors in system safety: Good people in bad systems. *Proceedings of the 2002 International Conference on Human-Computer Interaction in Aeronautics (HCI-Aero 2002)* (pp. 205–209). Menlo Park, CA: American Association for Artificial Intelligence Press.

McGraw, K. L., & Harbison-Briggs, K. (1989). *Knowledge acquisition: Principles and guidelines.* Englewood Cliffs, NJ: Prentice Hall.

Means, B., & Gott, S. P. (1988). Cognitive task analysis as a basis for tutor development: Articulating abstract knowledge representations. In J. Psotka, L. D. Massey, & S. A. Mutter (Eds.), *Intelligent tutoring systems: Lessons learned* (pp. 35–57). Hillsdale, NJ: Erlbaum.

Mieg, H. (2000). *The social psychology of expertise.* Mahwah, NJ: Erlbaum.

Militello, L. G., & Hutton, R. J. B. (1998). Applied Cognitive Task Analysis (ACTA): A practitioner's toolkit for understanding cognitive task demands. *Ergonomics, 41*, 1618–1641.

Militello, L., & Hoffman, R. R. (forthcoming). *Perspectives on cognitive task analysis.* Mahwah NJ: Erlbaum.

Militello, L., & Quill, L. (2006). Expert apprentice strategies. In R. R. Hoffman (Ed.), *Expertise out of context.* Mahwah, NJ: Erlbaum.

Naikar, N., & Sanderson, P. M. (2001). Evaluating system design proposals with work domain analysis. *Human Factors*, 43, 529–542.

Naikar, N., & Saunders, A. (2003). Crossing the boundaries of safe operation: A technical training approach to error management. *Cognition Technology and Work*, 5, 171–180.

Neale, I. M. (1988). First generation expert systems: A review of knowledge acquisition methodologies. *Knowledge Engineering Review*, 3, 105–146.

Novak, J. D. (1998). *Learning, creating, and using knowledge: Concept maps® as facilitative tools in schools and corporations*. Mahweh, NJ: Lawrence Erlbaum Associates.

Orr, J. (1996). *Talking about machines: An ethnography of a modern job*. Ithaca, NY: Cornell University Press.

Potter, S. S., Roth, E. M., Woods, D. D., and Elm, W. C. (2000). Bootstrapping multiple converging cognitive task analysis techniques for system design. In J. M. Schraagen and S. F. Chipman (Eds.), *Cognitive task analysis* (pp. 317–340). Mahwah, NJ: Erlbaum.

Prerau, D. (1989). *Developing and managing expert systems: Proven techniques for business and industry*. Reading, MA: Addison Wesley.

Raeth, P. G. (Ed.) (1990). *Expert systems*. New York: IEEE Press.

Rasmussen, J. (1985). The role of hierarchical knowledge representation in decision-making and system-management. *IEEE Transactions on Systems, Man, and Cybernetics*, SMC-15, 234–243.

Rasmussen, J. (1986). *Information processing and human-machine interaction: An approach to cognitive engineering*. Amsterdam: North-Holland.

Rasmussen, J. (1992). Use of field studies for design of workstations for integrated manufacturing systems. In M. Helander & N. Nagamachi (Eds.), *Design for manufacturability: A systems approach to concurrent engineering and ergonomics* (pp. 317–338). London: Taylor and Francis.

Rasmussen, J., Petjersen, A. M., & Goodstein, L. P. (1994). *Cognitive systems engineering*. New York: John Wiley.

Rasmussen, J., & Rouse, W. B. (Eds.) (1981). *Human detection and diagnosis of system failures*. New York: Plenum Press.

Rook, F. W., & Croghan, J. W. (1989). The knowledge acquisition activity matrix: A systems engineering conceptual framework. *IEEE Transactions on Systems, Man, and Cybernetics*, 19, 586–597.

Schmidt, L., & Luczak, H. (2000). Knowledge representation for engineering design based on a cognitive model. In *Proceedings of the IEA 2000/HFES 2000 Congress* (vol. 1) (pp. 623–626). Santa Monica, CA: Human Factors and Ergonomics Society.

Scribner, S. (1984). Studying working intelligence. In B. Rogoff & S. Lave (Eds.), *Everyday cognition: Its development in social context* (pp. 9–40). Cambridge: Harvard University Press.

Shadbolt, N. R., & Burton, A. M. (1990). Knowledge elicitation techniques: Some experimental results. In K. L. McGraw & C. R. Westphal (Eds.), *Readings in knowledge acquisition* (pp. 21–33). New York: Ellis Horwood.

Shanteau, J. (1992). Competence in experts: The role of task characteristics. *Organizational Behavior and Human Decision Processes*, 53, 252–266.

Shortliffe, E. H. (1976). *Computer-based medical consultations: MYCIN*. New York: Elsevier.

Simon, H. A., & Hayes, J. R. (1976). Understanding complex task instructions. In D. Klahr (Ed.), *Cognition and instruction* (pp. 51–80). Hillsdale, NJ: Erlbaum.

Spradley, J. P. (1979). *The ethnographic interview*. New York: Holt, Rinehart and Winston.

Stein, E. W. (1997). A look at expertise from a social perspective. In P. J. Feltovich, K. M. Ford, & R. R. Hoffman (Eds.), *Expertise in context* (pp. 181–194). Cambridge: MIT Press.

Sternberg, R. J., & Frensch, P. A. (Eds.) (1991). *Complex problem solving: Principles and mechanisms*. Mahwah, NJ: Erlbaum.

Suchman, L. (1987). *Plans and situated actions: The problem of human-machine communication*. Cambridge: Cambridge University Press.

Vicente, K. J. (1999). *Cognitive work analysis: Towards safe, productive, and healthy computer-based work*. Mahwah, NJ: Erlbaum.

Vicente, K. J., Christoffersen, K., & Pereklita, A. (1995). Supporting operator problem solving through ecological interface design. *IEEE Transactions on Systems, Man, and Cybernetics*, SMC-25, 529–545.

CHAPTER 13

Protocol Analysis and Expert Thought: Concurrent Verbalizations of Thinking during Experts' Performance on Representative Tasks

K. Anders Ericsson

The superior skills of experts, such as accomplished musicians and chess masters, can be amazing to most spectators. For example, club-level chess players are often puzzled by the chess moves of grandmasters and world champions. Similarly, many recreational athletes find it inconceivable that most other adults – regardless of the amount or type of training – have the potential ever to reach the performance levels of international competitors. Especially puzzling to philosophers and scientists has been the question of the extent to which expertise requires innate gifts versus specialized acquired skills and abilities.

One of the most widely used and simplest methods of gathering data on exceptional performance is to interview the experts themselves. But are experts always capable of describing their thoughts, their behaviors, and their strategies in a manner that would allow less-skilled individuals to understand how the experts do what they do, and perhaps also understand how they might reach expert level through appropriate training? To date, there has been considerable controversy over the extent to which experts are

capable of explaining the nature and structure of their exceptional performance. Some pioneering scientists, such as Binet (1893/1966), questioned the validity of the experts' descriptions when they found that some experts gave reports inconsistent with those of other experts. To make matters worse, in those rare cases that allowed verification of the strategy by observing the performance, discrepancies were found between the reported strategies and the observations (Watson, 1913). Some of these discrepancies were explained, in part, by the hypothesis that some processes were not normally mediated by awareness/attention and that the mere act of engaging in self-observation (introspection) during performance changed the content of ongoing thought processes. These problems led most psychologists in first half of the 20th century to reject all types of introspective verbal reports as valid scientific evidence, and they focused almost exclusively on observable behavior (Boring, 1950).

In response to the problems with the careful introspective analysis of images and perceptions, investigators such as John B.

Watson (1920) and Karl Duncker (1945) introduced a new type of method to elicit verbal reports. The subjects were asked to "think aloud" and give immediate verbal expression to their thoughts while they were engaged in problem solving. In the main body of this chapter I will review evidence that this type of verbal expression of thoughts has not been shown to change the underlying structure of the thought processes and thus avoids the problem of reactivity, namely, where the act of generating the reports may change the cognitive processes that mediate the observed performance. In particular, I will describe the methods of protocol analysis where verbal reports are elicited, recorded, and encoded to yield valid data on the underlying thought processes (Ericsson & Simon 1980, 1984, 1993).

Although protocol analysis is generally accepted as providing valid verbalizations of thought processes (Simon & Kaplan, 1989), these verbal descriptions of thought sequences frequently do not contain sufficient detail about the mediating cognitive processes and the associated knowledge to satisfy many scientists. For example, these reports may not contain the detailed procedures that would allow cognitive scientists to build complete computer models that are capable of regenerating the observed performance on the studied tasks. Hence, investigators have continued to search for alternative types of verbal reports that generate more detailed descriptions. Frequently scientists require participants to explain their methods for solving tasks and to give detailed descriptions of various aspects. These alternative reporting methods elicit additional and more detailed information than is spontaneously verbalized during "think aloud." The desire for increased amounts of reported information is central to the study of expertise, so I will briefly discuss whether it is possible to increase the amount reported without inducing reactivity and change of performance. The main sections of this chapter describe the methods for eliciting and analyzing concurrent and retrospective verbal reports and how these methods have

been applied to a number of domains of expertise, such as memory experts, chess masters, and medical specialists. The chapter is concluded with a broad overview of the issues of applying protocol analysis to the study of expert performance.

Historical Development of Verbal Reports on Thought Processes

Introspection or "looking inside" to uncover the structure of thinking and its mental images has a very long history in philosophy. Drawing on the review by Ericsson and Crutcher (1991), we see that Aristotle is generally given credit for the first systematic attempt to record and analyze the structure of sequences of thoughts. He recounted an example of series of thoughts mediating the recall of a specific piece of information from memory. Aristotle argued that thinking can be described as a sequence of thoughts, where the brief transition periods between consecutive thoughts do not contain any reportable information, and this has never been seriously challenged. However, such a simple description of thinking was not sufficiently detailed to answer the questions about the nature of thought raised by philosophers in the 17th, 18th, and 19th centuries (Ericsson & Crutcher, 1991).

Most of the introspective analysis of philosophers had been based on self-analysis of the individual philosophers' own thought. In the 19th century Sir Francis Galton along with others introduced several important innovations that set the groundwork for empirical studies of thinking. For example, Galton (1879, see Crovitz, 1970) noticed repeatedly that when he took the same walk through a part of London and looked at a given building on his path, this event triggered frequently the same or similar thoughts in memory. Galton recreated this phenomenon by listing the names of the major buildings and sights from his walk on cards and then presented a card at a time to observe the thoughts that were triggered. From this self-experiment Galton argued that thoughts reoccur with considerable frequency when the same stimulus is encountered.

Galton (1883) is particularly famous for the innovation of interviewing many people by sending out a list of questions about mental imagery – said to be the first questionnaire. He had been intrigued by reports of photographic memory and asked questions of the acuity of specific memories, such as the clarity and brightness of their memory for specific things such as their breakfast table. He found striking individual differences in the clarity or vividness, but no clear superiority of the eminent scientists; for example, Darwin reported having weak visual images. Now a hundred years later it is still unclear what these large individual differences in reported vividness of memory images really reflect. They seem almost completely unrelated to the accuracy of memory images and there is no reproducible evidence for individuals with photographic or eidetic memory (McKelvie, 1995; Richardson, 1988).

In one of the first published studies on memory and expertise Binet (1893/1966) reported a pioneering interview of chess players and their ability to play "blindfolded" without seeing a chess board. Based on anecdotes and his interviews Binet concluded that the ability required to maintain chess position in memory during blindfold play did not appear to reflect a basic memory capacity to store complex visual images, but a deeper understanding of the structure of chess. More troubling, Binet found that the verbal descriptions on the visual images of the mental chess positions differed markedly among blindfold chess players. Some claimed to see the board as clearly as if it were shown perceptually with all the details and even shadows. Other chess players reported seeing no visual images during blindfold play and claimed to rely on abstract characteristics of the chess position. Unfortunately, there was no independent evidence to support or question the validity of these diverse introspective reports. Binet's (1893/1966) classic report is a pioneering analysis of blindfold chess players' opinions and self-observations

and illustrates the problems and limits of introspection.

In a similar manner Bryan and Harter (1899) interviewed two students of telegraphy as they improved their skill and found evidence for an extended plateau for both as they reached a rate of around 12 words per minute. Both reported that this arrest in development was associated with attempts to move away from encoding the Morse code into words and to encode the code into phrases. Subsequent research (Keller, 1958) has found that this plateau is not a necessary step toward expert levels of performance and referred to it as the phantom plateau.

In parallel with the interviews and the informal collection of self-observations of expertise in everyday life, laboratory scientists attempted to refine introspective methods to examine the structure of thinking. In the beginning of the 20th century, psychologists at the University of Würzburg presented highly trained introspective observers, with standardized questions and asked them to respond as fast as possible. After reporting their answers, the observers recalled as much as possible about the thoughts that they had while answering the questions. They tried to identify the most basic elements of their thoughts and images to give as detailed reports as possible. Most reported thoughts consisted of visual and auditory images, but some participants claimed to have experienced thoughts without any corresponding imagery – *imageless thoughts*. The principle investigator, Karl Bühler (1907), argued that the existence of imageless thoughts had far-reaching theoretical implications and was inconsistent with the basic assumption of Wilhelm Wundt (1897) that all thoughts were associated with particular neural activity in some part of the brain. Bühler's (1907) paper led to a heated exchange between Bühler's introspective observers, who claimed to have observed them, and Wundt (1907), who argued that these reports were artifacts of inappropriate reporting methods and the theoretical bias of the observers. A devastating methodological conclusion arose from this controversy: the existence of imageless thoughts could not be resolved empirically by the introspective method. This finding raised fundamental doubts about analytic introspection as a scientific method.

The resulting reaction to the crisis was to avoid the problem of having to trust the participants' verbal reports about internal events. Instead of asking individuals to describe the structure of their thoughts, participants were given objective tests of their memory and other abilities. More generally, experimental psychologists developed standardized tests with stimuli and instructions where the same pattern of performance could be replicated under controlled conditions. Furthermore, the focus of research moved away from complex mental processes, such as experts' thinking, and toward processes that were assumed to be unaffected by prior experience and knowledge. For example, participants were given well-defined simple tasks, such as memorization of lists of nonsense syllables, e.g., XOK, ZUT, where it is easy to measure objective performance. In addition, experimenters assumed that nonsense syllables were committed to memory without any reportable mediating thoughts, and the interest in collecting verbal reports from participants virtually disappeared until the cognitive revolution in the late 1950s.

In one of the pioneering attempts to apply this approach to the study of expertise, Djakow, Petrowski, and Rudik (1927) tested the basic abilities of world-class chess players and compared their abilities to other adults. Contrary to the assumed importance of superior basic cognitive ability and memory, the international players were only superior on a single test – a test involving memory for stimuli from their own domain of expertise, namely, chess positions. A few decades later de Groot (1946/1978d) replicated chess players' superior memory for chess positions and found that correct recall was closely related to the level of chess skill of the player.

Many investigators, including the famous behaviorist and critic of analytic introspection, John Watson, are very critical of the accuracy of verbal descriptions of skilled activities, such as where one looks during a golf swing (Watson, 1913). He realized that many types of complex cognitive processes, such as problem solving, corresponded to ongoing processes that were inherently complex and were mediated by reportable thoughts. In fact, Watson (1920) was the first investigator to publish a study where a participant was asked to "think aloud" while solving a problem. According to Watson, thinking was accompanied by covert neural activity of the speech apparatus that is frequently referred to as "inner speech." Hence, thinking aloud did not require observations by any hypothetical introspective capacity, and thinking aloud merely gives overt expression to these subvocal verbalizations. Many other investigators proposed similar types of instructions to give concurrent verbal expression of one's thoughts (see Ericsson & Simon, 1993, for a more extended historical review).

The emergence of computers in the 1950s and 1960s and the design of computer programs that could perform challenging cognitive tasks brought renewed interest in human cognition and higher-level cognitive processes. Investigators started studying how people solve problems and make decisions and attempted to describe and infer the thought processes that mediate performance. They proposed cognitive theories where strategies, concepts, and rules were central to human learning and problem solving (Miller, Galanter, & Pribram, 1960). Information-processing theories (Newell & Simon, 1972) sought computational models that could regenerate human performance on well-defined tasks by the application of explicit procedures. Much of the evidence for these complex mechanisms was derived from the researchers' own self-observation, informal interviews, and systematic questioning of participants.

Some investigators raised concerns almost immediately about the validity of these data. For example, Robert Gagné and his colleagues (Gagné & Smith, 1962) demonstrated that requiring participants to verbalize reasons for each move in the Tower of Hanoi improved performance by reducing the number of moves in the solutions and improving transfer to more difficult problems as compared to a silent control

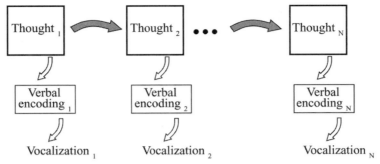

Figure 13.1. An illustration of the overt verbalizations of most thoughts passing through attention while a person thinks aloud during the performance of a task.

condition. Although improvements are welcome to educators, the requirement to explain must have changed the sequences of thoughts from those normally generated. Other investigators criticized the validity and accuracy of the retrospective verbal reports. For instance, Verplanck (1962) argued that participants reported that they relied on rules that were inconsistent with their observed selection behavior. Nisbett and Wilson (1977) reported several examples of experiments in social psychology, where participants gave explanations that were inconsistent with their observed behavior. These findings initially led many investigators to conclude that all types of verbal reports were tainted by similar methodological problems that had plagued introspection and led to its demise. Herb Simon and I showed in a review (Ericsson and Simon, 1980) that the methods and instructions used to elicit the verbal reports had a great influence on both the reactivity of the verbal reporting and on the accuracy of the reported information. We developed a parfticular type of methodology to instruct participants to elicit consistently valid non-reactive reports of their thoughts that I will describe in the next section.

Protocol Analysis: A Methodology for Eliciting Valid Data on Thinking

The central assumption of protocol analysis is that it is possible to instruct subjects to verbalize their thoughts in a manner that does not alter the sequence and content of thoughts mediating the completion of a task and therefore should reflect immediately available information during thinking.

Elicitation of Non-Reactive Verbal Reports of Thinking

Based on their theoretical analysis, Ericsson and Simon (1993) argued that the closest connection between actual thoughts and verbal reports is found when people verbalize thoughts that are spontaneously attended during task completion. In Figure 13.1 we illustrate how most thoughts are given a verbal expression.

When people are asked to think aloud (see Ericsson and Simon, 1993, for complete instructions), some of their verbalizations seem to correspond to merely vocalizing "inner speech," which would otherwise have remained inaudible. Nonverbal thoughts can also be often given verbal expression by brief labels and referents. Laboratory tasks studied by early cognitive scientists focused on how individuals applied knowledge and procedures to novel problems, such as mental multiplication. When, for example, one participant was asked to think aloud while mentally multiplying 36 by 24 on two test occasions one week apart, the following protocols were recorded:

OK, 36 times 24, um, 4 times 6 is 24, 4, carry the 2, 4 times 3 is 12, 14, 144, 0, 2 times 6 is 12, 2, carry the 1, 2 times 3 is 6,

7, 720, 720, 144 plus 720, so it would be 4, 6, 864.

36 times 24, 4, carry the – no wait, 4, carry the 2, 14, 144, 0, 36 times 2 is, 12, 6, 72, 720 plus 144, 4, uh, uh, 6, 8, uh, 864.

In these two examples, the reported thoughts are not analyzed into their perceptual or imagery components as required by Bühler's (1907) rejected introspectionist procedures, but are merely vocalized inner speech and verbal expressions of intermediate steps, such as "carry the 1," "36," and "144 plus 720." Furthermore, participants were not asked to describe or explain how they solve these problems and do not generate such descriptions or explanations. Instead, they are asked to stay focused on generating a solution to the problem and thus only give verbal expression to those thoughts that spontaneously emerge in attention during the generation of the solution.

If the act of verbalizing participants' thought processes does not change the sequence of thoughts, then participants' task performance should not change as a result of thinking aloud. In a comprehensive review of dozens of studies, Ericsson and Simon (1993) found no evidence that the sequences of thoughts (accuracy of performance) changed when individuals thought aloud as they completed the tasks, compared to other individuals who completed the same tasks silently. However, some studies have shown that participants who think aloud take somewhat longer to complete the tasks – presumably due to the additional time required to produce the overt verbalization of the thoughts.

The same theoretical framework can also explain why other types of verbal-reporting procedures consistently change cognitive processes, like the findings of Gagné and Smith (1962). For example, when participants explain why they are selecting actions or carefully describe the structure and detailed content of their thoughts, they are not able to merely verbalize each thought as it emerges, they must engage in additional cognitive processes to generate the thoughts corresponding to the required explanations

and descriptions. This additional cognitive activity required to generate the reports changes the sequence of generated thoughts (see Chi, Chapter 10, for another discussion of the differences between explanation and thinking aloud). Instructions to explain the reasons for one's problem solving and to describe the content of thought are reliably associated with changes in the accuracy of observed performance (Ericsson and Simon, 1993). Subsequent reviews have shown that the more recent work on effects of verbal overshadowing are consistent with reactive consequences of enforced generation of extensive verbal descriptions of brief experiences (Ericsson, 2002). Even instructions to generate self-explanations have been found to change (actually, improve) participants' comprehension, memory, and learning compared to merely thinking aloud during these activities (Ericsson, 1988a, 2003a; Neuman & Schwarz, 1998).

In summary, adults must already possess the necessary skills for verbalizing their thoughts concurrently, because they are able to think aloud without any systematic changes to their thought process after a brief instruction and familiarization in giving verbal reports (see Ericsson and Simon 1993, for detailed instructions and associated warm-up tasks recommended for laboratory research).

Validity of Verbalized Information while Thinking Aloud

The main purpose of instructing participants to give verbal reports on their thinking is to gain new information beyond what is available with more traditional measures of performance. If, on the other hand, verbal reports are the only source for some specific information about thinking, how can the accuracy of that information be validated? The standard approach for evaluating methodology is to apply the method in situations where other converging evidence is available and where the method's data can distinguish alternative models of task performance and disconfirm all but one reasonable alternatives.

Theories of human cognition (Anderson, 1983; Newell & Simon, 1972; Newell, 1990) proposed computational models that could reproduce the observable aspects of human performance on well-defined tasks through the application of explicit procedures. One of the principle methods applied by these scientists is an analysis of the cognitive task (see Chapter 11 by Schraagen for a discussion of the methods referred to as cognitive task analysis), and it serves a related purpose in the analysis of verbal protocols. Task analysis specifies the range of alternative procedures that people could reasonably use, in the light of their prior knowledge of facts and procedures, to generate correct answers to a task. Moreover, task analysis can be applied to the analysis of think-aloud protocols; for example, during a relatively skilled activity, namely, mental multiplication, most adults have only limited mathematical knowledge. They know the multiplication tables and only the standard "pencil and paper" procedure taught in school for solving multiplication problems. Accordingly, one can predict that they will solve a specific problem such as $36 \cdot 24$ by first calculating $4 \cdot 36 = 144$, then adding $20 \cdot 36 = 720$. More sophisticated adults may recognize that $24 \cdot 36$ can be transformed into $(30+6)(30-6)$ and that the formula $(a+b)(a-b) = a^2-b^2$ can be used to calculate $36 \cdot 24$ as $30^2-6^2 = 900-36 = 864$.

When adults perform tasks while thinking aloud the verbalized information must reflect information generated from the cognitive processes normally executed during the task. By analyzing this information, the verbalized sequences of thoughts can be compared to the sequence of intermediate results required to compute the answer by different strategies that are specified in a task analysis (Ericsson & Simon, 1993). The sequence of thoughts verbalized while multiplying $24 \cdot 36$ mentally (reproduced in the protocol examples above) agrees with the sequence of intermediate thoughts specified by one, and only one, of the possible strategies for calculating the answer.

However, the hypothesized sequence of intermediate products predicted from the task analysis may not perfectly correspond to the verbalizations. Inconsistencies may result from instances where, because of acquired skill, the original steps are either not generated or not attended as distinct steps. However, there is persuasive evidence for the validity of the thoughts that are verbalized, that is, that the verbalizations can reveal sequences of thoughts that match those specified by the task analysis (Ericsson & Simon, 1993). Even if a highly skilled participant's think-aloud report in the multiplication task only consisted of "144" and "720," the reported information would still be sufficient to reject many alternative strategies and skilled adaptations of them because these strategies do not involve the generation of both of the reported intermediate products. The most compelling evidence for the validity of the verbal reports comes from the use of task analysis to predict a priori a set of alternative sequences of concurrently verbalized thoughts that is associated with the generation of the correct answer to the presented problem.

Furthermore, verbal reports are only one indicator of the thought processes that occur during problem solving. Other indicators include reaction times (RTs), error rates, patterns of brain activation, and sequences of eye fixations. Given that each kind of empirical indicator can be separately recorded and analyzed, it is possible to examine the convergent validity established by independent analyses of different types of data. In their review, Ericsson and Simon (1993) found that longer RTs were associated with a longer sequence of intermediate reported thoughts. In addition, analyses show a close correspondence between participants' verbalized thoughts and the information that they looked at in their environment (see Ericsson & Simon, 1993, for a review).

Finally, the validity of verbally reported thought sequences depends on the time interval between the occurrence of a thought and its verbal report, where the highest validity is observed for concurrent, think-aloud verbalizations. For tasks with relatively short response latencies (less than 5 to 10 seconds), people are typically able to recall their sequences of thoughts accurately immediately after the completion of the task, and the validity of this type of retrospective reports remains very high. However, for cognitive processes of longer duration (longer than 10 to 30 seconds), recall of past specific thought sequences becomes more difficult, and people are increasingly tempted to infer what they must have thought, thus creating inferential biases in the reported information.

Other Types of Verbal Reports with Serious Validity Problems

Protocol analysis, as proposed by Ericsson and Simon (1980, 1984, 1993), specifies the constrained conditions necessary for valid, non-reactive verbalizations of thinking while performing a well-defined task. Many of the problems with verbally reported information obtained by other methods can be explained as violations of this recommended protocol-analysis methodology.

The first problem arises when the investigators ask participants to give more information beyond that which is contained in their recalled thought sequences. For example, some investigators ask participants *why* they responded in a certain manner. Participants may have deliberated on alternative methods; thus, their recalled thoughts during the solution will provide a sufficient answer, but typically the participants need to go beyond any retrievable memory of their processes to give an answer. Because participants can access only the end-products of their cognitive processes during perception and memory retrieval, and they cannot report why only one of several logically possible thoughts entered their attention, they must make inferences or confabulate answers to such questions.

In support of this type of confabulation, Nisbett and Wilson (1977) found that participants' responses to "why-questions" after responding in a task were in many circumstances as inaccurate as those given by other participants who merely observed these individuals' performance and tried to

explain it without any memory or first-hand experience of the processes involved. More generally, Ericsson and Simon (1993) recommended that one should strive to understand these reactive, albeit typically beneficial, effects of instructing students to explain their performance. A detailed analysis of the different verbalizations elicited during "think-aloud" and "explain" instructions should allow investigators to identify those induced cognitive processes that are associated with changes (improvements) in their performance.

A very interesting development that capitalizes on the reactive effects of generating explanations involves instructing students to generate self-explanations while they read text or work on problems (Chi, de Leeuw, Chiu, & LaVancher, 1994; Renkl, 1997). Instructing participants to generate self-explanations has been shown to increase performance beyond that obtained with merely having them "think aloud," which did not differ from a control condition (Neuman, Leibowitz, & Schwarz, 2000). The systematic experimental comparison of instructions involving explanations or "thinking aloud" during problem solving has provided further insights into the differences between mechanisms underlying the generation of explanations that alter performance and those that merely give expression to thoughts while thinking aloud (Berardi-Coletta, Buyer, Dominowski, & Rellinger, 1995).

The second problem is that scientists are frequently primarily interested in the general strategies and methods participants use to solve a broad class of problems in a domain, such as mathematics or text comprehension. They often ask participants to describe their general methods after solving a long series of different tasks, which often leads to misleading summaries or after-the-fact reconstructions of what participants think they must have done. In the rare cases when participants have deliberately and consistently applied a single general strategy to solving the problems, they can answer such requests easily by recalling their thought sequence from any of the completed tasks. However, participants typically employ multiple strategies, and their strategy choices may change during the course of an experimental session. Under such circumstances participants would have great difficulty describing a *single* strategy that they used consistently throughout the experiment, thus their reports of such a strategy would be poorly related to their averaged performance. Hence, reviews of general strategy descriptions show that these reports are usually not valid, even when immediate retrospective verbal reports after the performance of each trial provide accounts of thought sequences that are consistent with other indicators of performance on the same trials (see Ericsson & Simon, 1993, for a review).

Similar problems have been encountered in interviews of experts (Hoffman, 1992). When experts are asked to describe their general methods in professional activities, they sometimes have difficulties, and there is frequently poor correspondence between the behavior of computer programs (expert systems) implementing their described methods and their observed detailed behavior when presented with the same tasks and specific situations. This finding has led many scientists studying expertise (Ericsson, 1996a; Ericsson & Lehmann, 1996; Ericsson & Smith, 1991; Starkes & Ericsson, 2003) to identify a collection of specific tasks that capture the essence of a given type of expertise. These tasks can then be presented under standardized conditions to experts and less-skilled individuals, while their think-aloud verbalizations and other process measures are recorded.

In sum, to obtain the most valid and complete trace of thought processes, scientists should strive to elicit laboratory conditions where participants perform tasks that are representative of the studied phenomenon and where verbalizations directly reflect the participants' spontaneous thoughts generated while completing the task. In the next section I will describe how protocol analysis has been applied to study experts' superior performance on tasks representative of their respective domain of expertise.

Protocol Analysis and the Expert-Performance Approach

The expert-performance approach to expertise (Ericsson, 1996a; Ericsson & Smith, 1991) examines the behavior of experts to identify situations with challenging task demands, where superior performance in these tasks captures the essence of expertise in the associated domain. These naturally emerging situations can be recreated as well-defined tasks calling for immediate action. The tasks associated with these situations can then be presented to individuals at all levels of skill, ranging from novice to international-level expert, under standardized conditions in which participants are instructed to give concurrent or retrospective reports.

In this section I will describe the expert-performance approach and illustrate its application of protocol analysis to study the structure of expert performance. First, de Groot's (1946/1978) pioneering work on the study of expert performance in chess will be described, followed by more recent extensions in the domain of chess as well as similar findings in other domains of expertise. Second, the issue of developing and validating theories of the mechanisms of individual experts will be addressed and several experimental analyses of expert performance will be described.

Capturing the Essence of Expertise and Analyzing Expert Performance

It is important to avoid the temptation to study differences in performance between experts and novices because there are readily available tasks to measure such differences. Researchers need to identify those naturally occurring activities that correspond to the essence of expertise in a domain (Ericsson, 2004, Chapter 38). For example, researchers need to study how chess players win tournament games rather than just probing for superior knowledge of chess and test memory for chess games. Similarly, researchers need to study how doctors are able to treat patients with more successful outcomes rather than test their knowledge for medicine and memory of encountered patients. It is, however, difficult to compare different individuals' levels of naturally occurring performance in a domain because different individuals' tasks will differ in difficulty and many other aspects. For example, for medical doctors who primarily treat patients with severe and complex problems but with a relatively low frequency of full recovery, is their performance better than the performance of doctors who primarily treat patients with milder forms of the same disease with uniform recovery? Unless all doctors encounter patients with nearly identical conditions, it will be nearly impossible to compare the quality of their performance. The problem of comparing performers' performance for comparable tasks is a general challenge for measuring and capturing superior performance in most domains.

For example, chess players rarely, if ever, encounter the same chess positions during the middle part of chess games (Ericsson & Smith, 1991). Hence, there are no naturally occurring cases where many chess players select moves for the identical complex chess position such that the quality of their moves can be directly compared. In a path-braking research effort, de Groot (1946/1978) addressed this problem by identifying challenging situations (chess positions) in representative games that required immediate action, namely, the selection of the next move. De Groot then presented the same game situations to chess players of different skill levels and instructed them to think aloud while they selected the next chess move. Subsequent research has shown that this method of presenting representative situations and requiring generation of appropriate actions provides the best available measure of chess skill that predicts performance in chess tournaments (Ericsson, Patel, & Kintsch, 2000; van der Maas & Wagenmakers, 2005).

THE PIONEERING STUDIES OF CHESS EXPERTISE

In his pioneering research on chess expertise, de Groot (1946/1978) picked out chess positions that he had analyzed for a long time and established an informal task analysis. Based on this analysis he could evaluate the relative merits of different moves and encode the thoughts verbalized by chess players while they were selecting the best move for these positions.

The verbal protocols of both world-class and skilled club-level players showed that both types of players first familiarized themselves with the position and verbally reported salient and distinctive aspects of the position along with potential lines of attack or defense. The players then explored the consequences of longer move exchanges by planning alternatives and evaluating the resulting positions. During these searches the players would identify moves with the best prospects in order to select the single best move.

De Groot's (1946/1978) analysis of the protocols identified two important differences in cognitive processes that explained the ability of world-class players to select superior moves compared to club players. De Groot noticed that the less-skilled players didn't even verbally report thinking about the best move during their move selection, implying that they did not, in fact, think about it. Thus, their initial inferior representation of the position must not have revealed the value of lines of play starting with that move. In contrast, the world-class players reported many strong first moves even during their initial familiarization with the chess position. For example, they would notice weaknesses in the opponent's defense that suggested various lines of attack and then examine and systematically compare the consequences of various sequences of moves. During this second detailed phase of analysis, these world-class players would often discover new moves that were superior to all the previously generated ones.

MECHANISMS MEDIATING CHESS EXPERTISE

De Groot's analysis revealed two different mechanisms that mediate the world-class players' superiority in finding and selecting moves. The first difference concerns the best players' ability to rapidly perceive the relevant structure of the presented chess position, thus allowing them to identify weaknesses and associated lines of attack that the less-accomplished players never reported noticing in their verbal protocols. These processes involve rapid perception and encoding, and thus only the end products of these encoding processes are verbalized. There has been a great deal of research attempting to study the perceptual encoding processes by recording and analyzing eye fixations during brief exposures to reveal the cognitive processes mediating perception and memory of chess positions (see Gobet & Charness, Chapter 30). However, most of this research has not studied the task of selecting the best move but has used alternative task instructions, namely, to recall as many chess pieces as possible from briefly presented positions, or to find specific chess pieces in presented postions. These changes in the tasks appear to alter the mediating cognitive processes, and the results cannot therefore be directly integrated into accounts of the representative expert performance (Ericsson & Kintsch, 2000; Ericsson & Lehmann, 1996; Ericsson et al., 2000).

The second mechanism that underlies the superior performance of highly skilled players concerns a superior ability to generate potential moves by planning. De Groot's protocols showed that during this planning and evaluation process, the masters often discovered new moves that were better than those perceived initially during the familiarization phase. In a subsequent study Charness (1981) collected think-aloud protocols on the planning process during the selection of a move for a chess position. Examples of an analysis of the protocols from a club-level and an expert-level chess player are given in Figure 13.2. Consistent with these examples, Charness (1981) found that the depth of planning increased with greater chess skill. In addition, there is evidence that an increase in the time available for planning increases the quality of the moves selected, where move selection during regular chess is superior to that of speed chess with its limited time for making the next move (Chabris & Hearst,

2003). Furthermore, highly skilled players have been shown to be superior in mentally planning out consequences of sequences of chess moves in experimental studies. In fact, chess masters, unlike less-skilled players, are able to play blindfold, without a visible board showing the current position, at a relatively high level (Chabris & Hearst, 2003; Karpov, 1995; Koltanowski, 1985). Experiments show that chess masters are able to mentally generate the chess positions associated with multiple chess games without any external memory support when the experimenter reads sequences of moves from multiple chess games (Saariluoma, 1991, 1995).

In sum, the analyses of the protocols along with experiments show that expert chess players' ability to generate better moves cannot be completely explained by their more extensive knowledge of chess patterns. Recognition of patterns and retrieval of appropriate moves that they have stored in memory during past experiences of chess playing is not sufficient to explain the observed reasoning abilities of highly skilled players. As their skill increases, they become increasingly able to encode and manipulate internal representations of chess positions to plan the consequences of chess moves, discover potential threats, and even develop new lines of attack (Ericsson & Kintsch, 1995; Saariluoma, 1992). (For a discussion of the relation between the superior memory for presented chess positions and the memory demands integral to selecting chess moves, see Ericsson et al., 2000, and Gobet & Charness, Chapter 30.)

MEDICINE AND OTHER DOMAINS

The expert-performance approach has been applied to a wide range of domains, where skilled and less-skilled performers solve representative problems while thinking aloud. When the review is restricted to studies in domains that show reproducibly superior performance of experts, the think-aloud protocols reveal patterns of reports that are consistent with those observed in chess. For example, when expert snooker players are instructed to make a shot for a

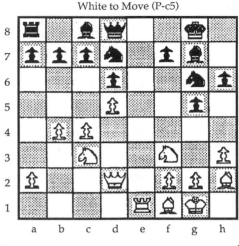

White to Move (P-c5)

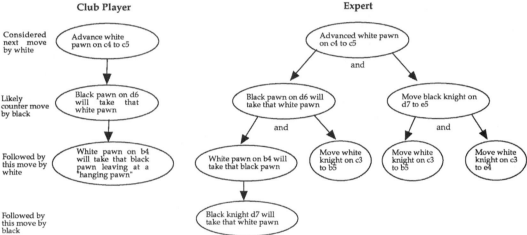

Figure 13.2. A chess position presented to chess players with the instruction to select the best next move by white (top panel). The think-aloud protocols of a good club player (chess rating = 1657) and a chess expert (chess rating = 2004) collected by Charness (1981) are shown in the bottom panel to illustrate differences in evaluation and planning for one specific move, P-c5 (white pawn is moved from c4 to c5), which is the best move for this position. Reported considerations for other potential moves have been omitted. The chess expert considers more alternative move sequences and some of them to a greater depth than the club player does. (From Ericsson, K. A., & Charness, N., 1994, Expert performance: Its structure and acquisition. *American Psychologist, 49(8),* 725–747, Figure 13.2 copyright American Psychological Association).

given configuration of pool balls, they verbalize deeper plans and more far-reaching exploration of consequences of their shots than less-skilled players (Abernethy, Neal, & Koning, 1994). Similarly, athletes at expert levels given protocols from dynamic situations in baseball (French, Nevett, Spurgeon, Graham, Rink, & McPherson, 1996) and soccer (Ward, Hodges, Williams, & Starkes,

2004) reveal a more complete and superior representation of the current game situation that allow them to prepare for future immediate actions better than less-skilled players in the same domains. In domains involving perceptual diagnosis, such as in the interpretation of Electrocardiograms (ECG) (Simpson & Gilhooly, 1997) and microscopic pathology (Crowley, Naus, Stewart,

& Friedman, 2003), verbal protocols reveal that the experts are able to encode essential information more accurately and are more able to integrate the information into an accurate diagnosis.

Most of the research on medical diagnosis has tried to minimize the influence of perceptual factors and has relied primarily on verbal descriptions of scenarios and patients. This research on medical expertise has shown that the process of generating a diagnosis becomes more efficient as medical students complete more of their medical training. The increase in efficiency is mediated by higher levels of representation that is acquired to support clinical reasoning (Boshuizen & Schmidt, 1992; Schmidt & Boshuizen, 1993). When studies present very challenging medical problems to specialists and medical students, the experts give more accurate diagnoses (Ericsson, 2004; Norman, Trott, Brooks, & Smith, 1994). The specialists are also more able to give complete and logically supported diagnoses (Patel & Groen, 1991) that appear to reflect higher-level representations that they have acquired to support reasoning about clinical alternative diagnoses (Ericsson & Kintsch, 1995; Ericsson et al., 2000; Patel, Arocha, & Kaufmann, 1994).

There are also studies showing differences in knowledge between experts and less-accomplished individuals that mediate successful task performance in experimental design of experiments in psychology (Schraagen, 1993) and detection of fraud in financial accounting (Johnson, Karim, & Berryman, 1991). The work on accounting fraud was later developed into a general theory of fraud detection (Johnson, Grazioli, Jamal, & Berryman, 2001). In this handbook there are discussions of the applications of verbal report methodology to study thinking in several different domains of expertise, such as medicine (Norman, Eva, Brooks, & Hamstra, Chapter 19), software design (Sonnentag, Niessen, & Volmer, Chapter 21), professional writing (Kellogg, Chapter 22), artistic performance (Noice & Noice, Cahpter 28), chess playing (Gobet & Charness, Chapter 30),

exceptional memory (Wilding & Valentine, Chapter 31), mathematical expertise (Butterworth, Chapter 32), and historical expertise (Voss & Wiley, Chapter 33).

The evidence reviewed in this section has been based primarily on findings that are based on averages across groups of experts. In the next section we will search for evidence on the validity of reported thoughts of individual experts as well as individual differences between different experts.

Individual Differences and Validity of Verbal Reports from Expert Performance

It is well established that to be successful in competitions at the international level, experts need to have engaged in at least ten years of intensive training – a finding that applies even to the most "talented" individuals (Ericsson Krampe, & Tesch-Romer, 1993; Simon & Chase, 1973). Consequently, researchers have not been surprised that verbal reports of experts and, thus, the corresponding sequences of reported thoughts, differ between expert performers – at least at the level of detailed thoughts. In the previous section I showed how protocols uncover many higher-level characteristics of expert performers' mediating mechanisms, such as skills supporting the expanded working memory (Ericsson & Kintsch, 1995). In this section I will discuss attempts to experimentally validate the detailed structure of the reported cognitive processes of individual expert performers.

The complexity of the knowledge and acquired skills of expert performers in most domains, such as chess and medicine, makes it virtually impossible to describe the complete structure of the expertise of an individual expert. For example, Allen Newell (personal communication) described a project in which one of his graduate students in the 1970s tried to elicit all the relevant knowledge of a stamp collector. After some forty hours of interviews, Newell and his student gave up, as there was no sight of the end of the knowledge that the expert had acquired. As it may be difficult, perhaps impossible, to describe all the knowledge and skills of experts, scientists should follow the recommendations of the expert-performance approach. Namely, they should focus on the reproducible structure of the experts' mechanisms that mediate their superior performance on representative tasks (Ericsson, 1996b). Consequently, I will focus on selected domains of expertise in which regularities in the verbal reports of different trials with representative tasks have been analyzed.

In the early applications of protocol analysis there were several studies that collected protocols from experts solving representative problems while thinking aloud. For example, Clarkson and Metzler (1960) collected protocols from a professional investor constructing portfolios of investments. Similar detailed analyses of individual experts from different domains have been briefly described in Ericsson and Simon (1993) and Hoffman (1992). These analyses were not, however, formally evaluated, and the proposed mechanisms were not demonstrated to account for reproducibly superior performance on representative tasks.

The most extensive applications of the expert-performance approach using protocol analysis to study individual experts have examined people with exceptional memory (Ericsson & Lehmann, 1996). In the introduction of this chapter I mentioned Binet's (1894) pioneering work studying individuals with exceptional memory for numbers. Several subsequent studies interviewed people with exceptional memory, such as Luria's (1968) Subject S and Hunt and Love's (1972) VP (see Wilding and Valentine, 1997, Chapter 31 for a review). However, the first study to trace the development of exceptional memory from average performance to the best memory performance in the world (in some memory tasks) was conducted in a training study by Chase and Ericsson (1981, 1982; Ericsson, Chase, & Faloon, 1980). We studied a college student (SF) whose initial immediate memory for rapidly presented digits was around 7, in correspondence with the typical average (Miller, 1956), but he eventually acquired exceptional performance for immediate memory and after

200 hours of practice was able to recall over 80 digits in the digit-span task. During this extended training period SF gave retrospective reports on his thought processes after most memory trials. As his memory performance started to increase he reported segmenting the presented lists into 3-digit groups and, whenever possible, encoding them as running times for various races because SF was an avid cross-country runner. For example, SF would encode 358 as a very fast mile time, 3 minutes and 58 seconds, just below the 4-minute mile. The central question concerning verbal reports is whether we can trust the validity of these reports and whether the ability to generate mnemonic running-time encodings influences memory.

To address that issue Bill Chase and I designed an experiment to test the effects of mnemonic encodings and presented SF with special types of lists of constrained digits. In addition to a list of random digits we presented other lists that were constructed to contain only 3-digits groups that could not be encoded as running times, such as 364 as three minutes and sixty four seconds, in a list (364 895 481...). As predicted his performance decreased reliably. In another experiment we designed digit sequences where all 3-digit groups could be encoded as running times (412 637 524...) with a reliable increase in his associated performance. In over a dozen specially designed experiments it was possible to validate numerous aspects of SF's acquired memory skill (Chase & Ericsson, 1981, 1982; Ericsson, 1988b). Other investigators, such as Wenger and Payne (1995), have also relied on protocol analysis and other process-tracing data to assess the mechanisms of individuals who increased their memory performance dramatically with practice on a list-learning task.

More generally, this method has been extended to any individual with exceptional memory performance. During the first step, the exceptional individuals are given memory tasks where they could exhibit their exceptional performance while giving concurrent and/or retrospective verbal reports. These reports are then analyzed to identify the mediating encoding and retrieval mechanisms of each exceptional individual. The validity of these accounts is then evaluated experimentally by presenting each individual with specially designed memory tasks that would predictably reduce that individuals' memory performance in a decisive manner (Ericsson, 1985, 1988b; Wilding & Valentine, 1998). With this methodology, verbal reported mechanisms of superior performance have been validated with designed experiments in a wide range of domains, such as a waiter with superior memory for dinner orders (Ericsson & Polson, 1988a, 1988b), mental calculators (Chase & Ericsson, 1982) and other individuals with exceptional memory performance (Ericsson, 2003b; Ericsson, Delaney, Weaver, & Mahadevan, 2004).

Exceptional memory performance for numbers and other types of "arbitrary" information appears to require that the expert performers sustain attention during the presentation (Ericsson, 2003b). The difficulty to automate memory skills for encoding new stimuli makes this type of performance particularly amenable to examination with protocol analysis. More generally, when individuals change and improve their performance they appear able to verbalize their thought processes during learning (Ericsson & Simon, 1993). This has been seen to extend to learning of experts and their ability to alter their performance through deliberate practice (Ericsson et al., 1993). There is now an emerging body of research that examines the microstructure of this type of training and how additional specific deliberate practice improves particular aspects of the target performance in music (Chaffin & Imreh, 1997; Nielsen, 1999) and in sports (Deakin & Cobley, 2003; Ericsson, 2003c; Ward et al., 2004) – for a more extended discussion see the chapter by Ericsson (Chapter 38) on deliberate practice.

Conclusion

Protocol analysis of thoughts verbalized during the experts' superior performance on representative tasks offers an alternative to the problematic methods of directed questioning and introspection. The think-aloud model of verbalization of thoughts has been accepted as a useful foundation for dealing with the problems of introspection (see the entry on "Psychology of Introspection" in the *Routledge Encyclopedia of Philosophy* by Von Eckardt, 1998, and entries on "Protocol Analysis" in the *Companion to Cognitive Science* [Ericsson, 1998] and the *International Encyclopedia of the Social and Behavioral Sciences* [Ericsson, 2001]. This same theoretical framework for collecting verbal reports has led to the accumulation of evidence that has led many behaviorists to accept data on cognitive constructs, such as memory and rules (Austin & Delaney, 1998). Consequently, the method of protocol analysis provides a tool that allows researchers to identify information that pass through expert performers' attention while they generate their behavior without the need to embrace any controversial theoretical assumptions. In support of this claim, protocol analysis has emerged as a practical tool to diagnose thinking outside of traditional cognitive psychology and cognitive science. For example, designers of surveys (Sudman, Bradburn, & Schwarz, 1996), researchers on second-language learning(Green, 1998) and text comprehension passages (Ericsson, 1988a; Pressley & Afflerbach, 1995), and computer software developers (Henderson, Smith, Podd, & Varela-Alvarez, 1995; Hughes & Parkes, 2003) regularly collect verbal reports and rely on protocol analysis.

The complexity and diversity of the mechanisms mediating skilled and expert performance is intimidating. To meet these challenges it is essential to develop methods to allow investigators to reproduce the experts' superior performance under controlled and experimental conditions on tasks that capture the essence of expertise in a given domain. Process tracing, in particular protocol analysis, will be required to uncover detailed information about most of the important mechanisms that are responsible for the superiority of the experts' achievement. Only then will it be possible to discover their structure and study their development and refinement with training and deliberate practice.

References

Abernethy, B., Neal, R. J., & Koning, P. (1994). Visual-perceptual and cognitive differences between expert, intermediate, and novice snooker players. *Applied Cognitive Psychology*, *18*, 185–211.

Anderson, J. R. (1983). *The architecture of cognition*. Cambridge, MA: Harvard University Press.

Austin, J., & Delaney, P. F. (1998). Protocol analysis as a tool for behavior analysis. *Analysis of Verbal Behavior*, *15*, 41–56.

Berardi-Coletta, B., Buyer, L. S., Dominowski, R. L., & Rellinger, E. R. (1995). Metacognition and problem solving: A process-oriented approach. *Journal of Experimental Psychology: Learning, Memory, & Cognition*, *21*, 205–223.

Binet, A. (1893/1966). Mnemonic virtuosity: A study of chess players. (Original paper appeared in 1893 and was translated by M. L. Simmel & S. B. Barron). *Genetic Psychology Monographs*, *74*, 127–162.

Binet, A. (1894). *Psychologie des grands calculateurs et joueurs d'echecs* [The psychology of great calculators and chess players]. Paris: Libraire Hachette.

Boring, E. B. (1950). *A history of experimental psychology*. New York: Appleton-Century Crofts.

Boshuizen, H. P. A., & Schmidt, H. G. (1992). On the role of biomedical knowledge in clinical reasoning by experts, intermediates and novices. *Cognitive Science*, *16*, 153–184.

Bryan, W. L., & Harter, N. (1899). Studies on the telegraphic language: The acquisition of a hierarchy of habits. *Psychological Review*, *6*, 345–375.

Bühler, K. (1907). Tatsachen und Probleme zu einer Psychologie der Denkvorgaenge: I. Ueber Gedanken [Facts and problems in a psychology of thinking: I. On thoughts]. *Archiv für die gesamte Psychologie*, *9*, 297–365.

Chabris, C. F., & Hearst, E. S. (2003). Visualization, pattern recognition, and forward search: Effects of playing speed and sight of the position on grandmaster chess errors. *Cognitive Science*, *27*. 637–648.

Chaffin, R., & Imreh, G. (1997). "Pulling teeth and torture": Musical memory and problem solving. *Thinking and Reasoning*, *3*, 315–336.

Charness, N. (1981). Search in chess: Age and skill differences. *Journal of Experimental Psychology: Human Perception and Performance*, *7*, 467–476.

Chase, W. G., & Ericsson, K. A. (1981). Skilled memory. In J. R. Anderson (Ed.), *Cognitive skills and their acquisition* (pp. 141–189). Hillsdale, NJ: Erlbaum.

Chase, W. G., & Ericsson, K. A. (1982). Skill and working memory. In G. H. Bower (Ed.), *The psychology of learning and motivation*, Vol. 16 (pp. 1–58). New York: Academic Press.

Chi, M. T. H., de Leeuw, N., Chiu, M.-H., & LaVancher, C. (1994). Eliciting self-explanations improves understanding. *Cognitive Science*, *18*, 439–477.

Clarkson, G. P., & Metzler, A. H. (1960). Portfolio selection: A heuristic approach. *Journal of Finance*, *15*, 465–480.

Crovitz, H. F. (1970). *Galton's walk: Methods for the analysis of thinking, intelligence, and creativity*. New York: Harper & Row Publishers.

Crowley, R. S., Naus, G. J., Stewart, J., & Friedman, C. P. (2003). Development of visual diagnostic expertise in pathology: An information-processing study. *Journal of the American Medical Informatics Association*, *10*, 39–51.

Crutcher, R. J. (1994). Telling what we know: The use of verbal report methodologies in psychological research. *Psychological Science*, *5*, 241–244.

de Groot, A. (1978). *Thought and choice and chess*. The Hague: Mouton. (Original work published 1946).

Deakin, J. M., & Cobley, S. (2003). A search for deliberate practice: An examination of the practice environments in figure skating and volleyball. In J. Starkes & K. A. Ericsson (Eds.), *Expert performance in sport: Recent advances in research on sport expertise* (pp. 115–135). Champaign, IL: Human Kinetics.

Djakow, I. N., Petrowski, N. W., & Rudik, P. A. (1927). *Psychologie des Schachspiels* [The psychology of chess]. Berlin: Walter de Gruyter.

Duncker, K. (1945). On problem solving. *Psychological Monographs*, *58*(5, Whole No. 270).

Ericsson, K. A. (1985). Memory skill. *Canadian Journal of Psychology*, *39*, 188–231.

Ericsson, K. A. (1988a). Concurrent verbal reports on reading and text comprehension. *Text*, *8*, 295–325.

Ericsson, K. A. (1988b). Analysis of memory performance in terms of memory skill. In R. J. Sternberg (Ed.), *Advances in the psychology of human intelligence*, Vol. 4 (pp. 137–179). Hillsdale, NJ: Erlbaum.

Ericsson, K. A. (Ed.) (1996a). *The road to excellence: The acquisition of expert performance in the arts and sciences, sports, and games*. Mahwah, NJ: Erlbaum.

Ericsson, K. A. (1996b). The acquisition of expert performance: An introduction to some of the issues. In K. A. Ericsson (Ed.), *The road to excellence: The acquisition of expert performance in the arts and sciences, sports, and games* (pp. 1–50). Mahwah, NJ: Erlbaum.

Ericsson, K. A. (1998) Protocol analysis. In W. Bechtel & G. Graham (Eds.), *A companion to cognitive science* (pp. 425–432). Cambridge, MA: Basil Blackwell.

Ericsson, K. A. (2001). Protocol analysis in psychology. In N. Smelser & P. Baltes (Eds.), *International Encyclopedia of the Social and Behavioral Sciences* (pp. 12256–12262). Oxford, UK: Elsevier.

Ericsson, K. A. (2002). Toward a procedure for eliciting verbal expression of nonverbal experience without reactivity: Interpreting the verbal overshadowing effect within the theoretical framework for protocol analysis. *Applied Cognitive Psychology, 16*, 981–987.

Ericsson, K. A. (2003a). Valid and non-reactive verbalization of thoughts during performance of tasks: Toward a solution to the central problems of introspection as a source of scientific data. *Journal of Consciousness Studies, 10*, 1–18.

Ericsson, K. A. (2003b). Exceptional memorizers: Made, not born. *Trends in Cognitive Sciences, 7*, 233–235.

Ericsson, K. A. (2003c). The development of elite performance and deliberate practice: An update from the perspective of the expert-performance approach. In J. Starkes & K. A. Ericsson (Eds.), *Expert performance in sport: Recent advances in research on sport expertise* (pp. 49–81). Champaign, IL: Human Kinetics.

Ericsson, K. A. (2004). Deliberate practice and the acquisition and maintenance of expert performance in medicine and related domains. *Academic Medicine, 10*, S70–S81.

Ericsson, K. A., Chase, W., & Faloon, S. (1980). Acquisition of a memory skill. *Science, 208*, 1181–1182.

Ericsson, K. A., & Crutcher, R. J. (1991). Introspection and verbal reports on cognitive processes – two approaches to the study of thought

processes: A response to Howe. *New Ideas in Psychology, 9*, 57–71.

Ericsson, K. A., Delaney, P. F., Weaver, G., & Mahadevan, R. (2004). Uncovering the structure of a memorist's superior "basic" memory capacity. *Cognitive Psychology, 49*, 191–237.

Ericsson, K. A., & Kintsch, W. (1995). Long-term working memory. *Psychological Review, 102*, 211–245.

Ericsson, K. A., & Kintsch, W. (2000). Shortcomings of article retrieval structures with slots of the type that Gobet (1993) proposed and modeled. *British Journal of Psychology, 91*, 571–588.

Ericsson, K. A., Krampe, R. Th., & Tesch-Römer, C. (1993). The role of deliberate practice in the acquisition of expert performance. *Psychological Review, 100*(3), 363–406.

Ericsson, K. A., & Lehmann, A. C. (1996). Expert and exceptional performance: Evidence on maximal adaptations on task constraints. *Annual Review of Psychology, 47*, 273–305.

Ericsson, K. A., Patel, V. L., & Kintsch, W. (2000). How experts' adaptations to representative task demands account for the expertise effect in memory recall: Comment on Vicente and Wang (1998). *Psychological Review, 107*, 578–592.

Ericsson, K. A., & Polson, P. G. (1988a). Memory for restaurant orders. In M. Chi, R. Glaser, & M. Farr (Eds.), *The nature of expertise* (pp. 23–70). Hillsdale, NJ: Erlbaum.

Ericsson, K. A., & Polson, P. G. (1988b). An experimental analysis of a memory skill for dinner orders. *Journal of Experimental Psychology: Learning, Memory, and Cognition, 14*, 305–316.

Ericsson, K. A., & Simon, H. A. (1980). Verbal reports as data. *Psychological Review, 87*, 215–251.

Ericsson, K. A., & Simon, H. A. (1984). *Protocol analysis: Verbal reports as data*. Cambridge, MA: Bradford books/MIT Press.

Ericsson, K. A., & Simon, H. A. (1993). *Protocol analysis: Verbal reports as data (revised edition)*. Cambridge, MA: Bradford books/MIT Press.

Ericsson, K. A., & Smith, J. (1991). Prospects and limits in the empirical study of expertise: An introduction. In K. A. Ericsson & J. Smith (Eds.), *Toward a general theory of expertise: Prospects and limits* (pp. 1–38). Cambridge: Cambridge University Press.

French, K. E., Nevett, M. E., Spurgeon, J. H., Graham, K. C., Rink, J. E., & McPherson, S. L. (1996). Knowledge representation and problem solution in expert and novice youth baseball players. *Research Quarterly for Exercise and Sport*, 67, 386–395.

Gagné, R. M., & Smith, E. C. (1962). A study of the effects of verbalization on problem solving. *Journal of Experimental Psychology*, 63, 12–18.

Galton, F. (1879). Psychometric experiments. *Brain*, 2, 148–162.

Galton, F. (1883). *Inquiries into human faculty and its development*. New York: Dutton.

Green, A. J. F. (1998). *Using verbal protocols in language testing research: A handbook*. Cambridge, UK: Cambridge University Press.

Henderson, R. D., Smith, M. C., Podd, J., & Varela-Alvarez, H. (1995). A comparison of the four prominent user-based methods for evaluating the usability of computer software. *Ergonomics*, 39, 2030–2044.

Hoffman, R. R. (Ed.) (1992). *The psychology of expertise: Cognitive research and empirical AI*. New York: Springer-Verlag.

Hughes, J., & Parkes, S. (2003). Trends in the use of verbal protocol analysis in software engineering research. *Behaviour & Information Technology*, 22, 127–140.

Hunt, E., & Love, T. (1972). How good can memory be? In A. W. Melton & E. Martin (Eds.), *Coding processes in human memory* (pp. 237–260). New York: Holt.

Johnson, P. E., Karim, J., & Berryman, R. G. (1991). Effects of framing on auditor decisions. *Organizational Behavior & Human Decision Processes*, 50, 75–105

Johnson, P. E., Grazioli, S., Jamal, K., & Berryman, R. G. (2001). Detecting deception: Adversarial problem solving in a low base-rate world. *Cognitive Science*, 25, 355–392.

Karpov, A. (1995). Grandmaster musings. *Chess Life*, November, pp. 32–33.

Keller, F. S. (1958). The phantom plateau. *Journal of the Experimental Analysis of Behavior*, 1, 1–13.

Koltanowski, G. (1985). *In the dark*. Coraopolis, PA: Chess Enterprises.

Luria, A. R. (1968). *The mind of a mnemonist*. New York: Avon.

McKelvie, S. J. (1995). The VVIQ and beyond: Vividness and its measurement. *Journal of Mental Imagery*, 19, 197–252.

Miller, G. A. (1956). The magical number seven, plus or minus two: Some limits of our capacity for processing information. *Psychological Review*, 63, 81–97.

Miller, G. A., Galanter, E., & Pribram, K. H. (1960). *Plans and the structure of behavior*. New York: Holt, Rinehart, and Winston.

Neuman, Y., & Schwarz, B. (1998). Is self-explanation while solving problems helpful? The case of analogical problem-solving. *British Journal of Educational Psychology*, 68, 15–24.

Neuman, Y., Leibowitz, L., & Schwarz, B. (2000). Patterns of verbal mediation during problem solving: A sequential analysis of self-explanation. *Journal of Experimental Education*, 68, 197–213.

Newell, A. (1990). *Unified theories of cognition*. Cambridge, MA: Harvard University Press.

Newell, A., & Simon, H. A. (1972). *Human problem solving*. Englewood Cliffs, NJ: Prentice-Hall.

Nielsen, S. (1999). Regulation of learning strategies during practice: A case study of a single church organ student preparing a particular work for a concert performance. *Psychology of Music*, 27, 218–229.

Nisbett, R. E., & Wilson, T. D. (1977). Telling more than we can know: Verbal reports on mental processes. *Psychological Review*, 84, 231–259.

Norman, G. R., Trott, A. D., Brooks, L. R., & Smith, E. K. M. (1994). Cognitive differences in clinical reasoning related to postgraduate training. *Teaching and Learning in Medicine*, 6, 114–120.

Patel, V. L., Arocha, J. F., & Kaufmann, D. R. (1994). Diagnostic reasoning and medical expertise. In D. Medin (Ed.), *The psychology of learning and motivation*, Vol. 30 (pp. 187–251). New York: Academic Press.

Patel, V. L., & Groen, G. J. (1991). The general and specific nature of medical expertise: A critical look. In K. A. Ericsson & J. Smith (Eds.), *Toward a general theory of expertise* (pp. 93–125). Cambridge, MA: Cambridge University Press.

Pressley, M., & Afflerbach, P. (1995). *Verbal protocols of reading: The nature of constructively responsive reading*. Hillsdale, NJ: Erlbaum.

Renkl, A. (1997). Learning from worked-out examples: A study on individual differences. *Cognitive Science*, 21, 1–29.

Richardson, J. T. E. (1988). Vividness and unvividness: Reliability, consistency, and validity of subjective imagery ratings. *Journal of Mental Imagery*, 12, 115–122.

Saariluoma, P. (1991). Aspects of skilled imagery in blindfold chess. *Acta Psychologica, 77*, 65–89.

Saariluoma, P. (1992). Error in chess: The apperception-restructuring view. *Psychological Research/Psychologische Forschung, 54*, 17–26.

Saariluoma, P. (1995). *Chess players' thinking.* London: Routledge.

Schmidt, H. G., & Boshuizen, H. (1993). On acquiring expertise in medicine. *Educational Psychology Review, 5*, 205–221.

Schraagen, J. M. (1993). How experts solve a novel problem in experimental design. *Cognitive Science, 17*, 285–309.

Simon, H. A., & Chase, W. G. (1973). Skill in chess. *American Scientist, 61*, 394–403.

Simon, H. A., & Kaplan, C. A. (1989). Foundations of cognitive science. In M. J. Posner (Ed.), *Foundations of cognitive science* (pp. 1–47). Cambridge, MA: MIT Press.

Simpson, S. A., & Gilhooly, K. J. (1997). Diagnostic thinking processes: Evidence from a constructive interaction study of electrocardiogram (ECG) interpretation. *Applied Cognitive Psychology, 11*, 543–554.

Starkes, J., & Ericsson, K. A. (Eds.) (2003). *Expert performance in sport: Recent advances in research on sport expertise.* Champaign, IL: Human Kinetics.

Sudman, S., Bradburn, N. M., & Schwarz, N. (Eds.) (1996). *Thinking about answers: The application of cognitive processes to survey methodology.* San Francisco, CA: Jossey-Bass.

van der Maas, H. L. J., & Wagenmakers, E. J. (2005). A psychometric analysis of chess expertise. *American Journal of Psychology, 118*, 29–60.

Verplanck, W. S. (1962). Unaware of where's awareness: Some verbal operants-notates, moments and notants. In C. W. Eriksen (Ed.), *Behavior and awareness – a symposium of research and interpretations* (pp. 130–158). Durham, NC: Duke University Press.

Von Eckardt, B. (1998). Psychology of introspection. In E. Craig (Ed.), *Routledge encyclopedia of philosophy* (pp. 842–846). London: Routledge.

Ward. P., Hodges, N. J., Williams, A. M., & Starkes, J. L. (2004). Deliberate practice and expert performance: Defining the path to excellence. In A. M. Williams & N. J. Hodges (Eds.), *Skill acquisition in sport: Research, theory and practice* (pp. 231–258). London, UK: Routledge.

Watson, J. B. (1913). Psychology as the behaviorist views it. *Psychological Review, 20*, 158–77.

Watson, J. B. (1920). Is thinking merely the action of language mechanisms? *British Journal of Psychology, 11*, 87–104.

Wenger, M. J., & Payne, D. G. (1995). On the acquisition of mnemonic skill: Application of skilled memory theory. *Journal of Experimental Psychology: Applied, 1*, 194–215.

Wilding, J., & Valentine, E. (1997). *Superior memory.* Hove, UK: Psychology Press.

Wundt, W. (1897). *Outlines of psychology* (Translated by C. H. Judd). Leipzig: Wilhelm Engelmann.

Wundt, W. (1907). Über Ausfrageexperimente und über die Methoden zur Psychologie des Denkens [On interrogation experiments and on the methods of the psychology of thinking]. *Philosophische Studien, 3*, 301–360.

Author Notes

This article was prepared in part with support from the FSCW/Conradi Endowment Fund of Florida State University Foundation. The author wants to thank Robert Hoffman, Katy Nandagopal, and Roy Roring for their valuable comments on an earlier draft of this Chapter.

CHAPTER 14

Simulation for Performance and Training

Paul Ward, A. Mark Williams, & Peter A. Hancock

Keywords: Simulation, Expert Performance, Training, Skill Acquisition, Aviation, Sport, Surgery.

Introduction

Many methods have been used to study experts. Traditionally, researchers have dissected performance into its constituent parts to isolate basic underlying mechanisms. Although this provides experimental control, task simplification and the use of novel and artificial tasks are antithetical to reproducing the "real-world" demands faced by actual domain experts. Changing the nature of the phenomenon under investigation may lead to a reduction, if not eradication, of the expert advantage. Cognitive anthropologists (see Clancey, Chapter 8) and Naturalistic Decision Making researchers (see Ross et al., Chapter 23), on the other hand, have argued that the most useful method of examining expertise is to capture performance as it occurs in the "natural" environment. However, critics have claimed that although this type of approach allows "real-world" perfor-

mance to be described, only minimal explanation is possible with regard to the underlying cognitive processes (e.g., Yates, 2001). Brehmer and Dörner (1993) concluded that field examination may not permit any definite conclusions to be drawn, whereas laboratory tasks are often too simplistic to reach any conclusions of interest. This leaves us in the invidious position that what is interesting is not explained and what is explained is not interesting. Simulation in its many guises may offer an excellent compromise.

The range and type of possible simulation environments is vast. Some are referred to as Computer-Aided Virtual Environment (CAVE) systems. Others include high fidelity simulations of complex systems (e.g., a commercial passenger jet simulator), scaled worlds (e.g., Military Operations in Urban Terrain [MOUT] facilities), synthetic environments (e.g., computational models of a task), virtual realities (e.g., immersive systems and head-mounted displays), augmented realities (e.g., supplementary systems such as navigational aids, BARS; see Goldiez, Ahmad, & Hancock, 2005), and simulated task environments (e.g., representative "real-world" tasks recreated using mechanical, video, or computer technology) (for a review, see Gray, 2002). Although these technologies have been developed primarily for purposes other than understanding complex performance, they can be put to that purpose.

In this chapter, we consider a narrow bandwidth of studies that fall under the general rubric of "simulated task environments," as well as "virtual reality," primarily because they have specifically addressed issues related to expert performance and skill development. Each study varies with respect to the degree of physical fidelity and ecological representativeness (Hoffman & Deffenbacher, 1993). However, psychological fidelity – the degree to which the system captures the real-world demands of the task, as well as the way in which it is implemented as an assessment and training tool – is likely to be of greater importance (e.g., Entin, Serfaty, Elliot, & Schiflett, 2001; Salas, Bowers, & Rhodenizer, 1998; Williams & Ward, 2003).

Our aim is to provide an overview of simulation tasks, environments, and technologies used to assess expert performance and train sport, medical surgery, and aviation skills. First, we describe the current state of expert-performance research conducted in a simulated task environment and highlight some factors constraining the development of paradigms and methods. Next, we summarize the development of simulation in each domain and emphasize pertinent issues in nurturing skill acquisition. We also address some misconceptions about simulation training by reviewing available procedures used to successfully train individuals under simulated conditions. We begin with a synopsis of expertise research and its development and the role of simulation in assessing expert performance.

Simulation for Performance: Assessing the Superior Performance of Experts

A bounty of research now exists on the nature of expertise and expert perfor-mance (e.g., Chi, Glaser, & Farr, 1980; Ericsson, 1996; Ericsson & Smith, 1991; Hoffman, 1992; Salas & Klein, 2001; Starkes & Ericsson, 2003). These researchers and others have arrived at different assumptions about expert cognition and have, thus, relied on divergent paradigms and methods to assess performance. Following de Groot's (1978/46) original work in chess, proponents of the early expertise approach designed classic structured and unstructured recall experiments to capture the memory feats of expert chess players (Chase & Simon, 1973). This work was motivated by the assumption that experts could circumvent short-term memory (STM) limitations by storing chunks in STM. However, subsequent research questioned the STM storage assumption, revealing that experts stored domain-specific information in accessible form in long-term memory (LTM) (e.g., Charness, 1976). Moreover, superior memory recall is likely to be an incidental by-product of their memory organization as opposed to a representative performance metric (see Chase & Ericsson, 1982). De Groot (1978/46) noted that other activities that better simulated the task requirements (e.g., selection of next best move) were actually better predictors of performance than memory recall (de Groot, 1978/1946).

As an alternative to the original expertise approach, and to counter the assumption that the knowledge elicited from so-called experts could account for expert-novice performance differences (see Fischhoff, 1989), Ericsson and Smith (1991) advocated the "expert-performance approach" in which researchers first identify tasks that truly capture expertise. Representative tasks can then be recreated in the laboratory where reliably superior performance can be assessed, experimental control maintained, and underlying mechanisms identified via the use of process-tracing methods. Although the expert-performance approach has been adopted in domains such as sport, music, games, and medicine (see Ericsson, 1996; Starkes & Ericsson, 2003), few researchers have fully embraced it or used simulation as a means of recreating the task. What follows is an overview of relevant expertise research using simulated task environments in sports, aviation, and surgery.

Expert Performance in Simulated Sports Tasks

The recall paradigm (Chase & Simon, 1973) was used by early researchers interested in experts who engaged in perceptually-demanding sports. Allard and colleagues (Allard, Graham, & Paarsalu, 1980; Allard & Starkes, 1980) investigated whether skill groups differed in their ability to recall patterns of play in basketball and volleyball, respectively. Varsity and intramural basketball players were presented with static, structured game-play and non-game scenarios and asked to recall player positions under time pressure. In line with the chess findings, varsity players recalled more positions than less-skilled players in the structured game condition only. In volleyball, no differences were found between national- and intramural-level players in either condition. Borgeaud and Abernethy (1987) modified Allard and Starkes' (1980) study by using dynamic film sequences in volleyball. They found distinct differences in expert and novice recall and concluded that simulating "real-world" perceptual characteristics of the task is likely to be a more informative way of studying expert-novice differences in sport.

The dynamic task used by Borgeaud and Abernethy (1987) and others (e.g., Williams, Davids, Burwitz, & Williams, 1993) recreated the typical viewpoint experienced during a game. However, the experimental task still required individuals to invoke a process (i.e., memory recall) that they otherwise may not have used, at least explicitly, during a typical game. Accordingly, recall tasks may provide only limited insight into the mechanisms underlying actual performance compared to more representative tasks that simulate "real-world" constraints.

In parallel with the memory-recall research, paradigms emerged that more closely simulated the actual perceptual-cognitive demands placed on an athlete. For instance, methods were devised to measure an individual's skill in anticipating an opponent's intentions (e.g., Haskins, 1965; Jones & Miles, 1978). Although this research was innovative for its time, participants were required to respond in a different modality (e.g., pen and paper, joystick) to that used during actual task performance, or information was presented in a fundamentally different manner (e.g., via static images, X's and O's representing offense and defense). For instance, using a video-based simulation and paper-and-pen response, Williams and Burwitz (1993) examined a key component of soccer goalkeeping – anticipating the direction of a penalty kick. Through the use of a temporal occlusion paradigm (a technique used to temporally limit the availability of visual information on which a decision could be made), they found that, compared to inexperienced players, experienced players could more accurately predict shot destination only when the simulation was occluded prior to striking the ball. No skill-based differences were observed thereafter (i.e., at/post foot-ball contact), indicating that only skilled players could anticipate the future consequences of action based on advance information available from key contextual cues, such as their opponent's posture.

Such tasks may capture different, or at least ancillary, cognitive processes instead of those used during actual task performance. A recent meta-analysis of sports-expertise research suggests that increasing the ecological representativeness of the action component resulted in a larger effect size (Thomas, 2003). Counter to this intuition, however, research from our laboratories shows that when the aim of the simulation is to recreate perceptual-cognitive demands of the task, participants need not necessarily be placed under associated perceptual-motor demands (Williams, Ward, Allen, & Smeeton, 2004). Consequently, even when part-task simulation is used, the crucial aspects of performance (i.e., ecological salience, see Hoffman & Deffenbacher, 1993) may still be captured, if not the "essence" of the task itself. Advances in measurement and simulation

Figure 14.1. Simulation of 1 v 1 soccer scenario used by Williams et al. (1994).

technology have enabled researchers to progressively increase the ecological representativeness of experimental tasks (see Abernethy, Thomas, & Thomas, 1993) and, in turn, increase the ability to capture "real-word" demands placed on the individual.

Williams and colleagues (Williams, Davids, Burwitz, & Williams, 1994; Williams & Davids, 1998) extended their initial research on expert anticipation by including an action component and recording eye-movement behavior. They were interested in soccer defenders' visual search characteristics while anticipating their opponents' intentions. They used a video-based simulation that incorporated a pressure-sensitive, movement-response system shown in Figure 14.1. Experienced soccer players responded significantly faster than novice performers in 11 player v 11 player, 3 v 3, and 1 v 1 simulations, confirming previous findings that experts' superior performance could be attributed, in part, to their ability to anticipate future events. The eye-movement data indicated that the expert search strategies are task dependent. In the 11 v 11 and 1 v 1 scenarios, experienced players used more fixations of shorter duration than novices. They

maintained awareness of player positions both on and off the ball (11 v 11), and spent considerably more time fixating on central areas of their opponents body (i.e., hip region) and the ball (1 v 1). In contrast, the inexperienced players were prone to "ball watching." In the 3 v 3 simulation, no differences in visual strategy were observed. Both groups fixated mainly on the player in possession of the ball. A subsequent spatial occlusion experiment revealed that experienced players employed a strategy in which they anchored foveal vision on one information source while also extracting information from the periphery.

Ward, Williams, and Bennett (2002) and Williams, Ward, Knowles, and Smeeton (2002) extended the soccer research to a tennis simulation, shown in Figure 14.2. Their results demonstrated that skilled regional-level players physically responded significantly faster to ground strokes played by a virtual opponent when compared to novice players. In contrast to soccer, skilled tennis players exhibited more fixations of longer duration than novices. However, much like the 1 v 1 soccer data, skilled players tended to fixate on central areas of the opponent's body (e.g., shoulders, hips), whereas novices spent more time fixating on the racket,

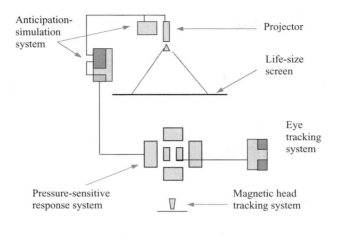

Figure 14.2. Illustration of the video-based anticipation simulation system adapted for use in Tennis by Ward et al. (2002) and Williams et al. (2002).

suggesting that skilled players were more adept at picking up earlier-occurring and more-informative movement cues. Ward et al. (2002) presented the same information (i.e., movements of the tennis opponent) in point-light form to determine the nature of the perceptual information extracted during simulated anticipatory performance. Novices shifted their attention solely toward the racket, whereas skilled players continued to extract information from the torso. While a performance decrement was observed in both groups under point-light conditions, the skill-based differences remained across conditions. The results suggested experts used the relative motion information available from the joint kinematics, as opposed to more superficial form cues, to direct their response.

Although sports researchers have used a number of minimally interactive video-based simulations to examine issues in expert performance, few have adopted alternative or, arguably, more-advanced interactive simulation. In a rare study Walls, Bertrand, Gale, and Saunders (1998) assessed dinghy sailing performance in competitive helmsmen. The simulator was comprised of a physical laser dinghy deck pivoting between two supports, dynamically controlled by a computer-operated pneumatic arm. Helming, sheeting, tacking, and boat trim were represented virtually using computer graphics. An illustration of the

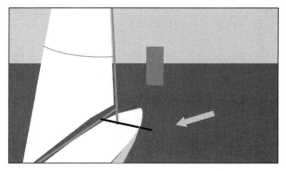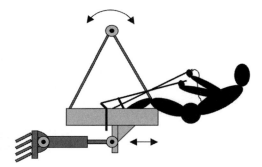

Figure 14.3. Graphic depiction of the dinghy-sailing simulator used by Walls et al. (1998).

simulator is provided in Figure 14.3. Participants had to sail upwind, tacking and then maneuvering the boat round a buoy while continually monitoring conditions to maintain control of the dinghy. Time to complete the simulated course was highly correlated with rankings of performance. The best sailors did not sail shorter distances, they were simply faster at completing the course. The implication is that more-skilled sailors were better at transforming the available visual information into necessary actions that allowed them to maintain control and maximize speed of the dinghy.

A number of virtual realities have been created that simulate the sporting environment, such as EasyBowling, a virtual bowling game machine; PCCAVEmash, an immersive table tennis game (see www.cad.zju.edu.cn/division/vrmm.html; Zheijiang University, China); and the Virtual Football Trainer, a CAVE-based American football simulation (see www-vrl.umich.edu/project/football/index.html; University of Michigan). However, simulations using this media have typically not been embraced by the sports science community to examine expert performance. An important question to ask is whether the increased physical fidelity and cost of such systems increases their benefit to performance compared to video- or PC-based simulations (see Salas et al., 1998).

Assessing the Skills of Expert Aviation Pilots using Simulation

The ability to recognize situations as familiar, make an appropriate strategic assessment, or maintain situation awareness (SA) under challenging conditions has become synonymous with skilled performance (e.g., Endsley, 1995). Aviation research has highlighted the need to increase pilot SA to lessen the risk of accidents, reduce fatality rates in landing and take-off, and improve performance (see Durso and Dattel, Chapter 20, this volume). However, our understanding of the cognitive mechanisms and processes that constitute or facilitate SA is limited. Moreover, although aviation simulation is perhaps more advanced than any other domain, relatively few attempts have been made to use simulated task environments to aid our understanding of the perceptual-cognitive or perceptual-motor bases of expert pilot performance.

As in the sports literature, a number of researchers have used both static tasks and dynamic simulations to examine performance. Doane, Sohn, and Jodlowski (2004) examined expert and novice pilots' ability to anticipate the consequences of flight actions (an integral aspect of long-term working memory and a higher-level component of SA; see Ericsson & Kintsch, 1995) using a static, simulated task environment. The task was to determine whether a change statement (i.e., the resultant main or side effects of a control movement) was consistent with the application of control movements on a simulated cockpit depiction of the current flight situation. Experts were typically quicker and marginally more sensitive to whether trials were consistent. Differences were significantly amplified when two control movements interacted with each other compared to when they were independent or when single control movements were presented.

Doane et al. (2004) argued that experts functionally increase their working memory capacity, enabling them to process simultaneously the interactive effects of main and side effects of control movements on the current situation more effectively, in contrast to processing control information independently or in sequence. In a variation of this study, Jodlowski and Doane (2003) examined whether long-term working memory skill (LT-WM; defined by these authors as difference scores between recall on structured and unstructured flight displays) or working memory (WM) capacity (e.g., reading span and spatial orientation) predicted performance on a similar static simulation. Expert instructor and student pilots' WM memory scores did not differ (but see Sohn & Doane, 2003), but experts did attain higher LT-WM scores than students, and this was a good predictor of their, but not novices', performance level. Results suggest that explanations based on LT-WM skill in recognizing meaningful displays were more informative than those based on WM capacity.

Although the definition of LT-WM used was somewhat restrictive, the results are consistent with Ericsson and Kintsch's (1995) LT-WM theory. Experts can overcome short-term working memory constraints by acquiring and applying superior indexing skills at encoding that result in a more accessible domain-specific retrieval structure. The static simulation tasks used in these experiments, however, are likely to have omitted key dynamic aspects of performance that are important for both capturing the ecologically salient aspects of expert performance and assessing experts' ability to build an accurate situation model (see van Dijk & Kintsch, 1983; Kintsch, 1988; Ericsson & Kintsch, 1995).

Jodlowski, Doane, and Brou (2003) extended their work to a dynamic flight simulation and examined pilots' ability to adapt to the changing constraints of routine and non-routine instrument flight situations. A personal computer-based aviation training device (PCATD), comprised of a Cirrus flight yoke and throttle, and a modified version of Microsoft Flight Simulator, was used to display a typical instrument panel. Participants flew seven simulated flight segments within predetermined bounds (i.e., $\pm$ 50 feet, $\pm$ 5 knots; $\pm$ 5°). On the next day, they flew the same seven plus an additional two segments involving a partial vacuum failure that affected the attitude indicator. The failure was announced on the final segment only.

Expert pilots with an average of over 2200 total hours of flight time were 20% more successful at staying within the specified bounds compared to apprentice pilots who had 89 hours of total flight time. When the failure was announced, skill groups did not significantly differ from each other (although we calculated a moderate effect size in favor of experts; Cohen's $d = 0.5$) and their performance was comparable to that in routine flight. When the failure was unannounced, both groups' scores were reduced by around 25%. The lack of an expert advantage for non-routine or unfamiliar situations implies that only routine, as opposed to adaptive, expertise was acquired (see Hatano & Ignaki, 1986). Although some researchers have intimated that experts acquire flexibility rather than rigidity with increased skill (see Feltovich, Spiro, & Coulson, 1997), only rarely has this distinction been empirically tested.

To examine expert pilots' attentional flexibility and monitoring skills, Bellenkes, Wickens, and Kramer (1997) assessed performance using a PCATD (e.g., see http://www.flyelite.com/faa-approved.php). The simulator displayed an on-screen virtual instrument panel and was controlled via a right side arm-mounted joystick. Participants flew similar segments to those mentioned in Jodlowski et al. (2003). Skilled flight instructors demonstrated superior tracking accuracy in the vertical and longitudinal axes but not on the lateral axis compared to student pilots. Less deviation from the desired flight path on each axis by flight instructors seemed to be a result of greater responsiveness to the changing constraints of the flight situation and was largely a function of greater flexibility in attention and control strategy. This conclusion was supported by the eye-movement data. Flight instructors sampled relevant instruments more frequently than student pilots who, in turn, distributed their time scanning each instrument.

In a comparison of United States Air Force pilots (experts) and Academy cadet pilots (apprentices), Kasarskis, Stehwien, Hickox, Aretz, and Wickens (2001) assessed participants' eye-movement behavior during simulated flight. Participants flew approaches and landings using a PCATD, starting on a 45° turn at 1000ft with the descent lasting around three minutes. Fly! software (Terminal Reality®) was used to depict both flight instruments and external environment, and a flight yoke was used to control pitch, roll, and airspeed. Experts' landing performance was less variable than the apprentices', and they employed significantly more fixations of shorter duration on the runway aim point and airspeed indicator. The authors suggested that this strategic monitoring difference between the groups afforded greater control and precision of the aircraft by experts. The experts' shorter dwell times were thought to reflect their skill level; they simply needed less time to extract relevant information.

In summary, the research suggests that expert pilots are better able to anticipate the consequences of the current situation. The higher visual search rate during important aspects of flight, and marginally more effective use of flight controls, indicates that experts develop superior monitoring and control skills that allow them to maintain awareness of the situation and adapt to the dynamic constraints of the environment. However, in situations that are not necessarily routine the reduction of expert performance to student levels indicates that expertise is highly context specific, not only to the domain itself but to particular aspects of the task.

From aviation, we now turn to research on surgical expertise using simulated tasks or virtual environments and highlight potential mechanisms implicated in expert performance.

Assessing Expert Skill via Surgical Simulation

Surgery is one of the most demanding of all performance tasks since, by definition, life-threatening circumstances are encountered in almost every incidence (see Norman, et al., Chapter 19, this volume). Mistakes, which in other domains could be considered negligible, are not simply dangerous here. They can be fatal. Given the costs of failure in this domain, the attainment and assessment of expert skills is vital. Objective performance assessment in the "real-world" is problematic for obvious reasons. Simulation allows such limitations to be circumvented by reproducing "real-world" task demands in a standardized setting.

Initial research examining performance on relatively low-tech simulators indicated that although basic skills transfer from one simulated task to another using the same system, there is little evidence that these skills improve surgical performance (Rosser, Rosser, & Savalgi, 1997; Strom, Kjellin, Hedman, Wredmark, & Fellander-Tsai, 2004). However, with the introduction of more advanced minimal access simulators, researchers have been able to recreate traditional clinical tasks used in educational contexts. Haluck, et al. (2001), for instance, used a laparoscopic simulator (Laparoscopic Impulse Engine, Immersion Corporation, see http://www.immersion.com/medical/products/laparoscopy/) to assess the ability of skilled surgical staff (experts) and medical students to navigate a virtual operating volume and identify six randomly placed arrows – a laparoscopic procedure consistent with those used by the Royal College of Surgeons (RCS) (see Torkington, Smith, Rees, & Darzi, 2001). Experts identified more arrows within the allotted timeframe and made fewer tracking errors than students. Although this study demonstrates experts' superior perceptual-motor skills during laparoscopic-type procedures, it is difficult to determine whether the perceptual-cognitive elements of the task, or the task as a whole, truly reflected the demands faced during surgical conditions, or simply whether some other skill set was being assessed.

Verner, Oleynikov, Holtmann, Haider, and Zhukov (2003) used the da Vinci robotic surgical system (see http://www.intuitivesurgical.com/products/da_vinci_html) to examine the coordination patterns of surgeons during a simulated procedure. Grip position and three-dimensional position and trajectory of the laparoscopic instrument were assessed as participants picked up and placed a bead onto a peg (another RCS-type training task) and then returned the surgical tool to its original position. Experts were quicker than novices at performing the task (approx. 7 v 11s, respectively), mainly due to the fact that experts spent less time during points of transition (i.e., picking up and placing the bead). Kinematic data indicated that novices were much slower and more variable. Experts were 15% and 50% faster than novices with their dominant and non-dominant hand, respectively. The lower variability of experts, and lack of difference between hands, is consistent with the literature on motor-skill acquisition and deliberate practice (see, Williams & Hodges, 2004; Ericsson, Krampe, & Tesch-Römer, 1993). As individuals refine their skills over time, their coordination improves, significantly reducing the variability with which an action is executed, allowing performance to be more reliably reproduced with greater control.

A few studies have begun to make use of simulation technologies that closely represent the stimuli, procedures, and actions that would be present or performed in the "real-world." Schijven and Jakimowicz (2003) compared surgeons with experience of performing over 100 clinical laparoscopic cholecystectomies (i.e., surgical excision of the gallbladder) with novice surgical residents and interns who had no experience in this procedure on a laparoscopic "clip-and-cut-cystic-artery-and-duct" task (for examples of the typical viewpoint during a simulated clip-and-cut task, see http://www.simbionix.com/LAP_Laparoscopic_Instruments.html). After a period of familiarization on the Xitact LS500 laparoscopic cholecystectomy simulator and hands-on task instruction, participants performed the task three times, attaining a sum "skill" score for each trial. Skilled surgeons' were approximately 13% better than novices for the second and final trials, and experts completed the task in half the time (approx. 100 v 210 s). Although these findings demonstrate the utility of simulation for medical performance assessment, the question is raised: by what specific mechanisms are experts able to consistently out-perform novice participants on such tasks? The next challenge for surgical simulation research is to employ process-tracing methodologies to determine the mechanisms implicated in superior performance (e.g., see Patel & Groen, 1986).

In an attempt to trace perceptual-cognitive processes during performance in a simulated environment, Law, Atkins, Kirkpatrick, Lomax, and Mackenzie (2004) assessed expert surgeons' and novice college students' eye-movements while performing a PC-based, laparoscopic simulation (http://www.immersion.com/medical/products/laparoscopy/; Immersion Corporation Laparoscopic Impulse Engine). In a simplified version of a laparoscopic task, participants guided a virtual tool with one hand toward a specified target. Expert surgeons were approximately 100s quicker than novices at reaching the target location, although this difference diminished to around 25s with practice. Expert surgeons visually fixated on the target far more and tracked the laparoscopic tool far less than their novice counterparts. Experts' performance was facilitated by centering their point of gaze around the target earlier in the tool movement, allowing the tool to be tracked in the periphery. In contrast, the novices tended to track the tool using the fovea and alternated the gaze more frequently between the tool and target.

The available surgical-simulation research suggests that experts demonstrate greater precision and speed through an enhanced ability to control and track laparoscopic tools. Experts also acquire a different perceptual or attention strategy to that of novices, which facilitates their superior level of control. Simulation has only recently been used as a medium to examine expert performance in surgery. Initial research suggests that simulated task environments are likely to be very conducive to improving our understanding of skilled performance.

We now turn to an overview of the use of simulation for training perceptual-cognitive and perceptual-motor skills and provide a summary of the development of simulation and training research in aviation, medicine, and sport.

Simulation for Training: Development and Research

Historically, training strategies have been based on intuition and emulation rather than on evidence-based practice (Williams & Ward, 2001; 2003). Researchers have often relied on mere exposure to simulation as opposed to using simulation as a means to deliver instruction. Today, however, empirically grounded methods exist that have demonstrated improvement. Staszewski and Davison (2000) developed a method they termed Cognitive Engineering Based on Expert Skill (CEBES) that applies the theory, principles, and methods of cognitive science to developing effective training. In this approach, an expert model is first derived from empirical evidence of how an expert performs a particular task, which in turn serves as a blueprint for training. Staszewski (1999) used this approach to derive an expert model of mine-detection clearance operations. Using an information-processing analysis of an expert while performing the task, the way in which an expert searched for, discriminated between, and accurately detected mines was decomposed into specific equipment manipulations and performance-specific perceptual-information, knowledge, and thought processes. This information provided the basis for the *content* on which participants were trained, and established methods of instruc-

tion and feedback were used to guide the mode of *delivery* in a simulated task environment (Staszewski & Davison, 2000). This method considerably improved soldier's mine-detection performance, and most encouragingly, the greatest improvement occurred on the most threatening types of mines when retested in the real world.

Training based on methods similar to those proposed by Stazsewski and others (e.g., Williams et al., 2002) is limited, particularly when it has taken place in a simulated environment. However, recent innovations have been employed that, when coupled with effective training procedures, offer support for the idea that simulation is an effective training tool. The next section provides an overview of a selection of studies from each domain. The history of simulation lies largely in the aviation domain, and so we begin with a summary of the development of flight simulation and its application to training.

The Development of Flight Simulation and its Application to Training

Flight simulation can be traced back almost as far as powered flight itself. One of the earliest simulators, the Link Trainer, was produced by Ed Link in 1929 and was first used by the Army Air Corps in 1934 (for a more detailed history of the Link Trainer, see http://www.link.com/history.html). The Link Trainer was used to reduce the number of pilot fatalities in the first few days of service; events that were attributed to a lack of experience in instrumented flight, night operations, and inclement weather (see Allerton, 2000). Development was typically spurred by technological advances and specific motives, such as the desire to familiarize military and commercial pilots with flying missions without actually having to fly, and to create affordable training environments to prepare apprentice pilots.

In the decades following introduction of the Link Trainer, technological advancement was the primary motivation for improvement. Systems moved from pneumatic to hydraulic, analog to digital, from the exclusion of visual displays entirely to the introduction of simple light projections, and finally toward high-end digital image generation. Although these advances have surpassed any other area of simulation, such development has occurred at a high financial cost. "State-of-the-art" simulations are now beyond the budget of most researchers. Furthermore, high-fidelity systems are rarely developed with sophisticated measurement in mind. Where systems can be adapted, the costs are often inordinate and such adaptations lend themselves to only a handful of research questions (see Gray, 2002; Hays, Jacobs, Prince, & Salas, 1992).

Hays et al. (1992) conducted a meta-analysis of experiments published between 1957 and 1986 to assess the effectiveness of flight simulation for improving trainee-pilot performance. From 247 simulation articles, only 19 on jet and seven on helicopter simulation were retained in the analysis. Over 90% of the effects supported the joint use of simulation and aircraft training over aircraft training alone. Small but positive effects were observed for jet, but not helicopter, simulation training when contrasted with aircraft training alone, and these effects were particularly pronounced for certain types of task, such as takeoffs, approaches, and landings. This finding is encouraging given the hazardous nature of landing and takeoff (see Kasarskis et al., 2001; Khatwa & Helmreich, 1999, see also Higgins, Chignell, & Hancock, 1989).

Hays and colleagues' analyses indicated that self-paced training to criterion was more effective than when practice was simply blocked. However, given the trend to train to criterion rather than assessing comparable degrees of different types of training under simulation (e.g., explicit vs. implicit instruction), it is unclear to what extent participants improvement is simply a function of the amount of time invested rather than the nature of training employed. In a number of reviews, researchers have concluded that simulation reduces the number of "air" training hours needed to attain criterion proficiency (Lintern, Roscoe, Koonce, & Segal,

1990; Smode, Hall, & Meyer, 1966). Typically, however, simulation-trained groups have spent more time in training overall compared to those trained in traditional aircraft training. After factoring in the typical cost of traditional training methods, the current results suggest that significant savings would be made by using simulation, making this a fiscally viable, albeit not necessarily time-efficient method of training. Roscoe and colleagues (e.g. Roscoe, 1971; Povenmire & Roscoe, 1971, 1973) pointed out that the efficiency of flight-simulation training is greater during the initial periods of learning. As training continues and performance improves, transfer gain significantly reduces in a negatively decelerating manner. To determine at what point simulation becomes ineffective, or at least less cost-effective, Povenmire and Roscoe (1971, 1973) suggested that incremental transfer functions need to be determined.

Taylor, Talleur, Emanuel, Rantanen, Bradshaw, and Phillips (2001, 2002) examined three different periods of PCATD simulation training; five hours (PCATD 5), 10 hours (PCATD 10), and 15 (PCATD 15) hours, and compared to a control group. Transfer-effectiveness ratios (see Povenmire & Roscoe, 1973) showed that PCATD training was generally effective and resulted in fewer trials in the airplane compared to the control group who received no PCATD training. Incremental transfer-effectiveness ratios suggested that the greatest amount of positive transfer was found in the PCATD 5 group. The additional training received by the PCATD 15 group failed to save any additional trials in the airplane compared to the PCATD 10 group. Overall, only limited additional time/trials were saved by the PCATD 10 group compared to the PCATD 5 group. The authors concluded that little additional benefit was found for PCATD simulation training beyond five hours. This finding questions the common conception that more is necessarily better (see Salas et al., 1998). In the future, researchers need to consider the relative performance improvement over time with training. When additional simulation training is ineffective or no longer cost-efficient, researchers need to examine whether or how the years of training required to reach expert performance levels can be circumvented.

Training Novice Surgeons through Simulation

Since the introduction of "Resusci Annie" (a half manikin designed for training cardiopulmonary resuscitation), and the use of motion pictures to simulate a medical evaluation scenario (Hubbard, Levitt, Schumacher, & Schnabel, 1965), medical simulation training has made considerable progress. A number of advanced mannequin-based (e.g., Human Patient Simulator, Mentice Procedicus, Sweden, see http://www.meti.com) and virtual reality simulators (e.g., Minimal Invasive Surgery Trainer in Virtual Reality; MIST-VR) now exist that allow practice to take place outside the operating room in a realistic environment, providing realistic force feedback and real-time modeling of physiological and hemodynamic parameters.

As in aviation, surgical training is expensive. Medical training programs have been shortened such that the skills previously acquired in the operating theatre now have to be acquired outside this traditional setting (McCloy & Stone, 2001). When real patients are used as teaching cases in invasive procedures, treatment time can be unduly prolonged, increasing patient discomfort and amplifying the risks of erroneous diagnoses and procedure-related morbidity (Colt, Crawford, & Galbraith, 2001). Minimally invasive or minimal-access surgery, including arthroscopy and laparoscopy, can markedly reduce the time needed for recovery compared to traditional surgery. The skills necessary for performing these procedures, such as the ability to use indirect visual information to guide tool manipulations, differ from more traditional approaches. Although traditional training methods have been used to overcome procedural differences, minimal-invasive simulation trainers offer an alternative, and potentially more effective, method of training surgery skills (e.g., McCloy & Stone, 2001; Torkington, Smith, Rees, &

Darzi, 2001). Although such innovations in technology could radically change the face of training in medicine, it should be noted that initial training is often conducted with the aim of attaining a basic level of proficiency, rather than attaining expert levels of performance per se.

Torkington et al. (2001) compared inexperienced medical students' performance, pre- and post-intervention, on a minimal-access box trainer; a validated laboratory-based device used to assess laparoscopic skill (see Taffinder, Sutton, Fischwick, McManus, & Darzi, 1998). Two training groups were compared to a control on their ability to grasp and cut five sutures in sequential order. The standard group received one hour of standardized minimal-access training (e.g., placing chick peas on golf tees) developed for the Royal College of Surgeons Basic Surgical Skills Course. The simulation group was trained on the assessment tasks using the Minimal Invasive Surgical Trainer (MIST; Mentice Procedicus, Sweden). The MIST is a virtual simulator that replicates laparoscopic surgery procedures using simple, real-time, 3D computer graphics. Both trained groups demonstrated a significant improvement in the speed and number of movements needed to manipulate the forceps and a reduction in the number of movements in the laparoscopic tool when compared to the control group. No differences were observed between the standard and simulation training groups, suggesting that simulation training was at least as effective as more traditional methods.

In an attempt to train an invasive endoscopic procedure via simulation, Colt et al. (2001) examined novice pulmonary and critical care fellows' ability to perform a flexible fiberoptic bronchoscopy (a procedure in which a bronchoscope is inserted through the nostril, and the nasopharynx, vocal cords, and tracheobronchial tree are inspected) using a PreOp Endoscopy Simulator (HT Medical Systems Gaithersburg, MD). Dexterity (i.e., contacts with bronchial wall and time in red out – when airway anatomy cannot be visualized because of improper tool positioning), speed, and accuracy (i.e., number of bronchial segments missed) of performance was measured pre- and post-training on the virtual trainer and an inanimate model. Eight hours of training were provided, including video instruction on the use of the simulator, instruction on tracheobronchial anatomy and flexible fiberoptic bronchoscopy techniques, supervised instruction, and unsupervised practice in the simulator. Trainees' speed and time in red out did not improve from pre- to post-test, but they missed fewer segments and made fewer contacts with the bronchial wall. Post-training performance approached that of a control group of skilled surgeons.

The absence of a placebo group and/or similarly skilled control group often makes it difficult to objectively determine whether the observed improvements merely reflect increased task familiarization, or are the result of a placebo effect. There have also been few attempts to determine whether simulation-trained skills transfer to the operating room. In a recent study, fourth-year surgical residents were trained in laparoscopic cholecystectomy procedures using standard methods as well as in the MIST (Seymour, et al., 2002; see also Gallagher & Satava, 2002). Participants were trained in a diathermy task; a medical technique used to generate heat in tissue through electric current. Training lasted approximately one hour until expert criterion levels were attained. Although comparative pre- or post-tasks were not employed to assess the absolute change in performance, transfer to the operating room was subjectively assessed by two attending surgeons. The transfer task required participants to perform a real surgical gallbladder excision. Simulation trained participants were six minutes (29%) faster in this procedure than residents who received standard training. In addition, the simulation group made fewer errors than the standard training group (1.19 v 7.38, respectively) and were much less likely to cause injury to the gallbladder or burn non-target tissue.

In a time when medical error is under close scrutiny (see Senate of Surgery report, 1998; Kohn, Corrigan, & Donaldson, 1999), these findings are likely to impact the future training of medical students. Kneebone (2003) noted that where technolog-ical advancement was once the primary focus of medical simulation, the emphasis has shifted toward the use of simulation in clinical learning environments such that domain-specific knowledge and perceptual-motor skills can be acquired in unison rather than in isolation. Caution is warranted until such systems have been effectively evaluated, standards have been derived, and measures of performance and methods of training have been refined and appropriately validated. Although some evidence of transfer to the operating room has been reported, the mechanisms by which performance improves and the nature of instruction and feedback provided have received only limited attention.

Using Simulation to Train Perceptual-Cognitive Skills in Sport

In sport, and in many other activities, training is typically the sole responsibility of the coach (see Section V.II, this volume). Training methods are passed down from coach to coach, and are usually based on tradition rather than scientific evidence. Although coaches typically invest much time in field-based training, many subscribe to the belief that some players are endowed with innate talent. This doctrine discourages coaches from explicitly investing time in the types of training that could be considered intangible (i.e., perceptual-cognitive skills such as anticipation and decision making). The research on training perceptual-cognitive skills using simulation, however, suggests that such skills are highly amenable to practice and instruction. Moreover, the research suggests that such skills are vital to successful performance (e.g., Helsen & Starkes, 1999; Ward & Williams, 2003). There have been a number of recent reviews on perceptual-cognitive skill training (e.g., Abernethy, Wann, & Parks, 1998; Williams & Ward, 2003). We provide a brief summary of this literature and of the evolution of sports simulation.

In an early attempt to create a simulated training environment to enhance perceptual-cognitive skill, film-based simulation and flash card training were used to improve high school American football players' ability to recognize patterns of play (Londerlee, 1967). Those trained using simulation were significantly quicker at recognizing patterns of play than those using flash cards. Given the use of a pattern-recognition test in this study and the qualitative difference between pattern recognition and real-world match performance, it is difficult to discern whether athletes would benefit from such training when transferring to the actual game. Moreover, methodological issues such as the absence of a pre-test and lack of placebo or control group render it difficult to assess the relative improvement in performance and the causal link between training and performance.

In the following years, a number of researchers capitalized on the availability of film and video technology to create improved simulations. Technological limitations and budgetary constraints restricted early studies to using response measures with low ecological representativeness (e.g., Day, 1980; Williams & Burwitz, 1993; McMorris & Hauxwell, 1997), however, a number of studies followed that incorporated realistic response modes. In contrast to the aviation research, much of this research focused on the training manipulation rather than on simulation per se.

A topical issue in the perceptual-cognitive skills-training research has been whether the observed performance improvement can be accurately attributed to the intervention used or whether the results are simply a consequence of task familiarity. Researchers across several domains have failed to appropriately distinguish between these two, often concurrent, influences. Only a handful of researchers have utilized a control group against which the performance of the experimental group could be compared (e.g., Singer, et al., 1994, Starkes & Lindley, 1994, Tayler, Burwitz, & Davids, 1994), and few have employed a placebo group to reject the hypothesis that training, irrespective of its content, is sufficient for improvement to occur.

Farrow, Chivers, Hardingham, and Sacuse (1998) trained novice tennis players using a film-based anticipation simulation, in which participants had to physically respond to a virtual tennis serve. The experimental group were trained to identify key postural cues to determine their relation to shot outcome and were given performance-based feedback. Participants in the placebo group watched professional tennis matches and were subsequently questioned about the action, whereas those in the control group merely participated in the pre- and post-test. Participants received training over a four-week period, totaling two hours, and performance was assessed pre- and post-treatment. The experimental group significantly reduced their response time, whereas the control and placebo groups did not improve from pre- to post-treatment. This study was one of the first to use a simulation-based training paradigm in which the results could be reliably attributed to the treatment effect. Moreover, this study exemplifies the utility of specifying the *content* of training, as opposed to merely exposing individuals to the training or simulation environment.

An important question remains in light of the results from Farrow et al. (1998): To what extent do these findings transfer from the simulator to the field? Building on expert data elicited from a prior study (Williams et al., 2002, Exp. 1), Williams et al. (2002, Exp. 2) assessed whether a simulation training program would result in "real-world" transfer. Using the same simulated task environment as that used to elicit expert-novice performance differences (Exp. 1), these authors assessed the pre- to post-training improvement of two experimental groups, a placebo and a control group. Participants were assessed on their ability to anticipate ground strokes played by a real (i.e., on-court) and virtual opponent. The experimental groups received 60 minutes of film-based simulation training (which highlighted the relationships between key cues, stroke kinematics, and shot outcome), as well as on-court training to couple new perceptual information with action-related information. The placebo group watched 60 minutes of a professional instruction video on stroke and match play, and the control group completed just the pre- and post-test. Only the experimental groups significantly improved their response time from pre- to post-test, and the greatest improvement was made when these groups transferred to the field. The superior performance of the experimental groups beyond that of a placebo or control indicate that improvement was not a result of task familiarity. Results suggest that the perceptual-cognitive skills-training method employed by these authors in a simulated task environment was effective in improving "real-world" performance (see also Williams, Ward, & Chapman, 2003).

Williams and colleagues (2002) also examined whether the nature of the delivery of the training content would differentially affect performance improvement. Two experimental training groups, explicit-instruction and guided-discovery, were contrasted. In addition to the perceptual simulation training and on-court practice received by both experimental groups, the explicit group received instruction with regard to relationships between important information cues and eventual shot placement. Explicit feedback and opportunities for practice as well as error detection and correction were provided throughout. The guided-discovery group, on the other hand, was directed to focus on potential areas of interest, to work out the relationships between key cues and shot outcome, and given equivalent opportunity for practice. No differences were found between the two experimental groups, although both groups significantly improved their performance beyond that exhibited by the placebo and control groups (also see Smeeton, Williams, Hodges, & Ward, 2005).

Summary

Simulation for Performance

Many forms of simulation have been used to study experts. At one end of the spectrum, static slide presentations and mannequin-based simulators have been used to recre-ate aspects of the task. At the other end, salient task demands have been captured through video-based simulations, desktop simulators, and virtual reality environments. Eye-movement technologies and experimental manipulations have been used during simulation to help identify processes and strategies that experts use to maintain superiority over less-skilled counterparts. However, differing results have promoted alternative interpretations. In sport, for instance, depending on the situation, soccer experts can exhibit either a high or low number of fixations of short and long duration, respectively, but also use an attention strategy that makes benefit of peripheral information extraction. In tennis, experts tend to use a search strategy with fewer fixations of longer duration compared to novices. This diversity across simulations is likely to indicate that experts flexibly employ effective strategies across divergent scenarios to extract meaningful information. In micro-game simulations of team sports (e.g., 1 v 1 in soccer) and in individual sports simulations (e.g., tennis), expert superiority appears to lie in the ability to pick up postural cues that are predictive of future events (e.g., hip/shoulder rotation in tennis), whereas in more macro-game team situations (e.g., 11 v 11 soccer, 5 v 5 basketball), experts are also likely to integrate option selection and pattern recognition strategies into their skill repertoire (Ward & Williams, 2003).

The research on assessing expert-novice differences in medical simulation indicates that this medium has been useful in identifying superior perceptual-motor skills. Experts typically demonstrate less movement variability with fewer positioning errors during task execution. Novice tool manipulation is slower and more variable. In line with the sports research, performance is aided by employing an attention strategy that centers the point of fixation on the target earlier in the movement, using peripheral visual information to track and guide the tool. In contrast, novices use a foveal strategy to aid aiming, focus on the tool throughout movement, and, as they approach the target, alternate fixations between the two, proving to be a costly strategy in terms of speed and accuracy.

In aviation, experts' superiority during simulated performance is typically accompanied by a search strategy that uses more fixations of shorter duration (cf. Sport). The suggestion is that experts required less time per fixation than non-experts to pick up meaningful information and to monitor and control the airspeed indicator. This was particularly evident during approach as airspeed changed, affording greater precision during touchdown. In general, experts typically viewed their instruments more frequently than novices and flexibly adapted their search as the task constraints change. However, expert strategies, including the ability to anticipate future consequences of the situation, may be limited to relatively routine operations (i.e., on tasks or under conditions in which performance is well practiced) and may not extend to unexpected events or high-uncertainty situations. Although much of this research has been conducted on relatively low- to moderate-fidelity simulators, the results suggest that simulation is an extremely useful tool for assessing "real-world," expert performance under standardized conditions.

Simulation for Training

Researchers examining simulation training have made only moderate use of expert empirical data as a basis for determining training content and delivery (see Staszewski & Davison, 2000; Williams et al., 2002). Traditionally, mere exposure and time spent in a simulator has been equated with effective (i.e., deliberate) practice, but the doctrine that "simulation is all you need for learning to occur" has recently been shown to be inaccurate. The way in which the simulation is implemented during training is of greater importance than the simulation itself. Salas and colleagues (1998) highlighted a number of misconceptions about simulation and training that have been implicitly addressed in this chapter. One of these suggests that greater financial investment in a simulator facilitates learning on

that simulator. There is little evidence to support this viewpoint. The research findings suggest that whereas increasing ecological representativeness with respect to the action component may increase the size of the effect, relatively lower-level simulations that capture the salient characteristics of the task are far more versatile for measuring and are very effective at improving performance, particularly for specific skill sets that are perceptual-cognitive in nature.

Technological advances in simulation have outpaced research that could contribute to our understanding of how skilled and less-skilled individuals learn or how training should be implemented using this medium. The cost-effectiveness and efficiency of advanced simulation and virtual reality systems will remain elusive until research is conducted that systematically addresses the content and delivery of the training program used in high-fidelity simulation training and comparisons are made to similar training programs in lower-fidelity systems. Research that has addressed the nature of the content and method of delivery of training in a simulated task environment indicates that there is much promise in using both explicit and implicit-type training programs (Williams et al., 2002).

A key question to ask, given the simulated nature of the environment, is whether training under simulated conditions is actually useful in improving "real-world" performance. The results on transfer of training from a simulated to the actual environment suggest that simulation can be very effective at improving performance on the criterion task. Structured programs that have trained individuals for as little as one hour have sometimes shown dramatic improvements in performance. However, as Salas et al. (1998) pointed out, "more" is not necessarily always "better," and transfer effectiveness may actually reduce with additional training time (Povenmire & Roscoe, 1973). Although performance improvement may be less pronounced after the first few hours of simulation training (see Taylor et al., 2001, 2002), performance improvement is typically a monotonic function of practice.

When a sustained investment in deliberate practice is maintained, performance will likely continue to improve (see Ericsson, 2003; Ericsson et al., 1993). The task for the scientist working in simulation training is to identify the training content and delivery methods that will continue to improve the trainees' performance and move them closer to excellence.

References

Abernethy, B., Thomas, K. T., & Thomas, J. R. (1993). Strategies for improving understanding of motor expertise (or mistakes we have made and things we have learned!). In J. L. Starkes & F. Allard (Eds.), *Cognitive issues in motor expertise* (pp. 317–356). Amsterdam: Elsevier Publishing.

Abernethy, B., Wann, J., & Parks, S. (1998). Training perceptual motor skills for sport. In B. Elliott (Ed.), *Training in sport: Applying sport science* (pp. 1–55). London: Wiley Publications.

Allard, F., Graham, S., & Paarsalu, M. L. (1980). Perception in sport: Basketball. *Journal of Sport Psychology, 2*, 14–21.

Allard, F., & Starkes, J. L. (1980). Perception in sport: Volleyball. *Journal of Sport Psychology, 2*, 22–53.

Allerton, D. J. (2000). Flight simulation: Past, present and future. *Aeronautical Journal, 104*, 651–663.

Bellenkes, A. H., Wickens, C. D., & Kramer, A. F. (1997). Visual scanning and pilot expertise: The role of attentional flexibility and mental model development. *Aviation, Space, and Environmental Medicine, 68*, 569–579.

Brehmer, B., & Dörner, D. (1993). Experiments with computer-simulated microworlds: Escaping both the narrow straits of the laboratory and the deep blue sea of the field study. *Computers in Human Behavior, 9*, 171–184.

Borgeaud, P., & Abernethy, B. (1987). Skilled perception in volleyball defense. *Journal of Sport Psychology, 9*, 400–406.

Charness, N. (1976). Memory for chess positions: Resistance to interference. *Journal of Experimental Psychology: Human Learning and Memory, 2*, 641–653.

Chase, W., & Ericsson, K. A. (1982). Skill and working memory. In G. H. Bower (Ed.), *The psychology of learning and motivation* (pp. 1–58). New York: Academic Press.

Chase, W. G., & Simon, H. A. (1973). Perception in chess. *Cognitive Psychology, 4*, 55–81.

Chi, M. T. H., Glaser, R., & Farr, M. (1980). *The nature of expertise.* Hillsdale, NJ: Erlbaum.

Colt, H. G., Crawford, S. W., & Galbraith, O. (2001). Virtual reality bronchoscopy simulation. *Chest, 120*, 1333–1339.

Day, L. J. (1980). Anticipation in junior tennis players. In J. Groppel & R. Sears (Eds.), *Proceedings of the International Symposium on the Effective Teaching of Racquet Sports* (pp. 107–116). Champaign, IL: University of Illinois.

Doane, S. M., Sohn, Y. W., & Jodlowski, M. T. (2004). Pilot ability to anticipate the consequences of flight actions as a function of expertise. *Human Factors, 46*, 92–103.

Endsley, M. (1995). Towards a theory of situation awareness. *Human Factors, 37*, 32–64.

Entin, E. B., Serfaty, D., Elliott, L. R., & Schiflett, S. G. (2001). DMT-RNet: An internet-based infrastructure for distributed multidisciplinary investigations of C2 performance. In *Proceedings of the 6th International Command and Control Research and Technology Symposium*, June 2001. Annapolis, MD.

Ericsson, K. A. (1996). *The road to excellence: The acquisition of expert performance in the arts and science, sports, and games.* Mahwah, NJ: Erlbaum.

Ericsson, K. A. (2003). How the expert-performance approach differs from traditional approaches to expertise in sports: In search of a shared theoretical framework for studying expert performance. In J. Starkes & K. A. Ericsson (Eds.), *Expert performance in sport: Recent advances in research on sport expertise* (pp. 371–401). Champaign, IL: Human Kinetics.

Ericsson, K. A., & Kintsch, W. (1995). Long term working memory. *Psychological Review, 102*, 211–245.

Ericsson, K. A., Krampe, R. Th., & Tesch-Römer, C. (1993). The role of deliberate practice in the acquisition of expert performance. *Psychological Review, 100*, 363–406.

Ericsson, K. A., & Smith, J. (1991). Prospects and limits of the empirical study of expertise: An introduction. In K. A. Ericsson & J. Smith (Eds.), *Toward a general theory of expertise: Prospects and limits* (pp. 1–38). New York: Cambridge University Press.

Farrow, D., Chivers, P., Hardingham, C., & Sacuse, S. (1998). The effect of video-based perceptual training on the tennis return of serve. *International Journal of Sport Psychology*, 29, 231–242.

Feltovich, P., Spiro, R., & Coulson, R. (1997). Issues of expert flexibility in contexts characterized by complexity and change. In P. J. Feltovich, K. M. Ford, & R. R. Hoffman (Eds.), *Expertise in context*. Menlo Park, CA: AAAI/MIT Press.

Fischhoff, B. (1989). Eliciting knowledge for analytical representation. *IEEE Transactions on Systems, Man, and Cybernetics*, 19, 448–461.

Gallagher, A. G., & Satava, R. M. (2002). Virtual reality as a metric for the assessment of laparoscopic psychomotor skills. *Surgical Endoscopy*, 16, 1746–1752.

Goldiez, B., Ahmad, A. M., & Hancock, P. A. (2005). Wayfinding and navigation in augmented reality. *Manuscript submitted for publication*.

Gray, W. (2002). Simulated task environments: The role of high-fidelity simulations, scaled worlds, synthetic environments, and laboratory tasks in basic and applied cognitive research. *Cognitive Science Quarterly*, 2, 205–227.

de Groot, A. (1978/1946). *Thought and choice in chess*. The Hague: Mouton.

Haskins, M. J. (1965). Development of a response-recognition training film in tennis. *Perceptual and Motor Skills*, 21, 207–211.

Hatano, G, & Ignaki, K. (1986). Two courses of expertise. In H. Stevenson, H. Azuma, & K. Hakuta (Eds.), *Child development and education in Japan*. New York: W. H. Freeman.

Hays, R. T., Jacobs, J. W., Prince, C., & Salas, E. (1992). Flight simulator training effectiveness: A meta-analysis. *Military Psychology*, 4, 63–74.

Haluck, R. S., Webster, R. W., Snyder, A. J., Melkonian, M. G., Mohler, B. J., Dise, M. L., & Lefever, A. (2001). A virtual reality surgical simulator trainer for navigation in laparoscopic Surgery. In J. D. Westwood et al. (Eds.), *Medicine meets virtual reality 2001: Outer space, inner space, virtual space* (pp. 171–177). Amsterdam: IOS Press.

Helsen, W. F., & Starkes, J. L. (1999). A multidimensional approach to skilled perception and performance in sport. *Applied Cognitive Psychology*, 13, 1–27.

Higgins, T. J., Chignell, M. H., & Hancock, P. A. (1989). Knowledge-based supervisory control

for aerospace applications. In P. A. Hancock & M. H. Chignell (Eds.), *Intelligent interfaces: Theory, research, and design*. North Holland: Elsevier.

Hoffman, R. R. (1992). *The psychology of expertise: Cognitive research and empirical AI*. New York: Springer-Verlag.

Hoffman, R. R., & Deffenbacher, K. A. (1993). An analysis of the relations of basic and applied science. *Ecological Psychology*, 5, 315–352.

Hubbard, J. P., Levitt, E. J., Schumacher, C. F., & Schnabel, T. G. (1965). An objective evaluation of clinical competence: New techniques used by the National Board of Medical Examiners. *New England Journal of Medicine*, 272, 1321–1328.

Jodlowski, M. T., & Doane, S. M. (2003). Event reasoning as a function of working memory capacity and long term working memory skill. In *Proceedings of the 25th Annual Meeting of the Cognitive Science Society*, July 31–August 2. Boston, MA: Cognitive Science Society.

Jodlowski, M. T., Doane, S. M., & Brou, R. J. (2003). Adaptive expertise during simulated flight. In *Proceedings of the Human Factors and Ergonomics Society 47th Annual Meeting*, October 10–17. Denver, Colorado: HFES.

Jones, C. M., & Miles, T. R. (1978). Use of advance cues in predicting the flight of a lawn tennis ball. *Journal of Human Movement Studies*, 4, 231–5.

Kasarskis, P., Stehwien, J., Hickox, J., Aretz, A., & Wickens, C. (2001). Comparison of expert and novice scan behaviors during VFR flight. Paper presented at the 11th International Symposium on Aviation Psychology. Columbus OH: The Ohio State University.

Khatwa, R., & Helmreich, R. (1999). Analysis of critical factors during approach and landing in accidents and normal flight. *Flight Safety Digest*. Alexandria, VA: Flight Safety Foundation.

Kintsch, W. (1988). The use of knowledge in discourse processing: A construction-integration model. *Psychological Review*, 95, 163–182.

Kneebone, R. (2003). Simulation in surgical training: Educational issues and practical applications. *Medical Education*, 37, 267–77.

Kohn, L. T., Corrigan, J. M., & Donaldson, M. (1999). *To err is human: Building a safer health system*. Washington, DC: Institute of Medicine.

Law, B., Atkins, M. S., Kirkpatrick, A. E., Lomax, A. J., & Mackenzie, C. L. (2004). Eye gaze patterns differentiate novice and experts in a virtual laparoscopic surgery training environment. *Proceedings of the eye tracking research & applications symposium on eye tracking research & applications* (pp. 41–48). New York: ACM Press.

Lintern, G., Roscoe, S. N., Koonce, J. M., & Segal, L. (1990). Transfer of landing skills in beginning flight training. *Human Factors*, 32, 319–327.

Londerlee, B. R. (1967). Effect of training with motion pictures versus flash cards upon football play recognition. *Research Quarterly*, 38, 202–207.

McCloy, R., & Stone, R. (2001). Science, medicine, and the future: Virtual reality in surgery. *British Medical Journal*, 323, 912–915.

McMorris, T., & Hauxwell, B. (1997). Improving anticipation of soccer goalkeepers using video observation. In T. Reilly, J. Bangsbo, & M. Hughes (Eds.), *Science and football III* (pp. 290–294). London: E. & F. N. Spon.

Patel, V. L., & Groen, G. (1986). Knowledge-based solution strategies in medical reasoning. *Cognitive Science*, 10, 91–116.

Povenmire, H. K., & Roscoe, S. N. (1973). Incremental transfer effectiveness of a ground-based general aviation trainer. *Human Factors*, 15, 534–542.

Roscoe, S. N. (1971). Incremental transfer effectiveness. *Human Factors*, 13, 561–567.

Rosser, J. C., Rosser, L. E., & Savalgi, R. S. (1997). Skill acquisition and assessment of laparoscopic surgery. *Archives of Surgery*, 132, 200–204.

Salas, E., Bowers, C. A., & Rhodenizer, L. (1998). It is not how much you have but how you use it: Toward a rational use of simulation to support aviation training. *The International Journal of Aviation Psychology*, 8, 197–208.

Salas, E., & Klein, G. (2001). *Linking expertise and naturalistic decision making (Expertise: Research and applications)*. Mahwah, NJ: Erlbaum.

Schijven, M., & Jakimowicz, J. (2003). Construct validity: Experts and novices performing on the Xitact LS500 laparoscopy simulator. *Surgical Endoscopy*, 17, 803–810.

Senate of Surgery (1998). *Response to the general medical council determination on the Bristol Case*. London: Senate Paper 5, The Senate of Surgery of Great Britain and Northern Ireland.

Seymour, N. E., Gallagher, A. G., Roman, S. A., O'Brien, M. K., Bansal, V. K., Anderson, D. K., & Satava, R. M. (2002). Virtual reality training improves operating room performance: Results of a randomized, double blinded study. *Annals of Surgery*, 236, 458–463.

Singer, R. N., Cauraugh, J. H., Chen, D., Steinberg, G. M., Frehlich, S. G., & Wang, L. (1994). Training mental quickness in beginning/intermediate tennis players. *The Sport Psychologist*, 8, 305–318.

Smeeton, N. J., Williams, A. M., Hodges, N. J., & Ward, P. (2005). The relative effectiveness of various instructional approaches in developing anticipation skill. *Journal of Experimental Psychology: Applied*, 11, 98–110.

Smode, A. F., Hall, E. R., & Meyer, D. E. (1966). *An assessment of research relevant to pilot training* (Vol. 11) (Technical Report No. AMRL-TR-66-196). Wright Patterson Air Force Base, OH: Aerospace Medical Research Laboratory.

Sohn, Y. W., & Doane, S. M. (2003). Roles of working memory capacity and long-term working memory skill in complex task performance. *Memory & Cognition*, 31, 458–466.

Starkes, J. L., & Ericsson, K. A. (2003). *Expert performance in sports: Advances in research on sports expertise*. Champaign, IL: Human Kinetics.

Starkes, J. L., & Lindley, S. (1994). Can we hasten expertise by video simulations? *Quest*, 46, 211–222.

Staszewski, J. (1999). Information processing analysis of human land mine detection skill. In T. Broach, A. C. Dubey, R. E. Dugan, & J. Harvey, (Eds.), *Detection and remediation technologies for mines and mine-like targets IV. Proceedings of the Society for Photo-Optical Instrumentation Engineers 13th Annual Meeting*, SPIE. Vol. 3710, 766–777.

Staszewski, J., & Davison, A. (2000). Mine detection training based on expert skill. In A. C. Dubey, J. F. Harvey, J. T. Broach, & R. E. Dugan (Eds.), *Detection and remediation technologies for mines and mine-like targets V. Proceedings of Society of Photo-Optical Instrumentation Engineers 14th Annual Meeting*, SPIE Vol. 4038, 90–101.

Strom, P., Kjellin, A., Hedman, L., Wredmark, T., & Fellander-Tsai, L. (2004). Training in tasks with different visual-spatial components does not improve virtual arthroscopy performance. *Surgical Endoscopy*, 18, 115–120.

Taffinder, N., Sutton, C., Fishwick, R. J., McManus, I. C., & Darzi, A. (1998). Validation of virtual reality to teach and assess psychomotor skills in laparoscopic surgery: Results form randomized controlled studies using the

MIST VR laparoscopic simulator. *Studies in Health Technology and Informatics, 50*, 124–130.

Tayler, M. A., Burwitz, L., & Davids, K. (1994). Coaching perceptual strategy in badminton. *Journal of Sports Sciences, 12*, 213.

Taylor, H. L., Talleur, D. A., Emanuel, T. W., Rantanen, E. M., Bradshaw, G. L., & Phillips, S. I. (2001). Incremental training effectiveness of personal computers used for instrument training. Paper presented at the 11th International Symposium on Aviation Psychology. Columbus, OH: The Ohio State University.

Taylor, H. L., Talleur, D. A., Emanuel, T. W., Rantanen, E. M., Bradshaw, G. L., & Phillips, S. I. (2002). Incremental training effectiveness of personal computers used for instrument training: Basic instruments. *Interim Technical Report ARL-02-4/NASA-02-2*. Moffett Field, CA: NASA Ames Research Center (Contract NASA NAG 2–1282).

Thomas, J. R. (2003). Meta analysis of motor expertise. Invited Motor Development Scholar Address presented at the North American Society for the Psychology of Sport and Physical Activity Conference. NASPSPA: Savannah, GA.

Torkington, J., Smith, S. G. T., Rees, B. I., & Darzi, A. (2001). Skill transfer from virtual reality to a real laparoscopic task. *Surgical Endoscopy, 15*, 1076–1079.

van Dijk, T. A., & Kintsch, W. (1983). *Strategies of discourse comprehension*. New York: Academic Press.

Verner, L., Oleynikov, D., Holtmann, S., Haider, H., & Zhukov, L. (2003). Measurements of the level of surgical expertise using flight path analysis from da Vinci Robotic Surgical System. *Medicine Meets Virtual Reality, 11*, 373–378.

Walls, J., Bertrand, L., Gale, T., & Saunders, N. (1998). Assessment of upwind dinghy sailing performance using a virtual reality dinghy sailing simulator. *Journal of Science and Medicine in Sport, 1*, 61–71.

Ward, P., & Williams, A. M. (2003). Perceptual and cognitive skill development in soccer: The multidimensional nature of expert performance. *Journal of Sport and Exercise Psychology, 25*, 93–111.

Ward, P., Williams, A. M., & Bennett, S. J. (2002). Visual search and biological motion perception in tennis. *Research Quarterly for Exercise and Sport, 73*, 107–112.

Williams, A. M., & Burwitz, L. (1993). Advance cue utilisation in soccer. In T. Reilly, J. Clarys, & A. Stibbe (Eds.), *Science and football II* (pp. 239–244). London: E. & F. N. Spon.

Williams, A. M., & Davids, K. (1998). Visual search strategy, selective attention, and expertise in soccer. *Research Quarterly for Exercise and Sport, 69*, 111–128.

Williams, A. M., Davids, K., Burwitz, L., & Williams, J. G. (1993). Cognitive knowledge and soccer performance. *Perceptual and Motor Skills, 76*, 579–593.

Williams, A. M., Davids, K., Burwitz, L., & Williams, J. G. (1994). Visual search strategies of experienced and inexperienced soccer players. *Research Quarterly for Exercise and Sport, 65*, 127–135.

Williams, A. M., & Hodges, N. J. (2004) (Eds.). *Skill acquisition in sport: Research, theory and practice*. London: Routledge.

Williams, A. M., & Ward, P. (2001). Developing perceptual skill in sport: The need for evidence-based practice. In A. Papaioannou, M. Goudas, & Y. Theodorakis (Eds.), *Proceedings of the 10th World Congress of Sport Psychology: Vol. 3. In the dawn of the new millennium* (pp. 159–161). Skiathos, Hellas: International Society of Sport Psychology.

Williams, A. M., & Ward, P. (2003). Perceptual expertise: Development in sport. In J. L. Starkes & K. A. Ericsson (Eds.), *Expert performance in sport: Advances in research on sport expertise*, (pp. 220–249). Champaign, IL: Human Kinetics.

Williams, A. M., Ward, P., Allen, D., & Smeeton, N. J. (2004). Developing perceptual skill in tennis using on-court instruction: Perception versus perception and action. *Journal of Applied Sport Psychology, 16*, 350–360.

Williams, A. M., Ward, P., & Chapman C. (2003). Training perceptual skill in field hockey: Is there transfer from the laboratory to the field? *Research Quarterly for Exercise and Sport, 74*, 98–103.

Williams, A. M., Ward, P., Knowles, J., & Smeeton, N. (2002). Anticipation skill in a real-world task: Measurement, training, and transfer in tennis. *Journal of Experimental Psychology: Applied, 8*, 259–270.

Yates, J. F. (2001). "Outsider": Impressions of naturalistic decision making. In E. Salas & G. Klein (Eds.), *Linking expertise and naturalistic decision making* (pp. 9–33). Mahwah, NJ: Erlbaum.

Part IV

METHODS FOR STUDYING THE ACQUISITION AND MAINTENANCE OF EXPERTISE

CHAPTER 15

Laboratory Studies of Training, Skill Acquisition, and Retention of Performance

Robert W. Proctor & Kim-Phuong L. Vu

For most investigations of expertise, conclusions are drawn about the knowledge representations and strategies of experts through observing their performance of tasks in natural or artificial settings, analyzing verbal protocols that they provide while performing the tasks, and using knowledge-elicitation methods. A major component of research on expertise involves comparing the performance of experts to that of novices on specific tasks in the laboratory. Level of expertise is a subject variable for which the prerequisite training and experience of the experts has occurred prior to task performance. Investigations of experts in a variety of domains with these methods have provided invaluable information about the nature of expert performance and knowledge, and the ways in which they differ from those of novices. However, because the acquisition of the experts' skills is completed prior to the investigation, issues concerning how this expertise was acquired and how it is maintained outside of the laboratory can be investigated only through self-reports. Although self-reports can yield substantial data, they are limited in their ability to provide detailed information about the changes in information processing and performance that occur as the skill develops and the conditions that optimize acquisition and retention of these skills.

Learning and retention have been studied extensively in the laboratory since the earliest days of psychology. For a large part of the 20th century, much of the efforts of experimental psychologists were centered on studying animal learning and human verbal learning (e.g., Leahey, 2003). This research resulted in an extensive database and numerous facts and principles concerning acquisition and retention, which are summarized in numerous sources (e.g., Bower & Hilgard, 1981; Crowder, 1976). There is also a long history of research on skill acquisition and retention in laboratory settings (e.g., Bilodeau & Bilodeau, 1969), which is the main focus of this chapter. Laboratory studies of skill acquisition offer the advantage of being able to control the conditions of training and testing so that effects of independent variables can be isolated and causal relations established. This method allows evaluation of alternative hypotheses and theories concerning the acquisition, retention, and transfer of skill. It is possible also to determine factors that influence the speed with which a skill can be acquired and its generalizability to other tasks and environments.

Various methods can be used to evaluate the nature of skill acquisition and retention in the laboratory. Functions relating performance to amount of practice can be measured, allowing implications to be drawn about the rate of skill acquisition and the changes in processing that accompany development of skill. Different schedules of practice and feedback can be compared to evaluate factors that influence immediate performance and learning. Retention tests can be conducted after delays of minutes, days, weeks, months, or years to establish that the differences evident during acquisition reflect differences in learning and to establish the durability of the acquired skill. Psychophysiological and brain-imaging techniques can be employed to assess neurophysiological changes that accompany skill acquisition.

Perhaps the most widely used technique is that of transfer designs (e.g., Speelman & Kirsner, 2001), in which participants practice a task and subsequently are transferred to another task that shares some features with the first task. Positive transfer is an indication that the skills acquired in the practice task are applicable to the transfer task, whereas negative transfer implies that their application cannot be prevented even though it interferes with performance. Through the use of transfer designs it is possible to determine exactly which processes have been affected by practice and the nature of the changes that have occurred.

A generally accepted rule is that a minimum of ten years of deliberate practice is required to attain expert performance in many domains (Ericsson & Smith, 1991). Although the amount of practice in laboratory studies of skill acquisition is necessarily considerably less than ten years, laboratory studies nevertheless can illuminate many aspects of skill acquisition and retention. One reason why is that for many simple tasks, performance asymptotes after relatively little practice and is retained at that level for a long period, implying that a durable skill has been acquired. Ericsson and Smith (1991) noted, "It is clear that the learning mechanisms that mediate increasing improvements from repeated practice trials must play important roles in the acquisition of expertise" (p. 27). But, they regard as shortcomings that the learning mechanisms "can account only for making the initial cognitive processes more efficient and ultimately automatic" (p. 27) and "do not take into account the acquisition of new cognitive structures, processes that are prerequisites for the unique ability of experts to plan and reason about problem situations" (p. 28). Although we agree that a major contribution of the laboratory studies is to show how performance improves with practice, which is an important part of expert performance, we describe several studies that also reveal development of new cognitive structures and changes in strategy.

Phases of Skill Acquisition

For virtually any task, performance improves with practice, with the greatest improvement occurring early in training. One issue is whether the improvement in performance reflects only quantitative changes (i.e., increased processing efficiency) or qualitative changes (i.e., changes in processing mode). In an early study, Bryan and Harter (1899) characterized improvement in performance at telegraphy as the development of a hierarchy of habits, reflecting increasingly higher-order chunking and automatization as the telegrapher became more skilled. They stressed the importance of automatization for expert performance, stating, "Only when all the necessary habits, high and low, have become automatic, does one rise into the freedom and speed of the expert" (p. 357).

The distinction between attention-demanding controlled processes early in practice and automatic processes later in practice is evident in many formulations of skill acquisition, including the influential one of Schneider and Shiffrin (1977). It is customary to distinguish three phases of skill acquisition, which Fitts (1964) referred to as *cognitive, associative,* and *autonomous* and Anderson (1982) called *declarative, knowledge compilation,* and *procedural.* In the first phase, task instructions are encoded in declarative representations and held in working memory. General interpretive procedures use these representations to generate behavior appropriate to the task. In the transitional phase, procedures specific to the task or skill are acquired that no longer require the interpretive procedures. In the final phase, further progression of skilled performance is achieved through a gradual strengthening of the procedures and tuning of the conditions that will trigger them. In this phase, some skills can become automatized.

Whereas Anderson's (1982) account of skill acquisition, like most others, attributes it to development of procedures, or associations, that become strengthened with practice, an alternative view is that skill acquisition reflects a change in processes. Logan (1988) proposed an instance theory of automatization, according to which execution of two processes – an algorithm based on task instructions and retrieval from memory of previously encoded instances – occurs in parallel. An assigned task is performed initially using an appropriate algorithm. With practice, specific instances of stimuli and their responses are encoded into memory, and performance can instead be based on retrieval of a prior instance. At first, retrieval is slow, but with practice under consistent conditions, it becomes much faster, resulting in a mix of trials on which performance is algorithm based and ones on which it is retrieval based. With sufficient experience, the retrieval process comes to be used on all trials. Thus, according to the instance theory, increasing automatization with practice is a consequence of a gradual shift from algorithm-based to memory-based performance.

One way to evaluate models of skill acquisition is to examine the functions relating response time (RT) to amount of practice. Accounts that suggest changes in modes of processing or strategies seem to imply that the learning curves will be discontinuous, although such accounts can generate smooth functions. Bryan and Harter (1899) reported discontinuities, called plateaus, which they attributed to acquisition of lower-order habits prior to higher-level habits. However, until recently, the prevailing view has been that the function is continuous. Newell and Rosenbloom (1981) concluded that across a variety of tasks, the reduction in RT with practice can be captured by a power law, as first proposed by Snoddy (1926):

$$\text{RT} = A + BN^{-\beta},$$

where N is the number of practice trials, B is performance time on the first trial, β is the learning rate, and A is the asymptotic RT after learning has been completed.

The power law of practice has become widely accepted as a benchmark that must be generated by any theory of skill acquisition (e.g., Logan, 1988). However, it recently has been challenged as being applicable only to averaged acquisition functions. Heathcote, Brown, and Mewhort (2000) fit power and exponential functions to the data from individual participants for 40 data sets. They found that the power function, for which the learning rate is a hyperbolically decreasing function of practice, did not fit the individual-participant data as well as the exponential function, for which the learning rate is constant at all levels of practice. Consequently, Heathcote and colleagues proposed a new exponential law of practice:

$$\text{RT} = A + Be^{-\alpha N},$$

where α is the rate parameter.

Whereas both the power and exponential laws assume that the acquisition functions are continuous, several authors have reported evidence that for some tasks, such as mental arithmetic problems, the functions for individual participants show abrupt changes (e.g., Haider & Frensch, 2002; Rickard, 2004). Much of this research has been conducted within the framework of Logan's (1988) instance theory and has been interpreted as indicating that the change from an algorithmic process to a retrieval process is discrete, rather than being a gradual shift in dominance of the parallel execution of algorithm and search strategies as proposed by Logan (Rickard, 2004). More generally, Delaney, Reder, Staszewski, and Ritter (1998) concluded that acquisition of skill and expertise is characterized by multiple strategy shifts that produce discontinuities in individual learning curves. They provided evidence that individual improvement in solution time for mental arithmetic problems with practice is characterized better by separate power functions for each specific strategy than by a single power function for the task.

Basic Information-Processing Skills

Research on the acquisition and retention of basic information-processing skills has been conducted using a variety of tasks. Although there is not a clean separation between skills involving perception, response selection, and motor control, it is convenient to organize studies around this distinction. (See also Rosenbaum, Augustyn, Cohen & Jax, Chapter 29.)

Perceptual Skill

Ahissar (1999) notes, "The extent of adult improvement in not only complex but also simple perceptual tasks is remarkable" (p. 124). Perceptual learning has been studied since the 1800s, with much of the work in the second half of the 20th century conducted from the ecological perspective (Gibson & Pick, 2000). According to this perspective, perceptual learning involves the individual becoming "tuned" to "pick up" information afforded by the environment. Interest in perceptual learning has increased considerably in the last decade (e.g., Fahle & Poggio, 2002), with an emphasis on examining the underlying cognitive and neural mechanisms. Understanding per-

ceptual learning is important not only for basic theory about skill acquisition but also for the acquisition and training of real-world skills that have substantial perceptual components, such as identification of abnormal features in X-ray images (Sowden, Davies, & Roling, 2000), wine tasting (Brochet & Dubourdieu, 2001), and discriminating the sex of baby chicks (Biederman & Shiffrar, 1987).

Goldstone, Schyns, and Medin (1997) specify five mechanisms involved in perceptual learning: (1) *Attention weighting* concerns shifts of attention from less-relevant to more-relevant dimensions. This is accomplished in part by (2) *detector creation*, for which functional units are established, each of which respond selectively to a specific type of input, and (3) *dimensionalization*, or the creation of ordered detector sets that represent objects by their distinct dimensions. These processes act to enable efficient selective attention to specific stimulus dimensions. (4) *Unitization* involves acquisition of higher-level functional units that can be activated by complex configurations of features, thus allowing stimuli to be processed as a whole. The final mechanism of perceptual learning identified by Goldstone et al. is (5) *contingency detection*: The contingencies between parts of stimuli are learned to allow more efficient extraction of information by, for example, changing scanning patterns.

FEATURE IDENTIFICATION

A major aspect of perceptual skill is learning to identify features that distinguish alternative stimuli or classes of stimuli. For example, Sowden et al. (2000) note, regarding perception of medical X-ray images, "The expert film reader apparently perceives features present in X-ray images that go unnoticed by the novice" (p. 379). Numerous studies have shown that training that emphasizes distinctive features is highly beneficial. Gibson (1947) reported an experiment in which cadets received 30 hours of training for distinguishing among slides of 40 different aircraft, using instructions that emphasized a set of distinctive features or the total form of each plane. Cadets who received the distinctive-feature instructions performed better on a subsequent recognition test than did those who received the total-form instructions. Biederman and Shiffrar (1987) found that novices could be trained to perform at a similar level to experts at classifying chicks as male or female, a skill that typically takes years to acquire, by using instructions and diagrams that emphasized the critical features for differentiating male and female chicks.

Although the tasks above required relatively complex discriminations, many simple perceptual tasks such as grating waveform discrimination and motion discrimination show substantial learning as well (Karni & Bertini, 1997). Transfer techniques have been used to determine the conditions to which each skill generalizes and to provide evidence about the neuronal mechanisms involved. Karni and Bertini note that an important characteristic of perceptual learning is a lack of broad transfer. Karni (1996) has proposed a model for which the central idea is that the acquisition of a skill is at the earliest level of the stream for processing the sensory information in which the relevant stimulus parameter can be represented. Karni and Bertini conclude that top-down mechanisms control perceptual learning because repeated exposure to a stimulus is not sufficient for learning to occur, but they note that perceptual learning has often been reported in the absence of explicit performance feedback (e.g., Fahle & Edelman, 1993).

AUTOMATICITY AND UNITIZATION

Research on skill acquisition and transfer has been conducted using search tasks for which participants must indicate whether a probe item is a member of a target set. For a memory search task, the participant receives a memory set of one to four target items (e.g., letters) and then one or more displays consisting of probe items that may or may not include the target. One response key is to be pressed if the probe item matches any of the target items and another if it does not. In visual search tasks, the displays contain one or more stimuli, and the participant is to indicate whether an item held in memory is in the display (or, to identify which of two possible targets is in the display). For hybrid memory-visual search tasks, the sizes of both the memory and the display sets are varied.

Schneider and Shiffrin (1977) and Shiffrin and Schneider (1977) established that a critical factor influencing the benefit of practice in search tasks is whether the target items in the memory set on one trial are never distractors on other trials (consistent mapping, CM), or whether the same items can be targets on some trials and distractors on others (varied mapping, VM) (see Figure 15.1). Initially, RT is slow, and it increases substantially as a linear function of the target set size. Practice with CM results in a large decrease in RT and elimination of the set-size effect. In contrast, practice with VM produces little improvement in performance. These results suggest that automaticity develops only when the mapping of stimuli to target and nontarget categories remains consistent. Shiffrin and Schneider concluded that automatic processes are fast and operate in parallel, whereas controlled processes are slow and operate serially.

Schneider and Chein (2003) list five additional phenomena for search behavior that reflect differences in controlled and automatic processing. (1) Controlled search requires considerable effort, whereas automatic search does not. (2) Controlled processing is more sensitive to stressors, such as fatigue, than is automatic processing. (3) Controlled processes can be modified easily, but automatic processes cannot. (4) Controlled processing results in explicit learning of task characteristics, whereas automatic processing does not. (5) Automatic attraction of attention to a stimulus is determined by the priority of the stimulus alone and not the context in which the stimulus occurs.

Letters and digits are already highly unitized when used as stimuli in experiments. To examine the acquisition of unitized representations, Shiffrin and Lightfoot (1997)

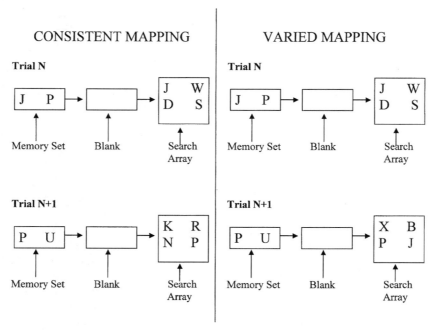

Figure 15.1. Illustration of a search task with consistent or varied mapping. With consistent mapping (left column), stimuli in the memory set for one trial are never distractors on other trials. With varied mapping (right column), stimuli in the memory set for one trial can be distractors on other trials (as illustrated by the letter *J* changing from a target on trial N to a distractor on trial N + 1).

used a visual search task with novel characters composed of line segments for which no single feature could be used to identify the target (see Figure 15.2), comparing learning for CM and VM tasks. At the beginning of training the slopes of the set-size functions for both tasks averaged approximately 100 ms for positive (target present) responses and 200 ms for negative (target absent) responses. The VM task received as much benefit of practice as the CM task, and both tasks continued to show relatively high slope values and 2:1 negative-to-positive

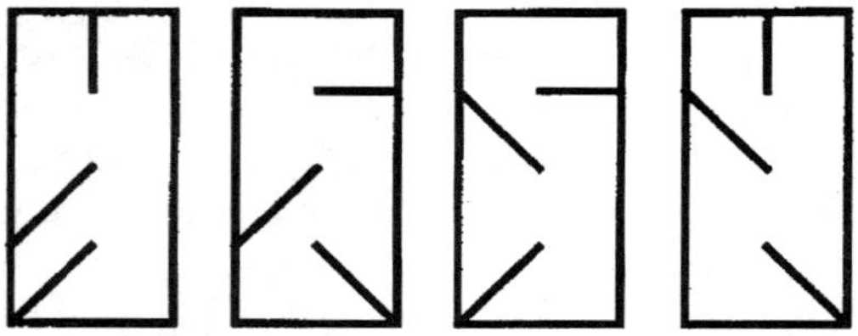

slope ratios suggestive of controlled search. Thus, no automatic attraction of attention developed under CM conditions for these novel stimuli, in contrast to the results obtained with familiar letter and digit stimuli. Shiffrin and Lightfoot concluded that the changes with practice were due to a unitization process that allowed a holistic representation for the stimuli to develop.

Response-Selection Skill

Response selection refers to processes involved in determining which response to make to a stimulus. The phenomena that can be attributed primarily to response-selection processes are stimulus-response compatibility (SRC) effects (Sanders, 1998), which are differences in performance as a function of the mapping of individual stimuli to responses and the overall relation between the stimulus and response sets (e.g., whether physical stimulus locations are mapped to keypresses or vocal location

Figure 15.2. Examples of the novel, conjunctively defined stimuli used in Shiffrin and Lightfoot's (1997) visual search study.

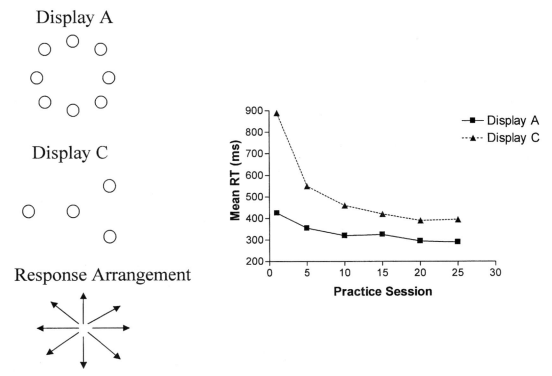

Figure 15.3. Left panel: Illustration of Displays A and C, and the response arrangement, used in Fitts and Seeger's (1953) study. Right panel: Mean reaction time as a function of practice session and display type.

names). In the simplest form of SRC study, left and right stimuli are mapped to left and right responses. RT is shorter with the mapping of right stimulus to right response and left stimulus to left response than with the opposite mapping. This element-level SRC effect is larger when the stimulus and response sets are both visuospatial or both verbal than when one set is visuospatial and the other verbal (Proctor & Wang, 1997), due to the higher compatibility of physical locations with manual responses and of location-words with vocal responses.

Most explanations attribute the benefit for the compatible mapping at least in part to intentional, controlled processing being faster for that mapping than for the incompatible mapping. According to some accounts, the compatible mapping also benefits from automatic activation of the corresponding response (e.g., Kornblum & Lee, 1995), which is the correct response for the

compatible mapping but not for the incompatible mapping. In network models, the controlled processing is represented as short-term stimulus-response associations defined by task instructions, and the automatic processing as long-term stimulus-response associations that are overlearned through years of experience (Zorzi & Umiltà, 1995).

PRACTICE WITH VARIOUS TASKS AND MAPPINGS

Most accounts of skill acquisition imply that SRC effects should disappear with practice, but numerous studies have shown that they do not. Fitts and Seeger (1953) had participants respond to eight possible stimuli by moving a stylus to one of eight response locations, arranged in a circle. Within each of 26 sessions, three displays were used that differed in their compatibility with the circular response array. In the first session, RT was 450 ms longer for the least compatible

Display C than for the most compatible Display A (see Figure 15.3). RT decreased across sessions, with the asymptotic difference between Displays C and A stabilizing at about 80 ms between sessions five and ten.

Dutta and Proctor (1992) had participants practice 1,200 trials with either a compatible or incompatible mapping of left-right stimuli to left-right response keys. The SRC effect was 72 ms initially and decreased to 46 ms at the end of practice. Dutta and Proctor also showed that two other types of SRC effects, one for orthogonal stimulus-response arrangements and another for two-dimensional symbolic stimuli, remained present across the same amounts of practice.

Proctor and Dutta (1993) examined whether the benefit of practice in two-choice tasks arises from participants learning associations between stimulus-response locations or stimuli and effectors. Participants practiced with a compatible or incompatible spatial mapping over three days, half with their hands in the natural adjacent positions and half with them crossed so that the right hand operated the left key and the left hand the right key. When transferred to one of the other mapping/placement conditions, positive transfer was evident only if the spatial mapping was the same in the transfer session as in the practice sessions and not if hand position was the same but spatial mapping different. With an incompatible spatial mapping, the practice benefit was evident even when participants switched periodically between crossed and uncrossed hand placements. These results imply that the improvement with practice in two-choice spatial tasks primarily involves faster selection of a location code.

Pashler and Baylis (1991) obtained similar benefits of practice on the speed of response selection for a task in which participants made keypresses with three fingers of one hand in response to stimuli from three categories (two letters, digits, and nonalphanumeric symbols). RT decreased by 150 ms over 750 practice trials. Each participant then performed 50 additional trials,

with two new members added to each category. Perfect transfer was obtained for the new category members, indicating that participants had learned category-to-response associations and not specific stimulus-to-response associations. Also, a change in the hand used for responding resulted in complete transfer, indicating that participants were not learning to make specific motor responses to the categories.

PRACTICE AND THE SIMON TASK

When stimulus location is irrelevant to the task, performance is better when stimulus and response locations correspond than when they do not (the Simon effect; Simon, 1990). For example, when instructed to respond to a green stimulus with a left keypress and a red stimulus with a right keypress, responses to the green stimulus are faster when it occurs in a left location than when it occurs in a right location, and vice versa for responses to the red stimulus. The Simon effect is typically attributed to automatic activation of the corresponding response produced via the long-term stimulus-response associations. As for SRC proper, the Simon effect is reduced but persists with practice. Simon, Craft, and Webster (1973) found that the Simon effect for high or low pitch tones presented in the left or right ear decreased from 60 ms initially to 35 ms after 1,080 trials. Similarly, Prinz, Aschersleben, Hommel, and Vogt (1995) had a single person perform 210 trials of an auditory Simon task in each of 30 sessions. The Simon effect decreased from 50 ms in the first three sessions to 20 ms over the last 20 sessions.

Although the Simon effect is not eliminated with practice, it can be eliminated or reversed by prior practice with an incompatible spatial mapping. Proctor and Lu (1999) had participants perform a two-choice visual SRC task with an incompatible mapping for 900 trials. When a Simon task was performed on the next day, the Simon effect reversed, yielding better performance on noncorresponding trials than on corresponding trials. Tagliabue,

Zorzi, Umiltà, and Bassignani (2000) showed that 72 trials with an incompatible mapping are sufficient to eliminate the Simon effect when the Simon task is performed immediately, a day, or a week after the practice session. Thus, when stimulus location is no longer relevant, the task-defined associations between noncorresponding locations continue to affect performance.

Tagliabue, Zorzi, and Umiltà (2002) provided evidence that this transfer effect occurs across modalities. Participants practiced with an incompatible mapping of left and right tones to keypresses and performed a visual Simon task after delays of five minutes, one day, or one week. The Simon effect was eliminated at all delays, leading Tagliabue et al. (2002) to conclude that the elimination is not due to modality-specific coding. Vu, Proctor, and Urcuioli (2003) replicated the findings from Tagliabue et al.'s (2000, 2002) studies, but found little influence of practice with a prior incompatible mapping when the transfer Simon task used auditory stimuli. One possible reason why the auditory Simon effect was unaffected by the prior practice is that the effect is larger at baseline than the visual Simon effect. Vu (2006) showed that the strength of the long-term stimulus-response associations is important in determining whether prior practice with an incompatible mapping affects the subsequent Simon task. When participants practiced 72 trials with an incompatible mapping of left-right (horizontal) or top-bottom (vertical) stimuli and transferred to a horizontal or vertical Simon task, the Simon effect was eliminated only for the horizontal practice and transfer condition. However, with 600 trials of practice, the Simon effect reversed when the practice and transfer conditions were both horizontal and was eliminated in all other conditions. These findings suggest that practice both changes the efficiency with which noncorresponding stimulus-response locations are processed and promotes learning of more general response-selection procedures (e.g., respond "opposite").

Motor Control

Many skills require proficiency not only at perception and response selection but also at motor control. Typically, the execution of movements must be coordinated with perceptual input and performed with appropriate timing and sequencing, as in playing the piano. Considerable research has been conducted on a variety of issues concerning practice and feedback schedules (Schmidt & Lee, 1999). Here, we concentrate on aspects of acquiring perceptual-motor skill in sequential tasks.

IMPLICIT LEARNING OF SEQUENTIAL EVENTS

Sequence learning is often studied in serial RT tasks because skill is acquired rapidly (see Clegg, DiGirolamo, & Keele, 1998). In a typical experiment, performance is measured for conditions in which spatial-location stimuli (and their assigned responses) occur in a repeating order and in which the events occur in a random order. Performance improves much more with repeating sequences than with a random order, and this benefit is often lost when the repeating pattern is modified. Sequence learning occurs not only when the sequence is deterministic, but also when it is probabilistic. It can occur without any instructions to look for sequential patterns, but there has been considerable debate about whether sequence learning can be implicit.

Willingham, Nissen, and Bullemer (1989) reported evidence for implicit learning. They asked participants who received a repeating sequence to indicate whether they were aware of the sequence and, if so, to report what it was. In addition, participants performed a generation task in which they were "to press the key corresponding to where they thought the next stimulus would appear" (p. 1049). Based on these measures, Willingham et al. divided the participants into groups with full, some, or no knowledge of the sequence. All groups benefited from practice with the repeating sequence, but the group with full knowledge benefited more than the other two groups (see Figure 15.4). However, when anticipatory trials

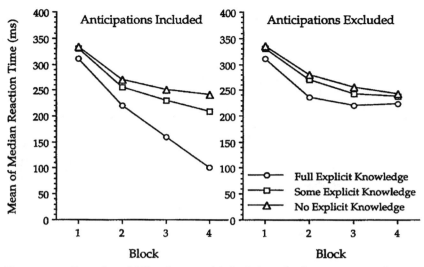

Figure 15.4. Data from Willingham et al.'s (1989) study showing mean of median reaction time as a function of practice block for groups with full, some, or no knowledge of the repeating sequence. From R.W. Proctor and A. Dutta, *Skill acquisition and human performance*, p. 173. Copyright 1995, Sage Publications. Reprinted with permission.

(RT < 100 ms) were removed, performance for the full-knowledge group was not significantly different from that for the some- and no-knowledge groups. This finding implies that sequence learning did not depend on explicit awareness, although awareness led to an anticipation strategy.

Researchers have questioned whether the generation task is an adequate measure of explicit-implicit knowledge, noting that it suffers from several methodological problems (e.g., Perruchet & Amorim, 1992). To circumvent the problems of this and other measures of explicit-implicit learning, Destrebecqz and Cleeremans (2001) adapted the process-dissociation procedure originally devised by Jacoby (1991) to study implicit memory. This procedure uses one generation test in which participants are to attempt to generate what they have been exposed to previously (inclusion instructions) and another in which they are to attempt to avoid doing so (exclusion instructions). After practice on a serial RT task using a repeating 12-element sequence, with a constant response-stimulus interval (RSI) of 0 or 250 ms, participants were asked to generate the sequence of trials. With inclu-

sion instructions, the proportion of the training sequence that was generated was above chance for both RSI groups. With exclusion instructions, the proportion of chunks generated by participants in the 250-ms RSI group was less than that under inclusion instructions and did not differ from chance, indicating that their learning was explicit. In contrast, the proportion generated by participants in the 0-ms RSI group did not differ from that under inclusion instructions. Consequently, Destrebecqz and Cleeremans concluded that learning of the sequence was implicit when there was not sufficient time between trials to prepare for the next event.

However, Wilkinson and Shanks (2004) reported three experiments using only a 0-ms RSI in which they were unable to replicate Destrebecqz and Cleeremans's (2001) findings. In all experiments, participants were able to avoid generating the sequence presented in the practice session under exclusion instructions. Wilkinson and Shanks suggest that a lack of power may have prevented this difference from being significant in Destrebecqz and Cleeremans's study. Regardless of whether sequence learning is truly implicit, it is clear that people are able to extract the sequential structure of events to which they are exposed without necessarily intending to do so.

Another issue in sequence learning concerns whether the representation that is learned is perceptual, motor, or stimulus-response associations. Several studies obtained results suggesting that the learning is not purely motor. Cohen, Ivry, and Keele (1990) trained participants on a serial RT task with repeating sequences for which the responses were keypresses of one of three fingers from a single hand. The sequence learning transfered well to a situation in which a single finger was used to press each of the three keys. Willingham et al. (1989) dissociated stimulus and response sequences by conducting a four-choice task in which one of four keypresses was made to a stimulus in one of four positions, but the relevant stimulus dimension was color. Learning was evident when the responses (and colors) followed a repeating sequence, but this learning did not transfer to a task for which stimulus location was relevant.

Willingham et al. (1989) also found no evidence of learning when stimulus location (which was irrelevant) followed a repeating sequence, suggesting that the sequence learning was not perceptual. Other studies have suggested a perceptual basis to sequence learning (e.g., Howard, Mutter, & Howard, 1992), but Willingham (1999) noted that participants in some of those studies showed substantial explicit knowledge and that artifacts associated with eye movements could have been responsible for the learning in others. He reported three experiments that provide strong evidence against a perceptual basis for sequence learning: Mere observation of a repeating stimulus sequence produced no benefit when participants who showed explicit knowledge were removed; transfer was robust from a training condition in which the stimuli were the digits 1–4 (mapped left-to-right to the responses) to one in which the stimuli were spatial locations; a less compatible spatial mapping in training (press the key to the right of the stimulus location) showed no transfer to a spatially compatible

mapping for which the sequence of stimulus locations was the same.

Given that the learned representation does not seem to be perceptual or specific to particular effectors, what is its nature? Willingham, Wells, Farrell, and Stemwedel (2000) proposed that a sequence of response locations is learned. They tested this proposition by configuring the four stimulus locations in a lopsided diamond arrangement (see Figure 15.5) that allowed them to have a left-to-right order along the horizontal axis. The arrangement was mapped compatibly to one of two keyboards on which participants responded using the index finger of their preferred hand. One keyboard was configured in a diamond shape and the other had the keys linearly arranged in a row. Participants who switched from one keyboard in the training phase to the other in the transfer phase showed no benefit from the repeating sequence. In another experiment, all participants used horizontal stimulus and response arrangements and performed with the hands in normal positions in the transfer phase. Participants who performed with their hands crossed during the training phase, such that the left hand operated the right keys and the right hand the left keys, showed no cost in the transfer phase relative to participants who performed only with the hands uncrossed, as long as the sequence of response locations remained unaltered. In contrast, when the sequence of finger movements was unaltered but the sequence of response locations changed, no transfer was evident.

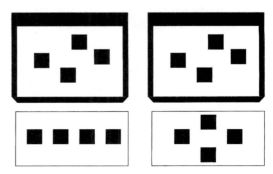

Figure 15.5. Illustration of the stimulus (top) and response (bottom) configurations used in Willingham et al.'s (2000, Experiment 1) study.

Although Willingham et al.'s (2000) results are consistent with an explanation in terms of stimulus-response associations, they rejected such an explanation based on the findings of Willingham (1999) that transfer was excellent when (a) the stimulus set was changed from digits to spatial locations but the response sequence remained the same or (b) the mapping was changed so that different spatial stimuli were mapped to the same response sequence. Consequently, they concluded that the evidence implicates a part of the motor system involving response locations but not specific effectors or muscle groups.

PROCEDURAL REINSTATEMENT

Healy, Bourne, and colleagues presented evidence that recall of perceptual-motor sequences depends on reinstatement at the retention test of the specific procedures used during training. Fendrich, Gesi, Healy, and Bourne (1995) showed participants a sequence of digits, with one group asked simply to read the digits, a second to enter the digits using the numeric keypad of a keyboard, and a third to enter the digits using the row of numbers at the top of the keyboard. A week later, participants were asked to enter old or new digit sequences using the row of numbers or the numeric keypad. After entering each sequence, participants were also asked to identify whether they recognized the sequence as "old." Fendrich et al. found that, for old sequences, recognition memory was better than in the read condition only when the sequence was entered using the same key layout as that used in practice. Thus, actually entering the sequence aided recognition of prior sequences only when they were produced with the same procedure during test as in practice.

Healy, Wohldmann, and Bourne (2005) provided additional evidence that the benefit of procedural reinstatement is specific to conditions in which the practice and transfer conditions are the same. They described results from a study in which participants moved a mouse controlling a cursor to a target location of a clock-face stimulus display. Each participant practiced in only one of four conditions. In the normal condition, left-right and up-down movements of the mouse produced cursor movements in the corresponding directions. In the up-down reversal condition, up-down mouse movements produced cursor movements in the opposite directions, whereas left-right movements produced cursor movements in the corresponding directions. Similarly, in the left-right reversal condition, the mouse-to-cursor relation was reversed for the left-right dimension but normal for the up-down relation. In the combined reversal condition, mouse movements along either dimension produced cursor movements in the opposite directions. Practice produced a benefit in performance when the same condition was performed after a one-week retention interval. However, there was minimal transfer from one condition to the others. The findings of Fendrich et al. (1995) and Healy et al. (2005) indicate that performance benefits when specific perceptual-motor procedures learned during practice are reinstated at test.

Skill at Complex Tasks

Complex tasks often have multiple elements that need to be executed successfully if performance is to be optimal. Issues that arise include whether extensive practice can eliminate limitations in performance of multiple tasks, how components of complex tasks should be trained to maximize subsequent performance of the whole task, and the nature of representations and processes for performing arithmetic and related tasks.

Multiple Tasks

When people are instructed to perform two tasks simultaneously, responses to at least one are typically slower than when each task is performed alone. Dual-task performance has been studied extensively using the psychological refractory period (PRP) effect paradigm (see Pashler & Johnston,

1998, and Lien & Proctor, 2002). In a typical PRP study, participants perform two tasks (T1 and T2), each of which requires a response to a stimulus. The stimulus (S1) for T1 is presented, followed after a variable interval (stimulus onset asynchrony; SOA) by the stimulus (S2) for T2. Instructions are to respond as rapidly as possible for both tasks, sometimes with an emphasis on making the response to T1 (R1) prior to that for T2 (R2). The PRP effect is that RT for T2 (RT2) is longer at short SOAs than at long SOAs, with the function relating RT2 to SOA often having a slope of –1 until a critical SOA, after which it asymptotes.

Most accounts attribute the PRP effect to a response-selection bottleneck (Pashler & Johnston, 1998): Stimulus identification for T1 and T2 can occur in parallel, as can response programming and execution, but response selection can be performed only for one task at a time. Consequently, selection of R2 cannot begin until selection of R1 is completed. According to the response-selection bottleneck model, variables that increase the time to identify S2 should interact underadditively with SOA (i.e., their effects should be smaller at short SOAs than long SOAs). This underadditive interaction is predicted because in the easiest identification conditions there is "slack" at short SOAs, during which the system is waiting to begin response selection for T2 after having identified S2. Consequently, much of the additional time for identification of S2 in the difficult condition can be "absorbed" by the slack without increasing RT2. In contrast, variables that have their influence on selection of R2 should have additive effects with SOA because the time for these processes cannot be absorbed into the slack. Results have generally conformed to these and other predictions of the bottleneck model (Pashler & Johnston, 1998).

Recently, the response-selection bottleneck model has been challenged on two fronts. One challenge is whether response selection is restricted to only one task at a time, as the bottleneck model assumes, or whether response selection is better characterized as a limited-capacity resource that can be divided in different amounts across two tasks, but at reduced efficiency compared to when the entire capacity is devoted to one task alone (e.g., Tombu & Jolicœur, 2003). The second challenge, which is more germane to present concerns, is whether the bottleneck is a structural limitation of the cognitive architecture, as both the bottleneck and resource accounts assume, or whether it reflects a strategy adopted by participants to satisfy the task demands (e.g., Schumacher et al., 2001).

If the PRP effect is due to a structural limitation, the effect should still be evident after extended practice. Several studies have found the PRP effect to persist across extended practice (e.g., Gottsdanker & Stelmach, 1971). However, despite the tendency for the PRP effect to persist, several recent studies have reported conditions under which the effect is small or possibly even absent after practice (e.g., Hazeltine, Teague, & Ivry, 2002; Levy & Pashler, 2001; Schumacher et al., 2001). Van Selst, Ruthruff, and Johnston (1999) noted that most of the studies showing little reduction in the PRP effect with practice used manual responses for both tasks, which creates output interference between the two tasks. Consequently, they conducted an experiment in which there was little overlap between the stimuli and responses for the tasks: T1 used four tone pitches, with the two lowest mapped to the vocal response "low" and the two highest to "high," and T2 used visually presented numbers and letters mapped to keypresses, made with the four fingers of the right hand. Six participants performed the tasks for 36 sessions of 400 trials each. A PRP effect of 353 ms was evident in the first session, and this effect was reduced to 40 ms by practice but eliminated entirely for only one subject. Van Selst et al. concluded that several aspects of their results indicated that a bottleneck was still present after extensive practice, and showed that the substantial decrease in the PRP effect could be attributed entirely to a reduction in RT1.

Ruthruff, Johnston, and Van Selst (2001) and Ruthruff, Johnston, Van Selst, Whitsell, and Remington (2003) presented additional evidence that the reduction of the PRP effect with practice is primarily due to a decrease in the duration of the bottleneck stage for T1. Ruthruff et al. (2001) tested the five participants from Van Selst et al.'s (1999) study for whom the PRP effect had not been eliminated, changing T1 so that it required "same"-"different" responses for pairs of tones instead of pitch judgments. The idea was that introducing a new T1 would slow R1, increasing the magnitude of the PRP effect. Consistent with this prediction, the initial PRP effect was 194 ms, a value considerably larger than the 50-ms effect obtained for those participants in the last session of the previous study. In contrast, when switched to a new T2, pressing one of two response keys to a visual letter X or Y, the PRP effect was only 98 ms.

Ruthruff et al. (2003) conducted further investigations of the participant from Van Selst et al.'s (1999) study for whom the PRP effect had been eliminated. Their hypothesis was that the bottleneck was latent for that participant, that is, the PRP effect was absent because the operations of the bottleneck stage for T1 were completed prior to that stage being needed for T2. To support this hypothesis they showed that a PRP effect was evident for that participant when negative SOAs were introduced for which T2 preceded T1 by up to 216 ms and when a new T1 (judging whether the third tone in a rapid series of three was higher or lower in pitch than the first) was paired with the old T2. On the whole, the experiments of Van Selst et al. (1999) and Ruthruff et al. (2001, 2003) suggest that the bottleneck is not eliminated by practice but only hidden. More recently, though, Ruthruff, Van Selst, Johnston, and Remington (in press) have found evidence that a few participants show evidence of bypassing the bottleneck after extensive practice under specific circumstances.

Part-Whole Transfer

Many complex tasks can be decomposed into distinct subtasks that are integrated when performing the whole task. One ques-tion is whether training should focus on the individual subcomponents first (part-whole training) or on the entire task (whole-task training). The logic behind part-whole train-ing is that a higher level of skill can be attained if participants are able to practice and master the individual components prior to integrating them in the whole task con-text. However, because participants are not exposed to the integrated task, the skills that they acquire while practicing the subcom-ponents may not transfer to it. Briggs and Naylor (1962) noted that the type of train-ing used should depend on the nature of the task complexity and organization. Part-whole training is most beneficial when the complexity of the whole task is high but the organization is low. That is, when the sub-components are not highly integrated, then part-whole training allows the participant to focus on mastering the skill for each subcom-ponent without being distracted by other subcomponents.

Frederiksen and White (1989) provided one notable demonstration of a benefit for part-whole training using the Space Fortress game. In that game, participants operate a spaceship with the goal of destroy-ing a fortress by shooting missiles at it while protecting the spaceship from dan-ger (e.g., avoiding shells fired at the space-ship from the fortress and navigating the ship to avoid mines). Frederiksen and White performed analyses regarding the skills/knowledge needed to perform certain individual components of the game and had one group of participants engage in part-whole training (practice with these individ-ual components alone for three days and with the whole game on the fourth day), and another group engage in whole-task training (practice with the whole game dur-ing the four days). After the practice ses-sion, both groups played the whole game for nine successive games, and mean game scores were obtained for each group (see Figure 15.6). For the first game, participants who received whole-task training scored a little over 500 more points than participants in the part-whole training group. However, beginning with Game 2, the participants in

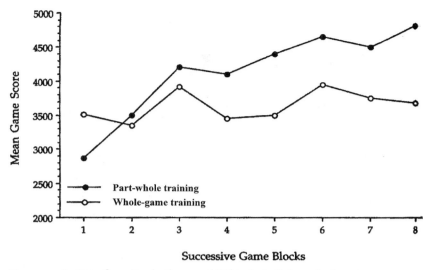

Figure 15.6. Data from Frederiksen and White's (1989) study showing mean game score as a function of part-whole training or whole-game training across successive game blocks. From R. W. Proctor and A. Dutta, *Skill acquisition and human performance*, p. 274. Copyright 1995, Sage Publications, Reprinted with permission.

the part-whole group performed much better than those in the whole-task training group. By Game 8, the part-whole training group scored about 1,300 more points that the whole-task training group.

The benefit of part-whole training suggests that higher-level skills can be attained with training of the easier component tasks first. However, several studies have shown that participants who engage in learning more difficult discriminations first show better transfer than those who engage in learning easier discriminations first to subsequent tasks containing both easy and difficult items (e.g., Doane, Alderton, Sohn, & Pellegrino, 1996). Doane et al. had participants determine whether two polygons were identical or not. The complexity of the polygons was defined by the number of vertices from which they were made, and the difficulty of the task was determined by the degree of similarity of the two polygons in the pair (see Figure 15.7). Doane et al. (1996, Experiment 1) had one group of participants practice first with easy discriminations and another group with difficult discriminations. After practice, the groups received both the easy and difficult discriminations

within a block. When presented with both types of discriminations, participants who first practiced difficult discriminations outperformed those who first practiced easy discriminations. In subsequent experiments, Doane et al. showed that this superior performance for the difficult-first group was due to both stimulus-specific knowledge and strategic knowledge.

Although Doane et al. (1996) found a benefit for practicing the more difficult discriminations first, Clawson, Healy, Ericsson, and Bourne (2001) showed that if the initial subset of stimuli is very difficult to learn, it will not yield superior performance on the full set. Clawson et al. gave participants 12 Morse codes to receive and translate into their corresponding letters. Six of the code-letter pairs were difficult items and six were easy. Clawson et al. evaluated the difference in performance accuracy for all items during acquisition immediately after the part-stimulus training and after a retention interval of four weeks. In contrast to the findings of Doane et al., training with the difficult stimuli first did not result in better performance with the full set of stimuli. Furthermore, after the four-week delay, the group

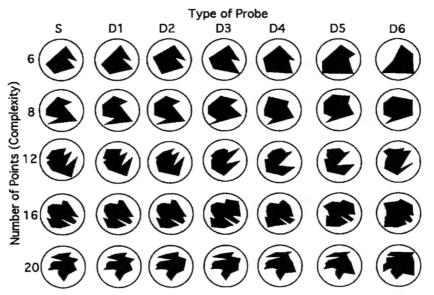

Figure 15.7. Illustrations of polygons used in Doane et al.'s (1996) study. S = referent polygon that was duplicated for same pairs; D = different polygon, with 1–6 representing decreasing similarity to referent polygon. One of the different polygons was presented with the referent polygon for different pairs. From "Acquisition and Transfer of Skilled Performance: Are Visual Discrimination Skills Stimulus Specific?" by S. M. Doane, D. L. Alderton, Y. W. Sohn, & J. W. Pellegrino, 1996, *Journal of Experimental Psychology: Human Perception and Performance*, 22, p. 1224. Copyright 1996, American Psychological Association. Reprinted with permission.

that initially received the difficult stimuli showed a decrease in accuracy, whereas the group that initially received the easy stimuli did not. Clawson et al. attributed this decrement in performance for the difficult-first training group to the fact that the Morse code reception task was extremely difficult, preventing participants from mastering the task during training.

Solving Arithmetic Problems

Basic arithmetic problems consist of an operator (add, subtract, multiply, divide) and operands (the numbers to which the operator is applied). Skilled performance on basic arithmetic tasks is not due primarily to more efficient application of the operator to the operands, but instead to retrieval of specific facts (e.g., $2 + 2 = 4$) from memory (Ashcraft, 1992). Under speed stress, for example, 70% – 90% of the incorrect

answers are table-related errors that would be correct for another problem that shares an operand with the current problem (e.g., Campbell & Graham, 1985). Campbell (1987) showed that such errors can be primed by prior problems. He had participants say the answers to single-digit multiplication problems (e.g., 7×9) as quickly as possible. Incorrect retrieval of a product (e.g., $7 \times 9 = $ "56") was more likely when the answer had been the correct product for a recent problem (7×8), and this priming of incorrect responses was restricted primarily to the table-related errors that would be most frequent without the prior priming event. Retrieval times for correct answers were also longer if strong false associates were activated by way of other problems. Campbell's study not only provided strong evidence of retrieval of answers via associations, it also showed no evidence for a contribution of general algorithmic procedures based on the operator. Specifically, participants were first pretested on all problems, then trained on half of the problems for several sessions, and finally retested on all problems. Only those problems that were practiced showed a benefit on the posttest, with performance being worse for the unpracticed problems on the posttest than it had been on the pretest.

Rickard, Healy, and Bourne (1994) had participants practice multiplication and division problems for 40 trial blocks, each of which included the 36 problems in the practice set. Immediately afterward, a test was given that included those problems as well as others that differed in the order of the operands and the format in which they were presented. Performance on the test was good if the operator and operands were the same as on a practiced problem, even if the order of the operands was changed, and was considerably poorer if any element other than operand order was changed. Rickard et al. interpreted their results as supporting an identical-elements model, according to which distinct knowledge representations exist for each unique combination of the digits that constitute a problem, arithmetic operator, and answer. Because there were only small effects of operand order and of which arithmetic symbol was presented, they concluded that this representation is relatively abstract. Problems with the same elements are presumed to access the same knowledge representation.

Rickard and Bourne (1996) conducted some additional tests of the identical-elements model. Experiment 1 was similar to that of Rickard et al. (1994), only with new problems added at the test phase. Consistent with the identical-elements model, problems with the same operators and operands were faster than those with changes or those that were completely new, with the latter conditions not differing significantly. In Experiment 2, in addition to the Arabic numeral format used in the previous experiments, a written verbal format was used (e.g., four × seven). Transfer tests showed both format-nonspecific and specific components, which

Rickard and Bourne interpreted as indicating that modality-independent representations of the type hypothesized by the identical-elements model and modality-specific perceptual representations were involved. One possibility they suggested is that number-fact retrieval is mediated by an abstract representation in most cases, but practice on a limited number of problems in the same input format may allow a more direct retrieval route to develop.

When unfamiliar pseudoarithmetic rules are learned in the laboratory, participants presumably cannot directly retrieve the answers but must perform algorithmic procedures. Sohn and Carlson (1998) proposed a procedural framework hypothesis according to which goals to apply operators can be instantiated abstractly to provide a framework for processing the operands. The hypothesis thus predicts that performance will be best when the operator is encoded first. To test this hypothesis, Sohn and Carlson had participants apply four Boolean rules (AND, NAND, OR, NOR) in a pseudoarithmetic format [e.g., #(0,1), where # indicates the AND rule and the correct response is 0]. Each participant performed six blocks of 48 trials during the acquisition phase and six blocks of 64 trials in the test phase. Within each block, the operator and operands could appear simultaneously, the operator could appear first, the operands first, or the operator could appear in the interval between the two operands. In both phases, all of the sequential presentation conditions showed faster responses than the simultaneous condition, but the operator-first display produced the largest benefit.

Conclusion

In his chapter, "Laboratory experimentation on the genesis of expertise," Shiffrin (1996) notes, "Laboratory studies of the development of expertise have a history as old as experimental psychology" (p. 338). He points out that although most current views of the development of expertise place an emphasis on practice, the evidence is primarily correlational. Shiffrin goes on to say, "I believe the establishment of the direction of causality will require laboratory experimentation, with appropriate controls" (p. 338). The studies we have described in this chapter provide good examples of the types of unique contributions that laboratory studies of skill acquisition and retention can make and the roles that these studies can play in our understanding of the nature of expertise and its development.

Although participants in laboratory research are not able to devote the ten years needed to achieve domain expertise, they are able to achieve a high level of skilled performance on many tasks over a short period of time. Performance of virtually any task improves with practice, regardless of whether the task has a perceptual, cognitive, or motoric emphasis and whether it is simple or complex, and this skill is often retained for long time periods. Practice functions aggregated across participants typically show continuous reductions in response time that can be characterized by power functions, but individual learning curves often show discontinuities suggestive of strategy shifts. Practice also substantially reduces the amount of attention and effort that must be devoted to task performance. Regardless of whether the benefit of practice is attributed to strengthening, chunking, or efficiency of retrieval, it seems to reflect a shift from attention-demanding controlled processing to a much more automatic mode. This shift is often most pronounced when the conditions of practice maintain a consistent mapping or direct the person's attention to critical features of the task. The resulting skill, in many cases, transfers only to tasks that are very similar to the original task, which is in agreement with the fact that expertise is largely domain-specific. Although development of automaticity does not ensure that expert levels of performance will be attained, automaticity does provide a necessary foundation. As Bryan and Harter (1899) took note of more than a century ago, "Automatism is not genius, but it is the hands and feet of genius" (p. 375).

Performance of a task results in learning that is often incidental, although the extent to which this learning can be truly implicit is still a matter of debate. Incidental learning can be of stimulus-response relations, general response selection rules, the sequential structure of events, the procedures for executing actions, and so on. As for experts within a particular domain, the benefits of this learning are lost when the task situation no longer conforms closely to the skill acquired by practice, and in some cases, performance may even show a cost. Although learning can occur without explicit intent, learning of all types, including even the most elementary forms of perceptual learning, can be influenced by attention.

For tasks that require manual responses, the learning often is not specific to particular effectors but is at the more abstract level of response locations. This point is illustrated by numerous studies that show essentially perfect transfer when the fingers used to operate the response keys are changed. One way to characterize these results is that the acquired skill is specific to particular action goals and not to the physical means by which these goals are achieved.

Task goals and strategies play an even more important role in more complex tasks such as dual-task performance and mental arithmetic. Having the procedures relevant to the task goals activated at the appropriate time facilitates task performance. Although the strategies developed to satisfy task goals may generalize farther than many of the specific procedures that are learned, they also may be relatively specific. For complex tasks, there can be a benefit of practicing the subcomponents, mastering each before performing the whole task. However, if part-task training does not promote learning of discriminations or coordination of task components required for whole-task performance, then part-whole training may not be particularly beneficial. Thus, the development of skill in a domain involves acquisition of higher-level strategies and goal structures in addition to the perceptual, cognitive, and motoric components.

Behavioral and neurophysiological studies of practice and transfer have converged to show that learning occurs not only at central levels of information processing but also at early and late levels. Regarding perceptual learning, Fahle and Poggio (2002) emphasize, "We now know for sure that even the adult primary sensory cortices have a fair amount of plasticity to perform changes of information processing as a result of training. . . . All cortical areas seem to be able to change and adapt their function both on a fast and a slow time scale" (p. xiii). Similarly, Sanes (2003) notes, "The historical and recent record provide incontrovertible evidence that many neocortical regions, including the motor-related areas, exhibit plasticity and are likely to contribute to motor-skill learning" (p. 225). An implication of these findings is that acquiring expertise in a domain is likely to involve fundamental cognitive and neural changes throughout most of the information-processing system.

Acknowledgment

The authors thank Alice F. Healy for helpful comments on an earlier draft of this chapter.

References

Ahissar, M. (1999). Perceptual learning. *Current Directions in Psychological Science, 8*, 124–128.

Anderson, J. R. (1982). Acquisition of cognitive skill. *Psychological Review, 89*, 369–406.

Ashcraft, M. H. (1992). Cognitive arithmetic: A review of data and theory. *Cognition, 44*, 75–106.

Biederman, I., & Shiffrar, M. M. (1987). Sexing day-old chicks: A case study and expert systems analysis of a difficult perceptual-learning task. *Journal of Experimental Psychology: Human Perception and Performance, 13*, 640–645.

Bilodeau, E. A., & Bilodeau, I. M. (Eds.) (1969). *Principles of skill acquisition*. New York: Academic Press.

Bower, G. H., & Hilgard, E. R. (1981). *Theories of learning* (5th ed.). Englewood Cliffs, NJ: Prentice-Hall.

Briggs, G. E., & Naylor, S. C. (1962). The relative efficiency of several training methods as a function of transfer task complexity. *Journal of Experimental Psychology, 64*, 505–512.

Brochet, F., & Dubourdieu, D. (2001). Wine descriptive language supports cognitive specificity of chemical senses. *Brain and Language, 77*, 187–196.

Bryan, W. L., & Harter, N. (1899). Studies on the telegraphic language: The acquisition of a hierarchy of habits. *Psychological Review 6*, 345–375.

Campbell, J. I. D. (1987). Network interference and mental multiplication. *Journal of Experimental Psychology: Learning, Memory, and Cognition, 13*, 109–123.

Campbell, J. I. D., & Graham, D. J. (1985). Mental multiplication skill: Structure, process, and acquisition. *Canadian Journal of Psychology, 39*, 338–366.

Clawson, D. M., Healy, A. F., Ericsson, K. A., & Bourne, L. E., Jr. (2001). Retention and transfer of Morse code reception skill by novices: Part-whole training. *Journal of Experimental Psychology: Applied, 7*, 129–142.

Clegg, B. A., DiGirolamo, G. J., & Keele, S. W. (1998). Sequence learning. *Trends in Cognitive Sciences, 2*, 275–281.

Cohen, A., Ivry, R. I., & Keele, S. W. (1990). Attention and structure in sequence learning. *Journal of Experimental Psychology: Learning, Memory, and Cognition, 16*, 17–30.

Crowder, R. G. (1976). *Principles of learning and memory*. Hillsdale, NJ: Erlbaum.

Delaney, P. F., Reder, L. M., Staszewski, J. J., & Ritter, F. E. (1998). The strategy-specific nature of improvement: The power law applies by strategy within task. *Psychological Science, 9*, 1–7.

Destrebecqz, A., & Cleeremans, A. (2001). Can sequence learning be implicit? New evidence with the process dissociation procedure. *Psychonomic Bulletin & Review, 8*, 343–350.

Doane, S. M., Alderton, D. L., Sohn, Y. W., & Pellegrino, J. W. (1996). Acquisition and transfer of skilled performance: Are visual discrimination skills stimulus specific? *Journal of Experimental Psychology: Human Perception and Performance, 22*, 1218–1248.

Dutta, A., & Proctor, R. W. (1992). Persistence of stimulus-response compatibility effects with extended practice. *Journal of Experimental Psychology: Learning, Memory, and Cognition, 18*, 801–809.

Ericsson, K. A., & Smith, J. (1991). Prospects and limits of the empirical study of expertise: An introduction. In K. A. Ericsson & J. Smith (Eds.), *Toward a general theory of expertise: Prospects and limits* (pp. 1–38). Cambridge, UK: Cambridge University Press.

Fahle, M., & Edelman, S. (1993). Long-term learning in vernier acuity: Effects of stimulus orientation, range and of feedback. *Vision Research, 33*, 397–412.

Fahle, M., & Poggio, T. (Eds.) (2002). *Perceptual learning*. Cambridge, MA: MIT Press.

Fitts, P. M. (1964). Perceptual-motor skill learning. In A. W. Melton (Ed.), *Categories of human learning* (pp. 243–285). New York: Academic Press.

Fitts, P. M., & Seeger, C. M. (1953). S-R compatibility: Spatial characteristics of stimulus and response codes. *Journal of Experimental Psychology, 46*, 199–210.

Fendrich, D. W., Gesi, A. T., Healy, A. F., & Bourne, L. E., Jr. (1995). The contribution of procedural reinstatement to implicit and explicit memory effects in a motor task. In A. F. Healy & L. E. Bourne, Jr. (Eds.), *Learning and memory of knowledge and skills: Durability and specificity* (pp. 66–94). Thousand Oaks, CA: Sage.

Frederiksen, J. R., & White, B. Y. (1989). An approach to training based upon principled task decomposition. *Acta Psychologica, 71*, 89–146.

Gibson, E. J., & Pick, A. D. (2000). *An ecological approach to perceptual learning and development.* Oxford, UK: Oxford University Press.

Gibson, J. J. (1947) (Ed.). *Motion picture research and testing* (Army Air Forces Aviation Psychology Program Research Reports, Report No. 7). Washington, DC: U.S. Government Printing Office.

Goldstone, R. L., Schyns, P. G., & Medin, D. L. (1997). Learning to bridge between perception and cognition. In R. L. Goldstone, D. L. Medin, & P. G. Schyns (Eds.), *Perceptual learning (The psychology of learning and motivation, Vol. 36*, pp. 1–14). San Diego, CA: Academic Press.

Gottsdanker, R., & Stelmach, G. E. (1971). The persistence of psychological refractoriness. *Journal of Motor Behavior, 3*, 301–312.

Haider, H., & Frensch, P. A. (2002). Why aggregated learning follows the power law of practice when individual learning does not: Comment on Rickard (1997, 1999), Delaney et al. (1998), and Palmeri (1999). *Journal of Experimental Psychology: Learning, Memory, and Cognition, 28*, 392–406.

Hazeltine, E., Teague, D., & Ivry, R. B. (2002). Simultaneous dual-task performance reveals parallel response selection. *Journal of Experimental Psychology: Human Perception and Performance, 28*, 527–545.

Healy, A. F., Wohldmann, E. L., & Bourne, L. E., Jr. (2005). The procedural reinstatement principle: Studies on training, retention, and transfer. In A. F. Healy (Ed.), *Experimental cognitive psychology and its applications* (pp. 59–71). Washington, DC: American Psychological Association.

Heathcote, A., Brown, S., & Mewhort, D. J. K. (2000). The power law repealed: The case for an exponential law of practice. *Psychonomic Bulletin & Review, 7*, 185–207.

Howard, J. H., Mutter, S. A., & Howard, D. V. (1992). Serial pattern learning by event observation. *Journal of Experimental Psychology: Learning, Memory, and Cognition, 18*, 1029–1039.

Jacoby, L. L. (1991). A process dissociation framework: Separating automatic from intentional uses of memory. *Journal of Memory & Language, 30*, 513–541.

Karni, A. (1996). The acquisition of perceptual and motor skills: A memory system in the adult human cortex. *Cognitive Brain Research, 5*, 39–48.

Karni, A., & Bertini, G. (1997). Learning perceptual skills: Behavioral probes into adult plasticity. *Current Opinion in Neurobiology, 7*, 530–535.

Kornblum, S., & Lee, J.-W. (1995). Stimulus-response compatibility with relevant and irrelevant stimulus dimensions that do and do not overlap with the response. *Journal of Experimental Psychology: Human Perception and Performance, 21*, 855–875.

Leahey, T. H. (2003). Cognition and learning. In D. K. Freedheim (Ed.), *History of psychology* (pp. 109–133). Volume 1 in I. B. Weiner

(Editor-in-Chief) *Handbook of psychology*. New York: Wiley.

Levy, J., & Pashler, H. (2001). Is dual-task slowing instruction dependent? *Journal of Experimental Psychology: Human Perception and Performance, 27*, 862–869.

Lien, M.-C., & Proctor, R. W. (2002). Stimulus-response compatibility and psychological refractory period effects: Implications for response selection. *Psychonomic Bulletin & Review, 9*, 212–238.

Logan, G. D. (1988). Toward an instance theory of automatization. *Psychological Review, 95*, 492–527.

Newell, A., & Rosenbloom, P. S. (1981). Mechanisms of skill acquisition and the law of practice. In J. R. Anderson (Ed.), *Cognitive skills and their acquisitions* (pp. 1–55). Hillsdale, NJ: Erlbaum.

Pashler, H., & Baylis, G. C. (1991). Procedural learning: Locus of practice effects in speeded choice tasks. *Journal of Experimental Psychology: Learning, Memory, and Cognition, 17*, 20–32.

Pashler, H., & Johnston, J. C. (1998). Attentional limitations in dual-task performance. In H. Pashler (Ed.), *Attention* (pp. 155–189). Hove, UK: Psychology Press.

Perruchet, P., & Amorim, M.-A. (1992). Conscious knowledge and changes in performance in sequence learning: Evidence against dissociation. *Journal of Experimental Psychology: Learning, Memory, and Cognition, 18*, 785–800.

Prinz, W., Aschersleben, G., Hommel, B., & Vogt, S. (1995). Handlungen als Ereignisse [Actions as events]. In D. Dörner & E. van der Meer (Eds.), *Gedächtnis: Trends, probleme, perspektiven* (pp. 129–168). Göttingen, Germany: Hogrefe.

Proctor, R. W., & Dutta, A. (1993). Do the same stimulus-response relations influence choice reactions initially and after practice? *Journal of Experimental Psychology: Learning, Memory, and Cognition, 19*, 922–930.

Proctor, R. W., & Lu, C.-H. (1999). Processing irrelevant location information: Practice and transfer effects in choice-reaction tasks. *Memory & Cognition, 27*, 63–77.

Proctor, R. W., & Wang, H. (1997). Differentiating types of set-level compatibility. In B. Hommel & W. Prinz (Eds.), *Theoretical issues in stimulus-response compatibility* (pp. 11–37). Amsterdam: North-Holland.

Rickard, T. C. (2004). Strategy execution and cognitive skill learning: An item-level test of candidate models. *Journal of Experimental Psychology: Learning, Memory, and Cognition, 30*, 65–82.

Rickard, T. C., Healy, A. F., & Bourne, L. E., Jr. (1994). On the cognitive structure of basic arithmetic skills: Operation, order, and symbol transfer effects. *Journal of Experimental Psychology: Learning, Memory, and Cognition, 20*, 1139–1153.

Rickard, T. C., & Bourne, L. E., Jr. (1996). Some tests of an identical elements model of basic arithmetic skills. *Journal of Experimental Psychology: Learning, Memory, and Cognition, 22*, 1281–1295.

Ruthruff, E., Johnston, J. C., & Van Selst, M. (2001). Why practice reduces dual-task interference. *Journal of Experimental Psychology: Human Perception and Performance, 27*, 3–21.

Ruthruff, E., Johnston, J. C., Van Selst, M., Whitsell, S., & Remington, R. (2003). Vanishing dual-task interference after practice: Has the bottleneck been eliminated or is it merely latent? *Journal of Experimental Psychology: Human Perception and Performance, 29*, 280–289.

Ruthruff, E., Van Selst, M., Johnston, J. C., & Remington, R. (in press). How does practice reduce dual-task interference: Integration, automation, or just stage-shortening? *Psychological Research*.

Sanders, A. F. (1998). *Elements of human performance*. Mahwah, NJ: Erlbaum.

Sanes, J. N. (2003). Neocortical mechanisms in motor learning. *Current Opinion in Neurobiology, 13*, 225–231.

Schmidt, R. A., & Lee, T. D. (1999). *Motor control and learning: A behavioral emphasis*. Champaign, IL: Human Kinetics.

Schneider, W., & Chein, J. M. (2003). Controlled & automatic processing: Behavior, theory, and biological mechanisms. *Cognitive Science, 27*, 525–559.

Schneider, W., & Shiffrin, R. M. (1977). Controlled and automatic human information processing: I. Detection, search, and attention. *Psychological Review, 84*, 1–66.

Schumacher, E. H., Seymour, T. L., Glass, J. M., Fencsik, D. E., Lauber, E. J., Kieras, D. E., & Meyer, D. E. (2001). Virtually perfect time sharing in dual-task performance: Uncorking the central cognitive bottleneck. *Psychological Science, 12*, 101–108.

Shiffrin, R. M. (1996). Laboratory experimentation on the genesis of expertise. In K. A. Ericsson (Ed.), *The road to excellence: The acquisition of expert performance in the arts and sciences, sports, and games* (pp. 337–345). Mawah, NJ: Erlbaum.

Shiffrin, R. M., & Lightfoot, N. (1997). Perceptual learning of alphanumeric-like characters. In R. L. Goldstone, D. L. Medin, & P. G. Schyns (Eds.), *Perceptual learning (The psychology of learning and motivation, Vol. 36*, pp. 45–81). San Diego, CA: Academic Press.

Shiffrin, R. M., & Schneider, W. (1977). Controlled and automatic human information processing: II. Perceptual learning, automatic attending, and a general theory. *Psychological Review, 84*, 127–190.

Simon, J. R. (1990). The effects of an irrelevant directional cue on human information processing. In R. W. Proctor & T. G. Reeve (Eds.), *Stimulus-response compatibility: An integrated perspective* (pp. 31–86). Amsterdam: North-Holland.

Simon, J. R., Craft, J. L., & Webster, J. B. (1973). Reaction toward the stimulus source: Analysis of correct responses and errors over a five-day period. *Journal of Experimental Psychology, 101*, 175–178.

Snoddy, G. S. (1926). Learning and stability: A psychophysiological analysis of a case of motor learning with clinical applications. *Journal of Applied Psychology, 10*, 1–36.

Sohn, M.-H., & Carlson, R. A. (1998). Procedural frameworks for simple arithmetic tasks. *Journal of Experimental Psychology: Learning, Memory, and Cognition, 24*, 1052–1067.

Sowden, P. T., Davies, I. R. L., & Roling, P. (2000). Perceptual learning of the detection of features in X-ray images: A functional role for improvements in adults, visual sensitivity? *Journal of Experimental Psychology: Human Perception and Performance, 26*, 379–390.

Speelman, C. P., & Kirsner, K. (2001). Predicting transfer from training performance. *Acta Psychologica, 108*, 247–281.

Tagliabue, M., Zorzi, M., Umiltà, C., & Bassignani, F. (2000). The role of LTM links and STM links in the Simon effect. *Journal of Experimental Psychology: Human Perception and Performance, 26*, 648–670.

Tagliabue, M., Zorzi, M., & Umiltà, C. (2002). Cross-modal re-mapping influences the Simon effect. *Memory & Cognition, 30*, 18–23.

Tombu, M., & Jolicœur, P. (2003). A central capacity sharing model of dual-task performance. *Journal of Experimental Psychology: Human Perception and Performance, 29*, 3–18.

Van Selst, M. A., Ruthruff, E., & Johnston, J. C. (1999). Can practice eliminate the psychological refractory period effect? *Journal of Experimental Psychology: Human Perception and Performance, 25*, 1268–1283.

Vu, K.-P. L. (2006). *Influences on the Simon effect of prior practice with spatially incompatible mappings: Transfer within and between horizontal and vertical dimensions*. Manuscript submitted for publication.

Vu, K.-P. L., Proctor, R. W., & Urcuioli, P. (2003). Effects of practice with an incompatible location-relevant mapping on the Simon effect in a transfer task. *Memory & Cognition, 31*, 1146–1152.

Wilkinson, L. & Shanks, D. R. (2004). Intentional control and implicit sequence learning. *Journal of Experimental Psychology: Learning, Memory, & Cognition, 30*, 354–369.

Willingham, D. B. (1999). Implicit motor sequence learning is not purely perceptual. *Memory & Cognition, 27*, 561–572.

Willingham, D. B., Nissen, M. J., & Bullemer, P. (1989). On the development of procedural knowledge. *Journal of Experimental Psychology: Learning, Memory, & Cognition, 15*, 1047–1060.

Willingham, D. B., Wells, L. A., Farrell, J. M., & Stemwedel, M. E. (2000). Implicit motor sequence learning is represented in response locations. *Memory & Cognition, 28*, 366–375.

Zorzi, M., & Umiltà, C. (1995). A computational model of the Simon effect. *Psychological Research, 58*, 193–205.

CHAPTER 16

Retrospective Interviews in the Study of Expertise and Expert Performance

Lauren A. Sosniak

"If we want to know how people become extraordinary adults, we can start with some of the latter . . . and then try to find out how they came to do it" (Gruber, 1982, p. 15). That is the premise for retrospective interviews in the study of expertise and expert performance.

As this *Handbook* makes quite clear, there is a large body of work that coalesces around what Gruber (1986), again, calls "an interest in . . . human beings . . . at their best" (p. 248). Only a very small portion of that work uses the method of retrospective interview. But findings from retrospective interview studies have been important in their own right and of significant use to others studying expert performance in other ways. My task in this chapter is to speak about studies using retrospective interviews, to highlight what we have learned from them, to note their strengths and limitations, and to consider where we might head next both in this tradition and as a result of work from this tradition.

In some respects I am well qualified to tackle this task. I served as research coordinator for the Development of Talent Project

(Bloom, 1985), work directed by Benjamin Bloom at the University of Chicago in the 1980s and carried out by a large research team. This series of studies has received widespread attention and to some degree has become emblematic of retrospective studies of expert performance.

Ironically, when we conducted the Development of Talent Project we did not think of ourselves as studying expertise. That was not the language we spoke. Apparently, it was not yet the language of the day. According to Glaser and Chi (1988), "The topic of expertise first appears in major textbooks in cognitive psychology in 1985, in John Anderson's second edition of *Cognitive Psychology and Its Implications*" (p. xvii). Of course that was the very same year we published the major account of the Development of Talent Project.

In 1985, when expertise was becoming known by that label and was becoming an important area of study in psychology, we, working from a department of education, wrote instead about the development of talent, about exceptional accomplishment, about reaching the limits of learning. Others, previously and since, have used the language of giftedness, human extraordinariness, genius, prodigious performance, and so on.

The particular language we use has consequences for what we investigate, how we investigate, and what we report as findings. But, as a set, the various words do represent an interest in human performance at its very best. And the words frequently are used interchangeably, irrespective of the theoretical orientation of the author. Consider, for example, the opening sentences in Michael Posner's (1988) chapter on "What is it to be an *expert*?": "How do we identify a person as *exceptional* or *gifted*? One aspect is truly *expert performance* in some domain" (p. xxix, all italics added). The various words used by different authors have more that unites them than divides them, and so this chapter includes them collectively.

In this chapter I also walk a fine line regarding method. Retrospective interview studies are, inherently, biographical studies. They mine life experiences. Yet they do not rely on standard biographical material. They rely on interviews, on allowing an individual to tell his or her life story shaped within the theoretical framework of the interviewer. Yet unlike most interviews done in the service of investigating expertise, these focus on more distant and less proximal events and experiences. In this chapter I ignore both biographical studies and the studies using retrospective verbal reports of near-term activities. These forms of research are tackled most ably elsewhere in this *Handbook* (e.g., Simonton, Chapter 18; Deakin, Côté & Harvey, Chapter 17).

My plan for the rest of this chapter is as follows: first, I will outline several of the retrospective interview studies that have informed research on expertise, beginning with the one I know best. Given, then, a body of information about expertise derived from retrospective interviews, I will discuss the strengths and weaknesses of the methodology and call attention to mechanisms researchers have used to strengthen their studies. I will move then to highlight the convergence of certain findings across studies of expertise and to a discussion of potentially fruitful directions for future work.

The Development of Talent Project

The Development of Talent Project (Bloom, 1985) was a study of groups of individuals who, though relatively young (under the age of 35), had realized exceptional levels of accomplishment in one of six fields: concert piano, sculpture, swimming, tennis, mathematics, and research neurology (two artistic fields, two psychomotor activities, and two academic/intellectual fields). The project explored the lives of 120 talented individuals in all, approximately 20 in each field. The plan was to search for regularities and recurrent patterns in the educational histories of groups of clearly accomplished individuals, hoping that such consistencies might shed light on how the development of high levels of talent is achieved.

We conducted retrospective, semi-structured, face-to-face interviews with the individuals who met criteria of exceptional achievement set by experts in their respective fields. We interviewed parents as well, by telephone, for corroborative and supplementary information. Data analysis was a process analogous to superimposing the unique histories one on the other, and identifying the patterns that were common across most cases. We did this first within each field and later across the fields.

One of the important findings from this study has to do with what we did *not* find. At the start of the project Bloom expected that the individuals we studied "would be initially identified as possessing special gifts or qualities and then provided with special instruction and encouragement" (Bloom, 1982, p. 520). But data from the study made it clear that this initial assumption of early discovery followed by instruction and support was wrong. The individuals in the sample for the Development of Talent Project typically did not show unusual promise at the start. And, typically, there was no early intention of working toward a standard of excellence in a particular field. Instead of early discovery followed by development, we found that the individuals were encouraged and supported in considerable learning before they were identified as special and then accorded even more encouragement and support. More time and interest invested in the talent field resulted in further identification of special qualities that in turn were again rewarded with more encouragement and support. Aptitudes, attitudes, and expectations grew in concert with one another, and were mutually confirming (Bloom, 1985; Sosniak, 1987).

As Bloom once told a reporter: "We were looking for exceptional kids and what we found were exceptional conditions" (Carlson, 1985, p. 49). The "exceptional conditions" we found can be summarized under the headings of opportunity to learn, authentic tasks, and exceptionally supportive social contexts (Sosniak, 2003).

Some of our findings about time (opportunity to learn) are well known. We confirmed what many researchers had suspected and some already had demonstrated: developing exceptional abilities takes a lot of time. We found, for example, that internationally recognized concert pianists worked for an average of 17 years from their first formal lessons to their first international recognition; the "quickest" in the group went from novice to tyro in a dozen years. For Olympic swimmers, 15 years elapsed, on average, between the time they began swimming just for fun and the time they earned a place on an Olympic team.

Although the sheer number of years the individuals spent acquiring knowledge and skill was impressive, the way time was distributed also was striking. We took note, for example, of the small amount of time the individuals spent in formal instruction – perhaps once a week, for many of their years of learning. And we were frequently jolted by the multiple and overlapping arenas for time spent learning: children and youth not only received instruction in a talent area, they also played at the talent quite informally, they read about and watched or listened to others working at the talent area, and they demonstrated their involvement with the talent area to others both publicly and privately. For the individuals who formed

the sample for the Development of Talent Project, the development of talent was a process of learning that grew from and threaded around their everyday lives. It was both formal and informal, structured and casual, self-conscious and matter-of-fact, special and ordinary, all at the same time. Time spent learning had a vertical dimension as well as a horizontal one, and an affective dimension as well as a cognitive one.

We also came to appreciate that the long-term process of developing talent was not simply a matter of becoming quantitatively more knowledgeable and skilled over time, or of working more intensely for longer hours. It was, predominantly, a matter of qualitative and evolutionary transformations. The individuals were transformed, the substance of what was being learned was transformed, and the manner in which individuals engaged with teachers and field-specific content was transformed. Students progressively adopted different views of who they were, of what their fields of expertise were about, and of how the field fitted into their lives (Sosniak, 1987). These transformations generally followed a pattern reminiscent of Whitehead's (1929) rhythms of learning – phases of romance, precision, and generalization.

The tasks the individuals were engaged with over time also seem to be particularly notable. Although tasks obviously changed over time, consistent with the amount of experience the individuals had with their field, they were stable in some key ways. Typically they were tasks that represented the field itself in its contemporary social construction. They were genuine, they were real in an everyday commonsense way. Children and youth did things they knew other people of various ages from various settings also were doing and had been doing for years.

Children and youth used materials that are part of our social technologies – they played pianos that adults used also, swam in Olympic-sized pools, read field-specific books and magazines that were created for the consuming public. Both the tasks the youth engaged in, and the materials they used to pursue their tasks, were connected to tasks valued by significant portions of society. And youth knew these tasks and materials were valued because they saw them being displayed – by others in their family, in their community, and in ever larger arenas.

Finally, and as a logical extension, we found that the development of talent appears to require enormously supportive social contexts. One of the lessons we learned from the project is that no one develops talent on his or her own, without the support, encouragement, advice, insight, guidance, and goodwill of many others. The many years of work on the way to international recognition involved increasing exposure to and participation in communities of practice for their respective talent fields.

Communities of practice are groups of people who share a substantive focus that is important to their lives, and who share a willingness to invest time and effort around work in that substantive area. Communities of practice offered *models* for development, and they offered *resources* for support, inspiration, and sustenance. Communities of practice created *standards* for work – for work by the novice, the knowledgeable layman, and for the expert. For participants in the Development of Talent Project, communities of practice modeled and inspired excellence, they defined and gave meaning to significant educative tasks, and they supported and sustained work over the long periods necessary for the development of talent. The youth and young adults in the Development of Talent Project were fortunate to be welcomed into, or to find their way into, communities that shaped and inspired their work. They had many varied opportunities to see themselves as a member of field-specific communities, to come to know the commitments, and to watch and live out for themselves the process of a community renewing itself.

Other Retrospective Interview Studies of Expertise and Expert performance

Another of the well-known series of studies in this genre was conducted three decades before the Development of Talent Project, by Anne Roe (1952), who used retrospective interviews (in part) to study the making of scientific talent. The central question that guided her work – *The making of a scientist* – asked "what kinds of people do what kinds of scientific research and why, and how, and when" (p. 1). Woven among the more specific questions she worked with were: "Are scientists different from other people? Is one kind of scientist characteristically different from another?" (p. 13).

Roe studied "sixty-four of the country's leading scientists," divided approximately equally among biologists, physicists, and social scientists. Her focus was on a sample representing "the *best* men in each field" (p. 20). (Yes, Roe studied men only. Apparently there was only one woman who, but for her gender, would have qualified to be part of the sample in biology.) Roe interviewed the scientists and administered several psychological tests – the Rorschach, the Thematic Apperception Test, and a set of timed intelligence tests – verbal, spatial, and mathematical.

Roe concluded her major report of her study with findings that emphasized personal and psychological characteristics. Her leading scientists largely came from families with professional fathers. They came from homes with select religious backgrounds (none were from Catholic homes). "What seems to be important in the home background is the knowledge of learning, and the value placed on it *for its own sake*, in terms of the enrichment of life, and not just for economic and social rewards" (p. 231). Roe noted that "[m]ore than is usual, these men were placed on their own resources" (p. 231), as a result of losing a parent early in life, suffering serious physical problems, being eldest sons.

Roe also found that "[m]ost of them were inveterate readers, and most of them enjoyed school and studying" (p. 231). They were, principally, products of public, not private, schools. Their early interests typically were consistent with the fields they would later take on vocationally, with physical scientists involved in "gadgeteering," for example, and the biologists interested in natural history. Their "[l]evel of intellectual functioning" (p. 233) was very high, with different patterns for the different scientific fields.

Roe also addressed the scientists' "general personality structure" at some length. She highlighted their curiosity, their "general need for independence, for autonomy, for personal mastery of the environment" (p. 235).

Harriet Zuckerman's (1977/1996) work – as reported, for example, in *Scientific elite: Nobel laureates in the United States* – represents a third important example of retrospective interviews in the study of expertise. In this instance, the central focus was on the sociology of science – "the stratification system in science, its shape, maintenance and consequences" (p. xxxii) – rather than a focus on the individuals for the purpose of learning more about their personalities or their educational experiences.

Zuckerman began her investigations by interviewing "forty-one of the fifty-six laureates then at work in the United States" (p. 4). Subsequently, she collected considerable additional information, including some additional interviews, for a larger sample of ninety-two, including "all American Nobel laureates from the first, Albert A. Michelson, who won the award in physics in 1907, to those who had won prizes by 1972" (p. 4). Zuckerman's research focus expanded over time, and ultimately centered on questions of "how [American laureates] are educated, recruited, sustained, and what contributions they have made to the advancement of science" (p. 5).

Zuckerman's work is finely detailed and engagingly written. Her primary focus on the world of elite science rather than on the development of the scientists themselves means that some significant parts of the book might not seem at first glance to inform studies of expertise. But those whose work emphasizes expertise as a co-construction between individuals and domains (cf., Csikszentmihalyi & Robinson, 1986; Feldman, 1986) will find much in the way of detail that both coalesces with other work and that can inform hypotheses for future

work. Even for those who focus more on the individual and less on the context there is much here that supplements and complements work done by Roe, Bloom, and others.

Zuckerman, like Roe before her, found that her elite scientists largely were products of middle-class families with professional fathers. The laureates' religious origins also dovetailed with Roe's scientists, with just 1 percent of the laureates from a Catholic background and with Jewish backgrounds somewhat overrepresented. Zuckerman reveals little about the laureates earliest years, but makes significant contribution to "the making of..." scientific expertise beginning with the information she reports about college enrollment and continuing through her discussion of the graduate school experience.

Zuckerman's account of masters and apprentices (chapter 4) is particularly important reading for a better understanding of a significant stage in the development of expertise. In this chapter Zuckerman provides important details about finding places to study, working with expert teachers, and becoming socialized into the world and the ways of the scientific elite.

There have been other retrospective interviews of expertise and expert performance that might be included in this chapter if we maintain a very broad approach to the language of expertise. For example, in an interesting twist on retrospective studies of expertise and expert performance, Subotnik et al. (1993) studied the adult lives of "grown-up high-IQ children from Hunter College Elementary School" (p. vii). Hunter was a "school for the intellectually gifted" (p. 20) in New York City, serving students from nursery school to grade six who entered with an IQ score of 130 or above (mean IQ 157). The Subotnik volume speaks to scholars interested in gifted education as it was conceived and practiced in the middle of the 20th century. However, for the purpose of better understanding expertise, the chief contribution this retrospective study makes is to remind us how difficult it is to identify youth who will realize exceptional adult accomplishment, and how poor

IQ is as a potential early indicator. As Subotnik and her colleagues report: "Although most of our study participants are successful and fairly content with their lives and accomplishments, there are no superstars, no Pulitzer Prize or MacArthur Award winners, and only one or two familiar names" (p. 11).

As I hope is obvious by now, studying "the making of..." one group or another of experts can take significantly different directions, even within the common methodological context of retrospective interviews. Certainly method shapes a study to a significant degree; however, the research question(s) guiding the work are much more influential, as should be the case.

Researchers, and the questions they ask, are products of their time and their own scholarly histories. Roe, a psychologist studying personality, asked the questions and made use of the instruments that were part of the zeitgeist when she was doing her work. Zuckerman, a sociologist, made significant contributions to work being conducted also by her mentors and colleagues in their common academic arena. Bloom reflected the interests of educators, especially with his concern for studying what he called "alterable variables" – variables that can be influenced through changes in teaching, parenting, schooling, and so on.

Still, despite the differences in the research question(s) guiding each study, there are commonalities in the data collected and in the findings reported that have important consequences for the study of expertise. I will turn to these commonalities shortly. But first it seems important to take note of the method of investigation itself, and the strengths and limitations of retrospective interviews.

Retrospective Interviews as a Necessary Although Imperfect Method for Studying Long-Term Development of Expertise

Retrospective interview studies represent an imperfect but necessary method of investigation for this field. These studies allow us to investigate questions about expertise that can not be explored with other methods, and they reveal aspects of expertise that we would be unlikely to uncovered in any other way. Retrospective interviews support a long-term perspective on the development of expertise, call attention to researchable opportunities for other investigations, and sometimes challenge the directions headed by researchers with a more time-constrained or data-limited focus.

Although all interview studies suffer from what participants are able and/or willing to report about their lives, well-prepared interviewers can prompt, provoke, notice things that seem inconsistent and probe further into those matters, use humor and surprise, and otherwise retrieve far more information about a person's life than even the interviewee might have believed he or she could report at the start. And retrospective interview studies allow an examination of experience through the learner's eyes, which may at times be quite different from what an outside observer thinks he or she is seeing.

Studies concerned with the development of exceptional talent over time have little choice but to make use of retrospective interviews. We have a body of knowledge, beginning with Simon and Chase (1973), clearly indicating that the development of expertise is a long-term process (see also Ericsson, Krampe, & Tesch-Römer, 1993). We also have a body of knowledge, beginning with the work of Terman (see, for example, Terman & Oden, 1959), clearly indicating that we do not yet know enough to be able to identify children or young adults whom we might logically follow for a decade or more to better understand development toward adult exceptional performance. As Wagner and Stanovich (1996) argue: "One cannot really do a prospective, developmental study of 50 million individuals to obtain an ultimate sample of 50 individuals whose level of performance is 1 in a million" (p. 190).

Even studies of prodigies (Feldman, 1986; Goldsmith, 2000), which begin with early demonstrated excellence in clear areas of expertise, have supported the general proposition that we do not yet have the appropriate markers to know whom to follow longitudinally. As Goldsmith (2000) writes:

> By and large, the children I have studied have not gained national attention for their work, although they are still young enough that they may yet do so in the future. Some have long since given up their original areas of achievement, so if they are to develop national visibility, it will be in some other domain of accomplishment. (p. 115)

The question, then, is not whether we need to use the method of retrospective interview in the study of expertise, but, rather, how best to use the method. The Roe, Zuckerman, and Bloom studies offer insights into mechanisms for enhancing reliability and validity in retrospective interview studies.

Defining a Sample

The Roe, Zuckerman, and Bloom studies all chose samples of (a) recognized experts (b) in numbers sufficient to allow for a study of groups rather than individuals. The quality of the people interviewed – the transparency of their expertise – mattered a great deal to all of the researchers. As Roe (1952) put it, in a sentiment shared across these studies, "if there were particular factors in the lives or personalities of men which were related to their choice of vocation, these factors should appear and possibly would appear most clearly in the men who had been most successful at the vocation" (pp. 20–21). For Zuckerman (1977/1996), "It seemed sensible to assume that Nobel prize-winners constituted a small sample of the most accomplished American scientists making up the scientific elite" (p. 3).

Extreme instances of accomplishment were thought to provide the clearest and most compelling findings. And relying on data from a set of expert performers, rather than focusing on individuals, also was considered important to the design. The assumption underlying the preference for studies of groups rather than the individual-case-study approach is that by studying a group

rather than an individual, researchers can harvest what is essential for the development of expertise and leave behind that which is idiosyncratic.

The process for identifying the specific people who would become part of the studied group by virtue of their exceptional accomplishment also was quite similar across the studies: it relied on other experts, specific to the fields of study. People with broad and deep knowledge of each field made decisions about what was most important in and to each field. For the Zuckerman study, for example, people Zuckerman did not know, who had served on Nobel Prize selection committees, defined for her the talented individuals she would study (every American who had been honored with the Nobel award in one of the sciences was included in the sample). For the Bloom project, older experts who were known for knowing about their fields defined the *criterion measures* for exceptional performance that would capture a sample of the younger talented individuals in the study; everyone who met the criteria set (winning certain competitions or awards, and so on) was invited to participate.

Some researchers argue against relying on social judgments and/or relying on a relativistic approach of looking for the "best" among a group to characterize expertise. According to Salthouse (1991), "[c]onsensual judgments of expertise should . . . be avoided, because they can be influenced by a variety of characteristics other than true competence, such as popularity or reputation" (p. 287). Sloboda (1991) argues that "we have to find a characterization of expertise that will allow any number of people (up to and including all) to be expert in a particular area" (p. 154). Generally, however, examining extreme cases as defined normatively by people who should be qualified to make such distinctions is widely accepted as a reasonable strategy, at least for certain domains of expertise where other measures of competence might not be available. Both Bloom and Zuckerman acknowledged that their samples may have excluded others who were similarly exceptional except for meeting a very particular criteria (e.g., a Nobel Prize, one of a defined set of piano competitions). But both Bloom and Zuckerman argued that although some talented people might have been excluded, there could be no doubt that those who were included were exceptional.

All three of the sets of studies tweaked the definition of sample in small ways. Both the Roe and Bloom studies set age ceilings for the individuals they would invite to participate. In the Bloom studies the age ceiling was set much lower (approximately age 35) than in the Roe study (61 years). Because the Bloom studies were focused on the educational experiences of the sample, rather than personality and intelligence characteristics of the sample, the age of the people interviewed had special importance. The aim was to identify a sample that had reached the age of demonstration of talent, rather than merely indication of potential, but at the same time the individuals should not be so far along in a "career" sense that they would be unlikely to remember their early experiences or might shade those recollections significantly in relation to subsequent events. The Bloom studies also included interviews with parents of the talented individuals in a further effort to capture early experiences and to help triangulate the information provided by the talented individuals themselves; the relatively young age of the talented individuals increased the likelihood that parents might be able and willing to contribute to the research.

Finally, all three of the sets of studies focused on American experts. Although this might seem a concession to the costs and other difficulties associated with scanning the world for the clearest instances of expertise, the Bloom study articulated a different rationale: the focus on Americans only would reduce the variation that might be associated with differences in the home and educational cultures in different parts of the world. I will have more to say about the "American" nature of these studies later in this chapter.

The Issue of Control / Comparison Groups

Retrospective interviews of such elite groups as these pose the ultimate challenge to the issue of control or comparison groups. Against whom should the small number of people reaching the highest rungs of a domain ladder be compared? Do we compare elite concert pianists, for example, with people who never took music lessons at all? With people who studied music briefly, but abandoned their studies before they left childhood? With a random sample of Americans stratified by age, geography, socioeconomic status? With people who "almost" made the elite and thus might be expected to have the closest relation in experiences to the elite group?

What difference does it make if we have no comparison group at all? A great deal, *perhaps*. Absent a control or comparison group, it is impossible to ascertain which of the findings, or to what extent any of the findings, tells anything about the development of exceptional talent. Absent a control or comparison group it is possible that anything and everything reported as findings about the development of talent could be so for many people who have never demonstrated exceptional talent of any sort. Yet a random sample control group makes no sense for a purposefully chosen elite study group, and the possibility of a matched sample on certain key criteria gets weighed down with the question of what to match for a long-term experience.

Roe, Zuckerman, and Bloom took overlapping approaches to the challenge of control or comparison groups. Roe created a "subsidiary study" to "check on how closely eminent men resembled other men in the same fields" (p. 214); for this study she administered a group Rorschach to more than 382 scientists at fourteen universities. Roe also made use of the naturally occurring divisions in science to study separately biologists (who were involved with basic research into normal life processes), physical scientists (both theoretical and experimental), and social scientists (psychologists and anthropologists), and then compared her experts in one domain with experts in another domain. Zuckerman did not create a formal "subsidiary study" but did take into account in her discussions a group of scientists who are said to hold "the forty-first chair. . . . 'uncrowned' laureates who are the peers of prize-winners in every sense except that of having the award" (p. 42).

The Bloom studies took advantage of the approach of comparing experts in one domain with experts in another domain and added an additional methodological element. Bloom created a spectrum of talents: psychomotor activities, artistic fields, academic/intellectual fields, and fields emphasizing interpersonal relations. Each portion of the spectrum was to be represented by two separate investigations, with fields that clearly belonged together in the spectrum but diverged in identifiably significant ways. Olympic swimmers and tennis players represented psychomotor activities, concert pianists and sculptors represented the arts, and mathematicians and research neurologists represented the academic/intellectual talents. (The last portion of the spectrum – interpersonal relations – ultimately was abandoned; we found ourselves unable at the time to specify appropriate talent fields and criteria for recognizing individual achievement.) Thus the Bloom studies involved six groups of talented individuals: each group would have its own story, pairs of fields should be related by many common considerations, and all six groups might share at least some significant elements of the development of talent (or so it was hoped).

Freeman (2000) points out that the Bloom studies (and this could be said as well for the Roe and Zuckerman studies) failed to make comparisons with siblings even as we concluded that family influences were significant. Freeman is correct. Although in the Bloom studies we did make mention of siblings from time to time, in relation to the talented individuals' own comparisons with their siblings or parents' comparisons for their own children, we did not set out to study siblings, and our comparisons

relied on what we were told in the course of our interviews without any predetermined intentional probing.

Freeman's larger point is the possibility for comparison groups created by some of the key findings in the studies. In this regard, as will become clearer shortly, another likely comparison group would be all of the individuals who studied with the same final "master" teacher (or in the same graduate school program) identified as so important across many studies.

The bigger error I think we may have made in the Bloom study (and this could be said as well for the Roe and Zuckerman studies also) was that we purposefully chose to study only Americans. Although this made conceptual and procedural sense, it did deny us the chance of using as a comparison group *people who had realized exceptional levels of talent under different conditions* (e.g., other countries' best pianists, best swimmers, best mathematicians, and so on).

Other Issues of Validity

We need to recognize that whether we use retrospective interviews or any other method to study a long-term process like the development of expertise, we cannot collect every bit of information that might, ultimately, be of value. As Freeman (2000) points out, "we have to recognize that we can never identify and measure the full context of anyone's life, even in the present, and interpretation of data can only be as well informed as possible" (p. 236).

The Roe, Zuckerman, and Bloom studies were theory driven. Of course, each relied on different bodies of knowledge for its theoretical framework. Theory-driven work is important because only in this way can we clearly focus our attention for data collection and analysis, and make reasonable efforts to look for both confirming *and* disconfirming evidence. Given the limits of data collection in all instances, working atheoretically would not help us build increasing bodies of knowledge and would be disrespectful of the time and trust that the talented individuals invest in our studies. Nevertheless, as social science theories evolve, prior work may come to look increasingly less meaningful and ridden with significant holes. Perhaps one way to compensate for this is to encourage the collection and reporting of data at the most descriptive and least inferential levels possible; others, then, might be able to take significant advantage of previous work even as theoretical frameworks change.

One further dilemma associated with studying experts and working backward is that we run the risk of confusing what was the case for the experts with what needs to be the case or might be the case in other circumstances. Retrospective interviews focused on experiences from many years back are particularly sensitive to challenges from social moments, or cohort effects. In other words, retrospective interviews conducted with adults who were youth in, say, the 1950s, run the risk of confusing elements important to the development of expertise with the circumstances of the times. For example, retrospective interviews that highlight intact families with certain child-rearing characteristics might tell as much about the social times as they tell about what it takes to become an expert. Again, this calls attention to the importance of multiple studies of the development of expertise under different conditions.

One specific aspect of a cohort effect seems not to be particularly problematic: how much people are able to recollect about their life experiences across their lifespans. Considerable research on autobiographical or recollective memory (e.g., Rubin, 1986, 1996; Rubin & Schulkind, 1997) indicates first that people have many more memories than can be captured in any set of interviews. Interestingly, the distribution of memories across the lifespan seems quite orderly: following a period of childhood amnesia for a person's earliest years, there seems to be simple retention for the most recent 20 to 30 years of a person's life, and, for people older than 35, a "bump" in the number of memories from ages 10 to 30. Of course the age of interviewees most appropriately should reflect the data the researchers are trying to collect. If data about early years matter a great deal, then we would want to

interview experts as young as is reasonable to do so; if the consequences of certain later-stage experiences are the research interest, then of course we want to interview when enough time has lapsed to be able to see a wide range of possible consequences.

Because people have many more memories than can be captured in interviews, and especially because in this body of work no single memory nor even any single participant is essential to data collection and analysis, the issue of recollective memory seems less problematic than other considerations for retrospective interview studies. For example, working with a coherent sample and then trying to collect supplementary and collaborative information (from parents, from previously conducted and published interviews, and from other data about peoples' lives) seem to be important methodological considerations. Similarly, the care taken in describing and analyzing data within cases and across cases, and looking thoughtfully for negative evidence for developing arguments, will distinguish studies that will hold up or at least continue to be useful over time. And it is important that studies be useful over time, be repeated and repeatable in some fashion over time, to help separate out important elements of the development of expertise from specific cohort or context effects.

Of course all methods for studying expertise have strengths and weaknesses. There are no methodologies inherently better than the others – *except in relation to the particular research question(s) proposed*. Ochse (1990, pp. 37–45) offers a succinct summary of different methodologies for studying "people who have achieved excellence" (p. 37), cites various studies done in each tradition, and notes the strengths and weaknesses of the different forms of study. Ochse argues for the importance of convergence of findings across different methodologies:

> *If consistent findings emerge from studies in which different methods were employed, one may with some confidence ascribe the correspondence to principles governing natural underlying regularities rather than repeated methodological errors. (p. 37)*

Common Patterns across Studies and Some Implications for Future Work

Notwithstanding all of the limitations of retrospective interviews in the service of studying expertise and expert performance, and the significant differences in the theoretical frameworks for the Roe, Zuckerman, and Bloom studies, there are findings that appear again and again in these studies and not infrequently in studies using other methods of investigation. The most obvious of the common findings relate to *time*. Multiple studies report specific, continued, long-term experience with a field before a person realizes exceptional accomplishment (see, for example, Simon & Chase, 1973; Ericsson, Krampe, & Tesch-Römer, 1993). This finding has led many of us, even from quite different theoretical orientations, to hypothesize that the central challenge of helping people develop exceptional abilities is that of creating and maintaining the *motivation* necessary to stay with a field for the many years it takes to develop expertise (Sosniak, 1987; Posner, 1988). See also Zimmerman, Chapter 39.

We do not yet seem to have research addressing how to help create and maintain long-term investments in learning. We do have evidence, however, that the long-term experience is not all of one kind, but, rather, involves a series of *phases of qualitatively different experiences* (Sosniak, 1987). Motivation undoubtedly needs to be understood as both an individual quality and as socially promoted, embedded in tasks and teaching and learning interactions, public performances, and so on. And motivation undoubtedly needs to be understood as it likely changes over time in relation to activities and experiences. Changes in motivation over time are suggested also in the work of Ericsson, Tesch-Römer, and Krampe (1990) and Ericsson and Charness (1994), who used a modified version of the phases from the Bloom studies to pursue investigations into the influence of practice on the development of expert performance.

The retrospective interviews that point to qualitatively different phases suggest additional research that might be profitable in the near term. My own puzzlement has to do with how individuals negotiate the *transition points*. How, for example, do children make the move from enjoying playful experiences with a field to becoming more deliberate, precise, and intense in their involvement? Can we learn to account for how and why some people make this transition and others are left behind or drop out entirely? Similarly, there seems to be a critical transition between developing serious competence and then moving further toward the limits of expertise. This seems to be the transition between precision and generalization in Bloom's work, the move to study with a master teacher in Zuckerman's work, and the "crisis" that Bamberger (1982) identifies in her work with prodigies. How and why do students of a field get so very far in developing competence and move no further?

An alternative point of view about the phases, however, might be that they are stunting growth, unnecessarily prolonging the development of expertise, and that students of a field might benefit by being introduced early to the final phase, which represents work as experts engage it. I am probably misinterpreting Bereiter and Scardamalia (1986) when they write "relative experts are not merely better at doing the same things that others do; they do things differently, and the same differences appear in various domains" (p. 16), but I read into their discussion of the qualitative differences the implication that we should, then, teach people from the start how to work as experts do. Ochse (1990) makes just this leap – from what experts know and do to what we should teach novices – when she supports teaching thinking styles rather than facts early in a student's experience based on work indicating that Nobel Prize winners testified that learning thinking styles was the most influential part of their work with master teachers (see p. 259).

It may indeed make sense to begin a student's education with what the most advanced learners teach us about their knowledge, skill, and ways of working. Certainly, it might make sense to focus on the underlying principles and processes of a field in even the earliest instruction. But it might also be the case that learners need significantly different activities and aims, different feedback and correctives, different standards of excellence, before they can make sense of and make use of the expectations and strategies associated with expert performance. Although I have argued elsewhere about the necessity of distinctly different phases of learning, this is, of course, a testable question that is as yet untested.

There does seem to be considerable agreement across retrospective interview studies and other investigations that people who demonstrate exceptional accomplishment have almost always had the experience of *studying with a master teacher* – a teacher who has considerable standing in the field and who has helped prepare others who are known for their accomplishments. There is evidence also that work with a master teacher is significantly different from earlier educational experiences. Zuckerman's reports of Nobel laureates' experiences with master teachers dovetail with reports from the Bloom studies.

Zuckerman writes about the match between a master teacher and a student as a "jointly operating process of self-selection by the future scientists and selective recruitment by the academic institutions" (p. 107). How the master and the apprentice get together, what they do together, and how some survive this experience while others fall by the wayside, would seem to be fruitful arenas for investigation.

Investigations into experiences with master teachers should be mindful of the fact that considerable learning has already taken place, and the only way to understand what happens with a master teacher is to know well what prepared the student for this teacher. In other words, students come to a master teacher with no small measure of expertise already. The type of expertise they come with, and how they arrived at it, may be as important in defining the mechanisms of developing exceptional talent as the learners' experiences with the master teachers.

Discussion about the long-term nature of developing talent, and the phases that may or may not be important aspects of that development, inevitably lead to a predominant point of view about the importance of an *"early start."* I have used "early start" in quotation marks because, although it summarizes findings within studies, it does not necessarily mean the same thing across studies. In the Bloom studies, for example, early start would refer to experiences that people who eventually became outstanding concert pianists or Olympic swimmers had before they were old enough even to enroll in elementary school. In the Zuckerman study, however, early start would mean earning one's doctorate at a younger age than the average scientist, and producing scientific publications in one's twenties.

The value of an early start undoubtedly is intricately linked with the demands and expectations of a particular domain of expertise. In domains that call for considerable physiological development, a *young* start might be particularly beneficial in order to catch developing bodies and minds at the most malleable times. In domains that call for significant advanced education, including doctoral studies and post-doctoral research experiences, an early start might logically be linked with choice of college, which then becomes a feeder into graduate programs and beyond.

The age at which one must begin work in a field surely is linked with moments that the field uses to recognize and honor its participants. And following from this, the age at which one must begin work in a field also likely is linked to the coherence and history of the field. Newly emerging fields (like research neurology when the Bloom studies were conducted) might allow for or even require different processes for the development of expertise than more firmly established and perhaps more closed fields. For reasons I still do not understand well, the development of exceptional research neurologists (in the Bloom studies) did seem to be different in important ways from, say, the concert pianists' experiences.

One further related finding that appears again and again across studies but may be an artifact of the domain or the larger culture has to do with the importance of *family influences* on providing early experiences and motivating learning over the long term. It seems reasonable to wonder if, in fields for which there is a strong societal press (certain sports, perhaps, or maybe even television news or entertainment reporting), the societal press may well have more power than anything parents might do or say. Or in circumstances where young children spend more time outside of the home than with parents, people outside the home might prove more influential than parents. It might be wise to think about family influences as a proxy measure for activities that dominate the lives of young children and for the ways children experience early activities.

In this regard it may become as important to know about the society in which the development of expertise takes place – or maybe especially the local community for the young child – as to know about the home in which a learner may get an initial start. Scholars like Feldman (1986) and Csikszentmihalyi and Robinson (1986), arguing the case for the coincidence or co-construction of expertise, point us in important directions for future research. For educators, especially, separating the family from the knowledge, skills, and dispositions that might develop early, and attending more to the youngsters' communities, would help us think about new ways of helping more people reach greater levels of expertise in more fields. It would do this by reducing the importance of being born into the right household and increasing the likelihood of choice and fit for children and the areas in which they might go on to exceptional accomplishment. Again, these are testable questions that call for studies of talent development under different conditions.

Further Challenges in Thinking about Future Research

For a great many reasons, then, it seems important that we conduct studies of the long-term development of expertise across a greater range of conditions and cultures. It seems important, also, that we conduct studies across a greater range of domains. Albert (1983) called attention to this last issue some time ago. What do we know about the long-term development of expertise in business, finance, law, public service, or social service? What do we know about the long-term development of expertise as playwrights or poets, teachers or preachers, engineers or architects or statisticians?

> *Since what we know obviously depends upon who is available for study as well as our techniques, interests, and values, this raises the possibility that the model we construct concerning creativity and eminence may be of limited generality. (Albert, 1983, p. viii)*

Ultimately, where we might head in future research will depend a great deal on our intentions and our theoretical orientations. Researchers interested in the long-term development of expertise likely will choose different domains to study and certainly will choose different methods of investigation than will researchers interested in the structure and characteristics of expert performance. Absent an interest in long-term development (or at least aspects of the long-term experience), retrospective interviews will not be the method of choice. It will become crucial, then, to ensure repeated syntheses of studies across domains and across methods of investigation in order that we do not end up following a trail that was created artificially by the fields we chose to study and the methods we chose to use for our studies.

I am hardly impartial in the discussion of what fields to study. As an educator I resonate with Sloboda's (1991) argument regarding the purpose for our studies:

> *One of the principal reasons for studying expertise is practical. Given that it would be socially desirable for certain manifestations of expertise to be more widespread than they are, we want to know what we can do to assist people to acquire them. (p. 156)*

To this end, I am interested not only in the long-term experience of learning but also in learning in domains that have particular social value. Given the enormous investment an individual must make in the development of expertise, and the considerable investment others make in the success of a single individual, I would argue for keeping our eye on fields in which expertise could serve simultaneously the individual and society.

Finally, I would like to suggest that an important challenge we face as we continue studying expertise, especially the development of expertise over the long term, is to beware of labeling levels of development below the ultimate as failures. Students who at some point in their development abandon a field in which they may have been selected as a potential elite or may have already demonstrated considerable expertise are not abandoning their talent. They may be choosing to devote their energies in other directions, but the talent they have developed already does not disappear. It is not lost and it is not wasted. In choosing to move in other directions, the individuals still carry with them both what they have learned and the experience of learning. And the ways they may use their knowledge and experience of learning create various other avenues of investigation, depending on the theoretical orientation of a researcher.

Expertise is not an endpoint, it is a continuum. Although retrospective interviews may concentrate on the ultimate expression of expertise because this allows us to study expertise most clearly, and although some scholars studying expertise might be interested only in that ultimate demonstration, we must remember not to devalue the many other levels of expertise that serve individuals and society well. There are limits on the number of people who can enter an Olympic contest or who can be considered the very most talented of living musicians. But there are no limits on the number of people who can value music and sports and so many other avenues for expression in their lives, who can value the opportunity to continue advancing their own personal bests, and who can make significant contributions to their communities through their considerable, although perhaps not exceptional, talent. In the best of worlds, retrospective inter-

view studies will allow us to frame and test meaningful opportunities for advancing the development of talent, however far, for ever-expanding numbers of individuals and, of course, for society.

References

Albert, R. S. (Ed.) (1983). *Genius and eminence: The social psychology of creativity and exceptional achievement*. Oxford: Pergamon Press.

Bamberger, J. (1982). Growing up prodigies: The midlife crisis. In D. Feldman (Ed.), *New directions for child development: Developmental approaches to giftedness and creativity*, no. 17. San Francisco: Jossey-Bass.

Bereiter, C. & Scardamalia, M. (1986). Educational relevance of the study of expertise. *Interchange*, 17(2), 10–19.

Bloom, B. S. (1982, April). The role of gifts and markers in the development of talent. *Exceptional Children*, 48(6), 510–521.

Bloom, B. S. (Ed.) (1985). *Developing talent in young people*. New York: Ballantine.

Carlson, B. (1985, Fall). Exceptional conditions, not exceptional talent, produce high achievers. *The University of Chicago Magazine*, 78(1), 18–19, 49.

Csikszentmihalyi, M. & Robinson, R. E. (1986). Culture, time, and the development of talent. In R. J. Sternberg & J. E. Davidson (Eds.), *Conceptions of giftedness* (pp. 264–284). Cambridge: Cambridge University Press.

Ericsson, K. A. & Charness, N. (1994). Expert performance: Its structure and acquisition. *American Psychologist*, 49(8), 725–747.

Ericsson, K. A., Krampe, R. Th., & Tesch-Römer, C. (1993). The role of deliberate practice in the acquisition of expert performance. *Psychological Review*, 100, 363–406.

Ericsson, K. A., Tesch-Römer, C., & Krampe, R. Th. (1990). The role of practice and motivation in the acquisition of expert-level performance in real life: An empirical evaluation of a theoretical framework. In M. J. A. Howe (Ed.), *Encouraging the development of exceptional skills and talents* (pp. 109–130). Leicester, UK: The British Psychological Society.

Feldman, D. H. (with Goldsmith, L. T.) (1986). *Nature's gambit: Child prodigies and the development of human potential*. NY: Basic Books.

Freeman, J. (2000). Teaching for talent: Lessons from the research. In C. F. M. van Lieshout & P. G. Heymans (Eds.), *Developing talent across the life span* (pp. 231–248). East Sussex: Psychology Press.

Glaser, R. & Chi, M. T. H. (1988). Overview. In M. T. H. Chi, R. Glaser, & M. J. Farr (Eds.), *The nature of expertise* (pp. xv–xxvii). Hillsdale, NJ: Erlbaum.

Goldsmith, L. T. (2000). Tracking trajectories of talent: Child prodigies growing up. In R. C. Friedman & B. M. Shore (Eds.), *Talents unfolding: Cognition and development* (pp. 89–122). Washington, DC: American Psychological Association.

Gruber, H. E. (1982). On the hypothesized relation between giftedness and creativity. In D. H. Feldman (Ed.), *Developmental approaches to giftedness and creativity* (pp. 7–29). San Francisco: Jossey-Bass.

Gruber, H. E. (1986). The self-construction of the extraordinary. In R. J. Sternberg & J. E. Davidson (Eds.), *Conceptions of giftedness* (pp. 247–263). Cambridge: Cambridge University Press.

Ochse, R. (1990). *Before the gates of excellence: The determinants of creative genius.* Cambridge: Cambridge University Press.

Posner, M. I. (1988). Introduction: What is it to be an expert? In M. T. H. Chi, R. Glaser, & M. J. Farr (Eds.), *The nature of expertise* (pp. xxix–xxxvi). Hillsdale, NJ: Erlbaum.

Roe, A. (1952). *The making of a scientist.* NY: Dodd, Mead & Company.

Rubin, D. C. (Ed.) (1986). *Autobiographical memory.* Cambridge: Cambridge University Press.

Rubin, D. C. (Ed.) (1996). *Remembering our past: Studies in autobiographical memory.* Cambridge: Cambridge University Press.

Rubin, D. C. & Schulkind, M. D. (1997). Distribution of important and word-cued autobiographical memories in 20-, 35-, and 70-year-old adults. *Psychology and aging, 12*(3), 524–535.

Salthouse, T. A. (1991). Expertise as the circumvention of human processing limitations. In K. A. Ericsson & J. Smith (Eds.), *Toward a general theory of expertise: Prospects and limits* (pp. 286–300). Cambridge: Cambridge University Press.

Simon, H. A. & Chase, W. G. (1973). Skill in chess. *American Scientist, 61,* 394–403.

Sloboda, J. (1991). Musical expertise. In K. A. Ericsson & J. Smith (Eds.), *Toward a general theory of expertise: Prospects and limits* (pp. 153–171). Cambridge: Cambridge University Press.

Sosniak, L. A. (1987). The nature of change in successful learning. *Teachers College Record, 88*(4), 519–535.

Sosniak, L. A. (2003). Developing talent: Time, task and context. In N. Colangelo & G. Davis (Eds.), *Handbook of gifted education* (3rd ed.) (pp. 247–253). New York: Allyn & Bacon.

Subotnik, R., Kassan, L., Summers, E., and Wasser, A. (1993). *Genius revisited: High IQ children grown up.* Norwood, NJ: Ablex.

Terman, L. M., & Oden, M. H. (1959). *Genetic studies of genius: The gifted group at mid-life.* Stanford, CA: Stanford University Press.

Wagner, R. K. & Stanovich, K. E. (1996). Expertise in reading. In K. A. Ericsson (Ed.), *The road to excellence: The acquisition of expert performance in the arts and sciences, sports, and games* (pp. 189–225). Mahwah, NJ: Erlbaum.

Whitehead, A. N. (1929). *The aims of education.* New York: Macmillan.

Zuckerman, H. (1977/1996). *Scientific elite: Nobel laureates in the United States.* New Brunswick: Transaction Publishers.

CHAPTER 17

Time, Budgets, Diaries, and Analyses of Concurrent Practice Activities

Janice M. Deakin, Jean Côté, & Andrew S. Harvey

Introduction

Time is an inescapable dimension of all human activity. What time of day, month, and year, for how long, before or after what other activity, how long before or after another given activity and how often, are questions answerable for all activities. The relevance of each question varies with one's perspective on the activity. Time-use methodology can provide rich, objective, and replicable temporal information to answer the questions posed, hence providing a basis for forming and/or collaborating empirical judgments. Coupled with other objective and subjective contextual information on each incident of an activity, time-use methodologies can generate invaluable information for understanding activities and human behavior. Time-use studies show how people use their time. Minimally, they show what activities people do, while maximally, they can show what people are doing, where they are, who they are with, and how they feel.

Time-use studies can use a variety of data-collection methods ranging from self-reported activities to observation reports. In expertise research, time spent in an activity needs to be considered at a minimum of two different levels: a macro and a micro level. These two different levels encompass different units of time and provide different information about an activity. For example, at a macro level a researcher interested in music expertise may want to assess a typical week of training by analyzing time spent on general activities, such as practice alone, practice with a teacher, playing with others, resting, and so forth. On the other hand, the same researcher may want to explore more in-depth (i.e. micro level) a specific activity consistently performed by expert musicians, such as practices with a teacher. Information gathered at the micro level could focus on: 1) objective variables such as time spent practicing particular pieces, listening to instruction, or discussing technique with an instructor, and/or 2) subjective variables such as the immediate rating of the activity in terms of concentration and enjoyment. The micro analysis of an activity is quantitatively and qualitatively different from the macro analysis of time spent in various activities and will result in the coding of different episodes. The decision regarding the level of analysis that one wants to investigate will determine a method of data collection that would be most appropriate. The diary method may be more appropriate to investigate time-use data at a macro level, whereas systematic observation may be more appropriate for the micro analysis of selected activities. After providing an historical perspective of time-use research and time-budget methods used in expertise research, this chapter will focus on the use of diary and observation methods as they relate to the investigation of expert performance.

Historical Perspective

Two of the earliest published accounts of time use are *How Working Men Spend Their Time* (Bevans, 1913) and *Round about a Pound a Week* (Pember-Reeves, 1913). Time-use research emerged in Europe in conjunction with early studies of living conditions of the working class in response to pressures generated by the rise of industrialization. Studies examined activities such as paid work, household work, personal care, leisure, and so on, in the daily, weekly, or yearly time budget of the population. They also examined how the time use varied among population groups such as workers, students, and housewives, and in the use of leisure time.

Most pre-World War II diaries originated in the Soviet Union, Great Britain, and the United States. One of the earliest landmark studies was undertaken in the Soviet Union (1924) by S. G. Strumilin (1980) for use in governmental and communal planning. In the United States, home economists started using time-use studies in the 1920s to study farm and rural women (Avery, Bryant, Douthitt, & McCullough, 1996; Kneeland, 1929). Work began at Cornell during the 1920s on a program to study household output in terms of time use (Walker & Woods, 1976). In the 1930s Lundberg and Komarovsky (1934) launched a new era in

the examination of leisure time and activities. As the foregoing suggests, such studies can be used to study both activities and population groups.

The Multinational Time Use Study in the mid-1960s directed by Alexander Szalai (1972) stands as a landmark in cross-national survey research and was unquestionably the most significant time-diary undertaking in the last century. The study examined the use of quantitative political, social, and cultural data from thirteen countries and sixteen different survey sites. This study had a profound effect on all subsequent collection of time-use data. Specifically, the coding scheme used in that study shaped those of all subsequent national time studies, and the wide range of analyses using the Multinational Study data has broadened the scope of data collectors and data analysts.

The United States, which had never collected official national time-use data, launched, through the Bureau of Labor Statistics, an ongoing study in January of 2003. The major national studies in the United States have been undertaken by the Institute of Social Research (ISR) at the University of Michigan (Juster, 1985) and by the Survey Research Center at the University of Maryland (Robinson & Godbey, 1997). The first general population survey conducted in Canada was undertaken in Halifax, Nova Scotia in 1971. The Halifax study was a time-space study that captured not only what people were doing, but also where they were, coded to a one-tenth kilometer grid (Elliott et al., 1976). The fist nationwide time use study in Canada was conducted in 1981(Kinsley & O'Donnell, 1983). As a part of that study, over 450 respondents to the 1971 Halifax study completed diaries, thus providing a ten-year panel of time use (Harvey & Elliott, 1983). Statistics Canada, as part of its General Social Survey program, collected diaries for approximately 9,000 Canadians in 1986, 1992, and 1998 (Fredrick, 1995; Harvey, Marshall, & Frederick, 1991).

In the last decade, there have been significant advances in time-use methodologies, including innovative applications to non-traditional topics of inquiry, and a variety of analysis strategies. The literature on time use have been remarkable in reflecting the interests of many different fields, including economics (Juster & Stafford, 1991; Goldschmidt-Clermont, 1987), business administration (Das, 1991; Grossin, 1993a, 1993b; McGrath & Rotchford, 1983), gerontology (Harvey & Singleton, 1989, Moss & Lawton, 1982), urban planning (Chapin, 1974; Gutenschwager, 1973), political science and occupational therapy (Larson, 1990; McKinnon, 1992; Pentland, Harvey, & Walker, 1998), nursing and medicine (Frankenberg, 1992), recreation and physical and health education (Rosenthal & Howe, 1984; Ujimoto, 1985), sociology and anthropology (Andorka, 1987; Elchardus & Glorieux, 1993, 1994; Garhammer, 1995), psychology (Block, 1990; Lawton, Moss, & Fulcomer, 1987), and expert performance (Ericsson, Krampe, & Tesch-Römer, 1993; Deakin & Cobley, 2003; Starkes, Deakin, Allard, Hodges, & Hayes, 1996).

Time-use methodologies provide hard, replicable data that are the behavioral output of decisions, preferences, attitudes, and environmental factors. It can be used to examine, describe, and compare role performance (Ross, 1990), cultures and lifestyles (Chapin, 1974), poverty (Douthitt, 1993), household and community economies (Knights & Odih, 1995), as well as social indicators such as quality of life and well-being (Japan, Ministry of Economic Planning, 1975).

Time Use and Expertise

Time and its use are central to contemporary discussions on the acquisition and retention of expert performance. Early attributions of superior performance to a set of general inherited capacities (e.g., Galton, 1869; Cattell & Drevdahl, 1955) diminished the need to evaluate the contribution of the *use of time* to the attainment of eminence. This predominantly genetic explanation of expert performance has given way to the pervasive belief that practice and other forms of preparation are essential prerequisites for the development of expertise. Understanding practice as a major independent variable in the acquisition of skill requires a concomitant understanding of time use in that process.

The study of expert performers affords us the opportunity to determine the characteristics that underlie their superior performance and examine the process by which those characteristics of performance are acquired. The uniqueness of this opportunity was eloquently stated by Starkes (2003) when she noted that "few human endeavors exist to which people dedicate so much time, energy, resources and effort – all with the goal of becoming quite simply the best they can be." Although she was speaking specifically of sport-related expertise, these characteristics are uniformly applicable to experts across a vast variety of domains, including chess (de Groot, 1946/1978; Chase & Simon, 1973; Simon & Chase, 1973), physics (Chi, Glaser, & Rees, 1982), music (Ericsson et al.,1993), and sports (Deakin & Cobley, 2003; Starkes et al. 1996).

Although time use *per se* was not the focus of the classic work on chess expertise (Chase & Simon, 1973), it was heavily implicated in their hypothesis that chess-specific pattern-recognition processes underlay the superior memory recall performance of the Grand Master player. They claimed that a minimum of ten years of preparation is required to develop and organize the necessary repertoire of domain-specific information to attain an international level of chess skill. Further, they suggested that a similar timeframe would be required in other domains. Subsequent studies crossing many domains have substantiated this claim (e.g., Bloom, 1985; Ericsson et al., 1993; Hayes, 1981; Helsen, Starkes, & Hodges, 1998; Krogius, 1976; Starkes et al., 1996). However, specific relationships between experience with activities in a domain and acquired performance have been uniformly weak (Ericsson et al., 1993). This suggests that maximal levels of performance are not attained merely as a function of extended experience, but rather by deliberate efforts to improve, further implicating the importance of elucidating the components of domain-related experience that are critical to performance improvement over time.

Ericsson and colleagues (1993) presented a theoretical framework for the acquisition of expert performance that implicated *deliberate practice* – "a highly structured set of activities, with the explicit goal of improving performance" (p. 368) – as the central factor in the determination of acquired performance. They defined deliberate practice as specific tasks "rated very high on relevance for performance, high on effort and comparatively low on inherent enjoyment" (p. 373). Their proposition that the expert could be differentiated from both less expert and novice performers solely on the extent of their involvement in deliberate practice formed the basis of an elegant series of studies undertaken with three groups of violin students (best, good, and music-teacher candidates) from the Music Academy of West Berlin. Ericsson et al. (1993) collected retrospective reports on when the musicians first became involved with the violin, the beginning of practice with the instrument, the number of music teachers they had studied under, and their involvement in competitions. Participants were asked to estimate the number of hours per week they had devoted to practicing alone with the violin for each year since they started to practice. The participants also completed daily diaries for a seven-day period, using ninety-six fifteen-minute intervals. All activities were then encoded by the participant using a thirty-item preestablished taxonomy. The purpose of the diary work was multidimensional. First, use of the taxonomy facilitated the calculation of total time spent in any one category of activity by addition across days. Second, it enabled the concurrent rating of each activity category on the defining attributes of deliberate practice (relevance, effort, enjoyment). Finally, the diary data could be contrasted with the retrospective data on time

estimates as a way of validating the retrospective data.

Ericsson et al. (1993) concluded that solitary practice was the only activity that met their definition of deliberate practice. Although both the "best" and "good" violinists spent a similar amount of time engaged in music-related activities, the only distinguishing activity was solitary practice, where the best violinists spent four hours per day each day of the week. When they considered next the estimates of time spent in solitary practice since the beginning of involvement from the retrospective recall data, they reported that by age eighteen, the best violinists had accumulated an average of about 7,500 hours of practice, which was reliably different from the good violinists, with 5,300 hours of practice. Both of these groups had accumulated more hours than the music-teacher group, who had accumulated 3,400 hours of practice at the same age. They concluded that the differential skill levels seen between these groups of violinists could be accounted for by the accumulated hours of solitary practice. Though the relationship between the amount of solitary practice and acquired performance has been demonstrated in chess (Charness, Krampe & Mayr, 1996) and music (Ericsson et al., 1993), it has been more problematic to identify domain-related activities that meet the definition of deliberate practice.

Retrospective reports and diaries of time use have been used extensively to examine the development of expert performance in sport. Starkes et al. (1996) first used the methodologies to examine the practice activities of skilled wrestlers and figure skaters with a view to validating the definition of deliberate practice in the sport environment, and to determine whether time spent in deliberate practice was monotonically related to acquired performance. Similar to Ericsson et al.'s (1993) protocol, a taxonomy of sport-related and everyday activities was compiled by asking participants to think back and report what activities they had participated in during their most recent "typical" week. They then kept a diary for seven days, with each day divided into fifteen-minute intervals. Daily entries were made at the end of each day, and all activities were encoded using the sport-specific taxonomy.

On the issue of identifying practice activities that met the requirement of being rated as highly relevant but not enjoyable, none were found. For both the wrestlers and figure skaters, all of the activities that were rated highest for relevance were also rated high for enjoyment. The second requirement – being high on relevance and high on effort – was apparent in both sets of data, with the top two activities for relevance also being rated high on concentration. Although, strictly speaking, no activities in these studies met the definition of deliberate practice, the strong positive relationship between relevance and concentration seen across domains was evident in these data. Interestingly, if the high-relevance/high-effort definition of deliberate practice is used, the top two deliberate-practice activities for each of the violinists, wrestlers, and figure skaters are perfectly consistent and include an activity that is identical to what must be done in the actual performance and work with a teacher or coach (Starkes et al., 1996).

The availability of both retrospective time estimates and diary data made it possible to examine the reliability of these time-use methodologies. For those wrestlers who took part in both the retrospective recall and diary studies, time-use estimates from their most recent year (retrospective recall) were compared to the time-use attributions of the diary week. For international wrestlers the correlation between a typical week and the diary week was 0.66 for wrestling related activities. Although their retrospective reports indicated that in a typical week they would have spent over seventeen hours in practice "with others," the data from the diary week indicated that they actually spent under eleven hours in that activity. Similarly, the less-expert club wrestlers reported spending the same amount of time on this activity in a typical week, but actually recorded spending under ten hours in this activity during the diary week. Ericsson et al. (1993) reported similar findings for

their musicians in that they too overestimated practice hours, suggesting that retrospective estimates reflected the amount of practice participants aspire to, rather than what was actually attained. Although the international wrestlers overestimated the amount of time they spent in some practice activities involving others, there was no difference in predicted time spent on other elements of practice. For example, correlations between the retrospective recall and diary data for the international wrestlers on strength training with others ($r = 0.98$), strength training alone ($r = 0.96$), and time spent attending wrestling practice ($r = 0.76$) were uniformly high and superior to those of the club-level wrestlers. Although these correlations support the validity of both time-use methodologies, diary data allows for an accurate assessment of time use in activities on a finer level of detail than does retrospective reports.

The question of differential accuracy in the estimation of time use across skill level led Deakin and Cobley (2003) to include a separate evaluation of time use through direct observation of practice in figure skating, in addition to the retrospective-recall and diary techniques. They reasoned that the inclusion of an observational assessment of practice sessions would provide data on the extent to which those elements of practice consistently rated as high on relevance and concentration or effort where represented in actual on-ice practice sessions. The study involved the recording of on-ice activities of three groups of skaters ($n = 24$) differing in skill level (elite or national team members, competitive skaters, and test skaters; see Deakin & Cobley, 2003 for details on participants and methodology). A log of the practice activities including the number and time spent in jump attempts, spins, lessons, program run-through, and rest time was recorded for each of three taped sessions per skater. In addition, a seven-day diary and a series of questionnaires were completed to provide estimates of time during a typical week spent in a variety of activities, including skating-related activities, sleep, education, and non-skating-related activities. Each skater was asked to rate the activities on a ten point scale in terms of their relevance to skill development.

Of central interest was whether time use during practice reflected the relative importance assessed to the element by the skaters, and whether the estimates of time use provided for a typical week were consistent with what was observed in the on-ice sessions. The practicing of jumps and spins were rated as being highly relevant to performance improvement by all groups of figure skaters, and all groups reported spending the highest proportion of their practice time on these elements. However, despite the lack of group differences in the assessment of relevance to improvement, the time-motion analyses revealed that the elite and competitive skaters spent 68% and 59% of their sessions practicing jumps, whereas the test group was engaged in those activities for only 48% of their on-ice time. Further, when rest time was expressed as a percentage of total session length by group, an inverse relationship with skill level emerged. Specifically, the elite group spent an average of 14% of their total on-ice practice time on rest, the competitive group spent 31%, and the test skaters, 46%. The analysis of rest time indicated that the elite skaters utilized their on-ice time more effectively than the other groups by practicing the critical elements for a higher proportion of their on-ice practice time and by resting less.

Inclusion of an observational time-motion analysis of practice in figure skating has provided another dimension to the determination of time use and to the applicability of retrospective estimation of the quantity of practice. Any interpretation of skaters' reports of cumulative practice must be made cautiously. Despite skaters' ability to accurately recall scheduled hours of practice, the relationship between scheduled hours and actual hours of practice is far from clear. Although the three groups of skaters in this study had spent a similar number of years practicing, the actual active practice time would be in the order of 13% to 46% lower than the reported hours of scheduled practice. Although at first glance this might seem

more problematic for the interpretation of retrospective reports than for diary data, another example of the bias toward the overestimation of practice elements raises similar concerns for diary data. The relationship between what skaters say they practice and what they actually practice was examined by asking each skater, immediately prior to beginning their practice session, the number and type of jumps and spins they were going to undertake in that particular session. Without exception skaters overestimated the number and difficulty-level of the jumps they undertook in practice. The examination revealed that all skaters spent considerably more time practicing jumps that existed in their repertoire and less time on jumps they were attempting to learn. Whereas it appears they aspired to work on increasingly difficult elements, they instead opted to execute elements that required less effort on their part for successful completion. For example, the elite skaters estimated attempting seven double jumps and twenty triple jumps per session, whereas they actually attempted an average of thirty doubles and six triples. This difference amounts to a three- to fourfold discrepancy between what they intend to do and what they are observed to do. The results of our investigation corroborate those of Ericsson et al. (1993) on this matter and highlight the question of the extent to which diary data on practice activities themselves may be influenced by aspired versus actual practice time.

The assessment of time use across concurrent activities by both direct observation and diary methodologies should elucidate the complex relationships between time, activities, and the attainment of expert performance. In the following section we provide specific details of diary and observational methodologies for the evaluation of how time is spent.

A Macro Analysis of Time Use: The Diary Method

The time diary provides one of the most comprehensive and accurate means of collecting data about time spent on specific categories of activities. The diary captures the sequence and duration of activities engaged in by an individual over a specified period. All activities during the period are recorded in sequence, including their start and completion times. One of the key strengths of the diary methodology is that it can exhaust all activities and all time during the selected period. A broad range of subjective and contextual data can also be collected at the same time, providing rich context for the individuals, the activities, and individual behaviour.

Diaries may be presented in a number of ways, each with different implications for implementation and data generation. The simplest is a *Stylized Activity List*. It provides an abbreviated list of activities. Respondents are then asked to estimate how much time they spent on each, say, during the previous day or week. Two particular problems are inherent in this approach. First, responses are heavily dependent on the respondent's ability to recall and accumulate time on each activity listed with essentially no external clues. Second, generally, by using selected activities it lacks the period of time constraint that aids reporting accuracy. However, such an instrument can get participation and duration for the listed activities.

A *Stylized Activity Log* improves on the above by capturing episodes, the basic building blocks of time use. Sometimes known as the quick diary, the log typically provides a vertical activity list and a horizontal time referent covering the twenty-four hours of the day, broken into ten- to thirty-minute units. Respondents can then indicate their activities over the day by drawing a line beside the activity and under the relevant time period. This approach provides much enhanced control over the quality of the time-use data since it requires the respondent to think through the day and to identify transitions from activity to activity. The stylized activity log is capable of providing significantly more information on time use than is provided by the stylized activity list. As indicated, it provides information on activity

episodes, what activities are done, and when. Thus, it is possible to derive an understanding of how an individual's day is organized. Forms of the stylized activity log have been used in the examination of expert performance to investigate how expert performers maximize the quality of their multiple practice sessions through managing their time in daily cycles (see Starkes et al., 1996).

Time-use studies report the state of selected details at each successive time point or period. The basic unit in a time-use study is the *episode*, a single diary entry with all attendant dimensions sought by the researcher. Although episodes are meaningful for analysis at one level, they are less useful at another. One may be interested in each episode of lessons, jump attempts, or program run-throughs during an on-ice training session for expert figure skaters. This would be accompanied by information on when, where, and with whom the practice occurred, as well as the overall allocation of time to skating over the study period. Thus, it is necessary to aggregate identical or similar episodes during the study period of interest into higher-level categories for more aggregated analysis.

The focal aggregation is typically an *activity*. What are relevant activities? How are they organized? Episode and activity organization is spelled out in a coding scheme. All such schemes have an implicit, if not explicit, theoretical or heuristic base. At the most fundamental level interest centres on the actual amount of time allocated to specific activities, such as those related to the domain under investigation (practice alone, lessons with a coach or teacher), those related to the demands of daily living (paid work, housework, childcare, education, rest), and other activities meaningful to the particular interests being examined. The activity list used in a time-use study can range from a few to hundreds of activities. The greater detail provides for an elaboration of activities, such as the type of practice undertaken, work done, television show watched, the type of book read, and so on. Although on the surface more detail is better, this is true only if there are sufficient

Participant Name:_____ Date: _____ Day of the week:_____

Time	What did you do?	Time Began	Time Ended	Location	List other persons with you
AM 7					
8					
9					
10					
11					
PM 12					
1					
2					
3					
4					
5					
6					
7					
8					
9					

Figure 17.1. Time-diary template

episodes of an identified activity for analysis. Thus, there are tradeoffs between detail and usability.

A diary survey typically consists of two parts. One is socio-demographic and includes other information useful in classifying and interpreting the material collected. This information can be treated as a fixed-length vector in a manner similar to that done in ordinary surveys. The second, time diaries, collect information on how time is being used and is most frequently collected as a vector that may or may not be of fixed length, dependent on the number of characteristics collected with a diary entry. Typically, studies collect what is being done, where, with whom, and sometimes what else is being done at the time (secondary/parallel activity). A sample of a partial diary consisting of a time period from 7 am to 9 pm in one hour blocks is presented in Figure 17.1. It provides only one example of the types of information that can be surveyed using a diary technique.

Unit of Analysis

Diary data allows one to generate estimates of how much time is devoted and by whom (i.e. by experts versus non-expert performers) to activities related (or not) to the domain of interest and to see how that time is structured with other activities such as work, rest, family/personal care, and free time over hours, days, or weeks. Data can be examined within and across the following units of analysis. When analysing time diaries the researcher has several possible units of analysis across which to evaluate the use of time.

RESPONDENTS

Though not a factor in the examination of time use when specific participants are of interest (i.e., expert – non expert), the respondent is the unit of analysis in national time-use surveys. In this instance the researcher is concerned with exhaustively capturing the dimensions of interest for the total time period being studied: what the respondent was doing, when, and with whom.

PARTICIPANTS

This is the primary unit of analysis in the examination of expert performance. Interest is focused on only those people who meet an a priori definition for inclusion in the study groups. Details on how long expert versus novice figure skaters spend on skating related activities during a diary day, week, or month would be collected on groups of participants.

DAY

The day becomes the unit of analysis if one is concerned with how behaviour varies from day to day. Weekdays and weekends are often examined in an attempt to measure anticipated inherent differences in behaviour. Capturing multiple days for the same person makes it possible to examine the effect behaviour on one day has on another day, or the recurrence of activities from day to day. Restriction of recording to one day per respondent greatly limits analytical controls and possibilities.

EPISODE

If the episode is taken as the unit of analysis, it becomes possible to determine various objective and subjective traits attached to the episode, such as the time of day at which episodes take place, the presence or absence of individuals (coaches, teachers, other participants, etc.), or the presence or absence of secondary activities. Evaluation of episodes allows for the examination of the sequence in which activities take place. For example, when do skaters take part in on-ice training relative to off-ice training, rest periods, and sleeping, and to what extent may the differences in daily routine between expert and non-expert skaters account for differential levels of performance across groups?

ACTIVITY

Time-budget data is typically analysed in terms of a finite set of activity categories, as outlined above. Thus, daily meals are combined into a category "eating." Similarly, elements of on-ice skating practice could be aggregated into on-ice practice, strength training, program choreography, or indeed total daily time devoted to all skating-related activities. The major advantage of dealing with the activity in its circumscribed nature is that it is simpler to deal with ninety-six or thirty-seven activities per respondent than to deal with an unknown number of activity episodes. Of the major national studies, the Japanese study, containing thirty-two activities, has the least detailed coding system. In contrast Finland and Norway coded ninety activities, whereas the 1981 Canadian study had 271 activities. In their evaluation of expert musicians (Ericsson et al., 1993) and athletes (Starkes et al., 1996), a thirty-item taxonomy was used to code the diary data. Regardless of the coding system used, there is agreement that primary activities must add to 1440 minutes per day.

WITH WHOM

Each dimension collected in a time slot provides the same opportunities for exploration as does the activity. Ideally, data should be collected reflecting social contact with at least the following categories: 1) alone, 2) coach/instructor, 3) training partners, 4) other participants, 5) parents, 6) siblings, 7) friends/relatives outside household, and 8) others outside the household. However, there is wide variety in the detail used to capture "with whom." One important aspect of the "with whom" coding is that a distinction must be made during capture and/or coding between "being in the presence of" and "acting with." The data should at a minimum permit the researcher to identify the time that the respondent was "acting with" others. It is suggested that respondent instruction is important for accurate reporting of "with whom."

DURATION

At what time does an activity start and end? At any given time (morning, 12 noon, 5 pm), what is being done? Many differences can occur regarding when and how long an activity is performed, and these can have important consequences on expertise development.

LOCATION

Though not central in the use of diary data or the examination of the development of expert performance, the collection of location data in general provides valuable information for use in coding the diaries, as well as providing important analytical information. A strong case can be made for the collection of geographic location information, if its collection is feasible (Elliott, Harvey, & Procos, 1976).

OTHER ASPECTS OF ACTIVITY

There are other aspects of an activity that can be examined when one considers the flexibility of the diary format. For example, assessing the subjective nature of an activity is important in the evaluation of practice activities undertaken by expert and non-expert performers. Is an activity more enjoyable or does it require more concentra-

tion than another, and how much effort is required in order to complete certain activities relative to others?

The diary method allows researchers to collect multi-dimensional data related to the use of time. At a macro level, diaries provide a general picture of how experts conduct their daily activities; however, it provides little information about the structure and context of a specific activity. For example, two people can engage in the same activity for the same amount of time, but the way they experience the activity can be very different and ultimately produce a different outcome. Systematic observation of experts and non-experts in various structured settings can provide a wealth of information about how teachers or coaches structure an activity and how participants experience the activity. Demarco, Mancini, Wuest, and Schempp (1996) suggested that various descriptive-analytic instruments of behavior have made significant contributions to the quality of teaching and coaching in education, physical education, and sport. Although systematic observation methods have not been used extensively in expertise research, it is a critical part of any study interested in human behaviors and issues that revolve around the use of time. The possibility of using systematic observation in expertise research is limited by the fact that observation can occur only in particular physical settings where targeted behaviors can be formalized, observed, and analyzed.

Micro-Analysis of Time Use: Systematic Observation

Systematic observation becomes a method of choice when researchers are interested in the consequences that repetitive and structured activities have on the development of expertise. Key questions at the heart of expertise research that can appropriately be answered by systematic observation relates to issues surrounding what activities are like, who performs them, and in what context they occur. This section will focus on two issues related to the use of systematic observation in expertise research: 1) what should be observed, and 2) how should behavior be observed?

The first decision to make in a systematic-observation study involves selecting the target information to observe. Johnson and Sackett (1998) suggest three broad categories of information common in activity studies: 1) actors (participants), 2) actions (activities), and 3) settings (location). The actors include the subject(s) of interest and other participants with whom he or she interacts. In expertise research, this would include making decision about observing the performer(s), the instructor, teacher, or coach, or the interactions between these actors.

Actions refer to the specific behaviors or activities of interest. In an expertise study, performers' behaviors could range from specific practice activities, such as practicing a new piece in music, to focusing on warm-up, technical, or tactical activities in a sport practice. Specific actions of a teacher or coach that could be linked to the development of expertise include providing technical instruction, strategies, feedback, and so forth. The theoretical or conceptual perspective of the study will most often determine the choice of behavior(s) to record. According to Hawkins (1982), behaviors that have the greatest "functional validity" should be the focus of observation. When observing experts, researchers have to make decisions about behaviors that truly perform a function for the individual's development of skills and performance. A useful approach to selecting behaviors that have high "functional validity" is to conduct a task analysis (Sulzer-Azaroff & Reese, 1982). In task analysis, a performer's practice activities or performance would be broken down into behavioral components so that each behavior usually exhibited in a practice can be observed and assessed.

Finally, the settings include the location of action and the details of the physical space in which the observation is taking place. For example, an expertise researcher could observe the settings of various practice activities and the physical facilities that could constrain or enhance expertise development.

The most probable useful focus of expertise research is on actors (i.e., performer or teacher). Once the actors have been selected, their actions and the setting in which they practice or perform becomes the content of the observation. More rarely, the focus of the observation would be on a specific action or setting. The selection of actor(s), behavior(s), and setting(s) will be directly linked to the research issue under investigation. If researchers are interested in how performers spend their time in practice, they could develop an observation code that would allow them to account for the various activities that a performer can get involved in when training. Another researcher could be interested in the behaviors of expert teachers and could use a behavior code that would include categories of behaviors such as instruction, feedback, modeling, and so forth. In sum, the selection of behaviors to be recorded is dependent on the research questions asked and the overall purpose of the study. Operationalization of the target behaviors will determine the quantitative measures to be gathered. Researchers (Foster, Laverty-Finch, Gizzo, Osantowski, 1999; Hawkins, 1982) have suggested various alternatives that can be summarized into four main choices: 1) frequency, 2) duration, 3) latency, and 4) quality measures.

Frequency

When focusing on frequency of behaviors, the researcher records each instance of the targeted behaviors. For instance, a researcher may keep tallies of a performer's practice of various skills or interaction with an instructor during practices. According to Foster et al. (1999), frequency counts are appropriate when "a) rates of behavior are important, b) the behavior occurs with a lot to medium frequency, and c) the target behavior is a discrete event with an easily identifiable beginning and end" (p. 427).

Duration

When focusing on duration, the researcher records how long each instance of a targeted behavior lasts using a stopwatch or a timer. For example, a researcher may be interested in recording the amount of time devoted to the practice of skills in a specific environment. Recording this dimension of a behavior is useful when the amount of time each episode lasts is more important than the actual occurrence of the episode.

Latency

Response latency or temporal location refers to time elapsed from the moment one has the opportunity to perform a behavior until the same person actually executes the behavior. For example, latency measures of expertise could entail measuring the time period between the beginning of a practice and the actual involvement of the performer in skill-development activities, or recording the time intervals between involvement in effortful activities during practices. Latency measures can provide expertise researchers with valuable information regarding the optimal structure of practices.

Quality

A specific behavior can be observed also in terms of its quality or intensity. For example, a specific practice behavior can be assessed in terms of its effort, concentration, or enjoyment. The challenge in assessing more subjective dimensions of a behavior, such as enjoyment and effort, involves finding observable indicators that can be used as valid measures of these psychological states. For example, one can infer a lower level of effort when observing athletes in practices that sit down to rest, joke around, or observe others train (Côté et al., in press). Alternatively, subjective ratings can be used during practices or at the end of a practice to evaluate the quality of specific activities. When using subjective rat-

ings it is important to provide the performers with clear anchors that trigger a memorable past experience that in turn acts as reference point (Côté et al., in press; Foster et al., 1999). For instance, when rating concentration, performers can be asked to identify the most mentally demanding activity they have ever been involved in during a practice and consider this level of concentration to correspond to 100% concentration. Then performers can be asked to identify an activity during practice where their concentration level had been non-existent or at its lowest level to correspond to 0% concentration. Using these two points of reference, performers can rate their concentration level for all their observed behaviors during a given practice.

In addition to determining the behaviors to be observed and the dimensions of behavior to be assessed, a researcher must select a procedure by which behavior is recorded. This issue focuses on the "how" of systematic observation.

Coding Strategies

Whether observing experts' behaviors live during practices or performances or from a videotape, the researcher must choose a procedure for converting observed behaviors or events into quantitative data. There are numerous strategies by which behaviors can be coded. Four procedures are in common use: event recording, duration recording, interval recording, and momentary time sampling (Darst, Zakrajsek, & Mancini, 1989; Foster et al., 1999; Hawkins, 1982).

EVENT RECORDING

This procedure consists of a tally of each occurrence of a defined behavior throughout the observation session. Event recording provides the researchers with data on the frequency of occurrence of a discrete behavior. Behaviors that could be measured through event recording include the number of times a performer has the opportunity to do a specific drill or an activity during a practice, the number of times a teacher presents verbal instruction during a lesson, or how often a performer arrives late to a scheduled practice. Overall, event recording provides a numerical account of the occurrence of behaviors.

DURATION RECORDING

This procedure is needed when the focus is on the amount of time spent in a particular activity or on the response latency to a specific stimulus. This recording procedure is useful, for example, to collect data on time spent by performers on relevant tasks during a practice, the time spent by a teacher or a coach to explain the technical aspect of a particular skill, or the amount of time spent between involvements in relevant learning activities during practice. In sum, duration recording provides a temporal account of the observed behaviors.

INTERVAL RECORDING

This procedure refers to observing behavior for short time periods (intervals) and making a decision as to what behavior best characterizes that time period. Darst et al. (1989) suggest interval lengths that usually vary between six and thirty seconds. Interval data provides neither frequency nor duration information; however, it can be used to estimate both. A problem with interval recording is when the observation system includes multiple categories and the intervals are so long that several behaviors can occur within the same interval; this situation forces the researcher to make a decision as to which behavior should be recorded. On the other hand, the advantage of this procedure is that it can record behavior that occurs frequently and has starting and stopping points that are difficult to detect (e.g., social interactions, teacher/coach observing during a practice). The data collected from interval recording are expressed as a percentage of intervals in which the behavior(s) occurred.

MOMENTARY TIME SAMPLING

This procedure is used to gather periodic data on an individual's behavior or the behavior of a group of people. With momentary time sampling, the behavior is recorded upon a signal that is emitted at constant time intervals. Contrary to interval recording, where observation starts at the beginning of the interval and continues throughout the entire interval, the observation in momentary time sampling occurs at the end of each interval. Darst et al. (1989) suggest using intervals ranging from one to ten minutes. The length of the intervals depends on the duration of the observation session and the number of sample behavior, needed. With momentary time sampling the researcher records the targeted behavior(s) when signaled. In other words, when receiving a signal, the observer scans the observed setting and records the presence or absence of an individual's behavior, or, if observing a group of people, records the number of people engaged in the specified behavior. Momentary time sampling procedure could be useful in expertise research to observe categories of behaviors such as effort, participation in an activity, or number of individuals on a team or in a class that are involved in a given activity. Data recorded from a momentary time sampling procedure are reported as percentage of total intervals or as percentage of individuals in a group that are engaged in a specific behavior.

Observation techniques in expertise studies allow researchers to investigate practices at a micro level of analysis that focuses on temporal matters such as frequency and duration of specific behaviors. Questions relevant to expertise researchers may concern how often a teacher provides instruction during a class (i.e., frequency), how long before an athlete shows signed of tiredness during a practice (i.e., latency), how much concentration is required to learn a new piece of music (i.e. quality), or how long a chess player spends between moves during a game (i.e., duration). The temporal dimensions that are descriptive of an expert learning environment can be uncovered with proper observation methods. Nevertheless, it is important that expertise researchers tailor their observation and quantification system to the unique properties and behaviors of the expertise environment under examination.

Diary and systematic observation are complementary methodologies in the examination of expert performance. The data each technique provides informs our understanding of both the macro- and microstructure of daily activities and their relevance to the advancement of expertise. Further, the multiple levels of analysis allow for direct and robust assessments of the validity and reliability of the diary data that relates specifically to the activities thought to be relevant to the development of expertise.

References

Andorka, R. (1987). Time budgets and their uses. *Annual Review of Sociology*, 13, 149–164.

Avery, R. J., Bryant, W. K., Douthitt, R. A., & McCullough, J. (1996). Lessons from the past. Directions for the future. In R. J. Avery (Ed.). Household time use: Research in the 21st century [Special Issue] *Journal of Family and Economic Issues*, 17(3/4), 409–418.

Bevans, G. E. (1913). *How working men spend their spare time.* New York: Columbia University Press.

Block, R. A. (1990). Models of psychological time. In R. A. Block (Ed.), *Cognitive models of psychological time* (pp. 1–35). Hillsdale, NJ: Erlbaum.

Bloom, B. S. (1985). *Developing talent in young people.* New York: Ballintine Books.

Cattell J. M., & Drevdahl, J. E. (1955). A comparison of the personality profile of eminent researchers with that of eminent teachers and administrators, and of the general population. *British Journal of Psychology*, 46, 248–261.

Chapin, R. S. (1974). *Human activity patterns in cities: Things people do in time and in space.* New York: Wiley.

Charness, N., Krampe, R. T., & Mayr, U. (1996). The role of practice and coaching in entrepreneurial skill domains: An international comparison of life-span chess skill acquisition. In K. A. Ericsson (Ed.), *The road to excellence: The acquisition of expert performance in the arts and sciences, sports, and games* (pp. 51–80). Mahwah, NJ: Erlbaum.

Chase, W. G., & Simon, H. A. (1973). The mind's eye in chess. In W. G. Chase (Ed.), *Visual information processing* (pp. 215–281). San Diego, CA: Academic Press.

Chi, M. T. H., Glaser, R., & Rees, E. (1982). Expertise in problem solving. In R. S. Sternberg (Ed.), *Advances in the psychology of human intelligence* (Vol. 1, pp. 1–75). Hillsdale, NJ: Erlbaum.

Côté, J., Baker, J., & Abernethy, B. (2003). From play to practice: A developmental framework for the acquisition of expertise in team sports. In J. Starkes & K. A. Ericsson (Eds.), *Expert performance in sports: Advances in research on sport expertise* (pp. 89–110). Champaign, IL: Human Kinetics.

Côté, J., Ericsson, K. A., & Beamer, M. (in press). Tracing the development of athletes using retrospective interview methods: A proposed interview and validation procedure for reported information. *Journal of Applied Sport Psychology.*

Darst, P. W., Zakrajsek, D. B., Mancini, V. H. (Eds) (1989). *Analyzing physical education and sport instruction.* Champaign, IL: Human Kinetics.

Das, T. L. (1991). Time: The hidden dimension in strategic planning. *Long Range Planning*, 24(3), 49–57.

Deakin, J. M., & Cobley, S. (2003). An examination of the practice environments in figure skating and volleyball: A search for deliberate practice. In J. Starkes & K. A. Ericsson (Eds.), *Expert performance in sports: Advances in research on sport expertise* (pp. 90–113). Champaign, IL: Human Kinetics.

Demarco, G., Mancini, G. M., Wuest, V. H., & Schempp, P. G. (1996). Becoming reacquainted with a once familiar and still valuable tool: Systematic observation methodology revisited. *International Journal of Physical Education*, 32(1), 17–26.

Douthitt, R. (1993). The inclusion of time availability in Canadian poverty measures. In Instituto Nazionale di Statistica (ISTAT) (Ed.), *Time use methodology: Toward consensus* (pp. 88–92). Rome: ISTAT.

Elchardus, M., & Glorieux, I. (1993). Towards a semantic taxonomy: Classifying activities on the basis of their meaning. In Instituto Nazionale di Statistica (ISTAT) (Ed.), *Time use methodology: Toward consensus* (pp. 250–276). Rome: ISTAT.

Elchardus, M., & Glorieux, I. (1994). The search for the invisible 8 hours: The gendered use of time in a society with a high labour force participation of women. *Time and Society*, 3(1), 5–27.

Elliott, D. H., Harvey, A. S., & Procos, D. (1976). An overview of the Halifax time-budget study. *Society and Leisure*, 3, 145–159.

Ericsson, K. A., Krampe, R. T., & Tesch-Römer, C. (1993). The role of deliberate practice in the acquisition of expert performance. *Psychological Review*, 100, 363–406.

Foster, S. L., Laverty-Finch, C., Gizzo, D. P., & Osantowski, J. (1999). Practical issues in self observation. *Psychological Assessment*, 11, 426–438.

Frankenberg, R. (1992). *Time, health and medicine*. London: Sage.

Fredrick, J. A. (1995). *As time goes by, time use of Canadians: General social survey*. Ottawa: Statistics Canada; Housing, Family and Social Statistics Division.

Galton, F., Sir (1869). *Hereditary genius: An inquiry into its laws and consequences*. London: Julian Friedman Publishers.

Garhammer, M. (1995). Changes in working hours in Germany: The resulting impact on everyday life. *Time and Society*, 4, 167–203.

Goldschmidt-Clermont, L. (1982). *Unpaid work in the household: A review of economic evaluation methods*. Geneva: International Labour Office.

Grossin, W. (1993a). *Le temps de la vie quotidienne*. Paris: Mouton.

Grossin, W. (1993b). Technology evolution, working time and remuneration. *Time and Society*, 2, 157–167.

Gutenschwager, G. A. (1973). The time budget: Activity systems perspective in urban research and planning. *Journal of the American Institute of Planners*, 39(6), 378–387.

Harvey, A. S., & Elliott, D. H. (1983). Time and time again. In M. C. Casserly (Ed.) & B. L. Kinsley (Vol. Ed.), *Explorations in time use series* (Vol. 6, p. 88). Ottawa: Canada Employment and Immigration Commission.

Harvey, A. S., Marshall, K., & Frederick, J. A. (1991). *Where does time go?* Ottawa: Statistics Canada; Housing, Family and Social Statistics Division.

Harvey, A. S., & Singleton, S. (1989). Canadian activity patterns across the life span: A time budget perspective. *Canadian Journal on Aging*, 8(3), 268–285.

Hawkins, R. P. (1982). Developing a behavior code. In D. P. Hartmann (Ed.), *Using observers to study behavior* (pp. 21–35). San Francisco: Jossey-Bass.

Hayes, J. R., (1981). *The complete problem solver*. Philadelphia, PA: Franklin Institute Press.

Helsen, W. F., Starkes, J. L., & Hodges, N. J. (1998). Team sports and the theory of deliberate practice. *Journal of Sport and Exercise Psychology*, 20, 260–279.

Japan Ministry of Economic Planning (1975). *An analysis of structure of living time: The pattern of use of time and the quality of life*. Tokyo: Authro (in Japanese).

Johnson, A., & Sackett, R. (1998). Direct systematic observation of behavior. In H. R. Bernard (Ed.), *Handbook of methods in cultural anthropology* (pp. 301–332). Walnut Creek, CA: Sage.

Juster, F. T. (1985). A note on recent changes in time use. In F. T. Juster & F. P. Stafford (Eds.), *Time, goods, and well-being* (pp. 313–332). Michigan: Institute for Social Research.

Juster, F. T., & Stafford, F. P. (1991). Comment. *Public Opinion Quarterly*, 55, 357–359.

Kinsley, B., & O'Donnell, T. (1983). *Marking time*. Ottawa: Canada Employment and Immigration Commission.

Kneeland, H. (1929). Women's economic contribution in the home. *Annals of the American Academy of Political and Social Science*, 143, 33–40.

Knights, D., & Odih, P. (1995). It's about time!: The significance of gendered time for financial services consumption. *Time and Society*, 4(2), 205–231.

Krogius, N. (1976). *Psychology in chess*. New York: RHM Press.

Larson, K. B. (1990). Activity patterns and life changes in people with depression. *American Journal of Occupational Therapy*, 44(10), 902–906.

Lawton, M. P., Moss, M., & Fulcomer, M. (1987). Objective and subjective uses of time by older people. *International Aging and Human Development*, 24(3), 171–188.

Lundberg, G. A., & Komarovsky, M. (1934). *Leisure: A suburban study*. New York: Columbia University Press.

McGrath, J. E., & Rotchford, N. L., (1983). Time and behaviour in organization. *Research in Organizational Behaviour*, 5, 57–101.

McKinnon, A. L. (1992). Time use for self-care, productivity, and leisure among elderly

Canadians. *Canadian Journal of Occupational Therapy*, 59(2), 102–110.

Moss, M. S., & Lawton, M. P. (1982). Time budgets of older people: A window on four lifestyles. *Journal of Gerontology*, 37(1), 115–123.

Pember-Reeves, M. (1913). *Round about a pound a week*. London: Bell.

Pentland, W., Harvey, A. S., & Walker, J. (1998). The relationships between time use and health and well-being in men with spinal cord injury. *Journal of Occupational Science*, 5(1), 14–25.

Robinson, J. P., & Godbey, G. (1997). *Time for life: The surprising ways Americans use their time*. State College: The Pennsylvania State University Press.

Rosenthal, L., & Howe, M. (1984). Activity patterns and leisure concepts: A comparison of temporal adaptation among day versus night shift workers. *Occupational Therapy in Mental Health*, 4(2), 59–78.

Ross, M. M. (1990). Time-use in later life. *Journal of Advanced Nursing*, 15, 394–399.

Szalai, A. (1972). *The use of time*. The Hague: Mouton.

Simon, H. A., & Chase, W. G., (1973). Skill in chess. *American Scientist*, 61, 394–403.

Starkes, J. L. (2003). The magic and the science of sport expertise. In J. L. Starkes & K. A. Ericsson (Eds), *Expert performance in sports: Advances in research on sport expertise* (pp. 3–17). Champaign, IL: Human Kinetics.

Starkes, J. L., Deakin, J. M., Allard, F., Hodges, N., & Hayes, A., (1996). Deliberate practice in sports: What is it anyway? In K. A. Ericsson (Ed.), *The road to excellence: The acquisition of expert performance in the arts and sciences, sports, and games* (pp. 81–106). Mahwah, NJ: Erlbaum.

Strumilin, S. G. (1980). Time-budgets of Russian workers in 1923–1924. In J. Zuzanek (Ed.), *Work and leisure in the Soviet Union: A time-budget analysis* (pp. 177–180). New York: Praeger (Originally pulished in Russian in the review *Planove khoziatvo*, No. 7).

Sulzer-Azaroff, B., & Reese, E. P. (1982). *Analyzing behavior analysis: A program for developing professional competence*. New York: Holt, Rinehard, and Winston.

Ujimoto, K. V. (1985). The allocation of time to social and leisure activities as social indicators for the integration of aged ethnic minorities. *Social Indicators Research*, 17, 253–266.

Walker, K. E., & Woods, M. E. (1976). *Time use: A measure of household production of family goods and services*. Washington, DC: Centre for the Family of the American Home Economics Association.

CHAPTER 18

Historiometric Methods

Dean Keith Simonton

Historiometric Methods

Of the many methods applicable to the scientific study of expertise and expert performance, historiometrics is perhaps the least well known and least frequently used. Therefore, before I can discuss the technique any further, it must first be defined. According to one monograph devoted specifically to the subject, "historiometrics is a scientific discipline in which nomothetic hypotheses about human behavior are tested by applying quantitative analyses to data concerning historical individuals" (Simonton, 1990, p. 3). This definition contains three central concepts:

1. *Historical individuals* are persons who have "made a name for themselves" or who have "left a mark on history" by some superlative achievement. Possibilities include recipients of the Nobel Prize, politicians elected President of the United States, world chess champions, and athletes who have won medals in the Olympics. It is this feature of historiometrics that makes it ideally suited for the study of expert performance. After all, such accomplishments

are presumed to require a high degree of expertise, and when expert performance attains world-class levels in many domains, the result will be awards, honors, and other forms of recognition. Of course, the adjective "historical" actually assumes an underlying dimension that is quantitative rather than qualitative (Simonton, 1990). An athlete who wins a gold medal in the Olympics represents a higher degree of achievement than one who is a national champion, just as the national champion represents a degree above an athlete with even more local eminence. Moreover, within each of these groups athletes can be differentiated according to whether they ranked first (gold), second (silver), third (bronze), or even lower down in ordinal position. In fact, in some domains of achievement, such as tennis and chess, objective ranking systems exist that place the leading competitors along an ordinal or interval scale (e.g., Elo, 1986; Schulz & Curnow, 1988).

2. *Quantitative analyses* consist of two features. First, historiometrics requires objective measurement of well-defined variables along a nominal, ordinal, interval, or

ratio scale. In this sense, historiometrics does not differ from psychometrics except that the measurement techniques are applied to historical individuals. Second, the measurements are subjected to statistical analyses using the full panoply of tools available for drawing inferences from correlational data. These two features set historiometrics apart from psychobiography and psychohistory, an approach to the psychological study of historical figures that entails qualitative rather than quantitative analysis (Elms, 1994; Runyan, 1982).

3. *Nomothetic hypotheses* concern general laws or regularities of human behavior. For example, a considerable research literature has grown around whether expert performance in various domains is described by a distinctive age curve (Simonton, 1988a). Thus, in the case of creative expertise, some have argued for a monotonic function like a learning curve (Ohlsson, 1992), whereas others have proposed a nonmonotonic, single-peaked function with a mid-career optimum (Lehman, 1953; Simonton, 1997). This aspect of historiometrics constitutes another characteristic that separates this method from psychobiography and psychohistory. The latter approach favors the idiographic rather than the nomothetic, that is, it attempts to explain the distinctive attributes of eminent personalities. I should also point out that the historiometric emphasis on the nomothetic almost invariably requires that the hypotheses be tested on large samples of historical individuals. Only in this way can the investigator be confident that the findings extend beyond the idiosyncrasies of any single research subject. As a consequence, single-case or $N = 1$ studies are rare in historiometric research (but see Simonton, 1989a, 1998a).

Now that the method has been defined, I would like to accomplish three tasks in the remainder of this chapter. First, I provide a brief history of the method. Second, I offer an overview of the diverse methodological issues involved in carrying out historiometric research. Third, I will review the main empirical findings that this approach

has obtained with respect to expertise acquisition and expert performance.

History

Although historiometrics is not as well known as other techniques, it can be considered the first scientific method that was applied to the objective and quantitative study of expertise and expert performance. To be specific, the first bona fide historiometric investigation was conducted by Adophe Quételet back in 1835. Quételet is best known for his pioneering applications of statistics and probability theory to social phenomena. Much of this work concentrated on establishing the normal curve as descriptive of the distribution of human traits around some central value representing the *homme moyen* (or "average person"). Yet his empirical investigations were by no means confined to establishing the ubiquity of this symmetric distribution. He was also intrigued with the question of how creative productivity is distributed across the career. To address this issue, he scrutinized the lifetime output of eminent French and English dramatists. By tabulating their dramatic works into consecutive age periods, he was able to discern the characteristic longitudinal distribution. In addition, Quételet directly examined the empirical relation between quantity and quality of creative output. Not only was he the first to apply quantitative and objective techniques to biographical and historical data, but he also did so with a methodological sophistication that was not to be surpassed for nearly a century (Simonton, 1997).

Unfortunately, Quételet's (1835) historiometric inquiry was buried in a larger work dealing with different topics, and so this particular contribution was largely ignored (Simonton, 1988a). Therefore, the first behavioral scientist to publish a truly influential historiometric study was not Quételet but rather Francis Galton. The specific work was *Hereditary Genius: An Inquiry into Its Laws and Consequences*, which was published in 1869, albeit as a significant expansion of an earlier historiometric study published as an article four years earlier (Galton, 1865). The main goal of Galton's investigation was to establish a biological basis for *natural ability*, the capacity underlying exceptional achievement in all its forms, including creativity, leadership, and sports. To accomplish this task, he collected extensive biographical data on the family pedigrees of eminent creators, leaders, and athletes, and then subjected these data to quantitative analysis. Unlike Quételet's study, Galton's investigation had both a short- and a long-term impact, thereby becoming one of the classics in psychology (Simonton, 2003b). In the short term, the work sparked a controversy among his contemporaries (e.g., Candolle, 1873) that led Galton (1874) to formulate the nature-nurture issue, one of the critical questions concerning the development of expertise (Ericsson, 1996; Simonton, 1999b). In the long term, the work inspired other historiometric inquiries into the role of genetics in exceptional achievement (e.g., Bramwell, 1948). In addition, Galton's research provided the impetus for James McKeen Cattell's innovations in the area of the measurement of differential expertise, as gauged by achieved eminence in a domain (e.g., Cattell, 1903).

Despite the fact that the research conducted by Quételet, Galton, and Cattell was clearly historiometric, it was not identified as such by these or any other researcher at the time. Instead, the investigations were labeled as "empirical," "scientific," or "quantitative." The method was not actually given a formal name until 1909, when Woods (1909) published an article in *Science* on "A New Name for a New Science." There he defined the technique as encompassing those investigations in which "the facts of history of a personal nature have been subjected to statistical analysis by some more or less objective method" (p. 703). This definition was followed by a 1911 article in the same journal on "Historiometry as an Exact Science," (Woods, 1911) in which he

claimed that the approach has some special value for research on the "psychology of genius." Somewhat surprisingly, Woods's own historiometric inquiries seldom dealt with this issue directly. Instead, his most important publications using this method were on the inheritance of intelligence and morality in royalty (Woods, 1906) and the influence of monarchs on their nation's welfare (Woods, 1913). Hence, subsequent historiometric research most germane to expertise and expert performance was conducted by others.

In this later work one investigation stands out well above the others: Catharine Cox's (1926) *The Early Mental Traits of Three Hundred Geniuses*. This study forms the second volume of Terman's (1925–1959) classic work *Genetic Studies of Genius*. Although the other four volumes concern a longitudinal study of over a thousand intellectually gifted children, Cox's is retrospective. Rather than collect data on gifted children and follow them into adulthood to see if they displayed world-class expertise, Cox gathered a sample of unquestionable geniuses – Napoleon, Luther, Newton, Descartes, Voltaire, Michelangelo, Beethoven, and so Forth – to determine whether they showed any signs of precocious intellect in childhood. After compiling a list of early intellectual achievements and applying the operational definition of the intelligence quotient as the ratio of mental to chronological age (times 100), she was able to obtain reasonably reliable estimates of IQ scores for nearly all those sampled. Significantly, Cox identified her study as an example of historiometrics. Not only was it an example, but it soon became an exemplar of the technique.

In fact, Cox's (1926) publication represents the climax of the early period of historiometric research. Subsequent investigations were seldom as ambitious, and few came anywhere close to the same level of methodological sophistication (see, e.g., Raskin, 1936). The only work to come close to the same level was Harvey Lehman's (1953) book *Age and Achievement*, which dealt with the same issue first investigated by

Quételet (1835) over a century earlier (see also Lehman, 1958, 1960, 1962, 1963, 1966a, 1966b). Nonetheless, historiometrics underwent something of a revival in the 1960s and 1970s. As a consequence, the first book summarizing historiometric findings with respect to genius, creativity, and leadership came out in 1984 (Simonton, 1984c), and in 1990 the first book totally devoted to explicating the methodological issues entailed in historiometric research appeared (Simonton, 1990). Other publications on historiometrics have appeared in the *Annual Review of Psychology* (Simonton, 2003c) and *Psychological Methods* (Simonton, 1999a), suggesting that the approach has become an accepted, even if relatively rare, methodology in psychological science.

Methodological Issues

As a scientific technique, historiometrics departs appreciably from other methods in the behavioral sciences (Simonton, 1999a, 2003c). It certainly differs from experimental approaches, whether laboratory or field, insofar as it depends on correlational data analyses. In this sense it has a close affinity with psychometrics. Even so, historiometrics and psychometrics dramatically differ on several key methodological parameters. As a result, it is necessary to treat some of the technical concerns that are especially prominent in this distinctive approach (see also Simonton, 1990). These issues pertain to sampling procedures, variable definitions, research designs, and methodological artifacts.

Sampling Procedures

Most psychological research relies on research participants who are anonymous and inherently replaceable. This is especially the case for investigations that draw their samples from college undergraduates who sign up as research participants in order to fulfill a course requirement. The specific identity of the participant is not relevant, and one participant is presumed to be essentially equivalent to any other. Historiometric research, in contrast, depends on what has been called *significant samples* (Simonton, 1999a). In this case, the individuals in the studies have known identities, and their identities are such that they cannot be said to be interchangeable with other participants. In particular, the participants are persons who have "made a name for themselves" by attaining eminence in some domain that presumes special expertise. Examples include famous or world-class creators, leaders, athletes, and performers (e.g., Elo, 1965; Oleszek, 1969; Schulz & Curnow, 1988; Simonton, 1975a; Simonton, 1977a; Zusne, 1976). Moreover, these luminaries have attained sufficient distinction to have substantial information about them readily available in archival sources, such as encyclopedias, histories, biographical dictionaries, autobiographies, and biographies. Accordingly, unlike what holds for any other general research method, historiometric samples can include individuals who are deceased. Indeed, it is not uncommon for a historiometric investigation to be confined to eminent achievers who have already finished out their life spans (e.g., Cox, 1926; Raskin, 1936; Simonton, 1975b). This capacity has critical implications for the study of expertise acquisition and expert performance because it becomes thereby possible to examine exceptional achievement across the entire life, from birth to death. It should be noted, too, that because the samples often consist of deceased celebrities, they cannot properly be called "participants," as is the current convention, but rather they must be referred to by the older term "subjects" (Simonton, 1999a).

Given the distinctive nature of historiometric samples, the next question is how to assemble the individuals who will become the research subjects. Sometimes the sample will be defined according to membership in well-defined groups of eminent achievers, such as all Nobel laureates in the sciences (e.g., Manniche & Falk, 1957; Stephan & Levin, 1993). The only limitation may be that some subjects will have to be deleted owing to the lack of necessary biographical data (see, e.g., Cox, 1926). Other times the domain of achievement is not so specifically defined, such as the expert performance displayed by "great generals," "illustrious scientists," "outstanding artists," or "famous composers." In such instances eligibility for the sample is more open-ended. The most common procedure in this case is to sample those individuals who attain the highest degree of eminence in the targeted domain of achievement (e.g., Simonton, 1977c, 1984a, 1980, 1991a). For example, in Cox's (1926) study the sample was derived from the most eminent historical personalities on Cattell's (1903) list, where eminence was based on the amount of space devoted to each person in standard reference works. Because most domains of expertise are not well defined, sampling according to eminence is a very common procedure. However, it does have one major disadvantage: By selecting only those subjects who attain the highest degree of distinction, the investigator necessarily truncates the amount of variance that will be exhibited by many relevant variables. This variance truncation will reduce the expected correlations that can be obtained between performance criteria and various predictor variables.

Variable Definitions

Historiometric inquiries into expertise generally must include two types of assessments. The first type concerns measures of actual performance and the second concerns indicators of acquisition.

PERFORMANCE MEASURES

Most commonly expertise is viewed as an attribute of individuals, and accordingly the assessment of expert performance is carried out at the level of individuals. In this case, individual attainment can be gauged in terms of (a) eminence as recorded by space allotted in reference works (Cattell, 1903; Cox, 1926; Galton, 1869; Simonton, 1976a), (b) the receipt of major honors such as the Nobel Prize or Olympic medals (Clark & Rice, 1982; Berry, 1981; Manniche & Falk, 1957; Zuckerman, 1977), (c) total lifetime productivity or the output of highly influential works (Murray, 2003; Simonton, 1977c, 1991b, 1992b), (d) objective scoring systems such as those used to rate chess players and athletes (e.g., Elo, 1986; Schulz & Curnow, 1988), (e) the attainment of high offices and positions, such as president, prime minister, pontiff, patriarch, or company CEO (Lehman, 1953; Sorokin, 1925, 1926), and (f) subjective assessments based on surveys of scholars and other experts (Simonton, 1977b, 1987c, 1992b). Occasionally, investigators have gauged historic individuals with respect to their display of multiple competencies, usually under the variable category of versatility (Cassandro, 1998; Simonton, 1976a; White, 1931).

However, sometimes historiometricians will adopt a more fine-grained analysis by taking particular achievements or events as the units of analysis. Performance is then gauged according to the differential impact or success of those units. Examples include the critical evaluations bestowed on motion pictures (e.g., Simonton, 2004b; Zickar & Slaughter, 1999), the frequency that an opera appears in the world's major opera houses (Simonton, 2000), and whether a battle resulted in victory or defeat for a particular general (Simonton, 1980). Finally, sometimes the analysis of singular acts of exceptional performance will be aggregated into consecutive periods of a career, such as decades. For instance, investigators might examine how the magnitude of performance changes as a function of age (Simonton, 1977a, 1984d, 1985). Alternatively, researchers might study how expertise in separate domains must be distributed across the career course so as to maximize impact or influence (Root-Bernstein, Bernstein, & Garnier, 1993; Simonton, 1992b).

ACQUISITION INDICATORS

Expert performance has numerous predictors, but certainly among the most crucial is the acquisition of the necessary competence in the first place. This acquisition has been accessed several ways. The easiest is to use an expert's chronological age as a gauge of accumulated domain-specific experience. This is the measure used in the huge literature on the relation between age and exceptional achievement (Dennis, 1966; Lehman, 1953; Quételet, 1835/1968, Simonton, 1988a). A more refined indicator is an individual's career age, that is, the length of time that he or she has been actively engaged in making contributions to a given achievement domain (Simonton, 1988a, 1997, 1998b). For example, in the sciences this may be defined as the years that have transpired since a person received his or her Ph.D. An even better measure for most purposes is the number of years that have transpired since an individual initiated formal training in the domain. Thus, expertise acquisition in classical composers has been assessed by the number of years that have elapsed since they first began music lessons (Hayes, 1989; Simonton, 1991b, 2000). Even more superior, perhaps, are studies that gauge acquisition according to the number of products or achievements within a domain, such as the number of films directed (Zickar & Slaughter, 1999), the number of symphonies composed (Simonton, 1995), and the battles fought or won (Simonton, 1980). Of course, all of these indicators are explicitly or implicitly temporal in nature. Therefore, sometimes historiometricians will assess other features of the expertise-acquisition process. For instance, an inquiry might focus on the influence of domain-specific mentors and role models, including both their number and their eminence (Simonton, 1977b, 1984a, 1992b, 1992c; Walberg, Rasher, & Parkerson, 1980).

Research Designs

Historiometric studies of expertise acquisition and expert performance have adopted a diversity of research designs. This diversity reflects the complexity of history-making achievements, a complexity that requires that the phenomenon be scrutinized from multiple perspectives. Nevertheless, most of the published research falls into one of the following three categories: cross-sectional, longitudinal, and mixed.

CROSS-SECTIONAL DESIGNS

Expertise exists in degrees and thus varies across individuals. At one extreme there are persons who are completely uninitiated in even the basic knowledge and skill, whereas at the other are individuals who display world-class competence – the recipients of prizes, medals, honors, and other forms of universal acclaim. Between these extremes are novices, who at least know the basics of the domain, and those persons who may attain professional status without reaching the highest levels of performance. Hence, expertise can often be conceived along a quantitative scale that defines a dimension on which individuals may vary. The goal of cross-sectional designs is to discover the factors that are responsible for this substantial variation. Of course, the underlying factors are both numerous and diverse (Simonton, 1987a). Yet certainly among the most critical are those factors that pertain to the acquisition of domain-relevant knowledge and skill. Hence, historiometricians have used cross-sectional designs to assess the following: (a) the eminence attained by artists or scientists as a function of the number and distinction of their teachers and mentors (Simonton, 1984a, 1992b, 1992c), (b) the probability of a general winning a battle as influenced by the amount of battle experience he has accumulated over the course of his military career (Simonton, 1980), (c) the magnitude of an opera's success as determined by previous compositions in similar and dissimilar genre (Simonton, 2000), (d) the degree to which the performance of a US president is contingent on prior experiences, such as executive experience as a state governor, legislative experience in Congress, or military experience as an army general (Simonton, 1987c).

LONGITUDINAL DESIGNS

An alternative procedure is to trace the course of expert performance across time. By conducting such a longitudinal analysis the investigator can trace the growth and decline in the capacity for exceptional achievement. This approach has two main forms: individual and aggregated. Individual designs scrutinize the performance of a single expert over the course of his or her career. An example is Ohlsson's (1992) demonstration that Isaac Asimov's output of books can be described according to a standard learning curve. See also Weisberg, chapter 42, for a case study approach. Such single-case designs have also been applied to such historic figures as Napoleon (Simonton, 1979), Shakespeare (Simonton, 1986b); Simanton, 1989b Beethoven (Simonton, 1987b), and Edison (Lehman, 1953). The obvious drawback to this approach is that the observed fluctuations in performance may be idiosyncratic to that particular person. There is no guarantee that the longitudinal results would generalize to a larger collection of experts drawn from the same domain. As a consequence, the vast majority of longitudinal studies utilize an aggregated design (Simonton, 1988a). In this case, performance is averaged across multiple experts, producing an overall career trajectory in which individual idiosyncrasies cancel out. The number of cases making up the aggregated analysis may run into the hundreds. This mode of analysis was first introduced by Quételet (1835/1968) and was most extensively used by Lehman (1953). It is difficult to identify a form of world-class expertise to which this design has not been applied. Examples include creativity, leadership, sports, and chess.

MIXED DESIGNS

Although aggregated longitudinal designs are widely used and have a long history, they suffer from a number of methodological problems (see later discussion). As a consequence, historiometricians have more recently applied mixed designs that integrate individual and aggregate levels of analysis. The first mixed design was cross-sectional time-series analysis (Simonton, 1977b). Here the performance data are tabulated across consecutive units of an individual's career, producing individual-level time series, but then the age functions are

estimated across multiple time series representing more than one career. This approach was first applied to the study of ten top classical composers (Simonton, 1977a), but was later applied to the careers of ten eminent psychologists (Simonton, 1985) as well as to the reigns of absolute monarchs in Europe (Simonton, 1984d) and Great Britain (Simonton, 1998a). A far more sophisticated procedure takes advantage of the latest advances in multi-level designs. An excellent example is Zickar and Slaughter's (1999) use of hierarchical linear modeling to assess the creative performance of distinguished film directors. The method permits the estimate of a typical career trajectory while at the same time obtaining estimates for each expert making up the sample.

Methodological Artifacts

By the very nature of the method, historiometric research is correlational rather than experimental. As a necessary repercussion, such research lacks the random assignment and variable manipulations required for the secure causal inferences found in laboratory and field experiments. Instead, controls must be implemented statistically, most often via a multiple-regression analysis (Simonton, 1990). That is, in addition to the substantive variables that are directly relevant to the hypothesis at hand, the investigator must include one or more control variables that permit statistical adjustment for potential artifacts. In particular, statistical controls help the researcher avoid the intrusion of spurious associations. These controls include such variables as birth year, life span, gender, nationality, and domain of expertise. For instance, one historiometric inquiry examined the ages at which scientists produce their first major contribution, their single best contribution, and their last major contribution (Simonton, 1991a). The specific issue was whether the location of these three career landmarks varied according to the specific scientific discipline. However, such interdisciplinary contrasts are contaminated by the fact that life expectancies are not constant across domains. Mathematicians in particular tend to live less long than scientists in other disciplines. Accordingly, the interdisciplinary differences had to be estimated after first controlling for life expectancy.

The specific source of spuriousness depends on the nature of the substantive question. What may be an essential control variable in one study may prove irrelevant in another. Nonetheless, certain research designs are especially vulnerable to artifactual results. A case in point is longitudinal designs that aggregate results across the careers of multiple cases. These designs are particularly susceptible to what has been called the *compositional fallacy* (Simonton, 1988a). This is a specific form of aggregation error (Hannan, 1971). That is, statistics that are aggregated across individuals may produce age curves that are not characteristic of any individual making up the sample. To illustrate, suppose that a sample of creators is used to tabulate the number of creative products produced in consecutive decades. Let us also assume that the sampled creators vary appreciably in life span. Then the total count of products in the later decades will be smaller than the total count in the earlier decades simply because there are fewer creators still alive in the later decades. Thus, even if there is not age decrement in performance at the individual level, there will still appear an artifactual decrement in the aggregated data. Furthermore, even if an individual-level age decline exists, that decline will be exaggerated at the aggregate level. This is a recurrent problem with many of the empirical findings reported in Lehman's (1953) classic work. Fortunately, methods exist to circumvent this bias. For instance, statistical adjustment of the totals might be implemented based on the number of individuals alive each period (Quételet, 1835/1968), or the sample might be confined to individuals who lived unusually long lives (Dennis, 1966; Lindauer, 1993).

Finally, it is important to recognize another methodological difficulty inherent in studies of the relation between age and expert performance (Adam, 1978; Schaie, 1986). The expected performance of an individual at a particular point in time is often presumed to be a function of three effects: (a) history, defined as the particular point in time (T); (b) cohort, defined as the individual's year of birth (B); and (c) age, defined as the person's chronological age $(T - B)$. Yet it should be obvious that these three effects are not linearly independent. Specifically, if history and cohort are given, then age is fixed. This linear dependence can introduce subtle problems in data analysis. For example, if a study is looking at the number of citations a scientist receives to work published in a given time period, and if variables are introduced for the scientist's age and year when the publications appeared, then it is impossible to also include a control for a scientist's birth year. This means that any variation across cohorts in output levels must be ignored. Because this limitation is mathematical rather than empirical it cannot be overcome by any statistical method.

Empirical Findings

Since Quételet's (1835/1968) pioneering study, historiometric research has come up with an impressive inventory of empirical results. These can be grouped into two categories, namely, those concerning the acquisition of expertise and those regarding expert performance. In each category I will begin by giving an overview of some of the central findings and then end by describing a particular historiometric study that addresses an issue in that category.

Expertise Acquisition

OVERVIEW

Early historiometricians were often interested in the developmental antecedents of exceptional achievement (e.g., Bowerman, 1947; Candolle, 1873; Cox, 1926; Ellis, 1926; Galton, 1869; Raskin, 1936). Indeed, one of the original arguments for the method was that it could provide important insights into the origins of genius and talent (Woods, 1911). Furthermore, many of the early empirical findings have been replicated and extended in more recent historiometric work (e.g., Goertzel, Goertzel, & Goertzel, 1978; Simonton, 1976a, 1984a; Walberg, Rasher, & Parkerson, 1980). The most critical of these results concern the following three factors (Simonton, 1987a).

First, world-class expertise tends to emerge from a distinctive *family background*. As already noted, Galton's (1869) classic inquiry was dedicated to showing that eminent achievers tended to come from distinguished family pedigrees (see also Bramwell, 1948). Although a significant portion of this tendency may reflect the influence of nurture rather than nature, the relevance of genetic endowment cannot be totally dismissed (Simonton, 1999b). For instance, notable individuals in certain domains of achievement are also more prone to come from family lineages in which the incidence rate of psychopathology is above the population average (Jamison, 1993; Juda, 1949; Karlson, 1970). Nevertheless, numerous historiometric investigations have documented how certain family circumstances serve as environmental factors that influence the acquisition of extraordinary expertise (Simonton, 1987a). These factors include socioeconomic class, early traumatic experiences, and birth order (Eisenstadt, 1978; Goertzel, Goertzel, & Goertzel, 1978; Raskin, 1936; Silverman, 1974; Sulloway, 1996). Interestingly, these factors work primarily by channeling a young person into a particular form of expertise. For instance, scientific creators, in comparison to artistic creators, are more likely to grow up in stable and conventional homes with highly educated parents who pursue professional occupations (Simonton, 2004a).

Second, genius and exceptional talent are associated with distinctive *education and training*. Galton's (1869) assertion that exceptional achievement is born rather than made is plain wrong. The literature on expertise acquisition suggests that it requires around a decade of committed training and practice to attain world-class expertise (Ericsson, 1996), an idea that has received endorsement from historiometric research as well (Hayes, 1989; Simonton, 1991b). This acquisition process can take

a multitude of forms, including formal education, private instruction, coaching or mentoring, exposure to domain-specific role models, and various forms of self-education, such as omnivorous reading (Raskin, 1936; Simonton, 1976a, 1984a, 1986a, 1992a; Walberg, Rasher, & Parkerson, 1980). Nonetheless, historiometric research also has pinpointed some important qualifications and complications regarding this "10-year rule" (Simonton, 1996a, 2000). To begin with, the specific nature of the instruction and training depends greatly on the type of expertise being acquired (Goertzel, Goertzel, & Goertzel, 1978; Raskin, 1936; Simonton, 1986a). For example, outstanding leaders require different educational experiences than do exceptional creators, and, within eminent creators, distinguished scientists need distinct educational experiences than do illustrious artists (Simonton, 2004a). In fact, there is evidence that in some domains of achievement it is possible to have too much formal education or scholastic success to be successful (Simonton, 1976a, 1986a). This can be viewed as a form of "overtraining" (Simonton, 2000). In addition, substantial individual differences exist in the amount of time used to master the domain-specific skills and knowledge that are needed for exceptional accomplishments (Cox, 1926; Raskin, 1936; Simonton, 1991b, 1992a). In particular, those who attain the highest levels of achievement are more likely to have undergone expertise acquisition at an accelerated rate.

Third and last, expertise of the highest order is most likely to appear in a particular *sociocultural context*. This reality is indicated by the fact that genius and talent are not randomly distributed across space and time but rather tend to cluster into particular geographical locations (Candolle, 1873; Charness & Gerchak, 1996; Yuasa, 1974) and historical periods (Kroeber, 1944; Murray, 2003; Simonton, 1988b, 1996b). The underlying causes of such clustering involve a host of cultural, social, political, economic, and cultural factors (Simonton, 2003a). For instance, a large portion of the temporal clustering of exceptional creators and leaders can be attributed to the availability of domain-specific role models (Murray, 2003; Simonton, 1975b, 1988b, 1992a). In particular, the number of great achievers in one generation is a positive function of the number in the preceding generation. In the specific area of creativity, some political environments tend to nurture creative development whereas others tend to discourage creative development (Simonton, 2003a). For example, exceptional creators are less likely to develop during times of political anarchy but are more likely to develop during periods of political fragmentation, when a civilization is divided into numerous independent states (Simonton, 1975b, 1976b). Of course, another critical factor underlying the appearance of certain forms of high achievement is the value or importance that a particular culture assigns to that activity at a given point in time (Candolle, 1873; Charness & Gerchak, 1996; Murray, 2003). Potential talent will not become fully realized in a milieu that discourages the corresponding domain of achievement.

ILLUSTRATION

To provide a better idea of how historiometric investigations can contribute to our scientific understanding of expertise acquisition, I will describe in somewhat more detail a specific study in this area (Simonton, 1991a). A major goal of the inquiry was to discern how individual differences in expertise acquisition are correlated with individual differences in expert performance. The particular domain under scrutiny was the composition of classical music. A sample of 120 eminent composers was obtained by taking those who had entries in two distinct reference works. The differential eminence of these composers was then assessed using six different sources, including their performance frequencies in concert halls, their ranking by musicologists, and the space devoted to them in various reference works. This composite eminence measure was shown to reflect a high degree of consensus regarding the creative achievements of these composers (see also Simonton, 1991c).

Next, two sets of substantive variables were defined.

First, for each composer determinations wre made of the total lifetime output, the maximum annual output rate, the age at maximum output, the age at first hit, the age at best hit, and the age at last hit, where a "hit" was a work that had obtained a secure place in the standard repertoire. These measures were all assessed two ways, namely, complete works (or compositions) and the individual themes (or melodies) making up those works. Two alternative definitions were used to take into consideration that works vary greatly in the magnitude of achievement, such as the contrast between a song and an opera. This contrast might be better captured by assessing the total amount of melodic material going into each work, a song having much fewer themes than an opera.

Second, for each composer the age at first formal music lessons was gauged, as well as the age at which composition began, including any juvenilia. These two measures were then combined with the assessment of age at first hit to create another set of variables: (a) musical preparation, or the age at first hit minus the age at first lessons and (b) compositional preparation, or the age at first hit minus the age at which composition was initiated. The first variable concerns how many years transpired between the onset of lessons and the first compositional success, whereas the second concerns how many years passed between the initiation of composition and the first success. Because age at first hit was defined two different ways (works and themes), there were actually two alternative indicators of musical and compositional preparation.

Finally, two control variables were also included, namely, the composer's birth year and the life span. The former allows adjustment for any historical trends whereas the latter permits adjustment for how long the composer lived, a factor that places an obvious constraint on lifetime output as well as the age at last hit.

These measures were subjected to a series of correlation and regression analyses, with each analysis executed twice to confirm that the same results emerged for both themes and works. The analyses revealed that the onset of lessons and composition bore a prominent connection with expert performance. In the first place, the earlier a composer began music lessons, the sooner the first hit appeared, the higher the maximum output rate, and the higher the total lifetime output. The same pattern appeared for both works and themes. Thus, the most precocious and prolific composers tend to begin lessons and composition at relatively young ages. Even more striking were the results for the two preparation measures. Both were *negatively* correlated with maximum output rate, total lifetime output, and ultimate eminence as a classical composer. In other words, the greatest composers spend fewer years in music training and compositional practice before they started to make lasting contributions to the classical repertoire. The abbreviated preparation period is all the more remarkable given that the composers had begun expertise acquisition at a younger and thus, presumably, less mature chronological age. This finding implies that there may exist individual differences in musical talent that allow the most productive and eminent composers to accelerate expertise acquisition in their early developmental years. Lesser composers, in contrast, take a much longer time in music training and compositional practice before they can launch their creative careers (Simonton, 1996a). Yet, ironically, they not only must take longer, but begin later, too – prolonging the acquisition process all the more.

This faster start for outstanding composers is not unique to classical music. The same pattern holds in other domains of creativity, such as the sciences (Simonton, 2002, 2004a). In addition, an early career commencement is associated with other key aspects of expert performance. Specifically, precocious impact is correlated with high annual productivity rates and total lifetime output (Lehman, 1946; Simonton, 1997). Hence, accelerated expertise acquisition is related with exceptional expert performance.

Expert Performance

Once an individual acquires his or her domain-specific expertise, how is that expertise manifested over the course of a career? More historiometric research has been dedicated to this question than to the issue of expertise acquisition. Again, I start with an overview of research findings and then turn to a specific illustration of the technique applied to this question.

OVERVIEW

The main thrust of research on this topic has been to determine the relation between age and outstanding achievement (Simonton, 1988a). As noted in the historical introduction, the first historiometric inquiry into this issue dates back to 1835 (Quételet, 1835/1968). Since then, a host of age-performance studies have been published concerning various domains of world-class expertise, such as leadership (Oleszek, 1969; Simonton, 1984c, 1998b), sports (Schulz & Curnow, 1988), and chess (Elo, 1965). Some of this diversity of domains is seen in Lehman's (1953) classic *Age and Achievement*. This compendium contains age-performance curves for achievements for the sciences, medicine, philosophy, music, literature, art, architecture, film, business, leadership, sports, and chess. Moreover, each of these areas of high accomplishment is usually broken down to numerous subdomains. For instance, the sports include baseball, football, ice hockey, boxing, golf, tennis, car racing, billiards, bowling, and rifle/pistol shooting. Nonetheless, the vast majority of Lehman's tables and graphs concern some form of creativity, an emphasis reflected in the general literature as well (Simonton, 1988a). Therefore, this brief overview will place the most stress on the key findings in the age function of world-class creative performance. This is necessary because the underlying causes of the age-performance curves often vary according to the domain of achievement. For example, the variables that account for the age curve in sports will not be the same as those that explain the curves in creativity, leadership, music performance, or chess. With that restriction in mind, we see that the historiometric work on the age-creativity relationship has arrived at the following four empirical generalizations (Simonton, 1988a, 1997):

1. The output of creative products in consecutive age periods is described by a curvilinear function. The output first rapidly increases to a single peak in the 30s or 40s and then gradually declines, producing an age decrement that approaches the zero output rate asymptotically. Most typically productivity in the final years of the career is about half the rate seen at the career peak.

2. The specific location of the peak as well as the magnitude of the post-peak decline varies according to the particular domain of creative achievement. In some fields such as lyric poetry and mathematics the peak arrives relatively early and the age decrement is usually large, whereas in fields like history and geology the peak comes later and the ensuing decline is minimal.

3. Properly speaking, the age functions just described are based on career age rather than chronological age. In any given field there will always appear considerable individual differences in the age at career onset (e.g., age at receiving a doctorate). Those with an accelerated onset (early bloomers) will have their career peak occur earlier in chronological age, whereas those with a delayed onset (late bloomers) will have their career peak appear later. The latter temporal shift is commonplace for those creators who exhibited a mid-life career change.

4. The age-performance curves are the same for both quantity and quality of output. That is, the production of total works independent of creative impact follows the same longitudinal form as the production of just those works that manage to exert some influence on the domain of creativity. As a consequence, a creator's best work is more likely to appear in those periods in which the most total work appears. In fact, the ratio of "hits" to total output per age period does not systematically change over time, a finding known as the *equal-odds rule* (Simonton, 1997).

It should be pointed out that many of the above results apply to other domains of outstanding achievement. For instance, the curvilinear function seen in creative domains has a very similar form in leadership, sports, and chess, where single-peaked functions are commonplace (Elo, 1965; Lehman, 1953; Schulz & Curnow, 1988). At the same time, the specific form of the curve, including the location of the peak and the post-peak decline, also varies from domain to domain. For example, the age for top performance in sports depends on the specific event (Lehman, 1953; Schulz & Curnow, 1988). On the other hand, some of the findings for creative achievement do not necessarily hold for other forms of world-class expert performance. A case in point regards the distinction between career and chronological age. To the extent that performance depends on physiological rather than psychological variables, the longitudinal curves will be defined in terms of chronological age. This qualification holds for some types of leadership and virtually all forms of sports (Schulz & Curnow, 1988; Simonton, 1998b).

ILLUSTRATION

A good example of historiometric research on expert performance is a recent study of top movie directors (Zickar & Slaughter, 1999). The specific goal was to determine the age-achievement function for 73 directors who made at least 20 feature-length movies for the Hollywood film industry. Because the investigators used a hierarchical linear model, the units of analysis existed at two levels, directors and films. The films for each director were evaluated according to the ratings they received from film critics, as recorded in two movie guides. A composite evaluation constituted the dependent variable for the investigation. The independent variable was the order of the film in the director's career. This order was introduced into the predictions equation in both linear and quadratic functions in order to test for the curvilinear single-peak function found in the literature on creative performance. In addition, acting quality was inserted as a control variable. This was gauged by the number of Academy Awards that each film received in the acting categories (two points for each lead role and one point for each supporting role).

In general, the cinematic performance of the 73 directors was described by a quadratic function. That is, the ratings the films received from critics first increased to a single peak and thereafter declined. The most typical outcome was for a significant decline in performance to set in after the tenth film. Nevertheless, there were substantial differences across directors in the specific form of this curve. For instance, those directors who had higher rates of cinematic output tended to reach higher levels in peak performance, an effect found for virtually all creative domains (Simonton, 1997). More surprising was the finding that directors who launched their careers with an exceptionally successful film were most likely to exhibit a linear decline in performance rather than rise to a yet higher peak. This subgroup probably represents directors whose initial performance was due to luck, and thus the subsequent decrement can be attributed to regression toward the mean.

Conclusions

Although historiometrics cannot be considered a mainstream method in the behavioral sciences, the earliest research on expert performance used this technique. Furthermore, the number of studies that have accumulated since 1835 is truly impressive (Simonton, 1988a). The resulting literature has produced an impressive body of empirical findings, particularly in those domains that entail creative expertise (Simonton, 1996a). Not only do we know a lot about the factors that underlie the acquisition of world-class expertise (Simonton, 1987a), but also we have learned even more about how that expertise manifests itself in adulthood performance (Simonton, 1988a). In fact, the cumulative results regarding the age-performance function in creative domains has become sufficiently rich and robust to provide the basis for complex

mathematical models that can account for the fine structure of careers (Simonton, 1984b, 1989a, 1997). Of course, there remain considerable gaps in our knowledge. This is particularly apparent in those domains outside creative achievement – most notably the diverse forms of leadership. In addition, even in domains pertaining to creativity we have much more to learn about the developmental correlates of expertise acquisition. Indeed, no matter what the domain, much more is known about expert performance than about how experts acquire the capacity to perform at world-class levels.

Admittedly, historiometric methods have certain features that militate against its wide usage in empirical research. As a correlational method, it lacks the power of causal inference that is enjoyed by experimental methods. Historiometrics also has to rely on biographical and historical data that is sometimes of questionable reliability. Furthermore, historiometric inquiries focus on a subject pool or "research participants" that depart significantly from the norm. Rather than anonymous college undergraduates earning extra credit points in introductory psychology classes, historiometric samples invariably consist of individuals whose achievements have earned them a place in the annals of history (Simonton, 1999a, 2003c). No wonder that historiometric research is rare in any area of psychological research, expertise or otherwise.

Nevertheless, the latter characteristic of historiometrics must also be viewed as one of its great assets. Any theory of expertise acquisition and expert performance must ultimately be able to account for those persons whose expertise reaches the highest possible levels. For example, a theory that explains how students solve science problems in laboratory experiments but not how real scientists earn Nobel Prizes must be considered woefully incomplete. Although other methods exist that permit the direct examination of eminent achievers, these have their own methodological limitations. For instance, Nobel laureates can certainly be subjected to intensive interview and assessment techniques (Roe, 1953;

Zuckerman, 1977). Yet these methods depend on the willingness of such notables to participate. It should also be recognized that some of the liabilities of historiometric studies are becoming progressively removed. In the first place, the historical record is becoming far richer and more complete, in addition to becoming more available in electronic form on the Internet and computer storage media. Even more importantly, the statistical techniques suitable for the analysis of correlational data are becoming more sophisticated and powerful, thereby mitigating some of the problems in nonexperimental causal inference. These statistics include structural equation and hierarchical linear models as well as time-series analyses. By applying these tools to the lives and careers of the leading figures in the major achievement domains, it should be possible to enhance our scientific understanding of both expertise acquisition and expert performance.

References

Adam, J. (1978). Sequential strategies and the separation of age, cohort, and time-of-measurement contributions to developmental data. *Psychological Bulletin, 85*, 1309–1316.

Berry, C. (1981). The Nobel scientists and the origins of scientific achievement. *British Journal of Sociology, 32*, 381–391.

Bowerman, W. G. (1947). *Studies in genius*. New York: Philosophical Library.

Bramwell, B. S. (1948). Galton's "Hereditary Genius" and the three following generations since 1869. *Eugenics Review, 39*, 146–153.

Candolle, A. de (1873). *Histoire des sciences et des savants depuis deux siècles*. Geneve: Georg.

Cassandro, V. J. (1998). Explaining premature mortality across fields of creative endeavor. *Journal of Personality, 66*, 805–833.

Cattell, J. M. (1903). A statistical study of eminent men. *Popular Science Monthly, 62*, 359–377.

Charness, N., & Gerchak, Y. (1996). Participation rates and maximal performance: A log-linear explanation for group differences, such as Russian and male dominance in chess. *Psychological Science, 7*, 46–51.

Clark, R. D., & Rice, G. A. (1982). Family constellations and eminence: The birth orders of Nobel Prize winners. *Journal of Psychology, 110*, 281–287.

Cox, C. (1926). *The early mental traits of three hundred geniuses*. Stanford, CA: Stanford University Press.

Dennis, W. (1966). Creative productivity between the ages of 20 and 80 years. *Journal of Gerontology, 21*, 1–8.

Eisenstadt, J. M. (1978). Parental loss and genius. *American Psychologist, 33*, 211–223.

Ellis, H. (1926). *A study of British genius* (rev. ed.). Boston: Houghton Mifflin.

Elms, A. C. (1994). *Uncovering lives: The uneasy alliance of biography and psychology*. New York: Oxford University Press.

Elo, A. E. (1965). Age changes in master chess performance. *Journal of Gerontology, 20*, 289–299.

Elo, A. E. (1986). *The rating of chessplayers, past and present* (2nd ed.). New York: Arco.

Ericsson, K. A. (1996). The acquisition of expert performance: An introduction to some of the issues. In K. A. Ericsson (Ed.), *The road to expert performance: Empirical evidence from the arts and sciences, sports, and games* (pp. 1–50). Mahwah, NJ: Erlbaum.

Ericsson, K. A. (Ed.). (1996). *The road to expert performance: Empirical evidence from the arts and sciences, sports, and games*. Mahwah, NJ: Erlbaum.

Galton, F. (1865). Hereditary talent and character. *Macmillan's Magazine, 12*, 157–166, 318–327.

Galton, F. (1869). *Hereditary genius: An inquiry into its laws and consequences*. London: Macmillan.

Galton, F. (1874). *English men of science: Their nature and nurture*. London: Macmillan.

Goertzel, M. G., Goertzel, V., & Goertzel, T. G. (1978). *300 eminent personalities: A psychosocial analysis of the famous*. San Francisco: Jossey-Bass.

Hannan, M. T. (1971). Problems of aggregation. In H. M. Blalock (Ed.), *Causal models in the social sciences* (pp. 473–508). Chicago: Aldine-Atherton.

Hayes, J. R. (1989). *The complete problem solver* (2nd ed.). Hillsdale, NJ: Erlbaum.

Jamison, K. R. (1993). *Touched with fire: Manic-depressive illness and the artistic temperament*. New York: Free Press.

Juda, A. (1949). The relationship between highest mental capacity and psychic abnormalities. *American Journal of Psychiatry*, 106, 296–307.

Karlson, J. I. (1970). Genetic association of giftedness and creativity with schizophrenia. *Hereditas*, 66, 177–182.

Kroeber, A. L. (1944). *Configurations of culture growth*. Berkeley: University of California Press.

Lehman, H. C. (1946). Age of starting to contribute versus total creative output. *Journal of Applied Psychology*, 30, 460–480.

Lehman, H. C. (1953). *Age and achievement*. Princeton, NJ: Princeton University Press.

Lehman, H. C. (1958, May 23). The chemist's most creative years. *Science*, 127, 1213–1222.

Lehman, H. C. (1960). Age and outstanding achievement in creative chemistry. *Geriatrics*, 15, 19–37.

Lehman, H. C. (1962). More about age and achievement. *Gerontologist*, 2, 141–148.

Lehman, H. C. (1963). Chronological age versus present-day contributions to medical progress. *Gerontologist*, 3, 71–75.

Lehman, H. C. (1966a). The most creative years of engineers and other technologists. *Journal of Genetic Psychology*, 108, 263–270.

Lehman, H. C. (1966b). The psychologist's most creative years. *American Psychologist*, 21, 363–369.

Lindauer, M. S. (1993). The span of creativity among long-lived historical artists. *Creativity Research Journal*, 6, 231–239.

Manniche, E., & Falk, G. (1957). Age and the Nobel prize. *Behavioral Science*, 2, 301–307.

Murray, C. (2003). *Human accomplishment: The pursuit of excellence in the arts and sciences, 800 B.C. to 1950*. New York: HarperCollins.

Ohlsson, S. (1992). The learning curve for writing books: Evidence from Professor Asimov. *Psychological Science*, 3, 380–382.

Oleszek, W. (1969). Age and political careers. *Public Opinion Quarterly*, 33, 100–103.

Quételet, A. (1968). *A treatise on man and the development of his faculties*. New York: Franklin. (Reprint of 1842 Edinburgh translation of 1835 French original.)

Raskin, E. A. (1936). Comparison of scientific and literary ability: A biographical study of eminent scientists and men of letters of the nineteenth century. *Journal of Abnormal and Social Psychology*, 31, 20–35.

Roe, A. (1953). *The making of a scientist*. New York: Dodd, Mead.

Root-Bernstein, R. S., Bernstein, M., & Garnier, H. (1993). Identification of scientists making long-term, high-impact contributions, with notes on their methods of working. *Creativity Research Journal*, 6, 329–343.

Runyan, W. M. (1982). *Life histories and psychobiography*. New York: Oxford University Press.

Schaie, K. W. (1986). Beyond calendar definitions of age, time, and cohort: The general developmental model revisited. *Developmental Review*, 6, 252–277.

Schulz, R., & Curnow, C. (1988). Peak performance and age among super athletes: Track and field, swimming, baseball, tennis, and golf. *Journal of Gerontology*, 43, 113–120.

Silverman, S. M. (1974). Parental loss and scientists. *Science Studies*, 4, 259–264.

Simonton, D. K. (1975a). Age and literary creativity: A cross-cultural and transhistorical survey. *Journal of Cross-Cultural Psychology*, 6, 259–277.

Simonton, D. K. (1975b). Sociocultural context of individual creativity: A transhistorical time-series analysis. *Journal of Personality and Social Psychology*, 32, 1119–1133.

Simonton, D. K. (1976a). Biographical determinants of achieved eminence: A multivariate approach to the Cox data. *Journal of Personality and Social Psychology*, 33, 218–226.

Simonton, D. K. (1976b). Philosophical eminence, beliefs, and zeitgeist: An individual-generational analysis. *Journal of Personality and Social Psychology*, 34, 630–640.

Simonton, D. K. (1977a). Creative productivity, age, and stress: A biographical time-series analysis of 10 classical composers. *Journal of Personality and Social Psychology*, 35, 791–804.

Simonton, D. K. (1977b). Cross-sectional time-series experiments: Some suggested statistical analyses. *Psychological Bulletin*, 84, 489–502.

Simonton, D. K. (1977c). Eminence, creativity, and geographic marginality: A recursive structural equation model. *Journal of Personality and Social Psychology*, 35, 805–816.

Simonton, D. K. (1979). Was Napoleon a military genius? Score: Carlyle 1, Tolstoy 1. *Psychological Reports*, 44, 21–22.

Simonton, D. K. (1980). Land battles, generals, and armies: Individual and situational determinants of victory and casualties. *Journal of Personality and Social Psychology*, 38, 110–119.

Simonton, D. K. (1984a). Artistic creativity and interpersonal relationships across and within generations. *Journal of Personality and Social Psychology, 46*, 1273–1286.

Simonton, D. K. (1984b). Creative productivity and age: A mathematical model based on a two-step cognitive process. *Developmental Review, 4*, 77–111.

Simonton, D. K. (1984c). *Genius, creativity, and leadership: Historiometric inquiries.* Cambridge, MA: Harvard University Press.

Simonton, D. K. (1984d). Leader age and national condition: A longitudinal analysis of 25 European monarchs. *Social Behavior and Personality, 12*, 111–114.

Simonton, D. K. (1985). Quality, quantity, and age: The careers of 10 distinguished psychologists. *International Journal of Aging and Human Development, 21*, 241–254.

Simonton, D. K. (1986a). Biographical typicality, eminence, and achievement style. *Journal of Creative Behavior, 20*, 14–22.

Simonton, D. K. (1986b). Popularity, content, and context in 37 Shakespeare plays. *Poetics, 15*, 493–510.

Simonton, D. K. (1987a). Developmental antecedents of achieved eminence. *Annals of Child Development, 5*, 131–169.

Simonton, D. K. (1987b). Musical aesthetics and creativity in Beethoven: A computer analysis of 105 compositions. *Empirical Studies of the Arts, 5*, 87–104.

Simonton, D. K. (1987c). *Why presidents succeed: A political psychology of leadership.* New Haven, CT: Yale University Press.

Simonton, D. K. (1988a). Age and outstanding achievement: What do we know after a century of research? *Psychological Bulletin, 104*, 251–267.

Simonton, D. K. (1988b). Galtonian genius, Kroeberian configurations, and emulation: A generational time-series analysis of Chinese civilization. *Journal of Personality and Social Psychology, 55*, 230–238.

Simonton, D. K. (1989a). Age and creative productivity: Nonlinear estimation of an information-processing model. *International Journal of Aging and Human Development, 29*, 23–37.

Simonton, D. K. (1989b). Shakespeare's sonnets: A case of and for single-case historiometry. *Journal of Personality, 57*, 695–721.

Simonton, D. K. (1990). *Psychology, science, and history: An introduction to historiometry.* New Haven, CT: Yale University Press.

Simonton, D. K. (1991a). Career landmarks in science: Individual differences and interdisciplinary contrasts. *Developmental Psychology, 27*, 119–130.

Simonton, D. K. (1991b). Emergence and realization of genius: The lives and works of 120 classical composers. *Journal of Personality and Social Psychology, 61*, 829–840.

Simonton, D. K. (1991c). Latent-variable models of posthumous reputation: A quest for Galton's G. *Journal of Personality and Social Psychology, 60*, 607–619.

Simonton, D. K. (1992a). Gender and genius in Japan: Feminine eminence in masculine culture. *Sex Roles, 27*, 101–119.

Simonton, D. K. (1992b). Leaders of American psychology, 1879–1967: Career development, creative output, and professional achievement. *Journal of Personality and Social Psychology, 62*, 5–17.

Simonton, D. K. (1992c). The social context of career success and course for 2,026 scientists and inventors. *Personality and Social Psychology Bulletin, 18*, 452–463.

Simonton, D. K. (1995). Drawing inferences from symphonic programs: Musical attributes versus listener attributions. *Music Perception, 12*, 307–322.

Simonton, D. K. (1996a). Creative expertise: A life-span developmental perspective. In K. A. Ericsson (Ed.), *The road to expert performance: Empirical evidence from the arts and sciences, sports, and games* (pp. 227–253). Mahwah, NJ: Erlbaum.

Simonton, D. K. (1996b). Individual genius and cultural configurations: The case of Japanese civilization. *Journal of Cross-Cultural Psychology, 27*, 354–375.

Simonton, D. K. (1997). Creative productivity: A predictive and explanatory model of career trajectories and landmarks. *Psychological Review, 104*, 66–89.

Simonton, D. K. (1998a). Mad King George: The impact of personal and political stress on mental and physical health. *Journal of Personality, 66*, 443–466.

Simonton, D. K. (1998b). Political leadership across the life span: Chronological versus career age in the British monarchy. *Leadership Quarterly, 9*, 195–206.

Simonton, D. K. (1999a). Significant samples: The psychological study of eminent individuals. *Psychological Methods, 4*, 425–451.

Simonton, D. K. (1999b). Talent and its development: An emergenic and epigenetic model. *Psychological Review, 106*, 435–457.

Simonton, D. K. (2000). Creative development as acquired expertise: Theoretical issues and an empirical test. *Developmental Review, 20*, 283–318.

Simonton, D. K. (2002). *Great psychologists and their times: Scientific insights into psychology's history*. Washington, DC: APA Books.

Simonton, D. K. (2003a). Creative cultures, nations, and civilizations: Strategies and results. In P. B. Paulus & B. A. Nijstad (Eds.), *Group creativity: Innovation through collaboration* (pp. 304–328). New York: Oxford University Press.

Simonton, D. K. (2003b). Francis Galton's *Hereditary Genius*: Its place in the history and psychology of science. In R. J. Sternberg (Ed.), *The anatomy of impact: What has made the great works of psychology great* (pp. 3–18). Washington, DC: American Psychological Association.

Simonton, D. K. (2003c). Qualitative and quantitative analyses of historical data. *Annual Review of Psychology, 54*, 617–640.

Simonton, D. K. (2004a). *Creativity in science: Chance, logic, genius, and zeitgeist*. Cambridge, England: Cambridge University Press.

Simonton, D. K. (2004b). Group artistic creativity: Creative clusters and cinematic success in 1,327 feature films. *Journal of Applied Social Psychology, 34*, 1494–1520.

Sorokin, P. A. (1925). Monarchs and rulers: A comparative statistical study. I. *Social Forces, 4*, 22–35.

Sorokin, P. A. (1926). Monarchs and rulers: A comparative statistical study. II. *Social Forces, 4*, 523–533.

Stephan, P. E., & Levin, S. G. (1993). Age and the Nobel Prize revisited. *Scientometrics, 28*, 387–399.

Sulloway, F. J. (1996). *Born to rebel: Birth order, family dynamics, and creative lives*. New York: Pantheon.

Terman, L. M. (1925–1959). *Genetic studies of genius* (5 vols.). Stanford, CA: Stanford University Press.

Walberg, H. J., Rasher, S. P., & Parkerson, J. (1980). Childhood and eminence. *Journal of Creative Behavior, 13*, 225–231.

White, R. K. (1931). The versatility of genius. *Journal of Social Psychology, 2*, 460–489.

Woods, F. A. (1906). *Mental and moral heredity in royalty*. New York: Holt.

Woods, F. A. (1909, November 19). A new name for a new science. *Science, 30*, 703–704.

Woods, F. A. (1911, April 14). Historiometry as an exact science. *Science, 33*, 568–574.

Woods, F. A. (1913). *The influence of monarchs*. New York: Macmillan.

Yuasa, M. (1974). The shifting center of scientific activity in the West: From the sixteenth to the twentieth century. In. N. Shigeru, D. L. Swain, & Y. Eri (Eds.), *Science and society in modern Japan* (pp. 81–103). Tokyo: University of Tokyo Press.

Zickar, M. J, & Slaughter, J. E. (1999). Examining creative performance over time using hierarchical linear modeling: An illustration using film directors. *Human Performance, 12*, 211–230.

Zuckerman, H. (1977). *Scientific elite*. New York: Free Press.

Zusne, L. (1976). Age and achievement in psychology: The harmonic mean as a model. *American Psychologist, 31*, 805–807.

Part V

DOMAINS OF EXPERTISE

Part V.A

PROFESSIONAL DOMAINS

CHAPTER 19

Expertise in Medicine and Surgery

Geoff Norman, Kevin Eva, Lee Brooks, & Stan Hamstra

Introduction

Expertise in medicine requires mastery of a diversity of knowledge and skills – motor, cognitive, and interpersonal – which makes it unlike many other fields of expertise, such as chess, bridge, computer programming, or gymnastics. Although some specialties such as pathology or surgery may emphasize one kind of skill or another, most clinicians must be skilled in all domains and must also master an enormous knowledge base drawn from areas as diverse as molecular biology, ethics, and psychology.

Perhaps paradoxically, despite the considerable effort required to achieve mastery, there is no formal equivalent of elite performance, which has been a topic of many other chapters in this book. Though there is stiff competition to enter medical school and only about 15% of Canadian applicants get a position, once in, better than 95% will graduate, get placement in a specialty (residency) program, and enter practice. Once certified competent, competition in practice is absent. Medicine has its legendary clinicians, but these are as rare as Olympic gold medalists and have not been systematically studied.

That is not to say that there are no measures of relative expertise. In some domains, particularly surgery, treatment success can be measured with indicators such as death, complications, or blood loss, and has been linked to physician characteristics like specialty certification (Ericsson, 2004; Norcini et al., 2002) and undergraduate training (Tamblyn et al., 2002). However, studies of clinical reasoning in medicine have tended to use a loose definition of expertise, partly, at least, because participants in reasoning studies tend to be in medical rather than surgical specialties and hence are less likely to have any documented measure of competence. Complicating the picture, "experts" may simply be graduate physicians or final year students, contrasted with learners at various stages, or specialists contrasted with general physicians. Though this approach clearly does not identify elite performance, it is usually the case that the measures show a strong gradient across levels of expertise, so the construct has some validity.

Medicine is also unique as a domain of expertise in that the formal knowledge base is both extensive and dynamic; approaches to therapy are constantly changing with the advent of new drugs, and "keeping up" is a significant hurdle to practitioners (Choudhry et al., 2005). In addition to the shifting sand of formal knowledge, successful practice requires an extensive period of practice, not unlike chess or music, and it is not unusual for subspecialists to undergo as much as six to nine years of apprenticeship before they enter independent practice. The interplay between the formal knowledge of medicine and experiential knowledge has emerged as a central issue in understanding medical expertise.

Not all of the domains of medicine are equally represented in the literature on medical expertise. Indeed, much of what we call medical expertise is really closer to medical diagnostic expertise, and, of this, much is confined to the diagnosis of problems in internal medicine. There are exceptions; much of our own work, for reasons that will become evident, has ventured into areas of visual diagnosis (radiology and dermatology). In this chapter, we will also examine some literature related to acquisition of motor skills in surgery. Still, the subject of our immediate concern is the physician's initial contact with a patient, where she gathers data by history taking and physical examination (and possibly lab tests) in order to arrive at a diagnosis. Although diagnosis usually leads to management, this latter aspect has rarely been studied and we know little about how clinicians choose among various therapeutic alternatives.

Historically, one can discern at least three broad approaches to the understanding of medical diagnostic expertise. Early studies took a process-oriented approach, viewing diagnosis as a general skill acquired by experts concurrently with their medical knowledge, but distinct from knowledge. This model was abandoned in the 1980s and replaced by a paradigm that explicitly recognized the centrality of knowledge. The new paradigm assumed that expertise lay in the extent and organization of knowledge. Finally, recent work has considered that expertise involves coordination among multiple kinds of knowledge.

The chapter loosely follows this historical development in our consideration of diagnostic expertise. However, recognizing that some domains of medicine, such as surgery, involve considerable psychomotor skill, we will address this kind of expertise separately. Finally, repeating a theme in other sections of the book, we will consider the relation between aging and medical expertise.

Medical Diagnosis as a General Skill

In the light of our current understanding of expertise, it may seem quaint that at one time expertise in medicine was equated to general thinking (clinical-reasoning) skills. Early research conducted in parallel at Michigan State University (Elstein, Shulman, & Sprafka, 1978) and McMaster University (Barrows et al., 1982; Neufeld et al., 1981) was predicated on the assumption that medical experts (operationally defined as peer-nominated practising physicians) possessed general strategies or skills to approach clinical diagnostic problems, and that medical students could acquire these skills. The studies had common features: participants were observed taking a patient history and conducting a physical examination with standardized patients (actors performing a patient presentation) in a realistic clinical setting. They were encouraged to think aloud, or were asked to review a videotape and recall their thoughts at the time. All the details were transcribed and mulled over by the researchers.

Two consistent findings emerged from these studies. First, there appeared to be a common strategy across all levels of expertise from first-year student to seasoned clinician. Within a few minutes of the beginning of the encounter, the clinician advanced one or more diagnostic hypotheses, and these hypotheses guided further search for (primarily confirming) information. There was little change in the process with increasing experience. Experts had higher diagnostic accuracy, not because of a different process, but because they knew more and organized their knowledge differently, which enabled them to generate and test more accurate diagnostic hypotheses (Feltovich et al., 1984; Neufeld et al., 1981). This observation is remarkably consistent with studies of chess expertise (Simon & Chase, 1973). But the most surprising finding was that success on one problem was a poor predictor of success on a second problem; the correlation across problems was typically of the order of 0.1 to 0.3, (Elstein et al., 1978), and the factors leading to variation in performance appear to be multiple. Collectively, these findings spelled the death knell for the idea of a general problem-solving process and led to a change in direction and a closer examination of the role of knowledge in expertise.

Medical Expertise as Amount of Knowledge

The new tradition began by adopting strategies that had proved successful in other domains (de Groot, 1978) based on memory for typical cases (for example, chess masters shown a mid-game position for five seconds can recall about 80% of the positions). Instead of actually doing diagnosis, clinicians in these studies read written cases, typically about a page long, then recalled what they had read.

Surprisingly, this method, which worked well elsewhere, led to few successes in the medical domain. Given unlimited time, novices could recall as much as experts (Muzzin et al., 1983), although experts appeared to acquire information more efficiently and attended to more critical information (Coughlin & Patel, 1987). However, intermediates (final-year medical students) appear to consistently recall more information than novices or experts (Schmidt & Boshuizen, 1993).

There are several possible explanations for this apparent anomaly. Reading a page of text takes much longer than the five second exposure to a mid-game chess position. Indeed, Schmidt and Boshuizen (1993) showed that superior recall of experts emerges with short exposure of as little as thirty seconds. Second, in other domains, differences with expertise may occur simply because being able to remember all the details is an adaptive strategy for chess and for medical students (who are often expected to recite details of clinical cases), but synthesizing all the details into a brief but coherent problem formulation, ignoring extraneous details, is a better description of medical experts (Eva, Norman, Neville, Wood, & Brooks, 2002).

There are, however, areas of medicine where it is necessary to keep all the data in mind. Nephrology requires an understanding of abnormal kidney function at a physiological level, which can be understood by examining the relations among as many as twenty numerical laboratory values. Norman, Brooks, and Allen (1989) were able to show a positive relation between expertise and recall; however, apparently this superiority occurs only when experts do not have clinical information available and hence can not infer possible diagnoses from clinical patterns (Verkoeijn et al., 2004).

Regardless, it is not clear what implications are to be derived from these findings. We may conclude, as did Simon and Chase (1973), that experts have large memory "chunks" and this superior memory (when it does occur) may reflect that expertise in medicine, as in chess (Burns, 2004), is an index of rapid pattern recognition related to experience with many cases. But it would appear that such observations yield little direction for improving the education of medical students.

It is not surprising therefore that, in view of the failure of recall measures to characterize knowledge, the focus again changed – this time to an examination of the type and organization of knowledge.

Medical Expertise and the Organization of Knowledge

In this section, we will review a number of perspectives on how knowledge is represented. But before we begin, a cautionary note about research method is in order. The standard approach to these studies is to assemble groups of experts and novices, engage them in some task, and examine the data for differences between the two groups. When differences are found, then the claim is made that therein lies the essence of expertise. There are fundamental problems with this inference. Experts differ from novices in many ways. The fact that a difference is found in some domain does not by itself justify the conclusion that the domain is a central cause of their superior performance. The measure under scrutiny may be a consequence of success rather than a cause, or some other variable may be "causing" differences on both this variable and better performance. Second, it is unlikely that experts represent knowledge in any single form, or even that any representation is, in some sense, more "basic" than any other. Experts, when interrogated, can provide everything from the probability that a child with ventricular septal defect has growth retardation, to the colour of the hair of the last child they saw with VSD (Hassebrock et al., 1988). It is likely that both forms of knowledge, and many more, are available to the expert.

With these reservations, what have we discovered about representations of knowledge? First, investigations have examined three broad kinds of knowledge: causal knowledge (essentially, understanding basic mechanisms), analytical knowledge (the formal relation between diagnoses and features – signs and symptoms – of various conditions), and experiential knowledge (the accumulation of a storehouse of prior cases that comes with experience) (Schmidt, Norman, & Boshuizen, 1990; Gruppen & Frohna, 2002).

Although this classification evolved within medical expertise, it also has equivalents in psychology more broadly. Causal knowledge is a relatively small but active area of cognition, associated with researchers like Kim and Ahn (2003). Analytical knowledge, as we have described it, might be aligned with "semantic memory" in the classical view of memory types, and with prototype theories of categorization (Rosch & Mervis, 1976). Experiential knowledge can be seen as a kind of episodic memory, from the classical view, and is closely associated with exemplar models of categorization (Medin, Altom & Murphy, 1984; Brooks, 1978).

Causal Knowledge: The Role of Basic Science

Medical students spend the first half of their time in school studying aspects of the basic mechanisms of disease, and the last half in wards and clinics with patients learning two kinds of knowledge: first, the formal clinical knowledge of signs and symptoms, predictive value of tests, and preferred management approaches, and second, the experiential knowledge of specific cases. One prominent research agenda has been to investigate how these various knowledge types contribute to the acquisition of expertise.

One of the first attempts to characterize the structure of knowledge was the prolific research program of Patel and Groen, beginning in the mid-1980s. Experts and students were given a written case and were then asked to explain the case in terms of processes or mechanisms. They may have access to a relevant basic science text, before or after the case (Patel & Groen, 1986), or they may just generate the elements from memory. The resulting verbal "think-aloud" protocols were then analyzed using the propositional-analysis methods of Kintsch (1974). Their conclusions were that experts showed greater diagnostic accuracy than novices, had more coherent explanations for the problems, were selective in the use of findings, and made more inferences from the data and fewer literal interpretations. However, experts used less basic science in their explanations than medical students, and experts made greater use of forward reasoning (for example, "The patient has retrosternal chest pain with radiation down the left arm and diaphoresis. It is likely a heart attack," as opposed to backward reasoning like "It might be a heart attack because the patient has crushing chest pain. Or it could be a fever, because she's sweating").

Schmidt and his colleagues (Boshuizen & Schmidt, 1992) used similar methods and arrived at similar conclusions, primarily that expert clinicians actually make little use of biomedical science in routine reasoning. However, their investigations have gone further. In order to explain both the absence of science in clinicians' protocols and the "intermediate effect," where intermediates recall more from case descriptions than experts or novices, they postulated that this knowledge is encapsulated but available in response to specific probe questions (Schmidt & Boshuizen,1993). That is, although experts may not mention the basic mechanisms in their case explanations, they have the information available and can recall it on demand.

A more microscopic look at expertise, within the causal framework, can reveal how concepts themselves are learned. Coulson, Spiro, and Feltovich (1997) did this by examining how misconceptions arise in medical practitioners. They identified a large number of factors that contribute to misconceptions, many related to the fact that practitioners might never have learned the pertinent basic science very well at all.

Perhaps the most intriguing finding of all of these studies is that the role of basic science in expertise *appears* to be minimal. However, this may be misleading. Schmidt's studies show that the knowledge is encapsulated but available with specific probes (Rikers, Loyens, & Schmidt, 2004). Coulson and colleagues (1997) showed that a subgroup of physicians will approach management using an understanding of basic science. Norman et al. (1994) showed empirically that, when faced with difficult diagnostic problems, experts revert to basic science.

Nevertheless, descriptive studies of experts and novices may underestimate the role that basic science plays in the acquisition of expertise. Woods, Brooks, and Norman (2005) have shown experimentally that students who learn a causal explanation for signs and symptoms are no more proficient in diagnosis of straightforward cases than a comparable group who simply learned the signs and symptoms of a disease. However, when the task is made more difficult – by imposing a delay in the test, changing the specific descriptions, or adding extraneous details – students who understand mechanisms show improved diagnostic performance, suggesting that understanding mechanisms may add coherence to the relation between signs and symptoms and diagnoses.

Of course, mechanistic basic science knowledge is not the only kind of knowledge that is learned in medical school. Although medical students begin their learning by an immersion into the basic sciences, they then move to a consideration of diseases and spend endless hours learning the "29 causes of anemia" or the signs and symptoms of Hashimoto's disease. It is reasonable, therefore, to assume that one dimension of expertise is the acquisition of elaborate rules relating signs and symptoms to diseases. Such knowledge may be of a simple list-like form, or may be more of a narrative form, such as an "illness script" (Feltovich & Barrows, 1984; Custers, Boshuizen, & Schmidt, 1996).

Another possibility is that the knowledge may be in more formal structures like schemas, which may resemble a mental "decision tree" from chief complaint to diagnosis. An observational study (Coderre, Mandin, Harasym, & Fick, 2003) examined the clinical reasoning of medical students and experts, categorizing the self-reports as "schema induction," "patter-recognition," and "hypothetico-deductive." The former two processes were more strongly associated with diagnostic success. Of course, the caution we expressed earlier should be exercised. It would seem unlikely that anyone used one approach exclusively. Moreover, it is not really possible to identify cause and effect.

Analytical Knowledge: Signs and Symptoms

This kind of knowledge representation is very close to prototype theories of concept formation (Rosch & Mervis, 1976), where category prototypes contain more features characteristic of the particular category and fewer features characteristic of other categories. Indeed, early work in medical expertise by Bordage and Zacks (1984) was guided explicitly by prototype theory and showed that medical knowledge of diseases within broader systems (e.g., diabetes as an endocrine disease) was consistent with prototype theory (e.g., prototypical diseases like diabetes were mentioned more often, identified faster, and viewed as more representative than less prototypical diseases like Hashimoto's disease). However, they found no particular linkage to expertise, except to show that experts classified prototypical diseases more rapidly and accurately than atypical diseases.

According to a number of authors (Gruppen & Frohna, 2002; Patel, Evans, & Groen, 1989), one critical element of expert reasoning is the problem representation. George Bordage's research program has attempted to characterize the quality of the representation using what he calls "semantic qualifiers" (SQs), which are standard representations, usually bipolar, of signs and symptoms (such as proximal vs. distal, large joint vs. small joint, recurrent vs. acute or chronic [Bordage & Lemieux, 1991]. In turn, he has characterized different levels of expertise related to how these SQs are organized: "Reduced" (few features with no linkages among features or between features and diagnoses), "Dispersed" (extensive but disorganized), "Elaborated" (extensive use of SQs with clear associations), and "Compiled" (rapid and correct summary). An increase in level from Reduced to Compiled has been shown to be associated with diagnostic accuracy (Bordage et al., 1997).

As with all inferences from observational studies, it is not clear whether this distinction is causally related to the better performance of experts – whether it reflects fundamental and stable differences in strategy associated with the acquisition of expertise (Bordage, 1997) or simply more extensive knowledge. An experimental intervention (Nendaz & Bordage, 2002) showed that students could be instructed to make greater use of semantic axes in their discourse, but this had no impact on diagnostic accuracy, suggesting the latter interpretation.

It is likely that clinicians, and good students, have direct access to remembered lists of features and diseases simply because they have spent much time learning such lists. Further, it is likely that these lists may use standard nomenclature (semantic axes) if for no other reason than this is the language of communication among professionals (Eva, Brooks, & Norman, 2001). It is less clear whether they have or use semantic axes in practice, and the evidence to date suggests that these are correlated with, but not causally related to, expertise.

Experiential Knowledge: The Role of Exemplars

A number of years ago, J. R. Anderson (1980) stated that "One becomes an expert by making routine what to the novice requires creative problem-solving ability." In reflecting on expert performance on routine problems in many domains, it certainly seems unlikely to us that, in most circumstances, any form of analytical, feature-by-feature, or causal knowledge is needed. Rather, we solve the problem the same way we always did, by rapidly, and unconsciously, recognizing its similarity to an already-solved problem. Just as the chess master has access to about 50,000 stored positions (Gobet & Simon, 2000), any expert has acquired her expertise in part by working through many examples that can now serve as a rich source of analogies to permit efficient problem solving. Complex or unusual problems may stimulate further analytical inquiry, but this is rarely required (Feltovich, Coulson, & Spiro, 1997).

Psychological exploration of the role of prior examples in everyday concept formation has led to "exemplar theory" (Medin,

Altom, & Murphy, 1984; Brooks, 1978). The basic notion is that every learned category is accompanied by a number of examples acquired through experience, and that these examples are still individually retrievable and provide support for the categorization of new cases that are similar to at least one prior example. Retrieval occurs rapidly and without any conscious application of rules. Since the process is not analytical and conscious, it may be stimulated by similarity based on features that are objectively irrelevant to the category.

Clearly, since the process is not amenable to introspection, the usual "think-aloud" strategies cannot be used. Instead, it is necessary to manipulate, in a limited way, prior experience and then examine its impact on subsequent problem solving. Commonly, therefore, the studies conducted in this tradition all rely on a practice phase, which involves exposure to particular exemplars, followed by a test phase where the influence of these specific examples is examined. This two-step process, with a requirement for multiple examples both during learning and testing, imposes real time constraints, and the studies commonly use visual domains such as dermatology or electrocardiology, which can be learned more quickly than written cases.

Initial studies in dermatology (Brooks, Norman, & Allen, 1991), using resident physicians in family medicine and slides of common dermatologic conditions, showed an increase of diagnostic accuracy of about 10% when preceded by a similar slide, both on immediate test and two weeks later. Subsequent studies, where more care was taken in matching the cases' similarity, show even larger effects: an increase in accuracy of about 40% with residents (Regehr et al., 1994) and 28 to 44% with medical students (Kulatanga-Moruzi, Brooks, & Norman, 2001).

Although these results are impressive, it is difficult to generalize beyond dermatology for several reasons. Dermatologic diagnosis is highly empirical, with little science to clearly and precisely explain why one lesion is pink and another red. Further, the images themselves are sometimes difficult to decompose into features. For that reason, another study was conducted on electrocardiographic (ECG) diagnosis (Hatala, Norman, & Brooks, 1999). With ECGs, the features, though still part of an overall image, are much more separable (for example, an ST segment elevated more than three mm.). The experimental manipulation was actually conducted on verbal information – the age, gender, and occupation of the patient – which was objectively irrelevant to the diagnosis. The test materials were designed to be ambiguous with two likely diagnoses. However, if the nonrelevant historical information were used to recall a prior example, this would lead to the incorrect diagnosis. Accuracy of residents dropped from 46% to 23% when the test-case historical data matched the prior (incorrect) example. The fact that the effect was observed with manipulation of information that was not diagnostically relevant suggests that the process was not available to critical reflection.

Whereas the studies to date provide a convincing case for an exemplar-based form of knowledge organization in the domains studied, it remains less certain how common this mechanism may be in other areas of medicine. However, there is no shortage of anecdotes, and some evidence (Hassebrock, Bullemer, & Johnson, 1988; van Rossum & Bender, 1990), that individual cases can be highly memorable.

These findings suggest that it takes many examples, and not just formal knowledge, to become an expert (a finding consistent with the 10,000-hours practice of chess masters [Simon & Chase, 1973]). But there is as yet very little evidence about how these experiences should be structured to enhance the efficiency of learning. A few studies have begun to examine the effectiveness of different sequences of examples, both within medicine and elsewhere. There is a clear advantage for starting from prototypes and moving to ambiguous examples (Avrahami, Kareev, Bogot, Caspi et al., 1997). Further, mixed practice, where examples from different confusable categories are interspersed, leads to large gains in efficiency over practice blocked into categories (Hatala, Norman, & Brooks, 2003).

The implications of these findings for instruction are not obvious. When one argues that expertise is critically dependent on the organization of knowledge, then it is tempting to speculate that the teacher should spend time teaching strategies of knowledge organization, thereby encouraging students to become compiled learners, to strive for global coherence, or and to use forward reasoning. In one experiment where this strategy was tried (Nendaz & Bordage, 2002), it emerged that the organization may be a consequence of knowledge, not a causal factor in the formation of knowledge or knowledge representations. And although "forward reasoning" has become a hallmark of expertise, there is some evidence that this represents a methodological artifact (Eva, Norman, & Brooks, 2002).

Moreover, it is unlikely that a search for the single representation (whether "mental" or theoretical) that fits all is appropriate. Far more likely, there are multiple forms of expert knowledge, and each may be used to greater or lesser degree depending on the situation. Indeed, recent experimental manipulations instructing novices to utilize multiple forms of knowledge do appear to enable gains in diagnostic accuracy (Ark, Brooks, & Eva, 2004). Experts (and novices) may invoke causal knowledge, rules relating features to diagnoses, or prior examples to solve the problem. So a better question is "How are these various forms of knowledge used in solving clinical problems?" For that, we turn to a limited body of research on the coordination of knowledge.

Coordination of Causal, Analytical, and Exemplar-based Processes

At one level, it is almost self-evident that multiple processes must be operating in medical reasoning, if not simultaneously, at least within the same problem. Although a physician may recognize a patient's problem within seconds or minutes, she then commonly goes through a more-or-less systematic search for additional data before she arrives at a conclusion, presumably based on the weighting of the features against internalized rules. Every so often, more likely for tough or unusual cases, the physician may well "go back to the basics" and reason things out from basic science principles.

The question, then, is whether these different strategies are invoked in response to different degrees of problem complexity, or alternatively, whether all are used to elicit additional evidence and hence decrease uncertainty. There is some evidence that physicians revert to reasoning based on basic science principles when confronted with particularly difficult cases (Norman et al., 1994). On the other hand, Patel and Groen (1986) claimed that experts in another discipline used more backward reasoning, but did not use more basic science when confronted with difficult cases.

The situation differs when we examine analytical, feature-based knowledge versus exemplar knowledge. In a series of studies in dermatology (Regehr et al., 1994; Kulatanga-Moruzi et al., 2001), independent effects of rule-based and exemplar-based reasoning was examined using a clever experimental design, so that performance was assessed on typical–similar, typical–dissimilar, atypical–similar, and atypical–dissimilar slides. Since typicality amounts to the presence of a large number of specified, individual features, an effect of typicality would be evidence of application of a rule, whereas an effect of similarity would result from recognition of a prior exemplar.

The results for both of the studies were similar: an effect of similarity amounting to an increase in accuracy of about 30 to 40%, and an effect of typicality of about 15%. There was no evidence of an interaction, suggesting that the two processes are independent, or additive. The effect of similarity was higher in residents than medical students, and the effect of typicality was higher in medical students, perhaps because medical students rely more on analytical rules, whereas with increasing experience, there is greater use of exemplar-based reasoning. A subsequent study (Kulatanga-Moruzi, Brooks, & Norman, 2004) tested expert dermatologists, general practitioners, and residents with a series of dermatology lesions in three forms – a verbal description, a description followed by a photo, and a photograph alone. Resident performance was best with the verbal description with or without the photograph, and worst with just the photograph. However, general practitioners and dermatologists did best with just the photograph, and worst with the verbal description. Again, this suggests that greater experience results in greater reliance on exemplar-based knowledge, and less on formal rules.

Expertise and the Acquisition of Technical Skills

Although the discussion so far has focused largely on expertise in terms of diagnostic ability, a significant component of medical practice also involves technical skill. However, there has been very little work on expertise in surgery and related technical fields. There are numerous reports of a positive relation between surgeon volume and patient outcome (e.g., Halm, Lee, & Chassin, 2002), but there are virtually no studies that address the direct assessment of expert surgical performance. Almost all of the related research has involved educational and training issues, such as the development of valid measures for curriculum evaluation or identification of trainees for remediation (e.g., Moorthy et al., 2004). These measures evolved from validation studies involving gross differences in relative performance (e.g., senior residents vs. novices), and thus are relatively insensitive to distinctions of expertise among practicing clinicians. But perhaps we can gain some clues about the process of *becoming* an expert by examining this literature, including transfer of learning and correlates of performance.

Learning and Transfer of Surgical Skills

A popular notion is that surgeons possess innate talent; however, the limited body of research touching on surgical expertise appears to be consistent with our earlier sections, as well as previous writing (Ericsson, 2004). We now have some evidence that surgical expertise is acquired and highly local. The ability to perform one task derives from specific practice with that task and does not generalize to other, even apparently similar, surgical tasks.

Recent transfer-of-learning research involves training within a given task and has been driven by developments in surgical simulators, ranging from simple inanimate bench models to computer-based virtual reality systems. Several studies (Anastakis et al., 1999; Matsumoto et al., 2002; Grober et al., 2004) have now shown that technical skills acquired on low-fidelity bench models transfer to improved performance on higher-fidelity models (such as human cadavers), as well as live patients in the operating room, both in laparoscopic surgery (Scott et al., 2000) and anaesthesia (Naik et al., 2001). In these studies, the authors identified essential constructs inherent in the relevant technical tasks and developed low-fidelity bench models to facilitate transfer of these constructs to the clinical setting. One interpretation of this is that transfer occurs because the low-fidelity models preserve the functional (process) aspects of training, and this appears to be more important than structure, at least in the case of surgery and related technical disciplines; that is, trainees are asked to "suspend disbelief" about the physical structure and focus on the process of the task. Once they learn the process components, it is apparently relatively trivial to transfer the task across physical structures.

However, transfer of learning across surgical tasks is a different story. For example, Wanzel et al. (2002) had novice trainees learn a simple two-flap Z-plasty (a procedure to rotate skin flaps along a Z-shaped line) and found that some trainees had difficulty in transferring to a more spatially-complex surgical task on the same physical model, again highlighting the specificity of process learning. An interesting additional finding was that those who had scored significantly lower on tests of visuo-spatial ability had more difficulty in the transfer task, leading to more questions about the correlates of surgical performance.

Correlates of Surgical Performance

Several studies have examined characteristics of surgical trainees in an attempt to predict performance in technical skills. By and large, demographic information (e.g., age, gender) (Schueneman et al., 1985; Risucci et al., 2001), medical school grades (Keck et al., 1979; Papp et al., 1997), and manual dexterity (Schueneman et al., 1985; Squire et al., 1989; Steele et al., 1992; Francis et al., 2001) fail to correlate with surgical ability. It is not surprising that variables such as medical school grades yield no relation to technical skill since these assessments by and large measure cognitive ability, which may have very little to do with technical competence.

But why not the manual dexterity test? A popular lay notion is that surgery requires fine psychomotor control. However, among surgeons, it has been hypothesized that visuo-spatial ability is significant (Grace, 1989; Cuschieri, 1995). Recent work on the relative importance of visuo-spatial and psychomotor ability has found strong correlations between scores on higher-level visuo-spatial tests (i.e., the ability to mentally manipulate and rotate complex three-dimensional objects) and efficiency of hand motion in novice surgical trainees, with Pearson correlations ranging from 0.40 to 0.58 (Wanzel et al., 2002; Wanzel et al., 2003). Surprisingly, manual dexterity did not correlate with hand motion, suggesting that efficient hand motion during surgery may be more closely related to planning and preoperative visualization than precise motor control during subtasks, thus calling into question the importance of a "steady hand."

Is surgical expertise therefore a matter of innate visuo-spatial abilities? We suspect not. Wanzel et al. (2002) found that residents' scores on selected visuo-spatial tests correlated strongly with performance on the Z-plasty. However, following ten minutes of supervised practice and feedback, partic-

ipants were retested on the Z-plasty, and those with low visuo-spatial test scores performed as well as the higher-scoring group. This suggests, at most, that the learning curves might be different. It appears that individuals with low visuo-spatial test scores may have more difficulty *initially* in performing a spatially complex surgical task, but that they can learn the task with minimal practice and training. In a follow-up study, expert craniofacial surgeons who perform spatially complex surgical tasks on a regular basis were found to have visuo-spatial test scores and manual dexterity around the norm (Wanzel et al., 2003), suggesting that their expertise is related less to complex spatial abilities or manual skills than repeated practice under the carefully controlled conditions of training during residency and fellowship.

It is conceivable that intimate knowledge of and experience with surgical tasks, when combined with competent intraoperative judgment, may overshadow any advantage afforded by superior visuo-spatial ability. The ultimate skill may not be related to the same mechanisms that mediate the initial performance. For novices, innate abilities may help in acquiring technical skills, whereas for experts, experience alone may significanctly determine the acquisition of technical skills independent of – or perhaps in spite of – innate abilities.

Aging and Medical Expertise

Despite three decades of research focused on the development and nature of medical expertise, little attention has been paid to the dynamic relationship between age and medical expertise. Krampe and Charness (Chapter 40) address the relationship in other domains, but as indicated at the beginning of this chapter, medical expertise has proven to be sufficiently unique that the impact of age in this specific context must be considered. As the average age of medical practitioners increases along with the population, delineation of expertise in this older and more experienced subgroup could, arguably, have a greater impact on health care than any educational innovations directed at facilitating the development of skills among new trainees.

The relation between age and expertise in medicine is unlike the curves in chess (Ericsson, 2000). In a variety of studies, older physicians consistently perform less well on knowledge tests than their younger colleagues, a trend that is more or less linear from the point of graduation (Choudhry et al., 2005). Recent work by one of the recertification bodies shows this trend is not directly linked to identifiable neuropsychological impairments (Turnbull et al., 2000).

Interestingly, however, an equally strong positive correlation has been observed between competence and years of experience when the clinical information provided to physicians is limited to the contextual information that one would receive early in a patient encounter (Hobus et al., 1987). Similarly, studies have shown that surgical success, as assessed by indicators such as mortality rates, is directly related to number of procedures performed (Halm, Lee, & Chassin, 2002). In one of the few studies examining management skill, Schuwirth et al. (2005) have shown a strong direct relation between experience and management.

These contrasting sets of findings, taken together, support the notion that physicians have multiple forms of knowledge (both formal and experiential) available to them and that the extent to which the latter form is emphasized may increase over the course of a career. Perversely, this suggests that expertise in medicine may be evidenced as much in knowing when to depart from clinical practice guidelines as it is in knowing what the guidelines contain. Indeed, a very recent study of hospital clinicians indicated that consultant approaches to drug therapy were more idiosyncratic than house officers, mainly because they were more holistic and adapted the prescribing to the individual patient, whereas juniors used a more formulaic approach (Higgins & Tully, 2005).

Nonetheless, it does appear to be the case that the benefits of exemplar-based processing can have a deleterious impact if relied on too heavily. Systematic consideration of the causes of poor performance in older physicians suggests that premature closure (i.e., excessive reliance on one's early impressions of a case) may be the primary source of difficulty for those with more experience (Caulford et al., 1994). In other words, more-experienced physicians appear more likely to accurately diagnose using pattern recognition, but as a result of increased reliance on this strategy, they also run the risk of being less flexible, failing to give due consideration to competing diagnoses (Eva, 2002). Historical work into the cost of experience confirms that the more one relies on automatic processing, the harder it is to exert cognitive control when problem solving (Sternberg & Frensch, 1992). More recently, Hashem, Chi, and Friedman (2003) have presented data supporting this idea, showing that medical specialists have a tendency to pull cases towards the domains in which they have the most experience.

This formulation views experience in medicine as a dynamic and evolving double-edged sword that draws on multiple types of knowledge and is influenced by contextual factors. If the initial hypotheses raised during a categorization task such as medical diagnosis tend to arise from automatic, experience-based processes, then a greater amount of experience should improve physicians' ability to generate plausible diagnoses during the early stages of a patient encounter. However, if later confirmation is more controlled and analytic and the controlled or deliberative aspects of memory decrease with aging, it seems plausible that aging physicians might be unlikely to retain conflicting details of case histories long enough to allow them to overrule their initial conception of clinical cases. This possibility is consistent with a large body of work published in the general psychology literature (Eva, 2002), but further research is required within medicine to determine the extent to which predictions that arise from this hypothesis are supported, and the extent to which the implications generated prove capable of improving the efficacy of efforts to maintain expertise.

Conclusions

Several central themes emerge from this review. First, as we indicated in the introduction, medical expertise explicitly involves coordination of both analytical and experiential knowledge. We are just beginning to understand the interplay between these two forms of knowledge. Extensive experience, which, among other things, amounts to acquisition of multiple examples, is an important component of medical expertise, as in many other domains reviewed in this book. But in medicine, it is insufficient as an explanation for what makes it possible for people to achieve expertise. Second, despite the unique features of medicine, some other commonalities emerge. Just as in sport or chess, certain lay notions of skill or talent find little support in this literature. General skills are as inadequate an explanation for surgical expertise as they are for violin expertise. Instead, cognitive processes and the knowledge on which they are based emerge as central to expertise in every domain of medicine.

Acknowledgments

This work was supported in part by grants from the Physicians' Services Incorporated Foundation of Ontario and the Natural Sciences and Engineering Research Council (NSERC) of Canada.

References

Anastakis, D. J., Regehr, G., Reznick, R. K., Cusimano, M. D., Murnaghan, J., Brown, M., & Hutchison, C. (1999). Assessment of technical skills transfer from the bench training model to the human model. *American Journal of Surgery*, 177, 167–170.

Ark, T. K., Brooks, L. R., & Eva, K. W. (2006). Giving learners the best of both worlds: Do clinical teachers need to guard against teaching pattern recognition to novices? *Academic Medicine*; In press.

Avrahami, J., Kareev, Y., Bogot, Y., Caspi, R. et al. (1997). Teaching by examples: Implications for the process of category acquisition. *Quarterly Journal of Experimental Psychology*, 50A, 586–606.

Anderson, J. R. (1980). *Cognitive psychology and its implications* (p. 292). San Francisco: W. H. Freeman.

Barrows, H. S., Norman, G. R., Neufeld, V. R., & Feightner, J. W. (1982). The clinical reasoning process of randomly selected physicians in general medical practice. *Clinical and Investigative Medicine*, 5, 49–56.

Bordage, G., & Zacks, R. (1984). The structure and knowledge in the memories of medical students and general practitioners: Categories and prototypes. *Medical Education*, 18, 406–416.

Bordage, G., & Lemieux, M. (1991). Semantic structures and diagnostic thinking of experts and novices. *Academic Medicine*, 66, S70–S72.

Bordage, G., Connell, K. J., Chang, R. W., Gecht, M. R., & Sinacore, J. M. (1997). Assessing the semantic content of clinical case presentations: Studies of reliability and concurrent validity. *Academic Medicine*, 72, S37–S39.

Boshuizen, H. P. A., & Schmidt, H. G. (1992). Biomedical knowledge and clinical expertise. *Cognitive Science*, 16, 153–184.

Brooks, L. R. (1978). Decentralized control of categorization: The role of prior processing episodes. In U. Neisser (Ed.), *Concepts and conceptual development* (pp. 141–174). Cambridge: Cambridge University Press.

Brooks, L. R., Norman, G. R., & Allen, S. W. (1991). The role of specific similarity in a medical diagnostic task. *Journal of Experimental Psychology: General*, 120, 278–287.

Burns, B. D. (2004). The effects of speed on skilled chess performance. *Psychological Science*, 15, 442–447.

Caulford, P. G., Lamb, S. B., Kaigas, T. B., Hanna, E., Norman, G. R., & Davis, D. A. (1994). Physician incompetence: Specific problems and predictors. *Academic Medicine*, 69, S16–S18.

Choudhry, N. K., Fletcher, R. H., & Soumerai, S. B. (2005). Systematic review: The relationship between clinical experience and quality of health care. *Annals of Internal Medicine*, 142, 260–273.

Coderre, S., Mandin, H., Harasym, P. H., & Fick, G. H. (2003). Diagnostic reasoning strategies and diagnostic success. *Medical Education, 37,* 695–703.

Coughlin, L. D., & Patel, V. L. (1987). Processing of critical information by physicians and medical students. *Journal of Medical Education, 62,* 818–828.

Coulson, R. L., Feltovich, P. J., & Spiro, R. J. (1997). Cognitive flexibility in medicine: An application to the recognition and understanding of hypertension. *Advances in Health Sciences Education, 2,* 141–161.

Cuschieri, A. (1995). Visual displays and visual perception in minimal access surgery. *Seminars in Laparoscopic Surgery, 2,* 209–214.

Custers, E. J., Boshuizen, H. P., & Schmidt, H. G. (1996). The influence of medical expertise, case typicality and illness script component on case processing and disease probability estimates. *Memory and Cognition, 24,* 384–399.

de Groot, A. D. (1978). *Thought and choice in chess.* The Hague: Mouton.

Elstein, A. S., Shulman, L. S., & Sprafka, S. A. (1978). *Medical problem solving: An analysis of clinical reasoning.* Cambridge, MA: Harvard University Press.

Ericsson, K. A. (2000). How experts attain and maintain superior performance: Implications for the enhancement of skilled performance in older individuals. *Journal of Aging and Physical Activity, 8,* 346–352.

Ericsson, K. A. (2004). Deliberate practice and the acquisition and maintenance of expert performance in medicine and related domains. *Academic Medicine, 79,* S70–S81.

Eva, K. W. (2002). The aging physician: Changes in cognitive processing and their influence on medical practice. *Academic Medicine, 77,* S1–S6.

Eva, K. W., Brooks, L. R., & Norman, G. R. (2001). Does 'shortness of breath' = 'dyspnea': The biasing effect of feature instantiation in medical diagnosis. *Academic Medicine, 76,* S11–S13.

Eva, K. W., Norman, G. R., & Brooks, L. R. (2002). Forward reasoning as a hallmark of expertise in medicine: logical, psychological, phenomenological inconsistencies. *Advances in Psychology Research, 8,* 25–40.

Eva, K. W., Norman, G. R., Neville, A. J., Wood, T. J., & Brooks, L. R. (2002). Expert / novice differences in memory: A reformulation. *Teaching and Learning in Medicine, 14,* 257–263.

Feltovich, P. J., Johnson, P. E., Moller, J. H., & Swanson, D. B. (1984). The role and development of medical knowledge in diagnostic expertise. In W. J. Clancey & E. H. Shortliffe (Eds.), *Readings in medical artificial intelligence: The first decade.* Reading, MA: Addison Wesley.

Feltovich, P. J., & Barrows, H. S. (1984). Issues of generality in medical problem solving. In H. G. Schmidt & M. L. DeVolder (Eds.), *Tutorials in problem-based learning.* Assen, the Netherlands: Van Gorcum.

Feltovich, P. J., Coulson, R. L., & Spiro, R. J. (1997). Issues of expert flexibilty in contexts characterized by complexity and change. In P. J. Feltovich, K. D. Ford, & R. R. Hoffman (Eds.), *Expertise in context: Human and machine.* Menlo Park, CA: AAAI / MIT Press.

Francis, N. K., Hanna, G. B., Cresswell, A. B., Carter, F. J., & Cuschieri, A. (2001). The performance of master surgeons on standard aptitude testing. *American Journal of Surgery, 182,* 30–33.

Gobet, F., & Simon, H. A. (2000). Five seconds or sixty? Presentation time in expert memory. *Cognitive Science, 24,* 651–682.

Grace, D. M. (1989). Aptitude testing in surgery. *Canadian Journal of Surgery, 32,* 396–397.

Grober, E. D., Hamstra, S. J., Wanzel, K. R., Reznick, R. K., Matsumoto, E. D., Sidhu, R. S., & Jarvi, K. A. (2004). The educational impact of bench model fidelity on the acquisition of technical skill: The use of clinically relevant outcome measures. *Annals of Surgery, 240,* 374–381.

Gruppen, L. D., & Frohna, A. Z. (2002). Clinical reasoning. In G. R., Norman, D. I., Newble, & C. P. M, van der Vleuten (Eds.), *International Handbook of Research in Medical Education* (pp. 205–230). Dordrecht: Kluwer.

Halm, E. A., Lee. C., & Chassin, M. R. (2002). Is volume related to outcome in health care? A systematic review and methodological critique of the literature. *Annals of Internal Medicine, 137,* 511–520.

Hashem, A., Chi, M. T. H., & Friedman, C. P. (2003). Medical errors as a result of specialization. *Journal of Biomedical Informatics, 36,* 61–69.

Hassebrock, F., Bullemer, P., & Johnson, P. E. (1988). When less is more: Selective memory of problem-solving experts. Paper presented at the annual meeting of the American Educational Research Association, New Orleans.

Hatala, R. M., Norman, G. R., & Brooks, L. R. (1999). Influence of a single example upon subsequent electrocardiogram interpretation. *Teaching and Learning in Medicine, 11*, 110–117.

Hatala, R. M., Norman, G. R., & Brooks, L. R. (2003). Practice makes perfect: The critical role of deliberate practice in the acquisition of ECG interpretation skills. *Advances in Health Sciences Education, 8*, 17–26.

Higgins, M. P., & Tully, M. P. (2005). Hospital doctors and their schemas about appropriate prescribing. *Medical Education, 39*, 184–193.

Hobus, P. P., Schmidt, H. G., Boshuizen, H. P., & Patel, V. L. (1987). Contextual factors in the activation of first diagnostic hypotheses: Expert-novice differences. *Medical Education, 21*, 471–476.

Keck, J. W., Arnold, L., Willoughby, L., & Calkins, V. (1979). Efficacy of cognitive/noncognitive measures in predicting resident-physician performance. *Journal of Medical Education, 54*, 759–65.

Kim, N. S., & Ahn, W. (2002). The influence of naïve causal theories an lay concepts of mental illness. *American Journal of Psychology, 115*, 33–65.

Kintsch, W. (1974). *The representation of meaning in memory*. Hillsdale, NJ: Erlbaum.

Kulatanga-Moruzi C., Brooks L. R., & Norman, G. R. (2001). Coordination of analytical and similarity based processing strategies and expertise in dermatological diagnosis. *Teaching and Learning in Medicine, 13*, 110–116.

Kulatanga-Moruzi, C., Brooks, L. R., & Norman, G. R. (2004). The diagnostic disadvantage of having all the facts: Using comprehensive feature lists to bias medical diagnosis. *Journal of Experimental Pychology: Learning, Memory and Cognition, 30*, 563–572.

Matsumoto, E. D., Hamstra, S. J., Radomski, S. B., & Cusimano, M. D. (2002). The effect of bench model fidelity on endourologic skills: A randomized controlled study. *Journal of Urology, 167*, 1243–1247.

Medin, D. L., Altom, M. W., & Murphy, T. D. (1984). Given versus induced category representations: Use of prototype and exemplar information in classification. *Journal of Experimental Psychology: Learning, Memory and Cognition, 10*, 333–352.

Moorthy, K., Munz, Y., Jiwanji, M., Bann, S., Chang, A., & Darzi, A. (2004). Validity and reliability of a virtual reality upper gastrointestinal simulator and cross validation using structured assessment of individual performance with video playback. *Surgical Endoscopy, 18*, 328–333.

Muzzin, L. J., Norman, G. R., Feightner, J. W., & Tugwell, P. (1983). Expertise in recall of clinical protocols in two specialty areas. *Proceedings of the 22nd Conference on Research in Medical Education* (pp. 122–127). Washington, DC: Association of American Medical Colleges.

Naik, V. N., Matsumoto, E. D., Houston, P. L., Hamstra, S. J., Yeung, R. Y. M., Mallon, J. S., & Martire, T. M. (2001). Fiberoptic orotracheal intubation on anesthetized patients: Do manipulation skills learned on a simple model transfer into the operating room? *Anesthesiology, 95*, 343–348.

Nendaz, M. R., & Bordage, G. (2002). Promoting diagnostic problem representation. *Medical Education, 36*, 760–766.

Neufeld, V. R., Norman, G. R., Barrows, H. S., & Feightner, J. W. (1981). Clinical problem solving by medical students: A longitudinal and cross-sectional analysis. *Medical Education, 15*, 315–322.

Norcini, J. J., Lipner, R. S., & Kimball, H. R. (2002). Certifying examination performance and patient outcomes following acute myocardial infarction. *Medical Education, 36*, 853–859.

Norman, G. R., Brooks, L. R., & Allen, S. W. (1989). Recall by experts and novices as a record of processing attention. *Journal of Experimental Psychology: Learning, Memory and Cognition, 15*, 1166–1174.

Norman, G. R., Trott, A. L., Brooks, L. R., & Smith, E. K. M. (1994). Cognitive differences in clinical reasoning related to postgraduate training. *Teaching and Learning in Medicine, 6*, 114–120.

Papp, K. K., Polk, H. C. J., & Richardson, J. D. (1997). The relationship between criteria used to select residents and performance during residency. *American Journal of Surgery, 173*, 326–329.

Patel, V. L., & Groen, G. J. (1986), Knowledge based solution strategies in medical reasoning. *Cognitive Science, 10*, 91–115.

Patel, V. L., Evans, D. A., & Groen, G. J. (1989). Biomedical knowledge and clinical reasoning. In D. A. Evans & V. L. Patel (Eds.), *Cognitive science in medicine: Biomedical modelling* (pp. 127–166). Mahwah, NJ: Erlbaum.

Regehr, G., Cline, J., Norman, G. R., & Brooks, L. R. (1994). Effect of processing strategy on diagnostic skill in dermatology. *Academic Medicine*, *i*, S34–S36.

Rikers, R. M., Loyens, S. M., & Schmidt, H. G. (2004). The role of encapsulated knowledge in clinical case representations of medical students and family doctors. *Medical Education*, 38, 1035–1043.

Risucci, D., Geiss, A., Gellman, L., Pinard, B., & Rosser, J. (2001). Surgeon-specific factors in the acquisition of laparoscopic surgical skills. *American Journal of Surgery*, 181, 289–293.

Rosch, E. H., & Mervis, C. B. (1976). Family resemblances: Studies in the internal structure of categories. *Cognitive Psychology*, 7, 573–605.

Schueneman, A. L., Pickleman, J., & Freeark, R. J. (1985). Age, gender, lateral dominance, and prediction of operative skill among general surgery residents. *Surgery*, 98, 506–515.

Schmidt, H. G., & Boshuizen, H. P. A. (1993). On the origin of intermediate effects in clinical case recall. *Memory and Cognition*, 21, 338–351.

Schmidt, H. G., Norman, G. R., & Boshuizen, H. P. (1990). A cognitive perspective on medical expertise: Theory and implications. *Academic Medicine*, 65, 611–621.

Schuwirth, L., Gorter, S., van der Heijde, D., Rethans, J. J., Brauer, J., Houben, H., van der Linden, S., van der Vleuten, C., & Scherpbier, A. (2005). The role of a computerized case-based testing procedure in practice performance assessment. *Advances in Health Sciences Education*, 10, 145–155.

Scott, D. J., Bergen, P. C., Rege, R. V., Laycock, Z. R., Tesfay, S. T., & Valentine, R. J., Euhus, D. M., Jeyarajah, D. R., Thompson, W. M., & Jones, D. B. (2000). Laparoscopic training on bench models: Better and more cost effective than operating room experience? *Journal of the American College of Surgeons*, 191, 272–283.

Simon, H. A., & Chase, W. G. (1973). Skill at chess. *American Scientist*, 61, 394–403.

Squire, D., Giachino, A. A., Profitt, A. W., & Heaney, C. (1989). Objective comparison of manual dexterity in physicians and surgeons. *Canadian Journal of Surgery*, 32, 467–470.

Steele R. J., Walder, C., & Herbert, M. (1992). Psychomotor testing and the ability to perform an anastomosis in junior surgical trainees. *British Journal of Surgery*, 79, 1065–1067.

Sternberg, R. J., & Frensch, P. A. (1992). On being an expert: A cost-benefit analysis. In R. Hoffman (Ed.), *The psychology of expertise: Cognitive research and empirical artificial intelligence*. New York: Springer-Verlag.

Tamblyn, R. M., Abrahamowicz, M., Dauphinee, W. D., Hanley, J. A., Norcini, J., Girard, N., Grand'Maison, P., & Brialovsky, C. (2002). Association between licensure examination scores and practice in primary care. *Journal of the American Medical Association*, 288, 3019–3026.

Turnbull, J., Carbotte, R., Hanna, E., Norman, G. R. et al. (2000). Cognitive difficulty in physicians. *Academic Medicine*, 75, 177–181.

Van Rossum, H. J. M., & Bender, W. W. (1990). What can be learned from a boy with acute appendicitis? Persistent effects of a case presentation on the diagnostic judgment of family doctors. Presented at the Fourth Ottawa Conference, Ottawa, Ontario.

Verkoeijn, P. P., Rikers, R. M., Schmidt, H. G., van de Wiel, M. W., & Kooman, J. P. (2004). Case representation by medical experts, intermediates and novices for laboratory data presented with or without a clinical context. *Medical Education*, 38, 617–627.

Wanzel, K. R., Hamstra, S. J., Anastakis, D. J., Matsumoto, E. D., & Cusimano, M. D. (2002). Effect of visual-spatial ability on learning of spatially-complex surgical skills. *Lancet*, 359, 230–231.

Wanzel, K. R., Hamstra, S. J., Caminiti, M. F., Anastakis, D. J., Grober, E. D., & Reznick, R. K. (2003). Visual-spatial ability correlates with efficiency of hand motion and successful surgical performance. *Surgery*, 134, 750–757.

Woods, N. N., Brooks, L. R., & Norman, G. R. (2005). The value of basic science. *Medical Education*, 39, 107–112.

CHAPTER 20

Expertise and Transportation[1]

Francis T. Durso & Andrew R. Dattel

There are more expert drivers in the United States than any other type of expert. A 35-year-old Los Angelino who commutes an hour to work and travels only minimally on weekends will have spent over 10,000 hours behind the wheel, a number sometimes held up as a threshold for expertise (Chase & Simon, 1973). If, however, instead of a time-based definition, one takes as the criterion for expertise performing a task better than someone with less experience, then our opening assertion about expert drivers in the United States is less apparent.

In the transportation domain, defining expertise in any absolute sense is nontrivial. Self-evaluations, as is often the case, place most drivers as above average (Waylen, Horswill, Alexander, & McKenna, 2004) and are at best weakly correlated with evaluations of a driving instructor (Groeger & Grande, 1996). If we searched the literature for "highly experienced" operators back to the turn of the last century, we would find a plethora of transportation studies, but they would not inform modern notions of expertise.

Instead, we chose to look at relative differences in experience. Table 20.1 details the participant characteristics for a number of the studies reviewed here, along with one modern-day classification scheme (Hoffman, 1996). Expertise is usually defined by number of years operating the vehicle, or miles driven, or hours flown by the operator. Table 20.2 shows a variety of comparisons in relative experience.

We begin by briefly considering the nature of transportation tasks and how experience affects performance in those tasks. From there, the chapter carves transportation into three underlying psychological components, attention, perception, and knowledge.

The Transportation Domain

The sheer number of operators controlling vehicles warrants a better understanding of these human-technical systems. Also, transportation offers a crucible in which basic laboratory findings can be tested and from which insights can be gleaned to inform basic theory.

Table 20.1. *Classification of participants used in studies cited in the chapter. The experience label borrows from Hoffman (1996)*

Experience label	Criteria from selected publications with a **Summary inclusion rule**	Sample publications considered in the chapter
Naivette: no experience or knowledge of the domain	No driving experience; no past drivers ed. Nonpilots	Mourant & Rockwell (1972) Tsang & Voss (1996)
Novice: A beginner; initial instruction	Student pilots (average of 32 flight hours)	Doane & Sohn (2004)
Apprentice: Undergoing instruction	ATC developmental <100 hours cross country 60 hours 361 hours ***in class OR under 400 hours flight time***	Seamster et al. (1993) Wiggins & O'Hare (1995) Sohn & Doane (2003) Schvaneveldt et al. (2001) Schvaneveldt et al. (1985)
Advanced apprentice/ Junior journeyman: Newly licensed with little experience	1 to 52 wk post-license 1 to 1.5 years driving <1 year FPL controller 101 to 1000 cross country 3 months post-license; 1047 miles <50 hours instrument 907 flight hours 2,000 km ***postlicense & (<2 year OR 2000 km) OR <1000 hours***	Duncan et al. (1991) Quenault & Parker (1973) Shinar et al. (1998) Seamster et al. (1993) Wiggins & O'Hare (1995) Chapman & Underwood (1998) Stokes et al. (1997) Sohn & Doane (2003) Wikman et al. (1998)
Journeyman/Expert	20 years licensed driver 5500 flight hours 25 years licensed driver 5 years as FPL controller 8000 miles for 5 years 200,000 km >1000 hours cross country 5 to 10 yrs; 79K miles drivers license; random licensed drivers Commercial license, instrument rating, & 1500 hours 4300 hours ***>5 years OR 4000 hours OR (1000 hrs + other feature) OR 40,000 miles***	Duncan et al. (1991) Tsang & Voss (1996) Shinar et al. (1998) Seamster et al (1993) Mourant & Rockwell (1972) Wikman et al. (1998) Chapman & Underwood (1998) Williams & O'Neill (1974) Stokes et al. (1997) Schvaneveldt et al. (1985) Schvaneveldt et al. (2001) Quenault & Parker (1973)
Experts/Exemplary journeymen	Instructor pilots trained to observe race car drivers license ***"Special" feature plus many years experience***	Schvaneveldt et al. (1985) Duncan et al. (1991) Williams & O'Neill (1974)

Table 20.2. Half-matrix showing relative comparisons extractable from articles considered in the chapter.

	Naïve/Novice	Apprentice	Advanced appren/ Jr Journeyman	Journeyman/ Expert
Naïve/novice				
Apprentice				
Advanced		Seamster et al. (1993)		
		Wiggins & O'Hare (1995)		
		Sohn & Doane (2003)		
Apprentice/ Junior journeyman				
Journeyman/ Expert	Mourant & Rockwell (1972)	Seamster et al. (1993)	Duncan et al. (1991)	
	Tsang & Voss (1996)	Wikman et al. (1998)	Seamster et al. (1993)	
		Schvaneveldt et al. (2001)	Shinar et al. (1998)	
		Schvaneveldt et al. (1985)	Chapman & Underwood (1998)	
		Quenault & Parker (1973)	Stokes et al. (1997)	
Expert/Master		Schvaneveldt et al. (1985)	Duncan et al. (1991)	Williams & O'Neill (1974)
				Duncan et al. (1991)
				Schvaneveldt et al. (1985)

The most notable feature of the crucible is that transportation takes place in a dynamic environment. Many studies of expertise take place in static or less than fully dynamic environments. Studies of expertise in chess, for example, are at best semi-dynamic. However, in transportation, the environment will change whether or not the operator takes an action. Expertise in modern dynamic environments (see Cellier, Eyrolle, & Marine, 1997, for a review) has been of interest since the 1970s with process control (DeKeyser & Piette, 1970), aviation (Bisseret, 1971), and driving (Mourant & Rockwell, 1972) drawing the attention of numerous researchers. Transportation offers complex embeddings of cognitive factors in an operator who is using technology that is embedded in a dynamic workplace that in turn is embedded in a social setting of a rich culture. This *terroir* is certain to add complexity to our theorizing about expertise. For example, in domains like chess, it is not surprising that expertise presents itself as heavily cognitive. In more dynamic domains with perceptual invariants in the environment and choices among tasks for the operator, the analyses may offer new insights into expertise.

The complexity of transportation also carries a price: Variables of interest, such as expertise for this volume, are entangled with other factors, such as aging. So, the expert driver and the experienced pilot found in the literature are typically older than the less-experienced ones. Of course, efforts can be made to control or assess confounding variables, and studies reported here often make attempts to equate groups on age either by matching or statistical control. However, these are not totally satisfactory, not only because the matching is rarely precise, but also because matching on age, for instance, can sometimes introduce other differences between experts and nonexperts. For example, other confounding variables may be introduced when people with ten years of driving experience are matched on age with drivers newly licensed. Thus, some studies forego methodological fixes for the confounding with age, interpretation relying instead on the anticipated opposite effects of growing older (poorer performance) and growing more expert (better performance). In fieldwork, alternative hypotheses can be eliminated, if not from each study, at least from the confluence of studies.

Overall, studying outcome variables, like safety, in transportation tasks (especially in the wild) will likely suggest multiple causes, only one of which will be experience. For example, drivers differ in their styles and willingness to accept risk. They also are able to engage in compensatory behaviors, allowing more distance by driving farther back when they believe their speed of reaction is slowed (e.g., Groeger, 2000). Thus, the relationship between experience and representative performance can be weak (see Ericsson, Chapter 38). Finally, the relationship between experience and a variable like safety raises the question: What kind of experience (McKinney & Davis, 2003)? Expertise in commercial flying is a function of the aircraft; an expert flying a regional jet may not be an expert flying a 757. On the other hand, train engineers are required additional training and certification for specific geographical areas rather than type of train. For our Los Angelena, the routine experience of her daily commute may be of little help if she must swerve to miss the statue of Jabba the Hutt that fell off of the truck in front of her.

Experience in Transportation

The value of experience in transportation tasks has been documented for a number of years and is reflected in everyday life in accident records and insurance rates. Research in transportation dates back to the early 20th century, with selection and aptitude tests of military (Henmon, 1919) and transport pilots (Snow, 1926). Research on experience and driving can be traced back at least to the work of Allgaier (1939), who showed that although reaction time and visual acuity were best for the younger driver, accident rates and traffic violations decreased with experience. World War II brought the need for more sophisticated and dependable equipment. The new field of human factors placed greater emphasis on the skills of the operators and their interaction with the equipment. That focus on the relationship between experience and performance skills continued.

For example, in a field study reported in 1973, Quenault and Parker studied apprentice drivers matched for age; the more-experienced apprentices (as much as a year of practice) showed better car control than the less-experienced ones (as little as a week of post-license practice). Further, all of these apprentices drove more poorly (e.g., near accidents) than older, experienced drivers. Advantages of experience continue to accumulate; for example, when Recarte and Nunes (1996) gave their participants the opportunity to control the accelerator to obtain a target speed, the group with no driving experience had a greater mean error than the groups with driving experience.

However, experienced operators do not always outperform less experienced ones (Duncan, Williams, & Brown, 1991; see Shanteau, 1992, for other examples). Every year, the public is baffled by incidents attributable to errors made by experienced airline pilots. For example, in March 2000, a Southwest Airlines flight overran the runway in Burbank, California stopping just feet from a gas pump. The captain had 11,000 flight hours. Although weather conditions were VFR (visual flight rules) and the winds were relatively calm at the surface, the pilot flew the approach at 50 mph above the recommended approach speed for the conditions and the type of airplane (NTSB, 2004).

More than anecdotes suggest that the relationship between experience and performance can be complicated in the domain of transportation. The literature on expertise and transportation also includes some studies that reach the interesting conclusion that recognized expert drivers do not necessarily have fewer accidents on public roads than would our hypothetical LA commuter. Duncan et al. (1991) compared experts, journeyman drivers, and advanced apprentices in an instrumented car over real-world urban and rural routes. The experts

were observers from Britain's Institute of Advanced Motorists and had held their license for an average of 18 years; journeyman drivers had held a license for about the same, 20 years; apprentices had received their license within the year. Mean ages were similar, between 35 and 41. Of interest to the current chapter are the findings that apprentices and experts were sometimes relatively similar to each other, with the normal journeyman drivers performing most poorly: Apprentices and experts checked mirrors comparably frequently and applied brakes comparably early, whereas journeyman drivers with 20 years experience infrequently checked the mirrors and braked significantly later. This disconnection between experience and performance can manifest for many reasons. Driving accident rates for those learning to drive have been reported at less than one in one hundred, whereas about one in five apprentices one year post license are involved in an accident (Forsyth, Maycock, & Sexton, 1995). Driving under supervision, or driving with less arrogance, or both may explain these results. Williams and O'Neill (1974) showed that licensed racecar drivers had more on-the-road accidents than did controls. Racecar drivers may be more risk tolerant, or the type of experience gained during a race does little for on-the-road safety.

Our approach to understanding these patterns of data relating experience is to consider how experience affects underlying psychological processes. Along the way, we stop to point out how basic research on expertise can be informed by applied work.

Attention

An excellent example of basic research being informed by applied work is the study of expert pilots in low-altitude flight. That work forces us to revisit our beliefs about the role of attention and resource management of skilled performance. Haber and Haber (2003) rightly view low-altitude air combat as at "the very edge of human perceptual and attentional capabilities" (p. 21). The pilot is flying close to the speed of sound, so near the ground that controlled flight into terrain (CFIT) is *the* primary concern, while trying to complete the mission and avoid being shot down.

Haber and Haber (2003) review possible sources of information that pilots could use to determine their altitude above ground level (AGL) and find that both preflight information (such as familiar size, experience with the route) and automatic perceptual processes (such as optic flow, vestibular information) are insufficient or even misleading in the determination of AGL. Instead, contrary to the reasonable expectation that such high-speed processing would rely on automatic processing, Haber and Haber effectively argue for the necessity of focused, controlled attention in these extreme situations.

Expertise in low-altitude military flying comes from explicit training and deliberate practice not only on the maneuvers unique to these environments, but also on task management and prioritization. For example, pilots learn about "free time" (time available for tasks before a CFIT is inevitable) learn about times required by tasks, and learn to abandon tasks failed during the free time so that ground clearance tasks regain priority. This training and resulting expertise on resource management is necessary before a pilot can be effective on an operational mission.

We know from the literature that expert performance on domain-relevant tasks is less constrained by resource limits than is novice performance (e.g., Chi, Glaser, & Farr, 1988; Ericsson & Smith, 1991). Most researchers would argue that resources are less constraining because tasks have become automated. Thus, in tasks more mundane than low-altitude combat, we see that expertise is a factor in resource allocation, but not necessarily by developing sophisticated techniques for performing tasks serially as Haber and Haber's pilots seem to do. In dynamic environments, freedom from constraints accompanies expertise, and this freedom may occur because of automatization

or because of more efficient management of controlled processes.

Although low-altitude combat is an extreme form of transportation, it does rely heavily on attentional components that are found in all transportation tasks. We cover two of them here, namely, performing tasks simultaneously (dual-task performance) and finding information in the environment (visual search).

Dual-Task Performance

Tsang and Voss (1996) looked at expertise in time-sharing by comparing pilots (who were presumed to be experts in time-sharing) with nonpilots. Pilots did, in fact, show a smaller decrement in performance in a dual task (horizontal tracking plus some other task (e.g., vertical tracking) than did nonpilots, and this was especially true for elderly participants (over 60 years). Thus, the results support the conclusion that experience can mitigate age decrements in dual-task performance. In addition, if we accept pilot experience as a surrogate for time-sharing expertise, the data support the notion that resource management is part of what develops with expertise. Other transportation tasks also require managing more than one subtask. An often-used classroom example is, of course, changing gears in a manual-shift car. Apprentices do indeed take longer to downshift than experts (Duncan et al., 1991). Experienced drivers have been shown not only to shift faster, but also to be unaffected by an additional cognitive load (randomly generating letters while driving; Duncan, Williams, Nimmo-Smith, & Brown, 1992). Shinar, Meir, and Ben-Shoham (1998) looked at experience with automatic and manual-shift cars in a field setting. The study took place in busy downtown Tel Aviv, presumably insuring a considerable number of gear changes. The dependent variable was success at detecting designated traffic signs (i.e., "Slow – Children on the Road" and "No Stopping"). Experienced drivers, those with a median driving experience of nine years, were unaffected by the type of transmission. Apprentices (Md = 1.4) who drove standard transmissions detected about 13% fewer signs than did their counterparts who drove automatic transmissions. It is worth noting that operators can be poor judges of whether a process requires attention or resource management, as Shinar et al.'s drivers did not realize changing gears was still a controlled process capable of interfering with other tasks.

As a final example of attention and resource management, consider the work by Seamster, Redding, Cannon, Ryder, and Purcell (1993), who studied expertise in air traffic control. They asked experts (supervisors or at least five years as certified professional controllers, CPC), intermediates (less than one year CPC), and developmentals (trainees) to identify the least costly means of resolving undesirable controller situations (e.g., situations leading to loss of aircraft separation). Transcriptions of controllers' discussion of actions, goals, consequences, and information were analyzed using cognitive task analysis (CTA; see Hoffman & Lintern, Chapter 12).

Seamster et al. (1993) reported evidence that experts were able to switch their attention to service less critical aspects of the situation, whereas apprentices continually went from one critical aspect to another. Thus, ATC experts seem to be better at time-sharing tasks. The CTA also revealed that experts used more strategies designed to manage workload.

Overall, apprentices seem to be more likely than experts to perform tasks serially or to time-share less efficiently. This difference seems to be in part because component tasks are not yet automatic for apprentices; expertise promotes performance that is less constrained by mental resources. This notion, that experts come to perform certain tasks automatically, seems to reach its limit however in some cognitively and perceptually extreme environments, such as low-altitude military combat. In fact, in those environments, because the automatic cues are untrustworthy, experts

seem to have some of the characteristics that less experienced journeymen exhibit in less-demanding situations: They process tasks serially and with focused attention. Recently, Beilock, Carr, MacMahon, and Starkes (2002), in work outside of transportation (i.e., golf), found empirical support for the contention that apprentices, and the weaker skills of experts, are helped by attending to the constituent steps of performance. However, such attentional monitoring hurts high-level skills. This finding can help explain the expertise and attention literature reviewed here, including the results of low-altitude combat pilots.

Overall, in addition to the development of more efficient or more automatic information processing, experts seem to have developed explicit resource management strategies that less-experienced operators have not. As with the development of automaticity, the efficient management of tasks can free resources, giving the expert additional capacity that the apprentice cannot extract. In complex dynamic tasks where there are multiple tasks, experts will spend time explicitly managing their tasks, whether as an air traffic controller on the ground, or a fighter pilot close to it.

We turn now to the task that is always one of the simultaneous tasks performed by transportation operators, scanning the environment through which they are moving.

Visual Search Behavior

It is well known by operators in dynamic environments that "scanning" for data or information is critical to success. In fact, scanning is often explicitly trained. In air traffic control, apprentice controllers are explicitly instructed to acquire a scan pattern across the radar display and other equipment that allows coverage of the scope without being lured into any particular problem in one part of the airspace. New drivers are explicitly taught to develop a scan pattern involving the road and the vehicle's mirrors. Similar training is required of pilots, that is, scanning the horizon and their instruments (e.g., Bellenkes, Wickens, & Kramer, 1997).

Experienced and inexperienced drivers have been thought to differ in some aspects of their eye-movement patterns. For example, some evidence exists that apprentices concentrate their search in a smaller area, closer to the front of the vehicle, than do journeymen who look at the focus of expansion (e.g., Mourant & Rockwell, 1972; cf. Wikman, Nieminen, & Summala, 1998). Beginners are thought to use foveal vision to keep the car on the road, whereas experienced drivers make better use of peripheral vision (Wikman et al., 1998).

Although reliable scanning differences are sometimes uncovered, scanning differences are often swamped by the variability in novice or apprentice data. This difference is not surprising if one assumes that novices have yet to develop the underlying cognitive representations that allow for good supervisory control. Greater variability in novices is often taken as an indication that automated processes have not been developed. Wikman et al. (1998), for example, suggest that automated performance is more stereotyped and consistent. More variable does not imply, however, more flexible. Crundall and Underwood (1998) found less-experienced drivers showed no differences when driving on a quiet rural road as compared to driving a busier multi-lane road. With experience, drivers develop particular scanning strategies for particular situations.

The difference in expert and novice scanning strategies can also bear on understanding resource management. If one views supervisory control as related to resource management, then we again observe support for a resource management deficit in nonexperts. Consider Wikman et al. (1998), who asked young apprentices and older, experienced drivers to drive an instrumented compact car on a 126 km route in three hours. During this time the participants were occasionally asked to timeshare with another task (e.g., dial their own number on a cellphone, search for soft music on the radio). Of interest here is the finding that apprentices' glances were more variable, and included a greater percentage of extreme (short or long) glances from the road to the shared task. Short looks are likely ineffective, and long looks dangerous. Forty percent of the male apprentices looked away from the road for over three seconds; experts never took their eyes off the road for this length of time. Disturbing is the possibility that this tendency to take longer fixations may be especially true in dangerous situations (Chapman & Underwood, 1998).

Thus, experts and apprentices seem to differ in their visual search patterns, but it is not always the case that expertise differences will be found in eye-movement patterns. Part of this difficulty may rest with the variability produced in the behaviors of novices, but this variability may be more than an inconvenience to statistical tests. This variability may reflect the processes that novices employ, the controlled nature of those processes, and may prove to be a fundamental characteristic of novice cognition in dynamic environments.

Perception

Although experienced and inexperienced operators may scan their environments differently, there is also evidence that experts and nonexperts perceive the world differently. It is likely that experts have learned to interpret not just informational cues, but also cue configurations and structural invariants in their dynamic environments that apprentices have not learned to perceive: The blurring of the passing landscape can substitute nicely for a glance at the speedometer. In an experiment where drivers viewed video clips photographed from inside a minibus, experienced drivers seemed to have no problem judging distance when switching back and forth between targets in a convex mirror (when the angle of convexity is appropriate) and objects in the direct visual field (Fisher & Galer, 1984). Thus, when it is said that experts and novices see the world differently, it can mean several things. An expert might notice things that an apprentice does not (e.g., an oil spot); an expert might interpret an object as a threat (e.g., to braking), whereas the apprentice may see the same object but not see it as threatering; or, both might see the object as a threat, but the expert sees also the solution (e.g., swerve). See Klein (1997) for a discussion of recognition-primed decision making.

Perceiving and interpreting patterns can be considered from a number of perspectives. Here we consider two overlapping areas of research: how well an operator can detect a problem (hazard detection), and how well an operator understands the situation (situation awareness).

Hazard Detection

If experts have freed resources by automating some constituent processes or by superior resource management, what might they do with those freed resources? The transportation literature suggests that one thing they do is apply the resources to hazard detection (Horswill & McKenna, 2004).

Horswill and McKenna (2004) point out that despite evidence from driving research that experience leads to automatic performance, this automaticity does *not* predict safer driving (e.g., Williams & O'Neill, 1974). In fact, it is difficult to find studies that suggest that driver skill, or better vehicle control skills, predict driver safety on public roads. Perhaps it is driver style – the desire to speed and take risks (Wasielewski, 1984) – rather than driver skill. Elander, West, and French's (1993) review of the literature admits a place for driver style but also argues for the speed of hazard detection as a factor in driver performance. Perhaps the vehicle-control skills develop quickly, leaving only the more cognitive aspects of driving, like hazard detection, with enough variance to account for differences in performance.

In a prototypical hazard-detection study, the participant sits in front of a monitor and presses a button when the situation presents a danger. The participant typically is not controlling the vehicle, a methodological nicety that eliminates differences in vehicle-control

skill and allows more precise focus on hazard detection. Provided that the experienced operators are substantially skilled (say ten years of experience), it is typical to find an expertise advantage. For example, McKenna and Crick's (1991) experienced drivers (more than ten years of experience) reacted faster to hazards than did drivers with less than three years of experience.

We noted above that experts seem to be less affected by load in a number of tasks, presumably because those tasks had become automatic, although efficient resource management of controlled processes was also sometimes implicated. There seems to be at least some evidence that hazard perception is not automatic, but rather is a controlled, effortful process. McKenna and Farrand (1999) studied drivers who completed a random letter-generation task during a hazard-perception test. Experienced drivers showed *more* interference on the hazard-perception task than did inexperienced drivers. If low-altitude military flight requires controlled processing (Haber & Haber, 2003) as we discussed earlier, it may be because hazard detection requires it. Processes responsible for skilled control of the plane itself may develop automaticity, but the processing of hazards may not. Perhaps there is simply not enough consistent mapping between some contextualized hazards and the appropriate response.

Hazard detection is a special case of gathering and interpreting cues from the environment. In this sense, expertise differences are ubiquitous. For example, Wiggins and O'Hare (1995) note evidence that experienced pilots acquire weather-related data from a menu-driven display more efficiently (less time, fewer returns to same information) than do apprentice or junior journeyman pilots. The groups also tend to differ in the weather cues they view as useful (Wiggins & O'Hare, 1995).

Chapman and Underwood (1998) conducted a study of apprentice and journeyman automobile drivers. Participants watched a video from the driver's perspective and were to indicate as soon as they saw any hazardous event, while reaction time and eye movements were recorded. No difference in latency between groups was found; however, apprentice drivers had longer fixations than experienced drivers during periods of hazardous events. They also found the experienced drivers had greater knowledge than apprentice drivers did about the potential location of threat-related information.

It seems that experienced drivers have a better awareness than less-experienced drivers of where potential hazardous situations may appear. Therefore, when a hazardous event is encountered, the experienced driver is able to react to the event accordingly without significant interference of other tasks of driving. Conversely, although the apprentice driver responds to the hazardous event as fast as the experienced driver, the apprentice's longer fixation is thought to reflect efforts at trying to understand the hazard. Consequently, this extra cognitive time will interfere with other driving tasks.

Situation Awareness (Understanding)

It is clear that detecting hazards is a critical part of understanding the environment in which one is operating. The understanding of a dynamic environment has come to be studied under the rubric of "situation awareness" (SA; Durso & Gronlund, 1999; Endsley, 1995; Endsley, Chapter 36).

Stokes, Kemper, and Kite (1997) found that experienced pilots (> 1500 hours) outperformed apprentice pilots (< 50 hours of instrument flight) in a situation-recognition task. The task required participants to listen to recorded dialogue between air traffic controllers and pilots. Participants listened to the recordings and then selected from an array of diagrams the situation that best represented the scenario being discussed. The experienced pilots were twice as likely to generate a plausible conceptualization of the dialogue. Experienced pilots were more adept than less-experienced pilots at creating an assessment of the situation, which Stokes et al. theorized was by integrating

and matching the dialogue into a preexisting schema.

The schema notion also appears in Randel, Pugh, and Reed (1996), who studied electronic-warfare technician operators on navy ships. The technician operator monitors a screen that shows radar emitters of hostile and friendly radar targets. He or she must monitor hostile and friendly traffic to keep a constant update of the changing environment. This experiment used the same software that is in the real fleet and simulated nearly identical displays. Situation awareness was measured by requiring the technician operators to reconstruct the locations of the hostile and friendly targets after the information on the screen was removed from view, a constrained processing task. The participants reconstructed the targets one-fourth of the way through the scenario and at the end of the scenario. Those who scored high on a job-relevant test recalled more targets than intermediates, and intermediates recalled more targets than low-scoring operators did. A higher percentage of hostile targets were recalled than the percentage of friendly targets. Skilled operators also outperformed intermediates and novices when verbally responding to situation-awareness questions about threats in the scenario. Randel et al. concluded that experts' repertoires of electronic-warfare situations, again a schema notion, can assist in determining the correct assessment of a new situation.

In a similar vein, Wiegmann, Goh, and O'Hare (2002) found that experienced pilots were better at integrating conflicting information than less-experienced pilots when flying a Frasca 142 flight simulator. More-experienced pilots recognized deteriorating weather conditions faster than did less-experienced pilots. Essentially, the more-experienced pilots were more efficient than less-experienced pilots in modifying a VFR model to acquire an Instrument Meteorological Conditions (IMC) model when encountering discrepancies. Additionally, Underwood, Crundell, and Chapman (in press) argue in their literature review that experienced drivers have developed schemata that guide their search during hazardous conditions.

Finally, there is evidence that expertise advantages in situation awareness are due, in part, to switching between domain-independent cognitive mechanisms, like working memory, and domain-dependent cognitive mechanisms. For example, Sohn and Doane (2003; see also Dattel and Sohn, 2003) investigated the relationship of working memory (WM) and expertise in groups of apprentice and expert pilots. They obtained measures of domain-independent spatial working memory and domain-specific working-memory skill. WM was measured using a rotation span task, and domain-specific working memory was measured by presenting participants with blocks of cockpit displays representing routine or implausible flight situations. Participants were presented with two snapshots of cockpit displays and were asked to recall one of the snapshots (randomly determined). Domain-specific WM was computed by subtracting delayed recall of the nonmeaningful pairs from recall scores for the meaningful pair. Finally, Sohn and Doane measured situation awareness by asking participants if a goal would be reached in the next five seconds given a presented cockpit configuration. Of interest here was the fact that, in some analyses, experts and apprentices seemed to rely differentially on general and domain-specific WM: As reliance on domain-specific working memory increased, reliance on general WM decreased. Again, there is evidence that, as with deficits due to aging, expertise can have compensatory effects for lower cognitive capacity, in this case smaller WM.

These abilities of experts to outperform less-skilled or less-experienced operators in tasks requiring assessment of the situation and detection of hazards undoubtedly depends on the underlying knowledge the operators bring to bear on their environment. We turn now to studies that address knowledge-representation issues more directly.

Knowledge

An answer to a question about expertise usually involves recourse to theoretical differences in the underlying knowledge representations of experts and novices (e.g., Glaser, 1987; cf., Ericsson, 2003). These differences can be of secondary interest, as when ecological psychologists claim that knowledge becomes attuned to affordances in the environment; or they can be of primary interest, as when cognitive psychologists claim that knowledge is added to and reorganized, but there is little denial that long-term changes in the operator are a critical aspect of expertise effects.

Knowledge Organization

Schvaneveldt et al. (1985) conducted an analysis of how apprentice pilots (Air Force undergraduate pilot trainees) and two groups of expert fighter pilots (Air Force instructors and National Guard pilots) organized air-to-air and air-to-ground fighter concepts. The participants judged all possible pairwise combinations of the terms for relatedness/similarity. Schvaneveldt et al. then submitted the matrix of judgments to multidimensional scaling (MDS) and Pathfinder-scaling algorithms to determine how pilots organized constructs. MDS places concepts in n-dimensional space such that the distance between concepts reflects their relatedness. Pathfinder links concepts represented by nodes in a graph or network such that the number of links or weights of those links between concepts reflects their relatedness. MDS revealed underlying dimensions along which experts' knowledge structures were organized, whereas Pathfinder offered interesting structural facets of expertise.

Schvaneveldt et al. (1985) found that experts tended to agree more with each other than with apprentices. Schvaneveldt et al. were able to point out specific deficits in the apprentices' structures, identifying well-defined, underdefined (missing connections), overdefined (extra connections), and misdefined (both over- and underdefined) concepts. Expert structures were not necessarily more complex than those of apprentices. In fact, the instructor pilots had a quite simple, "elegant" Pathfinder network. Thus, expertise seems not be accompanied by a more complex knowledge structure, but by a better organized one.

There are numerous knowledge structures that researchers have proposed as candidates for the "better organized one." We have already referred above to the schema notion. Like schemata, most of the knowledge structures attributed to experts seem to have a large top-down processing component. Even when no difference between experienced and less experienced pilots are found on a declarative knowledge test, experienced pilots were more able to apply their declarative knowledge when presented in open-ended scenarios in combination with procedural knowledge (Stokes et al., 1997). Thus, Stokes et al. suggested that apprentice pilots cannot apply knowledge learned in "ground school" to real-time situations as well as could the journeyman pilots, despite sufficient knowledge on a multiple-choice test.

We turn now to a particular schematic knowledge structure that has played a key role in thinking about dynamic environments, the "mental model," and its progeny, the situation models.

Mental and Situation Models

In a dynamic environment such as transportation, it is thought that the operator develops mental models that aid in planning, strategies, and decision making. Mental models of dynamic environments are schematic representations of the processes operating in the world (Gentner & Stevens, 1983). They contain information about causality and can give rise to judgments of probability. Durso and Gronlund (1999) argue that mental models of real-world dynamic systems are difficult to modify once they are developed, but together with the particular situation, they do give rise to "situation models" (see Endsley,

Chapter 36). Thus, a mental model can be viewed as a mental outline of expected events for a dynamic situation. By filling in particular information from the environment into the mental model, one mental model of a problem type can generate an endless number of specific situation models. For example, an air traffic controller has a mental model of the activity that occurs in her low-altitude sectors. She also knows the procedures for arrivals and departures, including procedures for "handing off" airplanes to other controllers and accepting airplanes from other controllers; and this general schematic information is represented in the mental model. A situation model about today's traffic in the west departure sector for DFW can be spawned from the mental model. Departure or arrival procedures for the specific airport that day, procedures for instantiating temporary flight restrictions, and expectation of a flight trajectory of a particular flight that flies to the same destination every day may be represented in the situation model along with all of the relevant information inherited from the parent mental model.

A highly developed mental model assists the operator in discriminating information that is relevant from that which is irrelevant. The operator who has a well-developed mental model should be more efficient at processing information because he or she knows the information to attend to and the information to ignore or discard. For example, in Stokes et al. (1997) where pilots listen to ATC radio communications, expert pilots recalled twice the number of concept words, but recalled less "filler" words than apprentices did. Stokes et al. take this as support for the idea that "[experts] are better able to make practical use of situational schemata to impose form on sensory data in real time" (p. 191).

Mental models also assist experts in anticipating what will happen next. For example, in an experiment where participants (with a student pilot's certificate or better) viewed displays of cockpit instruments and text, Doane and Sohn (2004) showed that novices were especially poor at predicting the result of multiple, meaningfully related control activities. Finally, superior mental models should generate superior situation models, and they do. For example, in Stokes et al. (1997), while listening to the transcriptions, the pilots were instructed to "build a mental picture" of the situation and then select from a set of diagrams that best represented the situation. Expert pilots outperformed the apprentice pilots in matching the correct diagram with the dialogue.

Strategies

Knowledge differences also manifest as differences in strategies. Experts seem to have more strategies overall and more abstract strategies from which to choose. This difference in turn allows experts to show more flexibility in their decision making and planning. For example, Wiggins and O'Hare (1995) found that when making diversion decisions, less-experienced pilots returned to the starting point and the more-experienced pilots were more likely to choose safe alternative routes. Strategies also come faster for those experts. The participants in that study had a series of menu items from which to choose. Each menu item contained categorized information about the scenario (e.g., weather information, landing-performance information). More-experienced pilots seemed to have a strategy developed before searching the menu. For example, they searched less of the menu items than the less-experienced pilots. In addition to searching more menu items, the less-experienced pilots were more likely to repeat reviews of the menu items. The less-experienced pilots seemed to be developing their strategy by searching the menu, as if the information in the menu were directing their strategy.

The CTA of air traffic controllers conducted by Seamster et al. (1993) also showed that apprentice, intermediate, and expert controllers differed substantially on the problem-solving techniques and strategies they employed. Seamster et al. had members from each group develop an air traffic problem and generate the most optimal solu-

tion. The scenario was presented to another member of the group who had to explain each step in solving the problem. The goals of the controllers were categorized into areas of importance. The category to receive the highest priority was a violation of minimum separation standards. The next highest priority was deviations from standard operating procedures, followed by situations that could lead to increased workload, and executing unnecessary requests of pilots.

Seamster et al. (1993) found that developmental controllers initially focused on solving potential airspace-violation problems. Only after these problems were solved did they begin to concentrate on solving deviations. Conversely, experts did not focus on solving violation problems to the extent that developmentals did. The experts were much more likely to solve violations and deviations alternately, and developmentals were more likely to solve violations sequentially followed by deviations. Seamster et al. suggested that apprentices' attention to the violations may be more cognitively demanding for them compared to experts and therefore reduced their cognitive resources and prevented them from attending to other problems and goals.

Seamster et al. (1993) also found that experts used fewer strategies than apprentices did when solving problem scenarios. The scenarios were rated at 65% complexity, a complexity level that should not overload apprentices. Despite Seamster et al.'s finding that experts use fewer strategies, the experts used a greater variety of strategies than did apprentices. Presumably, a smaller but more differentiated set of strategies allows experts to solve a wide range of problems.

Contributing to greater differentiation is the fact that experts employ more workload-management strategies than do apprentices. In fact, within experts, workload-management strategies were more frequent than planning strategies. Apparently, their experience obviated the need to rely on planning techniques and allowed more management strategies. Seamster et al. suggest that experience moderates the need to create planning strategies (see also Zsambok & Klein, 1997).

Schvaneveldt, Beringer, and Lamonica (2001) also studied prioritization, but with pilots rather than controllers. Schvaneveldt et al. asked apprentice pilots (M = 361 hrs) and expert pilots (M = 4,352 hrs) to rate the priority of various flight elements (e.g., track, vertical velocity) from "critical, frequently accessed, or both" to "not relevant or rarely accessed." Priority ordering changed as a function of phase of flight, but of relevance here is that expertise differences were found for specific flight elements. Experts differed most from apprentices in the final phases of flight – descent, approach, landing – with experts tending to give higher priority to the constituent elements of these phases than did apprentices. Although details of this analysis are beyond this review, the general point is that experts and nonexperts prioritize differently, especially in more difficult phases of flight. This also supports the earlier contention that in dynamic environments management of resources via prioritization is an important difference in expertise levels.

It is tempting to speculate that in dynamic environments, it may be less important that expertise brings increases in the number of available facts, but more important that it brings increases in the number of strategies – including workload-management strategies.

Future Travel

Understanding how experienced operators differ from less-experienced ones in transportation has importance for both basic and applied science. In this chapter, we have reviewed a number of findings from a variety of transportation domains including driving, flying, and supervising traffic. Although noncognitive hypotheses (e.g., driver style) compete with expertise as an explanation for operators' behaviors (e.g., safe highway driving), a consideration of the literature showed that there were clear expertise effects.

We have seen that the ability of experts to manage resources better than nonexperts has emerged as a recurrent theme. Experts efficiently move between tasks, prioritize subtasks differently, and

devote resources explicitly to management. Resource-management strategies are an explicit part of expertise in many transportation domains. They seem at least as important as the development of automaticity because much of what the expert does remains under controlled processing, and thus resources must be available at the appropriate time. Perhaps the most interesting such process is hazard perception, a keystone to situation awareness. Underlying all of this are differences in knowledge structures – models of the dynamic world – but there is at least some suggestion that expertise differences in knowledge may not be differences in networks of facts, but differences in compendiums of strategies.

Research explicitly on experience in transportation is relatively young, as are many of our modern modes of transportation. Thus, it is not surprising that sophisticated models of human expertise in transportation are only now emerging. For example, ADAPT developed by Doane and Sohn (2000) is able to predict accurately both expert and novice pilots' performance, visual attention, and control movements.

As sophisticated models develop, many of the same debates that we see in basic cognitive psychology will appear in the psychology of transportation. We see arguments for top-down, rule-based schematic structures as well as cognitive repertoires of separate cases; we see different views of the important control structures, long-term working memory versus working memory. Transportation research holds the promise to offer to basic cognitive research challenges to its fundamental assumptions. Ultimately, we believe that successful theories of expertise in transportation – in fact, expertise in any dynamic environment – will be fundamentally cognitive and they will have the management of cognitive resources at their core.

Finally, it seems fair to ask if the cognitive factors considered in this chapter suggest interventions that could aid in the development of expertise. How can we make drivers safer? First, drivers must be given the type of experience that is similar to the *atypical* experiences they will encounter on the highway. Most typical experiences are already likely to be easily and automatically handled by the unimpaired experienced driver. Explicit training on pattern detection and interpretation of hazards, the development of strategies, and the management of resources are likely targets for such deliberate practice (e.g., Ericsson, 2003; Ericsson, Krampe, & Tesch-Römer, 1993). Simulators, though once prohibitive, are well within the technological and financial constraints of the personal computer. Given that there is little reason to believe that the culprit for inferior driving is vehicle control, the PC is a fine simulator for training hazard detection, strategy selection, and resource management. Thus, we believe that a cognitive perspective combined with appropriate practice – specific and deliberate – can improve driving skills and make the drive for our LA commuter a little safer.

Footnote

1. We are grateful to Kate Bleckley, Ray King, Pat DeLucia, Anders Ericsson, and especially Robert Hoffman for comments on earlier versions of this chapter.

References

Allgaier, E. (1939). Experience counts: It takes more than physical ability to make a good driver. *Public Safety*, 15, 21.

Beilock, S. L., Carr, T., MacMahon, C., & Starkes, J. L. (2002). When paying attention becomes counterproductive: Impact of divided versus skill-focused attention on novice and experienced performance of sensorimotor skills. *Journal of Experimental Psychology: Applied*, 8, 6–16.

Bellenkes, A. H., Wickens, C. D., & Kramer, A. F. (1997). Visual scanning and pilot expertise: The role of attentional flexibility and mental model development. *Aviation, Space, and Environmental Medicine*, 68, 569–579.

Bisseret, A. (1971). Analysis of mental processes involved in air traffic control. *Ergonomics*, 14, 565–570.

Cellier, J. M., Eyrolle, H., & Marine, C. (1997). Expertise in dynamic environments. *Ergonomics*, 40, 28–50.

Chapman, P. R., & Underwood, G. (1998). Visual search of driving situations: Danger and experience. *Perception*, 27, 951–964.

Chase, W. G., & Simon, H. A. (1973). Perception in chess. *Cognitive Psychology*, 4, 55–81.

Chi, M. T. H., Glaser, R., & Farr, M. J. (1988). *The nature of expertise*. Hillsdale, NJ: Erlbaum.

Crundall, D., & Underwood, G. (1998). The effects of experience and processing demands on visual information acquisition in drivers. *Ergonomics*, 41, 448–458.

Dattel, A. R., & Sohn, Y. W. (2003). Novice-expert differences in flight situation awareness and action planning as a function of complexity. *Proceedings of the 15th Triennial International Ergonomics Association Meeting*. Seoul, Korea: The Ergonomics Society of Korea.

DeKeyser, V., & Piette, A. (1970). Analyse de l'activite des operateurs au tableau synoptique d'une chaine d'agglomeration. *Le Travail Humain*, 33, 341–352.

Doane, S. M., & Sohn, Y. W. (2004). Pilot ability to anticipate the consequences of flight actions as a function of expertise. *Human Factors*, 46, 92–103.

Doane, S. M., & Sohn, Y. W. (2000). ADAPT: A predictive cognitive model of user visual attention and action planning. *User Modeling and User-Adapted Interaction*, 10, 1–45.

Duncan, J., Williams, P., & Brown, I. (1991). Components of driving skill: Experience does not mean expertise. *Ergonomics*, 34, 919–937.

Duncan, J., Williams, P., Nimmo-Smith, I., & Brown, I. D. (1992). The control of skilled behavior: Learning, intelligence and distraction. In D. E. Meyer & S. Kornblum (Eds.), *Attention and performance XIV* (pp. 323–341). Cambridge, MA: MIT Press.

Durso, F. T., & Gronlund, S. D. (1999). Situation Awareness. In F. T., Durso, R. Nickerson, R. Schvaneveldt, S. Dumais, S. Lindsay, & M. Chi (Eds.), *The handbook of applied cognition*, (pp. 283–314). New York: John Wiley & Sons.

Elander, J., West, R., & French, D. (1993). Behavioral correlates of individual differences in road-traffic crash risk: An examination of methods and findings. *Psychological Bulletin*, 113, 279–294.

Endsley, M. R. (1995). Measurement of situation awareness in dynamic systems. *Human Factors*, 37, 65–84.

Ericsson, K. A. (2003). The search for general abilities and basic capacities: Theoretical implications from the modifiability and complexity of mechanisms mediating expert performance. In R. J. Sternberg (Ed.), *Psychology of abilities, competencies, and expertice* (pp. 93–125). New York: Cambridge University Press.

Ericsson, K. A., Krampe, R. T., & Tesch-Römer, C. (1993). The role of deliberate practice in the acquisition of expert performance. *Psychological Review*, 100, 363–406.

Ericsson, K. A., & Smith, J. (1991). *Toward a general theory of expertise*. Cambridge, MA: Cambridge University Press.

Fisher, J. A., & Galer, I. A. R. (1984). The effects of decreasing the radius of curvature of convex external rear view mirrors upon drivers' judgments of vehicles approaching in the rearward visual field. *Ergonomics*, 27, 1209–1224.

Forsyth, E., Maycock, G., & Sexton, B. (1995). *Cohort study of learner and novice drivers: Part 3, Accidents, offences and driving experience in the first three years of driving*. Transport and Road Research Laboratory, TRRL Report LR 111, Crowthorne, UK.

Gentner, D., & Stevens, A. L. (1983). *Mental models*. Hillsdale, NJ: Erlbaum.

Glaser, R. (1987). Thoughts on expertise. In C. Schooler & W. Schaie (Eds.), *Cognitive functioning and social structure over the life course* (pp. 81–94). Norwood, NJ: Ablex.

Groeger, J. A. (2000). *Understanding driving: Applying cognitive psychology to a complex everyday task*. Hove, UK: Psychology Press.

Groeger, J. A., & Grande, G. E. (1996). Self-preserving assessments of skills? *British Journal of Psychology*, 87, 61–79.

Haber, R. N., & Haber, L. (2003). Perception and attention during low-altitude high-speed flight. In P. S. Tsang & M. A. Vidulich (Eds.), *Principles and practice of aviation psychology* (pp. 21–68). Mahwah, NJ: Erlbaum.

Henmon, V. A. C. (1919). Air service tests of aptitude for flying. *Journal of Applied Psychology*, 3, 103–109.

Hoffman, R. (1996). How can expertise be defined? Implications of research from cognitive psychology. In R. Williams, W. Faulkner, & J. Fleck (Eds.), *Exploring expertise* (pp. 81–100). Edinburgh, Scotland: University of Edinburgh Press.

Horswill, M. S., & McKenna, F. P. (2004). Drivers' hazard perception ability: Situation awareness on the road. In S. Banbury & S. Tremblay (Eds.), *A cognitive approach to situation awareness: Theory, measurement, and application*. (pp. 155–175) Hampshire, UK: Ashgate.

Klein, G. (1997). An overview of naturalistic decision making applications. In C. E. Zsambok & G. Klein (Eds), *Naturalistic decision making* (pp. 49–60). Mahwah, NJ: Erlbaum.

McKenna, F. P., & Crick, J. L. (1991). *Hazard perception in drivers: A methodology for testing and training*. Final Report. Behavioural Studies Unit. Transport and Road Research Laboratory, Crowthorne, UK.

McKenna, F. P., & Farrand, P. (1999). The role of automaticity in driving. In G. B. Grayson (Ed.), *Behavioural research in road safety IX*. Transport and Road Research Laboratory, Crowthorne, UK.

McKinney, E. H., & Davis, K. J. (2003). Effects of deliberate practice on crisis decision performance. *Human Factors*, 45, 436–444.

Mourant, R. R., & Rockwell, T. H. (1972). Strategies of visual search by novice and experienced drivers. *Human Factors*, 14, 325–335.

NTSB (2004). Retrieved April 30, 2004 from the National Transportation Safety Board web cite: www.ntsb.gov.

Randel, J. M., Pugh, H. L., & Reed, S. K. (1996). Differences in expert and novice situation awareness in naturalistic decision making. *International Journal of Human-Computer Studies*, 45, 579–597.

Recarte, M. A., & Nunes, L. M. (1996). Perception of speed in automobile: Estimation and production. *Journal of Experimental Psychology: Applied*, 2, 291–304.

Schvaneveldt, R. W., Beringer, D. B., & Lamonica, J. A. (2001). Priority and organization of information accessed by pilots in various phases of flight. *The International Journal of Aviation Psychology*, 11, 253–280.

Schvaneveldt, R. W., Durso, F. T., Goldsmith, T. E., Breen, T. J., Cooke, N. M., Tucker, R. G., & DeMaio, J. C. (1985). Measuring the structure of expertise. *The International Journal of Man-Machine Studes*, 23, 699–728.

Seamster, T. L., Redding, R. E., Cannon, J. R., Ryder, J. M., & Purcell, J. A. (1993). Cognitive task analysis of expertise in air traffic control. *International Journal of Aviation Psychology*, 3, 257–283.

Shanteau, J. (1992). Competence in experts: The role of task characteristics. *Organizational*

Behavior & Human Decision Processes, 53, 252–262.

Shinar, D., Meir, M., & Ben-Shoham, I. (1998). How automatic is manual gear shifting? *Human Factors*, 40, 647–654.

Snow, A. J. (1926). Tests for transportation pilots. *Journal of Applied Psychology*, 10, 37–51.

Sohn, Y. W., & Doane, S. M. (2003). Roles of working memory capacity and long-term working memory skill in complex task performance. *Memory & Cognition*, 31, 458–466.

Stokes, A. F., Kemper, K., & Kite, K. (1997). Aeronautical decision making, cue recognition, and expertise under time pressure. In C. E. Zsambok & G. Klein (Eds.), *Naturalistic decision making* (pp. 183–196). Mahwah, NJ: Erlbaum.

Tsang, P. S., & Voss, D. T. (1996). Boundaries of cognitive performance as a function of age and piloting experience. *International Journal of Aviation Psychology*, 6, 359–377.

Underwood, G., Crundall, D., & Chapman, P. (in press). Cognition and driving. In. F. T. Durso, R. Nickerson, S. Dumais, S.Lewandowsky, & T. Perfect (Eds.), *Handbook of applied cognition (2nd)* Wiley: Chicester.

Wasielewski, P. (1984). Speed as a measure of driver risk: Observed speeds versus driver and vehicle characteristics. *Accident Analysis & Prevention*, 16, 89–103.

Waylen, A. E., Horswill, M. S., Alexander, J. L., & McKenna, F. P. (2004). Do expert drivers have a reduced illusion of superiority? *Transportation Research, F*, 323–331.

Wiegmann, D. A., Goh, J., & O'Hare, D (2002). The role of situation assessment and flight experience in pilots' decisions to continue visual flight rules flight into adverse weather. *Human Factors*, 44, 187–197.

Wiggins, M., & O'Hare, D. (1995). Expertise in aeronautical weather-related decision making: A cross-sectional analysis of general aviation pilots. *Journal of Experimental Psychology: Applied*, 1, 305–320.

Wikman, A. S., Nieminen, T., & Summala, H. (1998). Driving experience and time-sharing during in-car tasks on roads of different width. *Ergonomics*, 41, 358–372.

Williams, A. F., & O'Neill, B. (1974). On-the-road driving records of licensed race drivers. *Accident Analysis & Prevention*, 6, 263–270.

Zsambok, C. E., & Klein, G. (1997). *Naturalistic decision making*. Mahwah, NJ: Erlbaum.

CHAPTER 21

Expertise in Software Design

Sabine Sonnentag, Cornelia Niessen, & Judith Volmer

Keywords: software design, programming, computer program, debugging, communication, knowledge representation, Professionals.

Introduction

In this chapter, we review research evidence on expertise in software design, computer programming, and related tasks. Research in this domain is particularly interesting because it refers both to rather general features and processes associated with expertise (e.g., knowledge representation, problem-solving strategies) and to specific characteristics of high performers in an economically relevant real-world setting. Therefore, in this chapter we draw on literature from various fields, mainly from cognitive psychology, but also from work and organizational psychology and from the software-design literature within computer science.

Our chapter is organized as follows: In the first main section we provide a brief descrip-

tion of the domain and give an overview of tasks in software development. Next, we briefly describe the expertise concept and distinguish between a conceptualization of expertise as years of experience and expertise as high performance. The third main section is the core part of this chapter. In this section, we review empirical research on expertise in tasks such as software design, programming, program comprehension, testing, and debugging. Moreover, we describe how expert performers differ from non-experts with respect to knowledge as well as communication and cooperation processes. In the final section, we present directions for future research and discuss some practical implications.

Historical Context

Extensive research on expertise on software design and programming started in the early 1980s. For example, Jeffries, Turner, Polson, and Atwood (1981) as well as Adelson (1984) published influential studies on how experts differ from novices. These studies stimulated subsequent research and were often cited also in more general publications on expertise (e.g., Ericsson & Smith, 1991; Sternberg, 1996). Generally, research activity in the domain of software design and programming has been very lively and intensive (Hoffman, 1992). For many years, research on expertise in this domain was an important topic in the workshops on Empirical Studies of Programmers (Olson, Sheppard, & Soloway, 1987; Soloway & Iyengar, 1986). Since the 1990s, research interest seems to have shifted to investigations in more complex organizational settings (e.g., Campbell, Brown, & DiBello, 1992; Sonnentag, 1995; Turley & Bieman, 1995).

Studies on expertise in software design and programming do not aim only at scientific insight into the processes associated with expertise in a complex domain. Nowadays, as many countries' economy and people's life largely depend on information technology, the development and maintenance of high-quality software systems are of crucial relevance. Therefore, also with respect to practical implications it is important to examine how expert performance in software design and programming is achieved.

The Field of Software Design and Programming

The domain of software design and programming comprises distinct tasks, such as requirement analysis, software design, programming, testing, and debugging. It is the main goal of requirement analysis to specify the demands a new computer program or software system should meet. Ideally, future users of the computer system – or their representatives – should be involved in requirement analysis because they often have detailed knowledge about the tasks and processes the computer system should support. Software design aims at the description of the basic features of the future computer system and prescribes the functions the system should perform. During programming,

the functions specified during software design are translated into a computer program, that is, a set of grammatical rules that refer to calculations, procedures, or objects. A main challenge for software design is to ensure that a computer program meets the requirements and runs without errors. This asks for extensive testing and debugging (i.e., error correction).

Traditionally, software design and programming has been conceptualized as a rather linear process, starting from requirement analysis and moving then to testing and debugging, with design and programming as distinct intermediate phases. However, such a linear approach was not feasible in practice because often not all requirements can be specified in advance. Therefore, nowadays a more iterative view dominates the field (Sommerville, 2001).

From a more psychological perspective, many software-design tasks can be described as ill-defined problems (Simon, 1973). Ill-defined problems imply that problem specifications are incomplete and have to be decided on during the design process. Thus, ill-defined problems have no single correct solution. Software design and programming draws largely on syntactic, semantic, and schematic knowledge (Détienne, 2002). A broad range of different design and programming strategies have been distinguished, such as top-down versus bottom-up, forward versus backward development, or breadth-first versus depth-first (Détienne, 2002). Therefore, psychological research on software design and programming has focused mainly on designers' and programmers' cognitive processes.

However, it has been argued that professional software design and programming ("programming in the large") takes place in teams and other cooperative settings and, therefore, an exclusive focus on the cognitive processes of individuals can fall short when describing software design and programming (Curtis, 1986; Riedl, Weitzenfeld, Freeman, Klein, & Musa, 1991). To understand fully how high-quality software is produced research should also address communication and cooperation processes.

Before describing characteristics of expert software designers and programmers in detail, we introduce two conceptualizations of expertise.

Conceptualizations of Expertise in Software Design and Programming

As in many other domains, researchers in the domain of software design and programming have relied on various conceptualizations and operationalizations of expertise. Although at the conceptual level most researchers would probably agree with Ericsson and Smith's (1991) definition of expertise as "outstanding performance" (p. 2), in most empirical studies, expertise has been operationalized as years of experience. For example, Sonnentag (2001b) reported that 84 percent of all quasi-experimental studies on expertise in software development and programming published between 1981 and 1997 used an operationalization of expertise that referred to months and years of experience. In these studies, beginning students have been compared with graduate students or professional programmers (e.g., Jeffries et al., 1981). With respect to relatively inexperienced persons, it is plausible to equate years of experience with increasing expertise and to assume that expertise develops as a function of time spent within the domain.

However, when it comes to more-advanced software designers and programmers, long years of experience are not necessarily related to a high performance level (Sonnentag, 1995, 1998; Vessey, 1986). This result mirrors findings on expert performance in other domains where years of experience have been shown to be poor predictors of high performance (Ericsson, Krampe, & Tesch-Römer, 1993). Thus, at the professional level, high performers are not necessarily more experienced than moderate performers. Therefore, it is important to differentiate between the conceptualization of expertise as *(long) experience* and of expertise as *high performance*. Differences found between novices on the one hand and more-experienced programming students or software professionals on the other hand may not easily generalize to differences between highly performing and moderately performing software professionals (Sonnentag, 2000). Of course, there are also large variations within the group of inexperienced persons (ranging from novices, who are undergoing introductory training, to apprentices and journeymen) and within the group of moderate performers.

After now having defined the expertise concept, in the next section we will summarize research evidence on differences between experts and non-experts.

Empirical Studies on Software Design and Programming

In this section, we give an overview over results from empirical studies on expert software design and programming. More specifically, we describe differences between experts and non-experts in five areas: (1) requirements analysis and design tasks, (2) programming and program comprehension, (3) testing and debugging, (4) knowledge representation and recall, and (5) communication and cooperation. Major findings are summarized in Table 21.1.

We focus on studies that used a contrastive design comparing a group of experts with a group of non-experts (Voss, Fincher-Kiefer, Greene, & Post 1986) and on other studies in which study participants differed with respect to the level of expertise or performance. We excluded papers from our review that provided case studies of single experts without comparing them to non-experts (e.g., Campbell et al., 1992).

Requirement Analysis and Software Design

Requirements analysis aims at identifying the demands a future software system should meet. It includes tasks such as analysing the problem requirements, setting design goals, and decomposing the goals to come up with a software design representing

Table 21.1. Comparison between experts and non-experts in software design and programming

	Experienced persons – as compared to inexperienced persons	High performers – as opposed to moderate performers
Requirement analysis and design	• Spend more time and effort on problem comprehension • Spend more time on clarifying program requirements • Decompose design problems in small components in a top-down breadth-first manner	• Spend less time on problem comprehension • Adequate problem representation early in the design process
Program comprehension and programming	• Pursuit of abstract programming goals • Program comprehension based on abstract concepts	• Pursuit of abstract programming goals • Cross-referencing strategy
Testing and debugging	• Test for inconsistency • Hypothesis-driven procedure	• Active search for problems
Knowledge	• Knowledge organized in greater and more meaningful chunks • Knowledge of abstract concepts • Superior meta-cognitive knowledge	• Broader and more detailed knowledge base
Communication and cooperation	<not studied>	• Spend more time on communication and cooperation

a solution (Koubek, Salvendy, Dunsmore, & LeBold, 1989; Malhotra, Thomas, Carroll, & Miller, 1980). Early studies showed that there are considerable individual differences in software design and that activities tend to vary according to the design experiences of programmers (e.g. Jeffries et al., 1981; Weinberg & Schulman, 1974). Studies focused on the comparison of inexperienced programmers (e.g., students) and experienced programmers (e.g., professionals; Agarwal, Sinha, & Tanniru, 1996), rather than on the comparison of specific performance levels (e.g., Sonnentag, 1998).

In real-world design situations, an important part of the design process consists of analysing the requirements the new software system should comply with. These requirements are often ill defined and not clearly stated by clients or potential users. Thus, the first task of the software designer is to set and refine the design goals (Chevalier & Ivory,

2003; Malhotra et al., 1980). Similar to findings from early studies in physics problem solving (e.g., Chi, Feltovich, & Glaser, 1981), studies have indicated that experienced software designers spend more time on clarifying the program requirements compared to students (Batra & Davis, 1992; Jeffries et al., 1981). Moreover, within the web-design domain, professionals included more requirements in their web design than less-experienced designers (Chevalier & Ivory, 2003). Even when specific clients' requirements were not explicitly stated, professionals inferred more requirements of the client on the basis of their prior experience. In a study with performance level as expertise criterion, Sonnentag (1998) found no differences between high and moderate performers in analysing requirements in early phases of the design process. Moderate performers spent even more time analyzing requirements in later phases of the design process compared to high performers. High performers might have developed an adequate problem representation early in the design process, whereas moderate performers had to do additional requirement analysis on the later stages of the design process.

A lot of research has focused on the ability to decompose the design problem into smaller components. Here, a consistent result across many studies, albeit with very small samples, is that experts decomposed the design problem in a top-down and breadth-first manner (Adelson & Soloway, 1985). For example, Jeffries et al. (1981) described that experts decomposed a problem in major parts through a number of iterations. Also, advanced novices relied on such a top-down and breadth-first solution strategy, but with fewer iterations and therefore less detail.

A common assumption is that the decomposition process is guided by a knowledge representation, which is built up with experience and stored in long-term memory (Jeffries et al., 1981). When such a knowledge representation is not available, experts develop plans through a bottom-up, backward strategy (Rist, 1991). According to Rist (1986), experts have stored a broad range of programming plans that comprise knowledge of abstract and specific, language-dependent code fragments. This idea is supported by the study of Sonnentag (1998). When software designers were asked about strategies they would recommend to an inexperienced programmer working on the same design problem, high performers reported twice as many strategies as moderate performers. The studies of Davies (1991) showed that experienced programmers did not necessarily have more plans available, but focused on the most salient parts of the plan and flexibly switched between plans. In contrast, novices preferred a strategy with which plans are implemented in a more linear fashion.

With the emergence of new programming approaches (e.g., object-oriented programming), studies examined the role of knowledge in the design activity of experts using a new programming approach. These studies indicated that design strategies were influenced toward the specific language experiences (Agarwal et al., 1996). Though experts tried to obtain a deep understanding of a new language, they still used analogies to languages they knew when generating a program within a new framework (Campbell et al., 1992; Scholz & Wiedenbeck, 1992). Furthermore, research showed that when participants were experienced in one language (in object-oriented programming), complex plans were developed on the basis of the deep structure of this programming language. Inexperienced designers in object-oriented programming developed plans on the basis of functional similarity and showed more plan revisions (Détienne, 1995).

It thus seems that the knowledge base of experts is highly language dependent. However, experts also have abstract, transferable knowledge and skills. Agarwal et al. (1996) compared 22 computer scientists (more than two years of experience in process-oriented approaches) and 24 business students (limited knowledge in process-oriented modeling). When solving a design problem within a new non-process-oriented programming approach (here, object-oriented programming), experts did not differ from novices in the quality of solutions (structure and behavior of the program), and they showed even poorer performance on a finer level (processing aspects). Also Collani and Schömann (1995) examined the acquisition of a new programming language. In contrast to the study of Agarwal et al. (1996), the criterion for expertise was the programmers' performance. Their results supported the hypothesis that high performers possess language-independent abstract programming skills and knowledge that can be transferred faster and with less errors to the new programming framework.

The contrary results of the studies that defined expertise in terms of the length of experience versus performance can be explained by the different kinds of expertise: routine and adaptive expertise (Hatano & Inagaki, 1986). Individuals characterized by routine expertise show superior performance in well-known, often highly routinized tasks, whereas individuals characterized by adaptive expertise are able to master novel tasks and are successful in transferring existing knowledge and skills to unknown tasks or settings. For example, participants in the study of Agarwal et al. (1996) could have developed routine expertise through extended practice with process-oriented design, which has rigidifying effects on learning new skills and knowledge. On the other hand, the upper performance group in the study of Collani and Schömann (1995) might be characterized by the concept of adaptive expertise. Such experts have a deeper conceptual understanding of the domain that allows for a transfer of knowledge and skills to novel tasks (Hatano & Inagaki, 1986; Kimball & Holyoak, 2000). This might also lead to a faster in-depth requirement analysis that the high performers in the above mentioned study of Sonnentag (1998) have shown.

Most studies have focused on one aspect of the design activity. One exception is the study of Sonnentag (1998) that analysed a broad range of design activities: requirement analysis, feedback processing, planning, task focus, visualizations, and knowledge. According to the results, expertise in software design was characterized by more local planning activities, more feedback processing, less task-irrelevant cognitions, more solution visualizations, and more knowledge about design strategies experts would recommend to an imagined inexperienced colleague.

After the requirements have been analyzed and the software design has been produced, the concepts have to be implemented in computer programs. Therefore, in the next paragraphs we review research findings on differences between experts and nonexperts with respect to programming and program comprehension.

Programming and Program Comprehension

Programming refers to the process of "translating" specifications of a calculation or a procedure into a computer program.

Most studies on programming have compared relatively inexperienced students with more-experienced programmers (Bateson, Alexander, & Murphy, 1987; Davies, 1990; Soloway & Ehrlich, 1984). These studies clearly showed that more advanced programmers outperformed the relatively inexperienced students with respect to performance quality (Bateson et al., 1987; Soloway & Ehrlich, 1984) and solution time (Davies, 1990). When comparing high performers with moderate performers within a group of professional programmers, the high performers followed more abstract goals but did not differ with respect to other process features (Koubek & Salvendy, 1991).

Program comprehension is a necessary prerequisite for successfully completing programming tasks. Moreover, also testing and debugging tasks cannot be satisfactorily accomplished without understanding the program. In addition, program comprehension is of crucial importance in the context of professional software maintenance and software reuse. Nearly all empirical studies that have examined program comprehension have focused on the comparison between inexperienced and more-experienced persons (Adelson, 1984; Guerin & Matthews, 1990; Rist, 1996; Widowski & Eyferth, 1985; Wiedenbeck, Fix, & Scholtz, 1993). These studies showed that experienced persons perform better on program comprehension tasks and appear to be superior with respect to specific aspects of comprehension. For example, Adelson (1984) found that experienced programmers provided better answers to abstract questions than did students. Similarly, Rist (1996) reported that experienced graduates categorize programs according to programming plans. Thus, program comprehension of more-experienced persons is based on more-abstract concepts.

Pennington (1987) compared highly and poorly performing professional programmers. When trying to understand a program, high performers showed a "cross-referencing strategy" characterized by systematic alterations between systematically studying the computer program, translating it to domain terms, and subsequently verifying domain terms back in program terms. In contrast, poorer performers exclusively focused on program terms *or* on domain terms without building connections between the two "worlds." Thus, it seems that connecting various domains and relating them to each other is crucial for arriving at a comprehensive understanding of the program and the underlying problem.

Designing and programming software is only half of the story of software development. Finding and correcting errors in the software before introducing the software to the market is crucial. In the next paragraphs we will therefore summarize research evidence in the area of testing and debugging.

Testing and Debugging

Software testing aims at identifying inconsistencies and errors within computer programs. Debugging refers to the process of removing errors, so-called *bugs*, from a computer program. Empirical studies on testing and debugging have focused on comparisons between relatively inexperienced and more-experienced persons (Nanja & Cook, 1987; Teasley, Leventhal, Mynatt, & Rohlman, 1994; Weiser & Shertz, 1983). Not surprisingly, these studies illustrated that experienced students and professionals found more errors and detected the errors more quickly than did novices (Law, 1998; Weiser & Shertz, 1983). With respect to the testing processes, studies showed that experienced persons tested more for inconsistency (Teasley et al., 1994) and proceeded in a more hypothesis-driven and concept-oriented way (Krems, 1995). Thus, as students' programming experience increased, they seemed to work in a more systematic way.

Few studies have compared highly performing software professionals with those who perform at a moderate level. A thinking-aloud study showed that high performers needed less time for debugging, made fewer errors, searched more intensively for problems, and showed more information-evaluation activity (Vessey, 1986). Thus, it seems that high performers

have a better representation of the program and potential problems, which helps them to actively search for problems and to evaluate information. In the next paragraphs we discuss experts' knowledge and knowledge representations in greater detail.

Knowledge and Knowledge Representation

Knowledge and adequate knowledge representation are crucial in all phases of software development. Researchers have investigated knowledge and knowledge representation by using recall, problem-sorting, and other tasks. For example, study participants have been asked to recall program lines, either presented in a meaningful or in an arbitrary order (Barfield, 1986; McKeithen, Reitman, Rueter, & Hirtle, 1981). Again, most studies have contrasted inexperienced with more-experienced persons (Eteläpelto, 1993; McKeithen et al., 1981; Weiser & Shertz, 1983; Ye & Salvendy, 1994).

There is consistent evidence that novices and more-advanced students or professionals differ with respect to knowledge and knowledge representation. In recall tasks, more-experienced persons recalled more program lines, often only when the lines were presented in a meaningful order (Barfield, 1986, 1997; McKeithen et al., 1981), but sometimes also when presented in an arbitrary order (Bateson et al., 1987; Guerin & Matthews, 1990). Thus, it seems that experienced persons have organized their knowledge in greater and more meaningful "chunks" (Adelson, 1984; Ye & Salvendy, 1994). However, differences in chunking do not seem to be sufficient to explain experienced persons' better performance when recalling program lines presented in an arbitrary order.

Research has shown that professionals also possess more meta-cognitive knowledge than do students (Eteläpelto, 1993). Eteläpelto assessed students' and professional programmers' meta-cognitive knowledge during an interview that focused on a specific computer program and on the respondents' more general working strategies. Professional programmers' meta-cognitive knowledge was much more detailed and more comprehensive than students' knowledge. For example, a professional programmer provided a comment such as "The main program is not very well divided; the logic has been scattered over different parts of the program; the updating paragraph has too much in it. The control function of the program should be implemented in one paragraph; now the program has much depth in itself and scanning is difficult" (p. 248f.), whereas the students' comments were more general and diffuse. In addition, professional programmers expressed a clear idea about a good strategy of reading and comprehending computer programs. Thus, experienced persons know more about how to proceed when solving tasks in their domain.

When it comes to knowledge representation in highly versus moderately performing software professionals, high performers' superior knowledge seems not restricted to knowledge about how to solve rather narrowly defined software-design tasks (Sonnentag, 1998). Highly performing software professionals also possess more detailed knowledge about how to approach cooperation situations (Sonnentag & Lange, 2002). Thus, it seems that as work tasks become more comprehensive in real-world settings, high performers develop a more comprehensive representation of the entire work task, including necessary features of cooperation with coworkers.

In the next paragraphs we describe the role of communication and cooperation in expert performance in more detail.

Communication and Cooperation

Most research on experts has focused on specific activities in software design, such as design, programming, or testing in individual task settings. Nevertheless, some studies have addressed the question whether there are differences between high- and average-performing software professionals in cooperative work settings. Modern professional software development takes place mainly in project teams, suggesting that expertise in software design is not only a matter of knowledge and task strategies but also requires social and communicative skills.

Field studies suggest that high performers show better communication and cooperation competencies than moderate performers (e.g. Curtis, Krasner, & Iscoe, 1988; Kelley & Caplan, 1993; Sonnentag, 1995). In a field study with 17 software-development projects, Curtis et al. (1988) found that exceptional software designers showed superior communication skills. In fact, much of the exceptional designers' design work was accomplished while interacting with other team members. High performers spent a lot of time educating other team members about the application domain and its mapping into computational structures. Similarly, Sonnentag (1995), using a peer-nomination method in a study with 200 software professionals, showed that experts did not spend more time on typical software-development activities such as design, coding, or testing, but were more often engaged in review meetings and spent more time in consultations than did other team members. In a study at the Bell Laboratories, Kelley and Caplan (1993) compared top performers to average performers and found that differences could not be attributed to cognitive ability and that top performers considered interpersonal network abilities as highly important. Furthermore, top performers possessed better functioning interpersonal networks compared to average performers. Riedl et al. (1991) also observed highly developed interpersonal skills in expert software engineers. In a study on behavior in team meetings, Sonnentag (2001a) found that highly performing software professionals' involvement in cooperation situations differed, depending on situational demands. In highly structured meetings, no differences between highly and average performing software professionals were found, whereas differences were observed in poorly structured meetings. Thus, experts showed high adaptation to specific situational constraints and displayed cooperation competencies, particularly in difficult situations. Interestingly, high performers' communication behavior in unstructured cooperation situations mirrored their behavior when working on design problems in individual settings. More specifically, high performers showed process-regulating behavior such as planning or feedback seeking when the situation demands it, that is, when the meeting was unstructured, but not when it was highly structured.

What work strategies do exceptional software professionals recommend to an inexperienced colleague? This question was approached in a study with 40 software professionals (Sonnentag, 1998). In this study, high performers, more often than moderate performers, mentioned that the imagined inexperienced coworker should cooperate with others. Campbell and Gingrich (1986) demonstrated that this can be a useful strategy. They found that individual performance of software developers is facilitated significantly by a 15-minute talk with a senior designer about their task. These results hold for complex tasks, not just for simple ones, indicating that high task complexity makes it more necessary and more valuable for the programmer to communicate with a more senior person. In a more recent study, Ferris, Witt, and Hochwarter (2001) showed that social skill was more strongly related to job performance among programmers high in general mental ability (GMA) than for those with average or low levels of GMA. Thus, social skills in combination with high mental abilities – not high mental abilities by themselves – are related to the highest level of performance.

Several questions remain open since communication and cooperation processes in software design are rarely studied. It is not clear whether communication and cooperation competencies are a prerequisite of excellent software performance or a positive by-product of being an excellent software designer. Furthermore, third variables might cause the relationship between communication and cooperation competencies and excellent software performance (e.g., generalized problem-solving skills). Additional consideration of possible moderators, such as task or situational characteristics, might also illuminate this relationship, especially in professional software design with changing work requirements. In sum, more studies are needed to examine the causal relationships between expertise and communication skills and how these differences matter in complex real-world settings.

Directions for Future Research

Despite the growing research evidence on how experts differ from non-experts, several questions remain open that should be addressed in future research. In our view, the most important ones refer to: (1) the conceptualization of expertise, (2) the issue of causality, (3) the role of task and situational characteristics, (4) the role of motivation and self-regulation, and (5) the question of how expertise develops.

(1) THE CONCEPTUALIZATION OF EXPERTISE

Most studies on expertise in software design and programming refer to differences between inexperienced and more-experienced persons and compare beginning students with more-advanced students or professionals. Rather few studies examined how highly performing software professionals differ from software professionals performing less well (e.g., Koubek & Salvendy, 1991; Pennington, 1987; Sonnentag, 1998, 2001a; Vitalari & Dickson, 1983).

Of course, studies that contrast inexperienced with more-experienced persons provide useful insights about how skills may develop in a domain. However, it would be premature to assume that findings from comparisons between inexperienced and more-experienced persons can be easily generalized to differences within the group of professionals. Particularly in the domain of software design and programming, where specific knowledge becomes obsolete very quickly, long years of experience do not ensure high performance. Therefore, future studies should examine *professional* software designers and programmers and should operationalize expertise as high performance.

(2) THE ISSUE OF CAUSALITY

Most studies on expertise do not answer the question of causality because most empirical studies use a quasi-experimental or a correlational design. True experiments in which the independent variables are manipulated are very rare. Strictly speaking, without experimental manipulation it is impossible to falsify causal hypotheses. For example, although it is plausible that experts' pursuit of more abstract goals (Koubek & Salvendy, 1991) *leads* to their superior performance, it can not be ruled out that the focus on more abstract goals is a *consequence* of expertise. Similarly, experts' specific approach to communication and cooperation (Curtis et al., 1988; Sonnentag, 1995) may help them to arrive at their high performance level. However, experts' communication and cooperation processes might also be a consequence – or even only a by-product – of their superior performance. Because of their superior ability to master the intellectual demands of their tasks, experts might have more cognitive resources available to spend on communication. Thus, to arrive at a deeper understanding of the causal processes involved in expert performance, experiments are needed.

(3) THE ROLE OF TASK AND SITUATIONAL CHARACTERISTICS

Most studies have examined differences between experts and non-experts by using rather simple tasks with questionable external validity. Only a few studies looked at tasks that took two hours or longer to accomplish (exceptions are Sonnentag, 1998; Vitalari & Dickson, 1983). In real-world settings, software tasks can be laborious and time consuming, and therefore may involve other and more complex processes than those that have been examined. For example, future studies should use more-complex real-world tasks that require the coordination and prioritization of various subtasks. Expertise research should also pay more attention to the specific task demands placed on professional software developers. Particularly in areas such as web design and user-interface design, software designers have to deal with multiple constraints and must take economic, ergonomic, and domain-specific demands into account. Until now, there is not much insight into the strategies expert performers use in order to integrate multiple and sometimes conflicting constrains into their design. Future studies should address this gap.

Moreover, the role of specific task features and other situational characteristics that might enable or hinder expert performance has not been addressed systematically. There is some evidence that the differences observed between experts and non-experts are not obvious for all tasks and in all situations (Sonnentag, 2001a). For example, it might be that experts excel over non-experts only when working on complex tasks, but not when working on simpler tasks.

In addition, when completing tasks in real-world work settings, individuals are often faced with adverse and stressful conditions, such as work overload, time pressure, and role ambiguity (Fujigaki & Mori, 1997; Glass, 1997). It would be an interesting question for future research to study how experts and non-experts differ when confronted with stressful conditions. One may speculate that experts and non-experts differ in their perception on what constitutes stress and in how they deal with stressful conditions. Experts' und non-experts' differential reactions to stressful situations would imply that differences between the two groups become more evident under stressful conditions than under more relaxed conditions. Furthermore, Ericsson and Lehmann (1996) suggested that experts show a better adaptation to task constraints. This would imply that experts are not only less bothered by unfavorable situations but develop better ways to cope with them.

(4) THE ROLE OF MOTIVATION AND SELF-REGULATION

Expertise research has largely concentrated on cognitive issues associated with expert performance and has recently extended its focus to communication and cooperation skills. Until now, motivational and self-regulatory issues that might be highly relevant for high performance were beyond the research interest of most scholars in the field (But see Ericsson, Chapter 38). Empirical studies from other areas have shown that self-efficacy and the pursuit of difficult and specific goals are closely related to high performance levels (Latham, Locke, & Fassina, 2002; Locke & Latham, 1990; Stajkovic & Luthans, 1998). Moreover, it has been found that high performers verbalize less task-irrelevant cognitions during software design and focus more on the task at hand (Sonnentag, 1998). One interpretation is that high performers have superior self-regulatory skills that inhibit task-irrelevant thoughts. It would be a highly interesting avenue for future research to examine how motivation and self-regulation affect expert performance.

(5) THE QUESTION OF HOW EXPERTISE DEVELOPS

The question of how expertise develops is both highly interesting and practically relevant. However, our knowledge about how expertise in the software domain develops is very limited. Of course, as students progress from a novice level to a graduate student or even professional level, performance normally increases. However, within the group of software professionals, results on the empirical relationship between years of experience and performance are inconclusive. Although some studies have found positive relationships between years of experience and performance (Koubek & Salvendy, 1991; Turley & Bieman, 1995), others have not (Sonnentag, 1995, 1998; Vessey, 1986). There is some evidence that specific aspects of experience, such as its breadth and variety, are related to expert performance (Sonnentag, 1995). Ericsson et al. (1993) have argued that deliberate practice (i.e., regularly pursued purposeful and effortful learning and practice activities) is crucial for the achievement and maintenance of expert performance. Empirical studies have shown that deliberate practice indeed is related to high performance in domains such as music

or sports (Davids, 2000; Ericsson et al., 1993; Krampe & Ericsson, 1996) and also in more "classical" work settings such as insurance companies (Sonnentag & Kleine, 2000). We assume that deliberate practice might play also a core rule in the development of expert performance in software design and programming.

An issue closely related to the development of expertise refers to the distinction between routine and adaptive expertise (Hatano & Inagaki, 1986). In areas such as the software domain, where new tools and methodologies continuously emerge and where existing knowledge can become obsolete very quickly, more research on the development of adaptive expertise is particularly needed.

To adequately investigate the development of expertise in professional domains, longitudinal field studies are needed. Although retrospective studies can offer some interesting insights, only longitudinal studies that cover several years will allow conclusive answers about how expertise develops and unfolds over time.

Practical Implications

When it comes to practical approaches to promote expert performance in work settings, two major approaches have to be considered: (1) personnel selection and (2) training. Both approaches are based on the assumption that the characteristics typical for experts causally contribute to their superior performance. Most generally, personnel selection refers to organizational procedures and specific methods in order to select those individuals who may be well suited for a specific job. Based on the literature review provided in this chapter, personnel selection procedures – at least after some domain-specific training is accomplished – should include measures of knowledge and knowledge organization and of domain-specific problem-solving strategies that focus on abstract concepts and goals. In addition, assessments of communication and cooperation skills should be part of the personnel-selection process. In addition to more standardized tests (Stevens & Campion, 1999), group discussions or other teamwork assignments within an assessment center might be used. With respect to experience as a predictor in personnel selection, the situation is more complicated. Of course, for most jobs one would prefer to select individuals with professional experience over beginning students. However, when having to select individuals from a group of professionals – which would be more often the case – length of experience does not seem to be a very reliable predictor of expert performance. Other aspects of experience, such as experience variety, might be more helpful (Sonnentag, 1995).

In addition to personnel selection, training is a promising approach to the management of expert performance (Hesketh & Ivancic, 2002). Training should help individuals to develop adequate mental models of typical problems in the domain and to choose the most appropriate working strategy. Our literature review suggests that training should focus on domain-specific and meta-cognitive knowledge as well as on abstract planning and evaluation strategies. Effective communication and cooperation skills should be taught and deepened through practical exercises. In our view, it is important that training in communication and cooperation begins at the university because at present training in computer science and programming often relies exclusively on technical knowledge and skills and neglects communication and cooperation skills that seem to be particularly important for expert performance in professional settings.

References

Adelson, B. (1984). When novices surpass experts: The difficulty of a task may increase with expertise. *Journal of Experimental Psychology: Learning, Memory, and Cognition*, 10, 483–495.

Adelson, B., & Soloway, E. (1985). The role of domain experience in software design. *IEEE Transactions on software engineering*, 11, 1351–1360.

Agarwal, R., Sinha, A. P., & Tanniru, M. (1996). The role of prior experience and task characteristics in object-oriented modeling: An empirical study. *International Journal of Human-Computer Studies*, 45, 639–667.

Barfield, W. (1986). Expert-novice differences for software: Implications for problem-solving and knowledge acquisition. *Behaviour & Information Technology*, 5, 15–29.

Barfield, W. (1997). Skilled performance on software as a function of domain expertise and program organization. *Perceptual and Motor Skills*, 85, 1471–1480.

Bateson, A. G., Alexander, R. A., & Murphy, M. D. (1987). Cognitive processing differences between novice and expert computer programmers. *International Journal of Man-Machine Studies*, 26, 649–660.

Batra, D., & Davis, J. G. (1992). Conceptual data modelling in database design: Similarities and differences between expert and novice designers. *International Journal of Man-Machine Studies*, 37, 83–101.

Campbell, D. J., & Gingrich, K. F. (1986). The interactive effects of task complexitiy and participation on task performance: A field experiment. *Organizational Behavior and Human Decision Processes*, 38, 162–180.

Campbell, R. L., Brown, N. R., & DiBello, L. A. (1992). The programmer's burden: Developing expertise in programming. In R. R. Hoffman (Ed.), *The psychology of expertise* (pp. 269–362). New York: Springer.

Chevalier, A., & Ivory, M. Y. (2003). Web site designs: Influences of designer's expertise and design constraints. *International Journal of Human-Computer Studies*, 58, 57–87.

Chi, M. T. H., Feltovich, P. J., & Glaser, R. (1981). Categorization and representation of physics problems by experts and novices. *Cognitive Science*, 5, 121–152.

Collani, G. V., & Schömann, M. (1995). The process of acquisition of a new programming language (LISP): Evidence for transfer of experience and knowledge in programming. In K. F. Wender, F. Schmalhofer & H.-D. Boecker (Eds.), *Cognition and computer programming* (pp. 169–191). Norwood, NJ: Ablex.

Curtis, B. (1986). By the way, did anyone study any real programmers? In E. Soloway & S. Iyengar (Eds.), *Empirical studies of programmers* (pp. 256–262). Norwood, JN: Ablex.

Curtis, B., Krasner, H., & Iscoe, N. (1988). A field study of the software design process for large systems. *Communications of the ACM*, 31, 1268–1287.

Davids, K. (2000). Skill acquisitaion and the theory of deliberate practice: It ain't what you do it's the way you do it *International Journal of Sport Psychology*, 31, 461–466.

Davies, S. P. (1990). Plans, goals and selection rules in the comprehension of computer programs. *Behaviour & Information Technology*, 9, 201–214.

Davies, S. P. (1991). The role of notation and knowledge representation in the determination of programming strategy: A framework for integrating models of programming behavior. *Cognitive Science*, 15, 547–572.

Détienne, F. (1995). Design strategies and knowledge in object-oriented programming: Effects of experience. *Human-Computer Interaction*, 10, 129–169.

Détienne, F. (2002). *Software design. Cognitive aspects.* London, UK: Springer.

Ericsson, K. A., Krampe, R. T., & Tesch-Römer, C. (1993). The role of deliberate practice in the acquisition of expert performance. *Psychological Review*, 100, 363–406.

Ericsson, K. A., & Lehmann, A. C. (1996). Expert and exceptional performance: Evidence of maximal adaptation to task constraints. *Annual Review of Psychology*, 47, 273–305.

Ericsson, K. A., & Smith, J. (1991). Prospects and limits of the empirical study of expertise: An introduction. In K. A. Ericsson & J. Smith (Eds.), *Toward a general theory of expertise: Prospects and limits* (pp. 1–38). Cambridge: Cambridge University Press.

Eteläpelto, A. (1993). Metacognition and the expertise of computer program comprehension. *Scandinavian Journal of Educational Research*, 37, 243–254.

Feltovich, P. J., Spiro, R. J., & Coulson, R. L. (1997). Issues of expert flexibility in contexts characterized by complexity and change. In P. J. Feltovich, K. M. Ford, & R. R. Hoffman (Eds.), *Expertise in Context: Human and Machine* (pp. 125–146). Menlo Park, CA: MIT Press.

Ferris, G. R., Witt, L. A., & Hochwarter, W. A. (2001). Interaction of social skill and general mental ability on job performance and salary. *Journal of Applied Psychology*, 86, 1075–1082.

Fujigaki, Y., & Mori, K. (1997). Longitudinal study of work stress among information system professionals. *International Journal of Human-Computer Interaction*, 9, 369–381.

Glass, R. L. (1997). The ups and downs of programmer stress. *Communications of the ACM*, 40(4), 17–19.

Guerin, B., & Matthews, A. (1990). The effects of semantic complexity on expert and novice computer program recall and comprehension. *The Journal of General Psychology*, 117, 379–389.

Hatano, G., & Inagaki, K. (1986). Two courses of expertise. In H. Stevenson, A. Azuma, & K. Hakuta (Eds.), *Child development and education in Japan* (pp. 262–272). San Francisco: Freeman.

Hesketh, B., & Ivancic, K. (2002). Enhancing performance through training. In S. Sonnentag (Ed.), *Psychological management of individual performance* (pp. 247–265). Chichester: Wiley.

Hoffman, R. R. (1992). Bibliography: Expertise in programming. In R. R. Hoffman (Ed.), *The psychology of expertise: Cognitive research and empirical AI* (pp. 359–362). Hillsdale, NJ: Erlbaum.

Jeffries, R., Turner, A. A., Polson, P. G., & Atwood, M. E. (1981). The processes involved in designing software. In J. R. Anderson (Ed.), *Cognitive skills and their acquisition* (pp. 255–283). Hillsdale, NJ: Erlbaum.

Kelley, R., & Caplan, J. (1993). How Bell Labs creates star performers. *Harvard Business Review*, 71, 128–139.

Kimball, D. R., & Holyoak, K. J. (2000). Transfer and expertise. In E. Tulving & F. I. M. Craik (Eds.), *The Oxford handbook of memory* (pp. 109–122). Oxford: Oxford University Press.

Koubek, R. J., & Salvendy, G. (1991). Cognitive performance of super-experts on computer program modification tasks. *Ergonomics*, 34, 1095–1112.

Koubek, R. J., Salvendy, G., Dunsmore, H. E., & LeBold, W. K. (1989). Cognitive issues in the process of software development: Review and rappraisal. *International Journal of Man-Machine Studies*, 30, 171–191.

Krampe, R. T., & Ericsson, K. A. (1996). Maintaining excellence: Deliberate practice and elite performance in young and older pianists. *Journal of Experimental Psychology: General*, 125, 331–359.

Krems, J. F. (1995). Expert strategies in debugging: Experimental results and a computational model. In K. F. Wender, F. Schmalhofer, & H.-D. Boecker (Eds.), *Cognition and computer programming* (pp. 241–254). Norwood, NJ: Ablex.

Latham, G. P., Locke, E. A., & Fassina, N. E. (2002). The high performance cycle: Standing the test of time. In S. Sonnentag (Ed.), *Psychological management of individual performance* (pp. 201–228). Chichester: Wiley.

Law, L.-C. (1998). A situated cognition view about the effects of planning and authorship on computer program debugging. *Behaviour & Information Technology*, 17, 325–337.

Locke, E. A., & Latham, G. O. (1990). *A theory of goal setting and task performance*. Englewood Cliffs, NJ: Prentice Hall.

Malhotra, A., Thomas, J. C., Carroll, J. M., & Miller, L. A. (1980). Cognitive processes in design. *International Journal of Man-Machine Studies*, 12, 119–140.

McKeithen, K. B., Reitman, J. S., Rueter, H. H., & Hirtle, S. C. (1981). Knowledge organization and skill differences in computer programmers. *Cognitive Psychology*, 13, 307–325.

Nanja, M., & Cook, C. R. (1987). An analysis of the on-line debugging process. In G. M. Olson, S. Sheppard, & E. Soloway (Eds.), *Empirical studies of programmers. Second workshop* (pp. 172–184). Norwood, NJ: Ablex.

Olson, G. M., Sheppard, S., & Soloway, E. (Eds.) (1987). *Empirical studies of programmers: Second workshop*. Norwood, NJ: Ablex.

Pennington, N. (1987). Comprehension strategies in programming. In G. M. Olson, S. Sheppard, & E. Soloway (Eds.), *Empirical studies of programmers: Second workshop* (pp. 100–113). Norwood, NJ: Ablex.

Riedl, T. R., Weitzenfeld, J. S., Freeman, J. T., Klein, G. A., & Musa, J. (1991). What we have learned about software engineering expertise. *Proceedings of the Fifth Software Engineering Institute Conference on Software Engineering Education* (pp. 261–270). New York: Springer.

Rist, R. S. (1986). Plans in programming: Definition, demonstration and development. In E.

Soloway & R. Iyengar (Eds.), *Empirical studies of programmers*. Norwood, NJ: Abley.

Rist, R. S. (1991). Knowledge creation and retrieval in program design: A comparison of novices and intermediate student programmers. *Human-Computer Interaction*, 6, 1–46.

Rist, R. S. (1996). System structure and design. In W. D. Gray & D. A. Boehm-Davis (Eds.), *Empirical studies on programmers: Sixth workshop*. Norwood, NJ: Ablex.

Scholtz, J., & Wiedenbeck, S. (1992). Learning new programming languages: An analysis of the process and problems encountered. *Behaviour & Information Technology*, 11(4), 199–215.

Simon, H. A. (1973). The structure of ill-structured problems. *Artificial Intelligence*, 4, 181–204.

Soloway, E., & Ehrlich, K. (1984). Empirical studies of programming knowledge. *IEEE Transactions on Software Engineering*, 10, 595–609.

Soloway, E., & Iyengar, S. (Eds.) (1986). *Empirical studies of programmers*. Norwood, NJ: Ablex.

Sommerville, I. (2001). *Software engineering* (6th edition). Harlow, UK: Addison-Wesley.

Sonnentag, S. (1995). Excellent software professionals: Experience, work activities, and perceptions by peers. *Behaviour & Information Technology*, 14, 289–299.

Sonnentag, S. (1998). Expertise in professional software design: A process study. *Journal of Applied Psychology*, 83, 703–715.

Sonnentag, S. (2000). Expertise at work: Experience and excellent performance. In C. L. Cooper & I. T. Robertson (Eds.), *International Review of Industrial and Organizational Psychology* (pp. 223–264). Chichester: Wiley.

Sonnentag, S. (2001a). High performance and meeting participation. An observational study in software design teams. *Group Dynamics: Theory, Research and Practice*, 5, 3–18.

Sonnentag, S. (2001b). Using and gaining experience in professional software development. In E. Salas & G. Klein (Eds.), *Linking expertise and naturalistic decision making* (pp. 275–286). Mahwah, NJ: Erlbaum.

Sonnentag, S., & Kleine, B. M. (2000). Deliberate practice at work: A study with insurance agents. *Journal of Occupational and Organizational Psychology*, 73, 87–102.

Sonnentag, S., & Lange, I. (2002). The relationship between high performance and knowledge about how to master cooperation situations. *Applied Cognitive Psychology, 16*, 491–508.

Stajkovic, A. D., & Luthans, F. (1998). Self-efficacy and work-related performance: A meta-analysis. *Psychological Bulletin, 124*, 240–261.

Sternberg, R. J. (1996). Costs of expertise. In K. A. Ericsson (Ed.), *The road to excellence: The acquisition of expert performance in the arts and sciences, sports and games* (pp. 347–354). Mahwah, NJ: Erlbaum.

Stevens, M. J., & Campion, M. A. (1999). Staffing work teams: Development and validation of a selection test for teamwork settings. *Journal of Management, 25*, 207–228.

Teasley, B. E., Leventhal, L. M., Mynatt, C. R., & Rohlman, D. S. (1994). Why software testing is sometimes ineffective: Two applied studies of positive test strategy. *Journal of Applied Psychology, 79*, 142–155.

Turley, R. T., & Bieman, J. M. (1995). Competencies of exceptional and nonexeptional software engineers. *Journal of Systems and Software, 28*, 19–38.

Vessey, I. (1986). Expertise in debugging computer programs: An analysis of the content of verbal protocols. *IEEE Transactions on Systems, Man, and Cybernetics, 16*, 621–637.

Vitalari, N. P., & Dickson, G. W. (1983). Problem solving for effective systems analysis: An experimental exploration. *Communications of the ACM, 26*, 948–956.

Voss, J. F., Fincher-Kiefer, R. H., Greene, T. R., & Post, T. A. (1986). Individual differences in performance: The contrastive approach to knowledge. In R. J. Sternberg (Ed.), *Advances in the psychology of human intelligence* (Vol. 3, pp. 297–334). Hillsdale, NJ: Erlbaum.

Weinberg, G. M., & Schulman, E. L. (1974). Goals and performance in computer programming. *Human Factors, 16*, 70–77.

Weiser, M., & Shertz, J. (1983). Programming problem representation in novice and expert programmers. *International Journal of Man-Machine Studies, 19*, 391–398.

Widowski, D., & Eyferth, K. (1985). Comprehending and recalling computer programs of different structural and semantic complexity by experts and novices. In H.-P. Willumeit (Ed.), *Human decision making and manual control* (pp. 267–275). Amsterdam: Elsevier.

Wiedenbeck, S., Fix, V., & Scholtz, J. (1993). Characteristics of the mental representations of novice and expert programmers: An empirical study. *International Journal of Human-Computer Studies, 39*, 793–812.

Ye, N., & Salvendy, G. (1994). Quantitative and qualitative differences between experts and novices in chunking computer software knowledge. *International Journal of Human-Computer Interaction, 6*, 105–118.

CHAPTER 22

Professional Writing Expertise

Ronald T. Kellogg

Keywords: planning, translating, reviewing, deliberate practice, ten-year rule, flow states, working memory, long-term working memory, domain-specific knowledge, verbal ability, concrete language, strategies, rituals, work environment, work schedule.

Introduction

Writing extended texts for publication is a major cognitive challenge, even for professionals who compose for a living. Serious writing is at once a thinking task, a language task, and a memory task. A professional writer can hold multiple representations in mind while adeptly juggling the basic processes of planning ideas, generating sentences, and reviewing how well the process is going. This chapter will open with the question of how to define the concept of professional writing and an explanation of the demands that writing processes make on cognitive resources. The characteristics of professional-level writers and writing expertise are then enumerated and explored. In the final section, the acquisition of writing skill will be discussed, with comparisons and contrasts to other kinds of expertise highlighted. Much remains to be learned, but the lessons from the state-of-the-art research literature can be helpful to aspiring professional writers.

Defining Professional Writing

Defining expertise in writing is difficult because the task is ill structured (Simon, 1973) and because the types of texts generated by professionals are so varied. An expert in chess successfully checkmates the opponent, and the allowable moves in the game are defined clearly. By contrast, the writer's task is poorly structured with multiple goals that are described in very general terms (e.g., the text must be coherent), and the means to these ends are not well specified and agreed on. Further, professionals who write as part of their work have skill sets that do not necessarily overlap. Journalists, novelists, screen writers, poets, technical writers, and authors of everything from scientific tomes to cookbooks are only the beginning of the list of professional writers. Many professionals often devote considerable time and effort to writing, even though they define their job in other ways (e.g., professors, scientists, engineers, business managers, government bureaucrats, and diplomats). The jobs of career writers, those who compose on technical and professional subjects for a living, certainly differ from those of engineers and administrators in an organization (Couture, 1992). The scientific literature on professional writing samples from all of these domains, albeit too sparsely to draw many conclusions about how they differ. The focus of this chapter, therefore, is on the common elements of professional writing expertise, while recognizing that much more research in this area is possible.

Cognitive Demands of Writing

Hayes and Flower (1980) distinguished three basic processes of text production: planning ideas, translating ideas into text, and reviewing ideas and text. As will be discussed, these are not linear phases of text production, starting with planning and ending with reviewing. Instead, each process can be and often is invoked throughout all phases of text development, from prewriting to a final draft.

Planning includes generating concepts, organizing them, and setting goals to be achieved in the structure of the text. The products of planning fall along a continuum ranging from nonverbal imagery to abstract propositions and word images that are more readily translated to written text (Flower & Hayes, 1984). Sequences of word images or mental pre-texts are what Witte (1987) called "the last cheap gas" before the major cost of concretizing plans into written text. The only visible products of a writer's planning consist of diagrams, outlines, lists, and other "notebooks of the mind," to borrow John-Steiner's (1985) description. These externalized plans are typically cryptic and intended only for the writer's private use.

The translation of ideas into sentences and paragraphs yields a draft of a text that

the author intends to eventually be read and understood by others. Several linguistic processes, largely nonconscious, operate on images and propositions to generate a sentence, such as selecting words and assigning them to syntactic roles (Bock & Levelt, 1994). Besides translating ideas into a sentence, writers must also generate cohesive links among sentences, establishing coherence at both local and global levels in the text (McCutchen, 1984). For written output, graphemic representations must be specified for spelling each word (Caramazza, 1991). The motor transcription of words into written characters often closely follows sentence generation in time and is difficult to distinguish through natural observation alone. It can, therefore, be viewed as a subprocess of translating (Berninger & Swanson, 1994).

Reviewing the text involves reading and editing operations that detect faults at multiple levels of text structure, ranging from local matters of diction, spelling, or punctuation to the coherence of the whole text. It further involves editing ideas and other products of planning (e.g., lists, outlines, diagrams) prior to their conversion to sentences and extended text. The reading and editing processes are complex because so many things can go wrong in a plan or a text at so many different levels of structure (Hayes, Flower, Schriver, Stratman, & Carey, 1987). At the word level of a text, for example, the writer may detect problems with the graphemes used for spelling or with the shade of meaning conveyed. At the sentence level, grammatical errors, semantic ambiguities, alternative interpretations, and problems of reference must be evaluated. The writer must further address faulty logic, errors of fact, and other inconsistencies with world knowledge, on the one hand, and problems with text structure, incoherence, and disorganization, on the other. As if this were not enough, the writer must also consider the needs of the audience, looking for the right tone and degree of complexity.

As noted earlier, the basic processes of writing can be distinguished from the temporal phases of composing a text. The research literature clearly shows that planning, translating, and reviewing do not occur in a linear sequence in text production; rather, they occur and reoccur in complex patterns through prewriting, first draft, and subsequent draft or revision phases of composition (Kellogg, 1994). The interactions among planning, translating, and reviewing are responsible for the development of sophisticated descriptions, narratives, and arguments. During a prewriting phase, for example, the writer may plan, review the ideas and mental pre-text, and then plan some more to produce, say, an outline of topics to be included in a first draft. Although prewriting can be brief, experts approaching a serious writing assignment may spend hours, days, or weeks thinking about the task before initiating a draft.

During the first draft phase, writers continue to plan, generate sentences, read the developing text, and edit ideas and text. Although some writers try to produce a perfect first draft that requires only minor corrections, the first draft is typically revised through one or perhaps many subsequent drafts. Fitzgerald (1987) defined the revision phase of reworking the first draft as "identifying discrepancies between intended and instantiated text, deciding what could or should be changed in the text and how to make the desired changes, and . . . making the desired changes" (p. 484). In revision, as in the original drafting of a text, the writer may engage again in planning and translating as well as further reviewing.

Writing Expertise

We now turn to the specific skills that professional writers bring to their job. This is not intended as an exhaustive list but rather as a selection of the key characteristics of professional writers and their writing skills.

Problem Solving

Aspiring professional writers must be good at thinking through ill-structured problems (Hayes & Flower, 1980). Experienced writers struggle concurrently with two separate problems (Bereiter & Scardamalia, 1987). On the one hand, there is the problem of what to say. The writer mentally represents and manipulates beliefs and facts about the topic within the content "problem space." On the other hand, there is the different problem of how to say it. In the rhetorical "problem space," the writer finds ways to achieve the goals of the composition.

The importance of finding a good way to represent content and rhetorical intent can be seen in interviews with six professional essayists (Dowdy, 1984). For all of them, deciding on the topic, researching the topic, and constructing an integrating theme came first. Having a clear, concrete theme was important because it allowed the essayists to attach their ideas to it, thus interconnecting them. A necessary skill for a professional writer, therefore, is the ability to represent content and rhetorical problems, to explore these representations for satisfactory solutions during composition, and to update them as new insights are achieved (Scardamalia & Bereiter, 1991).

Language Use

Professional writers use language to activate extensive associations among verbal and imaginal representations in the reader (Sadoski & Pavio, 2001). It is the reader who finds a text meaningful, coherent, interesting, or persuasive. The words crafted by the author can potentially trigger the reader's long-term memory representations from the bottom up and motivate constructive processes from the top down. That is to say, the text both relates to what a reader already knows and stimulates new thinking at the same time. Deep comprehension of a text calls on the reader to construct a mental representation of what the text says and how this information integrates with other knowledge about the world (Kintsch, 1998). A shallow level of comprehension is fragmentary by comparison. Professional writers aim to engage the reader in such deep comprehension. How can their skill in doing so be characterized?

VERBAL ABILITY

Construction of a locally cohesive text depends heavily on verbal ability. Fluency in sentence generation and forging links among sentences depends on such linguistic expertise (McCutchen, 1984). Verbal protocols and theoretical analyses suggest that sentences are generated in phrases. Chenoweth and Hayes (2001) observed bursts of words separated by pauses, as writers constructed and then evaluated separate parts of a sentence. Of interest, they found that more-experienced writers (graduate students) generated twice as many words per burst (ten to twelve) compared with less-experienced writers (five to six words for undergraduates). The graduate students' superior verbal ability enabled the rapid retrieval of words, complete phrases, and complex grammatical structures from long-term memory, resulting in the large word bursts.

Both vocabulary size and diversity in word choice correlate positively with judgments of writing effectiveness (Grobe, 1981). High verbal ability also means that writers can tap into multiple syntactic structures for establishing cohesive ties between one clause and the next (McCutchen, 1984). Both word choice and grammatical markers prompt the reader to establish coherence, making an inference if needed, in their mental representation of the text (Givon, 1995). For example, consider the following sentence: Rick left *his bedroom* and stepped *into the living room, where* Mary was reading. *His, into,* and *where* are grammatical cues that guide the reader's sense of spatial relations, driven by the word choice of *his bedroom* and *the living room.*

CONCRETE LANGUAGE

More-memorable writing often results from concrete language usage because it permits verbal and imaginal coding by readers during comprehension (Sadowski & Paivio, 2001). Such dual coding strengthens memory for the text. Sadoski, Goetz, and Avila (1995) compared the recall of four texts that were matched for number of sentences, sentence length, cohesion, and rated comprehensibility. Two of the texts were equally familiar to the readers, but one used concrete language and the other used abstract language. The other two texts differed in familiarity, with abstract language used in the *more* familiar and concrete language used in the *less* familiar. The results showed that equally familiar texts were recalled better with concrete compared to abstract language. Strikingly, increasing familiarity for a text with abstract language did not help; it was recalled no better than an unfamiliar text written in concrete language.

Professional writers do not abolish abstractions from their texts; indeed at times abstract concepts can be rendered only using abstract words. They do, however, know how to provide readers with sufficient concrete references and graphic descriptions of context to make a text come alive in the reader's imagination.

Managing the Cognitive Load

Composing can place severe demands on working memory because the task requires temporarily maintaining numerous mental representations in planning ideas, translating sentences, and reviewing the results. The verbal protocols collected by Flower and Hayes (1980) indicated that: "A writer caught in the act looks... like a very busy switchboard operator trying to juggle a number of demands on her attention and constraints on what she can do" (p. 33). These demands have been further documented by measuring the time needed to respond to a secondary auditory probe during writing. It takes longer to detect the probe and respond while one is composing, compared with listening for the probe as a sole task. The degree to which responding slows down while writing reflects the concurrent demands of composing processes on working memory. Of interest, writing text causes very large delays in responding to the probes for college-level writers, much larger than that observed with learning and reading tasks (Kellogg, 1994). The delays when writing were comparable to those observed in earlier research with chess experts evaluating multiple moves in the middle stages of a game (Britton & Tessor, 1982).

A variety of cognitive strategies help the writer to cope with the cognitive demands of text production. Prewriting, drafting, and revising strategies are essential strategies. Preparing an outline as a prewriting strategy enables the writer to focus attention on translating ideas into text while drafting and can enhance productivity (Kellogg, 1988). Individuals who write in organizations as part of their job responsibilities frequently report the need to plan a lot mentally (98%), create notes and lists (95%), and prepare outlines (73%), especially for serious writing tasks that do not fit a routine schema (Couture & Rymer, 1993).

Highly successful writers have reported a wide range of prewriting strategies that can be expressed as styles (Cowley, 1958; Plimpton, 1963; 1989). "Beethovians" engage in few prewriting activities and prefer to compose rough first drafts immediately to discover what they have to say (Bridwell-Bowles, Johnson, & Brehe, 1987). Their drafting necessarily involves many rounds of revision. By contrast, "Mozartians" delay drafting for lengthy periods of time in order to allow time for extensive reflection and planning. They may also plan mental pretext that is later recalled and written down as a first polished draft. A variety of notational methods are used to externalize plans during prewriting, including tree diagrams, flow charts, boxes, arrows, doodles, and scribbles, as well as lists and outlines (John-Steiner, 1985).

Preparing a rough draft can help writers to reduce the number of processes juggled simultaneously by dissociating the author from an editing mindset (Glynn, Britton, Muth, & Dogan, 1982). However, professional writers who report attempting to produce a perfect first draft are just as productive as those who report starting with a rough draft (Kellogg, 1986). An intriguing strategy reported by some fiction writers is to dissociate the author into multiple characters, so to speak. The writer observes what the characters are doing and saying, in the writer's imagination, as a way of composing the text (Tomlinson, 1986). But again, listening to the characters dictate the story is not an essential feature of successful creative writers, though many do find daydreaming and even dreaming at night conducive to their work (Epel, 1993).

Domain Specificity

As noted earlier, writing expertise is highly domain dependent. In an important sense, then, the *professional writer* may be a rare individual indeed, when conceived as a generalist capable of writing across any number of domains (Carter, 1996). An outstanding journalist might be lost if they had to compose a scientific report. A scientist may be equally adrift in trying to write for the general public. Even within a profession, a writer often specializes in a specific rhetorical context. For example, the journalist who specializes in movie reviews for the *New Yorker* might well perform more like a novice in writing market analyses for the *Wall Street Journal*. There are indeed diverse, highly specific skills required by journalism, exposition, creative fiction, business writing, or technical writing. Professionalism in any one of these kinds of writing requires a progression beyond general writing skills, such as outlining, fluent sentence generation, and effective topic sentences, to domain-specific knowledge and skills.

For example, the expert must master the rhetorical style required in a given domain. Psychologists, for example, learn the rhetorical style mandated by the American Psychological Association *Publication Manual*, which contrasts with the *Chicago Manual of Style* used in the humanities (Madigan, Johnson, & Linton, 1995). Psychologists' conclusions must be hedged so as to avoid stepping beyond the limits of the data, creating an air of uncertainty that is atypical in the humanities. Disagreements are couched in terms of differences about appropriate methods or interpretations of data, never in the personal terms at times seen in literary criticism.

Rapid Access to Long-Term Memory

Domain-specific knowledge allows experts to escape, in part, the severe constraints on working memory that hinder effective writing in novices (McCutchen, 2000). Expertise allows the rapid, facile retrieval of representations from long-term memory as they are needed rather than requiring the thinker to maintain everything actively in short-term working memory (Ericsson & Kintsch, 1995). The ability of domain experts to use long-term memory as a kind of working memory could be the critical advantage they have over less-knowledgeable writers in achieving fluent production (McCutchen, 2000). For example, expertise in the game of baseball enabled writers to respond to auditory probes as they composed narratives of a half-inning significantly faster than was observed for control participants with little knowledge of the game (Kellogg, 2001).

Rapid retrieval from long-term working memory allows experts to take into account more ideas in planning a text relative to novices. For example, Geisler, Rogers, and Haller (1998) asked software engineering experts, advanced software engineering students, advanced technical communication students, and advanced chemistry students to list all the issues that needed to be resolved in designing an automated bus ticket issuing system. The experts listed 62% more ideas than the average of the other three groups combined. Compared to the advanced chemistry students, who performed the worst, the experts retrieved markedly more information about system issues (71%) and business issues (83%), for example.

Awareness of the Readership

Professional writers are able to craft their knowledge, through their writing, so that it is understandable to a specific audience. Knowledge crafting requires maintaining three representations in working memory simultaneously (Traxler & Gernsbacher, 1992). First, the ideas to be communicated must be formulated and held long enough to translate them into sentences. Second, the actual meaning of the sentences produced thus far must also be read and comprehended by the author. Third, the author ought to try to read the text from the perspective of the potential reader. This requires adopting the perspective of another individual and imagining how the reader would construe the text. Revision of the text can be limited to detecting mismatches between the author's intent and the text as it reads to the author. Professional revision, on the other hand, benefits further by the author trying to see the text as a reader would see it.

Hyland (2001) documented the ways in which academic writers anticipate readers' reactions to their arguments and counter them. A total of 240 published articles from leading journals in ten disciplines were analyzed for markers that initiate a dialogue between the writer and reader. For example, the writers posed real and rhetorical questions to engage the reader. They made direct references to the reader and to shared knowledge, and used second person pronouns and asides addressed to the reader.

Still, failures to craft knowledge for readers abound, from poorly written technical documentation (Hayes & Flower, 1986) to jargon-filled legal documents that are incomprehensible to the general public (Hartley, 2000). Professional writers hired to improve the clarity of documents do not always succeed (Duffy, Curran, & Sass, 1983). The ability to see the document from the reader's vantage point is a serious challenge that requires extended practice by professionals. Further, writers must at times anticipate the needs of multiple audiences, as when a technical article is read by a student as well as by a specialist. As a coping heuristic, professionals may write for someone close to them rather than for an imagined public audience. Of six scientific essayists, all claimed that they were not quite sure who their real audience was. Lewis Thomas wrote instead for members of his family to read, Jeremy Bernstein wrote for his friends, and Stephen Jay Gould said he wrote for himself (Dowdy, 1984).

Managing the Emotional Challenges

Professional writers, as with other practitioners of the creative arts, must be self-motivated to commit long hours to a lonely task of working with ideas and language rather than with other people. The emotional demands of writing are just as challenging as the cognitive demands (Brand, 1989). Experienced writers learn to self-regulate their emotions and behavior to stay on task and complete the work by losing themselves in their work, engineering their work environment, adhering to a work schedule, and practicing motivational rituals. Breakdowns in their efforts to regulate their emotions and behavior can, in serious cases, result in writer's block (Boice, 1994).

FLOW STATES

A common experience of experts engaged in their craft is feeling lost in the work. The writer looses a sense of ego and an awareness of the immediate surroundings. Hours can pass quickly as a skilled writer is absorbed in thought and language. Csikszentmihalyi (1990) referred to such absorption and the positive affect associated with it as a flow state of consciousness. Flow can be produced when an individual's aptitude and skills are well matched by the demands of any task and writing is no exception (Larsen, 1988). Clarity of purpose, a sense of mastery, and high intrinsic motivation further characterize flow. When the demands exceed one's capacity, on the other hand, then the consequence is anxiety and frustration. A mismatch in the opposite direction produces boredom.

Schere (1998) contrasted university professors of creative writing, fine arts, and engineering on a drawing versus writing task. As predicted, the creative writers reported a higher level of positive mood after completing the writing task compared with the drawing task. Brand and Leckie's study of professional writers (1989) also concluded that the opportunity to engage a task that fits the writer's capabilities enhances positive mood. Perry (1996) interviewed 33

poets and 29 fiction writers about the conditions that lead to flow. Entry into flow, she concluded, is chiefly facilitated by having a strong motivation to write. Believing that the writing task is intrinsically important is sufficient for many professional writers, but Perry found also that pay and other extrinsic motivators stimulate flow. By contrast, some evidence suggests that a writer's creativity can be diminished by extrinsic rewards (Amabile, 1985).

The positive affect of flow states can characterize the work of professional writers, but they also face frustrations, anxieties, and other negative emotions when the demands of the task temporarily exceed their capacities. Writer's block can be one consequence whereby production is sharply curtailed or stopped altogether (Boice, 1994). Perry (1996) documented that some writers force themselves during these periods "to produce line after line ... and the product of such reluctant writing sessions is often not up to what the writers consider their standard" (p. 275). Thus, judging from Perry's interviews, professionals manage to tolerate negative emotional states as well as enjoying the positive experience of flow. It is also important to recognize that procrastination can be beneficial when it reflects a real need to take more time (Murray, 1978). Extensive prewriting activities can be a way for professional writers to digest and understand their subject thoroughly before beginning a first draft.

ENVIRONMENTS, SCHEDULES, AND RITUALS

Where, when, and how writers work show enormous variability. However, many writers develop habitual ways of approaching their work such that they become necessary conditions for effective knowledge use. Perry's (1996) interviews with established creative writers and surveys of university faculty who produce scholarly publications (Boice & Johnson, 1984; Hartley & Branthwaite, 1989; Kellogg, 1986) converge on three points. All of the idiosyncratic habits of professional writers (1) focus attention inward by eliminating distractions, (2) may alter consciousness to facilitate entry in a flow state, and (3) help regulate the writer's emotional state to keep at the task.

For example, whereas some writers report that they find a quiet environment useful, others preferred background music or the bustle of a cafe. Whereas some must write with a word processor, others prefer longhand or a typewriter. Many choose to write at the same time each working day, but individuals differ from morning, afternoon, evening, late night, to early morning preferences. Work sessions of one to two hours correlate with productivity in scientific writing, but the relationship is weak ($r = .22$) and the variability is large, with some individuals writing four or more hours at a time (Kellogg, 1986). Successful poets also typically write for one or two hours, whereas most novelists typically report longer sessions of two to three or even four to six hours (Perry, 1996). Running or walking help some writers think through problems while away from the writing table (Oates, 2003; Kellogg, 1986). Others use meditation, coffee, cigarettes, alcohol, or other drugs to alter consciousness in the service of writing (Piirto, 2002).

BLOCKING

Writer's block, defined as a persistent inability to put thoughts on paper, can impede, if not end, the career of a professional writer. Boice (1985) found the thoughts of blocked academics were characterized by procrastination, dysphoria (e.g., burnout, panic, obsessive worries), impatience (e.g., thoughts of achieving more in less time or imposing unrealistic deadlines), perfectionism (e.g., thoughts reflecting an internal critic who allows no errors), and evaluation anxiety (e.g., fears of being rejected). Of interest, unblocked as well as blocked writers fretted about how difficult and demanding the task was for them.

Thus, professional writers not only know how to enter flow, but how to endure the intense negative feelings that often accompany the early stages of writing a text, when all can seem hopelessly incoherent. Learning to manage the emotional ups and downs

of writing is important for writers to avoid burning out and perhaps ending their career prematurely. Self-regulation through daily writing, brief work sessions, realistic deadlines, and maintaining low emotional arousal help professional writers stay with the task for the weeks, months, and years required (Boice, 1994; Zimmerman & Risemberg, 1997). Binge writing – hypomanic, euphoric, marathon sessions to meet unrealistic deadlines – is generally counterproductive and potentially a source of depression and blocking (Boice, 1997).

To summarize, there is a wide variety of skills and qualities that professional writers bring to their daily work. We now turn to what is known about the acquisition of those writing skills.

Skill Acquisition

Literacy is a fundamental goal of schooling in contemporary societies worldwide. Thus, unlike medical diagnosis, finance, and other skills for which practice begins in early adulthood for a select few, writing development starts in early childhood in industrialized nations. The foundations of literacy are established in toddlers with letter and word recognition and scribbling. By the time a child enters school, practice in handwriting is well underway, and children as young as four years of age distinguish writing from drawing (Lee & Karmiloff-Smith, 1996).

Deliberate Practice

Ericsson, Krampe, and Tesch-Römer (1993) defined the characteristics of deliberate practice as (1) effortful exertion to improve performance, (2) intrinsic motivation to engage in the task, (3) practice tasks that are within reach of the individual's current level of ability, (4) feedback that provides knowledge of results, and (5) high levels of repetition. They contrasted deliberate practice with work activities for pay or other external rewards and play activities that are enjoyable but have no goal for improving performance.

Deliberate practice can only be sustained for a limited amount of time each day because of the effort involved.

Signs of deliberate practice in writing can be seen in work habits and practice techniques. Successful writers often schedule only a few hours per day for composing, and avoid binges that lead to exhaustion (Boice, 1994; 1997). High levels of practice can be seen in the daily work schedules of prolific writers (Cowley, 1958; Kellogg, 1982; Plimpton, 1963).

It has long been known that composition instructors can coach writers through feedback. Apprenticeships in creative writing programs and schools of journalism rely on this method of practice. The Iowa Writer's Workshop, the earliest creative writing degree program in the United States, has from the outset emphasized learning by doing and immersing writers in feedback from others (Adams, 1993). As early as 1890, writers' clubs formed in Iowa City, where students and faculty could read and critique each others' work and practice their craft. Journalists, too, have always learned by doing, first in newspaper offices and later in formal university programs. From its beginning in 1908, the University of Missouri's School of Journalism has run a daily city newspaper for students to practice their skills with instruction and feedback from the faculty.

Well-known writers have reported valued practice techniques. As a college student, Joyce Carol Oates would write a novel in longhand, then turn the pages over, writing another novel on the flipside. Both novels would then be tossed in the trash. Since high school she began "consciously training myself by writing novel after novel and always throwing them out when I completed them" (Plimpton, 1989; p. 378). Her practice books would be modeled after specific works by authors she admired, such as Hemingway's *In Our Time*. Norman Mailer (2003) credited his eventual success as a writer to self-motivated practice.

I think from the time I was seventeen, I had no larger desire in life than to be a writer, and I wrote . . . I learned to write by writing. As I once calculated, I must have written more than a half a million words before I came to The Naked and the Dead. *(pp. 13–14)*

In his autobiography, Benjamin Franklin explained how he rewrote admired texts that he wished to emulate (Lemay & Zall, 1981). He took careful notes on a text and then several days later used these as retrieval cues to reconstruct the original in his own words.

Evidence of deliberate practice emerges from several ethnographic studies of professional writers (Henry, 2000; MacKinnon, 1993; Paradis, Dobrin, & Miller, 1985). Learning on the job, practicing to perfection, and viewing oneself as still developing in skill over the course of one's career are typical traits of these writers. Successful expository writers who meet weekly and monthly deadlines continue to develop their skills through immersion in a habitual, predictable task environment (Root, 1983).

Reading

Extensive reading is a powerful predictor of the amount of general knowledge that an individual accumulates in long-term memory (Stanovich & Cunningham, 1993). A composite measure of print exposure is strongly correlated with a composite measure of general knowledge ($r = .85$). This relationship remains statistically significant even after the effects of cognitive ability are removed. How much one knows depends on how much one reads.

Because a wide range of knowledge is so important for writers (Kellogg, 1994), it is not surprising that professional writers report reading extensively, even compulsively. Louis L'Amour, the prolific writer of novels about the American West, recounted in *Education of a Wandering Man* (1989) that he read hundreds of books as he traveled the world. Mark Singer, a staff writer at the *New Yorker* magazine, reads and re-reads the masters of nonfiction, such as E. B. White, Calvin Trillin, and John McPhree (Pearson,

1998). Truman Capote, when asked whether he read a great deal, responded:

> Too much. And anything, including labels and recipes and advertisements. I have a passion for newspapers – read all the New York dailies everyday, and the Sunday editions, and several foreign magazines too. The ones I don't buy I read standing at news stands. (Capote quoted in Cowley, 1958; p. 293)

Piirto (2002) concluded from her case studies that professional writers often begin reading early in childhood and read compulsively throughout their lifespan. The reading begins as a way to learn about the world. The reading later becomes more focused and intellectually challenging during the course of formal education, according to Piirto. As writers develop professionally, they read within the genre in which they work. For example, science fiction writers read science fiction, whereas romance writers read romances.

The Ten-Year Rule

Studies of chess players (Simon & Chase, 1973), musical composers (Hayes, 1985), and other domains (Ericsson et al., 1993) have suggested a rule of thumb that it takes at least a decade of intensive practice to achieve excellence. In the case of writing, the clock starts early, since spoken language and scribbling are developed in preliterate children (Lee & Karmiloff-Smith, 1996). By the age of 12 to 14 years, children have spent ten years mastering the mechanics of handwriting and spelling. Approximately during this same time frame, they advance from thinking in term of concrete events in the here and now to thinking in hypothetical, abstract terms. From studies that tracked the cohesion of texts produced by children at different ages, Scinto (1986) concluded that this advancement from concrete to abstract thinking is essential for writing cohesive texts. Although speech is proficient by the age of six, written fluency does not catch up until around the age of 12 years (Bereiter & Scardamalia, 1987).

The written production strategy of children is a simple one of egocentric knowledge telling (Bereiter & Scardamalia, 1987). An idea is retrieved from long-term memory and then told to the reader by writing it down. This process continues until the writer has no more ideas to retrieve and communicate. The heavy demands made on working memory by handwriting alone make it difficult for young writers to do much more than retrieve and translate (Bourdin & Fayol, 1994; McCutchen, 1996). They can maintain a representation of what they intend to write, but no more than this.

By contrast, Bereiter and Scardamalia (1987) characterized adult writing as knowledge transforming. What the writer thinks is transformed by the act of composition. The adult writer reads the evolving text and develops a representation of what it says to the author. Reflection on the existing text can prompt the writer to restructure the ideas stored in long-term memory, elaborating and reorganizing what the writer knows about the topic. Whereas knowledge-telling often produces a string of assertions linked by "and," knowledge-transforming yields complex argument structures and the use of cohesive devices to link clauses in a paragraph. The adult writer, therefore, maintains representations of the author's current intent and what the text says from the author's perspective.

After mastering handwriting and achieving written fluency at ages 12 to 14, approximately a decade of practice is needed to progress from knowledge-telling to knowledge-transforming. Bereiter and Scardamalia (1987) turned to graduate-student writing to illustrate knowledge-transforming. It is unknown how long it takes to advance further to knowledge-crafting, whereby professionals can mentally represent the text as it appears to the reader and respond to their needs adroitly. But several years are probably needed to acquire the domain-specific rhetorical skills and practice at crafting knowledge for a specific audience (Rymer, 1988).

Wishbow (1988) examined the biographies of 66 poets listed in the *Norton Anthology of Poetry*, locating their approximate starting date for reading and writing poetry. The earliest work to appear in Norton's came during the ten years after this date or later for 83% of the sample. The poets began reading and writing poetry in their early teens to early twenties. Thus, ten to twenty years of writing seemed to span their first scribbling as a toddler to their first masterpiece. T. S. Elliot wrote his masterpiece, *The Waste Land*, in his early 30s, about a decade after composing his first published poem (Gardner, 1993).

Not surprisingly, the earlier the writer starts the better. Childhood story writing was so commonly mentioned in Henry's (2002; p. 37) ethnographies that "people who were attracted to writing after childhood may even refer to themselves as 'late bloomers.'" A study of 986 creative writers found a significant correlation between the age of first publication and the number of works published in total for poets (Kaufman & Gentile, 2002). Replicating and extending Wishbow's findings, both poets and fiction writers developed mechanics and cognitive writing skills for 15 to 20 years before first publishing. Only 10% of the sample published prior to the age of 21. About half (49%) first published in their twenties and the remainder in their thirties or later.

Isaac Asimov's prolific career illustrates how productivity depends on decades of preparation and practice (see the Asimov web site, http:www.asimovonline.com/). His first book appeared in 1950. He published one, two, or three books a year for the next six years, but then gradually began to publish more than five books a year on a consistent basis from 1962 on. It took Asimov 19 years to publish his first 100 books, but only ten years to publish the second 100. His productivity then accelerated after approximately 30 years of practice at the craft. It took him only five additional years to bring his total to 300 books.

Conclusion

Professional writing reflects not just general writing ability but also expertise in a particular genre and domain. Thus, there are really many specific kinds of professional writers, but some features apply to them all. Extensive reading, high verbal ability, the skilled use of concrete language, and the ability to envision and respond to the readership are hallmarks of the writer's craft.

The other common features of professional writers also overlap with different kinds of expertise and figure prominently in a general theory of expertise (Ericsson & Smith, 1991). Strategies for managing the cognitive load on working memory are important for the writer as well as for professionals in computer programming, for example. Knowledge about the domain permits the rapid retrieval of information from long-term memory and minimizes the demands on short-term working memory, such as is observed in master chess players. The ten-year rule of expert skill acquisition applies to writers and, if anything, underestimates the number of years of deliberate practice required to reach professional levels of achievement. Writers, as with surgeons, musicians, and athletes, perform best in a flow state of consciousness. They all try to shape their surroundings, work schedules, and rituals in ways that foster flow. Self-regulation of the emotional demands of writing in these ways is necessary for a productive career, a feature shared in common with many professions. Much remains to be discovered about the skills of professional writers and longitudinal studies of their development would be particularly informative, but those aspiring to the role can learn from the findings reviewed here.

References

Adams, K. H. (1993). *A history of professional writing instruction in American colleges*. Dallas: Southern Methodist Press.

Amabile, T. M. (1985). Motivation and creativity: Effects of motivational orientation on creative writers. *Journal of Personality and Social Psychology, 48*, 393–399.

Asimov web site. (n.d.). Retrieved December 6, 2003 from http:www.asimovonline.com/.

Berninger, V. W., & Swanson, H. L. (1994). Modifying Hayes and Flower's model of skilled writing to explain beginning and developing writing. In E. C. Butterfield (Ed.), *Children's writing: Toward a process theory of the development of skilled writing* (pp. 57–81). Greenwich, CT: JAI Press.

Bereiter, S., & Scardamalia, M. (1987). *The psychology of written composition*. Hillsdale, NJ: Erlbaum.

Bock, J. K., & Levelt, W. (1994). Language production: Grammatical encoding. In M. Gernsbacher (Ed.), *Handbook of psycholinguistics* (pp. 945–984). San Diego: Academic Press.

Boice, R. (1985). Cognitive components of blocking. *Written Communication*, *2*, 91–104.

Boice, R. (1994). *How writers journey to comfort and fluency: A psychological adventure*. Westport, CT: Praeger.

Boice, R. (1997). Which is more productive, writing in binge patterns of creative illness or in moderation? *Written Communication*, *14*, 435–459.

Boice, R., & Johnson, K. (1984). Perception and practice of writing for publication by faculty at a doctoral-granting university. *Research in Higher Education*, *21*, 33–43.

Bourdin, B., & Fayol, M. (1994). Is written language production more difficult than oral language production: A working memory approach. *International Journal of Psychology*, *29*, 591–620.

Brand, A. G. (1989). *The psychology of writing: The affective experience*. New York: Greenwood Press.

Brand, A. G., & Leckie, P. A. (1989). The emotions of professional writers. *The Journal of Psychology*, *122*, 421–439.

Bridwell-Bowles, L., Johnson, P., & Brehe, S. (1987). Composing and computers: Case studies of experienced writers. In A. Matsuhashi (Ed.), *Writing in real time: Modeling production processes* (pp. 81–107). London: Longman.

Britton, B. K., & Tessor, A. (1982). Effects of prior knowledge on use of cognitive capacity in three complex cognitive tasks. *Journal of Verbal Learning and Verbal Behavior*, *21*, 421–436.

Caramazza, A. (1991). *Issues in reading, writing, and speaking: A neuropsychological perspective*. Dordrecht: Kluwer Academic.

Carter, M. (1996). What is *advanced* about advanced composition: A theory of expertise in writing. In G. A. Olson & J. Drew (Eds.), *Landmark essays on advanced composition* (pp. 71–80). Mahwah, NJ: Erlbaum.

Chenoweth, N. A., & Hayes, J. R. (2001). The inner voice in writing. *Written Communication*, *20*, 99–118.

Couture, B. (1992). Categorizing professional discourse: Engineering, administrative, technical/professional writing. *Journal of Business and Technical Communication*, *6*, 5–7.

Couture, B., & Rymer, J. (1993). Situational exigence: Composing processes on the job by writer's role and task value. In R. Spilka (Ed.), *Writing in the workplace: Now research perspectives* (pp. 4–55). Carbondale, IL: Southern Illinois University Press.

Cowley, M. (Ed.) (1958). *Writers at work: The Paris Review interviews* (Vol. 1). New York: Viking Press.

Csikszentmihalyi, M. (1990). *Flow: The psychology of optimal experience*. New York: Harper & Row.

Dowdy, D. (1984, March). The trying out of the essay: How six scientific essayists compose. Paper presented at the 35th annual meeting of the Conference on College Composition and Communication. New York. (ERIC Document Reproduction Service No. ED243150)

Duffy, T., Curran, T., & Sass, D. (1983). Document design for technical job tasks: An evaluation. *Human Factors*, *25*, 143–160.

Epel, N. (1993). *Writers dreaming*. New York: Carol Southern Books.

Ericsson, K. A., & Kintsch, W. (1995). Long-term working memory. *Psychological Review*, *102*, 211–245.

Ericsson, K. A., Krampe, R. T., & Tesch-Römer, C. (1993). The role of deliberate practice in the acquisition of expert performance. *Psychological Review*, *100*, 363–406.

Ericsson, K. A., & Smith, J. (Eds.) (1991). *Toward a general theory of expertise: Prospects and limits*. Cambridge: Cambridge University Press.

Fitzgerald, J. (1987). Research on revision in writing. *Review of Educational Research*, *57*, 481–506.

Flower, L. S., & Hayes, J. R. (1980). The dynamics of composing: Making plans and juggling constraints. In L. W. Gregg & E. R. Steinberg (Eds.), *Cognitive processes in writing* (pp. 31–50). Hillsdale, NJ: Erlbaum.

Flower, L. S., & Hayes, J. R. (1984). Images, plans, and prose: The representation of meaning in writing. *Written Communication*, *1*, 120–160.

Geisler, C., Rogers, E. H., & Haller, C. R. (1998). Disciplining discourse: Discourse practice in the affiliated professions of software engineering design. *Written Communication, 15*, 3–24.

Givon, T. (1995). Coherence in the text and coherence in the mind. In M. A. Gernsbacher & T. Givon (Eds.), *Coherence in spontaneous text* (pp. 139–160). Amsterdam: John Benjamins.

Glynn, S. M., Britton, B. K., Muth, D., & Dogan, N. (1982). Writing and revising persuasive documents: Cognitive demands. *Journal of Educational Psychology, 74*, 557–567.

Grobe, C. (1981). Syntactic maturity, mechanics, and vocabulary as predictors of quality ratings. *Research in the Teaching of English, 15*, 75–85.

Hartley, J. (2000). Legal ease and 'legalese.' *Psychology, Crime, and Law, 6*, 1–20.

Hartley, J., & Branthwaite, A. (1989). The psychologist as wordsmith: A questionnaire study of the writing strategies of productive British psychologists. *Higher Education, 18*, 423–452.

Hayes, J. R. (1985). Three problems in teaching general skills. In S. F. Chipman, J. W. Segal, & R. Glaser (Eds.), *Thinking and learning skills: Vol. 2. Research and open questions* (pp. 391–405). Hillsdale, NJ: Erlbaum.

Hayes, J. R., & Flower, L. S. (1980). Identifying the organization of writing processes. In L. W. Gregg & E. R. Steinberg (Eds.), *Cognitive processes in writing* (pp. 3–30). Hillsdale, NJ: Erlbaum.

Hayes, J. R., Flower, L. S., Schriver, K. S., Stratman, J., & Carey, L. (1987). Cognitive approaches in revision. In S. Rosenberg (Ed.), *Advances in applied psycholinguistics: Vol. 2. Reading, writing, and language processing* (pp. 176–240). New York: Cambridge University Press.

Hayes, J. R., & Flower, L. S. (1986). Writing research and the writer. *American Psychologist, 41*, 1106–1113.

Henry, J. (2000). *Writing workplace cultures: An archeology of professional writing.* Carbondale, IL: Southen Illinois University Press.

Hyland, K. (2001). Bringing in the reader: Addressee features in academic articles. *Written Communication, 18*, 549–574.

John-Steiner, V. (1985). *Notebooks of the mind: Explorations of thinking.* Albuquerque: University of New Mexico Press.

Kaufman, J. C., & Gentile, C. A. (2002). The will, The wit, The judgment: The importance of an early start in productive and successful creative writing. *High Ability Studies, 13*(2), 115–123.

Kellogg, R. T. (1986). Writing method and productivity of science and engineering faculty. *Research in Higher Education, 25*, 147–163.

Kellogg, R. T. (1988). Attentional overload and writing performance: Effects of rough draft and outline strategies. *Journal of Experimental Psychology: Learning, Memory, and Cognition, 14*, 355–365.

Kellogg, R. T. (1994). *The psychology of writing.* New York: Oxford University Press.

Kellogg, R. T. (2001). Long-term working memory in text production. *Memory & Cognition, 29*, 43–52.

Kintsch, W. (1998). *Comprehension: A paradigm for cognition.* Cambridge: Cambridge University Press.

Larsen, R. (1988). Flow and writing. In M. Csikszentmihalyi & I. S. Csikszentmihalyi (1988). *Optimal experience: Psychological studies of flow in consciousness* (pp. 150–171). Cambridge: Cambridge University Press.

Lee, K., & Karmiloff-Smith, A. (1996). The development of external symbol systems: The child as notator. In R. Gelman & T. Kit-Fong (Eds.), *Perceptual and cognitive development* (185–211). San Diego, CA: Academic Press.

Lemay, J. A. L., & Zall, P. M. (Eds.) (1981). *The autobiography of Benjamin Franklin: A genetic text.* Knoxville: Univerisity of Tennessee Press.

L'Amour, L. (1989). *Education of a wandering man.* New York: Bantam.

Madigan, R., Johnson, S., & Linton, P. (1995). The language of psychology: APA style as epistemology. *American Psychologist, 50*, 428–436.

Mailer, N. (2003). *The spooky art: Some thoughts on writing.* New York: Random House.

MacKinnon, J. (1993). Becoming a rhetor: Developing writing ability in a mature, writing intensive organization. In R. Spilka (Ed.), *Writing in the workplace: New research perspectives* (pp. 41–55). Carbondale, IL: Southern Illinois University Press.

McCutchen, D. (1984). Writing as a linguistic problem. *Educational Psychologist, 19*, 226–238.

McCutchen, D. (1996). A capacity theory of writing: Working memory in composition. *Educational Psychology Review, 8*, 299–325.

McCutchen, D. (2000). Knowledge, processing, and working memory: Implications for a theory of writing. *Educational Psychologist, 35*, 13–23.

Murray, D. M. (1978). Write before writing. *College Composition and Communication, 29*, 375–381.

Oates, J. C. (2003). *The faith of a writer: Life, craft, and art*. New York: Harper Collins.

Paradis, J., Dobrin, D., & Miller, R. (1985). Writing at Exxon ITD: Notes on the writing environment of an R&D organization. In L. Odell & D. Goswami (Eds.), *Writing in nonacademic settings* (pp. 281–307). New York: Guilford.

Pearson, M. (1998). Mr. Personalities: A conversation about the writing process with Mark Singer. *Creative Nonfiction, 9*, 118–125.

Perry, S. K. (1996). When time stops: How creative writers experience entry into the flow state. *Dissertation Abstracts International, 58* (8), 4484B. (UMI No. 9805789)

Piirto, J. (2002). *"My teeming brain": Understanding creative writers*. Cresskill, NJ: Hampton Press.

Plimpton, G. (Ed.) (1963). *Writers at work: The Paris Review interviews, second series*. New York: Penguin.

Plimpton, G. (Ed.) (1989). *Women writers at work: The Paris Review interviews*. New York: Penguin.

Root, R. L. (1983). The composing processes of professional expository writers. Paper presented at the 34th annual meeting of the Conference on College Composition and Communication. Detroit. (ERIC Document Reproduction Service No. ED232157)

Rymer, J. (1988). Scientific composing processes: How eminent scientists write journal articles. In D. A. Jollife (Ed.), *Advances in writing research, Volume 2: Writing in academic disciplines* (pp. 211–250). Norwood, NJ: Ablex.

Sadoski, M., & Paivio, A. (2001). *Imagery and text: A dual coding theory of reading and writing*. Mahwah, NJ: Erlbaum.

Sadoski, M., Goetz, E. T., & Avila, E. (1995). Concreteness effects in text recall: Dual coding

or context availability? *Reading Research Quarterly, 30*, 278–288.

Scardamalia, M., & Bereiter, C. (1991). Literate expertise. In K. A. Ericsson & J. Smith (Eds.), *Toward a general theory of expertise: Prospects and limits* (pp. 172–194). Cambridge: Cambridge University Press.

Schere, J. J. (1998). Effect of engaging in creative activity on the mood of artists and writers: An empirical test of flow theory. (Doctoral Dissertation, The California School of Professional Psychology). *Dissertation Abstracts International, 59* (06), 3074B.

Scinto, L. F. M. (1986). *Written language and psychological development*. Orlando: Academic Press.

Simon, H. A. (1973). The structure of ill-structured problems. *Artificial Intelligence, 4*, 181–210.

Simon, H. A., & Chase, W. G. (1973). Skill in chess. *American Scientist, 61*, 394–403.

Stanovich, K. E., & Cunningham, A. E. (1993). Where does knowledge come from? Specific associations between print exposure and information acquisition. *Journal of Educational Psychology, 85*, 211–229.

Tomlinson, B. (1986). Characters as co-authors: Segmenting the self, integrating the composing process. *Written Communication, 3*, 421–448.

Traxler, M. J., & Gernsbacher, M. A. (1992). Improving written communication through minimal feedback. *Language and Cognitive Processes, 7*, 1–22.

Wishbow, N. A. (1988). Studies of creativity in poets. (Doctoral Dissertation, Carnegie Mellon University). *Dissertation Abstracts International, 51*, 0491A.

Witte, S. P. (1987). Pre-text and composing. *College Composition and Communication, 38*, 397–425.

Zimmerman, B. J., & Risemberg, R. (1997). Becoming a self-regulated writer: A social cognitive perspective. *Contemporary Educational Psychology, 22*, 73–101.

CHAPTER 23

Professional Judgments and "Naturalistic Decision Making"

Karol G. Ross, Jennifer L. Shafer, & Gary Klein

This chapter looks at expertise from the perspective of the community of practice known as Naturalistic Decision Making (NDM). We provide an overview of the emergence of NDM, the underlying theoretical orientation, and key NDM research. We discuss the impact NDM has had on one particular domain of expert judgment, military decision making. We conclude by discussing applications and continuing research issues in NDM.

Emergence of Naturalistic Decision Making

The focus of NDM research is on expert practitioners trying to figure out what to do under difficult circumstances. The need to understand decision making in the context of time pressure, uncertainty, ill-defined goals, and high personal stakes was a major impetus for the emergence of NDM. The coalescence of NDM as a field of study was marked by the publication of *Decision*

Making in Action: Models and Methods (G. A. Klein, Orasanu, Calderwood, & Zsambok, 1993).[1]

Zsambok (1997) described how this publication brought together the contextual factors that defined NDM:

> *The identification of key contextual factors that affect the way real-world decision making occurs, in contrast to their counterparts in the traditional decision research paradigm, evolved as a major contribution of the 1989 NDM conference (Orasanu & Connolly, 1993). They are:*
> *1. Ill-structured problems (not artificial, well-structured problems). 2. Uncertain, dynamic environments (not static, simulated situations). 3. Shifting, ill-defined, or competing goals (not clear and stable goals). 4. Action/feedback loops (not one-shot decisions). 5. Time stress (as opposed to ample time for tasks). 6. High stakes (not situations devoid of true consequences for the decision maker). 7. Multiple players (as opposed to individual decision making). 8. Organizational goals and norms (as opposed to decision making in a vacuum). (p. 5)*

The primary theme of the Klein et al. (1993) volume was how traditional decision-making research did not provide much that was relevant to understanding professional judgment and decisions in the field. "To a great extent, the initial motivation for the NDM paradigm, as sometimes happens in scientific change, involved a reaction against the currently dominant paradigm, which in this case was the paradigm of Judgment & Decision Making (JDM) and the various models and approaches that fell under that banner" (Hoffman, 1995, p. 33).

A new view of decision making and judgment arose because NDM researchers were describing what they were seeing in stressful field conditions as professionals, including experts, applied their judgment. Early NDM research discovered that expert professional judgment was largely based on a process in which experts expend effort on situation assessment (figuring out the nature of the problem), then evaluate single options through mental simulation, and then arrive at a satisfactory answer or action. Qualitative analysis of professional judgment under stress in field conditions was a major departure from traditional research in decision making. Mainstream models of decision making at that time were not much help in understanding these new findings. Specifically, utility theory mandates a procedure for "good" judgment in which the decision maker lays out all of the alternative decision paths and iteratively evaluates each for costs and benefits. The successful professional judgment being observed in the field was radically different from the prescriptive processes of "good" decision making found in the literature at the time.

To put NDM in perspective, Cohen (1993) provided a discussion of three basic paradigms of decision-making research: the formal-empiricist paradigm (also known as classic decision making), the rationalist paradigm, and the naturalistic paradigm. The formal-empiricist paradigm lasted until the late 1960s. Its essential characteristic was that it was a normative (prescriptive) model of rational behavior. The decision maker chooses among concurrently available alternatives; there is an input-output orientation, a comprehensive information search, and a formal development of an abstract, context-free model amenable to quantitative testing (Lipshitz, 2001). The formal-empiricist paradigm focused on behavioral testing of formal models, not on understanding cognitive processes.

The rationalist paradigm overtook the classic decision making paradigm, but retained the essential characteristics in terms of normative (prescriptive) models as the standard for evaluating decision quality. The rationalist paradigm emphasized the concept of errors due to bias in unaided decision making. The rationalist paradigm also asserted that discrepancies in performance are the fault of the decision maker, not the model. Earlier efforts in classic decision making had sought to modify the model when discrepancies were found (Cohen, 1993). What was the motivation for the change in the paradigm? According to Kahneman and Tversky (1982a), the goal of the rationalist paradigm was to make the research more cognitive, that is, to expose intellectual limitations, reveal psychological processes, and map the use of intuition.

Lipshitz, Klein, Orasanu, and Salas (2001) asserted that the naturalistic or NDM paradigm places the expert at the center of the research focus. "Comprehensive choice was replaced by matching, input-output orientation was replaced by process orientation, and context-free formal modeling was replaced by context-bound informal modeling... researchers within the NDM framework embarked on the construction of descriptive models of proficient decision makers in natural contexts without relying on normative choice models as starting points" (Lipshitz, 2001, p. 333).

"The NDM paradigm liberates the study of proficiency from reliance on traditional, decision-analytic theories of problem-solving and the related normative prescriptions concerning 'proper' decision-making methods and training techniques" (Hoffman, 1995, p. 14). The essentials of NDM have remained the same since its emergence: proficient decision makers, situation-action matching decision rules, context-bound informal modeling, process orientation, and empirical-based prescription (Lipshitz et al., 2001). Lipshitz et al. point out, however, that the emphasis in NDM has also changed in certain respects over time. In early work, the emphasis was on shaping features of the field setting contexts, and expertise was a secondary factor. By the time of the second NDM conference in 1994, the decision maker was the distinguishing focus of NDM. Expertise had become a core of NDM research.

Expertise from the NDM Perspective

Expertise has been investigated from a number of theoretical perspectives, such as in the JDM literature. JDM has studied heuristics and biases in an attempt to demonstrate biases among expert populations (Tversky & Kahneman, 1982). Experts do not perform well when the tasks (e.g., probability juggling tasks) depart from the experts' "familiar" tasks, and recommendations for debiasing do not fit within the confines of their job. The JDM approach differs from an NDM approach, which emphasizes the domain specificity of expertise. Many studies have found that when experts perform in their domain in their natural context, bias is alleviated and experts yield good judgments (e.g., Borstein, Emler, & Chapman, 1999; Cohen, 1993; Keren, 1987; Shanteau, 1989; Smith & Kida, 1991).

The development of computer applications generated a huge literature devoted to capturing expertise. With the advent of expert systems, hundreds of projects sought to capture expertise and embed it in decision aids across many domains. Hoffman (1995) cites a number of studies that elicited expertise to create decision aids (Boose, 1986; Bramer, 1985; Coombs, Dawes, & Tversky, 1970; Keller, 1987; Waterman, 1986; Weiss & Kulikowski, 1984). This approach views expertise differently from the NDM paradigm in that it seeks to capture an objective expertise model as if there is one

ideal for a given domain. Situated cognition research also examines the nature of expertise, in works such as those of Suchman (1987) and Lave and Wenger (1991), which along with Winograd and Flores (1986) emphasize the contextual aspects of learning and performance and have provided the foundation for a plethora of studies in education and computer applications.

When NDM researchers study experts, they mean individuals who have achieved exceptional skill in one particular domain, and the NDM research has focused on understanding the process of developing and applying that expertise in context. Researchers have defined a number of variables of expertise that are important to NDM researchers (adapted from Phillips, Klein, & Sieck, 2004):

Perceptual skills – Experts have the ability to make fine discriminations. They see more in a situation than a novice by noticing cues a novice does not (see, for example, Klein & Hoffman, 1993).

Mental models – Experts have rich internal representations of how things work in their domain of practice (Rouse & Morris, 1986). These mental models allow them to learn and to understand situations more rapidly (Ross, Battaglia, Phillips, Domeshek, & Lussier, 2003).

Sense of typicality and associations – Experts have a large repertoire of patterns. They recognize what is typical in a situation (Ericsson & Simon, 1993) and they recognize complex patterns. They also recognize when things are not going as expected, that is, when there is an anomaly or something is missing.

Routines – Experts know how to get things done (Anderson, 1983). They have a wide repertoire of tactics. They don't just know about things; they know how to do things.

Declarative knowledge – Experts know more facts and details and have more tacit knowledge than novices do. Tacit knowledge is the operational knowledge inaccessible to consciousness. Much of expertise operates without conscious effort, and that tacit knowledge supporting expertise is not verbally encoded, nor easily articulated (B. W. Crandall, Kyne, Militello, & Klein, 1992).

Mental simulation – Experts run mental simulations to refine their course of action or to understand how a situation got to the point at which they found it (see G. A. Klein & Crandall, 1995).

Assessing the situation – Experts spend more time than novices understanding the dynamics of the situation. Novices spend more time deliberating over the course of action (Kobus, Proctor, Bank, & Holste, 2000).

Finding leverage points – Experts can find leverage points in a situation and capitalize on them to implement innovative strategies (G. Klein & Wolf, 1998). Leverage points are opportunities for making critical changes at relatively low effort (Ross et al., 2002).

Managing uncertainty – Experts have a range of strategies for managing uncertainty in the field (Lipshitz & Strauss, 1997; Schmitt & Klein, 1996).

Understanding one's own strengths and limitations (metacognition) – Experts are better self-monitors than novices (see, for example, Chi, Feltovich, & Glaser, 1981; Larkin, 1983).

Today, NDM encompasses a number of models and theories about how expertise works. For example, Cohen, Freeman, and Thompson (1997) describe the Recognition/Metacognition model, which describes a set of skills that supplement recognitional processes when making decisions in novel situations. Endsley (1995) developed a model of Situation Awareness, which involves three levels (perception, comprehension, and prediction) and mechanisms for selecting goals and actions. Serfaty, MacMillan, Entin, and Entin (1997) developed a mental model theory for studying expertise. G. A. Klein (1989) described

the Recognition-Primed Decision (RPD) Model developed from the observations of fireground commanders by Klein, Calderwood, and Clinton-Cirocco (1986). The RPD Model was the earliest model of expert decision making in the NDM paradigm, and we focus on it here.

The RPD Model

The RPD Model states that when it comes to high-stakes, time-pressured decisions, people do not use "rational choice" or utility analysis; instead, they rely on their experience. An expert confronted with a situation is able to recognize that this situation is typical, an instantiation of a prototype. This prototype is a cognitive package that includes the type of situation this is, what to expect from the situation (expectancies), suitable goals, typical courses of action (COAs), and relevant cues. Once the expert has this prototype in mind, he knows what he's facing and what to do next without going through elaborate analyses.

Recognition of a situation prototype can and often does lead directly to action that involves no comparison of options, because the situation prototype is linked to a COA that the expert already knows will work. In situations in which RPD is applicable there is often no time to seek the optimal solution; all that is required is one that will work. This principle of accepting what will work rather than continuing to look for what is ideal is called "satisficing" (coined by Herbert A. Simon, 1957).

There are also times when recognition of the situation prototype is not enough. If a situation is unusual or uncertain enough that the prepackaged COA needs evaluating, a second step to RPD can occur: mental simulation. Mental simulation is the process of consciously envisioning a sequence of events, such as imagining how a COA will play out. This allows a decision maker who knows enough to make accurate predictions to see what the consequences of a particular COA might be. The expert will use mental simulation to assess the worth of a particular COA. Satisficing also occurs in this step; all the expert needs is a COA that will work to meet his goals and fit the constraints of the situation. If the first COA evaluated is found wanting, the expert generates a second and so on, evaluating each in turn but never comparing options against each other.

The Origin of RPD

The RPD Model was first expressed in a study of fireground commanders (fireground comanders) (G. A. Klein et al., 1986). Klein et al. wanted to understand how decisions are really made. To do this, they eschewed the less meaningful, less time-pressured decision tasks of most laboratory studies and elected to study real decision makers who performed in naturalistic settings. They selected fireground commanders as their research domain because fireground decision making was a task with high time pressure, high stakes, and a wide range of contexts or situations. In order to understand how fireground commanders made their decisions, they interviewed the commanders about nonroutine or command-challenging past experiences ("critical incidents"). Since the interview was structured and not in real time, this was a quasi-naturalistic approach. They collected detailed retrospections on 32 critical incidents from 29 interviews with 26 officers. The officers interviewed were lieutenants, captains, and chiefs, with an average of 23.2 and no less than 12 years of experience. Data analysis found that approximately 80% of the commanders' decisions were recognition-based. In fact, some interviewees said that they never made "decisions" at all. Those statements were the catalyst for the development of the RPD Model:

> Their ability to handle decision points appeared to depend on their skill at recognizing situations as typical, as instances of general prototypes that they had developed through experience. The prototypes provided them with an understanding of the causal dynamics at work, suggested promising courses of action, and provided

them with expectations.... serial option evaluation model. Here, an option is generated, and then either implemented or rejected. If rejected, a second option is considered, and so forth. This may be described as a serial model of decision making, because although one or more options are considered, only one option is examined at a time. (G. A. Klein et al., 1986, p. 17)

RPD has been the subject of much study and refinement. Below we describe the key studies conducted by Klein and his collaborators that contributed to the further development of the RPD Model. One of the first replications, in the study of neonatal intensive care nurses, was also a test of the Critical Decision Method (CDM), a knowledge elicitation technique that was developed in tandem with and in order to study the RPD Model. The CDM has been found to be reliable and effective in uncovering expert knowledge and reasoning strategies (Hoffman, Crandall, & Shadbolt, 1998; see Hoffman & Lintern, Chapter 12).

Neonatal Intensive Care Nurses

Crandall and Calderwood (1989) studied highly experienced neonatal intensive care unit (NICU) nurses in order to test the emerging CDM. They used the method to elicit challenging incidents. Each nurse supplied two incidents, one to assess the CDM and one to examine the content of expert knowledge. This second incident always involved identification of sepsis (a serious condition in neonates), before the infant became critically ill. When Crandall and Calderwood analyzed the data, they found that experienced nurses relied heavily on the recognition of perceptual cues and patterns of cues to identify the early stages of sepsis. Many of these cues did not occur in the medical literature, and many of the medical literature's cues did not appear in the nurses' accounts. In addition, 16 randomly chosen cases were assessed for judgment processes. Of the 16 cases, ten were coded as recognition-primed, two as a blend of recognitional and analytic strategies, and two as analytic.

Chess Players

Klein, Wolf, Militello, and Zsambok (1995) studied eight highly skilled and eight medium-skilled chess players. Each participant viewed in-progress chess boards and spoke aloud about each move he considered, then selected the next move. Klein et al. found that the first move considered was of significantly higher quality, as judged by a chess Grand Master, than would be expected from a random sample of available moves (p < .0001). Skill level had only a small effect on move quality. And when the first move considered was weak, players discarded it quickly, suggesting this approach is still more efficient than generating a large option set to evaluate. Calderwood, Klein, and Crandall (1988) carried out a similar study, except that participants generated moves under either normal or time-pressured conditions. Calderwood et al. found that the highly skilled players generated moves of the same high quality even under time pressure, whereas the medium-skilled players did significantly worse under time pressure.

Platoon Commanders

Brezovic, Klein, and Thordsen (1987) wanted to understand decision strategies of novice and experienced tank platoon commanders. They studied 21 students and nine instructors at the Ft. Knox Armor Platoon Leader Training Course in a set of training exercises. They asked the instructors for a list of the most difficult decision situations in each exercise, and used this list in conjunction with the CDM to question the students. This yielded decision situations and option selections, accounts of the events surrounding those decision points, and performance ratings of students' behavior and justification of those ratings. The researchers found that students were aware of the same cues in each of several relevant categories that instructors were. Instructors always considered hypotheticals more than students did and were more likely to recall hypothetical actions or situation features in a decision point. Forty-two percent of the students' decisions were

recognitional, which they expected since the participants were inexperienced; this confirmed their hypothesis that people deliberate when they lack the experience to do RPD. Experts and novices were trying to do the same thing. The difference wasn't in strategies but in knowledge.

Design Engineers

Klein and Brezovic (1986) conducted CDM interviews with 50 professional system designers having an average of 9.5 years of experience. They found 76 decision points during the design of actual projects and determined decision-making strategies for each of them. These projects were carried out over the course of days or months, and therefore were not as time-pressured as the situations firefighters faced, but the highest frequency of decision-making strategy was recognitional matching (others were empirical deliberation, analytical deliberation, and other). In addition, the designers tended to avoid formal decision making; they were less interested in finding the best option possible than identifying the best option readily available and working to make it more effective.

In addition to the above studies, several independent researchers have found RPD a useful and accurate description of how experts really make decisions.

Electronic Warfare Technicians

Randel, Pugh, and Reed (1996) studied decision-making processes in 28 electronic warfare technicians with experience ranging from six months to seven years, who were classified as novices, intermediates, or experts using a Performance Assessment tool (Schuler, 1994). Each technician participated in the same 35-minute scenario. Randel et al. measured situation awareness with participant drawings of what was on the screen and verbal questionnaires after the scenario had been completed. They interviewed each participant for a major decision made during the scenario using the CDM. They also examined the number of details remembered from the scenario and information about the tactical situation, and asked participants to rate the scenario's difficulty on a five-point scale.

The results included a statistically significant effect for expertise level on situation awareness both with drawing accuracy ($p < .001$) and recall of platform knowledge ($p < .02$). Experts scored significantly higher ($p < .05$) on the tactical situation questions than the novices and intermediates, with the latter two not differing significantly. Participant expertise and rating of scenario difficulty were significantly correlated ($r = -0.4$), indicating that the more expert participants considered the scenario to be less difficult. The researchers analyzed the decisions by rating each one and assigning it to a decision type category. They found that experts and intermediates emphasized situation assessment, whereas novices emphasized deciding on a course of action; these differences were statistically significant ($p < .05$). Ninety-three percent of the decisions involved serial consideration, with no differences between groups, which conforms to the RPD Model.

Army Command and Control

R. Pascual and Henderson (1997) studied military Command and Control officers performing a variety of problem-solving and decision tasks in simulated planning and dynamic scenarios. Participants verbalized their actions but not the reasoning behind their actions. In debrief sessions, Pascual and Henderson used a modified version of the CDM to elicit decision strategies used, errors made, and contextual factors. They found that 87% of coded responses to the scenarios used an RPD strategy. They also found that different working methods were used by the more and the less experienced decision makers.

Offshore Installation Managers

Flin, Slaven, and Stewart (1996) studied managers of offshore oil installations, which are high-stakes environments where a mistake during an emergency can be catastrophic. The managers were responsible for any such emergencies (incidents). Flin et al. attempted to describe the managers' decision-making processes. They studied 14 managers and four deputy managers from two different operating companies. They gave each manager or deputy manager three scenarios, each depicting an emergency at an offshore installation. Each manager identified the first three critical decisions and the cues, goals, expectancies, and COAs relevant to each. Flin et al. found that the most experienced managers had emergency response schemata in place that they used to assess incidents and recognition-based rules that they used to manage those incidents.

Military Decision Making – A Case of NDM Impacting Professional Judgment

The impact of NDM on professional judgment can be seen most clearly in military decision making. Military decision making has traditionally been a prescribed analytic process. Below we describe how NDM research uncovered the limitations of the prescribed decision-making process and provided an alternative process to support how military commanders actually make decisions. This research led to changes in military doctrine, practice, and training.

Traditionally, training for military command and control – the heart of military decision making – was based on rational-analytic theories of decision making (e.g., Kahneman & Tversky, 1982b). Such research sought to eliminate bias and improve decision making by using prescribed analytic processes to yield optimal decisions. The research showed that people are not very good at finding optimal solutions (Kahneman & Tversky, 1972). To overcome supposed human limitations, the military developed analytical decision-making processes for structuring facts, generating courses of action, and evaluating options. Examples are the Military Decision Making Process (MDMP) (U.S. Army, 1997) and the U.S. Marine Corps Planning Process (MCPP) (U.S. Marine Corps, 2001).

The MDMP and MCPP are highly proceduralized and cumbersome to employ. Military commanders and some officers who have also become NDM researchers have reported that they tried hard to make these processes work in the field, but the process kept failing them. One way that military decision makers deal with the prescribed process when they go into the field is to abbreviate it. However, there is little guidance on how to achieve this abbreviation, since the current U.S. Army Field Manual (U.S. Army, 1997) includes general suggestions but no complete abbreviated process.

Research into the cognition of decision making provides an understanding of why and how the formal, analytic process must be modified in field practice. G. Klein (1997) and Lipshitz (1993) have shown that experienced decision makers working in their domain do not analyze a situation in terms of its components or generate a series of different courses of action as is prescribed in military decision making. Instead, experts use their domain knowledge to recognize the situation or aspects of the situation and retrieve a plausible, basic COA almost immediately (G. A. Klein, 1987; G. A. Klein et al., 1986).

The RPD Model, which was developed as a result of command and control work sponsored by the U.S. Army (G. A. Klein, 1987), helps us understand why a prescribed analytic process doesn't help military decision makers in the field. The RPD Model describes how decision makers can come up with a plausible COA as the first one they consider. Their knowledge base, training, and experience generally render them able to satisfactorily assess a situation, even if it is not exactly the same as previous situations encountered. When the typical aspects of a situation are recognized, a plausible COA usually comes to mind. That initial COA is based on the expert's recognition of aspects or patterns in the situation, and at times the entire situation. That recognition brings to mind associated, typical actions that are likely to work in that circumstance. Experienced decision makers then assess that course of action by mentally wargaming it, rather than contrasting it to other options on a set of abstract evaluation dimensions as the MDMP or MCPP would have them do. These findings have been generalized to a wide variety of tasks and specialties and have been replicated a number of times (Fallesen & Pounds, 2001; G. Klein, 1998; G. Klein, 2004; R. Pascual & Henderson, 1997).

Further, G. Klein et al. (1995) showed that skilled decision makers generated a good COA as the first one they considered. Johnson and Raab (in press) have recently replicated this finding and extended it, showing that when skilled decision makers abandoned their initial COA in favor of one they generated subsequently, the quality of that subsequent COA was significantly lower than their initial COA. Johnston, Driskell, and Salas (1997) showed that recognitional processes, now sometimes referred to as intuitive decision making, resulted in higher performance than analytical processes.

These findings call into question the very rationale of the MDMP and MCPP, which attempt to ensure good decision making by having planners generate three COAs and evaluate them analytically in order to find the best one possible. Officers with more expertise often had to work around the prescribed process to achieve their objectives. The staff who generate three COAs for their commander to review have often reported anecdotally that there is one main COA they are working on and two that are more like "straw men" just to satisfy the process. In reality, the commander and staff naturally produce a good basic COA after an initial assessment and work to make sure it is satisfactory for the purpose. An optimal plan is just not necessary and may, in fact, be counterproductive if we are to believe the expertise of General George S. Patton, who said: "A good plan, violently executed now, is better than a perfect plan next week."

Based on findings from research on the RPD Model and on several studies of military planning exercises, Schmitt and Klein (1999) developed the Recognitional Planning Model (RPM). The purpose was to codify the informal and intuitive planning strategies already used in the field by skilled planning teams observed in the Army and the Marine Corps in order to support the natural cognitive process of the experienced commander rather than force him to use a procedure that disrupts the power of his expertise.

Rather than trying to replace the MDMP, Schmitt and Klein sought to codify the way planners actually work. As a result, the RPM does not feel awkward or unnatural to planners. Rather, a typical comment is "we're already doing this." And that was exactly the intent: to codify the existing and effective practices and give the military a set of procedures that reflect their best practices as these have evolved over decades. The RPM strategy is for the commander to identify his preferred COA so the staff can work on detailing and improving it. Of course, for a strong COA the commander must bring experience to the mission to achieve good situational understanding specifically in relation to his goals. As the officer role-playing the commander in one experiment put it, "The RPM is built around the early identification of a base COA that's improved over time" (Ross et al., 2003, p. 5).

Comparison of the MDMP with the RPM yields several key distinctions (Ross, Klein, Thunholm, Schmitt, & Baxter, 2004; Ross et al., 2002). First, the rationales behind the two models are completely different (an analytic rationale called multi-attribute utility analysis for MDMP versus a recognition-primed decision rationale for RPM). Second, the research support for the basic assumption of the MDMP – that comparing several COAs will result in a superior COA compared to a simplified process – is weak. Third, the RPM is designed to build on experience and expertise whereas MDMP tries to use analytical procedures that can actually prevent or hamper experienced planners from using their ability to quickly assess a situation and come up with a plausible COA. Fourth, time pressure degrades the MDMP whereas the RPM is specifically adapted to time-constrained planning. The MDMP is rarely fully implemented in the field, whereas the RPM describes a "natural" strategy.

Ross et al. (2004) also compared the RPM with the description of an "abbreviated MDMP" provided in the U.S. Army Field Manual FM 101–5 (U.S. Army, 1997). Although the RPM and abbreviated MDMP both rely on a single COA, this is seen as a highly degraded strategy for the abbreviated MDMP, and the commander and staff are assumed to have followed all of the MDMP steps, although some may be performed "automatically." Thus, for the abbreviated MDMP, using a single COA is the last resort, whereas for the RPM it is the first resort. If more time becomes available, the abbreviated MDMP would restore some of the steps that were skipped or slighted. In the RPM, additional time would be used to do more wargaming or to enable subordinate units to increase their preparation.

The RPM has stimulated interest in the military ever since it was first described. On their own initiative, individual U.S. Army and Marine battalion commanders have experimented with the RPM and found it useful. The British military has been conducting experiments with the RPM (Blendell, Molloy, Catchpole, & Henderson, in preparation; R. G. Pascual, Blendell, Molloy, Catchpole, & Henderson, in preparation), so far demonstrating its face validity. The most stringent research on the RPM was performed by Thunholm (in press), who contrasted performance for division-level planning groups in the Swedish Army who used either a variant of the RPM or the Swedish Army's version of the MDMP. Thunholm found that the RPM permitted an increase in tempo of about 20% and plans that were of equivalent or higher quality than those generated using the MDMP. Plans were scored blindly by independent raters. Thunholm also observed that the RPM plans tended to be somewhat bolder and better adapted to situational demands than those emerging from the MDMP, which tended to be more constrained by an over-compliance with current doctrinal templates. Currently, the Swedish Army has adopted its variant of the RPM in the draft of the new field manual and the National Defence College provides training on tactical planning aided by that model only.

In addition to generating a new planning process, the RPD Model has also been the source of changes in military doctrine. Based on findings about the efficacy of the model, Field Manual 6-0 (U.S. Army, 2003) has formally recognized the power of recognitional decision making – termed intuitive decision making in the doctrine – on the battlefield.

> Because uncertainty and time drive most decisions, commanders emphasize intuitive decision making as the norm, and develop their subordinates accordingly. Emphasizing experienced judgment and intuition over deliberate analysis, the intuitive approach helps commanders increase tempo and develops the flexibility to deal with the uncertainty that follows. (U.S. Army, 2003, pp. 2–12)

The doctrine specifically cites NDM research as the source of the addition of intuitive decision making.

In the next section, we describe the impact that NDM, as an applied discipline, has had on the development and support of expertise in the field setting. The impact is manifested in training applications, organizational and process design, and system design.

NDM Applications

As a discipline having applications as well as a basic science aspect, NDM research forms the basis for training development, organizational and process change, and system design that support the exercise of expertise. NDM researchers have successfully implemented applications across a wide range of domains from military settings to healthcare to firefighting. We describe several applications of NDM to illustrate how research on expertise can help develop and support professional judgment in the field.

Decision Skills Training

Decision Skills Training (DST) addresses domain-specific training to accelerate the transition toward expertise. We define domain-specific training as the broad judgments and actions across a job, and not in terms of specific tasks. DST is based on the understanding of how expertise develops and functions in dynamic settings. The DST program was developed based on a survey of the literature on expertise (Chi, Glaser, & Farr, 1988; Ericsson, 1996; Ericsson & Charness, 1994; Glaser, 1996; G. A. Klein & Hoffman, 1993) to identify strategies that experts use in order to learn more rapidly and effectively. These strategies include the following: engaging in deliberate practice, so that each opportunity for practice has a goal and evaluation criteria; compiling an extensive experience bank; obtaining feedback that is accurate and diagnostic; building mental models; developing metacognitive skills; and becoming more mindful of opportunities for learning (Pliske, McCloskey, & Klein, 2001).

The training uses surrogate experiences carefully constructed from cognitive task analysis data that detail lived experiences in terms of cues, strategies, factors, and novice difficulties. These scenarios are designed so that novices can experience all of the following processes (Ross, Lussier, & Klein, 2005):

- Explore and reveal the limits of their mental models, including factual information and cause and effect relationships.
- Practice seeing and assessing cues and their associated patterns, generating expectancies, and identifying goals and typical actions.
- Envision the situation-specific mental models they have developed in the training context as it is played out.
- Receive feedback on what they are not recognizing or accounting for in their mental models and COAs.
- Compare their perceptions and decisions with others when the training is done in a small group setting.

The training is based on the premise that expert knowledge is largely tacit knowledge and can be difficult for the expert to share when asked. We cannot tell someone how to perform largely unconscious processes.

There is no lecture component on how to make decisions or what strategies to employ. Instead, we provide a carefully structured scenario-based context in which students perform and reflect on their performance. The situation is realistic enough that trainees can recognize cues and factors and assess how possible decisions will unfold. Trainees must respond to a dilemma that requires assessment of the situation and a decision. After the decision, a facilitator provides the trainees with structured discussion and reflection on their recognition and mental simulation processes using the DST learning tools.

Based on the review of the literature, the learning tools were developed to be used in conjunction with the low-fidelity simulation exercises. The learning tools include the Decision Making Critique, the Decision Requirements Exercise, the PreMortem Exercise, the Commander's Intent Exercise, and the Situation Awareness Calibration Exercise. These are described in detail in Pliske et al. (2001).

Organizational and Process Design

An example of organizational impact based on an NDM approach is described by Klinger and Klein (1999). The emergency response organization of a nuclear power plant was having problems with emergency drills, which are regulated by the Nuclear Regulatory Commission. Klinger and Klein studied team decision making in the emergency response organization. They gathered data through observation and interviews and used the Advanced Team Decision Making Model (Zsambok, Klein, Kyne, & Klinger, 1992) to understand the key functions that were causing most of the problems. Based on these data, they generated more than 100 recommendations to improve the organization's efficacy, more than 50 of which were put into place during the ten-month period of the project. None of the recommendations involved adding technology; some were to change the room layout, simplify communication channels, situate expertise within positions, and actually *reduce* the number of

staff from 80 to 35, which in part allowed expertise to be unencumbered by too many lines of communication. The nuclear power plant manager put the major recommendations into practice shortly before their annual drill. After watching the team in action, the Nuclear Regulatory Commission reduced the number of required drills at the plant down to one every two years. The estimated savings to the plant was about $1,000,000 per year.

Systems Design

Decision-Centered Design (Hutton, Miller, & Thordsen, 2003) is a systems engineering approach developed by NDM researchers that is based on understanding the expertise of users. Too often, technology does not support the exercise of expertise, or even interferes with it (G. Klein, 2004). Systems can interfere with expertise and reduce performance by presenting too much data; presenting high-level understanding, not low-level details; requiring people to use formal analyses; and discouraging people from seeking their own data. While systems can speed the learning curve by providing low-cost, rapid feedback and advice, this actually hinders the development of skills at seeking one's own feedback, which is critical to growing expertise (Schmidt & Wulf, 1997). Decision-Centered Design helps to shape the design of information technologies to support different aspects of expertise, such as making fine discriminations, anticipating events, seeking diagnostic data, detecting early signs of problems, and seeing the big picture.

People develop expertise as they search for information, as they learn to see patterns in the details, as they revise the categories in their mental models, and as they generate and carry out new courses of action. Technological aids that replace these processes can interfere with this development and learning. Using Decision-Centered Design to define the key decisions in a domain and specify these as design criteria makes the cognitive processes of the expert users the center of the design process. The

Decision-Centered Design process not only supports more usable designs for expert use, but allows expertise to develop naturally.

The process of Decision-Centered Design involves (1) domain familiarization, (2) knowledge elicitation, (3) data analysis, (4) knowledge representation, (5) system development, and (6) system evaluation. The core of the process is step (2), knowledge elicitation to determine what experts know, think, and do in performing their tasks. Decision-Centered Design yields a clear understanding of the cognitive challenges involved in the task of interest, including the requirements and the context of the tasks, and uses information from experts about those challenges to create systems that support cognitive performance (Stanard, Uehara, & Hutton, 2003).

Future Research

The future of NDM research and application is wide open. Research is becoming broader in the cognitive processes under study, making the term "decision making" seem limited as a title for this community of practice. Current research focuses on many of the cognitive elements that are found in the execution of expertise, such as the use of mental models, managing uncertainty, and sensemaking, or the process of assessing situations over time (see Hoffman, 2006). These cognitive elements are being referred to as macrocognition (which also includes cognitive elements such as identification of leverage points, mental simulation, adaptation or replanning, and maintaining common ground) to distinguish them from the type of *microcognitive* processes (such as attention and short-term memory) studied in the laboratory and also to maintain the emphasis on naturalistic field research (G. Klein, 2004). In addition, NDM practitioners confront many issues that need further study to refine and build on existing research.

Much of the early work in NDM contrasted traditional decision-making research and the paradigm underlying NDM. The debate has matured, but still continues as the quantitatively oriented decision research challenges the qualitatively oriented NDM research to meet more rigorous standards. Even within the community, researchers assert that NDM needs to focus on developing theory built on sound findings, tools, and principles based on more empirical studies using more rigorous (i.e., experimental) methodology (Lipshitz et al., 2001). Recommendations have been made to balance qualitative field studies with traditional experimental work and controlled observation. It is difficult for qualitative researchers to accept the strictures of the quantitative paradigm. The limitations of quantitative research often create blinders. It is certainly beyond the scope of this chapter to address the differences between qualitative and quantitative research rigor. But that argument needs to be addressed in the literature, and the possibility of NDM being more rigorous without becoming pseudo-quantitative should be investigated. An appropriate application of mixed qualitative-quantitative research designs may be an optimal solution.

Training applications based on the NDM perspective have the advantage and strength of potentially moving the trainee much more quickly along the path toward expertise. Training is a multimillion-dollar business in the commercial and military sectors, and the pursuit of physical fidelity is expensive. To understand what truly makes training a suitable surrogate experience is an important research goal both for creating the resource of expertise and using our training resource dollars wisely.

We have come to believe that the key issue for developing effective training is not physical fidelity, which seems centered around the engineer or researcher's view of development, but the establishment of what we call *cognitive authenticity* (Ross, Halterman, Pierce, & Ross, 1998; Ross & Pierce, 2000). By this term we mean the inclusion of the features that an expert would perceive in a specified domain to support building perceptual skills to recognize critical cues and factors in the problem-solving and decision-making processes. We use the term "authenticity" to reflect the requirement for an authentic experience by the user. Matching the level of expertise to the level of authenticity is an empirical question that must be considered to achieve the highest impact for training (Jacobson & Spiro, 1994).

NDM must consolidate findings across the variety of applications that have been developed to evaluate these products. This effort calls for the development of measures that are appropriate to the qualitative nature of NDM research. In both systems development and training development, measures are needed to help NDM researchers better understand whether performance is improving during learning or being supported during operations. Developing measures is difficult, especially when the researcher does not want to boil down cognitive processes into behavioral performance outcomes. The development of meaningful measures for assessing changes in naturalistic cognitive performance is a current topic of emphasis.

Expert judgment remains the essence of NDM. The descriptive models and applications that have emerged from the research are widely touted by practitioners in a variety of fields as having a profound impact on their performance and their ability to mentor novices. Researchers critical of NDM challenge the field to create methods and metrics that back up these anecdotal findings. NDM researchers continue to challenge themselves to refine and expand their understanding of expertise to better support the professionals who daily make time-pressured, high-stakes decisions under uncertain conditions.

Acknowledgment

Support for the preparation of this chapter was provided through SAIC's Prime Contract MDA972-03-9-0001K, under Subcontract 4400062705 to Klein Associates.

Footnote

1. This volume documented the first conference held for NDM researchers in 1989. The conference was sponsored by the Army Research Institute to bring together researchers studying complex decision making in real-world contexts. The conference had the express purpose of organizing a book to document decision-making research being carried out across a wide range of professional domains.

References

Anderson, J. R. (1983). *The architecture of cognition*. Cambridge, MA: Harvard University Press.

Blendell, C., Molloy, J. J., Catchpole, L. J., & Henderson, S. M. (in preparation). Defence Evaluation and Research Agency, Ministry of Defence, United Kingdom.

Boose, J. H. (1986). *Expertise transfer for expert system design*. Amsterdam: Elsevier.

Borstein, B. H., Emler, A. C., & Chapman, G. B. (1999). Rationality in medical treatment decisions: Is there a sunk-cost effect? *Social Sciences & Medicine, 49,* 215–222.

Bramer, M. (Ed.). (1985). *Research and development in expert systems*. Cambridge, UK: Cambridge University Press.

Brezovic, C. P., Klein, G. A., & Thordsen, M. (1987). *Decision making in armored platoon command* (Contract MDA903-85-C-0327 for U.S. Army Research Institute, Alexandria, VA). Fairborn, OH: Klein Associates Inc. [also published as DTIC No. ADA231775, http://www.dtic.mil].

Calderwood, R., Klein, G. A., & Crandall, B. W. (1988). Time pressure, skill, and move quality in chess. *American Journal of Psychology, 101,* 481–493.

Chi, M. T. H., Feltovich, P. J., & Glaser, R. (1981). Categorization and representation of physics problems by experts and novices. *Cognitive Science, 5,* 121–152.

Chi, M. T. H., Glaser, R., & Farr, M. J. (Eds.). (1988). *The nature of expertise*. Mahwah, NJ: Lawrence Erlbaum Associates.

Cohen, M. S. (1993). Three paradigms for viewing decision biases. In G. A. Klein, J. Orasanu, R. Calderwood, & C. E. Zsambok (Eds.), *Decision making in action: Models and methods* (pp. 36–50). Norwood, NJ: Ablex.

Cohen, M. S., Freeman, J. T., & Thompson, B. B. (1997). Training the naturalistic decision maker. In C. E. Zsambok & G. Klein (Eds.), *Naturalistic decision making* (pp. 257–268). Mahwah, NJ: Lawrence Erlbaum Associates.

Coombs, C. H., Dawes, R. M., & Tversky, A. (1970). *Mathematical psychology*. Englewood Cliffs, NJ: Prentice Hall.

Crandall, B., & Calderwood, R. (1989). *Clinical assessment skills of experienced neonatal intensive care nurses* (Contract 1 R43 NR0191101 for The National Center for Nursing, NIH). Fairborn, OH: Klein Associates Inc.

Crandall, B. W., Kyne, M., Militello, L., & Klein, G. A. (1992). *Describing expertise in one-on-one instruction* (Contract MDA903-91-C-0058 for U.S. Army Research Institute, Alexandria, VA). Fairborn, OH: Klein Associates Inc.

Endsley, M. R. (1995). Toward a theory of situation awareness in dynamic systems. *Human Factors, 37*, 32–64.

Ericsson, K. A. (1996). The acquisition of expert performance: An introduction to some of the issues. In K. A. Ericsson (Ed.), *The road to excellence: The acquisition of expert performance in the arts and sciences, sports, and games* (pp. 1–50). Mahwah, NJ: Lawrence Erlbaum Associates.

Ericsson, K. A., & Charness, N. (1994). Expert performance: Its structure and acquisition. *American Psychologist, 49*, 725–747.

Ericsson, K. A., & Simon, H. A. (1993). *Protocol analysis: Verbal reports as data* (2nd ed.). Cambridge, MA: MIT Press.

Fallesen, J. J., & Pounds, J. (2001). Identifying and testing a naturalistic approach for cognitive skills training. In E. Salas & G. Klein (Eds.), *Linking expertise and naturalistic decision making*. Mahwah, NJ: Lawrence Erlbaum Associates.

Flin, R., Slaven, G., & Stewart, K. (1996). Emergency decision making in the offshore oil and gas industry. *Human Factors, 38*, 262–277.

Glaser, R. (1996). Changing the agency for learning: Acquiring expert performance. In K. A. Ericsson (Ed.), *The road to excellence* (pp. 303–311). Mahwah, NJ: Erlbaum.

Hoffman, R. R. (1995). *A review of naturalistic decision making research on the critical decision method of knowledge elicitation and the recognition priming model of decision-making, with a focus on implications for military proficiency* (Prepared for the University of Nottingham under sponsorship of the Defense Research Agency-Farnborough and Epistemics, Ltd.).

Hoffman, R. R. (Ed.). (2006). *Expertise out of context: Proceedings of the Sixth International Conference on Naturalistic Decision Making*. Mahwah, NJ: Lawrence Erlbaum Associates.

Hoffman, R. R., Crandall, B. W., & Shadbolt, N. R. (1998). Use of the critical decision method to elicit expert knowledge: A case study in cognitive task analysis methodology. *Human Factors, 40*, 254–276.

Hutton, R. J. B., Miller, T. E., & Thordsen, M. L. (2003). Decision-centered design: Leveraging cognitive task analysis in design. In E. Hollnagel (Ed.), *Handbook of cognitive task design* (pp. 383–416). Mahwah, NJ: Erlbaum.

Jacobson, M. J., & Spiro, R. J. (1994). A framework for the contextual analysis of technology-based learning environments. *Journal of Computing in Higher Education, 5*, 3–32.

Johnston, J., Driskell, J. E., & Salas, E. (1997). Vigilant and hypervigilant decision making. *Journal of Applied Psychology, 82*, 614–622.

Kahneman, D., & Tversky, A. (1972). Subjective probability: A judgment of representativeness. *Cognitive Psychology, 3*, 430–454.

Kahneman, D., & Tversky, A. (1982a). On the study of statistical intuitions. *Cognition, 11*, 123–141.

Kahneman, D., & Tversky, A. (1982b). On the study of statistical intuitions. In D. Kahneman, P. Slovic, & A. Tversky (Eds.), *Judgment under uncertainty: Heuristics and biases*. Cambridge, MA: Cambridge University Press.

Keller, R. (1987). *Expert systems technology: Development and applications*. Englewood Cliffs, NJ: Prentice Hall.

Keren, G. (1987). Facing uncertainty in the game of bridge: A calibration study. *Organizational Behavior and Human Decision Processes, 39*, 98–114.

Klein, G. (1997). The current status of the naturalistic decision making framework. In R.

Flin, E. Salas, M. E. Strub, & L. Martin (Eds.), *Decision making under stress: Emerging themes and applications* (pp. 11–28). Aldershot: Ashgate.

Klein, G. (1998). *Sources of power: How people make decisions.* Cambridge, MA: MIT Press.

Klein, G. (2004). *The power of intuition.* New York: A Currency Book/Doubleday.

Klein, G., & Wolf, S. (1998). The role of leverage points in option generation. *IEEE Transactions on Systems, Man and Cybernetics: Applications and Reviews, 28,* 157–160.

Klein, G., Wolf, S., Militello, L., & Zsambok, C. E. (1995). Characteristics of skilled option generation in chess. *Organizational Behavior and Human Decision Processes, 62,* 63–69.

Klein, G. A. (1987). Applications of analogical reasoning. *Journal of Metaphor and Symbolic Activity, 2,* 201–218.

Klein, G. A. (1989). Recognition-primed decisions. In W. B. Rouse (Ed.), *Advances in man-machine systems research* (Vol. 5, pp. 47–92). Greenwich, CT: JAI Press, Inc. [also published as DTIC No. ADA240659].

Klein, G. A., & Brezovic, C. P. (1986). Design engineers and the design process: Decision strategies and human factors literature. *Proceedings of the Human Factors and Ergonomics Society 30th Annual Meeting, 2,* 771–775.

Klein, G. A., Calderwood, R., & Clinton-Cirocco, A. (1986). Rapid decision making on the fireground. *Proceedings of the Human Factors and Ergonomics Society 30th Annual Meeting, 1,* 576–580.

Klein, G. A., & Crandall, B. W. (1995). The role of mental simulation in naturalistic decision making. In P. Hancock, J. Flach, J. Caird, & K. Vicente (Eds.), *Local applications of the ecological approach to human-machine systems* (Vol. 2, pp. 324–358). Mahwah, NJ: Lawrence Erlbaum Associates.

Klein, G. A., & Hoffman, R. (1993). Seeing the invisible: Perceptual/cognitive aspects of expertise. In M. Rabinowitz (Ed.), *Cognitive science foundations of instruction* (pp. 203–226). Mahwah, NJ: Lawrence Erlbaum Associates.

Klein, G. A., Orasanu, J., Calderwood, R., & Zsambok, C. E. (Eds.). (1993). *Decision making in action: Models and methods.* Norwood, NJ: Ablex.

Klinger, D. W., & Klein, G. (1999). Emergency response organizations: An accident waiting to happen. *Ergonomics In Design, 7,* 20–25.

Kobus, D. A., Proctor, S., Bank, T. E., & Holste, S. T. (2000). *Decision-making in a dynamic environment: The effects of experience and information uncertainty* (No. 1832). Space and Naval Warfare Systems Center.

Larkin, J. H. (1983). The role of problem representation in physics. In D. Gentner & A. L. Stevens (Eds.), *Mental models.* Mahwah, NJ: Lawrence Erlbaum Associates.

Lave, J., & Wenger, E. (1991). *Situation learning-legitimate peripheral participation.* Cambridge, UK: Cambridge University Press.

Lipshitz, R. (1993). Converging themes in the study of decision making in realistic settings. In G. A. Klein, J. Orasanu, R. Calderwood, & C. E. Zsambok (Eds.), *Decision making in action: Models and methods* (pp. 103–137). Norwood, NJ: Ablex.

Lipshitz, R. (2001). Puzzle seeking and model-building on the fire ground: A discussion of Karl Weick's keynote address. In E. Salas & G. Klein (Eds.), *Expertise and naturalistic decision making* (pp. 337–345). Mahwah, NJ: Lawrence Erlbaum Associates.

Lipshitz, R., Klein, G., Orasanu, J., & Salas, E. (2001). Focus article: Taking stock of naturalistic decision making. *Journal of Behavioral Decision Making, 14,* 331–352.

Lipshitz, R., & Strauss, O. (1997). Coping with uncertainty: A naturalistic decision making analysis. *Organizational Behavior and Human Decision Processes, 66,* 149–163.

Orasanu, J., & Connolly, T. (1993). The reinvention of decision making. In G. A. Klein, J. Orasanu, R. Calderwood, & C. E. Zsambok (Eds.), *Decision making in action: Models and methods* (pp. 3–20). Norwood, NJ: Ablex.

Pascual, R., & Henderson, S. (1997). Evidence of naturalistic decision making in military command and control. In C. E. Zsambok & G. Klein (Eds.), *Naturalistic decision making* (pp. 217–226). Mahwah, NJ: Lawrence Erlbaum Associates.

Pascual, R. G., Blendell, C., Molloy, J. J., Catchpole, L. J., & Henderson, S. M. (in preparation). *An investigation of alternative command planning processes* (Defense Education and Research Agency paper prepared for the United Kingdom Ministry of Defence).

Phillips, J. K., Klein, G., & Sieck, W. R. (2004). Expertise in judgment and decision making: A case for training intuitive decision skills. In D. J.

Koehler & N. Harvey (Eds.), *Blackwell handbook of judgment & decision making* (pp. 297–315). Victoria, Australia: Blackwell Publishing.

Pliske, R. M., McCloskey, M. J., & Klein, G. (2001). Decision skills training: Facilitating learning from experience. In E. Salas & G. Klein (Eds.), *Linking expertise and naturalistic decision making* (pp. 37–53). Mahwah, NJ: Lawrence Erlbaum Associates.

Randel, J. M., Pugh, H. L., & Reed, S. K. (1996). Differences in expert and novice situation awareness in naturalistic decision making. *International Journal of Human-Computer Studies*, 45, 579–597.

Ross, K. G., Battaglia, D. A., Phillips, J. K., Domeshek, E. A., & Lussier, J. W. (2003). Mental models underlying tactical thinking skills. In *Proceedings of the Interservice/Industry Training, Simulation, and Education Conference 2003*. Arlington, VA: National Training Systems Association.

Ross, K. G., Halterman, J. A., Pierce, L. G., & Ross, W. A. (1998). *Preparing for the instructional technology gap: A constructivist approach*. Paper presented at the 1998 Interservice/Industry Training, Simulation, and Education Conference, Orlando, FL.

Ross, K. G., Klein, G., Thunholm, P., Schmitt, J. F., & Baxter, H. C. (2004). The recognition-primed decision model. *Military Review*, LXXIV, 6–10.

Ross, K. G., Lussier, J. W., & Klein, G. (2005). From recognition-primed decision making to decision skills training. In S. Haberstroh & T. Betsch (Eds.), *Routines of decision making* (pp. 327–341). Mahwah, NJ: Lawrence Erlbaum Associates.

Ross, K. G., McHugh, A., Moon, B. M., Klein, G., Armstrong, A. A., & Rall, E. (2002). *High-level cognitive processes in field research* (Year One Final Report under Contract 02TA2-SP1-RT1 for U.S. Army Research Laboratory under Cooperative Agreement DAAD19-01-2-0009). Fairborn, OH: Klein Associates Inc.

Ross, K. G., & Pierce, L. G. (2000). Cognitive engineering of training for adaptive battlefield thinking. In *IEA 14th Triennial Congress and HFES 44th Annual Meeting* (Vol. 2, pp. 410–413). Santa Monica, CA: Human Factors and Grgononics Society.

Rouse, W. B., & Morris, N. M. (1986). On looking into the black box: Prospects and limits on the search for mental models. *Psychological Bulletin*, 100, 349–363.

Schmidt, R. A., & Wulf, G. (1997). Continuous concurrent feedback degrades skill learning: Implications for training and simulation. *Human Factors*, 39, 509–525.

Schmitt, J. F., & Klein, G. (1996). Fighting in the fog: Dealing with battlefield uncertainty. *Marine Corps Gazette*, 80, 62–69.

Schmitt, J. F., & Klein, G. (1999). How we plan. *Marine Corps Gazette*, 83(10), 18–26.

Schuler, J. W. (1994). *AN/SLQ-32 Operator Training: Development of Performance Assessment Instrument (NPRDC-TN-94-13)*. San Diego, CA: Navy Personnel Research and Development Center.

Serfaty, D., MacMillan, J., Entin, E. E., & Entin, E. B. (1997). The decision-making expertise of battle commanders. In C. E. Zsambok & G. Klein (Eds.), *Naturalistic decision making* (pp. 233–246). Mahwah, NJ: Lawrence Erlbaum Associates.

Shanteau, J. (1989). Cognitive heuristics and biases in behavioral auditing: Review, comments, and observations. *Accounting Organizations and Society*, 14, 165–177.

Simon, H. A. (1957). *Models of man: Social and rational*. New York: John Wiley & Sons, Inc.

Smith, J. F., & Kida, T. (1991). Heuristics and biases: Expertise and task realism in auditing. *Psychological Bulletin*, 109, 472–489.

Stanard, T., Uehara, M. A., & Hutton, R. J. B. (2003). *Decision-centered design: Principles & processes* (Year one Report prepared through participation in the Advanced Decision Architectures Collaborative Technology Alliance [Contract #02TA1-SP3-RT2] sponsored by the U.S. Army Research Laboratory under Cooperative Agreement DAAD19-01-2-0009). Fairborn, OH: Klein Associates Inc.

Suchman, L. A. (1987). *Plans and situated actions: The problem of human-machine communication*. Cambridge, England: Cambridge University Press.

Thunholm, P. (in press). Military decision making under time-pressure: To evaluate or not to evaluate three options before the decision is made? *Organizational Behavior and Human Decision Processes*.

Tversky, A., & Kahneman, D. (1982). Causal schemas in judgments under uncertainty. In D. Kahneman, P. Slovic, & A. Tversky (Eds.), *Judgment under uncertainty: Heuristics and biases*. Cambridge, MA: Cambridge University Press.

U.S. Army. (2003). *Field Manual 6-0, Mission command: The command and control of army forces.* Washington, DC: U.S. Army.

U.S. Army. (1997). *Field Manual 101-5, Staff organization and operations.* Washington, DC: Department of the Army.

U.S. Marine Corps. (2001). *MCWP 5-1, Marine Corps planning process.* Quantico, VA: U.S. Marine Corps.

Waterman, D. A. (1986). *A guide to expert systems.* Reading, MA: Addison-Wesley.

Weiss, S., & Kulikowski, C. (1984). *A practical guide to designing expert systems.* Totowa, NJ: Rowman and Allanheld.

Winograd, T., & Flores, F. (1986). *Understanding computers and cognition: A new foundation for design.* Norwood, NJ: Ablex.

Zsambok, C. E. (1997). Naturalistic decision making: Where are we now? In C. E. Zsambok & G. Klein (Eds.), *Naturalistic decision making* (pp. 3–16). Mahwah, NJ: Erlbaum.

Zsambok, C. E., Klein, G., Kyne, M. M., & Klinger, D. W. (1992). *Advanced team decision making: A developmental model* (Contract MDA903-90-C-0117 for U.S. Army Research Institute for the Behavioral and Social Sciences). Fairborn, OH: Klein Associates Inc. [also published as DTIC No. 259512, http://www.dtic.mil].

CHAPTER 24

Decision-Making Expertise

J. Frank Yates & Michael D. Tschirhart

Picture basketball coach Don Smith, who desperately needs at least a couple of outstanding free throw shooters. Coach Smith's team has lost game after game in the waning seconds. That is because opposing teams easily regain possession of the ball by committing intentional fouls since they know that Smith's players make few of their free throws. Coach Smith is pondering how to recruit a new player who has already demonstrated his proficiency at the line. He is also trying to figure out how to train a current player to elevate his free throw performance to the level of an expert. Related to this second approach, Coach Smith also has what some would call "scientific" concerns. He wonders why none of his players is already an excellent free throw shooter. What exactly is involved in foul shooting expertise? How does one normally develop the skill? Why is it that some players acquire the ability but others do not? Are there certain constitutional factors, physical or psychological, that limit a player's potential at the free throw line? If so, what are they? And how can one detect them, so that resources are not

wasted "trying to make a silk purse from a sow's ear?"

Coach Smith's situation is by no means unique. In some form or another, it is replicated in countless circumstances where the focus is on making decisions rather than shooting free throws. Thus, instead of Coach Smith, our protagonist might be the managing partner in a medical practice, where the need is for new staff physicians who make excellent treatment decisions for their patients. It could be the head of a marketing division who is recruiting brand managers, ones who will make choices that improve market share. It could be a police department official who wants to assure that the officers retained after their probationary periods make wise choices in the heat of the moment. In all these cases, the fundamental questions are similar:

- *Identification*: How can we find people with high degrees of decision-making expertise?
- *Explanation*: How can we explain the presence or absence of such expertise?

- *Development*: How can we develop this kind of expertise?

Our original aims for this chapter were to survey, analyze, and summarize what the decision-making literature has to offer for questions like those above, with a special emphasis on the explanation question. A portion of the literature does indeed directly address expertise, but it is small. Moreover, our examination of the literature forced us to conclude that most research explicitly focused on decision-making expertise is incapable of providing answers that satisfy all major constituencies. Put another way, scholarship on this variety of expertise appears to be much less well developed than one might like or expect, a perception that is not unique to us (cf. Phillips, Klein, & Sieck, 2004).

We therefore modified our aims. Thus, in the chapter, we first offer our analysis of significant impediments to progress in research on decision-making expertise. We then describe a means of overcoming those impediments, an overarching way of thinking about decision making that makes clearer what decision-making expertise must entail. In the context of describing that perspective, we interpret some of the few major conclusions from earlier studies on decision-making expertise that seem firmly defensible. We also identify findings about aspects of decision behavior that have implications for expertise, although this is usually unrecognized. The analysis also identifies specific questions whose answers derived in future work should significantly accelerate progress toward a deep understanding of decision-making expertise.

Decisions

It is obvious what a free throw is in a basketball game. But things are murkier in the case of decision making; there is not universal agreement about what constitutes a decision. The resulting fuzziness has been burdensome for decision scholarship generally and for studies on decision-making expertise

in particular. Consider, for instance, the suggestion that scholarship on expertise in problem solving has been more productive than that on decision making (e.g., Orasanu & Connally, 1993). What can one make of such propositions if, as is often the case, decision making and problem solving are not clearly distinguished. (To anticipate, we view decision making as a special case of problem solving.)

To avoid such difficulties, it would help if investigators adhered consistently to a convention about what decisions are. Such a convention actually exists, although, as implied in the previous discussion, it is not universally followed. The convention is embodied in the following definition, which we assume for the remainder of the chapter (Yates, 2003, p. 24):

A "decision" is a commitment to a course of action that is intended to yield results that are satisfying for specified individuals.

There are several major decision varieties: "choices," which entail the selection of a subset from a larger collection of discrete alternatives (e.g., a class of ten new graduate students from a pool of 100 applicants); "acceptances/rejections," which are special cases of choices in which only one specific option (e.g., potential marriage partner) is acknowledged and must be accepted or not; "evaluations," which are statements of worth that are backed up by commitments to act (e.g., a $310,000 binding bid on a house); and "constructions," which are attempts to create ideal decision problem solutions given available resources (e.g., a department's budget or a plan for fighting a fire).

The present definition is a synthesis of how the decision idea has been understood implicitly in most scholarship on decision making, for example, in psychology, education, marketing, politics, operations, and the military. Individual investigators are sometimes inconsistent and imprecise in their use of the word "decision." But in our experience, when pressed, they almost never claim that the definition here differs significantly from how they understand the decision concept.

Several key features are packed into the decision definition:

- *Action*: Decisions ultimately are about people doing things – taking actions. Thus, when Jane Davis decides to purchase General Motors stock, the pertinent action is exchanging her money for GM shares.
- *Commitment*: Decisions need to be distinguished from the actions they implicate because, for instance, not all decisions are eventually executed. Hence, we recognize that a decision has been made as soon as there is a commitment to act in a particular way, as when Davis resolves to buy 100 GM shares.
- *Intention*: People cannot decide by accident, even though they sometimes decide haphazardly. That is, decision making is intentional behavior; it has a purpose. This is not to say, however, that unintended consequences do not sometimes (often?) occur or that deciders are always fully aware of how they arrive at their decisions, as when they decide according to "intuition."
- *Satisfying results*: Decision making is about achieving results that are experienced as satisfying (e.g., with high "utility"), not merely "correct" in some purely logical sense. The intentional character of decisions implicates their sought-after results (e.g., relief from arthritic pain in making a choice of medication). But other results that people care about are usually involved, too, ones recognized as "side effects" (e.g., liver damage from a medicine) or "process costs" (e.g., the time it takes to choose among alternative medications or the anxiety experienced when deliberating such choices).
- *Specified individuals*: People make decisions to serve the interests of particular individuals. Sometimes the targeted "beneficiary" is the decider alone, for example, when one is dining solo and choosing between the Szechuan chicken and the egg foo young. But at other times, the beneficiaries include others, for example, when a physician is choosing a pain reliever to prescribe for a particular patient. (The decider is nearly always among the intended beneficiaries of a decision, since people rarely seek to decide contrary to their own interests.) The specification of beneficiaries is critical, implicating what is arguably the single feature of decision problems that distinguishes them most sharply from more general problems – *differences among people in the values they attach to decision results*. The correct solution to an algebra problem is the correct solution for everybody. But, whereas Joe Payne regards the cobalt blue Phantom as the most beautiful car he has ever seen, Lew Walters sees it as "hideous" and therefore cringes at the mere idea of buying one. It is noteworthy that the implicit subjectivity represents a significant and challenging departure from most expertise scholarship, which prizes unambiguous performance criteria.

Decision Quality and Decision-Making Expertise

Even more than for the decision concept itself, ambiguity about notions of decision quality and expertise is a major hindrance to scholarship on decision-making expertise. Here we describe common views and their difficulties and propose an escape route.

The Satisfying-Results Perspective

It is plain for all to see when a basketball player is an expert free throw shooter. A successful shot is one that goes through the hoop. And an expert shooter is one who makes a high percentage of successful shots, even when the game is in the balance and the tension is palpable. In principle, there is no reason that decision quality and, correspondingly, decision-making expertise could not be conceptualized the same way. Thus, recalling that the aim of any decision is results that satisfy particular people, from a satisfying-results perspective, *a "high-quality decision" is one that does indeed achieve such satisfying results*. Consider a decision to prescribe Medication A over Medication B for Patient Lang. That would be the better decision if, taking pain relief, side effects, and all other results into account, Lang would, in fact, be more satisfied using Medication A. By extension, *an "expert decider" is a person who tends to make high-quality decisions*. So, according to this statistical ("tends") satisfying-results viewpoint, Dr. Lincoln is a more expert prescription decider than Dr. Thomas if, typically, Lincoln's patients get prescriptions that leave them more satisfied, on the whole, than Thomas's patients, all else being the same.

The Coherence Perspective

Perhaps surprisingly, the pure satisfying-results perspective is unpopular in traditional decision scholarship. Indeed, authors often go out of their way to caution against it, as when Hammond, Keeney, and Raiffa (1999, p. 110) write: "Although many people judge the quality of their own and others' decisions by the quality of the consequences – by how things turn out – this is an erroneous view." Research on outcome bias mirrors that sentiment. As described by Baron and Hershey (1988, p. 570), people exhibit "outcome bias" when they "take outcomes into account in a way that is irrelevant to the true quality of the decision." Elsewhere in their article (p. 569), Baron and Hershey remark that "Information that is available only after a decision is made is irrelevant to the quality of the decision," and presumably such information includes indications of decision results. There is good evidence that laypersons generally do conceive of decision quality in terms of outcomes, as implicated in the satisfying-results characterizations described here. Yates, Veinott, and Patalano (2003) asked people to bring to mind actual serious decisions of their own that they considered to have been "good" and "bad" ones. They then had those individuals explain why they put those decisions into the good and bad categories. By *far*, the most

commonly cited reason for describing decisions as "good" (95% of the time) was that those decisions yielded desirable outcomes. Similarly, decisions classified as "bad" ones were described (89% of the time) as having led to poor results.

Why have some scholars resisted people's apparently natural inclination to appraise decisions according to their outcomes? The main reason is the role of chance, as implicit in remarks by Ward Edwards (Edwards, Kiss, Majone, & Toda, 1984): "A good decision cannot guarantee a good outcome. All real decisions are made under uncertainty. A decision is therefore a bet, and evaluating it as good or not must depend on the stakes and the odds, not on the outcome" (p. 7). Writers often emphasize that the results of almost every decision-driven action depend at least partly on events outside the decider's control and awareness. Moreover, those events might well be beyond *anyone's* anticipation. Thus, in this view, it would be unfair and dysfunctional to castigate Dr. Lincoln for deciding to prescribe a medicine for Patient Lang that brings about a life-threatening but extremely rare allergic reaction.

So how do scholars antagonistic to the results perspective propose that people *should* appraise decisions (and, implicitly, decision-making expertise)? Apparently, they should do so according to the logical coherence of the procedures employed in making those decisions. Procedures are "logically coherent" if they do not contradict themselves or, equivalently, do not allow the decider to be self-contradictory in particular ways (cf. Yates, 1990, Chapters 5 and 9). As an extremely simple example, suppose that Jane says that she never wants to violate the transitivity principle, which says that, if A is preferred to B and B is preferred to C, then A must be preferred to C. Nevertheless, Jane likes Apartment 1 more than Apartment 2, Apartment 2 more than Apartment 3, but Apartment 3 more than Apartment 1. She is being logically incoherent.

In a perhaps extreme version of the coherence perspective, Edwards (Edwards, Kiss, Majone, & Toda, 1984) contended that the sole criterion for decision quality should be whether the process used to arrive at a decision mimics the maximization of expected utility: "No principle other than maximizing SEU deserves a moment's consideration" (p. 7). And in numerous laboratory studies of decision-making where the uncertainty is not explicitly acknowledged (e.g., Payne, Bettman, & Johnson, 1988), the coherence standard is often taken to be equivalent to additive utility or value maximization. Such expertise yardsticks are, incidentally, the ones implicit in several well-known decision-analytic methodologies. That is, the promise is that deciders (or, more importantly, their beneficiaries) would be well served by realizing such standards (e.g., Morris, 1977).

Implications for Expertise Questions

The satisfying results and the coherence perspectives are clearly different. This therefore poses a dilemma for addressing the expertise questions articulated at the outset of this chapter, most obviously the identification question. Suppose that one needs to identify expert deciders, for example, to hire them or to study them. The alternative perspectives suggest two different ways of doing that, and there is every reason to expect that those approaches would sometimes lead to different conclusions about who is actually an expert. Which conclusions would be right?

Interestingly, in terms of what happens in real life, this obvious question is actually moot. It is undoubtedly true that people commonly believe that some deciders – including professionals of various kinds – are either more or less expert than others. And those people almost certainly act on these beliefs, for example, in choosing to hire the services of individuals regarded as more expert than their peers. How do those beliefs arise and how are they justified? We are unaware of anyone pointedly trying to appraise expertise in terms of coherence. Nor have we seen full-fledged, legitimate attempts to assess decision-making expertise according to satisfying results in the kinds of complex, real-life situations for which people typically seek expertise. A

key reason is statistical. It is nearly impossible for people to defend statements like "Decider A's tendency for producing decisions with satisfying results is better than Decider B's" on the basis of large samples of observed cases. Instead, indications are that, when expertise beliefs are at all based on observations of results, those beliefs rest on fewer observations than statistical principles would demand. By default, then, the beliefs must be driven by other considerations.

An example: Extensive research has shown that people's judgment behavior is susceptible to strong primacy effects and that, under particular conditions, these effects result from "attention decrement" (e.g., Yates & Curley, 1986). Thus, people are inclined to observe a small number of cases, draw a conclusion on the basis of those cases, and then simply stop paying attention to pertinent facts that present themselves later. This phenomenon is plausibly related to the one Tversky and Kahneman (1971) dubbed "the belief in the law of small numbers," which suggests that people feel that attending to further cases beyond the first few is unnecessary as well as burdensome. In the present instance, these mechanisms suggest that our presumptions about a decider's expertise are dictated by the first few decisions we happen to associate with that person. If those decisions turn out well, we apply the label "expert." But if they turn out badly, the decider might well be called "inept." And that opinion is cast in stone since its underpinnings will not be revisited. It is worth noting that these effects implicate the sense in which the "outcome bias" label is sometimes justified. A process-control engineer would never dismiss a single product defect as irrelevant to conclusions about the quality of the manufacturing process that produced it. In the same way, it is unreasonable to say that people should ignore the results of a single decision when trying to infer the decider's expertise. The notion of "bias" enters the picture only when, in violation of principles like the law of large numbers, people use nothing more than a single case to draw *definitive* conclusions about long-term tendencies (Caplan, Posner,

& Cheney, 1991, provide a compelling illustration).

There are indications that beliefs about decision-making expertise are in large measure social constructions, too. In research on decision-making expertise, some investigators consider as experts individuals who have extensive experience, training, and/or professional and social standing, for example, practicing clinicians (Meehl, 1959) or senior military personnel (Tolcott, Marvin, & Lehner, 1989). In part, this practice seems to reflect a tendency to infer decision-making expertise from subject-matter expertise (e.g., the ability to recite standard psychiatric diagnostic categories). This is not unreasonable to the extent that subject-matter expertise is necessary for decision-making expertise, which it no doubt often is. For instance, it would be impossible for a layperson who knows nothing about the law to consistently make decent legal decisions on behalf of clients. Nevertheless, equating decision-making and subject-matter expertise effectively assumes that there is no such thing as decision-making expertise per se. This also implies that studies of expert deciders in one arena (e.g., law) offer no insight for decision-making expertise elsewhere (e.g., medicine); generalizability is nil.

Other researchers operationally define expertise according to consensus among peers (Shanteau, 1992). Thus, "experts" are people who already-acknowledged experts *say* are experts. Of course, this begs the question of how such self-sustaining impressions of expertise arise initially. As suggested earlier, these impressions plausibly are based at least partly on outcome observations, even if minimally. But they are also probably affected by such validity-vulnerable factors as personal style, which charlatans can easily "fake." Shanteau (1992, p. 257) put it nicely: "In short, to be accepted as an expert, it is necessary to act like one." This involves things like exhibiting self-confidence (bluster?) as well as good communication and persuasion skills. This conclusion agrees with the data of Yates, Price, Lee, and Ramirez (1996). These investigators found that many of their partici-

pants inferred consulting candidates' expertise at probability judgment according to their inclination to report extreme, that is, highly confident, opinions. They also found that many individuals demand that potential consultants be able to convincingly explain and justify their assessments; prospective principals give short shrift to empirical evidence of consultants' accuracy.

One worrisome possibility that the present analysis suggests is that our assumptions about who is or is not a decision-making expert might not be as good as we hope. (This is not to say that they are, in fact, erroneous, only that we do not know.) To the extent that this is true, we are not enjoying as many benefits of decision-making expertise as we might. There are troublesome research implications, too, concerning the decision-making expertise explanation and development questions. Some research designs for approaching such questions are predicated on identifying and studying large numbers of documented expert and nonexpert deciders. Those designs are precluded if certification is suspect, as it seems to be. Prospects for those designs are also compromised by sample size restrictions. Studies of decision-making expertise are conspicuous for their small sample sizes, which causes some observers to not take the research seriously. Consider, for instance, the six empirical expertise studies reported in the important collection edited by Zsambok and Klein (1997). The median number of participants in those studies, ones considered experts and otherwise, was only 20.5. One likely reason for such small numbers is the difficulty of finding and persuading busy experts to participate in research. All in all, it is clear that a good alternative to current perspectives and practices is essential. We now sketch what seems to be such an alternative.

The Process-Decomposition Perspective

In the process-decomposition perspective, the overall process of making a decision is partitioned into elements. If each element is executed well, this should contribute significantly to the adequacy of the resulting decision. (This is withstanding the real likelihood of the kinds of interactions emphasized in complex systems research, e.g., Sterman, 2002.) Ideally, there should be empirical evidence that, statistically, successful execution of an element does indeed increase the odds of decisions with satisfying outcomes. The process-decomposition perspective shares common ground with both the coherence and the satisfying-results perspectives. The standard coherence perspective focuses on just a couple of elements in normal decision processes. In that sense, it can be seen as a limited, special case of the process-decomposition perspective. No one claims that coherence harms the odds of good decision outcomes. Nevertheless, there have never been convincing demonstrations that coherence is sufficient to increase those odds substantially, which is what everyone wants decisions to do. Like the satisfying-results perspective, the process-decomposition perspective insists on efficacy demonstrations, even if they are only indirect or logical rather than empirical. It differs most sharply from the former point of view in its practicality. As we have seen, it is exceedingly difficult to appraise and study individuals' overall decision-making expertise. But it is often feasible to isolate and examine how people deal with specific process elements.

Decision processes can be decomposed into component processes in numerous different ways. But the particular decomposition to which we turn next has several attractions. Perhaps the most compelling, for present purposes, is that it is comprehensive. That is, it appears to encompass a great many of the activities implicated in virtually any decision situation. Thus, the following key inference makes sense: If a decider were to perform well on each element represented in the decomposition, we would be justified in expecting true decision-making expertise, even in the satisfying-results sense. Moreover, studies of such dimensional performance are directly informative about explanation and development questions regarding decision-making expertise. After all, if a decider is poor at some particular decision process element, this is itself a partial explanation of that individual's lack of overall decision-making proficiency. It also points to very specific things one can do to improve expertise, in the spirit of the "deliberate-practice" approach (Ericsson, Krampe, & Tesch-Römer, 1993).

Decision Processes as Cardinal Decision Issue Resolution

Decision-related writings in myriad fields (e.g., psychology, health care, management, finance, engineering, law, operations, anthropology, counseling, politics, and marketing) as well as analyses of hundreds of incidents indicate that a limited number of fundamental questions arise repeatedly in real-life decision problems. That is why the term "*cardinal* decision issues" is used to describe them (see Yates, 2003, for a more complete treatment of the "cardinal decision issue perspective"). In some instances, the issues go unrecognized by deciders themselves and thus are resolved by default, by whatever happens to be "natural" in the given situation. For instance, as we shall see, one cardinal issue concerns detecting that there is a decision problem in the first place. Suppose, say, driver James Lawson never senses growing deterioration in his car's transmission. Then he naturally makes no deliberate decision about how to deal with the impending disaster, and one day his car simply refuses to move. Regardless of their recognition, the cardinal issues are indeed somehow settled during the course of any decision episode. It therefore proves useful to characterize "decision processes" themselves as *the means by which the various cardinal issues are addressed for the decision problem at hand*.

There are ten cardinal issues, which are numbered for easy reference: 1) need, 2) mode, 3) investment, 4) options, 5) possibilities, 6) judgment, 7) value, 8) trade-offs, 9) acceptability, and 10) implementation. Detailed statements and illustrations of the issues appear below. But at this stage it is useful to put them in the context of the "big picture" of Figure 24.1, where the issues

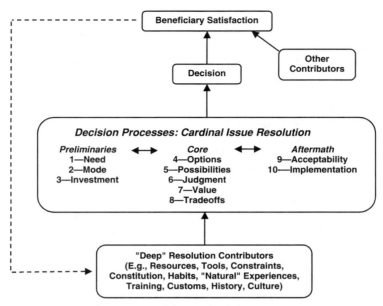

Figure 24.1. A big picture of the cardinal decision issue perspective.

are listed in the "Decision Processes" box. A tour of that big picture is useful.

Figure 24.1 mimics the kind of chart often sketched in root-cause analyses (see Robitaille, 2004). It starts with "Beneficiary Satisfaction" since that is the "point" of decision-making. We are ultimately interested in understanding (and sometimes influencing) contributors that, in cascade fashion, feed into that construct. The analysis acknowledges that, although decisions affect people's satisfaction with the results that ensue after a decision is made, so do "Other Contributors," factors unrelated to the decision. The decision is depicted as following from how the decider deals with each of the cardinal issues, "Decision Processes" as "Cardinal Issue Resolution."

Observe that the issues are grouped into categories that roughly correspond to when the issues arise in the typical decision episode. At the "core" of the overall decision process are the options, possibilities, judgment, value, and tradeoffs issues, matters that have received the most attention in decision research. But before those issues arise, usually the decider attends to several "preliminaries," the resolution of the need, mode, and investment issues, concern-

ing matters such as the resources assigned to the decision task. Ordinarily, deciders have reached their decisions (saying, for example, "So this is what we are going to do") once they have resolved the tradeoffs issue. In the "aftermath," often before anything else occurs, the acceptability and implementation issues take center stage, for example, how various other parties feel about how the decision was made. It is important to acknowledge that the stated order is indeed "rough." In real-life decision episodes, deciders often tentatively resolve issues but then revisit them later after confronting other issues (hence the double-headed arrows). Suppose, for example, that apartment seeker Linda Mathers, in addressing the options issue, identifies two possible places to rent. Later, in dealing with the tradeoffs issue, she realizes that picking Apartment A over Apartment B requires sacrifices that are too painful, and vice versa. She therefore returns to the options issue, attempting to find a third option that obviates such sacrifices.

The bottom portion of Figure 24.1 acknowledges that a decider's decision processes derive from a host of other, sometimes "deep," contributors that are important to understand in their own right, for example, unique personal experiences, constitutional factors such as inherited dispositions or abilities, training, and culturally transmitted local customs. The dotted arrow leading from "Beneficiary Satisfaction" to these contributors highlights the expectation that decision results – particularly bad results – are likely to instigate adjustments in how a decider does things, in a feedback loop.

Here we sketch and briefly illustrate the issues, with each articulated in the voice of deciders confronted with it. We also identify and discuss the implications of key expertise-significant ideas and findings associated with those issues. In addition, we identify specific and important addressable gaps in current understanding.

Issue 1 – Need: *"Why are we (not) deciding anything at all?"* The need issue is about whether and how decision problems are recognized at the outset. Suppose that a problem goes unacknowledged. Then necessarily there is no decision of any kind, and default consequences occur, a particular variety of "blindsiding." We already saw one illustration, the one in which driver Lawson was oblivious to the deteriorating transmission in his car.

Vigilance is one tack that deciders sometimes take to address the need issue. This is the sustained attempt to monitor for signals of threats and opportunities that warrant serious efforts to decide what, if anything, to do about them, as in the control room of a power plant. Over the past 50+ years, researchers have learned much about human vigilance, for example, how surprisingly rapidly it degrades (Howe, Warm, & Dember, 1995). Almost all vigilance research has examined the effects on performance of various aspects of the situation, not why one person might more successfully monitor signals than others. But some recent findings have identified various correlates of vigilance expertise. For instance, Rose, Murphy, Byard, and Nikzad (2002) found that false alarms in a vigilance task were associated with the Big Five dimensions of extraversion and conscientiousness. And Helton, Dember, Warm, and Matthews (1999) observed

that pessimists (vs. optimists) exhibited especially rapid vigilance declines. Results such as these suggest a side of expertise that is seldom discussed in any context – personality. That is, experts might perform particular tasks exceptionally well not (solely) because of cognitive capabilities but (also) because of temperament.

How well a decider maintains vigilance when actually trying is one thing. Whether the decider happens to notice good reasons for initiating decision-making efforts in the midst of performing other tasks is quite another, and arguably a more significant one. Consider, for instance, noticing subtle hints of customer taste changes in the normal course of commerce. We are unaware of research that has addressed differences in deciders' inclinations for doing this, which should be an important aspect of decision-making expertise. There is only a hint from the ancillary literature on problem finding and creativity that suggests the potential fruitfulness of decision-expertise scholarship on the problem. Rostan (1994) found that a significant distinction between "acclaimed" and merely "competent" artists and scientists was that, in an unstructured task, the former spent significantly more of their time finding problems.

Issue 2 – Mode: *"Who (or what) will make this decision, and how will they approach that task?"* Decision modes are qualitatively distinct approaches to deciding. The concern is with who decides and how those individuals address the various other cardinal issues that will be resolved in arriving at a decision. The mode issue per se is about how it is determined which of those modes is applied to the decision problem at hand.

A major part of the "who" mode distinction concerns whether and to whom people with the authority for making a decision defer at least part of their work to others, agents or consultants. "Agents" are parties (including possibly devices such as computers) who are granted the power to make a decision however they see fit, for example, a subordinate asked to make all hires in a particular unit. "Consultants" are parties who provide input to a decision procedure but who do not make the final decision, for example, a computer program that searches for and ranks job candidates but does not actually determine who gets a job. No decider can possibly have the substantive expertise required to make every kind of decision ideally. Thus, it seems apparent that deciders who are good at determining when there are significant advantages of using agents and consultants for particular purposes have an edge. That is, their expertise at the "who" side of the mode issue should pay off. There is consistent evidence that people generally have extraordinary confidence in the quality of their own decisions and that this confidence increases under particular conditions, for example, when they explain their decisions (e.g., Sieck & Yates, 1997). To the extent that this amounts to *over*confidence, this suggests that people generally defer to agents and consultants less often than they should. But if our earlier conclusions about the difficulty of assessing true decision-making expertise are correct, figuring out to whom one should defer is a formidable task. We are unaware of research that has even tried to identify, explain, or develop expertise on decision work deferral.

The "how" side of the mode issue is about the nuts and bolts of how deciders (as well as consultants) carry out their work. Several broad categories of possibilities are recognized, including (but not limited to) analytic, rule-based, automatic, and intuitive decision-making. The "analytic" label describes the broad category in which the decider effortfully seeks to figure out what action makes sense to do in a given decision situation. That mode is presumed to be necessary when the situation is unfamiliar. Most traditional decision scholarship (e.g., utility theory) addresses this mode. In "rule-based" decision-making, the decider applies rules of the following form: *If Conditions C hold, then take Action A.* Such rules are ubiquitous in business and medicine (e.g., "If the patient displays signs and symptoms X, Y, and Z, then treat as follows:...."). "Automatic" decision making is such that, if the decider recognizes particular conditions

(and not necessarily consciously), then a particular action spontaneously emerges, with negligible effort, control, and self-insight. This mode is common in high-speed, frequently repeated situations, for example, operating a vehicle or playing a sport such as basketball. "Intuitive" decision making is said to occur when the decider selects a course of action on the basis of considerations ("feelings") that the decider cannot articulate, perhaps because of fundamental weaknesses in the linkages between cognitive and affective psychological processes (Sadler-Smith & Shefy, 2004).

"How" decision modes differ most obviously in their efficiency. Deliberately pondering what to do, as in analytic decision-making, obviously takes far more time than deciding via any of the other modes. And, to the degree that a good decision maker is efficient, the application of various "how" modes is a significant dimension of decision-making expertise. Moreover, to the extent that expertise tends to (imperfectly) increase with experience, we should expect an association between mode use and measures of decision-making expertise beyond efficiency. Such associations have indeed been inferred. Probably the best-known example is embodied in research related to Klein's (1993) recognition-primed decision (RPD) model (see Ross et al., Chapter 23). Such work has repeatedly demonstrated that rule-based decision making is extremely common among highly experienced, recognized experts such as fire-ground commanders. Unfortunately, there is not yet a body of research that systematically addresses identification, explanation, and development questions as they apply to individual differences in expertise at shifting among "how" modes.

Issue 3 – Investment: *"What kinds and amounts of resources will be invested in the process of making this decision?"* The investment issue is about how and how well it is determined whether the "investment" of resources in the process of making a given decision is extensive or minimal, and in which particular resource categories. As implied in the mode issue discussion, if two deciders are otherwise equivalent, it clearly makes sense to say that the one who routinely expends fewer resources is more expert. As also suggested in that previous discussion, one means for minimizing decision-making costs – as yet unstudied systematically – is deliberate, strategic reliance on "cheap" modes such as rule-based and intuitive decision making.

Conceivably, deciders who require little time to decide do so because decision chores demand little of the mental resources they have available, compared to what others bring to the table. Such a possibility has been given little credence in view of results like those of Chase and Simon (1973), who compared the memory performance of chess masters and less-expert players. There was no indication that masters had generally superior pure memory skills. Instead, the inference drawn from such work is that experts are especially good at organizing or "chunking" pertinent information, which can facilitate effective memory performance in appropriate circumstances. Results like these as well as more recent research on the long-term working-memory concept (Ericsson & Kintsch, 1995) suggest a minimal role for capacity variations in explaining expertise, decision making and otherwise. But other research has been more favorable to the capacity view, finding reliable connections between performance on decision-related tasks, on the one hand, and measures of working-memory capacity (Dougherty & Hunter, 2003) and general cognitive facility (West & Stanovich, 2003), on the other.

Issue 4 – Options: *"What are the different actions we could potentially take to deal with this problem we have?"* If a decider never recognizes a certain alternative, then clearly the decider cannot commit to that alternative. Thus, the leaders of Ace Products cannot choose to market – or not market – Product C if that prospect never reaches their attention. The options issue is about how people come to "see," if not create, prospective solutions to their decision problems. It is essential to recognize that expert management of the options issue is not about

increasing the number of alternatives considered, a false assumption that many people make. The ideal "option consideration set" for a given problem consists of only a single alternative – the best one. Recognizing others is wasteful, requiring the decider to expend precious resources vetting alternatives that ultimately will (or should) be rejected. But recent work has demonstrated that the deliberation of large consideration sets can do more than simply waste time. It can also exact significant psychological costs, such as turmoil over the possibility of failing to pick the very best alternative (e.g., Schwartz et al., 2002).

There has been surprisingly little research that directly implicates expertise with respect to the options issue. One of the few decision articles on the subject was by Dougherty and Hunter (2003), who found that working-memory capacity was reliably related to the number of alternatives individuals could recall in a laboratory decision task. The creativity literature is the major nondecision literature most directly relevant to option-issue expertise since, by definition, highly creative individuals are especially good at crafting new and useful alternatives. Assuming their validity, creativity measures should be helpful in identifying this particular variety of decision-making expertise. So should measures of personality characteristics, such as openness to experience, that have been shown to be associated with creativity (e.g., Wolfradt & Pretz, 2001). Unfortunately, there is little in the literature immediately informative on the explanation and development expertise questions, for example, about where creativity originates, how creative people go about their work, or how their practices can be cultivated in others. Nevertheless, some possibilities seem implicit in other research. For instance, numerous studies have shown that creativity is enhanced by positive emotion (Fredrickson, 1998). This suggests that creative individuals might achieve some of their advantage by strategically arranging their work environments to exploit phenomena such as the creativity-emotion linkage.

Issue 5 – Possibilities: *"What are the various things that could potentially happen if we took that action – things they care about?"* This issue implicates another form of blindsiding, well illustrated by an actual case involving a popular assistant school superintendent. Only by accident was she discovered to have falsified her credentials (including degrees) when she was hired years earlier. The officials responsible for her appointment were stunned, saying things like: "It simply never occurred to us that she might not be who she said she was." More generally, the possibilities issue is about recognizing outcomes of prospective actions that are capable of occurring and which, if they did, would matter greatly. Note that the concern is not with whether those outcomes *would* occur, only whether they *could*. Thus, in the superintendent case, if the mere possibility of false credentials had come to mind, the deciders might well have made routine checks that would have precluded an embarrassing appointment.

Clearly, a truly expert decider would be good at anticipating possibilities. Yet, the possibilities issue as such has gone largely untouched in decision research. Nevertheless, work framed in other ways arguably has implications for it. This includes research demonstrating people's difficulty even imagining the sometimes bizarre behaviors of common real-life non-linear systems (Sterman, 2002). It also includes scholarship on stress. Numerous studies have shown that acute stress narrows the scope of attention. Thus, stress should induce the neglect of possibilities. But a decider who is stress resistant should be immune to such effects. This suggests that stress resistance should facilitate the handling of the possibilities issue and, thus, decision-making expertise, particularly in high-stress environments. There have been no direct tests of this proposition yet. But there are data consistent with it, such as indications that individuals who self-select and succeed in becoming air traffic controllers tend to be more stress resistant than other people (see the review by Yates, Klatzky, & Young, 1995).

Issue 6 – Judgment: *"Which of the things that they care about actually* would *happen if we took that action?"* Usually, this issue logically and temporally follows the possibilities issue. After the decider recognizes (accurately or otherwise) that some decision-relevant event *can* happen, the next task is judging whether it *would* happen. A "judgment" is *an opinion as to what was, is, or will be the state of some decision-relevant aspect of the world.* Accordingly, a judgment is "accurate" to the degree that there is a *close correspondence between that judgment and the actual pertinent state.* Clearly, judgments and decisions are distinct, but equally clearly, judgment accuracy imposes an upper bound on decision quality.[1] Many considerations go into crafting a bid on a business contract. But the eventual deal cannot possibly be fully satisfactory if it is predicated on false expectations about what the other party would do during the contract's life.

Much research that has been described as concerning decision making has really been about judgment. Consider, for instance, Shanteau's (1992) remarks on the "good decision performance" of weather forecasters, who actually make predictions of weather events rather than make decisions predicated on such predictions. Making the judgment-versus-decision distinction is useful for several reasons, including the fact that decision problems demand the consideration of much more than judgment problems. At the same time, however, as we shall see, judgments of various kinds assume roles in the resolution of several other cardinal decision issues beyond the judgment issue per se.

Partly because its adequacy is often easy to evaluate and analyze, judgment is the aspect of decision behavior that has been studied more extensively than any other. And the most consistent expertise conclusion has been this: *Subject matter experts often exhibit much worse judgment accuracy than most people expect.* Meehl (1959), for instance, found that clinical psychologists' diagnoses based on MMPI scores were less accurate than those derived from simple linear combinations of those scores. There have been many similar demonstrations since then. One of the most recent was Önkal-Atay, Yates, Şimga-Mugan, and Öztin's (2003) finding that, although professionals were generally more accurate at predicting foreign exchange rates than amateurs, in many individual comparisons, the opposite was true.

Several contributors to such occurrences have been hypothesized and, in some cases, documented. Some amount to artifacts of the testing conditions, for example, as in studies showing that auditors are minimally susceptible to known biases when making judgments in familiar professional contexts (Smith & Kida, 1991). Other contributors are apparently "real," including the fact that humans, unlike computers, necessarily cannot perfectly reliably execute any intended judgment policy (e.g., Dawes & Corrigan, 1974). An especially powerful contributor seems to lie in the very character of human judgment. Yates (1990) observed that there are two classes of judgment processes, formalistic and substantive. Formalistic procedures are similar to the application of rules such as those in probability theory or regression analysis. Significantly, such rules are indifferent to the content of judgment problems. Quite the opposite is true of substantive procedures, which entail the person attempting to envision how "nature" literally would (or would not) create the event in question. Pennington and Hastie's (1988) story model of juror decision making is a good illustration. In that model, jurors judge the likelihood of a defendant's guilt by how easily evidence fits into a narrative whereby the defendant committed the crime in question. The mental simulation process in Klein's (1993) RPD model is another illustrative substantive procedure. There are many indications in the literature that, as Yates (1990, pp. 209–210) argued, people resort to formalistic procedures only when they cannot use substantive ones, which are much more natural.

By definition, subject-matter experts know more than other people about the substance of a given area. This implies that they are also especially likely to apply substantive procedures when arriving at their judgments. Johnson's (1988) protocol data provide direct evidence for this expectation. Substantive procedures are a powerful but risky tool. The character of people's personal theories about how events (e.g., criminal acts) literally occur has little if any place for uncertainty, which should encourage overconfidence. Such theories also tend to be convoluted, since they seek to account for every local nuance in the abundant and interpretable information experts see. As Camerer and Johnson (1991) argued, this feature should manifest itself in configurality equivalent to interaction terms in statistical models, terms that tend to be unpredictive. This can actually harm the accuracy of experts' judgments by making them "noisy," laden with what amounts to random error, a phenomenon observed by Yates, McDaniel, and Brown (1991) in securities forecasting. A significant challenge for future research is the development of human-device systems that take effective account of the documented peculiarities as well as the complementary strengths of human experts and judgment algorithms.

Issue 7 – Value: "*How much would they really care – positively or negatively – if that in fact happened?*" The value issue is a special case of the judgment issue, albeit an exceptionally important special case. That is because it centers on what makes decision problems so distinctive and difficult – individual differences in what people like and dislike. In order for a decider to pursue actions that promise outcomes that the intended beneficiaries find satisfying – the goal of any decision-making effort – the decider must know those persons' tastes. That is, an expert decider must be outstanding at making judgments for which the target is how people feel about things. For instance, an expert designer, buyer, or casting director must be excellent at anticipating how much the typical potential customer would like or dislike any given "product."

There is extraordinary interest in the value issue these days in decision research, under the rubric of hedonic forecasting. Specifically, the concern is with the consistent errors people tend to make when trying to predict their own feelings about future occurrences, for example, winning a lottery, suffering paraplegia, or getting promoted (Loewenstein & Schakade, 1999). Unfortunately, there has been much less interest and systematic study of *expertise* in anticipating people's values, particularly other people's values. Nevertheless, work to date suggests that subject-matter experts are not always as good at the value issue as one might expect or hope. Consider the study by Wilson et al. (1997), involving interns and attending physicians caring for elderly patients. Only 4% of the interns knew their patients more than seven days, whereas almost half the attending physicians had known their patients more than six months. Nevertheless, the attending physicians (despite their confidence) were no more accurate than the interns at predicting patients' preferences for end-of-life care (e.g., lifelong tube feeding). Determining why accuracy sometimes fails to improve with experience is an important task on the research agenda. Part of the problem is likely to reside in the lack of attention and feedback.

Issue* 8 – *Tradeoffs: *"All of our prospective actions have both strengths and weaknesses. So how should we make the tradeoffs that are required to settle on the action we will actually pursue?"* This issue concerns the fact that in virtually all decision situations, deciders eventually arrive at this reality: Every alternative has drawbacks. Investing a company's funds in a new, untested product could provide unprecedented profits. On the other hand, it could also push the company into bankruptcy. To reach a decision, the company's leaders must trade off the prospect of great profit against the risk of ruin. Mainstream decision scholarship historically has been preoccupied with the tradeoffs issue. Expected utility theory, the undisputed point of reference for the field, is at heart about the trading off of outcome value and uncertainty (Yates, 1990, Chapter 9). Multiattribute utility theory and its variants seek to explain or guide the trading off of values for some outcomes against those for others (Keeney & Raiffa, 1976). And the discounted cash-flow rules at the core of so

many finance tools prescribe how to trade off outcome value against time (Higgins, 1998).

Behavioral decision research has been dominated by questions about deviations of people's actual decision behavior from what is predicted or prescribed by rules like the expected utility, additive utility, and discounting models. It is therefore perhaps surprising that there is virtually no literature on individual differences in adherence to those standards. And, accordingly, there has been virtually no discussion of expertise with respect to tradeoffs. This probably reflects an overly narrow conception of how deciders tend to deal with tradeoffs in real life. The dominant models just described presume a static, "pick among these" stance by the decider. Yet, there is evidence that a major tactic deciders use is, in effect, transforming tradeoffs problems into options problems (cf. Shafir, Simonson, & Tversky, 1993). Specifically, deciders sometimes seek to avoid having to make an onerous tradeoff altogether by finding or creating a new alternative that makes it unnecessary. Thus, instead of simply choosing between putting a new, untested product on the market and forgetting about it, a company's deciders might seek other alternatives, such as sharing the product's risk with a partner. Indeed, this approach seemed quite evident to Shapira (1995) in his study of risk taking among top executives. The executives appeared to believe that a major feature of managerial expertise was the ability to restructure risky alternatives such that they were less hazardous to one's company.

Issue* 9 – *Acceptability: *"How can we get them to agree to this decision and this decision procedure?"* In perhaps most of the situations where decision-making expertise matters, the decider is not a free agent. Instead, the decider must contend with the sentiments of many different people concerning two things, *what* is decided as well as *how* it is decided, the province of the acceptability issue.

Negotiations are the most familiar context where the acceptability issue figures significantly. Unless both parties accept a given proposal, there is no deal. Many deals fall through not only or even mainly because of the material aspects of a proposal but because of the character of the deliberations (e.g., the parties' perceptions of one another's integrity or respectfulness). Negotiation research and teaching are vibrant enterprises these days (cf. Thompson & Leonardelli, 2004). This is likely tied to the immediacy, transparency, and obvious importance of negotiator effectiveness. As soon as a negotiation is over, each party seems clearly better or worse off than before, and apparently because of the negotiators' skills or lack thereof. We are unaware of extensive research on negotiator expertise per se. But there are certainly popular assumptions that some negotiators (e.g., those entrusted with negotiating hostage releases) are more expert than others. And there is considerable work pointing toward negotiator behaviors or characteristics associated with their effectiveness and hence expertise, for example, their creativity (Kurtzberg, 1998).

The acceptability issue assumes significance beyond the realm of formal negotiations. Striking illustrations have played themselves out in courtrooms. American automakers have lost several major lawsuits because they mishandled the acceptability issue in design decisions. In one prominent case, jurors were repelled by testimony that the decision to limit costs on certain features rested partly on a decision analysis in which a dollar figure (based on actuarial records) was attached to lives that might be lost in accidents linked to those features. The jurors responded by forcing the company to pay billions in punitive damages (Fix, 1999). Such examples dramatically demonstrate the importance of expertise with respect to the acceptability issue. Unfortunately, there appear to have been no systematic efforts to identify and understand such expertise.

Issue 10 – *Implementation*: *"That's what we decided to do. Now, how can we get it done, or can we get it done, after all?"* This final cardinal issue arises in decision situations where the selected alternative entails a nontrivial "project" that must be executed

as opposed to a single action that is virtually synonymous with the decision itself (e.g., purchasing a shirt). What sometimes occurs is that the project proves to be difficult or even impossible to actually perform. A good example is a company that agrees to generous pension payments to its workers but ultimately discovers, years later, that it cannot afford those payments.

Disasters with respect to the implementation issue generally result from the mishandling of one or more of the other cardinal issues. For instance, in the pension illustration, the deciders plausibly did a poor job with the judgment and options issues, failing to anticipate increased employee longevity or to create contract options containing contingencies that take such increases into account. There has been little systematic research aimed at understanding how people, experts or otherwise, address the implementation issue, although this is changing (e.g., Dholakia & Bagozzi, 2002). But arguably relevant scholarship framed differently has existed for some time. This includes work highlighting cultural differences in priorities assigned to the issue. For instance, numerous Japanese businesses appear to have deliberately chosen to emphasize ease of decision implementation over decision-making speed (cf. Liker, 2004).

Closing Remarks

This review, built on the component analysis afforded by the cardinal issue perspective, has cited numerous results suggesting specific behaviors that plausibly contribute to decision-making expertise. Nevertheless, the review has also made it painfully obvious how much remains unknown about such behaviors. It also made clear how difficult it would be for any one person to consistently demonstrate excellence in resolving every one of the cardinal issues for any class of decision problem. This makes one suspect that true, across-the-board decision-making expertise is exceedingly rare. Yet, the present analysis is optimistic in that it points toward concrete and manageable questions for future fundamental as well as developmental research, including efforts to create collectives and human-device systems that decide with undeniable proficiency.

Acknowledgments

We are deeply grateful to Hannah Faye Chua, Georges Potworowski, Robert Hoffman, and Anders Ericsson for their invaluable comments and suggestions.

Footnote

1. Confusingly, the term "judgment" is sometimes applied to evaluation decisions in the literature, as when authors distinguish "judgment" and "choice" (e.g., Montgomery, Selart, Gärling, & Lindberg, 1994). The present use of the expression is older, more firmly established, and hence preferred.

References

Baron, J., & Hershey, J. C. (1988). Outcome bias in decision evaluation. *Journal of Personality and Social Psychology, 54*, 569–579.

Camerer, C. F., & Johnson, E. J. (1991). The process-performance paradox in expert judgment: How can experts know so much and predict so badly? In K. A. Ericsson & J. Smith (Eds.), *Toward a general theory of expertise: Prospects and limits* (pp. 195–217). New York: Cambridge University Press.

Caplan, R. A., Posner, K. L., & Cheney, F. W. (1991). Effect of outcome on physician judgments of appropriateness of care. *Journal of the American Medical Association, 265*, 1957–1960.

Chase, W. G., & Simon, H. (1973). Perception in chess. *Cognitive Psychology, 4*, 55–81.

Dawes, R. M., & Corrigan, B. (1974). Linear models in decision making. *Psychological Bulletin, 81*, 95–106.

Dholakia, U. M., & Bagozzi, R. P. (2002). Mustering motivation to enact decisions: How decision process characteristics influence goal realization. *Journal of Behavioral Decision Making, 15*, 167–188.

Dougherty, M. R. P., & Hunter, J. E. (2003). Hypothesis generation, probability judgment, and individual differences in working memory capacity. *Acta Psychologica, 113*, 263–282.

Edwards, W., Kiss, I., Majone, G., & Toda, M. (1984). What constitutes "a good decision?" *Acta Psychologica, 56*, 5–27.

Ericsson, K. A., & Kintsch, W. (1995). Long-term working memory. *Psychological Review, 102*, 211–245.

Ericsson, K. A., Krampe, R. Th., & Tesch-Römer, C. (1993). The role of deliberate practice in the acquisition of expert performance. *Psychological Review, 100*, 363–406.

Fix, J. L. (1999, July 13). Memos key in $4.9-billion verdict. *Detroit Free Press*, pp. 1Aff.

Fredrickson, B. L. (1998). What good are positive emotions? *Review of General Psychology, 2*, 300–319.

Hammond, J. S., Keeney, R. L., & Raiffa, H. (1999). *Smart choices*. Boston: Harvard Business School Press.

Helton, W. S., Dember, W. N., Warm, J. S., & Matthews, G. (1999). Optimism, pessimism, and false failure feedback: Effects on vigilance performance. *Current Psychology: Developmental, Learning, Personality, Social, 18*, 311–325.

Higgins, R. C. (1998). *Analysis for financial management*. Boston: Irwin McGraw-Hill.

Howe, S. R., Warm, J. S., & Dember, W. N. (1995). Meta-analysis of the sensitivity decrement in vigilance. *Psychological Bulletin, 117*, 230–249.

Johnson, E. J. (1988). Expertise and decision under uncertainty: Performance and process. In M. T. H. Chi, R. Glaser, & M. J. Farr (Eds.), *The nature of expertise* (pp. 209–228). Mahwah, NJ: Erlbaum.

Keeney, R. L., & Raiffa, H. (1976). *Decisions with multiple objectives: Preferences and value trade-offs*. New York: Wiley.

Klein, G. (1993). A recognition-primed decision (RPD) model of rapid decision making. In G. Klein, J. Orasanu, R. Calderwood, & C. Zsambok (Eds.), *Decision making in action: Models and methods* (pp. 138–147). Norwood, NJ: Ablex.

Kurtzberg, T. R. (1998). Creative thinking, cognitive aptitude, and integrative joint gain: A study of negotiator creativity. *Creativity Research Journal, 11*, 283–293.

Liker, J. K. (2004). *The Toyota Way*. New York: McGraw-Hill.

Loewenstein, G., & Schkade, D. (1999). Wouldn't it be nice? Predicting future feelings. In D. Kahneman, E. Diener, & N. Schwarz (Eds.), *Well-being: The foundations of hedonic psychology* (pp. 85–105). New York: Russell Sage Foundation.

Meehl, P. E. (1959). A comparison of clinicians with five statistical methods of identifying psychotic MMPI profiles. *Journal of Counseling Psychology, 6*, 102–109.

Montgomery, H., Selart, M., Gärling, T., & Lindberg, E. (1994). The judgment-choice discrepancy: Noncompatibility or restructuring? *Journal of Behavioral Decision-Making, 7*, 45–55.

Morris, W. T. (1977). *Decision analysis.* Columbus, OH: Grid, Inc.

Önkal-Atay, D., Yates, J. F., Şimga-Mugan, C., & Öztin, Ş. (2003). Professional vs. amateur judgment accuracy: The case of foreign exchange rates. *Organizational Behavior and Human Decision Processes, 91*, 169–185.

Orasanu, J., & Connally, T. (1993). The reinvention of decision making. In G. Klein, J. Orasanu, R. Calderwood, & C. Zsambok (Eds.), *Decision making in action: Models and methods* (pp. 3–20). Norwood, NJ: Ablex.

Payne, J. W., Bettman, J. R., & Johnson, E. J. (1988). Adaptive strategy selection in decision making. *Journal of Experimental Psychology: Learning, Memory, and Cognition, 14*, 534–552.

Pennington, N., & Hastie, R. (1988). Explanation-based decision making: Effects of memory structure on judgment. *Journal of Experimental Psychology: Learning, Memory, & Cognition, 14*, 521–533.

Phillips, J. K., Klein, G., & Sieck, W. R. (2004). Expertise in judgment and decision making: A case for training intuitive decision skills. In D. J. Koehler & N. Harvey (Eds.), *Blackwell handbook of judgment and decision making* (pp. 297–315). Malden, MA: Blackwell.

Robitaille, D. (2004). *Root cause analysis: Basic tools and techniques.* Chico, CA: Paton Press.

Rose, C. L., Murphy, L. B., Byard, L., & Nikzad, K. (2002). The role of the Big Five personality factors in vigilance performance and workload. *European Journal of Personality, 16*, 185–200.

Rostan, S. M. (1994). Problem finding, problem solving, and cognitive controls: An empirical investigation of critically acclaimed productivity. *Creativity Research Journal, 7*(2), 97–110.

Sadler-Smith, E., & Shefy, E. (2004). The intuitive executive: Understanding and applying 'gut feeling' in decision-making. *Academy of Management Executive, 18*, 76–91.

Schwartz, B., Ward, A., Monterosso, J., Lyubomirsky, S., White, K., & Lehman, D. R. (2002). Maximizing versus satisficing: Happiness is a matter of choice. *Journal of Personality and Social Psychology, 83*, 1178–1197.

Shafir, E., Simonson, I., & Tversky, A. (1993). Reason-based choice. *Cognition, 49*, 11–36.

Shanteau, J. (1992). Competence in experts: The role of task characteristics. *Organizational Behavior and Human Decision Processes, 53*, 252–266.

Shapira, Z. (1995). *Risk taking: A managerial perspective.* New York: Russell Sage Foundation.

Sieck, W., & Yates, J. F. (1997). Exposition effects on decision making: Choice and confidence in choice. *Organizational Behavior and Human Decision Processes, 70*, 207–219.

Smith, J. F., & Kida, T. (1991). Heuristics and biases: Expertise and task realism in auditing. *Psychological Bulletin, 109*(3), 472–489.

Sterman, J. D. (2002). All models are wrong: Reflections on becoming a systems scientist. *Systems Dynamics Review, 18*, 501–531.

Thompson, L., & Leonardelli, G. J. (2004, July/August). Why negotiation is the most popular business school course. *Ivey Business Journal,* http://www.iveybusinessjournal.com/.

Tolcott, M. A., Marvin, F. F., & Lehner, P. E. (1989). Expert decision making in evolving situations. *IEEE Transactions on Systems, Man, and Cybernetics, 19*, 606–615.

Tversky, A., & Kahneman, D. (1971). The belief in the "law of small numbers." *Psychological Bulletin, 76*, 105–110.

West, R. F., & Stanovich, K. E. (2003). Is probability matching smart? Associations between probabilistic choices and cognitive ability. *Memory & Cognition, 31*, 243–251.

Wilson, I. B., Green, M. L., Goldman, L., Tsevat, J., Cook, E. F., & Phillips, R. S. (1997). Is experience a good teacher? How interns and attending physicians understand patients' choices for end-of-life care. *Medical Decision Making, 17*, 217–227.

Wolfradt, U., & Pretz, J. E. (2001). Individual differences in creativity: Personality, story writing, and hobbies. *European Journal of Personality, 15*, 297–310.

Yates, J. F. (1990). *Judgment and decision making.* Englewood Cliffs, NJ: Prentice Hall.

Yates, J. F. (2003). *Decision management.* San Francisco: Jossey-Bass.

Yates, J. F., & Curley, S. P. (1986). Contingency judgment: Primacy effects and attention decrement. *Acta Psychologica, 62*, 293–302.

Yates, J. F., Klatzky, R. L., & Young, C. A. (1995). Cognitive performance under stress. In R. S. Nickerson (Ed.), *Emerging needs and opportunities for human factors research* (pp. 262–290). Washington, DC: National Academy Press.

Yates, J. F., McDaniel, L. S., & Brown, E. S. (1991). Probabilistic forecasts of stock prices and earnings: The hazards of nascent expertise. *Organizational Behavior and Human Decision Processes, 49*, 60–79.

Yates, J. F., Price, P. C., Lee, J.-W., & Ramirez, J. (1996). Good probabilistic forecasters: The "consumer's" perspective. *International Journal of Forecasting, 12*, 41–56.

Yates, J. F., Veinott, E. S., & Patalano, A. L. (2003). Hard decisions, bad decisions: On decision quality and decision aiding. In S. L. Schneider & J. C. Shanteau (Eds.), *Emerging perspectives on judgment and decision research* (pp. 13–63). New York: Cambridge University Press.

Zsambok, C. E., & Klein, G. (Eds.). (1997). *Naturalistic decision making.* Mahwah, NJ: Erlbaum.

CHAPTER 25

The Making of a Dream Team: When Expert Teams Do Best

*Eduardo Salas, Michael A. Rosen, C. Shawn Burke,
Gerald F. Goodwin, & Stephen M. Fiore*

The Making of a Dream Team: When Expert Teams Do Best

The original use of the phrase "Dream Team" was in reference to the US basketball team that won the gold medal at the 1992 Olympics in Barcelona. Team members included basketball greats (e.g., Michael Jordan, Magic Johnson, and Larry Bird) as well as Charles Barkley and seven more NBA All-Stars. This team of twelve proficient athletes who were at the top of their game seamlessly blended their talents such that they dominated the Olympic competition, beating their eight opponents by an average of 44 points.

On February 22, 1980 at the Olympic Winter Games in Lake Placid a highly skilled Russian hockey team, recognized as the best hockey team in the world, lost 4–3 to a young but skilled collegiate US hockey team. The US victory over the "undefeatable" Russian team in the semi-finals, whom they had just lost to 10–3 a week before in an exhibition match, put the US team in contention for the gold medal. The US hockey team, which had been seeded seventh in the 12-team tournament, went on to beat Finland (4–2) for the gold medal.

So what distinguishes these two teams from other teams? Teamwork? Individual expertise? Both? What led the original "Dream Team" to dominate the 1992 Olympics? Conversely, what led the star Russian team to lose to a team they had dominated only a week before? The above examples illustrate that it takes more than a set of experts to make an expert team. Examples of teams composed of individuals highly skilled in their task roles that have failed as teams, sometimes with disastrous consequences are not limited to sports, but abound within organizations (e.g., Hackman, 1990), industry, aviation, and medicine as well as the military (e.g. Cannon-Bowers & Salas, 1998; Salas, Stagl, & Burke, 2004).

The lack of understanding that exists within organizations concerning the creation and management of expert teams poses a challenge since, in recent decades the cognitive complexity and demanding nature of jobs has increased because of advances in technology. This has caused organizations to increasingly adopt team-based systems (Ilgen, 1994) in an effort to remain competitive and handle the cognitive demands placed on workers. In addition, the problem sets within organizations are often ambiguous, unstructured and ill defined, causing an increasing need for flexibility – adaptive expert teams. Because expert teams, in general, function in such dynamic, stressful, and complex environments, research that examines teams situated in their natural context has particular significance for understanding expert teams. Hence, this chapter focuses primarily on studies of teams in complex environments functioning in such areas as the military, business, aviation, and healthcare.

The focus of this chapter is on current scientific understanding of the performance of expert teams – what is it that these teams do, think, or feel that makes them expert. So, we present a brief review of the state-of-the-art in the study of performance of expert teams. We define an expert team as a set of interdependent team members, each of whom possesses unique and expert-level knowledge, skills, and experience related to task performance, and who adapt, coordinate, and cooperate as a team, thereby producing sustainable and repeatable team functioning at superior or at least near-optimal levels of performance. Expert teams are primarily characterized by high levels of team and task outcomes, achieved via the team's effective utilization of team member task-related expertise and the mastery of *team* processes. To that end, this chapter addresses three questions. First, what are the theories that are driving the research in the domain of expert teams? Second, what methods are being used to study expert teams? Third, given these things, what do we currently know about the performance of expert teams? We hope that in briefly addressing these three questions we get a glimpse at the making of a "dream team" – what are the cognitions, behaviors, and attitudes that we should strive for in high performing teams.

What Theories are Driving Expert Teams' Research?

There have been several advances in the study of teams within the past 25 years (see Guzzo & Dickson, 1996; Kozlowski & Bell, 2003; Salas et al., 2004); however, the literature often focuses on teams as a general topic and not expert teams specifically. By taking a multi-disciplinary approach and combining advancements within the team literature with that on individual expertise, we can begin to understand, create, and manage adaptive expert team performance in complex environments.

What has the literature told us so far? First, expert team members are able to combine their individual technical expertise and coordinate their actions to achieve a common goal in such a manner that performance seems fluid; the team as a whole creates a synergy greater than its parts (Salas et al., 2004). Second, expert teams need to possess routine expertise, that is, they need the ability to solve problems quickly and accurately and understand problems in terms of principles and concepts (Chi, Feltovich, & Glaser, 1981). Third, members must be able to flexibly apply existing knowledge structures such that when faced with a novel situation, members can make predictions about system functioning and invent new procedures based on these predictions (Hatano & Inagaki, 1986). Fourth, expert teams seem to hold shared mental models of the task, the situation, their teammates, and the equipment (Cannon-Bowers, Salas, & Converse, 1993; Orasanu & Salas, 1993), which promote implicit coordination. Finally, expert teams must possess adaptive expertise – the ability to invent new procedures based on knowledge and to make new predictions (Hatano & Inagaki, 1986). Smith, Ford, and Kozlowski (1997) further argue that the key to adaptive expertise is a deep conceptual understanding of the target domain such that declarative and procedural knowledge coalesce into strategic knowledge (i.e., why procedures are appropriate for certain conditions). Hatano and Inagaki (1986) argue that mindful processing and abstraction are critical to the formation of adaptive expertise.

Given these characteristics, advances in theory that serve as drivers to understanding expert teams can be broken down into five areas, those dealing with: (a) team effectiveness and teamwork, (b) team adaptability and decision making, (c) shared cognition, (d) team leadership, and (e) team affective states, such as collective efficacy and psychological safety. We briefly discuss these below.

TEAM EFFECTIVENESS AND TEAMWORK

Advances in understanding the components of team effectiveness serve to inform our knowledge about the creation of adaptive team expertise. Models and theories depict the relationship between input variables (e.g., team characteristics, individual characteristics), process variables (e.g., communication, coordination, decision making, back-up behavior, compatible cognitive structures, compensatory behavior, and leadership), and outcome variables (e.g., increased productivity, increased safety, increased job satisfaction) (e.g., Hackman, 1983; Gersick, 1988; Salas, Dickinson, Converse, & Tannenbaum, 1992; Marks, Mathieu, & Zaccaro, 2001; Salas, Stagl, Burke, & Goodwin, in press). In doing so, these input-process-output models illustrate the dynamic and multidimensional nature of teamwork and the importance of process variables in achieving team effectiveness (Guzzo & Dickson, 1996; Salas et al., in press).

Theoretical and empirical work has also further delineated what teams "think, do, and feel" (Salas & Cannon-Bowers, 2001). Team members must dynamically display critical knowledge (cognitions), skills (behaviors), and attitudes (feelings) while performing in complex environments. Teams are dynamic entities and evolve over time, during which they must master two tracks of skills: taskwork and teamwork (Gersick, 1988; Morgan, Glickman, Woodard, Blaiwes, & Salas, 1986; Kozlowski,

Gully, & Salas, 1996). Taskwork skills are those skills that members must understand and acquire for actual task performance, whereas teamwork skills are the behavioral and attitudinal responses that members need to function effectively as part of an interdependent team (Morgan et al., 1986). The implication for the creation of expert teams is that it is not sufficient that members be technical experts – they must also be experts in the social interactions that lead to adaptive coordinated action (i.e., teamwork) within the context of the technical expertise.

TEAM ADAPTATION AND DECISION MAKING

As noted one hallmark of expert teams is their ability to be adaptive and make timely decisions not only under stable, low-tempo, and information-rich conditions, but also in situations where information is dynamic and ambiguous, and decisions must be made quickly. Therefore, the literature on decision making provides a second theoretical foundation for the creation of expert teams (see Salas & Klein, 2001). Decision making has been defined as, "the ability to gather and integrate information, use sound judgment, identify alternatives, select the best solution, and evaluate the consequences" (Cannon-Bowers, Tannenbaum, Salas, & Volpe, 1995, p. 346). Moreover, within a team context decision making emphasizes skill in pooling information and resources in support of a response choice (Cannon-Bowers et al., 1995). Researchers have recently shown that the rational classical decision-making model (Bernoulli, 1738) does not reflect how decisions are actually made by experts in context (see Klein, 1993; Cannon-Bowers & Salas, 1998; Klein, 1996; Lipshitz, Klein, Orasanu, & Salas, 2001; Salas & Klein, 2001). Within operational environments where time is a premium, experts often trade decision accuracy for speed of decision because of the resource intensiveness of rational decision-making processes.

Experts operating in time-pressured situations typically look for patterns of situational cues. If, based on this pattern seeking,

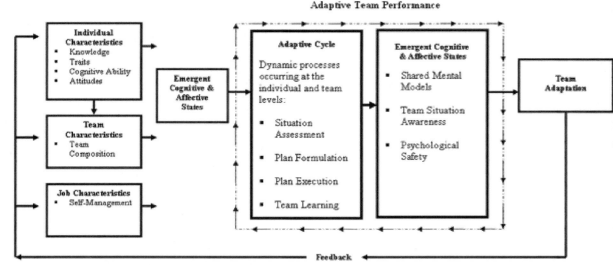

Figure 25.1. Team Adaptation Framework illustrating the relationship between input variables, emergent states, and the multiple phases of the team adaptation cycle (adapted from Stagl, Burke, Salas, & Pierce, 2006.)

the situation is perceived as being similar to one that the decision maker has encountered in the past, a similar decision is made (Klein, 1997). It has been argued that this type of decision making, recognition-primed decision-making (see Ross et al., Chapter 23), does not require a great deal of time or cognitive effort to accomplish, and may even reduce the vulnerability to stressors such as time pressure (Klein, 1997).

Adopting a multidisciplinary, multiphasic, multilevel perspective, Burke et al. (in press) recently advanced a theory of team adaptation. Figure 25.1 presents a framework of their theory. This framework does not represent a causal or testable model of adaptation, but is intended as a conceptual description of team adaptation. Burke et al. utilized an input-throughput-output model to describe a series of phases that unfold over time to emerge as adaptive team performance. Phase 1 is situation assessment, characterized by cue recognition and ascription of meaning to environmental patterns. Phase 2 is plan formulation, wherein the team pools cognitive resources and decides on a course of action. Phase 3 is plan execution, which relies heavily on the coordination mechanisms described later in this chapter. Team learning, phase 4, is the result

of an assessment of the team's performance and alters how the team will execute the earlier phases on the next pass through this adaptive cycle. As these phases unfold, the meaning, plans, and actions that ensue serve to update emergent affective (e.g., cohesion, viability) and cognitive states (e.g., shared mental models, shared situation awareness, psychological safety). In turn this reservoir of affect and cognition are drawn on by team members as they engage in the next phase of performance and in navigating future challenges. Thus, adaptive team performance is a recursive process that consists of several phases that reoccur across time (see Figure 25.1). This work is complemented by models of team regulation, in that they emphasize a team's incremental adjustment to situational change. DeShon et al. (2004) propose a multiple goal, multilevel model of individual and team regulation in which individual and team goals maintain separate feedback loops. The team's allocation of cognitive and behavioral resources will be influenced by discrepancies in the situation and team and individual goals. This gives rise to separate mirror regulatory mechanisms on the individual and team level that account for team learning, adaptation, and performance.

A challenge in decision making within team environments occurs when team members begin to experience stress and can't easily diagnose the situation because of the performance-degrading effects of stress. Normally higher-status members are less likely to take the advice of lower-status members. However, under stress three things happen. First, higher-status members are more willing to accept input from those with less expertise, but under these conditions low-status members generally aren't vocal in their viewpoints (Driskell & Salas, 1991). Second, attention tends to narrow, producing a form of tunnel vision (Salas, Cannon-Bowers, & Blickens-derfer, 1993). Third, explicit communication decreases as members become more focused on their own respective roles (Kleinman & Serfaty, 1989). Despite these challenges expert teams are adaptive and able to maintain coordination levels and corresponding effective decisions despite these conditions; they have behavioral and cognitive mechanisms in place that allow them to maintain high levels of performance.

SHARED COGNITION

Shared cognition has been used to refer to a number of related constructs (e.g., shared mental models, team situation awareness, common ground, team metacognition, transactive memory; Kelly, Badum, Salas, & Burke, 2005). Shared cognition has been increasingly used as an explanation for how the members of expert teams are able to interact with one another and adapt communication and coordination patterns while under stress (e.g., Campbell & Kuncel, 2001; Cannon-Bowers, Salas, & Converse, 1993; Cooke, Salas, Cannon-Bowers, & Stout, 2000; Ensley & Pearce, 2001; Entin & Serfaty, 1999; Hinsz, Tindale, & Vollrath, 1997; Klimoski & Mohammad, 1994; Orasanu, 1990). Shared cognition (in its various designations) has been argued to be the mechanism that allows teams to: (a) coordinate their action without explicit communication (Entin & Serfaty, 1999), (b) interpret cues in a similar manner, make compatible decisions, and take coherent or convergent

actions (e.g., Klimoski & Mohammad, 1994; Cooke et al., 2000; Mohammed & Dumville, 2001), and (c) make accurate predictions not only about the world in which the team is operating but about the team functioning that enables coordination (Rouse & Morris, 1986). Shared cognition, in the form of compatible mental models, as well as mutual performance monitoring are necessary precursors to effective team processes, such as back-up behavior, because they form the foundation for decisions of when a team member must step in to provide back up, who should step in, and what assistance is needed.

TEAM LEADERSHIP

The impact of leaders on individual, team, and organizational effectiveness is substantial (Zaccaro, Rittman, & Marks, 2001). Researchers have increasingly taken a functional perspective when examining team leadership (Fleishman, Mumford, Zaccaro, Levin, Korotkin, & Hein, 1991; Hackman, 2002; Zaccaro et al., 2001). From this perspective, leadership involves "social problem solving that promotes coordinated, adaptive team performance by facilitating goal definition and attainment" (Salas, Burke, & Stagl, 2004, p. 343) and is composed of four classes of leader responses to social problems: information search and structuring, information use in problem solving, managing personnel resources, and managing material resources (Salas et al., 2004). Although theoretical work in this area is continuing and a large leadership literature exists, research into the *functional* role of team leaders remains a glaring weakness (e.g. Salas et al., 2004). As the complexity of the social problems faced by leaders and teams increases, so does the need for adaptation. Research into shared leadership holds promise as a source for informing our understanding of the processes by which team leadership can contribute to expert team performance.

Shared leadership is "the transference of the leadership function among team members in order to take advantage of member strengths (e.g., knowledge, skills, attitudes, perspectives, contacts, and time available) as dictated by either environmental demands or the development stage of the team" (Burke, Fiore, & Salas, 2004, p. 105). Pearce and Sims (2002) have shown that shared leadership can be more effective than traditional vertical leadership (i.e., a rigid hierarchical authority structure). When leadership is shared, the team can adapt to situational demands by shifting leadership functions (the four broad categories of which are listed above), thereby more effectively moving toward the team goals. However, shared leadership does not presuppose the absence of a formal hierarchical leader. A formal leader can sometimes most effectively lead by setting the climate and team structure to facilitate the occurrence of shared leadership. The success of this shared leadership model depends on the fluidity with which leadership can be transferred – a type of coordination itself.

TEAM AFFECTIVE STATES: COLLECTIVE EFFICACY
AND PSYCHOLOGICAL SAFETY

In addition to the cognitive and performance aspects of teams discussed in the previous sections, recent research has highlighted the importance of a team's attitudes, perceptions, and beliefs and the roles that these factors play in team processes and outcomes. Self-efficacy has long been known to be related to motivation and performance at the individual level (Bandura, 1977). Translated to the group level, it describes the team's belief in the team's competence to handle specific environmental demands (Bandura, 1986). Zaccaro et al. (1995) define collective efficacy as "a sense of collective competence shared among individuals when allocating, coordinating, and integrating their resources in a successful concerted response to specific situational demands" (p. 309).

In addition to collective efficacy, team psychological safety has been identified as conducive to success when team learning is essential. Edmondson (1999) defined team psychological safety as "a shared belief that the team is safe for interpersonal risk taking" (p. 354). She argues that this construct comprises trust, but exceeds this to include a team environment where individual members feel at ease being themselves. Using teams within a manufacturing company, Edmondson (1999) showed that high levels of psychological safety led teams to view failure as a learning opportunity and to seek feedback from outside sources. Alternately, low levels of psychological safety led to an unquestioning acceptance of team goals for fear of reprisal from managers as well as a disinclination to seek help. Therefore, the author argued that a team's engagement in learning behavior is strongly tied to the team's level of psychological safety.

Thus far we have outlined the theoretical drivers central to understanding adaptive expert team performance. Research into team effectiveness and teamwork, team adaptability and decision making, shared cognition, team leadership, and collective efficacy and psychological safety serves to inform us of the processes by which individual and team competencies amalgamate into adaptive expert team performance. The following section will review the methods employed by researchers to examine expert teams.

What Methods are Being Used to Study Expert Teams?

In order to exhibit expert performance, an expert team must be engaged in tasks within their domain of expertise. Therefore, observational field studies are the dominant research tool used to study expert teams, although methodologies incorporating complex simulations and self-report survey methods are used as well. In the following sections, we briefly review these three methodological categories and present exemplar studies from the expert teams research.

OBSERVATIONS IN THE FIELD

Field observation studies are the mainstay of expert teams research. A sampling of the methods used to research expert teams include: retrospective analysis of critical incidents (e.g. Carroll, Rudolph, Hatakenaka, Widerhold, & Boldrini, 2001), interviews (e.g. Kline, 2005), and field observations (e.g. Edmondson, Bohmer, &

Pisano, 2001), including video recording task performance (e.g. Omodei, Wearing, & McLennon, 1997; McLennan, Pavlou, & Omodei, 2005). Observational studies are necessary to access information about how teams operate in their environments; however, observational studies lack the control imposed by experimental and quasi-experimental studies. See Lipshitz (2005) for a review of the issues of rigor in observational studies.

Patel and Arocha (2001) used observational methods to study a medical and a surgical intensive care unit (MICU, SICU, respectively). Specifically, they examined how the task and environmental constraints of the two units affected decision making. The primary source of data in the study was audiotapes of the morning rounds. The verbatim transcripts of the audiotapes were divided into episodes based on the discussion topic; then each episode was divided into a segment, or a particular aspect of care (e.g., lab tests, patient state) relevant to the episode; segments were further divided into propositions, or idea units. The coded transcripts were then categorized into decision types: findings (i.e., decision regarding patient-specific information), actions (i.e., decision regarding future procedures), and assessments (i.e., evaluation of tradeoffs between different treatments). Analysis of the data revealed that the MICU and SICU had markedly different communication patterns. The authors hypothesized that this was due to differing goals of the tasks performed in the two units. Similarly, by analyzing the transcripts coded for type of decision making (i.e., forward- or backward-driven inference), the research showed that there were differences between the units such that the MICU engaged in more deliberative decision making. This too was attributed to the differing environmental and task constraints in the two units.

SIMULATION

Simulation is an instrumental method for studying expert teams (Woods, 1993) in that it allows for experimental manipulation of environmental cues and presents an opportunity for collecting a wider variety of quantitative and qualitative data than is normally feasible in real-world field observation (Pliske & Klein, 2003). To be valid, the simulation must reach a level of functional quality that requires real-world expert teams to use their expertise, regardless of the level of fidelity (Lipshitz et al., 2001; Pliske & Klein, 2003). That is, in order to generalize findings of simulation research back to expert teams in a specific domain, the simulation must be engaging in such a way that it is relevant to members of expert teams from that domain.

Orasanu and Fischer's (1997) study of flight-crew decision-making performance is an example of the type of insights that can be gained into expert teams using simulation methods. Their methodology involved using a high-fidelity flight simulator to observe real-world flight teams handling problematic and routine in-flight situations. The scenario simulated several mechanical and weather conditions that required the crew to perform several critical tasks: (a) deciding whether to continue with a landing approach under risky conditions or perform a missed landing approach, (b) selecting an alternate airport to land at, and (c) coordinating extra functions during landing due to mechanical failures. By videotaping the sessions, the researchers had a record of expert team performance in action during critical situations. They did not have to rely on retrospective reports of what occurred and were therefore not reliant on the memories of team members. The authors used ethnographic and cognitive engineering techniques to analyze the data and to derive a set of decision strategies associated with more- and less-effective team performance. This work is representative of a growing body of research into expert teams using simulations (e.g. Roth, Woods, & Pople, 1992; Cohen, Freeman, & Thompson, 1998; Woods, 1993; Kanki, Lozito, & Foushee, 1989; Pascual & Henderson, 1997; Brun, Eid, Johnsen, Laberg, Ekornas, & Kobbeltvedt, 2005; McLennan, Pavlou, & Omodei, 2005; Smith-Jensch et al., 1998; Stokes, Kemper, & Kite, 1997).

SELF-REPORT

Studies employing a self-report methodology are common for investigating expert teams because they allow relatively quick access to information from large numbers of teams within a single domain (e.g. Jung & Sosik, 2002; Chidester, Helmreich, Gregorich, & Geiss, 1991). For example, Cannon and Edmondson (2001) used a method that combined self-report and interviews to investigate shared beliefs about failure in organizational work groups. They hypothesized that shared beliefs about failure can increase or decrease the severity of barriers to a team's productive self-examination of error and failure. Self-report surveys were used to assess three types of variables: antecedent (i.e., context support, clear direction, task motivation, and leadership coaching), behavior (i.e., beliefs about failure), and outcomes (i.e., work-group performance). These authors sampled 51 work groups within the same organization and using regression analysis showed that: (a) the antecedent variables of coaching and direction were significantly predictive of shared beliefs of failure, and (b) shared beliefs about failure within a team were significantly predictive of team performance.

Research employing these methods has produced a wealth of information about expert team performance. The remainder of the chapter is dedicated to distilling this growing literature into high-level characterizations of what is currently known about adaptive expert team performance.

When Do Expert Teams Do Best?

What has been learned about expert team performance in the last 20 years? A substantial amount of research has been conducted and much progress has been made, though the compartmentalized nature of the research can work to obfuscate an integrated view of the findings. What we do next is attempt to remedy this situation by extracting from the literature snapshots of teams when they function optimally – the characteristics of expert teams. We focus primarily on expert teams, but seek support from additional research where appropriate. Table 25.1 summarizes what we know (so far) about what expert teams do best. We briefly discuss these characteristics below.

Expert Teams Hold Shared Mental Models

Expert teams are composed of members who anticipate each other's needs. They are able to coordinate their action without necessarily or always engaging in overt communication because they share an experience of both explicit and subtle or tacit communication, arising from a shared knowledge of task structure and team processes. Orasanu (1990) has shown through observational studies that shared mental models distinguish effective and ineffective cockpit crews in that high-performing crews were able to communicate in a manner that allowed them to build a shared mental model of the situation (see also Cooke, Salas, Kiekel, & Bell, 2004; Ensley & Pearce, 2001; Moreland, 1999).

Expert Teams Optimize Resources by Learning and Adapting

Expert teams self-correct, compensate for each other, and reallocate functions as necessary. Edmondson et al. (2001) reported that surgical teams that successfully implemented new technology solutions were able to do so by means of effectively supporting the collective learning process (see also Kayes, 2004; Bunderson & Sutcliffe, 2003; Wong, 2004). The collective learning process was key in the team's development of new routines to guide use of the technology.

Expert Teams Engage in a Cycle or Discipline of Prebrief → Performance → Debrief

Expert team members provide feedback to each other. Expert teams are able to differentiate between higher and lower priorities and establish and revise team goals and plans accordingly. While working toward their goals, expert teams employ mechanisms

Table 25.1. Expert team performance effective processes and outcomes

Expert Teams . . .

Hold shared mental models
They have members who anticipate each other.
They can communicate without the need to communicate overtly.

Optimize resources by learning and adapting
They are self correcting.
They compensate for each other.
They reallocate functions.

Have clear roles and responsibilities
They mange expectations.
They have members who understand each others' roles and how they fit together.
They ensure team member roles are clear but not overly rigid.

Have a clear, valued, and shared vision
They have a clear and common purpose.

Engage in a cycle or discipline of prebrief → performance → debrief
They regularly provide feedback to each other, both individually and as a team.
They establish and revise ream goals and plans.
They differentiate between higher and lower priorities.
They have mechanisms for anticipating and reviewing issues/problems of members.
The periodically diagnose team "effectiveness," including its results, its processes, and its vitality (morale, retention, energy).

Have strong team leadership
They are led by someone with good leadership skills and not just technical competence.
They have team members who believe the leaders care about them.
They provide situation updates.
They foster teamwork, coordination, and cooperation.
They self-correct first.

Develop a strong sense of "collective," trust, teamness, and confidence
They manage conflict well; team members confront each other effectively.
They have a strong sense of team orientation.
They trust other team members' "intentions."
They strongly believe in the team's collective ability to succeed.
They develop collective efficacy.

Manage and optimize performance outcomes
They make fewer errors.
They communicate often "enough"; they ensure that fellow team members have the information they need to be able to contribute.
They make better decisions.
They have a greater chance of mission success.

Cooperate and coordinate
They identify teamwork and task work requirements.
They ensure that, through staffing and/or development, the team possesses the right mix of competencies.
They consciously integrate new team members.
They distribute and assign work thoughtfully.
They examine and adjust the team's physical workplace to optimize communication and coordination.

for anticipating and reviewing the issues and problems of the members. Similarly, expert teams deliberately self-diagnose elements of team effectiveness such as the team's results, its processes, and vitality issues such as morale, retention, and energy. Smith-Jentsch, Zeising, Acton, and McPherson (1998) showed through a case study that a US Navy combat information center (CIC) team realized high levels of performance by employing team self-correction and a cycle of prebrief, perform/observe, diagnose performance and debrief. The CIC team was able to identify teamwork-related problems, show immediate improvement on targeted goals, and generalize lessons learned, which resulted in sustained high levels of performance.

Expert Teams Have Clear Roles and Responsibilities

Expert teams are composed of individuals who manage their expectations by understanding each other's roles and how they work together to accomplish the team goals. Expert teams have clarity of team member roles, but not to the point of excess or rigidity in role definition. LaPorte and Consolini (1991) report on how air-traffic controllers are able to self-organize shifts in roles and responsibilities among themselves to meet the evolving workload conditions experienced throughout the day (see also Beauchamp, Bray, Eys, & Carron, 2002; Brun et al., 2005; Bliese & Castro, 2000).

Expert Teams Have a Clear, Valued, and Shared Vision

Expert teams have a clear and common purpose. Castka, Bamer, Sharp and Belohoubek (2001) argue that the success of high-performance teams is tied, in part, to the team members' thorough comprehension of the mission definition, vision, and goals (see also Pearce & Ensley, 2004; Campion, Medsker, & Higgs, 1993). In their ethnographic study, Castka et al. linked the effectiveness of a management team within a British manufacturing company to the clarity and focus of team goals.

Expert Teams Have Strong Team Leadership

Leaders of expert teams are not just technically competent; they possess quality leadership skills. In expert teams, team members believe that the leaders care about them. Leaders of expert teams provide situation updates, foster teamwork, coordination, and cooperation, and self-correct first (see Salas et al., 2004; Day, Gronn, & Salas, 2004; Pirola-Merlo, Hartel, Mann, & Hirst, 2002). Chidester, Helmreich, Gregorich, and Geis (1991) showed that cockpit crews led by pilots who were highly motivated and task oriented performed better when confronted with abnormal situations during a flight than did crews led by pilots with low motivation and task orientation.

Expert Teams Develop a Strong Sense of "Collective," Trust, Teamness, and Confidence

Members of expert teams are able to manage conflict appropriately by confronting each other effectively. Expert team members have a strong sense of team orientation and trust in the intentions of their fellow team members (see Salas et al., 2004; Edmondson et al., 2001; Edmondson, 1999; Cannon & Edmondson, 2001). They are confident in the team's ability to succeed and develop collective efficacy. Edmondson (2003) found that team leaders that created a sense of trust and minimized power differences were able to realize higher levels of adaptive performance in interdisciplinary medical action teams.

Expert Teams Manage and Optimize Performance Outcomes

Expert teams make better decisions and commit fewer errors. They are able to balance their communication so that team members have the appropriate and timely information they need to contribute to the team, thus creating a higher probability of mission success (Orasanu, 1990). Patel and Arocha (2001) showed how MICU and SICU teams manage information collection and flow in order to maximize decision-making performance relative to the specifics of the team task and the team goal.

Expert Teams Create Mechanisms for Cooperation and Coordination

Expert teams are able to identify all of the relevant teamwork and taskwork requirements and ensure that, through selection and training, the team is composed of individuals possessing the competencies necessary to successfully meet the team and taskwork requirements. Expert teams employ a deliberate method for integrating new team members so as to ameliorate the impact of membership change on performance. Similarly, work within expert teams is allocated in a thoughtful manner, balancing task characteristics with individual expertise as well as overall workload. Expert teams are also responsive to the impact of the physical environment in which the team operates and are cognizant of the effects that this physical space has on performance. That is, they deliberately try to alter their operating environment to optimize communication and coordination. Schaafstal, Johnston, and Oser (2001) identified coordination and cooperation as hallmarks of expert emergency-management (EM) teams. In the normal course of action, EM teams face decision-making situations fraught with informational uncertainty and stress; they also operate in a large multiteam system, interacting with EM teams from other organizations. This scenario demands highly refined coordination and communication skills, both within any one EM team, and between the EM teams comprising the larger multiteam system.

Concluding Remarks

A great deal has been learned about what expert teams do, think, and feel. Modern research has begun to show us what effective teams do when confronting complex, stressful, and difficult tasks. Clearly, effective teams perform fluidly and repeatedly and

manage to coordinate team-level actions, events, procedures, and communication protocols. Given the importance of teams in many current realms of human activity, research on team performance, team cognition, and expert teams will continue to reveal the mechanisms that support the achievement and maintenance of expert team performance, and based on a richer scientific understanding of those mechanisms, we can come to know how to compose, train, and manage more "dream teams."

Acknowledgment

We would like to thank Robert Hoffman for his detailed feedback and comments in an earlier draft. The views, opinions, and/or findings contained in this chapter are those of the authors and should not be construed as an official Department of the Army position, policy, or decision. This work was supported by funding from the US Army Research Institute for the Behavioral and Social Sciences (Contract #W74V8H-04-C-0025).

References

Bandura, A. (1977). Self-efficacy: Toward a unifying theory of behavioral change. *Psychological Review, 84*, 191–215.

Bandura, A. (1986). *Social foundations of thought and action: A social cognitive theory.* Engelwood Cliffs, NJ: Prentice-Hall.

Beauchamp, M. R., Bray, S. R., Eys, M. A., & Carron, A. V. (2002). Role ambiguity, role efficacy, and role performance: Multidimensional and mediational relationships within interdependent sport teams. *Group Dynamics: Theory, Research, and Practice, 6*, 229–242.

Bernoulli, D. (1738). Specimen theoriae novae de mensura sortis. *Commentarii Academiae Scientrum Imperialis Pertopolitanae, 5*, 175–192.

Bliese, P. D., & Castro, C. A. (2000). Role clarity, work overload and organizational support: Multilevel evidence of the importance of support. *Work & Stress, 14*, 65–73.

Brun, W., Eid, J., Johnsen, B. H., Laberg, J. C., Ekornas, B., & Kobbeltvedt, T. (2005). Bridge resource management training: Enhancing shared mental models and task performance? In H. Montgomery, R. Lipshitz, & B. Brehmer (Eds.), *How professionals make decisions* (pp. 183–193). Mahwah, NJ: Erlbaum.

Bunderson, J. S., & Sutcliffe, K. M. (2003). Management team learning orientation and business unit performance. *Journal of Applied Psychology, 88,* 552–560.

Burke, C. S., Fiore, S. M., & Salas, E. (2004). The role of shared cognition in enabling shared leadership and team adaptability. In C. L. Pearce & J. A. Conger (Eds.), *Shared leadership: Reframing the hows and whys of leadership* (pp. 103–121). Thousand Oaks, CA: Sage.

Burke, C. S., Stagl, K., Salas, E., Pierce, L., & Kendall, D. (in press). Understanding team adaptation: A conceptual analysis and model. *Journal of Applied Psychology.*

Campbell, J. P., & Kuncel, N. R. (2001). Individual and team training. In N. Anderson, D. S. Ones, H. K. Sinangil, & C. Viswesvaran (Eds.), *Handbook of industrial, work, and organizational psychology.* Thousand Oaks, CA: Sage Publications.

Campion, M. A., Medsker, G. J. & Higgs, A. C. (1993). Relations between work group characteristics and effectiveness: Implications for designing effective work groups. *Personnel Psychology, 46,* 823–847.

Cannon, M. D., & Edmondson, A. C. (2001). Confronting failure: antecedents and consequences of shared beliefs about failure in organizational work groups. *Journal of Organizational Behavior, 22,* 161–177.

Cannon-Bowers, J. A., Salas, E., & Converse, S. (1993). Shared mental models in expert team decision making. In N. J. J. Castellan (Ed.), *Individual and group decision making* (pp. 221–246). Hillsdale, NJ: Erlbaum.

Cannon-Bowers, J. A., Tannenbaum, S. I., Salas, E., & Volpe, C. E. (1995). Defining competencies and establishing team training requirements. In R. Guzzon & E. Salas (Eds.), *Team effectiveness and decision making in organizations.* San Francisco, CA: Jossey-Bass.

Cannon-Bowers, J. A., & Salas, E. (Ed.). (1998). *Making decisions under stress: Implications for individual and team training.* Washington, DC: American Psychological Association.

Carroll, J. S., Rudolph, J. W., Hatakenaka, S., Widerhold, T. L., & Boldrini, M. (2001). Learning in the context of incident investigation: Team diagnoses and organizational decisions

at four nuclear power plants. In E. Salas & Klein, G. (Ed.), *Linking expertise and naturalistic decision making* (pp. 349–366). Mahwah, NJ: Erlbaum.

Castka, P., Bamber, C., Sharp, J., & Belohoubek, P. (2001). Factors affecting successful implementation of high performance teams. *Team Performance Management, 7,* 123–134.

Chi, M., Feltovich, P., & Glaser, R. (1981). Categorization and representation of physics problems by experts and novices. *Cognitive Science, 5,* 121–152.

Chidester, T. R., Helmreich, R. L., Gregorich, S. E., & Geis, C. E. (1991). Pilot personality and crew coordination: Implications for training and selection. *The International Journal of Aviation Psychology, 1,* 25–44.

Cohen, M. S., Freeman, J. T., & Thompson, B. (1998). Critical thinking skills in tactical decision making: A model and a training strategy. In J. A. Cannon-Bowers and E. Salas (Eds.), *Making Decisions Under Stress: Implications for Individual and Team Training* (pp. 155–189). Washington, DC: American Psychological Association.

Cooke, N. J., Salas, E., Cannon-Bowers, J. A., & Stout, R. J. (2000). Measuring team knowledge. *Human Factors, 42,* 151–173.

Cooke, N. J., Salas, E., Kiekel, P. A., & Bell, B. (2004). Advances in measuring team cognition. In E. Salas & S. M. Fiore (Eds.), *Team cognition: Understanding the factors that drive process and performance.* Washington, DC: American Psychological Association.

Day, D. V., Gronn, P., & Salas, E. (2004). Leadership capacity in teams. *Leadership Quarterly, 15,* 857–880.

DeShon, R. P., Kozlowski, W. J., Schmidt, A. M., Milner, K. R., & Wiechmann, D. (2004). A multiple-goal, multilevel model of feedback effects on the regulation of individual and team performance. *Journal of Applied Psychology, 89,* 1035–1056.

Driskell, J. E., & Salas, E. (1991). Group decision making under stress. *Journal of Applied Psychology, 76,* 473–478.

Edmondson, A. C. (1999). Psychological safety and learning behavior in work teams. *Administrative Science Quarterly, 44,* 350–383.

Edmondson, A. C., Bohmer, R. M., & Pisano, G. P. (2001). Distrupted routines: Team learning and new technology implementation in hospitals. *Administrative Science Quarterly, 46,* 685–716.

Edmondson, A. C. (2003). Speaking up in the operating room: How team leaders promote learning in interdisciplinary action teams. *Journal of Management Studies, 40*(6), 1419–1452.

Ensley, M. D., & Pearce, C. L. (2001). Shared cognition as a process and an outcome in top management teams: Implications for new venture performance. *Journal of Organizational Behavior, 22*, 145–160.

Entin, E. E., & Serfaty, D. (1999). Adaptive team coordination. *Human Factors, 41*, 321–325.

Fleishman, E. A., Mumford, M. D., Zaccaro, S. J., Levin, K. Y., Korotkin, A. L., & Hein, M. B. (1991). Taxonomic efforts in the description of leader behavior: A synthesis and functional interpretation. *Leadership Quarterly, 4*, 245–287.

Gersick, C. J. (1988). Time and transition in work teams: Toward a new model of group development. *Academy of Management Journal, 31*, 9–41.

Guzzo, R. A., & Dickson, M. W. (1996). Teams in organizations: Recent research on performance and effectiveness. *Annual Review of Psychology, 47*, 307–338.

Hackman, J. R. (1983). *A normative model of work team effectiveness* (No. 2). New Haven, CT: Yale University.

Hackman, J. R. (Ed.). (1990). *Groups that work*. San Francisco, CA: Jossey-Bass.

Hackman, J. R. (2002). *Leading teams: Setting the stage for great performances*. Boston: Harvard Business School Press.

Hatano, G., & Inagaki, K. (1986). Two courses of expertise. In H. W. Stevenson & H. Azuma (Eds.), *Child development and education in japan* (pp. 262–272). New York: W. H. Freeman.

Hinsz, V. B., Tindale, R. S., & Vollrath, D. A. (1997). The emerging conceptualization of groups as information processors. *Psychological Bulletin, 121*, 43–64.

Ilgen, D. R. (1994). Jobs and roles: Accepting and coping with the changing structure of organizations. In M. G. Rumsey & C. B. Walker (Eds.), *Personnel selection and classification* (pp. 13–32). Hillsdale, NJ: Erlbaum.

Jung, D. I., & Sosik, J. J. (2002). Transformational leadership in work groups: The role of empowerment, cohesiveness, and collective efficacy on perceived group performance. *Small Group Research, 33*(3), 313–336.

Kanki, B. G., Lozito, S., & Foushee, H. C. (1989). Communication indices of crew coordination. *Aviation, Space, and Environmental Medicine, 60*, 56–60.

Kayes, C. D. (2004). The 1996 Mount Everest climbing disaster: The breakdown of learning in teams. *Human Relations, 57*, 1263–1284.

Kelly, B. C., Badum, A., Salas, E., & Burke, C. S. (2005). Shared cognition: Can we all get on the same page? Paper presented at the 20th Annual Conference for the Society of Industrial Organizational Psychology, Los Angeles, CA.

Klein, G. A. (1993). A recognition-primed decision (RPD) model of rapid decision making. In G. A. Klein, J. Orasanu, R. Calderwood, & C. E. Zsambok (Eds.), *Decision making in action: models and methods*. Norwood, NJ: Ablex.

Klein, G. (1996). The effect of acute stressors on decision making. In J. E. Driskell & E. Salas (Eds.), *Stress and human performance* (pp. 49–88). Mahwah, NJ: Erlbaum.

Klein, G. (1997). The current status of naturalistic decision making framework. In R. Flin, E. Salas, M. E. Strub, & L. Martin (Eds.), *Decision making under stress: Emerging themes and applications* (pp. 11–28). Aldershot: Ashgate.

Kleinman, D. L., & Serfaty, D. (1989). Team performance assessment in distributed decision-making. Paper presented at the Symposium on Interactive Networked Simulation for Training, Orlando.

Klimoski, R., & Mohammad, S. (1994). Team Mental Model: Construct or Metaphor? *Journal of Management, 20*, 403–437.

Kline, D. A. (2005). Intuitive team decision making. In H. Montgomery, R. Lipshitz, & B. Brehmer (Eds.), *How professionals make decisions* (pp. 171–182). Mahwah, NJ: Erlbaum.

Kozlowski, S. W., Gully, S. M., & Salas, E. (1996). Team leadership and development: Theory, principles, and guidelines for training leaders and teams. In M. M. Beyerlein, & A. Dougals (Eds.), *Advances in interdisciplinary studies of work teams: Team leadership* (Vol. 3, pp. 253–291). Greenwich, CT: JAI Press.

Kozlowski, S. W., & Bell, B. S. (2003). Work groups and teams in organizations. In W. C. Borman & D. R. Ilgen (Eds.), *Handbook of psychology: Industrial and organizational psychology* (Vol. 12, pp. 333–375). New York: John Wiley & Sons, Inc.

LaPorte, T. R., & Consolini, P. M. (1991). Working in practice but not in theory: Theoretical challenges of "high reliability organizations." *Journal of Public Administration Research and Theory*, 1, 19–48.

Lipshitz, R. (2005). There is more to seeing that meets the eyeball: The art and science of observation. In H. Montgomery, R. Lipshitz, and B. Brehmer (Eds.), *How Professionals Make Decisions* (pp. 365–378). Mahwah, NJ: Erlbaum.

Lipshitz, R., & Pras, A. A. (2005). Not only for experts: Recognition-primed decisions in the laboratory. In H. Montgomery, R. Lipshitz, & B. Brehmer (Eds.), *How professionals make decisions* (pp. 91–108). Mahwah, NJ: Erlbaum.

Lipshitz, R., Klein, G., Orasanu, J., & Salas, E. (2001). Rejoinder: A welcome dialogue – and the need to continue. *Journal of Behavioral Decision Making*, 14, 385–389.

Marks, M. A., Mathieu, J. E., & Zaccaro, S. J. (2001). A temporally based framework and taxonomy of team processes. *Academy of Management Review*, 26, 356–376.

McLennan, J., Pavlou, O., & Omodei, M. M. (2005). Cognitive control processes discriminate between better versus poorer performance by fire ground commanders. In H. Montgomery, R. Lipshitz, & B. Brehmer (Eds.), *How professionals make decisions: Expertise, research and applications* (pp. 209–221). Mahway, NJ: Erlbaum.

Mohammed, S., & Dumville, B. C. (2001). Team mental models in a team knowledge framework: Expanding theory and measure across disciplinary boundaries. *Journal of Organizational Behavior*, 22 (2), 89–103.

Moreland, R. L. (1999). Transactive memory: Learning who knows what in work groups and organizations. In L. L. Thompson & J. M. Levine (Eds.), *Shared cognition in organizations: The management of knowledge* (pp. 3–31). Mahwah, NJ: Erlbaum.

Morgan, B. B., Jr., Glickman, A. S., Woodward, E. A., Blaiwes, A. S., & Salas, E. (1986). *Measurement of team behaviors in a Navy environment* (No. 86-014). Orlando, FL: Naval Training Systems Center.

Omodei, M. M., Wearing, A. J., & McLennan, J. (1997). Head mounted video recording: A methodology for studying naturalistic decision making. In R. Flin, E. Salas, M. Strub, & L. Martin (Eds.), *Decision making under stress: Emerging themes and applications* (pp. 161–169). Aldershot: Ashgate.

Orasanu, J. (1990). *Shared mental models and crew decision making* (No. 46). Princeton, NJ: Cognitive Sciences Laboratory, Princeton University.

Orasanu, J., & Salas, E. (1993). Team decision making in complex environments. In G. A. Klein, J. Orasanu, R. Calderwood, & C. E. Zsambok (Eds.), *Decision making in action: Models and methods*. Norwood, NJ: Ablex Publishing.

Orasanu, J., & Fischer, U. (1997). Finding decisions in natural environments. In C. E. Zsambok & G. Klein (Eds.), *Naturalistic decision making* (pp. 434–458). Hillsdale, NJ: Erlbaum.

Pascual, R., & Henderson, S. (1997). Evidence of naturalistic decision making in military command and control. In C. E. Zsambok & G. Klein (Eds.), *Naturalistic decision making* (pp. 217–226). Mahwah, NJ: Erlbaum.

Patel, V. L., & Arocha, J. F. (2001). The nature of constraints on collaborative decision making in health care settings. In E. Salas & G. Klein (Eds.), *Linking expertise and naturalistic decision making* (pp. 383–405). Mahwah, NJ: Erlbaum.

Pearce, C. L., & Ensley, M. D. (2004). A reciprocal and longitudinal investigation of the innovation process: The central role of shared vision in product and process innovation teams. *Journal of Organizational Behavior*, 25, 259–278.

Pearce, C. L., & Sims, H. P. (2002). Vertical versus shared leadership as predictors of the effectiveness of change management teams: An examination of aversive, directive, transactional, transformational and empowering leader behaviors. *Group Dynamics: Theory, Research, and Practice*, 6, 172–197.

Pirola-Merlo, A., Hartel, C., Mann, L., & Hirst, G. (2002). How leaders influence the impact of affective events on team climate and performance in R&D teams. *Leadership Quarterly*, 13, 561–581.

Pliske, R., & Klein, G. (2003). The naturalistic decision-making perspective. In S. L. Schneider & J. Shanteau (Eds.), *Emerging perspectives on judgement and decision research* (pp. 559–585). New York: Cambridge University Press.

Roth, E. M., Woods, D. D., & Pople, H. E. (1992). Cognitive simulation as a tool for cognitive task analysis. *Ergonomics*, 35, 1163–1198.

Rouse, W. B., & Morris, N. M. (1986). On looking into the black box: Prospects and limits in the search for mental models. *Psychological Bulletin, 100*, 349–363.

Salas, E., Dickinson, T., Converse, S., & Tannenbaum, S. (1992). Toward an understanding of team performance and training. In R. Swezey & E. Salas (Eds.), *Teams: Their training and performance*. Norwood, NJ: Ablex Publishing.

Salas, E., Cannon-Bowers, J. A., & Blickensderfer, E. L. (1993). Team performance and training research: Emerging principles. *Journal of the Washington Academy of Sciences, 83*, 81–106.

Salas, E., & Klein, G. (Eds.). (2001). *Linking expertise and naturalisitc decision making*. Mahwah, NJ: Erlbaum.

Salas, E., & Cannon-Bowers, J. A. (2001). The science of team training: A decade of progress. *Annual Review of Psychology, 52*, 471–499.

Salas, E., Burke, C. S., & Stagl, K. C. (2004). Developing teams and team leaders: Strategies and principles. In D. Day, S. J. Zaccaro, & S. M. Halpin (Eds.), *Leader development for transforming organizations: Growing leaders for tomorrow* (pp. 325–355). Mahwah, NJ: Erlbaum.

Salas, E., Stagl, K. C., & Burke, C. S. (2004). 25 years of team effectiveness in organizations: Research themes and emerging needs. *International Review of Industrial and Organizational Psychology, 19*, 47–91.

Salas, E., Stagl, K. C., Burke, C. S., & Goodwin, G. F. (in press). Fostering team effectiveness in organizations: Toward an integrative theoretical framework of team performance. In W. Spaulding & J. Flowers (Eds.), *Modeling complex systems: Motivation, cognition and social processes*. Lincoln, NE: University of Nebraska Press.

Schaafstal, A. M., Johnston, J. H., & Oser, R. L. (2001). Training teams for emergency management. *Computers in Human Behavior, 17*, 615–626.

Smith, E. M., Ford, J. K., & Kozlowski, S. W. (1997). Building adaptive expertise: Implications for training design strategies. In M. A. Quinones & A. Ehrenstein (Eds.), *Training for a rapidly changing workplace: Applications of psychological research* (pp. 89–118). Washington, DC: American Psychological Association.

Smith-Jentsch, K., Zeisig, R. L., Acton, B., & McPherson, J. A. (1998). Team dimensional training: A strategy for guided team self-correction. In E. Salas & J. A. Cannon-Bowers (Eds.), *Making decisions under stress: Implications for individual and team training* (pp. 271–297). Washington, DC: American Psychological Association.

Stagl, K. C., Burke, C. S., Salas, E., & Pierce, L. (2006). Team adaptation: Realizing team synergy. In C. S. Burke, L. Pierce, & E. Salas (Eds.), *Understanding adaptability: A prerequisite for effective performance within complex environments* (pp. 117–141). Oxford, UK: Elsevier Science.

Stokes, A. F., Kemper, K., & Kite, K. (1997). Aeronautical decision making, cue recognition, and expertise under time pressure. In C. E. Zsambok & G. Klein (Eds.), *Aeronautical decision making, cue recognition, and expertise under time pressure* (pp. 183–196). Mahwah, NJ: Erlbaum.

Wong, S. S. (2004). Distal and local group learning: Performance trade-offs and tensions. *Organization Science, 15*(6), 645–656.

Woods, D. D. (1993). Process-tracing methods for the study of cognition outside of the experimental psychology laboratory. In G. A. Klein, J. Orasanu, R. Calderwood, & C. E. Zsambok (Eds.), *Decision making in action: Models and methods* (pp. 228–251). Norwood, NJ: Ablex.

Zaccaro, S. J., Blair, V., Peterson, C., & Zazanis, M. (1995). Collective efficacy. In J. E. Maddux (Ed.), *Self-efficacy, adaptation, and adjustment: theory, research, and application*. New York: Plenum.

Zaccaro, S. J., Rittman, A. L., & Marks, M. A. (2001). Team leadership. *Leadership Quarterly, 12*, 451–483.

Part V.B

ARTS, SPORTS, & MOTOR SKILLS

CHAPTER 26

Music

Andreas C. Lehmann & Hans Gruber

Research Approaches to Individual Differences in Music

Individual differences in musical achievement have at all times awed musicians and audiences alike. In former times, royalty and nobility invited outstanding musicians to perform in their salons. Today, the general public crowds the concert halls when certain celebrities perform while other concerts are scarcely attended. Sometimes, special attractions such as child prodigies or musical savants capture the attention of the mass media.

Scientific attempts to understand individual differences have existed for a long time. Barrington (1770) investigated Mozart's early performance achievements and described it in some detail. Such single-case studies are highly informative. However, they usually do not suffice for modern scientific standards. They merely document high achievements under controlled conditions and attribute them to exceptional levels of talent. Doubts can be expressed about the accuracy and reliability of the information presented in biographies of famous

musicians. More recent biographies mention skill acquisition explicitly from the perspective of musical talent research. This research explains exceptional performance as based in innate musical capacities.

Billroth's (1895) "Who is musical?" can be seen as a starting point for research on musical abilities in the 19th century. Later in the 1920s and 30s Seashore developed his "Measures of musical talents", which assessed subjects' perceptual discrimination abilities (Seashore, 1938/1967). With few exceptions, such as Wellek's attempt in 1939 to identify racial differences in musical abilities (Wellek, 1970), most music aptitude tests have tried to predict the potential for music performance (Boyle, 1992, for a review). Their overall success was limited, however, probably because the effects of talent tend to be confounded with the amount of previous training, which is rarely statistically controlled for. Generally, musically active children tend to score higher in such ability tests (Shuter-Dyson, 1999).

Another argument in favor of innate ability arises from musical dynasties, for example, the Bach, Corelli, Couperin, Garcia, and

Strauss families, which by their mere existence suggest a strong heritability of musical talents. Alas, the hope to identify heritability of excellence in families is not justified (see also discussion about Galton, 1979; e.g., Simonton, Chapter 18). Genetic background and environmental effects are mingled inevitably, and alternative explanations cannot be refuted. Older heritability explanations failed to take into account the genetic contribution of females in the genealogy or to the socio-historic fact that sons frequently followed in their fathers' professions (Farnsworth, 1969). Hence, there are different explanations for why many musicians have parents who are musically active (Gembris, 1998).

The home environment is obviously important for promoting musical excellence (Csikszentmihalyi, Rathunde, & Whalen, 1993; Sosniak, 1985). Also, the socio-economic conditions of a young musician's family constitute obvious factors that influence the choice of a teacher, the quality of the instrument played, and other possibilities awarded to the learner. An analysis of successful Polish musicians by Manturzewska (1995) revealed a common pattern of attitudes, value systems, and family structure in the musicians' families of origin. Families were emotionally stable, task oriented, and careful in selecting their children's friends, and they strongly supported the musical activities. These attitudes gain importance as they translate into behavioral consequences in the daily lives of musicians. For example, Csikszentmihalyi, Rathunde, and Whalen (1993) demonstrated that families of high-achieving children changed their lives to accommodate the needs of their talented offsprings, for example, by exempting them from household chores to give them additional time to practice. Biographies of famous musicians underline such practices: the cellist Jacqueline du Pre never did her own laundry and did not have any household responsibilities as an adolescent (Easton, 1989).

Taken together, it is difficult to obtain clear evidence on the role of innate abilities, despite the fact that giftedness features prominently in everyday discourse. On the other hand, much evidence exists that practice and other environmental factors have a large impact on changes in many variables related to music performance. Some researchers have expressed serious doubts whether it is even possible to identify specific innate characteristics that mediate the development of expertise (Ericsson, 2003). However, the goal of this chapter is not to work out the nature-nurture debate for music but to focus on the role of practice for the attainment of expert performance. In brief, we do not know whether practice is a *sufficient* condition for high achievement, but it is certainly a *necessary* one for invoking the cognitive, physiological, and psychomotor adaptations observed in experts.

Although practice is omnipresent during the development of expertise in music, its role and manifestation is not identical in all musical genres. Different musical styles are characteristic for specific musical cultures, and those different cultures have their respective types of practice. Most research on musical expertise has been conducted in the classical conservatoire tradition – also known as the "Western art music tradition". Investigations about expert performance in jazz music, popular music, or vernacular genres may yield somewhat different results (Berliner, 1994). For example, whereas an early start of training is typical for pianists and violinists in the classical music domain, jazz guitarists start much later (Gruber, Degner, & Lehmann, 2004), and so do most singers today (Kopiez, 1998). Despite some differences, important commonalities regarding phases of development or deliberate practice should exist regardless of the specific music style in question. These will be addressed below.

Increasing Performance through Practice

Practice: Investing the Time

The discussion about the role of training-induced changes in performance was triggered by Ericsson, Krampe, and Tesch-Römer (1993), who first introduced the concept of "deliberate practice." See also Ericsson, Chapter 38. Deliberate practice is a set of structured activities that experts in the domain consider important for improving performance; it is often strenuous and can therefore only be maintained for limited amounts of time per day without danger of psychological or physiological burnout. At the Berlin Academy of Music, Ericsson et al. (1993) investigated violin students from different degree programs that varied with regard to the instrumental proficiency required. The students were interviewed retrospectively about their practice and skill development. The amount of lifetime accumulated practice up to the point of the interview (or even the point of entry into the academy) was clearly related to the degree of level of performance attained. Less-proficient performers had practiced less than more-skilled ones. The lifetime trajectory of practice reported by the most promising group of students resembled that of musicians currently employed in Berlin orchestras. The results underline the predictive validity of the accumulated hours as an indicator of excellence, and are hence at odds with the everyday belief that some musicians – the "highly talented" ones – need not practice as much as the less talented, who have to compensate for lack of talent with excessive practice.

Although it may be difficult to refute claims by famous musicians not to have practiced much or to hate practice (Mach, 1981), the empirical evidence regarding contemporary musicians makes such claims rather suspicious. Musicians are likely to engage in conscious impression management when belittling practice in the classical tradition or, in the case of rock and popular musicians, to dismiss the role of formal instruction by emphasizing self-teaching, that is, autodidactic learning (Green, 2002).

The relation between innate abilities and practice probably is a complex one. According to Ackerman's (1986, 1990) theory of ability determinants of skilled performance, in which the change from controlled processing to automatized processing was discussed in terms of abilities versus practice, one could argue that in early phases of skill development general abilities play an important role, which is reduced later, if consistent task characteristics exist within the domain. These foster the development of compilation processes that are heavily influenced by practice. The more skilled a person is, the more specific components of information processing are relevant, so that the relation between general abilities and performance tends to disappear. The subjects in Ericsson et al.'s (1993) study might already have compensated ability differences through adaptation of practice. Thus, the role of talent could not be judged adequately. Additionally, experts might be most competent in selecting proper practice. At younger age levels, however, practice may not be as efficient, and a smaller amount of practice is accumulated. Therefore, practice time might be of less importance and ability of more importance in young musicians (Lehmann, 1997b, for a review).

Sloboda, Davidson, Howe, and Moore (1996) addressed this problem by replicating Ericsson et al.'s (1993) study. Students aged eight to eighteen from a music school were rated by their teachers with respect to musical achievement and promise. The students then were interviewed by the researchers about their practice history. In addition, many other data were collected, including a 42-week longitudinal recording of practice diaries. The results clearly support the deliberate-practice assumptions obtained from the study of adults. The least-proficient group of subjects had practiced less than the better-performing groups, and the students who dropped out of music lessons had practiced even less. In order to proceed from one level of performance to the next, the best groups' increase in practice was even larger than expected. Thus, already relatively early in instrumental music learning, the amount of practice is significantly related with level of performance.

Competing explanations could be that talented children practice more in a rage to master the skill (Winner, 1996), or that tangible progress and success keep children practicing. Although a proof in favor of one of these argumentations cannot easily be made, the latter is clearly better supported by research. The result that the amount of certain types of practice is related to level of performance was found in other domains as well.

It is noteworthy that the number of hours necessary for achieving particular levels of performance is not a constant across all musical instruments. Jørgensen (1997) showed that different instrumental groups practice very different numbers of hours. Pianists and violinists tend to be practice fanatics, logging the most hours, followed by other strings, organ, woodwinds and brass, closing with the singers at the bottom of the list. Such differences may result from different demands that instrumental performance imposes on the body. In the case of singers, different educational traditions may have an influence as well (Kopiez, 1998).

Although duration of practice is predictive of long-term success, it might be not as indicative of performance in the short run, for example, when learning a specific piece of music (Williamon & Valentine, 2000). Here, a player's prior knowledge with the music might influence practice times. For example, those who have not worked systematically on music by Bach may face problems that experienced Baroque performers do not (Lehmann & Ericsson, 1998).

Although time invested in practice is related to long-term level of performance, practice means different things for different musical styles and sub-skills. For musicians playing classical repertoire, a large portion of practice is solitary practice, working on instrumental technique and acquiring new pieces, assisted by more or less regular visits with a teacher. For jazz musicians, in addition to solitary practice, a substantial part of practice is communal practice with other musicians. Sitting in jam sessions, listening to others play, and copying performances by famous musicians from recordings all constitute activities that improve performance (Gruber et al., 2004). For singers and some instrumentalists, working

with an accompanist is an important practice activity. A conductor has to become familiarized with a piece first without the orchestra, silently reading and imaging the score and the desired interpretation before working with the ensemble. Deliberate practice is goal-directed, optimized practice, and responds to the typical demands imposed by the domain.

Investing the Effort

Ericsson et al. (1993) stressed that practice could lack inherent enjoyment because it requires much mental and physical effort. Musicians may enjoy their own improvement but dislike the actual practice activity. In a survey study on practicing, musicians indicated that performing in front of an audience was most enjoyable but highly effortful (Lehmann, 2002), whereas learning new pieces and working on difficult spots was most effortful but not enjoyable. Apparently, activities that resemble the target activity of performing seem more enjoyable than activities of a preparatory nature, even though the latter's relevance for improving skills is unquestioned. This result indicates that enhancing quality of practice requires substantial effort (Williamon, 2004, several chapters).

Ample advice from practitioners such as master teachers is readily available in books. Although the suggestions are grounded in lifelong experience, some recipes appear haphazard. Take, for example, the notion of "slow practice". Playing a section very slowly is often recommended among music teachers as a remedy for all sorts of problems. However, the piano teacher Matthay (1926), who was knowledgeable about psychological research, remarked that slow practice without actually imagining the upcoming note "is only a useless fetish" (p. 12). This implies that the quality of practice is not sufficiently defined by observable behavior (e.g., mere duration) but has to be judged by the co-occurrence of certain cognitive processes.

Many researchers in the field use verbal-report methodologies to get at these difficult-to-observe processes. For example,

Chaffin, Imreh, and Crawford (2002) published an extensive case study about solitary practice. In a naturalistic setting, they followed a performer practicing a new piece for performance and obtained retrospective and concurrent reports. The authors distinguished four stages of practice.

1. In the first, the musician tries to get the "big picture" of the piece. The first stage entails reading through the piece or more generally getting an aural representation of the entire piece. Practice strategies vary substantially: according to working habits of the musician, sight-reading, analyzing, or listening to recordings are preferred.

2. In the second stage, technical practice is undertaken to master the piece. During the second stage the piece is worked on in sections, which increase in length as practice progresses. The length of the section depends on the kind of problems encountered and analyses undertaken in the first stage. Whether the artistic interpretation is developed during the course of learning to play the piece or during anticipatory analytic processes might be a matter of individual preferences and habits (Hallam, 1995). During this elaborative stage of practice, the motor programs become largely automatic and the piece is being memorized.

3. Next, in the third stage the actual stage performance is tried out. During this stage, performance is prepared more directly by putting the pieces together and ironing out the seams between them. Memory, which up to then was more implicit, is now deliberately assisted by creating an internal map of the piece, knowing the order of the parts as well as points where the performer could restart in case of a memory lapse during performance. During this stage the piece is polished by slow playing, playing for an imagined or an informal real audience, refining interpretation details, and bringing all sections up to the correct tempo or even slightly above. As performance approaches, memory is repeatedly tried and tested using self-imposed constraints such as starting at the jump-points. If possible, the musician even practices under performance conditions, that is, in concert attire and in different locations. After some time, the returns of such final polishing and preparation work are diminishing; further practice is considered to be maintenance work.

4. The fourth stage, which sometimes extends over a long period of time between concerts or recordings, constitutes the maintenance of the piece.

Thus, practice is a systematic activity with predictable stages and activities. They all serve to establish a strong internal representation of the piece and the conditions under which the performance will take place.

Practicing is an effortful activity and a skill per se that has to be learned. Gruson (1988) demonstrated that experts differed from novices in their practice skill. A number of studies revealed that (adult) supervision during practice is important for beginning musicians (Davidson, Howe, Moore, & Sloboda, 1996; Lehmann, 1997a; Sosniak, 1985). In the simplest case, the adult or the supervisor ensures that time is spent with the instrument. Preferably, goals and feedback are provided. Research suggests that not all parents or tutors necessarily have to be musicians – everyone can hear wrong notes, encourage lovingly, or simply watch the clock. However, the mothers' previous experience with learning a musical instrument may influence their ideas about how much practice is necessary and their ability to support the child's practice (McPherson & Davidson, 2002). Written procedures have been found also to be helpful in structuring practice for beginners (Barry & Hallam, 2001). After the musicians have developed metacognitive skills, they can take over to regulate their practice themselves. A crucial factor for doing so is the motivation to invest effort and to engage in the process of self-regulation (McPherson & Zimmerman, 2002). Renwick and McPherson (2002) showed that children practicing by themselves engaged in elaborated activities when they were motivated by the piece, but simply played through the piece when disinterested in it. Similarly, when the goal is to master a certain piece or a specific difficulty, adults may work hard and use more practice strategies than when they want to enjoy themselves or relax rather than mastering the instrument (Lehmann & Papousek, 2003).

The Development of Musical Expertise

Stages and Phases

Demarcating points along the time line of acquisition of a new skill allows us to better conceptualize the process as a whole, and several stage and phase models have been proposed (see Proctor & Vu, Chapter 15). Fitts and Posner (1967), for example, in their well-known model describe skills as being first cognitive, then associative, and later autonomous, in essence requiring less and less cognitive mediation as skilled performance increases. Similar stages can be identified in Sudnow's (1993) phenomenological account of his learning to improvise jazz on the piano. First, he had to decide consciously which chord to use next and then how to distribute the chordal notes on the keyboard (voicing). Later his fingers seemed to find the right notes by themselves. Much later, his aesthetic decision of what to play seemed to trigger the correct chord sequences with associated voicings. Whereas the focus of attention in novices is directed toward technical, low-level aspects, experts attend to higher-level, strategic or aesthetic issues, a finding also demonstrated for composing (Colley, Banton, & Down, 1992) and improvising (Hargreaves, Cork, & Setton, 1991). For many musicians the earlier stages of skill development are successfully completed in (early) childhood.

Fitts and Posner's (1967) model is informative with regard to skill development of an individual, but it neglects the lifespan context. Bloom (1985) explicated how skills develop through life. First, the child is introduced to the domain in an informal phase, and it is here that children in "musi-

cal" households may be at an advantage. Then comes a phase during which formal tuition is sought. This stage extends until the young musician makes a full-time commitment to music in order to become a professional. In a later phase, once a professional status has been reached, the expert is working at trying to make a lasting contribution. For a musician, this would entail making sound recordings for major record labels, playing in prestigious concert halls (e.g., Carnegie Hall), or winning certain competitions (e.g., Frederic Chopin International Piano Competition). Vitouch (2005) described in detail how parts of the expertise may get lost in old age – one could call this "de-expertization" – and how experts like the piano soloist Horowitz possibly compensate for it. Interestingly the psychomotor adaptations do not decline inevitably with old age but can be maintained for a long time through continuous practice. Krampe and Ericsson (1996) demonstrated that older pianists were able to counteract losses in motor performance through practice, whereas non-pianists did not show this advantage. However, both groups suffered age-related declines in other cognitive domains (see also Krampe & Charness, Chapter 40).

The time needed for experts to develop sufficient skills for a professional career is sometimes estimated to be roughly a decade (Ericsson & Crutcher, 1990). Hayes (1989) demonstrated that this "10-year rule" also applies to composers in classical music, including Mozart. Works from Mozart's earliest phases were conspicuously underrepresented in selected lists of his recordings. Similarly, Weisberg (1999) demonstrated that it took The Beatles approximately a decade to acquire international reputation. Prior to writing their own songs they covered music by other bands. It is a futile effort to dwell on exact number of years, but it is important to note that even famous exponents of a domain take a long time to acquire their skills.

In order to compete successfully for scholarships, prizes, and media attention, instrumentalists in the classical music domain have to master the most demanding repertoire as teenagers. This requires either an early start for highly competitive instruments (e.g., violin) or the possibility of transfer of knowledge and skills from previously played instruments onto those instrument that do not allow such early start (e.g., string bass, oboe, trombone). Altogether, the development of expert performance can be seen as an adaptation to the typical task constraints of the domain (Ericsson & Lehmann, 1996), involving changes in cognitive, physiological, and perceptual-motor parameters that facilitate superior performance.

Cognitive Adaptations

Among the cognitive adaptations are aspects of memory and problem solving. The former can be seen in virtually all domains of expertise (Ericsson & Lehmann, 1996). Even when memorization is not their explicit goal, experts tend to have excellent long-term retention for domain-related material. For example, incidental memory for music just played correlated moderately with accompanying ability in classical pianists (Lehmann & Ericsson, 1996). Kauffman and Carlsen (1989) showed that musicians recalled musical material better than nonmusicians, especially when the material was structured according to rules of tonality (see our example concerning savants in later paragraph). Expert-novice differences decreased when tonality rules were violated or when random note sequences had to be recalled. This skill-by-structure interaction, demonstrated also in other domains, documents that experts' advantages are largely due to their knowledge and how their memory skills have adapted to the structure of the stimuli.

Acquired domain knowledge has been the most prominent explanation for the superiority of expert performance. Studies in many different domains showed that the essential factor of development of expertise is the accumulation of increasingly complex patterns in memory. It has been shown that expert knowledge can be retrieved quickly from long-term memory (Ericsson

& Kintsch, 1995). Chaffin and Imreh (2001) showed convincingly how a concert pianist developed sophisticated mental representations with associated retrieval structures that lead to successful performance of the rehearsed piece from memory even under high-stress conditions on stage. In addition, knowledge is represented in an elaborated format that allows quick access to relevant information and supports flexible reactions to domain-specific tasks, for example, in medicine by encapsulation of knowledge in procedural representations of earlier experiences with cases (Boshuizen & Schmidt, 1992).

A particularly impressive effect of the impact of knowledge for musical performance was found in studies with autistic savants. Despite the cognitive and communicative limitations that prevent them from functioning normally in everyday contexts, some autistic savants have exceptional musical skills and can play back music after only a few hearings. It can be demonstrated that these skills are based on knowledge-related generative processes (Miller, 1999; Sloboda, Hermelin, & O'Connor, 1985). When confronted with atonal music, the savants fail to imitate music but simply play haphazardly. Obviously, familiarity with the material and the genre mediates memory performance (Charness, Clifton, & MacDonald, 1988). The phenomenon of savants' music memory demonstrates that making use of one's knowledge about the structure of the stimulus is a quick and automatic process. Specialized knowledge of musical timbre and pitch even impacts early stages of perceptual processing that are not accessible to consciousness (Besson, 1997).

The study of individuals' cognitive representation of musical structure is important for understanding how music performance works (Palmer, 1997). It helps to understand why certain mistakes happen, and in which way a good use of the knowledge can be supported. But also from an educational point of view it is relevant to know how different learning processes or learning methods may result in different representations (Gruhn & Rauscher, 2002).

Musical knowledge comprises not only knowledge about musical pieces, but the cognitive mechanisms to represent and manipulate the relevant knowledge. Lehmann and Ericsson (1997) suggested a triangular model of mental representations for musicians. In brief, musicians first need to imagine their anticipated, desired outcome. Next, they have to represent their currently ongoing performance in order to compare it to their original plans. Finally, a mental representation is necessary of how a particular plan can be implemented on the instrument – how it feels. Woody (1999) investigated the connection between ongoing and desired performance (see Woody, 2003, concerning motor production representations). Pianists were asked to imitate the artistic, expressive features of a model musical performance, and verbal reports were recorded indicating which features they explicitly identified. Performance data showed that they imitated more accurately those features that they also correctly identified in their verbal reports. Also, researchers investigating African drummers found that rhythms in triple meter such as the Bolero-rhythm were notoriously difficult for experienced master drummers to imitate, who tried to assimilate the rhythms to African rhythmic prototypes (Kopiez, Langner, & Steinhagen, 1999). Thus, even seemingly automatic performance is mediated by complex cognition, even at high levels of proficiency.

In addition to knowledge-related cognitive adaptations we can also observe changes in the use of sophisticated metacognitive and self-regulation skills in musical learners. In a contrastive study addressing metacognitive components of expert performance, Gruber, Weber, and Ziegler (1996) analyzed top-level orchestra musicians and above-average amateur musicians. Judging retrospectively, experts indicated higher levels of aspiration along with a more positive attitude toward performance situations compared to the amateurs. As regards their current situation, experts rated themselves more effective in their learning behavior, but did not differ from the amateur players concerning their motivation. In a sec-

ond study, Gruber et al. (1996) surprisingly found that experts' competence and control beliefs were weaker concerning musical performance than regarding everyday life. This leads to an ambiguous situation. On the one side, early on experts practice effectively, look for challenging performance situations, and have aspirations. On the other side, once they work within their current community of experts, where they are only one among many, they neither perceive themselves as outstanding nor do they have superior self-concepts.

Physiological Adaptations

Everyone knows the minor physiological adaptations that happen in response to habitual usage of our bodies in everyday life. These adaptations are specifically localized, such as the growth of muscle after a few days of bike riding or the emergence of calluses on fingertips after starting to play the guitar or working in the yard. Musicians undergo a number of less obvious but highly telling adaptations. For example, Wagner (1988) found that degree of forearm rotation differed systematically between pianists (larger extent of inward rotation), violinists (larger outward rotation), and controls. However, the overall degree of rotation remained constant in all three groups but was shifted toward the respective habitual usages for the instrumentalists. Singers and brass players were found to have significantly larger vital and total lung capacities compared to controls (Sundberg, 1987). And the superior inhalation and expiration pressures in trumpet players were found only after several long notes were played (Fiz et al., 1993), demonstrating the highly contextual specificity of such changes.

Additional links between training and certain adaptations were uncovered in recent efforts to understand how the brain processes music, especially through the use of imaging techniques (Münte, Altenmüller, & Jäncke, 2002, for a review). The first study that received widespread attention was one that found that the cortical representation of the fingers of the left hand in string players was enlarged compared to that of the thumb (Elbert, Pantev, Wienbruch, Rock-stroh, & Taub, 1995). No changes occurred with the representations of the fingers of the right hand (the bowing arm). And this corti-cal reorganization was more pronounced for subjects who had started musical training at an earlier age.

Further studies, especially those compar-ing experts with novices, showed that cor-tical reorganization was not restricted to playing music but also occurred when lis-tening. Pantev, Roberts, Schulz, Engelien, & Ross (2001) learned that larger areas of the cortex were activated involuntarily when musicians listened to tones of instruments they played. Or, differences in the volume of gray matter in the motor as well as auditory and visuospatial brain regions were found when comparing professional musicians (keyboard players) to amateur musicians and non-musicians (Gaser & Schlaug, 2003). We can safely assume that music training and practice leads to substantial functional and structural changes in a person's brain and consequently alters processing capabilities.

Perceptual-Motor Adaptations

Instrumentalists require perceptual and motor skills different from those of non-musicians. For example, trilling on the piano requires ten to fourteen movements per second; tuning a violin needs the capa-bility of detecting slight frequency differ-ences. Motor researchers found that pianists were able to tap faster and more accu-rately than control subjects with their fin-gers, but that this advantage did not transfer to their heels (Keele, Pokorny, Corcos, & Ivry, 1985). How information is acquired with the senses also changes. For example, the minute movements of the eye (oculomotor activity) is modified considerably by train-ing, and beginning text readers' eye move-ments differ from that of advanced readers, a finding that has been replicated in music sight-reading (e.g., Goolsby, 1994). Future research in this area will most likely yield more precise results.

Finally, musicians develop a finer fre-quency and loudness discrimination than non-musician controls (Houtsma, Durlach,

& Horowitz, 1987). However, the improved discrimination of timbre and tones by musicians does not transfer to speech sounds (Münzer, Berti, & Pechmann, 2002). Musicians playing instruments that require fine tuning of individual notes during performance develop a more accurate dis-crimination for pitch height, whereas per-cussionists, whose work relies heavily on discriminating rhythms, show an improved perception of auditory duration (Rauscher & Hinton, 2003). Likewise, pianists require increased sensitive tactile discrimination, which proved to be related to the amount of practice undertaken (Ragert, Schmidt, Altenmüller, & Dinse, 2004). Taken to-gether, the increased acuity of the senses and adaptations of the motor system are restricted to the stimuli musicians typically encounter when playing their respective instruments. This indicates that the changes are highly specific, which makes the claim plausible that they are in large part linked to training and practice.

Outlook: Pushing the Limits

In this chapter, we have explored how music performance changes through practice. The debate is still open (and might remain indef-initely) about which "natural" limits of per-formance exist, and whether and how such limits can be pushed. Physiological factors might limit performance of selected individ-uals, but a number of environmental, histor-ical, and societal factors have been identi-fied that are likely to influence the upper bounds of performance at a given time in a given place.

A bitter taste regarding limits of expertise arises from the fact that most professional musicians suffer from medical problems. Hearing losses from overexposure to noise during practice or performance, as well as muscular-skeletal or neurological problems, are common (Brandfonbrener & Lederman, 2002). Interestingly, the ranking of instru-ments in order of prevalence of symptoms corresponds roughly to the intensity of prac-tice required to reach high levels of perfor-mance, with pianists, violinists, and guitarists at the top of the list. There may also exist an upper limit for attainable performance with regard to the neuroplastic changes (Lim & Altenmüller, 2003). Focal dystonia, a condition where, for instance, fingers start to perform involuntary movements when other fingers are activated, may be due to an overlap of expanded cortical representations (Elbert et al., 1998). The gradual enlargement of the cortical representations in the somatosensory cortex during acquisition of expertise might reach a limit when the separation between adjacent areas becomes blurred, resulting in uncontrollable coactivation of one finger through the use of another. It is obvious that research about physiological limits of musical performance and about interventions to overcome the limits (or remedy existing problems) is still at its very beginning. The same can be said about historical or societal constraints on musical performance.

It is interesting to study in the history of a domain how the demands imposed on musicians have changed over time (Lehmann & Ericsson, 1998). Everyone is aware of changed standards in sports, where records are kept about achievements that have to be matched and surpassed by following generations of athletes. (Even if they are not as obvious as world records in athletics, musical achievements offer similar trends – incidentally the young star pianist Yundi Li is making commercials for sportswear company Nike.) For example, the constraints of performance are related to the development of instruments. When the piano was invented in 1700, there was no specific way of playing it, and a standard repertoire did not yet exist. Later refinements of the instrument and the instrumental technique led to more complex compositions. A number of pieces exist that were deemed unplayable at the time of their composition, including examples even from the 20th century (e. g., "Etudes" for guitar by Villa-Lobos; "Hammerklavier" sonata for piano by Beethoven; "Etudes" for piano by Ligeti; "Caprices" for violin by Paganini). Nowadays many of these pieces are standard fare for adolescent performers. Such historical increases in levels of performance result from specialization, improved training and practice methods, and from the extrinsic rewards a society offers to those who try to make eminent contributions to the domain.

Similar to the domain of sports, where some disciplines are popular in certain countries but not in others, or where some countries provide incentives to reach the highest levels of performance, music is affected by societal factors. China, for example, has developed a highly competitive piano instruction system since the end of the Cultural Revolution; playing the piano is now a valued cultural practice. Being proficient at playing the piano affords girls the opportunity to marry into better situated families (similar to the situation in 19th-century Germany), and men receive the possibility to make a career (as piano teachers). It is estimated that 50 million Chinese are seriously playing the piano. The large number of highly qualified foreign students from Eastern European and Far Eastern countries entering performance degree programs in music academies in Western countries attests to this fact. At the same time, fewer and fewer families in the West are willing to surrender their children to a rigorous training starting in early childhood and to accept personal and financial disadvantages. Instead, broad ranges of competing activities and media use are offered to children. That indicates that the cultural environment and its value and reward systems promote the development or neglect of skills in a certain culture.

Research reported in this chapter predominantly deals with the Western art music tradition. To date, studies in non-European music genres are rare but would be interesting for many reasons. For example, Indian musicians are likely to show interesting problem-solving strategies because they perform mainly improvised music – as do musicians in the Middle East. Or Balinese musicians, who learn by ear an extensive repertoire, would offer insights into memory processes that are not mediated by music notation – as would to a certain degree European vernacular musicians in rock, popular, jazz, and folk music. New subdomains emerge that constitute touchstones for theories previously developed in the classical music domain. For example, one should ask what constitutes practice for a DJ? Thus, research in music expertise needs to take a broader look at music.

The fact that the *Annual Review of Psychology* has, over the last 15 years, published three articles on music (in 1991 one on perception, in 1997 one on performance, and in 2005 one on neuroscience) proves that music is a domain with a high appeal for studying a diversity of psychological topics. The combination of affective, perceptual, cognitive, and motor aspects in music making, along with its high cultural value, make it a prime candidate for the study of complex skills. Children are introduced to music very early on in their lives – earlier than in most other domains of expertise – at a time when their brains and bodies are malleable and training can be most effective. Therefore, we observe differences between musical experts and novices of stupefying magnitude. The universal nature of music as a grammar-based but non-semantic temporal phenomenon theoretically allows studies in all cultures and across time, adding to the appeal of music as a domain for expertise researchers. Finally, the potential connections to music education in and out of formal learning contexts make expertise research a fruitful area of research for those whose interests concern the effects of instruction and training.

Author Notes

We thank two reviewers and R. H. Woody for their insightful comments on a previous version of the paper. The first author is greatly indebted to Anders Ericsson and Neil Charness for starting him out on this fascinating topic during a postdoc at FSU.

References

Ackerman, P. L. (1986). Individual differences in information processing: An investigation of intellectual abilities and task performance during practice. *Intelligence, 10,* 101–139.

Ackerman, P. L. (1990). A correlational analysis of skill specificity: Learning, abilities, and individual differences. *JEP: Learning, Memory, and Cognition, 16,* 883–901.

Barrington, D. (1770). Account of a very remarkable young musician. *Philosophical Transactions of the Royal Society of London, 60,* 4–64.

Barry, N., & Hallam, S. (2001). Practice. In R. Parncutt & G. McPherson (Eds.), *Science and psychology of music performance* (pp. 151–166). Oxford: Oxford University Press.

Berliner, P. (1994). *Thinking in jazz.* Chicago: Chicago University Press.

Besson, M. (1997). Electrophysiological studies of music processing. In I. Deliege & J. Sloboda (Eds.), *Perception and cognition of music* (pp. 217–250). London: Taylor & Francis.

Billroth, T. (1895). *Wer ist musikalisch?* Nachgelassene Schrift. [Who is musical?] (Ed. by E. Hanslick). Berlin: Paetel.

Bloom, B. S. (1985). Generalizations about talent development. In B. S. Bloom (Ed.), *Developing talent in young people* (pp. 507–549). New York: Ballantine.

Boshuizen, H. P. A., & Schmidt, H. G. (1992). On the role of biomedical knowledge in clinical reasoning by experts, intermediates and novices. *Cognitive Science, 16,* 153–184.

Boyle, J. D. (1992). Evaluation of music ability. In R. Colwell (Ed.), *Handbook of research in music teaching and learning* (pp. 247–265). New York: Schirmer.

Brandfonbrener, A., & Lederman, R. (2002). Performing arts medicine. In R. Colwell & C. Richardson (Eds.), *The new handbook of research on music teaching and learning* (pp. 1009–1022). New York: Oxford University Press.

Chaffin, R., & Imreh, G. (2001). A comparison of practice and self-report as sources of information about the goals of expert practice. *Psychology of Music, 29,* 39–69.

Chaffin, R., Imreh, G., & Crawford, M. (2002). *Practicing perfection: Memory and piano performance.* Mahwah, NJ: Erlbaum.

Charness, N., Clifton, J., & MacDonald, L. (1988). Case study of a musical mono-savant. In L. Obler & D. Fein (Eds.), *The exceptional brain: Neuropsychology of talent and special abilities* (pp. 277–293). New York: Guilford.

Colley, A., Banton, L., & Down, J. (1992). An expert-novice comparison in musical composition. *Psychology of Music, 20,* 124–137.

Csikszentmihalyi, M., Rathunde, K., & Whalen, S. (1993). *Talented teenagers: The roots of success or failure*. Cambridge: Cambridge University Press.

Davidson, J. W., Howe, M. J. A., Moore, D. G., & Sloboda, J. A. (1996). The role of parental influences in the development of musical ability. *British Journal of Developmental Psychology*, 14, 399–412.

Easton, C. (1989). *Jacqueline du Pre: A biography*. New York: Summit.

Elbert, T., Candia, V., Altenmüller, E. O., Rau, H., Sterr, A., Rockstroh, B., Pantev, C., & Taub, E. (1998). Alteration of digital representations in somatosensory cortex in focal hand dystonia. *NeuroReport*, 9, 3571–3575.

Elbert, T., Pantev, C., Wienbruch, C., Rockstroh, B., & Taub, E. (1995). Increased cortical representation of the fingers of the left hand in string players. *Science*, 270, 305–307.

Ericsson, K. A. (2003). The search for general abilities and basic capacities. In R. J. Sternberg & E. L. Grigorenko (Eds.), *The psychology of abilities, competencies, and expertise* (pp. 93–125). Cambridge: Cambridge University Press.

Ericsson, K. A., & Crutcher, R. J. (1990). The nature of exceptional performance. In P. B. Baltes, D. L. Featherman, & R. M. Lerner (Eds.), *Life-span development and behavior* (Vol. 10, pp. 187–217). Hillsdale, NJ: Erlbaum.

Ericsson, K. A., & Kintsch, W. (1995). Long-term working memory. *Psychological Review*, 102, 211–245.

Ericsson, K. A., Krampe, R. T., & Tesch-Römer, C. (1993). The role of deliberate practice in the acquisition of expert performance. *Psychological Review*, 100, 363–406.

Ericsson, K. A., & Lehmann, A. C. (1996). Expert and exceptional performance: Evidence of maximal adaptations to task constraints. *Annual Review of Psychology*, 47, 273–305.

Farnsworth, P. R. (1969). *The social psychology of music*. Ames: Iowa University Press.

Fitts, P. M., & Posner, M. I. (1967). *Human performance*. Belmont: Brooks/Cole.

Fiz, J. A., Aguilar, J., Carreras, A., Teixido, A., Haro, M., Rodenstein, D., & Morera, J. (1993). Maximum respiratory pressures in trumpet players. *Chest*, 104, 1203–1204.

Galton, F. (1979). *Hereditary genius: An inquiry into its laws and consequences*. London: Friedman. (Original published 1869.)

Gaser, C., & Schlaug, G. (2003). Gray matter differences between musicians and nonmusicians. *Annals of the New York Academy of Sciences*, 999, 514–517.

Gembris, H. (1998). *Musikalische Begabung und Entwicklung*. [Musical ability and development] Augsburg: Wissner.

Goolsby, T. W. (1994). Profiles of processing: Eye movements during sightreading. *Music Perception*, 12, 97–123.

Green, L. (2002). *How popular musicians learn*. London: Ashgate.

Gruber, H., Degner, S., & Lehmann, A. C. (2004). Why do some commit themselves in deliberate practice for many years – and so many do not? Understanding the development of professionalism in music. In M. Radovan & N. Dordević (Eds.), *Current issues in adult learning and motivation* (pp. 222–235). Ljubljana: Slovenian Institute for Adult Education.

Gruber, H., Weber, A., & Ziegler, A. (1996). Einsatzmöglichkeiten retrospektiver Befragungen bei der Untersuchung des Expertiseerwerbs. [The use of retrospective inquiry in the study of expertise acquisition] In H. Gruber & A. Ziegler (Eds.), *Expertiseforschung. Theoretische und methodische Grundlagen* (pp. 169–190). Opladen: Westdeutscher Verlag.

Gruhn, W., & Rauscher, F. (2002). The neurobiology of music cognition and learning. In R. Colwell & C. Richardson (Eds.), *The new handbook of research on music teaching and learning* (pp. 445–460). New York: Oxford University Press.

Gruson, L. M. (1988). Rehearsal skill and musical competence: Does practice make perfect? In J. A. Sloboda (Ed.), *Generative processes in music* (pp. 91–112). Oxford: Clarendon.

Hallam, S. (1995). Professional musicians' approaches to the learning and interpretation of music. *Psychology of Music*, 23, 111–128.

Hargreaves, D., Cork, C., & Setton, T. (1991). Cognitive strategies in jazz improvisation: An exploratory study. *Canadian Journal of Research in Music Education*, 33, 47–54.

Hayes, J. R. (1989). *The complete problem solver*. (2nd ed.). Hillsdale, NJ: Erlbaum.

Houtsma, A. J., Durlach, N. I., & Horowitz, D. M. (1987). Comparative learning of pitch and loudness identification. *Journal of the Acoustical Society of America*, 81, 129–132.

Jørgensen, H. (1997). Time for practising? In H. Jørgensen & A. C. Lehmann (Eds.), *Does practice make perfect?* (pp. 123–140). Oslo: Norges Musikhogskole.

Kauffman, W. H., & Carlsen, J. C. (1989). Memory for intact music works: The importance for musical expertise and retention interval. *Psychomusicology, 8,* 3–19.

Keele, S., Pokorny, R., Corcos, D., & Ivry, R. (1985). Do perception and motor production share a common timing mechanism? *Acta Psychologica, 60,* 173–193.

Kopiez, R. (1998). "Singers are late beginners": Sängerbiographien aus Sicht der Expertiseforschung. Eine Schwachstellenanalyse. [Singers' biographies from the perspective of research on expertise. An analysis of weaknesses] In H. Gembris, R. Kraemer, & G. Maas (Eds.), *Singen als Gegenstand der Grundlagenforschung* (pp. 37–56). Augsburg: Wissner.

Kopiez, R., Langner, J., & Steinhagen, P. (1999). Afrikanische Trommler (Ghana) bewerten und spielen europäische Rhythmen African dicummers assess and play European rhythms. *Musicae Scientiae, 3,* 139–160.

Krampe, R. T., & Ericsson, K. A. (1996). Maintaining excellence: Deliberate practice and elite performance in young and older pianists. *JEP: General, 125,* 331–359.

Lehmann, A. C. (1997a). Acquired mental representations in music performance: Anecdotal and preliminary empirical evidence. In H. Jørgensen & A. C. Lehmann (Eds.), *Does practice make perfect?* (pp. 141–164). Oslo: Norges Musikhogskole.

Lehmann, A. C. (1997b). Acquisition of expertise in music: Efficiency of deliberate practice as a moderating variable in accounting for subexpert performance. In I. Deliège & J. A. Sloboda (Eds.), *Perception and cognition of music* (pp. 161–190). London: Psychology Press.

Lehmann, A. C. (2002). Effort and enjoyment in deliberate practice: A research note. In I. M. Hanken, S. G. Nielsen, & M. Nerland (Eds.), *Research in and for music education. Festschrift for Harald Jørgensen* (pp. 153–166). Oslo: Norwegian Academy of Music.

Lehmann, A. C., & Ericsson, K. A. (1996). Music performance without preparation: Structure and acquisition of expert sight-reading. *Psychomusicology, 15,* 1–29.

Lehmann, A. C., & Ericsson, K. A. (1997). Research on expert performance and deliberate practice: Implications for the education of amateur musicians and music students. *Psychomusicology, 16,* 40–58.

Lehmann, A. C., & Ericsson, K. A. (1998). The historical development of domains of expertise: Performance standards and innovations in music. In A. Steptoe (Ed.), *Genius and the mind: Studies of creativity and temperament in the historical record* (pp. 64–97). Oxford: Oxford University Press.

Lehmann, A. C., & Papousek, S. (2003). Self-reported performance goals predict actual practice behavior among adult piano beginners. In R. Kopiez, A. C. Lehmann, I. Wolther, & C. Wolf (Eds.), *Proceedings of the 5th Triennial Conference of the European Society for the Cognitive Sciences of Music* (pp. 389–392). Hannover: University of Music and Drama.

Lim, V., & Altenmüller, E. O. (2003). Musicians' cramp: Instrumental and gender differences. *Medical Problems of Performing Artists, 18,* 21–27.

Mach, E. (1981). *Great pianists speak for themselves.* London: Robson.

Manturzewska, M. (1995). A biographical study of the life-span development of professional musicians. In M. Manturzewska, K. Miklaszewski, & A. Bialkowski (Eds.), *Psychology of music today* (pp. 311–337). Warsaw: Fryderyk Chopin Music Academy.

Matthay, T. (1926). *On memorizing and playing from memory and on the laws of practice generally.* Oxford: Oxford University Press.

McPherson, G. E., & Davidson, J. W. (2002). Musical practice: Mother and child interactions during the first year of learning an instrument. *Music Education Research, 4,* 141–156.

McPherson, G. E., & Zimmerman, B. J. (2002). Self-regulation of musical learning: A social cognitive perspective. In R. Colwell & C. Richardson (Eds.), *The new handbook of research on music teaching and learning* (pp. 327–347). New York: Oxford University Press.

Miller, L. K. (1999). The savant syndrome: Intellectual impairment and exceptional skill. *Psychological Bulletin, 125,* 31–46.

Münte, T. F., Altenmüller, E. O., & Jäncke, L. (2002). The musician's brain as a model of neuroplasticity. *Nature Reviews: Neuroscience,* 3, 473–478.

Münzer, S., Berti, S., & Pechmann, T. (2002). Encoding timbre, speech, and tones: Musicians vs. Non-musicians. *Psychologische Beiträge, 44,* 187–202.

Palmer, C. (1997). Music performance. *Annual Review of Psychology, 48,* 115–138.

Pantev, C., Roberts, L. E., Schulz, M. Engelien, A., & Ross, B. (2001). Timbre-specific enhancements of auditory cortical representations in musicians. *Neuroreport 12,* 169–174.

Ragert, P., Schmidt, A., Altenmüller, E. O., & Dinse, R. (2004). Superior tactile performance and learning in professional pianists: Evidence for metaplasticity in musicians. *European Journal of Neuroscience, 19,* 473–478.

Rauscher, F. H., & Hinton, S. C. (2003). Type of music training selectively influences perceptual processing. In R. Kopiez, A. Lehmann, I. Wolther, & C. Wolf (Eds.), *Proceedings of the 5th Triennial Conference of the European Society for the Cognitive Sciences of Music* (pp. 89–92). Hannover: University of Music and Drama.

Renwick, J., & McPherson, G. E. (2002). Interest and choice: Student-selected repertoire and its effect on practising behavior. *British Journal of Music Education, 19,* 173–188.

Seashore (1938/1967). *The psychology of music.* New York: Dover.

Shuter-Dyson, R. (1999). Musical ability. In D. Deutsch (Ed.), *The psychology of music* (2nd ed., pp. 627–652). San Diego: Academic Press.

Sloboda, J. A., Davidson, J. W., Howe, M. J. A., & Moore, D. G. (1996). The role of practice in the development of performing musicians. *British Journal of Psychology, 87,* 287–309.

Sloboda, J. A., Hermelin, B., & O'Connor, N. (1985). An exceptional musical memory. *Music Perception, 3,* 155–170.

Sosniak, L. A. (1985). Learning to be a concert pianist. In B. S. Bloom (Ed.), *Developing tal-*

ent in young people (pp. 19–67). New York: Ballantine.

Sudnow, D. (1993). *Ways of the hand: The organisation of improvised conduct.* London: Routledge & Kegan Paul.

Sundberg, J. (1987). *The science of the singing voice.* De Kalb, IL: Northern Illinois University Press.

Vitouch, O. (2005). Erwerb musikalischer Expertise. [Acquisition of musical expertise] In T. H. Stoffer & R. Oerter (Eds.), *Allgemeine Musikpsychologie* (pp. 657–715). Göttingen: Hogrefe.

Wagner, C. (1988). The pianist's hand: Anthropometry and biomechanics. *Ergonomics, 31,* 97–131.

Weisberg, R. W. (1999). Creativity and knowledge. In R. J. Sternberg (Ed.), *Handbook of creativity* (pp. 226–250). Cambridge: Cambridge University Press.

Wellek, A. (1970). *Typologie der Musikbegabung im deutschen Volke* [Typology of musical abilities in the German people]. München: Beck. (Original published 1939.)

Williamon, A. (Ed.). (2004). *Musical excellence: Strategies and techniques to enhance performance.* Oxford: Oxford University Press.

Williamon, A., & Valentine, E. (2000). Quantity and quality of musical practice as predictors of performance quality. *British Journal of Psychology, 91,* 353–376.

Winner, E. (1996). The rage to master: The decisive role of talent in the visual arts. In K. A. Ericsson (Ed.), *The road to excellence* (pp. 271–302). Mahwah, NJ: Erlbaum.

Woody, R. H. (1999). The relationship between advanced musicians' explicit planning and their expressive performance of dynamic variations in an aural modeling task. *Journal of Research in Music Education, 47,* 331–342.

Woody, R. H. (2003). Explaining expressive performance: Component cognitive skills in an aural modeling task. *Journal of Research in Music Education, 51*(1), 51–63.

CHAPTER 27

Expert Performance in Sport: A Cognitive Perspective

Nicola J. Hodges, Janet L. Starkes, & Clare MacMahon

Introduction

The goal of this chapter is to present what is currently known about expert performance in sport. Research on expert performance in sport is a relatively recent area of inquiry covering only the last 30 years. Our view of its evolution is that there have been three overlapping phases in its development. During the 1970s and 1980s much of sport research employed recipient paradigms popular within experimental and cognitive psychology. Typical research of this time involved testing skilled and less-skilled or novice groups of athletes on sport-specific tests of recall and recognition, temporal and spatial occlusion of visual information, and anticipation (Abernethy, Thomas, & Thomas, 1993; Starkes, Helsen, & Jack, 2000). Again, following general trends in psychology verbal-protocol analyses of expert athletes were also published (Chiesi, Spilich, & Voss, 1979; McPherson, 1993a). At the end of the 1980s and early in the 1990s, developments in the recording and analyses of eye movements (Goulet, Bard, & Fleury, 1989; Vickers, 1992) and kinematic

data (Carnahan, 1993) made it feasible to examine the eye movements of expert performers in contrast with less-skilled individuals to determine what athletes focused on and how their eye-movement patterns differed from less-skilled athletes (for reviews see Starkes et al., 2000; Williams, Davids, &Williams, 1999). The focus until the 1990s was largely perceptual-cognitive and aimed at establishing where differences existed between experts and novices within a particular sport domain. One of the issues that plagued much of this early research was establishing who is an "expert" and what is an acceptable metric of expert performance (Starkes, 1993; Starkes et al., 2000).

Ericsson and Smith's (1991) publication was instrumental to the second phase in sport research in that it outlined three stages in examining expert performance: first, delineating aspects of expert versus novice performance in a specific domain; next, designing laboratory tasks that tap those measurable and reproducible aspects of expert performance and determine the underlying mechanisms responsible; and third, the development of a more generalized theory of expert performance. The goal now shifted from merely demonstrating expert-novice differences in a sport to developing laboratory tasks to elucidate the underlying mechanisms that afford consistent expert performance. As a result many studies over the past 15 years have demonstrated concerted efforts to examine the underlying mechanisms of expert performance in sport (see Starkes & Ericsson, 2003).

During this time Ericsson, Krampe, and Tesch- Römer's (1993) model of deliberate practice also had significant impact on research in sport. Over the past 12 years research on this model has been conducted in soccer, wrestling, figure skating, triathlon, swimming, netball, volleyball, and basketball (see Ward, Hodges, & Starkes, 2004). The deliberate-practice model has been examined more often in sport than in any other domain to date. See Ericsson, Chapter 38.

The last few years have seen the emergence of different paradigms in what we see as the third and most recent phase in the development of research on expert performance in sport. Ecological psychology, dynamical systems theory, and associated techniques are expected to play a more important role in the future in our understanding of performance in sport (see Beek, Jacobs, Daffertshofer, & Huys, 2003; Huys, Daffertshofer, & Beek, 2004). At present there are only a few studies available on expert performance using these techniques. A major advantage of these paradigms is that they view perception and action as inextricably linked and emphasize the continuous, time-dependent (emerging) nature of sporting activities. This focus on movement (not just cognition) as integral to performance is particularly appealing when one considers the level of movement skill inherent in world class sport performances.

Since the vast majority of existing research on the topic of expertise in sport has been approached from a cognitive perspective, that is the primary focus of this chapter. Given the volume of cognitive research available on sport, the complexity of issues

that have arisen, and the relatively short length of this chapter, our focus is to provide the reader with a brief overview of key issues and methods, as well as the major findings to date from a largely cognitive perspective.

The chapter is comprised of three main sections. In the first section, we introduce some unique issues that need to be considered when studying *sport* performance. The second section begins with a review of the historical roots of this area of research. In this second section, we first present the literature from a cognitive perspective, outlining the different research paradigms such as anticipation, the identification of perceptual features, recall and recognition, and decision making. This is followed by a discussion of perceptual training as one means of improving performance. A competing theoretical perspective is then presented with discussion of ecological psychology and the idea that perception is "educated." The second section concludes with presentation of research on the influence of practice for sport expertise. In the final section of the chapter we discuss and evaluate the first meta-analysis of sport-expertise research (Thomas, Gallagher, & Lowry, 2003).

Unique Features of Sport as a Performance Area

Sport performance demands proficiency in tasks that involve movement with severe time constraints, and very often interaction with moving objects and opponents. Though sports differ from what are commonly perceived as more cognitive tasks such as bridge and chess playing, there are also tremendous differences *among* sports. Witness the difference between a relatively slow-paced introspective game of golf and the fast-paced interceptive games of tennis or basketball. As well, the unique combination of requisite cognitive skill with movement skills may result in mismatches in the development of each area. For example, a young second baseman in baseball may understand the necessity to throw a ball to cut off a runner to home, but simply not be able to make that throw (Nevett & French, 1997). Finally, sport demands may differ depending on the role occupied by the performer as a player within a team, as a coach, or referee. For example, anticipating a player's next offensive move is an important skill for a player or a referee (who needs to get ahead of the play), but not very relevant to a coach. Adjusting a team's defensive strategy to deal with an opponent's offensive structure is most relevant to a coach and player but inconsequential for a referee. One's role in a sport is an important factor in determining the nature of skills that are critical. Likewise, one's role is often quite different in individual sports versus team sports. A football quarterback's role and skills are quite different from those required of a linebacker.

MOVEMENT

The most salient feature of sport is the central role that movement plays. Athletes perform movements that vary from the seemingly simple, such as running, to the extremely complex – such as a gymnastics bar routine. Moreover, many sports involve the coordination of movements between two or more athletes. This is the case in sports such as pairs figure skating, rowing, or team synchronized swimming. Elsewhere, a distinction has been made between *interactive* sports (basketball, soccer, ice hockey) that involve many interdependencies between players, and *coactive* sports (bowling, archery, golf) that are performed independently (Cratty, 1983). This distinction has been useful in determining the skill requirements and relative demands for communication that a sport presents. Some sports (rowing, swimming, track relays), however, demonstrate characteristics and thus demands of both (see Eccles & Tenenbaum, in press, for a review).

TIME CONSTRAINTS

A critically important aspect that must be taken into consideration in sport is the limit on performance imposed by inherent time constraints in a game. For open sports (see Poulton, 1957, for a discussion of open vs.

closed sports), often characterized as those in which athletes react to the movements of their opponents, the timing of action is critical to success. Not only do performers have to deal with deciding *when* to perform a skill, the actual *execution* of the skill also has time constraints. For example, an ice hockey player may be presented with an opportunity to score when the opposing team's goalie is temporarily out of position. However, the shooter has a time window of only milliseconds in which to select, prepare, and execute a successful shot. Once the hockey player has decided to take a shot, the action must follow instantaneously. The window of opportunity is wasted if the goalie is given the chance to prevent the shot, or the shooter's intentions are telegraphed to the goalie by a slow windup. One reason for this pressure is the systemic lag time intervening between an event and a decision to move (i.e., reaction time) and between this decision and its actual initiation and completion (i.e., movement time). This pressure on movement choice (response selection) and completion (response execution) is illustrated most clearly in fast ball sports. In sports such as tennis, squash, and baseball there is little or no time for a lag between movement choice and movement. In these sports, movement decisions must often be made based on early and incomplete information. For example, a baseball batter facing a 90-mph fastball must decide whether to swing or not before the ball has even left the pitcher's hand. In this scenario, there are constraints imposed by movement choice, movement timing, and coincidence anticipation.

DIFFERENT ABILITIES DEVELOP AT DIFFERENT RATES

The combination of movement demands, time constraints, and interaction with moving objects creates a need for both perceptual-cognitive and perceptual-motor skill for high-level sport performance (e.g., Starkes, Cullen, & MacMahon, 2004). Thus, an athlete's performance level depends on the development of these two interactive types of skills. This creates yet another unique situation in sport where a performer may have mismatches in the level of development of these two forms of skill. For example, an athlete may know *what* to do, but not *how* to do it (French, Nevett, Spurgeon, Graham, Rink, & McPherson, 1996; Nevett & French, 1997). This mismatch can result in either poor motor performance or a movement choice that is less than optimal.

DIFFERING ROLES

Although it has not received a great deal of attention within the literature, another unique aspect to sport is that individuals play different roles. Within a sport, the requisite skills for a soccer goalkeeper are quite different from those of a forward. Within track and field, a female sprinter has a very different skill set than a female javelin thrower. Likewise, one's role within a sport may differ such that the requisite skills for a coach (e.g., Côté et al., 1995; Salmela & Moraes, 2003) differ from those of judges and referees (e.g., Ste-Marie, 2003). Wheras a coach, athlete, and referee may operate within the same "sub-domain" or specific sport, there is evidence that the different task demands result in different skills and abilities (e.g., Allard, Deakin, Parker, & Rodgers, 1993; Williams & Davids, 1995). To date, however, the vast majority of the literature on expert performance in sport has dealt exclusively with athletes. A second issue creates problems for any empirical test of role. Most often, coaches and referees begin their career as athletes and thus have subsumed various roles throughout their athletic career.

TEAMS ARE MORE THAN A GROUP OF INDIVIDUALS

One aspect of team sports often ignored is that teams require successful processes of coordination and communication well beyond the skills required of individuals. Yet it is only recently that teams have been examined from the same social cognition approach that is common in industrial and organizational psychology. Eccles and Tenenbaum (2004) suggest that because team operations are performed by multi-ple or cooperating individuals these must be coordinated or integrated to achieve the best performance. Thus, the team must not only perform the task itself, but coordinate members' actions toward the task. In order to do so all team members must have shared mental models about the necessary behaviors of the team and its members, and have shared expectations. In addition there must be a general team knowledge of operations that is shared by everyone, yet more specific individual knowledge appropriate to certain positions or roles is also necessary. Although sport performance shares many similarities with industrial and military applications, to date the research on teams as process units is minimal. See Satas, Rosen, Burke, Goodwin, and Fiore, Chapter 25, for a review.

Historical Roots of the Expertise Approach in Sports

One of the earliest studies of perceptual-motor expertise was that of Bryan and Harter (1897; 1899) in their now-classic investigation of telegraphic skill (see Lee & Swinnen, 1993). The sending and receiving of messages via Morse code required correct production in the timing of signals and correct translation of incoming messages. Bryan and Harter observed that experienced operators were more accurate and consistent in their productions than the less experienced and showed qualitatively different strategies in receiving messages, delaying the copying of the message until some idea of content and meaning was conveyed. In comparison, the novice operators copied messages letter by letter.

Although Bryan and Harter did not specifically use the term "chunking" to discuss their findings (see Miller, 1956), they were one of the first to experimentally show that skill-based differences were a result of the (re)organisation of small units of information, such as letters, into larger units, such as words and phrases. Perceptual chunking ideas have been at the forefront of explanations for expert-novice differences in purely cognitive domains (Chase & Simon, 1973;

Ericsson & Polson, 1988) and also in sport (see, Starkes et al., 2000; Starkes, Cullen, & MacMahon, 2004; Tenenbaum & Bar-Eli, 1993; Williams, Davids, & Williams, 1999).

The ability to quickly and efficiently process domain-specific information has since been shown to be one of the defining features of expertise in sport, and hence explanations for skill-based differences in motor skills have been heavily grounded in cognitively-based theories of information-processing activities (e.g., Fitts, 1965; Fitts & Posner, 1967; Schneider & Shiffrin, 1977). Accordingly, the performer was seen as an intelligent receiver and translator of information resulting in various degrees of effective output or behavior. Time delays between a stimulus and a response, that is, the RT (reaction time) interval, provided a critical index of processing efficiency and skill. Three somewhat independent processing activities have been proposed to mediate the reception of information and motor behavior: stimulus identification, response selection, and response programming (see Schmidt & Lee, 1998), such that skilled performance has been interpreted at a specific level in terms of the type of processing activities engaged in at these various stages (e.g., Tenenbaum, 2003). At a more general level, differences in the processing activities of skilled and less-skilled performers in sport have been described on the basis of the verbally-mediated, cognitive, and conscious-awareness nature of the performance (e.g., Adams, 1971; Anderson, 1983; Fitts & Posner, 1967). These experimental findings, protocols, and theoretical approaches have been the foundation of much of the laboratory-based experiments designed to examine the mechanisms responsible for the expert advantage in sport, including the nature of the knowledge structures (e.g., McPherson, 1993b) and control processes (e.g., Beilock & Carr, 2001) underpinning expert performance. Some of the classic findings in this area will be presented next. See the reviews by Proctor and Vu, Chapter 15, and Rosenbaum et al., Chapter 29, for more detail.

The cognitive nature of the expert advantage in sport

ANTICIPATION AND DECISION MAKING

The exploitation of advance information through highly developed internal stores and effective organization of the motor system has been proposed to underlie fast behavioral responses in the environment. This results in what Abernethy describes as the time paradox wherein skilled performers operating under extreme time constraints appear to have "all the time in the world" (Abernethy, 1991). Recognition of familiar scenarios and the chunking of perceptual information into meaningful wholes and patterns speeds up processes related to stimulus identification. Processing activities associated with response selection can be reduced via knowledge and experience of previous stimulus-response situations and hence situational probabilities (e.g., Alain & Proteau, 1979, 1980; Nougier, Ripoll, & Stein, 1989; Ward & Williams, 2003). Finally, as motor learning improves, processes associated with motor programming become more efficient and the degree of programming necessary for motor-skill execution is reduced. In this way the whole action is merely parameterized or tuned based on prior experiences rather than constructed in terms of its individual components (see Schmidt, 1975; Schmidt & Lee, 1998).

In tennis (Goulet et al., 1988, 1989) and baseball (Paull & Glencross, 1997) the expert advantage has been evidenced through superior decisions and RTs in response to unfolding game scenarios. In cricket, squash, and badminton, Abernethy and Russell (1984) and Abernethy (1988, 1990) showed that skilled performers made more accurate decisions concerning stroke selection in cricket and shot direction in badminton and squash. Professional goalkeepers in soccer were better able and faster at predicting shot-location (Savelsburgh, Williams, van der Kamp, & Ward, 2002). Even as task complexity increases, as with the 11 versus 11 scenario in soccer, Williams et al. (1994) showed that skilled soccer players were faster and more accurate at verbalizing the future destination of the ball (see also Helsen & Pauwels, 1993).

IDENTIFYING PERCEPTUAL "STRUCTURE" THROUGH OCCLUSION STUDIES AND VISUAL SEARCH

There have been a variety of methods employed in sport to examine the specific nature of the information underlying the expert advantage in both speed and accuracy (faster and more accurate decisions/responses). One of the most common methods is that of occlusion as first operationalized by Abernethy and Russell (1984). They determined that information could be occluded either temporally (by specific periods of time in relation to ball contact for example) or spatially (via the removal of specific features or events within a display) (see Abernethy, 1988; Abernethy & Russell, 1984, 1987; Williams, et al., 1999; Williams, Ward, & Smeeton, 2004) With respect to temporal-occlusion studies, it has been shown that the expert advantage is most clearly observed when a structured game clip, for example, in tennis (e.g., Goulet et al., 1988, 1989) or in goal-keeping (e.g., Savelsburgh et al., 2002), is edited prior to ball-racquet or ball-foot contact. In these situations, experts are able to use advance visual cues to predict shot-type and direction, whereas the less-skilful players do not have this perceptual skill at their disposal. In this way, temporal-occlusion studies help to elucidate generally on the type of information used by skilled players to facilitate decision making. These findings have also held up in real-world occlusion tasks where portions of a volleyball serve have been occluded for the service receiver on a volleyball court (Starkes, Edwards, Dissanayake, & Dunn, 1995). Skilled volleyball players extract more information from advance visual cues and are better able to predict the landing position of a serve.

More-specific information can be gleaned through removal of various features of the display, and this is often accomplished through spatial occlusion of certain elements. For example, Abernethy and Russell (1987) showed that in badminton, when the arm and/or racquet was occluded during a display, the decision accuracy of the experts decreased to a level below that exhibited by the novice performers, showing the racquet to be a critical feature underlying the expert advantage.

A number of researchers have combined eye-movement recording techniques with temporal- or spatial-occlusion studies to gain a more precise picture of the nature of visual cues underlying the decision processes of experts (e.g., Helsen & Starkes, 1999; Goulet et al., 1989; Savelsburgh et al., 2002). Goulet et al. (1989) found that eye movements preceding decisions were focused on the shoulder and trunk area for skilled performers in tennis in comparison to the head for the less-skilled performers (see also Singer, Cauraugh, Chen, Steinberg, & Frehlich, 1996). Subsequent temporal occlusion in a second experiment showed that high accuracy levels could be maintained for the skilled performers even under situations where information was available only from the preparatory stage of the movement.

One of the benefits of eye-movement data is that a dynamic picture of the visual search patterns of skilled performers is provided as the action unfolds (Ward, Williams, & Bennett, 2002). It has generally been shown that skilled performers show relatively fewer fixations than novice performers (e.g., Abernethy, 1985), and that fixations are qualitatively different, with experts directed to areas of the display that are believed to be most informationally rich. A reduction in the number of fixations for skilled rather than less-skilled performers is in keeping with proposals that experts extract more information from one fixation than novices because of mechanisms of chunking (see also Ripoll, Kerlizin, Stein, & Reine, 1995; Allard & Starkes, 1993). More recently the smaller number of fixations by experts[*] has been linked to the idea of a perceptual pivot (see Huys & Beek, 2002; Williams & Davids, 1998; Williams & Elliott, 1999), where eye position is anchored, thus enabling a wide field of search of peripheral features; and second, to periods of "quiet eye" associated with movement preparation and a reduction of variability in the motor system (Vickers, 1996).

However, perhaps not surprisingly, visual search patterns can be relatively domain specific. Williams, Davids, Burwitz, and Williams (1994) showed that in 11 versus 11 soccer situations expert players showed more fixations (i.e., an increased search rate) than the less-skilled players, focusing on peripheral aspects of the display, including the position of other players, in comparison to novice performers, who tended to track the ball. Helsen and Pauwels (1993) also showed a difference in visual search patterns depending on the defensive or offensive nature of the decision (for a detailed review of the eye-movement data see Cauraugh & Janelle, 2002; Williams et al., 1999; Williams, 2002).

Although eye-movement fixations are potentially useful sources of information for determining the critical features underlying expert decisions, the validity of these methods has been questioned and the combination of multiple techniques to understand which cues afford the expert advantage has been recommended (e.g., Williams et al., 1999). For example, Ward, Williams, and Bennett (2002) removed all contextual cues from a tennis opponent by converting major joint centers into point light sources to determine whether the expert advantage in tennis was dependent on these cues. In keeping with previous literature, the relative motion information of the major joint centers displayed by the point lights provided enough information to show differences as a function of skill, and visual search behaviors did not differ across normal video and point-light displays. The conversion of data into minimal directional units of x and y coordinates affords easy editing and also enables the application of statistical data-reduction techniques, such as principal component analysis to aid in uncovering the common variance between the players and the ball. This analysis technique has been used by Post, Daffertshofer, and Beek (2000) to examine change over time in the acquisition of three-ball juggling, and Beek, Jacobs, Daffertshofer, and Huys (2003) have recommended using this technique to gain a further understanding of the control processes underlying expert performance. In summary, if the question is to determine the nature of the structural information underlying the expert advantage, especially in high-dimensional, team sports, a combination of the above techniques is believed to help understand *what* information is processed, in addition to *how*.

PERCEPTUAL TRAINING

From a practical standpoint, there has been considerable interest in the implications of the above findings for the training of perceptual skill (see Williams & Ward, 2003; Williams et al., 2004). Williams, Ward, Knowles, and Smeeton (2002) successfully improved the response time of tennis players, both in the laboratory and in the field, after perceptual-skills training interventions. Although this research has important implications for training and improving tactically-based decisions, the need to maintain the perception-action links during training has repeatedly been emphasized, in as much as the effectiveness of a decision is dependent on the associated accuracy and speed of the execution (i.e., motor efficiency). The need to maintain a degree of flexibility in the nature of the perceptual information affording action has also been recommended, at the expense of specific, prescriptive instruction methods and techniques that fail to provide sufficient variation in practice (see Beek et al., 2003). It is important to note that to date the effects of perceptual training have been assessed only in terms of immediate performance improvement and short-term retention. The long-term retention of performance improvements as a result of perceptual training has not been determined.

RECALL AND RECOGNITION

Recall and recognition paradigms, in addition to verbal reports, have alerted researchers to the memory structures and processing strategies underlying skilled performance (i.e., anticipation and decision making) in sport. These methods were based on the work of de Groot (1978), Charness (1976, 1979), and Chase and Simon (1973) in chess. Chase and Simon (1973) showed that experts in chess could be differentiated on their fast and accurate ability to perceive and recognize structured patterns of play, but not random placement of chess pieces. This finding highlighted the importance of domain-specific experience, rather than natural abilities associated with IQ and superior memory in general, underlying expertise. In sport, the historical and common attribution of performance to indices associated with talent, rather than experiential factors, meant that paradigms similar to that of Chase and Simon's could illuminate on the various contributions of domain-specific skills acquired as a result of practice.

Even though sports are often not perceived as being as highly cognitive in nature as chess, researchers have shown that strategic differences related to domain-specific knowledge structures, which have been coined "software" features, rather than physical "hardware" features, consistently differentiate across skill in sport (Starkes & Deakin, 1984). Recall of structured game sequences is better for high-level rather than low-level performers, across a variety of sports and with a variety of mediums (e.g., Abernethy, Neal, & Koning, 1994; Allard, Graham & Paarsalu, 1980; Borgeaud & Abernethy, 1987; Garland & Barry, 1991; Helsen & Pauwels, 1993; Nakagawa, 1982; Starkes, 1987; Starkes & Deakin, 1984; Williams, Davids, Burwitz, & Williams, 1993; Williams & Davids, 1995); incidental recognition tests of previously viewed structured game plays are improved for skilled rather than less-skilled performers (e.g., Allard et al., 1980; Garland & Barry, 1991; Williams & Davids, 1995; Williams et al., 1993); and domain-specific perceptual tests reliably differentiate expert and novice performers, in comparison to perceptual tests associated with physical features, such as static and dynamic visual acuity, simple visual RT, and central-peripheral awareness (e.g., Abernethy et al., 1994; Helsen

& Starkes, 1999; Starkes, 1987; Ward & Williams, 2003). Indeed, Reilly, Williams, Nevill, and Franks (2000) showed that anticipatory skill, related to domain-specific experience, was one of four important predictors of skill level among teenage soccer players, in addition to speed and agility. Although physical skills quite understandably differentiate across skill in sport, factors related to perceptual skill and cognitive development are at least equally important. Ward and Williams (2003) have shown also that these cognitive skills are acquired somewhat irrespective of cognitive development and maturational age (see also Abernethy, 1988). The degree of modification of cognitive abilities with practice has been the focus of much of the current expertise research in sports, as we detail later.

The ability to chunk information into meaningful wholes or patterns of tactical significance, via detailed and extensive task-specific memory structures, has been proposed to underlie early and accurate decision-making performance in sports (see Tenenbaum, 2003; Williams, et al. 1999), rather than being merely a consequence of experience with the game. For example, Williams and Davids (1995) showed that only skilled players, not physically disabled spectators matched for perceptual experience, showed superior recall on game structured scenarios. Likewise, Allard, Deakin, Parker, and Rodgers (1993) showed that coaches, athletes, and referees in basketball were differentially more skilled on those cognitive tasks that more directly tapped their role in the sport (i.e., referees were superior on tasks related to recognition and naming of violations, coaches better at recognizing schematic plays, etc.). Nevertheless, anecdotal information from coaches and certain other researchers (see Smeeton, Ward, & Williams, 2004) suggests that some transfer of perceptual skill is seen across sports with similar perceptual demands. Finally, high correlations between decision accuracy and recall (e.g., Helsen & Starkes, 1999) suggest that the memory structures associated with each underpin the expert perceptual-cognitive advantage in sport.

THE NATURE OF KNOWLEDGE AND CONTROL STRUCTURES

Performance differences between experts and novices for cognitive and perceptual-motor skills have traditionally been explained using terminology derived from Anderson's ACT (Active control of thought) or production system theory of skill acquisition (1982, 1983; see also French & Thomas, 1987; McPherson & French, 1991; McPherson, 2000; McPherson & Kernodle, 2003; Starkes & Allard, 1991). Accordingly, early in practice, declarative rules or knowledge structures underlie the slow and effortful decision making of novice performers. With practice, these rules become compiled into efficient productions, such that certain conditions evoke actions without the necessity for intervening processes associated with the bringing to mind of domain-specific, verbalizable knowledge. Based primarily on analysis of verbal protocols (see Ericsson & Simon, 1993) of children and adults in sports such as tennis and basketball, McPherson, French, Thomas, and colleagues have shown how factual knowledge (i.e., what to do) develops along with procedural knowledge (i.e., how to do it) and that skilled performers' plans, based on verbalizable goals, become transformed into more specific "if-then-do" or "condition-action" rules. These rules are then refined and improved as a function of extended practice, such that they become specific to the task and more tactical in nature as skill improves.

If knowledge does indeed become proceduralized as a function of skill and is thus supposedly non-verbalizable, then issues are raised with respect to the validity of verbal reports for skilled performers (see Abernethy, 1993, 1994). Additionally, whereas production-based terminology was formulated based on observations of change in cognitive-domains (such as learning a computer language), in motor skills, productions are no longer merely linked to the decision side but are highly dependent on execution. Therefore, motor-based productions are likely to be of quite a different nature to the internal representations governing the manipulation of thought. Although this issue has been addressed in the work of McPherson and colleagues (e.g., McPherson & Thomas, 1989), whereby response selection has been differentiated from execution, the highly cognitive-based level of explanation for these expertise effects might be over-stretched.

Production-based terminology and ideas have also been incorporated in recent research designed to examine notions of automaticity. The procedural or automatic stage of performing, whereby responses are executed without the need for problem solving and complex decisions, has been examined in relation to the nature of the control processes underlying skilled performance in golf and soccer (see Beilock et al., 2003; Beilock & Carr, 2001, for reviews). Beilock and colleagues have shown that manipulations, designed to encourage attention to aspects of performance that are believed to have become proceduralized (e.g., the dominant foot in soccer dribbling), cause decrements in performance in skilled athletes. These authors have argued that a control focus, characteristic of an earlier, less-effective and more-declarative level of performance, interferes with the procedural skill and hence control structures governing performance at high levels of skill. Indeed, whereas skilled performers are affected by this focus, novice performers are not.

The interpretation of these effects in production-system terminology, however, has been questioned. Perkins-Ceccato, Passmore, and Lee (2003) showed interactions of skill level with attentional focus in a golf putting task, whereby skilled golfers became more variable in their performance under focus manipulations designed to encourage attention to their arms and the swing, but not to the club, whereas the reverse was true for the novice performers. Rather than proceduralization of knowledge being responsible for these skill by attentional-focus interactions, another explanation might be found from theories and approaches that place less emphasis on cognitive processes and more on self-organizing principles operating within the motor system. Bernstein

(1967/1996) originally discussed the motor system in terms of distinct levels of control that interact on many levels but change in their control function as practice progresses and skill develops. Accordingly, skill and associated notions of automaticity are linked to the devolvement of control processes to lower levels of the action system (e.g., muscular-articular synergies) that can operate somewhat independently from higher levels (e.g., action plans) and that do not require cognitive involvement for efficient and effective results. Breakdowns in performance, therefore, may be a result of inappropriate levels of the motor system taking control of the movement (see also Beek, 2000).

COGNITIVE STRUCTURES OR THE EDUCATION OF PERCEPTION?

Highly cognitive information-processing explanations for the expert advantage in sport, which rely heavily on internal representations and cognitive processes mediating stimulus interpretation and action choice, have also been questioned by researchers influenced by the work of Gibson (1979) in ecological psychology (see Beek et al., 2003; Huys, Daffertshofer, & Beek, 2004). According to these researchers, learning and hence skilled performance is seen as a process of "educating attention," whereby specific sources of information, which inform action, are identified and functionally coupled to movement as skill progresses. Following from observations of extremely fast modifications to responses on the basis of vision during table-tennis and the long jump, for example (Bootsma & van Wieringen, 1990; Lee, Lishman, & Thomson, 1982), explanations for skilled performance were based on the tight couplings between perception and action (i.e., compensatory variability), rather than a reduction or change in processing activities. Although a reduction in the variability in movements is a common distinguishing characteristic of experts when compared to intermediate performers, it is the qualitative nature of this variability in relation to the task goal

that is important, rather than the general amount of variability per se (see Huys et al., 2004). The effective harnessing of variables that are non-functional is a feature of expert performance within the motor system generally, not just with the external environment. In cycling, Bernasconi and Kohl (1993) showed that distinct couplings emerged between respiration and cycle rate, which enabled the skilled performer more economical and effective control of their movements. In runners, Diedrich and Warren (1995) observed no correlation between step cycle and breathing for novice runners, but in expert runners there were specific respiration/step ratios (1:4, 1:3, 2:5, 2:3, 1:1) that were dependent on the tempo and incline of running. Similar, within-system couplings have also been observed in juggling between postural sway and arm movements (Huys et al., 2004). As with cycling and running these system couplings afford greater efficiency and economy in performance.

THE IMPORTANCE OF PRACTICE

Whereas explanations for the nature of the expert advantage in sport might differ with respect to the role of cognition, there is no disagreement across researchers as to the necessity of years of task-specific practice to acquire skilled performance. Research in support of this viewpoint was originally detailed by Ericsson et al. (1993). Individual differences across different levels of performance skill were shown to be closely related to deliberate practice hours and hence led the authors to conclude that "many characteristics once believed to reflect innate talent are actually the result of intense practice extended over at least 10 years" (p. 363) and that the role of heritability in attainment of high levels of skill might be limited to motivational factors. If one looks across the range of sport studies on practice or deliberate practice there is a correlation (sometimes high, sometimes low) between the *amount* of all types of reported practice and performance. This is consistent with the proposed *relation* between deliberate practice, albeit not equivalent (Ericsson, 2003).

Perhaps primarily because of enduring beliefs about the role of prior talent and abilities in sport, this proposal has received vibrant interest from researchers working within the sports field. Across a number of sports, ranging from figure skating to wrestling, from hockey to karate, sport-specific practice has been shown to be a significant predictor of skill-based differences in sport (see Starkes, Deakin, Allard, Hodges, & Hayes, 1996; Ward, Hodges, & Starkes, 2004, for reviews). Though these results are encouraging for the theory and speak to the role of practice in modifying physical attributes and skills, there have been reasons to question the ubiquitousness of these findings, particularly when performance and practice differences are examined at an individual level.

Hodges, Kerr, Starkes, Weir, and Nanandiou (2004) showed that the amount of variance that could be explained by estimates related to practice was domain specific in swimming and triathlon, such that the distance of the event mediated the amount of variance in performance times that could be explained by practice. In the 100 m and 200 m sprint events in swimming, only approximately 20% of the variance in times could be explained by practice-related variables, whereas gender accounted for approximately 40%. As for the 400 m, 1.5 km, and triathlon event comprising swimming, cycling, and running, these findings were reversed. Gender no longer played an important role in accounting for performance differences, whereas practice accounted for approximately 35 to 40% of the variance in performance times. It would seem that in the shorter, more-anaerobic events, physical factors related to height-and-muscle and to body-fat ratios limit performance, somewhat independently of practice. This is the first empirical evidence that non-practice specific factors play significant roles in predicting expert performance. It also appears to contradict strong interpretations of deliberate practice

theory. The issue of physical versus developmental causes underlying performance differences in sport clearly requires further analysis before more definitive conclusions can be drawn. Even though Hodges et al. (2004) have presented evidence that gender differences persist when practice-related variables are controlled, there is evidence that in other sports, particularly those that are less physically demanding (e.g., archery and bowling), gender differences are negligible once experience is controlled (e.g., Thomas, Schlinker, & Over, 1996). Similarly, Duffy, Baluch, and Ericsson (Submitted) failed to find that differences in physical stature (i.e., reach) for darts players differentiated across skill level. In their analyses of professional and amateur, male and female dart throwers Duffy, Baluch, and Ericsson (2004) found that the magnitude of gender differences in darts performance remained the same between professional and amateur throwers, thus explanations other than practice must account for this (p. 243).

Age-based interactions with practice have also been proposed to mediate skill performance such that Côté and colleagues (e.g., Côté & Hay, 2002; Baker, Côté, & Abernethy, 2003) argue that it is only after a decision to specialize (around 12 years of age) that sport-specific practice becomes a critical component and predictor of expertise. Before this period, diversity in physical experience and play are presumed to be important for later skill development. Despite these proposals, Hodges et al. (2004) showed a monotonic increase in the yearly amounts of practice for competitive swimmers that was highly related to performance times, even though their average start age was around six to eight years (see also Starkes et al., 1996; Ward, Hodges, & Starkes, 2004). Interactions with development have also been explored as a function of aging. The main finding has been that age-related declines in performance can be circumvented by specific and sustained practice, as evidenced through longitudinal practice records in comparison to cross-sectional comparisons (see Starkes, Weir, & Young, 2003; Young & Starkes, in press, for reviews).

Meta-analysis of sport expertise findings

A recent landmark meta-analysis by Thomas, Gallagher, and Lowry (2003) is the first to collate and examine sport-expertise research. The questions addressed were whether experts and novices differ on perceptual versus decision-making aspects of cognition, by level of expertise, by type of sport (team vs. individual), across age levels, according to levels of ecological validity of the test situation, according to levels of internal validity, and by gender. In addition the authors were interested in whether the importance of the ecological validity of the skill test varied by level of expertise and whether the importance of perceptual versus decision-making aspects of cognition varied by type of sport.

The authors located 66 published papers, of which 21 were eliminated because they did not include both expert and novice data, and another six studies lacked sufficient data to calculate effect size. Thirty-nine studies published between 1987 and 2002, or 87% of the literature available, were included. The meta-analysis included data on 1,112 experts and 1,287 novices. Perceptual and cognitive skills were found to be equally important in predicting expert performance in athletes. It appears that perception and decision making are both critical aspects of individual sport; however, cognitive skill was slightly more important for team-sport experts. The same findings hold true regardless of gender. In terms of design, adult expert-novice differences are typically larger than those found in children and adolescents and perhaps not unexpectedly level of experience influences the extent of expert-novice differences. When the expert group is comprised of international, national, or college-level athletes, differences across skill class are more likely to be observed than when the elite group is comprised of developmental-level athletes, such that national, interna-

tional, and college-level athletes are better than developmental-level athletes or others. Finally, greater ecological validity of the perception/decision task produced higher effect sizes for experts and novices, but it was a more important factor for higher levels of performance. The more expert you are as a performer, the more important ecological validity of the task becomes in assessing your performance.

On the basis of this analysis a number of recommendations can be made for future research. It is important that the research setting and technique focus on capturing the *basis* for superior performance, in terms of either the process of acquisition or cognitive structure involved. It is very important in sport research to be specific and define the level of expertise/performance one is studying, both in terms of years of experience and also in level of competition and performance attained. In terms of perceptual skill, adult high-performance athletes appear to focus attention on specific informative areas of a game and as a result they exhibit better recognition of game structure and better recall of game elements. In contrast, young athletes typically lack the knowledge to produce quality solutions and are unable to reliably separate relevant from irrelevant information. An interesting suggestion by the authors is that those children who become experts at relatively young ages have clearly derived *more from practice* than others. This is an important point worthy of future study.

This chapter provides an overview of the major approaches in sport expertise research. The complexity of this area is shown in the multiple research paradigms that have been applied, from visual search and decision making, to verbal protocol analysis, and from an examination of the automatic nature of performance, to the role of cognition. We have also presented different major theoretical approaches represented by cognitive and ecological psychology, with implications for skill training. The importance of practice to both of these approaches is shown in the section reviewing research on practice features in the acquisition of sport expertise. Bringing all of this research together, we discussed the meta-analysis of Thomas et al., (2003) which provides some directions for future research. Although the Thomas et al. meta-analysis demonstrates great consistency in many of the findings related to sport expertise, it is clear from the issues outlined earlier that we have far to go in understanding skilled performance in sport. Certainly expert sport performance is not a unitary entity but a complex interaction of perception, decision-making, and movement skill as well as one's role and the nature of the sport engaged in. The inherent complexity of sport, coupled with its real-world application, is both an intriguing quality and one that makes the domain ripe for research.

References

Abernethy, B. (1985). Cue usage in open motor skills: A review of available procedures in Motor Memory and Control. In D. G. Russell & B. Abernethy (Eds.) The Otago Symposium (p. 110–122). Dunedin, NZ: Human Performance Associates.

Abernethy, B. (1988). The effects of age and expertise upon perceptual skill development in a racquet sport. *Research Quarterly for Exercise and Sport*, 59, 210–221.

Abernethy, B. (1990). Expertise, visual search, and information pick-up in squash. *Perception*, 19, 63–7.

Abernethy, B. (1991) Visual search strategies and decision-making in sport. *International Journal of Sport Psychology*, 22, 189–210.

Abernethy, B. (1993). Attention. In R. Singer, M. Murphey, & L. Tennant (Eds.), *Handbook of research on sport psychology* (pp. 127–170). New York: McMillan.

Abernethy, B., Burgess-Limerick, R., & Parks, S. (1994). Contrasting approaches to the study of motor expertise. *Quest*, 46, 186–198.

Abernethy, B., Neal, R. J., & Koning, P. (1994). Visual-perceptual and cognitive differences between expert, intermediate, and novice snooker players. *Applied Cognitive Psychology*, 18, 185–211.

Abernethy, B., & Russell, D. G. (1984). Advance cue utilization by skilled cricket batsmen. *Australian Journal of Science and Medicine in Sport*, 15, 2–10.

Abernethy, B., & Russell, D. G. (1987). Expert-novice differences in an applied selective attention task. *Journal of Sport Psychology*, 9, 326–345.

Abernethy, B., Thomas, K. T., Thomas, J. T. (1993). Strategies for improving understanding of motor expertise (or mistakes we have made and things we have learned!!!). In J. L. Starkes & F. Allard (Eds.), *Cognitive issues in motor expertise* (pp. 317–358). Amsterdam: North-Holland.

Abernethy, B. (1994). The nature of expertise in sport. In S. Serpa, J. Alves, & V. Pataco (Eds.) *International perspectives on sport and exercise psychology* (pp. 57–68). Morgantown, WV.: FIT Press.

Adams, J. A. (1971). A closed-loop theory of motor learning. *Journal of Motor Behavior*, 3, 111–150.

Alain, C., & Proteau, L. (1979). Perception of objective probabilities in motor performance. In B. Kerr (Ed.) *Human performance and behavior* (pp. 1–5) Alberta Canada: Banff.

Alain, C., & Proteau, L. (1980). Decision making in sport. In C. H. Nadeau, W. R. Halliwell, K. M. Newell, & G. C. Roberts (Eds.), *Psychology of motor behavior and sport* (pp. 465–477). Champaign, IL: Human Kinetics.

Allard, F., Deakin, J., Parker, S., & Rodgers, W. (1993). Declarative knowledge in skilled motor performance: Byproduct or constituent? In J. L. Starkes & F. Allard (Eds.), *Cognitive issues in motor expertise* (pp. 95–107). Amsterdam: North-Holland.

Allard, F., Graham, S., & Paarsalu, M. L. (1980). Perception in sport: Basketball. *Journal of Sport Psychology*, 2, 14–21.

Allard, F., & Starkes, J. L. (1991). Motor-skill experts in sports, dance, and other domains. In K. A. Ericsson & J. Smith (Eds), *Toward a general theory of expertise: Prospects and limits* (pp. 126–152). Cambridge: Cambridge University Press.

Anderson, J. R. (1982). Acquisition of cognitive skill. *Psychological Review*, 89, 369–406.

Anderson, J. R. (1983). *The architecture of cognition*. Cambridge, MA: Harvard University Press.

Baker, J., Côté, J., & Abernethy, B. (2003). Sport specific training, deliberate practice and the development of expertise in team ball sports. *Journal of Applied Sport Psychology*, 15, 12–25.

Beek, P. J. (2000). Toward a theory of implicit learning in the perceptual-motor domain. *International Journal of Sport Psychology*, 31, 547–554.

Beek, P. J., Jacobs, D., Daffertshofer, A., & Huys, R. (2003). Expert performance in sport: Views from the joint perspectives of ecological psychology and dynamical systems theory. In J. L. Starkes & K. A. Ericsson (Eds.), *Expert performance in sports: Advances in research on sport expertise* (pp. 321–344), Champaign, IL: Human Kinetics.

Beilock, S. L., & Carr, T. H. (2001). On the fragility of skilled performance: What governs choking under pressure? *Journal of Experimental Psychology: General*, 130, 701–725.

Beilock, S., Carr, T., MacMahon, C., & Starkes, J. L. (2002). When paying attention becomes counterproductive: Impact of divided versus skill-focused attention on novice and experienced performance of sensorimotor skills. *Journal of Experimental Psychology: Applied*, 8, 6–16.

Bernasconi, P., & Kohl, J. (1993). Analysis of co-ordination between breathing and exercise rhythms in man. *Journal of Physiology*, 471, 693–706.

Bernstein, N. A. (1967). *The co-regulation of movements*. Oxford: Pergamon.

Bernstein, N. A. (1996). On dexterity and its development. In M. L. Latash & M. T. Turvey (Eds.), *Dexterity and its development* (pp. 3–244). Mahwah, NJ: Erlbaum.

Bootsma, R. J., & van, Wieringen P. C. W. (1990). Timing an attacking forehand drive in table tennis. *Journal of Experimental Psychology: Human Perception and Performance*, 16, 21–29.

Borgeaud, P., & Abernethy, B. (1987). Skilled perception in volleyball defense. *Journal of Sport Psychology*, 9, 400–406.

Bryan, W. L., & Harter, N. (1897). Studies in the physiology and psychology of the telegraphic language. *Psychological Review*, 4, 27–53.

Bryan, W. L., & Harter, N. (1899) Studies on the telegraphic language. The acquisition of the hierarchy of habits. *Psychological Review*, 6, 345–375.

Carnahan, H. (1993). The role of three dimensional analysis in the assessment of motor expertise. In J. L. Starkes & F. Allard (Eds.), *Cognitive issues in motor expertise* (pp. 35–53). Amsterdam: North-Holland.

Cauraugh, J. H., & Janelle, C. M. (2002). Visual search and cue utilisation in racket sports. In K. Davids, G. Savelsbergh, S. Bennett, & J. Van der Kamp (Eds.), *Interceptive actions* (pp. 64–89). London: E. & F. N. Spon.

Charness, N. (1976). Memory for chess positions: Resistance to interference. *Journal of Experimental Psychology: Human Learning and Memory*, 2, 641–655.

Charness, N. (1979). Components of skill in bridge. *Canadian Journal of Psychology*, 33, 1–16.

Chase, W. G., & Simon, H. A. (1973). The mind's eye in chess. In W. G. Chase (Ed.), *Visual information processing* (pp. 215–282). New York: Acasdemic Press.

Chiesi, H. L. O., Spilich, G. J., & Voss, J. F. (1979). Acquisition of domain related information in relation to high and low domain knowledge. *Journal of Verbal Learning and Verbal Behavior*, 18, 257–273.

Côté, J., & Hay, J. (2002). Children's involvement in sport: A developmental perspective. In J. M. Silva & D. Stevens (Eds.), *Psychological foundations in sport* (pp. 484–502). Boston, MA: Merrill.

Côté, J., Salmela, J. H., Trudel, P., Baria, A., & Russell, S. J. (1995). The coaching model: A grounded assessment of expert gymnastic coaches' knowledge. *Journal of Sport and Exercise Psychology*, 17, 1–17.

Cratty, B. J. (1983). *Psychology in contemporary sport: Guidelines for coaches and athletes (2nd Ed.)*. Englewood Cliffs, NJ: Prentice-Hall.

De Groot, A. (1978). *Thought and choice in chess*. The Hague: Mouton. (Original work published in 1946).

Diedrich, F. J., & Warren, W. H. (1995). Why change gaits? Dynamics of the walk-run transition. *Journal of Experimental Psychology: Human Perception and Performance*, 21, 183–202.

Duffy, L., Baluch, B., & Ericsson, K. A. (2004). Dart performance as a function of facets of practice amongst professional and amateur men and women players. *International Journal of Sport Psychology*, 35, 232–245.

Duffy, L., Baluch, B., & Ericsson, K. A. (Submitted). Gender differences in dart performance: The effects of physical size and differential recruitment rates. *Research Quarterly for Exercise and Sport*.

Eccles, D. W., & Tenenbaum, G. (2004). Why an expert team is more than a team of experts:

A cognitive conceptualization of team coordination and communication in sport. *Journal of Sport and Exercise Psychology, 26,* 542–560.

Ericsson, K. A., Krampe, R. T., & Tesch-Römer, C. (1993). The role of deliberate practice in the acquisition of expert performance. *Psychological Review, 100,* 363–406.

Ericsson, K. A., & Polson, P. G. (1988). A cognitive explanation of exceptional memory for restaurant orders. In M. T. H. Chi, R. Glaser, & M. J. Farr (Eds), *The nature of expertise* (pp. 23–70). Hillsdale, NJ: Erlbaum.

Ericsson, K. A., & Simon, H. A. (1993). *Protocol analysis: Verbal reports as data.* Cambridge, MA: MIT Press.

Ericsson, K. A. (2003). Development of elite performance and deliberate practice: An update from the perspective of the expert performance approach. In J. Starkes & K. A. Ericsson (Eds.) *Expert performance in sports: Advance in research on sport expertise.* (pp. 49–84). Champaign. Ill.: Human Kinetics.

Fitts, P. M. (1965). Factors in complex skill training. In R. Glaser (Ed.), *Training research and education* 177–197. New York: Wiley.

Fitts, P. M., & Posner, M. I. (1967). *Human performance.* Belmont, CA: Brooks/Cole.

French, K. E., Nevett, M. E., Spurgeon, J. H., Graham, K. C., Rink, J. E., & McPherson, S. L. (1996). Knowledge representation and problem solution in expert and novice youth baseball performance. *Research Quarterly for Exercise and Sport, 66,* 194–201.

French, K. E., & Thomas, J. R. (1987). The relation of knowledge development to children's basketball performance. *Journal of Sport Psychology, 9,* 15–32.

Garland, D. J., & Barry, J. R. (1991). Cognitive advantage in sport: The nature of perceptual structures. *American Journal of Psychology, 104,* 211–228.

Gibson, J. J. (1979). *An ecological approach to visual perception.* Boston, MA: Houghton-Mifflin.

Goulet, C., Bard, M., & Fleury, C. (1989). Expertise differences in preparing to return a tennis serve: A visual search information processing approach. *Journal of Sport and Exercise Psychology, 11,* 382–398.

Goulet, C., Flevry, M., Bard, C., Yerlès, M., Michaud, D., & Lemine, L. (1988). Analyses des indices visuels prélevés en réception de service au tennis. *Canadian Journal of Sport Sciences, 13,* 79-87

Helsen, W. F., & Starkes, J. L. (1999). A multidimensional approach to skilled perception and performance in sport. *Applied Cognitive Psychology, 13,* 1–27.

Helsen, W., & Pauwels, J. M. (1993). The relationship between expertise and visual information processing in sport. In J. Starkes & F. Allard (Eds.), *Cognitive issues in motor expertise* (pp. 109–134). Amsterdam: North-Holland.

Hodges, N. J., Kerr, T., Starkes, J. L., Weir, P., & Nanandiou, A. (2004). Predicting performance from 'deliberate practice' hours for triathletes and swimmers: What, when and where is practice important? *Journal of Experimental Psychology: Applied, 10,* 219–237.

Huys, R., & Beek, P. J. (2002). The coupling between point-of-gaze and ball movements in three-ball cascade juggling: The effects of expertise, pattern and tempo. *Journal of Sports Sciences, 20*(3), 171–186.

Huys, R., Daffertshofer, A., & Beek, P. J. (2004). The evolution of coordination during skill acquisition: The dynamical systems approach. In A. M. Williams & N. J. Hodges (Eds.), *Skill acquisition in sport: Research, theory and practice* (pp. 351–373). London: Routledge.

Lee, D. N., Lishman, J. R., & Thompson, J. A. (1982). Regulation of gait in long jumping. *Journal of Experimental Psychology: Human Perception and Performance, 8,* 448–459.

Lee, T. D., & Swinnen, S. P. (1993). Three legacies of Bryan and Harter: Automaticity, variability and change in skilled performance. In J. Starkes & F. Allard (Eds.), *Cognitive issues in motor expertise* (pp. 295–316). Amsterdam: North-Holland.

Miller, G. A. (1956). The magical number seven, plus or minus two: Some limits on our capacity for processing information. *Psychological Review, 63,* 81–97.

McPherson, S. L. (1993a). Knowledge representation and decision-making in sport. In J. L. Starkes & F. Allard (Eds.), *Cognitive issues in motor expertise* (pp. 159–188). Amsterdam: North-Holland.

McPherson, S. L. (1993b). The influence of player experience on problem solving during batting preparation in baseball. *Journal of Sport and Exercise Psychology, 15,* 304–325.

McPherson, S. L. (2000). Expert-novice differences in planning strategies during collegiate singles tennis competition. *Journal of Sport and Exercise Psychology*, 22, 39–62.

McPherson, S. L., & French, K. E. (1991). Changes in cognitive strategy and motor skill in tennis. *Journal of Sport and Exercise Psychology*, 13, 26–41.

McPherson, S. L. & Kernodle, M. (2003). Tactics, the neglected attribute of expertise: Problem representations and performance skills in tennis. In J. L. Starkes & K. A. Ericsson (Eds.), *Expert performance in sports: Advances in research in sport expertise* (pp. 137–168). Champaign, IL: Human Kinetics.

McPherson, S. L., & Thomas, J. R. (1989). Relation of knowledge and performance in boys' tennis: Age and expertise. *Journal of Experimental Child Psychology*, 48, 190–211.

Nakagawa, A. (1982). A field experiment on recognition of game situations in ball games: The case of static situation in rugby football. *Japanese Journal of Physical Education*, 27, 17–26.

Nevett, M. E., & French, K. E. (1997). The development of sport-specific planning, rehearsal and updating of plans during defensive youth baseball game performance. *Research Quarterly for Exercise and Sport*, 68, 203–214.

Nougier, V., Ripoll, H., & Stein, J. (1989). Orienting of attention with highly skilled athletes. *International Journal of Sport Psychology*, 20, 205–223.

Paull, G., & Glencross, D. (1997). Expert perception and decision making in baseball. *International Journal of Sport Psychology*, 28, 35–56.

Perkins-Ceccato, N., Passmore, S. R., & Lee, T. D. (2003). Effects of focus of attention depend on golfers' skill. *Journal of Sports Sciences*, 21, 593–600.

Post, A. A., Daffertshofer, A., & Beek, P. J. (2000). Principal components in three-ball cascade juggling. *Biological Cybernetics*, 82, 143–152.

Poulton, E. C. (1957). On predicting skilled movement. *Psychological Bulletin*, 54, 467–478.

Reilly, T., Williams, A. M., Nevill, A., & Franks, A. (2000). A multidisciplinary approach to talent identification in soccer. *Journal of Sports Sciences*, 18, 668–676.

Ripoll, H., Kerlirzin, Y., Stein, J. R., & Reine, B. (1995). Analysis of information processing, decision making, and visual strategies in complex problem solving sport situations. *Human Movement Science*, 14, 929–938.

Salmela, J. H., & Moraes, L. C. (2003). Development of expertise: The role of coaching, families, and cultural contexts. In J. L. Starkes & K. A. Ericsoon (Eds.), *Expert performance in sports: Advances in research on sport expertise* (pp. 275–294). Champaign, IL: Human Kinetics.

Savelsbergh, G. J. P., Williams, A. M., van der Kamp, J., & Ward, P. (2002). Visual search, anticipation and expertise in soccer goalkeepers. *Journal of Sport Sciences*, 20, 279–287.

Schmidt, R. A. (1975). A schema theory of discrete motor skill learning. *Psychological Review*, 82, 225–260.

Schmidt, R. A., & Lee, T. A. (1998). *Motor control and learning: A behavioral emphasis*. Champaign, IL: Human Kinetics.

Schneider, W., & Shiffrin, R. M. (1977). Controlled and automatic information processing: I. Detection, search, and attention. *Psychological Review*, 92, 424–428.

Singer, R. N., Cauraugh, J. H., Chen, O., Steinberg, G. M., & Frehlich, S. G. (1996). Visual search, anticipation, and reactive comparisons between skilled and beginning tennis players. *Journal of Applied Sport Psychology*, 8, 9–26.

Smeeton, N. J., Ward, P., & Williams, A. M. (2004). Do pattern recognition skills transfer across sports? A preliminary analysis. *Journal of Sports Sciences*, 22, 205–13.

Starkes, J. L. (1987). Skill in field hockey: The nature of the cognitive advantage. *Journal of Sport Psychology*, 9, 146–160.

Starkes, J. L. Motor experts: Opening thoughts. In J. L. Starkes & F. Allard (Eds.) *Cognitive issues in motor expertise* (pp. 3–16). Amsterdam: Elsevier.

Starkes, J. L., & Allard, F. (Eds.). (1993). *Cognitive issues in motor expertise*. Amsterdam: North Holland.

Starkes, J. L., Cullen, J., & MacMahon, C. (2004). A model of skill acquisition and retention of perceptual-motor performance. In A. M. Williams & N. J. Hodges (Eds.), *Skill acquisition in sport: Research, theory and practice* (pp. 259–281). London: Routledge.

Starkes, J. L., & Deakin, J. (1984). Perception in sport: A cognitive approach to skilled performance. In W. F. Straub & J. M. Williams (Eds.), *Cognitive sport psychology*, (pp. 115–128). Lansing MI: Sport Science.

Starkes, J. L., Deakin, J. M., Allard, F., Hodges, N. J., & Hayes, A. (1996). Deliberate practice in sports: What is it anyway? In K. A. Ericsson (Ed.), *The road to excellence: The acquisition of expert performance in the arts and sciences, sports, and games* (pp. 81–106). Mahwah, NJ: Lawrence Erlbaum.

Starkes, J. L., Edwards, P., Dissanayake, P., & Dunn, T. (1995) A new technology and fieldtest of advance cue usage in volley ball. *Research Quarterly for Exercise and Sport*, 66, 162–167.

Starkes, J. L., Helsen, W. F., & Jack, R. (2000). Expert performance in sport and dance. In R. N. Singer, H. A. Hausenblas, & C. M. Janelle (Eds.), *Handbook of sport psychology* (pp. 174–201). New York: John Wiley.

Starkes, J. L., Weir, P. L., & Young, B. (2003). Retaining expertise: What does it take for older expert athletes to continue to excel? In J. L. Starkes & K. A. Ericsson (Eds.), *Expert performance in sports: Advances in research on sport expertise* (pp 251–272). Champaign, IL: Human Kinetics.

Ste-Marie, D. (2003). Expertise in sport judges and referees: Circumventing information-processing limitations. In J. L. Starkes & K. A. Ericsson (Eds.), *Expert performance in sports: Advances in research in sport expertise* (pp. 169–190). Champaign, IL: Human Kinetics.

Tenenbaum, G. (2003). Expert athletes: An integrated approach to decision-making. In J. L. Starkes & K. A. Ericsson (Eds.), *Expert performance in sport: Advances in research on sport expertise* (pp. 191–218). Champaign, IL: Human Kinetics.

Tenenbaum, G., & Bar-Eli, M. (1993) Decision-making in sport: A cognitive perspective. In R. Singer, M. Murphey, & K. Tennant (Eds.), *Handbook of research on sport psychology* (pp. 171–192). New York: Macmillan.

Thomas, J. R., Gallagher, J., & Lowry, K. (2003). Developing motor and sport expertise: Meta-analytic findings. Paper presented at North American Society for the Psychology of Sport and Physical Activity, Savannah, Georgia.

Thomas, P. R., Schlinker, P. J., & Over, R. (1996). Psychological and psychomotor skills associated wioth prowess at ten-pin bowling. *Journal of Sports Sciences*, 14, 255–268.

Vickers, J. N. (1992). Gaze control in putting. *Perception*, 21, 117–132.

Vickers, J. N. (1996). Visual control while aiming at a far target. *Journal of Experimental Psychology: Human Perception and Performance*, 22, 342–354.

Ward, P., & Williams, A. M. (2003). Perceptual and cognitive skill development: The multidimensional nature of expert performance. *Journal of Sport and Exercise Psychology*, 25, 93–111.

Ward, P., Williams, A. M., & Bennett, S. J. (2002). Visual search and biological motion perception in tennis. *Research Quarterly for Exercise and Sport*, 73, 107–112.

Ward, P., & Williams, A. M. (2003). Perceptual and cognitive skill development in Soccer: The multidimensional nature of expert performance. *Journal of Sport and Exercise Psychology*, 25, 93–111.

Ward, P., Hodges, N. J., & Starkes, J. L. (2004). Deliberate practice and expert performance: Defining the path to excellence. In A. M. Williams & N. J. Hodges (Eds.), *Skill acquisition in sport: Research, theory and practice* (pp. 231–258). London: Routledge.

Williams, A. M. (2002). Visual search behaviour in sport. *Journal of Sports Sciences*, 20, 169–170.

Williams, A. M., & Davids, K. (1995). Declarative knowledge in sport: A byproduct of experience or a characteristic of expertise? *Journal of Sport and Exercise Psychology*, 7, 259–275.

Williams, A. M., & Elliott, D. (1999). Anxiety and visual search strategy in karate. *Journal of Sport and Exercise Psychology*, 21, 362–375.

Williams, A. M., & Ward, P. (2003). Developing perceptual expertise in sport. In J. L. Starkes & K. A. Ericsson (Eds.), *Expert performance in sports: Advances in research on sport expertise* (pp. 219–249). Champaign, IL: Human Kinetics.

Williams, A. M., Davids, K., & Williams, J. G. (1999). *Visual perception and action in sport*. London: E. & F. N. Spon.

Williams, A. M., Ward, P., & Smeeton, N. J. (2004). Perceptual and cognitive expertise in sport: Implications for skill acquisition and performance enhancement. In A. M. Williams & N. J. Hodges (Eds.), *Skill acquisition in sport: Research, theory and practice* (pp. 328–347). London: Routledge.

Williams, A. M., Davids, K., Burwitz, L., & Williams, J. G. (1993). Cognitive knowledge and soccer performance. *Perceptual and Motor Skills*, 76, 579–593.

Williams, A. M., Davids, K., Burwitz, L., & Williams, J. G. (1994). Visual search strategies of experienced and inexperienced soccer players. *Research Quarterly for Exercise and Sport*, 5, 127–135.

Williams, A. M., & Davids, K. (1998). Visual search strategy, selective attention, and expertise in soccer. *Research Quarterly for Exercise and Sport, 69,* 111–128.

Williams, A. M., Ward, P., Knowles, J. M., & Smeeton, N. J. (2002). Perceptual skill in a real-world task: Training, instruction, and transfer in tennis. *Journal of Experimental Psychology: Applied, 8,* 259–270.

Young, B., & Starkes, J. L. (in press). Lifespan analyses of track performance: Continued training moderates the age-related performance decline. *Experimental Aging Research.*

CHAPTER 28

Artistic Performance: Acting, Ballet, and Contemporary Dance

Helga Noice & Tony Noice

Acting

History

As an art form, acting dates back well over 2,500 years. Large choruses that performed dance-chant rituals called dithyrambs toured the Greek countryside celebrating the birth of Dionysus, god of wine and fertility. Some historians (e.g., Brockett, 1991) suggest that, although these group presentations sowed the seeds of theatre, only when a dithyramb leader named Thespis stepped forward and talked to members of his chorus (not as himself but as a character in the drama) did the art of theatre truly begin. Soon, writers contributed original dialogue to these presentations, and yearly competitions between dithyrambic groups were held in Athens at a 15,000-seat amphitheatre built for the purpose. Thus, the golden age of dramatic art was launched, showcasing the works of Aeschylus, Sophocles, Euripides, and Aristophanes.

When the Romans conquered Greece, playwrights such as Plautus and Terrance based most of their works on Greek models but made them far earthier, as they had to compete with such entertainments as gladiators fighting to the death and humans being fed to the lions. After the Romans, theatre more or less vanished until revived many centuries later by the Church for teaching religious principles (Cohen, 1994). The resulting awakening of public interest led to the Renaissance playwrights, most notably Shakespeare, who, in Hamlet's advice to the players, presented to all future generations the hallmarks of good acting: "... o'erstep not the modesty of nature. For anything so o'erdone is from the purpose of playing whose end was and is to hold, as 'twere, the mirror up to nature" (Shakespeare, 1604/1992, p. 137). Thus, from Sophocles to Shakespeare to Kushner, the form, set in ancient Greece, has remained remarkably intact: Actors, impersonating characters and using memorized dialogue in structured situations, perform "plays" in front of audiences assembled for that specific purpose.

What is Good Acting?

Of course, acting styles vary with each production and may range from gritty realism to highly artificial, robot-like interpretations that emphasize man's dehumanization. However, the majority of performances in today's theatre/film/television venues are in line with Hamlet's advice and are designed to lure audiences into accepting the portrayals as being true to life. Indeed, this requirement to make each performance uniquely real lies at the heart of professional acting. Only peripheral skills such as vocal projection or bodily flexibility are acquired through deliberate repetitive practice. The essence of acting consists paradoxically of successive attempts to refrain from repeating yesterday's rendition but to create the events anew at each moment of every performance (Noice & Noice, 1997a). The components of this expertise, and the research into those components, constitute the subject of this chapter.

Acquisition of Acting Expertise

In every era including the present, many outstanding actors have learned solely by observation and experience. In fact, the dominant approach to present-day actor training comes from the work of Russian actor-director-theorist Constantine Stanislavski (1936), who said he invented nothing but simply analyzed the acting of his day. He found that the worst actors were obviously feigning involvement in the dramatic situation but that the best seemed to be living in the present, experiencing what the character would experience. Stanislavski spent the rest of his life trying to codify that approach into a teachable system of acting so that what came naturally to the rare few could be reliably taught to others. The Stanislavski system and its offshoots form the basis of the majority of training programs in today's colleges and universities. The term *method acting* is often used to describe American variants of the Stanislavski system, but the phrase is subject to extreme interpretations, at times being applied only to director Lee Strasberg's view of Stanislavski's early writings, and at other times to any approach that results in truthful on-stage behavior (Vineberg, 1991). Nevertheless, an examination of today's most used acting textbooks

(Noice, A., 1995) reveals that the majority of training methods are rooted in the Stanislavski notion that good acting consists of determining the character's "spine" (the life purpose that motivates everything the character says and does) and, more importantly, each specific objective of the character at every moment in the play (Stanislavski, 1936). These concepts are seminal to the Stanislavski system, and succeeding generations of teachers have devised innumerable mental/physical exercises, explanations, and metaphors to explain the process (e.g., Adler, 1988; Guskin, 2003; Meisner & Longwell, 1987; Morris, 1985). Even those academic conservatory programs devoted primarily to classical theatre require this truthful playing of character objectives but place equal emphasis on technical matters such as voice projection, bodily flexibility, and use of heightened language.

However, some completely non-Stanislavski techniques have also received fairly wide acceptance. Probably the best known of these is "theatre games" (e.g., Spolin, 1963), an approach that teaches acting skills indirectly. For example, in a game called "gibberish," the intent is to remove the crutch of verbal meaning by forcing the actors to communicate their desires in nonsense strings of sound that they spontaneously generate in response to a given situation. Thus, they must use inflection, intonation, facial expression, and so forth to attain their goals without resorting to language, pantomime, or illustrative gestures typical of charades. The aim is to replace reliance on verbal meanings with goal-directed human conduct so that, when the dialogue is added, it will rest on a rich behavioral structure.

A less frequently used actor-training approach employs neutral and character masks. Wearing a neutral (i.e., expressionless) mask requires the actor to start from scratch when creating a new character instead of unwittingly imposing his or her own eccentricities on that creation, whereas wearing a character mask poses the challenge of generating real behavior that does not conflict with the fixed expression of the mask (for a complete discussion of masks and actor-training, see Rolf, 1977). Although masks have been used in performance from the beginnings of theatre in ancient Greece to current Japanese Noh performances, their use in actor training is relatively recent. Many historians credit Jacques Lecoq (1921–1999) for popularizing this instructional device (e.g., Rudlin, 2000).

In addition to the above, many theatre practioners have devised methods suited to their particular production needs. Bertold Brecht believed that theatre must serve a didactic purpose, which is best accomplished when the audience is not caught up in the action. Therefore, he instructed his actors to shun true emotional involvement and to remain at a distance from the characters so that the audience would not vicariously participate in the performance and thus be free to think about the issues raised (Barton, 1993). Musicals, ritual theatre, comedy improvisation, and many other theatrical forms all have instructional approaches designed to target needs quite different from those of traditional storytelling in theatre and film. However, it is essential to point out that whereas many college/professional training programs incorporate games, or masks, or dozens of other alternate approaches, the overwhelming majority of theatre education is still primarily Stanislavski-based (Noice, A., 1995).

Empirical Investigations into the Acting Process

RETENTION AND ACCESS TO ROLES

Actors report that the question they hear most often from theatregoers is, "How do you remember all those lines?" (Noice & Noice, 2002a). Therefore, it is hardly surprising that when cognitive psychologists began to investigate actors, they immediately focused on their memory processes.

Oliver and Ericsson (1986) performed one of the earliest such investigations when they tested actors currently performing Shakespearean roles in a professional repertory company. One of the main findings of those five linked experiments was that actors could reliably access individual words from anywhere in their very lengthy roles when given brief (one to four word) probes that provided little contextual information. (The authors of this chapter have informally replicated this effect over a number of years and have yet to find a professional actor currently performing a play who could not supply the remainder of a line of dialogue given any unique word from the role. Retrieval is no faster when the cue is from the beginning, as opposed to the middle or end of the play.) Oliver and Ericsson (1986) also found that the actors were successful at retrieval (although slower) when the probes and the targets crossed sentence boundaries (e.g., the first words of a sentence were used as probes and the actor's task was to retrieve the last words of the immediately preceding sentence). Testing actors who were playing roles in two different plays revealed that identifying the roles from which the probes were drawn affected response time but not accuracy. However, the methods by which this proficiency was acquired were not empirically investigated.

Intons-Peterson and Smyth (1987) did investigate some aspects of learning strategy but their research used non-professionals (student actors who were regarded as good memorizers). Two groups (acting students and non-acting students) were placed either in a gist or rote condition. They performed the same learn-by-repeating-aloud task with a prose passage, with the gist participants being allowed to read the passage over once before beginning and the rote participants being asked to start memorizing aloud immediately. These researchers found that rote instructions encouraged closer attention to exact wording, that most participants seemed to be using grammatical units as landmarks, and that the acting students attempted to find optimal length units.

In the pilot study for an ongoing series of experiments, Noice (1992) collected self-reports of professional actors of various ages, backgrounds, and education. These reports were categorized and analyzed. Results indicated that all the actors, before they gave any thought to memorization, stressed the notion of understanding the ideas behind the utterances, and the reasons the characters used those words to express those ideas. One of the actors summed up the process this way:

> We do things in reverse in the theater. We get the script, which is . . . at the end of the thought process: we have the lines there. Normally in life, you have an impulse and then a thought which you put into words. Well, I have the words, I get the words first in this finished script. And so I have to go back and find out what the thought was, to have you say those words. And more importantly, what was the impulse that created the thought that created the words, and usually it could be an emotional kind of thing. What is the reason for that thought? That's the way I have always thought of it. (Noice, 1992, pp. 420–421)

As intriguing as such statements were, they nevertheless represented actors' introspection into their own mental operations, a process that is always somewhat suspect. (See Ericsson, Chapter 13, for discussion of protocol analysis.) Therefore, some follow-up experiments employed the quantitative and qualitative analysis of concurrent or retrospective verbal protocols (Noice, 1991, 1993; Noice & Noice, 1994, 1996). The underlying tasks in these studies consisted of the actors being given a scene to prepare for an imaginary audition or performance. The actors worked their way through the scene, verbalizing all thoughts that occurred during the preparation phase, then performing free recall, cued recall, or summarization tasks. Analysis of the protocols revealed that, in almost every case, the primary concern was to extract from the literal text the true intentions of the assigned characters. Since most well-written plays employ subtlety and indirection, these thoughts rarely concerned the literal meaning of the words but rather an underlying meaning inferred by the actor. For example, when a character said, "I'm sure you can trust Storey," the actor thought "I'm trying to calm him down," and when a character said "He talks about you all the time," the actor thought "I'm flattering him" (Noice, 1991).

For comparison purposes, novices were given the same scenes to analyze. The overwhelming majority of the novices' verbalizations did not concern the intentions of the characters or the dramatic situation, but were either private ("I wonder how long this experiment will take?") or editorial ("The plot thickens"). From a quantitative standpoint, the actors retained significantly more of a theatrical script than the novices, even when the participants were told not to memorize the material, but to read it only for understanding. Yet when learning material other than theatrical scripts, actors fared no better than novices.

The overall picture that emerged from these studies was that actors regard their primary job as doing "for real" whatever the character is doing. So, if the dramatic situation calls for character A to plead with character B, the actor playing character A actually pleads with the actor playing character B. He or she does NOT try to look and sound "pleading," the plea must be genuine and made at the moment of utterance (Noice & Noice, 1994). Furthermore, the actor must pursue that intention truthfully at every performance (or during every take in a TV or film studio), which requires that the actor allow himself or herself to be influenced by the behavior of the other actors. This keeps the scene alive. The chemistry between the actors will vary subtly from performance to performance and affect how the intentions are played.

A further point that emerged from the protocols was that the fulfillment of the intention had to be "doable" at every performance. That is, the actor had to choose intentions that were not only implied by the script, but that could be executed regardless of circumstances, when feeling sick or well, on opening night with a career possibly riding on the outcome, or at the 300th performance of the role when torpor threatens.

An early step in role preparation is to segment the script into goal-directed units that actors call "beats" (Noice & Noice, 1993). These beats are chunks of dialogue, devoted to the fulfillment of a single intention. Most expertise investigations (e.g., Chase & Simon, 1973) show that experts generally form larger chunks of domain-specific information than novices. However, this "beat" study revealed that the experts' chunks were far smaller and far more diverse. This was because novices, when asked to divide the script into segments for the purpose of learning the text, almost uniformly made divisions where the topic of conversation changed. On the other hand, actors segmented the script into each separate intention of the assigned character, a process that required extensive elaboration, perspective taking, self-referencing, self-generation, distinctiveness, and other cognitive principles shown to benefit memory (see Noice & Noice, 1997a). Therefore, it is hardly surprising that, in the allotted 20 minutes, actors who analyzed the script on a micro-level remembered significantly more than the novices who processed it on a topic-by-topic basis.

The point that consistently emerged from these protocol studies was that virtually all actors appear to go through a two-stage process. The first (analytical) stage consists of examining the script in depth to determine the intentions of the characters. The second (rehearsal/performance) stage consists of what the researchers have called "active experiencing" (Noice & Noice, 1997b). This entails actually doing whatever the character is doing, whether it is taunting, interrogating, bullying, or any of the hundreds of common human transactions that might occur in the performance of a role. Proper application of this principle results in the actor experiencing the mental life of the character along with the concomitant feelings and appropriate physiological states.

To demonstrate the active experiencing principle, it is possible to carry out a thought experiment. First, one would become imaginatively involved in an intention, such as "to demand obedience." Obviously cognitive activity is present in terms of the specific nature of the demand, but also one's affect state will shift to a sense of strongly felt determination, and simultaneous physical changes will occur, such as a possible tightening of the jaw or a more belligerent stance. Each person will experience the situation slightly differently, but, in every case, the changes will be multi-modal: cognitive, affective, motoric. In addition to being a component of acting expertise, it has been shown that brief training in the use of active experiencing can produce enhanced recall in novice acting students and non-actors (Noice & Noice, 1997b).

Levenson, Ekman, and Friesen (1990) investigated the reverse of the active experiencing principle. That is, instead of using imagination to affect emotional and physiological changes, they coached participants to manipulate their faces into positions that resembled the outer expression of the inner experience. The researchers found that the participants then experienced the emotion consistent with that facial expression. However, the assumed facial poses were so blatant (amounting to grimaces) that they could not be used for most dramatic purposes. Toward the end of his life, Stanislavski experimented with a subtle form of this outside-in technique (usually referred to as "the method of physical actions") in which physically doing what the character would do leads to actively experiencing the character's inner life. For example, a physical action such as stroking a loved one's face so gently as to not wake her, is apt to generate feelings of tenderness in the actor (Stanislavski, 1961).

Further confirmation of the memory benefits of the active experiencing principle comes from a recent study by Scott, Harris, and Rothe (2001). Ninety-one female college students read the same long solo speech (twice through) from a contemporary play. All participants were then given one of five different 30-minute processing tasks – from answering questions about the character to improvising a scene in which the character might appear. Results showed greater recall (verbatim plus gist) for the improvisation group. The authors concluded that "a condition involving active experiencing at cognitive, affective, and motoric levels leads to better memory than other conditions that force deep processing but only on cognitive levels" (p. 303).

LONG-TERM RETENTION OF ROLES

Schmidt, Boshuizen, and van Breukelen (2002) tested the long-term recall of two semi-professional and two non-professional (but experienced) actors after a five-month performance hiatus. The researchers assessed both the amount of recall and the contribution of situational cues (spatial relationship with other actors, distances from stage props and set pieces, etc.). The actors were asked to perform the play, either exchanging dialogue while moving about as in a normal rehearsal, or sitting with their backs toward each other, producing the lines without spatial or other non-verbal cues. This alternating full-context and verbal-only rehearsal continued throughout the play. Results showed that after five months of disuse, the actors demonstrated 53% verbatim recall and 85% total recall (verbatim plus paraphrases). The paraphrases closely followed the textual meaning, suggesting that original learning was strongly meaning based, in line with much previous research (Noice & Noice, 1993). The researchers found a small but significant effect of full-context over verbal-only retrieval, and speculated that the small size might have been due to ceiling effects.

An earlier study on long-term retrieval of dialogue had been performed by Noice and Noice (2002b). They used fill-in-the-blank, standard recognition, and forced-choice recognition tasks to assess retention of previously performed roles. The fill-in-the-blank and forced-choice items were pretested to make sure that the missing words could not be guessed from context. Results showed that, for up to three years after the final performance, these full-time, professional actors had virtually perfect access to verbatim details of dialogue. After that, retention decreased, more with some actors than others, but in many cases was still remarkably high (e.g., 36% recall and 64% forced-choice recognition after 22 years).

ACTORS' GENERATION OF SITUATION-SPECIFIC AND TASK-SPECIFIC EMOTION

Denis Diderot (1830/1957) introduced the phrase "The actor's paradox" to describe the dichotomy of feeling versus feigning an emotion required in a play. Some modern theorists (e.g., Roach, 1985) believe this elliptical treatise was concerned with the notion of "double consciousness" (i.e., being able to create genuine situation-specific emotions while at the same time being able to deliberately execute pre-planned pauses, movements, gestures, etc.). Other interpretations are far more simplistic. Lee Strasberg summarized Diderot's view as "To move an audience, the actor himself must remain unmoved" (Diderot, 1830/1957, p. x). In an early investigation, Archer (1888) sent a questionnaire to the leading actors of his day and found that many of them endorsed the notion of dual consciousness. For example, the Victorian stage star, Fanny Kemble, said,

> The curious part of acting, to me, is the sort of double process which the mind carries on at once, the combined operation of one's faculties, so to speak, in diametrically opposite directions; for instance, in that very last scene of Mrs. Beverly, while I was half dead with crying in the midst of real grief, created by an entirely unreal cause, I perceived that my tears were falling like rain all over my silk dress. (Archer, 1888, p. 151)

Noice (2004) collected data for an investigation of actors' affective experiences onstage. Forty actors were tested right after their performances so the experiences were fresh in their minds. All participants were working under Equity (union) contracts, an important distinction with American actors because approximately 85% of union members are unemployed at any one time. Therefore, the sample was drawn from that small minority that can truly be called *currently active* professionals. The test instrument presented a visual analog scale that stood for polarities of affective experience on-stage. The left end represented only those affect states that might be felt if the actor were actually that character in the situation of the play. The right end represented only the affect states resulting from pursuing the craft of an actor who is portraying a character in front of an audience. The task consisted of placing an "X" at either extreme or somewhere in between that best indicated the mix of the two sources of emotion during performance.

Results showed that not a single actor placed an X at either extreme. The average mark was nearer to the character side (40% from the left end; SD 11.60), and the range of responses was skewed strongly to the right. That is, the greatest number of responders indicated that their feelings on-stage tended to be more character influenced than performance influenced.

The actors were also invited to offer feedback. The comments varied greatly but almost all referred to multiple sources of emotion, as in the following:

> I seem to alternate from one state to another. That is, I get immersed in the character side and experience real situational feelings but then I feel a rush of pleasure as an actor – sort of a self-congratulatory feeling that I am a good enough actor to actually experience private character feelings during a public performance. Then I regain some of my connection with the drama and get involved again until the pleasure of the involvement forces itself on my consciousness once more.

These results would suggest that the affect of an actor during performance is highly complex and includes feelings of both the actor-as-character and the actor-as-actor. Many actors also reported allowing emotional events outside the theatre to feed into and color their performances. In theatre jargon, this is called "Playing your day."

These results vary greatly from those obtained by Konijn (2000). She conducted two surveys by mail, one with Dutch/Flemish actors (response rate: 28%) and one with American actors (response rate: 11%). Her questionnaire listed 14 emotions that might be present in dramatic roles. Konijn charted the emotions on her list that actors reported actually experiencing and the ones they believed they portrayed to the audience, and found no significant correla-

tions between them. This finding casts doubt on the claim made by a very small minority of actors who assert that acting consists of totally becoming the character and experiencing only his or her feelings. However, Konijn not only rejects this extreme position, she goes far beyond her data to theorize that all on-stage affect consists solely of emotions resulting from the task of performing in front of an audience. This would appear to contradict the experience of almost all actors, not only those in our samples, but the hundreds who have described their processes in the theatre literature (e.g., Vilga, 1997). Even the avowedly technical "anti-method" actor, Laurence Olivier, reported that acting on-stage is "an emotional problem. You've got to feel it, a great test for the imagination" (Bee & Bragg, 1982).

Over a period of many years, Susana Bloch, a neuroscientist, investigated the intentional generation of emotion by physiological means. One study (Lemeignan, Aguilera-Torres, & Bloch, 1992) showed that, by duplicating the breathing patterns that accompany six emotions, actors can experience those emotions. Evidence for the efficacy of the procedure was based on three different measures: physiological arousal, self-appraisal, and independent observation by concealed viewers.

Using Actors' Expertise to Investigate Physiological and Psychological Issues

Because of their ability to generate an emotional state on demand, actors have often been recruited for experiments unrelated to theatre or film. Kelso, Weyhrauch, and Bates (1993) asked actors to perform action sequences that would later be used as models for AI programming of virtual reality scenarios that portrayed emotional situations. Reid and Mundell combined input from Carnegie Mellon's Theatre and AI faculty to create a storytelling robot receptionist for the Newell-Simon Hall (Watzman, 2004), and Futterman, Kemeny, Shapiro, Polonsky, and Fahey (1992) employed method-actors using emotional memory techniques in order to measure the influence of affect states on the immune system. They found that imaginatively produced affect states resulted in more variability in immunology than neutral states, with anxiety and happiness producing the highest variability and depression the lowest. Such explorations may have some interest to the expertise researcher inasmuch as they demonstrate the ability of actors to perform their tasks outside of a theatrical context even to the point of simultaneously experiencing invasive medical procedures.

Applied Issues

The many experiments that shed light on actors' processes prompted an intriguing question: Might actors' learning strategies benefit non-actors in terms of rapid assimilation and efficient retrieval of material? The first attempts to answer this question produced the surprising finding that memory was enhanced far less by the preliminary analytical work done on the script than by the rehearsal and performance components of the actor's role-learning process, referred to as the active experiencing principle (Noice & Noice, 1997b). The efficacy of this principle was verified by findings with non-actors under a wide variety of experimental procedures (Noice & Noice, 2004). Soon this inquiry became entwined with an entirely different branch of research: The effects of effortful activities on healthy cognitive aging, and delayed onset of Alzheimer's disease (e.g., Friedland et al., 2001; Wilson et al., 2002). This extensive body of research has shown the benefits of long-term cognitive and social activities, but little attention has been devoted to short-term interventions other than very narrowly targeted ones (e.g., examining the effect of mnemonics training on list learning). Recently, the "active experiencing" components of acting techniques were taught to older adults (average age 73 years) over a four-week period. Participants were pretested on word recall, working memory, problem-solving ability, and quality of life issues. Significant gains were found over no-treatment controls and over a comparison art-study group, recruited to control for non-content-specific effects (Noice, Noice, & Staines, 2004).

Implications of Acting Expertise on Theoretical Issues

LONG-TERM WORKING MEMORY

The picture of actors' memory processes that arises from much of the research cited in this chapter would appear to be a perfect fit with Ericsson and Kintsch's (1995) long-term working memory theory. That is, the actor possesses domain-specific information in LTM on human motivations and the myriad specific intentions that are used to act on those motivations. The text input is classified in terms of these intentions. ("In this section, I'm trying to soften him up. Then, in the next one, I go in for the kill.") These intentions then serve as efficient retrieval cues and the entire succession of intentions constitute a retrieval structure for the complete role. Thus, residing in LTM are both the exact dialogue and the necessary performance information (i.e., the reasons for uttering the dialogue). This theory would explain the ability of actors to access any part of the role with complete conviction given only minimal cues.

SUBJECT-PERFORMED TASKS

Researchers have frequently demonstrated that phrases such as "open the door" or "lift the pen" are better remembered when actually performed (with real or imaginary objects) than when acquired under standard verbal learning instructions (for reviews, see Cohen, 1989; Engelkamp & Zimmer, 1990; Nilsson, 2000). In these subject-performed tasks (SPTs), the movements actually duplicate the verbal phrases. Recent experiments with professional actors, student actors, and non-actors have shown that speeches accompanied by movements that do not duplicate their meaning are better recalled than speeches made while the participant is standing or sitting in one place (Noice & Noice, 1999, 2001; Noice, Noice, & Kennedy, 2000). The authors refer to this as the non-literal enactment effect and it occurs when the verbal material is related to the movement only at a higher-order level. For example, in a play, a husband might suspect that his wife had had lunch with her lover, so he asks her where she ate that day while he casually walks over to the bar and makes himself a drink. There is no literal connection between the stroll to the bar and the question about lunch, but there is a goal-directed one: They are both attempts to appear casual while trying to entrap the wife. Despite this difference, an SPT-type effect occurs, showing enhanced memory for verbal material accompanied by physical movement.

In a recent paper on SPTs, Koriat and Pearlman-Avnion (2003) argued that clustering observed after verbal or enactive encoding suggested that different encoding strategies resulted in different types of memory organization, which in turn produced different patterns of recall. However, that study examined only action phrases typical of SPT experiments (e.g., "hammer a nail"), and the results would not appear applicable to recall of non-literal dialogue that neither describes nor implies the accompanying action (e.g., a character saying, "I think that's remarkable, Big Daddy" while walking away from his father). However, the generation effect (Slamecka & Graf, 1978) might help explain enhanced recall for both standard enactment and non-literal enactment because the participants necessarily generate the accompanying movements.

THEORIES OF EMBODIED COGNITION

Art Glenberg and his associates (among others) have advanced a theoretical position in which cognitive activities (including speech acts) are viewed as evolutionary outcomes of our need to make our way in the physical world (e.g., Glenberg & Robertson, 1999). The findings of the various experiments on the non-literal enactment effect appear completely consistent with this theoretical view. (For a fuller discussion of the connections between actors' processes and embodied cognition see Noice & Noice, 2001; see also Scott et al., 2001.)

Dance

Acting and dance make both expressive and technical demands on the performer. However, an actor who exhibits mastery of voice projection, great fluidity of movement, and flawless retention of the longest scripts, but whose performances lack the juices of life, would probably never find employment in any professional theatre. On the other hand, although a great dancer must be both an artist and a technician, the technical component is absolutely indispensable. An audience may greatly admire Barishnikov's inner fire, but it is his ability to leap to phenomenal heights and appear to remain suspended in midair that truly dazzles viewers. Thus, the relatively greater contribution of practice-derived technical skill in dance becomes one defining difference between the two art forms.

History

Although dance has been an important aspect of our cultural heritage since the beginning of recorded history, it became a performance art with the birth of ballet in Europe during the Renaissance (Cass, 1993). In the 1300s and 1400s, various forms of dance performance emerged to entertain the nobility. This movement reached its peak in France during the 1600s, and by the next century, ballet had become a recognized genre of art. Soon, dance grew into the primary entertainment for much of Europe (Steeh, 1982). Ballet eventually reached Russia, where, under the Czars, lavish costumes, impressive scenery, and luxurious theatres characterized the form. In addition, dancers started to devote themselves to a strict schedule of rigorous rehearsals to achieve systematic technique (Burian, 1963). Spearheaded by its preeminence in Russia, ballet spread throughout the world. In America, a Russian émigré, the late George Balanchine, founded The School of American Ballet to train outstanding dancers for his New York City Ballet, currently one of the best-known and most respected companies in the world (Gottlieb, 2004). Its neoclassical style places strong emphasis on original choreography (Steeh, 1982).

America has made notable contributions to two other contemporary dance forms. The first, modern dance (whose most famous exponent was Martha Graham) rejected the restrictions of ballet and opted for an approach where there are no rules other than providing an aesthetically satisfying experience through movement, especially spontaneous movement. Training for modern dance can be as rigorous as for ballet. Each company (Martha Graham, Hanya Holm, Merce Cunningham, Paul Taylor, Alvin Ailey, etc.) teaches original techniques and methods designed to fulfill their originator's visions (Cheney, 1989).

The newest dance discipline, jazz, is the dominant form on Broadway. Its exponents usually study both ballet and modern dance, then specialize in the choreographic stylizations of Bob Fosse, Michael Bennet, Susan Strohman, and other musical theatre innovators. (The other well-known form of dance, tap, is more a sound-based than a movement-based art. Indeed, its most expert exponents frequently appear at musical venues such as the Newport Jazz Festival [Stearns & Stearns, 1968]).

Acquisition of Dance Expertise

It is widely agreed that dance training (particularly ballet) involves physically changing the body while it is still malleable, so most dancers start formal instruction between the ages of seven and nine. Approximately the first ten years of training are devoted to physical preparation that provides balance, posture, control, elevation, and the ability to initiate and terminate movements to match musical phrasing (De Mille, 1962). After that preparation phase, dancers generally seek out professional classes and start auditioning for dance companies (Loren, 1978).

Although ballet is often thought to be rigid and highly codified, there are actually many different training methods, including the Cecchetti (Italian), the Vaganova (Russian), the RAD (British), and the Balanchine (American). Each technique differs in its terminology, use of hands and arms, and methods of flowing from one state to another. Only the five different foot positions are common to almost all approaches (Craine & Mackrell, 2000).

Moreover, expertise in dance consists of many components, some clearly defined and some highly elusive. The Danish ballet star Eric Bruhn (1968) said,

> *Behind the discipline and the form, behind whatever is the specific thing you are trying to express, there must be a mind . . . it isn't that the body is so different – it didn't fall out from Mars or from the moon. It came from where everybody came from, only somewhere along the road the mind began to take it someplace. (p. 13)*

Empirical Investigations into the Dancing Process

As with acting, much of the early scientific inquiry of dance focused on memory processes. Starkes, Deakin, Lindley, and Crisp (1987) published a seminal paper that anticipated much of the investigation carried out during the following decades.[1] The most frequently cited finding was that, as with other experts, ballet dancers demonstrated superior memory for domain-specific information. Participants were shown a videotape of either structured or unstructured dance segments. The former was professionally choreographed, whereas the latter combined the identical movements randomly. The dancers were assigned to one of three conditions: verbal recall of the structured version, motor recall of the structured version, and motor recall of the unstructured version. The researchers reported an advantage for experts in verbal or motor recall of the structured version but found no differences in motor performance of the unstructured one, the usual finding in expertise studies.

However, some exceptions to such domain-specificity in dance have been noted. Starkes, Caicco, Boutilier, and Sevsek (1990) reported that experienced modern dancers remembered all sequences better than novices but did not display an advantage for structured sequences, suggesting that modern dance (which includes far fewer labeled structural movements than ballet) requires the ability to recall any type of movement sequence. The authors opined that this may have been accomplished by acquiring a flexible mental representation that incorporates the whole range of movements used in modern dance.

Solso and Dallob (1995) examined the possibility that experts acquire such a flexible mental representation by extracting prototypical information from a wide variety of movements. The investigators constructed a simple, prototypical "base" dance that was used to generate a series of ten dances. (None of the ten exactly matched the prototype.) Twenty professional dancers and 34 non-dancers learned these sequences to criterion (one rendition without mistakes). Then the participants learned an additional set of seven dances (three "old," three "new," and the original prototype). More (but not significantly more) experts falsely recognized the prototype as "old." The researchers suggested that the experts probably kinesthetically abstracted prototypical information from the original learning (but see also Jean, Cadopi, & Ille, 2001).

Problems in Applying Expert/Novice Procedures to Dancers

An inherent problem with expert/novice research is that non-dancers are often incapable of executing even rudimentary techniques, thus making meaningful comparisons impossible. One way researchers have circumvented this difficulty is by matching two groups in terms of training, but not of ability. For example Starkes et al. (1987) compared the dancers from the local ballet schools with dancers from the National Ballet School, which recruits outstanding students through worldwide auditions. Both groups had similar dance experience (experts = 5.1 years; novices = 4.7 years).

Poon and Rodgers (2000) used a comparable approach, assigning dancers from a University of Alberta Jazz Dance class to the novice group (average training: 7.87 years) and selecting dancers from local professional programs for the expert group (average training: 9.25 years). However, the researchers believed that previous

expert/novice experiments might not have fully uncovered the details of dancers' learning strategies because a test routine that was easy enough for a novice was too simple for an expert. Therefore, the investigators created different sets of dance sequences, judged by experienced dance instructors to clearly belong to the *easy* or *difficult* category. As predicted, the novice dancers lacked the sophisticated strategies necessary to cope with the difficult sequences and the expert dancers tended to abandon their usual strategies when faced with the simple ones. The researchers concluded that, in order to shed light on dancing expertise, stimuli would have to be created in which the relative difficulty of each sequence would be approximately the same when skill level was taken into consideration.

Mental Devices for Remembering Dance Patterns

Some dancers appear to encode steps by a process called "marking" in which they make small hand movements as they mentally rehearse a dance combination, resulting in superior retention while conserving energy (Starkes et al., 1987). Also, expert dancers employ multiple encoding devices, including using verbal labels to represent a series of movements (e.g., *step to the side, step together, step to the side* would be remembered simply as *chassé*; Poon & Rodgers, 2000).

The latter investigators also reported a difficulty endemic to expertise research with professionals. During the study, their novice group was always available but their expert group was cut in half by an unexpected rehearsal, resulting in the remaining expert dancers having to perform twice as many tasks as the novices in order for the researchers to complete their design.

Use of Imagery and Proprioception

In an attempt to see if the well known SPT (subject-performed task) effect extended to simple dance movements, Foley, Bouffard, Raag, and Disanto-Rose (1991, Experiment 1) found that both common and uncommon movements were remembered equally well as long as the participants (non-dancers) performed them or imagined themselves performing them. However, lower recall was found for uncommon movements when these non-dancers tried to learn them by observing or by imagining another person performing. The researchers speculated that the participants who were imagining themselves performing might have experienced greater enactive encoding of the sort responsible for the SPT effect (e.g., Engelkamp & Zimmer, 1990). In Experiment 2, using both dancers and non-dancers, the investigators found that neither the availability of verbal descriptions nor stored motor representations were necessary for memory to be enhanced by enactment, but they did find a domain-specific effect of imagery. That is, dancers reported greater ease in imagining themselves performing dance movements than novices did, although dancers and non-dancers considered themselves equal in general imagery ability (e.g., picturing a boat on a lake).

To investigate relative use of imagery among disciplines, Overby, Hall, and Haslam (1998) sent questionnaires to dance teachers, figure skating coaches, and soccer coaches. They found that, among the 44 dance teachers who responded, the majority employed both kinesthetic imagery and metaphorical imagery ("Imagine you're moving through water"). The teachers reported that such metaphorical imagery was highly effective in getting dancers to move slowly and smoothly from one location to another. Kinesthetic and metaphorical imagery were used far less by sports coaches.

In an experiment to investigate dependence on proprioception, Golomer and DuPui (2000) employed a precariously balanced seesaw attached to an accelerometer (otherwise known as a stabilometer). Dancers and non-dancers were assessed on their ability to remain upright with eyes open (vision dependent balance) and eyes closed (proprioceptive dependent balance). Results showed that dancers (particularly adult male dancers) depended more on proprioception and less on vision than non-

dancers. The investigators referred to this as *sensorimotor proprioception dominance*. Further evidence for proprioception comes from a study by Smyth and Pendelton (1994). They demonstrated that dancers' memories for dance patterns were disrupted by concurrent motor tasks or concurrent verbal tasks, suggesting that both types of information are implicated in performance.

Music Cues

Music and dance are integrally linked, with the former almost always accompanying the latter. Starkes et al. (1987, Experiment 1) examined the role that music played in producing a serial position effect for dance movements. They had experts and novices view dance sequences without accompanying music. In the subsequent recall phase, no evidence was found for a recency effect, so common in verbal-recall studies. In Experiment 2, they had experts view a sequence of eight ballet steps accompanied by music, then administered a recall task either with or without music. Music exerted a significant recall advantage especially on the most recent step of the sequence.

Poon and Rodgers (2000) reported that experts and novices differed in their handling of musical cues. The researchers collected verbal protocols based on 20- to 30-minute semi-structured interviews held immediately following the learning of new dance routines. The findings revealed that expert dancers made far greater use of music cues, attending to high and low notes, specific rhythmic phrases, and so on. The protocols showed also that experts used musical counts while creating fewer but larger chunks, which they learned separately, and not necessarily in the original order. All novices in the study tried to learn the first segment, then add on the second, and so forth. Furthermore, the novices tended to find the music distracting and either paid no attention or deliberately ignored it.

The Expressive Aspects

A dance performance is far more than a display of technique, yet there appears to be little consensus on methods of training for the expressive components. In ballet companies, young dancers frequently learn roles from older dancers who have previously performed them, a process that includes the interpretive aspects. Also, many dancers take separate acting classes on their own initiative (B. Doyle-Wilch, personal correspondence, July 16, 2004), but in response to a query, the associate chair of one of the country's larger college dance programs wrote, "We do not offer or require any form of acting classes within our dance programs" (R. Woodbury, personal correspondence, July 8, 2004).

Conclusion

Although many aspects of artistic performance are being clarified through empirical inquiry, much remains to be done. For example, great performing artists do not always give emotionally moving performances and lesser ones often do. Such differences cannot be ascribed to length or type of training, experience, motivation, or any other tangible factor, but are a continuing part of the mystery of artistic endeavor. Indeed, understanding the true nature of these complex arts will probably call for many more decades of interdisciplinary cooperation between actors/dancers and researchers in such disparate fields as expertise, memory, movement, emotion, and consciousness.

Footnote

1. There is also a large literature on movement in sports that is highly pertinent here (see Hodges, Starkes, & MacMahon, Chapter 27).

References

Adler, S. (1988). *The technique of acting.* New York: Bantam Books.

Archer, W. (1888). *Masks or faces?* London: Longmans, Green, & Co.

Barton, R. (1993). *Style for actors.* Mountain View, CA: Mayfield Publishing.

Bee, B. (Producer and Director), & Bragg, M. (Editor). (1982). *Laurence Olivier, a life.* [Video recording]. Chicago, IL: Public Media Video.

Brockett, O. G. (1991). *History of the theatre.* (6th ed.). Boston, MA: Allyn and Bacon.

Bruhn, E. (1968). *Beyond technique.* New York: Johnson Reprint Corporation.

Burian, K. V. (1963). *The story of world ballet.* London, England: Allan Wingate.

Cass, J. (1993). *Dancing through history.* Englewood Cliffs, NJ: Prentice-Hall.

Chase, W. G., & Simon, H. A. (1973). Perception in chess. *Cognitive Psychology, 4,* 55–81.

Cheney, G. (1989). *Basic concepts in modern dance: A creative approach.* Princeton, NJ: A Dance Horizons Book.

Cohen, R. (1994). *Theatre.* Mountain View, CA: Mayfield Publishing.

Cohen, R. L. (1989). Memory for action events: The power of enactment. *Educational Psychology Review, 1,* 57–80.

Craine, D., & Mackrell, J. (2000). *The Oxford dictionary of dance.* Oxford: Oxford University Press.

De Mille, A. (1962). *To a young dancer.* Boston: Little, Brown and Company.

Diderot, D. (1957). *The paradox of acting.* (W. H. Pollock, Trans.) New York: Hill and Wang. (Original work published 1830.)

Engelkamp, J., & Zimmer, H. D. (1990). Memory for actions events. A new field of research. *Psychological Research, 51,* 153–157.

Ericsson, K. A., & Kintsch, W. (1995). Long-term working memory. *Psychological Review, 102* (2), 211–245.

Foley, M. A., Bouffard, V., Raag, T., & Disanto-Rose, M. (1991). The effects of enactive encoding, type of movement, and imagined perspective on memory of dance. *Psychological Research, 53,* 251–259.

Friedland, R. P., Fritsch, T., Smyth, K. A., Koss, E., Lerner, A. J., Chen, C. H., et al. (2001). Patients with Alzheimer's disease have reduced activities in midlife compared with healthy control-group members. *Proceeding of the National Academy of Sciences, 98* (6), 3440–3445.

Futterman, A. D., Kemeny, M. E., Shapiro, D., Polonsky, W., & Fahey, J. L. (1992). Immunological variability associated with experimentally-induced positive and negative affective states. *Psychological Medicine, 22,* 231–238.

Glenberg, A. M., & Robertson, D. A. (1999). Indexical understanding of instructions. *Discourse Processes*, 28, 1–26.

Golomer, E., & Dupui, P. (2000). Spectral analysis of adult dancers' sways: Sex and interaction vision – proprioception. *International Journal of Neuroscience*, 105, 15–26.

Gottlieb, R. (2004). *George Balanchine: The ballet maker*. New York: Harper Collins.

Guskin, H. (2003). *How to stop acting*. New York: Faber and Faber.

Intons-Peterson, M. J., & Smyth, M. M. (1987). The anatomy of repertory memory. *Journal of Experimental Psychology: Learning, Memory, and Cognition*, 13 (3), 490–500.

Jean, J., Cadopi, M., & Ille, A. (2001). How are dance sequences encoded and recalled by expert dancers? *Current Psychology of Cognition*, 20 (5), 325–337.

Kelso, M. T, Weyhrauch, P., & Bates, J. (1993). Dramatic presence. *Presence*, 2 (1), 1–15.

Konijn, E. A. (2000). *Acting emotions: Shaping emotions on stage*. (B. Leach, Trans.) Amsterdam: Amsterdam University Press.

Koriat, A., & Pearlman-Avnion, S. (2003). Memory organization of action events and its relationship to memory performance. *Journal of Experimental Psychology: General*, 132 (3), 435–454.

Lemeignan, M., Aguilera-Torres, & Bloch, S. (1992). Emotional effector patterns: Recognition of expressions. *European Bulletin of Cognitive Psychology*, 12, 173–188.

Levenson, R. W., Ekman, P., & Friesen, W. V. (1990). Voluntary facial action generates emotion-specific autonomic nervous system activity. *Psychophysiology*, 27 (4). 363–394.

Loren, T. (1978). *The dancer's companion*. New York: Dial Press.

Meisner, S., & Longwell, D. (1987). *Sanford Meisner on acting*. New York: Vintage Books.

Morris, E. (1985). *Irreverent acting*. New York: Putnam Publishing.

Nilsson, L-G. (2000). Remembering actions and words. In E. Tulving & F. I. M. Craik (Eds.), *The Oxford handbook of memory* (pp. 137–148). New York: Oxford University Press.

Noice, A. A. (1995). *The application of learning and memory principles of cognitive science to an actor's ability to perform "in the moment."* (Doctoral dissertation, Wayne State University, 1995). *Dissertation Abstracts International Sec-

tion A: Humanities & Social Sciences*, 56 (5-A), 1586.

Noice, H. (1991). The role of explanations and plan recognition in the learning of theatrical scripts. *Cognitive Science*, 15, 425–460.

Noice, H. (1992). Elaborative memory strategies of professional actors. *Applied Cognitive Psychology*, 6, 417–427.

Noice, H. (1993). Effects of rote versus gist strategy on the verbatim retention of theatrical scripts. *Applied Cognitive Psychology*, 7, 75–84.

Noice, H., & Noice, T. (1993). The effects of segmentation on the recall of theatrical material. *Poetics*, 22, 51–67.

Noice, H., & Noice, T. (1994). An example of role preparation by a professional actor: A think-aloud protocol. *Discourse Processes*, 18, 345–369.

Noice, H., & Noice, T. (1996). Two approaches to learning a theatrical script. *Memory*, 4 (1), 1–17.

Noice, T., & Noice, H. (1997a). *Expertise of professional actors: A cognitive view*. Hillsdale, NJ: Erlbaum.

Noice, T., & Noice, H. (1997b). Effort and active experiencing as factors in verbatim recall. *Discourse Processes*, 23, 51–69.

Noice, H., & Noice, T. (1999). Long-term retention of theatrical roles. *Memory*, 7 (3), 357–382.

Noice, H., & Noice, T. (2001). Learning dialogue with and without movement. *Memory and Cognition*, 29 (6), 820–828.

Noice, T., & Noice, H. (2002a). A review of recent research on the expertise of professional actors. *High Ability Studies*, 13, (1), 7–19.

Noice, T., & Noice, H. (2002b). Very long-term recall and recognition of well-learned material. *Applied Cognitive Psychology*, 16, 259–272.

Noice, T., & Noice, H. (2004). A cognitive learning principle derived from the role acquisition strategies of professional actors. *Cognitive Technology*, 9 (1), 34–39.

Noice, H., Noice, T., & Kennedy, C. (2000). The contribution of movement on the recall of complex material. *Memory*, 8 (6), 353–363.

Noice, H., & Noice, T., & Staines, G. (2004). A short-term intervention to enhance cognitive and affective functioning in older adults. *Journal of Aging and Health*, 16 (4), 1–24.

Noice, T. (2004). [Phenomenology of acting.] Unpublished raw data.

Oliver, W. L., & Ericsson, K. A. (1986). Repertory actors' memory for their parts. *Proceedings of the Eighth Annual Conference of the Cognitive Science Society*, Amherst, MA (pp. 399–406). Hillsdale, NJ: Erlbaum.

Overby, L., Hall, C., & Haslam, I. (1998). A comparison of imagery used by dance teachers, figure skating coaches, and soccer coaches. *Imagination, Cognition and Personality*, 17 (4), 323–337.

Poon, P. P. L., & Rodgers, W. M. (2000). Learning and remembering strategies of novice and advanced jazz dancers for skill level appropriate dance routings. *Research Quarterly for Exercise and Sport*, 71 (2), 135–144.

Roach, J. R. (1985). *The player's passion: Studies in the science of acting*. Newark, NJ: University of Delaware Press.

Rolf, B. (1977). *Behind the mask*. Oakland, CA: Persona Books.

Rudlin, J. (2000). Jacques Copeau: The quest for sincerity. In A. Hodge (Ed.), *Twentieth Century actor training* (pp. 55–78). New York: Routledge.

Schmidt, H. G., Boshuizen, H. P. A., & van Breukelen, G. J. P. (2002). Long-term retention of a theatrical script by repertory actors: The role of context. *Memory*, 10 (1), 21–28.

Scott, C. L., Harris, R. J., & Rothe, A. R. (2001). Embodied cognition through improvisation improves memory for a dramatic monologue. *Discourse Processes*, 31 (3), 293–305.

Shakespeare, W. (1992). *Hamlet*. New York: Washington Square Press. (Original work published in 1604.)

Slamecka, N. Y., & Graf, P. (1978). The generation effect: Delineation of a phenomenon. *Journal of Experiment Psychology: Human Learning and Memory*, 4, 592–604.

Smyth, M. M., & Pendleton, L. R. (1994). Memory for movement in professional ballet dancers. *International Journal of Sport Psychology*, 25, 282–294.

Solso, R. L., & Dallop, P. (1995). Prototype formation among professional dancers. *Empirical Studies of the Arts*, 13 (1), 3–16.

Spolin, V. (1963). *Improvisation for the theater*. Evanston, IL: Northwestern University Press.

Stanislavski, C. (1936). *An actor prepares*. New York: Theatre Arts Books.

Stanislavski, C. (1961). *Creating a role*. New York: Theatre Arts Books.

Starkes, J. L, Deakin, J. M., Lindley, S., & Crisp, F. (1987). Motor versus verbal recall of ballet sequences by young expert dancers. *Journal of Sport Psychology*, 90, 222–230.

Starkes, J. L., Caicco, M., Boutilier, C., & Sevsek, B. (1990). Motor recall of experts for structured and unstructured sequences in creative modern dance. *Journal of Sport and Exercise Psychology*, 12, 317–321.

Steeh, J. (1982). *Story of ballet and other modern dance*. New York: Galahad Books.

Stearns, M., & Stearns, J. (1968). *Jazz dance*. New York: Schirmer Books.

Vilga, E. (1997). *Acting now*. New Brunswick, NJ: Rutgers University Press.

Vineberg, S. (1991). *Method actors*. New York: Schirmer Books.

Watzman, A. (2004) *Meet Valerie, Carnegie Mellon's first storytelling robotceptionists*. Retrieved March 11, 2004, from http://www.cmu.edu/cmnews/extra/040219_Valerie.html.

Wilson, R. S., Mendes de Leon, C. F., Barnes, L. L., Schneider, J. A., Bienias, J. L., Evans, D. A., et al. (2002). Participation in cognitively stimulating activities and risk of incident Alzheimer Disease. *The Journal of the American Medical Association*, 287 (6), 742–748.

CHAPTER 29

Perceptual-Motor Expertise

David A. Rosenbaum, Jason S. Augustyn,
Rajal G. Cohen, & Steven A. Jax

Introduction

If we consider perceptual-motor expertise as a subset of expertise in general, two questions immediately come to mind: (1) What can a focus on expertise in general contribute to the study of perceptual-motor expertise in particular, and (2) What can a focus on perceptual-motor skill contribute to the study of expertise more broadly? Excellent reviews have already addressed the first question (Starkes & Allard, 1993; Starkes & Ericsson, 2003). Less has been done in connection with the second question, which will be the focus of our presentation. (See also Proctor and Vu, Chapter 15.)

Our primary thesis is that the study of perceptual-motor expertise may have useful lessons for the study of expertise in general. The basis for this suggestion is that the study of perceptual-motor skill acquisition has witnessed rapid advances with different methodologies in the past several years. At the same time, it has seen intense debate about which of these methodologies is most appropriate. Describing this debate may be informative for researchers who study expertise in more complex tasks because it is reasonable to think that the debate will come knocking at their doors before long.

The methods pursued in the study of perceptual-motor expertise are associated with two perspectives: (1) Cognitive science (including cognitive psychology and neuroscience); and (2) Ecological psychology and dynamical systems analysis. Each of these perspectives has characteristic claims and techniques which compete for attention and support. Researchers in each tradition acknowledge that both approaches may be necessary, but methodological and theoretical differences often make synthesis between them difficult. This sometimes-uneasy relationship between these perspectives may signal how things will go in the study of more complex tasks.

Before turning to the substance of the chapter, we should post some disclaimers. First, this is not meant to be an exhaustive review. Other, more complete reviews of work on perceptual-motor skill acquisition have appeared elsewhere (e.g., Schmidt & Lee, 1999). Second, we have chosen to highlight the cornerstone concepts associated with each approach. This selectivity necessarily forces exclusion of useful findings. Third and finally, we use the term "expertise" in a way that is a bit unorthodox. Most investigators who study expertise argue that the study of the most accomplished practitioners of a skill provides a window into the factors that underlie the skill's development. We agree with this perspective but note that most tasks investigated by students of perceptual-motor skill are ones that can be mastered by virtually everyone (e.g., reaching for a glass of water). This makes their acquisition unremarkable, except for the fact that the apparent simplicity of these skills frequently eludes their mimicry by robotic systems. Still, even mundane skills such as reaching and grasping must be learned, and it seems reasonable to suspect that mechanisms supporting learning of commonplace skills will also support acquisition of skills commonly viewed as being more sophisticated.

Our review of perceptual-motor skill acquisition begins with some evidence for similarities between expertise in perceptual-motor skills and intellectual skills. Then we offer a brief review of neural plasticity before focusing on three concepts that have emerged from cognitive psychology: (1) Elements involved in the control of perceptual-motor activities are linked to one another; (2) Actions are guided by prediction of sensory feedback; and (3) Attention becomes less valuable as skill grows. Much of the classical and current work on the cognitive substrates of perceptual-motor expertise can be traced to these ideas. Last, we discuss the contributions from the ecological/dynamical systems approach.

Similarities between Perceptual Motor Skills and More Intellectual Functions

The gulf between a computer's ability to play chess and its inability to perform common acts of manual dexterity might lead one to believe that the systems underlying intellectual skill obey different principles than the systems underlying perceptual-motor skills. If that were true, the study of perceptual-motor expertise might bear little on the study of intellectual expertise and vice versa. However, the evidence from human performance reveals quite another picture. In fact, it is nearly impossible to find meaningful differences between the factors affecting the acquisition of perceptual-motor skills and those affecting the acquisition of intellectual skills (Rosenbaum, Carlson, & Gilmore, 2001; Schmidt & Bjork, 1992). That this is so is perhaps not surprising in view of the fact that the same neurophysiological principles support both kinds of learning. Nevertheless, we can go beyond a reductionist base to see common principles.

One similarity between intellectual and perceptual-motor skill is the short-term benefit of massed over spaced practice. Practicing a task *without* breaks leads to better performance immediately after practice than does practicing the same task *with* breaks, and this is true both for intellectual (Glenberg, 1997) and perceptual-motor tasks (Shea & Morgan, 1979). After several hours of consolidation the relative benefit of massed over spaced practice reverses when one assesses learning over the long term. Then, spaced practice leads to better long-term retention than does blocked or massed practice, and again this is true both for intellectual and perceptual-motor tasks. Magill and Hall (1990) provided a review of the relevant evidence for perceptual-motor skills, and Melton (1970), Landauer and Bjork (1978), and Rea and Modigliani (1985) wrote analogous reviews for intellectual skills.

A similar interaction exists between time of test and frequency of feedback. If participants are given frequent feedback about their performance on perceptual-motor tasks or on intellectual tasks, their performance in the *short term* is better than if they are given frequent feedback. However, their performance in the *long term* is better in both domains if they are given infrequent rather than frequent feedback during training. See Schmidt and Bjork (1992) for review.

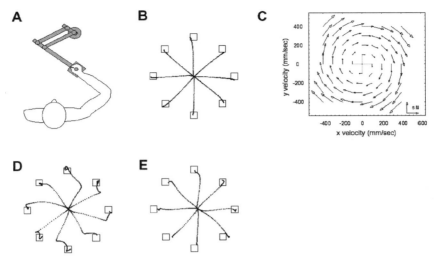

Figure 29.1. Adaptation to an artificial force field. (A). Overview of the subject grasping a handle connected to two joints powered by torque motors. (B). Normal handpaths in center-to-target or target-to-center movements. (C) Artificial force field. (D) Initial distortions of movements to the artificial force field. (E) Adapted movements, achieved five minutes later. From Brashers-Krug, T., Shadmehr, R., & Bizzi, E. (1996). Consolidation in human motor memory. *Nature*, 382, 252–255.

The phenomenon of consolidation also characterizes both the learning of perceptual-motor skills and the acquisition of more intellectual information. As is well known from studies establishing the existence of short-term memory, new memories for declarative information are fragile and only come to be crystallized after several hours of consolidation. Consolidation characterizes procedural learning as well as declarative learning, as shown in a study by Brashers-Krug, Shadmehr, and Bizzi (1996). Their participants learned to move a hand to targets in the horizontal plane while resisting velocity-dependent forces applied by a robot (Figure 29.1). After a few minutes, the participants could generate hand paths that were as straight as those they generated in normal circumstances. When the same participants returned to the task the next day, they performed *better* than they had at the end of training on the first day, reflecting consolidation. In contrast, participants who performed an interfering task immediately after the first task (moving against a manipulandum that pushed in the opposite direction from that encountered in the first task) showed no improvement on the second day. Finally, if a four-hour delay was interposed between performance of the primary and interfering tasks, consolidation was evident on the second day. Thus, some intervening period, perhaps as long as four hours, was needed for consolidation of this kind of procedural learning. Whether consolidation merely reflected recovery from fatigue is still an open question.

Reliance on instance retrieval or on computation is another property of perceptual-motor skill acquisition and the acquisition of more intellectual skill. As is well known from studies of mathematical problem solving, over the course of learning there is a shift from generation to recall of solutions (Logan, 1988, 2002). When asked, "What is the product of 13 times 13?" the novice problem-solver derives the result by applying the rules of multiplication. However, with practice the problem-solver recalls that the answer is 169. Cohen and Rosenbaum (2004) showed that a similar shift occurs in the everyday perceptual-motor task of taking hold of a vertical cylinder and moving it from one place to another.

A final piece of evidence for the commonality of intellectual and perceptual-motor skills comes from neuroscience. Early work by Holmes (1939) showed that damage to the cerebellum often resulted in reduced muscle tone, delayed movement initiation, motor planning errors, and tremor. These observations led to the view that the cerebellum controls and coordinates movement. Other work has shown that the cerebellum also subserves cognitive functioning (Fiez, 1996; Leiner, Leiner, & Dow, 1995). Cerebellar damage can lead to deficits in conditioning (Bracke-Tolkmitt, Linden, Canavan, & Diener, 1989) as well as disruptions in the analysis of temporal duration (Ivry & Keele, 1989). Brain-imaging studies have shown that the cerebellum is active during performance of tasks as varied as word generation (Petersen, Fox, Posner, Mintun, & Raichle, 1989), tactile discrimination (Gao, Parsons, Bower, Xiong, 1996), sequence learning (Jenkins, Brooks, Nixon, Frankowiak, & Passignham, 1994), and maintenance of information in working memory (Desmond, Gabrielli, Wagner, Binier, & Glover, 1997). Courchesne and Allen (1997) proposed that the cerebellum contributes to the prediction and preparation of sequences, broadly construed. Insofar as sequences can consist of symbols (the *sine qua non* of intellectual skills) or stimuli and responses (the *sine qua non* of perceptual-motor skills), the cerebellum may be viewed as an organ subserving both perceptual-motor skills and intellectual skills.

Neural Plasticity

For any skill to be learned, changes must occur in the nervous system. (see Hill and Schneider, Chapter 37.) Classically, neuroscientists have analyzed such changes at the level of the synapse (Hebb, 1949; Kandel, 1981; Lynch & Baudry, 1984). A great deal of work has extended this analysis to the study of changes in the functional properties of neural pools (Kaas, Merzenich, & Killackey, 1983). In contrast to older models of neuronal processes, there is growing consensus that such neural plasticity is a fundamental characteristic of brain organization.

Neural plasticity plays a role in perceptual-motor skill learning. Brain-imaging research has revealed enlargement of functionally relevant cortical areas in musicians who play stringed instruments such as the violin or cello (Elbert, Pantev, Wienbruch, Rockstroh, & Taub, 1995). These individuals have more brain tissue that responds to touch with the fingers of the left hand (the hand normally used for depressing the strings) than brain tissue that responds to touch with the fingers of the right hand (the hand that normally bows). Furthermore, the difference between left- and right-hand somatosensory areas grows with practice. Similar changes in neural representation occur as monkeys (Logothetis & Pauls, 1995) and humans (Gauthier, Skudlarski, Gore, & Anderson, 2000) develop perceptual expertise in recognizing objects.

These results fit with a view of the nervous system as a competitive arena in which perceptual-motor representations jockey for limited tracts of neural tissue. The findings also accord with hypotheses from cognitive psychology that posit inhibition among psychological elements (Dagenbach & Carr, 1994).

Elements of Motor Plans

The concept of associations among psychological elements has figured prominently in the study of perceptual-motor skill acquisition. The main questions about them are how the elements are assembled and how the assembly changes as skill develops.

One hypothesis regarding assembly is that elements underlying successive behaviors are linearly arranged such that one element triggers the next. For early behaviorists, the triggering signal was feedback: Performance of a movement caused by activation of element *i* generated feedback that activated element $i + 1$, and so on. This idea was refuted by Lashley (1951), who noted that feedback loops take too long to explain rapid performance, as in keyboard sequences of skilled pianists. He also observed, based on clinical work, that disruption of feedback loops does not prevent performance of basic movement sequences. Lashley argued that close examination of behavior suggested that successively executed movements cannot be triggered by immediate, prior activation of their associated control elements. Rather, the elements are activated well in advance. The ensemble of such activated elements constitutes a *plan* for ensuing action. By assuming plans for forthcoming action sequences, Lashley could account for the results just reviewed as well as errors in performance, such as slips of the tongue, that reflect knowledge of what will be said later. The spoonerism "...queer old dean" instead of the presumably intended "...dear old queen" is an example.

A rich set of data has been accumulated in support of Lashley's hypothesis. Among the relevant findings are changes in brain activity that reliably predict distinguishing properties of forthcoming actions (e.g., Jeannerod, 1988), changes in the time to initiate and complete movement sequences as a function of their length and complexity (e.g., Klapp, 1977; Rosenbaum, 1987), changes in the way early features of movement sequences are performed depending on what movements will be performed later (e.g., Cohen & Rosenbaum, 2004), and analyses of errors in speech (e.g., Dell, 1986; Fromkin, 1980), typewriting (Cooper, 1983), and other activities (Norman, 1981; Reason, 1990). Modern movement-recording techniques have also shown that ongoing movements are sufficiently overlapped in time that it is difficult to individuate successive movements, or even tell whether the order in which successive movements are completed comports with the order in which they were initiated. In this connection, Grudin (1983) showed that during typewriting, the fingers move toward their keys as soon as they can, such that in skilled typists, the fingers move in a blur, not in a neatly sequenced chain. Find-

ings such as these cannot easily be accommodated by a theory that holds that each movement is triggered by feedback from some previous movement. Instead, a plan is needed to enable the effectors to move to their targets with appropriate timing.

Many of the insights into the nature of perceptual-motor expertise were anticipated over a century ago by Bryan and Harter (1897, 1899), who suggested that perceptual-motor skill development relies on the formation of ever more inclusive routines. Low-level control elements are joined together by higher-level control elements, these higher-level control elements are in turn subsumed by still higher-order elements, and so on. The idea is familiar to computer programmers, who know that routines call lower-level subroutines, which in turn call other, still lower-level subroutines. One does not have to be a programmer nor subscribe to the computer metaphor of mind to appreciate that nested structures are vital for the control of behavior. The concept of the "chunk" introduced by Miller in his famous 1956 paper embraced the concept of subroutines while effectively sounding the death knell for the prevailing computer metaphor of the time – Shannon and Weaver's (1949) information theory. Chunking is the formation of successively embedded data structures used for storage of information or control of output. Shannon and Weaver's information theory held that data content could be meaningfully measured in terms of the number of binary ("yes/no") decisions needed to uniquely identify an event. As Miller pointed out, however, the number of items that can be held in immediate memory is not dictated by the number of such binary decisions but instead is determined by the number of meaningful elements or "chunks" into which participant can organize presentations. People can store seven plus or minus two nonsense syllables, but they can also store seven plus or minus two complex propositions comprised of scores of syllables, provided the propositions fit with people's experience. With proper training in memorizing random digits, people can boost their ostensive short-term memory

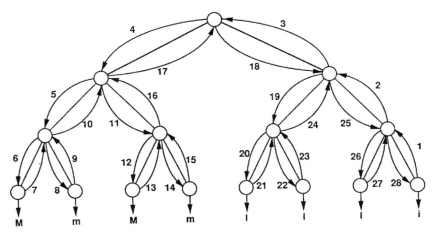

Figure 29.2. Tree-traversal model for rapid, repeated production of button presses made with the right middle finger (M), the left middle finger (m), the right index finger (I), and the left index finger (i). Numbers correspond to steps in the tree-traversal process beginning here after production of the final left index finger response (the rightmost terminal node).

capacity by an order of magnitude (Chase & Ericsson, 1981).

The idea of chunking, proposed in the late nineteenth century by Bryan and Harter (1897, 1899) and revitalized by Miller (1956), can be shown to lead to the Power Law of Learning (Newell & Rosenbloom, 1981). If the time to form a higher-level chunk grows with the number of chunks it subsumes, and if the formation of a higher-level chunk affords a reduction in the time to perform a task, then the time, T, to perform the task should decrease with the number of practice trials, P, in which the task is practiced. Moreover, the rate at which the time to perform the task decreases should in turn decrease over practice trials. Expressed mathematically, $T = a\,P^{-b}$, where a and b are nonnegative empirical constants.

If the psychological elements underlying perceptual-motor control are organized hierarchically, they may be unpacked in a regular fashion for purposes of production. According to this view, higher-order elements are unpacked into their immediate descendants, the descendants are in turn unpacked into their descendants, and so on. Provided there is a way of temporally ordering the unpacking of the descendants, one has a "tree-traversal" process (see Figure 29.2). Tree-

traversal routines are familiar to computer users. To get to a directory, one opens the directory in which it is contained. Alternatively, one could imagine that the terminal, or lowest-level, elements of the hierarchy are simply "read off" in sequence without involving higher units. The available evidence suggests that this is not what happens. For example, when people recall hierarchically organized keyboard sequences by keying them as rapidly as possible, the errors they make and the times between successive keystrokes are consistent with tree-traversal rather than rapid read-off of terminal nodes only (Povel & Collard, 1982; Restle, 1970; Rosenbaum, Kenny, & Derr, 1983; Simon, 1972). The same conclusion holds if the output medium is speech rather than keyboarding (Cooper & Paccia-Cooper, 1980).

The latter outcome reflects a similarity between performance and perception. As first shown by Sperling (1960), raw perceptual information is first entered in a limited-capacity buffer from which it is rapidly lost unless it is transferred to long-term storage. Unless the information is transferred and allowed to make contact with already formed meaning-bearing representations, there is little chance it will be available later (Kroll & Potter, 1984). The data reviewed in the last paragraph lead to a similar conclusion for motor output. If one supposes that there is a buffer for the output of motor commands, the buffer cannot be very large, for otherwise one would expect motor commands for extended sequences of forthcoming motor acts to be read off serially from the terminal elements of the hierarchy without access to higher-level elements. Instead, a very small set of terminal elements is available for output. Between these outputs, retrieval is needed from higher-level representations.

Responding to Feedback

The second major concept in the cognitive approach to perceptual-motor expertise concerns prediction and feedback. When one carries out a purposeful action, one typically seeks to effect perceptible changes in the environment. Whether the action is as mundane as lifting one's arm to stretch or as dramatic as raising one's arm to volunteer for a dangerous mission, there is a correspondence between the plan underlying the action and the feedback one expects as a result of it. Of course, in the case of volunteering for a dangerous mission, feeling one's arm rise up does not provide feedback about the success of the mission. By contrast, in the case of raising one's arm to stretch, feeling the arm ascend gives assurance that the intended movement occurred as planned. A challenge for theories of perceptual-motor skill is to understand how plans and feedback are integrated over these very different scales of experience. An equally important question is how the interaction of plans and feedback changes with practice.

For feedback to usefully guide behavior, one must have a representation of what feedback is expected given the action one intends to perform. In control theory, this representation is known as a *reference condition*. In effect, a reference condition is a prediction of what perceptual change will ensue as a result of forthcoming action. The development of perceptual-motor expertise builds on the capacity to make such predictions.

An important forerunner of current ideas about prediction was Helmholtz (1911), who argued that perception relies, at least in part, on unconscious inference: Given ambiguity about the objective source of proximal stimuli (e.g., images cast on the retina), one must engage in a kind of unconscious problem solving to discern the objective source. See Purves and Lott (2003) for a statistical version of this theory. An instance of unconscious inference that Helmholtz described was deciding whether the external environment moves when one's eyes move. Eye movements produce retinal image shifts, but so do movements of the external environment when the eyes are still. How, then, does one distinguish between these two events? Helmholtz and others following him (e.g., von Holst & Mittelstaedt, 1950) suggested that copies of eye-muscle motor commands are sent to perceptual centers and these signals are used to interpret subsequent visual input. One may think of this "efference copy" as providing a basis for predicting the perceptual consequences of imminent eye movements. In the case of initiating an eye movement when the retinal image is stationary, the eye movement should cause a sweep of the image across the retina. When such a predicted sweep occurs, the agent can be satisfied that the eye moved but the world did not.

Forming predictions about the perceptual consequences of voluntary actions helps explain other phenomena – for example, why we don't see the world go dark when we blink our eyes (Volkman, Riggs, & Moore, 1980) and why we can't tickle ourselves (Blakemore, Wolpert, & Frith, 1998). Other experimental demonstrations are similarly explained via prediction, including motor imagery, imitation of others' behavior, and the fact that reaction time is generally shorter for responses to stimuli that are similar to the perceptual effects the responses engender than to stimuli that are not similar to the responses' usual or learned perceptual effects. See Hommel, Musseler, Aschersleben, and Prinz (2001) for review.

Many studies indicate that people learn new perceptual-motor skills by forming ever more accurate predictions of the consequences of their actions. For example, when one adapts to novel force fields, as occurs in outer space or other unusual inertial environments (Dizio & Lackner, 1995), or when one takes hold of a heavy object such as a hammer (Sainburg, 2002), it is essential to alter one's motor commands to achieve the limb displacement one wants. Changing the motor commands solely in response to error is not adaptive in the long run, for then one's performance lags the intended outcome. Research on adaptation to artificial force fields has shown that human adults can indeed adapt to such fields by anticipating forces in different parts of the workspace, including, most impressively, parts of the workspace that were not previously visited. Generalizing to new regions has been shown to reflect true function learning rather than simple averaging of previously learned instances (Conditt, Gandolfo, & Mussa-Ivaldi, 1997; Goodbody & Wolpert, 1998), as is true of function learning in other tasks (Koh & Meyer, 1991; Lewandowsky, Kalish, & Ngang, 2002). Moreover, as shown by Körding and Wolpert (2004), predictions made during perceptual-motor skill learning are tuned to statistical properties of the environment. This finding comports with the observation that performers are sensitive to the variability of their own performance (Meyer, Abrams, Kornblum, Wright, & Smith, 1988; Worringham, 1993).

Attention

The third insight on expertise from cognitive psychology is that the role of attention changes as skill develops. The differential involvement of attention in skilled performance was made explicit in a three-stage model developed by Fitts and Posner (1967) and in a distinction made famous by Shiffrin and Schneider (1977) between controlled and automatic processes.

In the model of Fitts and Posner, an individual learning a new skill progresses through a cognitive stage, followed by an associative stage, followed by an automatic or "autonomous" stage. The cognitive stage is characterized by a relatively "intellectual" approach to task performance in which one is highly reliant on instructions and attends closely to cues and feedback. Performance is characterized by deliberate control of the separate elements of a skill and lacks the fluidity that characterizes later stages of performance. Such coordination develops during the associative stage, in which the elements of a skill become integrated into more elaborate procedures that may be rapidly and flexibly deployed. Finally, in the autonomous stage, performance becomes more independent of cognitive control and attention plays a diminishing role. At the same time, the performer becomes less vulnerable to interference from competing environmental cues.

A fundamental lesson of the Fitts-Posner model is that skill acquisition is accompanied by decreasing reliance on conscious cognitive control and focused attention. Shiffrin and Schneider presented a similar principle in their 1977 paper on controlled versus automatic processing. According to their model, controlled processes require attention, whereas automatic processes do not. Shiffrin and Schneider originally discussed this distinction with respect to memory tasks such as comparing a stimulus item against an array of similar items stored in memory (Schneider & Chien, 2003). However, many of the phenomena discussed in the literature on controlled versus automatic processes apply to a broad range of intellectual skills and perceptual-motor skills, again supporting the assertion that intellectual and perceptual-motor skill acquisition share fundamental properties.

Additional evidence for the role of attention in skill acquisition comes from Nissen and Bullemer (1987), who documented the critical role of attention during early perceptual-motor skill acquisition in a sequence-learning task. Participants in their experiment learned a sequence of button-pressing responses. In one condition participants performed only the sequence-learning task. In another condition participants simultaneously performed an attention-demanding auditory-monitoring task. Nissen and Bullemer found that participants in the dual-task condition were significantly diminished in their ability to learn the sequence as compared to participants in the single-task condition. Cohen, Ivry, and Keele (1990) extended this finding by showing that dual-task interference with sequence learning scales with sequence complexity. Similarly, Leavitt (1979) showed that novice hockey players were significantly impaired in basic hockey skills when they simultaneously performed a visual shape-monitoring task. By contrast, expert hockey players were unaffected by the secondary task. In a similar vein, Beilock, Weirenga, and Carr (2002) had novice and expert golfers putt while simultaneously monitoring a string of verbally presented words. Not only did novices putt less accurately during the secondary task, they also recognized fewer of the monitored words during a subsequent recognition memory task as compared to the expert golfers. These studies confirm the theoretical insights of Fitts and Posner (1967) and Shiffrin and Schneider (1977).

If attention is necessary for unskilled performance, to what should a skill-learner attend? Wulf, Lauterbach, and Toole (1999) had novice golfers practice a pitching stroke (in which the ball is lobbed a short distance onto the putting green) under one of two instructions. One instruction encouraged participants to focus on swinging their arms, whereas the other instruction encouraged participants to focus on swinging the club. The latter instruction, which provided an external focus for the golfer's attention, was associated with more accurate pitch shots than the former instruction. A similar result was obtained by Maddox, Wulf, and Wright (1999), who found that novice tennis players made more accurate forehand shots when they focused on the trajectory of the ball than when they focused on the contact between the ball and the racket. These data suggest that skill acquisition is facilitated by attending to the consequences of one's actions rather than to the actions themselves. Wulf and Prinz (2001) reviewed a number of studies that support this conclusion and proposed that attending to the elements of a skill causes an over-regulation of muscular degrees of freedom, which in turn limits one's ability to flexibly implement motor plans (cf. Riley, Stoffregen, Grocki, & Turvey, 1999).

Both empirical and phenomenological data attest to the valuable role of attention during early stages of perceptual-motor skill acquisition. But what of later stages of expertise? The Fitts-Posner model and the controlled-automatic distinction suggest that attention becomes unnecessary as skill grows. Allport, Antonis, and Reynolds (1972) found that skilled pianists could accurately sight-read musical scores while repeating words presented through headphones. In fact, too much attention can interfere with expert performance. The phenomenon of "choking" is a well-known example of the way in which one's mind can get in the way of performance. When athletes are asked what causes them to choke, they often report that thinking too hard about performance is what hurts them. Beilock, Carr, MacMahon, and Starkes (2002) documented the detrimental effects of such attention. When their golfing subjects were asked to attend to a specific element of their putting stroke, those participants were significantly less accurate than when they made putts without such attention.

Ecological Psychology and the Dynamical Systems Approach

The second approach covered in this chapter fits under the rubric of ecological psychology and dynamical systems analysis. These terms refer to perspectives that are traditionally linked, although their ancestries are quite different. The view associated with ecological psychology stems from the thinking of James Gibson (1950, 1966, 1979), who contested Helmholtz's notion that sensory input is so impoverished that the observer must engage in unconscious inference to perceive the environment. Gibson argued that owing to the physical properties of objects and the way those objects emit or reflect energy, sensory input is sufficiently rich and structured to afford direct perception of the external world. Thus, the surface of a pond, if sufficiently smooth, is immediately perceived by a water spider to afford walking, whereas that same surface is immediately perceived by a person to afford swimming. Consistent with Gibson's ideas, perceived properties of surfaces depend on the state of the perceiver. A person wearing a heavy backpack judges a hill as steeper than a person wearing a light backpack (Proffitt, Bhalla, Gossweiler, & Midgett, 1995). Similarly, a baby perched on the edge of a visual cliff (a deep recess with thick glass lying across it) hesitates to crawl across it, though the same infant may be impervious to the same degree of visual depth when his or her sensitivity is tested through other means (E. Gibson & Walk, 1960).

The partner of the ecological approach is dynamical systems analysis, an approach that stems from the use of differential equations to describe how systems change over time. Dynamical systems analysis is compatible with the ecological approach to perception and action because the ecological approach emphasizes a detailed (preferably quantitative) study of the physical environment and the physical capabilities of agents acting within it. Because dynamical systems analysis provides quantitative descriptions of time-varying events without appealing to causal explanations, it attracts advocates of ecological psychology, some of whom wish not only to avoid unconscious inference to explain perception but also to avoid mental representations. These individuals argue that reliance on mental representations begs the question of who views, hears, tastes, smells, or feels the representations – the well-known "homunculus" problem.

Setting aside the philosophical differences between supporters of ecological psychology and dynamical systems on one hand and cognitive psychology on the other, there is no question that the ecological/dynamical systems approach has enriched the study of perceptual-motor expertise. The range of behaviors probed under the rubric of ecological/dynamical systems extends beyond the domain of classical cognitive research, where participants typically recite word lists or press buttons in response to simple stimuli displayed on computer screens.

An example of a rich behavioral task that has been analyzed by students of the eco-

logical/dynamical systems approach is mastery of the Jolly Jumper by babies. The Jolly Jumper is a seat suspended from a beam by elastic bands. Babies can exploit the bands' elasticity to bounce up and down. Initially babies show no awareness that the seat affords bouncing. However, they eventually discover how to master the device by optimally timing leg flexions and extensions. The amplitude of the bounces grows over time while the variability of the bounce periods decreases (Goldfield, Kay, & Warren, 1993), an outcome which demonstrates *self-organization* because babies cannot be told what the Jolly Jumper lets them achieve nor how they should move to take advantage of this affordance. They simply learn, through trial and error, to exploit the mechanics of the mass-spring system of which they are a part. Such spontaneous discovery of affordances is not a capability that has been studied within traditional cognitive psychology.

Other behavioral tasks have been similarly studied within the ecological/dynamical systems approach. A partial list of such tasks includes juggling (Beek & Turvey, 1992), learning to use a ski simulator (Vereijken, Whiting, & Beek, 1992), learning to shoot a pistol (Arutyunan, Gurfinkel, & Mirskii, 1968), learning when it is safe to walk or slide down an inclined plane (Adolph, 1997), learning the physical composition of wielded objects (Carello & Turvey, 2004), learning how to swing two hand-held pendulums of different lengths and weights (Turvey, 1990), learning how to bounce a ball on a tennis racquet (Sternad, Duarte, Katsumata, & Schaal, 2001), and learning how to swing one's two index fingers back and forth at different frequencies and with different relative phases (Zanone & Kelso, 1997). Sophisticated mathematical techniques have been developed to characterize learning in these and related contexts (e.g., Newell, Liu, & Mayer-Kress, 2001).

Some comments are in order about the ecological/dynamical-systems approach to skill acquisition, especially because of the prominence this approach has gained. One comment pertains to the abstract nature of dynamical equations. Dynamical systems equations can model the time-varying properties of virtually any system. For example, the same family of equations describing the behavior of coupled oscillators can predict patterns of human inter-limb coordination and synchronization of pacemaker cells in the mammalian heart. This broad scope is made possible by using model parameters that transcend the specific structure of the phenomena that are modeled.

In our view, the abstractness of dynamical systems modeling is both positive and negative. On the positive side, dynamical system equations often yield impressive fits to the data. On the negative side, the functional interpretation of the equations may be unclear. One wonders what real-world objects or processes are represented by the terms in the equations. For example, Fajen and Warren (2003) modeled obstacle avoidance in walking by treating the walker as a point governed by attractors and repellors in the external environment. The attractors and repellors push and pull on the walker, metaphorically speaking, much as springs push and pull on an object to which they are attached. The dynamical equations associated with this metaphor provide a good fit to the data, but one wonders what to make of the metaphor. Clearly, there are no springs in the actual environment pulling walkers as they ambulate. Might it be preferable to postulate cognitively available and/or neurally realizable mental representations for attractors and repellors, along with physically realizable processes for interacting with them?

Pursuing such an approach in our lab, we have modeled reaching around an obstacle as a combination of reaching directly for a real target while simultaneously moving back and forth to a virtual target on the side. The combination of the two sets of motions – moving straight to the real target while "bouncing" to a virtual target and then back from it – yields a curved trajectory whose curvature depends on the location of the side target (Figure 29.3). This method of obstacle avoidance is computationally intensive, which makes it unappealing for those who prefer direct perception to number crunching or neural analogs thereof. Nonetheless, no matter how much one might wish obstacle avoidance to be computation-free, it

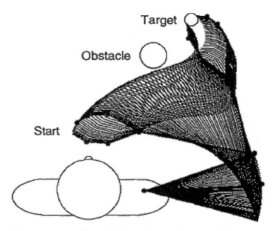

Figure 29.3. Simulation of grasping an object after circumventing another one. From Rosenbaum, Meulenbroek, Vaughan, and Jansen (2001).

rarely is. Otherwise, there would be fewer cases of spilled milk or broken bones.

A second concern about dynamical systems modeling is that it is unclear why any particular dynamical equation applies to one biological system and not another. The situation is exacerbated by the fact that similar biological systems sometimes exemplify different dynamical regimes, whereas very different biological systems sometimes exemplify the same dynamical regimes. These considerations led one of us to ask whether dynamical systems analysis is "just curve fitting" (Rosenbaum, 1998). The proposed answer was that curve fitting that uses flexible mathematical tools to model complex systems that could not be modeled otherwise is indeed justified or "just." Dynamical systems analysis has a rightful place, then, even if the ontological status of the terms of the equations is sometimes unclear.

Notwithstanding these concerns, we are enthusiastic about the rich set of behaviors and behavioral analyses that have been introduced by adherents to the ecological/dynamical systems approach. As a young field, ecological psychology and dynamical systems analysis will doubtless contribute in important ways to research on the acquisition and performance of complex perceptual-motor tasks. Indeed, several features of this general approach hold special promise. One is attention to physical constraints in performance. As mentioned earlier in connection with the Jolly Jumper, such behavior would not have been considered amenable to study within a traditional symbol-based approach. Other work, such as the modeling of bimanual pendulum swinging initiated by Turvey and colleagues (Turvey, 1990), has likewise built on well-established principles of physical mechanics to advance our understand of how coordination is achieved by balancing informational demands on the one hand and physical demands on the other. This perspective is largely attributable to Bernstein (1967), whose views on the study of action are in many ways analogous to Gibson's views on the study of perception. Much as Gibson argued that the physical environment affords directly perceivable opportunities for action, Bernstein argued that one's body, by virtue of how it physically interacts with the external world, provides exploitable opportunities for skillful performance.

Careful attention to the physical characteristics of perception and action has likewise advanced our understanding of skill acquisition. A classic case is a careful set of observations of pistol shooters. Arutyunyan, Gurfinkel, and Mirskii (1968) reported that *novice* shooters lock their wrists and elbows, making it difficult to compensate for changes in one or the other joint angle, but more-*expert* shooters free up those anatomical degrees of freedom so variations in wrist angle can be compensated for by variations in elbow angle, which leads to greater overall stability in the gun barrel. Research on bilateral finger oscillation has likewise revealed the key role played by muscular control and anatomical stability in the governance of bimanual coordination (Calvin et al., 2004).

Conclusions

Research on expertise will become more sophisticated as researchers develop more expertise themselves. One mark of expertise is having at one's disposal a rich set of available techniques. Here the study of

perceptual-motor expertise has shown what set of methodologies may become available in the years ahead. Researchers concerned with perceptual-motor expertise have been able to pursue multiple methods with some success because the problems they have studied are relatively simple, the tasks they analyze occur over relatively short time spans, and the activities they scrutinize can be performed by many populations. As a result, research on perceptual-motor expertise has witnessed significant strides in ways that may herald comparable advances in other branches of the study of expertise.

References

Adolph, K. E. (1997). Learning in the development of infant locomotion. *Monographs of the Society for Research in Child Development, 62, No. 3.*

Allport, D. A., Antonis, B., & Reynolds, P. (1972). On the division of attention: A disproof of the single channel hypothesis. *Quarterly Journal of Experimental Psychology, 24,* 225–235.

Arutyunyan, G. H., Gurfinkel, V. S., & Mirskii, M. L. (1968). Investigation of aiming at a target. *Biophysics, 13,* 536–538.

Beek, P. J., & Turvey, M. T. (1992). Temporal patterning in cascade juggling. *Journal of Experimental Psychology: Human Perception and Performance, 18* (4), 934–947.

Beilock, S. L., Carr, T. H., MacMahon, C., & Starkes, J. L. (2002). When paying attention becomes counterproductive: Impact of divided versus skill-focused attention on novice and experienced performance of sensorimotor skills. *Journal of Experimental Psychology: Applied, 8,* 6–16.

Beilock, S. L., Wierenga, S. A., & Carr, T. H. (2002). Expertise, attention, and memory in sensorimotor skill execution: Impact of novel task constraints on dual-task performance and episodic memory. *Quarterly Journal of Experimental Psychology: Section A, 55,* 1211–1240.

Bernstein, N. (1967). *The coordination and regulation of movements.* London: Pergamon.

Blakemore, S. J., Wolpert, D. M., & Frith, C. D. (1998). Central cancellation of self-produced tickle sensation. *Nature Neuroscience, 1,* 635–640.

Bracke-Tolkmitt, R., Linden, A., Canavan, A. G. M., & Diener, H. C. (1989). The cerebellum contributes to mental skills. *Behavioral Neuroscience, 103*, 442–446.

Brashers-Krug, T., Shadmehr, R., & Bizzi, E. (1996). Consolidation in human motor memory. *Nature, 382*, 252–255.

Bryan, W. L., & Harter, N. (1897). Studies in the physiology and psychology of the telegraphic language. *Psychological Review, 4*, 27–53.

Bryan, W. L., & Harter, N. (1899). Studies on the telegraphic language. *Psychological Review, 6*, 345–378.

Calvin, S., Milliex L, Coyle, T., & Temprado, J. J. (2004). Stabilization and destabilization of perception-action patterns influence the self-organized recruitment of degrees of freedom. *Journal of Experimental Psychology: Human Perception and Performance, 30*, 1032–1042.

Carello, C., & Turvey, M. T. (2004). Physics and psychology of the muscle sense. *Current Directions in Psychological Science, 13*, 25–28.

Chase, W. G., & Ericsson, K. A. (1981). Skilled memory. In J. R. Anderson (Ed.), *Cognitive skills and their acquisition* (pp. 141–189). Hillsdale, NJ: Erlbaum.

Cohen, A., Ivry, R. I., & Keele, S. W. (1990). Attention and structure in sequence learning. *Journal of Experimental Psychology: Learning, Memory, and Cognition, 16*, 17–30.

Cohen, R. G., & Rosenbaum, D. A. (2004). Where objects are grasped reveals how grasps are planned: Generation and recall of motor plans. *Experimental Brain Research, 157*, 486–495.

Conditt, M. A., Gandolfo, F., & Mussa-Ivaldi, F. A. (1997). The motor system does not learn the dynamics of the arm by rote memorization of past experience. *Journal of Neurophysiology, 78*, 554–560.

Cooper, W. E. (Ed.). (1983). *Cognitive aspects of skilled typewriting*. New York: Springer-Verlag.

Cooper, W. E., Paccia-Cooper, J. (1980). *Syntax and speech*. Cambridge: Harvard University Press.

Courchesne, E., & Allen, G. (1997). Prediction and preparation fundamental functions of the cerebellum. *Learning and Memory, 4*, 1–35.

Dagenbach, D., & Carr, T. H. (Eds.). (1994). *Inhibitory processes in attention, memory, and language*. San Diego: Academic Press.

Dell, G. S. (1986). A spreading activation theory of retrieval in sentence production. *Psychological Review, 93*, 283–321.

Desmond, J. E., Gabrielli, J. D., Wagner, A. D., Binier, B. L., & Glover, G. H. (1997). Lobular patterns of cerebellar activation of verbal working-memory and finger-tapping tasks as revealed by functional MRI. *Journal of Neuroscience, 17*, 9675–9685.

Dizio, P., & Lackner, J. R. (1995). Motor adaptation to coriolis force perturbations of reaching movements: Endpoint but not trajectory adaptation transfers to the nonexposed arm. *Journal of Neurophysiology, 74*, 1787–1792.

Elbert, T., Pantev, C., Weinbruch, C., Rockstroh, B., & Taub, E. (1995). Increased cortical representation of the fingers of the left hand. *Science, 270*, 305–307.

Fajen, B. R., & Warren, W. H. (2003). Behavioral dynamics of steering, obstacle avoidance, and route selection. *Journal of Experimental Psychology: Human Perception and Performance, 29*, 343–362.

Fiez, J. A. (1996). Cerebellar contributions to cognition. *Neuron, 16*, 13–15.

Fitts, P. M., & Posner, M. I. (1967). *Human performance*. Belmont, CA: Brooks/Cole Publishing Company.

Fromkin, V. A. (Ed.). (1980). *Errors in linguistic performance*. New York: Academic Press.

Gao, J. H., Parsons, L. M., Bower, J. M., & Xiong, J. (1996). Cerebellum implicated in sensory acquisition and discrimination rather than motor control. *Science, 272*, 545–547.

Gauthier, I., Skudlarski, P., Gore, J. C., & Anderson, A. W. (2000). Expertise for cars and birds recruit brain areas involved in face recognition. *Nature Neuroscience, 3*, 191–197.

Gibson, E. J., & Walk, R. D. (1960). The "visual cliff." *Scientific American, 202*, 63–71.

Gibson, J. J. (1950). *Perception of the visual world*. Boston: Houghton-Mifflin.

Gibson, J. J. (1966). *The senses considered as perceptual systems*. Boston: Houghton-Mifflin.

Gibson, J. J. (1979). *The ecological approach to visual perception*. Boston: Houghton-Mifflin.

Glenberg, A. M. (1997). What memory is for. *Behavioral and Brain Sciences, 20*, 1–55.

Goldfield, E. C., Kay, B. A., & Warren, W. H. (1993). Infant bouncing: The assembly and tuning of action systems. *Child Development, 64*, 1128–1142.

Goodbody, S. J., & Wolpert, D. M. (1998). Temporal and amplitude generalization in motor learning. *Journal of Neurophysiology, 79,* 1825–1838.

Grudin, J. G. (1983). Error patterns in novice and skilled typists. In W. E. Cooper (Ed.), *Cognitive aspects of skilled typewriting* (pp. 121–143). New York: Springer-Verlag.

Hebb, D. O. (1949). *The organization of behavior: A neuropsychological theory.* New York: John Wiley.

Helmholtz, H. von (1911). *Treatise on physiological optics.* (J. P. Southall, Ed. & Trans.) (3rd ed., Vols. 2 & 3). Rochester, NY: Optical Society of America.

Holmes, G. (1939). The cerebellum of man. *Brain, 62,* 1–30.

Hommel, B., Musseler, J., Aschersleben, G., & Prinz, W. (2001). The theory of event coding (TEC): A framework for perception and action planning. *Behavioral and Brain Sciences, 24,* 849–937.

Ivry, R. B., & Keele, S. W. (1989). Timing functions of the cerebellum. *Journal of Cognitive Neuroscience, 1,* 136–152.

Jeannerod, M. (1988). *The neural and behavioral organization of goal-directed movements.* Oxford: Oxford University Press.

Jenkins, I., Brooks, D., Nixon, P., Frackowiack, R., & Passingham, R. (1994). Motor sequence learning: A study with positron emission tomography. *Journal of Neuroscience, 14,* 3775–3790.

Kaas, J. H., Merzenich, M. M., & Killackey, H. P. (1983). The reorganization of somatosensory cortex following peripheral nerve damage in adult and developing mammals. *Annual Review of Neuroscience, 6,* 325–356.

Kandel, E. R. (1981). Nerve cells and behavior. In E. R. Kandel & J. H. Schwartz (Eds.), *Principles of neural science* (pp. 14–23). New York: Elsevier/North-Holland.

Kerr, B. A. & Langgolf, G. (1977). The speed of aiming moveents. *Quarterly Journal of Experimental Psychology, 29,* 475–481.

Klapp, S. T. (1977). Reaction time analysis of programmed control. *Exercise and sport sciences reviews, 5,* 231–253.

Koh, K., & Meyer, D. E. (1991). Induction of continuous stimulus-response associations for perceptual-motor performance. *Journal of Experimental Psychology: Learning, Memory, and Cognition, 17,* 811–836.

Körding, K. P., & Wolpert, D. M. (2004). Bayesian integration in sensorimotor learning. *Nature, 437,* 244–247.

Kroll, J. F., & Potter, M. C. (1984). Recognizing words, pictures, and concepts: A comparison of lexical, object, and reality decisions. *Journal of Verbal Learning and Verbal Behavior, 23,* 39–66.

Landauer, T. K., & Bjork, R. A. (1978). Optimal rehearsal patterns and name learning. In M. M. Gruneberg, P. E. Morris, & R. N. Sykes (Eds.), *Practical aspects of memory* (pp. 625–632). London: Academic Press.

Lashley, K. S. (1951). The problem of serial order in behavior. In L. A. Jeffress (Ed.), *Cerebral mechanisms in behavior* (pp. 112–131). New York: Wiley.

Leavitt, J. (1979). Cognitive demands of skating and stick handling in ice hockey. *Canadian Journal of Applied Sport Sciences, 4,* 46–55.

Leiner, H. C., Leiner, A. L., & Dow, R. S. (1995). The underestimated cerebellum. *Human Brain Mapping, 2,* 244–254.

Lewandowsky, S., Kalish, M., & Ngang, S. K. (2002). Simplified learning in complex situations: Knowledge partitioning in function learning. *Journal of Experimental Psychology: General, 131,* 163–193.

Logan, G. D. (1988). Toward an instance theory of automatization. *Psychological Review, 95,* 492–527.

Logan, G. D. (2002). An instance theory of attention and memory. *Psychological Review, 109,* 376–400.

Logothetis, N. K., & Pauls, J. (1995). Psychophysical and physiological evidence for viewer-centered object representations in the primate. *Cerebral Cortex, 5,* 270–288.

Lynch, G., & Baudry, M. (1984). The biochemistry of memory: A new and specific hypothesis. *Science, 224,* 1057–1063.

Maddox, M. D., Wulf, G., & Wright, D. L. (1999). The effect of an internal vs. external focus of attention on the learning of a tennis stroke. *Journal of Exercise Psychology, 21,* S78.

Magill, R. A., & Hall, K. G. (1990). A review of the contextual interference effect in motor skill acquisition. *Human Movement Science, 9,* 241–289.

Melton, A. W. (1970). The situation with respect to the spacing of repetitions and memory. *Journal of Verbal Learning and Verbal Behavior, 9,* 596–606.

Meyer, D. E., Abrams, R. A., Kornblum, S., Wright, C. E., & Smith, J. E. K. (1988). Optimality in human motor performance: Ideal control of rapid aimed movements. *Psychological Review, 95*, 340–370.

Miller, G. A. (1956). The magical number seven plus or minus two: Some limits on our capacity for processing information. *Psychological Review, 63*, 81–97.

Newell, A. M., & Rosenbloom, P. S. (1981). Mechanisms of skill acquisition and the law of practice. In J. R. Anderson (Ed.), *Cognitive skills and their acquisition* (pp. 1–55). Hillsdale, NJ: Erlbaum.

Newell, K. M., Liu, Y-T., & Mayer-Kress, G. (2001). Time scales in motor learning and development. *Psychological Review, 108*, 57–82.

Nissen, M. J., & Bullemer, P. (1987). Attentional requirements of learning: Evidence from performance measures. *Cognitive Psychology, 19*, 1–32.

Norman, D. A. (1981). Categorization of action slips. *Psychological Review, 88*, 1–15.

Petersen, S. E., Fox, P. T., Posner, M. I., Mintun, M., & Raichle, M. E. (1989). Positron emission tomographic studies of the processing of single words. *Journal of Cognitive Neuroscience, 1*, 153–170.

Povel, D-J., & Collard, R. (1982). Structural factors in patterned finger tapping. *Acta Psychologica, 52*, 107–124.

Proffitt, D. R., Bhalla, M., Gossweiler, R., & Midgett, K. (1995). Perceiving geographical slant. *Psychonomic Bulletin & Review, 2*, 409–428.

Purves, D., & Lott, R. B. (2003). *Why we see what we do: An empirical theory of vision.* Sunderland, MA: Sinauer Associates.

Rea, C. P., & Modigliani, V. (1985). The effect of expanded versus massed practice on the retention of multiplication facts and spelling lists. *Human Learning, 4*, 11–18.

Reason, J. (1990). *Human error.* Cambridge: Cambridge University Press.

Restle, F. (1970). Theory of serial pattern learning: Structural trees. *Psychological Review, 77*, 481–495.

Riley, M. A., Stoffregen, T. A., Grocki, M. J., & Turvey, M. T. (1999). Postural stabilization for the control of touching. *Human Movement Science, 18*, 795–817.

Rosenbaum, D. A. (1987). Successive approximations to a model of human motor programming. In G. H. Bower (Ed.) *Psychology of learning and motivation, Vol. 21* (pp. 153–182). Orlando, FL: Academic Press.

Rosenbaum, D. A. (1998). Is dynamical systems modeling just curve fitting? *Motor Control, 2*, 101–104.

Rosenbaum, D. A., Carlson, R. A. & Gilmore, R. O. (2001). Acquisition of intellectual and perceptual-motor skills. *Annual Review of Psychology, 52*, 453–470.

Rosenbaum, D. A., Kenny, S., & Derr, M. A. (1983). Hierarchical control of rapid movement sequences. *Journal of Experimental Psychology: Human Perception and Performance, 9*, 86–102.

Rosenbaum, D. A., Meulenbroek, R. G., Vaughan, J., & Jansen, C. (2001). Posture-based motion planning: Applications to grasping. *Psychological Review, 108*, 709–734.

Sainburg, R. L. (2002). Evidence for a dynamic dominance hypothesis of handedness. *Experimental Brain Research, 142*, 241–258.

Schmidt, R. A., & Bjork, R. A. (1992). New conceptualizations of practice: Common principles in three paradigms suggest new concepts for training. *Psychological Science, 3*, 207–214.

Schmidt, R. A. & Lee, T. D. (1999). *Motor control and learning – A behavioral emphasis (3rd Ed.).* Champaign, Illinois: Human Kinetics.

Schneider, W., & Chien, J. M. (2003). Controlled & automatic processing: Behavior, theory, and biological mechanisms. *Cognitive Science, 27*, 525–559.

Shannon, C., & Weaver, W. (1949). *The mathematical theory of communication.* Urbana, IL: University of Illinois Press.

Shea, J. B., & Morgan, R. L. (1979). Contextual interference effects on acquisition, retention, and transfer of a motor skill. *Journal of Experimental Psychology: Human Learning and Memory, 5*, 179–187.

Shiffrin, R. M., & Schneider, W. (1977). Controlled and automatic human information processing. II. Perceptual learning, automatic attending, and a general theory. *Psychological Review, 84* (2), 127–190.

Simon, H. A. (1972). Complexity and the representation of patterned sequences of symbols. *Psychological Review, 79*, 369–382.

Sperling, G. A. (1960). The information available in brief visual presentation. *Psychological Monographs, 74*, Whole No. 498.

Starkes, J. L. & Allard, F. (Eds.). (1993). *Cognitive issues in motor expertise*. Amsterdam: North-Holland.

Starkes, J. L., & Ericsson, K. A. (Eds.). (2003). *Expert peformance in sports: Advances in research on sport expertise*. Champaign, IL: Human Kinetics.

Sternad, D., Duarte, M., Katsumata, H., & Schaal, S. (2001). Bouncing a ball: Tuning into dynamic stability. *Journal of Experimental Psychology: Human Perception and Performance, 27*, 1163–1184.

Turvey, M. T. (1990). Coordination. *American Psychologist, 45, 8*, 938–953.

Vereijken, B., Whiting, H. T. A., & Beek, P. J. (1992). A dynamic-systems approach to skill acquisition. *Quarterly Journal of Experimental Psychology Section A: Human Experimental Psychology, 45*, 323–344.

Volkmann, F. C., Riggs, L. A., & Moore, R. K. (1980). Eyeblinks and visual suppression. *Science, 207*, 900–902.

von Holst, E., & Mittelstaedt, H. (1950). Das Reafferenzprinzip. *Die Naturwissenschaften, 37*, 464–474. (English translation in P. C. Dodwell [Ed.], [1980], *Perceptual processing: Stimulus equivalence and pattern recognition*. New York: Appleton-Century-Crofts.)

Worringham, C. J. (1993). Predicting motor performance from variability measures. In K. M. Newell & D. M. Corcos (Eds.), *Variability and motor control* (pp. 53–63). Champaign, IL: Human Kinetics.

Wulf, G., Lauterbach, B., & Toole, T. (1999). Learning advantages of an external focus of attention in golf. *Research Quarterly for Exercise & Sport, 70*, 120–126.

Wulf, G., & Prinz, W. (2001). Directing attention to movement effects enhances learning: A review. *Psychonomic Bulletin & Review, 8* (4), 648–660.

Zanone, P. G., & Kelso, J. A. S. (1997). Coordination dynamics of learning and transfer: Collective and component levels. *Journal of Experimental Psychology: Human Perception And Performance, 23*, 1454–1480.

Part V.C

GAMES AND OTHER TYPES OF EXPERTISE

CHAPTER 30

Expertise in Chess

Fernand Gobet & Neil Charness

Historical Background

Just like Drosophila – the fruit fly – is a model organism in genetics, chess has long served as a model task environment for research into psychological processes (Charness, 1992). Some of the earliest systematic work on individual differences in imagery (Binet, 1893/1966; 1894), memory (Djakow, Petrowski, & Rudik, 1927), and problem solving (de Groot 1946/1965) took place in the domain of chess. Cleveland (1907) was one of the first to identify the importance of complex units, now called chunks, in skilled play and speculated that intellectual abilities might be poor predictors of chess skill, even providing the score of a game played with a "mentally feeble" individual.

De Groot (1946/1965) ushered in the modern era of investigation using small groups of expert and grandmaster-level players in experimental studies. Of de Groot's many findings, it was the dissociation between thinking skills and perceptual-memory skills that laid the groundwork for subsequent research. When asking players to think aloud while they attempted to choose the best move in an unfamiliar position, de Groot discovered that, contrary to popular lore, the most-proficient players did not think further ahead than less-skilled practitioners. It was a different experimental task – memory for briefly presented chess positions – that markedly differentiated skill levels. De Groot found that skilled players proved to have strikingly superior memory for chess positions after brief presentations (two to fifteen seconds), compared to their less-proficient counterparts. De Groot interpreted these findings to support the importance of knowledge and perceptual organization principles over search algorithm differences in explaining how experts chose better moves.

Follow-up research by Chase and Simon (1973a, 1973b) revealed that the perceptual/memory advantage for skilled players was only obtained when they viewed structured chess positions. When pieces were randomly arranged on the board, there was little, if any, memory advantage for a Master player compared to a Class A player or compared to a novice player. This dissociation, a finding that has become a touchstone of the expert-performance approach in many other domains, suggested that acquired patterns, not innate abilities, accounted for skill differences. On the basis of these data and those gathered in other experiments and in simulation studies, Chase and Simon proposed their highly influential chunking theory of skilled performance in chess. That theory and its subsequent refinement has had a significant impact on expertise research in general and that on games in particular (see Gobet, de Voogt, & Retschitzki, 2004, for an extensive coverage on board games, and Charness, 1989, for a presentation of the data on bridge).

Brief Description of the Game and the Rating System

Chess is a game played by two opponents using an initial configuration, the starting position, consisting of 32 chess pieces placed on an eight-by-eight square chessboard. The rules of chess are sufficiently simple that children can be taught them at a very young age (four or five years old). Child prodigies are not uncommon and teenagers have been able to compete at the highest level. (Nineteen-year-old Ruslan Ponomariov was crowned World Champion in 2002.) Chess is sufficiently difficult to play well that it took about 40 years of effort by computer scientists to program computers to compete on an equal level with the best human players.

Another important feature for chess is the existence of a sophisticated measurement scale for evaluating chess skill based on performance in chess tournaments. The Elo rating scale, available since the mid-1960s (Elo, 1965; Elo, 1986), is open-ended, starting at a nominal value of zero and extending upward, with a nominal class interval (standard deviation) of about 200 rating points. The world's best players today hover above 2800 rating points with Grandmaster level at approximately 2500 rating points, International Master at about 2400 points, and Master at about 2200 points. This interval

level rating scale enables fine-grained examination of the relation between expertise and a variety of indicators of psychological processes. Measurement of expertise on this fine of a scale remains a central problem for many other domains discussed in this volume.

For instance, a psychometric approach to chess skill (e.g., Van der Maas & Wagenmakers, 2005) can capitalize on the chess rating scale to examine how well it correlates with different markers of psychological processes such as measures of memory, problem solving, and motivation. Early efforts at understanding skill in chess implicitly made use of this correlates approach for measures of attention (Tikhomirov & Poznyanskaya, 1966), imagery (Milojkovic, 1982; Bachmann & Oit, 1992), and personality (Charness, Tuffiash, & Jastrzembski, 2004).

In this chapter we focus on a process-model approach to understanding expertise in chess. Our goal is to shed light on the process of how players choose the best moves to play in a chess game, starting from early perceptual processes and tracing forward to the search processes first described by de Groot. We outline where skill differences arise within such processes. We describe computer simulation models that capture some of the features of skilled performance by chess players. We also describe how human players acquire the knowledge necessary to play chess expertly.

Information Processing Models of Choosing a Good Move: The Trade-Offs Between Knowledge and Search

The goal of a chess player is to choose the best possible move. Often, when playing through standard openings, the best move is dictated by knowledge from published analyses, such as the *Encyclopedia of Chess Openings*. Sometimes, detecting the best move in a sequence of exchanges of pieces is simple enough that even novices quickly find it. Much of the time, the best move is non-obvious and the player must decide based on a search process that evaluates a candidate move in terms of potential future positions reached via a branching tree of available moves for the two sides.

Search is difficult because of the enormous number of possible moves stemming from the opening position. Even Master players who can use well-tuned recognition processes to winnow the possible base moves down to three or four plausible alternatives at each point in the tree face a dilemma. The number of possible moves, computed as breadth raised to a power equal to depth, is 4^{76} moves, given that the average master game lasts about 38 moves or 76 plies (moves for each side). So, both computers and humans must search selectively among the alternatives using a variety of heuristics (Newell & Simon, 1972) to decide when a node reached in search can be properly evaluated.

Given the relatively slow rate at which moderately skilled players can generate analysis moves, estimated in Charness (1981b) to be about four moves per minute, it is obvious that much of the time that human players spend is not in generating all possible moves (perhaps taking a move per second) but in generating moves selectively and using complex evaluation functions to assess their value. Computer chess programs can achieve high-level play by searching many moves using fast, frugal evaluation processes that involve minimal chess knowledge to evaluate the terminal positions in search. Deep Blue, the chess program that defeated World Champion Garry Kasparov in a short match in 1997, searched hundreds of millions of positions per second. Today's leading microcomputer chess programs, which have drawn matches with the best human players, have sophisticated search algorithms and attempt to use more chess knowledge but still generate hundreds of thousands or millions of chess moves per second. Generally, chess programs rely on search more heavily than knowledge; for humans it is the reverse. Yet, each can achieve very high performance levels because knowledge and search can trade off (Berliner & Ebeling, 1989).

Because expert humans do so little search, yet still manage to find strong chess moves,

attention has shifted from investigating search processes to understanding the role of pattern-recognition processes in move selection. As de Groot noted, skilled players use their knowledge about chess configurations to generate plausible moves for limited searching. We now focus on understanding the perceptual mechanisms that support this rapid perception advantage.

Tracing Expertise Differences in Perception and Attention with Eye-Tracking Techniques

Jongman (1968) initiated work on perceptual skill differences by examining eye movements of expert and less-expert players, though his results became widely accessible with the re-analysis published by de Groot and Gobet (1996). These researchers showed that in a memorizing task, where players were given a few seconds to examine an unfamiliar chess position, better players fixated more on the edges of squares than weaker players did. Also, better players were more likely to have greater distances between fixations, implying that they were able to encode more widely about a fixation than weaker players. Experts also made shorter duration fixations than did weaker players implying faster encoding.

Reingold and colleagues confirmed the larger visual span for experts using a variety of tasks. Using a gaze-contingent paradigm that manipulated the number of visible squares, Reingold, Charness, Pomplun, and Stampe (2001) showed that more-skilled players needed a larger area around fixation to detect changes in successively displayed chess positions in order to match performance under unlimited view of the whole board. This was true only for structured, not random, chess positions. This result suggested that better players had a larger visual field from which they could extract chess relationships. In a second experiment, the authors noted that when players made a simple determination of whether a King was in check by an attacking piece on a minimized chessboard (three-by-three squares), experts required fewer fixations to decide, and these fixations were more likely to be between pieces (on empty squares), compared to intermediate-level players. (See also Fisk & Lloyd, 1988, and Saariluoma, 1985, for data on perceptual processes in simple decision tasks.)

In a choose-a-move task using full chessboards, Charness, Reingold, Pomplun, and Stampe (2001) demonstrated that experts made fewer fixations per trial and those fixations were more widely spaced out across the board and again, more likely to be between than on chess pieces. More important, for the first five fixations, experts were more likely to fixate on relevant squares (rated as relevant by a strong International Master player). This very early advantage (within the first second of exposure to a new position, given that fixations average about 250 milliseconds each for both experts and intermediate players) testifies to the importance of pattern-recognition processes in providing a better representational structure. Given this perceptual head start, experts also chose better moves and did so more quickly than their less-expert counterparts.

Reingold, Charness, Schultetus and Stampe (2001) used a Stroop-like interference task within a five-by-five square segment of a chessboard to demonstrate that expert players appear to extract chess relations in parallel, whereas weaker ones appear to shift attention and encode the same relations serially. In a two-attacker situation, supplying a cue about which piece to attend to provided an advantage in response time to less-skilled players, but no advantage to expert players because the latter appeared to encode both attack relations simultaneously.

In summary, experts rely on a rich network of chess patterns stored in long-term memory structures (or long-term working memory, Ericsson & Kintsch, 1995) to give them a larger visual span when encoding chess positions. They encode chess information far more quickly and accurately than non-experts. Within the first second of exposure to a new position, experts are examining salient squares on the chessboard and

extracting, in parallel, chess relationships critical to choosing good moves. In later sections we outline how CHREST, a computer simulation program, acquires and utilizes such chess patterns (templates and chunks).

Memory Processes

As early as Binet (1894), and in particular in de Groot's work, knowledge has been identified as a key component of chess expertise. In order to understand how knowledge (held in memory) mediates skill, a substantial amount of research has been carried out on chess players' memory. Domains of interest include memory for static positions, memory for moves and sequences of moves (discussed later in the section on blindfold chess), and the structure and contents of long-term memory (LTM), including the number of chunks necessary to reach expert performance. In many cases, experimentation has been carried out in concert with computational modeling.

MEMORY RECALL FOR POSITIONS: CHASE AND SIMON'S KEY RESULTS

Although both Binet and de Groot highlighted the key role of knowledge in chess expertise, one had to wait until Chase and Simon's work in 1973 to have a detailed theory of expert memory. Extending de Groot's study showing a striking skill effect in the recall of game positions, Chase and Simon carried out detailed analyses to identify what were the building blocks of chess knowledge. In a copy task, they analyzed the pattern of eye fixations on the stimulus board, as well as the way pieces were grouped during reconstruction. Comparing these results with those obtained in a recall task, they inferred that pieces placed within two seconds and sharing a number of semantic relations were likely to belong to the same chunk. (These results were replicated by Gobet & Simon, 1998, and Gobet & Clarkson, 2004.) They proposed that skill did not reside in differences in short-term memory (STM) capacity or encoding speed, but in the number of chunks held in LTM memory. These chunks give access to information such as what move to play, what plan to follow, and what evaluation to give to (part of) the position. Thus, their theory explained both why masters choose better moves in spite of their selective search (because chunks enable them to identify the key features of a position and guide search during look-ahead) and why they perform better in a memory task (because they can partition the position in relatively large groups of pieces, unlike weaker players who have to use more smaller groups, which overtax STM). Some of these ideas were implemented in a computer program, MAPP (Simon & Gilmartin, 1973), which simulated recall up to expert level.

PROBLEMS WITH THE CHUNKING THEORY LEAD TO THE TEMPLATE THEORY

A number of experiments have helped refined Chase and Simon's theory. Charness (1976) showed that the presence of an interfering task reduced recall only marginally, which runs counter to the assumption of a slow encoding in LTM. Several authors (Frey & Adesman, 1976; Cooke et al., 1993; Gobet & Simon, 1996a) have shown that players can remember multiple boards reasonably well, which again highlighted a weakness of the original chunking theory.

These results, as well as the fact that verbal protocols reveal that masters use larger structures than the chunks identified by Chase and Simon (e.g., de Groot, 1946; de Groot & Gobet, 1996; Freyhoff, Gruber, & Ziegler, 1992; Gobet, 1998a), led Gobet and Simon (1996a, 2000) to revise the chunking theory. Their template theory aimed to remedy these weaknesses while keeping the strengths of the original chunking theory. It also aimed to show how high-level, schematic structures (templates) can evolve from perceptual chunks. As with the chunking theory, chunks and now templates are crucial in explaining how players access relevant information by pattern recognition. The computer program CHREST (Chunk Hierarchy and REtrieval STructures) implements aspects of the template theory. CHREST consists of an STM, an LTM indexed by a discrimination net,

and a simulated eye. Each cognitive process has a time cost; for example, it takes 50 milliseconds to place a chunk in STM, and eight seconds to create a new chunk. During the learning phase, the program automatically acquires chunks and templates by scanning a database of positions taken from masters' games. During the testing phase, it is placed in the same experimental situation as human participants. The program has simulated various characteristics of players' eye movements (de Groot & Gobet, 1996), the details of reconstruction in recall experiments (Gobet, 1993; Gobet & Simon, 2000; Gobet & Waters, 2003), as well as the way novices learn to memorize chess positions (Gobet & Jackson, 2002). Beyond chess, variants of the program have been applied to memory for computer programs, use of diagrammatic representation in physics, concept formation, and children's acquisition of language (Gobet et al., 2001).

RANDOM POSITIONS

Whereas Chase and Simon (1973a, 1973b) found no skill difference in the recall of random positions, Gobet and Simon (1996b) show that later studies did in fact find such a difference, although the effect is rarely significant because of the low statistical power within these studies. This skill effect remains across a wide range of presentation times (from one second to 60 seconds; Gobet & Simon, 2000) and with positions where the location as well as the distribution of pieces is randomized (Gobet & Waters, 2003). These results are consistent with the chunking and template theories, which predict that strong players, who have more chunks, are more likely than weaker players to recognize some patterns even with random positions. Indeed, computer simulations (Gobet & Simon, 1996b; Gobet & Simon, 2000) confirmed these predictions.

NEW ESTIMATES OF THE VOCABULARY OF THE MASTER

Based on computer simulations with MAPP, Simon and Gilmartin (1973) estimated that one needed to acquire from 10,000 to

100,000 patterns to reach master level in chess. These estimates have led to several experiments, in part because Holding (1985) argued that a much smaller number was required if one assumed that the same chunk could encode the same constellation of pieces placed at different locations of the board. Saariluoma (1994) modified positions by swapping quadrants, and Gobet and Simon (1996c) modified positions by taking their mirror images along various axes of symmetry. Both found that these manipulations affected recall, which runs counter to Holding's predictions but supports the original chunking theory. Computer simulations with CHREST show that at least 300,000 chunks are required to reach Grandmaster level, even with the presence of templates, which were not part of the chunking theory.

RECOGNITION EXPERIMENTS

In the past, few studies have been carried out using a recognition paradigm (e.g., Goldin, 1978, 1979; Saariluoma, 1984). This pattern has not changed in recent years, and we could find only one study using this technique. McGregor and Howes (2002) presented positions for either nine or 30 seconds asked participants to evaluate them, and later carried out a recognition test. In one experiment, the positions presented during the recognition phase were distorted by shifting either all pieces or a single piece one square horizontally. Two further experiments used a priming technique during the recognition phase: a piece from the target position was shown for two seconds; this was followed by a second piece, and participants indicated whether they thought it was in the target position. The two pieces shared either a relation of attack/defence or a relation of proximity. McGregor and Howes found that Class A players used information about attack/defence more often that information about the location of pieces.

Problem-Solving Processes

Today's chess-playing programs benefit from the enormous progress in refining computer search algorithms. Running on off-the-shelf microcomputers, they are of world-championship caliber. One could argue that knowledge about human problem-solving processes in chess has lagged the efforts in artificial intelligence, though steady progress is evident. De Groot (1946/1965), Newell and Simon (1972), and Wagner and Scurrah (1971) have generated many of the explicit models that describe the heuristics used by humans to manage search.

DE GROOT'S STUDY

De Groot (1946) asked his participants to think aloud when choosing their next move in a problem position. The quantitative and qualitative measures he extracted from the verbal protocols provided important empirical information about chess players' thinking. We will use some of the main phenomena discussed by de Groot to organize this section.

MACROSTRUCTURE OF SEARCH IN CHESS

De Groot (1946) found few differences in the macrostructure of search between world-class grandmasters and relatively strong players (candidate masters). Surprisingly, during their search, players from both skill levels tended to search at similar depth, to consider the same number of positions, and to propose similar numbers of candidate moves. But there were differences as well: the grandmasters chose better moves than the candidate masters, they generated moves faster, they reached a decision faster, and, during their search, they examined moves and sequences of moves that tended to be more relevant.

Holding (1985) argued that de Groot's (1946) small sample (five grandmasters and five candidate masters) may have concealed existing skill differences. Supporting Holding's view, some skill differences were found with samples including weaker players (e.g., Charness, 1981b; Gobet, 1998b; Saariluoma, 1992). Charness (1981a) suggested that depth of search increases up to candidate master level, after which it stays uniform. Charness (1989) conducted a nine-year longitudinal investigation of a Canadian player who advanced (in power law fashion) from an average-level performance (1600 rating points) to International Master level performance (2300 rating points) and found no significant increase in depth of search. However, international masters and grandmasters sometimes carry out shallower search than masters (Saariluoma, 1990), perhaps indicating that they can tailor their search mechanisms to the demands of the position. Gobet (1997) carried out computer simulations with the SEARCH model (see below) and concluded that average depth of search keeps increasing with higher skill levels, but with diminishing returns (i.e., it follows a power law).

SELECTIVE SEARCH, MOVE GENERATION, AND PATTERN RECOGNITION

De Groot found that all players were highly selective in their search, rarely visiting more than one hundred nodes before choosing a move. Recent results support this view. Calderwood et al. (1988) showed that masters can make relatively good decisions even under time pressure (about five seconds per move). Gobet and Simon (1996d) found that world champion Kasparov, when playing simultaneous games against teams consisting of up to eight international masters and grandmasters, performed at a level that still placed him among about the six best players in the world. Gobet and Simon argued that, although Kasparov's performance was weaker than in normal games and showed more variability, it was higher than theories mainly based on search would predict (but see Lassiter, 2000, and Chabris & Hearst, 2003, for opposing views). Comparing the quality of play of world-class grandmasters in standard games (about three minutes per move, on average) and rapid games (less than 30 seconds per move, on average), Chabris and Hearst (2003) found that this decrease of thinking time by a factor of six only marginally affected the number of blunders per 1,000 moves (5.02 in classical games vs. 6.85 in rapid games). Although they took this as evidence for the role of search, a more natural interpretation of these results is that they show that a substantial decrease

in thinking time fails to increase the number of blunders substantially, which counts as direct support for theories emphasizing pattern recognition.

Proponents of search models often cite Holding and Reynolds' (1982) experiment as evidence that search and pattern recognition can be dissociated. Holding and Reynolds, who used semi-random positions as stimuli, first asked players to recall the position after an eight-second presentation, and then to choose what they thought would be the best move. They found that skill correlated with the quality of chosen move after a few minutes' deliberation, but not with the recall or the evaluation after brief presentation. Schultetus and Charness (1999) extended Holding and Reynolds' (1982) experiment with a crucial addition: they asked players to recall the position at the end of problem solving. Like in the original study, stronger players did not recall the position better after five seconds, but chose better moves. However, they also obtained better results in the recall performance following problem solving. Schultetus and Charness (1999) argue that these results are consistent with the hypothesis that pattern recognition underpins skill in chess. That is, in order to choose better moves, better players were able to form new relational patterns for the unusual piece placements. These new chunks provided the recall advantage after problem solving. Such results are also consistent with the Ericsson and Kintsch (1995) long-term working-memory perspective.

PROGRESSIVE DEEPENING

De Groot (1946) found that players were visiting the same branches of the search tree repeatedly, either directly or after visiting other branches. According to de Groot, this phenomenon of "progressive deepening" occurs both in order to compensate for limitations in memory and for propagating information from one branch of the search tree to another (de Groot, 1946; de Groot & Gobet, 1996). Gobet (1998b) found that skill affects how progressive deepening is carried out. The maximum number of immediate re-investigations (where the same base move is analyzed directly in the next episode) was proportional to players' strength, whereas the maximum number of non-immediate re-investigations (where the analysis of a base move and its reinvestigation is interrupted by the analysis of at least one different move) was inversely proportional to players' strength.

HIGH-LEVEL KNOWLEDGE AND PLANNING

De Groot (1946), who emphasized the role of conceptual knowledge in chess expertise, reported that players' descriptions of games were centered on key positions; this finding has been confirmed by recent research (e.g., Cooke et al., 1993; de Groot & Gobet, 1996; Saariluoma, 1995). The presence of these key positions enables masters to acquire what de Groot called a "system of playing methods," many of which are stereotypical. By applying this routine knowledge, masters can often find good moves with minimal look-ahead. Saariluoma (1990, 1992) tested this hypothesis with tactical positions and found that strong players tended to choose stereotyped solutions and missed shorter (but non-typical) solutions.

Saariluoma and Hohlfeld (1994) were interested in planning with strategic positions. They found that null moves (missing moves for one side) were common (about 12% of all moves). This result is similar to the 10% found in a previous study by Charness (1981a). In a second experiment, Saariluoma and Hohlfeld (1994) changed the nature of positions by relocating a key piece so that a combination possible before the transformation could not be carried out after. Eliminating the combination produced an increase of the number of null moves.

COMPUTATIONAL MODELS OF PROBLEM SOLVING

Simon and his colleagues developed a number of process models of problem solving in chess (Baylor & Simon, 1966; Newell & Simon, 1972), and two production systems at the boundary between cognitive science and artificial intelligence were written by Wilkins (1980) and Pitrat (1977). Gobet and Jansen (1994) describe a program that uses pure pattern recognition to select moves, without carrying out any search. This is presented more as a first step toward a full problem-solving program than as a theory of human problem solving. Gobet (1997) describes SEARCH, a probabilistic model that integrates pattern recognition and search. This model, which is a direct implementation of the template theory and which incorporates insights from previous theories (e.g., de Groot, 1946; Newell & Simon, 1972), does not play chess but computes several measures such as depth of search, rate of search, and the level of fuzziness in the mind's eye as a function of the skill level (i.e., number of chunks).

When generating moves from the stimulus position or later during look-ahead, the model uses either fast pattern recognition (chunks and templates) or slower heuristics. The same methods are used when the model evaluates positions at the end of a sequence of moves. The generation of an episode (sequence of moves) is stopped when the level of fuzziness in the mind's eye is too high, an evaluation has been proposed, or no move or sequence of moves has been proposed. It is assumed that information in the mind's eye decays at a constant rate, which interferes with search. Finally, the model has a time cost for every cognitive operation; for example, it takes two seconds to carry out a move in the mind's eye, and ten seconds to evaluate a position using heuristics.

The program predicts that depth of search follows a power law of skill. When simulating a small number of participants (as is typical in chess research), the program also shows substantial variability, as was found in Saariluoma's (1992) study, where international masters and grandmasters searched less than weaker masters.

Blindfold Chess

A number of studies have investigated blindfold chess, to which Binet (1894) had already devoted a lengthy study. In blindfold chess, a player carries out one or several games without the view of the board and the pieces; the moves are communicated through standard chess notation.

Ericsson and Oliver (1984; cited in Ericsson & Staszewski, 1989) investigated the nature of the representation for chess positions dictated move by move with a player of near Master strength. In a set of experiments they demonstrated that the retrieval structure utilized by the player was extremely flexible, permitting very fast responses about what piece was present (or if the square was unoccupied) to probes (square names in algebraic notation) of each square on the chessboard. In some cases the response time of about two seconds was faster than that obtained when the player looked at a chessboard position and was probed with the name of a square. They also found that when the player memorized two chess positions, responses to probes of the squares of the chessboard improved with successive tests from the same board at a much faster rate than in conditions where there were random probes or when probes alternated across boards. In further experiments they demonstrated that the representation structure was different for memory retrieval versus perceptually available retrieval conditions. Such flexibility in the encoded representation is necessary for being able to choose good moves when playing blindfolded. (See Gobet, 1998a, for a further discussion of these results.)

Saariluoma (1991) studied memory for move sequences using blindfold chess. He dictated one move every two seconds from three types of sequences: moves actually played in a game, random but legal moves, and random and possibly illegal moves. He found that masters could recall almost perfectly the position for the moves taken from actual games and legal random moves after 15 moves, but performed poorly with illegal random moves. With additional moves, the recall of legal random moves decreased much faster than that of game moves. Saariluoma proposed that legal random moves initially allow for a relatively good recall

because they only slowly produce positions where it is not possible to recognize chunks. These results are in line with Chase and Simon's (1973b), who studied memory for moves with plain view of the board.

In a series of experiments, Saariluoma (1991) and Saariluoma and Kalakoski (1997) systematically investigated memory for blindfold games. They presented one or several games aurally (dictating moves using the standard algebraic chess notation) or visually (presenting only the current move on a computer screen). Only a few of their results can be presented here: blindfold chess requires mainly visuo-spatial working memory, and makes little use of verbal working memory; differences in LTM knowledge (e.g., number of chunks) rather than differences in imagery ability underpin skill differences; abstract representations are essential (cf. also Binet's, 1894); and there is no difference between an auditory and a visual presentation. Campitelli and Gobet (2005) used blindfold chess to study how perception filters out relevant from irrelevant information. They found that irrelevant information affects chess masters only when it changes during the presentation of the target game.

Problem solving has also been studied using blindfold chess (Saariluoma & Kalakoski, 1998). In a task consisting in searching for the best move, they found that players memorized pieces better when these were functionally relevant. This difference disappeared in a task where players had to count the number of pieces. They also found that tactical combinations embedded in a game position were easier to solve than those contained in a random position. As with normal chess, visuo-spatial interfering tasks negatively affect problem-solving performance. Finally, Chabris and Hearst (2003) found that the number of blunders did not increase much when grandmasters played blindfold games as compared to games with the view of the pieces.

Campitelli and Gobet (2005) argue that most of the results found on blindfold chess can be explained by the template theory.

Building a Human Master

Prodigies: Born or Made, and the Issue of Critical Periods

In the last decade, psychology has seen renewed interest in the question of the roles of talent and practice, and the psychology of expertise is no exception. This section contains a brief review of topics related to this question that can be roughly classified in three headings: development, training and education, and neuroscience. A fair conclusion from the available evidence is that we still do not have data rich enough to determine how they might interact in the development of chess expertise.

DEVELOPMENTAL ISSUES

In a classic study on the role of knowledge on memory development, Chi (1978) found that, while non-chessplaying adults were better at memorizing digits than chessplaying children, they were worse at memorizing game positions. Thus, domain-specific knowledge can override developmental differences. Schneider et al. (1993) extended Chi's study by adding child novices and adult experts to the design; they also presented random positions and added a nonchess visuo-spatial control task. Adults and children offered the same pattern of results: experts' superiority was the largest with meaningful positions, was reduced with the random positions, and all but disappeared with the board control task (though absent in the first trial, skill effects were apparent in later trials).

LEARNING

Several longitudinal studies have trained novices to memorize chess positions (Ericsson & Harris, 1990; Saariluoma & Laine, 2001; Gobet & Jackson, 2002). Typically, learning follows a power function. Computer models based on chunking could simulate the data relatively well (Saariluoma & Laine, 2001; Gobet & Jackson, 2002). A power function of learning was also found in Fisk and Lloyd (1988), who studied how novices learn the movement of pieces in a pseudo-chess environment.

Didierjean, Cauzinille-Marmèche, and Savina (1999) were interested in how chess novices use reasoning by analogy in learning to solve chess combinations (smothered mates). The results show that transfer was limited to problems perceptually similar to the examples and did not extend to problems requiring the use of the abstract principle behind the solution of these problems.

TRAINING AND EDUCATION

Given the importance of deliberate practice in an entrepreneurial domain such as chess, one could expect that powerful training methods have been developed. There is not much about this topic in the literature, however. Gobet and Jansen (in press) show how educational principles that can be used in chess training can be derived from the template theory. The necessity of having a coach is debated in the literature; for example, Charness, Krampe, and Mayr (1996) found a bivariate but not a unique multivariate correlation between chess skill and the presence of a coach in one sample; however, Charness, Tuffiash, Krampe, Reingold, and Vasyukova (2005) did find it in another. Gobet, Campitelli, and Waters (2002) note that using computer databases and playing computers may provide more efficient training tools than traditional training practice based on books, which is consistent with the progressive replacement of the latter by the former in professional practice. This change in training and practice techniques may well explain Howard's (1999) observation that the number of young-players among the world's elite has increased in the last decades, which he takes as evidence that average human intelligence is rising overall. Another explanation is that as young-player populations increase, the best-trained individuals should reach higher levels of performance (Charness & Gerchak, 1996).

Do skills acquired in playing chess transfer to other domains? Gobet and Campitelli (in press) reviewed all the available publications. Most studies did not meet criteria of robust scientific research, but two well-controlled studies (Frank & d'Hondt, 1979; Christiaen & Verhofstadt-Denève, 1981) found that a chess-playing group outperformed a control group in verbal ability and school results, respectively. A limit of these two studies is that a large number of tests was used, which raises the possibility of type I errors.

INDIVIDUAL DIFFERENCES

Data about individual differences do not offer a clear pattern. There is evidence that chess skill correlates with measures of intelligence, both in children (Frank & d'Hondt, 1979; Frydman & Lynn, 1992; Horgan & Morgan, 1990) and adults (Doll & Mayr, 1987). However, whereas Frank and d'Hondt (1979) and Schneider, Gruber, Gold, and Opwis (1993) found that chess experts perform better than control in non-chess visuospatial tasks with children and teenagers, Djakow, Petrowski, and Rudik (1927), Doll and Mayr (1987), and Waters, Gobet, and Leyden (2002) failed to find such differences with adults. Note that all the above studies, with the exception of Frank and d'Hondt (1979), who had an experimental design, used quasi-experimental designs; therefore, the results are based on correlations, which are equivocal about the direction of causality (is intelligence a prerequisite to chess skill, or does chess playing improves one's intelligence?). The differing patterns between children and adults are consistent with developmental theories that propose differentiation of abilities across time. Early in development all forms of problem solving are dependent on fluid intelligence (search), but later in development crystallized intelligence (knowledge: templates and chunks) changes the way that problem solving is carried out.

NEUROSCIENCE

Based on the responses to a questionnaire sent to players rated in the US Chess Federation ranking list, Cranberg and Albert (1988) found that 18% of male chess players were not right-handers. This percentage is reliably higher than that in the general population (~11%).

Chabris and Hamilton (1992) carried out a divided visual-field experiment with male chess players and found that the right hemisphere was better than the left at parsing patterns according to the default rules of chess chunking, but that the left hemisphere was more efficient at grouping pieces together when these rules did not apply.

Several brain-imaging techniques have been employed to study chess skill (Atherton et al., 2003; Campitelli, 2003; Nichelli et al.; 1994; Onofrj et al., 1995; Amidzic et al., 2001). Overall, these studies suggest that frontal and posterior parietal areas, among other areas, are engaged in chess playing. These areas are known to be engaged in tasks requiring working-memory processes. There is also some evidence that chunks are encoded in temporal lobe areas, including the fusiform gyrus, parahippocampal gyrus, and inferior temporal gyrus. In a different line of research, Campitelli (2003) found that the left supramarginal gyrus and left frontal areas were involved in autobiographical memory in two chess masters.

The Role of Deliberate Practice and Tournament Experience

As appears to be true in other domains (see Ericsson, Chapter 38, in this volume), skill acquisition in chess requires a considerable investment. Few players reach Master level performance with less than 1000 hours of serious study (Charness, Krampe, & Mayr, 1996). Relying on responses to retrospective questionnaires, these investigators probed a large sample of tournament players from different countries focusing on how much time they spent in serious study alone (deliberate practice) versus that spent in tournament play and analysis of games with others. Other predictors for current skill level included variables such as current age, starting age, age when serious about chess, age when joining a chess club, presence of coaching, and size of chess library. The variables making independent contributions to explaining current chess rating were serious study alone, size of chess library, and current age. Tournament play was not statistically significant after taking deliberate practice time into account.

Not surprisingly, age was a negative predictor (older players tended to have lower ratings, averaging a loss of about five to six rating points per year), whereas deliberate practice and size of chess library were strong positive predictors, accounting in combination for nearly 70% of explained variance in current rating.

In an enlarged version of the first sample and in a new sample, Charness, Tuffiash, Krampe, Reingold, and Vasyukova (2005) showed a somewhat-different pattern of relationships, with both coaching and tournament play in addition to deliberate practice making independent predictions to current chess rating. For predicting a player's peak rating, the two practice variables accounted for most of the variance. Of course, this correlates approach suffers from the weakness that causality is not identifiable. Longitudinal research is needed to trace out how process variables covary with changes in rating.

Conclusion

The combination of empirical and theoretical work has identified and successfully characterized a rich range of phenomena from cortical activation patterns to eye-movement patterns and from memory for static chess positions to memory for sequences of moves (including blindfold chess). Many phenomena identified are central to the concerns of psychology, particularly to theories about individual differences, memory systems, developmental processes, and theories in cognitive science. The discovery of the strong relation between skilled perception processes and skilled problem solving has influenced theory development in many other domains. For instance, chess research has been useful in characterizing the trade-offs seen between memory, perception, and problem-solving performance, as well as in assessing the role of deliberate

practice in maintaining performance across the life span (Krampe & Charness, Chapter 40). Simulation work has proven useful in describing how aging processes interact with knowledge processes to predict memory performance (Mireles & Charness, 2002).

Nonetheless, many issues remain unresolved. It is not yet clear how deliberate practice and cognitive abilities jointly determine performance across the life span given the differing patterns seen in children, young adults, and older adults. Tighter links still need to be drawn between perceptual processes and search processes, particularly as a function of skill level. With the ready availability of modern tools (neuro-imaging, eye tracking, simulation) and in conjunction with reliable older ones (think-aloud protocol analysis), the future seems bright indeed for expanding our knowledge of expertise in chess.

References

Amidzic, O., Riehle, H. J., Fehr, T., Wienbruch, C., & Elbert, T. (2001). Pattern of focal gamma bursts in chess players. *Nature, 412*, 603.

Atherton, M., Zhuang, J., Bart, W. M., Hu, X., & He, S. (2003). A functional MRI study of high-level cognition. I. The game of chess. *Cognitive Brain Research, 16*, 26–31.

Bachmann, T., & Oit, M. (1992). Stroop-like interference in chess players' imagery: An unexplored possibility to be revealed by the adapted moving-spot task. *Psychological Research, 54*, 27–31.

Baylor, G. W., & Simon, H. A. (1966). A chess mating combinations program. *Proceedings of the 1966 Spring Joint Computer Conference, 28*, 431–447.

Berliner, H., & Ebeling, C. (1989). Pattern knowledge and search: The SUPREM architecture. *Artificial Intelligence, 38*, 161–198.

Binet, A. (1894). *Psychologie des grands calculateurs et joueurs d'échecs*. Paris: Hachette. [Republished by Slatkine Ressources, Paris, 1981.]

Binet, A. (1966). Mnemonic virtuosity: A study of chess players. *Genetic Psychology Monographs, 74*, 127–162. Translated from *Revue des Deux Mondes*, (1893), 117, 826–859.

Calderwood, R., Klein, G. A., & Crandall, B. W. (1988). Time pressure, skill, and move quality in chess. *American Journal of Psychology*, 100, 481–495.

Campitelli, G. (2003). *Cognitive and neuronal bases of expertise.* Unpublished doctoral dissertation, University of Nottingham, UK.

Campitelli, G., & Gobet, F. (2005). The mind's eye in blindfold chess. *European Journal of Cognitive Psychology*, 17, 23–45.

Chabris, C. F., & Hamilton, S. E. (1992). Hemispheric specialization for skilled perceptual organization by chessmasters. *Neuropsychologia*, 30, 47–57.

Chabris, C. F., & Hearst, E. S. (2003). Visualization, pattern recognition, and forward search: Effects of playing speed and sight of the position on grandmaster chess errors. *Cognitive Science*, 27, 637–648.

Charness, N. (1976). Memory for chess positions: Resistance to interference. *Journal of Experimental Psychology: Human Learning and Memory*, 2, 641–653.

Charness, N. (1981a). Aging and skilled problem solving. *Journal of Experimental Psychology: General*, 110, 21–38.

Charness, N. (1981b). Search in chess: Age and skill differences. *Journal of Experimental Psychology: Human Perception and Performance*, 7, 467–476.

Charness, N. (1989). Expertise in chess and bridge. In D. Klahr & K. Kotovsky (Eds.), *Complex information processing: The impact of Herbert A. Simon* (pp. 183–208). Hillsdale, NJ: Erlbaum.

Charness, N. (1992). The impact of chess research on cognitive science. *Psychological Research*, 54, 4–9.

Charness, N., & Gerchak, Y. (1996). Participation rates and maximal performance: A log-linear explanation for group differences, such as Russian and male dominance in chess. *Psychological Science*, 7, 46–51.

Charness, N., Krampe, R., & Mayr, U. (1996). The role of practice and coaching in entrepreneurial skill domains: An international comparison of life-span chess skill acquisition. In K. A. Ericsson (Ed.), *The road to excellence: The acquisition of expert performance in the arts and sciences, sports, and games* (pp. 51–80). Mahwah, NJ: Erlbaum.

Charness, N., Reingold, E. M., Pomplun, M., & Stampe, D. M. (2001). The perceptual aspect of skilled performance in chess: Evidence from eye movements. *Memory and Cognition*, 29, 1146–1152.

Charness, N., Tuffiash, M., & Jastrzembski, T. (2004). Motivation, emotion, and expert skill acquisition. In D. Dai & R. J. Sternberg (Eds.), *Motivation, emotion, and cognition: Integrative perspectives* (pp. 299–319). Mahwah, NJ: Erlbaum.

Charness, N., Tuffiash, M., Krampe, R., Reingold, E. M., & Vasyukova, E. (2005). The role of deliberate practice in chess expertise. *Applied Cognitive Psychology*, 19, 151–165.

Chase, W. G., & Simon, H. A. (1973a). Perception in chess. *Cognitive Psychology*, 4, 55–81.

Chase, W. G., & Simon, H. A. (1973b). The mind's eye in chess. In W. G. Chase (Ed.), *Visual information processing* (pp. 215–281). New York: Academic Press.

Chi, M. T. H. (1978). Knowledge structures and memory development. In R. S. Siegler (Ed.), *Children's thinking: What develops?* (pp. 73–96). Hillsdale, NJ: Erlbaum.

Christiaen, J., & Verhofstadt-Denève, L. (1981). Schaken en cognitieve ontwikkeling. *Nederlands Tijdschrift voor de Psychologie*, 36, 561–582.

Cleveland, A. A. (1907). The psychology of chess and of learning to play it. *American Journal of Psychology*, 18, 269–308.

Cooke, N. J., Atlas, R. S., Lane, D. M., & Berger, R. C. (1993). Role of high-level knowledge in memory for chess positions. *American Journal of Psychology*, 106, 321–351.

Cranberg, L., & Albert, M. L. (1988). The chess mind. In L. K. Obler & D. Fein (Eds.), *The exceptional brain. Neuropsychology of talent and special abilities* (pp. 156–190). New York: Guilford Press.

de Groot, A. D. (1946). *Het denken van den schaker.* Amsterdam: Noord Hollandsche.

de Groot, A. D. (1965). *Thought and choice in chess.* The Hague: Mouton.

de Groot, A. D., & Gobet, F. (1996). *Perception and memory in chess.* Assen (The Netherlands): Van Gorcum.

Didierjean, A., Cauzinille-Marmèche, E., & Savina, Y. (1999). Learning from examples: Case-based reasoning in chess for novices. *Current Psychology of Cognition*, 18, 337–361.

Djakow, I. N., Petrowski, N. W., & Rudik, P. A. (1927). *Psychologie des Schachspiels.* Berlin: de Gruyter.

Doll, J., & Mayr, U. (1987). Intelligenz und Schachleistung – eine Untersuchung an Schachexperten. *Psychologische Beiträge*, 29, 270–289.

Elo, A. E. (1965). Age changes in master chess performances. *Journal of Gerontology*, 20, 289–299.

Elo, A. E. (1986). *The rating of chessplayers, past and present*, (2nd ed.). New York: Arco chess.

Ericsson, K. A., & Harris M. S. (1990, November). Expert chess memory without chess knowledge: A training study. Paper presented at the 31st Annual Meeting of the Psychonomics Society, New Orleans.

Ericsson, K. A., & Kintsch, W. (1995). Long-term working memory. *Psychological Review*, 102, 211–245.

Ericsson, K. A., & Oliver, W. (1984, November). Skilled memory in blindfolded chess. Paper presented at the Annual Meeting of the Psychonomic Society, San Antonio, TX.

Ericsson, K. A., & Staszewski, J. J. (1989). Skilled memory and expertise: Mechanisms of exceptional performance. In D. Klahr & K. Kotovsky (Eds.), *Complex information processing: The impact of Herbert A. Simon* (pp. 235–267). Hillsdale, NJ: Erlbaum A.

Fisk, A. D., & Lloyd, S. J. (1988). The role of stimulus to role consistency in learning rapid application of spatial rules. *Human Factors*, 30, 35–49.

Frank, A., & d'Hondt, W. (1979). Aptitudes et apprentissage du jeu d'échecs au Zaire. *Psychopathologie Africaine*, 15, 81–98.

Frey, P. W., & Adesman, P. (1976). Recall memory for visually presented chess positions. *Memory & Cognition*, 4, 541–547.

Freyhoff, H., Gruber, H., & Ziegler, A. (1992). Expertise and hierarchical knowledge representation in chess. *Psychological Research*, 54, 32–37.

Frydman, M., & Lynn, R. (1992). The general intelligence and spatial abilities of gifted young Belgian chess players. *British Journal of Psychology*, 83, 233–235.

Gobet, F. (1993). *Les mémoires d'un joueur d'échecs*. Fribourg: Editions Universitaires.

Gobet, F. (1997). A pattern-recognition theory of search in expert problem solving. *Thinking & Reasoning*, 3, 291–313.

Gobet, F. (1998a). Expert memory: A comparison of four theories. *Cognition*, 66, 115–152.

Gobet, F. (1998b). Chess players' thinking revisited. *Swiss Journal of Psychology*, 57, 18–32.

Gobet, F., & Campitelli, G. (in press). Education and chess: A critical review. In T. Redman (Ed.), *Education and chess*.

Gobet, F., Campitelli, G., & Waters, A. J. (2002). Rise of human intelligence: Comments on Howard (1999). *Intelligence*, 30, 303–311.

Gobet, F., & Clarkson, G. (2004). Chunks in expert memory: Evidence for the magical number four . . . or is it two? *Memory*, 12, 732–747.

Gobet, F., de Voogt, A., & Retschitzki, J. (2004). *Moves in mind: The psychology of board games*. New York: Psychology Press.

Gobet, F., & Jackson, S. (2002). In search of templates. *Cognitive Systems Research*, 3, 35–44.

Gobet, F., & Jansen, P. J. (1994). Towards a chess program based on a model of human memory. In H. J. van den Herik, I. S. Herschberg, & J. W. Uiterwijk (Eds.), *Advances in computer chess 7* (pp. 35–60). Maastricht: University of Limburg Press.

Gobet, F., & Jansen, P. J. (in press). Training in chess: A scientific approach. In T. Redman (Ed.), *Education and chess*.

Gobet, F., Lane, P. C. R., Croker, S., Cheng, P. C. H., Jones, G., Oliver, I., & Pine, J. M. (2001). Chunking mechanisms in human learning. *Trends in Cognitive Sciences*, 5, 236–243.

Gobet, F., & Simon, H. A. (1996a). Templates in chess memory: A mechanism for recalling several boards. *Cognitive Psychology*, 31, 1–40.

Gobet, F., & Simon, H. A. (1996b). Recall of rapidly presented random chess positions is a function of skill. *Psychonomic Bulletin & Review*, 3, 159–163.

Gobet, F., & Simon, H. A. (1996c). Recall of random and distorted positions: Implications for the theory of expertise. *Memory & Cognition*, 24, 493–503.

Gobet, F., & Simon, H. A. (1996d). The roles of recognition processes and look-ahead search in time-constrained expert problem solving: Evidence from grandmaster level chess. *Psychological Science*, 7, 52–55.

Gobet, F., & Simon, H. A. (1998). Expert chess memory: Revisiting the chunking hypothesis. *Memory*, 6, 225–255.

Gobet, F., & Simon, H. A. (2000). Five seconds or sixty? Presentation time in expert memory. *Cognitive Science*, 24, 651–682.

Gobet, F., & Waters, A. J. (2003). The role of constraints in expert memory. *Journal of Experimental Psychology: Learning, Memory & Cognition, 29*, 1082–1094.

Goldin, S. E. (1978). Memory for the ordinary: Typicality effects in chess memory. *Journal of Experimental Psychology: Human Learning and Memory, 4*, 605–616.

Goldin, S. E. (1979). Recognition memory for chess positions: Some preliminary research. *American Journal of Psychology, 92*, 19–31.

Holding, D. H. (1985). *The psychology of chess skill*. Hillsdale, NJ: Erlbaum.

Holding, D. H., & Reynolds, R. (1982). Recall or evaluation of chess positions as determinants of chess skill. *Memory and Cognition, 10*, 237–242.

Horgan, D. D., & Morgan, D. (1990). Chess expertise in children. *Applied Cognitive Psychology, 4*, 109–128.

Howard, R. W. (1999). Preliminary real-world evidence that average human intelligence really is rising. *Intelligence, 27*, 235–250.

Jongman, R. W. (1968). *Het oog van de meester* (The eye of the master). Assen (The Netherlands): Van Gorcum.

Lassiter, G. D. (2000). The relative contributions of recognition and search-evaluation processes to high-level chess performance: Comment on Gobet and Simon. *Psychological Science, 11*, 172–173.

McGregor, S. J., & Howes, A. (2002). The role of attack and defense semantics in skilled players' memory for chess positions. *Memory & Cognition, 30*, 707–717.

Milojkovic, J. D. (1982). Chess imagery in novice and master. *Journal of Mental Imagery, 6*, 125–144.

Mireles, D. E., & Charness, N. (2002). Computational explorations of the influence of structured knowledge on age-related cognitive decline. *Psychology and Aging, 17*, 245–259.

Newell, A., & Simon, H. A. (1972). *Human problem solving*. Englewood Cliffs, NJ: Prentice-Hall.

Nichelli, P., Grafman, J., Pietrini, P., Alway, D., et al. (1994). Brain activity in chess playing. *Nature, 369*, 191.

Onofrj, M., Curatola, L., Valentini, G. L., Antonelli, M., Thomas, A., & Fulgente, T. (1995). Non-dominant dorsal-prefrontal activation during chess problem solution evidenced by single photon emission computer-ized tomography (SPECT). *Neuroscience Letters, 198*, 169–172.

Pitrat, J. (1977). A chess combinations program which uses plans. *Artificial Intelligence, 8*, 275–321.

Reingold, E. M., Charness, N., Pomplun, M., & Stampe, D. M. (2001). Visual span in expert chess players: Evidence from eye movements. *Psychological Science, 12*, 48–55.

Reingold, E. M., Charness, N., Schultetus, R. S., & Stampe, D. M. (2001). Perceptual automaticity in expert chess players: Parallel encoding of chess relations. *Psychonomic Bulletin and Review, 8*, 504–510.

Saariluoma, P. (1984). *Coding problem spaces in chess: A psychological study*. Commentationes scientiarum socialium 23. Turku: Societas Scientiarum Fennica.

Saariluoma, P. (1985). Chess players' intake of task-relevant cues. *Memory and Cognition, 13*, 385–391.

Saariluoma, P. (1990). Apperception and restructuring in chess players problem solving. In K. J. Gilhooly, M. T. G. Keane, R. H. Logie, & G. Erdos (Eds.), *Lines of thought: Reflections on the psychology of thinking* (Vol. II, pp. 41–57). New York: Wiley.

Saariluoma, P. (1991). Aspects of skilled imagery in blindfold chess. *Acta Psychologica, 77*, 65–89.

Saariluoma, P. (1992). Error in chess: The apperception-restructuring view. *Psychological Research, 54*, 17–26.

Saariluoma, P. (1994). Location coding in chess. *Quarterly Journal of Experimental Psychology, 47A*, 607–630.

Saariluoma, P. (1995). *Chess players' thinking: A cognitive psychological approach*. London: Routlege.

Saariluoma, P., & Hohlfeld, M. (1994). Apperception in chess players' long-range planning. *European Journal of Cognitive Psychology, 6*, 1–22.

Saariluoma, P., & Kalakoski, V. (1997). Skilled imagery and long-term working memory. *American Journal of Psychology, 110*, 177–201.

Saariluoma, P., & Kalakoski, V. (1998). Apperception and imagery in blindfold chess. *Memory, 6*, 67–90.

Saariluoma, P., & Laine, T. (2001). Novice construction of chess memory. *Scandinavian Journal of Psychology, 42*, 137–146.

Schultetus, R. S., & Charness, N. (1999). Recall or evaluation of chess positions revisited: The relationship between memory and evaluation in chess skill. *American Journal of Psychology, 112*, 555–569.

Schneider, W., Gruber, H., Gold, A., & Opwis, K. (1993). Chess expertise and memory for chess positions in children and adults. *Journal of Experimental Child Psychology, 56*, 328–349.

Simon, H. A., & Gilmartin, K. J. (1973). A simulation of memory for chess positions. *Cognitive Psychology, 5*, 29–46.

Tikhomirov, O. K., & Poznyanskaya, E. D. (1966). An investigation of visual search as a means of analyzing heuristics. *Soviet Psychology, 5*, 2–15.

Wagner, D. A., & Scurrah, M. J. (1971). Some characteristics of human problem-solving in chess. *Cognitive Psychology, 2*, 454–478.

Van der Maas, H. L. J., & Wagenmakers, E.-J. (2005). A psychometric analysis of chess expertise. *American Journal of Psychology, 118*, 29–60.

Waters, A. J., Gobet, F., & Leyden, G. (2002). Visuo-spatial abilities in chess players. *British Journal of Psychology, 93*, 557–565.

Wilkins, D. (1980). Using patterns and plans in chess. *Artificial Intelligence, 14*, 165–203.

CHAPTER 31

Exceptional Memory

John M. Wilding & Elizabeth R. Valentine

Historical Introduction

Interest in improving methods of memorizing has a long history. Before the widespread use of writing, poets and storytellers devised methods of making memorization and recall easier, using rhythm, imagery, and formulaic descriptions (Rubin, 1995). Non-experts, too, had to rely far more heavily on oral memory than in modern times.

Today equally impressive feats of memory are demonstrated regularly by experts in specific fields of knowledge (chess, music, medicine, literature, law, football, etc.), which embody far more information than was available to our ancestors. As with the poets and storytellers of an earlier age, long and varied exposure, together with motivation to achieve mastery, have enabled these experts to build up a body of information that makes new additions easier by embedding them in an already organized structure, often without conscious effort. Such an organized database is known as semantic memory and depends on the progressive addition and organization of material acquired over a lengthy period.

The focus of this chapter, however, is on individuals who display an unusual ability to memorize information, especially ability to memorize types of information that present particular difficulty for the majority, such as lists of numbers with no inherent structure. This form of expertise involves episodic memory, the ability to reproduce a prior input, event, or episode. Superior ability to retain episodic information will undoubtedly facilitate the development of semantic memory, but is probably not essential to it. Nor is it sufficient, since motivation and interest in the area of knowledge are equally or more important. Other chapters deal with the development of expertise depending on efficient semantic memory.

It has been known from Greek and Roman times that memory can be improved by certain techniques that orators adopted to aid them in their speech making. The Roman orator Cicero tells a story about the Greek poet Simonides who was reciting at a banquet. He was called outside to meet two men (said to be the mythical heroes, Castor and Pollux, who had adopted this method of saving his life). During his absence the roof of the building collapsed, killing everyone present. The bodies were unrecognizable but Simonides was able to recall where each guest had been sitting and was thereby inspired to invent the mnemonic method of loci, which is still widely used. In this method each item to be retained is associated with a location on a well-known route. When recall of the items is required, a mental walk is taken along the route, the locations serving as cues to recall the items in order.

The scientific study of superior memory ability begins with Binet's (1894) study of three experts in number recall. It was a further twenty years before a more detailed study appeared, of Rückle in Germany (Muller, 1911, 1913), and another twenty years before Susukita (1933, 1934) undertook a lengthy study of Ishihara in Japan. From the 1960s onward many more reports have appeared, some of them very detailed and much more precise in their testing of the processes involved. These include Luria's (1975) study of Shereshevskii (carried out in the 1930s but not available in English until 1975), Hunter's (1962, 1977) reports on the memory of Alexander Aitken, Hunt and Love's (1972) account of VP's memory, studies by Ericsson and his colleagues (e.g. Ericsson, 1985; Ericsson & Polson, 1988), Thompson et al.'s (1993) report on Rajan Mahadevan, and our own studies of TE, TM, and contestants at the World Memory Championships (Gordon et al., 1984; Wilding & Valentine, 1985, 1994a, 1994b). There is now therefore a substantial body of data available collected under controlled conditions, together with self-reports from experts on their methods. Theories have been developed and tested and a consensus is emerging about underlying processes.

One problem facing the study of exceptional memory performance is the location and identification of suitable individuals. Expert performers are by definition rare. Thus many of the studies in the literature (as seen above) are individual case studies. These have the disadvantage that one cannot be sure how far the results are generalizable to other cases. The rise of international memory championships has enabled the gathering of group data, but the contestants at such competitions tend to rely heavily on strategies, hence these samples may be somewhat biased to a particular type of memorizer.

Four main methods have been used in the study of superior memory: performance on experimental tasks, self-report on the methods used, psychometric analyses, and brain-imaging. Most studies have combined the first two of these. Self-reports provide unique insights into the methods employed by expert memorizers, but their reliability needs to be confirmed by objective performance data. Psychometric data have been used to explore relationships between memory and other individual difference variables such as intelligence, visual and verbal imagery, and personality factors. Lastly, the development of structural and functional brain-imaging opens up the possibility of examining both possible differences in brain structure in memory experts and brain activity during the process of memorizing, and hence of investigating the neurological basis of memory expertise.

Some Key Examples of Memory Expertise

Superiority in memory can be demonstrated in two main ways, firstly, by retrieval without error of a substantial amount of material, compared with frequent errors in the case of normal memory ability, and secondly, by retention of an unusually large proportion of the original material at some fixed interval afterwards, again in comparison with a control group. As pointed out earlier, this is known as episodic memory, in contrast to organized information in semantic memory.

One example of memory expertise where this distinction becomes blurred is the feat, popular among memory experts, of learning the expansion of the number pi to thousands of places. This requires long, dedicated exposure and the development of an organizational framework, as shown by the ability of many memory experts to locate a specific part of the sequence or expand a fragment of the original in response to a cue.

We offer now some of the most striking examples of memory expertise, which serve to raise the most insistent questions under investigation. Susukita presented the Japanese expert Ishihara with random sequences of numbers in rows and measured the time until he signaled he was ready to recall the list. For lists of 200 items Ishihara took an average of 1.7 seconds per item and made about 1% errors. For the longest list of 2400 items the time per item was 8.2 seconds and the error rate was 2%, so the list took some four hours to memorize. Ishihara described his method in detail. First, each numeral could be transformed into one of several syllables in Japanese and these could be combined into words. Second, he had a database of 400 images of places he knew. He associated the words with a succession of locations in one of these "foundations" as he called them. We will be returning frequently to these two basic processes of recoding items and embedding them in an already established structure.

The Russian neuropsychologist Alexander Luria first met the memory expert Shereshevskii (S) in the late 1920s and studied his memory intensively during the 1930s. He found that S's ability to retain sequences of spoken items was "virtually unlimited" and believed that this unusual memory was innate, not dependent on any technique. One of Luria's main arguments was derived from S's ability to memorize a number matrix. Luria believed that S retained a photo-like image of the matrix. However, Ericsson and Chase (1982) have noted that S took longer to recall columns than rows and longer to recall the matrix backwards than forwards. If he had been reading an image, there should have been little difference between these conditions. Many other experts tested on this task have shown a similar pattern and their descriptions of their method make no reference to an image. Instead they claim to code the matrix row by row, often recoding numbers into words. Recalling by columns involves retrieving each row, then one item from each row,

whereas reversing the order for backwards recall necessitates additional operations and hence more recall time, exactly as observed. Hence it seems likely that S was using some such method. Certainly he used the method of loci described above with other material, basing it on Gorky Street in Moscow. Luria argues that he adopted this method later only in order to organize the unusual spontaneous imagery that Luria assumed was the ultimate basis of his superiority, but there are indications that he may already have been using it when he first met Luria (see Wilding & Valentine, 1997, p. 23). Ericsson and Chase conclude that S's superior memory depended entirely on such methods, but this may be an oversimplification. Several observations made by Luria imply that there were a number of peculiarities about his memory, particularly the vivid imagery and synaesthesia that he experienced from a very early age. However, synaesthesia is not invariably associated with superior memory (Wilding & Valentine, 1997, pp. 25–26). In the case of S imagery was invariably evoked by surface characteristics of the input (particularly sounds) and impaired his ability to understand meaning or reference to a single object by different words (because the words evoked different images). Wilding and Valentine suggest that the dominance of surface characteristics of the input over meaning is reminiscent of some aspects of Asperger's syndrome, a milder form of autism, which is characterised by difficulty in interpreting meaning, social conventions, and "other minds."

In 1972 Hunt and Love published a study of VP, who demonstrated superior memory ability on a wide range of tasks. The authors obtained only general information on his methods. With numbers he searched for a meaningful association such as a date, then added further associations about events occurring on that date. With nonsense syllables he related them to one of many European languages he knew. However, other evidence suggested that he possessed some naturally superior ability. On a short-term memory-scanning task, he could decide equally quickly, regardless of list length, that a number had been present in a recently presented list. Normally decision time increases with list length, implying serial search through the list, but VP appeared to be able to scan all items simultaneously. Anecdotal evidence also suggested early superior memory for rail and bus timetables and the city map. VP, however, thought that his memory was the result of intensive training in rote memorization at school, so training and methods were probably also important.

One of the most interesting examples of superior memory is Alexander Aitken, Professor of Mathematics at Edinburgh University, described by Hunter (1962, 1977) in a largely anecdotal account. Aitken had a superior digit span (13 auditorily presented items and 15 visually presented items). He stated that he allowed associations to groups of items to "reveal themselves," based on his mathematical knowledge, and further structured these groups by rhythm, but he used no deliberate mnemonic methods. However, his abilities were not solely dependent on his mathematical expertise. Hunter (1996) reports that Aitken read Bartlett's (1932) "War of the Ghosts" story twice in 1934 and recalled it in 1960. Hunt and Love gave this story to VP and counted the number of nouns and verbs recalled (62% at immediate recall and 59% six weeks later). A control group with average memory ability recalled 45% initially and 32% after six weeks. Aitken recalled 58% after 26 years! He is thus the strongest candidate for a very superior, general, natural memory.

In contrast SF, an average undergraduate, was selected by Ericsson and Chase (Ericsson, Chase, & Faloon, 1980) to test whether digit span, normally around seven items, could be improved by practice. SF was a long-distance runner and devised the idea of encoding digit strings as running times such as "a good time for the mile," thereby constructing units composed of three or four digits. In later developments these units were combined into groups of three units, then pairs of these groups were combined into super-groups and so forth, thereby imposing a hierarchal structure on the whole

list. SF attained a span of 82 digits. Most of these were held in a more permanent form than fragile short-term memory, since suppressing auditory rehearsal affected only the final three or four digits. Another subject, DD, using dates or other meaningful recodings, attained a span of 101 digits. Wilding and Valentine (1997) have expressed some scepticism that this method alone can account completely for SF's achievement. Running times would not provide unambiguous cues for recall, even if he had many variations ("a very poor mile time," "an average mile time for the marathon," etc.). A tape of SF recalling at an early stage in his "career" refers to 12 mile times and six two-mile times in a single sequence. Some sequences could not be coded as times (89.6 seconds would be reported as 1 minute 29.6 seconds in athletics), so SF used ages ("a very old man") instead, but these codes are equally ambiguous. Both the tape and a protocol provided by Chase and Ericsson (1981) show many cases where no recoding occurred, implying that SF often fell back on rote recall. Finally, there is no indication of how SF could avoid confusion between successive sequences (nor any data on the frequency of such confusions). SF may not, therefore, have been quite so average as the experimenters believed. If nothing else, his drive to succeed was exceptional, as is revealed by his comments in the tape and protocol records, and might account for differences in performance across time for SF, DD, and for a woman who dropped out of digit-span training without achieving notable improvement.

In 1981 Rajan Mahadevan recalled 31,811 digits of pi without errors. (But Hideaki Tomoyori subsequently outdid this record by reciting 40,000 digits, using a story mnemonic; the names of digits in Japanese have a second meaning, which can be used readily to build such a story.) As pointed out earlier, such performances could be the result simply of sweat and tears, rather than any superior memory ability or methods. However, Thompson et al. (1993) demonstrated that Rajan could recall 43 digits presented auditorily and 28 (later 60) presented visually. His ability with letters was more modest (a span of 13 items) but still well above the norm. They argued that he had a natural ability to retain about 13 items, rather than the seven items of the normal span. They supported this by measuring how long Rajan took to begin recall after the end of list presentation, arguing that such a pause would remain constant as long as the list was within the natural memory span, but would rise once some recoding of the list became necessary because of the need to retrieve the additional codes. "Normal" subjects showed an increase in this measure once list length exceeded seven items, the average digit span, but Rajan showed no increase until list length exceeded 13 items.

Rajan cannot have been maintaining the items in a temporary short-term store, since he could remember them after being distracted, or recite them backwards; sometimes he retained them for 24 hours or more. However, he did not describe any form of recoding strategy analogous to those we have encountered above. Thompson et al. claim that he labelled each digit by its list position. When required to learn a 20 × 20 number matrix he said that he encoded row by row, together with the first column in order to retain the order of the rows. This was confirmed by the time pattern of his recall; the first column took much less time than other columns. However, there was no evidence in his time pattern when recalling the rows that he divided them up into smaller units.

Thompson et al. discuss in detail his memory for pi. In the display from which he learned, the numbers were laid out in rows of 100, separated into blocks of ten, every ten rows being separated from the next set of ten rows by a space; so it was possible to ask for the 13th item in the 5th row, for example. He was faster at locating the first five digits in a block of ten than the second five, suggesting that he had retained the display structure. Thompson et al. suggest that the blocks of ten digits formed units like words, created by sheer rote learning.

Recently Ericsson et al. (2004) have argued that Rajan's impressive digit span was primarily dependent on these units formed during his learning of pi. When given other symbols without this advantage, Rajan's performance was much worse than with digits, until he learned to convert these symbols into numbers. This conclusion may well be correct, but it leaves open the question of how Rajan had mastered pi without any apparent recoding strategy such as those used by Ishihara and Tomoyori. At the very least, highly unusual persistence and motivation were needed, and one has the suspicion that some superiority in normal memory is necessary in any individual who can persist with a task that is so unrewarding for the normal memorizer.

Wilding and Valentine (1997) describe a young female subject, JR, who showed remarkable memory ability without employing any well-practiced methods. She performed particularly well on immediate memory for faces and for names to faces, but her most impressive performance was in delayed recall without warning a week later. On the four tasks tested (memory for a story, faces, names, and words) she averaged 95% retention of her already high scores at immediate testing. A control group averaged 59% and the group of experts tested by these authors (Wilding & Valentine, 1994a) did only slightly better with 62% retention.

We have now described the most intriguing cases of unusual memory that raise some of the main questions. Other cases are described by Wilding and Valentine (1997). We will not discuss here the small number of cases of superior memory of a very specific kind, which appear to be independent of any strategy, such as for languages, music, visual imagery, and cases of autistic memory (see Wilding & Valentine, 1997, pp 47–51 for details).

Theoretical Issues

We now specify more precisely the main issues that have emerged in the course of the above survey.

- Is exceptional memory typically specific to a particular sub-process, type of task or material, or does it generalize across these?

- To what extent is exceptional memory superiority natural, or acquired by training in mnemonic methods, or both? If natural superiority occurs, are such cases interpretable as the tail of a normal distribution in memory ability or as qualitatively different from the normal population?
- If superiority can be acquired by training, what is the nature of successful training?
- How does such superiority relate to other individual differences, such as intelligence?
- What is the neurological basis of exceptional memory?
- Does training in mnemonic methods have practical benefits for everyday remembering, development of expertise in other areas, remediation of memory impairments, and so forth?

General or Specific?

All memory requires material to be encoded, stored, and retrieved, so a full understanding of exceptional memory requires the contribution of these different processes to be distinguished. Furthermore, memory is widely regarded as comprising a number of separate systems. We have already referred to the distinction between episodic memory and semantic memory, pointing out that when considering memory expertise we are primarily concerned with the former, the ability to reproduce in some way (by speech, writing, acting out, etc.) an earlier experience, whereas semantic memory is more properly considered as a component of other forms of expertise, such as knowledge in medicine, the arts, sport, and so forth.

However, many other distinctions have been made amongst subsystems in the brain that serve memory, particularly those dedicated to processing specific inputs (e.g., visual, auditory) or materials (e.g., faces, music). Wilding and Valentine (1997) have argued that, despite the evidence for separate memory systems that handle specific

types of input, there must be some central process that integrates information from separate systems. The amnesic syndrome, for example, typically affects memory over a wide range of material. Additional evidence in support of some overall memory ability can be drawn from correlational studies. Carroll (1993) has reviewed factor-analytic studies of cognitive abilities and concludes that there is "a general memory ability that affects . . . performances in a wide variety of tasks and behaviours involving memory" (p. 302). He suggests that there may also be separate abilities to learn over repeated exposure (to lay down long-term memories) and to retain information (Ingham, 1952). Wilding and Valentine (1997) also showed that memory for a wide range of material loaded on a single factor, whereas retention showed some tendency to load on a separate factor or factors. Wilding et al. (1999) showed that self-rating of memory ability correlated significantly, though not dramatically, with performance on a wide range of tasks and was also related to examination performance.

Thus it is possible, indeed likely, that memory efficiency may vary between individuals either within specific systems or overall, and hence exceptional ability may be either specific or general. Examples of unusual superiority in specific aspects of memory are rare, as indicated above. In the light of the preceding discussion individuals lying at the extreme end of the distribution of overall memory ability should show wide-ranging superiority. Alternatively, neural or genetic abnormality might produce performance that is so unusual as to appear qualitatively different from the norm. Also in some cases superiority with several types of material is clearly due to application of the same technique. The limited data available do not in general provide unequivocal evidence about the generality of the superiority exhibited since most of the studies tested mainly memory for numbers. Tests using numbers are popular because numbers are universal, have the same significance for all cultures, normally have no intrinsic meaning when combined into sequences, and permit load to be varied to any required degree.

In some of the cases we have discussed, however, memory ability was demonstrated over a wider range of material than numbers alone, notably by VP and Aitken, and to a lesser extent JR and S. Ishihara was proficient with both numbers and words (using a common strategy). On the other hand SF's superiority was restricted to numbers because he had not devised a strategy for use with letters; Rajan's performance was dazzling with numbers, less impressive with letters and other symbols, and otherwise quite moderate (Biederman et al., 1992), so his memory ability appears to have been relatively specific. Whether this is, as Ericsson et al. (2004) believe, because it was dependent on his prior learning of pi (itself requiring explanation) or because he had some inborn special facility with numbers, remains under debate.

Our conclusion to the first question is, therefore, that most often superior memory is quite general (as in the cases of VP and Aitken), but in some cases (described by Wilding & Valentine, 1997, p. 47 et seq.) it can be highly specific.

Natural or Acquired?

Many cases of memory superiority are clearly dependent on the use of special techniques, as already indicated. It does seem that highly impressive performance without the use of techniques is very rare indeed. The more difficult question is whether there are any cases where techniques can be completely ruled out as an explanation. The question also arises as to whether, where no technique is apparent, the individual represents a case drawn from the extreme tail of a normal distribution of ability or has some qualitatively different ability from the norm. Of the cases we have discussed, S, like autistic individuals, displays the most obvious abnormalities in the quality as well as the capacity of his memory. Aitken and JR present the most persuasive cases of natural all-round superiority, VP (and possibly Rajan) demonstrated natural ability aided

by already acquired knowledge and practice, and Ishihara and SF depended primarily on techniques, with the possibility of some preexisting natural facility on which to base them.

Wilding and Valentine (1994a), in their study of a group of memory experts, developed some criteria for distinguishing those relying on techniques from those who appeared to have a natural superiority. The tasks used were divided into "strategic," those readily amenable to techniques (on the basis of known methods, including those mentioned by the participants), and "non-strategic," those where techniques were inappropriate or not readily available because of task novelty. Tests for faces, names for faces, word lists, and telephone numbers were assigned to the first category and tests for a story, spatial and temporal positions of pictures, and snowflakes to the second. The eight participants in the study who performed best on the immediate memory tasks were divided into a group reliant on well-practiced mnemonic techniques ("strategic" memorizers; n = 5) and those denying any systematic use of such methods ("non-strategic" memorizers; n = 3). Results are shown in Figure 31.1. Strategic memorizers performed outstandingly well on strategic tasks but little better than a control group on non-strategic tasks. Non-strategic memorizers performed above average and equally well on both types of task, being worse than strategic memorizers on strategic tasks but better than them on non-strategic tasks. However, the overall superiority of non-strategic memorizers compared with an average control group, though substantial, was not outstanding, suggesting that very superior performance without using a technique is rare. There were also dramatic differences between the two groups in retention over a week, as shown in Table 31.1. This occurred even though three of the tasks tested after a delay (faces, names, and words) were strategic tasks (in the sense above) and produced superior immediate performance in the strategic group. Thus, despite the small number of cases, the differences were clear and the most striking evidence of

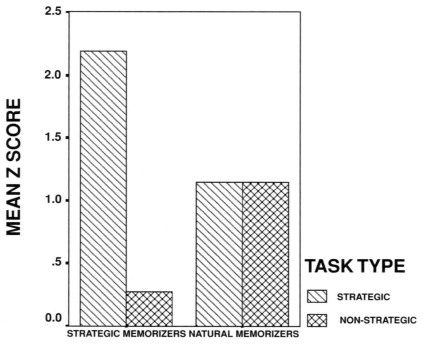

Figure 31.1. Mean z scores (compared with age-matched norms) on "strategic" and "non-strategic" tasks for strategic and natural memorizers.

superior natural memory seems to lie in retention.

Wilding and Marshall (2004) investigated the possibility of natural superiority in short-term memory, following the suggestion of Thompson et al. (1993) that Rajan Mahadevan had a natural short-term memory span of 13 items. As described earlier, the main evidence for this claim was derived from the delay before he started recall, which remained constant until list length exceeded

Table 31.1. Percentage recalled/recognized at immediate testing on four tasks and percentage of immediate recall/recognition retained over a week for strategic and non-strategic memorizers and a control group.

	Immediate test	Delayed test
Strategic memorizers	94	53
Natural memorizers	85	83
Control group	56	59

13 items, then rose. Wilding and Marshall took the same measure, but also recorded times to produce each item in lists of different length, testing four experts, all of whom had unusually long digit spans (14, 16, 18, and 21 items). Only one of them showed the same pattern as Rajan, with delay before recall constant up to a list length of eight items, then an increase in this delay. Hence Thompson et al.'s measure was not a useful criterion for natural memory span. Moreover, all four experts showed grouping of items, once list length exceeded about seven items, with groups separated by longer pauses at recall. Groups were two, three or four items in length in different cases, and in each case matched the recoding strategy described afterwards by the expert. Thus, in all four cases superior digit span seemed to depend on a mnemonic strategy; no evidence for any natural superiority was found.

We conclude that the most striking examples of superior memory are strategy dependent, but there is also evidence for a natural component. In the latter case, the ability demonstrated may be either qualitatively different from the norm or similar but more efficient.

The Nature of Successful Strategies

It is already apparent that various strategies have been practiced by different individuals that are highly successful when large amounts of unstructured or meaningless material are to be rapidly encoded and reproduced within a short period.

Chase and Ericsson (1981) have proposed three principles of skilled memory: meaningful encoding, retrieval structure, and speed-up. The first two encapsulate the key features of all mnemonic methods, and can be adopted very easily, though practice is required to make them efficient. However, as we have seen, they do not guarantee good retention, and one of the experts with whom we have discussed these issues emphasizes that they provide only a method of overcoming the initial problem of ensuring that the information is encoded and available at recall. Thereafter practice is required to ensure that this information can be achieved quickly and eventually automatically. This is the third process (speed-up) identified by Chase and Ericsson, and it is not, unlike the others, rapidly mastered but requires much practice to develop (Kliegl et al., 1987).

We have already seen examples of meaningful encoding in the descriptions of methods used by Ishihara (conversion of numbers to words), SF (conversion of numbers to running times), and VP (conversion of numbers to dates). Other variations are described by Wilding and Valentine (1997). In all these cases the basic principle is to select part of the input and retrieve a verbal or visual association, often learned for this specific purpose.

Once the input has been recoded, it is implanted into a structure. The method of loci is the best known and most widely used (Ishihara, S, several of our experts in our 1994 study, and all but one in a study by Maguire et al., 2003a). This structure is used to ensure that all items are inserted and has the advantage that order can be retained. Kalakoski and Saariluoma (2001) showed that the visuo-spatial knowledge of taxi drivers was better as a retrieval structure when recalling street names than semantic or alphabetical organization, suggesting that this type of structure has some special advantages. Creating a story is another possibility, though less reliable because the structure is neither permanent nor already known. These are examples of what Ericsson calls a retrieval structure, which he sees as principally designed to aid retrieval. However, it is equally important at encoding. Ericsson and Kintsch (1995, 2000) have in addition developed the concept of Long-Term Working Memory, mainly to explain the rapid access to relevant information of experts in fields such as chess. This is a more permanent store of readily available information that can be rapidly accessed via cues in short-term memory, as illustrated in several of the above cases.

These well-tried principles for aiding memory can, with ingenuity, be adapted to a variety of situations, provided that the units of information are clearly demarcated. However, their use in many real-life situations is limited because prior selection and organization are necessary and clear segmentation of the content, for example, of a philosophical argument, is not very easy.

Memory and Intelligence

Inevitably data on the IQ of memory experts are somewhat meager, and combining experts who do and do not use memory techniques confuses the picture. Maguire et al. (2003a) tested ten memory experts, all users of techniques, and ten matched controls (see below for details). They found no differences in general intelligence, measured by the National Adult Reading Test and the Matrix Subtest of the Wechsler Abbreviated Scale of Intelligence. However, the important question is whether natural memory superiority is related to IQ, and the available data are simply inadequate to reach any firm conclusion on this. Recorded cases of superior memory in learning-impaired individuals, such as autistics, would seem to suggest that memory ability is independent of IQ, but the underlying reasons for unusual memory in such cases are as yet poorly understood and seem to involve narrowly focused obsession and motivation in some cases, rather than pure memory ability. On the other hand, experts in specific fields of attainment, as already pointed out, show impressive knowledge of their field, but it is likely that this stems largely from motivation, exposure, and ability to select and organize information, and such abilities are undoubtedly related to general intelligence.

A considerable body of evidence demonstrates that the speed of processing in the brain is related to IQ. Salthouse (1985) suggested that the decline in memory with age could be due to decreasing speed of processing. On this view IQ and memory would in part depend on a single factor. Rabbitt (1993) and his colleagues confirmed the relation between performance on speeded processing and IQ but showed only weak relations between these measures and age. Memory, however, was strongly related to age and only weakly to IQ and processing speed. This is convincing evidence that memory and IQ are distinct constructs. See also Horn and Masunaga, Chapter 34.

Neurological Basis of Superior Memory

Although there is a fairly extensive literature on the neurological basis of normal memory, as yet few studies have investigated the neurological basis of superior memory. Maguire et al. (2003a) carried out structural and functional MRI on the brains of ten memory experts and ten controls matched for sex, age, and handedness. Participants were scanned while they attempted to memorize six-item sequences of three-digit numbers, faces, or snow crystals, the prediction being that these types of material would be differentially susceptible to the use of mnemonic strategies. Recognition was tested subsequently outside the scanner. A number of psychometric tests were also administered. There were no structural brain differences between the groups, so there was no evidence for brain plasticity as a function of

experience, as has been demonstrated in the case of musicians (e.g., Schlaug et al., 1995), Braille reading (Hamilton & Pascual-Leone, 1998), and navigational skills (Maguire et al., 2000). (In the case of the musicians, the structural changes were usually associated with early commencement of training, e.g., before the age of seven. However, Maguire et al.'s (2000) study of taxi drivers provided evidence for brain plasticity during adulthood.) The memory experts were much better than the controls on digits and somewhat better on faces, however, there was little difference on snow crystals. There were three main brain areas in which activity during memorizing occurred in the experts only: the medial parietal cortex, retrosplenial cortex, and right posterior hippocampus, areas known to be implicated in spatial memory and navigation (O'Keefe & Nadel, 1978; Maguire et al., 2003b). Nine out of the ten memory experts, but none of the controls, reported that they used the method of loci. Hence the neurological data concurred with the self-reports. These differences were not explicable in terms of superior performance by the experts, since the differences between groups in brain activity were maintained across tasks, whereas the difference in performance varied across tasks, being negligible for snow crystals. Nor were the differences explicable in terms of general cognitive ability, since there was no significant difference between the groups on tests of verbal and non-verbal intelligence. The experts, however, were superior on tests of working and long-term (though not visual) memory.

A question that remains to be answered is why there were no differences in any aspect of the brain recordings to match the differences in superiority of the experts for the different materials. Either the critical differences were too subtle to show in the measures taken, or some other difference remains to be uncovered.

Nyberg et al. (2003) used PET scanning to study brain activity in older and younger participants during training in acquisition and use of the method of loci. Younger participants and older ones who improved showed increased activity in occipito-parietal cortex and left retrosplenial cortex (see Maguire et al., 2003b). Only younger participants showed increased activity in dorsal frontal areas while using the method; these areas are associated with working-memory processes such as organization and image generation from words. The authors suggest two reasons for age-related deficits: basic resources (corresponding to frontal processing deficiency) and failure to engage in task-relevant cognitive processing (associated with posterior production deficiency). Both are presumably relevant for acquiring expertise.

Tanaka et al. (2002) used fMRI to study brain activity in abacus experts while they were retaining digits. Experts showed more activity in cortical areas relating to visuospatial working memory (bilateral frontal sulcus and superior parietal lobule) than in areas related to verbal working memory, whereas the reverse was true in non-experts. Thus, once again, experts seemed to utilize visuo-spatial representations more than non-experts in order to aid memory. (Also see Hill & Schneider, Chapter 37.)

Practical Applications of Memory Expertise

Effectiveness of mnemonic techniques for memory remediation has been reported in the elderly (for reviews see Camp, 1998; Verhaeghen & Marcoen, 1996; Verhaeghen, Marcoen, & Goossens, 1992) and in special needs populations (e.g., Mastropieri & Scruggs, 1989).

Yesavage and Rose (1983) examined the effect of training in the method of loci on immediate and delayed serial recall in the elderly. Effects were enhanced when the mnemonic training was preceded by concentration training (techniques designed to improve selective and sustained attention) and transferred to paired-associate learning. Anschutz et al. (1985) demonstrated that training older adults in the method of loci in a free-recall task transferred to the more ecologically valid task of memory for a grocery list in real-life shopping situations. Yesavage, Rose, and Bower (1983) investigated fac-

tors affecting instruction in a mnemonic to aid the learning of name-to-face associations (selecting a prominent facial feature and transforming the name into a concrete word) in the elderly. Both interactive imagery (forming an image to link the facial feature and the name) and semantic orienting (judging the pleasantness of the image association formed) enhanced name recall; semantic orienting also led to decreased forgetting in delayed recall.

Stigsdotter and Bäckman (1989; Stigsdotter, Neely, & Bäckman, 1993a, 1993b) investigated the effect of multifactorial memory training (training in the method of loci, attentional skills, and relaxation) on recall of concrete words in older adults. Improvement was sustained in testing three and one-half years later. The fact that a unifactorial group, trained only in the method of loci, performed as well as the multifactorial group in one of their studies suggests that training in encoding may be sufficient to produce long-term gains. The effects transferred to recall of objects but not recall of abstract words or subject-performed tasks, suggesting that generalization may be limited (Neely & Bäckman, 1995).

Kliegl, Smith, and Baltes (1989, 1990; Baltes & Kliegl, 1992) used improvement in serial word recall following training in the method of loci (reflecting "cognitive reserve capacity") to investigate the nature of age differences in cognitive performance. Though both younger and older participants showed substantial plasticity, differences between the age groups were magnified as a result of training. The new rank order of participants after training remained stable across subsequent practice sessions, suggesting that training substantially affected the way the task was performed. Also, consistent with the assumption of age-related decline in developmental reserve capacity, the unique variance in serial word recall associated with age group became more salient as training progressed. Fluid intelligence (as measured by digit symbol substitution) before training became a predictor of performance over the course of training.

Although a number of memory interventions have been developed for use with the pathological elderly, for example, those suffering from dementia (see Camp et al. 1996), the existing evidence suggests that mnemonics, which rely on internal processing rather than external aids and are aimed at enhancing explicit rather than implicit memory, are likely to be of limited use for such populations (Camp, 1998).

Future Directions

Although empirical work on memory expertise has continued, there has been little theoretical advance beyond development of Ericsson's (1985) framework, but more work is needed on the effectiveness and ease of application of different methods for different types of task. Patterns of improvement in memory performance as a result of training in mnemonics, particularly the method of loci, have been used to examine mechanisms underlying cognitive plasticity over the life span (Kliegl et al., 1989, 1990; Verhaeghen & Marcoen, 1996). This basic memory research, aimed at understanding the reasons underlying age differences, has been extended to the development of interventions for the normal and pathological elderly from a rehabilitation perspective, with increasing emphasis on external validity and applicability to everyday life. Probably the most striking advance in recent years has been the development of brain-imaging techniques. It is likely that these will lead to the most significant progress in the future. The study by Nyberg et al. (2003) (reviewed above) combines two of these approaches by examining the neural basis of facets of age-related changes in memory improvement as a function of mnemonic training.

References

Anschutz, L., Camp, C. L., Markley, R. P., & and Kramer, J. J. (1985). Maintenance and generalization of mnemonics for grocery shopping by older adults. *Experimental Aging Research, 11,* 157–160.

Baltes, P. B., & Kliegl, R. (1992). Further testing of limits of cognitive plasticity: Negative age differences in a mnemonic skill are robust. *Developmental Psychology, 28,* 121–125.

Bartlett, F. C. (1932). *Remembering.* Cambridge, UK: Cambridge University Press.

Biederman, I., Cooper, E. E., Mahadevan, R. S., & Fox, P. W. (1992). Unexceptional spatial memory in an exceptional memorist. *Journal of Experimental Psychology: Learning, Memory and Cognition, 18,* 654–657.

Binet, A. (1894). *Psychologie des Grands Calculateurs et Jouers d'Échecs.* Paris: Librairie Hachette.

Camp, C. J. (1998). Memory interventions for normal and pathological older adults. *Annual Review of Gerontology and Geriatrics, 18,* 155–189.

Carroll, J. B. (1993). *Human Cognitive Abilities: A Survey of Factor Analytic Studies.* Cambridge, UK: Cambridge University Press.

Chase, W. G., & Ericsson, K. A. (1981). Skilled memory. In J. R. Anderson (Ed.), *Cognitive Skills and Their Acquisition* (pp. 141–189). Hillsdale, NJ: Lawrence Erlbaum Associates.

Ericsson, K. A. (1985). Memory skill. *Canadian Journal of Psychology, 39,* 188–231.

Ericsson, K. A., & Chase, W. G. (1982). Exceptional memory. *American Scientist, 70,* 607–615.

Ericsson, K. A., Chase, W. G., & Faloon, S. (1980). Acquisition of memory skill. *Science, 208,* 1181–1182.

Ericsson, K. A., Delaney, P. F., Weaver, G., & Mahadevan, R. (2004). Uncovering the structure of a memorist's "basic" memory capacity: Toward a methodology for resolving theoretical issues in the study of exceptional memory. Unpublished paper.

Ericsson, K. A., & Kintsch, W. (1995). Long-term working memory. *Psychological Review, 102,* 211–245.

Ericsson, K. A., & Kintsch, W. (2000). Shortcomings of generic retrieval structures with slots of the type that Gobet (1993) proposed and modelled. *British Journal of Psychology, 91,* 571–590.

Ericsson, K. A., & Polson, P. G. (1988). A cognitive analysis of exceptional memory for restaurant orders. In M. Chi, R. Glaser, & M. Farr (Eds.), *The Nature of Expertise* (pp. 23–70). Hillsdale, NJ: Lawrence Erlbaum Associates.

Gordon, P., Valentine, E., & Wilding, J. (1984). One man's memory: A study of a mnemonist. *British Journal of Psychology, 75,* 1–14.

Hamilton, R. H., & Pascual-Leone, A. (1998). Cortical plasticity associated with Braille learning. *Trends in Cognitive Science, 2,* 168–174.

Hunt, E. B., & Love, T. (1972). How good can memory be? In A. W. Melton & E. Martin (Eds.), *Coding Processes in Human Memory* (pp. 237–250). New York: Wiley.

Hunter, I. M. L. (1962). An exceptional talent for calculative thinking. *British Journal of Psychology, 53,* 243–258.

Hunter, I. M. L. (1977). An exceptional memory. *British Journal of Psychology, 68,* 155–164.

Hunter, I. M. L. (1996). Remembering a story after 26 years. Unpublished paper.

Ingham, J. G. (1952). Memory and intelligence. *British Journal of Psychology, 43,* 20–32.

Kliegl, R., Smith, J., & Baltes, P. B. (1989). Testing-the-limits and the study of adult age differences in cognitive plasticity of a mnemonic skill. *Developmental Psychology, 25,* 247–256.

Kliegl, R., Smith, J., & Baltes, P. B. (1990). On the locus and process of magnification of age differences during mnemonic training. *Developmental Psychology, 26,* 894–904.

Kliegl, R., Smith, J., Heckhausen, J., & Baltes, P. B. (1987). Mnemonic training for the acquisition of skilled digit memory. *Cognition and Instruction, 4,* 203–223.

Kalakoski, V., & Saariluoma, P. (2001). Taxi drivers' exceptional memory of street names. *Memory and Cognition, 29,* 634–638.

Luria, A. R. (1975). *The Mind of a Mnemonist.* Harmondsworth, Middlesex: Penguin.

Maguire, E. A., Gadian, D. G., Johnsrude, I. S., Good, C. D., Ashburner, J., Frackowiak, R. S. J., & Frith, C. D. (2000). Navigation-related structural change in the hippocampi of taxi drivers. *Proceedings of the National Academy of Sciences of the United States of America, 97,* 4398–4403.

Maguire, E. A., Valentine, E. R., Wilding, J. M., & Kapur, N. (2003a). Routes to remembering: The brains behind superior memory. *Nature Neuroscience, 6,* 90–95.

Maguire, E. A., Spiers, H. J., Good, C. D., Hartley, T., Frackowiak, R. S. J., & Burgess, N. (2003b). Navigation expertise and the human hippocampus: A structural brain imaging analysis. *Hippocampus, 13,* 250–259.

Mastropieri, M. A., & Scruggs, T. E. (1989). Constructing more meaningful relationships: Mnemonic instruction for special populations. *Educational Psychology Review, 1,* 83–111.

Muller, G. (1911). Zur Analyse der Gedächtnistätigkeit und des Vorstellungsverlaufes. *Zeitschrift für Psychologie, Ergänzungsband, 5,* 7–367.

Muller, G. (1913). Neue Versuche mit Rückle. *Zeitschrift für Psychologie, 7,* 193–213.

Neely, A. S., & Bäckman, L. (1995). Effects of multifactorial memory training in old age: Generalizability across tasks and individuals. *Journal of Gerontology: Psychological Sciences, 50B,* P134–P140.

Nyberg, L, Sandblom, J., Jones, S., Neely, A. S., Petersson, K. M., Ingvar, M., & Bäckman, L. (2003). Neural correlates of training-related memory improvement in adulthood and aging. *Proceedings of the National Academy of Sciences, 100,* No. 23, 13728–13733.

O'Keefe, J., & Nadel, L. (1978). *The Hippocampus as a Cognitive Map.* Oxford: Oxford University Press.

Rabbitt, P. M. A. (1993). Does it all go together when it goes? The Nineteenth Bartlett Memorial Lecture. *Quarterly Journal of Experimental Psychology, 46A,* 385–434.

Rubin, D. C. (1995). *Memory in Oral Traditions.* New York: Oxford University Press.

Salthouse, T. A. (1985). *A Theory of Cognitive Aging.* Amsterdam: North Holland.

Schlaug, G., Jancke, L., Huang, Y. X., Staiger, J. F., & Steinmetz, H. (1995). Increased corpus-callosum size in musicians. *Neuropsychologia, 33,* 1047–1055.

Stigsdotter, A., & Bäckman, L. (1989). Multifactorial memory training with older adults: How to foster maintenance of improved performance. *Gerontology, 35,* 260–267.

Stigsdotter Neely, A., & Bäckman, L. (1993a). Maintenance of gains following multifactorial and unifactorial memory training in late adulthood. *Educational Gerontology, 19,* 105–117.

Stigsdotter Neely, A., & Bäckman, L. (1993b). Long-term maintenance of gains from memory training in older adults: Two 3½ year follow-up studies. *Journal of Gerontology, 48,* 233–237.

Susukita, T. (1933). Untersuchung eines ausserordentlichen Gedächtnisses in Japan (I). *Tohoku Psychologica Folia, 1,* 1–134.

Susukita, T. (1934). Untersuchung eines ausserordentlichen Gedächtnisses in Japan (II). *Tohoku Psychologica Folia, 2*, 15–42.

Tanaka, S., Michimata, C., Kaminaya, T., Honda, M., & Sadato, N. (2002). Superior digit memory of abacus experts: An event-related functional MRI study. *Neuroreport, 13*, 2187–2191.

Thompson, C. P., Cowan, T., & Frieman, J. (1993). *Memory Search by a Memorist*. Hillsdale, NJ: Lawrence Erlbaum Associates.

Verhaeghen, P., & Marcoen, A. (1996). On the mechanisms of plasticity in young and older adults after instruction in the method of loci: Evidence for an amplification model. *Psychology and Aging, 11*, 164–178.

Verhaeghen, P., Marcoen, A., & Goossens, L. (1992). Improving memory performance in the aged through mnemonic training – A meta-analytic study. *Psychology of Aging, 7*, 242–251.

Wilding, J., & Marshall, P. (2004). Superior digit span: Validation of reported strategies by the time structure of recall. Unpublished paper.

Wilding, J., & Valentine, E. (1985). One man's memory for prose, faces and names. *British Journal of Psychology, 76*, 215–219.

Wilding, J., & Valentine, E. (1994a). Memory champions. *British Journal of Psychology, 85*, 231–244.

Wilding, J., & Valentine, E. (1994b). Mnemonic wizardry and the telephone directory – But stories are another story. *British Journal of Psychology, 85*, 501–509.

Wilding, J., & Valentine, E. (1997). *Superior Memory*. Hove: Psychology Press.

Wilding, J., Valentine, E., Marshall, P., & Cook, S. (1999). Individual differences in memory ability and GCSE performance. *Educational Psychology, 19*, 117–131.

Yesavage, J. A., & Rose, T. L. (1983). Concentration and mnemonic training in the elderly with memory complaints: A study of combined therapy and order effects. *Psychiatry Research, 9*, 157–167.

Yesavage, J. A., Rose, T. L., & Bower, G. H. (1983). Interactive imagery and affective judgments improve face-name learning in the elderly. *Journal of Gerontology, 38*, 197–203.

CHAPTER 32

Mathematical Expertise

Brian Butterworth

Competence in mathematics is a basic requirement for effective citizenship in a modern numerate society (Cockcroft, 1982). Poor numeracy skills are known to be a serious handicap for paid employment in the US (Rivera-Batiz, 1992) and the UK (Bynner & Parsons, 1997). Indeed, the UK Basic Skills Agency has published a report suggesting that numeracy is more important even than literacy in terms of career prospects in the UK (Bynner & Parsons, 1997). And the trend is toward an even greater emphasis on numeracy: recent research for the British Science, Technology and Mathematics Council shows that "mathematical skills in the workplace are changing, with increasing numbers of people engaged in mathematics-related work, and with such work involving increasingly sophisticated mathematical activities" (Hoyles, Wolf, Molyneux-Hodgson, & Kent, 2002).

The level of competence routinely demanded in numerate cultures today would have been considered quite exceptional 200 years ago. How then does one distinguish today's expert from the normally competent

school-leaver who can handle numbers of arbitrary size, fractions and decimals, logarithms, equations with unknowns and negative roots, and some differentiation and integration? One could arbitrarily take the top n% of a standard test (like the SAT-M), but what should n be? Francis Galton, in *Hereditary Genius*, used obituaries from *The Times* of London and a biographical dictionary, *Men of our Time*, as the criteria of "eminence." This gave him an estimated proportion of 0.025% of the population. Really exceptional individuals, his class G, were about one-twentieth of these. He even designated a class X of people who were fewer than one in a million (Galton, 1979).

However, not every expert that we would wish to consider has taken the SAT-M, or been the subject of a *Times* obituary. The important criterion is that the candidate expert demonstrates "reproducible superior performance," preferably under something like laboratory conditions (Ericsson & Charness, 1994).

The focus of this chapter will be to attempt to identify the cognitive capacities, the disposition, and the training that equip someone to demonstrate "reproducible superior performance," particularly in calculation, since this is the only area of expertise in which there is much evidence.

There have been three extensive early reviews of exceptional mathematical abilities. The first was E. W. Scripture, a psychologist at Leipzig (Scripture, 1891). He reviewed in some detail the lives of 12 "arithmetical prodigies," including one mathematician of note, Carl Friedrich Gauss. From a "psychological analysis" of these lives, he identified five characteristics that seemed to distinguish the prodigies: the accuracy and "rapidity" of memory, "arithmetical association" (knowing lots of arithmetical facts and procedures), inclination, mathematical precocity, and "imagination" (visual imagery).

The second review, like Scripture's, was published in the *American Journal of Psychology*, and was by Frank D. Mitchell of "The Psychological Seminary of Cornell University" (Mitchell, 1907). Also like Scripture, he reviews the lives of prodigies, the same ones as Scripture plus a further case, the author. These are summarized in a table that lists the heredity, development, education, mental calculation, and memory of each prodigy. Mitchell takes the view that prodigious abilities grow out of counting, a verbal skill where the numbers are recited out loud initially, and internally thereafter. This has an implication for the "memory type" used by prodigies. In his own case and that of most of the prodigies he has analyzed, the memory is of the auditory type, reflecting this early experience since most of us begin to learn numbers through counting, which involves spoken words. Only between two and four of the prodigies he examined have memory of the "visual type."

The third review, by Alfred Binet (Binet, 1894), included reaction-time tests of two theatrical calculators of his day.

More recently, Barlow (1952) has written about mathematical prodigies in the context of other kinds of prodigy (Barlow, 1952). And there is an excellent reconsideration of the calculators studied by Scripture, Binet, and Mitchell, along with useful data on more recent calculators by Steven B. Smith in

The Great Mental Calculators: The Psychology, Methods, and Lives of the Calculating Prodigies (Smith, 1983). I shall be drawing heavily on this volume along with Scripture, Mitchell, and Binet for biographical details of calculating prodigies. Finally, one of the leading modern investigators has published a review of expert calculators (Pesenti, 2005).

Calculators have attracted also the attention of experimental psychologists usually focusing on a single case. The Polish calculator Salo Finkelstein was studied by Weinland and Schlauch (1937), who used sophisticated analyses of careful timing data from various mathematical tasks, but with no control subjects! The British mathematician Alexander Aitken was studied by Hunter (1962), and a more recent case, Rüdiger Gamm, by Pesenti and colleagues (Pesenti et al., 2001). Only Binet (1894) seems to have explored the general phenomenon, carrying out experiments on two professional theatrical calculators and comparing their results with other groups of practiced and unpracticed calculators. He took considerable pains to find the optimal way of timing the stimulus presentation and the response, in an age when there were no voice-activated relays. However, he was less careful in designing the experiments so that all the subjects received the same stimuli under the same conditions.

What is striking about all these students of exceptional mathematical abilities is their conviction that there is nothing special about mathematics as a cognitive domain. This may be contrasted with Gardner's popular theory of "multiple intelligences," one of which is "logico-mathematical" (Gardner, 1983).

The research on mathematical, especially numerical, abilities in general strongly suggests the existence of a domain-specific capacity. There are two main arguments in support of this.

First, specialized brain areas, especially the left angular gyrus and the intraparietal sulci, are active when mathematical activities are taking place (Donlan, 2003; Gruber, Indefrey, Steinmetz, & Kleinschmidt, 2001; Pesenti, Thioux, Seron, & De Volder, 2000). When these areas are damaged, selective impairment of calculation frequently occurs (Cipolotti & van Harskamp, 2001). Notice that the specialized number areas are distinct from the areas active in reasoning, which are in the prefrontal cortex (e.g., Goel & Dolan, 2004).

Second, there is evidence for an innate basis to this specialization. One strand of evidence supports the claim for numerical capacity in infants, even in the first few months of life, when neither language nor frontal-lobe functions such as reasoning have developed. They are able to respond discriminatively on the basis of numerosity (Antell & Keating, 1983; Starkey & Cooper, 1980) and can even mentally manipulate numerosities at six months by working out what would happen when an object is added or subtracted from an array (Wynn, 1992, 2000, 2002; Wynn, Bloom, & Chiang, 2002). These infant capacities are similar to ones observed in monkeys (Hauser, MacNeilage, & Ware, 1996), which suggests ancestral versions that may have evolved because the ability to recognize the numerosity parameter in the environment offers advantages in foraging, mating (Edwards, Alder, & Rose, 2002), and also in conflict with conspecifics (McComb, Packer, & Pusey, 1994). (See Butterworth, 1999, for a review.) Moreover, developmental disorder can lead to selective deficits in the acquisition of even these simple numerical concepts when intelligence, memory, and language are all at normal levels (Landerl, Bevan, & Butterworth, 2004).

However, even if it is accepted that we humans have inherited a specialized capacity for representing numerosities, it does not follow that this is normally distributed, such that some people have it to a greater degree than others, like height or IQ. It may be more like color vision – either it is normal, or it is defective in one of a small number of ways. In the same way that ability as a colorist may require normal color vision, the range of colorist abilities is not determined by better or worse color discrimination, so it is possible that calculating abilities require a normal numerical "starter kit," but the abstract and complex skills that make expert mathematicians and calculators is built by

other means on this basis. Smith (1983) compares it to juggling. "Any sufficiently diligent nonhandicapped person can learn to juggle, but the skill is actually acquired only by a handful of highly motivated individuals" (p. 6). Calculating prodigies themselves often say that their abilities come from their interest in numbers rather than from some special gift.

So our central question in this chapter is whether mathematical expertise, and in particular calculation expertise, depends on high cognitive abilities in non-numerical domains, such as reasoning and memory, or whether it can exist as a domain-specific achievement.

What Makes for Mathematical Expertise?

Francis Galton was quite clear that any kind of eminence depended on "natural ability," which was by-and-large inherited. "By natural ability, I mean those qualities of intellect and disposition, which urge and qualify a man to perform acts that lead to reputation. I do not mean capacity without zeal, nor zeal without capacity, nor even a combination of both of them, without an adequate power of doing a great deal of very laborious work."

Having compared divines, wrestlers, men of science, painters, poets, and others, he found that eminent people tended to have eminent parents and to produce eminent offspring. Of course, we are talking mostly about eminent men and their fathers, since it was difficult for women to achieve eminence. Overall, 31% of eminent men had an eminent parent. Some 26% of scientific men had scientific fathers, but 60% of scientifically eminent fathers have eminent sons (vs. 41% average). Galton speculates "descendants [are] taught . . . not to waste [their] powers on profitless speculation" (p. 320).

Although inherited characteristics are held to be the key, "it may be well to add a few supplementary remarks on the small effects of a good education on a mind of the highest order. A youth of abilities G, and

X, is almost independent of ordinary school education" (p. 43). He gives as an example D'Alembert, who was a "foundling... put out to nurse as a pauper baby to the wife of a poor glazier. The child's indomitable tendency to the higher studies, could not be repressed by his foster mother's ridicule and dissuasion, nor by the taunts of his schoolfellows, nor by the discouragements of his schoomaster, who was incapable of appreciating him, nor even by the reiterated deep disappointment of finding that his ideas, which he knew to be original, were not novel, but long previously discovered by others" (pp. 43–44). He records many other eminent men with a comparably unpromising history.

He pays particular attention to "Wranglers," students of mathematics at Cambridge University. Not only do these men have to pass the entrance examinations to Cambridge (not as difficult then as now, I believe), but they were ranked from the highest (Senior) to the lowest strictly according to the marks obtained in an exam. These ranged from less than 500 to over 7500. He was thus able to compare the Senior with the Second Wrangler, and he noted the enormous discrepancy often observed, with the Senior frequently achieving double the marks of the Second.

For Galton, this was a demonstration of the enormous range of inherited abilities. His tripartite theory of eminence – capacity, zeal, and power to work hard – is quite general and can be applied to any career. By capacity, he seems to have meant something like what we would now call intelligence or *g*. There was thus no special capacity for mathematics. He seeks to demonstrate this by analyzing the subsequent careers of top Wranglers. He notes that several were also classical scholars, and a few were both Senior Wranglers and the top classical prizemen of the year. Many achieved distinction in areas very different from mathematics, such as law, politics, or becoming headmasters of great schools.

His example of D'Alembert (1717–1783) reinforces this point. Not only was he a mathematician of great distinction, he was even better known as the co-editor with Denis Diderot of the *Encyclopedie*.

Intelligence

Ability in mathematics is widely seen as a marker for intelligence, and disability in mathematics in school is seen as a marker for low intelligence. This is not the place to discuss the general relationship between intelligence and mathematical ability but only to point out that severe disability can co-occur with good to superior IQ scores (Landerl et al., 2004).

In contrast to Galton, Mitchell (1907) noted that "Skill in mental calculation is, owing to the isolation of mental arithmetic already noted, independent of general education: the mathematical prodigy may be illiterate or even densely stupid, or he may be an all-round prodigy and veritable genius" (p. 131). Many expert calculators achieved eminence in a way that suggested exceptional cognitive abilities. These included the mathematicians Euler, Gauss, Aitken, and D'Alembert, and scientists and engineers such as Ampère, Bidder, and Mitchell himself.

Shakuntala Devi (born 1940) is in the Guinness Book of World Records for being able to multiply two 13 digit numbers in 28 seconds. She was tested formally by the psychologist A. R. Jensen, who showed that she was not much better than average on standard IQ tests, and was actually slower than average on some tests of speed of mental processing, which Jensen regards as a reliable measure of intelligence (Jensen, 1990). Dehaene comments that therefore "Devi's calculation were obviously not due to a global speed up of her internal clock: Only her arithmetic processor ran with lightning speed" (Dehaene, 1997).

Moreover, other prodigious calculators seemed to have been men of ordinary or even very low cognitive ability. Dase, who did calculations for Gauss and Schumacher, was "unable to comprehend the first elements of mathematics." One pair of twins with prodigious abilities for calendrical calculation were estimated to have IQs in the 60s and had great difficulties with simple arithmetic (Horwitz, Deming, & Winter, 1969). Mitchell (1907) noted that two prodigious calculators, Fuller (1710?–1790) and Buxton (1702–1772), "were men of such limited intelligence that they could comprehend scarcely anything, either theoretical or practical, more complex than counting" (pp. 98–99).

Hermelin and O'Connor reported a young man who was able to recognize and generate primes of up to five digits four or five times faster than a graduate with a math degree and also factorize these numbers faster and more accurately. What is extraordinary is that the man had a measured IQ of 67 and was unable to speak or understand speech (Hermelin & O'Connor, 1990). See Horn and Masunaga, Chapter 34, for further discussion of intelligence and expertise.

Memory

"The distinction often made between *memory* and *calculation*, with the implication that the great calculator is simply a little calculator with a big memory, using the same methods as his lesser rivals, is misleading; the process is always (in the "natural calculators") a true calculation, and memory for figures is important only in so far as it stands in the service of calculation" (Mitchell, 1907, p. 132).

Scripture (1891) distinguished "accuracy" and "rapidity" of memory from what he called "association." We would now call the former "working memory" and the latter long-term "semantic memory" (Cappelletti, Kopelman, & Butterworth, 2002). Calculators themselves stressed the importance of both being able to hold many items in mind as they were carrying out calculations, and also knowing many more facts about numbers than the average person.

Working memory

According to Smith (1983), George Parker Bidder (1806–1878), an exceptional calculator and a leading engineer of his time

(a collaborator with Robert Stephenson), was the first to explicitly draw attention to working-memory limitations on calculation. Bidder noted that "As compared with the operation on paper, in multiplying 3 figures by 3 figures, you have three lines of 4 figures each, or 12 figures in the process to be added up; in multiplying 6 figures into 6 figures, you have six lines of 7 figures, or 42 figures to be added up." In general, the difficulty in using the mental analogue of the written method increases by something in the order of $n^2 + n$ of the number of digits in an $n \times n$ problem (Smith, 1953, p. 53). For this reason, it very important for the calculator to develop techniques for reducing current load. Given that a three digit number was, for Bidder (and most calculating experts) a single item, a three-digit by three-digit calculation, working from the left (instead of the right, as is normal in the written method), requires no more than five items to be currently maintained. For the problem 358×464, assuming trailing zeros are stored at no cost, Bidder probably worked it out as shown in Figure 32.1.

Although there are many steps, the current load is kept small, and the routine is easy to practice.

Wim Klein (1912–1986), one of the fastest calculators, would write down intermediate results, which, he claimed, speeds up the process, an important element when there is an audience. Smith (1983) timed him multiplying two five-digit numbers. With writing down, it took 14 seconds, and without, 44 seconds.

Perhaps the most detailed psychological investigation of working memory comes from two studies of German calculating prodigy Rüdiger Gamm. Gamm is able to calculate the 9th powers and the 5th roots with great accuracy, and find the quotient of two primes to 60 decimal places. Even more extraordinary is that he started training for these feats when he was 20 years old. Before then, his mathematical abilities had been unexceptional.

Gamm, again like other experts, is able to solve multi-step problems very quickly and accurately. To solve 68×76 takes

Table 32.1.

Step	Numbers in memory	Number of items to be maintained	Calculation
1	358 464	2	
2	120000	3	400 × 300
3	20000	4	400 × 50
4	140000	3	120000 + 20000
5	3200	5	400 × 8
6	143200	4	140000 + 3200
7	18000	5	60 × 300
8	161200	4	143200 + 18000
9	3000	5	60 × 50
10	164200	4	161200 + 3000
11	480	5	60 × 8
12	164680	4	164200 + 480
13	1200	5	4 × 300
14	165880	4	164680 + 1200
15	200	5	4 × 50
16	166080	4	165880 + 200
17	32	5	4 × 8
18	166112	4	166080 + 32

(adapted from Smith, 1953, p. 54)

seven steps and six intermediate results. After some practice with the task, Gamm was taking around five seconds a problem with a high degree of accuracy. (Two digit squares, by contrast, took him just over a second because they were simply retrieved from memory.) Such a sequence of operations and data handling would put a considerable strain on normal working memory, yet all kinds of expertise show enormous gains in the temporary storage of task-relevant materials: musicians can recall tunes after a single hearing, chess masters can recall positions after a single tachistoscopic presentation as well as the whole game that they have just played, expert waiters can keep in mind the precise orders for up to 20 people without writing them down (at least until the customer has paid). Experts develop a kind of "Long-term Working Memory" (Ericsson & Kintsch, 1995).

"Long-term Working Memory"

As we have seen, one of the barriers to mental calculation is the limited capacity of working memory. Many exceptional calculators use and invent algorithms that minimize the load on working memory. It has also been suggested that one of the consequences of expertise is the ability to exploit the unlimited capacity of long-term memory in the service of the current task (Ericsson & Kintsch, 1995). It is as if experts "develop an ability to use long-term episodic memory to maintain task-relevant materials, rather as computers extend the capacity of RAM by using swap space on the hard drive to create a larger 'virtual memory'" (Butterworth, 2001, p. 12).

Language processing is a more familiar example of prodigious skill after years of daily practice enabling retention of information well beyond the span of short-term working memory. We can effortlessly retain meaningful sentences of 20 words or more, well beyond the span for unrelated words (about six) or words not in our language (about three). Several related accounts of this phenonemon propose cues in working memory for retrieving well-organized domain-specific information in long-term episodic memory (Butterworth, Shallice, & Watson, 1990). Pesenti and colleagues argue that Gamm has learned to use this LTWM facility to maintain task-related mathematical information.

It turned out that computation compared to retrieval of memorized number facts in both Gamm and the controls activated an extensive visual processing system bilaterally. According to the authors, this suggests that "during complex calculation, numbers are held and manipulated onto a visual type of short term representational medium." This contrasts with the more usual claim that "sub-vocal rehearsal is . . . required for mental arithmetic" (Logie, Gilhooly, & Wynn, 1994), but it would explain how it is possible for brain damage to reduce digit span to two and yet allow a patient to reliably add two orally presented three-digit numbers (Butterworth, Cipolotti, & Warrington, 1996). (See this volume for more on LTWM.)

We will see below that Gamm's use of LTWM is supported by analysis of neural acitivity.

Auditory and Visual Working Memory

Mitchell noticed that there seemed to be two types of working memory used in calculation, visual and auditory, depending on how numbers were initially learned. Most children learn about calculating by counting aloud using the names of numbers, names often some years before they understand written numerals (Gelman & Gallistel, 1978). There appear to be three main stages in the development of counting as an addition strategy:

1. *Counting all. For 3 + 5, children will count "one, two, three" and then "one, two, three, four, five" countables to establish the numerosity of the sets to be added, so that two sets will be made visible – for example, three fingers on one hand and five fingers on the other. The child will then count all the objects.*
2. *Counting on from first. Some children come to realise that it is not necessary to count the first addend. They can start with three, and then count on another five to get the solution. Using finger counting, the child will no longer count out the first set, but start with the word*

"Three," and then use a hand to count on the second addend: "Four, five, six, seven, eight."
3. *Counting on from larger. It is more efficient, and less prone to error, when the smaller of the two addends is counted. The child now selects the larger number to start with: "Five," and then carries on "Six, seven, eight." (Butterworth, 2005)*

However, many calculators report that their early experiences involved manipulables. Bidder described how he learned multiplication in the following way: "I used to arrange [peas, marbles, or shot] into squares, of 8 on each side, and then on counting them throughout, I found that the whole number amounted to 64" (Quoted by Smith, 1983, p. 212). It is probable that Bidder, like others who had early experience with manipulables, also used a kind of visual coding. Salo Finkelstein (born 1896), who seemed to have had a standard Polish mathematical education, without showing early signs of exceptionality, calculated by visualizing numbers on a freshly washed blackboard. His calculation ability seemed not to have equalled many other prodigies in terms of time or accuracy, but his ability to memorize numbers was. He was able to remember numbers up to about 28 digits following a one-second visual exposure; for 39 digits he needed a four-second exposure. He was adept at repeating in either direction with equal accuracy, which traditionally suggests a visual memory. However, he also used a wide variety of associations for substrings to help him, including numerical facts, such as the fact that 1.41 is the square root of 2, 2,592,000 is the number of seconds in a month, 10,592 is a familiar telephone number, and 2595 is the number of paragraphs of Spinoza's ethics (Smith 1983, Chapter 33).

Dehaene and colleagues (Dehaene & Cohen, 1995) have proposed that multidigit arithmetic of the sort carried out by calculators depends on visualizing the digits on a kind of mental blackboard. There is some evidence that neurological damage can lead to deficits in spatial cognition, which can lead to a kind of spatial "acalculia" where the patient has difficulty in maintaining the digits in columns accurately (Hécaen, Angelergues, & Houillier, 1961).

In the case of Gamm, it was possible to identify the brain areas active during calculation, and hence whether verbal or visual areas were active. It turned out that computation compared to retrieval of memorized number facts in both Gamm and the controls activated an extensive visual processing system bilaterally.

Domain-specificity in Memory

Gamm had a forward span of 11 digits (controls 7.2, SD = 0.8) and 12 digits backwards (controls 5.8, SD = 0.8), whereas his letter span was in the normal range (Pesenti, Seron, Samson, & Duroux, 1999).

Mondeux (1826–1861), a famous nineteenth-century calculator, was described by a contemporary as never having learned anything besides arithmetic; "Facts, dates, places, pass before his brain as before a mirror without leaving a trace" (quoted by Smith, 1983, p. 294)

Long-Term Working Memory (Ericsson & Kintsch, 1995), deployed by experts, is specific to the domain of expertise; thus, the musician, the chess master, and the waiter will be normal on for example digit span, (Ericsson & Kintsch, 1995). So, as Ericsson and Charness note, "exceptional memory is nearly always restricted to one type of material" (Ericsson & Charness, 1994).

"Management" and "Strengthening" Memories

Solving even a simple arithmetical problem can be broken down into separable components, which will include retrieving arithmetical facts from memory, retrieving procedures for calculating (such as borrowing and carrying), understanding the arithmetical concepts demanded by the problem, and creating a hierarchical set of goals and subgoals appropriate for reaching the solution. Charness and Campbell have shown that, in learning a new algorithm for multiplying double-digit numbers, the memory elements are strengthened by practice, but there is a larger effect from the overall

approach to the problem, particularly, from "increased efficiency in managing memory and accessing the next step in the procedure" (Charness & Campbell, 1988)

Convergent evidence for the compositionality of arithmetical task comes from neurological patients, whose arithmetical abilities can be selectively affected in very specific ways: the memories for facts alone can be lost, indeed the memories for facts from each of the four arithmetical operations can be selectively impaired (Cipolotti & van Harskamp, 2001; van Harskamp & Cipolotti, 2001); arithmetical procedures can be lost from memory (Girelli & Delazer, 1996; McCloskey & Caramazza, 1987); and the ability to apply arithmetical principles to problems can be selectively spared or affected (Delazer & Benke, 1997; Hittmair-Delazer, Semenza, & Denes, 1994).

It is, as has been noted above, that mathematical experts and calculating prodigies build up enormous stores of what Scripture called "associations" – numerical facts and procedures.

Perhaps the greatest of recent calculators, Wim Klein acquired the multiplication tables to 100 × 100 "from experience [he] got by factoring." However, he did set out to memorize the table of logarithms up to 150. This training enabled to him to achieve the world record in extracting roots. He could extract the 13th root of a 100-digit number in under two minutes by using a method that requires taking logarithms of the leftmost group of numbers.

Aitken, similarly, had an enormous store of number facts. For him the year 1961 evoked the thoughts 37×53, $44^2 + 5^2$, and $40^2 + 19^2$. He could also recite the first 100 decimal places of π (Hunter, 1962).

Like other calculating prodigies, Gamm taught himself a vast range of number facts. Most of us know our multiplication tables, and perhaps 50 simple additions (Ashcraft, 1995), but Gamm has learned tables of squares, cubes, roots, and so forth. Most of us know a few procedures for working out problems that we cannot retrieve from memory, whereas Gamm has an enormous store of procedures and shortcuts, some of which he has learned from books, others he has worked out for himself.

Motivation and Instruction

"Zeal" and "Inclination"

Most exceptional calculators seem to have been obsessed with numbers from the time they began to count. Jedediah Buxton kept a record of all the free drinks he received from demonstrating his calculating prowess, Thomas Fuller counted the hairs in a cow's tail, and Arthur Griffiths (1880–1911) kept track of the grains of corn he fed to the chickens: 42,173 over three years (Smith, 1953, p. 277). Srinivasa Ramanujan (1887–1920), a prodigious calculator and, according to G. H. Hardy (Hardy, 1969), a natural mathematical genius in the class of Euler or Gauss, would work at mathematics in the mornings before work, and often stayed up all night working on problems.

Calculators from an early age develop a kind of intimacy with numbers. When Bidder was learning to count to 100, the numbers became "as it were, my friends, and I knew all their friends and acquaintances" (Smith, 1983, p. 5). Klein told Smith that "Numbers are friends for me, more or less. It doesn't mean the same for you, does it, 3,844? For you it's just a three and an eight and a four and a four. But I say, 'Hi, 62 squared.'" In a famous story, Hardy visited Ramanujan in hospital and mentioned that the taxi in which he had come was number 1729, "A rather dull number." "No, Hardy! It is a very interesting number. It is the smallest number expressible as the sum of two cubes in two different ways" (C. P. Snow in his introduction to [Hardy, 1969]).

In some cases, there is an incident that awakens the interest. For Aitken, a teacher "chanced to say that you can use the factorization to square a number: $a^2 + b^2 = (a + b)(a - b) + b^2$. Suppose you had 47 – that was his example – he said you could take b as 3. So $(a + b)$ is 50 and $(a - b)$ is 44, which you can multiply together to give 2200. Then the square of b is 9, and so, boys, he said, 47 squared is 2209. Well, from that moment, that was the light, and I never went back" (Hunter, 1962).

In the case of Gamm, he said that at school he was "very bad at arithmetic" because the teachers never explained the concepts in ways he could understand. As a result he lost interest in mathematics until about the age of twenty, when he came across an algorithm for calendrical calculation. He practiced it for fun, and then entered for a TV competition where he could win bets by solving various calculations. See Zimmerman, Chapter 39, for more on motivational factors in the development of expertise.

The Role of Practice – 10,000 *Hours*

The highest level of expertise in violinists studied by Ericsson et al. (1993) requires 10,000 hours of practice (by the age of 20 years). In general, the level of expert performance was related directly (monotonically) to the amount of practice. Similarly, expert calculators spend a great deal of time learning numerical facts and procedures, though the exact amount has never been properly quantified. In preparation for the T.V. program, Gamm started to train up to four hours a day, learning number facts and calculation procedures. He now performs professionally. His expertise is rare enough to be a cause of wonder (the usual definition of prodigy).

Some of the best evidence for the pure effects of practice comes from an experiment carried out by Binet in which he compared the performance of two professional calculators, Inaudi and Diamandi, with cashiers from the Bon Marché department store in Paris, who had had 14-years experience of calculating (there were no mechanical calculators available in the 1890s), but who, presumably, showed no special early gift for mathematics. He compared how long it took them to carry out multidigit multiplications. Although the timing was about as accurate as it could have been without voice-activated relays, it is far from clear that the conditions were the same

Table 32.2.

	638×823	7286×5397
Inaudi	6.4 sec	21 sec
Diamandi	56 sec	2 min 7 sec
Best cashier	4 sec	13 sec

for each subject, and the different subjects were mostly given different problems to solve. However, they were given one identical 3-digit × 3-digit and one 4-digit × 4-digit problem. For these stimuli, the best cashier was better than either calculator: As can be seen at least one cashier was better than the professionals, but all were better than Binet's students. See Ericsson, Chapter 38, on the roles of experience and deliberate practice.

Education

Ericsson and colleagues have stressed the importance in reaching high levels of expertise of "optimal environments for ... children" and cite examples of parents who have designed such environments irrespective of objective evidence for innate talent in the children (Ericsson & Charness, 1994). One can think of the Polgar sisters in chess, the Williams sisters in tennis, Tiger Woods in golf, and so on; Mozart grew up in a musical household, and Picasso's father was himself a painter.

This optimal environment encourages "Deliberate practice" with its "individualized training on tasks selected by a qualified teacher" and its careful monitoring and feedback (Ericsson, Krampe, & Tesch-Römer, 1993).

However, there are numerous reports of calculating experts who had little education and were entirely, or almost entirely, self-taught. Zerah Colburn (1804–1840) was able at the age of six to calculate the number of seconds in 2,000 years (9,139,200) but "unable to read and ignorant of the name or properties of one figure traced on paper" (Scripture, 1891, p. 13). Even as an adult, "he was unable to learn much of anything, and incapable of the exercise of even ordinary intelligence or of any practical application" p. 16). Scripture inferred that "calculating

powers ... seemed to have absorbed all his mental energy."

Vito Mangiamele (born 1827) was the son of a shepherd who was unable to give the boy any instruction. According to Scripture, "By chance it was discovered that by methods peculiar to himself, he resolved problems that seemed at the first view to require extended mathematical knowledge" (p. 17), for example, "What satisfies the condition that its cube plus five times its square is equal to 42 times itself increased by 40?" ($x^3 + 5x^2 - 42x - 40 = 0$). He found the answer to this (5) in less than a minute when he was ten-years old.

Zacharias Dase (1824–1861) was an extraordinary calculator who, for a time, assisted Gauss in calculating tables. One distinguished mathematician credited him with "extreme stupidity." a view that seemed to be held also by his mathematician collaborators. He knew no geometry and never mastered a word of another language. "He had one ability not present to such a great degree in other ready reckoners. He could distinguish some thirty objects of a similar nature in a single moment as easily as other people can recognise three or four. The rapidity with which he would name the number of sheep in a herd, or books in book-case, or window-panes in a large house, was even more remarkable than the accuracy of his mental calculations" (Scripture, 1891, p. 20). According to Mitchell, he "could count some thirty objects at a glance" (p. 142), though it is not clear what this had to do with his calculating prowess.

Genetics

Galton's account of the parents and offspring of men of eminence did not examine the potential social and educational effects of growing up in a talented and well-connected family. Of course, there will be cases like D'Alembert, and those above, who have achieved eminence despite an apparently unhelpful upbringing.

Genetic studies support the idea of an innate domain-specific system for at least simple mathematics. A recent twin study of mathematical abilities showed that the concordance rates were 0.73 for monozygotic and 0.56 for dizygotic pairs (Alarcon, Defries, Gillis Light, & Pennington, 1997). Looking at the selective deficit of mathematical ability, dyscalculia, of the dyscalculic probands, 58% of monozygotic co-twins and 39% of dizygotic co-twins were also dyscalculic. In a family study, it was found that approximately half of all siblings of children with dyscalculia are also dyscalculic, with a risk five to ten times greater than for the general population (Shalev & Gross-Tsur, 2001).

Another line of research has attempted to assess whether sex-linked characteristics contribute to mathematical expertise. Benbow and colleagues have found in a host of studies a significant advantage for talented 12- to 13-year-old boys over girls at the upper end of the ability range, as measured by SAT-M (Scholastic Aptitude Test – Mathematics), whereas SAT-V (Verbal) showed no comparable difference (see Benbow, 1988, for a review). Benbow argues that the sex difference cannot be explained in terms of "environmental" hypotheses to do with attitudes, confidence, or teaching. She argues rather that a combination of biological differences between the sexes is the cause, in particular a more bilateral neural representation of cognitive functions in the female brain (see next section).

The differences between boys and girls in SAT-M performance appears to follow from the much larger variance in boys' scores, which would allow reliable differences at the top end of the range even if the mean score for girls were higher than for boys (Becker & Hedges, 1988). When one looks at the means, girls in England easily outperform boys in all subjects at all ages. There is one exception to this general rule: mathematics. Girls are only just outperforming boys (DfES, 2002).

On the other hand, Geary (Geary, 1996) reviewed a wide range of industrialized countries and showed that boys, on average, still outperform girls in mathematical problem solving. However, even in the USA

at 17 years the *average* difference between boys and girls is still only 1%. The most recent cross-national comparisons using the same tests in all countries, the Third International Maths and Science Survey (TIMSS) (Keys, Harris, & Fernandes, 1996), reinforces the overall picture that in most countries, including the USA, there is no statistical difference in the means, though there are enormous differences among countries, suggesting that educational and cultural factors are vastly more important than gender in the acquisition of mathematical skills.

Brain Systems for Mathematical Expertise

There is now extensive evidence that routine numerical tasks involve a fronto-parietal network (Pesenti et al., 2000), where the parietal components, perhaps especially the left intraparietal sulcus, are relatively specialized for numbers (Dehaene, Piazza, Pinel, & Cohen, 2003). It is certainly the case that damage to the left parietal lobe can severely affect calculation (Cipolotti & van Harskamp, 2001), though almost nothing is known about its effect on other mathematical domains.

More complex calculation in relatively non-expert subjects established that the neural basis of simple retrieval (e.g., $3 \times 4 = ?$), relative to a reading control, "engaged a left parieto-precentral circuit representing a developmental trace of a finger-counting representation that mediates, by extension, the numerical knowledge in adult," plus a naming network including the left anterior insula and the right cerebellar cortex (Zago et al., 2001). On the other hand, complex computation (e.g., 32×24) engaged, additionally, a left parieto-superior frontal network for holding multi-digit numbers in visuospatial working memory along with bilateral inferior temporal gyri, which is implicated visual mental imagery. Correlated activity in the left intraparietal sulcus and the precentral gyrus "may reflect the involvement of a finger movement representation network" in the calculation process.

This is not to say that these skilled adults are counting on their fingers, but it may be that the childhood use of fingers in learning to calculate somehow creates the neural substrate for later acquisition of numerical knowledge (Butterworth, 1999).

There have been very few studies of the brain systems of expert calculators. Benbow, O'Boyle, and colleagues (e.g., Alexander, O'Boyle, & Benbow, 1996; O'Boyle, Benbow, & Alexander, 1995; O'Boyle, Gill, Benbow, & Alexander, 1994; Singh & O'Boyle, 2004) have investigated mathematically gifted children and adolescents, with special reference to gender and brain organization. In general, they have found more right-hemisphere involvement in a range of tasks, though, curiously, mathematical tasks themselves have not been studied. Pesenti and colleagues have published data on the brain of an expert calculator carrying out mathematical tasks (Pesenti et al., 2001).

In a functional neuroimaging study, Pesenti and colleagues found that the prodigy Gamm's calculation processes recruited the same neural network as previously observed for both simple and complex calculation (Zago et al., 2001), *plus* a system of brain areas implicated in episodic memory, including right medial frontal and parahippocampal gyri, whereas those of control subjects did not (Butterworth, 2001; Pesenti et al., 2001). Functional brain imaging has established that speech-based working-memory storage, of the kind that supports standard digit-span tasks, involves the perisylvian language areas (Paulesu, Frith, & Frackowiak, 1993). So Gamm's activations here are quite different. As noted above, it has been suggested that experts develop a way of exploiting the unlimited storage capacity of long-term memory to maintain task-relevant information, such as the sequence of steps and intermediate results needed for complex calculation, whereas the rest of us still rely on the very limited span of working memory (Ericsson & Kintsch, 1995). Gamm's activations are consistent with his having developed LTWM for arithmetical calculations (Butterworth, 2001). See also Hill and Schneider, Chapter 37, concerning brain changes with expertise development.

Conclusions

Our starting point was Galton's tripartite theory of eminence: capacity, zeal, and the ability to do a very great deal of hard work.

Starting with capacity, it is clear that cases of individuals with exceptional mathematical, and especially calculating, ability show enormous variety of cognitive abilities. Some are highly intelligent, others averagely intelligent, yet others are classed by their peers (before standardized IQ testing) as stupid. So the kind of general intellectual capacity supposed by Galton does not seem to apply here. Nor does our survey support Gardner's (1983) idea of a distinct "logical-mathematical" intelligence, since many prodigies seem no better than average, and indeed many are much worse than average, in reasoning.

Zeal seems to be a characteristic common to all the prodigies described here. They are obsessed with numbers, treat them as familiar friends, and actively seek closer acquaintance with them.

They also seem to spend a great deal of time thinking and learning about numbers, presumably for many hours a day: all seem to have the capacity for very hard work. Extensive practice has an effect on memory, as would be expected, and it is quite specific. Exceptional calculators have acquired enormous repertoires of arithmetical facts and procedures, sometimes deliberately and sometimes by virtue of working with numbers so much. In some cases, excellent arithmetical memory goes hand in hand with very poor memory for other materials. Working-memory is frequently cited as a serious limitation on complex mental calculation, and eminent calculators learn or devise tricks to reduce working-memory load.

Is their exceptional ability confined to mathematics? Whereas some seem to excel only in calculation, others have shown eminence in fields other than mathematics. Although there appears to be specialized brain systems for numerical processing in the parietal lobes, which have an innate basis, this may have little or nothing to do with exceptional ability. This is confirmed by neuroimaging studies: exceptional calculators such as Gamm seem not to be activating the usual brain regions differently, but rather recruiting new regions outside the parietal lobes to support the current task. There is now ample evidence for activity-dependent plasticity: that is, that the functioning, and even the structure, of brain systems is shaped by practice and experience (Amunts et al., 1997; Pascual-Leone & Torres, 1993; Schlaug, Jancke, Huang, Staiger, & Steinmetz, 1995; Schlaug, Jancke, Huang, & Steinmetz, 1995).

Ericsson and Charness (1994) have stressed the role of systematic teaching for promoting the deliberate practice needed for the highest levels of expertise. This, at least in part, is because deliberate practice is not in itself rewarding. There are, in the biographies of mathematical prodigies, many counterexamples to this claim, where precocity in mathematics could be nurtured in a systematic way, whereas others appear to have acquired exceptional mathematical skills despite very unhelpful early conditions.

It may be that finding solutions to mathematical problems is, for the zealous, intrinsically rewarding. It may also be that the domain of mathematics is so ordered that it is propitious for unsupervised learning since it is easy to check an answer by using a different method. Many prodigies report external rewards also – amazing their friends and family. This may be especially relevant in the savant, or near-savant cases, where there may be few ways to gain the admiration of other people. Perhaps this is why parallels between music and mathematics are noticed. Both have intrinsic rewards that are propitious for unsupervised learning. In music, one can hear whether something sounds right or not – there is harmony or there is discord. And there are external rewards that do not require a teacher, namely, that other people readily appreciate good playing or singing.

Finally, are exceptional calculators born or made? There is ample evidence for zeal and hard work, and it may be that we are born with dispositions toward them. Charles Darwin, in a letter to Galton, wrote "I have always maintained that excepting fools, men did not differ much in intellect, only in zeal and hard work; I still think this an *eminently* important difference" (quoted by Ericsson & Charness, 1994). It may also be the case that some of us are born with a disposition to enjoy or even be obsessed with an orderly domain like mathematics. However, there is no evidence at the moment for differences in innate specific capacities for mathematics.

References

Alarcon, M., Defries, J., Gillis Light, J., & Pennington, B. (1997). A twin study of mathematics disability. *Journal of Learning Disabilities*, 30, 617–623.

Alexander, J. E., O'Boyle, M. W., & Benbow, C. P. (1996). Developmentally advanced EEG alpha power in gifted male and female adolescents. *International Journal of Psychophysiology*, 23, 25–31.

Amunts, K., Schlaug, G., Jancke, L., Steinmetz, H., Schleicher, A., Dabringhaus, A., et al. (1997). Motor cortex and hand motor skills: Structural compliance in the human brain. *Human Brain Mapping*, 5, 206–215.

Antell, S. E., & Keating, D. P. (1983). Perception of numerical invariance in neonates. *Child Development*, 54, 695–701.

Ashcraft, M. (1995). Cognitive psychology and simple arithmetic: A review and summary of new directions. *Mathematical Cognition*, 1, 3–34.

Barlow, F. (1952). *Mental Prodigies*. New York: Greenwood Press.

Becker, B. J., & Hedges, L. V. (1988). The effects of selection and variability in studies of gender differences. Commentary on Benbow (1988). *Behavioral and Brain Sciences*, 11(2), 183–184.

Benbow, C. P. (1988). Sex differences in mathematical reasoning ability in intellectually talented preadolescents: Their nature, effects, and possible causes. *Behavioral and Brain Sciences*, 11(2), 169–183.

Binet, A. (1894). *Psychologie des grands calculateurs et joueurs d'échecs*. Paris: Hachette.

Butterworth, B. (1999). The Mathematical Brain. London: Macmillan.

Butterworth, B. (2001). What makes a prodigy? *Nature Neuroscience*, 4(1), 11–12.

Butterworth, B. (2005). The development of arithmetical abilities. *Journal of Child Psychology & Psychiatry*, 46(1), 3–18.

Butterworth, B., Cipolotti, L., & Warrington, E. K. (1996). Short-term memory impairments and arithmetical ability. *Quarterly Journal of Experimental Psychology*, 49A, 251–262.

Butterworth, B., Shallice, T., & Watson, F. (1990). Short-term retention of sentences without "short-term memory." In G. Vallar & T. Shallice (Eds.), *Neuropsychological Impairments of Short-Term Memory*. Cambridge: Cambridge University Press.

Bynner, J., & Parsons, S. (1997). *Does Numeracy Matter?* London: The Basic Skills Agency.

Cappelletti, M., Kopelman, M., & Butterworth, B. (2002). Why semantic dementia drives you to the dogs (but not to the horses): A theoretical account. *Cognitive Neuropsychology*, 19(6), 483–503.

Charness, N., & Campbell, J. I. D. (1988). Acquiring skill at mental calculation in adulthood: A task decomposition. *Journal of Experimental Psychology: General*, 117(2), 115–129.

Cipolotti, L., & van Harskamp, N. (2001). Disturbances of number processing and calculation. In R. S. Berndt (Ed.), *Handbook of Neuropsychology* (2nd. ed., Vol. 3, pp. 305–334). Amsterdam: Elsevier Science.

Cockcroft, W. H. (1982). *Mathematics Counts: Report of the Committee of Inquiry into the Teaching of Mathematics in Schools under the Chairmanship of Dr. W. H. Cockcroft*. London: HMSO.

Dehaene, S. (1997). *The Number Sense: How the Mind creates Mathematics*. New York: Oxford University Press.

Dehaene, S., & Cohen, L. (1995). Towards and anatomical and functional model of number processing. *Mathematical Cognition*, 1, 83–120.

Dehaene, S., Piazza, M., Pinel, P., & Cohen, L. (2003). Three parietal circuits for number processing. *Cognitive Neuropsychology*, 20, 487–506.

Delazer, M., & Benke, T. (1997). Arithmetic facts without meaning. *Cortex*, 33, 697–710.

DfES. (2002). *GCSE/GNVQ National Summary Results*, from http://www.standards.dfes.gov.uk/performance/2002gcseresults.pdf?version=1.

Donlan, C. (2003). The early numeracy of children with specific language impairments. In A. J. Baroody & A. D. Dowker (Eds.), *The Development of Arithmetic Concepts and Skills: Constructing Adaptive Expertise* (pp. 337–358). Mahwah, NJ: Lawrence Erlbaum Associates.

Edwards, C. J., Alder, T. B., & Rose, G. J. (2002). Auditory midbrain neurons that count. *Nature Neuroscience*, 5(10), 934–936.

Ericsson, K. A., & Charness, N. (1994). Expert performance: Its structure and acquisition. *American Psychologist*, 49(8), 725–747.

Ericsson, K. A., & Kintsch, W. (1995). Long-term working memory. *Psychological Review*, 102, 211–245.

Ericsson, K. A., Krampe, R. T., & Tesch-Römer, C. (1993). The role of deliberate practice in the acquisition of expert performance. *Psychological Review*, 100, 363–406.

Galton, F. (1979). *Hereditary Genius: An Inquiry into its Laws and Consequences* (Originally published in 1869). London: Julian Friedman Publishers.

Gardner, H. (1983). *Frames of Mind: The Theory of Multiple Intelligences*. New York: Basic Books.

Geary, D. C. (1996). Sexual selection and sex differences in mathematical abilities. *Behavioral and Brain Sciences*, 19, 229 et seq.

Gelman, R., & Gallistel, C. R. (1978). *The Child's Understanding of Number* (1986 ed.). Cambridge, MA: Harvard University Press.

Girelli, L., & Delazer, M. (1996). Subtraction bugs in an acalculic patient. *Cortex*, 32, 547–555.

Goel, V., & Dolan, R. J. (2004). Differential involvement of left prefrontal cortex in inductive and deductive reasoning. *Cognition*, 93(3), B109–B121.

Gruber, O., Indefrey, P., Steinmetz, H., & Kleinschmidt, A. (2001). Dissociating neural correlates of cognitive components in mental calculation. *Cerebral Cortex*, 11, 350–359.

Hardy, G. H. (1969). *A Mathematician's Apology* (Originally published in 1940). Cambridge: Cambridge University Press.

Hauser, M., MacNeilage, P., & Ware, M. (1996). Numerical representations in primates. *Proceedings of the National Academy of Sciences, USA*, 93, 1514–1517.

Hécaen, H., Angelergues, R., & Houillier, S. (1961). Les variétés cliniques des acalculies au cours des lésions rétro-rolandiques: Approche statistique du problème. *Revue Neurologique*, 105, 85–103.

Hermelin, B., & O'Connor, N. (1990). Factors and primes: A specific numerical ability. *Psychological Medicine*, 20, 163–169.

Hittmair-Delazer, M., Semenza, C., & Denes, G. (1994). Concepts and facts in calculation. *Brain*, 117, 715–728.

Horwitz, W. A., Deming, W. E., & Winter, R. F. (1969). A further account of the idiot savants: Experts with the calendar. *American Journal of Psychiatry*, 126, 160–163.

Hoyles, C., Wolf, A., Molyneux-Hodgson, S., & Kent, P. (2002). *Mathematical Skills in the Workplace*. London: Institute of Education.

Hunter, I. M. L. (1962). An exceptional talent for calculative thinking. *British Journal of Psychology*, 53, 243–280.

Jensen, A. R. (1990). Speed of information-processing in a calculating prodigy. *Intelligence*, 14, 3.

Keys, W., Harris, S., & Fernandes, C. (1996). *Third International Mathematics and Science Study. First national Report. Part 1*. Slough: National Foundation for Educational Research.

Landerl, K., Bevan, A., & Butterworth, B. (2004). Developmental dyscalculia and basic numerical capacities: A Study of 8–9 Year Old Students. *Cognition*, 93, 99–125.

Logie, R. H., Gilhooly, K. J., & Wynn, V. (1994). Counting on working memory in arithmetic problem solving. *Memory & Cognition*, 22, 395–410.

McCloskey, M., & Caramazza, A. (1987). Dissociations of calculation processes. In G. Deloche & X. Seron (Eds.), *Mathematical Disabilities: A Cognitive Neuropsychological Perspective*. Hillsdale, NJ: Lowrence Erlbaum Associetes.

McComb, K., Packer, C., & Pusey, A. (1994). Roaring and numerical assessment in contests between groups of female lions, *Panthera leo*. *Animal Behaviour*, 47, 379–387.

Mitchell, F. D. (1907). Mathematical prodigies. *Amercian Journal of Psychology*, 18(1), 61–143.

O'Boyle, M. W., Benbow, C. P., & Alexander, J. E. (1995). Sex differences, hemispheric laterality, and associated brain activity in the intellectually gifted. *Developmental Neuropsychology*, 11(4), 415–443.

O'Boyle, M. W., Gill, H. S., Benbow, C. P., & Alexander, J. E. (1994). Concurrent finger-tapping in mathematically gifted males – evidence for enhanced right-hemisphere involvement during linguistic processing. *Cortex*, 30(3), 519–526.

Pascual-Leone, A., & Torres, F. (1993). Plasticity of the sensorimotor cortex representation of the reading finger in Braille readers. *Brain*, 116, 39–52.

Paulesu, E., Frith, C. D., & Frackowiak, R. S. J. (1993). The neural correlates of the verbal component of working memory. *Nature*, 362, 342–345.

Pesenti, M. (2005). Calculation abilities in expert calculators. In J. I. D. Campbell (Ed.), *Handbook of Mathematical Cognition* (pp. 413–430). Hove: Psychology Press.

Pesenti, M., Seron, X., Samson, D., & Duroux, B. (1999). Basic and exceptional calculation abilities in a calculating prodigy: A case study. *Mathematical Cognition*, 5, 97–148.

Pesenti, M., Thioux, M., Seron, X., & De Volder, A. (2000). Neuroanatomical substrates of Arabic number processing, numerical comparison and simple addition: A PET study. *Journal of Cognitive Neuroscience*, 12, 461–479.

Pesenti, M., Zago, L., Crivello, F., Mellet, E., Samson, D., Duroux, B., et al. (2001). Mental calculation expertise in a prodigy is sustained by right prefrontal and medial-temporal areas. *Nature Neuroscience*, 4(1), 103–107.

Rivera-Batiz, F. L. (1992). Quantitative literacy and the likelihood of employment among young adults in the United States. *The Journal of Human Resources*, 27(2), 313–328.

Schlaug, G., Jancke, L., Huang, Y. X., Staiger, J. F., & Steinmetz, H. (1995). Increased corpus callosum size in musicians. *Neuropsychologia*, 33, 1047–1055.

Schlaug, G., Jancke, L., Huang, Y. X., & Steinmetz, H. (1995). In-vivo evidence of structural brain asymmetry in musicians. *Science*, 267, 699–701.

Scripture, E. W. (1891). Arithmetical prodigies. *Amercian Journal of Psychology*, 4(1), 1–59.

Shalev, R. S., & Gross-Tsur, V. (2001). Developmental dyscalculia. Review article. *Pediatric Neurology*, 24, 337–342.

Singh, H., & O'Boyle, M. W. (2004). Interhemispheric interaction during global-local processing in mathematically gifted adolescents, average-ability youth, and college students. *Neuropsychology*, 18(2), 371–377.

Smith, S. B. (1983). *The Great Mental Calculators: The Psychology, Methods, and Lives of*

Calculating Prodigies. New York: Columbia University Press.

Starkey, P., & Cooper, R. G., Jr. (1980). Perception of numbers by human infants. *Science, 210*, 1033–1035.

van Harskamp, N. J., & Cipolotti, L. (2001). Selective impairments for addition, subtraction and multiplication. Implications for the organisation of arithmetical facts. *Cortex, 37,* 363–388.

Weinland, J. D., & Schlauch, W. S. (1937). An examination of the computing ability of Mr. Salo Finkelstein. *Journal of Experimental Psychology, 21,* 382–402.

Wynn, K. (1992). Addition and subtraction by human infants. *Nature, 358,* 749–751.

Wynn, K. (2000). Findings of addition and subtraction in infants are robust and consistent: Reply to Wakeley, Rivera, and Langer. *Child Development,* 71(6), 1535–1536.

Wynn, K. (2002). Do infants have numerical expectations or just perceptual preferences? Commentary. *Developmental Science,* 5(2), 207–209.

Wynn, K., Bloom, P., & Chiang, W. C. (2002). Enumeration of collective entities by 5-month-old infants. *Cognition,* 83(3), B55–B62.

Zago, L., Pesenti, M., Mellet, E., Crivello, F., Mazoyer, B., & Tzourio-Mazoyer, N. (2001). Neural correlates of simple and complex mental calculation. *Neuroimage,* 13(2), 314–327.

CHAPTER 33

Expertise in History

James F. Voss & Jennifer Wiley

Overviews of Expertise and of History

Expertise

Expertise, studied in a variety of domains, has referred to highly skilled performance in an activity such as violin playing or playing chess. Expertise has referred also to a person's knowledge and/or ability to perform representational tasks of a particular domain. The term also may be based on a reputation established by publications and/or lectures, or on a "certification" such as a PhD. In the present context, an expert in history is assumed to have a general and a specialized knowledge of history as well as facility in the skills of historical research and writing.

Although the study of expertise began in the late nineteenth century, the primary impetus occurred in the late twentieth century with the work on chess by de Groot (1965) and Chase and Simon (1973a, 1973b). This research, comparing expert, middle-range, and novice performance, demonstrated the importance of recognizing functionally related "chunks" of chess pieces.

Similarly, physics experts were superior to novices in their conceptual understanding of physics problems, which in turn led to their better problem solving (Chi, Feltovich, & Glaser, 1981; Larkin, McDermott, Simon, & Simon, 1980).

The nature of expertise in any domain involves an interaction of a person's knowledge (both domain-specific and general) and skills, and the characteristics of the domain that constrain performance. Some domains, because of their conceptual evolution, permit the use of mathematics, formal logic, or well-controlled experimentation. Such domains are generally termed "well structured," frequently dealing with problems having a single answer, readily identifiable constraints, and agreed-upon solutions. Other domains such as history and political science have conceptual structures that allow relatively little opportunity to use mathematics, formal logic, or controlled experimentation. Instead, reasoning and problem solving usually are verbal (not mathematical), with evidence for a solution presented as an argument, usually developed in relation to particular facts and interpretations. Such problems are termed "ill structured," having more than one possible answer, requiring identification of constraints, and having no agreed-upon solution.

With respect to the study of expertise in history, although centuries ago historians as a group were concerned about the quality and accuracy of their writings, the study of expertise in history as well as the social sciences emerged in the 1980s, the seminal papers being Voss, Greene, Post, and Penner (1983) in political science and Wineburg (1991) in history. Two suggestions are made regarding why and when these works emerged. One is that the study of expertise began in domains having well-structured problems, probably because such problems are relatively tractable and in many cases computer simulations of performance could be obtained. Political science and history, however, generally are concerned with ill-structured problems that have a large amount of potentially related information, and different experts may approach the same issue differently, depending on the expert's theoretical background, related knowledge, and other factors. Such solutions are usually verbal arguments, which typically do not have right or wrong answers, but the answers may vary in relative acceptability. Furthermore, evaluation may occur by examining the acceptability of the information provided *per se*, the extent to which the solution information supports the solution, and the quality of a counterargument or alternative solution that may be offered. The evaluator may be influenced also by the evaluator's own beliefs, theoretical orientation, or other factors. Thus, because of the nature of the domain, there is relatively little opportunity to profit from the benefits of quantitative analysis, which leads to relatively less certainty in subject-matter knowledge and more heterogeneity in constraint usage.

History

As expected, a number of definitions of history have been advanced. Stearns (1998) regards history as "change over time" (p. 281),

adding that such study has two components, continuity and causation, that is, the historian documents change and works to determine its causes.

Leinhardt, Stainton, and Virji (1994) developed a definition obtained from interviews with seven professional historians and two history teachers. The composite definition that Leinhardt et al. derived is "History is a process of constructing, reconstructing, and interpreting past events, ideas, and institutions from surviving or inferential evidence to understand and make meaningful who and what we are today. The process involves dialogues with alternative voices from the past itself, with recorders of the past, and with present interpreters. The process also involves constructing coherent, powerful narratives that describe and interpret the events, as well as skillful quantitative and qualitative information from a theoretical perspective" (p. 88). The above definitions emphasize change, reconstruction, and the importance of historiography, that is, the processes whereby the historian obtains and uses information.

The beginning of the study of history is usually marked by the writings of Herodotus (484–425 BC), which contain an account of the Persian-Greek Wars and related matters (Herodotus, 1987). Although his writings include some Homer-like mythological and religious components, Herodotus primarily wrote to provide a record for future readers. Thucydides (460–400 BC), also explicitly writing for the future, provided an account (1954) of the Peloponnesian War that matched Athens and Sparta. The war began in 431 BC, ending in 404 BC with the defeat of Athens. Thucydides focused on the military and political aspects of the war, considering social, cultural, and economic aspects when relevant. Moreover, by including speeches of leaders he provided examples of political rhetoric, with Pericles' funeral oration probably the most notable.

In a broader sense, a major contribution of these writers was to make history secular, that is, to consider human activity as causing events rather than seeing the forces of religion and myth as causes. In addition, the authors used a criterion of evidence for the historical accounts, namely, eyewitness testimony, including obtaining corroboration across witnesses.

From the time of Herodotus to the present, the field of history expanded substantially, and during this time, history frequently has been interpreted to support a particular ideological viewpoint. As examples, during the Middle Ages history was used by the Church to determine "God's Plan," during the Enlightenment it was used as a demonstration of progress, and during the nineteenth century as a means to support broad socio-cultural ideas of civilization's progress (Lemon, 2003).

Two historical developments of the twentieth century are noted. The field of social history developed, addressing more egalitarian topics related to the lives of everyday people. Second, the Covering Law, stated by Hempel (1942), constituted an attempt to subsume history under the theoretical framework of positivism, the atheoretical view of science emphasizing experimentation and the operation of laws. Under the Covering Law, history was regarded as event contingencies mediated by lawful relations, that is, event A was followed by event B because of a law operating to produce the relation.

The Covering Model raised a number of questions. Dray (1957), for example, argued that since each historical set of events is unique, there would need to be many laws of history. Moreover, historians generally have not found such laws, nor actually do they seek them (Mink, 1987). In addition, there is the importance of contextualization, that is, events occur in a context and the so-called meaning or importance of that event is often a function of that context. This would suggest a need for a law for each occurrence of A that is in a different context.

Finally, comparing the Herodotus period to the present, the study of history has not changed substantially, especially if compared, unfairly, to the technological changes in scientific investigation. Specifically, over time more and better sources have become available, but the basic means and

procedures have changed relatively little. As an example, in the Sixteenth century some historians were concerned about their methods and developed rules of writing historical accounts. These included avoidance of one's own or another person's religious, social, or patriotic biases, being detached when writing about recent events, writing in an appropriate manner and not for entertainment, and being sure to "stick to facts rather than inventing them" (Lemon, 2003, p. 119).

To this point we have provided some background in the fields of expertise and of history, and we turn now to the historian. The goal of the historian generally is to study a particular topic and provide a coherent, interpretive, and persuasive account stating a position that usually but not necessarily is a narrative. The contents of the narrative are usually concerned with the changes that took place in the topic being studied and what produced them. In the next section we delineate two inter-related tasks of the historian, obtaining information and writing a narrative.

Expertise in History: The Historian's Tasks

In this section we are inserting the first of ten Characteristics of History Experts (CHEs). Each CHE is a summary statement of the findings of expert or expert-related research in history or, in a few cases, a related discipline.

Obtaining Information

The historian may use many resources, including biographies, autobiographies, journals, other library sources, museum archives, letters, paintings, objects, birth and death records, and photographs, examining them for their reliability, validity, authenticity, and usefulness.

CHE 1

Historians evaluate sources emphasizing original and authentic information, using criteria different than novices. Historians also tend to have less intra-group variability in source evaluation than novices.

Wineburg (1991) had eight high school students and eight professional historians evaluate eleven sources pertaining to the Battle of Lexington. Eight written sources came from diaries (2), an autobiography, a deposition, a newspaper report, and a letter of protest, each written close to the time of the battle. The other two written excerpts were from a historical novel and a high school textbook, respectively, each written in the 1960s. The other three sources were paintings done, respectively, in 1775, 1859, and 1886.

"Think-aloud" protocols were obtained as well as rankings of each written document for its "trustworthiness as a source for understanding what happened on Lexington Green" (p. 75). The paintings were rated for "what most accurately depicts what happened on Lexington Green" (p. 75).

For the eight written documents, historians provided substantial within-group agreement, novices having less. There was poor agreement between the two groups, with experts, for example, rating one of the diaries as most trustworthy of the written sources and novices rating the textbook and novel excerpts as most trustworthy, which historians rated quite low. Rating the paintings for their description, analysis, relevance, and qualification, experts provided more information. History graduate students also were shown to evaluate information usefulness in a different way than psychology graduate students, with history students also demonstrating a more historian-like way of expressing and supporting their respective positions (Rouet, Favart, Britt, & Perfetti, 1997).

CHE 2

Experts use at least three heuristics in their analysis of sources, corroboration, sourcing, and contextualization (Wineburg, 1991).

Corroboration is the "act of comparing documents with one another," sourcing is the "act of looking first to the source of the document before reading the body of the text,"

and contextualization is the "act of situating a document in a concrete temporal and spatial context" (p. 77). Using both quantitative and qualitative indices, experts used the heuristics more frequently and more appropriately than novices. Wineburg speculated about a possible fourth heuristic, identifying absent evidence, which was also a more frequent strategy among experts. As Wineburg notes, the prior knowledge of the historian, both in general and in reference to specific expertise, is an important factor in the effective use of such heuristics.

The use of heuristics by historians raises a more general issue. Such heuristics, used as early as the Greek writings, provide the historian with a means of systematizing their inquiry, helping to constrain and interpret the material. In other words, the historian is improving the structure of an ill-structured task. These and findings reported later in this chapter support a conclusion of Ericsson and Lehmann (1996) that across a wide range of domains, one of the characteristics of expertise is the ability to adapt and use constraints.

CHE 3

When analyzing sources, historians develop mental representations of the events and activities discussed in the text (situation models) and also generate subtext.

Following cognitive text processing theory (e.g., Kintsch, 1988), Wineburg (1994), via the use of "think-aloud" protocols, studied how eight historians processed the written sources on the Battle of Lexington described above. Theoretically, each historian was presumed to have three mental representations derived from the text, namely, the text contents *per se*, the event, and the subtext. The text representation is of the contents of the text *per se*. The event model is the representation of the event as conceived by the historian, and the subtext, an elaboration of the situation model, is constructed by the reader, using whatever seems reasonable about the time and place of the text events, the intention of the author, the intended audience, and other factors. To construct the event representation the reader uses the preceding text contents as well as prior knowledge. Using knowledge and inferences based upon the event model, the reader may construct a subtext, possibly dealing with inferences about the author's goals and/or intentions, the motivations of the characters being discussed, or perhaps hidden assumptions about the actions. Historians' event and especially the subtext representations may vary depending on the background knowledge of the historian. As an example, one historian, in analyzing the diary of a British officer who wrote a description of what happened at the Lexington battle, indicated that given what the British army did immediately after the battle, the diary writer did not have time to write the diary until the next day, and he wrote the diary because he thought he may be questioned by his superior about his actions. Thus, he wrote the diary to show his actions in a favorable light. Subtext development has the difficulty of varying in the extent to which different historians would be in agreement.

CHE 4

Historians show expert-expert differences in performance based on differences in areas of specialization, but they show similarities in the use of domain-related skills.

Both Wineburg (1998) and Leinhardt and Young (1996) examined expert-expert differences. Wineburg presented two history experts with seven documents concerning statements by or about Abraham Lincoln and his attitudes concerning race. One expert's specialization was the Civil War and Abraham Lincoln, whereas the other expert's field was American History, the latter thus having substantial knowledge of the Civil War but not that of the first expert. Leinhardt and Young (1996) also provided historians with documents close to or in the particular historian's field of specialization.

Both studies demonstrated that experts specializing on the particular issue in question produced more extensive and detailed analysis of the documents. In addition, in the Wineburg (1998) study, the non-specializing

expert, through the application of general skills of the historian, was able to perform high-quality analyses but not at the specialized expert's level. Also, although both historians spoke of contextual aspects of the respective documents, such analysis was greater for the specializing expert. Furthermore, this result showed a greater development of subtext by the specialist, that is, this historian used his or her knowledge and beliefs to consider matters such as the intention of the text writer and for whom the text was intended. Finally, theoretically, Leinhardt and Young postulated that two schemas operate when historians read documents, an "identify" and an "interpret" schema, which in turn are related to procedures of analysis.

We want to mention in passing that an aspect of the historian's task that is virtually never studied in history or any other subject-matter domain is the ability of the expert to be adroit in selecting and defining the issue to be studied. Problem finding is the critical first step in problem solving (cf. Getzels, 1979), and expert historians must have skill at posing interesting yet researchable questions.

Narrative Construction and Analysis

Much has been written about the narrative, by historians, philosophers of history, literary critics, and psychologists. We next focus on the historical narrative and its purpose and use.

CHE 5

Historians have the goal of constructing narratives, based on evidence, that provide a reasonable account of particular historical events and actions. As such, narratives are rhetorical constructions aimed at building a case for a particular position in a manner persuasive to readers.

In his *Rhetoric*, Aristotle discussed arguments involving probability or plausibility rather than certainty. He described two types of argument structures employed for this purpose, the enthymeme, that is, a claim and a supporting reason, and the paradeigma or narrative (Aristotle, 1954; McGuire, 1990). In the narrative, the claim of the argument is the interpretation or conclusion of the author and the narrative is the supporting evidence. Within the narrative there may of course be other arguments, including extensive development of causal arguments. Moreover, the narrative may be written for a specific audience or a more general audience, as described by Perelman and Olbrechts-Tyteca (1969). Similarly, the historian may develop an argument in expository or categorical form. The use of these two types of argument within a discipline is current in other fields, such as Schum's (1993) distinction of temporal and relational arguments in jury decision making.

One of the issues raised by critics of the historical narrative is the relation of the historical narrative and the fictional narrative. One view is that the former is written to provide an accurate account based on the available evidence, whereas the latter is not based on evidence or seeking truth, except in the most abstract sense (cf. Mink, 1987). Although this comparison appears to be reasonable, historical narratives require further examination.

A historical narrative typically consists of organizing and interpreting actions and events and their consequences. But in doing so, to what extent does the historian "fill in the dots?" Hayden White (1987) has argued that a critical factor in historical narrative is "emplotment," that is, the events of the narrative take on meaning according to the development of the narrative's plot. Chronology is not enough, and the historian provides coherence and thematic content by generating the plot. To White the plot "endows them (real events) with illusory coherence" (White, 1987, p. xi), or similarly, he states "Reality wears the mask of meaning" (White, 1987, p. 21).

Mink (1987) argued that the narrative serves as a "cognitive instrument," and that it provides the historian with a valuable tool providing opportunity for interpretation. Mink also noted that the aggregation of historical information could occur via incorporation of narratives with one another, but that this seldom happens. Instead, Mink maintains that historic information increases via new discoveries and interpretations.

CHE 6

Narrative quality is related to five components: coherence, chronology, completeness, contextualization, and causation. Although not studied extensively, evidence suggests that narratives deficient in one or more of these characteristics may produce lower trustworthiness, the amount depending on the characteristics and the narrative contents.

What constitutes a "good" narrative has been studied empirically by Leinhardt, Stainton, Virji, and Odoroff (1994). The above five characteristics were those stated by seven professional historians when asked to indicate the qualities needed for a narrative to be "good."

Coherence, regarded as the most important characteristic, refers to the narrative's organization and focus on a central theme. Chronology refers to the reasonable and accurate discussion of the sequencing of events in time. Completeness, or exhaustivity, refers to the use of all available evidence that supports or opposes the expressed ideas and arguments. In practice this criterion is quite demanding because a writer must make judgments regarding what to include and what to omit. Contextualization refers to placing the narrative subject matter into a broader perspective, for example, writing about the causes of the 1991 Gulf War by framing it in the context of the interest of the United States to preserve its Middle East hegemony. Causation is demonstrating convincingly that events or actions produced particular consequences, thus providing coherence to the narrative as a whole and providing linkages of events and actions.

The importance of some characteristics of narrative quality was studied by Voss, Wiley, and Sandak (1999). Set in a legal context, fictional narratives were presented to college students, each narrative containing a murder. The texts included a baseline narrative, a narrative in which coherence and chronology together were degraded, and one in which causation was degraded by using fewer irrelevant (not pertaining to the murder) causal connectives than the baseline text. However, for all types of text the information pertaining to the respective murder was held constant. Participants were asked to regard each text as the summary of a prosecuting attorney and to rate (on a numerical scale) whether the defendant was guilty and also to rate the texts for cohesiveness and for quality.

The important result is that each of the degraded texts (coherence and chronology, and causality) produced not only lower ratings of text coherence and quality than the baseline text, but also yielded lower guilty ratings, that is, the poorer narratives were rated as having less convincing content, even though the murder-related contents were equivalent.

CHE 7

Historical narratives, although chronological, do not consist of linear chains; they typically have both narrative and expository components.

Voss, Carretero, Kennet, and Silfies (1994) asked two political science Soviet Union experts and 32 novices to write an essay on the collapse of the Soviet Union. The non-expert narratives, except those in which information was minimal, all contained narrative and expository components. This observation holds for most narratives in that there is a chronological flow that is marked by occasional sections, expository in nature, that provide rationales, explanations, elaborations, or speculations about some aspect of the narrative. Another finding is that there was a substantial difference in the approach of the two experts, with one describing the collapse in narrative form, providing a chronological account of the collapse interspersed with interpretive comments, the other expert producing an expository account listing and developing reasons for the collapse.

A related study on expository text was conducted by Schooler, Kennet, Wiley, and

Voss (1996) in which an expert and novices read two newspaper editorials, making comments as they read. Novices included political science or psychology graduate students. The expert, a political scientist, in reading the first few sentences, categorized the (anonymous) author of one editorial as a neo-realist, indicating problems he felt with that position. Although the graduate students of each discipline provided about the same number of evaluative comments, the political science graduate students supported their own positions more than the psychology graduate students, whereas the latter provided more comments about possible bias. Furthermore, only the political science graduate students used counterfactual reasoning. These findings support discipline-related expertise development at the graduate level.

CHE 8

Alternative narratives about a particular topic may be constructed for a variety of reasons, including differences in interpretation, information, and political-cultural factors.

We think of taking a course in school called "U.S. History." By the title it appears that the course contents constitute "The" history, the only history of the United States. But there are or could be multiple histories about virtually any topic addressed in the course. Why are there alternative histories? It is because each person writing a history bases it on his or her own particular perspective, which may include the person's knowledge, experience, beliefs, information available, theoretical orientation, and the time and place in which the individual lives.

CHE 8A

Alternative narratives may be written because of differential source use and interpretation.

One of the more interesting studies (Cronon, 1992) regarding alternative narratives involves a comparison of two books, each pertaining to the years of the Dust Bowl on the American Western Plains. Using much of the same information, one author wrote an upbeat book concerning its long-term effects while the other author wrote of it as a major disaster. Cronon notes that the matter does not simply concern the difference in conclusion, but that the stories told are also different, an issue leading Cronon into discussion of the historian and the constraints involved.

CHE 8B

Historians may produce alternative narratives because of differences in the time at which they write. Such differences may be due to the number and accuracy of sources as well as the cultural milieu of the time.

There are many examples of earlier and subsequent revisionist writings. In this regard, Lowenthal (2000) commented, "We are bound to see the Second World War differently in 1985 than in 1950 not merely because masses of new evidence have come to light but because the years have unfolded further consequences – the Cold War, the United Nations, the revival of the Japanese and German economies" (p. 78).

Historical events may be interpreted in terms of present conditions, but when this is done to an extreme, thereby apparently distorting events of the past, it is termed presentism. On the other hand, Levine (1989) pointed out that French historian Marc Bloch stated that "Misunderstanding of the present is the inevitable consequence of ignorance of the past, . . . But a man may wear himself out just as fruitlessly seeking to understand the past, if he is totally ignorant of the present" (pp. 671–672).

CHE 8C

Alternative narratives are found in countries in which the government and the citizens are not in agreement regarding historical-political-social thinking.

Alternative historical narratives also may coexist because of political-cultural factors. Wertsch and Rozin (1998), studying in the former Soviet Union, and Tulviste and Wertsch (1994), studying in Estonia, distinguished between an "official" history, a government-promoted history based on its

ideology, and an "unofficial" history, held by a number of the citizens, who nevertheless are quite knowledgeable about the "official" history. Moreover, an "official" history was organized and coherent, whereas an "unofficial" history was more piecemeal but in conflict with the "official" history. Wertsch and Rozin (1998) suggest three reasons for states to have an "official" history: to develop an instrument that shows the vision of the state, to foster community identity, and to produce loyalty to the state.

A related case is change in "official" histories when one set of government rulers replaces another. Ever since at least ancient Egypt it has been relatively common for new regime members to destroy statues, change names, burn records and pictures, and even kill family members of the old regime. Even today, in Russia, compared to the Soviet days, history books are being rewritten, there are few pictures and posters of Stalin and Lenin, and Leningrad is once more St. Petersburg.

Conflict between two "official" histories was shown in a study by Carretero, Jacott, and Lopez-Manjon (2002). Comparing history textbooks in Spain and Mexico, the Spanish text spoke of Columbus's discovery of America, whereas the Mexican text spoke of two cultures colliding. Similarly, whereas the Spanish text regarded Columbus as a leader and hero who endured hardship, the Mexican text hardly mentioned Columbus, emphasizing explorers as a group, and indicating that Columbus thought he was in Asia and at one time was put in chains.

CHE 8D

Alternative narratives are produced in classrooms by differences in students' cultural backgrounds.

Epstein (1998) reported that in a U.S. History class having a slightly greater number of white than Afro-American students, the teacher included more information about the role of Afro-Americans and women than typical U. S. History classes. Whereas students generally agreed that the teacher had done this, questionnaire and interview data indicated that Afro-Americans thought it was not enough, holding that the teacher should be Afro-American. The Americans identified as most important by Afro-American students were Martin Luther King, Malcolm X, and Harriet Tubman, whereas white students named George Washington, John F. Kennedy, and Martin Luther King Jr. Afro-Americans also rated the most important theme in U. S. History as Afro-American equality (66%) and nation building (13%), as opposed to nation building (56%) and equality (22%) for white students. Finally, the most important source for learning history was the family for Afro-American students; for white students it was the textbook, followed by the teacher. These findings are of course related to the "official" and "unofficial" history issue.

In another example of cultural differences, Barton (2001) found that whereas American students had a linear view of history, focusing on the expansion and growth of the United States, students of Northern Ireland considered history in terms of the changes over the centuries of the peoples that inhabited Northern Ireland, a view of history as a change of context or scene rather than linear development.

In this section we discussed the work of obtaining information and writing narratives. In the performance of such tasks, historians engage in a variety of mental activities, and we turn now to two such interrelated processing skills, reasoning and problem solving.

Reasoning and Problem Solving

By reasoning we mean the performance of an inferential process by which a person uses his or her knowledge to infer other information related to the initial knowledge (Voss, Wiley, & Carretero, 1995). The correctness or acceptability of the inference largely rests upon the proposition or information that justifies and connects the old and new information (Toulmin, 1958). As such, an inference can be an argument, A inferring C, justified by the statement B, connecting A and C. Furthermore, in history, as well as

most other disciplines, such inferences usually have plausibility or probability, but not certainty. Finally, these processes typically take place in the context of a goal, and reaching that goal may involve a number of such inferences, as well as assumptions and knowledge usage.

By problem solving, we mean addressing a domain-related question or problem and developing a solution or answer to it. As previously mentioned, the overall structure of a problem solution is an argument. Specifically, the problem statement constitutes a premise, the solution is viewed as the conclusion, and the steps to go from the initial statement to the goal or conclusion completes the argument. The solution process, by showing the movement from the initial state to the conclusion, serves to justify the conclusion. The form of the solution process in history or political science may be a narrative, an expository text, or a series of steps that would likely be in agreement with some model of problem solving. Evaluation of the solution, as stated, takes place by examining the quality of the evidence, the extent to which the evidence supports the solution, and the examination of opposing solutions.

CHE 9

Because of the conceptual nature of domains such as history, evidence or justification for a claim or conclusion usually is verbal. Moreover, such justification makes use of "weak" methods of reasoning and problem solving such as analogy, decomposition, and hypothesis or scenario generation and testing (thought experiments), as opposed to "stronger" solution methods such as mathematical proof and inference from well-controlled scientific experiments.

"Weak" methods (Newell, 1980), such as those mentioned above, typically do not lead to specific conclusions, as opposed to "strong" methods such as mathematics or logic that provide certainty. "Weak" methods also tend not to be taught in the classroom but are acquired as language structures from an early age. These methods are called "weak" because they do not lead to specific solutions, whereas "strong" methods do. Furthermore, as related to previous discussion, "strong methods" are generally used in relation to well-structured problems and "weak methods" in relation to ill-structured ones. It is not correct, however, to simply say that history is ill structured and physics is well structured. Tweney (1991), for example, in his study of Michael Faraday's discovery of electromagnetism, showed that Faraday's solution process was that of solving an ill-structured problem. So likewise may some history problems have known quantitative solutions, that is, they may be well structured. But in general, problems and issues of history are ill structured, and reasoning and problem solving take place by more informal means (Voss & Post, 1988).

The solving of ill-structured problems in political science has been studied by Voss et al. (1983). Using experts and novices with respect to knowledge of the Soviet Union, each person was asked to assume he or she was Head of the Ministry of Agriculture of the Soviet Union and, given the poor crop productivity, to say what he or she would do to improve it. (The research was conducted while the Soviet Union was in existence.) Individuals' "think-aloud" answers were tape-recorded, with expert protocols often being pages in length. In such an ill-structured problem the problem statement does not include a statement of the constraints of the problem.

The solving process of experts typically occurred in two phases, one of problem representation, which essentially is an analysis delineating the causes of the problem. The second, the solution phase, expresses how the problem should be solved and the justification of the solution. The problem representation may be developed in different ways. One expert began by describing the history of the problem, including a comparison showing that England developed a middle class, whereas Russia did not. He also discussed previous attempts at a solution in the Soviet Union and from this analysis generated the representation that the basic cause of poor crop productivity was a lack of modernization. This type of relatively

overarching representation is not uncommon for experts, as opposed to novices who tend to list specific problems. Other experts may not develop a problem history but may emphasize particular aspects of the problem such as political-economic factors. An important aspect of the representation process of experts is that in developing the representation they articulate some of the constraints that exist in relation to the particular problem, and it is not uncommon to attack one or more of the particular constraints in order to solve the problem.

Following representation development, a solution typically is stated. The expert who developed the representation of poor modernization went on to state that the solution was modernization, subsequently stating some of the ways to do this as well as some of the existing constraints. He stated that one would need to go to Gosplan (the Soviet economic planning agency) and argue to increase Soviet funds for agriculture, perhaps taking such funds from the military budget, a questionable possibility. He also suggested that since each family had a private plot, and since productivity on the private plots was greater that on the state farms, the private plots should be increased in size, and people should be allowed to sell the products at market. But this, he pointed out, was against government policy. This is an example of posting a constraint that negates one aspect of a solution. This expert mentioned other aspects of modernization, such as a better transportation system (because some grain rotted in silos) and the development of plastics (because a large amount of grain degenerated in wet paper bags). He also advocated putting people who knew about agriculture in charge of agricultural stations designed to help the farmers, rather than party members who knew little about agriculture. So, this expert provided a solution that involved different facets of modernization, although all of the possibilities could not be implemented.

The above example of an expert solution illustrates the following: first, the expert used a variety of weak methods including analogy, hypothesis generation and testing, and decomposition. Second, the expert attempted to improve on the solution process by using a strategy called "constraint satisfaction." The strategy adds power to the solving process by delineating the constraints that are particularly important to satisfy to obtain an acceptable solution.

A historical example that shows the importance of constraints in decision and problem-solving processes involves two examples of the United States going to war. When the Japanese bombed Pearl Harbor on December 7, 1941, President Roosevelt had virtually no choice in his decision to request war be declared on Japan. His actions were quite constrained. Indeed, probably any president or politician would have done the same thing. However, President George W. Bush's decision to invade Iraq was a choice made under much less constraint, that is, there were alternative actions possible and many people would likely agree that not all presidents or politicians would have made his decision, even if he himself perhaps felt constrained.

CHE 10

Causal reasoning in history faces at least two issues: the general absence of control groups and the presence of temporally antecedent events. Attempts to deal with these matters include, respectively, counterfactual reasoning and the categorization of prior events.

In good scientific experimentation, the results frequently provide reliable and verifiable evidence for the hypothesis under study, although such investigation does not produce certainty. Taking the experimental versus control design as the fundamental form of experimentation, history generally, as life, has no control groups; historical events happen once and control conditions do not exist (although simulations may be made). This lack of control and the fact that history is cumulative, that is, past events and actions are influencing today's events and actions, constitute two difficulties for causal analysis in history.

Counterfactual reasoning allows the historian to invent a hypothetical control condition, that is, "If X did not happen, would Y have happened?" when X and Y did happen. The quality of a counterfactual argument depends on the same three factors as other arguments, namely, the acceptability of the evidence, the extent to which the evidence is judged to support the claim, and the consideration of opposing evidence. However, people may differ in their evaluations, especially in relation to their own beliefs and knowledge. Tetlock and Belkin (1996), discussing the difficulties with such evaluation, suggest that successful evaluation of counterfactuals is tenuous. Tetlock (1999) presented 52 Soviet Union experts with seven counterfactuals involving hypothetical Soviet events. He presented the entire counterfactual, the If-Then statement, or only the antecedent If part of the statement. He also obtained measures of the political positions of the participants on a liberal-conservative scale. Ideological belief was related to agreement or disagreement with the If-Then statements, but not to the If only antecedents. Subsequently, participants were told that new evidence found in the Kremlin made it more likely that one of the counterfactuals is more likely to have been true. Individuals with positions not in agreement with that counterfactual asserted a much more critical analysis, using three means to attack the new information, namely, challenging the authenticity of the documents, challenging the representativeness of the documents, and questioning the competence and motives of the unknown investigator who found the new information. These results are thus in agreement with other findings demonstrating belief bias. Tetlock (1999) found a similar effect when experts were asked to predict events, that is, when shown to be wrong, experts felt high confidence in their prediction and defended themselves by use of similar bias procedures. Tetlock further pointed out that the results suggest that one reason why it is so difficult to learn from history is that there is the tendency to defend one's own position even when confronted by information that brings that position into question, rather than examining one's position for alternatives.

The above findings are not meant to suggest that the use of counterfactuals is always open to substantial bias. Breslauer (1996), for example, effectively argues that debates focused on counterfactuals have occurred when there is a quite substantial body of data available concerning the issue in question, when the issue suggests a discontinuity that is difficult to explain, and when there is political partisanship. For example, the collapse of the Soviet Union would likely be an interesting issue to deal with counterfactually since theoretically it was unexpected and the large amount of historical data on pre-Soviet days would suggest the possible operation of a number of important factors.

Pursuing the matter of learning from history, two political scientists (Holsti & Rosenau, 1977) collected data from over 2,000 individuals who worked in ten different occupations. The study, addressing lessons learned from the Vietnam War, had participants answer items pertaining to support of or opposition to the war at the beginning and the end, the individual's political belief system, and reasons for the outcome of the war. A relationship was found between a person's belief system and the particular reasons for the war's outcome, with hawkish people holding such reasons as not enough force was used early and that Vietnam was help from Russia and China, and with dovish people indicating that the spirit of the North Vietnamese was underestimated and the United States had unrealistic goals. Occupation also was related to belief system and outcome selection. These results also indicate the operation of belief in learning from history.

The second difficulty of causal thinking is exemplified by a quotation found in various places of history literature, namely, "If Cleopatra's nose would have been one-half inch longer, the history of Western Civilization would have been changed." The difficulty is that for any event, there are typically many preceding related events, thus raising the question of whether one, a number, or all of the preceding events should be considered as a cause (causes). Further, distant events are typically not considered as casual antecedents by lay people, as the causal importance of preceding events has been found to be inversely related to their distance from the event (Voss et al. 1994). Some writers (Mackie, 1965; Ringer, 1989) have delineated two classes of preceding events, namely, enabling conditions and causes. The former are antecedent conditions enabling events to occur. They are neither necessary nor sufficient to produce that event but may look necessary a posteriori. Ringer (1989) used the analogy of a driver hitting a sheet of ice and sliding into a ditch. The fact that the person made the trip and took the particular road and that the car is being driven at the appropriate speed are enabling conditions, with the ice being the cause of the car sliding. Within this general view, historical flow appears to happen such that at any point in time a set of conditions exists and some action is taken or occurs, as in a natural disaster, and conditions change. Or a government official takes an action that not only may but quite likely will lead to consequences that were not intended or anticipated. The historian attempts to make sense out of this chaos.

Concluding Comments

In this section we examine expertise research in history and, in so doing, relate it to expertise research in other subject-matter domains. Before summarizing what factors are important to expertise in history, we first ask whether there likely are any representative tasks in history that enable the investigator to do some type of measurement of such expertise. Not considering factual historical knowledge as a legitimate indicator, one is left with using tasks such as providing a substantial amount of information and asking that a historical account or analysis be written concerning a particular aspect of the information or perhaps some specific aspect of the information. Scoring would then be in terms of the use of skills of the historian as described above. Or, a number of historical accounts or analyses of the same topic could be provided, asking which account is best (or poorest) and why. Such tasks may be of some value at the undergraduate or graduate levels, but they probably would not be diagnostic for experts because skill performance likely would be quite high. However, as reported above, differences among experts could be found depending on subject-matter knowledge.

Similarly, especially in political interviews, historians are sometimes asked to predict what is likely to happen in a given situation in view of their knowledge of the past. Although some present situations may seem to be similar to particular past situations, these analogous occurrences are as weak as other analogies. That is, situations may seem similar at one level, but the similarity breaks down at some point. Indeed, situations in history usually have large differences. Occasionally in the literature you read "The past is unpredictable" or words to that effect, and when past events are not predictable given knowledge and perspective of the preceding actions and events, predictions of what is going to happen in the future is even more problematic. Indeed, it is more accurate to say that historians are more interested in providing an understanding or even explanation of the past than in trying to predict it.

Turning now to the major factors of historian expertise, the first factor of the expert historian that is noted is the person's subject-matter knowledge, especially that in his or her field of specialization, and to a lesser extent in related subject-matter. However, despite the demonstrated importance of subject-matter knowledge across virtually all domains, our understanding of the development of such knowledge is inadequate, in history as well as other domains. Longitudinal studies of knowledge development are especially needed, although there quite likely are many routes to expertise in a given domain and it may not be possible to identify necessary and/or sufficient conditions to become an expert. Moreover, although experts in a given subject-matter domain no doubt spend much time in study, the question is what are they learning and how are they organizing their knowledge rather than how much time is spent *per se*. The data we have in history suggest that particular characteristics of expertise begin to emerge in graduate school, such as defense of one's position, use of counterfactuals, and the development of techniques of historical analysis. Finally, with respect to history knowledge, we know of no studies that compare the knowledge of the historian to that of the non-professionally trained "history buff." Such a comparison may provide a better understanding of the nature of the historian's expertise.

A second knowledge-related factor is that the historian acquires a number of research skills. In addition to being excellent and prolific readers, historians also have research skills that focus on how to seek and find sources and extract the most authentic and high-quality information from them. However, the research conducted to the present on how historians engage sources is but scratching the surface. There is much more to learn about source seeking and evaluation and especially subtext generation. How does subtext generation facilitate historical understanding and how consistent is subtext generation from one historian to another? Similarly, how narratives are constructed is another issue requiring more study.

Up to this point we have discussed how historians and experts in other subject-matter domains have a high level of domain-specific knowledge and skill. Initially, it seems that the skills, methods, and procedures differ considerably across domains, and expertise is likely relatively domain-specific. What we argue, however, is that across domains there are similarities in the highest level of problem-solving and reasoning processes. What is consistent across domains is the existence of some problem or issue, and the person working in the domain has the goal of solving that problem. Furthermore, whatever the domain, the person needs to provide a solution that includes evidence providing support for that solution; in other words, he or she must present a convincing argument. This general argumentative structure is what is in common. What differs among domains are the standards for what constitutes an acceptable solution and the related matter of what in that particular domain constitutes appropriate evidence and justification, that is, the content of the inquiry and the nature and extent of proof that is appropriate for that content. In physics the solution may be justified by demonstration of the appropriate steps to a solution. In this domain, this evidence for solution is in a sense the proof. In history the same goal exists. The goal of the historian is to convince an audience that a narrative or perhaps an essay is highly acceptable, and this is done by providing a solution or answering a question with contents that provide evidence, which is done by verbal argument. Most often there is not a deductive argument or mathematical equation but a position that is being advanced and defended. As previously stated, a narrative often serves as the support and justification for the particular position. Thus, in history, the solution is not usually correct or incorrect but acceptable at some level. However, the similarity in goal structure and argument structure at a high level occurs across subject-matter domains with the lower-level specification of the specific domain goals, the solution, and the evidence or justification of the solution being essentially domain specific.

A final case is our own field, psychology. The subject matter of this domain is a combination of both informal and formal elements. We post constraints to make our problems more tractable. We search for regularities or laws. But ultimately, we are trying to explain human behavior, and that behavior is necessarily probabilistic. So, in essence, our field may be much closer to history that we might think initially. We may gather evidence, but the crux of our argument is the interpretation of data, and we build a narrative around the data. We test and operationalize them via experiments. As a result, one expert may say that experimental evidence supports a conclusion, whereas another may say that the study does not adequately test the hypothesis or lacks a control condition.

This divergence in expert opinion occurs because the domain of psychology is one in which answers cannot be demonstrated formally. For all the expertise research that has been conducted, little attention has been directed to our own field. Expertise in psychology requires skill in both the collection of empirical evidence and in appropriate informal reasoning about that evidence. As such, psychology would seem to be an excellent candidate for future investigation of expertise in academic domains.

Author Note

The authors thank Melinda Jensen for her assistance with this manuscript. During the preparation of this manuscript, the second author was supported by grant number REC 0126265 from the ROLE Program of the National Science Foundation. Any opinions, findings, and conclusions or recommendations expressed in this material are those of the author(s) and do not necessarily reflect the views of the National Science Foundation.

References

Aristotle (1954). *The Rhetoric and the Poetics of Aristotle.* (W. R. Roberts & I. Bywater, Eds. & Trans.). New York: Modern Library.

Barton, K. (2001). A socio-cultural perspective on children's understanding of historical change: Comparative findings from Northern Ireland and the United States. *American Educational Research Journal, 38(4),* 881–913.

Breslauer, G. W. (1996). Counterfactual reasoning in western studies of Soviet Politics and Foreign Relations. In P. Tetlock & A. Belkin (Eds.), *Counterfactual Thought Experiments in World Politics* (pp. 71–94). Princeton, NJ: Princeton University Press.

Carretero, M., Jacott, L., & Lopez-Manjon, A. (2002). Learning history through textbooks: Are Mexican and Spanish students taught the same story? *Learning and Instruction, 12,* 651–665.

Chase, W. G., & Simon, H. A. (1973a). Perception in chess. *Cognitive Psychology, 4,* 55–81.

Chase, W. G., & Simon, H. A. (1973b). The mind's eye in chess. In W. G. Chase (Ed.), *Visual Information Processing* (pp. 216–281). London: Academic Press.

Chi, M. T. H., Feltovich, P. J., & Glaser, R (1981). Categorization and representation of physics problems by experts and novices. *Cognitive Science*, 5, 121–152.

Cronon, W. (1992). A place for stories: Nature, history, and narrative. *Journal of American History*, 78, 1347–1376.

de Groot, A. D. (1965). *Thought and Choice in Chess*. The Hague: Mouton.

Dray, W. (1957). *Laws and Explanation in History*. London: Oxford University Press.

Ericsson, K. A., & Lehmann, A. C. (1996). Expert and exceptional performance: evidence of maximal adaptation to task constraints. *Annual Review of Psychology*, 47, 273–305.

Epstein, T. (1998). Deconstructing differences in African American and European American adolescents' perspectives on United States history. *Curriculum Inquiry*, 28, 397–423.

Getzels, J. W. (1979). Problem finding: A theoretical note. *Cognitive Science*, 3, 167–172.

Hempel, C. (1942). The function of general laws in history. *The Journal of Philosophy*, 39, 35–48.

Herodotus (1987). *The History*. (D. Grene, Trans.). Chicago: University of Chicago Press.

Holsti, O., & Rosenau, J. N. (1977). The meaning of Vietnam: Belief systems of American leaders. *International Journal*, 32, 452–474.

Kintsch, W. (1988). The role of knowledge in discourse comprehension: A construction–integration model. *Psychological Review*, 95, 163–182.

Larkin, J. H., McDermott, J., Simon, D., & Simon, H. (1980). Expert and novice performance in solving physics problems. *Science*, 208, 140–156.

Leinhardt, G., Stainton, C., & Virji, S. M. (1994). A sense of history. *Educational Psychologist*, 29, 79–88.

Leinhardt, G., Stainton, C., Virji, S. M., & Odoroff, E. (1994). Learning to reason in history: Mindlessness to mindfulness. In M. Carretero & J. F. Voss (Eds.), *Cognitive and Instructional Processes in History and the Social Sciences* (pp. 131–158). Hillsdale, NJ: Erlbaum.

Leinhardt, G., & Young, K. (1996). Two texts, three readers: Distance and expertise in reading history. *Cognition and Instruction*, 14(4), 441–486.

Lemon, M. C. (2003). *Philosophy of History*. New York: Routledge.

Levine, L. W. (1989). The unpredictable past: Reflection on recent American historiography. *The American Historical Review*, 94(1), 671–679.

Lowenthal, D. (2000). Dilemmas and delights of learning history. In P. N. Stearns, P. Seixas, & S. Wineburg (Eds.), *Knowing, Teaching & Learning History* (pp. 63–82). New York and London: New York University Press.

Mackie, J. L. (1965). Causes and conditions. *American Philosophical Quarterly*, 2, 245–264.

McGuire, M. (1990). The rhetoric of narrative: A hermeneutic critical theory. In B. K. Britton & A. D. Pellegrini (Eds.), *Narrative Thought and Narrative Language*. Hillsdale, NJ: Erlbaum.

Mink, L. O. (1987). *Historical Understanding*. Ithaca, NY: Cornell University Press.

Newell, A. (1980). One final word. In D. T. Tuma & F. Reif (Eds.), *Problem Solving and Education: Issues in Teaching and Research* (pp. 175–189). Hillsdale, NJ: Erlbaum.

Perelman, C., & Olbrechts-Tyteca, L. (1969). The New Rhetoric: A Treatise on Argumentation. (John Wilkinson & Purcell Weaver, Trans.) Notre Dame: University of Notre Dame Press.

Ringer, F. K. (1989). Causal analysis in historical reasoning. *History and Theory*, 28, 154–172.

Rouet, J-F, Favart, M., Britt, A., & Perfetti, C. A. (1997). Studying and using multiple documents in history: Effects of discipline expertise. *Cognition and Instruction*, 15, 85–106.

Schooler, T. Y. E., Kennet, J., Wiley, J., & Voss, J. F. (1996). On the processing of political editorials. In R. J. Kreuz & M. S. MacNealy (Eds.), *Empirical Approaches to Literature and Aesthetics* (pp. 445–459). Norwood, NJ: Ablex.

Schum, D. A. (1993). Argument structuring and evidence evaluation. In R. Hastie (Ed.), *Inside the Juror* (pp. 175–191). Cambridge: Cambridge University Press.

Stearns, P. N. (1998). Goals in history teaching. In J. F. Voss & M. Carretero (Eds.), *Learning and Reasoning in History* (pp. 281–293). London: Woburn Press.

Tetlock, P. E., & Belkin, A. (Eds.). (1996). *Counterfactual Thought Experiments in World Politics*. Princeton: Princeton University Press.

Tetlock, P. E. (1999). Theory-driven reasoning about possible pasts and probable futures: Are we prisoners of our preconceptions? *American Journal of Political Science, 43*, 335–366.

Thucydides (1954). *History of the Peloponnesian War*. New York: Penguin.

Toulmin, S. E. (1958). *The Uses of Argument*. Cambridge: Cambridge University Press.

Tulviste, P., & Wertsch, J. V. (1994). Official and unofficial histories: The case of Estonia. *Journal of Narrative and Life History, 4*, 311–329.

Tweney, R. D. (1991). Informal reasoning in science. In J. F. Voss, D. N. Perkins, & J. A. Segel (Eds.), *Informal Reasoning and Education* (pp. 3–16). Hillsdale, NJ: Erlbaum.

Voss, J. F., Carretero, M., Kennet, J., & Silfies, L. N. (1994). The collapse of the Soviet Union: A case study in causal reasoning. In M. Carretero & J. F. Voss (Eds.), *Cognitive and Instructional Processes in History and the Social Sciences* (pp. 403–429). Hillsdale, NJ: Erlbaum.

Voss, J. F., Greene, T. R., Post, T. A., & Penner, B.C. (1983). Problem-solving skill in the social sciences. In G. H. Bower (Ed.), *The Psychology of Learning and Motivation, 17* (pp. 165–213). New York: Academic Press.

Voss, J. F. & Post, T. A. (1988) On the solving of ill-structured problems. In M. T. H. Chi, R. Glaser, & M. I. Farr (Eds.), *The Nature of Expertise* (pp. 261–285). Hillsdale, NJ: Erlbaum.

Voss, J. F., Wiley, J., & Carretero, M. (1995). Acquiring intellectual skills. *Annual Review of Psychology, 46*, 155–181.

Voss, J. F., Wiley, J., & Sandak, R. (1999). On the use of narrative as argument. In S. R. Goldman, A. C. Graesser, & P. van den Broek (Eds.), *Narrative Comprehension, Causality, and Coherence: Essays in Honor of Tom Trabasso* (pp. 235–252). Mahwah, NJ: Erlbaum.

Wertsch, J. V., & Rozin, M. (1998). The Russian Revolution: Official and unofficial accounts. In J. F. Voss & M. Carretero (Eds.), *Learning and Reasoning in History* (pp. 39–60). London: Woburn Press.

White, H. (1987). *The Content of the Form: Narrative Discourse and Historical Representation*. Baltimore and London: Johns Hopkins University Press.

Wineburg, S. (1991). Historical problem solving: A study of the cognitive processes used in the evaluation of documentary and pictorial evidence. *Journal of Educational Psychology, 83*, 73–87.

Wineburg, S. (1994). The cognitive representation of historical texts. In G. Leinhardt, I. Beck, & C. Stainton (Eds.), *Teaching and Learning in History* (pp. 85–135). Hillsdale, NJ: Erlbaum.

Wineburg, S. (1998). Reading Abraham Lincoln: An expert/expert study in the interpretation of historical texts. *Cognitive Science, 22*, 319–346.

Part VI

GENERALIZABLE MECHANISMS MEDIATING EXPERTISE AND GENERAL ISSUES

CHAPTER 34

A Merging Theory of Expertise and Intelligence

John Horn & Hiromi Masunaga

Creations, new insights, and paradigm shifts emerge at junctures where different theories – different world views – meet, come in conflict, and are forced to accommodate. So it can be with a theory of expertise and a theory of human intelligence. Over the course of 20th-century research, the developments of these two "world views" have run along separately, rather like Leibnitz's clocks, each addressing much the same question – what are the major capabilities of the human and how do they come about – but neither speaking to the other. They have arrived at different conclusions, neither thoroughly correct, of course, but neither entirely wrong either. Now, we reason, if we put the two theories in newly-met dialog, we can drive off the odious irrelevancies of each in a distillation that captures the truthful essence of both – a new liquor: a theory that is more accurate than any that has gone before. That, immodestly, is what we present in what follows.

We deal with the question of how expertise fits within that part of human personality we describe with a theory of human intelligence. Thus, the larger perspective is

that of personality – a theory that describes what people do and explains why they do it. The principal descriptive concept of this theory is behavioral trait, a characteristic that persistently distinguishes one individual from another despite variation in the circumstances in which individuals are found.

The concept of behavioral trait is adopted by analogy from the concept of biological trait, with which it is easily confused. A behavioral trait is a way of behaving that emerges through learning over a course of development. It may be shaped partly by genetic predispositions, but it is shaped also through societal and cultural influences that involve learning. It becomes characteristic of an individual as development proceeds.

When a particular sample of people is drawn for study, people are at different levels of development and decline of a behavioral trait. One person is found to reason well relative to other persons, for example – at level R8, say, on a ten-point scale – and this characterizes that person (relative to other persons) over a stretch of time. As development proceeds the person may rise to a nearby level – say, R9 – that is then characteristic over a stretch of time, or the person may decline to a nearby level (R7) that becomes characteristic. The length of the "stretch of time" over which the trait is characteristic is estimated empirically through analyses of re-measure reliability.

There may be function fluctuation – that is, reliable (non-error) change over the stretch of time in a behavioral trait. A person characteristically R8, for example, may function at R9 in the morning and R7 in the evening. Also, there may be precipitous decline in a behavioral trait due to any of many possible circumstances, such as neuronal damage in any of several different parts of the brain. To establish such changes empirically requires study of period fluctuations in the trait, and the causes of these fluctuations.

Behavioral traits thus are at once somewhat stable and somewhat dynamic. They are characteristics that persistently distinguish one individual from another despite variation in the circumstances in which individuals are found, but they are ever changing as well.

Also important, behavioral traits are not absolutes; they are probabilistic patterns of behaviors. The patterns indicate constructs – that is, abstractions. The precise set of behaviors that indicate a behavioral trait in one individual can be different from the set of behaviors that indicate the same trait in other individuals. The behaviors of such different sets are all parts of the same pattern, however. That is why they indeed do indicate the same behavioral trait. To put it more concretely, not all people reasoning at a particular level get the same set of items correct in a reasoning test that measures that trait, but the different configurations of right answers that yield the same score nevertheless indicate the same amount of the trait.[1]

In what follows we will consider a trait theory of intelligence and seek to integrate it with a trait theory of expertise. The theory of intelligence that we will consider has become known as the extended theory of fluid (Gf) and crystallized (Gc) intelligence. We will refer to this as extended Gf-Gc theory. It is described in many publications in

psychology. Good examples are Flanagan and Harrison (2005), McArdle and Woodcock (1998), McGrew and Flanagan (1998), McGrew and Woodcock (2001), and Woodcock (1990). Tests – operational definitions of concepts – are described in these sources.

We have no particular name for the theory of expertise that we accommodate to the theory of intelligence. But the main ideas of this theory are well described in Ericsson (1996), Ericsson and Charness (1994), Ericsson and Kintsch (1995), Ericsson and Lehmann (1996) and Ericsson, Chapter 38.

Let us turn first to the theory of intelligence.

Extended Gf-Gc Theory of Intellectual Capabilities

The theory is a generalization of findings obtained in five kinds of research: (1) structural research: studies of the relationships and organization of abilities regarded as indicative of intelligence; (2) developmental research: studies of age differences and changes in cognitive capabilities; (3) physiological-function research: studies of the physiological – mainly neurological – correlates of cognitive abilities; (4) education-occupation research: studies of relationships between cognitive abilities and school and occupational performances; and (5) behavior-genetic research: twin and other family-comparison studies of the relationships between cognitive abilities and classifications representing consanguinity. More of the evidence on which the theory is based derives from structural and developmental research, than from the other three kinds of research.

Expertise theory, also, derives more from structural and developmental evidence than from the physiological evidence (but see Hill & Schneider, Chapter 37), education-occupational research, and behavior-genetic research. In this chapter major attention will be given to the structural and developmental evidence, although a few references will be made to some of the other kinds of evidence (see also Ackerman & Beier, Chapter 9).

The Structural Perspective

There have been thousands of studies, conducted over more than 100 years, of the covariations among tests, tasks, paradigms, and experiments designed to identify fundamental features of human intelligence. These studies indicate an astonishing number and variety of cognitive abilities. They range from abilities that seem to be elementary and narrow, to abilities that are broad and complex – abilities that clearly require development through extensive learning over long periods of time.

These apparent distinctions are somewhat misleading, however, because the observed behavior of what we call an ability depends on many abilities. There are no clearly discernable demarcations in the behavior that distinguish one ability from another.

For example, in a measure of backward-span memory, a person is asked to repeat, in the reverse of the order in which they were spoken, the names of seven numbers spoken at a measured pace. This may seem to be an elementary, narrow memory ability, but when we examine what a person must do to perform the task, it becomes apparent that several abilities are involved. One must comprehend the instructions, distinguish between the stimuli, and maintain awareness of those distinctions while at the same time reciting numbers in the asked-for order. Knowledge of number systems is involved. One person might group the numbers as odd or even; another might group them in sets of two or three; and others might organize them in other ways. In structural analyses it turns out that this "simple memory" task is substantially correlated with measures of "complex reasoning." The simple and the complex have much in common.

Inability to distinguish precisely the abilities producing the scores (measures) obtained with a particular ability test is a problem with all the abilities we measure. The outcome behaviors are a complex expression of many abilities.

We infer ability from correlates. Factor analysis is the method, par excellence, for summarizing correlates from which to infer an ability. From the evidence of such a summary we infer that a particular ability is dominant among all the abilities involved and give a name to that ability. In this manner we describe the organization among abilities in what we refer to as the structure of intellect. It's all a bit circular. That's the nature of structural evidence.

PRINCIPAL CLASSES OF ABILITIES

As just suggested, evidence of structure among cognitive abilities has come mainly from factor-analytic studies. More than a thousand of these studies have been conducted over the 100 years since Spearman (1904) created the first such study. The studies have been directed at determining the number of fundamental capabilities, as well as the nature of the capabilities, that describe measured individual differences in cognitive abilities thought to indicate intelligence. Summaries of the results of these factor-analytic studies indicate no fewer than 75 of what are called primary-ability factors.

These primary abilities are, for the most part, positively correlated, and factor analyses of selections among them indicate broad, second-order abilities. But these abilities, also, are usually positively correlated, and factor analyses of measures of these abilities indicate even broader third-order abilities, and these abilities, too, are positively correlated.

Carroll (1993) has done a tour-de-force summary of over 400 studies (477 data sets), showing that the reliable covariation among literally hundreds of ability tests[2] designed to measure important features of human intelligence can be described in terms of a system of more than 40 primary abilities and eight second-order factors of organization of the primary abilities.

The eight second-order factors – separate classes of abilities – are the principal descriptive concepts of extended Gf-Gc theory. They provide a sound basis for integrating a large proportion of the findings of developmental, physiological, education/ occupation, and behavior-genetic research. Defining features of these abilities can be summarized as follows:

- *Acculturation knowledge (Gc)*. These abilities indicate the extent to which an individual has incorporated the knowledge and language of the dominant culture. The abilities are explicitly taught in the curricula of schools, but more generally they are the abilities inculcated through acculturation. They are the abilities that are most prominently measured in what are accepted as IQ tests – such broadband tests as the Stanford-Binet and Wechsler. They are the abilities measured in school-readiness tests at all levels of schooling. For example, the scholastic aptitude tests required for admission to universities and colleges are primarily measures of Gc abilities.
- *Fluid reasoning (Gf)*. Identified as a common factor in company with the Gc common factor, the Gf abilities are primarily reasoning abilities and abilities that support reasoning. They are not as profoundly determined by factors of acculturation and social class as are the Gc abilities. They are measured in tasks requiring reasoning (inductive, conjunctive, and disjunctive), identifying relationships, comprehending implications, and drawing inferences in problems the form of which are novel, not dealt with in schools or other training programs or in the media. Also, the reasoning involved in the factor is required in an immediate situation, a rather short period of time – that is, not reasoning that extends over a long period of time, such as that involved in writing an article or constructing a machine or piece of art.
- *Short-term apprehension and retrieval (SAR)*. This is also referred to as short term memory and working memory. The abilities of this class are measured in a variety of tasks that indicate how many things one can, without rehearsal, hold in

the span of immediate awareness – i.e., for a minute or so.
- *Fluency of retrieval from long-term storage (TSR)*. This is also labeled long-term memory (Glm). These abilities indicate consolidation in learning – that is, abilities of reconstruction in associational retrieval of things associated hours, weeks, and years earlier. It can be measured with the same kinds of tasks used to measure SAR, except retrieval is called for after a substantially longer period of time. It can be measured also in various kinds of association tests – for example, associate (recall) words similar in meaning to a given word.
- *Visual processing (Gv)*. The tasks measuring these abilities involve visual closure and recognizing the way objects appear in space as they are rotated and flip-flopped in any of many different ways.
- *Auditory processing (Ga)*. These are abilities of comprehending patterns among sounds, recognizing such patterns under conditions of distraction or distortion, and maintaining awareness of order and rhythm among sounds.
- *Processing speed (Gs)*. Although involved in almost all intellectual tasks, the factor is measured most purely in rapid scanning and comparisons in tasks in which almost all people would get the right answer if the task were not highly speeded.
- *Quantitative knowledge (Gq)*. These are the quantitative thinking and problem-solving abilities of mathematics – the abilities measured in college-readiness tests such as the SAT and ACT. Although they are products of acculturation and indicate crystallized knowledge, their predictors and predictions are different from the predictors and predictions of Gc. There are good reasons to regard them as a second major class of crystallized abilities, distinct from Gc.

More detailed and scholarly descriptions of these abilities are provided in Carroll (1993), Flanagan and Harrison (2005), McArdle and Woodcock (1998), McGrew and Flanagan (1998), and Woodcock (1990).

The common factors indicating these classes of abilities have been identified in samples that differ in respect to gender, level of education, ethnicity, nationality, language, and historical period in this century. The abilities fully represent what is reliably measured in IQ tests and neuropsychological batteries. They are positively correlated but independent. Independence is indicated by structural evidence showing that a best-weighted linear combination of any set of seven factors (representing seven of the classes of abilities) does not account for the reliable covariance among the tests that define the eighth factor (representing a remaining class of abilities). More fundamentally, independence is indicated by evidence of distinct construct validities – the second-order factors have different relationships with other variables of developmental, physiological-neurological, educational-occupational, and behavior-genetic research.

No General Intelligence. A factor of general intelligence is notably lacking in this primary and second-order organization of abilities generally regarded as indicating human intelligence. The *g* – general common factor – is missing despite the fact that the idea is well entrenched in language, and many well-respected scientists (e.g., Carroll, 1993; Jensen, 1998; Estes, 1974) argue that one of the major achievements of psychological science is the discovery and measurement of general intelligence.[3] Quite simply, however, the evidence does not support this conclusion.

We will not review that evidence here. Such a review would require several pages of text that, in the present book, are better used for other matters. Horn (in press) has reviewed that evidence in a publication that will appear at about the same time as this book. Suffice it to note here that the principal hypothesis of Spearman's theory of g – the hypothesis that one and the same general factor is involved in all abilities indicating human intelligence – does not pass the critical test for one common factor that Spearman so importantly devised.

Process hypotheses of Spearman's theory are consistent with evidence

indicating the Gf second-order factor described above: indeed, Gf is much the same as the factor Spearman described as g. A study by Rimoldi (1951) first suggested this.

Rimoldi (1951) was especially careful to select variables to represent the essential capacities of intelligence – processes of Spearman's (1927) theory of g. He found that a model specifying one common factor would not fit the data. But a subset of tests – figure classifications, letter series, verbal analogies, and inferences – could be found to fit such a model. Such tests are among those that in subsequent studies were found to be indicative of Gf.[4]

In a similar way Horn (1989), following Rimoldi's lead, selected – from among the tests that had defined Gf – particular tests that also appeared to represent capabilities Spearman specified as essential for expression of g, and analyzed to see if a one-and-only-one common factor model would fit the intercorrelations. The results did show fit to a reasonable approximation, and thus indicated that batteries of tests that met the Spearman requirements could be assembled.

Specifically, for example, the intercorrelations among tests selected from the Horn, Donaldson and Engstrom (1981) studies to measure span of apprehension (measured with the Sperling [1960] paradigm), encoding and retention (maintaining awareness), comprehension of conjunctions (eduction of relations), drawing inferences (eduction of correlates), concentration and carefulness approximated a fit of the one-and-only-one common factor (RMSEA[5] = .067].

We have found similar approximations to Spearman's model with somewhat different post hoc selections of tests defining Gf in the various samples of previous research. In each case, when tests defining the Gc or Gv or TSR factors are added to the set of tests for which the Spearman model fits, the fit for the one-and-only-one common factor hypothesis becomes unacceptable.

There is thus good reason to suppose that the Gf concept captures much of the meaning of the g concept of Spearman's theory. But the evidence also indicates that

Gf does not represent a concept of general intelligence. It represents only one form of intelligence, not all the essential capabilities of intelligence.

THE DEVELOPMENTAL PERSPECTIVE

The case made up to this point for distinctions among different forms of intelligence is based on structural research. This case is made more compellingly by evidence derived from the other forms of research, particularly developmental and physiological research. Let us turn to a brief consideration of some of this work.

From about the third year of life onward, Gf and Gc can be identified as distinctly different abilities: the correlation between the two is approximately .65 whereas the internal consistencies of the factors are approximately .90 (see Horn, 1985, 1989, 1991 for reviews). The correlation between the two becomes smaller at successively later stages of development. In adulthood the correlation is found to be in a range of about .40 to .50 (with factor internal consistencies in a range of .80 to .90).

Gc correlates in a range of .40 to .60 with the educational or economic level of one's parents and with one's own educational or economic level at later ages. It correlates also with other indicators of social class. Gf, in contrast, correlates in a range of .20 to .45 with these same indicators of social class (Cattell, 1971; Horn, 1985, 2002).

The development of Gc abilities is associated with individual differences in the quality and amount of formal education, and with child-rearing that promotes the valuing of formal education and the attainment of the knowledge of the dominant culture. These educational and child-rearing conditions are in turn positively associated with the conditions of secure home, neighborhood, and school environments. The security of a child's attachment to a primary caregiver, particularly during the earliest periods of development, sets the stage for development of Gc (Burgess, Marshall, Rubin, & Fox, 2003; Shaver & Mikulincer, 2002). Such attachment enables curiosity about what is novel and a drive to investigate the

unfamiliar (Fagan & McGrath, 1981). Secure attachment thus is conducive to the development of Gc abilities.

Secure attachment also supports the development of the abilities of Gc in other ways. This was demonstrated in pioneering studies of Bowlby (1951) and Spitz (1946). They showed that secure attachment in the earliest periods of development generalizes to security in social interactions such as those required of a student in learning situations. This security leads to involvement in learning, which in turn promotes development of cognitive abilities such as those of Gc (Sroufe, 1977; Shaver & Mikulincer, 2002). Children who are securely attached, relative to those who are not, are found to be more enthusiastic, persistent, and involved in classroom learning; and they learn more and are able to firmly consolidate their learning.

In the studies of Harlow and his coworkers (e.g., Harlow & Suomi, 1970), rhesus monkeys that were more securely attached to a primary caregiver were better able to overcome neophobia, respond to curiosity, venture into the open field (a strange, somewhat frightening domain for a rhesus monkey), and deal with novelty.

Secure attachment facilitates neophilia. Even children who are highly predisposed to neophobia, but are raised under conditions that promote security, are able to respond to curiosity, explore novelty, and thus develop relatively high levels of Gc. Thus, fear of the novel need not inhibit the development of Gc.

On the other hand, the development of Gf abilities is more dependent on the basic adaptability of neophobia and has little association with factors that promote security in upbringing. Thus, in the development of Gf abilities, the factors that promote security have less influence than in the development of the Gc abilities, and in virtue of this, an adaptive neophobia will correlate with Gf.

It is likely that many factors determine the kind of security that enables one to deal with novelty and consequently develop cognitive abilities. Early-in-life secure attachment is only one such factor. We can not expect that it will account for a great amount of the covariances. Nevertheless, the evidence suggests that such attachment has substantial positive relationship with social class, education, acculturation, and the development of Gc abilities.

Much of the evidence on the distinction between the Gf and the Gc classes of abilities has come from studies of people of different ages in adulthood (cross-sectional research) and changes in the averages in repeated measurements of adults (longitudinal research). These two different kinds of research converge in indicating aging decline of Gf abilities, coupled with no decline or even improvement of Gc abilities (see also Krampe & Charness, Chapter 40).

Declining Capacities during Adult Development

The evidence of decline comes from both cross-sectional and longitudinal studies (Horn, 1991; Horn & Donaldson, 1980; McArdle, Ferrer-Caja, Hamagami, & Woodcock, 2002; McArdle, Prescott, Hamagami, & Horn, 1998; Salthouse, 2001; Schaie, 2000). These two kinds of studies control for and reveal different kinds of influences, and have different strengths and weaknesses (Horn & Donaldson, 1980). Yet in major respects the findings from the two kinds of studies are largely in agreement. The longitudinal findings suggest that the points in adulthood at which declines occur are later than is indicated by the cross-sectional findings, but the evidence of which abilities decline, and which decline more and less than others, is essentially the same.

The principal declines are in Gf, Gs, and SAR, which together are referred to as age-vulnerable abilities. The abilities that are particularly vulnerable to conditions associated with aging are also particularly vulnerable to conditions associated with brain damage (Horn, 1982, 1985 for early reviews). Some features of the neurological system decline (on average) with advancing age (Medina, 1996; Raz, 2000; Tisserand & Jolles, 2003; Hill & Schneider, Chapter 37).

SAR: Short-term Apprehension and Retrieval. The findings of many studies indicate decline with adulthood in a wide variety of tests measuring aspects of short-term memory (Backman, Small, Wahlin, & Larsson, 2000; Craik, 1977; 2000; Craik & Byrd, 1982; Craik & Trehub, 1982; Finkel, Reynold, McArdle, Gatz, & Pedersen, 2003; Lane & Zelinski, 2003; Schaie, 1996, 2000). The decline is smaller in tasks that require very short periods of retention; there are virtually no age differences for the Sperling (1960) kind of task, in which retrieval occurs over periods of only a few milliseconds. But for measures in which information is presented over periods of a few seconds and retrieval is required after short periods of up to a minute or two, age-related declines generally have been found. This is true of memory for information the subject could regard as meaningful, as well as for nonsense material, although age differences appear to be smaller for memory for the meaningful kind of information (Cavanaugh, 1997; Charness, 1991; Craik, 2000; Craik & Trehub, 1982; Ericsson & Delaney, 1998; Gathercole, 1994; Kaufman, 1990; Radvansky & Copeland, 2000; Radvansky, Copeland, & Zwaan, 2003; Salthouse, 1991a; Salthouse & Ferrer-Caja, 2003; Schaie, 1996). The more complex the memory task, and the more it requires that material be held in awareness while doing other things – as in definitions of working memory – the larger the negative relationship to age.

Tests of working memory also have substantial correlations with Gf. For example, the negative age relationship for backward-span memory, in which the subject must recall the to-be-remembered elements in the reverse of the order in which they were presented, is significantly larger (absolute value) than the negative age relationship for forward-span memory (Craik, 1977; Craik & Trehub, 1982; Masunaga & Horn, 2000, 2001; Horn et al., 1981; Salthouse, 1991b; Schaie, 1996), and the correlation of this test with Gf can be as large as its correlation with SAR (Masunaga & Horn, 2001).

Gs: Processing Speed. Most cognitive tests are speeded. The results of many studies suggest aging decline in speed of performance and in speed of thinking (Birren, 1974; Kausler, 1990; Christensen, 2001; Salthouse, 1992, 1993, 1994; Salthouse & Ferrer-Caja, 2003). Older adults are slower than their younger counterparts in both simple and choice reaction time (RT), although the magnitude of the differences, assessed in standard score units, are larger for choice RT. In studies in which young and old subjects are provided opportunity to practice a choice RT task, practice does not eliminate the age differences, and no noteworthy age-by-practice interactions are indicated (Madden & Nebes, 1980; Salthouse & Somberg, 1982).

Gf: Fluid Reasoning. The research findings are consistent in demonstrating steady decline of Gf over most of the period of adulthood. The decline is seen with measures of syllogisms and concept formation (Fisk & Sharp, 2002; McGrew, Werder, & Woodcock, 1991), in reasoning with metaphors and analogies (Salthouse, 1987; Salthouse, Kausler, & Saults, 1990), with measures of comprehending series, as in letter series, figural series, and number series (Horn, 1975, 1991; Noll & Horn, 1997; Salthouse, Kausler, & Saults, 1990), and with measures of mental rotation, figural relations, matrices, and topology (Cattell, 1979; Horn, 1977; McArdle, Hamagami, Meredith, & Broadway, 2000). In each case the evidence for Gf decline is cleanest if the elements of the reasoning test are novel or equally familiar to all – that is, if the test gives no advantage to those with greater knowledge of the culture.

Although many of the tests that have indicated the aging decline of Gf have a speeded component, the decline is also indicated very well by lowly-speeded tests that require resolution of high-level (difficult) complexities (Horn, 1991; Horn et al., 1981; Noll & Horn, 1997).

In these lowly-speeded tests the score indicating level of reasoning ability is the average level of difficulty of the problems correctly solved, not a count of the number of problems solved in some unit of time. The items are open-ended letter series, so

the participant must provide an answer, not merely select one from a multiple-choice set. Moreover, in the instructions the participant is taught that some problems do not have a solution, and if what appears to be a problem of that kind is encountered, the correct behavior is to mark "NC," representing "No correct solution," and go on to the next problem. Thus, when one does not work out a solution to a problem, there is little incentive to guess or to estimate a best bet for a solution. There is no reward for working quickly and no reward for guessing. And the score indicates merely average level of difficulty of the problems solved (independently of the number of problems attempted).

Under these conditions of measurement, decline with age from age 25 to age 65 years is approximately 1.1 standard deviation – that is, expressed in IQ units in which a standard deviation is 15, the decline is about 16.5 IQ points over 40 years of aging (about 4.1 IQ units for each ten years of aging).

Even though this lowly-speeded measure of Gf does not measure speed in providing answers, the Gs factor of cognitive speed accounts for about one-half of the decline. On first consideration, this evidence seems to indicate that some form of speed of thinking is involved in fluid reasoning. But we have found reasons to question this first consideration: the amount of decline in Gf that is associated with the Gs speed measure is completely accounted for by a measure of slow tracing that involves no speed in performance and in fact involves only the opposite of this, behaving as slowly as one possibly can. In the slow-tracing test the requirement is to trace a line as slowly as possible, and the shorter the line one traces in a unit of time, the larger the score.

These, short tracings (large scores) are positively correlated with fast matching and identifying in the Gs measure and with high level-of-difficulty scores on the letter-series measure of Gf. Moreover, each of these measures is negatively related to age over a range of from 25 to 65 years.

When the Gs measure is parted out of the Gf measure, the 16.5 IQ units of decline of Gf is reduced to about eight IQ units for the residual Gf (what is left after Gs is removed). But if the slow-tracing measure is parted out of Gf, the reduction in decline is approximately the same – from 16.5 to about eight IQ units when slow-tracing is removed – and the decline in Gf that is associated with Gs is reduced to near zero: the slow-tracing measure, which is not at all speeded, completely accounts for all the reduction in aging decline of Gf that is accounted for by the Gs measure.

The slow-tracing measure requires focused concentration – and so does the Gs measure. That is, although called a measure of speed, Gs requires focused concentration (in order to make many of the speeded responses). Thus, what seems to be involved in aging decline of Gf reasoning is a capacity for focusing attention and maintaining focused attention. This is measured in slow tracing, but also required in identifying relationships and working out their implications in solving difficult, highly novel reasoning problems of the kind that define Gf. This is probably the most important finding of the Horn et al. (1981) series of studies.

Capabilities that Do not Decline during Adult Development

In many of the studies in which age-related declines were documented, no evidence of decline was found (in the same samples of subjects) for reliable measures of Gc and TSR abilities – abilities indicating breadth of knowledge, consolidation in learning, and fluency of retrieval of information from the store of knowledge.

Gc: Acculturation Knowledge. As noted previously, the abilities of this class are often referred to as indicating what is most important about human intelligence. They are indicative of the extent to which an individual has incorporated the most valued features of the intelligence of a culture.

On average, over a period from early adulthood into the 60's, there is increase with age in these abilities (e.g., Botwinick, 1977, 1978; Cattell, 1971; Finkel et al., 2003; Harwood & Naylor, 1971; Horn, 1968, 1972, 1982, 1989, 1991; 1997; Horn & Cattell, 1967;

Horn & Hofer, 1992; Kaufman, 1990; McArdle et al., 2000; Rabbitt & Abson, 1991; Schaie, 1996, 2000; Stankov & Horn, 1980; Woodcock, 1990).

The results are more equivocal in suggesting whether or not Gc abilities continue to increase beyond 60 to 70 of age. Some findings suggest "yes," into the 80's (e.g., Harwood & Naylor, 1971), some suggest "no" (Schaie, 1996, 2000). Declines, indicated in averages, show up in the late 60's and are at first small but accelerating, so that in the 90's there is notable decline (Schaie, 1996, 2000).

If differences in years of formal education are statistically controlled, the increment of Gc through to the 70's is increased (Horn, 1968, 1972, 1989; Kaufman, 1990). The evidence does not make clear whether or not the declines beyond this age are reduced by control for education.

The standard deviations around the Gc averages increase as age increases. This means that though generally there is improvement with age in these abilities, the improvements for some individuals are much larger than for others, and for some people these abilities decline with age. The particular reasons why this occurs have not been well documented.

Generally the findings suggest two possibilities, both of which could be correct: (1) that whereas some people enter professions and adopt styles of life that require or otherwise encourage development of crystallized abilities, other people do not, and (2) that the tests used to assess abilities that are regarded as indicating Gc do not measure well in the areas of knowledge in which some people are invested. Both of these possibilities are relevant to the study of the development of expertise.

TSR: Tertiary Storage/Retrieval. Two different kinds of variables indicate this class of abilities. In one kind of variable subjects are required to retrieve information that was associated with other information several minutes or hours or days prior to the time when retrieval is requested. "Memory for Names" in the WJ-R (Woodcock, McGrew, & Mather, 2001) is a good example of this kind of measure. In the second kind of variable subjects are required to retrieve (or reconstruct), by association, information from stored knowledge. An example of such a measure is obtained with the "ideas" test. In this test subjects provide ideas similar to a given idea.

Tests for both kinds of measurement may be given under time limits, but time limits must be generous, such that subjects have ample time to provide nearly all the associations of which they are capable. Otherwise, the test will measure Gs and indicate aging decline, rather than aging increase.

The retrieval in both of the two kinds of measures of TSR relates to encoding and consolidation in learning, and to parameters that characterize individual differences in initial encoding and consolidation. These parameters also characterize the retrieval at later times (Bower, 1972, 1975; Estes, 1974).

One such parameter is facility in forming associations. This is prominent in the first kind of measure, where the assessment is over fairly short periods of time –although longer periods than in the measures of SAR. It indicates initial consolidation.

The second kind of measure indicates primarily long-retained consolidation of associations – consolidation that could have entered cognition at different times over one's history of learning and got stored in a system of categories (as described by Broadbent, 1966).

Both kinds of variables indicate facility in retrieving the consolidated and stored information, not the size and variety of the storage as such. This latter is indicated by Gc.

TSR thus indicates facility in retrieving the knowledge that primarily defines Gc. This facility is correlated with Gc, but the two factors are independent (as previously described) in the sense that the correlation between the two factors is well below their respective internal consistencies, and in the sense that they have different patterns of correlations with other variables. This means that people with a very large store of knowledge may not as readily access their stores as people with smaller stores.

Yet for the TSR class of abilities, as for Gc, the evidence indicates either improvement through age 60 years in adulthood, or if there is decline, it occurs late and is small, at least until the 80's (Horn, 1968; Horn & Cattell, 1967; Horn & Noll, 1997; McArdle et al., 2000; Schaie, 1996; Stankov & Horn, 1980; Woodcock, 1990).

Problems and Limitations of Extended Gf-Gc Theory

Extended Gf-Gc theory is based to a very considerable extent on results from studies of age differences and age changes in cognitive abilities. Indeed, it is largely an attempt to describe and explain cognitive ability development through the adulthood years. Regarded in that way, it appears to be notably inadequate in several ways.

For example, the ability declines described in the theory do not appear to characterize the adulthood development of which we are most aware in ourselves, in those with whom we most frequently interact, and in those we see and hear and read about in our various media of communication. Indeed, the declines described in the theory present a paradox: they suggest there are serious cognitive deficits in people otherwise regarded as exemplars of high intellect in our society – the professors, scholars, researchers of our major universities and research institutes, the CEO's of major businesses and others making the major decisions and inventions in these institutions, the writers and commentators and pundits of our media of communication, the politicians, our representatives in congress, our presidents and their cabinets, and so forth. These people in the most responsible positions in almost all our major institutions are usually adults well along on the age-decline curves described in extended Gf-Gc theory.[6]

How can it be that these people have notably declined in reasoning and memory abilities that are regarded as indicating essential features of human intelligence? If true, how can it be that we don't see this in their everyday behavior (or if we do, how can it be that we continue to entrust them with the most responsible and difficult jobs requiring intelligence in our society)? There indeed seems to be a paradox here. What is wrong? Our everyday observations? Are these older people really demented? Or are the findings and the theory deceiving us? Is there something wrong with the tests? Is there something wrong with the sampling of people in the research studies? Are the people we know and the people we hear about exceptions to what is going on with the rest of the populace?

We don't have really good answers to these questions. There is probably some truth in each answer that comes readily to mind. The older people in high-level positions probably have not lost the most important capabilities of human intelligence; there is probably something wrong with the tests; the samples of the various studies generally did not include the CEO's, professors, and so forth, alluded to above, and thus the samples are probably not truly representative of the smarter segments of our society. But also our friends and the folks at the highest levels in our institutions *do* sometimes appear to be fairly obtuse, the tests of the research *do* appear to measure some important aspects of intelligence, and samples of subjects used in the research *do* represent a segment of our society. Also, there is the well-replicated evidence indicating that normal aging is associated with loss of neuronal basis for cognitive abilities (see Hill & Schneider, Chapter 37). There probably is some decline in important cognitive capabilities; however, much of it may not be seen in everyday observations.

But there is reason to believe that in the research on which extended Gf-Gc theory is based, we have not measured some of the capabilities that best characterize the intelligence of adult humans. We have seen that the Gc abilities of breadth of knowledge and the TSR abilities of retrieval (or reconstruction) of knowledge on average increase – and for some increase a great amount – through a major part of adulthood. These measures thus would seem to be indicative of that high level of intelligence we expect to find and think we see in those older people who

hold positions in our society that appear to require the highest levels of intellect.

There are some problems, however, with the assumption that the measures of Gc and TSR abilities obtained in research really indicate the high levels of cognitive capability that are attained in adulthood. We can see these problems when we look carefully at the measures of Gc that are used in research.

First, these measures provide only a rather paltry sample of the abilities that, in theory, define Gc. This concept represents a much broader and diverse range of knowledge – the intelligence of the dominant culture – than is (or probably can be representatively) sampled with the sets of tests used in research. There is no battery of tests for which there is compelling evidence that it representatively samples the knowledge of the concept of Gc. The full set of the achievement tests of the WJ-R (Woodcock et al., 2001) is currently probably the most nearly representative battery of such tests. It takes three hours to administer, more time than can be allocated to measure one factor in almost any research.

Second, even tests such as those of the WJ-R battery, and certainly tests of the kind that have typically been used in the research on which the extended Gf-Gc theory is based (e.g., vocabulary, similarities, general information, esoteric-word analogies), measure only the elementary knowledge, the beginning knowledge, in the various fields of human culture. The measures sample only surface knowledge in a number of fields, not in-depth knowledge in any field. The Gc factor is thus more indicative of a dilettante grasp of the intelligence of the culture than it is an indication of what a scholar understands. The latter is not only more similar to what we mean by intelligence when we opine that middle-aged and elderly CEO's, scientists, writers, and so forth are highly intelligent, it is also more characteristic of what is actually meant by the concept of Gc.

Thus, the operational definition of Gc in the extant research is not quite adequate. As development of cognitive abilities proceeds through childhood into adulthood, people develop greater in-depth comprehension, in-depth knowledge, in-depth understandings; in consequence of this, they reason better and are better problem-solvers. This is what characterizes what we refer to as intelligence in adults; this is what some older adults have more of than younger adults. But this is not what is well measured in Gc and TSR.

It is more nearly what is studied in research on expertise, including its relationship to aging (see also Krampe & Charness, Chapter 40). Let us turn to a consideration of what is measured in research on expertise.

Theory of Expertise

The main argument at this point is that (1) the abilities that represent the quintessential expressions of human intellectual capability come to fruition in mature adulthood (not in childhood or even early adulthood), and (2) the measures on which current theories of intelligence are based do not assess these abilities, or at least do not do so at the high levels that truly characterize adult intelligence. Now we advance the argument that research on expertise more nearly indicates what these abilities are and what the intellectual capacities of humans become in adulthood.

There are different kinds of expertise, and some do not at all represent aspects of human intelligence, just as there are many abilities that were not considered in building the evidence on which Gf-Gc theory is based. As we restricted consideration of abilities to cognitive abilities in discussing the theory of human intelligence, so we here restrict consideration of expertise to what we may call "cognitive expertise" in describing how expertise fits within a scientific understanding of human intellectual capabilities.

Just as we found it useful to classify the research on the nature of intelligence as structural and developmental, so it is useful to classify research on expertise as structural and developmental. The structural research has been directed at identifying and measuring different aspects and levels of exper-

tise – showing what it is. The developmental research has been directed at describing how expertise comes about – showing how it develops. In what follows we will give first consideration to the structure of cognitive expertise, then move on to consider how expertise develops. Ours must be a rather cursory view of these matters. Other chapters in this volume provide a more comprehensive look (see many of the chapters in Section III of the handbook).

Principal Attributes of Cognitive Expertise

We will first identify abilities that consistently characterize expertise and differentiate experts from novices (see also Feltovich, Prietula, & Ericsson, Chapter 4. Then we will consider the relations of these to the kinds of abilities that have been addressed in the theory of intelligence.

Expert Knowledge. Descriptions of expert abilities begin with an account of the breadth and depth of the knowledge the expert possesses in the domain of the expertise (Barnett & Koslowski, 2002; Charness, 1981a, 1981b, 1991; Colonia-Willner, 1998; de Groot, 1978; Ericsson & Kintsch, 1995; Ericsson, 1996; Hershey, Walsh, Read, & Chulef, 1990; Patel & Arocha, 1999; Walsh & Hershey, 1993). The expert has greater in-depth domain knowledge (see Chi, Chapter 10). As the level of expertise increases, this knowledge increases and the elements of the knowledge become better organized and integrated. The resulting knowledge system provides the expert with a basis for selecting, organizing, representing, manipulating, and interpreting information in the environment. Some of the experts' reasoning is knowledge-based (Charness, 1981a, 1981b, 1991; Colonia-Willner, 1998; Crook, 2002; de Groot, 1978; Ericsson, 1996; Ericsson & Kintsch, 1995), and these processes are supported by the expanded working memory that provides flexible access to generated inferences and intermediate results (Charness & Bosman, 1990; Ericsson & Delaney, 1998; Ericsson & Kintsch, 1995; Gobet & Simon, 1996; McGregor & Howes, 2002; Morrow, Menard, Stine-Morrow, Teller, & Bryant 2001; Weber, 2003).

In sum, the expert has great knowledge in the area of expertise, and this provides a firm foundation for the acquisition of expanded working memory that supports the experts' reasoning about potential courses of action.

Expert Reasoning. The knowledge-based reasoning of expertise has been described by a number of researchers (e.g., Barnett & Koslowski, 2002; Crook, 2002; Charness, 1981a, 1981b, 1991; Colonia-Willner, 1998; de Groot, 1978; Ericsson, 1996; Ericsson & Kintsch, 1995; Hershey et al., 1990; Lighten & Sternberg, 2002; Patel & Arocha, 1999; Proffitt, Coley, & Medin, 2000; Rikers et al., 2002; Walsh & Hershey, 1993). Expert reasoning is best described as inferential and deductive (Charness, 1981a, 1991; Ericsson, 1996, 1997; Hershey et al., 1990),whereas Gf reasoning is best described as inductive (Cattell, 1971). In conceptualizing a problem, the expert is able to comprehend its structure and represent the most relevant relations before generating alternative courses of action, whereas novices generate a large number of options that often lack high relevance to the solution (Walsh & Hershey, 1993).

For example, chess experts chose the next move by first encoding the structure of the current chess position, drawing on their vast knowledge, and then evaluating alternative moves through planning consequences. In contrast, a person of low expertise, using only Gf reasoning, selects the next move by generating and evaluating the various move possibilities that can be seen in the immediate situation (de Groot, 1978). Even when experts encounter a problem they have not encountered before, their acquired representations allow them to "see" interesting moves and evaluate outcomes of these moves by planning and relying on their acquired chess skills. The novice will be forced to generate moves from scratch and will explore moves suggested by the immediately perceptible configuration of the chess pieces. Expert reasoning proceeds from the general – comprehension of essential relations, knowledge of relevant principles – to develop specific alternative courses of action, whereas novice reasoning is stimulated by the salient attributes of a presented situation or problem.

There has been some, but very limited, study of tests of deductive reasoning within the tradition associated with extended Gf-Gc theory. Perhaps the closest approximation to the kinds of tasks that have been studied in expertise research is tests of reasoning, such as mathematical word-problem tests or general reasoning tests. When the covariance of test scores of these reasoning tests is analyzed, factor analyses show an involvement of both Gf and Gc (Carroll, 1993; Horn et al., 1981).

These findings do not reflect the high-level reasoning associated with expert performance, because these tests require limited knowledge of mathematics for successful performance, and the samples of participants are not chosen to represent high levels of expertise. To identify high levels of reasoning ability, it would be necessary to construct tests with complex, novel problems that would challenge expert performers with extensive experience of the associated problems. These kinds of tests have not yet been constructed and studied by researchers who developed extended Gf-Gc theory.

Expert Memory. Researchers studying expertise have described a form of expanded working memory (de Groot, 1946, 1978; Ericsson & Kintsch, 1995; Ericsson & Staszewski, 1989; Holding, 1985; Koltanowski, 1985; McGregor & Howes, 2002; Morrow et al., 2001; Weber, 2003; Feltovich et al. Chapter 4), which differs from the short-term working memory (STWM) that is the essence of SAR and is central to extended Gf-Gc theory. This expanded working memory is illustrated by the ability of a chess expert in blindfold chess (see also Gobet & Charness, Chapter 30).

In playing blindfold chess, the expert is never able to literally see the chess board or the chess pieces. All the outcomes of sequences of plays must be kept accessible in working memory. The number of alternative move sequences that the chess expert must consider mentally is of the order of 30 to 40, at least – much more than the seven plus or minus two, that is generally accepted to be the limit of the capacity of short-term working memory (STWM).

Similar superior memory (see also Wilding & Valentine, Chapter 31) has been documented in studies of experts playing multiple games of chess simultaneously. Cooke, Atlas, Lane, and Berger (1993) and Gobet and Simon (1996) demonstrated that highly skilled chess players can not only recall information from up to nine chess positions, presented one after the other as rapidly as one every five seconds without pause, but can also back-through numerous sequences (more than seven) to previous positions. There are no such demonstrations of memory feats in the tests used to define the forms of memory that indicate SAR.

Ericsson (1996), Ericsson and Kintsch (1995), and Ericsson and Delaney (1998) reasoned from the evidence that the "storage" in which the "work" of the working memory of experts is carried out must be a different form of storage than the storage of STWM. Ericsson and Kintsch referred to the memory of this different form of storage as long-term memory working memory (LTWM). We note that it operates in the short-term and refer to it as expertise working memory (ExpWM).

ExpWM differs in four important ways from the STWM that has been most extensively studied in cognitive psychology and in the research on which extended Gf-Gc theory is based: (1) the amount of information that is stored is larger, (2) the information is less affected by disruption and distraction – there is more effective resumption of performance after a disruption, and more is retained under multiple-task demand, (3) the order of recall is more flexible – it can differ from the order of presentation, and (4) information is encoded in long-term memory and thus can be retrieved when recall is requested unexpectedly (Ericsson, 1998). The results and analyses of Ericsson and Kintsch (1995) and Masunaga and Horn (2001) are consistent in indicating these differences between ExpWM (LTWM) and STWM.

The span of ExpWM is substantially larger than the seven-plus-or-minus-two span of STWM. As we have mentioned, chess experts hold as many as 40 elements in the span of immediate apprehension. Similarly, Masanga and Horn (2001) found that experts in playing the game of GO held more than seven units in the span of immediate apprehension.

Experts are able to recall presented elements equally well in orders that are different from the presented order. For example, in a series of chess moves expert chess players can recall the moves nearly as well from the last to the first move as from the order in which the moves were made. In experiments demonstrating the features of STWM, on the other hand, recall of elements in the order in which they were presented is considerably better than recall in the reverse of this order (e.g. Anderson, 1990). Whereas the limit for forward span STWM is seven plus or minus two, the limit for backward span is four plus or minus one.

Experts in chess can play multiple games of chess at one time, and do very well in all the games, whereas if one is required to keep track of the meaning of sentences while also remembering the last word of each sentence, memory for the last word is likely to be very poor.

When experts are unexpectedly asked to recall information about a complex task in their domain of expertise, their memory is not only more accurate and more complete than that of less-skilled performers, it is also considerably more accurate than when one is unexpectedly required to recall material of STWM, For example, if someone unexpectedly asked you about a telephone number you dialed a moment or two before, you are not likely to retrieve it, whereas if an expert is unexpectedly asked about the last moves in a chess match, he's likely to remember the moves with considerable accuracy.

In sum, ExpWM is notably different from STWM (and more generally, SAR).

The Development of Expertise

High-level expertise in such domains as mathematics, physics, medical diagnosis, financial planning, music, sports, and the games of GO and chess is attained through a form of practice that a number of investigators have described as "deliberate and well-structured" (Anderson, 1990, Ericsson, Krampe, & Tesch-Römer, 1993, Ericsson & Lehmann, 1996, Walsh & Hershey, 1993 – see Ericsson, Chapter 38).

Deliberate, Well-Structured Practice. This type of practice is focused, programmatic, carried out over extended periods of time, guided by conscious performance monitoring, evaluated by analyses of level of expertise reached, identification of errors, and procedures directed at eliminating errors. Specific goals are set at successive stages of expertise development. It involves appropriate, immediate feedback about performance. The feedback can be obtained from objective observers – human teachers and coaches – or it can be self-generated by comparing one's own performance with examples of more-advanced expert performance. Such objective feedback helps the learner to become aware of the standards of expertise, to internalize how to identify and correct errors, to set new goals, to focus on overcoming weaknesses, and to monitor progress (Ericsson, 1996, 1998).[7]

Deliberate and well-structured practice builds on setting goals that go beyond one's current level of performance and thus may lead to failures or even lowered performance. Aspiring expert performers come to view failures as opportunities to improve (Ericsson et al., 1993; Ericsson, 1998, 2002). This is dramatically illustrated in acquisition of expertise in sports. An example is given by Deakin and Cobley (2003), who found that elite figure skaters spent more time on challenging jumps than their less-elite counterparts. The elite skaters made more attempts at jumps they had not mastered but were needed to move up in level of expertise. They repeatedly failed jumps and fell on the ice, but ultimately they reached a higher plateau of excellence.

The path to expertise is not fully monotonic. Plateaus are reached at which the person is comfortable and confident. But it's necessary to move off such plateaus to advance. This involves some discomfort and considerable effort. It may involve unlearning some aspects of what had brought one to a comfort-level of expertise. Good teaching/coaching may be necessary and, in any case, can be very helpful. Ericsson (2002) instructs students aiming to acquire expertise to avoid arrested development associated with automatization. He argues that maintaining conscious effort helps one to deliberately refine the cognitive skills required to exceed a current level of performance.

When practice is well-structured and deliberate, the amount of practice is important. Ericsson et al. (1993) found that top-level expert violinists by age 20 had put in an average of more than 10,000 hours of practice, compared to an average of 5,000 hours put in by violinists who were not among the top experts. Other researchers, cited above, have found similar differences between top-level experts and those not so expert (see Ericsson, Chapter 38). But, again, length and amount of practice alone do not determine top-level performance: what is most important is that the practice be "deliberate and well-structured."

Adult Development. As we have indicated, expertise is developed through deliberate practice over lengthy periods of time. Deliberate practice is also necessary to maintain the expertise attained (Anderson, 1990; Ericsson et al., 1993; Krampe & Ericsson, 1996; Krampe & Charness, Chapter 40; Walsh & Hershey, 1993). Just how long it takes to reach the highest levels of expertise varies with individuals, with domain of expertise, and with factors pertaining to deliberate and well-structured practice. Many researchers argue that it takes ten years of focused practice to attain sufficient cognitive expertise to be able to win at international tournaments in chess and other established domains of expertise (Simon & Chase, 1973). The "10-year-rule" represents a very rough estimate, and most researchers regard it as a minimum, not an average (Ericsson, Chapter 38).

It takes years to reach the highest levels of expertise. Some of this, perhaps most of it, has to be in adulthood. Therefore, the abilities of expertise should increase, on average, in adulthood, not decline.

The evidence, although limited, is in line with this prediction. The pinnacle of cognitive expertise is rarely reached by people in their 20's, but more often it is in one's 30's or 40's or even later. The most outstanding contributions to science, literature, and the arts are made by adults, sometimes youngish adults, to be sure, but more often middle-aged adults and even adults in their 50's, 60's, and 70's. The most advanced levels of expertise in chess, GO, and financial planning have been attained by middle-aged adults (Charness & Bosman, 1990;, Krampe, & Mayr, 1996; Ericsson & Charness, 1994; Kasai, 1986; Walsh & Hershey, 1993).

Charness (1981a, 1981b, 1991) found that age was correlated near zero with level of ratings of chess skill, and that measured capabilities such as depth of search,[8] efficiency of chunking in memory, and rapidity in evaluating an end-game position were positively correlated with level of expertise but not with age.

Rabbitt (1993) found that in a sample of novices, crossword-puzzle-solving ability was positively correlated with test scores indicating Gf ($r = 0.72$) and negatively correlated with age ($r = -0.25$), but in a sample of experts at different levels of expertise, this ability correlated near zero with Gf and positively with age ($r = 0.24$).

Krampe and Ericsson (1996) studied a sample of classical pianists who ranged from amateurs to concert performers with an international reputation, and who ranged in age from the mid-20's to the mid-60's. They obtained cognitive speed measures comparable to those that assess the Gs factor of extended Gf-Gc theory, and they obtained cognitive speed measures pertaining to music and piano playing – that is, within the domain of expertise. Older pianists were notably slower than younger counterparts in the Gs measures – just as in most of the research indicating aging decline of vulnerable abilities – but, independently of age, experts performed better than amateurs on all music-related speeded tasks, that is, speed was positively related to expertise but the relationship to age was not significantly different from zero. The single

best predictor of performance on all music-related tasks was the amount of practice participants had maintained during the previous ten years. Sixty-year-old expert pianists who maintained deliberate practice (over ten hours/week) performed piano-related tasks at a superior level comparable to the level attained by younger expert pianists (Krampe & Ericsson, 1996).

Charness et al. (1996) and Krampe (2002) found that chess-playing skill was most strongly related to the recent level of deliberate practice, not age. Baltes (1997) found that in domains of their specialization, older adults accessed information more rapidly than younger adults. Among architects of different ages and levels of expertise, Salthouse, Babcock, Skovronek, Mitchell, & Palmon (1990) found that at every age, high-level experts consistently scored above low-level experts in visualization abilities, and elderly high-level experts scored higher than youthful-low-level experts.

Deliberate, well-structured practice is required to maintain high levels of expert performance (Bahrick, 1984; Bahrick & Hall, 1991; Kramer & Willis, 2002; Krampe & Ericsson, 1996; Walsh & Hershey, 1993). If expertise abilities are not used, they decline. To the extent that regular quality practice is maintained, expertise abilities do not decline with age in adulthood.

Thus, generally the findings indicate that expertise abilities can be maintained as age increases in adulthood – that is, if they are used and if there is sustained deliberate practice. Ericsson (2000) argues that aging decrease in expert performance is largely attributable to "older individuals' decisions to reduce the frequency of engagement in challenging activities and decrease the intensity of maintained deliberate practice" (p. 371).

The Relation between Expertise Abilities and Extended Gf-Gc Theory

There is thus the suggestion that (1) expertise abilities better indicate the human's intellectual capacities than do the abilities thus far measured in the research on which the current theory of intelligence is based, (2) these intellectual capacities are different from the capacities thus far measured and represented in extended Gf-Gc theory, (3) these capacities come to greatest fruition in adulthood, and (4) these capacities therefore do not decline in adulthood – at least not in the vital first one-half of the adulthood period of development.

These arguments are, in effect, the principal hypotheses evaluated in a recent study by Masunaga and Horn (2001). In this study, indicator measures of the ability traits of expertise deductive reasoning (ExpDR), expertise working memory (ExpWM), and expertise cognitive speed (ExpCS) were constructed. The ExpDR indicators were designed to indicate a form of reasoning that characterizes adult intelligence. The ExpWM indicators were designed to be the same as the memory tests that define STWM, and the ExpCS tests were like those used to measure Gs, except in each case the elements of the tests were those dealt with in a domain of expertise. The analyses of the study were directed at determining, first, whether such variables indicate factors of intelligence that are distinct from the age-declining Gf, SAR, and Gs factors of extended Gf-Gc theory and, second, whether the patterns of relationship to age for putative expertise abilities were the same as, or different from, the patterns seen for the Gf, SAR, and Gs indicators of human intelligence.

This research studied expertise in playing the game of GO, utilizing Japanese players. In Japan[9] this game is very widely played – and practiced – and thus provides a kind of participant-sampling laboratory for study of this kind of expertise. Many people of all ages strive to become experts in GO, and there are notable differences in the ages at which people start, and in the time span over which they strive, to gain expertise (somewhat similar to golf in the United States). Although many people learn the rudiments of the game in adolescence, most of the development of expertise occurs in adulthood, often extending into old age. All the reigning GO professionals (analogous to

Grandmasters in chess) are adults, usually middle aged, but some of them would be classified as old.

The game is a competition between two players. One player deploys black stones, the other white stones. In turn each player places a stone at the intersection of grid lines on a board marked with 19 by 19 such lines. The object of the game is to place stones in such a way that one's stones surround the largest portion of the territory on the board, and thus surround the opponent's stones, but at the same time ensure that one's own territory and stones are not surrounded by the opponent's stones. The rules of the game are simple, but expertise in GO is very complex – at least as complex as chess. There are millions of combinations of possible stone placements and a huge number of possible strategies and contingencies to take into account in placing the stones. This involves complex and difficult reasoning, memory, and other indicators of human intelligence. It is extremely difficult to become expert in the game. It is estimated by those who have become experts that it takes at least ten years of concerted effort to reach the apex in GO (Kasai, 1986; Reitman, 1976).

A factor analysis of the measures of GO-expertise abilities and cognitive-ability tests indicated that ExpDR and ExpWM abilities were distinct from Gf, SAR, and Gs. The results did not, however, distinguish an ExpCS that differs from Gs. Experts were faster than novices in dealing with tasks involving stimuli from their domain of expertise, but the individual differences in the measures that involved these stimuli were largely accounted for by individual differences in Gs.

A further analysis of the separate ExpDR and ExpWM factors examined the effects of age on these expertise abilities and compared them with aging effects for the Gf and SAR indicators of human intelligence. As outlined previously, the principal hypothesis predicted that the expertise reasoning and working memory would not decline with age in adult experts when deliberate, well-structured practice was maintained during adulthood. At lower levels of expertise the tests of ExpDR and ExpWM would measure Gf, SAR, or Gs, and thus performance on these tests would show a similar age decline as Gf, SAR, or Gs (as reviewed in the first section of this paper). These findings would yield a level-of-expertise-by-age interaction for ExpDR and ExpWM with age-related declines with age at lower levels of expertise and no declines at high levels of expertise.

An ANOVA with expertise and age (13 age groups ranging from an average of above 25 to an average of 75 years of age) revealed a reliable age-by-expertise interaction for both ExpDR and ExpWM. The comparable interaction effects for the indicators of Gf, SAR, and Gs were of trivial magnitude and not significantly different from zero, thus signaling that the interaction effect was for expertise abilities of intelligence, but not for conventional abilities of extended Gf-Gc theory. These findings were consistent with the hypotheses described above and, in fact, the means for older persons at higher levels of expertise were generally larger than the means for younger people at lower levels of expertise.

The expertise abilities-by-age interactions were found to be positively related to skill rating in playing GO. These results are not notably altered by entering – as covariate controls – the abilities of extended Gf-Gc theory, although Gf and STWM were found to have small negative (suppressor) relations. Gf was found to be slightly negatively related to skill rating in GO, but the Gf-by-age interaction was positive, suggesting that those who best retain their Gf with advancing age perform at a relatively high level, whereas those who show declines in Gf perform at a lower level.

Summary and Conclusions

Abilities regarded as indicating important features of human intelligence are numerous and diverse, but findings from structural, developmental, physiological, educational/occupational and behavior-genetic studies indicate (empirically) that the many particular abilities the human is capable of developing fall into a relatively small number of different classes. These classes represent different ways in which neural capacities and learning interact over extended periods of development – in both childhood and adulthood – to produce cognitive ability traits (see also Hill & Schneider, Chapter 37). The neural capacities are laid down genetically, but are altered by environmental influences that directly affect physiological/neural structure and function. The environmental/learning influences are large in number and diverse, but acculturation learning influences are particularly important in shaping cognitive ability traits.

Four classes of abilities emerge from the interactions of neural dispositions and learning influences that operate over the course of development – Gc, TSR, ExpDR and ExpWM. These abilities reflect individual differences in acculturation and learning in different domains in which one can become expert. The Gc class of crystallized knowledge abilities indicate dilettante breadth of knowledge of the culture. The TSR abilities indicate fluency in tertiary retrieval of information from this knowledge store. The ExpDR abilities indicate expert deductive reasoning in particular domains in which advanced expert knowledge is built up. The ExpWM abilities indicate wide-span working-memory abilities in the domains in which one becomes expert. To the extent that one works at developing and maintaining these abilities, they increase throughout the lifespan.

Classes of reasoning abilities (Gf), short-term apprehension and retention abilities (SAR), and Gs abilities of cognitive processing speed are relatively little shaped by influences focused on acculturation or learning of particular forms of expertise. The reasoning abilities are similar to the abilities Spearman described as representing apprehension, eduction of relations, and eduction of correlates. He argued that these capacities are the *sine qua non* of all the abilities of human intelligence. It has not been found, however, that these capacities, as measured, represent anything that is general to all the abilities that are accepted as indicating important features of human intelligence. Measured Gf does not represent the concept of general intelligence that Spearman described under the heading of g: it represents a more limited form of intelligence – one among other forms of intelligence.

In the earliest period of development, neophobic and neophilic reaction patterns promote cognitive ability development. In conjunction with the extent to which secure attachment is established in infancy and early childhood, neophobia and neophilia activate primitive attention-maintaining and reasoning capacities to produce the awareness concepts and problem-solving capabilities that constitute early intelligence. Neophobia promotes the development of abilities that influence one to avoid unfamiliar, often dangerous conditions. Secure attachment in the earliest years of life enables the child to approach unfamiliar conditions, which in turn enables neophilia and promotes abilities that encourage exploration and manipulation of unfamiliar things. Individual differences in secure attachment are associated with many of the factors that promote acculturation. These influences, operating throughout development, produce the distinction between the Gc and TSR abilities, on the one hand, and the Gf, SAR, and Gs abilities, on the other hand.

The Gf, SAR, and Gs abilities increase with age in childhood and adolescence but decline in adulthood. One important aspect of this decline is loss of ability to maintain focused attention. Measured in tasks that require one to behave as slowly as possible, this ability accounts for a substantial part of the decline in Gs speed of processing information, SAR retention, and the complex reasoning of Gf.

The Gc and TSR abilities increase with acculturation, and this accumulates through childhood and adulthood. The Gc and TSR abilities thus indicate aspects of intelligence that reach their peaks in adulthood and in that sense characterize intelligence of adults, but neither well represents the feats of reasoning and memory that appear in adulthood and are most indicative of intellec-

tual capabilities of the human. Reasoning at the highest levels of which humans seem capable involves use of extensive, integrated bodies of knowledge. Gc does not represent this knowledge. It indicates only dilettante breadth of knowledge. Extensive, integrated, deep knowledge is found in particular kinds of expertise. Gq, representing the abilities of mathematical/quantitative thinking, is indicative of such knowledge in one domain of expertise.

The TSR abilities indicate fluency in accessing (recreating) information such as that in the Gc store of knowledge. TSR abilities also come to fruition in adulthood and thus help characterize adult intelligence. These are not, however, the abilities for flexibly maintaining large amounts of information in the span of immediate awareness that most characterize intelligence in adulthood. These abilities – the ExpWM abilities – are indicated in displays of expertise.

Also lacking in the Gc and TSR descriptions are the reasoning abilities that are most characteristic of adult intelligence. These abilities are not well represented by the Gf abilities, which decline in adulthood. Measures of Gf abilities are designed to minimize the influences of acculturation and learning in any particular domain in which one might become expert. Yet reasoning at the highest levels involves using best selections of information and problem-solving skills from bodies of knowledge that are difficult to acquire and require considerable time to acquire – that is, the bodies of knowledge of domains of expertise. Deductive reasoning with this kind of information – ExpDR – is characteristic of the intelligence of adults.[10]

Expertise deductive reasoning (ExpDR) and expertise working memory (ExpWM) capabilities are distinguishable in adulthood, are indicative of human intelligence, and are different from somewhat comparable Gf and SAR abilities that heretofore – in extended Gf-Gc theory – were regarded as capturing the essence of the reasoning and memory capabilities of human intelligence. Whereas Gf and SAR decline with age in adulthood at all levels of expertise, ExpDR and ExpWM increase with level of expertise, and to the extent that there is deliberate, well-structured practice to develop and maintain expertise, these abilities increase with age in adulthood. These abilities exemplify more nearly than the others the full capacity of human intelligence.

Footnotes

1. There is an assumption here that different items of reasoning are the same. One can conceive of specifying behavioral traits without this assumption, but in practice it is fundamental to the definition of all behavioral traits of personality. This is as true of the trait constructs of expertise theory as it is of the trait constructs of theory of intelligence. The characteristic behaviors that indicate one grand master in chess, for example, are not precisely the same as the characteristic behaviors that indicate another grand master at the same level.

2. Among the tests designed to measure abilities of human intelligence are tests of reasoning of various forms – induction, deduction, conjunctive, disjunctive, eduction of relations, eduction of correlates –, tests of many forms of problem-solving, tests of abstracting, concept formation, concept attainment, learning, knowledge, comprehension, decoding, encoding, communication, creativity, insight, sensitivity to problems, originality, associational fluency, expressional fluency, word naming, figural fluency, flexibility, associative memory, free recall, nonsense memory, visual memory, auditory memory, visualization, perceiving spatial relations, visual closure, visual integration, spatial scanning, sound localization, loudness discrimination, pitch discrimination, resistance to auditory distraction, judging rhythm, temporal integration, perceptual (visual, auditory, tactile) speed, reaction time speed, choice reaction time speed, semantic processing speed, and information processing speed.

3. Which is often referred to as Spearman's g, in recognition that Spearman was first to propose a testable theory of general intelligence, which, however, he designated with the letter g in order to escape from a number of undesirable and not-needed connotations of the word as it is used in everyday parlance.

4. Tests omitted in this selection can be seen to be indicative of Gc and Gv. Rimoldi found that

three factors were required to fit the intercorrelation data at the second order.

5. Root mean square error of approximation RMSEA, Browne & Cudeck, 1993; Steiger, 1990.

6. Expressed in IQ units the decline of fluid reasoning from age 25 to age 65 years is no less than 15 points. Thus the average IQ in this form of intelligence descends from 100 to below 85. Granted that CEO's, Senators, Professors, etc. would have started at higher levels than other folks – say in the 130's in IQ units – still the evidence of decline suggests that they would be back to fairly ordinary levels of intellect by the time they reached the exalted levels at which they are found in the real world of work and responsibility.

7. While it seems that generally feedback is best supplied by a good teacher/coach, Charness (1981a, b; 1991) and Ericsson (1996) have found instances in developing expertise in chess in which self-directed practice, using books and studying sequences of moves made by expert players, could be as effective as teacher/coach-directed practice.

8. Described as the point at which a player can no longer retain accurate information about projected changes in position.

9. It was comprised of 263 male GO players between 18 to 78 years of age, at 48 levels of expertise, drawn with the aid and sponsorship of the Japanese GO Association, which conducts examinations that enable individuals to establish (officially) their level of GO expertise (which members of the Association do about once a year on average).

10. Human intelligence also involves broad classes of abilities that are tied to particular organizations of visual processes (Gv) and auditory processes (Ga). These were not considered in any detail in this chapter.

References

Anderson, J. R. (1990). *Cognitive psychology and its implications* (3rd ed.). New York: W. H. Freeman.

Backman, L., Small, B. J., Wahlin, A., & Larsson, M. (2000). Cognitive functioning in very old age. In F. I. M. Craik & T. A. Salthouse (Eds.), *The handbook of aging and cognition* (2nd ed, pp. 499–558). Mahwah, NJ: Erlbaum.

Bahrick, H. P. (1984). Semantic memory content in permastore: Fifty years of memory for Spanish learned in school. *Journal of Experimental Psychology: General*, 113, 1–29.

Bahrick, H. P., & Hall, L. K. (1991). Lifetime maintenance of high school mathematics content. *Journal of Experimental Psychology: General*, 120, 20–33.

Baltes, P. B. (1997). On the incomplete architecture of human ontogeny: Selection, optimization, and compensation as foundation of developmental theory. *American Psychologist*, 52, 366–380.

Barnett, S. M., & Koslowski, B. (2002). Adaptive expertise: Effects of type of experience and the level of theoretical understanding it generates. *Thinking & Reasoning*, 8(4), 237–267. *Journal of Experimental Psychology: General*, 120, 20–33.

Birren, J. E. (1974). Translations in gerontology – From lab to life: Psychology and speed of response. *American psychologist*, 29, 808–815.

Botwinick, J. (1977). Aging and intelligence. In J. E. Birren & K. W. Schaie (Eds.), *Handbook of the psychology of aging* (pp. 580–605). New York: Van Nostrand Reinhold.

Botwinick, J. (1978). *Aging and behavior: A comprehensive integration of research findings*. New York: Springer.

Bower, G. H. (1972). Mental imagery and associative learning. In L. W. Gregg (Ed.), *Cognition in learning and memory* (pp. 213–228). New York: Wiley.

Bower, G. H. (1975). Cognitive psychology: An introduction. In W. K. Estes (Ed.), *Handbook of learning and cognitive processes*, vol. 1. New York: Lawrence Erlbaum Associates.

Bowlby, J. (1951). Maternal care and mental health. *Bulletin of the World Health Organization*, 3, 355–533.

Broadbent, D. E. (1966). The well-ordered mind. *American Educational Research Journal*, 3, 281–295.

Browne, M. W., & Cudeck, R. (1993). Alternative way of assessing model fit. In K. A. Bollen & J. S. Long (Eds.), *Tesing structural equation modles (pp. 136–162)*. Thousand Oaks, CA: Sage.

Burgess, K. M., Marshall, P. J., Rubin, K. H., & Fox, N. A. (2003). Infant attachment and temperament as predictors of subsequent externalizing problems and cardiac physiology. *Journal of Child Psychology & Psychiatry*, 44, 819–831.

Carroll, J. B. (1993). *Human cognitive abilities: A survey of factor-analytic studies*. New York: Cambridge University Press.

Cattell, R. B. (1971). *Abilities: Their structure, growth and action*. Boston: Houghton-Mifflin.

Cattell, R. B. (1979). Are culture-fair intelligence tests possible and necessary? *Journal of Research and Development in Education*, 12, 1–13.

Cavanaugh, J. C. (1997). *Adult development and aging*, 3rd ed. New York: ITP.

Charness, N. (1981a). Search in chess: Age and skill differences. *Journal of Experimental Psychology: Human Perception and Performance*, 7(2), 467–476.

Charness, N. (1981b). Visual short-term memory and aging in chess players. *Journal of Gerontology*, 36(5), 615–619.

Charness, N. (1991). Expertise in chess: The balance between knowledge and search. In K. A. Ericsson & J. Smith (Eds.), *Toward a general theory of expertise* (pp. 39–63). New York: Cambridge University Press.

Charness, N., & Bosman, E. A. (1990). Expertise and aging: Life in the lab. In T. M. Hess (Ed.), *Aging and cognition: Knowledge organization and utilization* (pp. 343–386). New York: Elsevier.

Charness, N., Krampe, R., & Mayr, U. (1996). The role of practice and coaching in entrepreneurial skill domains: An international comparison of life-span chess skill acquisition. In K. A. Ericsson (Ed.), *The road to excellence* (pp. 51–80). Mahwah, NJ: Lawrence Erlbaum Associates.

Christensen, H. (2001). What cognitive changes can be expected with normal ageing? *Australian & New Zealand Journal of Psychiatry*, 35(6), 768–775.

Colonia-Willner, R. (1998). Practical intelligence at work: Relationship between aging and cognitive efficiency among managers in a bank environment. *Psychology & Aging*, 13(1), 45–57.

Cooke, N. J., Atlas, R. S., Lane, D. M., & Berger, R. C. (1993). Role of high-level knowledge in memory for chess positions. *American Journal of Psychology*, 106, 321–351.

Craik, F. I. M. (1977). Age differences in human memory. In J. E. Birren & K. W. Schaie (Eds.), *Handbook of the psychology of aging*. New York: Van Nostrand Reinhold.

Craik, F. I. M. (2000). Age-related changes in human memory. In D. C. Park & N. Schwarz (Eds.), *Cognitive aging: A primer* (pp. 75–92). Philadelphia: Taylor & Francis.

Craik, F. I. M. & Byrd, M. (1982). Aging and cognitive deficits: The role of attentional resources. In F. I. M. Craik & Trehub, S. (Eds.), *Aging and cognitive processes* (pp. 191–211). New York: Plenum.

Craik, F. I. M. & Trehub, S., Eds. (1982). *Aging and cognitive processes*. New York: Plenum.

Crook, J. A. (2002). How do expert mental health nurses make on-the-spot clinical decisions? A review of the literature. *Journal of Psychiatric & Mental Health Nursing*, 8(1), 1–6.

Deakin, J. M., & Cobley, S. (2003). A search for deliberate practice: an examination of the practice environments in figure skating and volleyball. In J. Starkes and K. A. Ericsson (Eds.), *Expert performance in sport: Recent advances in research on sport expertise* (pp. 115–135). Champaign, IL: Human Kinetics.

de Groot, A. D. (1946). *Het denken vun den schaker [Thought and choice in chess]*. Amsterdam: North-Holland.

de Groot, A. D. (1978). *Thought and choice in chess*. Oxford, England: Mouton.

Ericsson, K. A. (1996). The acquisition of expert performance. In K. A. Ericsson (Ed.), *The road to excellence* (pp. 1–50). Mahwah, NJ: Lawrence Erlbaum Associates.

Ericsson, K. A. (1997). Deliberate practice and the acquisition of expert performance: An overview. In H. Jorgensen & A. C. Lehmann (Eds.), *Does practice make perfect?: Current theory and research on instrumental music practice* (pp. 9–51). NMH-publikasjoner.

Ericsson, K. A. (1998). The scientific study of expert levels of performance: General implications for optimal learning and creativity. *High Ability Studies*, 9, 75–100.

Ericsson, K. A. (2000). How experts attain and maintain superior performance: Implications for the enhancement of skilled performance in older individuals. *Journal of Aging and Physical Activity*, 8, 346–352.

Ericsson, K. A. (2002). Attaining excellence through deliberate practice: Insights from the study of expert performance. In M. Ferrari (Ed), The pursuit of excellence through education. The educational psychology series (pp. 21–55).

Ericsson, K. A. & Charness, N. (1994). Expert performance. *American Psychologist*, 49, 725–747.

Ericsson, K. A. & Delaney, P. F. (1998). Working memory and expert performance. In R. H. Logie & K. J. Gilhooly (Eds.), Working mem-

ory and thinking. Current issues in thinking & reasoning (pp. 93–114). Hove, England UK: Psychology Press/Erlbaum (UK) Taylor & Francis.

Ericsson, K. A. & Kintsch, W. (1995). Long-term working memory. *Psychological Review*, 105, 211–245.

Ericsson, K. A., Krampe, R. T., & Tesch-Romer, C. (1993). The role of deliberate practice in the acquisition of expert performance. *Psychological Review*, 100(3), 363–406.

Ericsson, K. A., & Lehmann, A. C. (1996). Expert and exceptional performance: Evidence of maximal adaptation to task constraints. *Annual Review of Psychology*, 47, 273–305.

Ericsson, K. A., & Staszewski, J. (1989). Skilled memory and expertise: Mechanisms of exceptional performance. In D. Klahr & K. Kotovsky (Eds.), Complex information processing (p. 235–268). Hillsdale, NJ: Lawrence Erlbaum Associates.

Estes, W. K. (1974). Learning theory and intelligence. *American Psychologist*, 29, 740–749.

Fagan, J. F., & McGrath, S. K. (1981). Infant recognition memory and later intelligence. *Intelligence*, 5, 121–130.

Finkel, D., Reynold, C. A., McArdle, J. J., Gatz, M., & Pedersen, N. L. (2003). Latent growth curve analyses of accelerating decline in cognitive abilities in late adulthood. *Developmental Psychology*, 39(3), 535–550.

Fisk, J. E. & Sharp, C. (2002). Syllogistic reasoning and cognitive ageing. Quarterly *Journal ofExperimental Psychology: Human Experimental Psychology*, 55A (4), 1273–1293.

Flangan, D. P., & Harrison P. L. (Eds). (2005). *Contemporary intellectual Assessment: Theories, tests, and issues*(2nd ed). New York: Guilford Press.

Gathercole, S. E. (1994). The nature and uses of working memory. In P. Morris & M. Gruneberg (Eds.), *Theoretical aspects of memory* (pp. 50–78). London: Routledge.

Gobet, F., & Simon, H. A. (1996). Templates in chess memory: A mechanism for recalling several boards. *Cognitive Psychology*, 31, 1–40.

Harlow, H. F., & Suomi, S. J. (1970). Nature of love: Simplified. *American Psychologist*, 25, 161–168.

Harwood, E., & Naylor, G. F. K. (1971). Changes in the constitution of the WAIS intelligence pattern with advancing age. *Australian Journal of Psychology*, 23, 297–303.

Hershey, D. A., Walsh, D. A., Read, S. J., & Chulef, A. S. (1990). The effects of expertise on financial problem solving: Evidence for goal-directed problem solving scripts. *Organizational Behavior and Human Decision Performance, 46,* 77–101.

Holding, D. H. (1985). *The psychology of chess skill.* Hillsdale, NJ: Lawrence Erlbaum Associates.

Horn, J. L. (1968). Organization of abilities and the development of intelligence. *Psychological Review, 75,* 242–259.

Horn, J. L. (1972). The structure of intellect: Primary abilities. In R. M. Dreger (Ed.), *Multivariate personality research* (pp. 451–511). Baton Rouge: Claitor Publishing.

Horn, J. L. (1975). Psychometric studies of aging and intelligence. In S. Gershon & A. Raskin (Eds.), *Aging, Vol. 2, Genesis and treatment of psychologic disorders in the elderly* (pp. 19–43). New York: Raven.

Horn, J. L. (1977). Human abilities: A review of research and theory in the early 1970's. *Annual Review of Psychology, 27,* 437–485.

Horn, J. L. (1982). The aging of human abilities. In B B. Wolman (Ed.), *Handbook of developmental psychology* (pp. 847–870). Englewood Cliffs, NJ: Prentice Hall.

Horn, J. L. (1985). Intellectual ability concepts. In R. J. Sternberg (Ed.), *Advances in the psychology of human intelligence, vol. 3* (pp. 35–77). Hillsdale, NJ: Lawrence Erlbaum.

Horn, J. L. (1989). Cognitive diversity: A framework for learning. In P. L. Ackerman, R. J. Sternberg, & R. Glaser (Eds.), *Learning and individual differences: Advances in theory and research* (pp. 61–114). New York: Freeman.

Horn, J. L. (1991). Measurement of intellectual capabilities: A review of theory. In K. S. McGrew, J. K. Werder, & R. W. Woodcock (Eds.), *Woodcock-Johnson technical manual* (pp. 197–246). Allen, TX: DLM.

Horn, J. L. (1997). A basis for research on age differences in cognitive capabilities. In J. J. McArdle, & R. Woodcock (Eds.), *Human cognitive abilities in theory and practice.* Chicago, IL: Riverside.

Horn, J. L. (2002). Selections of evidence, misleading assumptions, and oversimplifications: the political message of The Bell Curve. In J. Fish (Ed.). *Race and Intelligence: Separating Science from Myth* (pp. 297–325). Mahwah, NJ: Lawrence Erlbaum Associates.

Horn, J. L. (in press). Understanding Human Intelligence: Where have we come since Spearman? In R. C. MacCallum & R. Cudeck (Eds.), *One hundred years after Spearman.* Mahwah, NJ: Erlbaum.

Horn, J. L. & Cattell, R. B. (1967). Age differences in fluid and crystallized intelligence. *Acta Psychologica, 26,* 107–129.

Horn, J. L. & Donaldson, G. (1980). Cognitive development in adulthood. In O. G. Brim & J. Kagan (Eds.), *Constancy and change in human development* (pp. 445–529). Cambridge, MA: Harvard University Press.

Horn, J. L., Donaldson, G., & Engstrom, R. (1981). Apprehension, memory and fluid intelligence decline in adulthood. *Research on Aging, 3,* 33–84.

Horn, J. L. & Hofer, S. M. (1992). Major abilities and development in the adult period. In R. J. Sternberg & C. A. Berg (Eds.), *Intellectual development* (pp. 44–99). New York: Cambridge University Press.

Horn, J. L. & Noll, J. (1997). Human cognitive capabilities: Gf-Gc theory. In Flanagan, Genshaft, & Harrison (Eds.), *Contemporary intellectual assessment* (pp. 53–91). New York: Guilford Press.

Jensen, A. R. (1998). *The g Factor: The Science of Mental Ability.* London: Praeger.

Kasai, K. (1986). Tgo de atama ga yoku nara hon [Becoming smart with Go]. Tokyo, Japan: Shikai.

Kaufman, A. S. (1990). *Assessing adolescent and adult intelligence.* Boston: Allyn and Bacon.

Kausler, D. H. (1990). *Experimental psychology, cognition, and human aging.* New York: Springer.

Koltanowski, G. (1985). *In the dark.* Coraopolis, PA: Chess Enterprises.

Kramer, A. F., & Willis, S. L. (2002). Enhancing the cognitive vitality of older adults. *Current Directions in Psychological Science, 11,* 173–177.

Krampe, R. T. (2002). Aging, expertise and fine motor development. *Neuroscience & Biobehavioral Review, 26,* 769–776.

Krampe, R. T., & Ericsson, K. A. (1996). Maintaining excellence: Deliberate practice and elite performance in young and older pianists. *Journal of Experimental Psychology: General, 125*(4), 331–359.

Lane, C. J., & Zelinski, E. M. (2003). Longitudinal hierarchical linear models of the Memory

Functioning Questionnaire. *Psychology and Aging*, 18, 38–53.

Lighten, J. P., & Sternberg, R. J. (2002). Thinking about reasoning: Is knowledge power? *Korean Journal of Thinking & Problem Solving*, 12(1), 5–25.

Madden, D. J., & Nebes, R. D. (1980). Aging and the development of automaticity in visual search. *Developmental Psychology*, 16, 277–296.

Masunaga, H. & Horn, J. L. (2000). Characterizing mature human intelligence: Expertise development. *Learning and Individual Differences*, 12, 5–33.

Masunaga, H. & Horn, J. L. (2001). Expertise and age-related changes in components of intelligence. *Psychology and Aging*, 16(2), 293–311.

McArdle, J. J., Ferrer-Caja, E., Hamagami, F., & Woodcock, R. W. (2002). Comparative longitudinal structural analysis of the growth and decline of multiple intellectual abilities over the life span. *Developmental Psychology*, 38, 115–142.

McArdle, J. J., Hamagami, F., Meredith, K. P., & Broadway, K. P. (2000). Modeling the dynamic hypotheses of Gf-Gc theory using longitudinal life-span data. *Learning & Individual Differences*, 12(1), 53–79.

McArdle, J. J., Prescott, C. A., Hamagami, F., & Horn, J. L. (1998). A contemporary method for developmental-genetic analyses of age changes in intellectual abilities. *Developmental Neuropsychology*, 14, 69–114.

McArdle, J. J. & Woodcock, R. (Eds.) (1998). *Human Cognitive Abilities in theory and practice*. Chicago, IL: Riverside.

McGregor, S. J., & Howes, A. (2002). The role of attach and defense semantics in skilled players' memory for chess positions. *Memory & Cognition*, 30(5), 707–717.

McGrew, K. S., & Flanagan, D. P. (1998). *The Intelligence Test Desk Reference (ITDR)*. Boston: Allyn and Bacon.

McGrew, K. S., Werder, J. K., & Woodcock, R. W. (1991). *Woodcock-Johnson technical manual*. Allen, Texas: DLM.

McGrew, K. S., & Woodcock, R. W. (2001). *Technical Manual. Woodcock-Johnson III*. Itasca, IL: Riverside Pulbishing.

Medina, J. J. (1996). *The clock of ages*. Cambridge, UK: Cambridge University Press.

Miller, G. A. (1956). The magical number Seven, plus or minus two. *Psychological Review*, 63, 81–97.

Morrow, D. G., Menard, W. E., Stine-Morrow, E. A. L., Teller, T, & Bryant, D. (2001). The influence of expertise and task factors on age differences in pilot communication. *Psychology & Aging*, 16(1), 31–46.

Noll, J., & Horn, J. L. (1997). Age differences in processes of fluid and crystallized intelligence. Chapter 4 in J. J. McArdle & R. Woodcock (Eds.), *Human cognitive abilities in theory and practice* (pp. 263–281). Chicago, IL: Riverside Press.

Patel, V. & Arocha, J. (1999). Medical expertise and cognitive aging. In D. C. Park (Ed). *Processing of medical information in aging patients: Cognitive and human factors perspectives* (pp. 127–143). Mahwah, NJ: Lawrence Erlbaum Associates, Inc.

Proffitt, J. B., Coley, J. D., & Medin, D. L. (2000). Expertise and category-based induction. *Journal of Experimental Psychology: Learning, Memory, & Cognition*, 26(4), 811–828.

Rabbitt, P. (1993). Crystal quest: A search for the basis of maintenance of practice skills into old age. In A. Baddeley & L. Weiskrantz (Eds.), *Attention: Selection, awareness, and control* (pp. 188–230). Oxford, England: Clarendon Press.

Rabbitt, P., & Abson, V. (1991). Do older people know how good they are? *British Journal of Psychology*, 82, 137–151.

Radvansky, G. A., & Copeland, D. E. (2000). Functionally and spatial relations in memory and language. *Memory & Cognition*, 28, 987–992.

Radvansky, G. A., Copeland, D. E., & Zwaan, R. A. (2003). Brief report: Aging and functional spatial relations in comprehension and memory. *Psychology and Aging*, 18, 161–165.

Raz, N. (2000). Aging of the brain and its impact on cognitive performance: Integration of structural and functional findings. In F. I. M. Craik & T. A. Salthouse (Eds.), *The handbook of aging and cognition* (2nd Ed, pp. 1–90). Mahwah, NJ: Erlbaum.

Reitman, J. (1976). Skilled perception in GO: Deducing memory structures from inter-response times. *Cognitive Psychology*, 8, 336–356.

Rikers, R. M., Schmidt, H. G., Boshuizen, H. P. A., Linssen, G. C. M., Wesseling, G., & Paas, F. G. W. C. (2002). The robustness of medical expertise: Clinical case processing by medical experts and sub-experts. *American Journal of Psychology*, 115(4), 609–629.

Rimoldi, H. J. A. (1951). The central intellective factor. *Psychometrika*. 16, 75–101.

Salthouse, T. A. (1987). The role of representations in age differences in analogical reasoning. *Psychology and Aging*, 2, 357–362.

Salthouse, T. A. (1991a). *Theoretical perspectives on cognitive aging*. Hillsdale, NJ: Lawrence Erlbaum.

Salthouse, T. A. (1991b). Expertise as the circumvention of human processing limitations. In K. A. Ericsson & J. Smith (Eds.), *Toward a general theory of expertise: Prospects and limits* (pp. 286–300). New York: Cambridge University Press.

Salthouse, T. A. (1992). *Mechanisms of age-cognition relations in adulthood*. Hillsdale, NJ: Lawrence Erlbaum Associates.

Salthouse, T. A. (1993). Speed medication of adult age differences in cognition. *Developmental Psychology*, 29, 727–738.

Salthouse, T. A. (1994). The nature of influence of speed on adult age differences in cognition. *Developmental Psychology*, 30, 240–259.

Salthouse, T. A. (2001). Structural models of relations between age and measures of cognitive functioning. *Intelligence*, 29(2), 93–115.

Salthouse, T. A., Babcock, R. L., Skovronek, E., Mitchell, D. R. D., & Palmon, R. (1990). Age and experience effects in spatial visualization. *Developmental Psychology*, 26, 128–136.

Salthouse, T. A., & Ferrah-Caja, E. (2003). What needs to be explained to account for age-related effects on multiple cognitive variables? *Psychology and Aging*, 18, 91–110.

Salthouse, T. A., Kausler, D. H., & Saults, J. S. (1990). Age, self-assessed health status, and cognition. *Journal of Gerontology*, 45, 156–160.

Salthouse, T. A. & Somberg, B. L. (1982). Isolating the age deficit in speeded performance. *Journal of Gerontology*, 37, 59–63.

Schaie, K. W. (1996). *Intellectual development in adulthood: The Seattle longitudinal study*. Cambridge: Cambridge University Press.

Schaie, K. W. (2000). The impact of longitudinal studies on understanding development from young adulthood to old age. *International Journal of Behavioral Development*, 24, 257–266.

Shaver, P. R., & Mikulincer, M. (2002). Attachment-related psychodynamics. *Attachment & Human Development*, 4, 133–161.

Simon, H. A., & Chase, W. G. (1973). Skill in chess. *American Scientist*, 61, 394–403.

Spearman, C. (1904). "General Intelligence," objectively determined and measured. *American Journal of Psychology*, 15, 210–293.

Spearman, C. (1927). The abilities of man: Their nature and measurement. London: Macmillan.

Sperling, G. (1960). The information available in brief visual presentations. *Psychological Monographs*, 74, 498.

Spitz, R. A. (1946). Hospitalism; a follow-up report on investigation described in Volume I, 1945. *Psychoanalytic Study of the Child*, 2, 113–117.

Sroufe, L. A. (1977). Wariness of strangers and the study of infant development. *Child Development*, 48, 731–746.

Stankov, L. & Horn, J. L. (1980). Human abilities revealed through auditory tests. *Journal of Educational Psychology*, 72, 21–44.

Steiger, J. H. (1990). Structural model evaluation and modification: An interval estimation approach. *Multivariate Behavioral Research*, 25, 173–180.

Tisserand, D. J. & Jolles, J. (2003). On the involvement of prefrontal networks in cognitive ageing. *Cortex*, 39, 1107–1128.

Walsh, D. A. & Hershey, D. A. (1993). Mental models and the maintenance of complex problem-solving skills in old age. In J. Cerella, J. Rybash, W. Hoyer, & M. Commons (Eds.), *Adult information processing: Limits on loss* (pp. 553–584). San Diego: Academic Press.

Weber, N. (2003). Expert memory: The interaction of stimulus structure, attention, and expertise. *Applied Cognitive Psychology*, 17, 295–308.

Woodcock, R. W. (1990). Theoretical foundations of the WJ-R measures of cognitive ability. *Journal of Psychoeducational Assessment*, 8, 231–258.

Woodcock, R. W., McGrew, K. S., & Mather, N. (2001). Woodcock-Johnson III. Itasca, IL: Riverside Publishing.

CHAPTER 35

Tacit Knowledge, Practical Intelligence, and Expertise

Anna T. Cianciolo, Cynthia Matthew,
Robert J. Sternberg, & Richard K. Wagner

The drive to excel has long challenged humans to push their bodies, minds, and technologies in the determined pursuit of success. People have demonstrated their devotion to excellence through the years of effort and practice they have been willing to invest in accomplishing their goals (Ericsson, Krampe, & Tesch-Römer, 1993). For example, Simon and Chase (1973) observed that no one had ever attained the rank of Grandmaster in chess without at least a decade of intense preparation. This observation has since been extended to many domains, including music, sports, and academia (Bloom, 1985; Ericsson et al., 1993; Ericsson, Chapter 38). Despite folk tales about extraordinary performances by very young individuals, it is clear that the most eminent individuals in any field do not exhibit expert levels of performance prior to an extended period of preparation.

Exploration of the nature of expertise and how it develops has interested scholars, professionals, and laypeople alike, and has involved a wide range of theoretical and methodological approaches. One of the enduring debates over many years of study is whether the development of expertise is largely attributable to unusual characteristics of individuals, often thought of in terms of largely inherited talents, or of their learning histories (see Horn & Masunaga, Chapter 34). Because expertise is acquired over many years, perhaps as a result of more intense, sustained, and programmatic application of the identical mechanisms that underlie average levels of attainment (Ericsson et al., 1993), the study of expert performance is directly relevant to the study of typical human development. Indeed, the study of the development of expertise may represent an opportunity to observe developmental mechanisms operating at maximum efficiency.

On the flip side, the study of typical human developmental mechanisms may shed some light on the nature and development of expertise. Our research has been devoted, in part, to creating a better understanding of the cognitive mechanisms that allow people to develop and use the practical intellectual abilities required for success in everyday life. As such, our work represents a link between the study of typical human development and the exploration of expertise. Of particular interest to us is the way in which people use their intellectual capabilities to adapt to and succeed in particular environments. Expertise, whether demonstrated in such everyday feats as reading and writing, or in the exceptional accomplishments of artists, athletes, and scholars, reflects the outcome of people's active engagement in the world around them.

In this chapter, we discuss a psychological approach to exploring expertise that is based on the theory of practical intelligence and tacit knowledge (Sternberg, 1988; 1997; Wagner & Sternberg, 1985). This approach represents an attempt to explain the cognitive mechanisms underlying the human ability to adapt to, select, and shape environments in the pursuit of personally valued goals and success in life. We briefly outline our conceptualization of expertise; then we describe the fundamental role that practical intelligence and tacit knowledge are theorized to play in expert performance. We then describe the scientific exploration of practical intelligence and tacit knowledge – their nature, measurement, and relation to expertise. Finally, we discuss a variety of approaches used to enhance practical intelligence and tacit knowledge and suggest some directions for future research.

What Is Expertise? A Prototype View

The most common psychological approach to defining expertise is to rely on an empirical definition based on individual differences. That is, an expert is defined as someone whose level of performance exceeds that of most others.' For example, Ericsson and Smith (1993) observed that some individuals stand apart from the majority. These scholars view the central goal of the study of expertise as finding out what distinguishes these outstanding individuals from the less outstanding in some domain of activity. Approximately thirty years of research, explicitly devoted to studying the cognitive basis of expertise, has produced a rich and varied source of perspectives for conceptualizing such distinguishing

characteristics (Sternberg, 1994; see also Feltovich, Prietula, & Ericsson, Chapter 4). Among the characteristics explored are general information-processing capabilities, such as strategizing and problem solving, the nature, quantity, and organization of expert knowledge (e.g., Chase & Simon, 1973; Larkin, McDermott, Simon, & Simon, 1980), and, more recently, cognitive complexity (Day & Lance, 2005).

However, definitions of expertise based on individual differences preclude the recognition of expertise demonstrated by the majority of individuals when they succeed in their everyday lives. Another perspective on expertise, the triarchic perspective (Sternberg, 1988, 1997), takes a broader, developmental approach, and posits that success in life is determined by one's analytical, creative, and practical abilities, which improve with practice and experience. The value of the triarchic perspective to the broader, psychological study of expertise is that it provides an opportunity to rethink fundamental issues including what is an appropriate definition of expertise (see also Evetts, Mieg, & Felt, Chapter 7).

A prototype view of expertise represents an integration of all these perspectives, and others as well (Sternberg, 1994; Chapter 7 of this volume). Specifically, the prototype view of expertise maintains that expertise is relatively domain specific and that the attributes of experts may be specific to a time and place, Chapter 4. This view maintains the importance of domain-general information-processing capabilities, such as problem solving, while recognizing that expertise and its requisite knowledge, skills, and abilities are defined quite differently, depending on the environment in which people develop and express their expertise. Importantly, the prototype view of expertise recognizes the diversity of skills that can lead to successful performance, and that expertise can be thought to exist in degrees rather than in an all-or-none fashion.

Conceptualizing expertise as a domain-specific prototype – a confluence of general information-processing capabilities, knowledge depth and organization, and environmental opportunity – requires an understanding of how general psychological mechanisms interact with acquired knowledge and situational constraints to produce expertise in a given domain. The theory of practical intelligence and tacit knowledge (Sternberg, 1988, 1997; Wagner & Sternberg, 1985) explicitly addresses the interchange between information-processing capability and experience in particular environmental contexts, making it an important source of insight into expertise. Specifically, the theory posits that the development of practically intelligent behavior, a critical aspect of success in everyday life, occurs through a cycle of inquiry, knowing, and action, that is, a cycle of engaging the environment, acquiring tacit knowledge, and performing in a practically intelligent manner.

What Is Tacit Knowledge?

The word "tacit" is used to characterize exchanges that are carried out without the use of words or speech, and to describe shared arrangements that have arisen without explicit agreement or discussion (*Oxford American Dictionary*, 2001). Tacit knowing therefore represents a person-environment exchange that is not articulated and that arises without explicit attempt to link environmental stimulation to phenomenological experience. Although the idea that people's actions are subject to unconscious influences dates back to Sigmund Freud in the late 1800s, scientist and philosopher of science Michael Polanyi (1958, 1966) was among the first to discuss formally the concept of tacit knowledge, noting its influence on perception and scientific thinking.

Specifically, Polanyi (1966) argued that "we can know more than we can tell" (p. 4) and that tacit knowledge underlies a wide range of skills, from tool use to application of the scientific method. Polanyi (1958, 1966) claimed that when humans use a tool (e.g., a hammer), for example, they are unaware of how the sensations the tool is producing on their palm (i.e., their grip) correspond to the action of the tool (e.g., the direction and velocity of the striking surface). Such knowledge remains tacit as people solely attend instead to the actions of the tool. In effect, the tool becomes an extension of the person, such that the person cannot articulate how she uses the tool any more than she can articulate how she uses her own hand. Polanyi (1958) also emphasized the experiential nature of tacit knowledge – that it must be passed on by example and practice, often implicitly.

Since Polanyi's work, scholars from domains as diverse as linguistics (Dahl, 2000), cognitive psychology (Reber, 1989; Reber & Lewis, 1977), differential psychology (Wagner & Sternberg, 1985), and organizational management (Nonaka & Takeuchi, 1995) have independently worked toward understanding the nature and acquisition of tacit knowledge. These concepts have proven to be useful, if sometimes controversial (see, e.g., Gottfredson, 2003; Stadler & Roediger, 1998), for understanding how people accomplish much of what they do. This chapter will focus primarily on the work of psychologists Robert J. Sternberg and Richard K. Wagner and their colleagues, who have explored extensively the nature, measurement, and acquisition of tacit knowledge as it relates specifically to individual differences in practically intelligent behavior and expertise.

Wagner and Sternberg (1985) defined tacit knowledge as "knowledge that usually is not openly expressed or stated . . . is not directly taught or spoken about, in contrast to knowledge directly taught in classrooms" (pp. 438–439), with the qualification that "we do not wish to imply that this knowledge is inaccessible to conscious awareness, unspeakable, or unteachable, but merely that it is not taught directly to most of us" (p. 439). Sternberg and his colleagues have also emphasized that tacit knowledge is action oriented and procedural in nature, essentially a complex set of condition-action statements (see, e.g., Sternberg, Forsythe, Hedlund et al., 2000). Wagner and Sternberg (1985) have presented tacit knowledge as an enabler of practically intelligent behavior, which, in turn, is believed to be a critical aspect of expertise.

What Is Practical Intelligence?

Practical intelligence is defined as the ability to acquire tacit knowledge from everyday experience and to apply this knowledge to handling everyday practical problems in which the information necessary to determine a solution strategy is often incomplete (see, e.g., Sternberg, Forsythe, Hedlund et al., 2000). Practical intelligence is a component of Sternberg's (1988, 1997) wide-ranging triarchic theory of successful intelligence, which posits three distinct aspects of human intelligence: analytical, creative, and practical. Following Neisser's (1976) distinction between academic and naturalistic intelligence, Wagner and Sternberg (1985) put forth practical intelligence and domain-specific tacit knowledge as a partial explanation for the less-than-perfect correlation between tests of general, or academic, intelligence and measures of occupational performance or other everyday, practical endeavors. This view does not discount the importance of so-called "general ability." Rather, it emphasizes that general ability is an important part of a story, but not the whole story, of the nature of abilities (see also Horn & Masunaga, Chapter 34).

The tight coupling of practical intelligence and tacit knowledge reflects Sternberg's (1998) conceptualization of human ability as a form of developing expertise in that demonstrated ability is viewed as improving with experience and knowledge. Sternberg (1988) describes the acquisition of tacit knowledge and consequent enhancement of practical intelligence as driven by knowledge-acquisition components. Knowledge-acquisition components characterize the executive cognitive processes involved in the often unconscious manipulation of information found in novel situations in order to learn from experience (Sternberg, 1988). These three cognitive processes are (a) selective encoding, (b) selective combination, and (c) selective comparison. *Selective encoding* is the selection of information from the environment that is relevant to understanding the current situation or to solving the problem at hand. *Selective combination* is the integration of multiple pieces of selectively encoded information into a unified whole that creates a meaningful pattern and, eventually, a knowledge structure. *Selective comparison* is the comparison of newly formed patterns of information or knowledge structures to previously formed knowledge structures. Accurate selective encoding, selective combination, and selective comparison results in an increased body of tacit knowledge and, consequently, more practically intelligent behavior (see Sternberg, 1988).

Practical Intelligence, Tacit Knowledge, and Other Constructs

Of critical importance to the existence of a psychological construct is its distinctiveness from other, related constructs. Constructs potentially overlapping with practical intelligence include general (or fluid) intelligence, crystallized intelligence, and such non-ability constructs as personality and motivation (Jensen, 1993; Horn & Masunaga, Chapter 34). Constructs potentially overlapping with tacit knowledge include job knowledge (Schmidt & Hunter, 1993) and procedural knowledge (Hedlund, Forsythe, Horvath, Williams, Snook, & Sternberg, 2003). We briefly address the theoretical distinction between practical intelligence and tacit knowledge and each of these constructs.

General Intelligence

Although the exact nature of general intelligence is yet unknown, it is commonly defined as the highly general capability to process information and is believed to have specific neurological substrates (see, e.g., Duncan, Seitz, Kolodny et al., 2000). To the extent that neurological functioning undergirds all mental activity, practical intelligence should show some relation to general intelligence (See also, Hill & Schneider, Chapter 37). Practical intelligence is theoretically distinct from general intelligence, however, in that general intelligence is viewed as a relatively stable characteristic of individuals, whereas practical intelligence is viewed as developing with effort and experience (Sternberg, 1998). Moreover, the development of practical intelligence – through the acquisition of tacit knowledge – occurs via an interaction between an individual's existing level of competency and an environmental context. One's level of general intelligence is believed to exist largely independently of one's knowledge and experience.

Crystallized Intelligence

Crystallized intelligence has been defined as the outcome of "experiential-educative-acculturation influences" (Horn & Cattell, 1966, p. 254) on one's biological capacity. Tests of crystallized intelligence commonly assess vocabulary, reading comprehension, and other verbal skills. Practical intelligence resembles crystallized intelligence through their shared dependence on experience and similar developmental aspects. In contrast to crystallized intelligence, however, practical intelligence is applied to identifying and solving problems that often do not have one correct solution strategy or clearly right answer.

Personality and Motivation

Because practical intelligence is theorized to develop through effortful experience, it can be argued that acquiring tacit knowledge and improving practical intelligence are in part functions of non-ability constructs relating to performance, such as personality and motivation. With some probing, this argument can be made for the other psychological constructs listed above, including general intelligence as it is typically measured. Practical intelligence is theorized to be distinct from personality and motivation because it characterizes a person's use of his experiences for learning and performance and not, in particular, his drive to succeed or typical pattern of responding to external events.

Job Knowledge

Job knowledge typically is conceptualized as declarative knowledge, such as of facts and concepts required for successful job performance, and commonly is taught explicitly (e.g., Hunter, 1983; Ree, Caretta, & Teachout, 1995). However, occupational expertise requires more than implementation of facts and concepts learned in formal training, such that employees can solve novel problems and think proactively (see, e.g., DuBois & Shalin, 1995). Tacit knowledge specific to particular job domains, in contrast, is not explicitly taught, but is learned on the job. It facilitates occupational expertise by bridging the gap between formal training and operational experience (see, e.g., Sternberg & Horvath, 1999). Tacit knowledge can therefore be viewed as job-related knowledge, to the extent that it facilitates job performance (DuBois & Shalin, 1995); but tacit knowledge need not be job related (Sternberg & the Rainbow Project Collaborators, 2005).

Procedural Knowledge

In contrast to declarative knowledge of facts and concepts, procedural knowledge is knowledge of how to execute some task (Anderson, 1982). Procedural knowledge typically is viewed as the end state of a learning process for tasks that can be automatized with practice, such as typing and other psychomotor skills (Ackerman, 1988; Anderson, 1982; Fitts & Posner, 1967). Like procedural knowledge, tacit knowledge is action oriented, gained from experience, applied unconsciously, and often difficult to verbalize. However, tacit knowledge is not viewed as an automatic response produced from repeated exposures to the same patterns of stimuli. Rather, it is viewed as an adaptive intellectual resource stemming from the active interaction between individuals and their dynamic environment.

Of course, making compelling distinctions between practical intelligence and tacit knowledge and other psychological constructs requires empirical evidence, which, in turn, requires valid measurement. Below we describe the varied efforts to measure practical intelligence and tacit knowledge that have been made both by Sternberg and his colleagues and other independent researchers.

Measurement of Practical Intelligence and Tacit Knowledge

In the interest of triangulating on the construct of practical intelligence via converging operations (Garner, Hake, & Eriksen, 1956; Sternberg, 2001), Sternberg and his colleagues have developed diverse methods of assessing practical problem solving and tacit knowledge. These methods range from more traditional testing formats, featuring multiple-choice questions, to in-depth case-study scenarios requiring short essay-like responses. They can be administered using paper-and-pencil or computerized materials. The domain areas of expertise covered by these assessments range from quite specific, including business management (Wagner & Sternberg, 1991), sales (Wagner & Sternberg, 1989), and military leadership (Hedlund, Horvath, Forsythe et al., 1998), to more general, including everyday living and entry-level business skills (Sternberg & the Rainbow Project Collaborators, 2004). Scholars working independently of Sternberg and his colleagues, but with a shared interest in tacit knowledge and successful performance, have developed their own assessments of tacit knowledge in areas as diverse as academia (Somech & Bogler, 1999), auditing (Tan & Libby, 1997), and even driving (Legree, Heffner, Psotka, Martin, & Medsker, 2003). Below we describe the general formats of the different methods of assessment used to measure practical intelligence and tacit knowledge.

Traditional Test Formats

Assessments of practical intelligence featuring a traditional test design (i.e., multiple-choice questions, essays) are relatively few in number, but can be found on the various forms of the Sternberg Triarchic Abilities Test (STAT; Sternberg, 1991; Sternberg, Castejón, Prieto, Hautamäki, & Grigorenko, 2001; Sternberg & the Rainbow Project Collaborators, 2005). The STAT is designed to measure the three major abilities – creative, analytical, and practical – posited by Sternberg's triarchic theory of successful intelligence (Sternberg, 1988, 1997). Each of the three major-ability subscales is further divided into three parts defined by content: quantitative, verbal, and figural. Therefore, assessment of practical intelligence using the STAT involves three different tests of practical thinking: practical-quantitative, practical-verbal, and practical-figural. Scores on these tests are the number of problems correctly answered.

Practical-Quantitative problems require examinees to use mathematical reasoning that is situated in an everyday context, such as manipulating a recipe, in order to select correct answers from four alternatives. In practical-verbal problems, the examinee must read a short description of an everyday problem typical in the life of an adolescent and choose the best solution to the problem among four alternatives. Practical-Figural problems require examinees to use a map to select from four alternatives the optimal route to get from one place to another. A practical essay sometimes is featured on the STAT and requires examinees to state a problem in their life and present three practical solutions for solving it.

Tacit-Knowledge Inventories

Tacit-knowledge inventories are perhaps the most common method for assessing tacit knowledge. Tacit-knowledge inventories use a situational-judgment testing format (McDaniel & Nguyen, 2001), typically to assess highly domain-specific tacit knowledge. Examinees taking a tacit-knowledge inventory are presented with a series of brief vignettes, each of which depicts a practical problem that must be solved, and provides a set of solution alternatives. Examinees must rate each of the solution alternatives for its perceived effectiveness or quality using a Likert scale [usually a scale of 1 (very bad) to 7 (very good), but sometimes a scale of 1 (very bad) to 9 (very good)]. Figure 35.1 depicts an example vignette from the Tacit-Knowledge Inventory for Managers (Wagner & Sternberg, 1991). Scores on tacit-knowledge inventories are derived using a variety of means (see Sternberg, Forsythe,

You and a coworker jointly are responsible for completing a report on a new product by the end of the week. You are uneasy about this assignment because he has a reputation for not meeting deadlines. The problem does not appear to be lack of effort. Rather, he seems to lack certain organizational skills necessary to meet a deadline and also is quite a perfectionist. As a result, too much time is wasted coming up with the "perfect" idea, project, or report. Your goal is to produce the best possible report by the deadline at the end of the week. Rate the quality of the following strategies for

meeting your goal on a 1- to 7-point scale.

—Divide the work to be done in half and tell him that if he does not complete his part, you obviously will have to let your immediate superior know it was not our fault.
—Politely tell him to be less of a perfectionist.
—Set deadlines for completing each part of the report and accept what you have accomplished at each deadline as the final part of that report.
—Ask your superior to check up on your progress on a daily basis (after explaining why).
—Praise your coworker verbally for completion of parts of the assignment.
—Get angry with him at the first sign of getting behind schedule.
—As soon as he begins to fall behind, take responsibility for doing the report yourself, if need be, to meet the deadline.
—Point out firmly, but politely, how he is holding up the report.
—Avoid putting any pressure on him because it will just make him fall even more behind.
—Offer to buy him dinner at the end of the week if you both meet the deadline.
—Ignore his organizational problem so you don't give attention to maladaptive behavior.

Figure 35.1. Example TKIM Vignette

Hedlund et al., 2000), each of which represents the degree to which an individual's ratings correspond to (or deviate from) the average ratings of some comparison sample, usually a group of experts.

Case-Study Scenarios

Case-study scenarios provide detailed, in-depth information about a practical problem situation as it develops over time, followed by a set of open-ended questions designed to assess knowledge-acquisition components and practical problem-solving skills, two important aspects of behaving in a practically intelligent way (Sternberg, 1988). This method of assessing tacit knowledge draws from approaches commonly used in managerial assessment and education, including in-basket tests, which require prioritizing and responding to job relevant materials (e.g., memos and reports) in a limited amount of time, and case studies, which involve critiquing and/or solving a detailed case description. Case-study scenarios consist of a brief summary of a situation, followed by a detailed description of the particulars as they unfold over the near term. Supporting documents such as memos, transcriptions of verbal/e-mail exchanges, relevant reports, and other related materials are also provided. Though fictitious, case-study scenarios are designed to represent realistically practical problems

Overview

You are 2nd LT Pete Quandry and have recently taken over an infantry platoon with 30 soldiers and 4 Bradleys. Because you have just come on board as a PL (*Platoon Leader*), you need to learn a lot about weapon systems and procedures. The former PL left nothing on paper to help you get oriented...

The platoon is currently in a state of flux because PSG Joe Forte just left. SSG Ed Newell, a squad leader, has been promoted from among his peers without a change in rank to replace him... Apparently, your company commander CPT Powers was very dissatisfied with the previous PL but had a lot of respect for the former PSG because he kept the soldiers in line...

He (CPT Powers) clearly has high expectations of you and the platoon and has already given you responsibility for a new tactical mission...

Background

Apparently, CPT Powers found it so frustrating to work with the former PL that he often communicated directly with PSG Forte. PSG Forte had the reputation for being highly demanding and directive with the platoon. See attachment 1...

The Platoon has a mix of experienced and newly enlisted soldiers. Several were in combat together. Attachment 2 is an early interaction with PSG Newell about the Platoon.

You have some serious concern about platoon performance because during a recent FTX, you observed that the soldiers piled out of the vehicles and lit cigarettes rather than setting up a secure perimeter as their battle drill dictated...

One week before the Mission

On Monday morning this week you discover that one of the leader books was not up to date in the garrison...

On Tuesday, there was an accident with one of the Bradleys in a training exercise...

This morning (Wednesday) you meet with PSG Newell to discuss details of the upcoming mission and your concerns about platoon performance...

You only have a few days left to motivate your troops and prepare for the mission.

Figure 35.2. Abridged Military Leadership Case-Study Scenario

that might be encountered in a particular domain. Figure 35.2 presents an abridged example of a case-study scenario used to measure tacit knowledge for military leadership.

Case-study scenarios – derived from interviews with subject-matter experts – simulate the complexity of actual problem situations by including multiple issues, previous actions taken, and some relevant information needed to understand and solve a complex problem. Relative to tacit-knowledge inventories, case-study scenarios more closely simulate actual problem solving, and therefore target a greater number of the general cognitive mechanisms involved

in practically intelligent behavior. However, case-study scenarios take more time to complete than tacit-knowledge inventories, and scoring methods are somewhat more subjective and time consuming.

Research Findings on Practical Intelligence and Tacit Knowledge

The general results from exploring the constructs of practical intelligence, tacit knowledge, and their measurement have indicated that practical intelligence does not overlap substantially with general intelligence, crystallized intelligence, or personality. Importantly, the cause for this lack of overlap does not appear to be differences in the amount of domain-specific knowledge featured on the assessments of each construct; tacit knowledge also does not overlap substantially with technical job knowledge. Practical intelligence and tacit knowledge *do* show a noteworthy relation to everyday expertise in varied settings and is revealed using diverse performance criteria.

Practical Intelligence, Tacit Knowledge, and Other Psychological Constructs

Several studies have indicated the distinctiveness of practical intelligence and tacit knowledge from other psychological constructs. For example, scores on tacit-knowledge inventories show relatively weak correlation with measures of general and crystallized intelligence, typically below .20[1] (Cianciolo, Antonakis & Sternberg, 2004; Legree et al., 2003; Tan & Libby, 1997; Wagner, 1987; Wagner & Sternberg, 1985, 1990; though see Colonia-Willner, 1998, for slightly higher correlations), indicating the partial but incomplete overlap of these constructs. In one study of rural Kenyan children (ages 12–15), scores on a tacit-knowledge inventory for natural herbal medicines correlated negatively with tests of both general and crystallized intelligence ($r = -.16$ and $-.31$, respectively), reflecting the conflicting priorities of rural life and academic achievement in some African villages (Sternberg, Nokes, Geissler et al., 2001). Tacit knowledge has also been shown to be largely unrelated to several aspects of personality, including sociability, social presence, self-control, and achievement via conformity ($r = .14$, .29, .19, and $-.05$, respectively; Wagner & Sternberg, 1990).

The lack of relationship between scores on tacit-knowledge inventories and measures of intelligence or personality do not appear to be due to a heavy reliance on domain-specific knowledge in the tacit-knowledge inventories. Tan and Libby

(1997) found a correlation of .22 between technical knowledge for auditing and scores on an auditing tacit-knowledge inventory, suggesting that although tacit knowledge is an aspect of job knowledge, the two constructs are clearly not the same thing. Furthermore, using inventories of relatively domain-general tacit knowledge (e.g., everyday living, entry-level business), Cianciolo, Grigorenko, Jarvin, Gil, Drebot, and Sternberg (in press) still found correlations below .20 with tests of intelligence (.14–.20 with tests of fluid intelligence and .03–.19 with tests of crystallized intelligence). In addition, Cianciolo et al. (in press) found that a higher-order latent factor (practical intelligence), marked by the relatively domain-general tacit-knowledge inventories, correlated .34 with fluid intelligence and .20 with crystallized intelligence.

Tacit Knowledge and Expertise

In research conducted by multiple scholars, tacit knowledge has shown a notable relationship to many diverse demonstrations of expertise. That is, individuals scoring better on measures of tacit knowledge (usually tacit-knowledge inventories) have tended to show higher levels of performance, as measured by various criteria, and vice versa.

For example, Wagner (1987) administered a tacit knowledge for psychology inventory to a sample of ninety college psychology professors and found a correlation of .44 between scores on the inventory and the number of citations reported in the *Social Sciences Citation Index* in 1982 and 1983. Tacit knowledge was greater in psychology departments ranked higher for the scholarly quality of their faculty; the correlation between tacit knowledge and ratings of faculty quality was .48.

Wagner (1987) also found that tacit knowledge increased with level of professional development. That is, he found a significant linear trend ($p < .001$) in scores on the tacit-knowledge inventory with the highest scores (indicating greatest deviation from experts) earned by undergraduate students, intermediate scores earned by graduate students, and lowest scores earned by faculty. Wagner (1987) found this same significant linear trend in a sample of managers, business students, and undergraduates.

Wagner and Sternberg (1985, 1990) further have shown that tacit knowledge plays an important role in business management. In one study, Wagner and Sternberg (1985) administered an early version of the Tacit-Knowledge Inventory for Managers (TKIM, Wagner & Sternberg, 1991) to fifty-four business managers and found that scores on the inventory correlated .46 with salary and .34 with the level of the company where the participating manager was employed (i.e., whether the company was among the top companies in the Fortune 500 list). Wagner and Sternberg (1985) also found that in a sample of twenty-nine bank managers, scores on the tacit-knowledge inventory correlated notably with a variety of indicators of management success. Specifically, they found that tacit knowledge correlated .48 with the percentage of salary increases, .56 with ratings of success in generating new business, .29 with ratings of personnel management capability, and .39 with ratings of ability to implement company policy. In a later study of forty-five business managers taking part in a leadership-development program, Wagner and Sternberg (1990) examined the correlation between scores on the TKIM and performance ratings on two management simulations conducted as part of the program. The correlation between TKIM scores and performance ratings was .61, with the TKIM outpredicting several measures of general cognitive ability and personality.

Tan and Libby (1997) have also explored the relationship between tacit knowledge and expertise in a business setting, but with a special focus on financial auditors. They studied 100 auditors at the ranks of staff, senior, manager, and partner employed by the Singapore office of a major accounting firm. A tacit-knowledge inventory for auditing based on the TKIM (Wagner & Sternberg, 1991), but specialized for audi-

tors, was administered to all four ranks of auditor. The solution-alternative quality ratings of the staff, senior, and manager employees were then compared to those of the partners, who served as the expert criterion. As predicted, Tan and Libby found that level of tacit knowledge for auditing distinguished top and bottom performers at the higher rank of manager ($t = 1.72, p = .05$), but not at the lower ranks of senior ($t = 0.82, p = .21$) and staff ($t = 0.23, p = .41$). The opposite pattern was found for technical knowledge. Tacit knowledge became more important for success as the emphasis of job demands shifted away from the application of technical skills to the handling of complex practical problems, such as competing goals and career management (Tan & Libby, 1997; see also Colonia-Willner, 1998).

Exploring military applications, Hedlund, Forsythe, Horvath, Williams, Snook, and Sternberg (2003) studied the tacit knowledge for military leadership of 562 commissioned Army officers at the platoon, company, and battalion levels of command. Officers at each level of command filled out a Tacit Knowledge for Military Leadership inventory (TKML; Hedlund et al., 1998) relevant to their particular level of command. In addition, supervisors, peers, and subordinates rated participating officers on their leadership effectiveness. Hedlund et al. (2003) found that tacit knowledge was independent of subordinate ratings at both the company and battalion levels of command (subordinates did not rate platoon leaders), and of peer ratings at the platoon and battalion levels of command. However, significant correlations between tacit knowledge and supervisor ratings were found at the platoon and battalion levels of command, with an especially notable correlation at the battalion level ($r = .48$). Mirroring Tan and Libby's (1997) findings, lower correlations were found between tacit knowledge and supervisor ratings at the level of platoon leader (.17) and company commander (.05).

Legree et al. (2003) worked with 551 enlisted Army personnel, studying the relationship between tacit knowledge for safe driving and accident history. Legree et al.'s Safe Speed Knowledge Test featured fourteen "scenarios" that briefly depicted various combinations of driving conditions, including weather (e.g., snow, clear, light rain), traffic (heavy, light), or emotional states (angry, stressed), among others. Participants estimated how much they would adjust their speed (in one mph increments) in each scenario, ranging from no adjustment to slowing down twenty miles per hour. Performance scores on the Safe Speed Knowledge Test were derived by calculating the absolute difference between an individual's speed adjustments and the average speed adjustments of the experimental sample (see Legree, 1995), then reflecting this difference such that larger scores indicated greater tacit knowledge. Tacit-knowledge scores showed a strong relationship to driver at-fault crash rates. Specifically, individuals scoring within one standard deviation of the mean distance score were 2.3 times more likely to be involved in a crash as individuals scoring more than one standard deviation above the mean. Individuals scoring more than one standard deviation below the mean distance score were five times more likely to be involved in a crash.

Enhancing Expertise through Development of Practical Intelligence and Tacit Knowledge

Given that practical intelligence, through tacit-knowledge acquisition and improved problem-solving skills, is believed to be developable (Sternberg, 1998), research has also been devoted to exploring methods for making this development happen. Wagner and Sternberg (1990) have noted two ways in which one's body of tacit knowledge can be enhanced: (1) making tacit knowledge explicit and sharing it, and (2) improving people's ability to engage their environments and learn from experience. Substantial research and program development have also been devoted to improving people's practical problem-solving skills, some of

which has been conducted by Sternberg and his colleagues. We summarize below these diverse research and development efforts.

Making Tacit Knowledge Explicit: Communities of Practice

Methods to make tacit knowledge explicit are at the heart of a number of accepted practices recognized for their potential benefit to personal and professional development. These practices include psychotherapy, which involves uncovering tacit knowledge that may be maladaptive, and mentoring, which involves the articulation of why a particular action should be taken at a particular time. Although some may reject the notion that tacit knowledge can be made explicit, its potential to contribute to the development of expertise has been explored and advocated by a number of scholars from a variety of theoretical perspectives (Argyris, 1993; Brown & Duguid, 1991; Schön, 1983 Sternberg, Forsythe, Hedlund et al., 2000; Wenger, 1998). The central belief shared by these scholars, and others, is that because most of the relevant know-how that distinguishes different levels of expertise is acquired through experience, methods that stimulate the process of thinking about what one is doing and why, and talking about it with others, will facilitate the development of expertise.

Communities of practice, defined as groups of people who informally come together to exchange knowledge and experience in a shared domain of interest, have been increasingly recognized as an effective mechanism to develop expertise through sharing tacit knowledge (Gerardi, Nicolini, & Odella, 1998; Lesser & Storck, 2001; Nonaka & Takeuchi, 1995; Wenger, 2000; Wenger & Snyder, 2000). They are distinguished from workgroups and teams in that the nature of membership is self-selection versus assignment by an organizational authority, and the purpose of membership is to develop capability, and build on and exchange knowledge rather than accomplish a more specific task or assignment.

Examples of professional or trade associations akin to communities of practice can be found throughout human history, for example, in the artisan guilds in the Middle Ages (Lave & Wenger, 1991; see also Amirault and Branson, Chapter 5). What distinguishes them today is that they are not only common among independent practitioners but also are being formed in the context of large organizations. Enabled by advances in information technology, modern communities of practice range in format from regularly scheduled meetings to listservs to online discussion forums. Though typically communities of practice are self-organizing, increasingly, organizations are sponsoring their development to cultivate needed capabilities and are enjoying substantial return on investment, accomplished through increased productivity and innovation (Crager & Lemons, 2003). Below we describe some contemporary examples of communities of practice, with particular attention to how they facilitate making tacit knowledge explicit and sharing it.

ARMY STRUCTURED PROFESSIONAL FORUMS

Changes in the global political environment require that the Army adapt quickly to a broader range of missions, from warfighting to peacekeeping, while supported by state-of-the-art information technology. In response to this need, the Army is sponsoring the development of a web-enabled knowledge-sharing system called the Battle Command Knowledge System to provide Army leaders and soldiers with specific, relevant knowledge and information to prepare them to rapidly develop expertise. Structured professional forums – communities of practice more broadly designed to be resources for professional self-development and community growth – are a critical component of this knowledge system (Kilner, 2002).

One such structured professional forum, *CompanyCommand.mil* (see Dixon, Allen, Burgess, Kilner, & Schweitzer, 2005), was initially developed as a volunteer effort by two Army captains to create a website where company commanders could informally share their knowledge. Now formally recognized and endorsed by senior Army leadership, *CompanyCommand.mil* is defined as an "ongoing professional conversation about leading soldiers and building combat-ready units," where former and experienced company commanders share leadership-related stories, ideas, and tools with current and future commanders. In addition, commanders with a question or problem invite the advice of those who may have knowledge on the topic. When participants receive feedback that challenges their thinking, they are encouraged to reflect on their underlying assumptions and ultimately assess their thinking, which promotes the development of practical problem-solving ability (Cianciolo, et al. 2004).

CIVILIAN COMMUNITIES OF PRACTICE

Sponsorship and support for communities of practice can also be found in a wide range of other private and public sector organizations (Crager & Lemons, 2003; Lesser & Storck, 2001). Although the type of organization and the particular area of expertise may differ, these communities of practice share the same objective – to create knowledge and stimulate innovation by sharing experience and expertise across similar projects or products. For example, at Hewlett-Packard, product-delivery consultants across the country hold monthly teleconferences to solve problems they share in connection with a particular software product (Wenger & Snyder, 2000). Pepperdine University Educational Technology has developed a community of practice to capture and transfer knowledge generated by participants engaged in the EdTech Doctoral program using group memory software. Although its design is derived from the perspective of social-learning theory, the importance of capturing and transferring tacit knowledge is emphasized (Adams & Freeman, 2000).

RESEARCH ON COMMUNITIES OF PRACTICE

Although the financial value of communities of practice to organizations has been demonstrated (Crager & Lemons, 2003), there has been relatively little investigation into how both individual- and organizational-level expertise develop from sharing tacit knowledge (though see Lesser & Storck, 2001). A recent investigation of the impact of Army structured professional forums on individual leader competency and professionalism, unit effectiveness, and organizational performance has begun to illuminate metrics and assessment methods for capturing expertise as it relates to the intellectual and social capital developed through activity in an online discussion forum (Cianciolo, Heiden, Prevou, & Psotka, 2005). This study represents only the beginning of the research that must be conducted to understand how the organization and its individuals leverage tacit knowledge to improve performance.

Facilitating Tacit-Knowledge Acquisition

Facilitating tacit-knowledge acquisition is a more indirect approach to enhancing one's body of tacit knowledge than is sharing explicit tacit knowledge (see also, Hoffman & Lintern, Chapter 12). However, this indirect approach can be expected to have more lasting effects on one's practical intelligence. Explicit tacit knowledge, shared in communities of practice, eventually becomes outdated, sometimes very rapidly, as the mores of cultures shift (e.g., by becoming multiethnic) or as the operational environment changes (e.g., by introducing new technological capability). Learning how to acquire tacit knowledge, however, never becomes outdated.

Approaches to facilitating tacit-knowledge acquisition target the three cognitive processes thought to underlie knowledge-acquisition: selective encoding, selective combination, and selective comparison (Sternberg, 1988). Specifically, instruction is designed to draw students' attention to how the relevant information in the environment or from previous experience can be selected to guide decision making and problem solving, how relevant information can be combined to form patterns meaningful to under-standing the problem at hand, and how the knowledge acquired from past experience can be compared to new knowledge to inform decisions and action. It is believed that as students reflect on how they are using information from the environment and from experience to solve problems, they will come to value their experiences as opportunities for learning (Cianciolo et al., 2004).

In one study using this approach, Sternberg, Wagner, and Okagaki (1993) worked with five groups of fifteen college students and explored how different instructional conditions affected the difference in tacit-knowledge inventory scores before and after intervention. One group of students served as a control in the experiment, receiving no intervention, and each of the three experimental groups received instruction on how to use one of the three knowledge-acquisition components while completing a tacit-knowledge-acquisition task. The fifth group of students served as a second control, completing the knowledge-acquisition task, but without an instructional intervention.

The knowledge-acquisition task required participants to play the role of a personnel manager and to evaluate three fictional job candidates for sales positions, opting to hire none, one, two, or three of the candidates. On the basis of three fictional interview transcripts and a description of the hiring company, participants were asked to evaluate the candidates for their ability to manage themselves, to handle the tasks and problems that arise in sales positions, and to handle business relationships with customers, peers, and superiors. To facilitate selective encoding, participants in the first experimental group were cued with relevant information during the knowledge-acquisition task and were provided with relevant rules-of-thumb. To facilitate selective combination, participants in the second experimental group were also cued with relevant information and provided with rules-of-thumb, but were additionally provided with a structured note-taking sheet to help link the information to evaluation criteria. Participants in the third experimental group were also cued with relevant information and provided with rules-of-thumb, but to facilitate selective comparison participants in this group also received an evaluation that had been completed by a "predecessor" in the company such that they could benefit from someone else's experience.

Sternberg et al. (1993) found that participants in the two control groups showed less gain from pre-test to post-test (performance on a tacit-knowledge inventory for sales) than the experimental groups (average gain for control groups was 5.6; for experimental groups it was 15.27). Further, the experimental groups who received instruction on selective encoding and selective combination showed notably greater gain than the experimental group who received instruction on selective comparison (16.8, 19.7, and 9.3, respectively). The results from this brief intervention indicate that efforts to improve tacit-knowledge acquisition and, by extension, practical intelligence, can be successful.

The method of this research is not altogether isolated from other efforts to stimulate people's intellectual curiosity and critical thinking (see also Zimmerman, Chapter 39). Its theoretical heritage can be traced to philosopher John Dewey (1933), who believed that reflective thought – the critical analysis of one's ideas and behaviors – was an important aspect of good thinking skills and effective problem solving. Dewey's work has influenced the thinking of numerous philosophers (e.g., Ennis, 1987; Lipman, 1993) and psychologists (e.g., Andrade & Perkins, 1998; Bransford, Sherwood, Vye, & Rieser, 1986; Nickerson, 1989) who have sought to understand and enhance problem-solving and experience-based learning. These scholars have used a wide range of methods to facilitate inquisitiveness and experience-based learning – from using stories to engage children in the philosophical analysis of problems (Lipman, 1993) to training the particular cognitive processes involved in insight and learning from context (Davidson & Sternberg, 1984; Sternberg, 1987) to exploring complex problems by discussing multiple points of view (Paul, 1987).

Perkins and his colleagues (Andrade & Perkins, 1998; Grotzer & Perkins, 2000) have recently explored an approach called Cognitive Reorganization, which is designed to teach school children to think more deeply about problems before solving them, to monitor their thinking more closely, to be more open, careful, and organized about their thinking, to draw on multiple resources for thinking, and to make better connections between past, present, and future thinking experiences. Because of difficulties in conducting and evaluating programs designed to teach thinking skills (see Grotzer & Perkins, 2000), however, a definitive conclusion has not yet been reached whether these programs have lasting effects. In the evaluation studies that have been conducted, the results have been mixed but generally positive, suggesting that facilitating inquisitiveness and critical thinking in an attempt to enhance intelligent behavior is not a misguided endeavor (Bransford et al., 1986).

Developing Practical Intelligence

Another attempt to improve practical intelligence, Practical Intelligence for School (PIFS; Williams, Blythe, White, Li, Sternberg, & Gardner, 1996; Williams, Blythe, White, Li, Gardner, & Sternberg, 2002), targeted practical thinking skills directly in an effort to boost school achievement. Based on Sternberg's (1988, 1997) triarchic theory of successful intelligence and Gardner's (1983, 1999) theory of multiple intelligences, PIFS was a comprehensive theory-based program designed to enhance middle-school students' (fifth and sixth graders) scholastic achievement. Middle-school students were a focus in this intervention because differences in practical intelligence for school begin to appear during the middle-school years and at that time set the stage for future differences in school performance.

To develop students' practical thinking skills, the PIFS program was organized around five themes: knowing why, knowing self, knowing differences, knowing process, and revisiting, and targeted four domain areas: reading, writing, homework, and testing. In each of the four domain areas, students participated in a set of lessons that featured exercises to engage practical thinking along the five themes. For example, in the topic of writing, PIFS students are taught to discover why writing is important both in and out of school (knowing why), to recognize their personal strengths and weaknesses in writing (knowing self), to distinguish between different styles and strategies of writing (knowing differences), to understand the role of planning and organization in the writing process (knowing process), and to recognize the importance of revising (revisiting). Stand-alone exercises were applied to homework and testing skills. Students explored, for example, the purposes for homework, their personal homework practices, differences in homework requirements for different classes, and strategies for improving the effectiveness of the homework process and homework quality.

The PIFS program took place over a two-year period and was implemented in both Connecticut and Massachusetts. To maintain an ecologically valid implementation, the PIFS researchers encouraged participating teachers to integrate PIFS instruction into their teaching in a manner that best suited their instructional needs. Thus, PIFS lessons were either infused into ongoing classroom activity or administered as stand-alone instruction. At the end of each year, teachers and researchers evaluated students' practical thinking skills and academic achievement via a set of practical and academic assessments. Performance on these assessments was compared to performance on similar assessments given at the beginning of the year in order to evaluate gains in development. At the end of Year 2, students participating in the PIFS program showed significantly greater gain in scores on practical assessments of reading ($F = 19.37, p < .001$), writing ($F = 25.33, p < .001$), homework ($F = 27.89, p < .001$), and test-taking ($F = 10.36, p < .01$) and on academic assessments of reading ($F = 13.63, p < .001$), writing ($F = 16.49, p < .001$), and testing ($F = 5.71, p < .05$) than non-PIFS students (Williams et al., 2002). Long-term benefits of the PIFS program have not been assessed.

Future Directions for Practical Intelligence/Tacit Knowledge Research

An extensive amount of research has been committed to exploring the nature, measurement, and predictive validity of practical intelligence and tacit knowledge. Because of the potential practical and theoretical importance of these constructs, they have been investigated by a wide range of scholars including Sternberg and his colleagues but also several independent researchers. There remains, however, much interesting work to be done in order to more fully understand the nature of tacit knowledge and practical intelligence and their development. For example, large-scale investigations of the construct validity and predictive efficacy of practical intelligence and relatively domain-general tacit-knowledge measures within the context of multiple cognitive ability tests and non-ability assessments (e.g., personality inventories) should be conducted.

Another area of interest involves the conceptualization and measurement of tacit knowledge as it is acquired and applied dynamically during decision making and problem solving. Although practical intelligence and tacit knowledge are viewed as modifiable (Sternberg, 1998), most measures of tacit knowledge do not require examinees to work through practical problems as they develop over time and as a result of particular actions. The case-study scenarios recently developed by Sternberg and his colleagues represent a major effort to address this area of interest. However, efforts to capture tacit knowledge as it is acquired and applied in real time also can be informed by theories of social judgment and decision making (Brehmer & Joyce, 1988), whose primary focus includes identifying the environmental conditions that people use as the basis for judgment and action.

Briefly, social judgment theorists attempt to mathematically model the basis of human judgment and action by identifying the environmental cues linked to particular states of the world and how people use these cues to inform their judgments about these states of the world. Conceptualized as the adaptive use of environmental cues in particular situations, expert tacit knowledge can be identified and measured using these sophisticated performance-modeling techniques, which can be embedded into complex, dynamic tasks, such as command and control simulations (see, e.g., Rothrock & Kirlik, 2003).

Identifying experts' tacit knowledge using performance modeling also offers an alternative to relying on traditional methods for eliciting tacit knowledge. To date, the elicitation of tacit knowledge has relied on the verbalized recollections of experts, which provide unreliable information regarding the actual conditions (or environmental cues) that triggered particular actions (Nisbett & Bellows, 1977; Nisbett & Wilson, 1977). Moreover, mathematical modeling of tacit knowledge may provide some insight into what specifically is learned when tacit knowledge is acquired, thus making it easier to make tacit knowledge explicit or to facilitate tacit-knowledge acquisition.

Because much has been discovered regarding the nature and measurement of tacit knowledge, the development of tacit knowledge and practical intelligence is an area particularly ripe for research and is of special interest to leadership-development professionals. In leadership development, there is movement toward embedding tacit knowledge acquisition into the work context through methods that stimulate reflection on experience and action, such as executive coaching and "stretch assignments" (Day, 2000). Methods that facilitate the transfer of tacit knowledge from senior executive to junior manager are also commonly featured in leadership-development planning, including classes taught by senior executives that focus on sharing stories about pivotal leadership experiences and lessons learned. Other methods include mentoring, which provides junior managers an opportunity to observe, interact, and reflect on senior executives in action.

Although the use of various leader-development methods aimed at facilitating tacit-knowledge acquisition in professional development is theoretically compelling, there appears to be limited published empirical research to support claims of their effectiveness. Moreover, it is still unclear which of these methods, if any, actually facilitate the acquisition of tacit knowledge and in turn the development of expertise. In particular, the distinction between cognitive versus social learning processes involved in the development of experience-based learning, as suggested by social learning approaches (Gherardi, Nicolini, & Odella, 1998; Lave & Wenger, 1991), needs to be explored and understood (see also Evetts, Mieg, & Felt, Chapter 7; Mieg, Chapter 41). Research is also needed to test the effectiveness of methods currently in use and the conditions under which they may be effective. One important question that warrants examination is whether distinct methods are required for the development of novices, as compared to journeymen or experts, who may need to "unlearn" or modify outdated tacit knowledge. Another potentially useful area for research is the identification of the individual-differences factors that may influence the effectiveness of one particular method over another.

Conclusion

Although it is a delight to be awed by artistic, athletic, or intellectual excellence, or to be struck by the brilliance of everyday adaptation, the general psychological mechanisms underlying the nature and development expertise need not, indeed do not, remain a mystery. The theory of practical intelligence and tacit knowledge (Sternberg, 1988, 1997; Wagner & Sternberg, 1985) has provided one means for understanding expert performance by illuminating the complex, ever-shifting person-environment interaction that allows for success in everyday life. This approach to understanding expertise complements many of the other approaches discussed in this handbook, by serving as an integration of multiple perspectives and maintaining an inclusive conceptualization of what it means to be an expert. There is yet much work to be done to fully explore tacit knowledge, practical intelligence, and expertise, but this work represents exciting movement forward in the quest to understand a phenomenon that has, in one form or another, inspired us all.

Acknowledgments

Preparation of this chapter was supported by the U.S. Army Research Institute. Although we are grateful to this agency for its support, the ideas expressed in this chapter are solely those of the authors and do not represent any official position or policy on the part of ARI. We wish to thank Dr. Paul Feltovich and the anonymous reviewer whose thoughtful review and helpful comments significantly improved our discussion. Send correspondence to Anna T. Cianciolo, Command Performance Research, Inc., 1201 Waverly Dr., Champaign, IL, 61821.

Footnote

1. For consistency of presentation and ease of interpretation, the signs of the correlation coefficients from some studies have been reflected, where appropriate, such that "greater" levels of tacit knowledge (i.e., less deviation from the criterion comparison group) correspond to "greater" levels of other variables of interest.

References

Ackerman, P. L. (1988). Determinants of individual differences during skill acquisition: Cognitive abilities and information processing. *Journal of Experimental Psychology: General, 117*, 288–318.

Adams, E. C., & Freeman, C. (2000). Communities of practice: Bridging technology and knowledge assessment. *Journal of Knowledge Management, 4*, 38–42.

Anderson, J. R. (1982). Acquisition of cognitive skill. *Psychological Review, 89*, 369–406.

Andrade, H. G., & Perkins, D. N. (1998). Learnable intelligence and intelligent learning. In R. J. Sternberg & W. M. Williams (Eds.), *Intelligence, instruction, and assessment.* (pp. 67–94). Mahwah, NJ: Erlbaum.

Argyris, C. (1993). *Knowledge for action.* San Francisco, CA: Jossey-Bass.

Bloom, B. S. (Ed.) (1985). *Developing talent in young people.* New York: Ballentine Books.

Bransford, J., Sherwood, R., Vye, N., & Rieser, J. (1986). Teaching thinking and problem solving: Research foundations. *American Psychologist, 41*, 1078–1089.

Brehmer, B., & Joyce, C. R. B. (1988). *Human judgment: The SJT view.* New York: Elsevier.

Brown, J. S., & Duguid, P. (1991). Organizational learning and communities-of-practice: Toward a unified view of working, learning, and innovation. *Organization Science, 2*, 40–57.

Chase, W. G., & Simon, H. A. (1973). Perception in chess. *Cognitive Psychology, 4*, 55–81.

Cianciolo, A. T., Antonakis, J., & Sternberg, R. J. (2004). Practical intelligence and leadership: Using experience as a "mentor." In D. V. Day, S. Zaccaro, & S. Halpin (Eds.), *Leader development for transforming organizations – Growing leaders for tomorrow* (pp. 211–236). Mahwah, NJ: Erlbaum.

Cianciolo, A. T., & Grigorenko, E. L., Jarvin, L., Gil, G., Drebot, M., & Sternberg, R. J. (in press). *Tacit knowledge and practical intelligence: Advancements in measurement and construct validity.* Learning & Individual Differences.

Cianciolo, A. T., Heiden, C., Prevou, M. I., & Psotka, J. (2005). Evaluating Army structured professional forums: Innovations in understanding and assessing effectiveness. *Proceedings of the Interservice/Industry Training, Simulation, and Education Conference (I/ITSEC).* Arlington, VA: National Defense Industrial Association.

Colonia-Willner, R. (1998). Practical intelligence at work: Relationship between aging and cognitive efficiency among managers in a bank environment. *Psychology & Aging, 13*, 45–57.

Crager, J., & Lemons, D. (2003). *Consortium Learning Forum best-practice report: Measuring the impact of knowledge management.* Houston, TX: American Productivity & Quality Center.

Dahl, T. (2000). Text summarisation: From human activity to computer program. The problem of tacit knowledge. *Journal of Linguistics, 25*, 113–131.

Davidson, J. E., & Sternberg, R. J. (1984). The role of insight in intellectual giftedness. *Gifted Child Quarterly*, 28, 58–64.

Day, D. V. (2000). Leadership development: A review in context. *Leadership Quarterly*, 11, 581–613.

Day, D. V., & Lance, C. E. (2004). Understanding the development of leadership complexity through latent growth modeling. In D. V. Day, S. Zaccaro, & S. Halpin (Eds.), *Leader development for transforming organizations – Growing leaders for tomorrow* (pp. 41–69). Mahwah, NJ: Erlbaum.

Dewey, J. (1933). *How we think: A restatement of the relation of reflective thinking to the educative process*. Boston, MA: Heath.

Dixon, N. M., Allen, N., Burgess, T., Kilner, P., & Schweitzer, S. (2005). *CompanyCommand: Unleashing the power of the Army profession*. West Point, NY: Center for the Advancement of Leader Development and Organizational Learning.

DuBois, D., & Shalin, V. L. (1995). Adapting cognitive methods to real-world objectives: An application to job knowledge testing. In P. D. Nichols, S. F. Chipman, & R. L. Brennan (Eds.), *Cognitively diagnostic assessment*. (pp. 189–220). Hillsdale, NJ: Erlbaum.

Duncan, J., Seitz, R. J., Kolodny, J., Bor, D., Herzog, H., Ahmed, A., Newell, F. N., & Emslie, H. (2000). A neural basis for general intelligence. *Science*, 289, 457–460.

Ennis, R. H. (1987). A taxonomy of critical thinking dispositions and abilities. In J. B. Baron & R. J. Sternberg (Eds.), *Teaching thinking skills: Theory and practice* (pp. 9–26). New York: W. H. Freeman.

Ericsson, K. A., Krampe, R. T., & Tesch-Römer, C. (1991). The role of deliberate practice in the acquisition of expert performance. *Psychological Review*, 100, 363–406.

Ericsson, K. A., & Smith, J. (Eds.) (1993). *Toward a general theory of expertise: Prospects and limits*. Cambridge, UK: Cambridge University Press.

Fitts, P., & Posner, M. I. (1967). *Human performance*. Belmont, CA: Brooks/Cole.

Gardner, H. (1983). *Frames of mind: The theory of multiple intelligences*. New York: Basic.

Gardner, H. (1999). *Intelligence reframed: Multiple intelligences for the 21st century*. New York: Basic.

Garner, W. R., Hake, H. W., & Eriksen, C. W. (1956). Operationism and the concept of perception. *Psychological Review*, 63, 149–159.

Gherardi, S., Nicolini, D., & Odella, F. (1998). Toward a social understanding of how people learn in organizations. *Management Learning*, 29, 273–297.

Gottfredson, L. S. (2003). Dissecting practical intelligence theory: Its claims and evidence. *Intelligence*, 31, 343–397.

Grotzer, T. A., & Perkins, D. N. (2000). Teaching intelligence. In R. J. Sternberg (Ed.), *Handbook of intelligence* (pp. 492–515). New York: Cambridge University Press.

Hedlund, J., Forsythe, G. B., Horvath, J. A., Williams, W. M., Snook, S., & Sternberg, R. J. (2003). "Identifying and assessing tacit knowledge: Understanding the practical intelligence of military leaders. *Leadership Quarterly*. 14, 117–140

Hedlund, J., Horvath, J. A., Forsythe, G. B., Snook, S., Williams, W. M., Bullis, R. C., Dennis, M., & Sternberg, R. J. (1998). "Tacit knowledge in military leadership: Evidence of construct validity," Technical Report 1080, U.S. Army Research Institute for the Behavioral & Social Sciences, Alexandria, VA.

Horn, J. L., & Cattell, R. B. (1966). Refinement and test of the theory of fluid and crystallized general intelligences. *Journal of Educational Psychology*, 57, 253–270.

Hunter, J. E. (1983). A causal analysis of cognitive ability, job knowledge, job performance, and supervisor ratings. In F. J. Landy, S. Zedeck, & J. Cleveland (Eds.), *Performance measurement and theory* (pp. 257–275). Hillsdale, NJ: Erlbaum.

Jensen, A. R. (1993). Test validity: g versus "tacit knowledge." *Current Directions in Psychological Science*, 2, 9–10.

Kilner, P. (2002). Transforming army learning through communities of practice. *Military Review, May–June*, 21–27.

Larkin, J. H., McDermott, J., Simon, D. P., & Simon, H. A. (1980). Expert and novice performance in solving physics problems. *Science*, 208, 1335–1342.

Lave, J., & Wenger, E. (1991). *Situated learning: Legitimate peripheral participation*. Cambridge, UK: Cambridge University Press.

Legree, P. J. (1995). Evidence for an oblique social intelligence factor established with a Likert-based testing procedure. *Intelligence*, 21, 247–266.

Legree, P. J., Heffner, T. S., Psotka, J., Martin, D. E., & Medsker, G. J. (2003). Traffic crash involvement: Experiential driving knowledge and stressful contextual antecedents. *Journal of Applied Psychology, 88*, 15–26.

Lesser, E. L., & Storck, J. (2001). Communities of practice and organizational performance. *IBM Systems Journal, 40*, 831–841.

Lipman, M. (1993). Promoting better classroom thinking. *Educational Psychology, 13*, 291–304.

McDaniel, M. A., & Nguyen, N. T. (2001). Situational judgment tests: A review of practice and constructs assessed. *International Journal of Selection and Assessment, 9*, 103–113.

Neisser, U. (1976). General, academic, and artificial intelligence. In L. B. Resnick (Ed.), *The nature of intelligence* (pp. 135–144). Hillsdale, NJ: Erlbaum.

Nickerson, R. S. (1989). On improving thinking through instruction. *Review of Research in Education, 15*, 3–57.

Nisbett, R. E., & Bellows, N. (1977). Verbal reports about causal influences on social judgments: Private access versus public theories. *Journal of Personality & Social Psychology, 35*, 613–624.

Nisbett, R. E., & Wilson, T. D. (1977). Telling more than we can know: Verbal reports on mental processes. *Psychological Review, 84*, 231–259.

Nonaka, I., & Takeuchi, H. (1995). *The knowledge-creating company: How Japanese companies create the dynamics of innovation.* New York: Oxford University Press.

Oxford American Dictionary. (2001). New York: Oxford University Press.

Paul, R. W. (1987). Dialogical thinking: Critical thought essential to the acquisition of rational knowledge and passions. In J. B. Baron & R. J. Sternberg (Eds.), *Teaching thinking skills: Theory and Practice* (pp. 127–148). New York: W. H. Freeman.

Polanyi, M. (1958). *Personal knowledge: Towards a post-critical philosophy.* Chicago, IL: University of Chicago Press.

Polanyi, M. (1966). *The tacit dimension.* New York: Doubleday.

Reber, A. S. (1989). Implicit learning and tacit knowledge. *Journal of Experimental Psychology: General, 118*, 219–235.

Reber, A. S., & Lewis, S. (1977). Implicit learning: An analysis of the form and structure of a body of tacit knowledge. *Cognition, 5*, 333–361.

Ree, M. J., Caretta, T. R., & Teachout, M. S. (1995). Role of ability and prior job knowledge in complex training performance. *Journal of Applied Psychology, 80*, 721–730.

Rothrock, L., & Kirlik, A. (2003). Inferring rule-based strategies in dynamic judgment tasks: Toward a noncompensatory formulation of the lens model. *IEEE Transactions on Systems, Man, and Cybernetics – Part A: Systems and Humans, 33*, 58–72.

Schmidt, F. L., & Hunter, J. E. (1993). Tacit knowledge, practical intelligence, general mental ability, and job knowledge. *Current Directions in Psychological Science, 2*, 8–9.

Schön, D. A. (1983). *The reflective practitioner: How professionals think in action.* New York: Basic Books.

Somech, A., & Bogler, R. (1999). Tacit knowledge in academia: Its effects on student learning and achievement. *The Journal of Psychology, 133*, 605–616.

Stadler, M. A., & Roediger, H. L. (1998). The question of awareness in research on implicit learning. In M. A. Stadler & P. A. Frensch (Eds.), *Handbook of implicit learning* (pp. 105–132). Thousand Oaks, CA: Sage.

Sternberg, R. J. (1987). Most vocabulary is learned from context. In M. G. McKeown & M. E. Curtis (Eds.), *The nature of vocabulary acquisition* (pp. 89–105). Hillsdale, NJ: Erlbaum.

Sternberg, R. J. (1988). *Beyond IQ: A triarchic theory of human intelligence.* New York: Cambridge University Press.

Sternberg, R. J. (1991). Theory-based testing of intellectual abilities: Rationale for the Triarchic Abilities Test. In H. A. Rowe (Ed.), *Intelligence: Reconceptualization and measurement* (pp. 183–202). Hillsdale, NJ: Erlbaum.

Sternberg, R. J. (1994). Cognitive conceptions of expertise. *International Journal of Expert Systems, 7*, 1–12.

Sternberg, R. J. (1997). *Successful intelligence.* New York: Plume Books.

Sternberg, R. J. (1998). Abilities are forms of developing expertise. *Educational Researcher, 27*, 11–20.

Sternberg, R. J., Castejon, J. L., Prieto, M. D., Hautamaki, J., & Grigorenko, E. L. (2001). Confirmatory factor analysis of the Sternberg Triarchic Abilities Test in three international samples. *European Journal of Psychological Assessment, 17*, 1–16.

Sternberg, R. J., Forsythe, G. B., Hedlund, J., Horvath, J. A., Wagner, R. K., Williams,

W. M., Snook, S. A., & Grigorenko, E. L. (2000). *Practical intelligence in everyday life*. Cambridge, UK: Cambridge University Press.

Sternberg, R. J., & Horvath, J. A. (Eds.) (1999). *Tacit knowledge in professional practice: Researcher and practitioner perspectives*. Mahwah, NJ: Erlbaum.

Sternberg, R. J., Nokes, K., Geissler, P. W., Prince, R., Okatcha, F., Bundy, D. A., & Grigorenko, E. L. (2001). The relationship between academic and practical intelligence: A case study in Kenya. *Intelligence, 29*, 401–418.

Sternberg, R. J., & Rainbow Project Collaborators. (2005). Augmenting the SAT through assessments of analytical, practical, and creative skills. In W. J. Camara & E. W. Kimmel (Eds.), *Choosing students: higher education tools for the 21st century* (pp. 159–176). Mahwah, NJ: Erlbaum.

Sternberg, R. J., Wagner, R. K., & Okagaki, L. (1993). Practical intelligence: The nature and role of tacit knowledge in work and at school. In J. M. Puckett, & H. W. Reese, (Eds.), *Mechanisms of everyday cognition* (pp. 205–223). Hillsdale, NJ: Erlbaum.

Tan, H., & Libby, R. (1997). Tacit managerial versus technical knowledge as determinants of audit expertise in the field. *Journal of Accounting Research, 35*, 97–113.

Wagner, R. K. (1987). Tacit knowledge in everyday intelligent behavior. *Journal of Personality & Social Psychology, 52* (6), 1236–1247.

Wagner, R. K., & Sternberg, R. J. (1985). Practical intelligence in real-world pursuits: The role of tacit knowledge. *Journal of Personality & Social Psychology, 49*, 436–458.

Wagner, R. K., & Sternberg, R. J. (1989). *Tacit Knowledge Inventory for sales: Written*. Unpublished test.

Wagner, R. K, & Sternberg, R. J. (1990). Street smarts. In K. E. Clark & M. B. Clark (Eds.), *Measures of leadership* (pp. 493–504). West Orange, NJ: Leadership Library of America.

Wagner, R. K., & Sternberg, R. J. (1991). *Tacit Knowledge Inventory for managers*. San Antonio: The Psychological Corporation.

Wenger, E. C. (1998). *Communities of practice: Learning, meaning, & identity*. Cambridge, UK: Cambridge University Press.

Wenger, E. C. (2000). *Communities of practice and social learning systems*. Organization, 7, 225–246.

Wenger, E. C., & Snyder, W. M. (2000). Communities of practice: The organizational frontier. *Harvard Business Review, January–February*, 139–145.

Williams, W., Blythe, T., White, N., Li, J., Gardner, H., & Sternberg, R. J. (2002). Practical intelligence for school: Developing metacognitive sources of achievement in adolescence. *Developmental Review, 22*, 162–210.

Williams, W., Blythe, T., White, N., Li, J., Sternberg, R. J., & Gardner, H. (1996). *Practical intelligence for school handbook*. New York: Harper Collins.

CHAPTER 36

Expertise and Situation Awareness

Mica R. Endsley

In thinking about expertise, we often focus on skilled physical performance (e.g., the world-class tennis player or gymnast) or skilled decision making (e.g., the chess grandmaster). In addition to these aspects of performance, however, situation awareness (SA), an up-to-date understanding of the world around them, forms a critical cornerstone for expertise in most domains, from driving to aviation to military operations to medical practice. The characteristics that allow people to develop high levels of SA often develop silently alongside more observable features like skilled physical performance, even in tasks such as sports that are considered primarily physical in nature.

Take for example the following excerpt from a magazine story about Wayne Gretzky, an all-time leading hockey scorer who set or tied 49 different National Hockey League records, including most goals, most points, and most assists.

Gretzky doesn't look like a hockey player....His shot is only average – or, nowadays, below average ... Gretzky's gift, his genius even, is for seeing... To most

fans, and sometimes even to the players on the ice, hockey frequently looks like chaos: sticks flailing, bodies falling, the puck ricocheting just out of reach. But amid the mayhem, Gretzky can discern the game's underlying pattern and flow, and anticipate what's going to happen faster and in more detail than anyone else in the building. Several times during a game you'll see him making what seem to be aimless circles on the other side of the rink from the traffic, and then, as if answering a signal, he'll dart ahead to a spot where, an instant later, the puck turns up. (McGrath, 1997)

Although undoubtedly Wayne Gretzky possessed the important physical skills associated with the sport of hockey, this article points out that the critical attribute that placed him head and shoulders above his contemporaries was mental – his ability to understand what was happening in the game and to anticipate where the puck would be. This superior situation awareness allowed him to be "ahead of the game" and outmatch bigger, faster, and better players.

Similar stories can be found in other sports (for example, football, basketball, or tennis – see also Hodges et al., Chapter 27) in which anticipating the actions of one's teammates, one's opponents, and where the ball is going are key to effective individual and team performance. The importance of situation awareness can be found even in a relatively straightforward sport such as golf, which at first glance might appear to be only a matter of a mechanical match between the golf swing and the distance and bearing to the hole. Even in this sport situation awareness has a role, however. Expert players will walk the course ahead of time to take in key situational features that make one course play differently from another. In the 2004 Masters Golf Tournament, Phil Mickelson won by sinking a putt on the last hole. Credited as critical to that putt was the fact that the player immediately previous to Mickelson putted from almost the exact same location. This allowed Phil Mickelson to "read" the hole – observing the winds and very slight variations of the grass and grades of the slope between the ball and the hole. He consciously worked to develop the best SA possible before taking his swing.

Situation awareness plays an even more important role in other domains, such as military operations, piloting, or air traffic control, where there are many factors to keep track of and these factors can change quickly and interact in complex ways. Effective decision making depends on high levels of SA, and thus so does effective performance. In this chapter I will discuss the ways in which SA is critical to expert performance and the factors that allow it to improve with the development of expertise in a domain. Studies from several different arenas will be presented to highlight the many difficulties that novices have in developing good SA and to show how SA improves as performers develop expertise.

Situation Awareness

A general definition of SA, which has been found to be applicable across a wide variety of domains, describes SA as "*the perception of the elements in the environment within a volume of time and space, the comprehension of*

their meaning and the projection of their status in the near future" (Endsley, 1988). This definition of SA will be further discussed in terms of the three levels of SA embodied within it.

Level 1 SA – Perception

The perception of relevant information from the environment forms the first level of SA (see also Rosenbaum, Augustyn, Cohen, & Jax, chapter 29). Without basic perception of important information (through visual, auditory, tactile, or other means), the odds of forming an incorrect picture of the situation increase dramatically. In highly complex and demanding environments, novices may have significant difficulty in knowing which information is most important or in accessing needed information in a timely manner to form Level 1 SA. Even with considerable expertise, this can be quite challenging. Jones and Endsley (1996), for example, found that 76% of SA errors in pilots could be traced to problems in perception of needed information (due to either failures or shortcomings in the system or problems with cognitive processes).

Level 2 SA – Comprehension

Situation awareness involves more than simple perception of information – it also demands that people understand the meaning and significance of what they have perceived (Level 2 SA). Thus it encompasses how people combine, interpret, store, and retain information, integrating multiple pieces of information and arriving at a determination of its relevance to the person's goals. This is analogous to having a high level of reading comprehension, as compared to just reading words. Twenty percent of SA errors in pilots have been found to involve problems with Level 2 SA (Jones & Endsley, 1996).

Level 3 SA – Projection

At the highest level of SA, the ability to forecast future situation events and dynamics (Level 3 SA) marks individuals who have the highest level of understanding of the

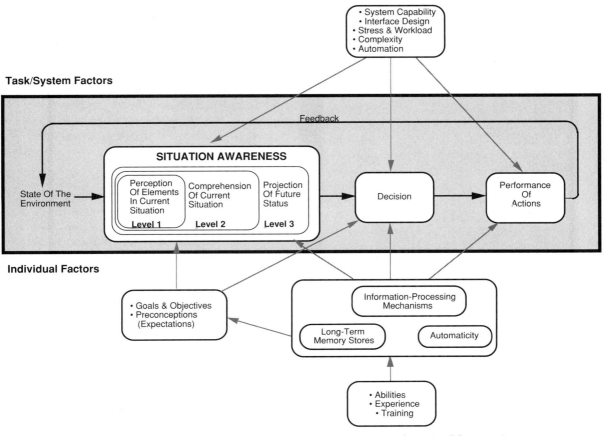

Figure 36.1. Model of Situation Awareness in Dynamic Decision Making (Endsley, 1995)

situation. This ability to project from current events and dynamics to anticipate future events (and their implications) allows for timely decision making. Experts rely heavily on future projections as a hallmark of skilled performance (Yates & Tschirhart, Chapter 24).

SA Model

The model of SA in Figure 36.1 shows how SA feeds into decision making and performance in an on-going cycle (Endsley, 1995). Key features of the environment affect how well people are able to obtain and maintain SA, including:

(1) The capability of the system for providing the needed information (e.g., relevant sensors, data transmission capabilities, networking, etc.).

(2) The design of the system interface, determining which information is available to the individual, along with the format of the displays for effectively transmitting information.

(3) System complexity, including number of components, inter-relatedness of those components, and rate of change of information, affecting the ability of the individual to keep up with needed information and to understand and project future events.

(4) The level of automation present in the system, affecting the ability of the individual to stay "in-the-loop," aware of what is happening and understanding what the system is doing.

(5) Stress and workload that occur as a function of the task environment, the system interface, and the operational domain, each of which can act to decrease SA.

In addition to these external factors, the model points out many features of the individual that determine whether a person will develop good SA, given the same environment and equipment as others. These features include:

(1) Perceptual processing and limited attention – As human capacity for attention is limited, the ability of the individual to apply conscious focalized attention to all relevant information is severely constrained in most domains. Information from different modalities may be more readily processed in parallel (Wickens, 1992), thereby somewhat reducing this effect; however, the limits of attention for taking in needed information forms a significant problem for SA.

(2) Limited working memory – Much of SA requires working memory for storing, integrating, and processing perceived information and maintaining the current internalized model of what is happening. As working memory is constrained, critical information may be forgotten or may not be properly integrated to develop Level 2 or 3 SA.

(3) Goal-driven processing, alternating with data-driven processing – Goals can be thought of as ideal states of the system or environment that the individual wishes to achieve. In a top-down goal-driven process, the person's goals and plans will direct which aspects of the environment are attended to in the development of SA. This creates significant efficiencies in information processing. Conversely, in a bottom-up, data-driven process, the individual's attention is directed across all relevant information (perhaps in a fixed scan pattern) and will be captured by salient features or by key information that can indicate to the individual that different plans will be necessary to meet goals or that different goals should be activated. An ongoing cycling between goal-driven and data-driven processing is a key feature underlying SA.

(4) Expectations – Expectations play an important role in SA, affecting where people will look for information and how they interpret what they perceive.

(5) Pattern-matching to schema & use of mental models – Mental models and schema provide cognitive mechanisms for interpreting and projecting events in complex domains. These long-term memory structures can be used to significantly circumvent the limitations of working memory.

It is worth noting that though the three levels of SA represent increasingly better SA, they do not necessarily indicate fixed, linear stages. In a linear progression, a person needs to see or hear a piece of information (Level 1 SA), interpret what it means (Level 2 SA), and then project what will happen next (Level 3 SA). This is from a data-driven perspective. In reality, however, a simple 1–2–3 data driven progression is not an efficient processing mechanism in a complex and dynamic system, which is where expertise and goal-driven processing come into play.

The model recognizes that many times people are goal driven. Based on their goals or their current understanding or projections (Levels 2 and 3 SA), individuals will look for data to either confirm or deny their assessments or will search for missing information (look for Level 1 data). This is an iterative process, with understanding driving the search for new data and new data combining to build understanding, as represented by the feedback arrow in the model in Figure 36.1.

Inherent in any discussion of SA is also a notion of what is important. For a given individual, SA requirements are based on the goals and decision tasks related to their job or role. The air traffic controller does not need to know everything (e.g., the copilot's shoe size and spouse's name), but does need to know a great deal of information related to the goal of safely separating aircraft within his or her sector. A doctor has just as great a need for situation awareness; however, the things she needs to know about will be quite different, dependent on a different set of goals and decision tasks. Because the things

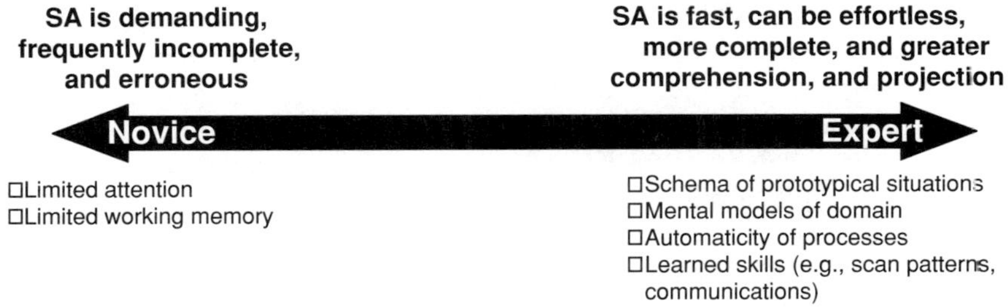

SA is demanding, frequently incomplete, and erroneous

SA is fast, can be effortless, more complete, and greater comprehension, and projection

◄ **Novice**

Expert ►

□Limited attention
□Limited working memory

□Schema of prototypical situations
□Mental models of domain
□Automaticity of processes
□Learned skills (e.g., scan patterns, communications)

Figure 36.2. Factors effecting SA in Novices and Experts in a Domain

that people need to perceive, comprehend, and project are by nature domain specific (based on their role and tasks), high levels of SA and thus expertise in one domain will not necessarily translate into high levels of SA or expertise in another domain (see also Feltovich, Prietula, & Ericsson, Chapter 4).

Role of Expertise in Situation Awareness

Based on this model of SA, expertise in a particular domain has a significant role in allowing people to develop and maintain SA in the face of high volumes of information transfer and system complexity. This can best be explained in terms of two divergent ends of a continuous spectrum, as represented in Figure 36.2.

Novices

In the most extreme case, a person who is completely new to the systems and situations in a particular domain (e.g., a person learning to drive or fly for the first time) will be considerably overloaded in seeking to gather information, understand what it means, and formulate correct responses. Novices will be severely hampered in their efforts by both limited attention and limited working memory. Lacking other mechanisms, they will have to think through each piece of data and try to process it in working memory along with other pieces of data. Reading each gauge, or listening to audio input and interpreting that data, will impose a significant burden in even mildly complex

systems. Proper understanding of the significance of what is perceived will likely be error prone as well, as a novice would not have the experience base from which to interpret those cues. So a new driver, pilot, or power plant operator simply remains far behind the demand curve in taking in and processing the information that forms the basis for good SA in these dynamic environments.

The process is further compromised by inefficiency. Novices lack the knowledge of when each piece of information is really most important (see also Feltovich et al., Chapter 4). Scan patterns tend to be sporadic and non-optimal. They may neglect certain key information or over-sample other information unnecessarily. This problem is not just a matter of needing to learn a set way of taking in information. Without knowledge of the underlying relationships among system components, novices do not realize what information to seek out following receipt of other information. Seeing rising temperatures, for example, does not lead to the immediate shifting of attention to system pressure to determine whether an explosion is imminent.

Thus, the prototypical novice is quickly overloaded, inefficient, and error prone in developing SA. Decision making and performance are highly compromised as a result. Luckily, development of expertise in a particular domain significantly reduces these problems through a number of mechanisms.

Expertise

The model also details how with increasing experience in a particular domain people are able to develop a number of mechanisms that help to overcome these significant hurdles. The first of these is a mental model of the systems being operated and the operational domain (see also Ross, Shafer, & Klein, Chapter 23). For example, a pilot develops not only a mental model of how the aircraft operates, including its many subsystems and its aerodynamic performance in the physical environment, but also a mental model of flight operations, including air traffic control (ATC) procedures and expected behaviors associated with interacting with ATC and other pilots.

Mental models have been succinctly defined as *"mechanisms whereby humans are able to generate descriptions of system purpose and form, explanations of system functioning and observed system states, and predictions of future states"* (Rouse & Morris, 1985). They are generally used to describe a person's representation of some physical system (e.g., how an engine or computer works), but also can concern other types of systems (e.g., how a university or business works). Mental models embody stored long-term knowledge about these systems that can be called on to direct problem solving and interaction with the relevant system when needed. They may even be borrowed to shed light on similar systems. Mental models, although they grow and evolve with experience, largely represent static knowledge about the system – its significant features, how it functions, how different components affect others, and how its components will behave when confronted with various factors and influences – as opposed to the more transient knowledge that is called SA.

Mental models are highly useful in the process of developing SA (Endsley, 1988, 1995). A well-developed mental model provides several advantages.

(1) Knowledge regarding which aspects of the system are relevant in a given situation. This knowledge is critical for directing attention in taking in and classifying information in the perception process, making that process much more efficient, particularly in a situation where there is a large amount of information to potentially be processed.

(2) A means of integrating various elements to form an understanding of their meaning (Level 2 SA). Understanding the significance of perceived system information is often very difficult without a mental model. *Is a temperature of 104 good, bad, or indifferent? Does this temperature mean the patient is in a critical or non-critical state?* Also, understanding is often not just a matter of interpreting one piece of data but rather is a function of the integration of multiple pieces of data. A physician will often consider multiple factors about the patient to determine a diagnosis, for example. Mental models provide the basis for interpreting perceived information (singularly or together) in terms of the individual's goals to form Level 2 SA.

(3) A mechanism for projecting future states of the system, based on its current state and an understanding of its dynamics (Level 3 SA). Similarly, the projection of future system states is very difficult without a mental model. *If the temperature of a car is in the red zone, what is likely to happen?* An experienced mechanic or driver has the knowledge base to project a cracked engine block, whereas an inexperienced person would not. In some cases, these projections could result from fairly simple pieces of knowledge (rules), but in other cases they would require a far more detailed understanding of the nature of the system's components and their interactions with each other. Accurately projecting what the enemy in a battle is likely to do requires a very detailed mental model of not only the battlefield (terrain features, weather, obstacles), but also of the enemy (objectives, capabilities, doctrine, culture, tactics, techniques, and procedures).

Over time, people will encounter many situations and from these will develop a set of prototypical situations, or schema, in memory. Schema can be thought of as prototypical states of the mental model (i.e., patterns consisting of the state of each of the relevant elements for that schema or situation type). By pattern matching between the current situation and this schema, people can instantly recognize known classes of situations. *"Oh, this is just like what happened last month."* These prototypical situations can be learned through direct experience or vicariously through formal training or the case studies and storytelling that are endemic in many professions. *"This is just like what happened to the aircrew in the Azores accident."* A critical feature of this schema is that new situations need not be exactly like previously encountered situations to achieve a match. Rather, only a few critical cues may be required to lead to a match or a near match.

Pattern matching to learned schema provides a considerable short-cut for SA and decision making. Rather than processing data to determine Level 2 or 3 SA (requiring working memory or exercising the mental model), that information is already a part of the schema and must merely be recalled. Klein has called this "recognition-primed decision making" (Klein et al., 1986). Newell has called it the "big switch," (Newell, 1973). The critical factors for achieving good SA through this mechanism are recognizing the critical cues that are used for pattern matching and having a good stock of such schema in memory. In addition, it appears that some people are better at pattern matching than others, and this attribute has been shown to be correlated with SA (Endsley & Bolstad, 1994).

A third relevant characteristic of expertise is the development of automaticity (see also Feltovich et. al, Chapter 4). Automaticity is normally considered in terms of physical tasks (e.g., riding a bicycle, steering the car while shifting gears and operating the clutch and fuel peddle simultaneously in a standard automobile). In these cases, as the physical actions are performed more autonomously, less conscious attention and effort are required of the individual (see also Hill & Schneider, Chapter 37). Tasks that initially completely absorbed the attention resources of the individual eventually are performed with little if any conscious thought at all. The decrease in demand on mental resources associated with automaticity of physical tasks provides a boon for SA, leaving more attention and working memory for attending to information and forming SA. Thus freed up from needing to concentrate on the demands of steering and shifting, the driver can give more attention to detecting potential traffic hazards, for example.

Automaticity may also be considered in relation to more cognitive tasks. With a fixed pairing of stimulus to response, even more complex cognitive behaviors can develop to a level of automaticity (e.g., braking following the detection of tail lights or a red traffic light in front of you, and pressing the gas pedal when the traffic light turns green). A highly experienced driver may begin to process these cues and convert even cognitive portions of driving to a level of automaticity with little conscious awareness or attention, freeing up the mind for other important matters such as conversation with a passenger, thinking about what to have for dinner, or daydreaming. Such a state can be quite common for experienced drivers operating in very familiar environments (e.g., the drive from home to work each day).

As SA requires "awareness" of information by definition, SA in such a situation may be fairly low, even though performance may be adequate (no wrecks are occurring). A reasonable question might be, is SA really necessary in that situation or in general? I believe the answer is yes. The reason that SA is always required is that good performance involves not just the known "normal" situations, but also the many abnormal situations that can and do occur. People operating at this level of cognitive automaticity are not as attentive to cues that are outside the learned "routine." Thus, if there is a new stop sign on that well-learned route home, people often will run right through without stopping because they are not alert to this important situational element. If on a particular day they intend to stop at the store on their way home from work, they may drive right past the store, seeing the store sign but not triggering the significance of its presence.

The low SA associated with cognitive automaticity is likely to negatively affect performance when the situation falls outside the bounds of the learned routine. For this reason experts in various domains take extra steps to guard against the deleterious effects of automaticity. Pilots, for example, run procedural checklists to make sure they check each item they are supposed to and do not lapse into automaticity in checking critical information.

Finally, with experience in a domain, people learn many specific skills that are relevant to efficiently and effectively obtaining critical information. Pilots learn to communicate with ATC and to scan their instruments to make sure their knowledge of the situation does not get out of date. Air traffic controllers learn how to scan their radar maps efficiently, based on traffic patterns in the sector. Military officers learn how to gather and disseminate key information on the radio, how to listen for information that is relevant to them while ignoring other information, and where to post troops as listening and observation posts to insure that key information is gathered and passed on in the first place. The development of SA is not just passive, waiting for key information to be presented, but rather is an active process. The information that is available to military pilots, for example, is dependant on how they set up and operate their radar (search patterns, where the radar is focused, modes), what frequency they tune their radios to, and when they request information from others. Thus, their actions determine what information they will obtain. All of these are examples of learned skills, specific to each domain, that improve with expertise and that contribute to higher SA among experts.

Running the Gamut

It is worth noting that the mechanisms underlying good SA in experts are very domain specific (see also, Feltivich et al. Chapter 4). They may promote good SA in the learned domain (e.g., brain surgery), but will not likely transfer to good SA in another domain (e.g., aircraft piloting). And even within a domain, when very novel situations are encountered, these mechanisms are of limited value. Relevant schema will not be present and the expert's mental model may be incomplete for the novel situation at hand. The risk for the expert in such a situation may be over-pattern matching – trying to use an inappropriate schema – or stretching the mental model beyond its limits to accommodate the new situation.

Therefore, SA in very novel situations may be hampered by the same factors that hamper novices, even for people who are generally considered to have a high level of expertise in that domain. The experienced pilot who has never encountered or been trained for a particular anomaly will be challenged to process information in working memory to determine what is happening, and may be inefficient in searching for relevant information to solve the problem, in much the same way as when she was a novice pilot (although it is likely that she will not be as bad off as a complete novice).

Most people do not operate at the level of novice all the time or expert all the time, but rather move around in between, using combinations of cognitive mechanisms depending on the situation at hand and the availability of key constructs (e.g., mental models and schema).

In order to understand these differences better, we will review a few case studies that explore how SA varies as a function of expertise.

SA and Expertise in Aviation Pilots

Much research on SA has focused on aviation, primarily in the realm of the military or commercial aviation pilot. These pilots are typically very carefully selected through a number of screening tests and highly trained. The training is rigorous – anyone not meeting the bar gets "washed out" early on – and is ongoing, with most pilots being required to demonstrate prowess on a variety of maneuvers and emergency tasks on an annual or semi-annual basis. Consequently, most of the SA research has concentrated on a population that is well along the continuum towards the expertise end of the scale.

In addition to benefiting from the additional cognitive structures discussed previously, anecdotal evidence indicates that experienced military pilots who are very good at SA engage in several practices or skills that are beneficial (Endsley, 1989, 1995; Ericsson, Chapter 38). First, they "think ahead of the aircraft" during the flight. They are continually engaged in projecting what might happen, allowing them to be ready for events if they materialize. Amalberti and Deblon (1992) found that these pilots report they spend much of their discretionary time engaged in projection and "what-if" type thinking. They also engage in extensive pre-mission planning and briefings that form a basis for what they expect to encounter during the mission. These expectations can lead to faster, more accurate SA when they are correct, but also can lead to significant SA errors if they are wrong (Jones & Endsley, 1996).

In a study comparing less-experienced general aviation (GA) pilots (mean experience level = 720 hours), more-experienced airline pilots (mean experience level = 6036 hours), and line check airmen, considered to be among the best commercial pilots (mean experience level = 12,370 hours), Prince and Salas (1998) noted two key differences among the groups. First, the amount of preflight preparation increased as a function of experience, with more experienced pilots focusing on planning and preparation specific to the flight and gathering as much information as possible about the conditions and flight elements. Second, there was more focus on understanding and projection at higher levels of expertise. GA pilots described themselves as passive recipients of information with an emphasis on information in the immediate environment (Level 1 SA). Line pilots dealt more at the level of comprehension (Level 2 SA) and emphasized their active role in seeking out information. Check airmen were more likely than the other groups to focus on Level 3 SA, seeking to be proactive. They dealt with a large number of details and the complex relationships between factors in this process.

GA pilots are typically far less experienced and have less training than commercial and military pilots. These much less-experienced and less-current pilots account for the vast majority of aviation accidents and fatalities; 94% of all U.S. civil aviation accidents and 92% of U.S. civil aviation fatalities involve GA pilots (NTSB, 1998). This accident rate has remained fairly stable for nearly two decades (AOPA, 1997). A 1989 NTSB review of 361 GA accidents concluded that 97% of the probable causes were due to pilot error (NTSB, 1989). Trollip and Jensen (1991) attribute these pilot error accidents to the following factors, in order of frequency:

- loss of directional control
- poor judgment
- airspeed not maintained
- poor preflight planning and decision making
- clearance not maintained
- inadvertent stalls
- poor crosswind handling
- poor in-flight planning and decision making

Most of these issues indicate problems with pilot SA.

Endsley et al. (2002) conducted a more in-depth analysis of SA problems in low-time GA pilots. To do this, they examined 222 incident reports at a popular flight school that contained reported problems with SA. These reports were stratified into four different experience levels: (1) students working on a private pilot's license, which typically requires 40 to 60 flight hours, (2) students working on an instrument pilot qualification whose experience levels are typically 75 hours and more, (3) students working on a commercial pilot license whose experience levels are usually 200 hours and more, (4) students working on a multiengine rating whose experience levels are typically 200 hours and more.

Overall, the least experienced group, those working on their private pilot's license, experienced the greatest proportion of incidents involving SA problems and the more-experienced groups encountered the least. The total number of incidents/flight hours

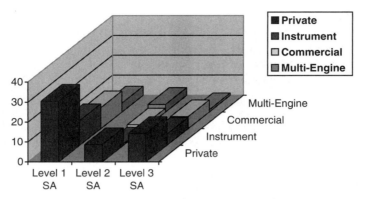

Figure 36.3. SA Error Causal Factors across Pilot Groups.

in the time period was significantly different between each student group.

As shown in Figure 36.3, these SA errors were also distributed differently across the three levels of SA. Significantly more Level 1 SA errors were found in the lower experience level groups and fewer in the most experienced group. None of the four groups was significantly more or less likely to experience Level 2 SA errors, but there were significantly fewer Level 3 SA errors in the multiengine student group and significantly more in the other three groups. The lower overall SA error rate observed for the most experienced group was due to a decrease in Level 1 and Level 3 SA errors, but not Level 2 SA errors.

Overall, a number of problems were noted as particularly difficult, leading to the SA problems found across this group of relatively inexperienced GA pilots.

(1) Distractions and high workload. Many of the SA errors could be linked to problems with managing task distractions and task saturation. This may reflect the high workload associated with tasks that are not learned to high levels of automaticity, problems with multitasking, or insufficiently developed task-management strategies. These less experienced pilot groups had significant problems in dealing with distractions and high workload,

(2) Vigilance and monitoring deficiencies. Though associated with overload in about half of the cases, in many incidents vigilance and monitoring deficiencies were noted without these overload problems. This may reflect insufficiently learned scan patterns, attentional narrowing, or an inability to prioritize information.

(3) Insufficiently developed mental models. Many errors in both understanding perceived information and projecting future dynamics could be linked to insufficiently developed mental models. In particular, the pilots had significant difficulties with operations in new geographical areas, including recognizing landmarks and matching them to maps, and understanding new procedures for flight, landings, and departures in unfamiliar airspace. They also had significant difficulties with understanding the implications of many environmental factors on aircraft dynamics/behaviors. Pilots at these relatively low levels of experience exhibited problems with judging relative motion and rates of change in other traffic.

(4) Overreliance on mental models. Reverting to habitual patterns (learned mental models) when new behaviors were called for was also a problem for the low-experience group. They failed to understand the limits of learned models and how to properly extend these models to new situations.

In a further study, Endsley et al. (2002) conducted challenging simulated

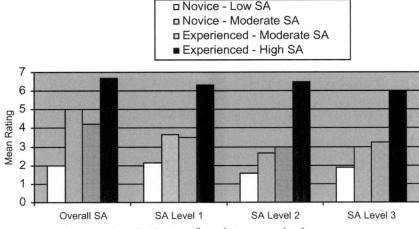

Figure 36.4. SA Ratings for pilots across the four groups

flight scenario studies with both inexperienced and experienced GA pilots. The inexperienced group included ten private pilots with a mean GA flight experience level of 109 hours (range 41 to 300). The experienced group included ten flight instructors with a mean GA flight experience level of 1790 hours (range 300 to 9000). Experienced pilot observers completed a rating form during each flight, indicating whether twelve key expected behaviors were never, sometimes, or always performed, and rating each pilot's SA and performance on a 1 to 7 scale.

In general, the experienced group outperformed the inexperienced group; however, closer examination showed that the groups were not internally consistent. Therefore, for purposes of analysis, they were redistributed into four groups, based on observer SA ratings:

(1) Novice pilots with low SA (scores of 1, 2, or 3 on the overall SA scale),

(2) Novice pilots with moderate SA (scores of 4 or 5),

(3) Experienced pilots with moderate SA (scores of 4 or 5), and

(4) Experienced pilots with high SA (scores of 6 or 7).

The mean SA scores of these four groups are shown in Figure 36.4 with the high-scoring experienced pilots clearly outscoring the other groups at all levels.

The pilots who scored better on SA within the novice and experienced groups were not necessarily those with the most flight hours. In the novice category, two of the more experienced GA pilots (180 and 300 hours) were rated as among the seven having low SA, and of the three novice pilots with moderate SA, two were fairly low-time pilots (55 and 80 flight hours). In the experienced category, while all of the very high-time pilots (more than 1000 hours) were rated as having high SA, so were two pilots with only 450 hours. Of the four experienced pilots who were rated as having only moderate SA, one had 730 flight hours of experience. Flight hours were therefore not significantly predictive of the group.

In examining the key behaviors performed, those pilots who were scored as having better SA (in both the novice and experienced categories) all received much higher ratings for aircraft handling/psychomotor skills, cockpit task management, cockpit task prioritization, and ATC communication/coordination than did the pilots who were rated as having lower SA. A step-wise regression model, accounting for 91.7% of the variance in SA score across all pilots, included aircraft handling/psychomotor skill and ATC communication and coordination.

Aircraft handling might normally be considered a manual or psychomotor task, not one significantly involved in a cognitive construct like SA. This finding is in agreement with previous studies, however, which have found a relationship between psychomotor skills and SA, presumably because of issues associated with limited attention (Endsley & Bolstad, 1994; O'Hare, 1997). The development of higher automaticity on this task helps free up attention resources needed for SA. The observers noted significant problems with basic flight skills in the novice pilots and indicated they were quickly overloaded by their tasks. Keeping up with ATC communications was also noted as challenging for many of the novice GA pilots. They had to ask for many repeats, which used up their attentional resources. These issues were less of a problem for the experienced pilots.

So whereas it might be easy to consider the development of physical skills associated with task performance as separate from cognitive skills like SA, these studies suggest that developing these physical skills to automaticity in order to off-load attentional demands may be an important prerequisite for developing high levels of SA (see also, Feltovich et al., Chapter 4). Expertise in SA may not be possible as long as an individual must concentrate on the performance of the physical tasks involved.

Among the experienced pilots with high SA, good aircraft-handling skills and good task prioritization were noted frequently. Their performance was not perfect, but this group seemed more able to detect and recover from their own errors than others. Many were noted as flying first and only responding to ATC clearances or equipment malfunctions when they had the plane under control. The experienced pilots who were rated as having only moderate SA were more likely to have been noted as having difficulty in controlling the simulated aircraft and poorer prioritization and planning skills. Thus, in addition to physical performance (aircraft handling), skills associated with task prioritization appear to be important for high levels of SA. As many environments

where SA is important involve multi-tasking among competing goals, demands, and tasks, this has been noted as an important skill (Endsley & Bolstad, 1994). A skill set associated with multi-tasking, planning, and prioritization is important. These skills appear to develop or to be enabled through increasing levels of expertise in the domain.

Overall this study illuminated the considerable workload problems that inexperienced pilots face. Basic flight control and ATC communications quickly overloaded them and left little attention available for maintaining SA. Attentional narrowing and fixation added to this problem. Among GA pilots with more experience, task prioritization and task management skills were also important markers associated with the pilots rated as having better SA. This group had the additional resources (or knowledge bases) to think ahead of the aircraft and plan for contingencies.

SA and Expertise in Army Infantry Officers

In a very different domain from general aviation, SA is important for army operations. The battlefield commander must have a clear and up-to-date assessment of the enemy, his own troops, and the battlefield environment. SA provides the foundation for military decision making, and the framework within which all plans and actions are conceived. Rather than obtaining SA from a largely engineered world like the pilot does, the battlefield commander is directly imbedded in a natural and more variable world, with fewer direct indications of needed information. The intentions and activities of others may be very difficult to discern. One's own troops are generally widely dispersed. Noise, heat and cold, fatigue, poor weather, smoke, and rugged terrain are common challenges. Enemy forces intentionally practice denial of information, misinformation, and deception that must be detected and interpreted correctly. Decision making in the face of uncertain, missing, and conflicting information is common. To develop SA, army officers have traditionally employed numerous techniques for gathering intelligence information to guide their activities (which increasingly may involve sensors, imagery from satellites, and unmanned air vehicles or human intelligence sources), sending out scouts or placing listening and observation posts in key locations, and establishing procedures for radio and networked communication among distributed forces.

Strater et al. (2001a) undertook a study to determine differences in SA between inexperienced and experienced army platoon leaders. The platoon leader is typically the entry level officer position, thus its new officers are considered to be novices in the Army hierarchy. Their study involved fourteen infantry officers: seven lieutenants and seven captains. None of the lieutenants had prior experience serving as platoon leaders, although they had just completed their initial platoon leader training course, whereas all captains were experienced in serving as platoon leaders.

In the study, each participant conducted two missions in a virtual reality simulator with a combination of live and digital teammates acting against a scripted threat. The actions of the participants were recorded and their SA was measured at three points during each scenario using the situation awareness global assessment technique (SAGAT). At each freeze point, the accuracy of their assessment of the situation was assessed on thirteen different factors. In addition, the behavior of the participants was rated by an experienced army officer using the situation awareness behavioral rating scale (SABARS).

The SAGAT scores of the two groups are shown in Figure 36.5, with the more-experienced group (captains) demonstrating higher levels of SA overall than the inexperienced lieutenants. These findings show an interesting effect of experience on platoon leader SA. Although more-experienced officers demonstrated superior Level 1 SA in identifying the locations of both their own troops and enemy troops, as would be expected, the more important story involves the subsequent cognitive

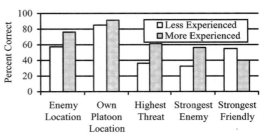

Figure 36.5. SAGAT mean scores by experience level.

processes – the transformation of the information into higher-level SA. More-experienced officers identified the strongest enemy and the highest enemy threat (level 2 SA) with greater accuracy than officers with less experience, whereas less-experienced officers demonstrated superior performance at identifying the strongest friendly elements.

Thus, not only did experienced leaders demonstrate higher levels of SA on certain factors, as might be expected, but SA also proved to be qualitatively different depending on level of experience (see also, Feltovich et al., Chapter 4). That is, with increasing levels of experience, platoon leaders shift their focus from concentrating on friendly disposition to focusing more on enemy disposition. Other research has also found that experienced officers concentrate more on the enemy situation than on the friendly situation (Shattuck et al., 2000). Thus, it appears that increasing expertise is important not only for helping people take in the correct information, but also in prioritization of internal focus for processing that information to form the higher levels of SA.

In terms of their SA-related behaviors, the experienced officers were rated higher on the factor of gathering information/following procedures (uses assets to effectively assess environment, utilizes a standard reporting procedure, identifies key elements, sets appropriate levels of alert, assesses information received, gathers follow-up information when needed, monitors company net, assesses key finds and unusual events) and focuses on the big picture (communicates key information to squad leaders, communicates to squads over-all situation and Commander's intent, solic-its information from commanders, monitors company net, asks for pertinent intelligence information, communicates key information to commander).

In addition to improvements in how they distributed their attention, these find-ings indicate that with experience, the pla-toon leaders are significantly improving the skill sets associated with gathering infor-mation from the battlefield environment and communicating with others. Commu-nicating information both up and down the echelon is important not only for building other team members' SA, but also because such activities prompt the delivery of rele-vant information back to the platoon leader. These skills are critical for the development of SA in the infantry environment.

In a second follow-up study, Strater, Jones and Endsley (2001b) surveyed Forty-three individuals (both officers and enlisted) who train new platoon leaders. Issues that were rated as a frequent problem by more than 25% of the respondents are shown in Table 36.1. Problems in communication posed a major problem for new platoon leaders, ranging from not requesting infor-mation to not communicating key informa-tion. In addition, there were significant prob-lems reported in gathering information on the combat-readiness status of the opposing force and one's own troops.

Comprehension problems were also noted as frequent problems for SA, includ-ing failing to assemble bits of informa-tion together into a coherent picture and not specifying alternate courses of action (COAs), along with not understanding task priorities, the impact of load and travel on fatigue, and the importance of soldier positioning to minimize fratricide. A continuation of Level-1 problems was noted with detecting information about the enemy. Instructors rated understanding enemy strengths and weaknesses, likely areas of strategic significance to the enemy, and enemy expectations of friendly actions as major problem areas for SA in new platoon leaders.

With regard to Level 3 SA, lack of con-tingency planning was identified as a prob-lem area, as was failure to project the usage rate of ammunition and supplies. Problems with SA regarding the opposing force were also found at the projection level, as train-ers noted that new platoon leaders had diffi-culty projecting a likely enemy COA, as well as their disposition around heavy weapons.

Like the inexperienced pilots, inexperi-enced platoon leaders appear to have many difficulties with forming good SA. Poor skills for gathering information are particularly problematic in this domain, as very little information presents itself otherwise. It was found that the officers often were not com-municating key information because they assumed they knew what was going on, or that the information did not need to be passed on.

The studies also indicate that novice pla-toon leaders suffer greatly from not having good mental models or schema. They are quickly overwhelmed by information, are slow to grasp which information is impor-tant, and do not know where to look for important follow-up information. Without this schema, they also fared poorly in inte-grating information to understand its signif-icance and in projection and contingency planning.

SA and Expertise in Driving

Driving provides a fertile ground for SA research because of its ubiquitous nature in modern society. Drivers of various levels of expertise are readily available (although experience is often confounded with age in the general population). A number of researchers have performed studies exam-ining hazard awareness, a form of Level 3 SA, in drivers at various levels of exper-tise. The researchers determine how far in advance drivers will anticipate or project a potential road hazard. These studies have shown a significant negative correlation between the lead time for predicting a haz-ard in a simulated driving task or traffic video and drivers' reported accident rates

Table 36.1. SA problems for new platoon leaders (% reporting)

Level 1 SA: Failure to Correctly Gather/Detect the Critical Information in the Situation

Not detecting information because of attentional narrowing	27%
Not utilizing a standard reporting procedure	30%
Not carrying out standard operating procedure	28%
Poor intelligence information owing to:	
Not requesting pertinent intelligence	31%
Not employing squads tactically to gather needed information	30%
Not determining reliability/timeliness of intelligence information	26%
Poor communication caused by:	
Not requesting information from squad leaders	30%
Not requesting information from commander	30%
Not communicating key information to commander	35%
Not communicating key information to squad leaders	30%
Not communicating key information to other platoons	44%
Not monitoring company net	28%
Not communicating overall situation/Commander's Intent to squads	28%
Not determining own combat readiness status	
Experience and training	26%
Timing/location of direct/indirect fire support	30%
Not determining combat readiness status of opposing forces	
Number and severity of casualties	37%
Physical fatigue	30%
Mental fatigue	31%
Movement and current position of troops	28%
Weapons types, characteristics and quantities available	33%
Location of direct/indirect fire support	44%
Ammo and supplies availability	33%
Availability of reinforcements	37%
Heavy weapons location	40%
Past behavior and tactics	25%
Impact of current and future weather factors	26%

Level 2 SA: Failure to Comprehend the Situation (although basic information is detected)

Not assembling bits of information together to form a coherent picture	29%
Not specifying alternate/supplemental plans/courses of action	32%
Not developing an understanding of:	
Task priorities	33%
Impact of soldier load and distance traveled on troop fatigue	33%
Positioning soldiers to minimize the risk of fratricide	25%
Enemy strengths and weaknesses	29%
Likely areas of strategic significance to enemy	27%
Enemy expectations of friendly actions	34%

Level 3 SA: Failure to Project the Future Situation (though current situation is understood)

Lack of contingency planning	39%
Failure to project the following:	
Usage rate of ammunition and supplies	36%
Likely enemy COA from available information	33%
Location of enemy troops around heavy weapons	32%
Failure to effectively perform the necessary mission tasks	
Poor mission planning	27%
Poor responses to unexpected/unplanned events	36%
Poor time management	45%
Poor task prioritization	28

(Currie, 1969; McKenna & Crick, 1991, 1994; Pelz & Krumpat, 1974). This finding holds even after age and miles driven are controlled (McKenna & Crick, 1991; Quimby et al., 1986).

In using this approach to study expertise in drivers, McKenna and Crick (1991) found that experienced drivers (more than ten years of experience) reacted significantly faster to hazards than novice drivers (less than three years of experience), and detected significantly more hazards. When they compared drivers with the same number of years of experience, half of whom were considered experts (class 1 police drivers in the UK) who had completed an advanced driving course that included hazard awareness training, they again found an advantage for those with more expertise as defined by this training.

Horswill and McKenna (2004) examined possible reasons for the superior hazard awareness of experienced drivers. While they acknowledge that some of the effect may be due to a change in response bias with experience (i.e., a lower response threshold for indicating that something is a hazard), they present compelling evidence that this explanation cannot explain all of the differences associated with expertise. They also cite evidence that novice drivers tend to focus closer to the front of their vehicle, use their mirrors less frequently, and fixate in smaller areas compared with more experienced drivers. In addition, more-experienced drivers were found to better adjust their scanning patterns to the road type (Mourant & Rockwell, 1972) and to have better search models regarding where to look for hazards (Underwood et al., 2002). Horswill and McKenna conclude *"experienced drivers are conducting a more efficient and effective search for hazards rather than simply lowering their criterion for what constitutes a hazard."*

In addition, McKenna and his colleagues have demonstrated that hazard awareness is a cognitively demanding task, and not one prone to high levels of automaticity. The superior hazard-detection performance of experts suffers from exposure to a concurrent memory task (McKenna & Farrand, 1999). Though the physical vehicle control portions of the driving task may become automatized, the cognitive activities involved in predicting hazards appear to continue to require significant cognitive resources. This is consistent with reports from pilots that projection takes up a considerable portion of their discretionary time. They furthermore conclude that when drivers' attention is redirected to other tasks (e.g., cell phone usage), they lose much of the advantage that their superior projection skills provide.

Although this body of research focuses primarily on Level 3 SA for the driving task, it provides a rich set of data showing that expertise and SA are tightly linked in ways that extend well beyond simple intake of information. And whereas other measures of driving (e.g., vehicle control skills) have failed to effectively discriminate real-world performance (likelihood of an accident), the hazard awareness aspect of SA has been found to have significant predictive ability, to the extent that it is now incorporated as a part of the driving test in Australia and the UK (Horswill & McKenna, 2004). Similar to the research from the aviation and military domains, this body of work also finds significant problems with efficient intake of information in less-experienced drivers. In addition, it appears that SA forms a central and conscious task for expert drivers, who may be freed up to develop SA by improved automaticity on physical tasks and enabled by effective mental models for organizing and directing information search and interpretation.

Conclusions

These studies illustrate the significant problems that novices have in building SA. They suffer from poor information-management strategies, including poorly directed information-seeking behaviors and scan patterns that will allow them to detect the most important information from amongst the large number of possibilities.

Their ability to process the information they perceive and to understand its significance to their goals is also quite limited. They may often fail to appreciate the importance or meaning of even the information that they do acquire. In that their cognitive resources are often overloaded with carrying out the necessary psychomotor and communications tasks, they remain significantly behind the ball in developing needed SA.

By contrast, those with increasing levels of expertise exhibit superior strategies for gathering information, both proactively and as a follow-up to information already received. They show superior abilities to grasp quickly the significance of information and to project what is going to happen, allowing them to be in the right place in the sports arena or the battlefield, to have solutions ready to execute in the cockpit, or to avoid road hazards while driving. Although the act of understanding and projecting can become quick and often effortless, i.e, a clear comprehension of the situation springing readily to mind, evidence also shows that experts spend considerable effort at the task of situation assessment. *Actively projecting and planning for contingencies* forms the *hallmark of expertise in* dynamic decision *making.*

It should be noted that much of what has been said here about the role of expertise on SA has much in common with the more general literature on the effect of expertise on cognitive performance (e.g., Ericsson & Lehmann, 1996; Feltovich et al., Chapter 4). This is because SA is not a new cognitive construct that has not been a part of the cognition in other research. Rather, SA has been integral to many of the domains in which expertise has been historically studied, even if it has not been specifically identified as such.

Historically, rather than evolving from psychology laboratories, the term "situation awareness" arose naturally from domain experts in aviation who speak of "getting SA" or trying to "keep SA," dating back as far as World War II (Press, 1986). Similar terms have been found to exist in other domains as well. Air traffic controllers, for instance, talk about "the picture" with an almost identical meaning.

The case for SA, as an area of study, is that it provides a focal point around which experts integrate the information they gather in order to perform their tasks. This integration, and future projections made possible by the mechanisms underlying their expertise, is critical to performance in these complex and demanding domains. By stopping to consider SA, therefore, a richer picture of expert performance can be generated and a more focused approach to developing systems that support SA has been possible.

Expertise undoubtedly also involves other skills, including prowess at physically carrying out the needed tasks (for example, throwing the ball, driving the car, or flying the plane) and forming effective decision strategies. In addition, the ability to develop and maintain situation awareness is a significant contributor to the high levels of performance exhibited by experts in the many domains where dynamic situations must be mastered and understood in order to perform well.

Acknowledgements

This work was conducted with the support of the Advanced Decision Architectures Collaborative Technology Alliance sponsored by the U.S. Army Research Laboratory under Cooperative Agreement DAAD19-01-2-0009.

References

Amalberti, R., & Deblon, F. (1992). Cognitive modeling of fighter aircraft process control: A step towards an intelligent on-board assistance system. *International Journal of Man-machine Systems*, 36, 639–671.

AOPA. (1997). Nall report: "General aviation accident trends and factors for 1996." Fredrick, MD: Aircraft Owners and Pilots Association Air Safety Foundation.

Currie, L. (1969). The perception of danger in a simulated driving task. *Ergonomics*, 12(6), 841–849.

Endsley, M. R. (1988). Design and evaluation for situation awareness enhancement. In *Proceedings of the Human Factors Society 32nd Annual Meeting, Human Factors Society* (pp. 97–101). Santa Monica, CA: Human Factors and Ergonomics Society.

Endsley, M. R. (1989). Pilot situation awareness: The challenge for the training community. In *Proceedings of the Interservice/Industry Training Systems Conference (I/ITSC)* (pp. 111–117), Ft. Worth, TX: American Defense Preparedness Association.

Endsley, M. R. (1995). Toward a theory of situation awareness in dynamic systems. *Human Factors*, 37(1), 32–64.

Endsley, M. R., & Bolstad, C. A. (1994). Individual differences in pilot situation awareness. *International Journal of Aviation Psychology*, 4(3), 241–264.

Endsley, M. R., Bolstad, C. A., Garland, D., Howell, C., Shook, R. W. C., Costello, A., et al. (2002). "Situation awareness training for general aviation pilots: Final report" (No. SATECH 02-04). Marietta, GA: SA Technologies.

Ericsson, K. A., & Lehmann, A. C. (1996). Expert and exceptional performance: Evidence of maximal adaptation to task constraints. *Review Annual of Psychology*, 47, 273–305.

Horswill, M. S., & McKenna, F. P. (2004). Drivers hazard perception ability: Situation awareness on the road. In S. Banbury & S. Tremblay (Eds.), *A cognitive approach to situation awareness: Theory, measurement and application*. Aldershot, UK: Ashgate Publishing.

Jones, D. G., & Endsley, M. R. (1996). Sources of situation awareness errors in aviation. *Aviation, Space and Environmental Medicine*, 67(6), 507–512.

Klein, G. A., Calderwood, R., & Clinton-Cirocco, A. (1986). Rapid decision making on the fire ground. In *Proceedings of the Human Factors Society 30th Annual Meeting* (pp 576–580), Santa Monica, CA: Human Factors Society.

McGrath, C. (1997, March 13). New York Times Magazine.

McKenna, F., & Crick, J. L. (1991). *Hazard perception in drivers: A methodology for testing and training*. Transport Research Laboratory Report No. 313. Crowthorne, U.K.

McKenna, F., & Crick, J. L. (1994). *Developments in hazard perception*. London, UK: Department of Transport.

McKenna, F., & Farrand, P. (1999). The role of automaticity in driving. In G. B. Grayson (Ed.), *Behavioural research in road safety ix*. Crowthorne, UK: Transport Research Laboratory.

Mourant, R. R., & Rockwell, T. H. (1972). Strategies of visual search by novice and experienced drivers. *Human Factors*, 14(4), 325–335.

Newell, A. (1973). Artificial inteligence and the concept of mind. In R. C. Schank & K. M. Colby (Eds.). *Computer models of thought and language (pp. 1–60)* San Francisco, W. H. Frelman.

NTSB. (1989). General aviation accidents involving visual flight rules flight into instrument meteorological conditions (No. NTSB/SR-89/01). Washington, DC: Author.

NTSB. (1998). "1997 U.S. Airline fatalities down substantially from previous year; general aviation deaths rise." NTSB press release 2/24/98 (No. SB 98–12). Washington, DC: Author.

O'Hare, D. (1997). Cognitive ability determinants of elite pilot performance. *Human Factors*, 39(4), 540–552.

Pelz, D. C., & Krumpat, E. (1974). Caution profile and driving record of undergraduate males. *Accident Analysis and Prevention*, 6, 45–58.

Press, M. (1986). Situation awareness: Let's get serious about the clue-bird. Unpublished Manuscript.

Prince, C., & Salas, E. (1998). Situation assessment for routine flight and decision making. *International Journal of Cognitive Ergonomics*, 1(4), 315–324.

Quimby, A. R., Maycock, G., Carter, I. D., Dixon, R., & Wall, J. G. (1986). "Perceptual abilities of accident involved drivers" (No. Research Report 27). Transport and Road Research Laboratory. Crowthorne, UK.

Rouse, W. B., & Morris, N. M. (1985). "On looking into the black box: Prospects and limits in the search for mental models" (No. DTIC #AD-A159080). Atlanta, GA: Center for Man-Machine Systems Research, Georgia Institute of Technology.

Shattuck, L., Graham, J., Merlo, J., & Hah, S. (2000). Cognitive integration: An investigation of how expert and novice commanders process battlefield data. In M. E. Benedict (Ed.), *Proceedings of the Fourth Annual Federated Laboratory Symposium on Displays and Interactive Displays Consortium*. Adelphi, MD: U.S. Army Research Laboratory.

Strater, L. D., Endsley, M. R., Pleban, R. J., & Matthews, M. D. (2001a). "Measures of platoon leader situation awareness in virtual decision making exercises" (No. Research Report 1770). Alexandria, VA: Army Research Institute.

Strater, L. D., Jones, D. G., & Endsley, M. R. (2001b). "Analysis of infantry situation awareness training requirements" (No. SATech 01–15). Marietta, GA: SA Technologies.

Trollip, S. R., & Jensen, R. S. (1991). *Human factors for general aviation*. Englewood, CO: Jeppesen Sanderson.

Underwood, G., Chapman, P., Bowden, K., & Crundall, D. (2002). Visual search while driving: Skill and awareness during inspection of the scene. *Transportation Research, Part F(5)*, 87–97.

Wickens, C. D. (1992). *Engineering psychology and human performance* (2nd ed.). New York: Harper Collins.

CHAPTER 37

Brain Changes in the Development of Expertise: Neuroanatomical and Neurophysiological Evidence about Skill-Based Adaptations

Nicole M. Hill & Walter Schneider

Introduction

As humans acquire skills there are dramatic changes in brain activity that complement the profound changes in processing speed and effort seen in behavioral data. These changes involve learning, developing new representations, strategy shifts, and use of wider cues and approaches. Experts differ from novices in terms of their knowledge, effort, recognition, analysis, strategy, memory use, and monitoring (e.g., see Chi, Chapter 2; Feltovich, Prietula, & Ericsson, Chapter 4). In the last decade, there have be major advances in our ability to noninvasively track human brain activity. There are now over a hundred experiments tracking learning or expert performance. Patterns are beginning to emerge that show that learning and skilled performance produce changes in brain activation – and different types of changes – depending on the brain structure and the nature of the skill being learned.

In this chapter, we will review the changes that occur in the brain as skill is acquired. We will detail the anatomy and processes involved. We will provide a brief summary of the methods employed. We will review the nature of learning of skills, resource utilization, and performance of experts. The reader who wishes to learn more details regarding these methods might examine a current introductory chapter (Schneider & Chein, 2003) or current textbooks of cognitive neuroscience (Gazzaniga, Ivry, & Mangun, 2002), brain imaging (Jezzard, Mathews, & Smith, 2001), and cognitive neuroscience modeling (O'Reilly & Munakata, 2000).

An Example of Changes in Brain Activation during One Hour of Skill Acquisition

It is important to realize that most of the issues involved in behavioral skill development are associated with changes in brain activity. Our brains are always active as we perform any task and even when we are at rest. Any change in human behavior, such as skill acquisition, must have some physical cause that involves either a *functional* change in the brain activation or a *structural* change in the size of brain tissue.

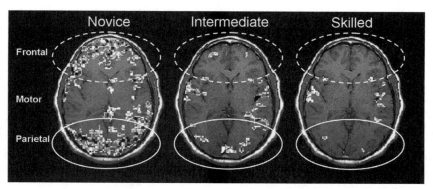

Figure 37.1. Activation of the brain, as a function of practice, in three periods of learning a motor tracking task. This is a maximum projection image, with white areas showing the activation of any cortical area either above or below the illustrated brain slice. The image is an axial (aerial) view of the head, where the top of the image corresponds to the front (nose) of the head and the bottom corresponds to the back of the head. The frontal areas (dashed ellipse) and parietal attention control areas (solid ellipse) show dramatic reductions in activation. The motor areas (middle of images) shares fairly preserved activation.

The understanding of brain mechanisms is synergistic with the understanding of the behavioral mechanisms. Let us illustrate with an example of how skill changes behavior and brains. Through the functional magnetic resonance imaging (fMRI) technique, we can collect brain data and relate that to the behavioral changes observed both in the brain scanner and as a consequence of prior behavioral training. With fMRI, we can compare activation across conditions with millimeter spatial resolution and one second temporal resolution.

Figure 37.1 provides a series of activation patterns that shows how brain activity changes as a skill is acquired, relative to initial untrained performance. The brain activity changes dramatically over the course of sixty minutes of practicing a simple tracking task. With this task, learning occurs rapidly enough to see changes in brain activation within one scanning session. In the first twenty minutes of task performance, many areas of the brain are active. With every ten minutes of practice, brain activation decreases, ultimately reducing by 85% over the course of the first hour.

Subject behavioral performance improves with reductions in tracking error, faster responding with less tracking delay, and as the session continues, tracking becomes less

effortful. As the behavioral changes occur, there are also quantitative and qualitative changes in the cortical activity.

The predominant change is a reduction of brain activation, but changes differ substantially across areas. There is a near drop out of activity in the frontal (anterior) parts of the brain that are involved in task control and working memory (solid ellipses). There are substantial reductions in the posterior part of the brain (parietal cortex) related to attentional control (dashed ellipses). The motor (center region) and perceptual areas (not visible in the brain slice) are involved in making responses and detecting stimuli respectively, and they will remain active because they are necessary for task performance during novice and skilled performance.

One must be cautious about overinterpreting dramatic imaging data, especially with regards to training and brain plasticity (see Poldrack, 2000, for a detailed explanation). When comparing across individuals or time, differences in brain activity can occur for many reasons. Imaging takes a snapshot at a particular point in time. It is difficult to determine if any contrast is stable or due to differences ranging from genetics, experience, strategy, motivation, or changes in baseline.[1]

There are a variety of patterns of change in activation seen in skill acquisition experiments, depending on the nature of the task, practice levels, task difficulty, and nature of control conditions (see Kelly & Garavan, 2005, for a recent review). The patterns include: brain activity decreases in the control network (see next paragraph), maintenance of activity in the perceptual and motor areas, and occasionally increases of brain activity or shifts in activity to new regions. Throughout the chapter we will review examples of changes in brain function (that is, changes in the activity patterns), and we will relate these patterns to the task parameters, behavioral responses, and level of experience in performing the task.

The most common pattern is **reduced control network activation with maintained perceptual motor activity** (note Kelly & Garavan, 2005, refer to this a "processing efficiency change"). The control network is a group of brain areas that are believed to work together to scaffold learning when performing a new task. This network (see "Network of Specialized Processing Regions") comprises a set of discrete cortical areas controlling goal processing, attention, and decision making. One would expect to see those (learning-related) areas active early in practice and then decrease activity, possibly even dropping out, as skill is acquired. This is the expected pattern for perceptual motor tasks, in which stimulus properties and (motor) response properties remain consistent or unvarying throughout performance (see "Controlled and Automatic Processing during Learning" section). A second pattern is one of **increased cortical tissue devoted to the task after very long periods of training** (e.g., expanded hippocampus for taxi drivers). And a third pattern is **functional reorganization.** As the term implies, there is a reorganization of active brain areas; that is, different brain areas are active in different stages of learning. The engagement and disengagement of brain regions reflects the fact that unique regions are involved in the various types of processing. As a skill is acquired, different strategies are used, and therefore new areas become active to perform the underlying processing (e.g., in mir-

ror reading, early practice involves mental rotation of the letters, and late performance involves recognition of the rotated word and recall of the meaning without slow algorithmic rotation).

Overview of Brain Anatomy and Functional Change

To understand the changes of the brain with skill acquisition it is useful to take a structural/functional view of the brain. We will provide a short overview of the architecture of the brain (i.e., the structure or anatomy), that will illustrate the hierarchical nature of perceptual processing by reviewing the visual system (specifically the occipitotemporal pathway), and then comment about brain misconceptions.

The Bare Basics of the Cerebrum

The cerebrum of the brain is divided into five lobes; occipital, parietal, temporal, insular, and frontal. Generally speaking,[2] the function of each lobe is the following:

1. The occipital lobe is involved in visual processing.

2. The parietal lobe participates in visual processing by coding spatial information, and it is involved in attentional control and somatosensory processing (bodily sensation).

3. The temporal lobe also contributes to visual processing at the level of object formation (and face processing) and is involved in coding auditory and verbal information and memory storage.

4. The insular lobe is involved in emotional processing, taste, and learning.

5. The frontal lobe is involved in executive function, reasoning, effort and emotional coding, conceptual information and rules, motor control, speech, and smell.

Network of Specialized Processing Regions

The brain is a network of hierarchically organized specialized modules. If one moves a

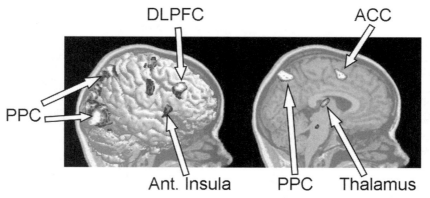

Figure 37.2. Major parts of the Control Network supporting skill acquisition and cognitive control. These areas include dorsolateral prefrontal cortex (DLPFC), anterior cingulate/pre-supplementary motor areas (ACC), posterior parietal cortex (PPC), anterior insula, and thalamus. These areas appear to be domain general and decrease in activation as automaticity develops.

centimeter in the brain, typically the tissue does something distinctively different than the neighboring region.

The brain has many **domain specific representational areas** connected in a quasi-hierarchical fashion. There are an estimated 500–1000 specialized processing regions (Worden & Schneider, 1995). A complex process, such as visual processing, occurs in over thirty distinguishable processing regions (Felleman & Van Essen, 1991), including those for detecting lines, colors, shapes, structure (e.g., houses, faces), motion, and spatial relationships. These representation areas appear to be quasi hierarchically connected. There are reciprocal connections between these regions, allowing information flow to be both bottom-up and top-down. Information is coded in the pattern of activity, with any one region encoding many exemplars and types of stimuli (Ishai, Ungerleider, Martin, Schouten, & Haxby, 1999). These representation areas include input (visual, audition, somatsensory, gustatory) and output motor areas. These areas can be mapped with nearly millimeter precision, showing *retinotopic* (a retinal [eye] based coordinate map in the visual [occipital] cortex), *tonatopic* (a map of acoustical frequencies in the auditory [temporal] cortex), *somatotopic* (a map of bodily sensation in the associative [parietal] cortex), and *motor* (map of muscle control of the

body) functions. As information processing flows to higher levels, its spatial localization reduces and object specialization increases (e.g., moving from lines covering 0.1° visual area in V1 [the initial visual processing region located in the occipital lobe] to faces of individuals anywhere in the visual field in the fusiform cortex [a later visual processing region located in the temporal lobe]).

The brain contains a small number of **domain general control areas** that appear to be involved in many tasks and that modulate cortical activity (see Schneider & Chein, 2003, for details). There is initial evidence to suggest some specialization of function within the different areas. However, these areas work as a tightly coupled unit (e.g., typical correlations between activation in respective areas range from 0.8–0.95). The major areas are listed below, and a subset is shown in Figure 37.2:

- attentional control – posterior parietal cortex (PPC)
- process monitoring, decision making, conflict management – anterior cingulate cortex/pre-supplementary motor area (ACC/pre SMA)
- goal processing and tasks switching – dorsolateral prefrontal cortex (DLPFC)
- emotional processing – amygdula
- episodic coding of association – parahippocampus and hippocampus

- smooth sequential processing – cerebellum
- reinforcement and motor control – basal ganglia

The existence of a *single domain general control architecture*, controlling a large number of *domain specific representation regions*, has strong implications regarding the understanding of skill acquisition and performance. Activation of the control network might differ between tasks and cause conflict when two tasks are performed simultaneously (e.g., the perceptual detection of a novel line angle and completion of a sentence in a language task might conflict if both tasks need activation of domain general comparison operations). Competing activation in the specific representational areas would be a problem only if two tasks utilized the same modality-specific region. For example, two tasks involving motion judgments would interfere with each other, causing performance to deteriorate, but a consistent[3] motion detection task and an auditory frequency detection task could be performed concurrently.

MISCONCEPTIONS ABOUT THE BRAIN AND EXPERTISE

There are three common misconceptions/myths about the brain that are worth refuting before proceeding in the review:

Misconception 1 – More Brain Implies Better Performance. This is perhaps best illustrated by the popular myth that most people "use only 10% of their brain" (see Beyerstein, 1999) and, by implication, that "using more would be better." The brain has many specialized areas, and for any specific task only a small subset is active. This is analogous to muscles. At any one point in time only a small subset of muscles are active in a normal person. In fact, if most of the muscles were active (as in generalized dystonia), a person would be out of control. If much of the brain is active (as in a severe epileptic seizure), one is completely dysfunctional. Another similarity to muscles is that in some cases more is better, but often it is not (e.g., a skilled skier makes very small focused muscle changes to control direction relative to the novice who

makes frequent erratic changes in muscle tone). In learning to row, training results in a decrease in muscle activation, and coherence increases as stroke rate and power increase (Lay et al., 2002). In the brain, having many areas process an input reduces the availability of those areas to process other stimuli. For example, early mirror reading involves large areas of visual representation to encode the visual input, rotate the individual letters, reassemble the rotated letters, and then recognize the word. However, after practice, a small area can recognize the rotated string directly as a visual object (e.g., "ɘʌol") and map it to its meaning, leaving large areas of the visual system available for other tasks.

Misconception 2 – Plasticity Is Limited in Adulthood. There is substantial evidence of changes in connection strength and neuron size for adult subjects. The elderly can learn skills (see Krampe & Charness, Chapter 40), and there is substantial evidence that normal elderly still have cortical plasticity (Buonomano & Merzenich, 1998) and exhibit substantial changes in activation with practice (Karni et al., 1998; Kolb & Whishaw, 2003). Cognitive (i.e., dual-task) training has been demonstrated to increase plasticity in the prefrontal brain regions that exhibit the greatest atrophy in aging population (Erickson et al., 2005c).

Misconception 3 – Left/Right Brain Specialization Is a Major Factor in Learning and Performance. It is true that the brain has specialization (e.g., language tends to be more left dominant). However, most functions appear both on the left and right side of the brain. The brain is far more specialized from front to back (e.g., emotion [front], motor, somatosensory [middle], spatial, visual [back]). The key benefit from brain mapping is not simple location (e.g., left/right or anterior/posterior). Rather, it is the understanding of the hierarchal stages of each of the representation systems and how those interact with executive, emotional, and memory processing that elucidates brain function. Practice will cause changes in the brain areas dedicated to the processing of *what* is specifically practiced (see also Ericsson, Chapter 38). People *do* vary in language and holistic processing, and there is left/right laterality of that processing, but there is little special status for the global feature of being on the left or right.

Next we will preview the six patterns of learning-related brain changes that will be elaborated further in the chapter.

THEMES IN LEARNING LITERATURE, BRAIN PROCESSING, AND BRAIN STRUCTURE

There are **six themes** evident in the learning literature (Kelly & Garavan, 2005; Poldrack, 2000; Schneider & Chein, 2003; see also Feltovich et al., Chapter 4). First, **learning is localized and very specialized,** with different portions of the brain showing dynamic change and location change depending on the task. Second, in general, **learning and processing occur in the same cortical locations**. Third, **learning can produce both increases and decreases in the areas of activation,** influencing both the richness of the representation and the efficiency of processing. Fourth, **in some tasks there is a reorganization of the task that involves different brain regions when alternate strategies[4] are used** (e.g., shifting from performing a math algorithm to using recall to produce an answer). Fifth, **behaviorally relevant objects and other stimuli are uniquely processed by experts** (i.e., faces for everyone, birds for bird watchers, ballet movements for professional ballet dancers). Sixth, **learning can produce detectable morphological changes,** such that extended training can enlarge the amount of grey matter dedicated to processing the type of information that has been trained. The remainder of the chapter will illustrate these themes in three major sections. Section one, "Controlled and Automatic Processing during Learning," will introduce the reader to the dual processing account of skill acquisition, by briefly reviewing the longstanding behavioral effects and the theory's recent extension into characterizing the underlying neural substrates. Within this section, themes 1 and 2 will be illustrated in cognitive laboratory tasks that involve several sessions of training. Section two, "Practice Effects on

Brain Activation in Working Memory Tasks and Dual-Tasks," will extend Section one into working memory and dual-task paradigms. Themes 1–4 will be illustrated in cognitive and motor laboratory tasks that involve a range of training, from minutes to sessions. Finally, Section three, "Perceptual-Motor Learning and Expertise," will review visual processing, motor learning, kinematics, navigation, reading, and music training. Themes 4–6 will be illustrated primary through the study of real-world skills that develop over many years of practice. The themes will be stressed throughout the text; however, we recommend that the reader briefly review them (see above) before proceeding.

Controlled and Automatic Processing during Learning

Skill acquisition involves creating representations and altering control routines. In this section, we will focus on the control routines. Skill acquisition involves priority learning, learning to code stimuli according to their importance (see Feltovich, Prietula, & Ericsson, Chapter 4, on "Expertise Involves Selective Access of Relevant Information"). Through this learning, critical stimuli (determined by learned priority) ultimately transmit information to stimulus processing regions and trigger control area responses. For example, in the cocktail party effect, hearing one's name in a nearby conversation can draw attention, despite competing background noise and focused attention on the current conversation. This is because one's name has become a high priority stimulus that one learns to automatically orient towards over time. (See Proctor & Vu, Chapter 15; Ericsson, Chapter 38, on traditional models of skill acquisition, such as Fitts & Posner, 1967).

Many of the practice effects of learning can be interpreted within the traditionally behavioral framework of automatic processing and controlled processing (Schneider & Shiffrin, 1977; Shiffrin & Schneider, 1977; Feltovich et al., Chapter 4, on "Expertise

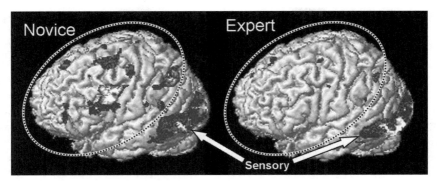

Figure 37.3. Activation early and late in a consistent search task. The dark areas (and dark areas with bright centers) illustrate regions that are active. The ellipses highlight the frontal and parietal areas. There is a substantial reduction in activation in these areas as skill is acquired and more automatic processing develops. The visual areas (lower right parts of the images) show continued activation early and late in practice with the sensory processing continuing even while controlled processing decreases.

Involves Automated Basic Strokes"), with recent extensions to cortical processing (Schneider & Chein, 2003, CAP2 model). Novice performance is assumed to involve high-effort use of the **domain general network** of control processing through attentional routines. The same pieces of brain tissue perform key tasks such as attention, comparison, and decision across different representation modalities (e.g., visual, auditory or motor). **Controlled processing** typically occurs in novel or varied tasks (see "varied mapping" in next paragraph), when one must compare stimuli and release responses based on information stored in working memory. **Automatic processing** typically occurs for well-practiced, consistent tasks where the responses can occur with little effort. These are representation-specific operations (e.g., the visual mapping "ɘʌol" to "love" will not transfer to the reversed phonemes [sounds] of the word "love").

The classic example of a controlled process is visual search of a varied set of objects (see Schneider & Shiffrin, 1977). For example, in a category search task, subjects respond if a word is a member of a category (e.g., respond to animal or vehicle). If the memory set alters from trial to trial and there is a *varied mapping* (VM) (e.g., responding to animals on some trial and ignoring vehicles,

and other trials the opposite) the reaction times are over 200ms per comparison (Fisk & Schneider, 1983). In contrast, if the categories are *consistently mapped* (CM) (e.g., always responding to animals and ignoring vehicles), reaction time is uninfluenced by the number of categories compared (e.g., slope 1ms) once there is extensive practice. The *novice* search task (both CM and VM) involves goal processing, memory, attention, decision making parts of the control network, representation patterns of the visual input, and memory of the targets. The *practiced* CM search task involves automatic processing in which modules transmit representations to the next stage without involvement of the control network (Figure 37.3).

Controlled and automatic processing show dramatically different and complementary processing benefits and disadvantages (see Schneider & Chein, 2003). Controlled processing has characteristics that allow rapid acquisition, easy alteration of process,[5] and modification of memory, but it is a slow, serial, high-effort mode of processing that deteriorates under high workload and stressors (e.g., sleep deprivation, stress, and alcohol). Automatic processing has the complementary weakness and strengths. Automatic processing shows slow acquisition over hundreds of trials, is difficult to alter, does not modify memory, is fast and parallel, is low effort, and is robust to high workload and stressors. The CAP2 model (for an in-depth coverage of the model, we refer the reader to Schneider & Chein, 2003) provides a connectionist implementation of controlled and automatic processing and interprets interactions in the control and data network and likely brain areas involved in each function. The transition from controlled to automatic processing occurs in this model as the data modules become capable of transmitting their output without mediation by the control system.

From a neural perspective, the development of automatic processing should result, with practice, in reductions in the same regions that support controlled processing (Chein & Schneider, in press; Schneider & Detweiler, 1988; Kelly & Garavan, 2005; Jansma et al., 2001; Schneider & Chein, 2003). To determine if a *specific group of brain areas* are commonly modulated as a function of practice, a meta-analysis of brain-imaging studies that utilized practice was performed (Chein & Schneider, in press; Schneider & Chein, 2003). Study selection was restricted to *consistent* tasks in which novice performance was contrasted to practiced (i.e., minimum of ten minutes) performance of an explicitly acquired skill. The meta-analysis revealed activity in a reliable network (that we refer to as the "control network") of brain regions. This putative control network includes lateral frontal, medial frontal, posterior parietal cortices, and the thalamus. According to the theory, such a network should be engaged in novel learning situations and should reduce activity or "drop-out" as a function of extensive consistent practice.

Automatic processing occurs as the control-network regions are released, *leaving task-specific processing regions engaged* to support task performance (Chein & Schneider, in press; Schneider & Chein, 2003; see also, Feltovich et al., Chapter 4 on "Expertise is Limited in its Scope and Elite Performance does not Transfer"). Two fMRI studies have varied consistency of learned associations and demonstrated that

consistency and practice can modulate cortical activity (Chein & Schneider, in press; Jansma, Ramsey, Slagter, & Kahn, 2001) when acquiring skilled performance. Jansma et al. (2001) trained a working-memory consonant item-recognition task under consistent (i.e., target and distractor items are always from distinct sets) and variable conditions (i.e., targets and distractor sets are redefined on every trial by selection from a common pool of items) and found that practice produced reductions in activity only for the consistent task.

The control network appears to be domain general. In a study by Chein, McHugo, and Schneider (in prep), early in practice both an auditory task and a visual spatial task had activated a network of common areas in frontal, cingulate and parietal cortex. In addition there were task specific areas (occipital cortex for the visuospatial task and temporal lobe for the auditory task) that were unique to the type of task being performed. In both tasks, with consistent practice the control network dropped out. It is important to note that at the millimeter level of cortical tissue, *very different tasks initially activated the same cortical control areas* to provide scaffolding to perform and learn the task. The same tissue (i.e., the control network brain regions) was controlling different representation areas, each of which was later able to perform its task automatically.

In a separate study, a paired-associate task, in which all training was kept consistent, demonstrated engagement of the same network and subsequent practice-related reductions for both verbal and non-verbal (i.e., novel shapes that are difficult to assign verbal labels) associates (Chein & Schneider, in press).

In varied mapping tasks, activation resembled initial, untrained levels, both early and late in practice (Chein, McHugo, & Schneider, in prep). There was no evidence of practice-related increases of activation or reorganization. These studies demonstrate that consistent practice, but not variable practice, results in processing efficiency or activity reduction, in the same regions that support untrained performance.

Furthermore, some ancilliary task-related processing regions (such as motor cortex if the task requires a button – press response) continue to activate without regard to consistency of practice.

In summary, the shift from controlled to automatic processing can occur on a relatively short time scale.[6] The changes in behavioral performance (i.e., increases in accuracy and/or decreases in reaction time) are associated with underlying changes in brain processing (i.e., decreases in brain regions responsible for learning and control). This shift only occurs through practice of consistent tasks. Furthermore, brain regions involved in motor and perceptual processing remain active even with practice, as ongoing processing in these areas is necessary for task performance. Finally, automated consistent tasks show no evidence of functional reorganization or practice-related activation increases in the control network regions.

The next section will explore practice effects in working memory and dual-task paradigms. In these studies, outcomes are mixed; that is, practice-related activation increases, practice-related activation decreases, and as well as practice-related activation increases and decreases are all reported. Although the controlled and automatic processing perspective focuses on practice-related brain-activation decreases, practice-related activation maintenance, as well as practice-related activation reorganization, are consistent with the theory in cases of variable tasks that require manipulation of working memory (Jansma et al., 2001; Schneider & Chein, 2003).

Practice Effects on Brain Activation in Working Memory Tasks and Dual-Tasks

In this section we will look at practice effects in cognitive tasks that employ online-learning or working memory and tasks that involve learning to process multiple sub-tasks concurrently, that is, dual-task learning. Although these studies were not designed to investigate automatic processing shifts

(see prior section), parallels can be made in terms of behavioral improvement and neural response. Furthermore, these tasks were trained under a range of practice, both "briefly" (i.e., for 30 minutes) and "extensively" (i.e., several weeks), and produced similar results.

BASIC WORKING MEMORY (WM) OVERVIEW

The working memory model is composed of three major parts, an executive control system and two slave processing systems, one involved in visuospatial information and the other involved in phonological information (Baddeley & Hitch, 1974). Distinct from both short-term and long-term memory, this system is involved in processing and maintaining information over brief delays and in manipulating information. WM tasks have three phases, encoding of stimuli, delay (where no stimulus is present and the associated codes must be maintained and/or manipulated), and retrieval (of codes or transformed codes) to enable responding.

PRACTICE AND WORKING MEMORY

Working memory tasks have been frequently studied using behavioral measures and in brain imaging (Baddeley, 2003; Cabeza & Nyberg, 2000), but only recently have studies investigated the impact of training in these tasks. Imaging studies have reported practice-related increases and decreases in neural activity, as well as shifts in activation location (for review, see Kelly & Garavan, 2005; Poldrack, 2000). Increases may result from strengthening of existing activation or from spatial expansion. Decreases in activity, conversely, may reflect the reduction in the strength of existing activation or a reduction in spatial extent. Whereas increases are believed to reflect the buildup of cortical representations, decreases are believed to result from greater neural efficiency, where only a subset of the initial neurons continue to respond to a particular stimulus or support the performance of a particular task. A shift in the location of activity reflects a reorganization of regions used to support performance. The reorganization may reflect a shift in processing or strategy usage as a result of practice. The level of practice, the period of imaging in proportion to practice amount, the task domain, and task characteristics (such as stimulus-response relationships) influence the dynamics of activation. The majority of experiments involving practice of cognitive tasks report practice-related decreases or reorganization, while motor learning tasks (see motor learning section) tend to report practice-related increases (see below).

Garavan, Ross, Li, and Stein (2000) varied the amount of practice for participants in a visuospatial delayed-match-to-sample task (dot location). Prefrontal and parietal areas, typically implicated in working-memory function (Cabeza & Nyberg, 2000; Carpenter, Just, & Reichle, 2000), were activated during the initial performance of this task. Brain imaging, after both brief and extended practice (80 vs. 880 trials; Garavan et al. 2000), showed reduced activation in these regions. Performance after practice was not associated with increased activation in any other regions, which suggests *processing efficiency* as the source of the reduction as opposed to a *functional reorganization*, where practiced task performance would be supported by regions differing from unpracticed performance. Similar findings were obtained by Landau, Schumacher, Garavan, Druzgal, and D'Esposito (2004), who found that the initial activity in frontal, temporal, parietal, and occipital cortex during a face working-memory[7] task was reduced with practice. The reductions occurred within a single brain-imaging session, subsequent to only thirty minutes of behavioral training, which demonstrated that the decreased magnitude of activation can occur rapidly. Other investigators have found initial increases in activation, with subsequent reductions after extended training. Hempel et al. (2004) trained participants on a verbal n-back task twice daily for two weeks. At two weeks, performance improvements accompanied increases in right superior parietal lobe and right intraparietal sulcus, followed by stable performance and activation decreases after four weeks of practice.

Not all studies report practice-related activation reductions in working memory tasks. Olesen, Westerberg, and Klingberg (2004) trained subjects in a visuospatial span task and monitored this activation in fMRI on five occasions, once per week. The increases found in frontal and parietal regions were interpreted as evidence of cortical plasticity occurring on a slower time scale through extensive training, akin to the "slow learning" changes reported in the motor-learning literature (Karni et al., 1995). Additionally, the experimental training resulted in improved performance on several untrained neuropsychological tests (i.e., spatial tasks, including the Raven's Progressive Matrices, a task that involves reasoning). Olesen et al. (2004) suggest that extended WM training may improve processing capacity, which is necessary for high-level performance on a neuropsychological test battery.

Olesen et al. (2004) and Klingberg et al. (2002) used adaptive training (tasks in which difficulty is adjusted for individual performance) over a longer time scale. The increases in neural activity reported by Olesen may reflect this continual increase in task difficulty, the extensive amount of training conducted relative to other studies, and/or the specifics of the task. Extensive training alone is not likely to account for the increases. At four weeks, Hempel et al. (2004) report *decreases* in n-back training, whereas Karni et al. (1995) report *increases* in activity in finger opposition sequence performance. The increases are consistent with other studies of sequence learning (Karni et al, 1995; Hazeltine, Grafton, & Ivry 1997; Honda et al, 1998), suggesting a distinction between practice on motor and cognitive tasks.

Most of the reviewed studies report decreased working memory activation with task practice, whether the experiment employed "short" training regiments (thirty minutes) "long" training regiments (weeks), or both. One study of visuospatial span (Olesen et al., 2004) did find practice related increases with long training; however, although the task is a working memory task, it is also a sequence task (in which participants had to perform both forward and backward sequences), and the neural response was similar to sequence learning paradigms (which typically contrast new [or transformed] and old sequences [Hazeltine et al., 1997; Honda et al, 1998]) and the finger opposition paradigm ([Karni et al., 1995]; see the motor learning section). This suggests a distinction between motor and cognitive tasks in which motor task practice leads to functional increases of activation, whereas cognitive task practice leads to functional decreases reflecting neural efficiency. Cognitive task decreases of activation are not restricted to working memory tasks per se; decreases were also found in the studies of automatic and controlled processing.

DUAL-TASK METHODOLOGY

An important aspect of skilled performance is the ability to perform multiple tasks at one time. Dual-task performance is an area of interest because of its potential to inform understanding of attention limitations, learning, and executive processing, both through behavioral investigations and more recently in brain-imaging studies. Dual-tasks paradigms employ the performance of two or more tasks in close temporal proximity (see Meyer & Kieras, 1997; Pashler, 1994; Schneider & Detweiler, 1988). Simultaneous performance that is untrained typically results in decreases in accuracy and increases in reaction time relative to isolated task performance. Although all dual-tasks report this concurrent performance cost at some point in training, a distinction is made between dual-tasks that employ *short, variable time lags* (i.e., interstimulus interval, ISI) between component tasks, known as psychological refractory periods (PRP; short ISI < 300 msecs), and those dual-tasks that use relatively *longer, fixed time lags* (typically > 1 second). In PRP tasks, reaction time increases for the second task response in the short-lag condition, relative to the long-lag condition, because short ISIs force the performer to use overlapping task processing,[8] which is a limited resource (that is, for short ISI RT2 > long ISI RT2). PRP tasks are also

typically given response priorities because one task is designated as the primary task while the other is designated the secondary task. The PRP effect is immutable with practice unless performers are allowed to respond without regard to task designation (remove the primary and secondary task-response designation). Non-PRP dual-tasks (ISI > 1 second) do not have immutable concurrent performance costs because practice results in the speeding of processing, so that the performer can learn to respond to each task quickly in isolation, as long as there are no structural limitations (such as having only one response finger) (see Meyer & Kieras, 1997).

There are a variety of patterns of activation seen when contrasting single- and dual-task conditions. This is not surprising when one considers the range of paradigms that are referred to as dual-tasks. A dual-task can be composed of subtasks that involve *concurrent* component tasks (such as PRP tasks) or temporally *separated* component tasks. The subtasks are sometimes "simple" tasks, such as detection or discrimination, or more "complex" tasks, such as spatial rotation or reading comprehension.

Generally speaking, dual-tasking typically involves more effort and time sharing than the single task performance. And motivation and practice history (both single- and dual-task) must be considered when comparing single- and dual-task performance. All of these factors must be interpreted with caution when reviewing dual-task effects in a behavioral study, and the issues are further complicated in a brain-imaging study. For example, in fMRI, threshold selection can cause an area to appear active only under dual-task performance, when in fact it is active, but to a lesser extent, under single-task conditions. In addition, a region that is below threshold because of lack of statistical power may in fact be above threshold due to greater demand for the region in a dual-task setting. Alternatively, time sharing *between two areas* while dual-tasking can result in an area that was active in a single task to drop below threshold during dual-task performance. Typically, however, areas engaged in single tasks are still active in dual-tasks, with equal or greater activity in dual-task conditions.

An early dual-task study by D'Esposito, Detre, Alsop, and Shin (1995) found that concurrent performance of two non-working memory tasks engaged dorsolateral prefrontal cortex (DLPFC) and anterior cingulate cortex (ACC), though these areas were not active during component-task performance. Increasing the difficulty in one of the component tasks (spatial rotation) did not result in activity increases in either of these areas. Together these patterns were interpreted as evidence of DLPFC and ACC as candidate areas for task coordination, an executive function.

Since this study, dual-task specific prefrontal activity has been a contested issue. Adcock et al. (2000) used the same task as D'Esposito et al. (1995), auditory semantic categorization and spatial rotation, to serve as a replication and added another task, face matching, to further test the concept of domain general dual-task specific processing. Both the replication dual-task pair and the new dual-task pair activated prefrontal areas; however, component tasks also engaged these areas to a lesser extent when performed in isolation. The contradictory finding (regarding component-task prefrontal activity) with the original study may be the result of insufficient power or threshold selection (Bunge et al., 2000) such that the prefrontal activity appeared dual-task specific in the D'Esposito study. Furthermore, these purported dual-task areas (DLPFC and ACC) are very commonly reported in single-task experiments (see Cabeza & Nyberg, 2000), and multiple researchers, using a variety of tasks, have not found dual-task specific areas (Adcock, Constable, Gore, & Goldman-Rakic, 2000; Bunge, Klingberg, Jacobsen, & Gabrieli, 2000; Erickson et al., 2005c), though dual-task performance can result in the further activation of areas involved in single-task processing. Alternatively, it has been suggested that concurrent performance may result in the modulation of single-task brain regions (Adcock et al., 2000; Bunge et al., 2000; Erickson et al., 2005c).

Dual-task performance, however, does not always result in brain activity increases. When component tasks compete for the same processing resources, concurrent activation of the same tissue can result in dual-task reductions (Bunge et al., 2000; Just, et al., 2001; Klingberg, 1998). Klingberg (1998) found that auditory and visual working memory tasks activate overlapping areas in prefrontal, cingulate, and inferior parietal cortex that are not sensory modality specific. Furthermore, concurrent performance results in a lesser activation in the face of increasing working memory demand. Jaeggi, et al. (2003) found similar DLPFC and inferior frontal increases in both single-task and dual-task performance when load was parametrically varied in a two n-back tasks. However, the increase in activation as a consequence of load was less for the dual-task, compared to the summed single-task activation. This also suggests that concurrent performance does not necessarily require specific dual-task processing regions.

Recent imaging studies suggest that dual-task specific processing occurs when tasks involve interfering processing (Herath, Klingberg, Young, Amunts, & Roland, 2001; Jiang, 2004; Marcantoni, Lepage, Beaudoin, Bourgouin, & Richer, 2003; Stelzel, Schumacher, Schubert, & D'Esposito, 2005; Szameitat, Schubert, Muller, & von Cramon, 2002; Szameitat, Lepsien, von Cramon, Sterr, & Schubert, 2005). These tasks employ the psychological refractory period paradigm in which a short ISI[9] results in longer response times for the secondary task.[10] Activation of inferior frontal regions were found when concurrent-task performance resulted in interference (i.e., ISI > 300 msec). Interference in these studies was attributed to different sources (motor effector, Herath et al., 2001; perceptual attention [when attending to the periphery of both tasks], Jiang, 2004; central processing, Szameitat, Schubert et al., 2002; Szameitat, Lepsien et al., 2005; stimulus-response modality incompatibility, Stelzel et al., 2005). Herath et al. 2001, found inferior frontal gyrus (IFG) activation only when there was a concurrent performance cost (i.e., only during the shorter ISI). However, recent work by Erickson et al. (2005c) suggests that right IFG activity is not specific to dual-task interference but, alternatively, is associated with preparing to make multiple responses (whether in the context of a single or dual-task) and not actual coordinated performance. This area was engaged by *single-task performance* when comparing mixed single-task trials (i.e., interspersed with dual-task trials) to pure single-task trials (i.e., exclusively single-task trials) in a mixed event related design.[11] Furthermore, this area *was not engaged* by dual-task performance, suggesting that the area is sensitive to "*preparing* to perform multiple tasks" as opposed to the actual performance of multiple tasks.

Two of the studies employing psychological refractory period paradigm (Herath et al., 2001; Szameitat et al., 2002) found dual-task specific prefrontal activity that was *spatially distinct* from the component-task activity, which also activated prefrontal regions. The inconsistent dual-task specific prefrontal activation may potentially be attributable to whether concurrent performance results in a performance deficit and to the level of component task complexity. Although differences in task complexity and performance appear to factor into prefrontal activity, the extent of the impact is a matter of speculation. Further research is necessary to elucidate the role of prefrontal cortex in task coordination and interference.

DUAL-TASK PRACTICE EFFECTS

Few studies have investigated the effects of practice on dual-task related neural activity (Erickson et al., 2005a; Erickson et al., 2005b; Hill & Schneider, 2005). Erickson et al. (2005a) found that untrained dual-task performance engaged the same areas as the component tasks (letter and color discrimination), but to a greater extent. This study is consistent with those that do not report specific prefrontal dual-task processing regions (Adcock et al., 2000; Bunge et al., 2000). After extensive dual- and

single-task training outside of the scanner, most regions decreased in activity except for dorsolateral prefrontal cortex. An increase in left DLPFC was associated with mixed single-task (single-task trials interspersed with dual-task trials) performance for participants that received behavioral training.[12] Bi-lateral DLPFC activity was found for the dual-task condition. These areas were not significantly active at session one. Erickson et al. (2005b) regard the training increase as a shift in processing, where DLPFC begins to support task coordination as a result of training.

Hill and Schneider (2005) found widespread decreases in activity as a result of training an object-word visual search dual-task and a pattern-letter visual search dual-task. These decreases included prefrontal areas, and no areas were found to increase activity with training, suggesting processing efficiency of performance. The training decreases were predicted based on prior work (Chein, McHugo & Schneider, in prep; Chein & Schneider, in press; Schneider & Chein, 2003) demonstrating practice-related reductions when developing automatic processing for consistent tasks (see "Controlled and Automatic Processing during Learning" section).

Differences in activation dynamics between the studies potentially reflect differences in task design and training history. Hill and Schneider (2005) extensively trained *all single-tasks* prior to any scanning, effectively scanning changes related to naïve versus experienced dual-task performance (participants were unpracticed on dual-task performance at scan one). Conversely, scan sessions of Erickson et al. (2005a) reflect untrained task performance (both single and dual-task) compared to trained task performance. The difference in the direction of DLPFC may reflect different assessment points of learning. In addition, the Erickson et al. (2005a, 2005b) dual-task involved simultaneous concurrent letter and color discrimination (ISI = 0), where the Hill and Schneider (2005) dual-task involved continuous rapid visual search (nine search locations changing five times per second);

however, simultaneous targets did not occur in this design (targets could appear at any time during the minute search window as long as they occurred at least two seconds after the prior target). Although participants were instructed to give equal task priority in both studies, Erickson et al. (2005c) subjects tended to respond to the color discrimination task first. PRP interference occurs when one task is instructed to be given response priority or if this strategy is employed by the performer (Meyer & Kieras, 1997). The DLPFC activity may reflect interference related to strategy choice of responding in a fixed order.

In summary, dual-tasks that use a psychological refractory period design elicit inferior frontal activation under conditions of high interference, when the ISI is short. The neural effect of practice on these designs is an unexplored area; however, since practice does not attenuate behavioral interference, inferior frontal cortex would likely maintain activation with training. Dual-tasks with longer, fixed ISI (non-PRP tasks) generally do not report dual-task specific prefrontal (or otherwise) activity, suggesting no general locus for task coordination, an executive process. These tasks tend to have complex subtasks, and therefore it may be difficult to find particular areas engaged in task coordination processing. Dual-tasks that contrast the effects of practice have generally found decreases for inital-task-engaged brain regions; however, one study reports a DLPFC increase. Practice must be employed in more studies to determine the conditions under which practice-related increases would arise. For a discussion of skilled individuals engaging in high-level "real-word" multiple-task environments (such as pilots), see Durso and Dattel (Chapter 20).

Previous sections have looked at performance and brain changes in laboratory cognitive tasks under conditions of short to moderate amounts of training. The final sections will look at performance and brain changes that occur over longer amounts of practice for basic perceptual and motor skills. Examples are face processing, which is developed normally through experience, and music skill, which occurs through intentional training.

Perceptual-Motor Learning and Expertise

Much of human skill acquisition and expertise involves perceptual-motor learning (see Chapter 29 on perceptual-motor expertise by Rosenbaum, Augustyn, Cohen, & Jax). Learning can occur at many levels within the processing hierarchy, depending on the nature of the task. In the case of vision, training has resulted in improved ability to perform discrimination in various tasks (texture segregation, motion discrimination, line orientation, etc.). In some cases, such as line orientation, learning of the trained orientation is specific to the trained location. The failure to transfer learning to other locations argues that the learning occurs early in the processing stream (that is, V1, the locus of initial visual processing in occipital cortex) where receptive fields are small, tightly tuned to a specific orientation, and topographically organized. This is remarkable because early visual processing regions were traditionally considered fixed in the adult brain. The specificity of learning (i.e., does training transfer to untrained location, quadrant, or eye) has demonstrated that perceptual learning can occur at different levels of the processing hierarchy. The specificity effects, however, have not always been consistent (i.e., sometimes transfer occurs and other times it does not), even when training the same type of perceptual task. Note, in a hierarchy of areas, learning can occur at multiple potential levels that show differential transfer (e.g., attend to the lower left oriented line or an oriented line anywhere in the visual field).

The nature of attention and task difficulty can influence the specificity of what is learned in a discrimination task. According to Reverse Hierarchy Theory (Ahissar & Hochstein, 2004), difficult tasks (short vs. long ISI and/or fine vs. course line discrimination) are learned with a high degree of specificity. According to this view, learning is driven by attention, with learning occurring first at the top of the processing hierarchy, then proceeding to the lower levels. Skill on a specific discrimination task also constrains learning such that the performers have improved their signal-to-noise ratio at the lower processing levels and can perform difficult discriminations. Less-skilled performers have poor signal-to-noise ratios at low levels and use high-level representation, providing more generalization and perhaps faster learning, but without the very high levels of performance. Note, in a hierarchical attention network (see Olshausen, Anderson, & Van Essen, 1993), proficiency allows the performer to determine the optimal level of processing given the difficulty of the discrimination.

Learning to perceive phonemes, faces, chess patterns, music, or radiology images all involve multi-level perceptual learning. A simple illustration is the inability even to find word boundaries in a spoken language that is unfamiliar. With experience, phonemes, words, and phrases become units of processing (see Feltovich et al., Chapter 4, "Expertise Involves Larger Cognitive Units"). Imaging data show changes in cortical processing at multiple levels of processing as perceptual discrimination improves (Karni & Sagi, 1991).

In the following we will see how high-level visual areas represent and process objects in the temporal lobe and other brain regions. Visual processing begins in occipital cortex in the back of the brain. As we move forward into the temporal cortex, neurons become responsive to larger receptive fields and more complex configurations of stimuli. Along this pathway, perceptual discrimination develops into object-based representation (that is, entities with specific meaning) through *reciprocal* interactions between high-level and low-level processing regions.

Face Processing

Humans are required to process faces on a daily basis, and it has been suggested they develop greater expertise in this processing than in any other domain (Haxby, Hoffman, & Gobbini, 2000). Neuroimaging studies implicate a visual area in the right mid-fusiform gyrus (though sometimes bilateral) that increases its activity when faces are detected (Kanwisher, McDermott, & Chun, 1997; McCarthy, Puce, Gore, & Allison, 1997). This area has been termed the Fusiform Face Area (FFA) because although it is responsive to other objects, it is most responsive to faces (Kanwisher et al., 1997; Haxby et al., 2000). Imaging studies have demonstrated this greater response to faces, without regard to format (photos and line drawing) and without regard to familiarity (i.e., not more responsive to famous faces) (Gorno-Tempini & Price, 2001; Gorno-Tempini et al., 1998). FFA activation is greater for faces than for hands, animals, objects, and scenes (Aguirre, Singh, & D'Esposito, 1999; Haxby et al., 2000; Ishai et al., 1999; Kanwisher et al., 1997; Kanwisher, Tong, & Nakayama, 1998; Yovel & Kanwisher, 2004). Imagined faces also elicit activation in this area (Kanwisher & O'Craven, 2000). It is undisputed that right FFA responds greatest to faces; however, it has been suggested that this area is not specifically modulated for face processing per se, but for processing visual items for which an individual has developed high levels of expertise and familiarity that can be categorized on the individual level[13] (Tarr & Gauthier, 2000; Feltovich et al., Chapter 4, "Expertises Is Limited in its Scope"). Support for this argument comes from fMRI studies that demonstrate an FFA response to items that are learned at high levels of expertise, such as cars, birds, and "greebles," artificial animal-like stimuli (Gauthier & Tarr, 1997; Gauthier, Skudlarski, Gore, & Anderson, 2000; Gauthier & Tarr, 2002). All of these items are visual, classifiable at the individual level (like faces), and only elicit FFA responses in an individual who has developed expertise for these items.

The FFA response to non-face objects has sparked a debate as to whether this area is a module for face detection (Kanwisher, 2000; Kanwisher et al., 1997;

Kanwisher et al., 1998; Yovel & Kanwisher, 2004), an area of visual expertise (Gauthier & Tarr, 1997; Gauthier et al., 2000; Tarr & Gauthier, 2000), or one area in a network of regions responsible for the distributed-representation of faces and other learned objects. The distributed-representation view claims that all objects produce a pattern of activation across a series of visual areas that codes the learned category (Haxby et al., 2000; Haxby, Gobbini, Furey, Ishai, Schouten, & Pietrini, 2001). The intricacies of this debate are beyond the scope of this chapter, but as a consequence they have produced evidence that humans process all faces as members of an expert class of objects[14] in a small localized area of cortex (e.g., the faces areas in cortex represent less than 1% of the brain). The processing is not unique to one stimulus class but to a range of related stimuli (e.g., faces and other objects).

FFA appears to activate differently, based on experience with different types of faces. Athough FFA is not further activated by famous faces (Gorno-Tempini & Price, 2001; Gorno-Tempini et al., 1998), one study found greater FFA activation for most subjects for same-race faces, compared to faces from other races, presumably because of greater experience with same-race faces (Golby, Gabrieli, Chiao, & Eberhardt 2001); for a critique see Phelps, 2001). This processing area is also sensitive to inversion effect, considered a sign of expert-level object processing,[15] an impairment in recognition for upside-down objects (Yin, 1969; Yin, 1970). Brain-imaging studies have found that inverted faces elicit the same or slightly less FFA activation compared to upright faces (Kanwisher et al. 1998); however, inverted faces further activate object-sensitive regions to a greater extent than upright faces, presumably reflecting that they are processed more like objects (Aguirre, Singh, & D'Esposito 1999; Haxby et al., 1999). In other words, object sensitive regions are highly responsive to inverted faces compared to non-inverted faces, and since the same pattern is exhibited for inverted objects compared to non-inverted

objects, one can argue that faces are treated like objects by object-processing regions.

Existence of the specialized area for face processing is also supported from studies of prosopagnosia patients, who have impairment in identifying individuals through facial recognition (Moscovitch, Winocur, & Behrmann, 1997). This disorder occurs both congenitally and as a consequence of stroke. These patients do not have a general problem with (visual) identification, as they can identify and name individual face parts such as noses, and they can identify people through other cues such as voices. Prosopagnosia patients, however, are not impaired in face inversion presumably because they process inverted faces more like objects (Yin, 1970). Since object inversion is specific to objects for which someone has developed expertise, this may reflect a shift in processing once a class of objects is extremely well learned.

Object Processing

In addition to face processing, humans spend a great deal of time processing other types of objects. The ventral occipito-temporal cortex is activated when viewing pictures of objects, houses, and scenes, compared to textures, noises, or scrambled objects (for a review see Grill-Spector 2003). Many brain-imaging studies have contrasted faces and objects to differentiate processing between these complex visual items (Aguirre et al., 1999; Gauthier et al., 2000; Haxby et al., 2001; Ishai et al., 1999; Malach et al., 1995; McCarthy et al. 1997). There are areas that respond to both parts and whole objects. Object parts elicit responses from object-sensitive regions (Lerner Hendler, Ben-Bashat, Harel, & Malach, 2001), in contrast to the fusiform face area, which is not responsive to face parts. Temporal lobe areas perform object processing. These areas are more sensitive to greater complexity (i.e., these cells are not simple, single feature detectors; they are most responsive to configurations of features; see "Network of Specialized Processing Regions" section) and exhibit some activity to object scrambling, which has been interpreted as evidence that object representation is based on component features (Grill-Spector et al., 1998; Lerner et al, 2001). Recall that objects are typically learned at the basic level (e.g., chairs, chairs, and more chairs, though there is some amount of individual level categorization – "bar stool" versus "armchair"), whereas faces are identified on a highly individualized level (e.g., Mary, Albert, Samantha, Jennifer, Sue, Jean, and David). Some objects (birds, cars, dogs[16]) can support the development of face-like individual level expertise and elicit responses in face-processing regions in individuals who have acquired this expertise through intentional learning; however, most objects are not learned at an expert level, as compared to faces, and are processed differently as such (i.e., object sensitive regions respond to object scrambling, face sensitive regions do not respond to face scrambling).

Experience with objects, however, does impact their processing in other ways. Object recognition in ventral occipito-temporal cortex is *invariant to size* and location (Grill-Spector et al., 1999). Human behavioral work demonstrates that the ability to recognize backwards-masked objects improves with specific practice, and ability transfers when trained objects are *modulated in size* Furmanski & Engel (2000). Monkey single-unit studies (e.g., recording electrical activity from individual units (neurons), to understand neuronal responsiveness)[17] of inferotemporal (IT) neurons have demonstrated that IT neurons develop view-point invariance to objects that *prior to training* were meaningless and unfamiliar (Logothesis, Pauls, & Poggio, 1995). Other studies confirm that IT increases its responsiveness to trained objects (Kobatake, Wang, & Tanaka, 1998) as well as learned patterns (Sakai & Miyashita 1991; 1994).

Recent work implicates these neurons in visual object expertise (i.e., face, acquired bird expertise, etc.; Baker, Behrmann, & Olson, 2002; for comments see Connor, 2002). Baker et al. (2002) performed discrimination training on monkeys to determine if training enhances IT selectivity (i.e.,

tendency to respond to fewer or specifically one thing). Although there was some enhanced selectivity for individual object parts,[18] there was a notable enhancement for "configurations of parts," that is, whole objects. Importantly, this study showed that the specific enhancement in selectivity for trained objects is not due to differences in the strength of response between trained and untrained stimuli. *Selectivity allows objects to be coded at the individual level* (see face-processing section, i.e., specific to a particular category example) instead of at the basic level (i.e., at the category level without regard to a specific example). The former is the hallmark of expertise. Typically objects are not coded at this level. For example, an individual without specific experience studying birds should not be able to identify many subtypes relative to an expert. The Baker et al. (2002) result (i.e., a neuron that is selective to an individual item) suggests a mechanism by which bird watchers may develop selectivity as they learn to identify individual types of birds.

Although the temporal lobe is clearly involved in object learning, training influences frontal cortical areas as well. A recent monkey study by Rainer and Miller (2000) showed that training enhances specificity in PF neurons. Though novel objects elicited a greater PF response than familiar objects, with training neural activity became more narrowly tuned for familiar objects in these neurons. Training also results in a PF representation that is robust to the effects of stimulus degradation. In addition, Freedman, Riesenhuber, Poggio, and Miller (2001) demonstrated that PF neurons are important in learning new object categories.

In summary, objects such as faces and other highly behaviorally relevant objects (i.e., relevant for the task at hand, such as birds are behaviorally relevant to bird watchers) receive specialized processing in the visual-processing stream. In the motor sections we will present further examples of how behaviorally relevant movements (i.e., finger movements for violinist) and stimuli (i.e., words for readers) are represented uniquely in the cortex. We will also see that practice with these items will sometimes result in structural expansions of cortex.

Word Reading

Learning to read is a key skill in our modern society. It involves developing new representations in a variety of cortical areas. Of particular importance is the Visual Word Form Area (VWFA), an area of left fusiform gyrus that appears sensitive to words that are specifically presented visually. The basic findings with regard to this area have been reviewed by McCandliss, Cohen, and Dehaene (2003) and will be summarized below. VWFA is insensitive to visual variation such as changes in case, font, and even location (i.e., no difference in response to left or right hemisphere presented words). It is insensitive to lexical properties of words such as word frequency, and it even responds to pseudowords as long as these words are well formed according to regularities of the language system. This area is also responsive to non-word objects for which a person has achieved visual expertise such as faces. Therefore VWFA has been suggested as an area specifically implicated in word-form processing as a result of developed expertise in processing behaviorally relevant stimuli. A recent meta-analysis of imaging cross-cultural language processing (Bolger, Perfetti, & Schneider, 2005) provides support by demonstrating that VWFA is consistently activated across word tasks and writing systems (both eastern and western). Furthermore, lesions to the VWFA region have resulted in impairments in recognizing and naming words and pronounceable nonwords, but are relatively spared in the identification of digits, objects, and, in some cases, letters themselves. This is a disorder known as pure alexia. Thus, the role of processing visually abstract forms of candidate words has been ascribed to this region (McCarthy & Warrington, 1990; Miozzo & Caramazza, 1998). However, owing to the complex vasculature of the brain, pure alexia stemming from the inferior temporal region rarely ever occurs (Price & Devlin, 2003).

What are the areas that support reading change as a function of proficiency? A cross-sectional fMRI study (subjects ranged in age between six and twenty-two) found a shift in brain regions associated with an implicit word-processing task as reading ability develops (Turkeltaub, Gareau, Flowers, Zeffiro, & Eden, 2003). As reading began to reflect knowledge of abstract word properties (semantics and phonological properties) and was less supported by rote memorization of words based on visual features and context (i.e., "stop" in a stop sign), readers demonstrated increased activation in left middle temporal and inferior frontal gyri and decreases in right inferotemporal regions.

Brain plasticity in the reading circuit can be observed even in adult subjects after short periods of training. In a novel orthography training experiment, Bolger, Schneider, and Perfetti (2005) trained subjects to learn to read eighty words written in Korean script. Pilot studies conducted with training on only sixteen words found increases in cortical activation occur rapidly: a 0.7% increase in BOLD signal from learning trials one through four to trials thirteen through sixteen (Bolger, 2005). After four sessions (twenty words/session) of training, the response in the VWFA increased significantly and with greater learning in a componential (i.e., learning letter-sound correspondences) compared with a holistic (i.e., learning of the whole word) training approach to the material.

How people attend and process stimuli alters what cortical areas show plasticity. Sandak et al. (2004) explored the effects of orthographic, phonological, and semantic pseudowords training on overt naming ability. Orthographic training involved making judgments about consonant and vowel patterns in pseudowords, phonological training involved making rhyme judgments in pseudowords, and semantic training involved learning novel semantic associations to pseudowords. Phonological and semantic training resulted in equivalent (but superior when compared to orthographic training) performance on reading ability. Despite comparable behavioral performance, phonological and semantic training effects were driven by different neural processes. Phonological training modulates VWFA processing. The reported reduction in activation was interpreted as reflecting efficient processing in this region.

Studies have shown the structural connectivity of white matter fiber tracts to be deficient in poor versus skilled readers (Klingberg et al., 2000). Similarly, functional-connectivity studies of correlated cortical activity have revealed stronger connectivity between angular gyrus with inferior frontal and ventral fusiform regions as a function of reading skill (Horwitz et al., 1998). Pugh et al. (2001) conducted their own functional-connectivity study of the angular gyrus comparing normal to impaired readers. Their findings reveal that in dyslexics connectivity in the angular gyrus region is weak for word and pseudoword reading.

The reading literature illustrates some anatomical mechanisms of learning in the brain. Processing is localized and very specialized, with VWFA showing word encoding, learning, and processing occurring in the same area. Learning produces both increases in activation early in practice and decreases as reading becomes more automatic (i.e., if processing rate is controlled). Words are processed in specialized areas by experts, and learning can produce detectable morphological changes. In addition, the training studies show that the nature of the practice (e.g., phonological or semantic encoding) impacts where the plastic change takes place.

Motor Learning

Motor areas can *rapidly* change as a result of skilled movement practice and improved performance. Primary motor cortex or M1 is notable for plastic change with *very extensive experience and practice* (for a review see Sanes & Donoghue, 2000). M1 motor representations are experience dependent and highly modifiable under changing environments. For example, blind individuals with knowledge of Braille have enlarged M1 representation for their (reading) index finger (Pascual-

Leone et al, 1993; Pascual-Leone and Torres, 1993). Perhaps most dramatically, structural damage, such as a facial nerve lesion, resulted in the rat primary motor cortex (M1) shifting representation to a new group of muscles (representing the forelimb) within one to three hours of the insult (Huntley, 1997).

Primary motor cortex learning effects have been investigated extensively with sequence learning paradigms. An early functional magnetic resonance imaging study (Karni et al, 1995) found that M1 modulates its response to trained finger-thumb opposition sequences according to the level of practice. Early in practice, M1 is sensitive to order, initially being more responsive to the first sequence and later being more responsive to the second sequence, within one session of training. Karni has referred to the reversal of order effect as the fast learning phase. However, after four weeks of training M1 is more responsive to the trained sequence, compared to the untrained sequence, regardless of practice order – termed the slow learning phase. In addition to slow and fast learning, M1 is believed to be involved in consolidation or in performance improvements that occur subsequent to practice (Ungerleider, Doyon, & Karni, 2002). The consolidation process is time dependent; disruption of M1 by repetitive Transcranial Magnetic Stimulation (rTMS) immediately after practice diminishes the effects of training (Muellbacher et al., 2002). rTMS of control brain[19] regions and of M1 six hours after training does not mitigate the effects of practice. M1 consolidation effects are evidence that this region is involved in early learning processing; however, consolidation blocking has been found in other regions. This has been regarded as evidence for a distributed network of areas involved in early phases of motor learning, particularly the learning of complex motor skills (Baraduc, Lang, Rothwell, & Wolpert, 2004).

Although brain-imaging work implicates M1 in sequence learning, (Karni et al., 1995), single-unit research suggests that M1 is involved in movement execution but is insensitive to temporal order aspects of skilled movement (Tanji & Shima;

1994). Single-unit recording in the monkey implicates supplementary motor area (SMA) and pre-supplementary motor area (pre-SMA) involvement in sequence learning. Neuron response properties in these regions are sensitive to *particular* trained sequences and rank orders (i.e., "always respond to the second action"); additionally, they are sensitive to movement interval and movement initiation, both with regard to specific movement types and sequence completion (Tanji & Shima, 1994; Shima & Tanji, 2000). The distributions of neural responsiveness for the aforementioned functions vary between SMA and pre-SMA, as does the specific selectivity for each function (for example in the case of rank-order neurons, their response may be exclusive to the second action, or they may respond to both the first and second action but not the third). More pre-SMA neurons (10%) as compared to SMA neurons (2%) respond during the initiation of a new sequence, suggesting a role in the early stages of learning for pre-SMA. Injecting pre-SMA with muscimol to produce a reversible lesion resulted in a disruption of performance (in terms of button press errors) for novel but not learned sequences (Nakamura, Sakai, & Hikosaka 1999). Injection of SMA produced a similar pattern (i.e., disruption occurring only for novel sequence performance); however, this was not a significant effect. Furthermore, in another study, pre-SMA neurons became less active as sequences become automated (Nakamura, Sakai, & Hikosaka 1998). Together these studies provide evidence that pre-SMA is involved in sequence learning.

Body Kinematics

Complex motor actions, such as those involved in dance and martial arts (see Noice and Noice, Chapter 28), are coded differently by an observer, depending on the observer's own expertise executing the specific movements (Calvo-Merino, Glaser, Grèzes, Passingham, & Haggard, 2005). Regions sensitive to motor expertise include bilateral pre-motor cortex and intraparietal sulcus, right superior parietal lobe, and left posterior superior temporal sulcus. These areas respond more strongly when an expert observer *views* a movement that was *specifically acquired previously by the observer (e.g., seeing a dance move that the observer had learned to perform)*. Therefore, the brain is sensitive to complex acquired movement, such that passive viewing of another individual performing behaviorally relevant movement results in specialized processing and representation. Studies of the macaque "mirror" neurons provide a mechanism for this viewer-based processing of relevant movement. Mirror neurons discharge when the monkey performs an action or observes another monkey or human perform this action, hence their name, and have been proposed to exist in humans (Gallese & Goldman, 1998; Rizzolatti et al., 1996). In the monkey these neurons are known to exist in premotor and parietal cortex. According to Calvo-Merino et al. (2005), the human mirror system appears to code for "complete action patterns" that are in an individual's motor repertoire, as opposed to movements that are highly familiar to the observer. They scanned professional ballet dancers, professional capoeira martial artists, and control subjects with no specific movement expertise as these individuals passively viewed video-taped movements from both disciplines. They were able to demonstrate the mirror system's expertise specificity, which even distinguishes ballet and capoeira, despite similar kinematics for males. Even though whole movements were somewhat similar (sub-movements can be identical) the expert brain is sensitive enough to discriminate between acquired movements in the studied discipline and similar movements in the non-studied discipline. In other words, if the participants were expert performers, such as a ballet dancer, their brain had a greater response to viewing ballet movements when compared to viewing capoeira, even though there is similarity in the types of movements being performed in both disciplines (see also, Feltovich et al., Chapter 4, on "Expertise is Limited . . ."). It is important to stress that Calvo-Merino et al. (2005) argue that expertise is operating at the level of being able to perform the movement and not just being familiar with the movement (i.e., this suggests that there is a difference between the brain of a professional dancer and an avid dance enthusiast) that appears to drive these regions. Female and male ballet dancers code ballet movements differently based on the "gender" of the movement; that is, in classical ballet certain movements are only performed by men, and other movements only by women, but many movements are gender neutral. For example, men never learn to dance "on point," that is, stand on their toes. Although no dancer can perform all movements, all dancers are highly familiar with viewing all movements through rehearsals, classes, and performances. Left parietal cortex is less responsive in female ballet dancers when they view "male" ballet movements. A skilled movement, in this case gender-matched specific movements, modulate the level of envoked representation by the expert brain. Therefore, the ability and personal experience with performing these specialized movement patterns appear to be critical to the difference in representation of the movements. These results show brain specializations that enable the encoding of observed actions into one's own action systems in a way that may potentially enable replication of the observed actions.

Automotive Spatial Navigation

Brain areas supporting spatial navigation are sensitive to expertise with regard to function and structure (see Durso & Dattel, Chapter 20). One example of a spatial navigation expert is a taxi driver. These highly skilled individuals have to know large metropolitan areas and how to reach locations in the most efficient manner. London taxi drivers rigorously train, on average for two years, to pass a series of exams about street names and their locations, which is required for their taxi license. Their extensive experience learning navigation has been suggested to produce functional and structural changes (Maguire, Frackowiak, & Frith, 1997; Maguire et al., 2003). Functional MRI revealed increased right posterior hippocampus (RPH) activation with successful recall of routes around

London (Maguire et al., 1997). Grey matter volume in this region (as well as left posterior hippocampus; LPH) was subsequently shown to be greater in the expert (driver) population, compared to a non-expert control group (increase relative to non-drivers: RPH = 1.936%, LPH = 1.506%; Maguire et al., 2000) and another control group ranging in navigational expertise but without specific taxi driving experience (Maguire et al., 2003).[20] Posterior right hippocampal grey matter volume is positively correlated with taxi driving experience (r = 0.6; p < 0.05) in drivers, but there was no associated grey matter relationship in non-drivers. Haguire and colleagues suggest that the structural differences in taxi drivers are based on acquired experience and *not* innate ability that might cause high performers to seek out this profession. Correlation analysis shows that individuals skilled in "wayfinding" (new route development) activated anterior hippocampus during novel routes but activated the head of the right caudate when following well-learned routes (Hartley, Maguire, Spiers, & Burgess, 2003). This distinction is not found in individuals who perform poorly at wayfinding.

Expert drivers use these two areas dependent on the task at hand; the hippocampus is purported to form a modifiable cognitive map supporting new route development, whereas the caudate supports fast, automatic navigation of well-learned routes. Furthermore, these areas have been proposed to support learning in a complimentary fashion (Hartley et al., 2003) in other task domains (classification learning, Poldrack et al., 2001; mirror reading, Poldrack & Gabrieli, 2001). These studies demonstrate that expertise provides the flexibility to choose the optimal strategy for successful completion of a given task (cf. Feltovich, Spiro, & Coulson, 1997). These different strategies rely on different brain structures for their execution.

Music Training

Music expertise is an important topic in skill acquisition (see Lehmann & Gruber, Chapter 26) in which mastery has been shown to produce changes in brain regions that support both motor and auditory functions. Analogous to the section on ballet dancer expertise (see "Body Kinematics" section), trained musicians code behaviorally relevant movements uniquely in their given discipline. And consistent with the information presented in the motor learning section, we again see that movement practice results in the expansion of motor cortex. This section will briefly review motor related changes. (For extensive reviews, including related changes in the auditory cortex, see Gaser & Schlaug, [2003]).

Increased cortical representation, specific to the muscles engaged in the task at hand, is associated with playing musical instruments. For example, the fingers on the left hand of violinists have reliably larger cortical representation compared to the same hand in non-musicians (Elbert, Pantev, Wienbruch, Rockstroh, & Taub, 1995). There are no right-hand differences between musicians and non-musicians, consistent with the fact that the right-hand fingers do not move independently when playing the violin, unlike the left hand. This increased representation reflects cortical reorganization that is more dramatic in individuals who began musical study at an early age. Furthermore, a training study found that both physical and mental piano practice has resulted in increased M_1 representation for the trained hand, but only in novice players (Pascual-Leone et al., 1995). Experienced players have already developed M_1 representations for relevant movements in their acquired domain.

In addition to increasing M_1 representation, music training may influence how digits are represented (Small, Hlustik, Chen, Dick, Gauthier, & Solodkin, 2005). Although thumb movement resulted in a "predictable"[21] M_1 activation for all subjects, non-dominant left-hand individual finger movements were predictable in right M_1 for violinists but not non-musicians. Conversely, non-musicians showed the opposite pattern, in which dominant right-hand finger movements were the only ones to produce predictable left M_1 activation. Dominant-hand M_1 predictability was not found in the violinist. Musical training did not result in a difference in primary somatosensory cortex for musicians and non-musicians. This preliminary work suggests that the relative distribution of M_1 activity for individual digits is sensitive to experience and *typically encodes* individual movements in the *dominant hand* (i.e., the hand with the greater dexterity). However, violin-specific, highly individuate finger training impacts the "default state" of M_1 encoding (i.e., contralateral[22] M_1 typically encodes individual movements in the dominant hand), which results in a *predictable* contralateral M_1 *encoding the non-dominant left hand* of violins. Presumably this reorganization reflects representation of movement at a task-specific level, modulated by practice. In other words, M_1 representation reflects behavioral relevance. The learning is specific (e.g., to the hand and type of motor action).

Finally, in a recent study, music training has been demonstrated to induce structural changes (increased myelination in white matter tracts) in professional pianist (Bengtsson et al., 2005). Several areas show this increased myelination, but most areas correlated with childhood practice (i.e., practice occurring at age sixteen years or younger). Furthermore, practice-related myelination thickening was greater for childhood practice than adulthood practice.

Music training results in structural changes (expansion and increased myelination). Primary and secondary motor areas are considerably less active in professional musicians (Jäncke et al., 2000). This suggests that in terms of functional differences, training produces greater efficiency with regard to processing in experts. Therefore, expertise results in a savings in processing in a music-related motor task.

Other Types of Expertise Discussed in This Handbook

In their chapter on exceptional memory, Wilding and Valentine (Chapter 31) discussed the imaging studies by Maguire et al. (2003) comparing the world's memory experts' to control participants' brain activation during memorization. They found that the differences in brain activation during different memory tasks could be completely accounted for by the superior strategies that the world experts reported using (similar to taxi drivers; Hartley et al., 2003). The same study did not find any anatomical differences in the brains of the world experts compared to the control participants,[23] which suggests that the difference in memory performance can be explained in terms of acquired skill (Ericsson, 2003; Chapter 13).

Of additional interest, Butterworth (Chapter 32) describes the evidence on brain activation during routine and challenging mathematical calculations. He reviews evidence that fronto-parietal networks support the performance of routine numerical tasks (Pesenti, Thioux, Seron, & De Volder, 2000) with left intraparietal sulcus being specialized for numerical processing (Dehaene, Piazza, Pinel, & Cohen, 2003). The brain of an expert calculator named Gamm is also discussed. Similar to the taxi driver study of Hartley et al. (2003), Pesenti et al. (2001) found that experts use different brain systems to support their calculations and also could exhibit flexibility in strategy choice (supported by different brain regions) to solve their problems.

In summary, in addition to processing efficiency, enriched representations, and structural expansions, experts can flexibly use strategies, by recruiting the associated brain regions, to solve a range of problems, whereas novice performers can not.

Conclusion

The development and execution of skills has profound effects on the nature of brain processing. The brain is a plastic structure that can change the amount of area and the activity of areas as a function of training, effort, and strategy. There are hundreds of specialized areas of the brain. Training has differential effects on the domain general control areas and the domain specific representational areas. The presence of a single domain general control network that supports novice and variable performance represents a severe resource limit for performing novel or varying tasks and working memory dependent tasks (see also Feltovich et al., Chapter 4, "Expertise is an Adaptation"). This network provides the scaffolding to support new learning and to maintain working memory variables and operations in order to allow varying the nature of the performance and strategy shifts in cognitive processing. In consistent tasks, as processing becomes more automatic, the domain general activity decreases or drops out.

The specific nature of the representational areas suggests that both training and performance will be sensitive to the strategy and nature of the training. What is learned is based on which representational areas are active during training. Typically, as practice develops, activity decreases, and there are rarely new areas that develop in laboratory studies of skill acquisition. This suggests that training causes local changes in the specific representational areas that support skilled performance. In studies of extensive training, there is ample evidence for changes in cognitive processing as well as structural changes in the nervous system.

Brain training has analogies and differences to muscle training. Working a specific brain area can increase the representation space and make processing more focused. If one wants to strengthen a brain area, one needs to attentively activate those areas to alter the neurons in that area. Training of the domain specific areas typically decreases activity as processing gets more focused; however, it can cause increases in some motor tasks as well as some tasks involving exceptional memory. The domain general areas might be analogous to cardiovascular training in muscle training (e.g., training endurance transfers across many sports). However, the specific training (e.g., shooting in basketball and hitting in baseball) is unlikely to activate the same areas or representation and do not lead to transfer.

Cognitive neuroscience is in a synergistic research development with skill-based research. We know that training dramatically effects performance and brain activity. We are now beginning to relate those changes to better understand both the brain and skilled performance.

Footnotes

1. FMRI data is not an absolute value and therefore the signal is always assessed as a percent change relative to a baseline or control condition. One can determine whether a location differs in activation over time (e.g., active when stimulus present but not during resting periods).

2. This is not a comprehensive list of functions. Often performance relies on dynamic interactions among various regions, both within and across lobes. Furthermore, there are regions outside the cerebrum, namely, the brain stem, cerebellum, and spinal cord, that make important contributions to the performance of skills.

3. See "Controlled and Automatic Processing during Learning" section.

4. Evidence will also be presented that experts are more flexible in their strategy utilization.

5. That is, performance characteristics can be flexibly modified on the fly.

6. This shift typically involves no more than several sessions of training for simple cognitive tasks such as visual search paradigms (where one searches for targets in a display containing distractor items), as opposed to several years of training for learning a musical instrument or high-level chess mastery.

7. The task involved recognition of faces presented at encoding after a delay period. Load was varied to compare low-load (one to two faces) with high-load (three to four faces) conditions.

8. This is referred to as processing bottlenecks, which means that a specific process must be performed serially. Serial processing produces interference (increased RT) when in a dual-task environment. The nature of locus of such bottlenecks is a matter of debate (Meyer & Kieras, 1997; Pashler, 1994; Schneider & Detweiler, 1988; Shiffrin, 1988).

9. The paper uses the term "SOA" for stimulus onset asynchrony instead of "ISI" for inter-stimulus interval.

10. Marcantoni et al. (2003) uses another interference paradigm, rapid serial visual presentation (RSVP).

11. Dual task and single tasks were scanned in a mixed event-related design allowing blocks to contain pure (i.e., exclusively) single-task, pure dual-task, and mixtures of single- and dual-task trials. This design allowed the activity associated with individual trial types to be contrasted against any other trial, regardless of block, such that differences in dual-task performance when planning to perform exclusively a dual-task trial versus a mixture of dual- and single-task trials could be addressed.

12. A control group was employed to control for non-training specific effects in dual-task activity.

13. Most objects, such as "tables," are classified at the basic level. Faces are considered relatively unique because they are processed at the individual level, which is with regarded to particular examples.

14. The authors are not presenting this information in support of the Gauthier et al. (2000) visual-expertise interpretation. It should be noted that some of these findings have been contested or interpreted as both support for and evidence against this FFA-individual-level-expertise model. The work is mentioned because it pertains to differential processing of expert or experienced-based items.

15. Dog experts, compared to novices for instance, exhibit dog-inversion decrements in identification (Diamond & Carey, 1986).

16. To clarify, being familiar with a few specific types of birds or even an individual bird (i.e., a pet parrot) does not grant this level of expertise. To develop face-like expertise for a non-face object category such as birds, one must become extremely knowledgeable in identifying many bird subtypes. This expertise-based processing would develop only in an avid bird watcher and not the typical individual who can identify a few varieties of birds and/or may own birds as pets.

17. Much of our understanding of the visual system traditionally comes from invasive monkey physiology studies. Since the advent of non-invasive brain imaging techniques, we have been able to confirm that the human

visual system works in a highly similar way. Single-unit recording studies allow us to determine the response properties of individual neurons; however, because this technique is invasive, it is typically not performed on humans, with the rare exception being patients undergoing neurological surgical procedures.

18. Selectivity enhancement for object parts has been demonstrated also when features are diagnostic (Sigala & Logothetis, 2002).

19. "Control brain regions" does not refer to the control network, but rather other brain regions serving as experimental controls.

20. Overall hippocampal size does not differ between drivers and non-drivers, because non-drivers have an increase in anterior hippocampi regions relative to drivers.

21. A split-half correlation analysis was preformed, based on a technique developed by Haxby et. al., (2001), on primary motor and somatosensory cortex (respectively M1 and S1). Digit movement was defined more predictably for a particular region, in this case M1, if the movement-specific activity correlated better with itself across the two halves of the data than with any other digit movement.

22. In the motor system, the right side of the body is controlled by the left side of the brain and vice versa.

23. Taxi-drivers do have morphological expansions based on experience, see "Automotive Spatial Navigation" section for an explanation.

References

Adcock, R. A., Constable, R. T., Gore, J. C., & Goldman-Rakic, P. S. (2000). Functional neuroanatomy of executive processes involved in dual-task performance. *Proceedings of the National Academy of Sciences*, 97(7), 3567–3572.

Aguirre, G. K., Singh, R., & D'Esposito, M. (1999). Stimulus inversion and the responses of face and object-sensitive cortical areas. *Neuroreport*, 10, 189–194.

Ahissar, M., & Hochstein, S. (2004). The reverse hierarchy theory of visual perceptual learning. *Trends in Cognitive Sciences*, 8(10), 457–464.

Baddeley, A. (2003). Working memory and language: An overview. *Journal of Communications Disorders*, 36, 189–208.

Baddeley, A. D., & Hitch, G. J. (1974). Working memory. In G. A. Bower (Ed.), *Recent Advances in Learning and Motivation*, Vol. 8 (pp. 47–89). New York: Academic Press.

Baker, C. I., Behrmann, M., & Olson, C. R. (2002). Impact of learning on representation of parts and wholes in monkey inferotemporal cortex. *Nature Neuroscience*, 5(11), 1210–1216.

Baraduc, P., Lang, N., Rothwell, J. C., & Wolpert, D. M. (2004). Consolidation of dynamic motor learning is not disrupted by rTMS of primary motor cortex. *Current Biology*, 14(3), 252–256.

Bengtsson, S. L., Nagy, Z., Skare, S., Forsman, L., Forssberg, H., & Ullen, F. (2005). Extensive piano practicing has regionally specific effects on white matter development. *Nature Neuroscience*, 8(9), 1148–1150.

Beyerstein, B. L. (1999). Whence cometh the myth that we only use ten percent of our brains? In S. D. Sala (Ed.), *Mind Myths: Exploring Everyday Mysteries of the Mind and Brain* (pp. 1–24). Chichester, UK: Chichester, UK.

Bolger, D. J. (2005). [Pilot fMRI data of learning a novel orthography.] Unpublished raw data.

Bolger, D. J., Perfetti, C. A., & Schneider, W. (2005). Cross-cultural effect on the brain revisited: Universal structures plus writing system variation, *Human Brain Mapping*, 25, 92–104.

Bolger, D. J., Schneider, W., & Perfetti, C. A. (2005). *The Development of Orthographic Knowledge: A Cognitive Neuroscience Investigation of Reading*. Paper presented at the 12th Annual Meeting of the Society for the Scientific Study of Reading, Toronto, Ontario.

Bunge, S. A., Klingberg, T., Jacobsen, R. B., & Gabrieli, J. D. E. (2000). A resource model of the neural basis of executive working memory. *Proceedings of the National Academy of Sciences*, 97(7), 3573–3578.

Buonomano, D. V., & Merzenich, M. M. (1998). Cortical plasticity: From synapses to maps. *Annual Review of Neuroscience*, 21, 149–186.

Cabeza, R., & Nyberg, L. (2000). Imaging cognition ii: An empirical review of 275 pet and fMRI studies. *Journal of Cognitive Neuroscience*, 12(1), 1–47.

Calvo-Merino, B., Glaser, D. E., Grèzes, J., Passingham, R. E., & Haggard, P. (2005). Action observation and acquired motor skills: An fMRI study with expert dancers. *Cerbral Cortex, 15*, 1243–1249.

Carpenter, P. A., Just, M. A., & Reichle, E. D. (2000). Working memory and executive function: Evidence from neuroimaging. *Current Opinion in Neurobiology, 10*, 195–199.

Chein, J. M., McHugo, M., & Schneider, W. (in preparation). The transition from controlled to automatic processing in simple search tasks as revealed with fMRI. Manuscript in preparation.

Chein, J. M., & Schneider, W. (in press). *Neuroimaging studies of practice-related change: fMRI and meta-analytic evidence of a domain-general control network for learning.* Cognitive Brain Research.

Connor, C. E. (2002). Representing whole objects: Temporal neurons learn to play their parts. *Nature Neuroscience, 5*(11), 1105–1106.

D'Esposito, M., Detre, J. A., Alsop, D. C., & Shin, R. K. (1995). The neural basis of the central executive system of working memory. *Nature, 378*(6554), 279–281.

Dehaene, S., Piazza, M., Pinel, P., & Cohen, L. (2003). Three parietal circuits for number processing. *Cognitive Neuropsychology, 20*, 487–506.

Elbert, T., Pantev, C., Wienbruch, C., Rockstroh, B., & Taub, E. (1995). Increased cortical representation of the fingers of the left hand in string players. *Science, 270*(5234), 305–307.

Erickson, K. I., Colcombe, S. J., Wadhwa, R., Bherer, L., Peterson, M. S., Scalf, P. S., Kim, J. S., Alvarado, M., & Kramer, A. F. (2005a). *Training-induced plasticity in older adults: Effects of training on hemispheric asymmetry.* Unpublished manuscript, Urbana.

Erickson, K. I., Colcombe, S. J., Wadhwa, R., Bherer, L., Peterson, M. S., Scalf, P. S., Kim, J. S., Alvarado, M., & Kramer, A. F. (2005b). *Training induced changes in dual-task processing: An fMRI study.* Unpublished manuscript, Urbana.

Erickson, K. I., Colcombe, S. J., Wadhwa, R., Bherer, L., Peterson, M. S., Scalf, P. S., & Kramer, A. F. (2005c). *Neural correlates of dual-task performance after minimizing task-preparation.* Unpublished manuscript, Urbana.

Felleman, D. J., & Van Essen, D. C., (1991). Distributed hierarchical processing in primate cerebral cortex. *Cerebral Cortex, 1*, 1–47.

Feltovich, P. J., Spiro, R. J., & Coulson, R. L. (1997). Issues of expert flexibility in contexts characterized by complexity and change. In P. J. Feltovich, K. M. Ford, & P. R. Hoffman (Eds.), *Expertise in Context* (pp. 125–146). Menlo PK, CA: AAAI/MIT Press.

Fisk, A. D., & Schneider, W. (1983). Category and word search: Generalizing search principles to complex processing. *Journal of Experimental Psychology: Learning, Memory, and Cognition, 9*(2), 177–195.

Fitts, P., & Posner, M. I. (1967). *Human Performance.* Monterey, CA: Brooks/Cole. Fitts, P., & Gibson, E. J. (1969). *Principles of Perceptual Learning and Development.* Englewood Cliffs, NJ: Prentice Hall. Fitts, P., & Welford, A. T. (1968). *Fundamentals of Skill.* London: Methuen.

Freedman, D. J., Riesenhuber, M., Poggio, T., & Miller, E. K. (2001). Categorical representation of visual stimuli in the primate prefrontal cortex. *Science, 291*, 312–316.

Furmanski, C. S., & Engel, S. A. (2000). Perceptual learning in object recognition: Object specificity and size invariance. *Vision Research, 40*, 473–484.

Gallese, V., & Goldman, A. (1998). Mirror neurons and the simulation theory of mind-reading. *Trends in Cognitive Science, 2*(12), 493–501.

Garavan, H., Ross, T. J., Li, S. J., & Stein, E. A. (2000). A parametric manipulation of central executive functioning. *Cerebral Cortex, 10*, 585–592.

Gaser, C., & Schlaug, G. (2003). Gray matter differences between musicians and nonmusicians. *Annals of the New York Academy of Sciences, 999*, 514–517.

Gauthier, I., Skudlarski, P., Gore, J. C., & Anderson, A. W. (2000). Expertise for cars and birds recruits brain areas involved in face recognition. *Nature Neuroscience, 3*(2), 191–197.

Gauthier, I., & Tarr, M. J. (1997). Becoming a "greeble" expert: Exploring mechanisms for face recognition. *Vision Research, 12*, 1673–1682.

Gauthier, I., & Tarr, M. J. (2002). Unraveling mechanisms for expert object recognition: Bridging brain activity and behavior. *Journal of Experimental Psychology: Human Perception and Performance, 28*(2), 431–446.

Gazzaniga, M. S., Ivry, R. B., & Mangun, G. R. (2002). *Cognitive Neuroscience: the Biology of the Mind* (Second Edition). New York: W. W. Norton & Company.

Golby, A. J., Gabrieli, J. D., Chiao, J. Y., & Eberhardt, J. L. (2001). Differential responses in the fusiform region to same-race and other-race faces. *Nature Neuroscience, 4*(8), 845–850.

Gorno-Tempini, M. L., & Price, C. J. (2001). Identification of famous faces and buildings: A functional neuroimaging study of semantically unique items. *Brain, 124,* 2087–2097.

Gorno-Tempini, M. L., Price, C. J., Josephs, O., Vandenberghe, R., Cappa, S. F., Kapur, N., Frackowiak, R. S. J., & Tempini, M. L. (1998). The neural systems sustaining face and proper-name processing. *Brain, 121,* 2103–2118.

Grill-Spector, K. (2003). The neural basis of object perception. *Current Opinion in Neurobiology, 13,* 159–166.

Grill-Spector, K., Kushnir, T., Edelman, S., Avidan-Carmel, G., Itzchak, Y., & Malach, R. (1999). Differential processing of objects under various viewing conditions in the human lateral occipital complex. *Neuron, 24,* 187–203.

Grill-Spector, K., Kushnir, T., Hendler, T., Edelman, S., Itzchak, Y., & Malach, R. (1998). A sequence of object-processing stages revealed by fMRI in the human occipital lobe. *Human Brain Mapping, 6,* 316–328.

Hartley, T., Maguire, E. A., Spiers, H. J., & Burgess, N. (2003). The well-worn route and the path less traveled: Distinct neural bases of route following and wayfinding in humans. *Neuron, 37,* 877–888.

Haxby, J. V., Gobbini, M. I., Furey, M. L., Ishai, A., Schouten, J. L., & Pietrini, P. (2001). Distributed and overlapping representations of faces and objects in ventral temporal cortex. *Science, 293,* 2425–2430.

Haxby, J. V., Hoffman, E. A., & Gobbini, M. I. (2000). The distributed human neural system for face perception. *Trends in Cognitive Sciences, 4*(6), 223–233.

Haxby, J. V., Ungerleider, L. G., Clark, V. P., Schouten, J. L., Hoffman, E. A., & Martin, A. (1999). The effect of face inversion on activity in human neural systems for face and object perception. *Neuron, 22,* 189–199.

Hazeltine, E., Grafton, S. T., & Ivry, R. (1997). Attention and stimulus characteristics determine the locus of motor-sequence encoding. A pet study. *Brain, 120,* 123–140.

Hempel, A., Giesel, F. L., Garcia Caraballo, N. M., Amann, M., Meyer, H., Wustenberg, T., Essig, M., & Schroder, J. (2004). Plasticity of cortical activation related to working memory during training. *American Journal of Psychiatry, 161*(4), 745–747.

Herath, P., Klingberg, T., Young, J., Amunts, K., & Roland, P. (2001). Neural correlates of dual task interference can be dissociated from those of divided attention: An fMRI study. *Cerebral Cortex, 11,* 796–805.

Hill, N. M., & Schneider, W. (2005). Changes in neural activation related to dual-task practice: Evidence for a domain general learning network. Poster presented at the 11th annual meeting of Human Brain Mapping. Toronto, ON.

Honda, M., Deiber, M. P., Ibanez, V., Pascual-Leone, A., Zhuang, P., & Hallett, M. (1998). Dynamic cortical involvement in implicit and explicit motor sequence learning. A pet study. *Brain, 121,* 2159–2173.

Horwitz, B., Rumsey, J. M., & Donohue, B. C. (1998). Functional connectivity of the angular gyrus in normal reading and dyslexia. *Proceedings of the National Academy of Science of the United States of America, 95,* 8939–8944.

Huntley, G. W. (1997). Correlation between patterns of horizontal connectivity and the extend of short-term representational plasticity in rat motor cortex. *Cerebral Cortex, 7,* 143–156.

Ishai, A., Ungerleider, L., Martin, A., Schouten, J. L., & Haxby, J. V. (1999). Distributed representation of objects in the human ventral visual pathway. *Proceedings of the National Academy of Sciences of the United States of America, 96,* 9379–9384.

Jäncke, L., Shah, N. J., & Peters, M. (2000). Cortical activation in primary and secondary motor areas for complex bimanual movements in professional pianists. *Cognitive Brain Research, 10,* 177–183.

Jaeggi, S. M., Seewer, R., Nirkko, A. C., Eckstein, D., Schroth, G., Gronerm R., & Gutbrod, K. (2003). Does excessive memory load attenuate activation in the prefrontal cortex? Load-dependent processing in single and dual task: functional magnetic resonance imaging study. *NeuroImage, 19,* 210–225.

Jansma, J. M., Ramsey, N. F., Slagter, H. A., & Kahn, R. S. (2001). Functional anatomical correlates of controlled and automatic processing. *Journal of Cognitive Neuroscience, 13,* 730–743.

Jezzard P., Matthews, P. M., & Smith, S. M. (2001). *Functional MRI: An introduction to methods.* Oxford: Oxford University Press.

Jiang, Y. (2004). Resolving dual-task interference: An fMRI study. *Neuroimage, 22,* 748–754.

Just, M. A., Carpenter, P. A., Keller, T. A., Emery, L., Zajac, H., & Thulborn, K. R. (2001). Interdependence of nonoverlapping cortical systems in dual cognitive tasks. *Neuroimage, 14,* 417–426.

Kanwisher, N. (2000). Domain specificity in face perception. *Nature Neuroscience, 3*(8), 759–763.

Kanwisher, N., McDermott, J., & Chun, M. M. (1997). The fusiform face area: A module in human extrastriate cortex specialized for face perception. *Journal of Neuroscience, 17*(11), 4302–4311.

Kanwisher, N., & O'Craven, K. (2000). Mental imagery of faces and places activates corresponding stimulus-specific brain regions. *Journal of Cognitive Neuroscience, 12*(6) 1013–1023.

Kanwisher, N., Tong, F., & Nakayama, K. (1998). The effect of face inversion on the human fusiform face area. *Cognition, 68,* B1–B11.

Karni, A., Meyer, G., Jezzard, P., Adams, M. M., Turner, R., & Ungerleider, L. G. (1995). Functional MRI evidence for adult motor cortex plasticity during motor skill learning. *Nature, 377,* 155–158.

Karni, A., & Sagi, D. (1991). Where practice makes perfect in texture discrimination: Evidence for primary visual cortex plasticity. *Proceedings of the National Academy of Science of the United States of America, 88*(11), 4966–4970.

Karni, A., Meyer, G., Rey-Hipolito, C., Jezzard, P., Adams, M. M., Turner, R., & Ungerleider, L. G. (1998). The acquisition of skilled motor performance: Fast and slow experience-driven changes in primary motor cortex. *Proceedings of the National Academy of Sciences of the United States of America, 95,* 861–868.

Kelly, A. M. C., & Garavan, H. (2005). Human functional neuroimaging of brain changes associated with practice. *Cerebral Cortex, 15*(8), 1089–1102.

Klingberg, T. (1998). Concurrent performance of two working memory tasks: Potential mechanisms of interference. *Cerebral Cortex, 8,* 593–601.

Klingberg, T., Forssberg, H., & Westerberg, H. (2002). Training of working memory in children with adhd. *Journal of Clinical and Experimental Neuropsychology, 24*(6), 781–791.

Klingberg, T., Hedehus, M., Temple, E., Salz, T., Gabrieli, J. D., Moseley, M. E., & Poldrack, R. A. (2000). Microstructure of temporo-parietal white matter as a basis for reading ability: Evidence from diffusion tensor magnetic resonance imaging. *Neuron, 25,* 493–500.

Kobatake, E., Wang, G., & Tanaka, K. (1998). Effects of shape-discrimination training on the selectivity of inferotemporal cells in adult monkeys. *Journal of Neurophysiology, 80,* 324–330.

Kolb, B., & Whishaw, I. Q. (2003). *Fundamentals of Human Neuropsychology* (Fifth Edition). New York: Worth Publishers.

Landau, S. M., Schumacher, E. H., Garavan, H., Druzgal, T. J., & D'Esposito, M. (2004). A functional mri study of the influence of practice on component processes of working memory. *Neuroimage, 22,* 211–221.

Lay, B. S., Sparrow, W. A., Hughes, K. M., & O'Dwyer, N. J. (2002). Practice effects on coordination and control, metabolic energy expenditure, and muscle activation. *Human Movement Science, 21,* 807–830.

Lerner, Y., Hendler, T., Ben-Bashat, D., Harel, M., & Malach, R. (2001). A hierarchical axis of object processing stages in the human visual cortex. *Cerebral Cortex, 11*(4), 287–297.

Logothetis, N. K., Pauls, J., & Poggio, T. (1995). Shape representation in the inferior temporal cortex of monkeys. *Current Biology, 5,* 552–563.

Maguire, E. A., Frackowiak, S. J., & Frith, C. D. (1997). Recalling routes around London: Activation of the right hippocampus in taxi drivers. *The Journal of Neuroscience, 17*(18), 7103–7110.

Maguire, E. A., Gadian, D. G., Johnsrude, I. S., Good, C. D., Richard, J. A., Frackowiak, S. J., & Frith, C. D. (2000). Navigation-related structural change in the hippocampi of taxi drivers. *Proceedings of the National Academy of Science United States of America, 97*(8), 4398–4403.

Maguire, E. A., Spiers, H. J., Good, C. D., Hartley, T., Frackowiak, S. J., & Burgess, N. (2003). Navigation expertise and the human hippocampus: A structural brain imaging analysis. *Hippocampus, 13,* 250–259.

Malach, R., Reppas, J. B., Benson, R. R., Kwong, K. K., Jiang, H., Kennedy, W. A., Ledden, P. J., Brady, T. J., Rosen, B. R., & Tootell, R. B. (1995). Object-related activity revealed by functional magnetic resonance imaging in human occipital cortex. *Proceedings of the National Academy of Sciences of the United States of America, 92*(18), 8135–8139.

Marcantoni, W. S., Lepage, M., Beaudoin, G., Bourgouin, P., & Richer, F. (2003). Neural correlates of dual task interference in rapid visual streams: An fMRI study. *Brain and Cognition*, 53, 318–321.

McCandliss, B. D., Cohen, L. G., & Dehaene, S. (2003). The visual word form area: Expertise for reading in the fusiform gyrus. *Trends in Cognitive Sciences*, 7(7), 293–299.

McCarthy, G., Puce, A., Gore, J. C., & Allison, T. (1997). Face-specific processing in the human fusi-form gyrus. *Journal of Cognitive Neuroscience*, 9(5), 605–610.

McCarthy, R., & Warrington, E. K. (1990). The dissolution of semantics. *Nature*, 343(6259), 599.

Meyer, D. E., & Kieras, D. E. (1997). A computational theory of executive cognitive processes and multiple-task performance: Part I. Basic mechanisms. *Psychological Review*, 104, 2–65.

Miozzo, M., & Caramazza, A. (1998). Varieties of pure alexia: the case of failure to access graphemic representations. *Cognitive Neuropsychology*, 15(1–2), 203–238.

Moscovitch, M., Wincour, G., & Behrmann, M. (1997). What is special about face recognition? Nineteen experiments on a person with visual object agnosia and dyslexia but normal face recognition. *Journal of Cognitive Neuroscience*, 9(5), 555–604.

Muellbacher, W., Ziemann, U., Wissel, J., Dang, N., Kofler, M., Facchini, S., Borrojerdi, B., Poewe, W., & Hallett, M. (2002). Early consolidation in human primary motor cortex. *Nature*, 415, 640–644.

Nakamura, K., Sakai, K., & Hikosaka, O. (1998). Neuronal activity in medial frontal cortex during learning of sequential procedures. *Journal of Neurophysiology*, 80, 2671–2687.

Nakamura, K., Sakai, K., & Hikosaka, O. (1999). Effects of local inactivation of monkey medial frontal cortex in learning of sequential procedures. *Journal of Neurophysiology*, 82(2), 1063–1068.

O'Reilly, R. C., & Munakata, Y. (2000). *Computational Explorations in Cognitive Neuroscience: Understanding the Mind by Simulating the Brain*. Cambridge, MA: MIT Press.

Olesen, P. J., Westerberg, H., & Klingberg, T. (2004). Increased prefrontal and parietal activity after training of working memory. *Nature Neuroscience*, 7, 75–79.

Olshausen, B. A., Anderson, C. H., & Van Essen, D. C. (1993). A neurobiological model of visual attention and invariant pattern recognition based on dynamic routing of information. *Journal of Neuroscience*, 13(11), 4700–4719.

Pashler, H (1994). Dual-task interference in simple tasks: Data and theory. *Psychological Bulletin*, 116, 220–244.

Pesenti, M., Thioux, M., Seron, X., & De Volder, A. (2000). Neuroanatomical substrates of Arabic number processing, numerical comparison and simple addition: A PET study. *Journal of Cognitive Neuroscience*, 12, 461–479.

Pesenti, M., Zago, L., Crivello, F., Mellet, E., Samson, D., Duroux, B., Seron, X., Mazoyer, B., & Tzourio-Mazoyer, N. (2001). Mental calculation expertise in a prodigy is sustained by right prefrontal and medial-temporal areas. *Nature Neuroscience*, 4(1), 103–107.

Phelps, E. A. (2001). Faces and races in the brain. *Nature Neuroscience*, 4(8), 775–776.

Poldrack, R. A. (2000). Imaging brain plasticity: Conceptual and methodological issues. *Neuroimage*, 12, 1–13.

Poldrack, R. A., Clark, J., Paré-Blagoev, E. J., Shohamy, D., Moyano, J. C., Myers, C., & Gluck, M. A. (2001). Interactive memory systems in the human brain. *Nature*, 414, 546–550.

Poldrack, R. A., & Gabrieli, J. D. E. (2001). Characterizing the neural mechanisms of skill learning and repetition priming. Evidence from mirror reading. *Brain*, 124, 67–82.

Price, C. J., Devlin, J. T. (2003). The myth of the visual word form area. *Neuroimage*, 19, 473–481.

Pugh, K. R., Mencl, W. E., Jenner, A. R., Katz, L., Frost, S. J., Lee, J. R., Shaywitz, S. E., & Shaywitz, B. A. (2001). Neurobiological studies of reading and reading disability. *Journal of Communication Disorders*, 39, 479–492.

Rainer, G., & Miller, E. K. (2000). Effects of visual experience on the representation of objects in the prefrontal cortex. *Neuron*, 27, 179–189.

Rizzolatti, G., Fadiga, L., Matelli, M., Bettinardi, V., Paulesu, E., Perani, D., & Fazio, F. (1996). Localization of grasp representations in humans by pet: 1. Observation versus execution. *Experimental Brain Research*, 111, 103–111.

Sakai, K., & Miyashita, Y. (1991). Neural organization for the long-term memory of paired associates. *Nature*, 354(6349), 108–109.

Sakai, K., & Miyashita, Y. (1994). Visual imagery: An interaction between memory retrieval and focal attention. *Trends in Neuroscience*, 17(7), 287–289.

Sandak, R., Mencl, W. E., Frost, S. J., Rueckl, J. G., Katz, L., Moore, D. L., Mason, S. A., Fulbright, R. K., Constable, R. T., & Pugh, K. R. (2004). The neurobiology of adaptive learning in reading: A contrast of different training conditions. *Cognitive, Affective, & Behavioral Neuroscience*, 4(1), 67–88.

Sanes, J. N., & Donoghue, J. P. (2000). Plasticity and primary motor cortex. *Annual Review of Neuroscience*, 23, 393–415.

Schneider, W., & Chein, J. M. (2003). Controlled & automatic processing: Behavior, theory, and biological mechanisms. *Cognitive Science*, 27, 525–559.

Schneider, W., & Detweiler, M. (1988). The role of practice in dual-task performance: Toward workload modeling in a connectionist/control architecture. *Human Factors*, 30(5), 539–566.

Schneider, W., & Shiffrin, R. M. (1977). Controlled and automatic human information processing I: Detection, search, and attention. *Psychological Review*, 84(1), 1–66.

Shiffrin, R. M. (1988). Attention. In R. C. Atkinson, R. J. Herrnstein, G. Lindzey, & R. D. Luce (Eds.), *Stevens' Handbook of Experimental Psychology, 2nd Edition* (pp. 739–811). New York: Wiley.

Shiffrin, R. M., & Schneider, W. (1977). Controlled and automatic human information processing II: Perceptual learning, automatic attending, and a general theory. *Psychological Review*, 84(2), 127–190.

Shima, K., & Tanji, J. (2000). Neuronal activity in the supplementary and presupplementary motor areas for temporal organization of multiple movements. *Journal of Neurophysiology*, 84, 2148–2160.

Sigala, N., & Logothetis, N. K. (2002). Visual categorization shapes feature selectivity in the primate temporal cortex. *Nature*, 415, 318–320.

Small, S., Hlustik, P., Chen, E., Dick, F., Gauthier, J., & Solodkin, A. (2005). *Distributed population codes in the primary motor cortex of violinist*. Paper presented at the 11th Annual Meeting of the Organization for Human Brain Mapping, Toronto, Ontario.

Stelzel, C., Schumacher, E. H., Schubert, T., & D'Esposito (in press). The neural effect of stimulus-response modality compatibility on dual-task performance: an fMRI study. *Psychological Research*.

Szameitat, A. J., Lepsien, J., von Cramon, D. Y., Sterr, A., & Schubert, T. (in press). Task-order coordination in dual-task performance and the lateral pre-frontal cortex: an event-related fMRI study. *Psychological Research*.

Szameitat, A. J., Schubert, T., Muller, K., & von Cramon, D. Y. (2002). Localization of executive functions in dual-task performance with fMRI. *Journal of Cognitve Neuroscience*, 14(8), 1184–1199.

Tanji, J., & Shima, K. (1994). Role for supplementary motor area cells in planning several movements ahead. *Nature*, 371(6496), 413–416.

Tarr, M. J., & Gauthier, I. (2000). FFA: A flexible fusiform area for subordinate-level visual processing automatized by expertise. *Nature Neuroscience*, 3(8), 764–769.

Turkeltaub, P. E., Gareau, L., Flowers, D. L., Zeffiro, T. A., & Eden, G. F. (2003). Development of neural mechanisms for reading. *Nature Neuroscience*, 6, 767–777.

Ungerleider, L. G., Doyon, J., & Karni, A. (2002). Imaging brain plasticity during motor skill learning. *Neurobiology of Learning and Memory*, 78, 553–564.

Worden, M., & Schneider, W. (1995). Cognitive task design for fMRI. *International Journal of Imaging Systems and Technology*, 6, 253–270.

Yin, R. K. (1969). Looking at upside-down faces. *Journal of Experimental Psychology*, 81(1), 141–145.

Yin, R. K. (1970). Face recognition by brain-injured patients. A dissociable ability? *Neuropsychologia*, 8, 395–402.

Yovel, G., & Kanwisher, N. (2004). Face perception: Domain specific, not process specific. *Neuron*, 44, 889–898.

CHAPTER 38

The Influence of Experience and Deliberate Practice on the Development of Superior Expert Performance

K. Anders Ericsson

There are several factors that influence the level of professional achievement. First and foremost, extensive experience of activities in a domain is necessary to reach very high levels of performance. Extensive experience in a domain does not, however, invariably lead to expert levels of achievement. When individuals are first introduced to a professional domain after completing their basic training and formal education, they often work as apprentices and are supervised by more-experienced professionals as they accomplish their work-related responsibilities. After months of experience, they typically attain an acceptable level of proficiency, and with longer experience, often years, they are able to work as independent professionals. At that time most professionals reach a stable, average level of performance, and then they maintain this pedestrian level for the rest of their careers. In contrast, some continue to improve and eventually reach the highest levels of professional mastery.

Traditionally, individual differences in the performance of professionals have been explained by an account given by Galton (1869/1979, see Ericsson, 2003a, for a description). According to this view, every healthy person will improve initially through experience, but these improvements are eventually limited by innate factors that cannot be changed through training; hence attainable performance is constrained by one's basic endowments, such as abilities, mental capacities, and innate talents. This general view also explains age-related declines in professional achievement, owing to the inevitable degradation of general capacities and processes with age (see also Krampe & Charness, Chapter 40). More recently, researchers of expert performance have found that there are many types of experience and that these different types have qualitatively and quantitatively different effects on the continued acquisition and maintenance of an individual's performance (Ericsson, 1996, 2002; Ericsson, Krampe, & Tesch-Römer, 1993). This framework proposes that some types of experience, such as merely executing proficiently during routine work, may not lead to further improvement, and that further improvements depend on deliberate efforts to change particular aspects of performance.

In this chapter I will review evidence on the effects of experience and deliberate practice on individual differences in the acquisition of skilled and expert performance. I will first describe the traditional account of individual differences in performance based on experience and innate talent. Then I will review evidence on the effects of various types of experience on performance, especially the effects of deliberate practice. In the last half of the chapter, I will discuss how deliberate practice can account for the changes in the structure of the mechanisms that mediate the superior performance of experts.

The Traditional View of Skill Acquisition and Professional Development: History and Some Recent Criticisms

Ideas about how experience and training can explain individual differences in attained level of performance have a long history. The contemporary view of lifespan development (Denney, 1982) is based on the assumption that children develop their abilities during childhood and can reach their innate potential under favorable experiential conditions. Further, the general view is that the individual's potential is limited by innate biological capacities that will ultimately constrain the highest level of achievement. Sir Francis Galton is often recognized for articulating this view in the 19th century. His pioneering book, *Hereditary Genius* (Galton, 1869/1979), presented evidence that height and body size were determined genetically. Most importantly, he argued that innate mechanisms also regulated size and characteristics of internal organs, such as the nervous system and the brain, and thus must similarly determine mental capacities. Galton (1869/1979) clearly acknowledged the need for training and practice to reach high levels of performance in any domain. However, he argued that improvements of performance for mature adults are rapid only in the beginning of training and that subsequent increases diminish, until "Maximal

performance becomes a rigidly determinate quantity" (p. 15). According to Galton, the relevant heritable capacities determine the upper bound for the performance that an individual can attain through practice, and reflect the immutable limit that "Nature has rendered him capable of performing" (p. 16). According to Galton, the characteristics that limit maximal performance after all benefits of training have been gained must, therefore, be innately endowed. Galton's arguments for the importance of innate factors for attaining the highest levels of performance were compelling and, thus, have had a lasting impact on our culture's view of ability and expertise.

Contemporary theories of skill acquisition (Anderson, 1982; Fitts & Posner, 1967) are consistent with Galton's general assumptions about basic unmodifiable capacities and with observations on the general course of professional development. When individuals are first introduced to a skilled activity such as driving a car, typing on a computer, or playing golf, their primary goal is to reach a level of proficiency that will allow them to perform these everyday tasks at a functional level. During the first phase of learning (Fitts & Posner, 1967), beginners try to understand the requirements of the activity and focus on generating actions while avoiding gross mistakes. This phase is illustrated in the lower arrow in Figure 38.1. In the second phase of learning, when people have had more experience, noticeable mistakes become increasingly rare, performance appears smoother, and learners no longer need to focus as intensely on their performance to maintain an acceptable level. After a limited period of training and experience – frequently less than 50 hours for most everyday activities such as typing, playing tennis, and driving a car – an acceptable level of performance is typically attained. As individuals adapt to a domain during the third phase of learning, their performance skills become automated, and they are able to execute these skills smoothly and with minimal effort (as is illustrated in the lower arrow in Figure 38.1). As a consequence of automatization, performers lose the ability to control

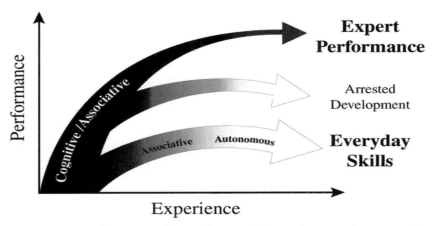

Figure 38.1. An illustration of the qualitative difference between the course of improvement of expert performance and of everyday activities. The goal for everyday activities is to reach as rapidly as possible a satisfactory level that is stable and "autonomous." After individuals pass through the "cognitive" and "associative" phases, they can generate their performance virtually automatically with a minimal amount of effort (see the gray/white plateau at the bottom of the graph). In contrast, expert performers counteract automaticity by developing increasingly complex mental representations to attain higher levels of control of their performance and will therefore remain within the "cognitive" and "associative" phases. Some experts will at some point in their career give up their commitment to seeking excellence and thus terminate regular engagement in deliberate practice to further improve performance, which results in premature automation of their performance. (Adapted from "The scientific study of expert levels of performance: General implications for optimal learning and creativity" by K. A. Ericsson in *High Ability Studies*, 9, p. 90. Copyright 1998 by European Council for High Ability.)

the execution of those skills, making intentional modifications and adjustments difficult (see Hill & Schneider, Chapter 37). In the automated phase of learning, performance reaches a stable plateau, and no further improvements are observed – in agreement with Galton's (1869/1979) assumption of a performance limit.

Similar phases of acquisition and automatization have been shown to account for development in professional domains, such as telegraphy (Bryan & Harter, 1897, 1899) and typing (Book, 1925a, 1925b). Whereas initial proficiency in everyday and professional skills may be attained within weeks and months, development to very high levels of achievement appear to require many years or even decades of experience. In fact, Bryan and Harter claimed already in 1899 that over ten years are necessary for becoming an expert. In their seminal theory of

expertise, Simon and Chase (1973) proposed that future experts gradually acquired patterns and knowledge about how to react in situations by storing memories of their past actions in similar situations. Hence, performance is assumed to improve as a consequence of continued experience. Chase and Simon's (1973) research on chess masters extended the pioneering work by de Groot (1946/1978) and demonstrated that the masters' recall for briefly presented regular game positions was vastly superior to less-skilled players. Simon and Chase (1973) argued that the masters must have acquired some 50,000 chunks or patterns to enable them to retrieve the appropriate moves for the current position in a chess game. They highlighted the parallels between reaching this highly skilled performance in chess and acquiring other cognitive skills, such as speaking a foreign language with its large vocabulary of many thousands of words. They found that players must have played chess for at least ten years before they are able to win international chess tournaments. In a similar vein, every healthy child requires many years of experience of listening and speaking before they are able to master their first language with its extensive vocabulary.

Some scientists started to consider the possibility that expertise was an automatic consequence of lengthy experience, and they considered individuals with over ten years of full-time engagement in a domain to be experts. These scientists typically viewed expertise as an orderly progression from novice to intermediate and to expert, where the primary factors mediating the progression through these stages were instruction, training, and experience. Thus, the primary criteria for identifying experts were social reputation, completed education, accumulated accessible knowledge, and length of experience in a domain (over ten years) (Chi, Glaser, & Farr, 1988; Hoffman, 1992).

Several reviews over the past decade (Ericsson et al., 1993; Ericsson & Kintsch, 1995; Ericsson & Lehmann, 1996; Ericsson & Smith, 1991; Vicente & Wang, 1998) have raised issues about this characterization of expertise. Most importantly, when individuals, based on their extensive experience and reputation, are nominated by their peers as experts, their actual performance is occasionally found to be unexceptional. For example, highly experienced computer programmers' performance on programming tasks is not always superior to that of computer science students (Doane, Pellegrino, & Klatzky, 1990), and physics professors from UC Berkeley were not always consistently superior to students on introductory physics problems (Reif & Allen, 1992). More generally, level of training and experience frequently has only a weak link to objective measures of performance. For example, the length of training and professional experience of clinical psychologists is not related to their efficiency and success in treating patients (Dawes, 1994), and extensive experience with software design is not associated with consistently superior proficiency on

presented tasks (Rosson, 1985; Sonnentag, 1998). Similarly, when wine experts are required to detect, describe, and discriminate characteristics of a wine without knowledge of its identity (i.e., seeing the label on the bottle), their performance is only slightly better than those generated by regular wine drinkers (Gawel, 1997; Valentin, Pichon, de Boishebert, & Abdi, 2000). More generally, reviews of decision making (Camerer & Johnson, 1991; Shanteau & Stewart, 1992) show that experts' decisions and forecasts, such as financial advice on investing in stocks, do not show a reliable superiority over novices and thus must not improve simply with added experience. Similar absence of improvement by experienced individuals considered experts has been documented in several other areas (Ericsson & Lehmann, 1996; Ericsson, 2004). There are even examples, such as diagnosis of heart sounds and x-rays by general physicians (Ericsson, 2004) and auditor evaluations (Bédard & Chi, 1993), in which performance decreases systematically in accuracy and consistency with the length of professional experience after the end of formal training.

Once it is clear that social and simple experience-based indicators of expertise do not guarantee superior performance, an alternative approach is required. Ericsson and Smith (1991) proposed that the focus should not be on socially recognized experts, but rather on individuals who exhibit reproducibly superior performance on representative, authentic tasks in their field. For example, the focus should be on physicians who can diagnose and treat patients in a superior manner, on chess players who can consistently select the best moves for chess positions, and on athletes and musicians who exhibit superior performance in competitions. The first step in a science of expert performance requires that scientists be able to capture, with standardized tests, the reproducibly superior performance of some individuals, and then be able to examine this performance with laboratory methods, as will be described in the next sections (see also, Ericsson, Chapter 13, for a more detailed treatment).

Reproducibly Superior Performance and Experience

In many domains of expertise, individuals have been interested in assessing and comparing levels of performance under fair and controlled circumstances. For thousands of years athletes have competed under highly standardized conditions in track and field events, such as running, jumping, and throwing. These competitive conditions approach the controlled conditions generated in modern studies of performance in the laboratory. In a similar manner, musicians, dancers, and chess players have a long history of displaying their performance under controlled conditions during competitions and tournaments. Such competitions, together with similar tests, such as auditions, serve several purposes beyond identifying the best performers and presenting awards. For younger and developing performers, successful performance at competitions and auditions is necessary to gain access to the best teachers and training environments.

Ericsson and Smith (1991) discussed how one could use similar techniques to measure various types of professional expertise. We argued that a complete understanding of the structure and acquisition of excellence will be possible only in domains in which experts exhibit objectively superior performance, in a reproducible manner, for the representative activities that define the essence of accomplishment in a given domain (Ericsson, 1996, 2002). Expert performers are accustomed to performing in response to external demands, such as during emergencies in their professional practice, or at competitions and exhibitions. If they are able to reproduce their performance repeatedly on these types of occasions as well during training, they should be able to reproduce them even under laboratory conditions, a finding confirmed by recent research (Ericsson & Lehmann, 1996).

Unfortunately, expert performance occurs naturally in complex and unique contexts, where the conditions of performance differ between performers, making comparison difficult. For example, musi-cians select their own pieces of music for their performance. Similarly, the sequence of moves in a chess game is never the same and, thus, players never encounter the exact same positions during the middle game. Fortunately, most domains of expertise require that experts be able to exhibit superior performance for presented *representative* situations. Ericsson and Smith (1991; Ericsson, 1996) proposed a way to find representative situations that capture the essence of expert performance in a domain and call for immediate action. They also described general methods for recreating these situations in the laboratory and then instructing experts and less skilled individuals to reproduce their performance under controlled laboratory conditions, so that investigators can identify the responsible mediating mechanisms.

Representative tasks that have been found to capture the essence of expertise in three domains are illustrated in Figure 38.2 (see treatments of these and other fields in Sections 5). In each example, the measured performance is closely related to the naturally occurring performance. To study chess expertise, players at different skill levels are asked to generate the best move for the same chess positions that have been taken from actual games between chess masters, which are not publicly available. Different typists are presented the same material and asked to type as much as possible during a fixed time period. Musicians are asked to play familiar or unfamiliar pieces of music while being recorded, and are then asked to repeat their performance exactly. When musicians are instructed to repeat their original performance, experts' consecutive renditions show much less variation than renditions by less-skilled musicians and, by implication, experts exhibit greater control over their performance.

When a review of evidence is restricted to only the reproducible superior performance of experts, obtained under directly comparable conditions, it is possible to examine several claims about the relation between expert performance and experience that generalize across domains. First, extensive

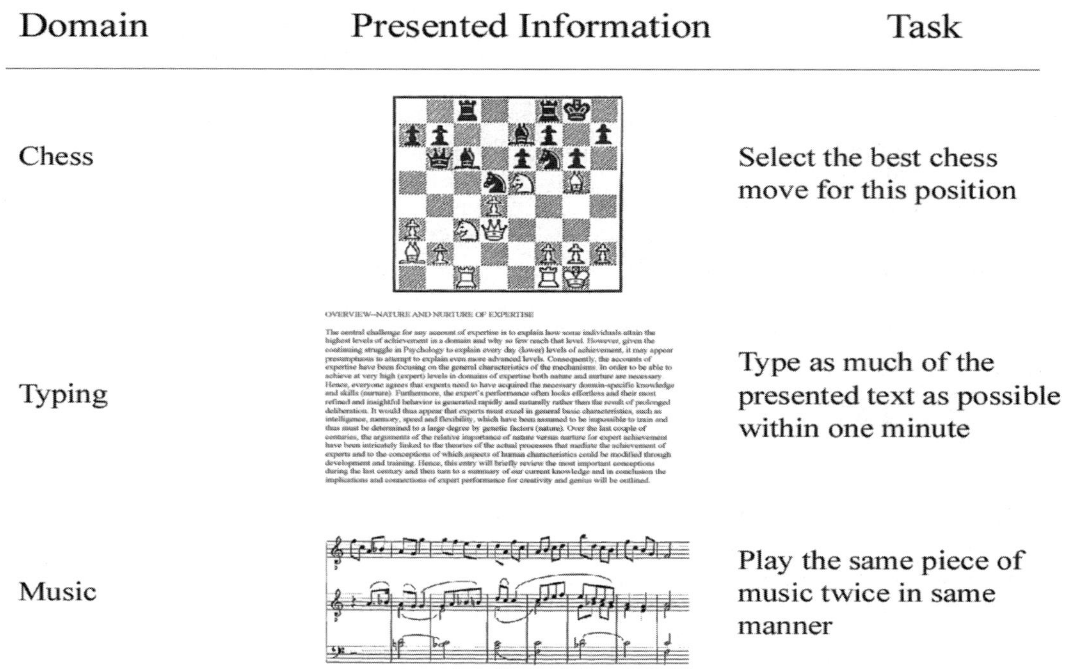

Domain	Presented Information	Task

Chess

Select the best chess move for this position

Typing

Type as much of the presented text as possible within one minute

Music

Play the same piece of music twice in same manner

Figure 38.2. Three examples of laboratory tasks that capture the consistently superior performance of domain experts in chess, typing, and music. (From "Expertise," by K. A. Ericsson and Andreas C. Lehmann, 1999, *Encyclopedia of Creativity*. Copyright by Academic Press.)

experience is shown to be necessary to attain superior expert performance. Second, only some types of domain-related experience are shown to lead to improvement of performance. In addition, many thousands of hours of specific types of practice and training have been found to be necessary for reaching the highest levels of performance.

The Necessity of Domain-Specific Experience for Attaining Reproducibly Superior Performance

Reviews (Ericsson, 1996, 2004 Ericsson & Lehmann, 1996) show that extended engagement in domain-related activities is necessary to attain expert performance in that domain. The availability of standardized tests allows us to measure the level of performance during development and to compare these longitudinal data to uniform adult standards. Hence, we can describe the development of expert performance as a function of age and years of experience, as fol-

lows. First, longitudinal assessments of performance reveal that all individuals improve gradually, as illustrated in Figure 38.3. There is no objective evidence that a child or adult is able to exhibit a high level of performance without any relevant prior experience and practice. Similarly, there is no evidence for abrupt improvements of reproducible performance when it is tested on a monthly or yearly basis. When the performance of child prodigies in music and chess are measured against adult standards, they show gradual, steady improvement over time. Second, elite performance keeps improving beyond the age of physical maturation – the late teens in industrialized countries (Ulijaszek, Johnston, & Preece, 1998) – and is, thus, not directly limited by the functional capacity of the body and brain. Peak performance of experts is nearly always attained in adulthood – many years, and even decades, after initial exposure to the domain, as illustrated in Figure 38.3. The age at which performers typically reach their highest level of

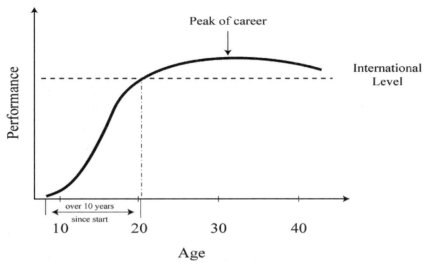

Figure 38.3. An illustration of the gradual increases in expert performance as a function of age, in domains such as chess. The international level, which is attained after more than around ten years of involvement in the domain, is indicated by the horizontal dashed line. (From "Expertise," by K. A. Ericsson and Andreas C. Lehmann, 1999, *Encyclopedia of Creativity*. Copyright by Academic Press.)

performance in many vigorous sports is the mid- to late 20s. For the arts and science, it is a decade later, in the 30s and 40s (see Schulz & Curnow, 1988, and Simonton, 1997 chapter 18, for reviews). The continued and often extended development of expertise past physical maturity shows that additional experience is necessary to attain one's highest level of performance.

Finally, the most compelling evidence for the role of vast experience in expertise comes from investigators who have shown that, even for the most talented individuals, ten years of experience in a domain (ten-year rule) is necessary to become an expert (Bryan & Harter, 1899) and to win at an international level (Simon & Chase, 1973). Subsequent reviews have shown that these findings extend to international-level success in music composition (Hayes, 1981), as well as to sports, science, and the arts (Ericsson, Krampe, & Tesch-Römer, 1993). A closer examination of the evidence for the ten-year rule shows that the number ten is not magical. In fact, the number of years of intense training required to become an internationally acclaimed performer dif-

fers across domains. For example, elite musicians (disregarding the biased standards for child prodigies) need closer to 20 to 30 years of training and often peak when they are around 30 to 40 years old. Further, outstanding scientists and authors normally published their first work at around age 25, and their best work follows around ten years later (Raskin, 1936).

Other investigators have pointed to potential exceptions to the ten-year rule. Some of the exceptions are so close to the ten-year rule that they support the necessity for around ten years to win at the international level. For example, famous chess player Bobby Fischer required nine years of intense chess study before being recognized as a grand master in chess at age 16 (Ericsson et al, 1993). Other examples suggest clearer violations. Very tall basketball players (around seven feet) have been able to reach the highest professional ranks in less than ten years of training – in around six years. Research on training of memory experts has shown that individuals can reach the highest level in the world after less than a couple of years training (Ericsson, 2003b;

Ericsson, Delaney, Weaver, & Mahadevan, 2004). More generally, people are able to reach world-class levels in fewer than ten years in activities that lack a history of organized international competition. In addition, there is solid evidence that the highest levels for performance in a given domain are not stable but sometimes continue to increase over historical time as a function of progressively higher and more effective levels of training and practice.

Increases in Performance over Historical Time: The Relation between Performance and Improved Methods of Practice

In virtually every aspect of human activity there have been increases in the efficiency and level of performance. Over centuries and millennia, across domains of expertise, people have developed methods for accumulating and preserving discovered knowledge and skills and produced tools and refined their technique of application. Hence, they have assembled a body of organized knowledge that can be transferred from the current to the next generation through instruction and education (Ericsson, 1996; Feldman, 1994). It is no longer necessary for individuals to discover the relevant knowledge and methods by themselves. Today's experts can rapidly acquire the knowledge originally discovered by the pioneers. For example, in the 13th century Roger Bacon argued that, using the then-known methods of learning (self-study), it would be impossible to master mathematics in less than 30 to 40 years (Singer, 1958). Today, the roughly equivalent material (calculus) is taught in highly organized and accessible form in every high school. Today the development of expert levels of achievement requires instruction by teachers that helps performers gain access to the body of domain-specific knowledge, which is expressed and accumulated in terms of predefined concepts, notation systems, equipment, and measurement devices. The increases in the level of expert performance over historical time are often taken for granted in science and sports, but

the improvements in instrumentation and equipment make it difficult to find comparable tasks over large time-spans in which performance can be directly compared. However, in domains with fewer changes in tools and instruments, such as music performance with the piano and violin, today's performers readily master music that was considered unplayable by the best musicians in the 19th century. They can match or often even surpass the technical virtuosity of legendary musicians and music prodigies of the past, such as Wolfgang Amadeus Mozart (Lehmann & Ericsson, 1998).

In sports, the increases in performance over time are well known, and even today world records are broken on a regular basis. In some events, such as the marathon, swimming, and diving, many dedicated amateurs and college athletes perform at a much higher level in the 21st century than the gold medal winners of the early Olympic Games. For example, after the IVth Olympic Games in 1908, organizers almost prohibited the double somersault in dives because they believed that these dives were dangerous, and no human would ever be able to control them. More generally, record-breaking levels of performance are nearly always originally attained by only a single eminent performer. However, after some time, other athletes are able to design training methods that allow them to attain that same level of performance. Eventually, these training methods become part of regular instruction, and all elite performers in the domain are expected to attain the new higher standard. Perhaps the most well-known example is Roger Bannister's first ever sub-four-minute mile. The earlier record for the mile had been viewed as the ultimate limit for performance, but after Bannister broke the four-minute barrier, several other runners were able to do so within a couple of years (Denison, 2003). Over time, differences in practice methods have become so great that Olympic swimmers from early in the last century would not even qualify for swim teams at today's competitive high schools (Schulz & Curnow, 1988). In some competitive domains, such as baseball, it is sometimes difficult to demonstrate the increased level of today's performers because both the level of the pitcher and batter has improved concurrently (Gould, 1996). In spite of the increases in the average level of elite performance over historical time, the variability in individual differences in athletes' performance remains large – a topic that will be addressed in the next section.

From Experience to Designed Practice

Many individuals seem satisfied in reaching a merely acceptable level of performance, such as amateur tennis players and golfers, and they attempt to reach such a level while minimizing the period of effortful skill acquisition. Once an acceptable level has been reached, they need only to maintain a stable performance, and often do so with minimal effort for years and even decades. For reasons such as these, the length of experience has been frequently found to be a weak correlate of job performance beyond the first two years (McDaniel, Schmidt, & Hunter, 1988). In addition, extensive watching is not the same as extensive playing. Williams and Davids (1995), for example, found large differences in the ability to anticipate events in soccer between players and avid spectators. The select group of individuals who eventually reach very high levels do not simply accumulate more routine experience of domain-related activities, but extend their active skill-building period for years or even decades, both forward and backward in time. In particular, from retrospective interviews of international-level performers in many domains, Bloom (1985a; see chapter by Sosniak, Chapter 16) showed that elite performers are typically introduced to their future realm of excellence in a playful manner at a young age. As soon as they enjoy the activity and show promise compared to peers in the neighborhood, their parents help them seek out a teacher and initiate regular practice. Bloom and his colleagues (Bloom 1985b) demonstrated that performers that reach an international level

have received remarkable support by their parents and teachers (see also Mieg, Chapter 41). The parents of the future elite performers were even found to spend large sums of money for teachers and equipment, and to devote considerable time to escorting their child to training and weekend competitions. In some cases, the performers and their families even relocate to be closer to the chosen teacher and the training facilities. Based on their interviews, Bloom (1985a) argued that access to the best training resources was necessary to reach the highest levels.

At the same time the best training environments are not sufficient to produce the very best performers, and there are substantial individual differences even among individuals in these environments. Can differences in the amount and type of domain-related activities that individuals engage in explain individual differences in music performance, even among the best performers? Expert violinists at the music academy in Berlin kept a weekly diary on how much time they spent during a week on different activities (Ericsson et al., 1993). All groups of expert violinists were found to spend about the same amount of time (over 50 hours) per week on music-related activities. However, the best violinists were found to spend more time per week on activities that had been specifically designed to improve performance, which we call "deliberate practice." A prime example of deliberate practice is the expert violinists' solitary practice, in which they work to master specific goals determined by their music teacher at weekly lessons. The same groups of expert violinists, along with a group of professional violinists from world-class symphony orchestras, were also interviewed to estimate the amount of deliberate practice in which they had engaged during their musical development. Even among these elite groups we were able to find that the most accomplished musicians had spent more time in activities classified as deliberate practice during their development. Figure 38.4 shows that these differences were reliably observable before their admittance to the academy at around age 18. By the age of 20, the best

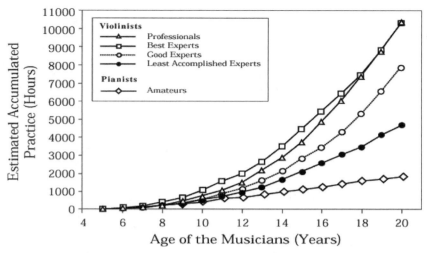

Figure 38.4. Estimated amount of time for solitary practice as a function of age for the middle-aged *professional* violinists (triangles), the *best* expert violinists (squares), the *good* expert violinists (empty circles), the *least accomplished* expert violinists (filled circles), and *amateur* pianists (diamonds). (From "The role of deliberate practice in the acquisition of expert performance," by K. A. Ericsson, R. Th. Krampe, and C. Tesch-Römer, 1993, *Psychological Review*, 100(3), p. 379 and p. 384. Copyright 1993 by American Psychological Association. Adapted with permission.)

musicians had spent over 10,000 hours practicing, which averages 2,500 and 5,000 hours more than two less-accomplished groups of musicians at the same academy, respectively (Ericsson et al., 1993). In comparison to amateur pianists of the same age (Krampe & Ericsson, 1996), the best musicians from the academy and the professionals had practiced 8,000 more hours.

The core assumption of deliberate practice (Ericsson, 1996, 2002, 2004; Ericsson et al., 1993) is that expert performance is acquired gradually and that effective improvement of performance requires the opportunity to find suitable training tasks that the performer can master sequentially – typically the design of training tasks and monitoring of the attained performance is done by a teacher or a coach. Deliberate practice presents performers with tasks that are initially outside their current realm of reliable performance, yet can be mastered within hours of practice by concentrating on critical aspects and by gradually refining performance through repetitions after feed-

back. Hence, the requirement for *concentration* sets deliberate practice apart from both mindless, routine performance and playful engagement, as the latter two types of activities would, if anything, merely strengthen the current mediating cognitive mechanisms, rather than modify them to allow increases in the level of performance. Research is currently reevaluating claims that some individuals can improve their level of performance without concentration and deliberate practice. Even the well-known fact that more "talented" children improve faster in the beginning of their music development appears to be in large part due to the fact that they spend more time in deliberate practice each week (Sloboda, Davidson, Howe & Moore, 1996). In a recent study of singers Grape, Sandgren, Hansson, Ericsson, and Theorell (2003) revealed reliable differences of skill in the level of physiological and psychological indicators of concentration and effort during a singing lesson. Whereas the amateur singers experienced the lesson as self-actualization and an enjoyable release of tension, the professional singers increased their concentration and focused on improving their performance during the lesson.

In other domains it has been more difficult to isolate practice activities that meet all the criteria for deliberate practice in music. In sports, several studies have found a consistent relation between attained performance and amount of practice (Helsen, Starkes, & Hodges, 1998; Hodges & Starkes, 1996; Starkes et al., 1996). In recent reviews of deliberate practice in sports (Côté, Ericsson, & Law, 2005; Ericsson, 2003c; Ward, Hodges, Williams, & Starkes, 2004), several issues have been discussed concerning the relation between different domain-related practice activities and improvements in performance. In a study of insurance agents, Sonnentag and Kleinc (2000) found that engagement in deliberate practice predicted higher performance ratings.

For example, whereas solitary training was found to distinguish elite and less-skilled performers in some sports, the amount of time spent in team-related deliberate practice activities correlates reliably with skill level in team sports (Helsen et al., 1998; Ward et al., 2004). Contrary to some evidence suggesting that playful activities, sporting diversity, and late specialization are associated with elite level sport, a quasi-longitudinal study by Ward et al. (2004) demonstrated that elite-level youth soccer players did not spend more time in playful activities or in other sports or activities than their less-skilled counterparts, nor did they specialize any later. Instead, while less-skilled players spent the majority of their time in "play," elite players spent significantly longer per week and accrued more total time in deliberate practice. They perceived themselves to be more competent than the less-skilled players, and rated one of their parents as the most influential person in their career.

Rare longitudinal studies of elite performers (some of them world class, Schneider, 1993) have found that the most potent variables linked to performance and future improvements of performance involved parental support, acquired task-specific (in this case, tennis) skills, and motivational factors including concentration. Similarly in chess, Charness and his colleagues (Charness, Krampe, & Mayr, 1996; Charness, Tuffiash, Krampe, Reingold, & Vasyukova, 2005) found that the amount of solitary chess study was the best predictor of chess skill, and when this factor was statistically controlled, there was only a very small benefit from the number of games played in chess tournaments. Similar findings have been obtained by Duffy, Baluch, and Ericsson (2004) for dart throwing. In a particularly interesting study McKinney and Davis (2004) examined successful handling of emergency situations during flying by expert pilots. They found that if prior to the emergency event the expert pilots had practiced the same emergency situation in the simulator, they were reliably more successful in dealing with the actual event. More generally, Deakin, Côté, and Harvey (Chapter 17) review evidence on methods for recording the amount and structure of deliberate practice, using diary methods and other kinds of observations.

In this handbook several chapters discuss the role of deliberate practice in relation to self-regulated learning (Zimmerman, Chapter 39), to successful training in simulators (Ward, Williams, & Hancock, Chapter 14), to maintained performance in older experts (Krampe & Charness, Chapter 40), and in creative activities (Weisberg, Chapter 42). Other chapters review evidence on the relation between deliberate practice and the development of expertise in many domains, such as professional writing (Kellogg, Chapter 22), music performance (Lehmann & Gruber, Chapter 26), sports (Hodges, Starkes, & MacMahon, Chapter 27), chess (Gobet & Charness, Chapter 30), exceptional memory (Wilding & Valentine, Chapter 31), and mathematical calculation (Butterworth, Chapter 32). The next section will focus on the microstructure of deliberate practice and how it leads to changes in the mechanisms that mediate expert performance.

Deliberate Practice and the Acquisition of Complex Mechanisms Mediating Expert Performance

The fundamental challenge for theoretical accounts of expert performance is to propose how expert performers can avoid reaching a performance asymptote within a limited time period, as predicted by contemporary theories of skill acquisition and expertise (Anderson, 1982; Fitts & Posner, 1967), and keep improving their performance for years and decades.

In the introduction of this chapter, the stages of everyday skill acquisition were described. At the first encounter with a task, people focus on understanding it and carefully generating appropriate actions, as illustrated in the lower arm of the previously discussed Figure 38.1. With more experience, individuals' behaviors adapt to the demands of performance and become increasingly automatized, people lose conscious control over the production of their actions and are no longer able to make specific intentional adjustments to them. For example, people have difficulty describing how they tie their shoelaces or how they get up from sitting in a chair. When the behaviors are automatized, mere additional experience will not lead to increased levels of performance.

In direct contrast to the acquisition of everyday skills, expert performers continue to improve their performance with more experience as long as it is coupled with deliberate practice. The key challenge for aspiring expert performers is to avoid the arrested development associated with automaticity and to acquire cognitive skills to support their continued learning and improvement. By actively seeking out demanding tasks – often provided by their teachers and coaches – that force the performers to engage in problem solving and to stretch their performance, the expert performers overcome the detrimental effects of automaticity and actively acquire and refine cognitive mechanisms to support continued learning and improvement, as shown in the upper arm of Figure 38.1. The expert performers and their teachers identify specific goals for improving particular aspects of performance and design training activities that allow the performer to gradually refine performance with feedback and opportunities for repetition (deliberate practice). The performers will gradually acquire mechanisms that increase their ability to control, self-monitor, and evaluate their performance in representative situations from the domain and thus gain independence from the feedback of their teachers (Ericsson, 1996, 2002; Glaser, 1996). Although the overall structure of these mechanisms reflects general principles, the detailed structure and practice activities that mediate their acquisition will reflect the demands of that particular activity and thus differ from one domain of expertise to another.

According to the expert-performance approach (Ericsson, 1996, 2002, 2004), skill acquisition is viewed as an extended series of gradual changes of the physiological and cognitive mechanisms that allow the observable performance to show associated improvements. The acquisition of expert performance can thus be described as a series of relatively stable states, where each state has a set of mechanisms that mediate the execution of the associated performance (see Figure 38.5). The primary differences between two adjacent states can be physiological, where the subsequent states differ in the level of strength, endurance, or speed of critical muscular systems. Alternatively, the difference between the mechanisms of the two adjacent states might be primarily cognitive. For example, the performer might be better able to represent and monitor internal and external states during performance, which in turn allows the performer to generate and select better actions, or initiate and complete actions faster, or execute motor actions more consistently and accurately.

Another fundamental challenge to a theoretical account of the acquisition of expert performance involves describing plausible explanations of how a certain type of practice activity (deliberate practice) can change any complex State[I] into the directly following complex State [I + 1]. First, the practice activities that mediate improved

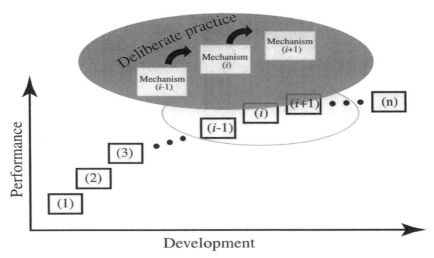

Figure 38.5. A schematic illustration of the acquisition of expert performance as a series of states with mechanisms for monitoring and guiding future improvements of specific aspects of performance.

physiological function will be discussed, followed by a description of how practice can improve performance by changes in cognitive mechanisms that mediate performance and further learning.

Improving Adaptations by Straining Physiological Systems

Measurable increases in physical fitness do not simply result from wishful thinking. Instead people have to engage in intense aerobic exercise that pushes them well beyond the level of comfortable physical activity if they are to improve their aerobic fitness (Ericsson, 2003a; Ericsson et al., 1993; Robergs & Roberts, 1997). Specifically, in order to increase their aerobic fitness young adults have to exercise at least a couple of times each week, for at least 30 minutes per session, with a sustained heart rate that is 70% of their maximal level (around 140 beats per minute for a maximal heart rate of 200). When the human body is put under exceptional strain, a range of dormant genes in the DNA are expressed and extraordinary physiological processes are activated. Over time the cells of the body, including the brain (see Hill & Schneider, Chapter 37) will reorganize in response to the

induced metabolic demands of the activity by, for example, increases in the number of capillaries supplying blood to muscles and changes in metabolism of the muscle fibers themselves. These adaptations will eventually allow the individual to execute the given level of activity without greatly straining the physiological systems. To gain further beneficial increases in adaptation, the athletes need to increase or change their weekly training activities to induce new and perhaps different types of strain on the key physiological systems. For example, improvements of strength are attained when individuals lift weights to induce brief maximal efforts of the targeted muscle groups. More generally, athletic training involves pushing the associated physiological systems outside the comfort zone to stimulate physiological growth and adaptation (Ericsson, 2001, 2002, 2003a, 2003c, 2003d). Furthermore, recent reviews (Gaser & Schlaug, 2003; Hill & Schneider, Chapter 37; Kolb & Whishaw, 1998) show that the function and structure of the brain is far more adaptable than previously thought possible. Especially, early and extended training has shown to change the cortical mapping of musicians (Elbert, Pantev, Wienbruch, Rockstoh, & Taub, 1995), the development of white matter in the brain (Bengtsson et al., 2005), the development of "turn out" of ballet dancers, the development of perfect pitch, and flexibility of fingers (Ericsson & Lehmann, 1996).

In sum, elite performers search continuously for optimal training activities, with the most effective duration and intensity, that will appropriately strain the targeted physiological system to induce further adaptation without causing overuse and injury.

The Acquisition of Mental Representations for Performance and Continued Learning

One of the principal challenges to continued improvement of expert performance is that the acquired representations and mechanisms mediating expert performance must be modifiable to allow gradual changes that incrementally improve performance. They need to allow for improvements of specific aspects of the performances as well as for the coordination of necessary adjustments required by the associated changes. The experts' mental representations thus serve a dual purpose of mediating the superior expert performance while also providing the same mechanisms that can be incrementally altered to further enhance performance after practice and training. Finally, individuals must engage in deliberate-practice activities to continue to stretch their performance. The dual role of representations has been most extensively documented in chess and typing (Ericsson, 1996, 2002, 2004). Chess players rely on planning out consequences of potential moves in order to select the best move during matches in a tournament. During deliberate practice, the same chess players will rely on the same planning mechanisms to improve their ability to select the best moves. Similarly, typists rely on the same representations during performance and when they attempt to increase their speed of typing during deliberate practice. After these two examples of deliberate practice, broader issues of deliberate practice in a wide range of domains will be discussed.

CHESS

Expertise in chess was proposed by Simon and Chase (1973) to be a prototype for many domains of expertise. In his pioneering work on chess expertise, de Groot (1946/1978) uncovered the detailed processes that allow world-class chess players to analyze chess positions and to find their best move for each position. He instructed expert and world-class players to "think aloud" while they selected the best move in a set of unfamiliar chess positions taken from games by chess masters (see Figure 38.2). Subsequent reviews related to this research showed that the quality of the selected moves was closely associated with the performers' play in tournaments and, therefore by inference, captured the essence of chess skill (Ericsson, Patel, & Kintsch, 2000). De Groot's (1946/1978) analysis of experts' "think aloud" protocols revealed that they first formed a rapid impression of the chess position in order to retrieve potential moves from memory. These promising moves were then evaluated by mentally planning the consequences of potential options. During the course of this exercise, even the world-class players would discover better moves, indicating that they continued to improve.

A major challenge for successful planning and chess skill is that the chess players be able to represent the chess positions in working memory in a manner that allows evaluation and flexible exploration of sequences of moves. The skills required to represent and manipulate chess positions in long-term memory appear to develop slowly as a function of increased chess skill (Ericsson & Kintsch, 1995; Ericsson, et al., 2000). Consequently, more-skilled chess players have been shown to be able to plan more thoroughly and to represent chess positions more effectively. In addition, their memory for briefly presented chess positions is vastly superior to those of less-skilled players (Gobet & Charness, Chapter 30). However, this superior recall performance is limited to representative chess positions and disappears almost completely when chess positions are randomly rearranged.

The central challenge to an account of the continued improvement of a chess experts' ability is to understand how they plan and select the best action in a given game situation. Chess players typically practice this task by studying chess openings and analyzing published games between the very best chess players in the world. They typically analyze the games by playing through the games, one move at a time, to determine if their selected move matches to the corresponding move originally selected by the masters. If the master's move in the studied chess game differed from their own selection, this would imply that their planning and evaluation must have overlooked some aspect of the position. It is important to note that this learning process allows the player to diagnose the source of suboptimal moves and thus make a local change that improves the selection of related moves, without causing interference with other aspects of the existing skill.

By more careful and extended analysis, the chess expert is generally able to discover the reasons for the chess master's superior move. Serious chess players spend as much as four hours every day engaged in this type of solitary study (Charness et al., 1996, 2005; Ericsson et al., 1993). By spending additional time analyzing the consequences of moves for a chess position, players can increase the quality of their selections of moves. With more study, individuals refine their representations and can access or generate the same information faster. As a result, chess masters can typically recognize a superior move virtually immediately, whereas a competent club player requires much longer to find the same move by successive planning and evaluation rather than recognition. The same type of improvement, based on deliberate practice and increased depth of planning, can explain gradually increased performance in a wide range of domains, such as billiards, golf, music, and surgery (Ericsson, 2004).

TYPING

If chess is viewed as one of the most intellectually challenging tasks, then typing is typically viewed as a diametrically different, mundane, habitual activity. Many adults are able to type, yet there are often large individual differences in the speed attained. The standardized measure of typing speed involves having skilled typists and unskilled participants type passages from a collection of unfamiliar texts as fast as they can without making errors. High-speed films of finger movements show that the faster typists start moving their fingers toward their desired locations on the keyboard well before the keys are struck. The superior typists' speed advantage is linked to their perceptual processing of the text beyond the word that they are currently typing (Salthouse, 1984). By looking ahead in the text to identify letters to be typed, they can prepare future keystrokes in advance. This evidence for anticipation has been confirmed by experimental studies where expert typists have been restricted from looking ahead. Under such conditions their typing speed is dramatically reduced and approaches the speed of less-skilled typists.

In sum, the superior speed of reactions by expert performers, such as typists and athletes, appears to depend primarily on cognitive representations mediating skilled *anticipation* (see also, Endsley, Chapter 36), rather than faster basic speed of their nervous system (Abernethy, 1991). For instance, expert tennis players are able to anticipate where a tennis player's shots will land, even before the player's racquet has contacted the ball (Williams, Ward, Knowles, & Smeeton, 2002). Eye movements of expert tennis players show that they are able to pick up predictive information from subtle, yet informative, motion cues, such as hip and shoulder rotation, compared to their novice counterparts. They can also use later-occurring and more-deterministic cues, such as racket swing, to confirm or reject their earlier anticipations.

Research on instruction in typing (Dvorak, Merrick, Dealey, & Ford, 1936) has so far provided the best initial insights into how speed of performance can be increased through deliberate practice that alters and improves the representations mediating anticipation and coordination of finger movements. The key empirical observation is that people can increase their typing speed by exerting full concentration toward improvement. Regular typists can typically maintain this level of concentration for only 15 to 30 minutes per day. When typists concentrate and strain themselves to type at a faster rate (typically around 10 to 20% faster than their normal speed), they strive to anticipate better, possibly by extending their gaze further ahead.

The increased tempo also brings out keystroke combinations for which the typists are comparatively slow, thus restricting a fluent higher speed. These challenging combinations can then be trained in special exercises and incorporated into the typing of regular text. This is in order to assure that any modifications can be integrated with the representations mediating typical typing tasks. By increasing anticipation and successively eliminating weaknesses, typists can increase their average speed in practice at a rate that is still 10 to 20% faster than their new average speed attained after such practice. The general approach of finding methods to push performance beyond its normal level – even if that performance can be maintained only for a short time – offers the potential for identifying and correcting weaker components that will improve performance as well as for enhancing anticipation.

A Broader View of Expert Performance and Deliberate Practice

The theoretical framework of deliberate practice asserts that improvement in performance of aspiring experts does not happen automatically or casually as a function of further experience. Improvements are caused by changes in cognitive mechanisms mediating how the brain and nervous system control performance and in the degree of adaptation of physiological systems of the body. The principal challenge to attaining expert level performance is to induce stable specific changes that allow the performance to be incrementally improved.

Once we conceive of expert performance as mediated by complex integrated systems of representations for the planning, analysis, execution, and monitoring of performance (see Figure 38.5), it becomes clear that its acquisition requires a systematic and deliberate approach. Deliberate practice is therefore designed to improve specific aspects of performance in a manner that assures that attained changes can be successfully measured and integrated into representative performance. Research on deliberate practice in music and sports shows that continued attempts for mastery require that the performer always try, by stretching performance beyond its current capabilities, to correct some specific weakness, while preserving other successful aspects of function. This type of deliberate practice requires full attention and concentration, but even with that extreme effort, some kind of failure is likely to arise, and gradual improvements with corrections and repetitions are necessary. With increased skill in monitoring, skilled performers in music focus on mastering new challenges by goal-directed deliberate practice involving problem solving and specialized training techniques (Chaffin & Imre, 1997; Ericsson, 2002; Gruson, 1988; Nielsen, 1999).

In their research on sports, Deakin and Cobley (2003) found that ice skaters spend a considerable portion of their limited practice time on jump-combinations they have already mastered, rather than working on the yet-to-be-mastered combinations, where there is the largest room for improvement. More generally, they found that with increasing levels of attained skill the skaters spent more time on jumps and other challenging activities that had the potential to improve performance.

Practice aimed at improving integrated performance cannot be performed mindlessly, nor independently of the representative context for the target performance. In addition, more-accomplished individuals in the domain, such as professional coaches and teachers, will always play an essential role in guiding the sequencing of practice activities for future experts in a safe and effective manner. Research on self-regulated learning (Zimmerman, Chapter 39) has documented effective study methods that are related to superior academic performance, especially in high schools. More recent work has shown that engagement in study methods consistent with deliberate practice has been found to predict achievement in both undergraduate college students (Plant, Ericsson, Hill, & Asberg, 2005) as well as in students in medical school (Moulaert, Verwijnen, Rikers, & Scherpbier, 2004).

The deliberate-practice framework can also explain the necessity for further deliberate practice in order for individuals simply to maintain their current level of skill. It is well known that athletes and musicians who reduce or stop their regular practice will exhibit a reduced level of performance – a maintained level of challenge and strain appear necessary to preserve the attained physiological and cognitive adaptations. The same type of account has been developed to explain age-related reductions in music performance and how they can be counteracted by maintained levels of deliberate practice (Krampe & Ericsson, 1996; see Krampe and Charness, Chapter 40).

Concluding Remarks: General Characteristics of Deliberate Practice

The perspective of deliberate practice attributes the rarity of excellence to the scarcity of optimal training environments and to the years required to develop the complex mediating mechanisms that support expertise. Even children considered to have innate gifts need to attain their superior performance gradually, by engaging in extended amounts of designed deliberate practice over many years. Until most individuals recognize that sustained training and effort is a prerequisite for reaching expert levels of performance, they will continue to misattribute lesser achievement to the lack of natural gifts, and will thus fail to reach their own potential.

The effects of mere experience differ greatly from those of deliberate practice, where individuals concentrate on actively trying to go beyond their current abilities. Consistent with the mental demands of problem solving and other types of complex learning, deliberate practice requires concentration that can be maintained only for limited periods of time. Although the detailed nature of deliberate practice will differ across domains and as a function of attained skill, there appear to be limits on the daily duration of deliberate practice, and this limit seems to generalize across domains of expertise. Expert performers from many domains engage in practice without rest for only around an hour, and they prefer to practice early in the morning when their minds are fresh (Ericsson et al., 1993). Elite musicians (Ericsson, 2002) and athletes (Ericsson, 2001, 2003c) report that the factor that limits their deliberate practice is primarily an inability to sustain the level of concentration that is necessary. Even more interestingly, elite performers in many diverse domains have been found to practice, on the average, roughly the same amount every day, including weekends, and the amount of practice never consistently exceeds five hours per day (Ericsson, 1996; Ericsson et al., 1993). The limit of four to five hours of daily deliberate practice or similarly demanding activities holds true for a wide range of elite performers in different domains, such as writing by famous authors (Cowley, 1959; Plimpton, 1977), as does their increased tendency to take recuperative naps. Furthermore, unless the daily levels of practice are restricted, such that subsequent rest and nighttime sleep allow the individuals to restore their equilibrium, individuals often encounter overtraining injuries and, eventually, incapacitating "burnout." In some domains of sports, such as gymnastics, sprinting, and weight lifting, the maximal effort necessary for representative performance is so great that the amount of daily deliberate practice is even further limited by factors constraining the duration of production of maximal power and strength.

The scientific study of deliberate practice will enhance our knowledge about how experts optimize the improvements of their performance (and motivation) through a high level of daily practice they can sustain for days, months, and years. The emerging insights should be relevant to any motivated individual aspiring to excel in any challenging domain (Ericsson, 2004). Although we are already gaining understanding about how performers improve with deliberate practice and reach expert levels, it is unlikely that we will ever be able to fully understand and predict future innovations. We may be able to reproduce the path of development that elite performers have taken to reach their highest levels of performance in the past. We may also be able to help performers in one domain of expertise, such as surgery, learn about the best training methods that have been developed in domains with a longer tradition, such as violin performance. We may even be able to work in collaboration with world-class performers who are working on improving their performance to new and undiscovered heights. At the highest levels of expert performance, the drive for improvement will always involve search and experimentation at the threshold of understanding, even for the masters dedicated to redefining the meaning of excellence in their fields.

References

Abernethy, B. (1991). Visual search strategies and decision-making in sport. *International Journal of Sport Psychology, 22*, 189–210.

Anderson, J. R. (1982). Acquisition of cognitive skill. *Psychological Review, 89*, 369–406.

Bédard, J., & Chi, M. T. H. (1993). Expertise in auditing. *Auditing, 12*, (Suppl.), 1–25.

Bengtsson, S. L., Nagy, Z., Skare, S., Forsman, L., Forsberg, H., & Ullén, F. (2005). Extensive piano practicing has regionally specific effects on white matter development. *Nature Neuroscience, 8*, 1148–1150.

Bloom, B. S. (1985a). Generalizations about talent development. In B. S. Bloom (Ed.), *Developing talent in young people* (pp. 507–549). New York: Ballantine Books.

Bloom, B. S. (Ed.) (1985b). *Developing talent in young people*. New York: Ballantine Books.

Book, W. F. (1925a). *Learning to typewrite*. New York: The Gregg Publishing Co.

Book, W. F. (1925b) *The psychology of skill*. New York: The Gregg Publishing Co.

Bryan, W. L., & Harter, N. (1897). Studies in the physiology and psychology of the telegraphic language. *Psychological Review, 4*, 27–53.

Bryan, W. L., & Harter, N. (1899). Studies on the telegraphic language: The acquisition of a hierarchy of habits. *Psychological Review, 6*, 345–375.

Camerer, C. F., & Johnson, E. J. (1991). The process-performance paradox in expert judgment: How can the experts know so much and predict so badly? In K. A. Ericsson and J. Smith (Eds.), *Towards a general theory of expertise: Prospects and limits* (pp. 195–217). Cambridge: Cambridge University Press.

Chaffin, R., & Imreh, G. (1997). "Pulling teeth and torture": Musical memory and problem solving. *Thinking and Reasoning, 3*, 315–336.

Charness, N., Krampe, R. Th., & Mayr, U. (1996). The role of practice and coaching in entrepreneurial skill domains: An international comparison of life-span chess skill acquisition. In K. A. Ericsson (Ed.), *The road to excellence: The acquisition of expert performance in the arts and sciences, sports, and games* (pp. 51–80). Mahwah, NJ: Erlbaum.

Charness, N., Tuffiash, M. I., Krampe, R., Reingold, E., & Vasyukova E. (2005). The role of deliberate practice in chess expertise. *Applied Cognitive Psychology, 19*, 151–165.

Chi, M. T. H., Glaser, R., & Farr, M. J. (Eds.) (1988). *The nature of expertise*. Hillsdale, NJ: Erlbaum.

Côté, J., Ericsson, K. A., & Law, M. (2005). Tracing the development of athletes using retrospective interview methods: A proposed interview and validation procedure for reported information. *Journal of Applied Sport Psychology, 17*, 1–19.

Cowley, M. (Ed.) (1959). *Writers at work: The Paris review interviews*. New York: Viking.

Dawes, R. M. (1994). *House of cards: Psychology and psychotherapy built on myth*. New York: Free Press.

Deakin, J. M., & Cobley, S. (2003). A search for deliberate practice: An examination of the practice environments in figure skating and volleyball. In J. Starkes & K. A. Ericsson (Eds.), *Expert performance in sport: Recent advances in research on sport expertise* (pp. 115–135). Champaign, IL: Human Kinetics.

de Groot, A. (1978). *Thought and choice in chess* (Original work published in 1946). The Hague: Mouton.

Denison, J. (2003). *Bannister and beyond: The mystique of the four minute mile.* Breakaway books.

Denney, N. W. (1982). Aging and cognitive changes. In B. B. Wolman (Ed.), *Handbook of developmental psychology* (pp. 807–827). Englewood Cliffs, NJ: Prentice Hall.

Doane, S. M., Pellegrino, J. W., & Klatzky, R. L. (1990). Expertise in a computer operating system: Conceptualization and performance. *Human-Computer Interaction, 5,* 267–304.

Duffy, L. J., Baluch, B., & Ericsson, K. A. (2004). Dart performance as a function of facets of practice amongst professional and amateur men and women players. *International Journal of Sport Psychology, 35,* 232–245.

Dvorak, A., Merrick, N. L., Dealey, W. L., & Ford, G. C. (1936). *Typewriting behavior.* New York: American Book Company.

Elbert, T., Pantev, C., Wienbruch, C., Rockstroch, B., & Taub, E. (1995). Increased cortical representation of the fingers of the left hand in string players. *Science, 270,* 305–307.

Ericsson, K. A. (1996). The acquisition of expert performance: An introduction to some of the issues. In K. A. Ericsson (Ed.), *The road to excellence: The acquisition of expert performance in the arts and sciences, sports, and games* (pp. 1–50). Mahwah, NJ: Erlbaum.

Ericsson, K. A. (2001). The path to expert performance: Insights from the masters on how to improve performance by deliberate practice. In P. Thomas (Ed.), *Optimizing performance in golf* (pp. 1–57). Brisbane, Australia: Australian Academic Press.

Ericsson, K. A. (2002). Attaining excellence through deliberate practice: Insights from the study of expert performance. In M. Ferrari (Ed.), *The pursuit of excellence in education* (pp. 21–55). Hillsdale, NJ: Erlbaum.

Ericsson, K. A. (2003a). The search for general abilities and basic capacities: Theoretical implications from the modifiability and complexity of mechanisms mediating expert performance. In R. J. Sternberg & E. L. Grigorenko (Eds.), *Perspectives on the psychology of abilities, competencies, and expertise* (pp. 93–125). Cambridge: Cambridge University Press.

Ericsson, K. A. (2003b). Exceptional memorizers: Made, not born. *Trends in Cognitive Sciences, 7,* 233–235.

Ericsson, K. A. (2003c). The development of elite performance and deliberate practice: An update from the perspective of the expert-performance approach. In J. Starkes & K. A. Ericsson (Eds.), *Expert performance in sport: Recent advances in research on sport expertise* (pp. 49–81). Champaign, IL: Human Kinetics.

Ericsson, K. A. (2003d). How the expert-performance approach differs from traditional approaches to expertise in sports: In search of a shared theoretical framework for studying expert performance. In J. Starkes & K. A. Ericsson (Eds.), *Expert performance in sport: Recent advances in research on sport expertise* (pp. 371–401). Champaign, IL: Human Kinetics.

Ericsson, K. A. (2004). Deliberate practice and the acquisition and maintenance of expert performance in medicine and related domains. *Academic Medicine, 10,* s70–S81.

Ericsson, K. A., Delaney, P. F., Weaver, G., & Mahadevan, R. (2004). Uncovering the structure of a memorist's superior "basic" memory capacity. *Cognitive Psychology, 49,* 191–237.

Ericsson, K. A., & Kintsch, W. (1995). Long-term working memory. *Psychological Review, 102,* 211–245.

Ericsson, K. A., Krampe, R. Th., & Tesch-Römer, C. (1993). The role of deliberate practice in the acquisition of expert performance. *Psychological Review, 100,* 363–406.

Ericsson, K. A., & Lehmann, A. C. (1996). Expert and exceptional performance: Evidence on maximal adaptations on task constraints. *Annual Review of Psychology, 47,* 273–305.

Ericsson, K. A., Patel, V. L., & Kintsch, W. (2000). How experts' adaptations to representative task demands account for the expertise effect in memory recall: Comment on Vicente and Wang (1998). *Psychological Review, 107,* 578–592.

Ericsson, K. A., & Smith, J. (1991). Prospects and limits in the empirical study of expertise: An introduction. In K. A. Ericsson & J. Smith (Eds.), *Toward a general theory of expertise: Prospects and limits* (pp. 1–38). Cambridge: Cambridge University Press.

Feldman, D. H. (1994). *Beyond universals in cognitive development* (2nd. Ed.). Norwood, NJ: Ablex.

Fitts, P., & Posner, M. I. (1967). *Human performance*. Belmont, CA: Brooks/Cole.

Galton, F., Sir (1869/1979). *Hereditary genius: An inquiry into its laws and consequences* (Originally published in 1869). London: Julian Friedman Publishers.

Gaser, C., & Schlaug, G. (2003). Brain structures differ between musicians and non-musicians. *Journal of Neuroscience, 23*, 9240–9245.

Gawel, R. (1997). The use of language by trained and untrained experienced wine tasters. *Journal of Sensory Studies, 12*, 267–284.

Glaser, R. (1996). Changing the agency for learning: Acquiring expert performance. In K. A. Ericsson (Ed.), *The road to excellence: The acquisition of expert performance in the arts and sciences, sports, and games* (pp. 1–50). Mahwah, NJ: Erlbaum.

Gould, S. J. (1996). *Full house: The spread of excellence from Plato to Darwin*. New York: Harmony books.

Grape, C., Sandgren, M., Hansson, L.-O., Ericson, M., & Theorell, T. (2003). Does singing promote well-being?: An empirical study of professional and amateur singers during a singing lesson. *Integrative Physiological & Behavioral Science, 38*, 65–71.

Gruson, L. M. (1988). Rehearsal skill and musical competence: Does practice make perfect? In J. A. Sloboda (Ed.), *Generative processes in music* (pp. 91–112). Oxford, UK: Clarenden Press.

Hayes, J. R. (1981). *The complete problem solver*. Philadelphia, PA: Franklin Institute Press.

Helsen, W. F., Starkes, J. L., & Hodges, N. J. (1998). Team sports and the theory of deliberate practice. *Journal of Sport and Exercise Psychology, 20*, 12–34.

Hodges, N. J., & Starkes, J. L. (1996). Wrestling with the nature of expertise: A sport specific test of Ericsson, Krampe and Tesch-Römer's (1993) theory of "Deliberate Practice." *International Journal of Sport Psychology, 27*, 400–424.

Hoffman, R. R. (Ed.) (1992). *The psychology of expertise: Cognitive research and empirical AI*. New York: Springer-Verlag.

Krampe, R. Th., & Ericsson, K. A. (1996). Maintaining excellence: Deliberate practice and elite performance in young and older pianists. *Journal of Experimental Psychology: General, 125*, 331–359.

Kolb, B., & Whishaw, I. Q. (1998). Brain plasticity and behavior. *Annual Review of Psychology, 49*, 43–64.

Lehmann, A. C., & Ericsson K. A. (1998). The historical development of domains of expertise: Performance standards and innovations in music. In A. Steptoe (Ed.), *Genius and the mind* (pp. 67–94). Oxford, UK: Oxford University Press.

McDaniel, M. A., Schmidt, F. L., & Hunter, J. E. (1988). Job experience correlates of job performance. *Journal of Applied Psychology, 73*, 327–330.

McKinney, E. H., & Davis, K. J. (2004). Effects of deliberate practice on crisis decision performance. *Human Factors, 45*, 436–444.

Moulaert, V., Verwijnen, M. G. M., Rikers, R., & Scherpbier, A. J. J. A. (2004). The effects of deliberate practice in undergraduate medical education. *Medical Education, 38*, 1044–1052.

Nielsen, S. (1999). Regulation of learning strategies during practice: A case study of a single church organ student preparing a particular work for a concert performance. *Psychology of Music, 27*, 218–229.

Plant, E. A., Ericsson, K. A., Hill, L., & Asberg, K. (2005). Why study time does not predict grade point average across college students: Implications of deliberate practice for academic performance. *Contemporary Educational Psychology, 30*, 96–116.

Plimpton, G. (Ed.) (1977). *Writers at work: The Paris review. Interviews, Second Series*. New York: Penguin.

Raskin, E. (1936). Comparison of scientific and literary ability: A biographical study of eminent scientists and letters of the nineteenth century. *Journal of Abnormal and Social Psychology, 31*, 20–35.

Reif, F., & Allen, S. (1992). Cognition for interpreting scientific concepts: A study of acceleration. *Cognition and Instruction, 9*, 1–44.

Robergs, R. A., & Roberts, S. O. (1997). *Exercise physiology: Exercise, performance, and clinical applications*. St. Louis, MO: Mosby-Year Book.

Rosson, M. B. (1985). The role of experience in editing. *Proceedings of INTERACT '84 IFIP Conference on Human-Computer Interaction* (pp. 45–50). New York: Elsevier.

Salthouse, T. A. (1984). Effects of age and skill in typing. *Journal of Experimental Psychology: General, 113*, 345–371.

Schneider, W. (1993). Acquiring expertise: Determinants of exceptional performance. In K. A. Heller, J. Mönks, & H. Passow (Eds.), *International handbook of research and development of giftedness and talent* (pp. 311–324). Oxford, UK: Pergamon Press.

Shanteau, J., & Stewart, T. R. (1992). Why study expert decision making? Some historical perspectives and comments. *Organizational Behaviour and Human Decision Processes, 53,* 95–106.

Schulz, R., & Curnow, C. (1988). Peak performance and age among superathletes: Track and field, swimming, baseball, tennis, and golf. *Journal of Gerontology: Psychological Sciences, 43,* 113–120.

Simon, H. A., & Chase, W. G. (1973). Skill in chess. *American Scientist, 61,* 394–403.

Simonton, D. K. (1997). Creative productivity: A predictive and explanatory model of career trajectories and landmarks. *Psychological Review, 104,* 66–89.

Singer, C. (1958*). From magic to science.* New York: Dover.

Sloboda, J. A., Davidson, J. W., Howe, M. J. A., & Moore, D. G. (1996). The role of practice in the development of performing musicians. *British Journal of Psychology, 87,* 287–309.

Sonnentag, S. (1998). Expertise in professional software design: A process study. *Journal of Applied Psychology, 83,* 703–715.

Sonnentag, S., & Kleine, B. M. (2000). Deliberate practice at work: A study with insurance agents. *Journal of Occupational and Organizational Psychology, 73,* 87–102.

Starkes, J. L., Deakin, J., Allard, F., Hodges, N. J., & Hayes, A. (1996). Deliberate practice in sports: What is it anyway? In K. A. Ericsson (Ed.), *The road to excellence: The acquisition of expert performance in the arts and sciences, sports, and games* (pp. 81–106). Mahwah, NJ: Erlbaum.

Ulijaszek, S. J., Johston, F. E., & Preece, M. A. (Eds.) (1998). *The Cambridge encyclopedia of human growth and development.* Cambridge, UK: Cambridge University Press.

Valentin, D., Pichon, M., de Boishebert, V., & Abdi, H. (2000). What's in a wine name? When and why do wine experts perform better than novices? *Abstracts of the Psychonomic Society, 5,* 36.

Vicente, K. J., & Wang, J. H. (1998). An ecological theory of expertise effects in memory recall. *Psychological Review, 105,* 33–57.

Ward. P., Hodges, N. J., Williams, A. M., & Starkes, J. L. (2004). Deliberate practice and expert performance: Defining the path to excellence. In A. M. Williams & N. J. Hodges (Eds.), *Skill acquisition in sport: Research, theory and practice* (pp. 231–258). London, UK: Routhledge.

Williams, M., & Davids, K. (1995). Declarative knowledge in sport: A by-product of experience or a characteristic of expertise? *Journal of Sport & Exercise Psychology, 17,* 259–275.

Williams, A. M., Ward, P., Knowles, J. M., & Smeeton, N. J. (2002). Anticipation skill in a real-world task: Measurement, training, and transfer in tennis. *Journal of Experimental Psychology: Applied, 8,* 259–270.

Author Notes

This research was supported by the FSCW/Conradi Endowment Fund of Florida State University Foundation. The author wants to thank Andreas Lehmann, Len Hill, Robert Hoffman, and Paul Ward for the helpful comments on earlier drafts of the chapter.

CHAPTER 39

Development and Adaptation of Expertise: The Role of Self-Regulatory Processes and Beliefs

Barry J. Zimmerman

The attainment of expertise in diverse fields requires more than nascent talent, initial task interest, and high-quality instruction; it also involves personal initiative, diligence, and especially practice. Both the quality and quantity of an expert's practice have been linked directly to acquisition and maintenance of high levels of performance (Ericsson, 1996, Ericsson, Chapter 38). Regarding its quality, the practice of experts is characterized by its conscious *deliberate* properties – namely, a high level of concentration and the structuring of specific training tasks to facilitate setting appropriate personal goals, monitoring informative feedback, and providing opportunities for repetition and error correction (Ericsson, Krampe, & Tesch-Römer, 1993). Deliberate attention (i.e., strategic awareness) is believed to be necessary to overcome prior habits, to self-monitor accurately, and to determine necessary adjustments.

Although a skilled teacher typically structures these desirable dimensions of practice episodes, a student must implement them on his or her own before returning to the teacher for evaluation and new assignments. Expert musicians rated both lessons with their teacher and their solitary practice as two keys to their improvement, but only the latter was solely under their control (Ericsson, Krampe, & Tesch-Römer, 1993). Interestingly, the quantity of deliberate practice, but not total amount of music-related activity, was predictive of the musicians' acquisition and maintenance of expert performance. Ericsson (2003) has discussed a person's attempts to acquire expertise as deliberate problem solving because they involve forming a cognitive representation of the task, choosing appropriate techniques or strategies, and evaluating one's effectiveness. These properties of deliberate practice (e.g., task analysis, goal setting, strategy choice, self-monitoring, self-evaluations, and adaptations) have been studied as key components of self-regulation (Boekaerts, Pintrich, & Zeidner, 2000; Schunk & Zimmerman, 1998; Winne, 1997; Zimmerman & Schunk, 2001). Self-regulation is defined formally as self-generated thoughts, feelings, and actions that are strategically planned and adapted to the attainment of personal goals (Zimmerman, 1989). Feedback from one's performance is used cyclically to make strategic adjustments in future efforts.

In this chapter, I review research on the development of personal expertise in diverse areas of functioning, such as music, writing, and sport, with particular attention to the role of self-regulatory processes and supportive self-motivational beliefs. Expertise involves self-regulating three personal elements: one's covert cognitive and affective processes, behavioral performance, and environmental setting. These triadic elements are self-regulated during three cyclical phases: forethought, performance, and self-reflection (see also Feltovich, Prietula, & Ericsson, Chapter 4, "Expertise is Reftective"). Then I discuss research on phase differences in self-regulatory processes and motivational beliefs of novices and experts, and finally, I describe the development of expertise through multi-phase self-regulation training.

Expertise is defined as a sequence of mastered challenges with increasing levels of difficulty in specific areas of functioning (Ericsson, 2003). In this chapter, the terms *expert* and *novice* refer to high or low positions respectively on this continuum of task difficulty, without limiting the term *expertise* to the pinnacle of performance. Expertise involves more than self-regulatory competence; it also involves task knowledge and performance skill. Self-regulatory processes can assist a person to acquire both knowledge and skill more effectively, but improvements in one's use of self-regulatory processes will not immediately produce high levels of expertise. What then is the role of self-regulatory processes in the development of expertise?

A Social Cognitive View of Self-Regulation

From this perspective, expertise develops from both external support and self-directed practice sessions. A child's acquisition of expertise in both common and more esoteric activities emerges from modeling, instruction, monitoring, and guidance activities by his or her parents, teachers, and peers within the social milieu of the family, the school, and the community. In his classic study of

talented concert pianists, sculptors, mathematicians, neurologists, Olympic swimmers, and tennis players, Bloom (1985) found that their parents not only nurtured the child's initial interest and provided or arranged high-quality instruction, they also emphasized the importance of dedicated practice: "To excel, to *do one's best*, to *work hard*, and to *spend one's time constructively* were emphasized over and over again" (p. 10). Because high levels of skill must be practiced and adapted personally to dynamic contexts, aspiring experts need to develop a self-disciplined approach to learning and practice to gain consistency (Nicklaus, 1974). As children attain higher levels of performance, parents and teachers gradually eliminate external supports (Glaser, 1996). Parental activities that foster children's self-regulatory control of learning have been found to increase the social and cognitive competence of the children (e.g., Brody & Flor, 1998; see also Horn & Masunaga, Chapter 34).

Social cognitive researchers view self-regulatory competence as involving three elements: self-regulating one's covert personal processes, behavioral performance, and environmental setting (Bandura, 1986). Successful learners monitor and regulate these triadic elements in a strategically coordinated and adaptive manner. Because each of these triadic elements fluctuates during the course of learning and performance, it must be monitored and evaluated using a separate self-oriented feedback loop, which is depicted in Figure 39.1 (Zimmerman, 1989).

During *behavioral self-regulation*, an individual self-observes and strategically adjusts his or her overt performance, such as when a tennis player double faults when serving and decides to adjust his or her ball toss. With *environmental self-regulation*, a person observes and adjusts his or her environmental conditions or outcomes, such as when a golfer has trouble with sun glare and decides to wear sunglasses. During *covert self-regulation*, an individual monitors and adjusts cognitive and affective states, such as when a basketball player begins to "choke" under pressure and decides to

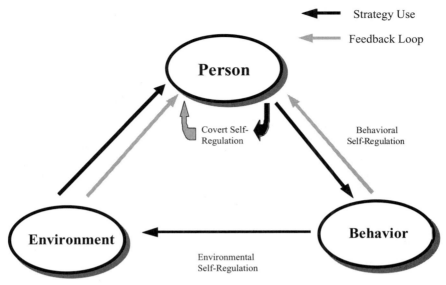

Figure 39.1. Triadic forms of self-regulation. From "A social cognitive view of self-regulated academic learning," by Barry J. Zimmerman, 1989, *Journal of Educational Psychology*, 81, p. 330. Copyright 1989 by the American Psychological Association. Adapted with permission.

form a relaxing mental image to counteract the pressure. For all three self-regulatory elements, people's accuracy and constancy in self-monitoring of outcomes positively influence the effectiveness of their strategic adjustments and the nature of their self-beliefs, such as perceptions of self-efficacy – their self-belief in their capability to perform effectively (Schunk, 1983b; Zimmerman & Kitsantas, 1997). The latter belief, in turn, is a major source of motivation to self-regulate one's functioning (Bandura, 1997; Zimmerman, 1995), and its cyclical role during self-regulation, along with that of other key self-motivational beliefs, is discussed next.

A Cyclical Phase View of Self-Regulatory Processes and Motivational Beliefs

Bloom's (1985) study revealed that talented youth were distinguished by their initial attraction to their field from first exposure and by their increasing practice time. Their successes led them or their parents to seek instruction from master teachers. But why does the initial task interest of these talented youths' lead to self-

enhancing cycles of motivation, whereas the initial task interest of their undistinguished peers fails to sustain dedicated learning and practice? To explain self-enhancing cycles of learning, social cognitive researchers (Bandura, 1991; Zimmerman, 2000) have proposed that self-regulatory processes are linked to key self-motivational beliefs during three cyclical phases: forethought, performance control, and self-reflection (see Figure 39.2).

The forethought phase involves learning processes and motivational beliefs that precede and can enhance efforts to learn, practice, and perform. The performance phase involves use of processes to improve the quality and quantity of learning, practice, and performance, and the self-reflection phase involves processes that occur after efforts to learn, practice, or perform that influence a learner's cognitive and behavioral reactions to that experience. These self-reflections, in turn, influence a person's forethought processes and beliefs regarding subsequent learning, which completes the self-regulatory cycle. Although all learners attempt to self-regulate their personal functioning in some way, developing experts

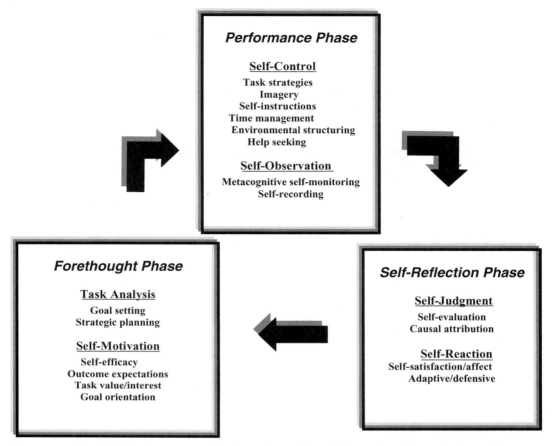

Figure 39.2. Phases and subprocesses of self-regulation. From "Motivating self-regulated problem solvers," by B. J. Zimmerman & M. Campillo, 2003, in J. E. Davidson & R. J. Sternberg (Eds.), *The nature of problem solving* (p. 239). New York: Cambridge University Press. Copyright by Cambridge University Press. Reprinted with permission.

focus *proactively* on learning processes (i.e., as a means to an end) during the forethought and performance control phases, rather than only *reactively* on personal outcomes during self-reflection (Cleary & Zimmerman, 2001). We address these issues next.

FORETHOUGHT PHASE

To prepare to perform at their desired level, aspiring learners or their instructors analyze the learning tasks in order to set appropriate practice goals and plan an effective strategy for attaining those goals (Ericsson, 1996). The self-regulatory process of *goal setting* refers to specifying intended actions or outcomes (Locke & Latham, 2002). Research

on women volleyball players (Kitsantas & Zimmerman, 2002) has shown that experts set more specific technique or processes goals for themselves than non-experts. For example, experts reported technique goals such as "toss the ball properly," whereas non-experts reported general goals such as "concentrate," and novice learners fail to set goals for themselves at all. In other research, learners who set a combination of process and outcome strategies performed better than learners who set singular goals (Filby, Maynard, & Graydon, 1999; Kingston & Hardy, 1997). Process goals refer to improving one's strategy or technique, whereas outcome goals refer to enhancing the results of performance, such as points won or applause from an audience. An exclusive focus on outcome goals can detract from one's technique on an athletic task (Zimmerman & Kitsantas, 1996), and coaches often try to alter this mind-set. For example, to reduce the pressure on European team members of the 2004 Ryder Cup, the successful captain, Bernhard Langer, advised them to avoid looking at the scoreboard unless their team was way ahead (Anderson, September 19, 2004).

Strategic planning refers to decisions about how one can accomplish a particular goal, and there is evidence that experts select more technique-oriented strategies. For example, Natalie Coughlin is an extraordinary American swimmer who broke four world records during 2002 and was a gold medallist in the 2004 Olympics in Athens. She credits her success to her staunch work ethic and her strategic planning. Her practice strategy focuses on swimming technique rather than brute effort. "There's so much technique involved in swimming... You're constantly manipulating the water. The slightest change of pitch in your hand makes the biggest difference" (Grudowski, August, 2003, p. 73). As a result of her disciplined practice strategy, she could complete each leg of her races with fewer but more efficient strokes, which gives her exceptional stamina. In support of Coughlin's strategic planning, researchers have found that learners' use of technique-oriented strategies significantly improves their athletic and academic learning (Zimmerman & Kitsantas, 1996; 1999).

The willingness of talented youths to engage in effective forms of goal setting and strategy use depends on their high levels of motivation (Bloom, 1985), and coaches and expert performers have ranked desire to succeed as the most important factor for eventual success in a domain (Starkes, Deakin, Allard, Hodges, & Hayes, 1996). Social cognitive researchers have identified four key self-motivational beliefs that underlie efforts to self-regulate: self-efficacy, outcome expectations, task interest/ valuing, and goal orientation. Expert basketball free-throw shooters have reported higher *self-efficacy* beliefs – in their capability to perform effectively – than non-experts or novices (Cleary & Zimmerman, 2001). Learners with high self-efficacy beliefs have been found to set higher goals for themselves (Zimmerman, Bandura, & Martinez-Pons, 1992) and are more committed to those goals than learners with low self-efficacy beliefs (Locke & Latham, 2002). For example, the American actress Geena Davis took up archery as an adult. She has developed such a high level of skill that she was invited to try out for the 2000 U.S. Olympic team, but she narrowly missed being selected. She described the role of her self-efficacy beliefs in motivating her practice efforts in the following way, "You have to be very self-motivated. You have to have faith in yourself and believe in your abilities" (Litsky, 1999, August 6, p. D4).

Outcome expectations refer to self-motivational beliefs about the ultimate ends of learning, practice, and performance, such as Geena Davis' hope of making the Olympic team. Because successful learners view strategic processes as effective means to an end, they are motivated more by the attraction of positive outcomes of these processes than by the fear of adverse outcomes (Pintrich, 2000). Outcomes that reflect increases in one's learning competence have been found to increase the perceived *value* of a task (Karniol & Ross, 1977; Zimmerman, 1985). Because of their valuing of a task, experts are more motivated to continue striving, even in the absence of tangible rewards (Kitsantas & Zimmerman, 2002). Geena Davis described her growing task interest from practicing in the following way, "I guess I just got hooked. It is really fun to try to see how good you can get, and I don't know how good that is. I haven't maxed out. I haven't peaked. I'm trying to get better" (Litsky, 1999, August 6, p. D4).

A mastery or learning *goal orientation* refers to self-motivational beliefs about valuing learning progress more than achievement outcomes (Ames, 1992). There is evidence that students with strong learning goals display higher levels of cognitive engagement and performance on learning tasks than students with weak learning goals (Graham &

Golen, 1991; Nolen, 1988). The tennis champion Monica Seles described her learning goal orientation in the following way: "I really never enjoyed playing matches, even as a youngster. I just love to practice and drill and that stuff. I just hate the whole thought that one [player] is better than the other. It drives me nuts" (Vecsey, 1999, p. D1).

PERFORMANCE PHASE

Experts' advantageous goals, strategic planning, and motivational beliefs during the forethought phase lead to the self-controlled and self-observed implementation of these strategies, methods, or techniques during the performance phase. However, forethought phase task analyses that are superficial or inaccurate, like those of many novices, can lead to ineffective or even counterproductive efforts to control performance phase processes. Because strategies vary in their situational effectiveness, they must be constantly self-observed and adjusted, which is the second class of performance phase processes.

The first *self-control* process to be discussed is *self-instruction*. This form of self-talk refers to vocal or subvocal guidance of one's performance, and there is evidence of its effectiveness in enhancing academic (Meichenbaum, 1977; Schunk, 1986) and athletic (Hardy, Gammage, & Hall, 2001) expertise. For example, with athletes who have trouble controlling their negative outbursts, Loehr (1991), a sports psychologist at the elite Nick Bolletierri Tennis academy, recommended listing all of their negative responses and finding a positive alternative for each one, such as saying "let it go" or "come on" (p. 47) when they lose a point. However, self-directive verbalizations must be adapted to task outcomes and generally should be faded as a skill is mastered (Meichenbaum, 1977), or they can limit further improvement (Zimmerman & Bell, 1972).

The self-regulatory process of *imagery* is used to create or recall vivid mental images to assist learning and performance (Paivio, 1986). Approximately 80 to 85% of expert athletes, such as the diver Greg Louganis, the decathalete Bruce Jenner, the golfer Jack Nicklaus, and the tennis player Chris Evert, consider mental imagery to be an asset in their training (Loehr, 1991). Athletic performers who imagine themselves as successful have reported higher levels of motivation and performance than those who do not use this technique (Munroe, Giacobbi, Hall, & Weinberg, 2000). Donald Murray (1990), a Pulitzer Prize-winning writer, used imagery in similar fashion: "I see what I write and many times the focus of my writing is in my image" (p. 97).

Task strategies refer to advantageous methods for learning or performing particular tasks. In the domain of academic learning, an extensive number of task strategies, such as mnemonics, cognitive maps, note-taking, and outlines, have been found to be effective (e.g., Schneider & Pressley, 1997; Weinstein & Mayer, 1986). For example, as his task strategy, the American author Irving Wallace (1971) prepared extensive notes and outlines before he began writing. Often task strategies are domain specific in their scope and are context specific in their effectiveness. For example, the concert pianist Alicia de la Rocha used the practice strategy of playing difficult passages very slowly and very softly to improve her technique (Mach, 1991). As her technique on a passage became proficient, she modified her strategy and began practicing at normal speed. This illustrates the issue discussed earlier: The utility of a particular strategy needs to be carefully monitored to ensure its optimal utilization.

Time management refers to estimating and budgeting one's use of time (Zimmerman, Greenberg, & Weinstein, 1994), and experts often structure their practice and work time carefully. For example, to improve the quantity and quality of his writing, the German poet Goethe recommended, "Use the day before the day. Early morning hours have gold in their mouth" (Murray, 1990, p. 16). Although professional writers differ in the timing of their optimal states for writing (such as the morning), those who structure their writing time have reported evidence of its effectiveness (Wallace & Pear,

1977). Among student instrumental musicians, high achievers in annual competitions have reported a greater amount of practice time than low achievers (McPherson & Zimmerman, 2002). Thus, time management can involve regulation of both the quality and quantity of time use.

In research on students' academic homework (Zimmerman & Kitsantas, 2005), the quality of students' study time was highly correlated with its quantity, and both indices were highly predictive of students' grade point average.

It should be noted that implementation of these self-control strategies often involves significant others, such as parents and teachers. The self-regulatory process of adaptive *help seeking* is defined as choosing specific models, teachers, or books to assist oneself to learn (Newman, 1994). For example, parents often structure practice environments for talented youth, and master teachers coach students how to improve their practice techniques (Bloom, 1985). High academic achievers are not asocial in their methods of practice, but, rather, selectively seek instructional assistance in a self-initiated adaptive manner. By contrast, low achievers are reluctant to seek help because of their lack of planning and their resultant fear of adverse reactions from help-givers (Karabenek, 1998). Among expert musicians, the concert pianist Janina Fialkowska frequently sought out Arthur Rubinstein as an exemplary model. "He couldn't tell me how to do something, but he could demonstrate how it should sound . . . So when I'd play something that wasn't up to par, he became very exasperated, and believe me he became exasperated very easily. Then he'd kick me off the bench and play it the way he thought it should be played" (Mach, 1991, pp. 79–80).

Environmental structuring, which refers to selecting or creating effective settings for learning or performance, is another important self-control process. For example, students who had difficulty concentrating during studying were taught how to create an effective study environment where daydreaming, eating, or other off-task behav-

iors were excluded and where a structured study method and self-reinforcement were included (Fox, 1962). All the students in the study reported increases in their grade points of at least one letter grade. These favorable results of environmental structuring were replicated a decade later (Beneke & Harris, 1972). Experts are very sensitive to the impact of their surroundings on quality and quantity of their functioning. For example, the French poet and novelist Cendrars described his need to write in a quiet undistracted place, such as an enclosed room with the window shade pulled down. The American bike racer Lance Armstrong prepared himself to win the Tour de France in the mountainous sections of the racecourse by sleeping in a low oxygen tent to adapt himself physiologically to those conditions ahead of time (Lehrer, 2001, July 30).

The key *self-observation* processes during the performance phase are metacognitive monitoring and self-recording, which refer respectively to mentally tracking or physically recording one's performance. Experts observe the implementation and effectiveness of their self-control processes and outcomes more systematically than non-experts or novices (Kitsantas & Zimmerman, 2002).

Metacognitive self-monitoring is difficult for novices because the amount of information involved in complex performances can easily overwhelm and can lead to inconsistent or superficial tracking. Experts are selective in their cognitive self-monitoring during practice because of the specificity of their learning, practice, and performance goals (Abrahams, 2001). Experts' recall of information about a completed task has been found to be more accurate and complete than that of novices and less accomplished individuals in the same domain (Ericsson & Kintsch, 1995). Experts are also more likely to recall pertinent or substantial information that is pitched at a higher level of abstraction (see also Feltovich et al., Chapter 4, "Expertise Involves Functional, Abstracted Representations").

The legendary golfer Bobby Jones (1966) described his method of monitoring as follows, "It has never been possible for me to think of more than two or three details of the swing and still hit the ball correctly . . . The two or three are not always the same, sometime a man's swing will be functioning so well he need worry about nothing" (p. 203).

Experts can improve the accuracy of their self-observations by *self-recording* their progress (see also, Deakin, Côté, & Harvey, Chapter 17). Literary experts, such as Trollope (1905) and Hemingway (Wallace & Pear, 1977), were acutely aware of the value of self-recording in enhancing the quantity of their literary output and consistently utilized this technique. A person's records are more effective if they track not only his or her performance but also the conditions that surround it, and the results that it produces (Zimmerman & Paulsen, 1995; Ericsson, 1996). Unfortunately, novices often self-record in a cursory and inaccurate way (Hallam, 1997). However, it should be noted that record keeping can be time consuming, and as a result, its effectiveness needs to be monitored carefully. After a skill has been mastered to a personally acceptable level, people can often cease record keeping unless problems arise (Zimmerman & Paulsen, 1995).

SELF-REFLECTION PHASE

Experts increase the accuracy of their feedback by generating self-evaluative standards for themselves (Hamery, 1976). *Self-evaluation* judgments compare self-observed information with one of three types of standards or criteria: (a) a self-improvement criterion (e.g., comparing current efforts to one's best previous effort), (b) a social comparison criterion (e.g., comparing one's efforts to those of competitors), or (c) a mastery criterion (e.g., comparing one's performance to a national record). Self-evaluations are not automatic outcomes of performance but, rather, depend on an individual's selection and interpretation of an appropriate criterion (Bandura, 1991). When self-evaluative standards are too high or too low, people's learning and performance is diminished (Schunk, 1983a). For example, the legendary golfer Ben Hogan (1957) warned about the dangers of setting unrealistically high standards. "I had stopped trying to do a great many difficult things perfectly because it had become clear in my mind that this ambitious over-thoroughness was neither possible nor advisable or even necessary" (p. 113). Conversely, individuals who fail to set challenging standards for themselves have displayed lower levels of performance than persons who challenged themselves (Locke & Latham, 2002).

A second self-judgment that is hypothesized to play a pivotal role in self-reflection involves the *causal attribution* of errors. For example, when errors are attributed to uncontrollable sources, such as an opponent's luck, learners display negative self-reactions and diminished attainment of skill. By contrast, when errors are attributed to controllable sources, such as one's strategies, learners experience positive self-reactions and increased skill (Zimmerman & Kitsantas, 1999). Expert golfers have exhibited this favorable pattern of attributions when discussing differences between good and bad rounds. They tend to discount the possibility that chance factors played an important role (Kirschenbaum, O'Connor, & Owens, 1999) and instead attribute their errors to personally controllable processes, such as poor concentration, tenseness, poor imagination and feel (McCaffrey & Orlick, 1989). The swimmer Natalie Coughlin put it this way, "In general, I'm pretty inwardly focused . . . I like to concentrate on my stroke and do my race, because that's all I can control" (Grudowski, August, 2003, p. 73). Novices are prone to attributing causation for errors to such uncontrollable sources as a lack of ability, task difficulty, or bad luck Cleary & Zimmerman, 2001; Kitsantas & Zimmerman, 2002). These unfortunate attributions occur because of novices' poor self-regulatory processes and beliefs during the forethought and performance phases, such as vague goal setting, non-strategic efforts to learn, and low perceptions of self-efficacy (Bandura, 1991).

Self-evaluation and attribution self-judgments are closely linked to two key self-reactions: self-satisfaction and adaptive inferences. Perceptions of *self-satisfaction* or dissatisfaction and associated emotions, such as elation or depression, regarding one's practice or performance influence the courses of action that people pursue, such as expertise in writing (Zimmerman & Bandura, 1994). In general, self-satisfaction reactions are positively related to subsequent sources of motivation (e.g., Zimmerman & Kitsantas, 1997; 1999), but there is anecdotal evidence that expert writers increase their self-evaluative standards as they progress, which initially decreases their satisfaction. For example, the American novelist William Faulkner warned that a writer "must never be satisfied with what he (sic) does. It never is as good as it can be" (Stein, 1959, p. 123). Clearly, self-satisfaction is not an automatic outcome of performance; rather, it depends on people's self-judgment standards as well as their forethought goals.

Adaptive or *defensive inferences* refer to self-reactions about how to alter one's self-regulatory approach during subsequent efforts to learn or perform. There is evidence (Kitsantas & Zimmerman, 2002) that experts are more adaptive, rather than defensive, in their self-reactions, preferring to adjust their strategy rather than to avoid the task. Adaptive inferences guide learners to new and potentially more effective forms of performance self-regulation, whereas defensive inferences serve primarily to protect the person from future dissatisfaction and aversive affect (Garcia & Pintrich, 1994). Personal adaptations can lead to extraordinary outcomes, such as those of the bike racer Lance Armstrong. After a life-threatening bout with cancer and physical debilitation from chemotherapy, Armstrong had to alter his bicycle training methods to minimize pedal resistance (which taxes leg strength), so he adapted by increasing pedal speed (which taxes aerobic capacity). As he improved his aerobic capacity, this adaptation became an advantage over his competitors, especially in mountainous stretches of the racecourse (Lehrer, 2001).

Adaptive inferences during practice experiences are affected by other self-reflection phase beliefs, such as attributions and perceptions of satisfaction with one's progress, as well as by forethought phase self-efficacy beliefs and by performance phase self-control strategies. By attributing errors to specific learning methods, experts sustain their self-satisfaction and foster variations in their methods until they discover an improved version (Cleary & Zimmerman, 2001). In contrast, novices' attribution of unfavorable results to uncontrollable factors leads to dissatisfaction and undermines further adaptive efforts. In this way, the strategic process goals of experts lead cyclically to greater self-satisfaction and more effective forms of adaptation. The latter outcomes were correlated with their forethought self-motivational beliefs, goals, and strategy choices regarding further efforts to learn (Kitsantas & Zimmerman, 2002).

Research on Experts' Use of Cyclical Self-Regulatory Processes

Although there is extensive evidence that successful learners display greater self-regulation and stronger motivational beliefs (Schunk & Zimmerman, 1998; Boekaerts, Pintrich, & Zeidner, 2000), research on experts' and novices' athletic practice is limited to date(see also Hodges, Starkes, & MacMahon, Chapter 27). Several empirical studies have been conducted recently using athletic experts whose performance was exemplary at a school level but not at a state, national, or international level. Thus, the terms expert and novice refer to high or low positions respectively on this continuum of task difficulty in this research. In particular, in an investigation of the practice methods of basketball free-throw shooters, Tim Cleary and I studied individual differences in the self-regulation of three groups of high school boys: basketball experts, non-experts, and novices (Cleary & Zimmerman, 2001). These relative *experts* made more than 70% of their free-throws during varsity basketball games, whereas *non-experts* made less than 55% of their shots in those games. By contrast, *novices* had not played basketball on organized teams during high school. The non-expert group was added to the classical expert-novice design to provide better control of a variety of background variables, such as basketball playing experience, and familiarity with the game that novices typically lack. Our methodology, called *microanalysis*, employs specific questions that address well-established psychological processes at key points during the act of performing, such as self-efficacy and attribution beliefs. Each participant is separately observed, and researchers develop context-specific information by intensive qualitative and quantitative analyses. In this study, the boys were questioned regarding their forethought phase goals, strategy choices, self-efficacy beliefs, and intrinsic interest, as well as their self-reflection phase attributions and feelings of satisfaction as they practiced their free-throw shooting.

There were no significant differences between experts and non-experts in their frequency of practice, playing experience, and knowledge of free-throw shooting techniques, but there were significant differences in their *methods* of self-regulation during practice. As expected, novices differed from experts and non-experts on all variables except age. It was found that experts set more specific goals, selected more technique-oriented strategies, made more attributions to strategy use, and displayed higher levels of self-efficacy than either non-experts or novices. When asked to self-reflect after two consecutive misses, free-throw experts were more mindful of their specific, technique-oriented flaws than boys in the other two groups. Although 60% of the experts indicated that they needed to focus on their techniques (i.e., "to keep my elbow in," "to follow through") in order to make the next shot, only 20% of the non-experts and 7% of the novices mentioned this type of strategy. Non-experts preferred strategies related to the rhythm of shooting and general focus strategies (e.g., "to concentrate" or "to try harder") for a majority (i.e., 53%) of their responses. Unfortunately, these self-reflections do not correct faulty techniques because they divert attention away from essential athletic form processes.

To see if the results were consistent with a cyclical model, we analyzed relations among the boys' use of self-regulatory processes.

We found that goal setting was correlated with choice of strategy. Athletes who set outcome-specific goals (e.g., "to make ten out of ten") were more likely to select specific technique-oriented strategies (e.g., "to follow through"), whereas those athletes setting outcome-general goals (e.g., "to make them") were more likely to select general technique strategies (e.g., "to concentrate on my form"). It appears that teaching athletes to set specific goals can lead to their selection of specific strategies to achieve those goals.

A key finding about the self-reflection phase was that the boys' attributions of errors to strategies were predictive of the boys' forethought strategy selections during further efforts to learn. For example, boys who attributed their failure to specific techniques (i.e., "I missed the last two shots because my elbow was going to the left") were more likely to select a specific technique-oriented strategy to improve their shooting accuracy (e.g., "I need to keep my elbow in"). Overall, this study revealed highly significant differences in the quality of self-regulation during self-directed practice efforts by high school basketball players of varying ability. Experts were more focused on specific shooting processes during goal setting, strategic planning, and self-reflecting than non-experts or novices, and they were more self-efficacious about their performance.

In a study of college women's volleyball practice, Anastasia Kitsantas and I (2002) selected a group of *experts* from the university varsity volleyball team and a group of *non-experts* from the university volleyball club (i.e., who had been on the club team for at least three years). The group of novices had not ever participated in volleyball as an organized sport but had played it informally. The three groups of women were questioned regarding their forethought phase goals, strategy choices, self-efficacy beliefs, and intrinsic interest, as well as their self-reflection phase attributions and feelings of satisfaction as they practiced their volleyball serves. It was found that experts displayed better goals, planning, strategy use, self-monitoring, self-evaluation, attributions, and adaptation than either non-experts or novices. Experts also reported higher self-efficacy beliefs, perceived instrumentality, intrinsic interest, and self-satisfaction about volleyball serving than either non-experts or novices. The combined 12 cyclical measures of self-regulation explained 90% of the variance in the women's volleyball serving skill. Clearly, experts differed greatly in self-regulation of their practice methods.

Development of Greater Expertise through Multi-Phase Self-Regulatory Training

Although there was unambiguous evidence of superior self-regulation during athletic practice by experts, the causal role of these self-regulatory processes and beliefs in the development of expertise is another issue. To develop free-throw expertise of male and female college students, Cleary, Zimmerman, and Keating (in press) trained them to shoot basketball free-throws more effectively during their physical education classes. The participants assigned to a *three-phase self-regulation group* were instructed to set technique goals (a forethought phase process), self-record (a performance phase process), and to make strategic attributions and adjustments following missed free throws (self-reflection phase processes). Setting technique goals involved focusing on properly executing the final four steps of the shooting process (i.e., grip, elbow position, knee bend, follow through) rather than on shooting outcomes. The examiner showed the participants a cue card delineating the process goal. This group was then taught how to use a self-recording form in order to monitor the step(s) of the strategy that they were focusing on while shooting the shots. This recording form also allowed the participants to monitor whether they missed any shots, the reasons for the missed shots, and strategies needed to make the next shot. In addition to this self-reflection phase training, the participants were taught how to link poor shots with one or more of the shooting techniques taught in the study. The participants assigned to the *two-phase self-regulation group* received the same forethought phase goal setting and performance phase self-recording training as the three-phase group, but they were not instructed how to self-reflect. The *one-phase self-regulation group* received instruction in only the forethought phase process of goal setting. There was also a *practice-only control group* and a *no-practice control group*, which did not receive self-regulation training. All of the participants were randomly assigned to one of the five conditions and were tested and trained individually by an experimenter.

It was expected that one-phase training would influence subsequent phases of self-regulation, and two-phase training would influence self-reflection phase self-regulation to some degree due to the cyclical dependence of later phase processes on earlier phase processes, but we expected that total phase training, including explicit training in self-reflection phase processes, would be optimal. Thus, a positive linear relationship was predicted between the students' free-throw shooting performance and the number of self-regulatory phases in which they were trained.

The results revealed that there were no gender differences in learning and that there was in fact a linear relationship between amount of phase training and two key measures of learning: free-throw shooting accuracy and shooting adaptation. A more sensitive measure of shooting accuracy than simple making or missing the basket was developed. It involved earning one to five points for each shot according to the following criteria: (a) five points for swishing the shot (not hitting any part of the rim), (b) four points for making the shot after hitting the rim, (c) three points for hitting the front or back of the rim but not making the shot, (d) two points for hitting the side of the rim and not making the shot, and (e) one point for completely missing the rim or hitting the backboard first. A missed shot hitting the front or back of the rim earned more points (i.e., three points) than a missed shot hitting the sides of the rim (i.e., two points) because the former indicated greater accuracy. Shooting adaptation referred to the frequency of improvements on the next shot following a poor shot.

The group means ranged in order from lowest to highest as was predicted: no practice control group, practice-only control group, one-phase training, two-phase training, and three-phase training. This suggested that not only did the participants who received multiple-phase self-regulation training show greater accuracy when shooting, but they were also able to improve on poor shots with a more successful throw on a more consistent basis than those individuals who received only one-phase or no self-regulation training. Furthermore, the three-phase group and the two-phase group took significantly fewer practice shots than both the one-phase and practice-only control groups, perhaps because they were called on to self-record their shooting techniques at various points during the practice session. Thus, the *quality* (i.e., defined in terms of self-regulatory sophistication) of these novices' practice methods proved to be more important than the *quantity* of their practice (i.e., number of shots taken) (see also Ericsson, Chapter 38).

This study focused particular attention on the effects of self-regulation training on the participants' self-reflective phase self-judgments (i.e., attributions and self-evaluations) and self-reactions (i.e., adaptive inferences) to missed free throws because they reveal how these learners think about their failures as well as their ability to improve future performances. Learners who received three-phase training displayed the most adaptive motivational profile. For example, they evaluated their performance based on personal processes (e.g., use of correct strategy or personal improvement) more frequently (60%) than all other groups: two-phase group (10%), one-phase group (20%), practice-only control group (20%), and the no-practice control group (10%). This is consistent with the self-regulation cyclical phase hypothesis that using a process criterion to evaluate performance is linked to learning or mastery goal orientation, which has been found to be related to a variety of motivational and achievement variables in

sports (Fox, Goudas, Biddle, Duda, & Armstrong, 1994; Williams & Gill, 1995) and academic functioning (Ames, 1992; Pintrich, 2000).

In terms of causal attributions and adaptive inferences, significantly more members of the multi-phase training group focused on specific shooting techniques or strategies following missed free throws, such as "not keeping my elbow in" and "not touching my elbow to my side as I shot the ball." In contrast, participants from the one-phase training group or the practice control group often attributed their misses to general, non-technique factors, such as a lack of concentration or ability. These technique attributions and adaptive inferences were associated with more accurate shooting performance on the posttest and greater shooting adaptation during practice. Thus, these inexperienced free-throw shooters' ability to improve their poor free-throw shots during practice was related to deficiencies in attributions and adapting these techniques during subsequent shot attempts. Focusing on controllable processes is important because it helps athletes become more aware of what and how they are doing something rather than simply their level of attained outcomes (Cleary & Zimmerman, 2001; Clifford, 1986).

In another study of multi-phase self-regulatory training, Anastasia Kitsantas and I (Zimmerman & Kitsantas, 1997) examined the effects of multiple goal setting and self-recording on the dart-throwing performance and self-reflections with novice high school girls. Girls in a *process goal* group focused on practicing strategy steps for acquiring high-quality dart-throwing technique (e.g., the take-back, release, and follow-through positions). By contrast, girls in an *outcome goal* group focused on improving their scores. The "bullseye" on the target had the highest numerical value and the surrounding concentric circles declined in value. Previous research had demonstrated that process goals were more effective than outcome goals with novice dart throwers (Zimmerman & Kitsantas, 1996). From a multiple goal perspective, girls who *shifted goals* from processes to outcomes when automaticity was achieved should acquire more skill during practice than girls who adhere to only one goal (see Zimmerman, 2000). Automaticity was operationally defined as performing the strategy steps without error for a specified number of dart-throwing trials.

Self-recording was taught to half of the girls in each goal group. Girls in the process-monitoring group recorded any strategy steps they may have missed on each practice throw, whereas girls in the outcome-monitoring group wrote down their target scores for each throw. Girls in the shifting-goal group changed their method of self-monitoring when they shifted goals. Before being asked to practice on their own, all of the girls were taught strategic components of the skill. Thus, the experiment compared the effects of process goals, outcome goals, and shifting goals as well as self-recording during self-directed practice.

The results were supportive of the multiple goal hypothesis: Girls who shifted goals from processes to outcomes surpassed classmates who adhered solely to either process or outcome goals in posttest dart-throwing skill. Girls who focused on outcome goals exclusively were the lowest in dart-throwing skill. Self-monitoring assisted learning for all goal-setting groups. In addition to their superior learning outcomes, girls who shifted their goals displayed superior forms of self-reflection than girls who adhered to either process or outcome goals exclusively. The former girls attributed more errors to controllable causes (i.e., to strategy use) and reported greater self-satisfaction than the latter girls. The girls in the shifting-goal condition also exhibited superior forethought phase motivational beliefs: These girls reported more positive self-efficacy beliefs and greater interest in the dart throwing than girls who adhered exclusively to either process or outcome goals.

The same researchers conducted another study of the effects of multiple-goal training and self-recording on the writing skill of girls attending an academically challenging high school (Zimmerman & Kitsantas, 1999). The design of this study closely paralleled the dart-throwing study, but in this case, the task involved revising a series of writing problems drawn from a sentence-combining workbook. These exercises involved transforming a series of simple and often redundant kernel sentences into a single non-redundant sentence. For example, the sentences: "It was a ball. The ball was striped. The ball rolled across the room" could be rewritten as "The striped ball rolled across the room." The entire group of experimental participants was initially taught a three-step writing revision strategy that involved identifying key information, deleting duplicate information, and combining the remaining words.

During a practice session following training, girls in a process goal group focused on implementing the strategy for revising each writing task, whereas girls in an outcome goal group focused on decreasing the number of words in the revised passage, which was the main outcome criterion. Process goals, which focused on strategy steps, had been found to be more effective than outcome goals in prior writing research (Schunk & Swartz, 1993). As in the dart-throwing study (Zimmerman & Kitsantas, 1997), the most effective goal setting condition was expected to involve shifting from process goals to outcome goals when automaticity in performance was achieved. Half of the girls in each goal group were asked to self-record during practice. Girls in the process-monitoring group recorded strategy steps they missed on each of a series of revision problems, whereas girls in the outcome-monitoring group wrote down the number of words used on each problem. Girls in the shifting-goal group changed their method of self-monitoring when they shifted goals.

The results were supportive of a multiple goal hypothesis. Girls who shifted forethought phase goals from processes to outcomes surpassed the writing revision skill of girls who adhered exclusively to process goals or to outcome goals. Girls who focused on outcomes exclusively displayed the lowest writing skill of the three goal groups. As in the dart-throwing study, self-recording enhanced writing skill for all goal-setting groups. Forethought phase goals significantly increased the girls' performance phase writing skill and also their self-reflection phase attributions to strategy use and their self-satisfaction reactions. Performance phase self-recording also enhanced the girls' writing skill and self-reflection phase attributions and their self-satisfaction. The latter two self-reflection phase processes were predictive of increases in the girls' task interest and self-efficacy beliefs regarding subsequent efforts to learn (i.e., their forethought). These findings provided further evidence of causality in cyclical relations among self-regulatory processes and self-motivational beliefs.

The benefits of training in self-regulatory processes are not limited to novice learners and regular students. Semi-professional cricketers (Thelwell & Maynard, 2003) were trained in goal setting, self-talk, mental imagery, concentration, and activation self-regulation strategies to improve their batting and bowling skills. Goal setting involved both process and outcome (i.e., multiple) goals. Self-talk referred to positive self-statements, task-relevant cues, and personal goals. Mental imagery dealt with forming mastery images of oneself designed to enhance both motivation and execution of the skill. Concentration involved ignoring distracting cues, especially when one's performance suffers, and focusing on task-relevant cues. This superior concentration was expected to enhance the cricketers' self-confidence, which is similar to self-efficacy judgments (Thelwell & Maynard, 2002). Activation strategies involved trying to create a mental and physical state of optimal relaxation and alertness when performing.

These strategies were taught to an experimental group of cricketers between two seasons, during hour-long, weekly training sessions for 12 weeks. A control group of cricket players were trained in team building or fielding activities during the training sessions. Three types of dependent measures were studied. First, the cricketers' batting or bowling scores during the matches were analyzed as an objective measure of perfor-

mance. Second, several coaches rated the cricketers' performance for each match as a subjective measure. Third, the players rated their strategy use with five scales: imagery ability, mental preparation, self-confidence, concentration, and activation.

It was discovered that the experimental training group significantly surpassed the control group in their level of performance, according to both the objective and subjective measures. In addition, these cricket players displayed significantly greater consistency in their performance during the season according to subjective but not objective measures of performance. Finally, cricket players in the experimental group also reported significantly higher levels of strategy use for each of the five scales of strategy use, which included a measure of self-confidence. Clearly, training in the optimal use of self-regulatory processes improved the performance of what many might regard as quite expert athletes. It appears that self-regulatory training can benefit individuals across a wide range of expertise.

Conclusion

This chapter dealt with the role of self-regulatory processes in the development of expertise. Although a child's initial interest in a field of endeavor usually grows from and is supported by parents and teachers, his or her ultimate level of expertise depends on self-disciplined practice and performance. Experts from diverse disciplines, such as sport, music, and writing, rely on well-known self-regulatory processes to practice and perform. Variants of these self-regulatory processes can also assist aspiring learners to acquire both knowledge and skill more effectively. For example, free-throw shooters who set specific practice goals, monitored their improvements in performance, and adjusted their shooting strategy appropriately learned more quickly than free-throw shooters who practiced without employing these self-regulatory processes (Cleary & Zimmerman, 2001).

However, increases in one's use of self-regulatory processes will not immediately produce expert levels of knowledge and skill. Indeed, learners' selection of goals and strategies will depend on their levels of task knowledge and performance skill, such as when the Olympic swimmer Natalie Coughlin self-regulated subtle hand positions to improve her performance (Grudowski, August, 2003), whereas a high school swim team member might focus on improving a more obvious skill. Many training texts, such as for skiing (Tejada-Flores, 1986), have organized knowledge and skills into hierarchical levels, such as basic, intermediate, and advanced, to help learners set goals and monitor their performance more effectively. Clearly, expertise involves more than self-regulatory competence; it also involves greater task knowledge and performance skill.

The use of a cyclical phase model of self-regulation to investigate differences in the practice methods of experts, non-experts, and novices has been limited to date, but the initial results appear promising. Recall that the terms expert and novice refer to high or low positions respectively on this continuum of task difficulty in this research. Multi-phase self-regulation training that is designed to enhance the quality of one's practice improved not only skill acquisition but also key sources of motivation that underlie continued striving to learn, such as perceptions of self-efficacy or confidence and valuing of the intrinsic properties of the task. The importance of such motivation to the development of expertise was emphasized by Csikszentmihalyi, Rathunde, and Whalen (1993) in their study of the roots of success and failure with talented teenagers: "Unless a person wants to pursue the difficult path that leads to the development of talent, neither innate potential nor all the knowledge in the world will suffice" (pp. 31–32).

References

Abrahams, J. (2001, March). And the winner is . . . you. *Golf Magazine, 43* (3), 92–100.

Anderson, D. (2004, September 19). Another deep hole and not enough rope. *New York Times, Sp,* 7.

Ames, C. (1992). Achievement goals and the classroom motivational climate. In D. H. Schunk & J. L. Meece (Eds.), *Student perceptions in the classroom* (pp. 327–348). Hillsdale, NJ: Lawrence Erlbaum Associates.

Bandura, A. (1986). *Social foundations of thought and action: A social cognitive theory.* Englewood Cliffs, NJ: Prentice Hall.

Bandura, A. (1991). Self-regulation of motivation through anticipatory and self-reactive mechanisms. In R. A. Dienstbier (Ed.), *Perspectives on motivation: Nebraska symposium on motivation* (Vol. 38, pp. 69–164). Lincoln: University of Nebraska Press.

Bandura, A. (1997). *Self-efficacy: The exercise of control.* New York: W. H. Freeman.

Beneke, W. M., & Harris, M. B. (1972). Teaching self-control of study behavior. *Behavior Research and Therapy, 10,* 35–41.

Bloom, B. (1985). *Developing talent in young people.* New York: Ballantine Books.

Boekaerts, M., Pintrich, P. R., & Zeidner, M. (Eds.) (2000). *Handbook of self-regulation* (pp.13–39). San Diego, CA: Academic Press.

Brody, G. H., & Flor, D. L. (1998). Maternal resources, parenting practices, and youth competence in rural, two-parent African American families. *Developmental Psychology, 32,* 696–706.

Cleary, T. J., & Zimmerman, B. J. (2001). Self-regulation differences during athletic practice by experts, non-experts, and novices. *Journal of Applied Sport Psychology, 13,* 185–206.

Cleary, T. J., Zimmerman, B. J., & Keating, T. (in press). Training physical education students to self-regulate during basketball free throw practice. *Research Quarterly for Exercise and Sport.*

Csikszentmihalyi, M., Rathunde, K., & Whalen, S. (1993). Talented teenagers: The roots of success and failure. New York: Cambridge University Press.

Clifford, M. (1986). Comparative effects of strategy and effort attributions. *British Journal of Educational Psychology, 56,* 75–83.

Ericsson, K. A. (1996). Acquisition of expert performance: An introduction to some of the issues. In K. A. Ericsson (Ed.), *The road to excellence* (pp. 1–50) Mahwah, NJ: Lawrence Erlbaum Associates.

Ericsson, K. A. (2003). The acqusition of expert performance as problem solving. Construction and modification of mediating mechanisms through deliberate practice. In J. E. Davidson & R. J. Sternberg (Eds.), *The nature of problem solving* (233–262). New York: Cambridge University Press.

Ericsson, K. A., & Kintsch, W. (1995). Long term memory. *Psychological Review, 102*, 211–245.

Ericsson, K. A., Krampe, R. Th., & Tesch-Römer C. (1993). The role of deliberate practice in the acquisition of expert performance. *Psychological Review, 100*, 363–406.

Filby, W. C. D., Maynard, I. W., & Graydon, J. K. (1999). The effect of multiple-goal strategies on performance outcomes in training and competition. *Journal of Applied Sport Psychology, 11*, 230–246.

Fox, L. (1962). Effecting the use of efficient study habits. *Journal of Mathematics, 1*, 76–86.

Fox, K., Goudas, M., Biddle, S., Duda, J., & Armstrong, N. (1994). Children's task and ego goal profiles in sport. *British Journal of Educational Psychology, 64*, 253–261.

Garcia, T., & Pintrich, P. R. (1994). Regulating motivation and cognition in the classroom: The role of self-schemas and self-regulatory strategies. In D. H. Schunk & B. J. Zimmerman (Eds.), *Self regulation of learning and performance: Issues and educational applications* (p. 127–153). Hillsdale, NJ: Lawrence Erlbaum Associates.

Glaser, R. (1996). Changing the agency for learning: Acquiring expert Performance. In K. A. Ericsson (Ed.), *The road to excellence* (pp. 1–50) Mahwah, NJ: Lawrence Erlbaum Associates.

Graham, S., & Golen, S. (1991). Motivational influences on cognition: Task involvement, ego involvement, and depth of information processing. *Journal of Educational Psychology, 83*, 187–194.

Grudowski, M. (August, 2003). The girl next door is hungry. *Men's Journal, 12* (7) 72–73.

Hallam, S. (1997). Approaches to instrumental music practice of experts and novices: Implications for education. In H. Jorgensen & A. C. Lehmann (Eds.), *Does practice make perfect: Current theory and research on instrumental music practice* (pp. 89–108). Oslo, Norway: Norges musikkhogskole.

Hemory, D. (1976). *Another hurdle: The making of an Olympic champion*. New York: Taplinger.

Hardy, J., Gammage, K., & Hall, C. (2001). A descriptive study of athlete self-talk. *The Sport Psychologist, 15*, 306–318.

Hogan, B. (with Warren, H.). (1957). *Five lessons: The modern fundamentals of golf*. New York: Simon & Schuster.

Jones, R. T. (1966). *Bobby Jones on golf*. New York: Doubleday.

Karniol, R., & Ross, M. (1977). The effects of performance-relevant and performance-irrelevant rewards on motivation. *Child Development, 48*, 482–487.

Karabenek, S. A. (1998). *Strategic help-seeking: Implications for learning and teaching*. Mahwah, NJ: Lawrence Erlbaum Associates.

Kingston, K. M., & Hardy, L. (1997). The effects of different types of goals on the processes that support performance. *The Sport Psychologist, 11*, 277–293.

Kirschenbaum, D. S., O'Connor, E. A., & Owens, D. (1999). Positive illusions in golf: Empirical and conceptual analyses. *Journal of Applied Sport Psychology, 11*, 1–27.

Kitsantas, A., & Zimmerman, B. J. (2002). Comparing self-regulatory processes among novice, non-expert, and expert volleyball players: A microanalytic study. *Journal of Applied Sport Psychology, 14*, 91–105.

Lehrer, J. (2001, July 30). *The News Hour with Jim Lehrer*. Televised program on the Public Broadcasting System.

Litsky, F. (1999, August 6). Geena Davis zeros in with bow and arrows. *New York Times*, D4.

Locke, E. A., & Latham, G. P. (2002). Building a practically useful theory of goal setting and task motivation: A 35-year odyssey. *American Psychologist, 57*, 705–717.

Loehr, J. E. (1991). *The mental game*. New York: Plume.

Mach, E. (1991). *Great contemporary pianists speak for themselves* (Vols. 1–2). Toronto, Canada: Dover.

McCaffrey, N., & Orlick, T. (1989). Mental factors related to excellence among top professional golfers. *International Journal or Sports Psychology, 20*, 256–278.

McPherson, G. E., & Zimmerman, B. J. (2002). Self-regulation of musical learning: A social cognitive perspective. In R. Colwell & C. Richardson (Eds.), *The new handbook of research on music teaching and learning* (pp. 327–347). New York: Oxford University Press.

Meichenbaum, D. (1977). *Cognitive behavior modification: An integrative approach*. New York: Plenum Press.

Munroe, K. J., Giacobbi, P. R., Hall, C. R., & Weinberg, R. (2000). The four W's of imagery use: Where, when, why, and what. *The Sport Psychologist, 14,* 119–137.

Murray, D. M. (1990). *Learn to write* (3rd ed.). New York: Holt, Rinehart & Winston.

Newman, R. S. (1994). Academic help seeking: A strategy of self-regulated learning. In D. H. Schunk & B. J. Zimmerman (Eds.), *Self-regulation of learning and performance: Issues and educational applications* (pp. 283–301). Hillsdale, NJ: Lawrence Erlbaum Associates.

Nicklaus, J. (with Bowden, K.). (1974). *Golf my way*. New York: Simon & Schuster.

Nolan, S. (1988). Reasons for studying: Motivational orientations and study strategies. *Cognition and Instruction, 5,* 269–287.

Paivio, A. (1986). *Mental representations: A dual coding approach*. New York: Oxford University Press.

Pintrich, P. R. (2000). Multiple goals, multiple pathways: The role of goal orientation in learning and achievement. *Journal of Educational Psychology, 92,* 544–555.

Schneider, W., & Pressley, M. (1997). *Memory development between two and twenty* (Chapter 7). Mahwah, NJ: Lawrence Erlbaum Associates.

Schunk, D. H. (1983a). Goal difficulty and attainment information: Effects of children's achievement behaviors. *Human Learning, 1,* 107–117.

Schunk, D. H. (1983b). Progress self-monitoring: Effects on children's self-efficacy and achievement. *Journal of Experimental Education, 51,* 88–105.

Schunk, D. H. (1986). Verbalization and children's self-regulated learning. *Contemporary Educational Psychology, 11,* 347–369.

Schunk, D. H., & Swartz, C. W. (1993). Goals and progressive feedback: Effects on self-efficacy and writing achievement. *Contemporary Educational Psychology, 18,* 337–354.

Schunk, D. H., & Zimmerman, B. J. (1998). *Self-regulated learning: From teaching to self-reflective practice*. New York: Guilford.

Starkes, J. L., Deakin, J., Allard, F., Hodges, N. J., & Hayes, A. (1996). Deliberate pratice in sports: What is it anyway? In K. A. Erics-son (Ed.), *The road to excellence* (pp. 81–106). Mahwah, NJ: Lawrence Erlbaum Associates.

Stein, J. (1959). William Faulkner. In M. Cowley (Ed.), *Writers at work: The Paris review interviews* (pp. 119–141). New York: Viking Press.

Tejada-Flores, L. (1986). *Breakthrough on skis*. New York: Vintage Books.

Thellwell, R. C., & Maynard, I. W. (2002). Anxiety – performance relationships in cricketers: Testing the zone of optimal functioning hypothesis. *Perceptual and Motor Skills, 87,* 675–589.

Thellwell, R. C., & Maynard, I. W. (2003). The effects of a mental skills package on "repeatable good performance" in cricketers. *Psychology of Sport and Exercise, 4,* 377–396.

Trollope, A. (1905). *An autobiography.* New York: Dodd Mead.

Vecsey, G. (1999, September 3). Seles feels windy blast from past. *New York Times*, D1.

Wallace, I. (1971). *The writing of one novel*. Richmond Hill, Canada: Simon & Schuster of Canada.

Wallace, I., & Pear, J. J. (1977). Self-control techniques of famous novelists. *Journal of Applied Behavior Analysis, 10,* 515–525.

Weinstein, C. E., & Mayer, R. E. (1986). The teaching of learning strategies. In M. C. Wittrock (Ed.), *Handbook of research on teaching* (pp. 315–327). New York: Macmillan.

Williams, L., & Gill, D. L. (1995). The role of perceived competence in the motivation of physical activity. *Journal of Sport and Exercise Psychology, 1,* 363–378.

Winne, P. H. (1997). Experimenting to bootstrap self-regulated learning. *Journal of Educational Psychology, 89,* 397–410.

Zimmerman, B. J. (1985). The development of "intrinsic" motivation: A social learning analysis. In G. J. Whitehurst (Ed.), *Annais of child development* (pp. 117–160). Greenwich CT: JAI Press.

Zimmerman, B. J. (1989). A social cognitive view of self-regulated academic learning. *Journal of Educational Psychology, 81,* 329–339.

Zimmerman, B. J. (1995). Self-efficacy and educational development. In A. Bandura (Ed.), *Self-efficacy in changing societies* (pp. 202–231). New York: Cambridge University Press.

Zimmerman, B. J. (2000). Attaining self-regulation: A social cognitive perspective. In M. Boekaerts, P. Pintrich, & M. Zeidner (Eds.),

Handbook of selfregulation (pp. 13–39). San Diego, CA: Acadernic.

Zimmerman, B. J., & Bandura, A. (1994). Impact of self-regulatory influences on attainment in a writing course. *American Educational Research Journal, 29*, 845–862.

Zimmerman, B. J., Bandura, A., & Martinez-Pons, M. (1992). Self-motivation for academic attainment: The role of self-efficacy beliefs and personal goal setting. *American Educational Research Journal, 29*, 663–676.

Zimmerman, B. J., & Bell, J. A. (1972). Observer verbalization and abstraction in vicarious rule learning, generalization, and retention. *Developmental Psychology, 7*, 227–231.

Zimmerman, B. J., & Campillo, M. (2003). Motivating self-regulated problem solvers. In J. E. Davidson & R. J. Sternberg (Eds.), *The nature of problem solving* (pp. 233–262). New York: Cambridge University Press.

Zimmerman, B. J., Greenberg, D., & Weinstein, C. E. (1994). Self-regulating academic study time: A strategy approach. In D. H. Schunk & B. J. Zimmerman (Eds), *Self regulation of learning and performance: Issues and educational applications* (pp. 181–199). Hillsdale, NJ: Lawrence Erlbaum Associates.

Zimmerman, B. J., & Kitsantas, A. (1996). Self-regulated learning of a motoric skill: The role of goal setting and self-monitoring. *Journal of Applied Sport Psychology, 8*, 69–84.

Zimmerman, B. J., & Kitsantas, A. (1997). Developmental phases in self-regulation: Shifting from process to outcome goals. *Journal of Educational Psychology, 89*, 29–36.

Zimmerman, B. J., & Kitsantas, A. (1999). Acquiring writing revision skill: Shifting from process to outcome self-regulatory goals. *Journal of Educational Psychology, 91*, 1–10.

Zimmerman, B. J., & Kitsantas, A. (2005). Homework practices and academic achievement: The mediating role of self-efficacy and perceived responsibility beliefs. *Contemporary Educational Psychology, 30*, 397–417.

Zimmerman, B. J., & Paulsen, A. S. (1995). Self-monitoring during collegiate studying: An invaluable tool for academic self-regulation. In P. Pintrich (Ed.), *New directions in college teaching and learning: Understanding self-regulated learning* (No. 63, Fall, pp. 13–27). San Francisco, CA: Jossey-Bass.

Zimmerman, B. J., & Schunk, D. H. (Eds.) (2001). *Self-regulated learning and academic achievement: Theoretical perspectives* (2nd ed.), Mahwah, NJ: Lawrence Erlbaum Associates.

Author Note

I would like to thank K. Anders Ericsson and Paul Feltovich for their helpful comments regarding an earlier draft of this chapter.

CHAPTER 40

Aging and Expertise

Ralf Th. Krampe & Neil Charness

Introduction

Outstanding accomplishments by older individuals, such as the wisdom of elderly statesmen, the virtuoso performances of older musicians, or the swan-song oeuvres of famous composers have been the subject of admiration throughout human history. Commonsense or folk psychology rarely considers such achievements as incompatible with older age. On the contrary, in the public's opinion advanced age has been identified with maturity or heightened levels of experience that complement the exceptional talents or gifts that had presumably enabled outstanding individuals to surpass ordinary people in the first place. Allegedly, these dispositions are the driving force leading to high achievements, and the presumed stability of related capacities is believed to guarantee that outstanding individuals' superior skills remain at their disposition throughout adulthood. In traditionalist cultures (as in Germany or Japan) such appreciations of early achievement and seniority overshadow actual accomplishments and remain an integral part of society and job promotion until this day.

The scientific study of interindividual differences and the experimental investigation of human performance in normal adults portray a less optimistic picture of adult development, at least in the normal population. Ubiquitous findings of negative age-graded changes in psychometric ability factors and reduced speed or accuracy in most cognitive-motor tasks have motivated theories of broad decline, like the notion of general, age-related slowing (Salthouse, 1985a). In the light of these findings, the accomplishments by older experts and the high performance levels in many older professionals present a puzzle. Thus, the central questions in the context of aging and expertise are whether older experts are exempted from general age-related declines and how they can maintain their performances into older age (see also Horn & Masunaga, Chapter 34).

We start out with a brief historical sketch of scientific concepts related to ability and the relationship of these to adult development. We then detail the concept of general, age-related slowing and its relations to the different theoretical accounts for expert performance in later adulthood. Our subsequent review of age-comparative studies in different domains makes a strong case for the dominance of acquired skills and mechanisms in expert performance. In the final sections, we focus on deliberate practice as the prime means to improvement and its role in maintaining expertise as people age. Particularly, we focus on the trade-offs that may be critical to expertise in advancing age: between deliberate practice, and its potential to maintain performance, and aging processes that work to degrade performance.

Historical Background

Commonsense notions, which typically attribute high achievement to innate dispositions, had their scientific origin in the 19th-century writings of Sir Francis Galton (1979). Galton emphasized three precursors of exceptional achievements, namely, natural (innate) capacity, zeal, and the power to work hard. It was Galton's first assertion that received prime attention in later theorizing, and two conceptual trends are noteworthy in this context. In certain areas, most notably in music and the arts, the notion of innate talent became increasingly associated with highly specific dispositions that required only little external stimulation to emerge in those rare, gifted individuals so endowed (Winner, 1982). Simultaneously, Galton's legacy of emphasizing innate, interindividual differences as prerequisites of extraordinary accomplishments was also echoed in 20th-century conceptions of intelligence. For the pioneers of intelligence research, notably Binet and Stern, the concept of intelligence denoted stable, interindividual differences in general abilities and capacities that were relevant to acquiring new skills and learning in novel situations. In the minds of the general public to this day, having a high IQ is synonymous with being smart and having a large potential for successfully coping with learning and

with all kinds of professional and everyday challenges.

In their attempts to identify such general dispositions, researchers in psychometric intelligence focused on presumably content-free measures of basic cognitive functioning, like processing speed, abstract reasoning, or spatial abilities in figural transformation tasks. These basic capacities were assumed to be the building blocks of complex skills. Presumably the most influential theory in this context was Cattell and Horn's investment theory (Cattell, 1971; Horn, 1982), which posits that primary mental abilities are invested into the development of more complex abilities (see for related proposals, Krampe & Baltes, 2003). From this perspective, innate dispositions towards certain primary abilities have the potential to draw some individuals toward specific domains and, furthermore, provide them with both a head start and a continued performance advantage over "less gifted" individuals. As an example, above-average abilities in spatial visualization might attract certain individuals to professions like architecture or graphics design (e.g., Lindenberger et al., 1992; e.g., Salthouse et al., 1990).

Empirical research in the second part of the 20th century was partly successful in supporting the first of Galton's premises. Tests of intellectual abilities proved to be valid correlates of academic achievement (specifically, high-school grades), job training, and job performance at the point of entry (Schmidt & Hunter, 1998). Modern behavioral genetics (Plomin, 1990; Plomin & Rende, 1991) established converging estimates of about 50% heritability[1] for general intelligence (the g-factor; see also Horn & Masunaga, Chapter 34). The program fared less well when it came to specific abilities and their relevance to different occupational specializations. Heritability estimates observed for specific capacities are lower than those for general intelligence (g), even if different reliabilities are controlled for. Particularly, research in areas that were believed to represent prime exemplars of specific talents produced disconcerting results. For example, professional musicians showed remarkably poor performances on tests of musical talent (Howe et al., 1999; Sloboda, 1991). Coon and Carey (1989) found reliable estimates of heritability in their study with identical and fraternal twins, who performed tasks similar to those in standardized musicality tests. However, heritability estimates were markedly smaller in those twins who had undergone systematic musical training.

Besides the domain-specificity problem, the Coon and Carey findings also point to another problem of ability tests that had enormous impact on current theorizing about abilities, age, and expertise, namely, the role of continued training. Different from their success in predicting achievement during academic training, psychometric-ability test measures show only weak to moderate correlations with performance in practicing professionals like medical doctors (Baird, 1985). In their meta-analysis Hulin, Henry, and Noon (1990) showed that this phenomenon generalizes to other domains: Correlations between intellectual abilities and job performance at the time of entry were systematically reduced if levels of performance at longer time intervals after the end of formal training were considered. The increasing relevance of domain-specific knowledge and skills over general abilities has also been demonstrated for older professionals.

For example, although older bank managers show normal age-related decline on psychometric ability measures, their degree of professional success depended mainly on acquired tacit knowledge about the bank environment (Colonia-Willner, 1998). Tacit knowledge (Wagner & Sternberg, 1991; Cianciolo, Mathew, Wagner, & Sternberg, Chapter 35) refers to practical knowledge about business culture and interpersonal relations that enables managers to work effectively. It is measured with a test that presents scenarios, followed by different solutions that are to be rated. Degree of concordance of solution ratings with expert manager ratings is assessed.

Several laboratory training studies demonstrated changes in the correlational patterns between psychometric-ability factors and performance change across different stages of skill development (Ackerman, 1988; Fleishman, 1972; Labouvie et al., 1973; see also, Proctor & Vu, Chapter 15). Specifically, general intelligence (g) emerged as a factor at early stages of skill acquisition (Fitts, 1964), when understanding the nature of the task is a critical requirement (Anderson, 1982). Later stages and performance after practice tends to be less correlated with g, but to show substantial relations to interindividual differences in factors closer to the skill under investigation. For example, in his training study using an air-traffic control task, Ackerman (1988) found that g, as well as more specific ability factors, indeed correlated with pre-test levels of performance. Subsequently, these correlations were reduced to non-significance with the notable exception of perceptual speed (measured through the digit-symbol substitution test), which gained in strength and remained the only reliable correlation with post-training performance after ten sessions. At a more general level, the contribution of specific over general psychometric abilities also appears to depend on individuals' overall level of cognitive functioning, with g having its strongest expression in participants scoring within lower values of g (Detterman & Daniel, 1989).

Taken together, these findings demonstrated that there exists a reliable impact of general psychometric intelligence at early stages of learning a new skill and in individuals performing at relatively low levels of competence. A sizeable portion of interindividual differences in this capacity can be traced to genetic (i.e., inherited and innate) factors. Levels of experience and other age-correlated factors attenuate or decrease the effects of those ability factors that may be relevant at earlier stages of skill acquisition. The psychometric study of abilities and their relevance for complex skills provided an invaluable starting point for the systematic investigation of the processing mechanisms that underlie expert performance. To understand the mechanisms and preconditions of expert performance in later adulthood, we need to consider some general age-related changes in processing.

General Processing Speed, Intellectual Abilities, and Aging

The dominant finding in cognitive-aging research with normal adults is that accuracy and speed of memory processes, as well as most types of cognitive-motor performance, undergo systematic age-related declines from young to older adulthood. Older adults in their 7th decade of life typically need about 1.6 to 2 times as long to process the same tasks as young adults in their 20s. Similar findings have been reported in the domain of fine-motor control and movement production (for an overview, see Krampe, 2002). As a general finding, negative age-effects tend to be more pronounced if tasks require more complex processing, like recall versus recognition or unimanual versus bimanual movement coordination. Large-scale cross-sectional studies with psychometric-test batteries consistently reveal considerable age graded declines in performance IQ (e.g., perceptual-motor speed, timed reasoning tasks) during adulthood, starting as early as age 30 (Kaufman, 2001).

The ubiquity of negative age effects in speeded performance has nurtured the development of general factor accounts, such as models of general, age-related slowing (Cerella, 1985, 1990), the processing-speed mediation of adult-age differences in cognition (Salthouse, 1985b, 1996), or the information-loss model of age-related slowing (Myerson et al., 1990). Reduced working-memory capacity or slowing of retrieval and storage to and from working memory (Salthouse, 1991c), deterioration of neural interconnectedness (Cerella, 1990), or the ability to ignore irrelevant information (Hasher et al., 1991) have been proposed as candidate mechanisms underlying general age-related performance declines. Some domains of cognitive functioning appear to be less affected by aging than others, presumably because of the compensatory effects of accumulated knowledge, for instance, in tasks requiring lexical decisions (Cerella & Fozard, 1984; Lima et al., 1991). Negative age effects are ameliorated or absent in knowledge-based tasks if performance is adjusted for age-related decrements in general speed (Hertzog, 1989; Schaie, 1989).

The bottom line is that "normal" aging tends to reduce the speed and efficiency of cognitive, perceptual, and psychomotor functions. From the assumption that these processes form the building blocks for, or integrate components of expert performance, one would expect such age-related reductions to affect professional competence. Contrary to such expectations, the relationship between age and productivity in work settings is near zero or slightly positive in cross-sectional studies as seen in two meta-analyses (McEvoy & Cascio, 1989; Waldman & Avolio, 1986). The evidence from experimental and psychometric research does leave the possibility that knowledge and experience can compensate age-related declines in knowledge-rich domains like chess or medical diagnosis (see also Horn & Masunaga, Chapter 34). Neural net simulation work (Mireles & Charness, 2002) provides a biologically oriented explanation about how acquired structured knowledge may even protect working-memory function, such as that of Long Term Working Memory (Ericsson & Kintsch, 1995), from expected age-related changes in neural network integrity that govern learning rate, forgetting rate, and quality of signal-noise ratio. However, maintained levels of professional skill or expertise in domains with extreme demands on speed and accuracy, such as air-traffic control, piloting, or virtuosi musical performance, pose a more difficult explanatory problem. In the next section we detail theoretical accounts that have addressed these issues.

Theoretical Accounts of Expert Performance in Older Age

Three alternative accounts have been proposed in the literature to reconcile the observed age-related declines in basic cognitive-motor abilities in normal adults with the evidence for superior performances in older experts and professionals (Charness & Bosman, 1990; Krampe & Baltes, 2003; Salthouse, 1991b). The first account maintains that older experts have always been superior in skill-relevant abilities, such that their advantages at any age could be attributed to interindividual differences with long-term stability that already existed prior to expertise acquisition. Such explanations have been termed "preserved differentiation" (Salthouse et al., 1990) or "a priori disposition accounts" (Krampe & Baltes, 2003) in the literature. The second position assumes that the process of acquiring expertise involves gradual improvements in those abilities that constrain normal performance (like working-memory span) such that expertise should transfer to some (but not necessarily all) broader cognitive functions. Finally, the third account posits that outstanding performance rests on specific mechanisms that enable experts to circumvent the process limitations constraining performance in normal individuals (Chase & Ericsson, 1982). According to the deliberate-practice model (Ericsson & Charness, 1994; Ericsson et al., 1993; Ericsson & Lehmann, 1996; Ericsson, Chapter 38) these mechanisms must be acquired through individual efforts directed at the long-term adaptation to internal (e.g., age-related changes in cognitive functions) and external (e.g., task-domain, professional environment) constraints.

When applied to aging and expertise, the deliberate-practice account implies that older experts must actively maintain those specific mechanisms that are vital to their domain, and we refer to this set of assumptions as the "maintenance-through-deliberate-practice" account (Charness et al., 1996; Krampe & Ericsson, 1996). This position maintains that expertise in later adulthood is not merely the outcome of achievements during younger ages. Rather, older experts must continuously invest deliberate effort into the development of their skills, while adapting to the constraints imposed by aging. One specific variant of the maintenance-through-

deliberate-practice account is that older experts actually acquire specific mechanisms to compensate for age-related deterioration in critical skills.

Studies that tried to disambiguate between the three accounts for expert performance in later adulthood typically addressed one or more of the following questions: (1) Do older experts, who excel in their domains, also differ from normal, age-matched individuals in terms of cognitive abilities, such as general processing speed? (2) Does outstanding performance in a particular domain also convey an advantage in near transfer domains that are subject to age-related decline in the normal population? (3) Does the level of maintained performance in older experts depend on individual investment into critical activities, like deliberate practice?

Cognitive Abilities, Age, and Expertise: Empirical Evidence

The assumption that interindividual (and presumably innate) differences in basic cognitive-motor functions are natural precursors to, or contribute to interindividual differences in, expert performance can indeed be found in the literature (Keele & Hawkins, 1982). Given that such basic components also overlap with measures of performance-IQ as measured by psychometric tests, an argument can be made that interindividual differences in psychometric intelligence or relatively broad abilities are causally linked to the ultimate levels of performance. Findings from several studies that compared experts and amateurs appeared to be in line with related assumptions. As examples, maximum finger tapping rate is correlated with overall typing speed (Book, 1924; Salthouse, 1984) or level of accomplishment in pianists or typists (Keele et al., 1985; Krampe & Ericsson, 1996; Telford & Spangler, 1935). Likewise, timing capacity (the variability in controlling successive movements) is more efficient in professional musicians than in amateurs and controls (Keele et al., 1985; Krampe et al., 2002). These results, however, could also reflect near transfer as hypothesized by the expertise-driven specific abilities account. Given general age-related changes in performance-IQ and basic cognitive-motor speed, age-comparative studies with individuals differing in levels of expertise provide a special route to further disentangle these issues – through systematic comparisons of interindividual differences in general cognitive abilities, near transfer tasks, and expertise-specific functions.

Age-comparative studies with individuals differing in their levels of expertise have been conducted in such diverse domains as typewriting (Bosman, 1993; Salthouse, 1984), chess (Charness, 1981a, 1981b; Charness et al., 1996), bridge (Charness, 1983, 1989), GO (Masunaga & Horn, 2001), piloting (D. Morrow et al., 1994; D. G. Morrow et al., 2001), mastermind (a game requiring identification of hidden patterns of colored pegs on a pegboard) (Maylor, 1994), crossword-puzzle solving (Hambrick et al., 1999; Rabbitt, 1993), management skills (Colonia-Willner, 1998; Walsh & Hershey, 1993), and music (Krampe & Ericsson, 1996; Meinz, 2000) (see also Chapters in Section V). The general picture emerging from these studies is that older experts show "normal" (i.e., similar to non-expert controls) age-graded declines in general measures of processing speed, cognitive abilities as measured through psychometric tests, and performance on unfamiliar materials. At the same time, older experts show reduced, if any, age-related declines in the efficiencies or the speed at which they perform *skill-related* tasks. Thus, the evidence from age-comparative expertise studies speaks largely for the proposition that expert performance at any age relies more on specific rather than general cognitive mechanisms (see also Feltovich, Prietula & Ericsson, Chapter 4). Consequently, models of expertise have departed from the assumption that the same set of abilities that underlie performance in psychometric intelligence tests can also account for the ultimate level of expertise attained or the level of expertise maintained in later adulthood.

Findings from laboratory research on older experts generally correspond with the dominant finding in occupational psychology, namely, that age and skilled performance are poorly correlated. There are, however, a number of reasons why the existing literature may be inadequate to detect age-related declines in work productivity. These include weaknesses in existing studies, such as restricted age ranges, restricted job types, and uncertain reliability and validity in the productivity measures (Salthouse & Maurer, 1996). The demonstration of expertise moderation for age-effects also faces severe methodological problems. Field-study designs, using regression-analytic techniques on stratified age samples, have considerable power to detect age-related changes that generalize across larger age ranges. However, their statistical power to detect age-by-expertise interactions is limited and requires huge sample sizes (typically more than a thousand, assuming medium-sized effects). To this end (McClelland & Judd, 1993), Lindenberger and Pötter (1998) demonstrated that moderator analyses, using hierarchical regression or structural equation modeling techniques, suffer from a confirmation bias towards general factor models (like general age-related performance declines), and that their power to detect age-differential changes is limited.

Although these considerations seem to favor the extreme-group approach, related studies are susceptible to the criticism of different selection criteria for young and older participants. In typical age-by-expertise designs there is no overlap in biographical ages between young and older groups, respectively, and frequently, accomplished experts are compared with novices or amateurs with limited amounts of formal instruction or professional training. Arguably, older experts in these studies could represent the survivors of an age-graded winnowing process by which individuals with stronger age-related declines in relevant capacities, or those who have been less motivated to continuously invest in the development of their skills, have dropped from their fields of expertise or have been promoted to less-challenging positions. Related selection processes occur in societal contexts, which are rarely considered in expertise studies. For example, older employees are more likely to be in stable positions than younger ones who switch jobs more frequently (Swaen et al., 2002), and some societies, for example, Germany, take radical measures to promote early retirement for those older individuals who feel overwhelmed by occupational challenges. Employers make extensive use of this mechanism to rid themselves of older employees suspected of declining productivity.

Despite some limitations of the pertinent studies, we argue that the most likely reason for the age-graded stability of performance in older experts is that increased age brings with it increased job-specific knowledge and skills. These assets do not come for free, however. To support the claim that the continuation of deliberate practice throughout one's career is a necessary prerequisite for expert performance in later adulthood, it is necessary to establish its compensatory effects over and above age-related changes in general processing capacities. We now turn to studies that provide evidence along these lines.

Deliberate Practice and Expertise Maintenance in Later Adulthood

The "maintenance-through-deliberate-practice" account is subject to at least one alternative explanation, which equally acknowledges the specificity of skilled mechanisms. It is feasible that experts acquire the critical skills in their domain at younger ages and that related mechanisms remain available throughout later adulthood. Thus, deliberate practice may well be the key factor in the acquisition phase, whereas comparatively little individual effort and investment is necessary to maintain high levels of performance thereafter. The belief that prolonged experience and usage of once-acquired knowledge and skills suffices to sustain lifelong expertise is widely believed

among the public and is also held among some older experts themselves.

Krampe and Ericsson (1996) studied expert and amateur pianists of different ages, with a combination of experimental and psychometric measures of ability, along with self-report and diary data recording time investment in deliberate practice and other activities. The expertise-related abilities tested comprised virtuoso skills like maximum repetitive tapping and speeded multi-finger sequencing tasks, but also non-speeded tasks such as memorization of sequences and (rated) expressive musical interpretation. In line with results for typists and chess experts, the authors found that older professional pianists showed normal age-related declines in measures of general processing speed, such as choice reaction time and speed of digit-symbol substitution. However, though age-effects within the amateur group, with regard to expertise-related measures of multiple-finger coordination speed, were similar to those pertaining to the general speed measures (e.g., choice reaction time), they were reduced or fully absent in the expert sample. Taken together these findings led to postulation of an age-by-expertise dissociation of mechanisms underlying general processing versus expertise-specific processing.

Krampe and Ericsson (1996) argued that this dissociation reflects older experts' selective maintenance of acquired, expertise-specific mechanisms. Expertise-specific mechanisms in skilled piano performance comprise the sequencing of rapid finger movements (Rosenbaum et al., 1983), bimanual coordination and hand independence (Krampe et al., 2000), and the efficient executive control of varying motor patterns (Krampe, 2002; Krampe et al., 2005), all of which enable experts to optimally prepare their movements in advance and perform in a fluent, seemingly effortless fashion (MacKay, 1982). The selective maintenance interpretation in the Krampe and Ericsson study rests on data pertaining to older experts' investments in deliberate practice at different stages of their development. Consistent with this view, the authors showed that the extent to which levels of performance in speeded-expertise tasks was maintained in old age depended on the amounts of deliberate practice invested at the later stages of life, namely, in the 5th and 6th decade. At the same time measures of general processing speed did not account for the interindividual differences in levels of maintained expertise in the expert group. In contrast, such measures correlated with performance in the amateur group, suggesting that the basis of expertise is decoupled from general abilities, particularly if later adulthood is considered (Krampe & Baltes, 2003).

In a similar vein, Charness and colleagues (Charness et al., 1996; Charness et al., 2005) found that chess ratings (based on chess tournament performance) in a large sample of rated players, covering ages from 20 to 80 years, depended far more on amounts of deliberate practice than on chronological age (standardized coefficients in a regression equation were − .38 for age and .62 for deliberate practice). The effects of deliberate practice were even more pronounced in the older players, as seen in a regression analysis that showed an interaction of age and current deliberate practice in predicting current skill level. It appeared that older players needed more current deliberate practice than younger players to reach equivalent skill levels, again pointing to the need for continued investment in maintenance of skills at advanced ages. However, a second interaction suggested a trend toward diminishing returns from deliberate practice later in life. Increasing amounts of cumulative deliberate practice did not reap the same gains in skill level for older players. Effects such as those just reported regarding the effects of maintenance practice have also been demonstrated in the domain of sports (Ericsson, 1990; Starkes et al., 1996; Hodges, Starkes, & MacMahon, Chapter 27)

Expert Mechanisms as Compensatory Means for Age-Related Decline

One of the most fascinating theoretical perspectives on outstanding perfor-

mance in older age is the idea that older experts compensate for age-related declines in certain capacities through the development of compensatory, specific, higher-level mechanisms. This idea motivated the "molar-equivalence-molecular-decomposition approach" (Charness, 1981a; Over & Thomas, 1995; Salthouse, 1984; Westerman et al., 1998). This approach entails the study of samples of people in which correlations between age and overall levels of performance (e.g., overall typing speed, rated chess performance) are essentially zero (molar equivalence). Based on the decomposition of a complex expertise into component processes (molecular decomposition), investigators then use differential patterns of age-related changes among subprocesses to establish evidence for compensatory mechanisms.

The first evidence that pointed to compensatory mechanisms came from a study on age and chess expertise conducted by Charness (1981a, 1981b). He found that the quality of the chess moves subjects selected for an unfamiliar chess position was unrelated to age and closely linked to skill level (current chess rating on the ELO-scale). Detailed analysis of think-aloud protocols revealed that older experts engaged in less extensive search (i.e., they generated fewer potential moves in a move selection task) than their younger counterparts did, but they nonetheless came up with moves of comparable quality. One possible interpretation of these findings is that older players compensate for age-related declines in search and retrieval speed with more refined knowledge-based processes related to move selection.

The molar-equivalence-molecular-decomposition approach was also applied by Salthouse (1984, 1991b) in his study with typists. He found that across age groups basic components of movement proficiency, such as the rate of repetitively typing the same letter, showed a moderate correlation to overall typing speed, accounting for 42% of the variance. In contrast, measures reflecting complex expertise-related mechanisms, like the speed of typing letters with alternate hands or the eye-hand span (i.e., the number of letters they looked ahead prior to executing the actual keystrokes), accounted for more than 70% of the interindividual differences in overall typing speed. Note that repetitive tapping rate, like other measures of general processing speed, showed typical age-related decline in this sample, whereas the correlation between age and overall typing speed was essentially zero. Interestingly, older expert typists showed larger eye-hand spans compared with their younger counterparts. Salthouse argued that the successful maintenance of typing skills in his older expert typists relied on cognitively complex mechanisms, namely, extensive anticipation as illustrated by older skilled typists' longer eye-hand spans (see also Endsley, Chapter 36). More recently, Bosman (1993) argued that older typists might indeed compensate for their age-related declines in basic motor speed through their extended eye-hand spans.

The studies by Charness and Salthouse broke new ground in that they suggested that older experts attain the same level of performance as young experts by means of different mechanisms. Compensation in the narrow sense implies that older experts rely on mechanisms that are not part of young experts' repertoire. A related, but slightly different interpretation, assumes that aged experts rely differentially on different component processes, preferably with an emphasis on those that can be easier maintained at advanced ages. The latter view is closer to the *selective skill maintenance* interpretation forwarded by Krampe and Ericssson (1996), who argued that older expert pianists maintain their levels of performance by selectively training existing skills. In either case, deliberate practice is necessary to detect weaknesses and to develop existing or new skills. As a general point, cross-sectional analyses of expert mechanisms face the challenge to determine whether older individuals deliberately adopted compensatory mechanisms in response to aging, or whether their performance at younger ages was already superior and associated mechanisms were better preserved, owing to a slower age-related decline or owing to deliberate activities to maintain these critical capacities.

The concept of compensation also features prominently in extant frameworks of adaptive aging, like the model of selection, optimization, and compensation (Baltes & Baltes, 1990). The SOC model depicts compensation as the acquisition and use of novel or alternative means to counter losses in certain functions (like using a wheelchair or a hearing aid). As an example for compensatory strategies in expert performance, Baltes and Baltes cite from the biographical self-report of the famous pianist Arthur Rubinstein. He claimed that his compensatory means for age-related decline in movement speed was to slow down prior to difficult passages to create a more impressive contrast. In their application of the SOC framework to expertise, Krampe and Baltes (2003) describe how the *selection* of critical activities (practice) over alternative engagements (e.g., leisure or school) shape developmental trajectories. At the level of the individual life course, such selective processes can be viewed to mitigate or compensate for age-related changes, a perspective that illustrates how related interpretations depend on theoretical context and scope.

The reported benefits of sustained maintenance practice for older experts and the possibility of developing compensatory strategies or mechanisms appear to be good news for the successful mastery of everyday life and professional competence in the elderly. Some qualifications of this optimistic view are in place. Three constraints of successful skill maintenance must be considered to evaluate the patchwork findings in the area. The first constraint relates to the nature of deliberate-practice activities, that is, whether critical abilities remain intact if only exercised in everyday life or the normal course of professional work and what these critical abilities are in the first place. A second constraint arises from differential sensitivities of different skill components to age-related declines. Finally, there is some evidence suggesting that the capacity to engage in skill-sustaining deliberate-practice activities might itself be constrained by advancing age. In the following sections we detail these constraints, along with a discussion of those empirical studies that challenge the deliberate-practice perspective or certain aspects thereof.

Deliberate Practice, Experience, and Domain Specificity of Maintained Skills

Not all studies found a mitigation of age-related decline by expertise, and some studies that observed superior levels of performance in older experts found them to excel in domain-specific as well as domain-general skills. Moreover, several attempts to link expert performance to previous engagement in skill-related activities were unsuccessful.

Studies of age-related changes in everyday cognitive functioning and leisurely activities tend to support the claim that age-related losses in basic cognitive abilities result in deficiencies in more specific skills. For example, in their study of memory for baseball game descriptions, Hambrick and Engle (2002) found similar age-related differences among individuals with high versus low levels of domain-relevant knowledge (i.e., no mitigation). The authors identified interindividual differences and age-related declines in working memory as the critical factors. Similarly, earlier studies on elderly adults' everyday problem-solving skills found that much of the variance could be accounted for by psychometric measures of speed or working memory (Allaire & Marsiske, 1999; Willis & Marsiske, 1991). However, in a more recent study, Allaire and Marsiske (2002) demonstrated that measures of specific reasoning skills (atuned to the ill-defined nature of everyday settings) make for better predictors than psychometric markers. Though certainly relevant to everyday reasoning and memory, it is questionable whether the tasks investigated in these studies meet the criteria of expert performance and whether participants were sufficiently motivated to maintain their skills at exceptional levels.

Age-related changes in professional skills were studied by Salthouse and colleagues (Salthouse, 1991a; Salthouse et al., 1990). They investigated whether professionals (architects) who presumably exercised spatial-ability skills throughout their careers can maintain them into old age. Spatial-ability measures are quite age sensitive, with psychometric tests showing strong age-related and longitudinal decline. The Salthouse et al. studies showed robust age-related decline in spatial ability, even in older architects who were still practicing. Similarly, two studies, which investigated perception and memorization of musical materials in musicians from wide experience and age ranges, found no (Meinz & Salthouse, 1998) or little (Meinz, 2000) evidence that simple amounts of experience can attenuate negative age effects.

Whereas the absence of reliable attenuation effects in these studies can be partly attributed to the design features (regression-analytic approaches to field-design-typical, continuous age variation) discussed earlier, another critical aspect relates to the measures of previous engagement used. The concept of deliberate (maintenance) practice is in marked contrast to a notion of simple "experience" or "exercise," which merely implies continued usage of once-acquired skills (Ericsson, Chapter 38; Feltovich et al., chapter 4). Deliberate-practice efforts are distinguished by a systematic analysis of weaknesses and the invention of specific methods to overcome these suboptimal aspects (Ericsson et al., 1993; Ericsson & Lehmann, 1996). Older amateur pianists in the Krampe and Ericsson (1996) study had up to 40 years of "experience" in playing the piano. In contrast, the amount of *deliberate practice* accumulated by this group was less than half of that estimated for young experts, who were 35 years younger on average. In line with the results reported by Meinz and Salthouse (1998), age effects in these amateurs corresponded to general age-related slowing in speeded IQ measures, and measures of deliberate practice failed to add to the prediction of performance.

Another aspect of successful maintenance relates to the domain specificity of practice in professional contexts and its limited transfer to other skills or abilities (see Feltovich et al., Chapter 4, "Expertise is Limited in Scope and Elite Performance does not Transfer"). For example, the aforementioned studies by Meinz and colleagues assessed sight-reading performance in musicians. Sight-reading is a highly specific skill that has high ecological relevance to certain (e.g., accompanists and cembalo players) musicians only, whereas most performers are expected to rely on their memories for intensively prepared pieces (Lehmann & Ericsson, 1993, 1996). Similarly, Lindenberger et al. (1992) found that negative age effects in imagery-based memory performance in a sample of older graphic designers were attenuated, but not eliminated. Arguably, the memory task (the Method-of-Loci) presented a case of medium transfer with respect to the occupational expertise of older graphic designers.

Another complication is that the relative importance of component skills (and presumably the degree to which they are exercised) can differ among experts from a larger age range. Salthouse and colleagues (1990) found that the occupational relevance that participants attributed to the experimental tasks in their study correlated negatively with age, suggesting that different types of skilled processes are required for young and older architects. In line with the latter assumption, expert pianists' diary data in the study by Krampe and Ericsson (1996) showed a larger amount of professional activities in older, compared with young experts, but also a pronounced shift in focus (e.g., less practice and more teaching).

Domains like piloting or air-traffic control maximally tax experts' skills to act on unpredictable events, or their task-sharing abilities. Morrow et al. (2003) observed poorer air-traffic control message-recall performance of older pilots compared to younger pilots. However, when the task was changed to a realistic one that allowed note taking, the age-related differences in performance disappeared. Similarly, simulator-based flying accuracy, in response to air-traffic control instructions,

showed age deficits that were mediated by age-related differences in working-memory measures and speed of processing (Taylor et al., 2005). Positive expertise effects on flying performance were also observed and attributed to deliberate-practice differences. However, expertise did not interact with age to reduce age-related differences. These findings point to potential limitations of individual adaptation in less-predictable settings or to increasing difficulties to counter age-related changes through training.

In sum, professional experience or staying on the job does not guarantee that the relevant capabilities remain intact in older age. Rather, the available evidence suggests that maintaining skills is as effortful as acquiring them in the first place, and benefits become increasingly more specific, that is, limited to those skills that are actively practiced and maintained.

Differential Sensitivities of Skills to Age-Related Decline

Anecdotal reports cite the famous piano virtuoso, Wilhelm Backhaus, as explaining that he intensified his etude exercises when he reached his 50s, because at that point he felt that his technical skills required systematic maintenance practice. Indeed, it seems plausible that certain aspects of skilled performance are more affected by age than other aspects, require more intensive maintenance practice, or both. Unfortunately, empirical evidence related to these issues is sparse.

Whereas the speed of repetitive single-finger movements (maximum tapping rate) tends to be reduced in normal older compared with young adults (for an overview, Salthouse, 1985b), Krampe and Ericsson (1996) observed only modest age-related declines in two samples of amateur pianists (and no such declines in the experts). Similarly, older amateur musicians performed as well as their young counterparts when performing simple rhythm tasks at a large range of tempos (Krampe et al., 2001). These findings suggest that certain basic motor components can be maintained with relatively small amounts of practice or that they can be sustained by merely "exercising" a real-life skill. In contrast, complex cognitive-motor functions, particularly those that involve bimanual coordination, sequencing operations, or executive control, show more pronounced declines in both normal adults and skilled amateurs (Krampe et al., 2002; Krampe et al., 2005). This suggests that mere experience cannot compensate for negative age effects, or in turn, that increased amounts of deliberate practice are required to this end.

Another critical factor determining the need for maintenance practice is the degree to which the skill under consideration relies on specialized, pragmatic knowledge. Age effects in the expert pianist group in the Krampe and Ericsson (1996) study were significantly reduced when participants performed complex sequences from memory, compared with a condition in which pianists sight-read the tasks, suggesting that older professionals benefitted from their vast knowledge related to harmonic relations or melodic patterns during encoding. In addition, older experts and older amateurs showed similar levels of performance in a musical interpretation task, which involved a piece that posed little challenge in terms of speed or technical virtuosity. This latter finding suggests that those skill components that relate to specialized knowledge can be maintained through experience, at least to some degree. The prominent role of pragmatic knowledge in the development of expertise was also evident in a study of chess players conducted by Charness et al. (1996). These authors found a significant contribution to skill level from the number of chess books owned by participants, which was independent of age and amounts of deliberate practice.

Age-Related Constraints on Improvement through Practice

Common belief holds that expertise, but also age, should lead to growing knowledge about optimal and efficient practice methods. Indeed, older expert pianists reported that they find it easier to develop musical interpretations of new pieces and that their practice is more efficient compared to when they were younger (Krampe, 1994).

Somewhat different from this positive self-perception in older experts, laboratory training research suggests that cognitive plasticity (i.e., learning rates as well as the ultimate outcomes of what individuals achieve through practice) decrease in later adulthood (Kliegl et al., 1989), particularly after the age of 70 (Singer et al., 2003; Yang et al., 2006). Consistent with laboratory research, in part because the studies reviewed contained many instances of lab research, meta-analyses of job-related training, age, and performance show moderate to strong negative correlations (Callahan et al., 2003; Kubeck et al., 1996). That is, older adults seem to benefit less from training than younger ones (Kubeck et al., 1996), or they require specific types of training (self-paced training) to approach the degree of benefit found for young adults (Callahan et al., 2003). Such studies may not generalize well to acquiring and maintaining expertise because training methods used were not individualized for the most part, and were certainly not geared to promoting high-level performance. Nonetheless, they may speak to increasing difficulty expected for older experts, who have to learn new techniques that are possibly unrelated to past ones. As mentioned above, Charness et al. (1996) also found a weak interaction between age and deliberate practice, suggesting a diminishing return for cumulative deliberate practice for older chess players.

It is necessary to draw some distinctions to understand the disconnect that sometimes occurs between the images of aging seen in laboratory performance and real world performance. An important distinction is that between speeded performance and non-speeded performance. For instance, except perhaps in assembly-line work, most regulated jobs do not require people to work as quickly as possible for long periods of time. A related distinction is that of usual and maximal performance. It seems unlikely that many jobs in the economy require maximal output during working hours. However, most laboratory research stresses human performance to the maximum, by requiring that people respond as quickly and as accurately as possible for a long series of repetitive trials on novel tasks (see also Proctor & Vu, Chapter 15). Whereas this makes good sense from the point of view of testing the limits of human adaptability, it may provide a distorted view of performance likely to be observed in most ordinary work settings.

Nonetheless, when we examine maximal performance in real settings, the most usual pattern observed is a backward inverted J-shaped function (Simonton, 1996). For instance, in a highly competitive environment, chess playing, within a very elite sample of Grandmasters, Elo (1965, 1986) observed that there was a rapid rise in ability during the teenage and young adult years and then about a one-standard-deviation decline in tournament performance from the peak years of the mid-30s to age 65.

Another activity in which outstanding performance can be fruitfully examined is sports, where the clash between opponents provides strong feedback about superiority and inferiority and where the financial incentives to excel are extremely high. Multimillion-dollar contracts are not unusual for top professionals in soccer, basketball, baseball, and football. In those domains, it is rare to play at top form beyond the fourth decade (Schulz & Curnow, 1988; Schulz et al., 1994). Here too we do not usually have easy access to training regimens for participants, so it is difficult to know to what extent reduced motivation to maintain intense training or biological/physiological factors are responsible for decline.

One age-related constraint on practice activities that has, until recently, received too little attention relates to changes in bodily and health conditions. Deliberate practice is considered to be among the most effortful activities by experts (Ericsson et al., 1993), and there is tentative evidence that aging professionals in particular must compromise between skill development and bodily constraints. Older expert pianists' diary data

in the Krampe and Ericsson (1996) study revealed increased amounts of time spent on health and body care or medical consultation compared with young pianists. Such findings are typical in age-comparative time-budgeting studies.

One potential explanation is that the time it takes individuals to recuperate from challenging practice activities increases with age, and thus limits the total amounts of time that can be invested into the maintenance of expertise. The increasing impact of bodily functions and health condition on learning ability and cognitive functioning in older age is also evident from two recent lines of investigations. Work by Kramer and colleagues (Kramer et al., 1999; Kramer & Willis, 2002) demonstrated that some intellectual abilities, most notably those reflecting executive functions, can be improved by aerobic exercise. There is also growing evidence from dual-task research that in older age there exists an increasing demand of bodily functions for cognitive resources, which in turn can no longer be invested into intellectual activities (Krampe & Baltes, 2003; Rapp et al., 2005; Woollacott & Shumway-Cook, 2002). Although this opens the perspective that optimizing one's physical health can support continued maintenance practice, both lines of research also point to growing constraints on further improvement, which are inescapable eventually.

Does Expertise Provide General Benefits at Advanced Ages?

There is by now little disagreement in the literature that acquired, domain-specific mechanisms support expert performance at any age. From this perspective, we would expect little transfer or benefits to general intellectual abilities. In line with this assumption, Hambrick et al. (1999) found similar factor structures for intellectual abilities in individuals who had spent considerable time on crossword-puzzle solving, as have others for non-specialist adults. However, in contrast to these studies, there are some cross-sectional results that hint at positive domain-general cognitive outcomes of training or practicing in a specific domain. Clarkson-Smith and Hartley (1990) examined a sample of adults for whom leisure-activity information was available and found that bridge players were more likely than non-bridge players to have better general reasoning abilities and working-memory abilities. A similar advantage in domain-related and domain-unrelated working memory was found for "Skat" players by Knopf, Preussler, and Stefanek (1995). Skat is a card game somewhat similar to bridge.

One difficulty in interpreting such cross-sectional research is that prior ability profiles, such as superior general working-memory capacity, may influence who initially participates in and persists with such mentally demanding activities. However, some longitudinal research studies also point in the direction of general gains in cognition for intellectually stimulating work environments. For instance, Schooler, Mulatu, and Oates (1999) showed that stimulating work environments were particularly beneficial for older adults, though the effects are better described as reciprocal than causal. Similarly, cognitive abilities in later life were superior when people had engaged earlier in intellectually stimulating leisure activities (Schooler & Mulatu, 2001).

A conservative interpretation of the available evidence is that long-term investment into expertise portrays beneficial effects at a more general level, rather than supporting direct transfer at the level of cognitive mechanisms. For example, the necessity to sustain intense practice regimes and coordinate them with other professional demands might well motivate high accomplishments in one domain, and they also tend to provide individuals with resources (e.g., salaries) to optimize other life domains (health, recuperation). Along these lines, Krampe and Baltes (2003) proposed that reciprocal effects emerge at the level of meta-cognition or life-management, in ways such as learning-to-learn, optimal time-budgeting of daily activities, or the personal belief that pursuing long-term goals pays off eventually.

Summary and Conclusions

The evidence reviewed in this chapter illustrates that general cognitive abilities, as measured through psychometric tests, are poor correlates of expert performance in older age. There is also accumulating evidence that accomplishments in later adulthood do not merely reflect the success of initial learning. More likely, older experts must actively maintain specific skills through deliberate practice efforts. Such maintenance efforts do not transfer to the more general cognitive abilities typically assessed in IQ tests. The potential for maintenance through deliberate practice is not limited to purely knowledge-based performance, but rather extends to skills involving speed and accuracy.

For some time, researchers have started to express concerns about the decontextualization of tests designed in the IQ-based tradition and standard laboratory tasks as valid indicators of competencies and cognition in the elderly (Dixon & Baltes, 1986; Sternberg & Wagner, 1986). Subsequently, research strategies changed from searching for correlates or causes of age-related decline to identifying mechanisms that support successful aging in those individuals who maintain competencies at high levels, like older experts. As a result, more ecologically based approaches, focusing on everyday competencies and real-life expertise, have emerged, which also attempt to incorporate expert performance in a revised concept of intelligence (Horn & Masunaga, 2000; Krampe & Baltes, 2003; Sternberg, 1999; Horn & Masunaga, Chapter 34).

At the level of societies and culture, declining birth rates and continued increases in life expectancy in industrialized countries have forced a rediscovery of older adults in their 60s and even 70s as valuable participants in the work force. Some industries are investing in knowledge-preservation projects to try to maintain institutional expertise when their aging experts retire (Hoffman, Shadbolt, Burton & Klein, 1995; Hoffman & Lintern, Chapter 12). Considerable efforts are now being made by industry and applied researchers to design interventions suitable for developing older adults' potentials and supporting opportunities for their lifelong learning (Charness et al., 2001). The good news emerging from research on expertise and learning is that older adults can maintain high levels of skill through their own deliberate efforts, at least up to the third age (i.e., until age 70). To this end, societies' protective mechanisms, that typically guarantee that older employees are more likely to be in stable positions than younger ones (Swaen et al., 2002), provide a context for these individuals to selectively maintain relevant skills. However, to the extent that job demands change over time, obsolescence of skills becomes a risk, (Sparrow & Davies, 1988) unless, we would argue, people continue to engage in deliberate practice. There are, however, limits imposed on the continued investment of resources into skill development that emerge at even more advanced ages (the fourth age), that ultimately constrain an individuals' participation in the long-distance race to achieve and maintain high-level expertise.

Footnote

1. Heritability estimates in behavioral genetics are based on correlations of criterion measures (e.g., IQ-test performances) between samples that are genetically related. Specifically, heritability denotes the proportion of interindividual differences (the variance of the criterion measure) that can be accounted for by kinship.

References

Ackerman, P. L. (1988). Determinants of individual differences during skill acquisition: Cognitive abilities and information processing. *Journal of Experimental Psychology: General*, 117, 288–318.

Allaire, J. C., & Marsiske, M. (1999). Everyday cognition: Age and intellectual ability correlates. *Psychology and Aging*, 14, 627–644.

Allaire, J. C., & Marsiske, M. (2002). Well- and ill-defined measures of everyday cognition:

Relationship to elders' intellectual ability and functional status. *Psychology and Aging*, 17, 101–115.

Anderson, J. R. (1982). Acquisition of cognitive skill. *Psychological Review*, 89, 369–406.

Baird, L. L. (1985). Do grades and tests predict adult accomplishment? *Research in Higher Education*, 23, 3–85.

Baltes, P. B., & Baltes, M. M. (1990). Psychological perspectives on successful aging: The model of selective optimization with compensation. In P. B. Baltes & M. M. Baltes (Eds.), *Successful aging: Perspectives from the behavioral sciences* (pp. 1–34). Cambridge, NY: Cambridge University Press.

Book, W. F. (1924). Voluntary motor ability of the world's champion typists. *Journal of Applied Psychology*, 8, 283–308.

Bosman, E. A. (1993). Age-related differences in the motoric aspects of transcription typing skill. *Psychology and Aging*, 8, 87–102.

Callahan, J. S., Kiker, D. S., & Cross, T. (2003). Does method matter? A meta-analysis of the effects of training method on older learner training performance. *Journal of Management*, 29, 663–680.

Cattell, R. B. (1971). *Abilities: Their structure, growth, and action*. Boston, MA: Houghton Mifflin.

Cerella, J. (1985). Information processing rates in the elderly. *Psychological Bulletin*, 98, 67–83.

Cerella, J. (1990). Aging and information processing rates in the elderly. In J. E. Birren & K. W. Schaie (Eds.), *Handbook of the psychology of aging* (3rd ed., pp. 201–221). San Diego, CA: Academic Press.

Cerella, J., & Fozard, J. L. (1984). Lexical access and age. *Developmental Psychology*, 20, 235–243.

Charness, N. (1981a). Aging and skilled problem solving. *Journal of Experimental Psychology: General*, 110, 21–38.

Charness, N. (1981b). Search in chess: Age and skill differences. *Journal of Experimental Psychology: Human perception and Performance*, 7, 467–476.

Charness, N. (1983). Age, skill, and bridge bidding: A chronometric analysis. *Journal of Verbal Learning and Verbal Behavior*, 22, 406–416.

Charness, N. (1989). Expertise in chess and bridge. In D. Klahr & K. Kotovsky (Eds.), *Complex information processing: The impact of*

Herbert A. Simon (pp. 183–208). Hillsdale, NJ: Erlbaum.

Charness, N., & Bosman, E. A. (1990). Expertise and aging: Life in the lab. In T. M. Hess (Ed.), *Aging and cognition: Knowledge organization and utilization* (pp. 343–385). North-Holland: Elsevier Science Publishers B.V.

Charness, N., Krampe, R. T., & Mayr, U. (1996). The role of practice and coaching in entrepreneurial skill domains: An international comparison of life-span chess skill acquisition. In K. A. Ericsson (Ed.), *The road to excellence: The acquisition of expert performance in the arts and sciences, sports, and games* (pp. 51–80). Mahwah, NJ: Erlbaum.

Charness, N., Park, D. C., & Sabel, B. A. (2001). *Communication, technology and aging: Opportunities and challenges for the future.* New York: Springer.

Charness, N., Tuffiash, M., Krampe, R., Reingold, E. M., & Vasyukova, E. (2005). The role of deliberate practice in chess expertise. *Applied Cognitive Psychology, 19,* 151–165.

Chase, W. G., & Ericsson, K. A. (1982). Skill and working memory. In G. H. Bower (Ed.), *The psychology of learning and motivation* (Vol. 16, pp. 1–58). San Diego, CA: Academic Press.

Clarkson-Smith, L., & Hartley, A. A. (1990). The game of bridge as an exercise in working memory and reasoning. *Journal of Gerontology, 45,* P233–P238.

Colonia-Willner, R. (1998). Practical intelligence at work: Relationship between aging and cognitive efficiency among managers in a bank environment. *Psychology and Aging, 13,* 45–57.

Coon, H., & Carey, G. (1989). Genetic and environmental determinants of musical ability in twins. *Behavioral Genetics, 19,* 183–193.

Detterman, D. K., & Daniel, M. H. (1989). Correlations of mental tests with each other and with cognitive variables are highest for low IQ groups. *Intelligence, 13,* 349–359.

Dixon, R. A., & Baltes, P. B. (1986). Toward life-span research on the functions and pragmatics of intelligence. In R. J. Sternberg & R. K. Wagner (Eds.), *Practical intelligence: Nature and origins of competence in the everyday world* (pp. 203–235). New York: Cambridge University Press.

Elo, A. E. (1965). Age changes in master chess performances. *Journal of Gerontology, 20,* 289–299.

Elo, A. E. (1986). *The rating of chessplayers, past and present* (2nd ed.). New York: Arco.

Ericsson, K. A. (1990). Peak performance and age: An examination of peak performance in sports. In P. B. Baltes & M. M. Baltes (Eds.), *Successful aging: Perspectives from the behavioral sciences* (pp. 164–196). New York: Cambridge University Press.

Ericsson, K. A., & Charness, N. (1994). Expert performance: Its structure and acquisition. *American Psychologist, 49,* 725–747.

Ericsson, K. A., & Kintsch, W. (1995). Long-term working memory. *Psychological Review, 102,* 211–245.

Ericsson, K. A., Krampe, R. T., & Tesch-Römer, C. (1993). The role of deliberate practice in the acquisition of expert performance. *Psychological Review, 100,* 363–406.

Ericsson, K. A., & Lehmann, A. C. (1996). Expert and exceptional performance: Evidence on maximal adaptations on task constraints. *Annual Review of Psychology, 47,* 273–305.

Fitts, P. (1964). Perceptual-motor skill learning. In A. W. Melton (Ed.), *Categories of human learning* (pp. 243–285). San Diego, CA: Academic Press.

Fleishman, E. A. (1972). On the relation between abilities, learning, and human performance. *American Psychologist, 27,* 1017–1032.

Galton, F., Sir. (1979). *Hereditary genius: An inquiry into its laws and consequences.* London: Julian Friedman Publishers. (Originally published in 1869).

Hambrick, D. Z., & Engle, R. W. (2002). Effects of domain knowledge, working memory capacity and age on cognitive performance: An investigation of the knowledge-is-power hypothesis. *Cognitive Psychology, 44,* 339–387.

Hambrick, D. Z., Salthouse, T. A., & Meinz, E. J. (1999). Predictors of crossword puzzle proficiency and moderators of age-cognition relations. *Journal of Experimental Psychology: General, 128,* 131–164.

Hasher, L., Stoltzfus, E. R., Zacks, R. T., & Rympa, B. (1991). Age and inhibition. *Journal of Experimental Psychology: Learning, Memory, & Cognition, 17,* 163–169.

Hertzog, C. (1989). Influences of cognitive slowing on age differences in intelligence. *Developmental Psychology, 25,* 636–651.

Hoffman, R. R., Shadbolt, N. R., Burton, A. M., & Klein, G. (1995). Eliciting knowledge from experts: A methodological analysis.

Organizational Behavior and Human Decision Processes, 62, 129–158.

Horn, J. L. (1982). The theory of fluid and crystallized intelligence in relation to concepts of cognitive psychology and aging in adulthood. In F. I. M. Craik & S. Trehub (Eds.), *Aging and cognitive processes* (pp. 237–278). New York: Plenum.

Horn, J. L., & Masunaga, H. (2000). New directions for research into aging and intelligence: The development of expertise. In T. J. Perfect & E. A. Maylor (Eds.), *Models of cognitive aging. Debates in psychology.* (pp. 125–159). New York: Oxford University Press.

Howe, M. J. A., Davidson, J. W., & Sloboda, J. A. (1999). Innate talents: Reality or myth? *Behavioral and Brain Sciences, 21*, 399–442.

Hulin, C. L., Henry, R. A., & Noon, S. L. (1990). Adding a dimension: Time as a factor in the generalizability of predictive relationships. *Psychological Bulletin, 107*, 328–340.

Kaufman, A. S. (2001). WAIS-III IQS, Horn's theory, and generational changes from young adulthood to old age. *Intelligence, 29*, 131–167.

Keele, S. W., & Hawkins, H. L. (1982). Explorations of individual differences relevant to high level skill. *Journal of Motor Behavior, 14*, 3–23.

Keele, S. W., Pokorny, R. A., Corcos, D. M., & Ivry, R. (1985). Do perception and motor production share common timing mechanisms: A correlational analysis. *Acta Psychologica, 60*, 173–191.

Kliegl, R., Smith, J., & Baltes, P. B. (1989). Testing-the-limits and the study of adult age differences in cognitive plasticity of a mnemonic skill. *Developmental Psychology, 25*, 247–256.

Knopf, M., Preussler, W., & Stefanek, J. (1995). "18, 20, 2." – Does expertise in skat compensate for age-related deficits in working memory? *Swiss Journal of Psychology – Schweizerische Zeitschrift Fuer Psychologie – Revue Suisse de Psychologie, 54*, 225–236.

Kramer, A. F., Hahn, S., McAuley, E., Cohen, N. J., Banich, M. T., Harrison, C., et al. (1999). Exercise, aging, and cognition: Healthy body, healthy mind? In W. A. Rogers & A. D. Fisk (Eds.), *Human factors interventions for the health care of older adults* (pp. 91–120). Mahwah, NJ: Erlbaum.

Kramer, A. F., & Willis, S. L. (2002). Enhancing the cognitive vitality of older adults. *Current Directions in Psychological Sciences, 11*, 173–177.

Krampe, R. T. (1994). *Maintaining excellence: Cognitive-motor performance in pianists differing in age and skill level.* Berlin, Germany: Edition Sigma.

Krampe, R. T. (2002). Aging, expertise and fine motor movement. *Neuroscience and Biobehavioral Reviews, 26*, 769–776.

Krampe, R. T., & Baltes, P. B. (2003). Intelligence as adaptive resource development and resource allocation: A new look through the lenses of SOC and expertise. In R. J. Sternberg & E. L. Grigorenko (Eds.), *The psychology of abilities, competencies, and expertise* (pp. 31–69). New York: Cambridge University Press.

Krampe, R. T., Engbert, R., & Kliegl, R. (2001). Age-specific problems in rhythmic timing. *Psychology and Aging, 16*, 12–30.

Krampe, R. T., Engbert, R., & Kliegl, R. (2002). The effects of expertise and age on rhythm production: Adaptations to timing and sequencing constraints. *Brain and Cognition, 48*, 179–194.

Krampe, R. T., & Ericsson, K. A. (1996). Maintaining excellence: Deliberate practice and elite performance in young and older pianists. *Journal of Experimental Psychology: General, 125*, 331–359.

Krampe, R. T., Kliegl, R., Mayr, U., Engbert, R., & Vorberg, D. (2000). The fast and the slow of skilled bimanual rhythm production: Parallel versus integrated timing. *Journal of Experimental Psychology: Human Perception and Performance, 26*, 206–233.

Krampe, R. T., Mayr, U., & Kliegl, R. (2005). Timing, sequencing, and executive control in repetitive movement production. *Journal of Experimental Psychology: Human Perception and Performance, 31*, 379–397.

Kubeck, J. E., Delp, N. D., Haslett, T. K., & McDaniel, M. A. (1996). Does job-related training performance decline with age? *Psychology and Aging, 11*, 92–107.

Labouvie, G. V., Frohring, W. R., & Baltes, P. B. (1973). Changing relationship between recall performance and abilities as a function of stage of learning and timing of recall. *Journal of Educational Psychology, 64*, 191–198.

Lehmann, A. C., & Ericsson, K. A. (1993). Sight-reading ability of expert pianists in the context of piano accompanying. *Psychomusicology, 12*, 182–195.

Lehmann, A. C., & Ericsson, K. A. (1996). Performance without preparation: Structure and acquisition of expert sight-reading and accompanying performance. *Psychomusicology*, 15(1–2), 1–29.

Lima, S. D., Hale, S., & Myerson, J. (1991). How general is general slowing? Evidence from the lexical domain. *Psychology and Aging*, 6, 416–425.

Lindenberger, U., Kliegl, R., & Baltes, P. B. (1992). Professional expertise does not eliminate negative age differences in imagery-based memory performance during adulthood. *Psychology and Aging*, 7, 585–593.

Lindenberger, U., & Pötter, U. (1998). The complex nature of unique and shared effects in hierarchical linear regression: Implications for developmental psychology. *Psychological Methods*, 3, 218–230.

MacKay, D. G. (1982). The problems of flexibility, fluency, and speed-accuracy trade-off in skilled behavior. *Psychological Review*, 89(5), 483–506.

Masunaga, H., & Horn, J. (2001). Expertise in relation to aging changes in components of intelligence. *Psychology & Aging*, 16, 293–311.

Maylor, E. A. (1994). Ageing and the retrieval of specialized and general knowledge: Performance of masterminds. *British Journal of Psychology*, 85, 105–114.

McClelland, G. H., & Judd, C. M. (1993). Statistical difficulties of detecting interactions and moderator effects. *Psychological Bulletin*, 114, 376–390.

McEvoy, G. M., & Cascio, W. F. (1989). Cumulative evidence of the relationship between employee age and job performance. *Journal of Applied Psychology*, 74, 11–17.

Meinz, E. J. (2000). Experience-based attenuation of age-related differences in music cognition tasks. *Psychology and Aging*, 15, 297–312.

Meinz, E. J., & Salthouse, T. A. (1998). The effects of age and experience on memory for visually presented music. *Journals of Gerontology: Psychological Sciences*, 53B, P60–P69.

Mireles, D. E., & Charness, N. (2002). Computational explorations of the influence of structured knowledge on age-related cognitive decline. *Psychology & Aging*, 17, 245–259.

Morrow, D., Leirer, V., Altiteri, P., & Fitzsimmons, C. (1994). When expertise reduces age differences in performance. *Psychology and Aging*, 9, 134–148.

Morrow, D. G., Menard, W. E., Stine-Morrow, E. A. L., Teller, T., & Bryant, D. (2001). The influence of expertise and task factors on age differences in pilot communication. *Psychology and Aging*, 16, 31–46.

Morrow, D. G., Ridolfo, H. E., Menard, W. E., Sanborn, A., Stine-Morrow, E. A. L., Magnor, C., et al. (2003). Environmental support promotes expertise-based mitigation of age differences on pilot communication tasks. *Psychology and Aging*, 18, 268–284.

Myerson, J., Hale, S., Wagstaff, D., Poon, L. W., & Smith, G. A. (1990). The information-loss model: A mathematical theory of age-related cognitive slowing. *Psychological Review*, 97, 475–487.

Over, R., & Thomas, P. (1995). Age and skilled psychomotor performance: A comparison of younger and older golfers. *International Journal of Aging & Human Development*, 41(1), 1–12.

Plomin, R. (1990). The role of inheritance of behavior. *Science*, 248, 183–188.

Plomin, R., & Rende, R. (1991). Human behavioral genetics. *Annual Review of Psychology*, 42, 161–190.

Rabbitt, P. M. A. (1993). Crystal quest. A search for the basis of maintenance of practised skills into old age. In A. Baddeley & L. Weiskrantz (Eds.), *Attention: Selection, awareness, and control*. Oxford, UK: Clarendon Press.

Rapp, M., Krampe, R. T., & Baltes, P. B. (2005). Adaptive task prioritization in aging: Selective ressource allocation to postural control is preserved in Alzheimer disease. *American Journal of Geriaric Psychiatry* 14(1), 52–61.

Rosenbaum, D. A., Kenny, S., & Derr, M. (1983). Hierarchical control of rapid movement sequences. *Journal of Experimental Psychology: Human Perception and Performance*, 9, 86–102.

Salthouse, T. A. (1984). Effects of age and skill in typing. *Journal of Experimental Psychology: General*, 113, 345–371.

Salthouse, T. A. (1985a). Speed of behavior and its implications for cognition. In J. E. Birren & K. W. Schaie (Eds.), *Handbook of the psychology of aging* (pp. 400–426). New York: Van Nostrand Reinhold.

Salthouse, T. A. (1985b). *A theory of cognitive aging*. Amsterdam: North Holland Press.

Salthouse, T. A. (1991a). Age and experience effects on the interpretation of orthographic drawings of three-dimensional objects. *Psychology and Aging*, 6, 426–433.

Salthouse, T. A. (1991b). Expertise as the circumvention of human processing limitations. In K. A. Ericsson & J. Smith (Eds.), *Toward a general theory of expertise: Prospects and limits* (pp. 286–300). New York: Cambridge University Press.

Salthouse, T. A. (1991c). Mediation of adult age differences in cognition by reductions in working memory and speed of processing. *Psychological Science, 2,* 179–183.

Salthouse, T. A. (1996). The processing-speed theory of adult age differences in cognition. *Psychological Review, 103,* 403–428.

Salthouse, T. A., Babcock, R. L., Skovronek, E., Mitchell, D. R. D., & Palmon, R. (1990). Age and experience effects in spatial visualization. *Developmental Psychology, 26,* 128–136.

Salthouse, T. A., & Maurer, T. J. (1996). Aging, job performance, and career development. In J. E. Birren & K. W. Schaie (Eds.), *Handbook of the psychology of aging* (4th ed., pp. 353–364). New York: Academic Press.

Schaie, K. W. (1989). Perceptual speed in adulthood: Cross-sectional and longitudinal studies. *Psychology and Aging, 4,* 443–453.

Schmidt, F. L., & Hunter, J. E. (1998). The validity and utility of selection methods in personnel psychology: Practival and theoretical implications of 85 years of research findings. *Psychological Bulletin, 124,* 262–274.

Schooler, C., & Mulatu, M. S. (2001). The reciprocal effects of leisure time activities and intellectual functioning in older people: A longitudinal analysis. *Psychology and Aging, 16,* 466–482.

Schooler, C., Mulatu, M. S., & Oates, G. (1999). The continuing effects of substantively complex work on the intellectual functioning of older workers. *Psychology and Aging, 14,* 483–506.

Schulz, R., & Curnow, C. (1988). Peak performance and age among superathletes: Track and field, swimming, baseball, tennis and golf. *Journal of Gerontology: Psychological Sciences, 43,* 113–120.

Schulz, R., Musa, D., Staszewski, J., & Siegler, R. S. (1994). The relationship between age and major league baseball performance: Implications for development. *Psychology and Aging, 9,* 274–286.

Simonton, D. K. (1996). Creative expertise: A life-span developmental perspective. In K. A.

Ericsson (Ed.), *The road to excellence* (pp. 227–253). Mahwah, NJ: Erlbaum.

Singer, T., Lindenberger, U., & Baltes, P. B. (2003). Plasticity of memory for new learning in very old age: A story of major loss? *Psychology and Aging, 18,* 306–317.

Sloboda, J. A. (1991). Musical expertise. In K. A. Ericsson & J. Smith (Eds.), *Toward a general theory of expertise. Prospects and limits* (pp. 153–171). Cambridge, MA: Cambridge University Press.

Sparrow, P. R., & Davies, D. R. (1988). Effects of age, tenure, training, and job complexity on technical performance. *Psychology and Aging, 3,* 307–314.

Starkes, J., Deakin, J., Allard, F., Hodges, N. J., & Hayes, A. (1996). Deliberate practice: What is it anyway? In K. A. Ericsson (Ed.), *The road to excellence: The acquisition of expert performance in the arts and sciences, sports, and games* (pp. 81–106). Mahwah, NJ: Erlbaum.

Sternberg, R. J. (1999). Intelligence as developing expertise. *Contemporary Educational Psychology, 24,* 359–375.

Sternberg, R. J., & Wagner, R. K. (1986). *Practical intelligence: Nature and origins of competence in the everyday world.* Cambridge, MA: Cambridge University Press.

Swaen, G. M. H., Kant, I., van Amelsvoort, L. G. P. M., & Beurskens, A. J. H. M. (2002). Job mobility, its determinants, and its effects: Longitudinal data from the maastricht cohort study. *Journal of Occupational Health Psychology, 7,* 121–129.

Taylor, J. L., O'Hara, R., Mumenthaler, M. S., Rosen, A. C., & Yesavage, J. A. (2005). Cognitive ability, expertise, and age differences in following air-traffic control instructions. *Psychology and Aging, 20,* 117–133.

Telford, C. W., & Spangler, H. (1935). Training effects in motor skills. *Journal of Experimental Psychology, 18,* 141–147.

Wagner, R. K., & Sternberg, R. J. (1991). Tacit knowledge: Its uses in identifying, assessing, and developing managerial talent. In J. Jones, B. Steffy, & D. Bray (Eds.), *Applying psychology in business: The manager's handbook* (pp. 333–344). New York: Human Sciences Press.

Waldman, D. A., & Avolio, B. J. (1986). A meta-analysis of age-differences in job-performance. *Journal of Applied Psychology, 71,* 33–38.

Walsh, D. A., & Hershey, D. A. (1993). Mental models and the maintenance of complex problem-solving skills in old age. In J. Cerella, J. Rybash, W. Hoyer, & M. Commons (Eds.), *Adult information processing: Limits on loss* (pp. 553–584). San Diego, CA: Academic Press.

Westerman, S. J., Davies, D. R., Glendon, A. I., & Stammers, R. B. (1998). Ageing and word processing competence: Compensation or compilation. *British Journal of Psychology, 89,* 579–597.

Willis, S. L., & Marsiske, M. (1991). Lifespan perspective on practical intelligence. In T. E. Tupper & K. D. Cicerone (Eds.), *The neuropsychology of everyday life: Issues in development and rehabilitation* (pp. 183–197). Boston, MA: Kluwer Academic Publishers.

Winner, E. (1982). *Invented worlds: The psychology of the arts.* Cambridge, MA: Harvard University Press.

Woollacott, M., & Shumway-Cook, A. (2002). Attention and the control of posture and gait: A review of an emerging area of research. *Gait and Posture, 16,* 1–14.

Yang, L., Krampe, R. T., & Baltes, P. B. (2006). Basic forms of cognitive plasticity extended into the oldest-old: Retest learning, age, and cognitive functioning. *Psychology and Aging,* in press.

CHAPTER 41

Social and Sociological Factors in the Development of Expertise

Harald A. Mieg

We have serious difficulties when it comes to explaining what really defines an "expert" – a difficulty that goes beyond the explanatory range of defining experts by their individual performance. Take, for example, people who provide political advice or consult multinationals. What would qualify them as experts? How can we assess their performance? How can we disentangle their individual expert contribution and the success of the enterprise or party they work for? We cannot understand these cases if we don't consider what Hoffman, Feltovich, and Ford (1997) concluded: the "minimum unit of analysis" is the "expert-in-context" (p. 553)(see also Clancey, Chapter 8).

For the purpose of this chapter on social and sociological factors in the development of expertise, I assume that an expert has to be regarded as the connection between a *person and a function*. The function indicates the social context of the expert performance. In the following, I use a broad notion of function that includes both the pertinent duties and the effects of expert performance, such as the duties and work of a doctor, as well as the effect of music on its audience. In short: I understand function as defined by what an audience, patient, or customer would pay for.[1] The function of medical therapy is to render a sick person healthy. The function of music is to please the audience (as entertainment) or peer professionals (as being excellent). My definition of function as "what would be paid for" says that there is a potential interest in a particular expert performance, by the patient, the audience, or other sorts of clients.

In this chapter, I will first introduce an *expert role approach* that is mainly based on attribution theory and will provide an understanding of the social "functions" of experts. The key to understanding expert roles is to take into account the layperson or client. In other words, to look at expert roles as forms of *interaction* between the expert and his or her client or an audience. In society, "expert" means that you are regarded or addressed as such by someone else. This social conception of expert differs from other ones discussed in this handbook, such as the expert as an outstanding individual nominated by peers (see

Chi, Chapter 2) and the expert defined by his/her superior performance (See Ericsson, Chapters 13, 38).

In the second part, the expert role approach will help us understand the work of experts in various social contexts – organizations, professions, society. We will see that professions play a decisive role in setting and controlling quality standards of expert performance (see also Evetts, Mieg, Felt, Chapter 7).

The third part of this chapter will be devoted to mediating mechanisms in the development of expertise, such as socialization. Particularly, we will take a look at the assertion that the best context for the socialization of experts is the "bourgeois" middle-class home.

Expert Roles: From Relative Expertise to Professionalism

Living in a western society, we might come into the following situations:

- asking someone on the street for directions to the station
- consulting a doctor
- speaking in court as an appointed expert on asbestos
- instructing a child how to lace its shoes
- watching a broadcast discussion with scientists on safety regimes for nuclear power plants.

These situations differ in various aspects: the persons and consequences involved; the frequency and probability of the event; its general social significance. Even the perspective differs: in some of the situations we are asking somebody, in others we are answering in some way. In whatever way the situations may differ, they share their form: *somebody explains a matter (what, how, and/or why) to someone else*. In the following, I will call this form "The expert"-interaction or, simply, "The expert."

This first part of the chapter examines "The expert"-interaction, thereby revealing the social functions of the use of experts. The

starting point is the observation that there are *relative experts*. In other words: the depth of knowledge and skill necessary to provide an explanation depends on what is required in a particular context. If I visit a town I have never been to before and want to know the direction to the station, I might ask a person on the street who looks or behaves like a possible resident of that town. In this case I suppose that a resident knows his or her town through personal experience and is able to provide me with reasonable instructions on how to get to the station.

There are many open questions regarding the role of relative experts and beyond. In this first part, I will examine "The expert"-interaction by taking five steps to answer such questions as:

1) What makes a relative expert an interesting case of an expert?

2) What are the constituents of "The expert"-interaction? How does context come into play?

3) Is there a general function of experts or "The expert"-interaction, respectively, that explains "The expert"-interaction with a relative expert as well as with doctors and other professionals?

4) What are the social and psychological mechanisms driving this interaction? Particularly: where does trust in experts come from?

5) Is a relative expert a somewhat "deficient" expert, or are there basically different expert roles?

We will see that we can distinguish various types of experts or expert roles, relative experts and professionals being only two of them. These expert roles share a general *social form*, "The expert," that allows us to easily address and "use" people as experts even in unstructured or strange situations, such as when we are strangers in a town or a knowledge domain – that is, when we are the laypersons. A particular challenge will accompany us throughout the chapter: What about the criteria of expert performance? Do we need them to identify experts?

Table 41.1. Experts (and expert perfromance)

Classical examples of experts	Experts as well	Examples of relative experts
Chess masters (winning chess games)	Entrepreneurs (rising an enterprise)	Star Wars film experts (knowing Star-Wars film)
Medical doctors (medical diagnosis)	Master chefs (cooking)	Law student (e.g., advising a psychology student)
Scientists (scientific analyses)	Aborigines (native Australian art)	Residents (e.g., knowing their town)
Musicians (superior musical performances)	Astrologers (horoscopes)	Politicians (e.g., serving as minister of foreign affairs)
Athletes (setting records in sports)	Computer freaks (hacking)	Corporate communications employee (presenting the company)

On Relative Experts, Other Experts, and Expert-Performance Criteria

Almost anyone can – under certain circumstances – act as an expert. This is based on the fact that the level of knowledge and skill differs in our society, as well as the level of knowledge and skill necessary to serve a function in a context. If you are a student of psychology and in trouble with your landlord, you may turn to a friend who studies law. In this situation your friend acts as an expert on law – a status he or she would never have in the law community.

In Table 41.1 we see on the left side some examples of experts that are classic to the study of expertise, particularly chess masters and medical doctors. On the right side we see examples of more or less relative experts, such as the resident or the law student. I have also included the example of a Star Wars film expert whom we might see in a TV game show. Hoffman, Shadbolt, Burton, and Klein (1995) reported that there are studies on expertise where psychologists relied on "the participation of preschool children who were avid fans of 'Star Wars' films" (p. 131). Other examples include the politician who serves as a minister of foreign affairs and usually is not a professional diplomat, or as a minister of transport without having mastered any university studies on that topic. However, in his or her political party, the politician has become the expert on foreign affairs or transportation by virtue of working on that topic or even by denomination.

The last example in the list is the corporate communications employee. In general, this person does not really know the plans, strategies, and decision constraints of the company's board members, nor the industrial-technological processes or scientific background a company's production is based on. However, this person's function is to present the company in the public and to answer questions by guests or journalists. More specifically, the function of the corporate communication employee is to act as a *gatekeeper* who prevents the working force behind the scene from being involved in public queries. This person definitely is a *relative* expert as to everything going on in the company and might be an expert in an absolute sense regarding his or own job in corporate communications. The middle column of Table 41.1 contains a list of experts more or less seldomly cited in literature on expertise, such as entrepreneurs, master chefs, aborigines, astrologers, or computer freaks who are expert hackers. Each of them can act or be addressed as an expert in certain contexts. I have arranged this list in order to show the importance (or problem) of *expert-performance criteria*. In the case of entrepreneurs, a broad and open set of criteria has to be applied (innovativeness, financial success, seize of the company, public impact etc.). Astrology lies outside the scope of today's accepted sciences, and hacking outside accepted social practices. However, there are astrologers, as well as occultists and pendulum specialists, who have been used as court-appointed experts (Dippel, 1986). In cases where a client sues an astrologer because of an unqualified horoscope, a neutral astrology expert has to testify the standards for deriving horoscopes. What we see is that there are communities that define standards that might not be known or transparent to the public. This is true for astrology as well as aboriginal art; aboriginals have to appear in Australian courts as experts in cases of unauthorized reproduction of aboriginal art (Antons, 2004). This is particularly true for sciences (listed in the left column of Table 41.1); usually only members of a particular scientific community can really assess the research of a colleague. Even when it comes to cooking, a domain where everyone has a minimum of at least passive experience, the criteria for excellence are not comprehensive for everyone and are set by a community of chefs and "gourmet" critics. In a later part of this chapter, we will see that professions play an important role in setting and controlling the criteria of expert performance (see also Evetts, Mieg, & Felt, Chapter 7).

Agnew, Ford, and Hayes (1997) put the provocative question of why we would deny expert status to snake-oil salesmen, TV evangelists, and chicken sexers when granting it to geologists, radiologists, and computer scientists:

> What do snake oil salesmen, TV evangelists, chicken sexers, small motor mechanics, geologists, radiologists, and computer scientist's all have in common? They all meet the minimum criterion of expertise, namely they all have a constituency that perceives them to be experts. (Agnew, Ford, & Hayes 1997, p. 219)

Moreover, they insist on the point that "expert" denotes a role "that some are selected to play on the basis of all sorts of criteria, epistemic and otherwise" (p. 220). There are, they add, "many niche-specific characteristics and performance criteria" (loc cit.).

To summarize: relative experts also have to be regarded as "true" experts in their particular contexts. "Expertise" in itself seems to be relative to the performance criteria applied in a particular context.

Constituents of "The Expert"-Interaction

From a psychological point of view, expertise may be studied without respect to social contexts. From a social or sociological point of view, expertise and experts are relational notions: to be an expert always means to be an expert in counterdistinction to non-experts, i.e., to laypersons. The dichotomy between experts and laypersons often implies not only a gradient of expertise, but also gradients in other social dimensions, such as prestige, privileges, and power (see also Evetts et al., Chapter 7).

Evidence for understanding "expert" as a form of interaction comes from applied linguistics. From this point of view, the distribution of expertise in interaction has to be regarded as a joint construct achieved by the participants. An empirical study on the "constitution of expert-novice in scientific discourse" showed some basic features of "The expert"-interaction (Jacoby & Gonzales, 1991):

- The dual and *relative* character of an expert in relation to a non-expert: "the constitution of a participant as expert at any moment in ongoing interaction can also be a simultaneous constitution of some other participant (or participants) as less expert, and [. . .] these interactionally achieved identities are only candidate constitutions of Self and Other until some next interactional move either ratifies or rejects them in some way" (p. 149);

- The phenomenon of *shifting* expert status: "the same individual can be constituted as an expert in one knowledge domain, but constituted as a novice when traversing to some other knowledge domain. Secondly, within a single knowledge domain, the same individual can be constituted now as more knowing, now as less knowing. Finally, in either of these two situations, the valence of expertise may shift with a change of recipients" (p. 168).

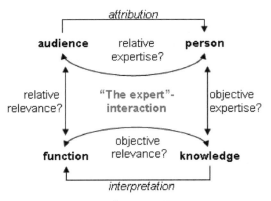

Figure 41.1. "The expert"-interaction.

Figure 41.1 shows the constituents of "The expert"-interaction: a person is addressed as an expert in front of an audience – a client, a layperson, a jury, a TV audience, and so forth. The person is addressed because he or she might have *knowledge* relevant to a certain *function*, for instance tackling a certain problem. The function slightly varies with the context: The patient consults the doctor, seeking relief from his or her neck pains; a jury is comprehensively informed by an expert on the health risks caused by asbestos in a particular industrial plant; or the stranger simply wants to know the direction to the station.

Figure 41.1 is just an extension of the expert-lay dichotomy that lies at the core of "The expert"-interaction. On the left side, there is the lay audience with an open function, for instance a problem to be tackled. On the right hand side, there is an individual with knowledge or skills. The main constituting process is the *attribution* of the expert status to that person by the audience. Another process involved consists in the *interpretation* of the function in the light of expert knowledge. Even the resident of a town, when asked on the street for directions to the station, has to interpret his or her function: How detailed can the answer be? Is it helpful to include information about the public transportation system? Might it be more effective to accompany the stranger for part of the way? Similarly, the expert on asbestos has to provide an interpretation of the problem to be dealt with. An interpreta-

tion on the basis of an epidemiological model displaying risk classes might provide the jury with a different (weaker) impression of the health risk than a toxicological interpretation that shows direct causal links between the presence of asbestos and toxic effects.

There are always some question marks we can put behind the attribution of "expertise": Is the "expert" really more capable than the audience (relative expertise)? Does the "expert" really have the specific knowledge required (objective expertise)? Is this kind of knowledge really suitable when it comes to tackling the identified problem (objective relevance)? Today, sciences have developed an internal differentiation that often makes it impossible to discern which scientist is an expert for what type of problem. It might be useless to consult THE expert on asbestos (material characteristics, usage, etc.) if he or she cannot provide any answer on the toxicological effects on humans.

To summarize: "The expert"-interaction is based on the expert-lay dichotomy and the knowledge gradient that is characteristic of this dichotomy. "The expert"-interaction involves the attribution of expertise to a person (= expert) by an audience (= layperson). From that perspective, "The expert"-interaction can look like one of many forms of the division of labor, the expert executing specialized work. What is special about using experts?

Expertise as Human Capital

Gary S. Becker speaks of *human capital*, which is created by investments – education, training, medical care, and so forth (1993, p. 16). Expertise can be regarded as a form of human capital. Human capital is capital in the sense that it can be invested in industries to raise productivity. The long periods of persisting growth in per capita income in the USA, Japan, and some European countries presumably are, as Becker states, due to "the expansion of scientific and technical knowledge that raises the productivity of labor and other inputs in production" (1993, p. 24). If this is true, we can assume that the contribution of human experts to the increase in productivity is crucial and not limited to engineering the technical basis of industries.

What is the advantage from understanding expertise as human capital? Isn't that simply another way of speaking of the division of labor? The notion of the division of labor could invoke ideas of a preestablished categorization of possible occupations. From this point of view, experts are specialists for specific problems. In this case, it would be best to educate everyone at the place he or she will go to work for the rest of their lives. However, this would underestimate the dynamics of productive knowledge in our societies.

Understanding expertise as human capital implies the following:

- Expertise is personalized: Expertise is embodied in persons. This has the advantage that we can exchange types of knowledge by exchanging experts. It is much easier to exchange a doctor than to change the medical system.
- Expertise is priced: To select or exchange experts, their expertise has to be valued. The value of human expertise is expressed (measured) by prices paid in labor markets or prizes won in professional competitions.

To fully understand the social function of experts as human capital (in the broad sense of function introduced at the outset of this chapter), let us take a short look at some basics of the psychology of expertise (see also Feltovich, Prietula, & Ericsson, Chapter 4):

- Expertise seems to be a form of cognitive/behavioral adaptation to a particular domain of tasks, hence it is domain-specific.
- To become an expert requires massive domain-specific training and practice – deliberate practice (see Ericsson, Chapter 38).

From this point of view, expertise is based on focused experience and training. The social function of using experts is the *time-efficient use of knowledge*, based on the expert's routine through experience.

I argue that the simplicity and usefulness of "The expert"-interaction is based on a simple fact: the criteria for finding the expert result from an extension or *generalization* of one's own experience. By addressing someone as an expert we need to suppose only that this person has obtained knowledge we could obtain ourselves, supposing we had the time to do so. This is quite obvious in the case of asking someone on the street for directions to station. We need to assume only that a normal resident (we address as expert) has had enough time to develop a sufficient picture of the geography of his or her town. After being informed about the directions to the station, we can, ourselves, act as "experts" and instruct others (e.g., our children) how to get to the station.

Everyone knows a story about how "The expert"-interaction can fail, here is one more: A scientist came to Berlin for the first time; he wanted to attend a conference at the Technical University. In the morning, his colleague from Berlin picked him up at the hotel and walked with him to the University. This was a nice but long walk of more than half an hour passing through a spacious urban park (Tiergarten). The next day, the visiting scientist used exactly this way to get from the hotel to the University. After two or more days, he was accompanied by other scientists staying at this hotel and attending the same conference. Sometimes they really had to hurry through the park because they left the breakfast table too late. Another day, the colleague from Berlin picked him up at the hotel again, but this time he went a much shorter way, not crossing the park. Now the visiting scientist realized that the first time his colleague from Berlin wanted to talk to him and had therefore chosen this long deviation through the park. He himself had assumed that this colleague from Berlin (as a relative expert on this area) showed him (the layperson) a reasonable way from the hotel to the Technical University.

We can say: *The core of the expert's role consists of providing experience-based knowledge that we could attain ourselves if we had enough time to undertake the necessary learning.* In other words: the particular gain from using an expert is the relatively fast utilization of the expert's compressed experience *any* reasonable person could make if she or he had enough time to do so (cf. Mieg, 2001). The important remaining question is: How do we identify experts of subjects where we lack any experience? Why do we trust experts even (or particularly!) in fields where most of us are complete laypersons, for instance in the diagnosis of brain tumors, asbestos, or international trade regulations?

To summarize: Expertise can be regarded as human capital. The question of how such capital is valued led us to recognize the *time* investment in the development of expertise. From this we can derive the core social function of the expert's role: It consists of the relatively fast utilization of the expert's compressed experience that *any* reasonable person could attain if she or he had enough time to do so.

The Social and Psychological Mechanisms of "The Expert"-Interaction: "The Expert" as a Social Form and a Result of a Personal Causal Attribution

The inquiry into social and psychological mechanisms of "The expert"-interaction will show that the roles of different kinds of experts, relative experts as well as professionals, share one social *form*, "The expert." This social form is linked to a certain assumption of truth.

The notion of a "social form" was introduced by Georg Simmel, a sociologist at the beginning of the 20th century. As he remarked, we can always differentiate between the contents of a social situation and its form:

> Any social phenomenon is composed of two elements which in reality are inseparable: on the one hand, an interest, a purpose, or a motive; on the other, a form or a mode of interaction among individuals through which, or in the shape of which, that content attains social reality. (1971, p. 24)

In all the examples cited above, we have a common form, but the interests involved can vary considerably. Providing explanation needn't be the main intent of the person asked: The person on the street may

be in a hurry and unwilling to stop; the doctor's main purpose might be to keep his practice running; the appointed expert's dominant motivation might be not to say anything wrong; the mother instructing her child might not want to have to lace her daughter's shoes herself; and the scientists may want to present themselves in the discussion as favorably as possible. Nevertheless, all of them provide explanations for someone else.

"The expert" is a social form, in the same way that "division of labor" and "hierarchy" are social forms. Social forms can be characterized as

- extreme generalizations of interactions we find in many societies
- being independent from the kind of use or the motives connected to this use.

Compared to "division of labor" or "hierarchy," "The expert" is a simple social form, easy to recognize. A person asked on the street about the directions to the station would have difficulties in understanding this interaction as a form of division of labor. What would be the shared task? "The expert" is a social form of its own, open to many kinds of use and motives: This may be the expert's "representation of self" (Goffman, 1959), as well as the pure motivation to help a stranger lost in a town.

Crucial to interaction – we are still following Simmel – is that "every interaction is properly viewed as a kind of exchange" (1971, p. 43). And, exchange in some sense creates value, Simmel says.

> What one expends in interaction can only be one's own energy, the transmission of one's own substance. Conversely, exchange takes place not for the sake of an object previously possessed by another person, but rather for the sake of one's own feeling about an object, a feeling which the other previously did not possess. The meaning of exchange, moreover, is that the sum of values is greater afterwards than it was before and this implies that each party gives the other more than he had himself possessed. (p. 44)

There is a specific value attached to "The expert"-interactions, *truth*. In this context truth means: A sentence such as "This or that is the shortest way to the station" is true if (and only if) this or that is actually the shortest way to the station. Truth is an option that can potentially be realized in every interaction with experts who have sufficient knowledge to share it. When we say that the value "truth" is attached to the social form "The expert," this does not mean that every client or person asking for information expects the expert to tell the truth. But, even if someone who is generally suspicious of scientific knowledge – be it modern medicine or political sciences – asks a scientist about the current trends or information on the state of the art, this person would nevertheless expect most scientists to truthfully explain the state of the art in that particular science to the best of their knowledge – unless they had financial incentives to bias their assessments. The origin of this truth presupposition in experts, I would argue, lies in the extension or generalization of one's own experience: "True" is what I could know myself if I had enough time to undertake the necessary experience (as the expert did).

The power of the social form "The expert" can be seen clearly in unstructured contexts, such as in a group of people who are unfamiliar with one another and meet only once. This is the situation we encounter in experimental groups. Garold Stasser and colleagues have studied the effects of expert role assignment in groups. A common experimental design is the hidden profile: Some group members have unshared information that is necessary to complete the group task (see, e.g., Stasser, 1992). In these studies, unshared information is a basis for the definition of expertise, expertise signifying "that a person has access to more information in a specific domain than others in the group" (Stewart & Stasser, 1995, p. 619). It can be shown that the explicit assignment of particular expert roles to the group members who have unshared information increases the chance that this piece of information will contribute to the group's work. The

assignment of expert roles seems to serve as a source of *social validation*, that is, the veracity of the information introduced by one group member is confirmed by another (p. 627).

The studies by Simmel and Stasser are backed by the attribution theory. *Attribution theory* reveals much of what is said as a result of the attribution that is inherent to "The expert"-interaction. It was founded by the psychologist Fritz Heider. His starting point was the question: How does a person interpret the actions of another person? Thus he started by investigating commonsense psychology. Heider wrote:

> In everyday life we form ideas about other people and about social situations. We interpret the actions of other people and we predict what they will do under certain circumstances. Though these ideas are usually not formulated, they often function adequately. (1958, p. 5)

Attribution theory basically distinguishes two main, dichotomous sources of attributed causality: the *person* or the *situation*. A personal attribution is an internal attribution, a situational attribution is an external one. Persons, as well as situations, have invariant (dispositional) or variable properties (see Weiner, 1986): A personality trait would be a dispositional personal property; pure luck would be a variable situational factor. Usually, we regard expertise as based on experience and training, thus expertise is a *personal dispositional* characteristic.

Two implications of the attribution theory are of particular importance for "The expert"-interaction:

- There is a tendency to overestimate individual expertise and neglect the context owing to the so-called "fundamental attribution error" (Ross, 1977).
- This personalized attribution of expertise reduces the perceived *uncertainty*, implying certainty (truth) as well as, to some extent, trust.

The *fundamental attribution error* consists in "the tendency for attributers to underestimate the impact of situational factors and to overestimate the role of dispositional factors" (p. 183). This error of overestimating dispositional factors (such as personality traits) and neglecting situational factors (such as role-relationships or group influences) is quite common in everyday "commonsense" psychology. The commonsense psychologist "too readily infers broad dispositions and expects consistency in behavior or outcomes across widely disparate situations and contexts" (p. 184). Thus, personal causal attribution is mostly a dispositional attribution. Persons are "inventors," "reformers," "criminals," "bad risks" – or "experts." It is not a surprise, therefore, that information and explanations provided by an expert are easily attributed to a stable dispositional property of that person – his or her expertise. The context of expertise is systematically faded out.

As Heider remarked, causal attributions to invariant dispositional properties "make possible a more or less stable, predictable, and controllable world" (1958, p. 80). Therefore, experts are more or less stable, predictable, and controllable sources of knowledge. From a psychological perspective, we can say that such causal attributions serve an "illusion of control" (Langer, 1983; Mieg, 2001, pp. 60–61). From a sociological perspective, the attribution of expertise to experts *reduces uncertainty*. Our modern societies are too complex, they exceed our ability to extrapolate the scope of personal experience and knowledge. Therefore, we need social structures and social forms that reduce uncertainty and thereby create trust (cf. Luhmann, 1979). The social form "The expert" is a perfect example of this mechanism of reducing uncertainty. By supposing truth (in "The expert"-interaction), we also suppose *certainty* that dispenses us from checking facts on our own.

To summarize: "The expert"-interaction involves a *personal* attribution of expertise to a person, the "expert," thereby utilizing a common social form, "The expert." The use of experts makes possible (at least the illusion of) a more or less stable, predictable, and controllable world.

Figure 41.2. Professional work according to Abbott (1988).

A Typology of Experts

Today, the social form "The expert" has been institutionalized, the main version being professionals and professions (see also Evetts et al., Chapter 7). Or in the words of Andrew Abbott: "Professionalism has been the main way of institutionalizing expertise in industrialized countries" (1988, p. 323). Abbott analyzed professional work and described the following sequence:

- *Diagnosis*: "assembles clients' relevant needs into a picture and then places this picture in the proper diagnostic category" (1988, p. 41).
- *Inference*: "takes the information of diagnosis and indicates a range of treatments with their predicted outcomes" (p. 40).
- *Treatment*: "Like diagnosis, treatment imposes a subjective structure on the problems with which a profession works" (p. 44).

Figure 41.2 provides an impression of the sequence of professional work. We can use Abbott's analysis to sketch expert roles. These expert roles define concrete versions of the general social form "The expert," indicating that somebody explains a matter (what, how, and/or why) to someone else. Modern role theory considers roles as means for acquiring resources (Platt, 2001, p. 15094). Hence, in contrast to the mere social form "The expert," expert roles can be actively utilized by experts and "exploited." Table 41.2 provides a typology of expert roles, distinguishing four types and taking reference to the analysis of professional work in Figure 41.2. Starting on the right hand side, we have *relative* experts who deliver particular information. They

Table 41.2. A Typology of expert roles

	Professionals	*Formal experts/ Decision experts*	*Researchers/Analysts*	*Relative experts/ Local "system experts"*
Function (cf. Fig. 41.2)	Complete professional task	inference / formal decision support	diagnosis / analysis	local information
Performance criterion	effectiveness & efficiency	effectiveness	validity	validity

are addressed as experts in specific circumstances, but not because they are scientists or professionals. For example: In every organization there seems to be a person who – without any authority – knows "everything and everyone" and whom we can ask anything regarding the organization's informal structure. Relative experts can also be experts by role assignment, for instance in teams where each member is responsible for a specific part of the team's work. In some contexts, such as environmental issues, a sort of non-scientific "lay expert" comes into play to support science, so-to-say *system experts* (Mieg, 2000, 2001). They are the individuals who know the local conditions of the human-environment system they live in, for instance a town, very well.

In Figure 41.2, the function of relative experts might be, if at all, subsumed under diagnosis. If we want a full diagnosis, we have to consult an expert *researcher* or analyst. They define a separate expert role. The performance criterion for research is validity, or at least, supposed validity. In general, the public appearance of scientists provides a perfect example of this type of expert (cf. Kurz-Milcke & Gigerenzer, 2004): A researcher presents an analysis that focuses on the parts of a problem that can be analyzed with some certainty and refuses to speculate on topics where little evidence from research exists. However, we should not forget that today researchers are normally professionals, employed in the science system or by industry. The researcher or analyst is, so to say, the extension of a relative expert, providing not only information but also

an understanding of principles, connections, and evidence. In short, researchers provide knowledge.

Let us now turn to professionals. Abbott claims that the core of the professional's work is inference (as in Fig. 41.2). Inference, says Abbott, is a "purely professional act" (1988, p. 40). A professional can easily outsource diagnosis and treatment to specialists. In fact, a normal doctor who runs his or her own practice uses the help of specialized firms or coworkers for the analysis of blood and tissue. And in some cases the doctor will prescribe treatments that have to be executed by others, for example, nurses or parents of a sick child. However, the inference of a particular medical treatment from a particular diagnosis is the doctor's job. In complicated or unusual cases, the doctor can delegate the inference to a colleague (not a subordinate!). But the delegation of *all* inference problems would be the end of the doctor's practice. Table 41.2 also includes a type of experts who solely focus on inference. These experts are called *formal* experts or decision experts (Otway & von Winterfeldt, 1992). These experts provide formal knowledge, for example, on mathematics or decision theory; their task is the support of decision making and methodology. Therefore, their work should be judged by its effectiveness: Do we effectively come to a sound decision with the help of formal decision advice? Conflict mediation and formalized risk management, for example, in the finance industry, can be subsumed under this category. However, the role of a pure formal expert seems to be ephemeral: Professionals hesitate to delegate the inference task or to publicly cooperate with such decision-making experts. Who, as a professional, wants to see his or her expert judgment explained to the public by a formal expert? Therefore, experts desiring to be recognized and consulted as formal experts have to professionalize themselves, for instance as specialized consultants or "risk professionals" (Dietz & Rycroft, 1987).

An expert's role also determines the scope of *accountability* for the expert's work. Professionals account for the complete professional task, including treatment. Relative experts account only for the information they provide, researchers for the correctness of their analyses. If we take into account what is said about human capital and personal causal attributions (in previous section), we can say that experts represent not only units of expertise (as human capital) but also *units of accountability* for the application of expertise in accordance to their expert role.

To summarize: We have started our analysis of expert roles in this chapter with the example of asking someone on the street for directions to the station. We have seen that this simple case of relative expertise contains all the elements of "The expert"-interaction, that is, the situation where we consult an expert, including expertise as a form of human capital. We concluded with a typology of expert roles.

Contexts of Expertise

I will review expert roles in three of the most important social contexts: the organizational context, the professional context, and the societal context. The general sociological perspective on experts, highlighting professions and the context of science, has already been addressed in Chapter 7. The study of the organizational context of expert work would fill a separate book. Therefore, I can focus only on specific aspects of expertise in context: the division of labor (organizational context), the definition of performance criteria (professional context), and

the question "Can we trust in experts?" (societal context).

Organizational Context: The Division of Labor

In general, organizations are forms of labor division. Max Weber (1979) regarded rationally administered divisions of labor as *bureaucracies*, impersonal organizations of tasks and specialists. From a more modern perspective, companies and similar organizations are considered resource pools that assemble human, financial, material, and other resources (see, e.g., Engeström, 1991). In both versions, the organization involves a connected distribution of relative expertise. The success of such an organization depends on the art of combining the resources in an effective way. We can reveal the particular distribution of expertise by assessing who is used as a source for what sort of information and know-how in an organization (e.g., Stein, 1992).

Studies in organizational psychology have shown that groups and other organizational structures can learn. They develop a kind of memory, *transactive memory* (Wegner, 1987), that is a coordinated and distributed storage of knowledge. Transactive knowledge is based on the fact that we can use other people as "external memory," for instance, by asking a colleague about details on meetings we have missed. A large part of a secretary's job consists of reminding his or her superiors of appointments. Transactive memory is "a property of a group" (p. 191), which can be a family or a company.

A central mechanism in transactive memory is the attribution of expertise. This has been demonstrated in experiments with coworkers or work groups in laboratory settings (see Hollingshead, 2001). Best group performances (in most times recall tasks) were found where expertise was clearly attributed to particular group members. Moreover, transactive memory seems to be most differentiated when the group members possess different areas of expertise and incentives to remember different information.

Describing a company as defined by the division of labor probably provides too weak a picture, neglecting the influence of internal struggles for power (Crozier, 1964). Moreover, it is doubtful whether companies that are organized as efficient combinations of relative expertise are the successful ones in any industries. For instance, long-term studies in Silicon Valley showed that a philosophy of employing only excellent candidates in managerial positions, irrespective of the organizational fit of their projects, seems to pay out most (Baron & Hannan, 2002).

Professions: The Power of Defining Performance Criteria

For more than 80 years, professions have been a matter of sociological interest (e.g., Abbott, 1988; Freidson, 2001; Evetts et al., Chapter 7). Professions are often characterized as privileged, *autonomous* occupational groups, each profession having gained control of a specific, socially relevant section of work. A profession can define standards for professional education and control entry into a market. Doctors and lawyers are considered to be the most prominent professions, having developed in the late Middle Ages. More recently established professions include, for example, architects, accountants, and engineers.

According to Andrew Abbott (1988), professions have to be seen within a system. The system is centered around work and consists of professions and their links ("jurisdiction") to particular tasks. The professions compete with one another for control of particular tasks. The "currency" of this competition is knowledge (p. 102). Today, professional work is based on abstract knowledge backed by science. According to Abbott, abstract knowledge is productive because it can be used to define new tasks and to take over jurisdiction for these tasks. Currently, we can observe the struggle of genetic biologists and medicine regarding the jurisdiction for genetic consulting. The medical profession defines genetic consulting as part of the doctor's therapeutic work; genetic biologists understand it as the transposition of scientific genetic analysis into practice.

There has been a discussion on role conflicts of professionals in organizations (as organizations tend to restrict the autonomy of professional work (Hall, 1968; Mieg, 2000, 2001); this is, so to say, a struggle for the power of defining performance, defined by the organization or by the profession. Today, consumer movements and public discussion on the status of professions drive professions into redefining their professional standards in a more explicit and transparent manner, thus redefining themselves (cf. Evetts, 2003).

Experts and Society: Trust in Experts?

Trust in experts is personalized trust as well as institutionalized trust. According to Anthony Giddens (1990), trust in expert systems is perhaps the core dilemma of modernity ("expert systems" here referring to networks of experts). Because of the complexity of modern societies, we cannot but rely on expert judgment and expert services in many domains of life. However, societies have to ensure control of experts. According to Niklas Luhmann, trust in general serves to reduce social uncertainty and can be considered a functional equivalent of power (Luhmann, 1979). Francis Fukuyama emphasizes that trust is a form of social capital (Fukuyama, 1995), regulating social order as well as financial markets. The beginning of the 21st century brought along some spectacular cases of misled trust in experts in the financial sector, for example, the Enron case and the failures of accounting firms on the one hand, and the cases of financial analysts who promoted the products of their clients, pushing stock prices ever higher, on the other.

These cases of misled trust in experts also highlight a common practice, the *legitimizing use* of experts (Mieg, 2001). Companies, for instance, make use of experts for advertising or public-relation purposes. The experts certify the quality of certain products or services. In the domain of national and international politics, the legitimizing use of experts is ubiquitous. We find all administrations using expert panels in order to demonstrate the severity of problems and the necessity of administrative work, thus creating a demand for bureaucratic staff and funds (as Jasanoff [1994] describes it for the relation between the Environmental Protection Agency [EPA] and its Science Advisory Board). And, of course, we find experts who directly play into politics, promoting themselves, as in the case of the IPCC, the Intergovernmental Panel on Climate Change. The IPCC has itself become a powerful international expert system with an impact on academic course programs and scientific fund raising by supporting international climate politics.

An intriguing case of experts and trust can be found in courts. In US trials, experts are a type of witness. The expert can testify on almost anything that is helpful and relevant to the trial (Rossi, 1991). Experts in US trials, as introduced here, are a helpful means to the parties involved in a trial. The adversary process prevents the jury from undue deference to experts. In practice, many of the critical aspects of using experts – such as, What qualifies a person as an expert? or What data form the basis for an expert's opinion? – are left to cross-examination by the lawyers. It is in the interest of each party to examine the experts of the adversary party and demonstrate lack of evidence if this proves to be the case. There is also the possibility of employing a "court-appointed expert" (Federal Rule of Evidence 706). However, they are employed very infrequently. Appointment of experts through the court transcends the adversary system of common law. Thus the social form "The expert" comes into play again and the consequences of "The expert"-interaction have to be taken into account. A survey revealed that "juries and judges alike tend to decide cases consistent with the advice and testimony of court-appointed experts" (Cecil & Willging, 1993, p. 52):

> The most dramatic illustration of dominance by a court expert occurred in a case in which a large number of workers claimed

damages due to working conditions. At the behest of the court, a physician examined all of the workers and reported findings for each plaintiff. The physician's court-appointed status was disclosed to the jury, and the judge reported "the jury discounted the experts for each side." In fact, in each individual case, the jury followed the findings of the court-appointed expert, finding sometimes for the plaintiff and sometimes for the defendant. (loc. cit., p. 54)

Statutory judicial frameworks, such as in France and Germany, tend to systematize and differentiate legal matters, including actors and functions. In statutory systems, the role of the expert in the court is more systematized than in common law. In German law, for example, the expert is considered as a "judicial clerk" or "clerk of the judge" who, under the supervision of the judge, helps the court interpret and understand a case.

To summarize: Expert roles and the attribution of expertise serve an important function in organizations as well as in society. However, the social form "The expert" has its own dynamics that can run into conflict with organizational or public constraints, as we saw in the case of experts in court. This raises awareness for expert-performance criteria.

Mediating Processes in the Development of Expertise

Having discussed the contexts of expertise and expert work, we can now turn to the question of the contexts that nourish the development of expertise. I will start with the process of socialization and then introduce some selected more or less psychological approaches. We will leave the discussion of the social form "The expert" and come to what Simmel had called "content": expertise. Thereby, we return to the more classical examples of expertise (see also pertinent Chapters in Section V), such as chess, the medical profession, or sports, for the simple reason that these activities have gained a certain social function. However, we should not forget that the very challenging cases, the ones where individual expertise and social context are interwoven, such as in entrepreneurs or politicians, are not addressed here.

Socialization

The main mediating socio-psychological process during the development of expertise is *socialization*. "Socialization generally refers to the process of social influence through which a person acquires the culture or sub-culture of his or her group, and in the course of acquiring these cultural elements the individual's self and personality are shaped" (Gecas, 2001, p. 14525). Classic sociology considered socialization as a process of internalizing social roles (e.g., Parsons, 1955). Modern sociology views socialization as the formation of identities (Gecas, 2001). As the acquisition of expertise is based on deliberate practice and long-term training, we can expect socialization to exert a strong impact on the development of expertise.

Socialization takes place in different social contexts – family, schools, peer groups, work, and so forth. The importance of these contexts varies during the lifetime of a person.

THE FAMILY CONTEXT

In general, parents are the most effective "agents of socialization" when they express a "high level of support or nurturance combined with the use of inductive control" (Gecas, 2001, p. 14527). In the development of "extraordinary minds," the orderly life in a "bourgeois" family is a favorable environment (Gardner, 1998).

Families have always played an important role in nurturing high levels of expertise. Famous examples are families of musicians such as the Bach family or the Mozart family, where the parents trained their children from an early age. These German musicians' families appeared with the Kapellmeister profession, that is, conductors-composers who could make a living by working for one of many small princedoms that coexisted on German territory after the Thirty Year's War (1618–1648).

Families can create their own particular subculture with its own system of val-ues and rewards. Such a subculture exists, for instance, in some families of physicians that have for generations maintained a culture of values and routines – such as family music – as well as an ethics of personal care for patients and the community. These family subcultures even survived the former German Democratic Republic (1949–1990) that tried to wipe out the traditional health system based on an autonomous medical profession (Hoerning, 2003).

THE SCHOOL CONTEXT

Schools are an important element in an education system. They transmit not only essential skills and knowledge but also cultural norms for excellence. This transmission often happens via "narratives," story-like mental models representing how life may be (Ferrari, 2002).

In some states, primary schools are part of an encompassing system of talent screening and selection. This was, for instance, the basis for the extraordinary success of physical education in the former German Democratic Republic. In the post-1970 German Democratic Republic, every 6th young boy and every 18th young girl had to start training in one of the specialized national sports training centers (Trainingszentren), which formed the basis of a system of sports schools, sports research institutes, and competitions (Teichler & Reinartz, 1999).

PEER GROUPS

"Peer groups are voluntary associations of status equals and are based on friendship bonds" (Gecas, 2001, p. 14528). Among youths, peer groups play an important role in forming and reinforcing the self-identities of their members. Peer groups can function as a fertile soil for the development of skills in team sports (e.g., basketball, soccer) and in the dramatic or performing arts (e.g., music bands, acting). We should also not forget the *ethnic* context, such as the socialization context of immigrant children in the USA (Rumbaut & Portes, 2001). Families and peers play an important role in transmitting impacts within ethnic groups. In some ethnic groups, children of immigrants display an extraordinary ambition in striving for social and professional success.

ADULT SOCIALIZATION

Much of adult socialization is role specific and occurs in a work environment. As to the development of expertise, the most important socialization contexts are institutes of higher education (universities, professional schools) and professional cultures such as in professions (see also Evetts et al., Chapter 7) and expert organizations (universities, hospitals, law firms). Professional cultures function as "communities of practice" (Lave, 1991) or, sociologically, via the formation of a "habitus" (Bourdieu, 1979), that is, a certain group-specific style of life and logic of work.

Whereas in former times the extended family exerted a considerable influence even on adult socialization by providing resources and opportunities for qualified work, adult socialization today depends much more on individual decisions in some subcultures. Personal networks play an important role and enhance the development of individual competence, particularly "weak ties" to people in higher positions (Granovetter, 1973). Another phenomenon of modern times is dual-career couples, couples where both partners work in the same domain. This is quite a common phenomenon in scientific professions.

POLITICAL CULTURE

We also have to take into account the political context that translates into the school and family contexts. This is particularly true for totalitarian states. The development of sports in the former German Democratic Republic and the promotion of chess in the former Soviet Union were driven by an explicit political will to educate people, thereby steering societal change, and to demonstrate the superiority of socialism at an international level. In Leningrad alone the number of registered chess players rose from 1,000 in 1923 to 140,000 in 1928 after the Soviet Third All-Union Congress in 1924 had officially declared chess "a political weapon" (Hallman, 2003).

Which is the dominant socialization context? A recent study on American elites (Lerner, Nagai, & Rothman, 1996) shows that, in comparison to the general public, the American elite is still "disproportionately drawn from middle- and upper-class backgrounds" (p. 25). This is particularly true for the political elite and lawyers (as a leading profession), where more than two-thirds come from a family with an upper-class, white-collar background. However, a great percentage of the American elite stems from lower-class families, for instance 36% in the military (p. 26). Putnam (1976) claimed that two independent factors might lead to elite status: (i) education and (ii) high social status. New data suggest that either education, alone, or high social status in combination with education, can predict elite status (Lerner et al., 1996, p. 29).

Some Mediating Socio-Psychological Factors

From a psychological point of view, socialization implies quantities of mediating submechanisms; hence, developmental psychology as a whole would be applicable. I just want to mention examples of three types of approaches. They differ in how they focus on the relationship between the individual and the context (or the person and the social function) in the development of expertise.

A Focus on the Individual

Psychology, in general, focuses on individual prerequisites of expertise. For instance, Alfred Adler (1912) considered *compensation* as the psychological mechanism of setting fictitious goals of superiority by which the children strive to overcome feelings of inferiority. Adler mentioned painters and authors who suffered from eye complaints as children and musicians who succeeded in compensating for ear anomalies. More recently, the concept of *self-efficacy* has been advanced by Alfred Bandura (1997). Perceived self-efficacy governs "what you believe you can do with what you have under a variety of circumstances"

(p. 37). Bandura demonstrated the positive influence of self-efficacy on performance in various domains (see also Zimmerman, Chapter 39).

Individual and Context

The works of Jean Piaget, Lev Vygotsky, and Sylvia Scribner stand for a series of classical studies on *socio-cognitive development*. Piaget (1936/1953) described stages of cognitive child development. Vygotsky (1934/1962) introduced the concept of the *zone of proximal development*, this zone describing the difference between what a child can do unguided, on the one hand, and with guidance, on the other. Scribner expanded Vygotsky's socio-cultural approach to adult cognition. In studies on adult cognition, such as "working intelligence" (Scribner, 1984/1997), she showed how the development of particular cognitive capabilities is linked to work-specific experience (see also Clancey, Chapter 8).

The Context

In 1960, Donald T. Campbell wrote a paper on the "blind variation and selective retention in creative thought as in other knowledge processes," arguing that the set of creative personalities is subject to variation and selection. In a similar vein, I argued (Mieg, 2001) that by using an expert, we use the specific experience of someone else (the expert) in order to solve a problem or to find an explanation. Particularly in domains with poor expert decision performance (cf. Shanteau, 1992), such as financial markets or business consulting, experts can be used like *hypotheses* (like "heuristics") that work successfully as long as a certain work environment does not change. When environments change, we can test new approaches by exchanging the expert.

TO SUMMARIZE

The study of mediating processes in the development of expertise shows the importance of connecting the psychological to the sociological perspective. One of the most challenging scientific puzzles still to be solved is the relationship between socialization, levels of cognitive development, and transitions between task contexts (school, positions) that shape and provoke the development of expert performance. There are promising approaches, such as the selection-optimization-compensation model of aging by Paul Baltes (1997), or the "time-span capacity" model of managerial work by Elliott Jaques (1976), both first steps toward a comprehensive theory of human expertise.

Footnote

1. In German, we would use the word "Leistung" (see Mieg & Pfadenhauer, 2003).

References

Abbott, A. (1988). *The system of professions*. Chicago: University of Chicago Press.

Adler, A. (1912). *Über den nervösen Charakter* [The neurotic constitution]. München: Bergmann.

Agnew, N. M., Ford, K., M., & Hayes, P. J. (1997). Expertise in context: Personally constructed, socially selected and reality-relevant? In P. J. Feltovich, K. M. Ford, & R. R., Hoffman (Eds.), *Expertise in context: Human and machine* (pp. 219–244). Menlo Park, CA: AAAI Press.

Antons, C. (2004). Folklore protection in Australia: Who is expert in aboriginal tradition? In E. Kurz-Milcke & G. Gigerenzer (Eds.), *Experts in science and society* (pp. 85–103). New York: Kluwer Academic.

Baltes, P. B. (1997). On the incomplete architecture of human ontogeny: Selection, optimization, and compensation as foundation of developmental theory. *American Psychologist*, 52, 366–380.

Bandura, A. (1997). *Self-efficacy: The exercise of control*. New York: W. H. Freeman.

Baron, J. N., & Hannan, M. T. (2002). *Organizational blueprints for success in high-tech start-ups: Lessons from the Stanford project on emerging companies*. Stanford, CA: Graduate School of Business, Stanford University.

Becker, G. S. (1993). *Human Capital* (3rd ed.). Chicago: The University of Chicago Press.

Bourdieu, P. (1979). *La distinction* [Distinction]. Paris: Minuit.

Campbell, D. T. (1960). Blind variation and selective retention in creative thought as in other knowledge processes. *Psychological Review*, 67(6), 380–400.

Cecil, J. S., & Willging, T. E. (1993). *Court-appointed experts: Defining the role of experts appointed under Federal Rule of Evidence 706*. Federal Judicial Center.

Crozier, M. (1964). *The bureaucratic phenomenon*. Chicago: University of Chicago Press.

Dietz, T. M., & Rycroft, R. W. (1987). *The risk professionals*. New York: Russell Sage Foundation.

Dippel, K. (1986). *Die Stellung des Sachverständigen im Strafprozeß* [The legal position of experts in criminal cases]. Heidelberg: R. V. Decker's.

Engeström, Y. (1991). Developmental work research: Reconstructing expertise through expansive learning. In M. Nurminen & G. R. S. Weir (Eds.), *Human jobs and computer interfaces*. Amsterdam: North-Holland.

Evetts, J. (2003). Professionalization and professionalism: Explaining professional performance initiatives. In H. A. Mieg & M. Pfadenhauer (Eds.), *Professionelle Leistung – Professional Performance* (pp. 49–69). Konstanz: UVK.

Ferrari, M. (Ed.). (2002). *The pursuit of excellence through education*. Mahwah, NJ: Erlbaum.

Freidson, E. (2001). *Professionalism: The third logic*. Cambridge, UK: Polity.

Fukuyama, F. (1995). *Trust: The social virtues and the creation of prosperity*. London: Hamish Hamilton.

Gardner, H. (1998). *Extraordinary minds. Portraits of exceptional individuals and an examination of our extraordinariness*. London: Phoenix.

Gecas, V. (2001). Socialization: sociology of. In N. Smelser (Ed.), *International encyclopedia of the social & behavioral sciences* (pp. 14525–14530). Amsterdam: Elsevier.

Giddens, A. (1990). *The consequences of modernity*. Cambridge, UK: Polity Press.

Goffman, E. (1959). *The presentation of self in everyday life*. New York: Anchor Books.

Granovetter, M. S. (1973). The strength of weak ties. *American Journal of Sociology*, 78(6), 1360–1380.

Hall, R. H. (1968). Professionalization and bureaucratization. *American Sociological Review*, 33, 92–104.

Hallman, J. C. (2003). *The chess artist*. New York: Thomas Dunne.

Heider, F. (1958). *The psychology of interpersonal relations*. Hillsdale, NJ: Erlbaum.

Hoerning, E. (2003). Ärztinnen und Ärzte in der DDR [Doctors in the GDR]. In H. Mieg & M. Pfadenhauer (Ed.), *Professionelle Leistung – Professional Performance* (pp. 111–145). Konstanz: UVK.

Hoffman, R. R., Feltovich, P. J., & Ford, K. M. (1997). A general framework for conceiving of expertise and expert systems in context. In P. J. Feltovich, K. M. Ford, & R. R. Hoffman (Eds.), *Expertise in context: Human and machine* (pp. 543–580). Menlo Park, CA: AAAI.

Hoffman, R. R., Shadbolt, N. R., Burton, A. M., & Klein, G. (1995). Eliciting knowledge from experts: A methodological analysis. *Organizational Behavior and Human Decision Processes*, 62(2), 129–158.

Hollingshead, A. B. (2001). Cognitive interdependence and convergent expectations in transactive memory. *Journal of Personality and Social Psychology*, 81(6), 1080–1089.

Jacoby, S., & Gonzales, P. (1991). The constitution of expert-novice in scientific discourse. *Issues in Applied Linguistics*, 2(2), 149–181.

Jaques, E. (1976). *A general theory of bureaucracy*. London: Heinemann.

Jasanoff, S. (1994). *The fifth branch*. Cambridge, MA: Harvard University Press.

Langer, E. J. (1983). *The psychology of control*. Beverly Hills, CA: Sage.

Lave, J. (1991). Situating learning in communities of practice. In L. B. Resnick, J. M. Levine, & S. D. Teasley (Eds.), *Perspectives on socially shared cognition* (pp. 63–82). Washington, DC: American Psychological Association.

Lerner, R., Nagai, A. K., & Rothman, S. (1996). *American elites*. New Haven: Yale University Press.

Luhmann, N. (1979). *Trust and power*. Chichester: John Wiley. (German original in 1968.)

Mieg, H. A. (2000). University-based projects for local sustainable development: Designing expert roles and collective reasoning. *International Journal of Sustainability in Higher Education*, 1, 67–82.

Mieg, H. A. (2001). *The social psychology of expertise*. Mahwah, NJ: Erlbaum.

Mieg, H. A., & Pfadenhauer, M. (Eds.). (2003). *Professionelle Leistung – Professional Performance: Positionen der Professionssoziologie* [Professional performance: Approaches to the sociology of professions]. Konstanz: UVK.

Kurz-Milcke, E., & Gigerenzer, G. (Eds.). (2004). *Experts in science and society*. New York: Kluwer Academic.

Otway, H., & von Winterfeldt, D. (1992). Expert judgment in risk analysis and management: Process, context, and pitfalls. *Risk Analysis*, 12(1), 83–93.

Parsons, T. (1955). Family structure and the socialization of the child. In T. Parsons & R. F. Bales (Eds.), *Family, socialization, and interaction Processes*. Glencoe, IL: Free Press.

Piaget, J. (1953). *Origin of intelligence in the child*. London: Routledge (French original in 1936.).

Platt, G. M. (2001). Status and role, social psychology of. In N. Smelser (Ed.), *International encyclopedia of the social & behavioral sciences* (pp. 15090–15095). Amsterdam: Elsevier.

Putnam, R. D. (1976). *The comparative study of political elites*. Englewood Cliffs, NJ: Prentice Hall.

Ross, L. (1977). The intuitive psychologist and his shortcomings: Distortions in the attribution process. In L. Berkowitz (Ed.), *Advances in Experimental Social Psychology* (pp. 173–220). New York: Academic Press.

Rossi, F. F. (Ed.). (1991). *Expert witnesses*. Chicago: American Bar Association.

Rumbaut, R. G., & Portes, A. (Eds.). (2001). *Ehnicities: Children of immigrants in America*. Berkeley, CA: University of California Press.

Scribner, S. (1997). Studying working intelligence. In E. Tobach et al. (Eds.), *Mind and social practice: Selected writings of Sylvia Scribner* (pp. 338–366). Cambridge: Cambridge University Press. (Originally & published in 1984.)

Shanteau, J. (1992). The psychology of experts. In G. Wright & F. Bolger (Eds.), *Expertise and decision support* (pp. 11–23). New York: Plenum.

Simmel, G. (1908). *Soziologie: Untersuchungen über die Formen der Vergesellschaftung* [Sociology: Studies on the forms of sociation]. Leipzig: Duncker & Humblot.

Simmel, G. (1971). *On individuality and social forms* (trans. by K. H. Wolff, ed. by D. N. Levine). Chicago: The University of Chicago Press.

Stasser, G. (1992). Pooling of unshared information during group discussion. In S. Worchel, W. Wood, & J. A. Simpson (Eds.), *Group process and productivity* Newbury Park, CA: Sage.

Stein, E. W. (1992). A method to identify candidates for knowledge acquisition. *Journal of Management Information Systems*, 9, 161–178.

Stewart, D. D., & Stasser, G. (1995). Expert role assignment and information sampling during collective recall and decision making. *Journal of Personality and Social Psychology*, 69(4), 619–628.

Teichler, H. J., & Reinartz, K. (1999). *Das Leistungssportsystem der DDR in den 80er Jahren und im Prozeß der Wende* [Training systems in professional sports in the GDR in the 1980s and subsequent to German unification]. Schorndorf: Verlag Karl Hofmann.

Vygotsky, L. S. (1962). *Thought and language*. Cambridge: MIT Press. (Russian original in 1934.)

Weber, M. (1979). *Economy and society* (Vol. I, G. Roth & C. Wittich, Trans.). Berkeley, CA: University of California Press.

Wegner, D. M. (1987). Transactive memory: A contemporary analysis of the group mind. In B. Mullen & G. R. Goethals (Eds.), *Theories of group behavior* (pp. 185–208). New York: Springer.

Weiner, B. (1986). *An attributional theory of motivation and control*. New York: Springer.

CHAPTER 42

Modes of Expertise in Creative Thinking: Evidence from Case Studies

Robert W. Weisberg

Introduction

The study of expertise has in the last several decades become an area of interest to scholars from a broad range of disciplines. In much of the research literature, *expertise* is taken to mean *consistent superior performance, resulting from deliberate practice* (Ericsson, 1996, 1998, Chapter 38). Deliberate practice is the intentional repeated execution, usually under the instruction of a coach, of skills directly relevant to improving the performance in question. The study of expertise can be traced in psychology to de Groot's (1965) study of chess playing, although expertise has been of interest to psychologists since the beginning of scientific psychology (see Shiffrin, 1996, Feltovich, Prietula, & Ericsson, Chapter 4). Examination of the development and functioning of expertise now encompasses a wide range of domains, including medical diagnosis; problem solving in physics; radiologists' skill in reading X-rays; swimming, tennis, soccer, and other athletic domains; performance of classical music; and the perhaps unlikely domain of memory span for digits (see chap-

ters in Ericsson, 1996, and in this volume, especially those in Section V, for representative studies and reviews).

The present chapter examines the question of whether expertise plays a role in creativity, where *creativity* is defined as the *goal-directed production of novelty* (Weisberg, 1993). A creative product (an *innovation*) emerges when an individual intentionally produces something new in attempting to meet some goal (Weisberg, 1993, 1999, 2003). The *creative process* – or *creative thinking* – consists of the cognitive processes that play a role in production of innovations. A *creative individual* is one who produces innovations.

Until relatively recently, researchers studying expertise did not specifically consider whether expertise might underlie creative achievement. In addition, there has been little interest in this issue among researchers studying creativity (for exceptions, see Hayes, 1989, and Weisberg, 1999, 2003). Ericsson (1998, 1999) has made a valuable contribution by analyzing how expertise and creativity might be linked (see also Weisberg, 1999). He proposed that expertise facilitates creative thinking because deliberate practice enables the would-be creator to develop new techniques or skills, which allow him or her to go beyond what had previously been accomplished. We can derive three testable hypotheses from Ericsson's proposal: (1) expertise is necessary for creative accomplishment; (2) creative advances develop as the result of new techniques and skills; (3) creative advances extend the boundaries of the field of endeavor.

The present chapter examines the support for those three hypotheses. The first section of the chapter provides further elaboration on the definitions of relevant concepts, in order to eliminate several possible points of confusion and to clarify possible roles of expertise in creativity. I then consider several possible objections to the notion that expertise might be relevant to creativity, in order to place the present investigation in a broader context. The next section of the chapter responds in broad terms to those objections. I then review in detail several case studies of seminal creative advances that provide evidence relevant to the three hypotheses outlined above. The results of the analyses of the case studies indicate that expertise can play several roles in creative advances. In the final section of the chapter, possible limitations on the role of expertise in creative accomplishment are discussed. I recently presented evidence that can be taken as support for the hypothesis that expertise is necessary for creative thinking (e.g., Weisberg, 1999, 2003, 2006); the analysis in this chapter examines the limits of that claim.

Further Questions of Definition

One difficulty in examining the role of expertise in creative thinking is that the terms *expert* and *expertise* have meanings in the research literature that are different from ordinary language, and this can cause confusion. As noted, in much of the literature, an expert is someone who exhibits consistent superior accomplishment as the result of deliberate practice. In ordinary conversa-

tion, we also use the term *expert* to refer to a person who exhibits a high degree of competence, but we do so irrespective of how that competence was acquired. In this chapter I will use *expertise* in the ordinary sense, to refer to the capacity to perform consistently at a superior level, without regard to how that capacity was acquired. In a number of places I examine the specific role of practice in innovation, but when I use the term *expert* or *expertise* without modification, I am including practice and study under one umbrella (see also Weisberg, 1999).

Some clarification is also needed concerning my definition of *creativity* – goal-directed production of novelty – and related concepts. Most researchers who study creativity usually include the *value* of an innovation as a criterion for calling it creative. (See chapters in Sternberg, 1999 for numerous examples.) Including positive value in the definition of "creative" means, for example, that a candidate solution must actually solve the problem in order to be called creative. Similarly, an invention must carry out the task for which it was designed; a scientific theory must be useful; and a work of art must find an audience. Researchers who include value in their definition of creative do so in order to be able to rule out simply bizarre products from consideration as innovations (e.g., the word salad of a schizophrenic, produced perhaps in response to a problem). However, if we include *intentional* production of novelty in the definition, it also precludes the schizophrenic's word salad, since no one in schizophrenic episode would be able to deal intentionally with a problem.

I believe that including value in the definition also clouds several important issues (Weisberg, 1993, Chapter 8; 2003, 2006). Most critically, including *value* as part of the definition of *creative* means that if, for example, an audience comes to value a previously ignored work of art, the attribution of *creative* to the work, and, *ipso facto*, to the artist who produced it will change: a previously noncreative artist will become creative (even after death). Conversely, an artist may, if his or her work falls out of favor, become noncreative. Such changes mean that we could never develop theories of creative thinking because the data base on which we build our theories will be constantly changing. That is, we would have to add the new people who became creative since we formulated our conclusions and subtract those who have become noncreative. We would then have to reexamine our data base to determine if any previously formulated conclusions are no longer valid. This is obviously an untenable situation for researchers.

In my work (e.g., Weisberg, 1993, 2003, 2006), I differentiate between a *creative* product (a goal-directed innovation) and one that is *valued, influential, significant,* or *important,* which I use as near synonyms. With a work of art, the audience's reaction determines whether or not it will be valued. In the case of inventions, scientific theories, and solutions to problems, the effectiveness of the innovation is critical in that determination. We thus can have *valued and nonvalued innovations*; even if an innovation is of no value, however, it is still creative. In the present context, the specifics of the definition are not of critical concern since all the innovations to be discussed in this chapter are undoubtedly of the highest value. However, it is important to clarify the definition now so that no one will object that ignoring the value of a product might have affected the conclusions drawn concerning creative thinking.

Expertise and Creativity

Domain-Specific versus General Modes of Expertise

Recent research studying creative thinking has indicated that innovations can develop in at least two ways. Case studies of creative thinking at the highest levels (e.g., Weisberg, 1999, 2003, 2004, 2006) have indicated that creative ideas can be built relatively directly on the past, as creative individuals use what they know about the domain in question as the basis for creating something new. In such situations, what one can call *domain-specific expertise* serves as the

basis for transfer of knowledge to the new situation, where that knowledge serves as the foundation for innovation. Second, research that has studied undergraduates solving laboratory problems has found that creative products can also come about as the result of an individual's analysis of a problematic situation in which he or she is not an expert in the sense discussed earlier (e.g., Fleck & Weisberg, 2004; Perkins, 1981; Weisberg & Suls, 1973). In such cases, creative thinking may not depend on domain-specific experience, but rather on *general expertise*, what we also call general knowledge, such as logical-reasoning ability or mathematical ability. This distinction between domain-specific versus general expertise is similar to the distinction between *strong* versus *weak* methods of problem solving (Newell, 1973 Feltovich et al., Chapter 4).

One example of the role of general expertise in problem solving and, therefore, in creative thinking comes from a study by Fleck and Weisberg (2004; see also Weisberg, 1980, Chapter 9; Weisberg & Suls, 1973), who examined the processes underlying solution of the Candle Problem. In this problem, the individual is asked to attach a candle to a wall or a similar vertical surface and is supplied with a box of tacks or fasteners and a book of matches. One solution that has been of particular interest to researchers is the *box solution*, that is, the use of the tack box as a shelf or container for the candle. This solution is not produced by a majority of people attempting the problem, and when it is produced, it is usually not produced as the first solution proposed by an individual. Research examining the fine grain of the processes involved in attempting to solve the candle problem indicates that the box solution often develops in response to difficulties that arise when the individual tries to attach the candle directly to the wall, as requested in the instructions. If the individual tries to use melted wax as an adhesive to attach the candle, for example, he or she may find that the candle is too heavy. This failure may lead the individual to search for something to use to hold up the candle – a shelf or candle holder. This search can result in the box being used. In this example, the problem solver presumably had no deep expertise attaching candles to walls. However, most people know enough about the properties of candles, fasteners, and shelves, and possess enough general skill working with their hands, that they can fashion a shelf out of a tack box as needed. In implementing the box solution to the Candle Problem, then, true domain-specific expertise may not be available. However, more general expertise is used.

Similarly, Perkins (1981) examined processes underlying solution of the Antique Coin Problem:

> *A museum curator is approached by an archeologist offering to sell him an ancient coin. The coin had an authentic appearance and was marked with the date 544 B.C. The curator had dealings with this man before, but this time he called the police. Why?*
> **Solution:** *The coin had to be fake. It was dated 544* **B.C.** *How could the person fashioning the coin know that Christ would be born 544 years later?*

Perkins found that solution of this problem came about as a result of the individual's realizing the impossibility of someone predicting when anyone would be born. That is, the individual recognized the contradiction inherent in the dating on the coin. So, here too we see that there was no direct transfer of domain-specific expertise to the problem, since most of us are not expert in antiquities and/or forgery; and even if we were, it is not clear how that domain-specific expertise would help to solve this problem. However, as with the Candle Problem, the person's general expertise, that is, the ability to discern contradictions in a situation, was used in solving the problem.

In conclusion, we have just examined two laboratory situations in which general knowledge served as the basis for creative responses to problems. As noted earlier, however, research has indicated also that sometimes an expert is able to apply his or her domain-specific expertise directly to a problem, as when an expert radiologist is faced with a new X-ray to interpret. In that case, the expert can use domain-specific expertise in solving the problem he or she is facing. Problem-solving exercises used in laboratory studies are relatively simple and bare of information, which may account for why general expertise can suffice to solve them. Creative thinking in the real world, in contrast, occurs in complex, information-rich environments. It therefore becomes of interest to determine if there are examples of creative advances in "real-world" settings in which general knowledge, independent of domain-specific information, plays the leading role.

Modes of Expertise: Degrees of Specificity in Transfer of Knowledge

We have now sketched what we can call two different modes of expertise: domain-specific versus general. As a concrete example of how one might see these different modes of expertise in real-world creative advances, consider a situation in which investigators are attempting to determine the structure of some important organic macromolecule, say, an important protein. Figure 42.1A represents different sorts of information that might be brought to bear on this question, ranging from what they know about that specific molecule when they begin, to what they learn from their own and others' investigations of the properties of that molecule, to what they learn from studies of other macromolecules that might be relevant to understanding the molecule of interest, and so forth. As presented in Figure 42.1A, we have an ever-widening range of knowledge that, as the area widens, becomes relevant only at a more general level. That is, if mathematics or logic is brought to bear on the problem, it is only at a very general level, because of the nature of the expertise that we have developed in those domains (Bassok & Holyoak, 1989). One may not agree with the specific set of domains outlined in Figure 42.1A, or the order of generality portrayed there, but the specifics are not relevant to the discussion. The point to be gleaned from Figure 42.1A is that we can discuss modes

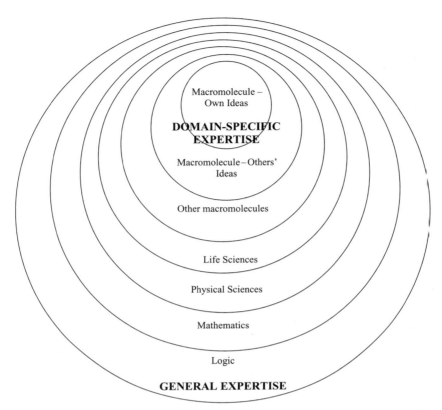

Figure 42.1A. Outline of use of expertise in a hypothetical example of scientific creativity: Determining the structure of an important organic macromolecule.

of transfer of knowledge or expertise, from domain-specific to general, when discussing creative advances, so that findings from case studies and laboratory studies can be integrated.

Figure 42.1B presents the same sort of analysis applied to a hypothetical example from painting, a domain in artistic creativity. Let us say that an artist has been stimulated by the death of a loved one, and he or she begins to create a painting in response. Here too we can outline a set of ever-more-general domains of expertise that might be brought to bear on this project, beginning with the artist's feelings concerning love and death and his or her earlier works concerned with those issues. The domain broadens to include the artist's own works on a broader range of topics and works of other artists, both works addressing love and death as well as other topics. We then go more broadly to include influences from other arts,

both specifically involving love and death and more general, and so forth, until at the broadest level we might see the incorporation of science, logic, and mathematics. Again, the specific details of the scheme in Figure 42.1B are not of concern here; the important point is that one can outline a movement away from domain-specific expertise to more-general aspects of expertise that can be brought to bear on the problem faced by the hypothetical artist. In the case of a person who possesses general expertise, we sometimes use the terms *knowledge* or *general knowledge* to describe the state of the person.

The purpose of this chapter is to consider various case studies of seminal creative advances, to determine in each case if expertise was brought to bear in producing the innovation and, if so, to determine the domain specificity or generality of that expertise. It should also be noted that

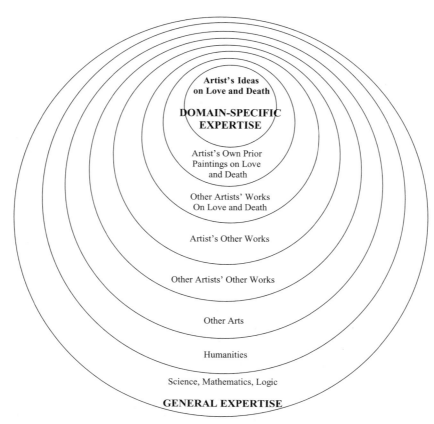

Figure 42.1B. Example of use of expertise in a hypothetical example of artistic creativity.

Figures 42.1A and 42.1B make clear that, when we discuss domain-specific versus general expertise, we are in actuality talking about a continuum, ranging from information directly relevant to the specifics of the problem at hand, through less directly relevant but still domain-specific information, to information relevant on a more general level to the problem, and so forth. It is also not necessary for the present discussion that we specify exactly how each example of expertise is to be classified. All that is needed is that we be able to make gross differentiations among examples of expertise of different degrees of domain specificity. As will be seen in the discussion of the case studies in the chapter, that will be possible.

Before turning to a consideration of the possible role of the various modes of expertise in creativity, it will be useful to discuss the opposite view, that is, the idea that

expertise cannot be the basis for creativity. This view, from my perspective, postulates *tension* of several types between expertise and creativity, so I refer to it as the *tension view*. The tension view has a long history in psychology (e.g., James, 1880) and has many advocates today (e.g., Csikszentmihalyi, 1996; Simonton, 1999; Sternberg, 1996). Thus, it is important to consider reasons why theorists have rejected expertise as the basis for creativity.

Skepticism about Expertise and Creativity: The Tension View

There are a number of different arguments that might lead one to believe that expertise and creativity are unrelated or even that expertise might be an impediment to creativity (Ericsson, 1996, 1998;

Weisberg, 1999). First, the concept of expertise involves an "automatic" mode of responding, where the individual does not think about what he or she is doing. An example is driving a car, which most of us carry out expertly and automatically, without thought. This sort of automatic responding would seem to be incompatible with creative thinking, which involves conscious deliberate processing, although automaticity in performance may free up cognitive capacity for deliberation (see also, Hill & Schneider, Chapter 37; Endsley, Chapter 36, this volume). Second, many researchers believe that *talent* (a constellation of inherited skills that makes a person especially suited to excel in a specific domain), rather than expertise based on experience and practice, plays a critical role in enabling superior levels of achievement (Sternberg, 1996; Winner; 1996, Horn & Masunaga, Chapter 34, this volume). If so, then concentrating on experience and practice with regard to expertise and its role in creativity is misdirected. Finally, it is believed by many researchers, as well as by many in our society, that creative thinking requires that one not rely on the past, as exemplified by knowledge and habit (e.g., Csikszentmihalyi, 1996; Simonton, 1999). This view is captured by the ubiquitous idea that creativity requires that we think "outside of the box." Expertise, however, involves encapsulation of the past, so expertise would seem to be in conflict with the needs of the creative thinker (e.g., as in the restrictive effects of "problem-solving set" and related phenomena; see Luchins & Luchins, 1959; Scheerer, 1963; for a different perspective, see Feltovich, Spiro, & Coulson, 1997; Weisberg, 1980, ch. 9).

In contrast to those beliefs concerning the possible negative relationship between expertise and creativity, Ericsson (e.g., 1996, 1998) has recently proposed that expertise and creativity are intimately connected. Concerning the notion of automaticity and lesser creativity in certain domains, Ericsson proposed that domains such as athletic performance, performance of classical music, and medical diagnosis are more *open* than many realize and, therefore, can require

creative thinking. If an expert musical performer (see also Lehmann & Gruber, Chapter 26), for example, is told by a conductor that her playing of a piece should be less emotional, she will adjust her performance to achieve that end. One could argue that this ability to adjust one's behavior to demands arising in the situation is an example of creative thinking. So, by this view, conclusions from research on expertise might be broadly relevant to creative thinking.

In addition, expertise does not include just mindless, automatic processing (although it usually involves some degree of automated processing)(see also Hill & Schneider, Chapter 37, this volume). The expert acquires a rich, highly complex conceptual structure that is used consciously to represent and reason about situations. Evidence for such a structure can be seen in the ability of chess masters to play several games at once while blindfolded, that is, solely from memory (see also Gobert & Charness, Chapter 30, this volume). In order to carry out such a task, the expert must have available a rich and detailed representation of each game so that it can be remembered and effective moves can be made. Experts in other domains show similar abilities. For example, musical performers sometimes have prodigious memories for the pieces in their performance repertoires. The expert thus uses a detailed analysis of the situation that he or she is facing in order to exercise conscious adaptive processing. Only as the result of experience and practice will an individual possess the detailed representations of a situation needed to support creative thinking. Furthermore, there is evidence that raises questions concerning the role of talent in superior levels of achievement, at least in the domain of performance of classical music (e.g., Sloboda, 1996), which indirectly supports the importance of expertise. Finally, in contrast to the idea that creativity always involves rejecting the past ("think outside the box"), there is, as noted, evidence that creative thinking can build on the past: new ideas can come about as the result of an individual's building on old ideas (e.g., Weisberg, 1999, 2003, 2004, 2006). It is an empirical question as to whether creative achievements necessarily build on the past, but finding that some do is compatible with the hypothesis that expertise plays a part in creative thinking.

Ericsson (1998, 1999) also discusses how expertise and creativity are related. Deliberate practice is the basis of expertise, which, in turn, is responsible for consistent superior performance that is creative. By this argument, many creative thinkers exhibit expertise: for example, Mozart, Picasso, and Dickens produced numerous masterworks; Edison produced numerous inventions; and Einstein and Darwin each made multiple scientific contributions. Ericsson also examines why deliberate practice might be crucial in the development of expertise (1996, 1998). He notes that in all the domains for which objective measurements of performance are available, performance levels have consistently increased over the years. As an example, Olympic levels of performance from the mid-20th century are now achieved by high-school athletes. This has presumably come about because, among other things (e.g., changes in nutrition and overall levels of health), training methods have improved. Deliberate practice is necessary because the athlete, through a coach, must take advantage of the accumulated knowledge of previous generations concerning optimal training (see also Hodges, Starkes, & MacMahon, Chapter 27, this volume).

Ericsson proposes that creative innovations are the highest levels of achievement in any domain because the creative individual goes beyond the boundaries of the domain and redefines it (1996, 1998). Expertise facilitates creative thinking because deliberate practice enables the would-be creator to develop new techniques or skills, that allow him or her to go beyond what had previously been accomplished in the domain. Such innovations are in Ericsson's view analogous to an elite athlete's setting a new performance standard. Ericsson makes this analogy clear: he discusses the competitions that musical performers enter, which are analogous to athletic events (i.e., with winners and losers), and he also discusses similar "competitive" aspects of creative domains, such as artists' or scientists' competition for an audience for their works (Ericsson, 1999). On this analysis, the study of great creative achievements is continuous with the study of expertise.

In conclusion, there are a number of reasons to believe that expertise might play a role in creative accomplishment. We now turn to a consideration of several case studies to investigate in more detail the relationship between creativity and the modes of expertise outlined earlier.

The Ten-Year Rule in Creative Thinking

One of the seminal findings from the study of expertise has been codified as the *Ten-Year Rule*. Chase and Simon (1973) proposed that rule to summarize their finding that the development of superior (master-level) chess performance demands approximately ten years of practice and study of the game. The Ten-year Rule has been verified in many domains, and, most importantly for the present discussion, there is evidence that it holds in the development of creative thinking. Hayes (1989) assessed the role of what he called "preparation" in creative achievement. He examined the career development of important creators in several fields – composition of classical music, painting, and poetry – and calculated the amount of time between an individual's beginning his or her career and the production of a *masterwork*. Information on when the person's career began came from biographies. A masterwork was defined objectively: in poetry, it was a poem reprinted in one of several respected anthologies; in painting, it was a work discussed in one of several respected histories of art; in classical music, it was a work for which at least five recordings were available. Hayes found that masterworks were produced only after approximately ten years into the individual's career. Furthermore, even the most precocious individuals, such as Mozart, required many years before producing a masterwork (see also

Gardner, 1993). These results indirectly support the notion that expertise is important in creativity since it would be expected that developing expertise would take time.

One limitation to Hayes's (1989) investigation is that, because he presented data summarized across large groups of individuals, he presented no information concerning the specific activities that occurred during the pre-masterwork years. Thus, although Hayes's results are consistent with the hypothesis that expertise is necessary for creativity, they do not provide specific information concerning the actual development of expertise in any individuals. Accordingly, I now turn to several case studies of creative achievements of the first rank from the arts, science, and invention to investigate in more detail the question of the necessity of expertise in creativity. We will find in those studies a range of uses of expertise. Some of the cases correspond directly to what would be expected on the basis of the Ten-Year Rule, with innovation dependent on domain-specific expertise and deliberate practice playing a critical role in the development of that expertise. In other cases, explicit practice may not be seen, but a critical role is nonetheless played by domain-specific expertise. Finally, in two cases, seminal creative advances may have come about by a combination of domain-specific and general modes of expertise.

Case Studies of Creative Thinking

Musical Composition

THE YOUNG MOZART

I recently examined in detail the career development of Mozart (Weisberg, 1999, 2003), who, sometimes along with Picasso, is often cited by researchers as the prototype of the creator whose abilities are impossible to understand without invoking a concept like talent or giftedness. Sternberg (1996) discussed Mozart's accomplishments in the context of a critique of research on expertise, specifically of the notion that practice might be more important than talent in determining the level of achievement

reached by an individual. Practice may be important in musical performance or swimming, but, according to Sternberg, expertise researchers may have ignored domains in which talent is more important than practice (e.g., musical composition or painting). According to Sternberg, practice cannot account for the "extraordinary early achievements" of Mozart or Picasso.

> Why was Mozart so damn good? . . . What made Picasso so good so young? (p. 350) . . . [W]hat Mozart did as a child most musical experts will never do nor be able to in their lifetimes, even after they have passed many times over the amount of time Mozart could possibly have had for deliberate practice as a child. (p. 351) . . . We fail to see evidence all around us–scholarly and common-sensical–that people differ in their talents, and that no matter how hard some people try, they just cannot all become experts in the mathematical, scientific, literary, musical, or any other domains to which they may have aspired. (p. 352) . . . The truth is that practice is only part of the picture. Most physicists will not become Einstein. And most composers will wonder why they can never be Mozart. (p. 353)

One piece of evidence that raises questions for Sternberg's view of Mozart is Hayes's finding that the Ten-Year Rule holds even for him (and, as we shall see, it holds also for Picasso). As noted, Hayes's analysis provides no information about the years before the first masterwork. Based on the hypothesis that expertise is necessary for creativity, and on the expertise literature, one might expect to find Mozart developing his skills over those years, as reflected, for example, in increasing production of compositions and in their increasing quality. There should also be evidence for the occurrence of deliberate practice during the formative years.

In order to test those expectations, I looked in detail at Mozart's development, in three ways (Weisberg, 2003). I examined the number of compositions produced during the various years of Mozart's career (Hayes, 1989) and found that his output increased over the first ten years or so of his career, supporting the notion that he was mastering his craft. Second, I measured the quality of Mozart's early compositions by determining the average number of recordings for each composition for each year. The quality of Mozart's compositions increased over the early years of his career, which also supports the idea that he was honing his skill. Finally, there is evidence that Mozart was carrying out deliberate practice over those years under the direction of his father, a professional musician of some repute. Consider Mozart's earliest piano concertos, the first four written at the ripe old age of 11, and the next three written when he was 16. Those works contain no original music by Mozart: they are simply arrangements of music of other composers. Mozart's father may have used others' music as the basis for practice by the young man in writing for groups of instruments. Furthermore, if some of the *published* works by the young Mozart are based completely on the works of others, then Mozart's *private* tutelage from his father must also have centered on study of works of others. So Mozart learned his craft over many years, under the watchful eye of a professional teacher. This training is not different from that received today in schools of music by aspiring composers.

These results call into question Sternberg's (1996) claim that most composers will never approach the accomplishments of Mozart's early years. We have just seen that a number of Mozart's early compositions show no originality on his part. Many of his other early works, which do contain his own music, have been more or less ignored by musicians and audiences, which means that those works are not "so . . . good." They have nothing distinctively "Mozartian" about them. Thus, whereas it is no doubt true that most composers will not match Mozart's ultimate achievements, his early achievements are matched by many composers as they advance through music school. Recent analyses of the career development of other seminal classical composers – Bach, Beethoven, and Haydn – supports the findings from Mozart (Weisberg & Sturdivant, 2006). The pattern of pro-

ductivity over the early years for Beethoven and Haydn, for example, mirrored that of Mozart. There was an increase in quantity and quality of compositions, indicating that those individuals too were developing the skill of writing music. Kozbelt (2004) has also examined Mozart's career in detail, as well as the careers of other classical composers, and he has also found increases in quality of work over their careers in a majority of them. (For further discussion of the importance of talent versus practice and expertise in music, see Sloboda, 1996.)

In conclusion, studies of the development of classical composers support the claim that domain-specific expertise was being used as the basis for composition. If one developed an analysis similar to that in Figure 42.1B for classical composition, based on the case studies just discussed, one would place the influence of expertise relatively close to the domain-specific core of the diagram.

THE BEATLES

Evidence for the Ten-Year Rule in creative thinking also comes from a study of the development of the Lennon-McCartney songwriting team, whose songs for The Beatles broke new ground in popular music in the 1960s (Weisberg, 1999, 2003). The Beatles' career trajectory corresponds in several ways to the findings from the studies of acquired expertise. When The Beatles hit the big time in 1963, they had already been working together for several years, and they had spent thousands of hours playing together. So there was a period of apprenticeship before The Beatles made a significant contribution to pop music. Although this early period did not involve deliberate practice in the sense of formal tutelage under the supervision of a teacher, Lennon and McCartney began their careers by immersing themselves in the works of others. A large majority of the songs played by The Beatles in their early years were cover versions of hits recorded by others. This immersion in the works of others served as a kind of unstructured "practice." In addition, there was more explicit practice. Lennon and

McCartney spent much of their early years together in active collaboration, in which any new information concerning musical structure acquired by either (e.g., if either learned new chords on the guitar) was shared and served as the basis for explorations of new possibilities of composition (Everett, 2001).

It should also be noted that several additional years passed before Lennon and McCartney made their major contributions to popular music. The very earliest songs written by The Beatles were not big hits, and most of them are forgotten, except by collectors. Most of those songs were only recorded late in their career, when their early music became interesting because of what The Beatles had become, not necessarily because of the quality of the songs themselves. The most significant music produced by The Beatles is usually considered to be the "middle-period" albums *Rubber Soul* (1965), *Revolver* (1966), and *Sergeant Pepper's Lonely Hearts Club Band* (1967), created approximately ten years into their career (Reising, 2002). The Beatles' development thus supports the notion that domain-specific expertise was important in their achievements, and, comparable to the results for Mozart and other classical composers, deliberate practice seems to have been involved.

INCREASING QUALITY IN MUSICAL COMPOSITION
VERSUS THE EQUAL-ODDS RULE

The finding that the quality of musical compositions increased over composers' careers in classical and popular music is relevant to Simonton's (1999) influential *Darwinian* theory of creative thinking, in which the creative process occurs in two stages, analogous to the stages in Darwin's theory of organic evolution through natural selection. In evolution, the first stage is *blind variation*, as random changes occur in the genetic material from one generation to the next. Those variations result in organisms with differing reproductive capabilities, which therefore will be differentially successful in passing their genetic material to the next generation. Another way to put this is to say that

the environment *selectively retains* some of those blind variations at the expense of others. Simonton has applied this view to creative thinking, assuming that two stages are involved there also. The first stage, involving production of new ideas, involves random combinations of old ideas. The second process, selective retention, selects and preserves only some of those variations, those which meet a criterion for acceptability.

If random combination of ideas is the first step in creative ideation, then expertise becomes at least irrelevant and perhaps an impediment to creativity. Along those lines, Simonton has presented evidence for what he calls the *equal-odds rule* as support for the role of a random process in the first stage of creative thinking. On the basis of a random process as the core of the first stage, Simonton's theory predicts that the probability of a creator's producing a masterwork should stay constant over a career. The equal-odds rule is in conflict with the notion that expertise is critical in creative thinking. Assuming that expertise serves as the basis for creative thinking, leads to the expectation that creative people should develop their skills over time. The results presented in the last few sections, which demonstrated just such a development in musical composition, thus contradict the equal-odds rule.

Those results leave us with the question of why Simonton found evidence for the equal-odds rule, whereas the results emphasized here (e.g., Hayes, 1989; Kozbelt, 2004; Weisberg, 2003; Weisberg & Sturdivant, 2006) do not support it. The answer is not clear at this point, but the different conclusions might be due to different data bases used by different investigators. For example, Simonton bases some of his analyses on surveys of classical works compiled 50 years ago, whereas Weisberg and Studivant and Kozbelt use more recent (and perhaps more thorough) tabulations of works. This might contribute to the different conclusions. At the very least, it seems that the equal-odds rule can be called into question (see Kozbelt, 2004, for further discussion).

Let us now turn to a different artistic domain – the visual arts – in order to examine the generality of the conclusion that domain-specific expertise is at the core of innovation.

Visual Arts

PAINTING: PICASSO'S *guernica*

In May–June 1937, Picasso created what was to become one of the best-known paintings of the 20th century: *Guernica*. The creation of that masterwork was stimulated by the bombing on April 27, 1937 of the Basque town of Guernica, in northern Spain. The bombing was carried out by the German air force, allies of Franco's fascist forces in the Spanish Civil War. The town per se seemed to have little strategic value (see Chipp, 1988, for discussion), and the Germans' action was looked on by many as an act of terrorism. When news reports of the bombing began to reach Paris over the next few days, Picasso, a Spaniard who had been living in Paris for more than 30 years, dropped his on-going project, which was a painting of an artist and model in the studio. That painting was to appear in the Spanish government's pavilion at an international exposition (a world's fair) to be held in Paris in June of 1937. Over the next six weeks or so, he produced a new work, called *Guernica*, which was put on display instead. The Spanish government was losing the Civil War, and Picasso's painting became a great antiwar and antifascist statement.

For the student of creativity, Picasso's working method for *Guernica* is particularly illuminating because he dated and numbered all the preliminary sketches – some 45 in all – that he produced while working out the details of the masterwork. I have analyzed the development of *Guernica* in detail elsewhere (Weisberg, 2004), based on the sketches, and several conclusions are relevant to the present discussion. From the beginning, as can be seen in the first sketch Picasso produced, on May 1, 1937, he had the overall structure of the painting worked out: one can see the main characters in the same layout as they appear in the final painting. This raises the question of where that structure and those characters came from, and similar characters organized in a similar

manner can be seen in at least one other work produced by Picasso in the mid-1930s. So Picasso built the structure of *Guernica* on the foundation of his own earlier work, that is, on his domain-specific expertise. That expertise also included knowledge of the work of other artists: a number of the specific characters in *Guernica* can be traced to works of others, including Goya, a Spaniard whose work was particularly important to Picasso. (See Weisberg, 1999, 2004, 2006, for further discussion.)

One can also find evidence for practice in Picasso's career development, which reveals a pattern similar to that seen in Mozart. Picasso's father was a painter, as well as a teacher of painting, so Picasso, like Mozart, was exposed from an early age to training from a professional (Weisberg, 1999). In addition, Picasso attended art school, and some of his early works that have been preserved show him practicing drawing eyes and facial profiles, as well as the human body in difficult poses. This is concrete evidence of the young artist carrying out deliberate practice. In addition, the Ten-Year Rule also applies to Picasso: the first works that show a unique Picasso style did not occur until more than ten years into his career (Weisberg, 1999). This analysis of Picasso also calls into question the claims made by Sternberg (1996) concerning the extraordinary level of Picasso's early development. Again, it is not absurd to say that the paintings produced by Picasso over the first ten years of his career are also matched by most painters as they work their way through art school. Pariser (1987), in an analysis of the juvenilia of several painters known for precocity, including Picasso, Klee, and Toulouse-Lautrec, concluded that they all went through stages of development that were the same as those traversed by all painters.

In sum, Picasso's overall development accords with the Ten-Year Rule, and *Guernica* was based on his domain-specific expertise: he began with information from previous works, his own and those of others, and used that as the basis for the creation of a new work. The outline in Figure 42.1B can be applied to Picasso's situation in creating

Guernica, and, to summarize Picasso's thought processes in producing that innovation, we would put a notation close to the center of the diagram. As noted earlier, the adequacy of the precise structure of Figure 42.1B is not at issue here. However that structure is depicted, it seems clear that Picasso's creation of *Guernica* was another example of domain-specific expertise serving in creative thinking. We now turn to a more seminal advance, from the domain of sculpture.

CALDER'S MOBILES

Abstract wind-driven hanging wire sculpture – the *mobiles* with which we all are now so familiar – were created in the early 1930s by Alexander Calder (1898–1976), a young American artist living in Paris (Marter, 1991; Weisberg, 1993, 2006); no one had ever seen anything like them before. Examination of this case study allows us to consider the role of expertise in what one could call a radical innovation, that is, one that seems to make a break with the past.

When he created the first mobiles, Calder had been a sculptor for several years. He was born into an artistic family, and he and his sister spent much time during their childhoods carrying out artistic and construction projects of various sorts. In addition, Calder was trained as a mechanical engineer, which gave him more formal exposure to mechanisms of various sorts, as well as developing further his construction skills. Calder's early sculptures, which usually represented people or animals, were often constructed out of wire and involved movement. In the 1920s, Calder constructed a "circus," with a cast of miniature performers made out of wire, bits of wood and cork, and pieces of cloth. There were three rings, in which an animal trainer and his wild charges, as well as trapeze artists, a sword swallower, and acrobats and clowns were put through their paces by the artist. Calder developed ways of having the miniature people and animals move, so the trapeze artists, for example, would swing on the trapeze and then "leap" from one trapeze to another in a death-defying maneuver. He had also earned money during the 1920s designing "action" toys, involving movement, for American manufacturers. Many of those toys can be seen in altered form in the *Circus*, which became a hit in Parisian art circles.

Around 1930, Calder's work took a radical turn, becoming *abstract* or *non-representational*; that is, one could no longer see people or animals in the pieces he created. This relatively sudden shift in style seems to have been triggered by Calder's visiting the studio of Piet Mondrian (Calder, 1966), another of the many young artists living in Paris at that time, who had met Calder though a visit to see Calder's *Circus*. Mondrian was a painter whose most well-known work is completely non-representational, using grids made out of black lines on a white canvas, with some of the spaces in the grid filled in with blocks of primary colors (blue, yellow, red). When Calder saw Mondrian's abstract works, he is said to have remarked to Mondrian that the works should move. Soon thereafter, Calder began to paint in an abstract style, similar to Mondrian's, but he quickly turned to wire sculpture, with which he was more comfortable. He produced several abstract works of sculpture and soon added movement, usually using electric motors. Motorized sculptures were difficult to keep working (the mechanisms kept breaking), and, even when they did work, the possible movements were restricted, and soon became repetitious and boring. Calder then decided to structure the sculptures so that they would be moved by the wind, a simpler and more reliable, as well as a less-predictable, source of movement, and so the first mobiles were created.

In analyzing Calder's creation of mobiles, we see further support for the role of domain-specific expertise in innovation. Many of his early sculptures, including the *Circus* and the action toys, were made out of wire and involved movement; also, some of his early representational works were designed to swing in the air. Those aspects of his own work – his domain-specific expertise – served as the basis for mobiles. The switch to an abstract subject matter was stimulated by Mondrian. So here we see an artist building on his own work, and changing it radically in subject matter on the basis of exposure to work by others. Since familiarity with Mondrian's work was part of Calder's expertise as an artist, we once again see evidence for domain-specific expertise in creative thinking. Calder's shift from motorized to wind-driven abstract sculpture might have been derived from either domain-specific or general expertise. If his earlier wind-driven hanging sculptures served as the basis for the shift when motorized sculpture proved unsatisfactory, then the switch was the result of domain-specific expertise. On the other hand, if the switch to wind as the motive force for the sculpture was the result of Calder's mechanical skills and reasoning ability, then it was the result of more general expertise. At this time, not enough information is available to distinguish between those two possibilities.

Concerning the specific question of the role of practice in Calder's achievements, his career development is consistent with those already discussed and provides further evidence for the Ten-Year Rule in creative accomplishment. As noted earlier, Calder was raised in an artistic family (his mother was a painter, and his father and grandfather sculptors), and their life was full of art (Marter, 1991). From childhood, Calder was strongly encouraged to participate in artistic activities. He and his older sister developed methods of drawing, with encouragement of their parents, and the two children together worked on many projects. Calder made "jewelry" for his sister's dolls, and his use of wire as an artistic material can be traced to his childhood. Those childhood years can be looked on as providing practice in the development of the skills he used later in producing his innovative wire sculptures. After graduating with his engineering degree, he attended art school, where he received more formal lessons in drawing and painting. So we have here another example of an individual whose development is consistent with what might be expected on the basis of the expertise view.

POLLOCK'S POURED PAINTINGS

In the late 1940s, Jackson Pollock began to produce a series of paintings that had a revolutionary effect on American art (Landau, 1989). Pollock's advance centered on his development of a new technique for applying paint to canvas: instead of using the traditional brush or palette knife, Pollock poured paint directly from the can onto the canvas, which was lying flat on the floor, or dripped or flicked paint with a stick. Pollock's *dripped* or *poured* paintings, constructed out of looping and swirling lines of paint of various thicknesses and textures, were totally nonrepresentational in subject matter. In the 1950s, Pollock's works were hailed by many critics as breakthrough works that helped to establish American art as the equal of the best of Europe. Pollock's radical new technique was directly developed out of his expertise. In the 1940s, the WPA sponsored artists' workshops in New York City, one of which was directed by David Alfaro Siqueiros, a Mexican painter who was living in New York and who, along with his compatriots Diego Rivera and José Orosco, had established a presence in the contemporary art scene. Siqueiros and his colleagues were Communist in their politics, and one of their goals as artists was to bring art down from what they saw as its exalted position among the elite and to make it more accessible to the masses. One way to bring this about was to use modern materials – including industrial paints available in cans, in place of traditional oil paints in tubes – and to replace traditional methods of painting, including the brush, with modern methods, such as airbrushing paint onto canvas.

One set of techniques explored in the workshop sessions was dripping, pouring, and throwing paint on canvas. Siqueiros had produced a work several years before that used those techniques in a primitive way, and the members of his workshop experimented with them. As one example, Pollock collaborated with several other young artists on a work that involved dripping paint on canvas. Pollock then took those primitive efforts and on his own developed a technique that he could use with great skill to produce dynamic lines of various textures. He then used those lines to weave highly textured compositions of great dynamism, sometimes on a large scale, which many people responded to with emotion. Thus, Pollock's radical new technique seems to have been a direct development out of his experience. As a result of those works, Pollock became the leader of the group of artists that came to be known as the Abstract Expressionists or the New York School and who served to raise American art to the level of the equal of Europe.

EXPERTISE AND CREATIVITY IN THE VISUAL
ARTS: SUMMARY

In conclusion, we have seen that the development of innovation in the case studies in visual arts that we have examined is parallel to that in the music case studies: domain-specific expertise played a critical role in all of them. Thus, there is consistency across different domains in the arts. We now turn to case studies in science and technology in order to examine further the finding that domain-specific expertise is of central importance in creative thinking. We have also not found any unequivocal examples of general expertise playing a role in real-world innovation, comparable to that found in the laboratory problem-solving results (e.g., Fleck & Weisberg, 2004; Perkins, 1981; Weisberg & Suls, 1973).

Science and Technology

THE DOUBLE HELIX

Early in 1953, Watson and Crick published the double-helix model of the structure of DNA, the genetic material (the discussion of the double helix is based on Olby, 1994; Watson, 1968; Weisberg, 1993, 2006). A number of research teams were at that time trying to determine that structure, because it was believed – correctly, as it turned out – that understanding the structure of the genetic material would enable scientists to understand how it replicated. It was assumed that this knowledge would ultimately allow scientists to control developmental processes, and we have all seen the astounding advances

that can be traced to Watson and Crick's model of the structure of DNA, ranging from new drugs to cloned organisms. Formulating the double helix was a creative act of the first order.

Watson and Crick collaborated at the Cavendish Laboratory at Cambridge University. Watson, an American who had recently earned a Ph.D. in genetics, arrived in the fall of 1951. Crick, who had been trained as a physicist but who had switched to biology after World War II, was already at the Cavendish, carrying out graduate-level work. Soon after Watson's arrival, he and Crick realized that they were both interested in solving the problem of the structure of DNA, and a close collaboration developed. They decided early on that they would attempt to build a model of the molecule. The general method of model building was adopted from Linus Pauling, a world-famous chemist who had had great success with model building in his recent research.

Watson and Crick also adopted a more specific strategy from Pauling, who had recently published a structural model of the protein alpha-keratin, which makes up hair, horn, and fingernails, among other things. Pauling's model of alpha-keratin was in the form of a helix (the *alpha-helix*), and Watson and Crick assumed, based on Pauling's work, that DNA was also helical. This was not an unreasonable assumption to make, since DNA and alpha-keratin are analogous in several ways: both are large organic molecules, constructed out of smaller elements that repeat again and again, in different combinations. Proteins are constructed out of *peptide* units, and DNA is made out of *nucleotides*. Thus, Watson and Crick used information from a closely related area – from their domain-specific expertise – as the foundation on which they constructed their model.

Those two strategic assumptions made by Watson and Crick – model building and starting with helical structures – led to several advantages on their part. First, they began to examine all the available information from the perspective of what each piece could tell them about the helical structure of DNA. That meant that they did not have to spend time examining information that might have taken them offtrack. Since DNA turned out to be helical in shape, Watson and Crick moved far along the correct path to the answer without having expended undue amounts of time and effort. In addition, Watson and Crick were in contact with Maurice Wilkins, who was also working on the structure of DNA. Wilkins told them that he believed that DNA was helical in structure and that it was thicker than a single strand. He also provided Watson and Crick with some experimental results that supported that view. Wilkins did not at that time build models of possible structures of DNA, as he was less committed to that strategy than were Watson and Crick. This lack of commitment to building models may have resulted in Wilkins being left behind by Watson and Crick.

The creation of the double-helix model of DNA was obviously a much more complex process than has been outlined here (for further discussion, see Olby, 1994, Watson, 1968, and Weisberg, 2003, 2006). Many other specific pieces of information had to be determined before a specific model could be constructed, such as how many strands were in the molecule; how the strands were structured; how far apart the strands were; the angle, or *pitch* of the helical spiral; how the strands of the helix were held together, and so forth. However, the answers to those questions do not introduce any issues that will change the present conclusions, especially the principal one, that the double helix, a creative product of the first rank, was firmly built on the domain-specific expertise of Watson and Crick.

In conclusion, we see here evidence for the critical role of domain-specific expertise in a seminal example of creative thinking in science. The example in Figure 42.1A can be used to outline the development of DNA just discussed. We see that all of what has just been summarized would fall near the center of the diagram – at the domain-specific area. I now turn to case studies in invention to examine further the generality of this finding.

THE WRIGHT BROTHERS' INVENTION OF THE AIRPLANE

The Wright brothers' first successful powered flights, on December 17, 1903, at Kitty Hawk, NC, came after several years of intense work (Weisberg, 2006). Wilbur and Orville Wright's interest in flying was kindled (or rekindled, since they had had some interest in flying machines earlier in their lives) by news accounts of the death of Otto Lilienthal in August 1896, in a gliding accident (Heppenheimer, 2003). Lilienthal, a German engineer, had for several years been experimenting with gliders of his own design as part of a project to produce a powered flying machine. Lilienthal's gliders had wings shaped like those of bats, and he flew by hanging suspended from the wing. The gliders were controlled by Lilienthal moving his body, thereby shifting the center of gravity of the apparatus, to counteract the lifting force of the wing. During one flight, a gust of wind brought up the front of the wing of the glider, and the craft stalled (it stopped moving, thereby losing *lift*, the capacity to stay aloft). Lilienthal was unable to bring the glider under control by shifting his weight, and it crashed, breaking his back. He died the next day. Lilienthal's death was reported in newspapers and magazines, and the Wrights read about it. It was not until 1899, however, that Wilbur Wright wrote to the Smithsonian Institution to inquire about any available information recounting research on flight. He received a list of the materials, including several books, and he also received several pamphlets published by the Smithsonian.

There were several research projects on flight beyond that of Lilienthal that were described in the materials the Wrights received (Weisberg, 2006). Octave Chanute, a retired engineer, was heading a team carrying out research using gliders, and several investigators had worked on powered flying machines, including Samuel P. Langley, the Secretary of the Smithsonian. The Wrights thus acquired information as the result of their study of other inventors' work, and this domain-specific expertise played a role in their own work. As an example, the biplane (two-wing) configuration of the gliders with which they began their work, and also of their powered Flyer, were similar to that of Chanute's gliders. However, perhaps more important for the Wrights, was what they perceived of as *missing* from the work of other would-be inventors of the airplane. On reading the accounts of those projects, the Wrights were most struck by the fact that none of those would-be inventors had attempted to tackle what to the Wrights was the most pressing problem in building a flying machine: development of a system that would enable the pilot to control the aircraft in the air.

As an example of the lack of focus on a control system, the steam-powered airplanes – called *aerodromes* – that Langley had under development had wings and a tail designed to automatically keep them stable in response to changes in wind velocity and direction (Heppenheimer, 2003, p. 88). There were no controls to enable the pilot to actively control the craft. Chanute's gliders were constructed similarly. There was concern on the part of many of the early researchers that a pilot would not be able to respond quickly to changes in wind direction and speed and thus would be useless in an emergency. The Wrights, in contrast, felt that the issue of control was so important that a method had to be devised so that a human would be able to pilot the craft.

The Wrights' belief in the necessity for control, and in the ability of a human to carry out that task, may have arisen from their experiences with bicycles (Heppenheimer, 2003, p. 88). The Wrights had built and sold bicycles of their own design, so they were well versed in the specifics of bicycling. Bicycles as vehicles are analogous to airplanes in important ways, because both require relatively complex control on the part of the "pilot." A person riding a bicycle makes constant adjustments to speed, body position, and orientation of the front wheel (through the handlebars) in order to maintain equilibrium and to proceed in the chosen direction. However, and this is most important, the rider also at times deliberately upsets equilibrium, most specifically, in order to turn:

one steers the front wheel in the direction one wishes to go by moving the handlebars, but one also leans to the side that one is turning to, so that the bicycle tilts (banks) to the inside of the turn. That is, one begins to *fall* when one is making a turn. The experienced rider keeps the bicycle's speed high enough so that it leans into the turn but does not fall; a novice rider when making a turn is likely to go too slowly and will have to put his or her inside foot on the ground to prevent a fall. When the turn is completed, the rider reestablishes equilibrium by straightening the front wheel and sitting straight on the bicycle.

The Wrights surmised that control of a plane in flight might be like control of a moving bicycle. One might say that the Wrights thought of the airplane as a bicycle with wings (Heppenheimer, 2003, p. 89). Thus, the Wrights' belief in the need for a system to enable a pilot to control an aircraft in flight was the outgrowth of their expertise with bicycles. Other researchers conceived of an airplane as a boat in the air, which is controlled very differently. Langley, for example, designed his aerodromes with a rudder at the rear, like that of a boat, to control turns. It should be noted, however, that some individuals who preceded the Wrights in speculating about the possibility of human-powered flight had also considered riding bicycles as analogous to piloting an aircraft. James Means, a commentator on the flight scene, predicted (in a book that was on the Smithsonian list sent to Wilbur Wright and probably read by the brothers) that the airplane would be perfected by "bicycle men," because to fly is like "wheeling": "To learn to wheel one must learn to balance. To learn to fly one must learn to balance" (quoted in Heppenheimer, 2003, p. 88). Lilienthal had written to Means in praise of Means's analysis of the relationship between riding a bicycle and flying. If we analyze this aspect of the Wrights' thinking based on the outlines presented in Figure 42.1A and 42.1B, their use of the bicycle as the basis for conceiving of control in flight would be classified as being based on relatively domain-specific expertise since both are modes of transportation, although one is land based and the other is not (Weisberg, 2006).

The Wrights then relatively quickly developed an idea for a control system based on observations they had made of birds in flight, another example of domain-specific expertise (Weisberg, 2006). Here too, there were precedents in the community of researchers with which the Wrights were familiar. L.-P. Mouillard had written a book in which he discussed bird flight and urged others to observe birds gliding effortlessly on air currents (Heppenheimer, 2003), and Lilienthal carried out observations of birds. In a magazine article on Lilienthal that had appeared in the United States, the author noted that Lilienthal's observations of birds in flight had led him to conclusions about the optimal shape of the wings for his gliders. The Wrights had read this article and had also read elsewhere about bird flight.

It is also possible that the Wrights – and many others interested in the possibility of human flight – were led to study birds because, if one wants to learn how to fly, one should study the behavior of an organism that already knows how. That is, use of information gleaned from birds would be another example of relatively specific transfer (Weisberg, 2006), and indeed one could argue that birds are "closer" to flying machines than bicycles are. The Wrights reported that they had observed birds gliding on wind currents, with their wings essentially motionless, in a dihedral or V shape. The animals could be seen sometimes being tilted to one side or the other by changing winds and air currents (the V would no longer be vertical), and somehow making adjustments that allowed them to return to level flight. Close observation indicated that the birds responded to changes from level flight by altering the orientations of their wing tips. By moving the tips of their wings in opposite directions, the birds essentially turned themselves into windmills, and were turned by the wind back toward level flight.

The Wrights' discovery of birds' use of their wing tips to control their orientation led them to develop a mechanical system whereby the pilot could control mov-

able surfaces, analogous to the birds' wing tips, through metal rods and gears (Heppenheimer, 2003). The system was designed to allow the pilot to move the wing tips up and down in opposite directions and to tilt the machine when necessary, either to maintain equilibrium in the face of wind gusts, or to disturb equilibrium intentionally in order to bank into a turn. This is an example where they used their expertise as mechanics – general expertise – to implement the birds' system in human materials. However, the rod-and-gear system was too heavy to be practical. They then, again, used their mechanical expertise to develop a system wherein the pilot, lying prone on the lower wing of a two-winged glider (a biplane), controlled the orientation of the wing tips, through wires that he could pull in one direction or another by swinging his hips in a cradle to which the wires were attached. The pilot's movement caused the wires to pull one set of wing tips up and the other down, which was called *wing warping*. An early version of a wing-warping system was developed by the Wrights at their home in Dayton, Ohio, during the summer of 1899. They tested it on a five-foot wingspan biplane kite model that they built. The person flying the kite was able to warp the wings by pulling on two sets of strings, one of which controlled each set of wing tips. They found that the system worked as they hoped. When the pilot's hip cradle was incorporated in their first glider in 1900, it added little weight to the machine and worked well enough that it was used to control all their gliders (1900–1902) and the first powered flying machine (1903).

We have seen what we can designate as three stages in the Wrights' development of a control system for their aircraft – (1) deciding that there was a need for a control system, (2) using birds' control of their wing tips as an example of a control system, (3) implementing the system – were outgrowths of different aspects of their expertise. The first two stages, which were dependent on the bicycle and bird flight, respectively, were the results of domain-specific expertise. The final stage, implementation of a method for controlling the wing tips of their aircraft, seems to have been independent of domain-specific expertise since they did not have any experience constructing a flight-control system analogous to that of birds. That is, the wing-warping system was based on the Wrights' general expertise as mechanics and carpenters, which in turn was based on years of construction projects, as well as their experiences as manufacturers of bicycles.

In conclusion, the accomplishments of the Wright brothers provide evidence that the two modes at the ends of the continuum of expertise as outlined earlier may play roles in major creative accomplishments. We will see further evidence of creative thinking based on both modes of expertise in the next case study, which examines a seminal invention produced by one of the most prolific inventors who ever lived.

EDISON AND THE LIGHT BULB

On New Year's Eve of 1879, Thomas Edison opened his Menlo Park, NJ, laboratory to the public so that they could see and marvel at the electric lighting system that had been installed there. This demonstration culminated several years' work in Edison's laboratory. In Edison's light bulb, electric current was passed through a thin filament of carbon ("the burner"), which was enclosed inside a glass bulb, in a vacuum. The current flowing through the carbon caused it to heat to the point of glowing or "incandescence."

Edison is usually referred to as *the* inventor of the light bulb, but there had been numerous earlier attempts to produce an incandescent electric light bulb, and he was aware of that work (Friedel & Israel, 1986; Weisberg, Buonanno, & Israel, 2006). Almost all of those earlier attempts used either carbon or platinum as the burner, but there were difficulties with each of those elements. When carbon was heated to a temperature sufficient to produce light, it would quickly oxidize (burn up), rendering the bulb useless. In order to eliminate oxidation, it was necessary to remove the carbon burner from the presence of oxygen, and many of the earlier workers had placed the carbon burner in a vacuum produced by a vacuum pump. The vacuum pumps then available could not produce anything near a complete vacuum, so the burner could not be protected, and the bulbs quickly failed. Platinum burners presented a different problem: their temperature had to be controlled very carefully because if the burner got too hot, it would melt and crack, thereby rendering the bulb useless. As with the Wrights, Edison began his work relatively knowledgeable about what had been done before, that is, other researchers' failures.

Edison started his electric-light work in 1877 with a carbon burner in a vacuum. This work, built directly on the past, was not successful: the burner oxidized. Since he knew of no way to improve the vacuum, Edison abandoned work on the carbon burner. About a year later, he carried out a second phase of work on the light bulb, this time with platinum burners, again building directly on what had been done in the past. In order to try to stop the platinum from melting, Edison's bulbs contained "regulators," devices like thermostats in modern heating systems, to regulate the temperature of the platinum and keep it from melting (Friedel & Israel, 1986). Edison had seen regulators in electric-lighting circuits designed by others. However, it proved impossible to control the temperature of the platinum burner. Thus, one could summarize Edison's early work on the light bulb by saying that it was based on domain-specific expertise, that is, relatively direct transfer of information from the same domain. Unfortunately, Edison's work also suffered the same fate as the earlier attempts on which it was based.

In response to the failure with platinum burners, Edison tried to determine exactly why they failed. He observed the broken burners under a microscope, and he and his staff concluded that the melting and cracking was caused by escaping hydrogen gas, which platinum under normal conditions had absorbed from the atmosphere. The hydrogen escaped when the platinum was heated, causing holes to form, which facilitated melting and cracking of the burner. Edison reasoned that the platinum might be stopped from cracking if the hydrogen could be removed slowly. He reasoned further that the platinum would first have to be heated slowly in a vacuum, which would allow the hydrogen to escape without destruction of the burner. The removal of the hydrogen from the platinum burners did make them last longer and burn brighter, but they still overheated and melted (Friedel & Israel, 1986, pp. 56–57; p. 78).

In the summer of 1879, Edison and his staff attempted to develop more efficient vacuum pumps in order to make the platinum-burner bulb work. They eventually produced a pump that was a combination of two advanced vacuum pumps, products of different manufacturers. The idea of combining two vacuum pumps was presented in an article by de la Rue and Muller (Friedel & Israel, 1986, pp. 61–62), and so is another example of strong expertise or near transfer. Even this combined pump, which produced a nearly complete vacuum (Friedel & Israel, 1986, pp. 62, 82), did not solve the basic problem: the platinum filaments would last for only a few hours and would tolerate only a minimal amount of electrical current before cracking.

In October, 1879, Edison began to experiment again with carbon as a burner. The return to carbon followed directly from Edison's situation: the platinum bulb was not successful; an improved vacuum pump was available; and Edison's earlier attempts with carbon had failed, owing to incomplete vacuums. On October 22, Edison's assistant Charles Batchelor conducted experiments using a "carbonized" piece of cotton thread – thread baked in an oven until it turned into pure carbon – placed inside of an evacuated bulb. Batchelor experimented with a variety of carbon materials throughout the day, and at 1:30 AM the next morning he attempted once again to raise a carbonized cotton thread to incandescence (Friedel & Israel, 1986, p. 104). This light burned for a total of 14½ hours, with an intensity of 30 candles, more than enough to be useful. In early November, 1879, Edison filed for an electric light patent with the U.S. patent office. The light was given its public debut on New Year's Eve.

In summarizing the role of Edison's expertise in his invention of the light bulb (Weisberg et al., 2006), we can see, in a parallel to the Wright brothers, that a broad range of Edison's expertise played a role. Edison began by trying to build on the past, so his initial work depended on his domain-specific expertise. His impasse with platinum, however, led him to examine carefully the failed burners. There was no direct precedent for this, but it is a response to an impasse that seems not untypical, based on people's general knowledge: if something is not working in the way you expect it to, examine it carefully to determine why. Based on his analysis of the problems with platinum burners and how they might be overcome, Edison turned to the development of an efficient vacuum pump. Edison's new pump came from an idea available in the literature, so domain-specific expertise played a role here. When platinum was still not viable, the availability of the improved vacuum may have stimulated a return to carbon and ultimate success. In conclusion, Edison's achievement, which resulted in his overcoming the problem with carbon that had defeated earlier workers, was the result of his analysis of why the platinum burners were failing, followed by his attempt to correct it by building a new vacuum pump. Domain-specific expertise played a role only in the latter achievement, so here, as with the Wright brothers, general expertise might have been necessary for creativity.

Case Studies: Summary

The case studies discussed in this chapter are summarized in Table 42.1. In each case, we can see a role played by domain-specific expertise. In two cases, aspects of the advances that were based on general, rather than domain-specific, expertise are also pointed out. Various aspects of the case studies will be discussed further as we examine the more general implications of the results summarized in Table 42.1 for the understanding of the role of expertise in creativity.

Table 42.1. Summary of case studies

Case study	*How did creative advance come about?*
Mozart	**Domain-specifi expertise:** Study of musical works of others; formal teaching; practice.
The Beatles	**Domain-specific expertise:** Study of musical works of others; informal teaching; practice.
Picasso's *Guernica*	**Domain-specific expertise:** Picasso's previous works for structure and characters; some characters from other artists.
Calder's Mobiles	**Domain-specific expertise:** Calder's previous works as the basis for the medium (wire sculpture) and for movement; nonrepresentational style from exposure to Mondrian's work.
Pollock's Poured Paintings	**Domain-specific expertise:** Pouring and dripping paint demonstrated at Siqueiros's workshop; Pollock's group practice with technique.
Double Helix	**Domain-specific expertise:** Pauling's modeling and alpha-helix; Wilkins's information about DNA.
Wright Brothers' Airplane	**Domain-specific expertise:** Bicycles as the basis for need for control; birds as an example of a flight-control system. **General Expertise:** Specific control system of their own, based on general mechanical skills.
Edison's Light Bulb	**Domain-specific expertise:** Built on unsuccessful work by others; used idea in article as basis for improved vacuum pump. **General expertise:** Analysis of failed platinum burners led to need for improved vacuum pump.

Expertise and Creativity

Ericsson (1996, 1998) proposed that creative advances are the highest expressions of expertise. From this proposal we derived three hypotheses. First, expertise is necessary for creativity. Second, innovations come about as the result of extensions of technique resulting from practice. Third, creative advances based on expertise redefine their domains. We can now test those hypotheses in a reasonably rigorous way by examining specifics of the case studies. However, before we do so, it is necessary to note that, based on the discussion in this chapter, those three hypotheses are ambiguous; in this chapter, the term *expertise* refers to a continuum of states of knowledge and/or skill, ranging from what we have called domain-specific expertise to general expertise. Therefore, in discussing the support for each of the three hypotheses, I will consider in some detail the question of the level of expertise involved.

Creativity and Expertise: Is Expertise Necessary for Creativity?

Support for this hypothesis would come about from a demonstration that no creative advances came about without the creators possessing expertise. The results from the relatively few case studies discussed in this chapter are obviously only the beginning of an examination of the potentially relevant data. Given that caution, we can conclude that the results of the present analyses supported the hypothesis that expertise is necessary for creativity, since expertise played a role in each of the case studies. However, as just noted, we have to be clear about how expertise functioned in each case. Mozart and The Beatles used study and practice of the musical works of others as the basis for development of their first works. Picasso used his own earlier work as the basis for the structure and some of the characters for *Guernica*, as well as adapting characters from other artists. Calder also used domain-specific expertise of two sorts: (1) his previous use of wire and motion in sculpture were critical in his development of mobiles; (2) the nonrepresentational content of the new sculpture came from Mondrian. That is, a critical component of Calder's innovation came from others, as did Pollock's. Watson and Crick's domain-specific expertise – their knowledge of Pauling's work served as the foundation for their own work in two ways: construction of models and attempts to model helical structures. The Wrights used information from several related domains – bicycles; birds' flight – as the basis for their work, perhaps because at that time there was little in the way of useful information available in aviation. Finally, Edison built on earlier work, but in a negative way: he began within the framework of earlier attempts (domain-specific expertise) and devised a way to overcome the problem of oxidation of the carbon burners (based on general and domain-specific expertise).

Turning to the more specific question of whether domain-specific or general expertise is necessary for creativity, it seems that domain-specific expertise may be necessary because in all the case studies considered here the innovations depended at least in part on domain-specific expertise. Based as well on the present case studies, general expertise is not always necessary for creativity, because in a majority of the cases the innovations did not seem to depend on general expertise (see Table 42.1). It might be the case that if an individual possesses detailed-enough domain-specific expertise, general expertise may not be called on.

An important related question concerns whether either domain-specific or general expertise is *sufficient* for creativity. We saw that the Wrights and Edison had to go beyond domain-specific expertise in order to successfully complete their work, so domain-specific expertise was not sufficient for them. Two additional pieces of evidence that might be relevant here come from the case of DNA. First, we saw that Wilkins provided Watson and Crick with some pieces of information that played a role in their creating their successful model. The fact that Wilkins himself did not create

the double helix may indicate that domain-specific expertise may not be sufficient for creativity. Similarly, and perhaps potentially more important in this context, Pauling, who was a world-renowned expert in analysis of the structure of complex organic macromolecules through modeling, also was not successful in determining the structure of DNA. In a parallel with the discussion of Wilkins, Pauling's failure to discover the double helix can be interpreted as indicating that domain-specific expertise may not be sufficient for creative achievement.

However, there is a critical assumption underlying such a conclusion: one must assume that the expertise of Wilkins and Pauling concerning DNA was equivalent to that of Watson and Crick. I have argued elsewhere (Weisberg, 1993; 2006) that the reason that Watson and Crick were successful when others, including Wilkins and Pauling, were not was because only Watson and Crick possessed all the information necessary for the construction of the double helix. So the reason that Wilkins and Pauling each failed was not because each of them lacked some sort of ingredient – a "creative spark" perhaps – that played a critical role in their creative thinking. Rather, the reason Wilkins and Pauling each failed was because each of them did not know what Watson and Crick did.

In conclusion, the present results paint a complicated answer to the question of whether domain-specific expertise is sufficient for creativity. Analysis of more case studies may help to provide more illumination on this question.

Creative Advances and the Extension of Technique

The second hypothesis was that creative advances come about through extensions of technique, in an analogy to the achievement of new performance standards by elite athletes. This hypothesis is not strongly supported by the case studies since most of the creative breakthroughs examined here, even those that depended on domain-specific expertise and deliberate practice, did not require that the innovator go beyond existing technique. Pollock's development of his dripping or pouring technique was a creative advance that went beyond existing techniques (Weisberg, 1993, 2003), but is was the only example of such an advance in the case studies that we examined. Calder's nonrepresentational sculpture, for example, was *simpler* than his representational work. Essentially the same technique was used – twisted pieces of wire – but the *content* was changed (and simplified). Similarly, *Guernica* was not based on new technical developments on Picasso's part.

Also, some radical artistic advances do not involve any "technique" at all. As an example, consider the use of "found objects" in painting and sculpture, which involves incorporating objects found in the environment into a work of art or, even more radically, presenting a *found* object by itself as a work of art. The most striking example of such a practice was Marcel Duchamp's *Bicycle Wheel*, which was a "sculpture" consisting of a bicycle wheel and the fork in which it spins, mounted on a painted kitchen stool. Similarly, Duchamp's *Fountain* consisted of a urinal, which he had signed "R. Mutt," sitting on a base (not mounted on the wall). The purpose behind Duchamp's use of those objects is not of relevance here. The critical point for us is that those "works of art" (and they are displayed in museums and are discussed in texts and histories of art – see, e.g., Arnason, 1986, p. 229 – so they are "works of art") require nothing in the way of technique acquired through practice.

The important conclusion to arise from those examples is that creative advances are not analogous to a new performance standard set by an elite athlete. When we say that an innovation *goes beyond the borders of some domain*, one may conclude that one is talking about the innovation surpassing the old, in a quantitative manner, along some dimension. That is not the way to analyze the relation between the old and the new, however. An innovation is *different* than the past but not necessarily *better*; this is in contrast to an ice-skater's five-revolution jump, say, which *is* better than one with four. Pollock's

poured paintings and Calder's nonrepresentational sculptures, for example, did not go *beyond* anything in a quantitative sense, they were simply new and different than existing forms. Creators – artists, for example – are usually not competing in a quantitative sense, as athletes are (even though, as noted earlier, works of art sometimes receive prizes). A better analogy might be to think of artists as *explorers*, each of whom takes a different path through heretofore unknown territory. One innovation is thus not better than another; it does not go further along the same path (as an athlete does when he or she jumps higher than anyone else, for example). Rather, the innovation takes a *different* path, so a direct quantitative comparison is not appropriate.

It is also interesting to note that old styles of art and music, and old ideas in science and invention, sometimes come back into favor, although perhaps not in identical form, which means that the old has not been surpassed, it has just been put aside for a while until it becomes relevant again. Examples of such "recyclings" include the development of the neoclassical style in classical music of the 1980s, as well as the realistic-based styles of painting that developed after the ascension of the modern nonrepresentational art of the 1950s and 1960s. Also, Edison's return to carbon burners in his lightbulb is an example of a previously rejected idea coming back, although the time frame was considerably shorter than that which usually occurs when old ideas are recycled. In conclusion, the analogy made by Ericsson between expertise in "performance" domains, such as athletics, and creative domains might not be that useful, musical and artistic competitions notwithstanding.

Do Creative Advances Based on Expertise Redefine Domains?

The final hypothesis is that acquiring expertise enables creative thinkers to redefine their domains. It should first be noted in response that not all creative advances redefine their domains. Most importantly, some creative advances based on domain-specific expertise do redefine their domains, but others do not. As one example, Mozart's music did not redefine the domain; it is usually appreciated as the highest example of the classical ideal. It is interesting in this context to compare the career development of Mozart with that of Beethoven. Earlier discussion indicated that Mozart's career development corresponded to the Ten-Year Rule: he developed in a way that provides evidence for the acquisition of expertise based on deliberate practice. A similar developmental path was taken by Beethoven, who received musical training starting at an early age, although not as early as Mozart. However, if we compare the works of Mozart with those of Beethoven, Mozart's works are not seen as revolutionary, whereas Beethoven is looked on as an innovator who changed the domain of music (Solomon, 1977). So we have here two creative individuals, each of whom had acquired expertise through deliberate practice, each of whom produced numerous masterworks, but only one of whom redefined the field.

Watson and Crick's formulation of the double helix also did not redefine the domain; it opened up new areas of exploration, but the problem of the structure of the genetic material was one that had been of interest to geneticists for years. Similarly, Picasso's *Guernica*, though undoubtedly a masterpiece, did not change the course of painting. It was a novel extension of Picasso's work until that point, but it did not represent a radical change technically or stylistically in what he was doing. Also, *Guernica* did not radically affect the work of other artists in the way that Picasso and Bracque's development of Cubism, for example, did. In the years following Picasso and Braque's pioneering Cubist works, artists all over the world adopted that radically new style of representation (Arnason, 1986). Edison's light bulb also did not redefine the domain; he overcame obstacles that earlier would-be inventors of the incandescent light were aware of, and his success was due to perfecting already existing mechanisms (i.e., the vacuum pumps).

Calder's mobiles, with their nonrepresentational style and wind-driven movement, redefined the domain of sculpture. No one had ever seen sculptures like those before. The nonrepresentational style came from Calder's familiarity with Mondrian's work, and movement had been part of Calder's work almost since he began to make art. So Calder's expertise was critical in this redefinition of the domain, although, as noted earlier, not through the development of new technique. Pollock's poured paintings did redefine painting, and they did so through the development of a new technique. (However, that new technique was not "better" than the existing technique.) The foundation for the new technique came from Pollock's exposure to Siqueiros's ideas in the workshop, as well as more informally, and through Pollock's interactions with other young artists who were also influenced by Siqueiros's ideas. The Wright brothers' flying machine also redefined the domain. Their principal innovation – an active control system – was one that no other researchers had considered, and their realization of that system was what redefined the domain. The crucial step in the Wrights' redefinition of the domain was their initial conclusion that a system was needed, which came from their experience with bicycles, so the redefinition of the field was based on their expertise.

The discussion to this point is summarized in Table 42.2, which uses two dimensions to analyze the creative achievements that have been discussed. The first dimension is the specificity of the expertise involved in the innovation, and the second is whether or not the innovation redefined the field. Based on the case studies discussed in this chapter (admittedly a small sample), it seems that domain-specific expertise is a necessary but not sufficient condition for redefinition of a domain.

CREATIVITY AND EXPERTISE: CONCLUSIONS
AND REMAINING QUESTIONS

As the discussion in this chapter makes clear, research on expertise raises issues that are important in the study of creative thinking.

Table 42.2. Case studies: Relationship between expertise and redefinition of the domain

Did the achievement redefine the domain?	How was the achievement brought about?	
	Domain-specific expertise (Including outside information from same domain)	General expertise
No	Mozart Picasso's *Guernica* DNA (Pauling's modeling and alpha-helix) Edison's Light Bulb (began with others' unsuccessful bulbs; combined vacuum pumps)	Edison's analysis of failures of platinum
Yes	Beatles' "Middle-Period" Works Calder's Mobiles (non-representational style from Mondrian) Pollock's Poured Paintings (pouring, spilling, and throwing paint as mode of application; Siqueiros workshop) Wright Brothers (bicycles for need for control system; bird flight for example of a control system)	Wright Brothers' implementation of specific wing-warping control system

The review in this chapter has indicated that a complex relationship exists between creativity and expertise. In some cases, there seems to be a close parallel between high-level creative achievement and domain-specific expertise, and the Ten-Year Rule may closely describe the basis for creative achievement. One difference between many creative achievements and those that occur in domains studied in the expertise literature is that expertise in, for example, elite athletic performance or medical diagnosis produces advances that go beyond previous levels of performance in a quantitative manner. Creative achievements, on the other hand, even radical and groundbreaking ones, typically do not go beyond the old in a quantitative way. Radically new approaches are not important because they are *better* than old approaches; they are important because they are *different*. Thus, although in this chapter we derived many important conclusions concerning creative thinking by examining case studies through the lens of expertise, it is important to keep in mind that there are limitations to the overlap between the two areas of study. Expertise in swimming is not the same as expertise in molecular genetics, and the differences between them may be as important as the similarities.

References

Arnason, H. H. (1986). *History of modern art. Painting. Sculpture. Architecture. Photography.* (3rd ed.). Englewood Cliffs, NJ: Prentice-Hall.

Bassok, M., & Holyoak, K. J. (1989). Interdomain transfer between isomorphic topics in algebra and physics. *Journal of Experimental Psychology: Learning, Memory, and Cognition, 15,* 153–166.

Calder, A. (1966). *Calder. An autobiography with pictures.* New York: Pantheon.

Chase, W. G., & Simon, H. A. (1973). The mind's eye in chess. In W. G. Chase (Ed.), *Visual information processing* (pp. 215–281). New York: Academic Press.

Chipp, H. B. (1988). *Picasso's "Guernica."* Berkeley, CA: University of California Press.

Csikszentmihalyi, M. (1996). *Creativity. Flow and the psychology of discovery and invention.* New York: Harper Collins.

de Groot, A. (1965). *Thought and choice in chess.* The Hague: Mouton.

Ericsson, K. A. (1996). The acquisition of expert performance: An introduction to some of the issues. In K. A. Ericsson (Ed.), *The road to excellence. The acquisition of expert performance in the arts and sciences, sports, and games* (pp. 1–50). Mahwah, NJ: Erlbaum.

Ericsson, K. A. (1998). The scientific study of expert levels of performance: General implications for optimal learning and creativity. *High Ability Studies, 9,* 75–100.

Ericsson, K. A. (1999). Creative expertise as superior reproducible performance: Innovative and flexible aspects of expert performance. *Psychological Inquiry, 10,* 329–333.

Everett, W. (2001). *The Beatles as musicians. The Quarry Men through "Rubber Soul."* New York: Oxford.

Feltovich, P. J., Spiro, R. R., & Coulson, R. L. (1997). Issues of expert flexibility in contexts characterized by complexity and change. In P. J. Feltovich, K. M. Ford, & R. R. Hoffman (Eds.), *Expertise in context* (pp 125–146). Menlo Park, CA: AAAI/MIT Press.

Fleck, J. I., & Weisberg, R. W. (2004). The use of verbal protocols as data: An analysis of insight in the candle problem. *Memory & Cognition, 32,* 990–1006.

Friedel, R., & Israel, P. (1986). *Edison's electric light. Biography of an invention.* New Brunswick, NJ: Rutgers University Press.

Gardner, H. (1993). *Creating minds. An anatomy of creativity seen through the lives of Freud, Einstein, Picasso, Stravinsky, Eliot, Graham, and Gandhi.* New York: Basic.

Hayes, J. R. (1989). Cognitive processes in creativity. In J. A. Glover, R. R. Ronning, & C. R. Reynolds (Eds.), *Handbook of creativity* (pp. 135–145). New York: Plenum.

Heppenheimer, T. A. (2003). *First flight. The Wright brothers and the invention of the airplane.* Hoboken, NJ: Wiley.

James, W. (1880). Great men, great thoughts, and the environment. *Atlantic Monthly, 46,* 441–459.

Kozbelt, A. (2004). Reexamining the equal odds rule in classical composers. In J. P. Frois, P. Andrade, & J. F. Marques (Eds.), *Art and science. Proceedings of the XVIII Congress of the International Association of Empirical Esthetics,* 540–543. Lisbon, Portugal: IAEA.

Landau, E. (1989). *Jackson Pollock.* New York: Abrams.

Luchins, A. S., & Luchins, E. H. (1959). *Rigidity of behavior.* Eugene, OR: University of Oregon Press.

Marter, J. (1991). *Alexander Calder.* Cambridge, MA: MIT Press.

Newell, A. (1973). Artificial intelligence and the concept of mind. In R. C. Shank & K. M. Colby (Eds.), *Computer models of language and thought.* San Francisco: W. H. Freeman.

Olby, R. (1994). *The path to the double helix. The discovery of DNA.* New York: Dover.

Pariser, D. (1987). The juvenile drawings of Klee, Toulouse-Lautrec, and Picasso. *Visual Arts Research, 13,* 53–67.

Perkins, D. N. (1981). *The mind's best work.* Cambridge, MA: Havard.

Reeves, L. M., & Weisberg, R. W. (1994). Models of analogical transfer in problem solving. *Psychological Bulletin, 116,* 381–400.

Reising, R. (2002). *Every sound there is. The Beatles' "Revolver" and the transformation of rock and roll.* Burlington, VT: Ashgate.

Scheerer, M. (1963). On problem-solving. *Scientific American, 208,* 118–128.

Shiffrin, R. M. (1996). Laboratory experimentation on the genesis of expertise. In K. A. Ericsson (Ed.), *The road to excellence. The acquisition of expert performance in the arts and sciences, sports, and games* (pp. 337–346). Mahwah, NJ: Erlbaum.

Simonton, D. K. (1999). *Origins of genius. Darwinian perspectives on creativity.* New York: Oxford.

Sloboda, J. (1996). The acquisition of musical performance expertise: Deconstructing the "talent" account of individual differences in musical expressivity. In K. A. Ericsson (Ed.), *The road to excellence. The acquisition of expert performance in the arts and sciences, sports, and games* (pp. 107–126). Mahwah, NJ: Erlbaum.

Solomon, M. (1977). *Beethoven.* New York: Schirmer.

Sternberg, R. J. (1996). Costs of expertise. In K. A. Ericsson (Ed.), *The road to excellence. The acquisition of expert performance in the arts and sciences, sports, and games* (pp. 347–354). Mahwah, NJ: Erlbaum.

Sternberg, R. (Ed.) (1999). *Handbook of creativity.* New York: Cambridge.

Watson, J. D. (1968). *The double helix: A personal account of the discovery of the structure of DNA.* New York: New American Library.

Weisberg, R. W. (1980). *Memory, thought, and behavior.* New York: Oxford.

Weisberg, R. W. (1993). *Creativity: Beyond the myth of genius.* New York: Freeman.

Weisberg, R. W. (1999). Creativity and knowledge: A challenge to theories. In R. J. Sternberg (Ed.), *Handbook of creativity* (pp. 226–250). New York: Cambridge University Press.

Weisberg, R. W. (2003). Case studies of innovation. In L. Shavinina (Ed.), *International handbook of innovation*. New York: Elsevier Science.

Weisberg, R. W. (2004). On structure in the creative process: A quantitative case-study of the creation of Picasso's *Guernica*. *Empirical Studies in the Arts*, 22, 23–54.

Weisberg, R. W. (2006). *Creativity: Understanding innovation in problem solving, science, invention, and the arts*. Hoboken, NJ: John Wiley.

Weisberg, R. W., Buonanno, J. & Israel, P. (2006). Edison and the Electric Light: A Case Study in Technological Creativity. Unpublished manuscript, Temple University.

Weisberg, R. W., & Sturdivant, N. (2006). *Career development of classical composers: An examination of the "equal-odds" rule*. Unpublished manuscript, Temple University, Philadelphia PA.

Weisberg, R. W., & Suls, J. M. (1973). An information-processing model of Duncker's candle problem. *Cognitive Psychology*, 4, 255–276.

Winner, E. (1996). The rage to master: The decisive role of talent in the visual arts. In K. A. Ericsson (Ed.), *The road to excellence. The acquisition of expert performance in the arts and sciences, sports, and games* (pp. 271–301). Mahwah, NJ: Erlbaum.

Author Note

Thanks are due to Anders Ericsson, Paul Feltovich, Dean Simonton, and Laurence Steinberg for comments on an earlier version of this chapter.

Author Index

Sanborn, A., 733, 740
Sandak, R., 574, 584, 670, 682
Sandblom, J., 548, 550, 551
Sanders, A. F., 270, 285
Sanderson, P. M., 209, 222
Sandgren, M., 692, 702
Sanes, J. N., 283, 285, 671, 682
Sass, D., 400
Satava, R. M., 255, 260, 261
Saults, J. S., 594, 611
Saunders, A., 215, 222
Saunders, N., 247, 248, 262
Sautu, R., 107, 123
Savalgi, R. S., 250, 261
Savelsbergh, G. J. P., 475, 476, 486
Savina, Y., 532, 535
Scalf, P. S., 657, 664, 665, 666, 678
Scardamalia, M., 82, 86, 297, 300, 400, 402
Schaafstal, A. M., 193, 194, 195, 196, 201, 449, 453
Schaal, S., 514, 520
Schadewald, M., 26, 29
Schaffer, S., 115, 123
Schaie, K. W., 326, 333, 593, 595, 596, 611, 726, 741
Scheerer, 767
Scheflen, A. E., 130, 144
Schempp, P. G., 312, 316
Schere, J. J., 402
Scherpbier, A. J. J. A., 349, 353, 699, 702
Schiebinger, L., 117, 123
Schiflett, S. G., 244, 259
Schijven, M., 251, 261
Schkade, D., 434, 437
Schlauch, W. S., 554, 568
Schlaug, G., 465, 468, 548, 551, 565, 567, 674, 678, 695, 702, 703
Schleicher, A., 565
Schliemann, A. D., 26, 29
Schlinker, P. J., 481, 487
Schmalhofer, F., 384, 386
Schmidt, A. M., 442, 450, 465, 470
Schmidt, F. L., 33, 38, 616, 631, 691, 702, 724, 741
Schmidt, H. G., 25, 26, 28, 29, 235, 238, 241, 349, 350, 351, 352, 353, 463, 467, 494, 503, 599, 610
Schmidt, J. A., 52, 67
Schmidt, L., 211, 222
Schmidt, R. A., 273, 285, 413, 475, 486, 505, 506, 519
Schmitt, J. F., 406, 410, 411, 418
Schnabel, T. G., 254, 260
Schneider, J. A., 496, 503
Schneider, S. L., 438
Schneider, W., 16, 24, 29, 31, 38, 46, 53, 54, 59, 60, 66, 67, 267, 269, 285, 286, 475, 486, 512, 513, 519, 532, 533, 538, 588, 597, 641, 653, 656, 658, 659, 660, 661, 663, 665, 670, 676, 677, 678, 679, 685, 693, 695, 703, 710, 721, 769
Scholtz, J., 377, 378, 386, 387
Schömann, M., 377, 384
Schön, D. A., 133, 144, 623, 631
Schooler, C., 736, 741
Schooler, T. Y. E., 575, 583
Schouten, J. L., 656, 667, 668, 677, 679
Schraagen, J. M. C., 15, 46, 185, 192, 195, 196, 197, 199, 200, 201, 205, 206, 229, 235, 241
Schriver, K. S., 401
Schroder, J., 662, 679
Schubert, T., 664, 665, 676, 682
Schueneman, A. L., 348, 353

Schuler, J. W., 408, 418
Schulkind, M. D., 296, 301
Schulman, E. L., 340, 341, 376, 387
Schultetus, R. S., 526, 529, 537, 538
Schulz, M., 465, 470
Schulz, R., 319, 322, 323, 329, 330, 333, 689, 690, 703, 735, 741
Schum, D. A., 574, 583
Schumacher, C. F., 254, 260
Schumacher, E. H., 59, 67, 277, 285, 662, 680
Schümann, 377, 378
Schunk, D. H., 705, 707, 710, 712, 715, 717, 721, 722
Schuwirth, L., 349, 353
Schvaneveldt, R. W., 180, 184, 356, 357, 365, 367, 368, 370
Schwartz, B. J., 50, 51, 63, 172, 179, 182, 228, 230, 240, 431, 437
Schwartz, W. B., 43, 55, 66
Schwarz, N., 237, 241, 437
Schweitzer, S., 624, 630
Schyns, P. G., 268, 284
Scinto, L. F. M., 402
Scott, A. C., 97, 102
Scott, C. L., 493, 497, 503
Scott, D. J., 347, 353
Scribner, S., 142, 205, 222, 758, 760
Scripture, E. W., 554, 557, 562, 567
Scruggs, T. E., 549, 551
Scurrah, M. J., 528, 538
Seah, C., 144
Seamster, T. L., 192, 201, 356, 357, 361, 367, 368, 370
Seashore, 457, 470
Seeger, C. M., 271, 284
Seely, 623
Seely-Brown, 48
Segal, L., 253, 261
Seitz, R. J., 616, 630
Selart, M., 436, 437
Semenza, C., 560, 567
Senate of Surgery, 255, 261
Senge, P. M., 130, 144
Serfaty, D., 206, 215, 221, 244, 259, 406, 418, 443, 451
Seron, X., 554, 560, 563, 567, 675, 681
Setton, T., 462, 468
Sevsek, B., 498, 503
Sexton, B., 370
Seymour, N. E., 255, 261
Seymour, T. L., 59, 67, 277, 285
Shadbolt, N. R., 97, 102, 170, 176, 180, 182, 183, 192, 198, 200, 206, 209, 215, 220, 222, 407, 416, 736, 745, 759
Shadmehr, R., 507, 517
Shafer, J. L., 15, 52, 54, 138, 206, 216, 243, 403, 442, 637, 640
Shaffer, L. H., 53, 67
Shafir, E., 434, 437
Shafto, P., 175, 184
Shah, N. J., 674, 679
Shakespeare, W., 489, 503
Shalev, R. S., 563, 567
Shalin, V. L., 185, 192, 199, 200, 201, 617, 630
Shallice, T., 558, 566
Shamir, B., 448, 453
Shanks, D. R., 274, 286
Shannon, C., 509, 519

Subject Index

abacus, 53, 549
Abelard, Peter, 74
abilities, 155. *See also* cognitive abilities; natural ability
  age-vulnerable, 593
  attention not focused specifically to level of, 161
  attenuated by age-correlated factors, 725
  characterizing expertise, 598
  complex, 724
  developing at different rates, 473
  differential patterns of, 34
  expertise as a form of, 616
  expertise decoupled from, 730
  mathematical, 554, 563
  in mature adulthood, 598
  practical intelligence and general, 616
  practice as compensation for differences, 459
  principal classes of, 589–591
  producing scores on a particular ability test, 589
  selectivity of arithmetical, 560
  skilled performance and determinants of, 459
  supporting reasoning, 590
  task-specific confidence in, 158
  traditional notion of student aptitude as, 79
ability predictors
  of individual differences, 162
  matching with criteria, 157
absent evidence identification, 572
absolute expertise, 21, 22
absorption in writing, 395
Absorption personality trait, 159
abstract concepts
  program comprehension based on, 378
  rendering, 392
abstract disciplines, 71
abstract goals, 378

abstract language, 392
abstract questions, 25
abstract representations
  essential in blindfold chess, 531
  retrieving appropriate material from memory, 52
  slow acquisition of, 52
abstracted features, 54
abstraction
  aiding utilization of knowledge and reasoning, 52
  of events, 54
  hierarchy, 188, 196
  levels of, 210
  in metacognition recall, 711
Abstraction-Decomposition matrices
  as an activity-independent representation, 210
  including processes, 210
  interactions with experts, 215
  representing the work domain, 214
  tutorial examples of, 210
  in WDA, 209
abstraction-decomposition space, 211
academic achievement
  African village priorities and, 621
  practical thinking skills and, 627
academic intelligence, naturalistic intelligence and, 616
academic learning. *See also* learning
  performance phase of, 710
  practice methods in, 711
  task strategies in, 710
  technique-oriented strategies in, 709
  time management in, 711
academic performance, prediction for children and adolescents, 155
academic qualifications, 22
academic success, too much formal, 327

computational models
  of human performance, 229
  of problem solving, 530
computer applications, expertise research and, 405
computer chess programs. *See* chess programs
computer databases as efficient chess training tools,
  532
computer files, 140
computer models, incorporating the knowledge of
  experts in, 12
computer programmers. *See also* programmers
  experienced performance not always superior to
    students, 686
  recall of experts compared to novices, 51
computer programming. *See* programming
computer programs
  implementing human problem solving models, 11
  performing challenging cognitive tasks, 226
  strategy of reading and comprehending, 380
computer science
  collaboration with cognitive psychology, 42
  study of expertise in, 14
computer simulations
  confirming chunking and template predictions, 527
  with MAPP,
    527
  of performance, 570
computer software developers, 237
computer system
  decomposition for a course on, 196
  users ideally involved in requirement analysis, 374
computer users, 131
computer-based education, expertise as goal state, 46
computer-based information systems, 138
computer-based models, emulating experts'
  performance, 12
computers
  as efficient chess training tools, 532
  judgment policy execution by, 433
  processing "symbols and symbol structures", 42
conative traits, 155, 158
concentration
  for deliberate practice, 699
  increasing typing speed, 698
  mnemonic training and, 549
  points of reference for, 314
  requirement for, 692
  self-regulatory training and, 718
  strong positive relationship with relevance, 307
concept formation
  measures of, 594
  prototype theories of, 344
Concept Map(s), 211–213
  about cold fronts in Gulf Coast weather, 213
  composing, 212
  eliciting forecasting knowledge, 217
  knowledge models, 215
  screen shot of, 212
Concept Mapping, 211–213
  for the elicitation of domain knowledge, 214
  representing practitioner knowledge of domain
    concepts, 214
  strength of, 217
Concept Mapping interviews
  articulation by domain experts, 216
  demonstrating comfort with the notion of a "mental
    model", 217

triggering recall of previously-encountered tough
  cases, 215
concept networks, data collected in, 141
concept-centered mode of reasoning, 55
concepts. *See also* abstract concepts; analytic concepts
  central to human learning and problem solving, 226
  in Concept Maps, 211
  learning, 343
conceptual foundations period of cognitive systems
  engineering, 193
conceptual framework, or model, of an expert system,
  91
conceptual structure, expertise as, 767
conceptualization of expertise, 381
concert piano. *See* pianists
concert violinists. *See* violinists
conclusion of a problem statement, 577
concrete entities, higher number cited by novices, 181
concrete instances, 48
concrete language in text, 392
concrete questions, novices better at answering, 25
concrete words, recalled by older adults, 549
concurrent component tasks, 663
concurrent measure for identifying exceptional
  experts, 21
concurrent performance, 664
concurrent-validation assessment, 150
condition in a production rule, 92
condition-action rules, 479
condition-action statements, tacit knowledge as, 615
conditional sentence, 92
The Conditions of Learning, 80
confabulation of answers, 230
confidence
  of deciders in quality of decisions, 430
  expert team efficacy and, 448
  personal theories in decision making and over-,
    433
  for a rule, 93
confidential knowledge of some professionals, 108
configuration class of expert systems, 94
conflict management in the brain, 656
confounding variables in the transportation domain,
  358
congruence, maximization of, 162
conscientiousness, 429
Conscientiousness personality trait, 159
conscious cognitive control, 512
conscious effort, maintaining, 601
consciousness
  actor emotional double, 494
  flow state of in writing, 395
consensual judgments, avoiding, 293
consequences, prediction of, 512
consistent mapping. *See* CM
consistent practice, 660
consistent search task, 659
consolidation
  blocking, 671
  of experts' representations, 180–181
  perceptual-motor skill learning and, 507
consolidation process of M1, 671
consonant item-recognition task, 660
constant relationship between stimulus and response,
  32
constant time of exposure model, 80–81
constituency perceptions of experts, 746

distinguished from calculation, 557
distribution across a lifespan, 296
in the domain of chess, 523
domain-specificity in, 560
driver hazard detection and, 648
effects on the test-retest method, 148
efficiency, 544
efficiency in managing, 560
eidetic, 225
enactment and physical movement, 497
encoding of, 544
examining people with exceptional, 236
exceptional, 539–550
expert knowledge demonstrations of, 539
expert skill-by-structure interactions and, 463
expertise and, 225
expertise as accumulation of patterns in, 463
expertise conceptual complexity and, 767
experts storing of past actions, 685
improvement methods, 539
improvement methods from Greek and Roman
    times, 539
intelligence and, 547–548
limitations of aids, 547
load in calculation, 557
loaded on a single factor, 544
management of, 560
in mathematical expertise, 557
musical performance and, 461
in musical practice and performance, 461
of organizations as transactive, 753
principles of skilled, 547
rapidity of, 554
recoding and embedding items, 541
retrieving specific facts from, 280
role in early learning, 156
of Shereshevskii (S), 541
short-term working, 558
strengthening of, 560
memory ability
    evidence in support of some overall, 544
    as independent of IQ, 547
    over a wider range of material than numbers alone,
        545
    self-rating of, 544
memory chunks. See chunks
memory expertise. See also expertise
    future directions in, 550
    key examples of, 540–543
    practical applications of, 549–550
memory experts. See also experts
    comparing to control participants' brain activation,
        675
    identification of, 540
    IQ of, 547
    reaching the highest level in the world after two
        years, 689
Memory for Names, 595
memory patterns, expertise as accumulation of, 463
memory performance. See also performance
    decision making and, 431
    of decision making experts, 431
    differences explained in terms of acquired skill,
        675
    mechanisms mediating, 11
    reanalyzing in terms of experts and non-expert
        chunks, 172
    of savants, 463

memory processes
    age-related decline, 726
    in chess, 526–528
memory remediation, effectiveness of mnemonic
    techniques, 549
memory research, future directions in, 550
memory retrieval
    versus perceptually available retrieval conditions,
        531
    representative structure different for, 531
memory search task, identifying probe items, 269
memory skills
    acquired by experts, 54
    validating numerous aspects of, 236
memory span, natural, 546
memory speed, long-term and expertise, 394
memory structures, underlying skilled performance,
    477
memory studies, history of modern, 540
memory superiority
    as natural or acquired, 545
    theoretical issues, 543–549
memory tasks, studying performance on, 11
memory techniques, distinguishing from a natural
    superiority, 545
memory tradeoffs, chess research characterizing, 534
memory training, 549
memory type, used by prodigies, 554
memory-visual search tasks, sizes of display sets in
    hybrid, 269
men. See also males
    becoming scientific fathers, 555
    music societal factors and, 466
mental arithmetic, sub-vocal rehearsal required for,
mental calculators, validation of, 237
mental capacities
    determined by innate mechanisms, 684
    found not to be valid predictors of attainment of
        expert performance, 10
    individual differences in, 10
    tests of individual differences in, 10
mental devices for dance pattern memory, 499
mental imagery. See imagery
mental models. See also model(s)
    assisting experts in anticipating what will happen
        next, 366
    assisting in discriminating relevant information, 366
    aviation student pilot situation awareness errors
        and, 642
    continual updating of the current situation, 52
    cultural norms of excellence transmission and,
        756
    in decision skills training, 412
    definition, 638
    driver physical automaticity and, 648
    of dynamic environments, 366
    expert teams shared, 440
    of experts, 405
    future state projections and, 638
    in learning process, 413
    in naturalistic decision making, 405
    notion of, 217
    perceived information interpretation and, 638
    shared by team members, 474
    situation awareness and, 638
    as situation awareness mechanism, 638
    situation projections and, 636
    superior generating superior situation models, 367